Conservation and Management of Rare and Endangered Plants

In Fond Memory of
Jeff Tuttle

Calaveras County District Attorney
2000 to 2010

Calaveras County Public Defender
1996 to 2000

Calaveras County Counsel
1977 to 1994

Calaveras High School
Student Body President, 1968-69

President, Calaveras County Bar Association;
President, Calaveras County Historical Society

Conservation and Management of Rare and Endangered Plants

Proceedings of a California Conference on the Conservation and Management of Rare and Endangered Plants

Edited by THOMAS S. ELIAS

Foreword by JIM NELSON

Based on a conference held at the Capital Plaza
Holiday Inn, Sacramento, California
5-8 November 1986

A Publication of the California Native Plant Society

Main entry under title:

Conservation and Management of Rare and Endangered Plants

    Includes bibliographies and index.

    1. Rare plants—California.   2. Endangered plants—California.

    3. Conservation—plants.   4. Management—rare plants.

    I. Elias, Thomas S., 1942-   . II. The California Native Plant Society

ISBN 0-943460-11-5 (cloth)

ISBN 0-943460-12-3 (paper)

Library of Congress Catalog Card Number 87-71025

The California Native Plant Society

Sacramento, California

Copyright © 1987 The California Native Plant Society

All rights reserved

Printed in the United States of America

Contents

Foreword ix
Introduction x

Background
California's Endangered Plants and the
CNPs Rare Plant Program
  James P. Smith, Jr. 1
The Potential for Permanent Plant
Protection
  Faith Thompson Campbell 7

Legal Aspects of Endangered Plant Conservation
The Federal Listing of Rare and
Endangered Plants: What Is Involved and
What Does it Mean?
  Jim Bartel 15
Rare Plant Conservation by
State Governments
  Linda R. McMahan 23
Endangered Plants and California State
Laws
  Susan A. Cochrane 33
A List Is a List ... or Is It?
  Richard P. York 39
Using the California Endangered Species
Act Consultation Provisions for Plant
Conservation
  Earl W. Cummings 43

California Endangered Plants— Today and Tomorrow
Conservation of Rare Plants on Public
Lands in California
  Edward L. Hastey 51
Sensitive Plant Management on the
National Forests in California
  Zane G. Smith, Jr. 61
Government Funding of Research,
Protection and Management of Rare Plants
in California
  Stephen J. Nicola 67
Rare and Endangered Species Management
in the California State Park System
  James Barry 73
Endangered Plants Along California
Highways: Considerations for Right-of-
Way Management
  Craig Martz 79

The Designation Process for a Research
Natural Area
  Gary Schoolcraft 85
Plant Exploration in California, the
Frontier Is Still Here
  James Shevock & Dean Wm. Taylor 91
Research Needs for Rare Plant
Conservation in California
  Timothy C. Messick 99
California's Most Endangered Plants
  Richard P. York 109

California's Endangered Habitats
Serpentine Endemism and Rarity
  Arthur K. Kruckeberg 121
Is *Quercus lobata* a Rare Plant?
Approaches to Conservation of Rare Plant
Communities That Lack Rare Plant
Species
  Robert F. Holland 129
Implications of Ecological Theory for Rare
Plant Conservation in Coastal Sage Scrub
  Walter E. Westman 133
Rare Plants in the Arroyo de la Cruz
Endemic Area, San Luis Obispo County,
California
  David J. Keil & Malcolm G. McLeod 141
The Problem of the Salmon Mountain
  J. O. Sawyer 155

Survey and Assessment Techniques
Rare Plant Surveys: Techniques for Impact
Assessment
  James R. Nelson 159
Determining Population Sizes of Narrowly
Endemic but Locally Common Plants in
the Red Hills, California
  *William B. DaVilla, Dean Wm. Taylor,
  R. Doug Stone & John W. Willoughby* 167
Predicting the Habitat Geography of
Sensitive Plants and Community Types
  Mona M. Myatt 173
The California Natural Diversity Data
Base—A Common Denominator
  James R. Shevock & Linda L. Hennessy .. 181

Impact of Exotic Species
The Displacement of Native Plants
by Exotics
  Elizabeth McClintock 185

Feral Hog Management at Golden Gate
National Recreation Area
    Alison G. Willy 189

Management of Feral Pigs at Pinnacles
National Monument: Why and How
    Steven H. DeBenedetti 193

Effects of Livestock Grazing on Two Rare
Plant Species in the Red Hills, Tuolumne
County, California
    John W. Willoughby 199

Case Studies

Threats to San Diego Vernal Pools and a
Case Study in Altered Pool Hydrology
    Ellen T. Bauder 209

Cactus Collection Factors of Interest to
Resource Managers
    *Peter S. Bennett, R. Roy Johnson
    & Michael R. Kunzmann* 215

Endangered Status of *Collomia rawsoniana*
(Polemoniaceae), Western Sierra Nevada,
California
    *Dean Wm. Taylor, John C. Stebbins
    & William B. DaVilla* 225

Effects of Wet-Season Management Burns
on Chaparral Vegetation: Implications for
Rare Species
    V. Thomas Parker 233

Endangerment Status of the Grass Tribe
Orcuttieae and *Chamaesyce hooveri*
(Euphorbiaceae) in the Central Valley
of California
    *R. Douglas Stone, Glenn L. Clifton,
    William B. DaVilla, John C. Stebbins
    & Dean Wm. Taylor* 239

Electrophoretic Analysis of Variation in
Native Monterey Cypress (*Cupressus
macrocarpa* Hartw.)
    M. Thompson Conkle 249

Bureau of Land Management's Efforts to
Conserve *Pediocactus peeblesianus* var
peeblesianus (Cactaceae)
    Mary Butterwick 257

The Ecology and Management of Three
Rare Salt Marsh Species of Humboldt Bay
    Gail A. Newton 263

The Endangered Sandhills Plant
Communities of Santa Cruz County
    Michael S. Marangio & Randall Morgan 267

Rare and Endangered Plant Successes in
San Luis Obispo County
    Malcolm G. McLeod 275

Status of Five Rare Plants Species in
Sequoia and Kings Canyon National Parks
    Larry L. Norris 279

Rare Plant Conservation in the
Southwestern Cape
    E. L. Gawith & N.J. Schmeidler III 283

Point Loma Lichens—Now and Then
    Charis C. Bratt 289

Evolutionary Relationships of *Holocarpa
macradenia*
    Rexford Palmer 295

Agave arizonica: An Endangered Species,
A Hybrid, or Does it Matter
    Rick DeLamater & Wendy Hodgson 305

Ecology and Population Dynamics

Attributes of Plant Populations and Their
Management Implications
    Bruce M. Pavlik 311

Ecology and Endangered Status of *Silene
invisa* Populations in the Central Sierra
Nevada, California
    Dean Wm Taylor & Rexford E. Palmer 321

What Constitutes a Good Year for an
Annual Plant? Two Examples from the
Orcuttieae
    Robert F. Holland 329

Ecology of the Serpentine Vegetation in the
San Francisco Bay Region
    Niall F. McCarten 335

Ecology and Distribution of *Poa marcida*
Hitch. in Northwestern Oregon
    *Rexford Palmer, Ronald Vanbianchi,
    Larry Schofield & Susan Nugent* 341

Population Dynamics of *Erysimum
menziesii*, a Facultative Biennial Mustard
    Ken S. Berg 351

Studies of the Population Biology of Prairie
Bush-clover (*Lespedeza leptostachya*)
    Welby R. Smith 359

Population Dynamics of the Tecate Cypress
    Anthony T. Dunn 367

Nurse Plant Ecology of Threatened Desert
Plants
    Gary P. Nabhan 377

Monitoring and Land Use Planning

Autecological Monitoring of Endangered
Plants
    Bruce M. Pavlik 385

Monitoring the Geyser's Panicum
(*Dichanthelium lanuginosum* var. *thermale*)
at the Little Geysers, Sonoma County,
California
    Barbara M. Leitner & Sally deBecker 391

Monitoring Rare Plant Populations in the
Knoxville Area of California
    Glen Clifton & Joe Callizo 397

Innovative Programmatic Approaches to
Resource Conservation
  Peter Grenell 401

Is Bonding Any Guarantee in Ecological
Management?
  Deborah Hillyard 405

Species Management

Strategies for Protecting Rare Plants from
Oil Development: A Santa Barbara County
Perspective
  Ann M. Howard 409

Transplantation of Sensitive Plants as
Mitigation for Environmental Impacts
  Lauren A. Hall 413

The 1986 Santa Cruz Tarweed Relocation
Project
  Neil A. Havlik 421

A Management Plan for Rare Plants in the
Red Hills of Tuolumne County, California
  Reynaud M. Farve 425

Management of *Hemizonia arida*
(Asteraceae) by the California Department
of Parks and Recreation
  Mark R. Faull 429

Endangered Species Management in
Southern California Coastal Salt Marshes:
A Conflict or an Opportunity
  Patrick V. Dunn 441

Assessment and Management of
Arctostaphylos pallida Eastwood
  David Amme & Neil Havlik 447

Development of Management Plans for
Sensitive Plant Species
  Bruce E. Dawson 455

Recovery of Endangered and Threatened
Plants in California: The Federal Role
  Monty D. Knudsen 461

Approach to Rare Plant Management at
Golden Gate National Recreation Area
  Terri Thomas 471

Species Recovery and Restoration

The Ring Mountain Restoration Plan
  Stan Strahan & Gregory J. Wolley 477

Guadalupe Dunes Revegetation Program
  Jacqueline L. Bowland 487

Habitat Reclamation for Endangered
Species on San Bruno Mountain
  Thomas S. Reid & Raymond C. Walsh 493

Habitat Characteristics of Willowy
Monardella in San Diego County:
Site Selection for Transplants
  Gerald A. Scheid 501

Methods of Increasing Native Populations
of *Erysimum menziesii*
  Jean Ferreira & Suzanne Smith 507

The Effects of Controlled Burnings on
Three Rare Plants
  Robert Boyd 513

Pediocactus knowltonii Recovery Efforts
  Peggy Olwell, Anne Cully,
  Paul Knight & Steve Brack 519

Genetic Conservation Issues in Land
Restoration: Open Forum Discussion
  Jean Ferreira & Deborah Hillyard 523

A Restoration of California:
A Practical Guide
  Wayne Tyson 525

Mineral Acquisition in Native Plants
  T.V. St. John 529

Revegetation of Rare and Endangered
Species: The Role of the Propagator
and Grower
  J. Michael Evans & Jeffrey W. Bohn 537

Germination and Seedling Establishment of
the Ione Buckwheat
  Rodney G. Myatt 547

Current Conservation Activities

Endangered Species in Botanic Gardens
  Donald A. Falk 553

Can Threatened and Endangered Species
be Maintained in Botanic Gardens?
  Thomas S. Elias 563

The California Nature Conservancy's
Landowner Contact and Registry Program:
Voluntary Protection for Rare Plant Sites
  Lynn Lozier 567

Habitat Restoration by a Non-Profit Organization:
A Case Study
  Phyllis M. Faber 573

San Clemente Island:
Remodeling the Museum
  R. Mitchel Beauchamp 575

Assessment and Monitoring of Rare Plants
in Alberta, Canada
  Clifford Wallis & Lorna Allen 579

Population Size and Preserve Design

Genetic Structure and the Conservation of
California's Endemic and Near-Endemic
Conifers
  F. Thomas Ledig 587

Concepts of Preserve Design:
What We Have Learned
  Deborah B. Jensen 595

Island Biogeography and Preserve Design
of an Insular Rare Plant Community
    Tim Krantz 605

Establishment of a Vernal Pool Preserve in
San Diego County
    John P. Rieger 615

Educational Awareness

Opportunities of Involvement in
Endangered Plant Education
    Kay Antunez de Mayola 619

Conservation Ethics, Animals, and
Rare Plant Protection
    Rolf W. Benseler 623

Acknowledgements 630

Foreword

DEVELOPMENT OF THE ENDANGERED PLANT CONFERENCE

For over twenty years California botanists have been concerned about the losses of rare plants and their habitats. Over these past two decades both the state and federal government passed legislation that provided some legal protection for rare plants, but these frequently failed to prevent trends of decreasing populations. The continuing decline of rare species has been an ongoing topic for discussion and a continuing source of frustration for many botanists.

Much has been learned about the rare plants themselves in recent years. The work of agency biologists, consultants, students, university researchers, amateur botanists and hobbyists have all contributed to our knowledge. But the dissemination of information has been slow and inefficient. The establishment of natural heritage programs has done much to improve the sharing of information among biologists, but is not entirely satisfactory due to the inherent need of these programs to focus on data sets rather than management issues. Even the data handled by heritage programs often do not tell the complete story. The existing scientific literature fails to fill this void as articles dealing with conservation and management issues are scattered through numerous journals and often excluded from botanical journals for lack of rigorous scientific approaches or because of a slant towards the management of resources rather than more basic botanical research.

While there exists a lack of media for sharing information, there is also an increasing need for an information exchange between all who were involved in the many aspects of rare plant conservation. Discussions during the California Native Plant Society conservation workshops in 1983 and 1984 made this need plainly evident. In June of 1985, a proposal for this conference was prepared and presented to fifteen agencies and private organizations. By September the conference had sufficient support to make the commitment to go forward.

The primary objectives of the conference were to:
1. Review the effects and the seriousness of man's activities on rare and endangered plants.
2. To identify effective techniques for the management and conservation of rare plants.
3. To identify practical recommendations for achieving more effective mitigation measures and long-term management of rare species.
4. To disseminate information to botanists, agency personnel, land developers and the public in general.

In addition, it was felt that
1. The Conference should be state-wide in scope, and open to any interested persons.
2. Proceedings should be published as promptly as possible following the conference.
3. There should be invited speakers (including politicians and agency administrators) who can give a "view from the top" as well as specialized concurrent sessions of contributed papers.
4. The conference should allow adequate time for direct interaction among participants to encourage direct exchange of information and the development of new ideas and approaches to conservation problems.

The conference attracted nearly 800 participants from the United States and Canada. Requests for information on the conference have been received from every state as well as Canada and England.

Clearly it was a timely meeting on a topic of great interest to many biologists. While this conference and proceedings cannot solve all of our information needs on the management and conservation of rare and endangered plants, it is hoped that this conference and its proceedings will serve as a lasting contribution.

JAMES R. NELSON

Introduction

The conservation of rare plants in California is a paradox. Over 5,000 species of native vascular plants and about 1,000 introduced species have naturalized and become components of the native flora. Such diversity of vegetation exceeds that of any other state, including Hawaii. Actually, California contains nearly one-third the total number of vascular plants native to the United States and Canada combined. California is also the most populous state with many major commercial and agricultural centers, compounded with rapidly spreading residential and recreational developments. Not surprisingly, California also has the greatest number of plants (approximately 680) which are in need of some form of protection. Despite the economic and population growth of this state, very few California plants have become extinct.

This encouraging fact is the result of early, concerted efforts by many people, private institutions, state and federal agencies, and industries working together to preserve and protect the rich and diverse natural heritage of this state. The California Native Plant Society has led in identifying the need and in forming the public and governmental agencies. Its publication, the *Inventory of Rare and Endangered Vascular Plants of California,* a fourth edition to be published later this year, has been and continues to be a basic reference to the species in need of conservation efforts.

Participation and attendance at this conference exceeded the expectations of the planners and organizers. It has become the largest conference ever held in North America (over 800 attending) to address rare and endangered plants. This fact, together with the numerous projects relating to the conservation and management of rare plants in the state is evidence that California is a leader in the United States and the world in the conservation of natural resources.

The papers in this proceedings are organized into subject areas patterned largely after the conference. The order has been changed somewhat to bring together related papers in this work. The number of papers submitted for publication to these proceedings exceeded our expectation by 50%. In the interest of disseminating as much information as possible and as quickly as possible, we decided to have the participants submit camera-ready copy for publication. Manuscripts were received in varying conditions and with a wide range of type styles and print quality despite efforts to standardize. While attempts have been made to bring them into a standard format, minor inconsistencies exist between papers. The organizers of the conference felt it more important to publish the papers in as timely a manner as possible rather than bringing them all into an identical format.

I wish to thank the many contributors who did submit papers. Ms. Marilyn Finn retyped much of the text and, together with Ms. Lisa Hedien and Ms. Dulce Arias, assisted with reformatting some of the pages. Dr. Kit Tan prepared the Index and also assisted in several ways. To them, I am extremely grateful and appreciative.

THOMAS S. ELIAS

California's Endangered Plants and the CNPS Rare Plant Program

James P. Smith, Jr. [1]

Abstract: Almost eight thousand ferns, fern allies, conifers, and flowering plants may be found in California. This large and complex assemblage is noted for its high degree of endemism and for its rare and endangered plants. Climate, topography, geology, soil types, genetic structure within populations, and biological interactions are often cited as the basis for these features of our flora. For almost 20 years the California Native Plant Society has been studying our state's rare plants and it has made the results available through its inventories, status reports, and informed scientific opinions and testimony.

I hope to accomplish two goals in my time with you this afternoon. The first is to provide a transition to some of the more specific talks that you will be hearing later in the symposium. I hope to do this by making some general remarks about the flora of California and to provide an overview of its rare and endemic plants. My second task is to tell you about the Rare Plant Program of the California Native Plant Society and of our efforts to learn about and to conserve our states endangered flora.

One of California's greatest natural treasures is its flora. The very numbers themselves are impressive. There are about 7700 species, subspecies, and varieties of ferns, fern allies, conifers, and flowering plants in our state. They are placed in about 1150 genera and in 170 to 175 families. Texas has more families and genera, but only about 5500 taxa. By comparison, Arizona has about 3400 species and Indiana has a flora of 2300 vascular plant species.

Early students of California floristics and plant geography recognized that we were dealing with a complex flora. It was made up of both northern and southern components and of both temperate and xeric elements. It was that greatest of all students of the California flora, Willis Linn Jepson, who stated definitively that the assemblage of plants that was most characteristic of our state extended beyond its borders. He wrote in the introduction to his 1925 <u>Manual</u>, "From the standpoint of plant provinces, the term California must be defined in a sense different from that of its political boundaries." In setting forth the differences, Jepson said, "Of the various physical features which distinguish the northern margins of the California province, the Rogue River is of the greatest importance." What we now refer to as the California Floristic Province does not extend east of the Sierra Nevada-Cascade axis. As Jepson put it, "There are, then, excluded the Colorado and Mojave deserts and the desert slopes in the south, and also the interior plateaus, slopes and ranges belonging to the Great Basin and extending from Inyo County to Modoc County and thence to eastern Siskiyou County." The California Floristic Province, an area of approximately 324,000 km^2 has more kinds of vascular plants than the central and northeastern United States and adjacent Canada combined, even though that area is ten times larger.

ENDEMISM

A striking feature of the vascular plants of the region is that almost half of them are endemic, plants that are restricted to a particular locality or habitat. The degree of endemism (47.7 per cent) is unparalleled in a continental flora. Peter Raven has calculated that 63.3 per cent of the annual dicots are endemic! Because we often apply a narrow definition of endemism obscures some important considerations. Very few plants, the common reed (<u>Phragmites australis</u>) might be considered an example, are really widespread or cosmopolitan. Most higher plants, one estimate placing it at about 90 per cent, are endemic; anywhere from a continent to a spot so small that the distribution of a plant is a single locality that is visible in its entirety. Douglas-fir (<u>Pseudotsuga menziesii</u>) is endemic to North America; coast redwood (<u>Sequoia sempervirens</u>) to California and Oregon; <u>Orcuttia viscida</u>, which has no common name, is restricted to a particular habitat in Sacramento County. The Catalina mountain-mahogany (<u>Cercocarpus traskiae</u>), which one of our speakers has

---

[1] Vice President for Rare Plants, California Native Plant Society; Professor of Botany, Humboldt State University, Arcata, CA.

labeled California's rarest trees, is known from a half dozen or so plants that are threatened by feral herbivores. All are endemics, just at different scales.

Stanley Cain suggested in 1944 there were two kinds of endemics: youthful ones where we may be observing populations that have yet to reach the limits of their natural biological barriers and relictual ones where the plants are headed toward extinction and that we are seeing their last gasps after a long evolutionary history. Stebbins and Major referred to these two categories as neoendemics and paleoendemics, respectively.

They noted that the distribution of endemics was uneven in the ten floristic subdivisions that they recognized in their 1965 paper. Neoendemics were most common in intermediate habitats in southern California, the Sierra Nevada, and the Central Coast; that the greater the variety of habitats, the higher the degree of endemism, and that low mountains contain more endemics than do high mountains. They also pointed out that at each end of the state there is a major concentration of relictual species, those plants that are the only representative or one of two species of that genus in our state and that are physically isolated from their relatives to the east by some distance. Curiously, a strong correlation exists between these relict species and a comparatively high level of precipitation during the warm season. Northwest California and southwest Oregon satisfy this criterion rather nicely. In research that John Sawyer and I have recently completed, we found there are 282 endemics, although not all of them are paleoendemics or relictual species.

It has been suggested that one the significant features of narrow endemics is that they are genetically depleted or depauperate. Indeed, some recent studies of enzyme diversity in rare and endemic plants point to very little genetic diversity in some populations. On the other hand, the California bigtree (Sequoiadendron giganteum) demonstrates that even a paleoendemic may have a wealth of diversity. Twenty-five distinct variants have been recognized in this California endemic. As Ledyard Stebbins noted in 1980, "There appears to be no recognizable correlation, either positive or negative, between the amount of genetic variation within a population of plant species and the rarity or commonness of the species as a whole."

RARITY

Related to the concept of endemism is that of rarity. Please note immediately that the former does not imply the latter. In our context, the term rare implies that the plant is unusual, uncommon, seldom encountered, few in number, forming a small or scattered group. For many of us, rareness has both a relative quantity and quality about it. For this reason many people expect a rare plant to be both infrequent and to have a certain elegance about it. We all know how awkward it is to use common names such as the clammy-bracted mudweed or the foetid lousewort for a rare and endangered plant. The words themselves work against us and sometimes so does the appearance of the plant. You can't be serious about saving that ugly thing! It's just an old weed.

Again, scale is an important consideration. A plant may be rare in the sense that the species is represented by a single population. But a particular species may be quite rare in one part of its range, but widespread elsewhere. The black crowberry (Empetrum nigrum) is rare in California, occurring only in Del Norte and Humboldt Counties, but it is widespread outside the state.

In her 1981 study, Deborah Rabinowitz recognized seven forms of rarity, noting that there were several ways in which species can become rare and that the consequences of rarity may be equally diverse. She noted that when we are talking about categories of rarity, we are taking stock of the geographic range of a species, its habitat specificity, and its local population size.

The current edition of the CNPS Inventory of Rare and Endangered Vascular Plants of California lists 950 taxa that are rare and/or endangered. It also contains an additional 499 uncommon plants of limited distribution. The occurrence of these plants is very uneven throughout the state. Sutter County has only five plants in the Inventory, while the top ten counties are San Bernardino (170 plants), San Diego (162), Siskiyou (153), Inyo (123), San Luis Obispo (113), Monterey (110), Riverside (105), and Del Norte with 98 plants.

Why does California have so many rare plants, especially so many that are endemic, and why are they so unevenly distributed? Could it be that our information about the occurrence of rare plants is an artifact. Could it be that they are found where there are roads and trails, universities, research stations; the kinds of places where botanists like to go on their vacations. I would hope that we could arrive at a more satisfying explanation.

First we have a large cast of characters to work with. Remember there are about 7700 flowering plants, gymnosperms, ferns, and fern allies, with the number of species per genus being relatively high. These plants live in our peculiar climate, a regime of dry summers and cool, wet winters. Only in the Mediterranean Basin, Chile, and parts of Australia and South Africa do we find similar climates. Each of these areas is famous for its array of rare plants. As Raven and Axelrod noted in 1977, our relatively mild climate and the mountains which insulate us from the more extreme fluctuations characteristic of a continental climate mean that the area has acted as a refuge for plants from the Tertiary. Microclimates provide the stage for even more diversification.

A second factor is topography. Within the boundaries of California are the extremes of low, tropical subdesert to habitats above timberline. A third factor is the richness of geological formations and the resulting diversity of soil types.

While climate, topography, and geology are important components of an explanation, whether taken singly or in concert, they are not sufficient. For instance, the same highly restricted serpentine barren, and we will hear much more about them from that great serpentophile Arthur Kruckeberg a little later, may yield a rare and endemic _Streptanthus_ and may also be the home of a widespread annual species of the same genus. Several recent workers have suggested that only a synthetic theory that recognizes multiple causes for rarity will prove satisfactory. Stebbins has proposed a model that takes into account the various ecological factors, the genetic structure of populations, and the past history of the evolutionary lines concerned in his "gene pool/niche interaction theory," a complex title for a complicated biological situation. We must also recognize the role of predators and the interactions of plants with other organisms, such as pollinators and fungi.

THE CNPS RARE PLANT PROGRAM

Given the richness and beauty of our flora and that many of our state's citizens point to it as one of the features that makes California "California," it is not surprising that the study of rare plants would be one of the major educational, scientific, and conservation efforts of the California Native Plant Society.

It all started in 1968 when G. Ledyard Stebbins, who was President of CNPS at the time, put together a card file of California vascular plants having a distribution of less than one hundred miles, based upon the data in Munz, _A California Flora_. Stebbins enlisted the aid of several individuals in this fledgling effort. Chief among them were Roman Gankin and W. Robert Powell. Over the next three years, Gankin would compile a list of almost 800 plants. This was the basis of the first official CNPS list. It appeared in 1971 and was made up of 520 plants. Three other lists were prepared in 1973 and 1974, these under the direction of Bob Powell, the new CNPS Rare Plant Project Director.

From the beginning, the CNPS studies have relied on first-hand knowledge derived from herbarium and field studies. Documentation was essential. So was critical review by field botanists. When I use the term "botanist," I wish to make it clear that I mean both the amateur and the professional student of plants. Our entire program has benefited greatly from the generous and competent efforts of the amateur.

Almost fifteen years ago, the Society began making photographs or photocopies of herbarium labels on rare plant specimens in collections around the state. The early phase of this effort, along with plotting plant locations on topographic maps, was funded by the Office of Planning and Research of the State of California. A contract, arranged in large part by Leslie Hood, Director of CNACC, provided the initial support to hire botanists to do this work. Thousands of specimens were photographed and hundreds of locations plotted. This detailed mapping and the confirmation of the continued existence of plants and the changes in population size continue today.

In July 1974, a number of botanists from around the state gathered on the University of California, Davis campus for a rare plant evaluation and mapping session. It was an exciting meeting-- an occasion to share our mutual knowledge, ignorance, hopes, and frustrations concerning California's rare and endangered vascular plants.

A major result of all of this appeared in December of that same year-- the first edition of the CNPS _Inventory of the Rare and Endangered Vascular Plants of California_. Edited by W. Robert Powell, it was a detailed compilation of rare plant data. It became the most widely used reference on the subject; a prime source of information for consultants, conservationists, botanists, and the staffs of county, state, and federal agencies.

In its main list were 704 plants of primary concern, taxa that were very rare and rare and endangered. A second list of 556 plants constituted a group of rare, but not presently endangered, plants. An appendix listed 134 plants that were not rare nor endangered, but which were of limited distribution.

Even before the publication of the first edition, it was recognized that attempts to classify plants solely on the basis of the degree to which they were threatened was too restrictive. The concept of rarity was interfering with that of endangerment. While it had been observed that, with few exceptions, endangered plants were also rare plants, some taxa of more widespread occurrence were endangered and their numbers diminished because of commercial and private exploitation for horticultural use. Many of the lilies, cacti, orchids, succulents, and insectivorous plants fall into this category. People like to take them home, plant them, and then watch them die.

In an attempt to address this problem, CNPS developed what was at first a scheme that would allow for the independent coding of four coordinate elements. In its current form, that code takes into account three of them: rarity, endangerment, and distribution. Rarity is a judgement of the extent of the plant, both in terms of the number of individuals and the nature and extent of distribution. The scoring of endangerment recognizes that a particular plant may or may not be threatened with extinction in some or all of its range. To this vocabulary we add the new term threatened, which you will also be hearing about later. The coding of distribution allows us to recognize that a plant may be endemic to California, but also to speak to its occurrence outside of the state. Then, as now, more distribution information was also presented in terms of counties and the United States Geological Survey topographic quadrangle maps.

Inventories have a major drawback. They are inevitably out-of-date by the time they are published. Errors, omissions, and inconsistencies needed correcting. A large volume of new rare plant data had been gathered, much of it provided by the users themselves. Field studies, carried out by Forest Service, Fish and Wildlife Service, and Bureau of Land Management botanists, were a second important source of new information. So were CNPS members in the chapters around the state. Another source of data was also generated by the Society itself. Beginning in 1977, CNPS contracted with the U. S. Forest Service and with the California Department of Fish and Game to prepare several hundred status reports on rare and endangered plants. These invaluable summaries of up-to-date information were prepared under the supervision and editorship of Alice Q. Howard and R. Jane Cole.

In late 1979, the whole process repeated itself. There was a second U. C. Davis conference. About fifty botanists helped to amend and to correct provisional lists that had been prepared for the proposed second edition of the CNPS Inventory. It appeared in May 1980. There were several changes in format. This time, 1383 taxa were arrayed in four lists, the first one titled "Presumed Extinct in California". This was done in an effort to bring special attention to 44 plants that were then known from historic collections only. Of course, it then became a challenge to see if any of them could be rediscovered and several of them were! I should also point out that the California Department of Fish and Game adopted the second edition of the Inventory as its list of species-of-concern.

The effort needed to produce a new edition of the Inventory, to prepare status reports, and to issue Supplements, along with many other aspects of our rare plant program, made one thing very clear. CNPS had become the victim of its own success. What had started out as a stack of index cards in 1968 had become the largest rare plant data base in the United States. The quantity of information was so great that it was overwhelming the ability of a volunteer organization to process it. Although there had been some limited use of a Burroughs 6700 computer to produce the first edition of the Inventory, CNPS was still relying heavily on manual files and volunteer labor. Could we continue to be effective under those circumstances?

Early in 1980, the Rare Plant Program faced another very serious problem. For years our rare plant files and maps had been housed at the University of California, Davis; first at the Arboretum and later at the Institute of Ecology. Now that space was no longer available and we had to relocate our office.

Offers for space came in from a variety of sources: universities, consulting firms, the Endangered Plant Program of the California Department of Fish and Game, and from a newly established group, the California Natural Diversity Data Base (CNDDB). This new organization was the result of a cooperative effort between The Nature Conservancy and the Department of Fish and Game. Each option was weighed carefully and after much debate the Society signed a contract with the Natural Diversity Data Base. And, for the first time in our Rare Plant Program, CNPS hired a full-time botanist, Rick York, who has been with us ever since, as many of you know from your contacts with the CNPS Rare Plant Office. By combining our efforts, the goals of both organizations could be met and duplication could be avoided. An important benefit to us was the computerization of our rare plant data. Back then such terms as relational data bases, interactive graphics, and digitizing were all part of a strange new language. Today we know them as techniques for allowing us to manipulate the way in which data are stored, retrieved, and presented. Through the generosity of CNPS members, the Rare Plant Program was also able to purchase a microcomputer, printer, and software. Having had editorial responsibilities in both the second and the third editions of the Inventory, I cannot tell you how much difference having that microcomputer has made.

The CNPS-CNDDB contract was to last for one year, but soon after it went into effect discussions proceeded about the possibility of turning this into a more permanent relationship. The combined effort had been a success from the start, as seen in the increased contribution and use of rare plant data and by the productive collaboration of the staff botanists. Since that time the relationship has continued and has flourished, in no small part because of the abilities of Rick York, Deborah Jensen, Susan Cochrane, and others. Our most recent agreement with the department, signed just a few months ago, recognizes not only our continuing cooperative efforts with the Data Base, but also with other entities, especially the Endangered Plant Program and its botanist, Susan Cochrane.

Why has CNPS expended so much time, energy, and money to gather all of this rare plant information? There is, to be sure, the intellectual satisfaction that derives from the knowledge itself. However, compilation is not, in and of itself, the goal. The data are a means for accomplishing one of the Society's major goals-- the preservation of rare plants and their habitats. The California Native Plant Society's responsibilities are best served by complete and accurate information upon which to make sound judgments and recommendations.

I like to think that our Rare Plant Program has contributed directly to a number of successes, such as the passage of the Native Plant Protection Act. This legislation, sponsored by Senator John Nejedly, required the California Department of Fish and Game to establish criteria for determining whether a native plant was rare or endangered, to inventory plants, to list them, and to make it unlawful to import or take, possess or sell them within the state. The work of CNPS rare plant people, especially that of Alice Howard, made a difference.

It has become axiomatic to say that if you want to save rare plants, you must save their habitats, a generality which some experts believe should be examined more critically. Saving specific areas has always been one of the Society's principal efforts. Many names come to mind-- Vine Hill, Butterfly Valley, Huckleberry Trail, the Lanphere-Christensen Dunes, Ring Mountain, Ione, San Bruno Mountain, San Luis Island, Ford Ord, the Presidio of San Francisco, the Nipomo Dunes. And the successes, especially at the chapter level in working out conservation easements, fashioning mitigation plans, affecting the language in local coastal plans have all benefited from our data base of rare plant information.

Although there are gaps to be filled, errors to be corrected, and refinements to be made, the information is there, in an increasingly accurate and accessible form. The challenge for all of us is to use it wisely.

SUGGESTED READINGS

Ayensu, E. S.; DeFilips, R. A. Endangered and threatened plants of the United States. Washington, D. C.: Smithsonian Institution and the World Wildlife Fund; 1978. 403 p.

Drury, W. H. Rare plant species. Rhodora 82:49-75; 1980.

Harper, J. L. The meaning of rarity. In: Synge, H., editor. The biological aspects of rare plant conservation. New York, NY: John Wiley & Sons; 1981; 189-203.

Hood, L. What's next for endangered plants? Fremontia 4(1):14-16; 1976.

Howard, A. Q. The legal position of rare plants today. Fremontia 5(4):17-21; 1978.

Jepson, W. L. A manual of the flowering plants of California. Berkeley, CA: University of California Press; 1925: 3,4; 11-14.

Kruckeberg, A. R.; D. Rabinowitz. Biological aspects of endemism in higher plants. Annual Review of Ecology and Systematics 16:447-479; 1985.

Lewis, H. The origin of endemics in the California flora. In: Valentine, D. H. Taxonomy, phytogeography and evolution. New York, NY: Academic Press; 1972; 179-188.

Morse, L. E.; Henifen, M. S. Rare plant conservation: geographical data organization. Bronx, NY: New York Botanical Garden; 1981. 377 p.

Powell, W. R. The CNPS Inventory-- a progress report. Fremontia 5(4):28, 29; 1975.

Powell, W. R.; Duncan, T.; Howard, A. Q. The California Native Plant Society Rare Plant Project. In: Morse, L. E.; Henifin, editors. Rare plant conservation: geographical data organization. Bronx, NY: New York Botanical Garden; 1981; 193-198.

Prance, G. T.; Elias, T. S. Extinction is forever: threatened and endangered species of plants in the Americas and their significance in ecosystems today and in the future. Bronx, NY: New York Botanical Garden; 1977. 437 p.

Rabinowitz, D. Seven forms of rarity. In: Synge, H., editor. The biological aspects of rare plant conservation. New York, NY: John Wiley & Sons; 1981; 205-217.

Rabinowitz, D. Biologists' attitudes toward rare species. Plant Science Bulletin 31(6):41, 42; 1985.

Raven, P. H. The importance of preserving species. Fremontia 11(1):9-12; 1983.

Reveal, J. L.; Broome, C. R. Plant rarity-- real and imagined. The Nature Conservancy News 29(2):4-8; 1979.

Simmons, J. B.; Beyer, R. I.; Brandham, P. E.; Lucas, G.; Parry, V. T. H. Conservation of threatened plants. New York, NY: Plenum Press; 1976. 336 p.

Smith, J. P., Jr.; York, R. Inventory of rare and endangered vascular plants of California. Special Publication No. 1. Third edition. Berkeley, CA: California Native Plant Society; 1984. 174 p.

Stebbins, G. L. Why are there so many rare plants in California? I. Environmental factors. Fremontia 5(4):6-10; 1978a.

Stebbins, G. L. Why are there so many rare plants in California? II. Youth and age of species. Fremontia 6(1):17-20; 1978b.

Stebbins, G. L. Rarity of plant species: a synthetic viewpoint. Rhodora 82:77-86; 1980.

Stebbins, G. L.; Major, J. Endemism and speciation in the California flora. Ecological Monographs 35:1-35; 1965.

Synge, H. The biological aspects of rare plant conservation. New York, NY: John Wiley & Sons; 1981. 558 p.

York, R.; Smith, J. P., Jr.; Cochrane, S. New developments in the rare-plant program. Fremontia 9(4):11-13; 1982.

The Potential for Permanent Plant Protection

Faith Thompson Campbell [1]

Abstract: To ensure "permanent" protection for plant species, we must implement a comprehensive conservation program which emphasize reserves and regulation of human exploitation. *Ex Situ* programs can supplement *in situ* measures, but cannot in themselves ensure the persistence and natural evolution of plant species and communities.

Governments are best suited to carrying out such a program, especially on the global scale. Governments also influence related processes of economic development and population growth.

Conservationists, including members of the California Native Plant Society, should actively pressure governments to act.

I appreciate the opportunity to participate in the Conference on Endangered and Rare Plants. This gathering provides a wonderful opportunity to further conservation of endangered plants not just here, but throughout the country and around the world.

I have been asked to address the prospects for "permanent" plant protection. By this, I understand that our goal is to ensure the ability of plant species and communities to persist and evolve over thousands and millions of years in the future -- until some natural development such as a change in the Sun's power puts an end to Earth as we know it. We cannot succeed completely; some plant species will become extinct. However, by working hard to overcome the obstacles, I think we can ensure long-term protection for a high proportion of currently extant plant species.

For several reasons, I believe we must stress actions by governments and focus on *in situ* conservation techniques.

Governments are the institutions which will determine whether life itself will persist on this planet. On the broadest level, we must somehow persuade every government, not just our own, that the immense destruction to the biosphere that would result from nuclear war or world-wide chemical warfare is just too high a price to pay for "national security". We must further convince governments and economic interests that slower but inexorable processes can have similar catastrophic effects. These include major climatic changes caused by the buildup of "greenhouse" gases or destruction of the ozone layer and exhaustion of the biosphere by the demands of a rapidly rising human population.

We must also induce governments to devote considerably more resources to specific conservation programs if we are to have any hopes of saving a reasonable sample of the earth's floral diversity. I say this because governments are best suited to implementing major *in situ* conservation programs. Furthermore, they are as "permanent" as any human institutions other than churches, and have more resources than those, such as universities and conservation organizations, which have an interest in protecting biological diversity.

In emphasizing the importance of governmental action, I do not want to imply that there is not room for considerable non-governmental effort. Indeed there is room for much more of this activity. Non-governmental institutions have and probably will continue to lead the way in many areas. They can establish and maintain reserves and such *ex situ* facilities as botanical gardens and seed banks; promote and apply vital scientific research; and train conservationists in a wide variety of skills. To me, however, their most important role is to build the political determination to *do* something effective to counter the extinction crisis.

---

[1] Natural Resources Defense Council Washington, D.C.

What does such an effective program include? I believe that it must encompass a broad range of techniques, but the emphasis must be on in situ methods. Despite the inevitable compromises, I believe that this approach holds the greatest promise.

First, if my opening assumption is correct -- that our shared goal is to preserve plant species as functioning, evolving components of ecosystems and not as some museum piece -- only in situ techniques have any chance of even partial success. Ex situ programs, valuable as they are for other purposes, simply do not protect functioning natural ecosystems.

Second, reserves allow the species to continue to evolve -- a natural process in itself and one which generates additional biological diversity.

Third, on site conservation allows protection of the maximum range of known and unknown species. I assume we are not such chauvinists as to be indifferent to the survival of members of other kingdoms. In reality, of course, we often do not known enough about functioning ecosystems to decide what the ideal reserve would be. Furthermore, reserves are established with borders that do not conform to ecosystem boundaries. External pollutants stray into the reserve and wreak their havoc. Nevertheless, our chances of preserving a wide range of species appear to be much greater with this approach.

In situ conservation serves other purposes as well, such as preserving beautiful or inspiring sites.

To a certain extent, reserves can take care of themselves after certain threats are removed. Such threats include over-collecting, pollutants at levels the target species or communities cannot withstand, absence of large herbivores or wildfire or some other factor which cannot be restored. Management to control these threats should be less expensive than intensive management in a garden of each species or even groups of species.

Finally, if there are sufficient numbers and volume of such reserves, they can help ensure the continuation of the "ecological services" which we all take advantage of -- the oxygen, carbon and nitrogen cycles; cleansing of surface water; prevention of soil erosion; provision of pollinators for our crops and yard plants, etc.

Indeed, often there are compatible human uses of the area, if they are carefully managed.

In situ conservation is not without costs, of course. There are numerous expenses involved in the establishment and maintenance of reserves, expecially systems involving large numbers of sizable reserves. How large an area do we mean when we suggest reserves encompassing "entire ecosystems"? These costs include not just the cash outlays for land acquisition and staff salaries, but also the opportunity costs of not using those reserve areas for other purposes which have social value and which may have a higher worth calculated in strictly economic terms. These opportunity costs will probably become more difficult to counter as the human population continues to grow and as over-exploitation reduces productivity of other areas.

A further complication is that the beneficiaries of the conservation action may not be the same people as those who pay the most direct costs. For example, conservationists in the United States call for the establishment of large reserves in remaining areas of tropical forests. We recognize the value of protecting those plants and other species, and believe -- I contend rightly -- that the long-term benefits will accrue to all people. But to the landless peasant of northeastern Brazil, the denial of an opportunity to farm a patch of Amazon forests -- even if only for a few years -- is much more immediate than a long-term, generalized payoff resulting from the conservation of biological diversity.

So the major weakness of in situ conservation is that we just cannot do it right. We lack the scientific knowledge to know what is necessary. Equally important, we lack the political ability to do what is necessary.

Ex situ conservation methods, I believe are important primarily as supplements to in situ approaches. Their principal advantage is in providing easy access to genetic materials for research and manipulation. Collections can assemble geographically and ecologically diverse species of interest for a particular purpose. Laboratory and other facilities are available to permit careful experimentation. At the present time, such collections are dominated by plants of interest in agriculture, but the system should be expanded to include plants valuable in horticulture, medicine, or industry. These collections enable people to utilize botanic diversity efficiently and with little impact on remaining wild populations. This is a valuable goal, but it does not constitute "permanent protection".

Research on living collections can strengthen conservation in the wild by answering questions about the species' biological needs and ecological relationships and by providing propagative material for reintroduction. These are certainly important contributions. But care must be taken to minimize adaptation of the captive material to the conditions of the greenhouse -- and away from natural ecosystems.

Another particularly valuable contribution of living collections is public education. Our success in conserving the world's flora will depend on public support, which is still far from adequate. Most Americans don't even know that plants can be "endangered," much less comprehend why they should care. Botanical gardens and arboreta can help generate the emotional commitment that is essential to success.

Finally, the expense of establishing and maintaining plant collections falls to a greater extent on people who choose to shoulder the burden.

As I said before, however, I believe that _ex situ_ methods of conservation should serve primarily to complement _in situ_ techniques. The primary reason is that plant species are not the only biological values that should be conserved. Whatever our underlying purpose in conserving species -- a spiritual belief in the right to life, aesthetic enjoyment, or a conviction that human life depends on a healthy ecosystem and utilization of the "products" derived from particular species -- saving individual species of plants is not going to be sufficient.

Ex situ conservation has other disadvantages too. Some are technical -- for example, certain species are extremely difficult or impossible to maintain either in growing collections or in seed banks. Freezers and greenhouses can suffer catastrophic losses due to power failures or other accidents. Furthermore, long-term, constant care and maintenance of adequate records are expensive and sponsoring institutions may lose interest. These risks can be reduced by establishing duplicate collections at several sites. But this increases the expense. Furthermore, it is impossible to establish enough collections to house a large proportion of the earth's plant species.

It would be particularly hard to obtain funding for the many species which have no currently perceived economic value.

If we agree that governments must carry the bulk of the conservation task, where do we stand in bringing this about?

Over the past decade, a steady stream of books, articles, television documentaries, and conferences have raised enormously public awareness of threats to biological diversity. Scientists and public administrators have joined to fashion strategies for action -- the IUCN World Conservation Strategy of 1980 and the World Resources Institute/World Bank tropical forest strategy of 1985 are just two examples. Activists are engaging in product boycotts and street marches.

But so far we have not stimulated a great increase in commitment by the United States government or others around the world. We lack a comprehensive program at either the national or international level to conserve biological diversity. Worse, we seem stuck in a period of reduced expectations and inertia. We can't even reauthorize the Endangered Species Act.

We do have pieces of a program, but these pieces need to be strengthened and the gaps between them should be filled.

Domestically, the Endangered Species Act is the most important component of the existing patchwork program. Its importance stems first from its relative strength and its specific statement that species "are of esthetic, ecological, educational, historical, recreational, and scientific value to the nation and its people" and that said species and the habitats on which they depend should be conserved.

Second, the Endangered Species Act was the first statute to give the federal government authority to conserve plant species.

The language of the statute is strong, but not perfect. One problem is that it provides for the listing of species, subspecies, and geographic populations of vertebrates, but only of species and subspecies of invertebrates and plants. It requires all federal agencies to "utilize their authorities" to protect listed species and to avoid any actions which are likely to jeopardize a species' continued existence or adversely modify its critical habitat. However, it has little power over actions by private parties or non-federal agencies. Furthermore, Section 7 is said by the federal government to apply only inside the United States, not abroad. Although a lawsuit is now pending, it may take Congressional amendment to extend Section 7 abroad, and such a move appears highly unlikely in the present climate. Finally, the Act prohibits killing, harassing, collecting, or possessing all listed faunal species, but prohibits only collecting listed plant species from federal lands and interstate and international commerce in them.

Recent efforts to strengthen the legal protection for plant species by outlawing malicious destruction of plants and collecting from non-federal lands without the permission of the landowner were defeated by the Congress.

The Endangered Species Act has been further weakened by its implementation. Few agencies put much effort into recovery efforts for listed species. The Environmental Protection Agency has virtually ignored the law in approving pesticides for use on crops and rangeland. Development projects have been pushed through despite their likely or certain damage to endangered species. Compromises are a political fact of life -- but we must try to ensure that they do not result in the extinction of species and the undermining of the purposes of the Act. Strong public support will help us to prevail in contests with particular development projects.

The power of public action can be demonstrated by the implementation of the Act for plants. This has never been as strong as that for animals. Pressure on Congress in 1982 resulted in a speed-up in listing plant species, which now proceeds on an equitable basis. This year we have focused Congressional attention on law enforcement, which has been abysmal. I would remind you that while habitat loss is by far the greatest cause of extinction, over-collecting is a severe threat for some types of plants. Even when eager would-be "rescuers" or "owners" are not finishing off some isolated population, the cumulative impacts of wholesale collecting may represent a significant drain on the species and this activity should be regulated. One couple in Michigan, recently convicted for illegal sale of ladyslipper orchids, had brokered the sale of up to 100,000 plants per year in some years.

The Fish and Wildlife Service has the lead responsibility in protecting terrestrial endangered species, including plants. Nevertheless, endangered species constitutes only about 7% of the service's overall operating budget, and this may decline further under the pressures of Gramm-Rudman-Hollings. Most National Wildlike Refuges continue to be established and managed for the production of game animals. Only two -- Ash Meadows and Antioch Dunes -- include plants as a significant management component.

The U.S. has no nationwide program to identify and protect biologically significant sites. One result is that centers of endemism such as Ash Meadows have been allowed to slip from government ownership and to be threatened by development. It required considerable political muscle and money borrowed by The Nature Conservancy to restore protection to part of this area.

The National Park Service has a protectionist philosophy, but units in the system were chosen for their recreational and scenic values and only incidentally for their biological riches. If units of the National Park system ever become major reservoirs of biological diversity, it will probably be because we have decimated the biological diversity of other public and private lands.

Our other public lands, managed primarily by the Bureau of Land Management and the Forest Service, do shelter considerable numbers of endangered species, including plants. These agencies have a clear legal responsibility to protect endangered species, yet they undermine this goal through their policies, their budgets, and their staffing levels. BLM has at least 122 federally listed species, 45 of them plants. Twenty-five percent are found in California. There are another 700 - 1,000 "candidate" species on the land managed by BLM, including 600-800 plant species. The Forest Service has 125 listed species plus 12 proposed species, 11% of them in California. Another 700 candidates, 80% of them plants, are found on the national forests and grasslands. These agencies, especially BLM, have completely inadequate budgets for managing wildlife -- $15 million and $50 million respectively. Most of this money is spent on mammals and birds. The agencies' staffs are small, and include a paltry number of botanists -- 7 for BLM, 16 for the Forest Service. Lobbying of Congress and pressure on these agencies has resulted in increased attention to plants. BLM and Forest Service biologists have developed "wish-lists" of projects that include significant botanical components. Congress this year instructed both agencies to increase their botanical staffs. Especially coming at a time of fiscal constraint and a hostile administration, these small but significant improvements show that political pressure does make a difference.

The public land agencies have a few, low-profile programs to identify and set aside areas of particular biological richness. The Research Natural Area program is 60 years old; 8 federal land-managing agencies participate. There are at least 446 RNAs totaling over 4.5 million acres. Some, however, are quite small -- even one acre; many are 100 acres or less. In addition, BLM may designate areas of critical environmental concern -- which of course are not limited to areas of biological importance. Designation of areas under both programs varies considerably depending on the proclivities of the BLM or Forest Service managers on the ground. California has a political climate favoring such designations, so it has the most ACECs - 102 - and a significant number of RNAs -- more than 35. However, these small "islands", even if properly sited and managed, cannot protect biological diversity by themselves in the face of continued mismanagement of the surrounding public lands. Unfortunately, the BLM's and the Forest Service's single-minded dedication to commodity production, especially livestock and timber, causes considerable damage to the public's biological resources. Congress must be persuaded to end the taxpayer subsidies that encourage this destruction.

Other programs can complement the lagging federal effort. The Nature Conservancy, University of California, and other institutions operate their own system of reserves. Many states have natural area programs. But all these efforts need to be broadened -- and they would benefit from coordination as well. At a minimum, the Federal Interagency Committee which coordinated the land-managing agencies' programs of ecological reserves should be revived and representatives of the private and state players included.

"Our" piece of the earth -- the United States -- is a wonderful garden, but the majority of the planet's floral species exist elsewhere. A program to provide "permanent" protection for plants must therefore include international efforts.

Again, we have pieces of a program, but it needs to be broadened.

The most direct way to contribute to conservation abroad is to put your own money and expertise to work. World Wildlife Fund and The Nature Conservancy carry out projects abroad. The former sponsors field research and conservation projects. TNC is creating "heritage-like" data centers in several American countries.

Some U.S. government agencies also do conservation work in other countries. The Fish and Wildlife Service and National Park Service have tiny programs designed to help train and provide technical help to their counterparts in the Western Hemisphere and India. I believe that it would significantly help conservation if we could obtain funding from Congress to expand these programs into Africa and the rest of Asia.

Several international treaties have been adopted to promote conservation; a few include plants explicitly. The treaty with the largest membership is the Convention on International Trade in Endangered Species of Wild Fauna and Flora (CITES), with over 90 party countries. CITES seeks to prevent over-exploitation from decimating wild populations. To control trade, CITES requires a person who wishes to import or export certain kinds of plants to obtain a permit from the exporting country. If the plant is a wild-collected specimen of a species considered "endangered" and listed in Appendix I, that person must obtain an import permit as well. The need to implement CITES led Congress to include plants in the U.S. Endangered Species Act of 1973.

CITES is controversial for several reasons, among them the inclusion of all cacti and orchids on the appendices, the requirement that propagated plants also be documented, and the bureaucratic hassles, in this country and abroad, associated with seeking permits. Time does not permit me to discuss CITES in detail, but I will say that over-exploitation is an important factor in endangering certain species of plants. Dr. Edward Anderson studied 23 species of Mexican cacti this summer on a grant from the World Wildlife Fund. He reports that 61% of the species he studied are threatened primarily by over-collecting; another 17% are threatened by a combination of over-collecting and habitat loss.

CITES does suffer from poor implementation in this country and abroad. From my perspective, inadequate law enforcement means that too many traders still escape punishment for violating treaty protections. Many hobbyists and dealers complain about bureaucratic bungling and red tape. Some bureaucracy is inevitable. However, as long as the government is not deterring cheaters, you get the hassles but conservation is not advanced. I urge you to join in pressing for better implementation and more aggressive enforcement.

A regional treaty, the Western Hemisphere Convention, seeks to protect "in their native habitat representatives of all species of (party countries') native flora and fauna" and "regions and natural objects of aesthetic, historic, or scientific value, and areas characterized by primitive conditions." Negotiated in 1940, the treaty has been signed by 19 countries. It provides the foundation for several Latin American countries' conservation laws and the basis for the FWS and NPS Technical Assistance Programs that I mentioned before.

Some other treaties and agreements, such as the World Heritage Convention and Man and the Biosphere Program, have promoted protection of natural areas, especially in the developing world. Neither is expressly intended to protect centers of endemism, however. The United States' participation in both programs has fluctuated in recent years, thus undermining what good they can do.

As I noted at the beginning, these treaties and programs are pieces, not a comprehensive whole. We need a comprehensive package that would result in creation and maintenance of a global network of reserves protecting centers of endemism and effective regulation of human use of wild species. The International Union for Conservation of Nature and Natural Resources (IUCN) tries to lead the process by setting priorities, stimulating coordinated action, and funding some projects. IUCN is hampered in this work by its small staff and few funds. The California Native Plant Society is a member of IUCN. It might wish to help lobby the government to provide a voluntary contribution to the IUCN.

The greatest obstacle to realization of a global conservation program is not scientific, but economic. Who will pay for creating and maintaining reserves and regulating harvest? Even more difficult, who will provide alternative livelihoods for the people who would be displaced? Some estimate that we need $100 million per year. Several ideas are circulating; some would cancel various countries' debts in exchange for conservation projects, others would have the developed countries contribute to a conservation fund, perhaps in exchange for "access" to genetic resources. The very premise is controversial, and the details will be extremely difficult to work out. It is vital that we continue to press for progress.

To have any chance of success in the long term, conservation must be linked to equitable and ecologically sustainable economic development in the third world and to slowing the growth in human population. If these problems are not successfully addressed, the struggles of the vast majority to scrape out a bare existence or to better themselves will overwhelm reserves and deny funding to other conservation programs. On the other side of the coin, development assistance must be carried out in a more ecologically sensitive manner. There is still time to steer development to less harmful sites and more productive forms -- but a decade or two from now, such choices will no longer be available.

There has been some progress on this front. Thanks to pressure from the Natural Resources Defense Council and other environmental organizations, the U.S. Agency for International Development now conducts environmental assessments of virtually all its projects. We continue our pressure on AID to incorporate concern about biological diversity into these evaluations. New legislation requiring special protection for tropical forests recently passed Congress. We also seek AID funding for projects explicitly designed to conserve biological diversity. AID already has authority to assist in the establishment and maintenance of sanctuaries and reserves, enforcement of anti-poaching measures, and identification and cataloguing of animal and plant species. Unfortunately, AID has hesitated to fund such projects, so we have persuaded Congress to order AID to spend $2.5 million on such projects in the current fiscal year.

Congress has also responded to environmental organizations' criticism of other development agencies, particularly the World Bank and various regional banks, for their very poor environmental record. Congressional instructions to the U.S. representatives to these banks, highly publicized hearings, and other tactics have resulted in some reluctant changes at the World Bank which we hope will now pick up speed. There has been less progress at the Inter-American Development Bank, but we continue to apply pressure.

These foreign assistance programs lack public support in the United States and consequently suffer disproportionate budget cuts. I contend that conservationists cannot allow this to continue. Our hopes for saving a significant proportion of the earth's plant (and animal) species are tied too closely to developing countries' struggles. I believe that we should become strong, vocal advocates for economic development assistance -- as long as it is environmentally sensitive.

Even worse is the plight of programs to slow population growth. These have been caught in the debate over abortion. As a result, funding for AID's population program has fluctuated. More worrisome is a policy denying support to foreign non-governmental organizations if they so much as counsel people about abortion. The U.S. has also cut off funds to the major non-governmental organization active around the world, The International Planned Parenthood Federation; and to the United Nations Fund for Population Activities. Probably even worse is the poisonous atmosphere surrounding the subject; some members of Congress just do not want to be seen supporting population programs.

I would like to conclude with a frankly political message. Conservation -- of plants or of anything else -- is a political act. Our success will be determined just as much, if not more, in the political as in the scientific arena. True, we do not yet know everything we need to know about what is threatened, how it is threatened, and how best to conserve it. But we cannot wait for answers.

I suggest that every conference on conservation should contain a political component that every participant should attend. Each conference, meeting, even book, article, or video on the subject, should aim at developing or promoting a plan of action. That plan should be coordinated with, and aim to further, at least one of the numerous existing plans that lack nothing in inspiration and credibility, but that nevertheless languish. Said plans should include ways of reaching out beyond the choir, of educating people who have never heard of endangered plants or biological diversity. They should include a coordinated program to raise the issues generally, and the specific plan of action, with elected officials.

The California Native Plant Society potentially has a leadership role because your membership is so large and you are located in a state with such political clout at the national level. As a society, you cannot become involved in partisan politics -- but you can educate your members about the issues and the California delegation's position on the. And individual members should consider becoming more involved in the political process. At the very least, you should vote as if life on Earth depended on the outcome. Because it does.

The Federal Listing of Rare and Endangered Plants: What Is Involved and What Does It Mean?

Jim A. Bartel [1]

Abstract: A discussion of the Endangered Species Act of 1973, as amended, is presented to clarify misconceptions and misinformation regarding this important Federal law. Focusing primarily on listing (Section 4) and interagency cooperation (Section 7), topics discussed include: assessment of status of non-listed plants; history and development of candidate species list (notice of review); listing procedures and priorities; data needs for proposing species; protection afforded candidate, proposed, and listed plants; and a brief overview of the consultation process.

The Senate and House of the 93rd Congress of the United States passed the "Endangered Species Act" (ESA) on the 19th and 20th of December 1973 respectively. Signed by President Nixon eight days later, the ESA repealed much of the "Endangered Species Conservation Act of 1969", which replaced the "Endangered Species Preservation Act of 1966". Designed by Congress to slow or stop anthropogenic extinctions of "various species of fish, wildlife, and plants in the United States", the ESA also protects foreign species and species threatened by non-human causes (Drabelle 1985). As a result, this new law extended Federal protection for the first time to plants and animals other than vertebrates, mollusks, and crustaceans (Bean 1983). Although amended several times since its passage in 1973, the ESA remains essentially intact.

Although the authorities of the ESA have been discussed in other articles and books (Bean 1983 and 1986, Bartel 1984, Drabelle 1985, Smith 1986), considerable confusion remains within the botanical community regarding Federal listing nomenclature and procedures pursuant to Section 4 of the ESA, as amended (Publ. L. 93-205, 16 U.S.C. 1531 et seq.). Recent journal articles erroneously reporting the "status" of particular plants under the ESA illustrate this widespread confusion (Barkworth and Linman 1984, Becking 1986). Moreover, many individuals, uncertain of the legal ramifications of Federal listing, have confused protections accorded non-listed plants by some Federal agencies (i.e., U.S. Forest Service, Bureau of Land Management, Fish and Wildlife Service) on lands under their jurisdiction with mandates of the ESA. Additional requirements and restrictions provided by State and local law point to the need for further clarification on the provisions of the ESA.

TERMINOLOGY

The words "endangered" and "threatened" are often used loosely or interchangeably as pronouns or adjectives within a variety of reports and articles. Nonetheless, crucial legal differences exist between listed "endangered" and "threatened" species, "proposed" endangered and threatened species, and "candidate" species under the provisions of the ESA and its implementing regulations (Bartel 1984). Discrimination between these terms is essential because the level of protection afforded these three groups varies greatly (Bartel 1984).

Section 3 (16 U.S.C. 1532) of the ESA defines an "endangered species" as any species, including "subspecies" [50 CFR 424.02 (k)], that is in "danger of extinction throughout all or a significant portion of its range" [50 CFR 424.02 (e)]. The U.S. Fish and Wildlife Service (Service) considers "varieties" to be "subspecies" and, thus, "species" under the ESA (Federal Register 43:17912-17913). This section of the ESA further defines "threatened species" as any species "likely to become an endangered species within the foreseeable future throughout all or a significant portion of its range [50 CFR 424.02 (m)]. "Federally-listed" or "listed", often used in conjunction with "endangered" or "threatened", indicates that a species has been the subject of a proposed and final rule or regulation in the Federal Register.

---

[1] Staff Botanist and Section 10 Coordinator, Fish and Wildlife Service, U.S. Department of Interior, Sacramento, CA

"Proposed" endangered and threatened species are those species for which a proposed regulation has been published in the Federal Register, but not a final rule.

"Candidate" means any species being considered by the Service for listing as an endangered and threatened species, but not yet the subject of a proposed rule [50 CFR 424.02 (b)]. Within the notice for plants, as well as vertebrates and invertebrates, the Service defined candidate species as those taxa either in category 1 or 2. Category 1 candidates are "taxa for which the Service currently has on file substantial information on biological vulnerability [relating to autecology and distribution] and threat(s) to support the appropriateness of proposing to list the taxa as endangered or threatened species." The development and publication of proposed rules for these plants will take several years (Bartel 1984). Category 2 candidates are "[t]axa for which information now in the possession of the Service indicates that proposing to list them as endangered or threatened species is possibly appropriate, but for which substantial data on biological vulnerability and threat(s) are not currently known or on file to support the immediate preparation of rules." Thus, the two categories delimit level of information and not degree of threat or biological vulnerability.

The non-candidates (plants previously considered candidates and included on past lists), which constitute category 3, have been excluded because these taxa are known to be extinct (3A), taxonomically invalid or not meeting the Service's definition of a "species" (3B), or too widespread or not threatened at this time (3C).

HISTORY OF CANDIDATE SPECIES LISTS

Recognizing a special need to conserve endangered and threatened plants, Congress through Section 12 of the ESA directed the Secretary of the Smithsonian Institution, in conjunction with other affected agencies, to review and report on species of plants that are now or may become endangered or threatened and to describe methods for their conservation, including recommendations for new legislation or amendments to existing legislation. Congress set a deadline of 1 year from the date of enactment of the ESA for the receipt of this report. On 9 January 1975, the Secretary of the Smithsonian Institution delivered the required report (House Document 94-51), which identified 3,187 vascular plants for the United States (including Hawaii) as "extinct", "endangered", or "threatened". House Document 94-51, however, did not confer any legal status to these species.

The Smithsonian report detailed also nine recommendations for the conservation of plants. Within these recommendations, the Smithsonian discussed the need for the Secretary of Interior (Secretary) to report and publish proposed lists of endangered and threatened plants in the Federal Register. As a result, the Service published a notice of review (Federal Register 40:27823-27924) on 1 July 1975. Accepting the Smithsonian report as a "petition" under Section 4(c)(2) of the ESA, the notice indicated the Service was reviewing taxa named in the report for possible inclusion in the list of endangered and threatened species. This notice followed a notice published in April 1975 (Federal Register 40:17612), which named four plants. Although these notices employed the words "endangered" and "threatened", they did not confer legal status.

The Smithsonian Institution and World Wildlife Fund published a book revising the Smithsonian report in 1978 (Ayensu and DeFillips). Accepted as a petition by the Service in 1983 (Federal Register 48:6752), Ayensu and DeFillips' (1978) book included revised lists and discussed the status of various lists, value in maintaining plant diversity, causes of rarity, habitats of endangered and threatened plants, several conservation measures, and eight suggested priorities for government action.

The Service subsequently proposed as endangered some 1,700 vascular plants on 16 June 1976 (Federal Register 41:24524-24572). Although many of these proposed plants were eventually given endangered status in later rulemakings, the 1978 amendments to the ESA (Publ. L. 95-632) mandated the withdrawal of proposals after two years. As a result, the proposed status for the remaining plants published in the 1976 rule was withdrawn on 10 November 1979 and published (Federal Register 44:70796) on 10 December 1979.

On 15 December 1980, the Service issued a comprehensive notice of review that superseded all prior notices (Federal Register 45:82479-82569). This notice introduced the three, currently-used and previously-discussed categories for non-listed plants. The Service published a supplement on 28 November 1983 (Federal Register 48:53639-53670) and eventually an update to the 1980 notice on 27 September 1985 (Federal Register 50:39525-39584).

The Service intends to keep all notices of review current with periodic revisions. These notices serve as a convenient centralized source of information on future listings, public notifications, and data requests for the Service. Notices also solicit comments and additional information on candidate species (50 CFR 424.15).

LISTING PROCEDURES

Background

Section 4 of the ESA (16 U.S.C. 1533) sets forth, among other things, procedures for the listing of species, designation of critical habitat, and maintenance of lists of endangered and threatened wildlife and plants. To carry out the purposes of the ESA, the Service and National Marine Fisheries Service (NMFS) of the National Oceanic and Atmospheric Administration proposed rules implementing listing and critical habitat requirements on 15 August 1979 (Federal Register 44:47862-47868).[2] The subsequent passage of the 1979 amendments to the ESA (Publ. L. 96-159) effected modest changes in the final regulations published on 27 February 1980 (Federal Register 45:13009-13026) from the proposed rules. After the passage of the the 1982 amendments, the Service and NMFS revised the Section 4 regulations with the publication of proposed rules on 8 August 1983 (Federal Register 48:36061-36069) and final regulations on 1 October 1984 (Federal Register 49:38899-38912).

Any species or taxonomic group of species (e.g., genus, subgenus) can be listed under the ESA. The Service and NMFS "shall rely on standard taxonomic distinctions and the biological expertise of [their respective Departments] and the scientific community concerning the relevant taxonomic group [50 CFR 424.11 (a)]." As required by the 1982 amendments, listing will be based solely on "the best available scientific and commercial information regarding a species' status, without reference to possible economic or other impacts of such determination [50 CFR 424.11 (b)]."

---

[2] Except those marine species given the Secretary of Commerce via an executive reorganization in 1970, listing authority rests with the Secretary of Interior. The Secretary of Commerce delegated his authority to NMFS while the Secretary of Interior delegated his authority to the Service.

Factors for Listing, Delisting, or Reclassifying Species

The Service, as required by the ESA and Section 4 regulations, employs one or any combination of five factors in the development of rules to list or reclassify species. These factors are "(1) [t]he present or threatened destruction, modification, or curtailment of [the species] habitat or range; (2) [o]verutilization for commericial, recreational, scientific, or educational purposes; (3) [d]isease or predation; (4) the [i]nadequacy of existing regulatory mechanisms; or (5) [o]ther natural or manmade factors affecting its existence [50 CFR 424.11 (c)]."

Listed species may be delisted if the best available data indicate that the species is either (1) extinct, or not endangered or threatened (as defined by the above five factors) because (2) it has been recovered or (3) the original classification data were in error.

Critical Habitat

The ESA defines "critical habitat" as either "specific areas within the geographical area occupied by the species ...[at the time of listing that are] ...essential to the conservation of the species and which may require special management considerations or protection; and specific areas outside the geographical area occupied by the species...[at the time of listing that]...are essential to the conservation of the species (16 U.S.C. 1533)." "Critical habitat shall be specified to the maximum extent prudent and determinable at the time a species is proposed for listing [50 CFR 424.12 (a)]." If a plant species is threatened by collection or the designation of critical habitat would not benefit the species, critical habitat designation is not "prudent". If required analyses of the impacts of designation are lacking or biological data are insufficient, critical habitat designation is not "determinable". Critical habitat shall be based on physical and biological features essential to its conservation and management [50 CFR 424.12 (b)].

Petitions

Any interested person may submit a written petition to the Secretary of Interior or Service requesting the listing, delisting, or reclassification of a plant species. The petition, which should contain the petitioner's name, address, signature, telephone number (if any), and affiliation (if any), must clearly state the requested action. Suggestions of candidates to consider or other comments received in response to notices of review will not be considered petitions (Bartel 1984). The Service will acknowledge receipt of the petition within 30 days. Within 90 days, the Service must find whether the petition presents substantial scientific or commercial information indicating the petitioned action is warranted. If insufficient, the Service publishes a notice in the Federal Register indicating as such. If petition data are sufficient and listing may be warranted, the Service shall publish a finding within 120 days in the Federal Register and indicate whether a status review is necessary. If after 12 months and/or the completion of a status review the Service determines that the action is warranted, the Service must publish within 13 months in the Federal Register either a rule proposing the species as either endangered or threatened, or a notice that the action is warranted but precluded by staffing and time constraints and/or by higher listing priorities. If after the original published finding a status review concludes the action is not warranted, the Service must publish a notice within 13 months in the Federal Register indicating as such.

Because the Service considers House Document 94-51, Ayensu and DeFillips (1978), and all Federal Register plant notices to be petitions, nearly all plant species warranting listing under the ESA have been "petitioned". Thus, subsequent petitions received by the Service will be determined to be "second petitions" and are not subject to the above petition procedures. Submitters of second petitions will receive a written response from the Service informing him/her of the prior action with the first petition.

Proposed Rules and Public Comment

A notice published in the Federal Register proposing a species for listing, delisting, or reclassification "shall contain the complete text of the proposed rule, a summary of the data on which the proposal is based (including, as appropriate, citation of pertinent information sources), and shall show the relationship of such data to the rule proposed [50 CFR 424.16 (b)]." If the rule proposes to designate or revise critical habitat, the notice must appropriately discuss critical habitat and contain necessary maps. The notice must also include a summary of the five factors affecting the species and/or its critical habitat.

Aside from the Federal Register notice, the Service must notify appropriate Federal and State agencies; counties in which the species is believed or known to occur; appropriate scientific organizations; and local authorities, private individuals, and organizations known to affected by the proposed rule. The Service must also "[p]ublish a summary of the proposed regulation in a newspaper of general circulation in each area...in which the species is believed to occur [50 CFR 424.16 (c)(1)(vi)]."

The Service must allow at least 60 days for public comment following the publication of a rule proposing the listing, delisting, or reclassification of a species; and/or designation or revision of critical habitat. Other proposed rules must allow 30 days for public comment. With "good cause", the Service may extend or reopen the public comment period upon the publication of notice in the Federal Register detailing the basis for doing so [50 CFR 424.16 (b)(2)]

The Service must "hold at least one public hearing if any person so requests within 45 days of publication of a proposed regulation [50 CFR 424.16 (b)(3)]." A Federal Register notice describing the location and time of the hearing shall be published by the Service no later than 15 days prior to the hearing date.

Within one year of the publication of a proposed rule, the Service shall publish one of the following in the Federal Register; (1) a final rule determining a species as either endangered or threatened, and/or designating or revising critical habitat, (2) a finding that such revision should not be made, (3) a notice withdrawing the proposed rule because available data do not justify the proposed action, or (4) a notice extending for six months the 1-year period because of substantial disagreement among scientists regarding the sufficiency and accuracy of available data relevant to the proposed action [50 CFR 424.17 (a)].

Final Rules

Aside from updating those items discussed within the proposed rule (see above), the final rule must summarize public comments and recommendations received in response to the proposed regulation. In addition, if the Service publishes a final rule contrary in whole or part to comments from a State agency or if the Service fails to adopt a regulation for which a State agency petitioned, the final rule must provide written justification for the Service's action or failure to act on the petition. All needed revisions in the description of critical habitat and accompanying maps also must be made in the final rule. The final becomes effective 30 days after its publication in the Federal Register.

The Service shall analyze for the Secretary the economic impacts of designating critical habitat. As a result, the Secretary may exclude portions of critical habitat if the benefits of exclusion outweigh the benefits of designation (50 CFR 424.19).

Emergency Rules

Despite the laborious procedures described above, Section 4(b)(7) of the ESA permits the immediate issuance of a regulation implementing any action when any emergency poses a "significant risk to the well-being of a species...of plant [50 CFR 424.20 (a)]." Citing the reasons for the regulation, emergency rules take effect upon publication in the Federal Register and expire after 240 days unless the listing procedures detailed above have been completed during that period. The Service must notify affected State agencies of the emergency rule. Only one California plant has been the subject of an emergency rule (Federal Register 50:31187-31190), the Loch Lomond coyote-thistle (Eryngium constancei).

Periodic Review

The Service shall conduct a review of each listed species at least once every five years. The review will ascertain whether any species should be delisted or reclassified. The results of this review are published by the Service in the Federal Register.

Listing Priorities

On 21 September 1983, the Service published listing priority guidelines in the Federal Register. The Service developed a table with 12 priority categories for listing and reclassification from threatened to endangered (table 1).

Even with table 1, the numerous plant species falling within the top three categories necessitate the use of additional criteria to develop a list of "high-priority" candidates. For example, because of the mandates of Section 7 of the ESA (see discussion below), plants threatened by Federal actions should be listed before plants threatened solely by private activities. Such internal priorities reduce so-called "symbolic" listings, where only private actions (over which the ESA has no control) jeopardize a plant. In addition, because of the provisions of Section 9 of the ESA (see below), plants threatened by collection should be listed prior to plants unaffected by collection.

Table 1--Priorities for listing or reclassification from threatened to endangered.

Threat Magnitude	Immediacy	Taxonomy	Priority
High	Imminent	Monotypic genus	1
		Species	2
		Subspecies	3
	Non-Imminent	Monotypic genus	4
		Species	5
		Subspecies	6
Moderate to Low	Imminent	Monotypic genus	7
		Species	8
		Subspecies	9
	Non-Imminent	Monotypic genus	10
		Species	11
		Subspecies	12

The Service also developed a table with six priority categories for delisting and reclassification from endangered to threatened (table 2).

Table 2--Priorities for delisting and reclassification from endangered to threatened.

Management Impact	Petition Status	Priority
High	Petitioned Action	1
	Unpetitioned Action	2
Moderate	Petitioned Action	3
	Unpetitioned Action	4
Low	Petitioned Action	5
	Unpetitioned Action	6

Data Needs For Proposing Species

As discussed in the 1985 notice of review for plants, the Service seeks information on all vulnerable plant taxa, including those not listed in past notices. Degree and immediacy of threats, and distribution data for each taxon are of the highest priority because of the Service's need to accurately determine status, priority for listing, and appropriate candidate category. In addition, the Service requests information on the source and nature of threats, recent or forthcoming taxonomic or nomenclatural changes, appropriate common or vernacular names, errors in historical distributions, and any other relevant data.

PROTECTION AFFORDED PLANTS UNDER THE ESA

Candidate Species

Candidate species do not enjoy any protection under the ESA. Because of Congressional testimony given in 1985 detailing declines in candidate taxa, Congress likely will direct the Service to "monitor" the status of candidates and emergency list where appropriate (Bean 1986). As stated earlier, some Federal agencies accord some level of protection or management consideration to candidates; however; such policies are not mandatory under the ESA nor should they be confused with its legal mandates.

Because many candidate plants likely are more "endangered" or "threatened" than some listed endangered and threatened species, the Service provides "technical assistance" to Federal and State agencies, upon request, on the appropriate conservation and management of candidate species. In addition, interagency or conservation agreements between the Service and other Federal agencies can be developed to protect candidate flora, like the agreements reached with the Forest Service on the Shirley Meadows mariposa (Calochortus coeruleus var. westonii) and Rawson's flaming-trumpet (Collomia rawsoniana).

Proposed Species

Proposed species are granted limited protection under the ESA. Essentially proposed taxa must be addressed by Federal agencies in biological assessments [a document required by Section 7 of the ESA for certain Federal projects or actions (50 CFR 402.12)]. Also, Federal agencies must confer with the Service regarding any action or project "likely to jeopardize the continued existence" of a proposed species (50 CFR 402.10). This "conference", like the technical assistance for candidates, is only an advisory process. The Service typically reviews project plans and researches species information to determine the effects of a Federal action on a proposed species. As indicated above, any recommendations to modify or abandon the project and/or undertake protective measures for proposed species are not mandatory on the Federal agency conferring with the Service.

Listed Endangered or Threatened Species

Listed endangered and threatened plants enjoy the full protection and authorities of the ESA. Section 4(f) requires the Service to develop recovery plans for all endangered or threatened plants. These plans direct Service recovery monies and help procure the services of appropriate public and private agencies in efforts to recover listed species.

Section 5 of the ESA permits Federal agencies within the Department of Interior (e.g., Bureau of Land Management, Park Service, and Fish and Wildlife Service) and Forest Service to implement a program to conserve listed plants via "the land acquisition and other authority of under the Fish and Wildlife Act of 1956, as amended, the Fish and Wildlife Coordination Act, as amended, and the Migratory Bird Conservation Act, as appropriate" to acquire by purchase, donation, or otherwise endangered or threatened plant habitat [16 U.S.C. 1534 (a)]. More importantly, this section allows these Federal agencies to use funds from the Land and Water Conservation Fund Act of 1965, as amended, for habitat acquisition.

Section 6 of the ESA enables the Service to enter into management and conservation agreements with State agencies. The former permits a State to administer or manage any area established for the conservation of a listed species. The latter enables the Service to financially assist State agencies (e.g., California Department of Fish and Game) in the development of programs for the conservation of endangered and threatened species. Such actions typically funded by the Service include research, species management, and other recovery activities described in recovery plans. According to Smith (1986), 21 states have cooperative agreements for plants.

Section 7, the interagency cooperation portion of the ESA, provides the most significant protection of its 14 sections. Section 7(a)(1) allows Federal agencies, in consultation with the Service, to use their respective resources in furtherance of the purposes of the ESA by carrying out programs for the conservation of listed species. Section 7(a)(2) requires Federal agencies, in consultation with the Service, to ensure "that any action authorized, funded, or carried out by such agency...is not likely to jeopardize the continued existence of any listed species or result in the destruction or adverse modification of [critical] habitat". If a proposed activity affects a listed species and the activity is contingent on one or more Federal actions, as described above, formal consultation is initiated by the affected Federal agencies.

To clarify this complicated section of the ESA, the Service and NMFS published final procedural regulations governing interagency cooperation under Section 7 on 3 June 1986 (Federal Register 51:19925-19963). These regulations discuss in detail conferences on proposed species and proposed critical habitat, early consultation (an optional process designed to avoid conflicts between listed species or critical habitat and proposed Federal actions), biological assessments (information or a document prepared by or for a Federal agency that evaluates the effects of a proposed action on listed or proposed species), informal consultation (an optional process that includes all discussions and correspondence between the Service and a Federal agency prior to formal consultation), and formal consultation (a process between the Service and a Federal agency resulting in the issuance of a "biological opinion").

Formal consultation and its resulting biological opinion may eventuate in a required modification or rarely an abandonment of a proposed Federal action (i.e., project) affecting a listed plant or animal, when such activity is likely to jeopardize the species. Where only Federal authorization is needed, private development can be affected too by Section 7. For example, development of vernal pools, an isolated wetland according to the provisions of the Clean Water Act, may require an individual Section 404 permit from the Army Corps of Engineers if a listed species is affected (see Bartel and Knudsen 1984). Although a Federal agency or State governor in which the agency action will occur can seek an exemption, typically the "reasonable and prudent alternatives" resulting from a "jeopardy opinion" are binding on the Federal agency. Nonetheless, because of the relatively few plants (24) listed in California (table 3), formal consultations for plants are not a common event.

Section 9 of the ESA prohibits the removal and reduction to possession (i.e., collection) of endangered and threatened plants from lands under Federal jurisdiction. Plants, however, do not enjoy the full protection against "take" [i.e., harass, harm (which includes significant habitat modification or degradation) pursue, hunt, shoot, wound, kill, trap, capture, or attempt to engage in any such conduct] accorded animals under this section. Nevertheless, as with animals, Section 9 makes illegal the international and interstate transport, import, export, and sale or offer for sale of endangered and threatened plants.

Table 3--Federally-listed and proposed plants in California

San Mateo thornmint (Acanthomintha obovata subsp. duttonii)-E   (18 Sep 85)
large-flowered fiddleneck (Amsinckia grandiflora)-E   (8 May 85)
McDonald's rock-cress (Arabis mcdonaldiana)-E   (24 Apr 79)
Presidio manzanita (Arctostaphylos pungens var. ravenii)-E   (26 Oct 79)
Truckee barberry (Berberis sonnei)-E   (6 Nov 79)
San Benito evening-primrose (Camissonia benitensis)-T   (12 Feb 85)
San Clemente Island Indian paintbrush (Castilleja grisea)-E   (11 Aug 77)
spring-loving centaury (Centaurium namophilum)-T   (20 May 85)
slender-horned spineflower (Centrostegia leptoceras)-PE   (9 Apr 86)
salt marsh bird's-beak (Cordylanthus maritimus ssp. maritimus)-E   (28 Sep 78)
palmate-bracted bird's-beak (Cordylanthus palmatus)-E   (1 Jul 86)
Santa Cruz cypress (Cupressus abramsiana)-E   (8 Jan 87)
San Clemente Island larkspur (Delphinium kinkiense)-E   (11 Aug 77)
Santa Barbara Island liveforever (Dudleya traskiae)-E   (26 Apr 78)
Santa Ana River woolly-star (Eriastrum densifolium ssp. sanctorum)- PE   (9 Apr 86)
Contra Costa wallflower (Erysimum capitatum var. angustatum)-E   (26 Apr 78)
Loch Lomond coyote-thistle (Eryngium constancei)-E*   (23 Dec 86)
Ash Meadows gumplant (Grindelia fraxino-pratensis)-T   (20 May 85)
San Clemente Island broom (Lotus dendroideus var. traskiae)-E   (11 Aug 77)
San Clemente Island bushmallow (Malocothamnus clementinus)-E   (11 Aug 77)
Amargosa niterwort (Nitrophila mohavensis)-E   (20 May 85)
Eureka Dunes evening-primrose (Oenothera avita ssp. eurekensis)-E   (26 Apr 78)
Antioch Dunes evening-primrose (Oenothera deltoides ssp. howellii)-E   (26 Apr 78)
San Diego mesa mint (Pogogyne abramsii)-E   (28 Sep 78)
pedate checkerbloom (Sidalcea pedata)-E   (31 Aug 84)
Eureka dunegrass (Swallenia alexandrae)-E   (26 Apr 78)
slender-petaled mustard (Thelypodium stenopetalum)-E   (31 Aug 84)
Solano grass (Tuctoria mucronata)-E   (28 Sep 78)

E	=	endangered species
T	=	threatened species
PE	=	proposed endangered species
*	=	originally emergency listed as endangered on 1 Aug 85
(11 Aug 77)	=	published date of final rule

Section 10 of the ESA enables the Service to "permit" acts otherwise prohibited by Section 9. Such permits for plants are granted "for scientific purposes or to enhance the propagation or survival of the affected species". Moreover, such permits can be issued to establish "experimental populations", an introduced and separate population of an endangered or threatened species. "Essential" experimental populations (those whose loss appreciably reduces the likelihood of the survival of the species in the wild) are treated as threatened species while all other experimental populations, referred to as "non-essential", are accorded only proposed status.

I hope this discussion will answer most questions concerning this important law, the Endangered Species Act of 1973. Nonetheless, persons wishing additional information on specific sections or certain applications of the ESA should write: U.S. Fish and Wildlife Service, Endangered Species Office, 2800 Cottage Way, Room E-1823, Sacramento, CA 95825-1846.

REFERENCES

Ayensu, Edward S.; DeFilipps, Robert A. Endangered and threatened plants of the United States. Washington: Smithsonian Institution and World Wildlife Fund, Inc.; 1978 403 p.

Barkworth, Mary E.; Linman, Judy. Stipa lemmonii (Vasey) Scribner (Poaceae): A taxonomic and distributional study. Madroño 31:48-56; 1984 January.

Bartel, J. A. The federal program. In: Smith, James Payne, Jr., editor; York, Richard, data entry and management. Inventory of rare and endangered vascular plants of California. Berkeley: California Native Plant Society; 1984:xii-xiii.

Bartel, Jim A.; Knudsen, Monty D. Federal laws and vernal pools. In: Jain, Subodh; Moyle, Peter. Proceedings, vernal pools and intermittent streams symposium; 1981 May 8-9; Davis, CA. Inst. Ecology Publ. 28; Univ. Calif. Davis, CA 1984 263-268.

Bean, Michael J. The evolution of national wildlife law. New York: Praeger Publishers; 1983. 449 p.

Bean, Michael J. The endangered species program. In: Eno, Amos S., project director; Di Silvestro, Roger L., editor; Chandler, William J., research director. Audubon Wildlife Report 1986. New York: National Audubon Society; 1986:346-371.

Becking, Rudolf W. Hastingsia atropurpurea (Liliaceae: Asphodeleae), a new species from southwestern Oregon. Madroño 33:175-181; 1986 July.

Drabelle, Dennis. The endangered species program. In: Eno, Amos S., project director; Di Silvestro, Roger L. Audubon Wildlife Report 1985. New York: National Audubon Society; 1985:72-90.

Smith, E. LaVerne. Federal protection for plants. Public Garden 1:12&22; 1986 January.

Rare Plant Conservation by State Government: Case Studies From the Western United States

Linda R. McMahan [1]

Abstract: The 12 western states contain over half of the rare plants of the continental United States. Six western states have endangered plant laws or desert plant protection laws, and several additional states are considering plant conservation legislation. Six western states have completed cooperative agreements with the Fish and Wildlife Service to conserve rare plants, 11 have established Heritage Programs, and 5 have natural areas laws. Although a few states began conservation programs early in this century, most programs were enacted in the 1970s and 1980s.

Perhaps the first state law passed to protect a native plant was the 1918 Massachusetts law prohibiting the digging or injuring of the mayflower (Epigaea repens). The fine was set at $50.00, but could be doubled if the offense occurred at night or if the offender was in disguise.

We have come a long way since 1918. Now, half of the states have laws protecting native plants. These, added to the federal Endangered Species Act, natural areas laws, and private conservation programs may soon provide comprehensive conservation programs for our nations rare plants.

Here, I will summarize some of these efforts, focusing on the western 12 states of Arizona, California, Colorado, Idaho, Montana, Nevada, New Mexico, Texas, Utah, Washington, and Wyoming.

RARE PLANTS IN THE WEST

The 12 states making up approximately the western half of the U.S. are important states for rare plants; over half of the rare and endangered plants of the continental U.S. grow within their borders.

A 1985 Federal Register notice (Fish and Wildlife Service 1985) lists 2,869 plant taxa as already protected by the U.S. Endangered Species Act or as candidates for listing. The numbers of taxa that occur in each states and the percentages of the total number are:

[1] Senior Program Officer for Botany, Center for Plant Conservation, Jamaica Plain, MA.

State or Commonwealth	No. of [1] Taxa	Pct. of [2] Total
Hawaii	780	27.2
California	694	24.2
Florida	199	6.9
Oregon	147	5.1
Texas	144	5.0
Utah	121	4.2
Arizona	106	3.7
Puerto Rico	100	3.5
Alabama	97	3.4
Georgia	96	3.3
Nevada	87	3.0
North Carolina	87	3.0
Tennessee	71	2.4
Colorado	66	2.3
South Carolina	64	2.2
Virginia	59	2.1
Washington	48	1.7
New Mexico	43	1.5
Idaho	40	1.4
Kentucky	32	1.1
Maryland	31	1.1
Illinois	31	1.1
Wyoming	31	1.1
Alaska	30	1.0
New York	30	1.0
Missouri	28	1.0
Arkansas	26	0.9
Mississippi	25	0.9
New Jersey	25	0.9
Louisiana	24	0.8
Indiana	23	0.8
West Virginia	22	0.8
Ohio	21	0.7
Wisconsin	21	0.7
Pennsylvania	20	0.6
Virgin Islands	17	0.6
Delaware	16	0.6
Michigan	16	0.6
Minnesota	16	0.6
Montana	16	0.6
Oklahoma	15	0.5
Iowa	13	0.5
Maine	13	0.5
Connecticut	10	0.3

Massachusetts	10	0.3
Kansas	9	0.3
New Hampshire	9	0.3
Vermont	8	0.3
District of Col.	4	0.1
Rhode Island	4	0.1
North Dakota	3	0.1
South Dakota	3	0.1
Guam	2	0.1
Nebraska	1	>0.1

[1] Nos. add to more that 2,869 because many taxa occur in more than one state. Column includes categories of listed, proposed, and candidates for listing, including extinct taxa.

[2] Pcts. add to more than 100 since many taxa occur in more than one state.

The distinctiveness of the western states is most apparent on the continent: the distribution of rare plants in the continental U.S. is centered in the Southwest and the Southeast (fig. 1). The "top 10" continental states for rare plants include 6 western states, and California clearly dominates:

Continental States in "Top 10"	Pct.[1] of Rare Plants
*California	35.2
Florida	10.1
*Oregon	7.4
*Texas	7.3
*Utah	6.1
*Arizona	5.4
Alabama	4.9
Georgia	4.9
*Nevada	4.4
North Carolina	4.4

*Western states.
[1] Based on 1,970 taxa.

REASONS FOR WESTERN PLANT RARITY

Mosaic of Habitats

Although the western states tend to be larger geographically than eastern states, size alone cannot explain the discrepancy since mid-western states are also large but have relatively few nationally rare plants. Two articles by G. Ledyard Stebbins (1978a; 1978b) from *Fremontia* explain some of the environmental and biological factors for California; many are true for other parts of the West as well. Stebbins cites

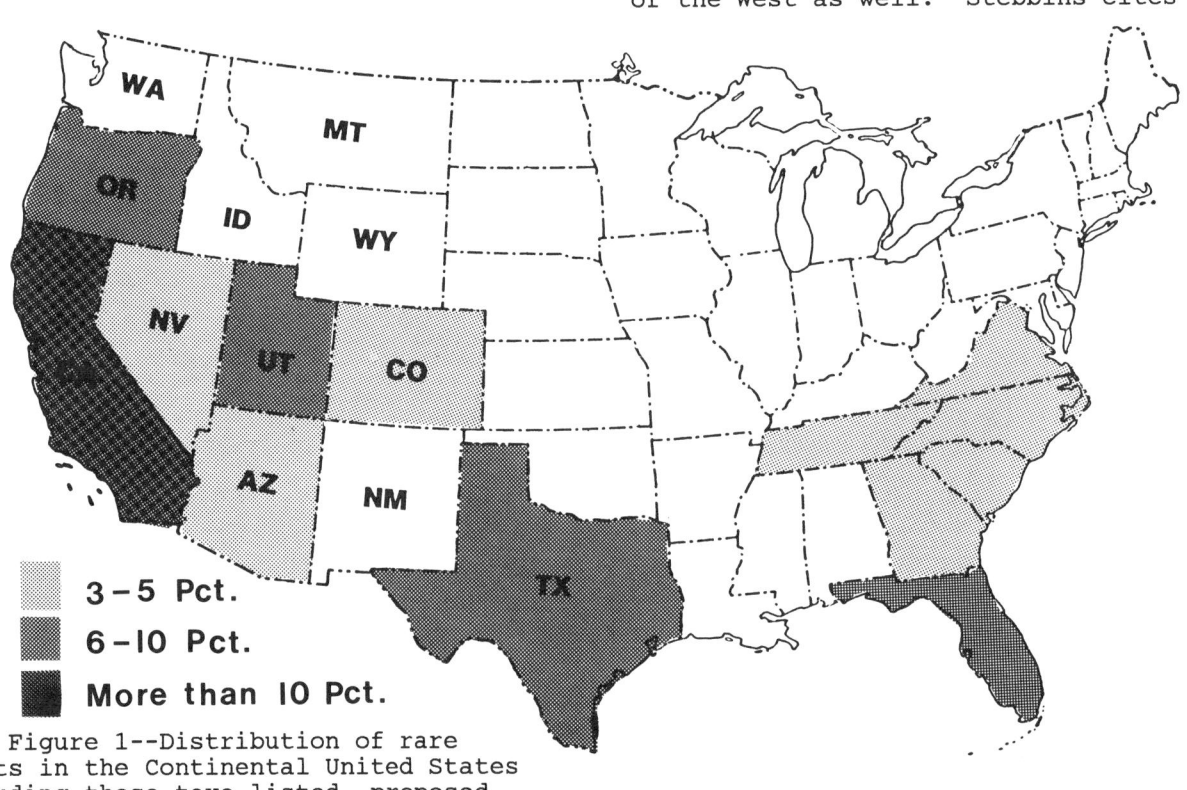

Figure 1--Distribution of rare plants in the Continental United States including those taxa listed, proposed, and candidates for listing under the U.S. Endangered Species Act.

the great diversity of climate, topography, and geology as largely responsible for California's plant rarity. All are factors that lead to a mosaic of plant habitats. He characterizes the number of California rare plants as a "mother lode" of scientific treasures (1978b), a phrase we could apply to much of the West.

High Proportion of Federal Land

Another factor leading to the special character of the West is the high proportion of federal land compared with other parts of the United States (Geological Survey 1970). The high proportion of federal land in the West lends increased importance to the U.S. Endangered Species Act, especially its prohibitions against collecting on federal lands and the requirement that federal agencies take endangered and threatened species into account when entering projects on lands under federal jurisdiction. Details of the effects of the Act are covered elsewhere in these proceedings.

Collecting for the Horticultural Trade

Collecting of desert plants has been particularly troublesome in the Southwest. Indeed, collecting led to the passage of some of the first plant conservation laws in the West as I will describe in the next section. Collecting problems were described early in this century; however, publicity about collecting reached its height in the 1970s (McMahan, in press). One 1929 article (Anon.) decried the "fast disappearing native flora of Southern California" due to collecting, particularly of cacti and Joshua trees.

Other Factors

In addition to collecting, the western states face the traditional pressures of development and competing land use, particularly grazing, timber production, and mining, much of which occurs on federal land. The states have developed other strategies to deal with these pressures, as has the federal government through the U.S. Endangered Species Act. I will summarize the state efforts in the next section.

PLANT CONSERVATION LAW OF THE STATES

The high number of rare plants, large amount of federal land, collecting problems, paired with rapid development, lead to special problems for the western states that wish to conserve their floral heritage.

The number of states with rare plant conservation laws has been increasing during this century, particularly since the early 1970s and the passage of federal protection under the U.S. Endangered Species Act (McMahan, 1980). Several authors have summarized plant conservation laws over the past decade (The Nature Conservancy 1977; The Nature Conservancy 1978; Johnston 1978; Kartesz 1977; Chambers 1978; Reveal 1978; McMahan 1980; McMahan 1984; Fitzgerald 1986).

Early History of Western Laws

Concern over collecting appears to have led to most of the early western laws. A series of articles in Desert Plant Life from 1929 and 1933 chronicle the development of the first laws of California and Arizona. A 1929 article describes new California legislation to regulate taking of desert plants in selected counties (Anon. 1929.

Arizona also passed a law in 1929 prohibiting the removal of desert foliage from public lands. The governor had issued a proclamation including the following: "My attention has again been called to the wholesale despoliation of desert flora of Arizona by commercial firms engaged in transporting these plants outside the state, particularly to California."

The problem with the first Arizona law was that it did not apply to private lands, and commercial firms soon found the loophole. They simply carried written permission from one or more private land owners and claimed that all the plants in their possession were from these lands; proving otherwise was difficult (Anon. 1932). The governor called for all law enforcement officials and interested private citizens to be vigilant in trying to end the problem. Frank Schilling (1932), president of the Desert Forum of Pasadena, cited cases of abuse of the Arizona law. He stated "If Arizona is to save her cactus forests, and this applies to other states as well, it will be necessary to immediately enact more stringent laws regulating the collecting of specimens."

In March of 1933, Arizona amended its law to cover private land and to require both landowner permission and a state permit (Anon. 1933). Although the law has been amended several times since then, many of its provisions stand almost as they were enacted in 1933.

Similar desert plant legislation was passed in Nevada and New Mexico during the early 1930s; however, enforcement programs in these two states have received less publicity than in Arizona and California.

A summary of the dates of plant conservation legislation by western states (except natural areas laws) shows activities scattered over this decade, with concentrations of activity in the 1970s and 1980s:

State (Type of Law)	Year First Passed	Year Last Updated
Arizona		
(Desert Plant)	1929	1981
California		
(Desert Plant)	1929	N.I.
(Native Plant)	1977	--
(Endangered Sp.)	1984	--
Colorado	none	--
Idaho	none	--
Montana	none	--
Nevada		
(Desert Plant)	1931	N.I.
(Native Plant)	1957	N.I.
New Mexico		
(Desert Plant)	1933	N.I.
(Endangered Sp.)	1985	--
Oregon		
(Wild Flower)	1963	--
Texas		
(Endangered Sp.	1981	1985
Utah	none	--
Washington	none	--
Wyoming	none	--

N.I. = No. Information

The 1970s

In the 1970s California passed a law that mirrored the U.S. Endangered Species Act (Howard 1978). Several states, including Washington, Montana, Oregon, and Colorado had passed natural areas laws to help monitor rare plants or preserve rare plant habitat. Several states began Heritage Programs in cooperation with The Nature Conservancy. Although the western states were slowly passing plant conservation legislation, they were generally behind the activities of states in other parts of the country, particularly the Midwest In the 1980s, however, the western states are showing increasing activity on the legislative front.

The 1980s

The 1980s have seen a new surge of plant conservation activities around the country. Many states, including Texas, New Mexico, Illinois, Tennessee, Maine, and Pennsylvania have passed rare plant legislation, bringing the total of 25 states, including 24 on the Continent (fig. 2) and Hawaii. Other states such as Texas, Vermont, Florida, and Virginia have upgraded existing laws, and in several states (e.g. Washington, Oregon, New York, Utah, New Jersey, Indiana) private organizations or governments are working to pass rare plant legislation.

Other events also show the increasing attention provided to rare plants by state governments. In 1979, The Nature Conservancy had established 21 Heritage Programs (McMahan 1980, quoting Robert Jenkins), By October 1986, The Conservancy had established Heritage Programs in 40 states and Proto-Heritage Programs in another 3 (fig. 3; including Hawaii) (The Nature Conservancy 1986). In 1984, 13 states (including Hawaii) had cooperative agreements with the U.S. Fish and Wildlife Service to conserve rare plants of the state. By October 1986, largely due to the efforts of Bruce Manheim at the Environmental Defense Fund, 23 states had entered into either full or limited cooperative agreements for plants with the U.S. Fish and Wildlife Service, making them eligible for federal funding of their plant conservation programs (fig. 4) (Manheim 1986).

STATE BY STATE SUMMARIES

Table 1 summarizes selected provisions of existing legislation in the western states. Following is a summary of some of the recent activities in each western state.

Arizona

The Arizona law requires dealers to obtain permits to collect certain plants and to tag them until sale or until leaving the state. The law also prohibits taking of certain other plants, such as all species of Pediocactus and Sclerocactus. Larry Richards (1986), an Arizona Native Plant Law Specialist, reports that amendments prepared by the Arizona Commission of Agriculture will soon be before the Arizona legislature to make the law "shorter and clearer" for the benefit of enforcement personnel.

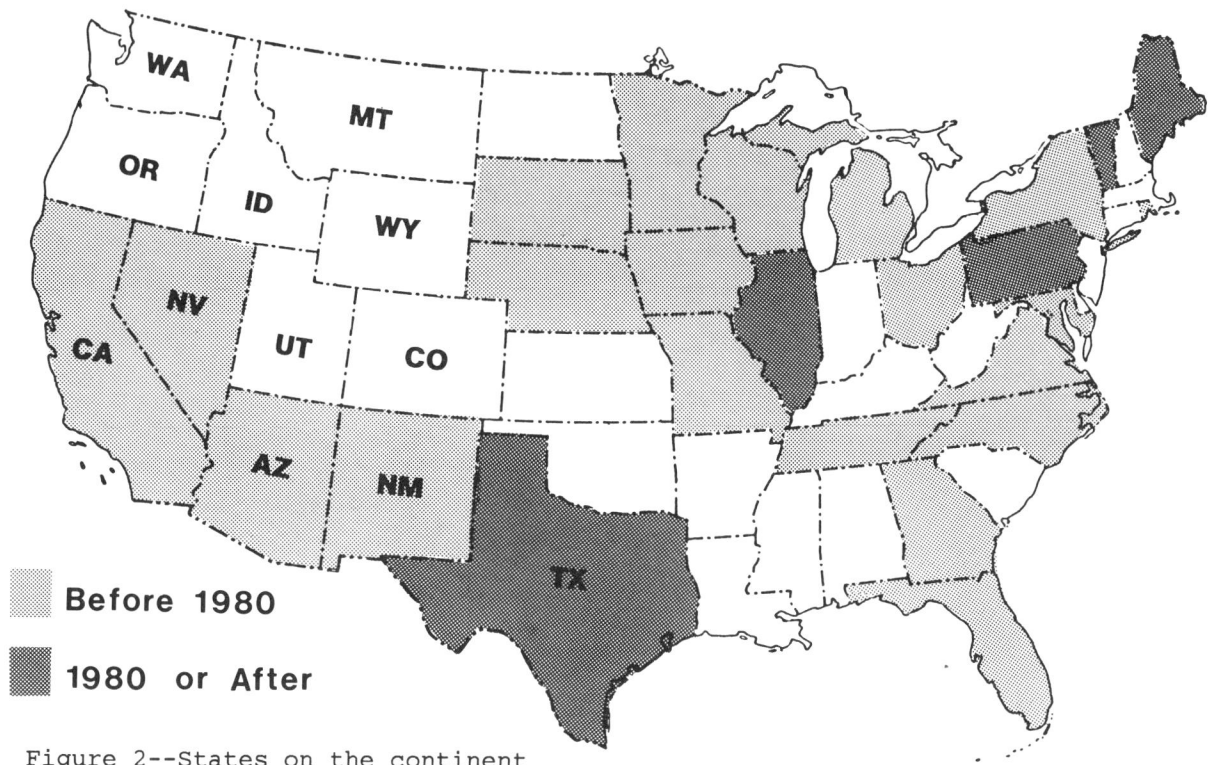

Figure 2--States on the continent having endangered species or desert plant legislation in 1980 and 1986.

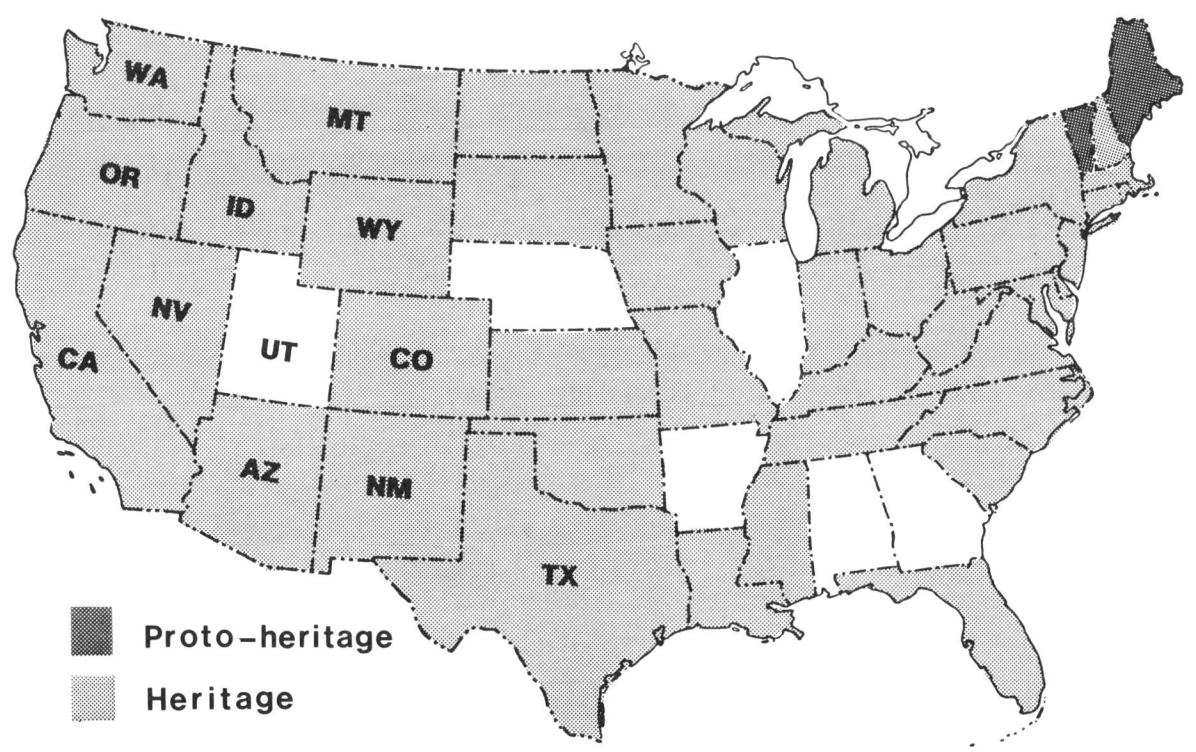

Figure 3--States having Heritage Programs or Proto-Heritage Programs in cooperation with The Nature Conservancy in October 1986.

New provisions responding to past abuses would prohibit interfering with actions of enforcement officials, or disposing or moving plants "on hold" for investigations or evidence. The Commission is also seeking authority to license dealers of native plants. Mr. Richards provided the following approximate figures for violations in the past two fiscal years:

	Fiscal Year (Jul. 1-Jun. 30)	
	1984-85	1985-86
No. Investigations	124	155
No. Citations	17	21
No. Convictions	8	13
No. Warnings Issued	25	51
No. Plants Salvaged fr. Private Land	274	596
No. Plants Confiscated	169	212
Approx. Market Value	$4225	$7965
Fines Collected	$2760	$1506

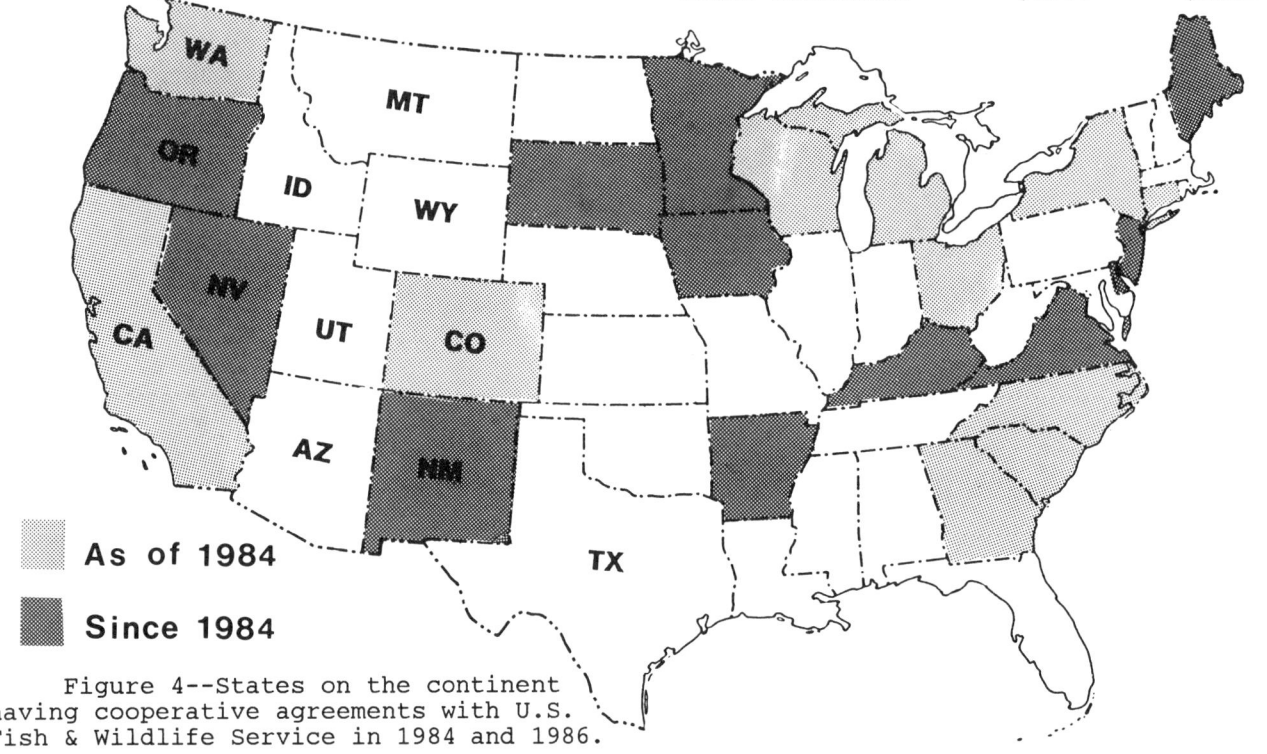

Figure 4--States on the continent having cooperative agreements with U.S. Fish & Wildlife Service in 1984 and 1986.

Table 1--Selected provisions of state endangered species acts, native plant acts, and desert plant acts of the western states.

State (Type of Law)	Listing Authority	Prohibit Taking		Permitting Authority	Exceptions[1]
		Public Land	Private Land		
AZ (Desert Plant)	yes	yes	yes[2]	yes	4,8
CA (Desert Plant)	yes	yes	yes[2]	yes	1,3,4,5
(Native Plant)	yes	yes	yes	yes	2,3,6,7
(End. Species)	yes	yes	yes	yes	10
NV (Native Flora)	yes	yes	yes	yes	9
NM (Desert Plant)	no	yes	yes	yes	--
(End. Species)	yes	yes	yes	yes[3]	--
TX (End. Species)	yes	yes	yes	yes	2

[1] 1 = utilities; 2 = agriculture; 3 = forestry; 4 = clearing land; 5 = fire control; 6 = nursery stock; 7 = work necessary to protect life and property; 8 = fewer than 5 plants or less than one cord of wood; 9 = native Indians; 10 = refers to exceptions in the native plant law.

[2] Requires a permit from the state in addition to landowner permission.

[3] For scientific use or for propagation.

California

California has what appears to be the most comprehensive rare plant legislation in the West provided by overlapping coverage of an endangered species act, amended in 1984 to include plants, a native plant law, and a desert plant law. A 1985 natural areas law completes the coverage. Susan Cochrane (1986) of the California Department of Fish and Game reports that the department keeps track of three categories of plants - endangered, threatened, and rare. The Act requires consultation by other state agencies for their projects, a provision requested by developers who wished to deal with only one agency on state projects (Cochrane 1986). The Department of Agriculture regulates the nursery trade under the desert plant law.

Colorado

Colorado's authority over rare plants is based on the Colorado Natural Areas Act, passed in 1977. The state has designated a list of rare plants under this act. Efforts to pass an endangered plant law in the state have so far been unsuccessful (Fitzgerald 1986).

Idaho

Idaho has a 1972 law prohibiting the digging, export, or sale of certain wildflowers growing within the right of way of a public highway. I have no record of other plant conservation in the state.

Montana

The primary legislation in Montana is the Natural Areas Law of 1974. The legislature has recently passed a law to transfer authority for rare plants to the state library (Manheim 1986).

Nevada

A Nevada law amended in 1979 gives the state's Division of Forestry authority over rare species and commercial collecting. The New Mexico Native Plant Society has been active in preparing the rare plant list for the state (Pinzl, 1979; Anon. 1981). Since a large proportion of land in Nevada is federally owned, any state efforts rely heavily upon federal cooperation.

New Mexico

New Mexico conserves plants under the Plant Protection Act administered by the Department of Agriculture; this law regulates collecting plants for sale from public and private lands. In 1985, the New Mexico Department of Natural Resources helped in the passage of endangered species legislation to "give enabling legislation for what they had already been doing," according to Cathy Carruthers (1986), Director of the Resource Management and Development Division. They worked from a bill drafted by Bruce Manheim at the Environmental Defense Fund. One of their goals was to become eligible for Section 6 funding under the federal Endangered Species Act. The state shorted the bill and worked with cattle growers and miners on minor amendments to address their concerns. The bill was sponsored by Vernon Kerr, a member of the conservative coalition in New Mexico, who helped greatly with its passage. The Department sought support on its own from the more liberal members of the legislature.

Oregon

The Native Plant Society of Oregon (McAvoy 1986) and other conservation groups are leading that state's efforts to pass an endangered plant law to replace an outmoded and unenforced (Chambers 1976) law regulates the sale of certain native wildflowers or the removal of plants growing on public land. The Society has drafted a more sweeping bill and has gained support from the Natural Heritage Advisory Council and Division of State Lands,. Representative Paul Hostika from Eugene has offered the use of a legislative aid to help draft a bill for introduction to the legislature. The Native Plant Society will look for a sponsor after the November elections.

Texas

According to George Adams (1985), a lawyer in the Texas Parks and Wildlife Department, recent strengthening amendments to that state's endangered plant law were sought directly by the legislative sponsors who considered the prior law to be too weak. The Act now regulates taking and sale of listed plants. The recent amendments increased penalties and extended protection to private lands. The Department issues permits for scientific and commercial collecting, and amends the list of plants covered by the law.

Utah

The Utah Native Plant Society has been working with the state on efforts to set up a plant conservation program, particularly those managed by the Division of State Lands (Manheim 1986). A bill to do this was tabled in the 1985 legislative session. State conservationists hope this legislation will qualify the state for a limited authorities cooperative agreement with the U.S. Fish and Wildlife Service to make them eligible for federal funding.

Washington

Presently Washington has legislation protecting roadside wildflowers. Mark Sheehan (1986) of the Washington Natural Heritage Program reports that an endangered species law covering both plants and animals was introduced last legislative session but was killed in the House Rules Committee. Mark attributes the failure to the concerns expressed by special interest groups. There are plans to reintroduce the bill this coming January after consultation with timber and agricultural representatives. The bill will probably prohibit taking without the landowner's permission and will permit taking for scientific reasons. It may be split into two bills - one for plants and the other for animals. Mark noted that the Northwest is a "place of contrasts." Oregon, for example, is often perceived as strongly environment, but Washington is ahead on a system of natural preserves.

Wyoming

Wyoming has no plant conservation laws that I know of, although it does have a Heritage Program.

Acknowledgments: I thank the following people for responding to my questions about recent activities in the western states: Julie Kierstead, Ester McAvoy, Bruce Manheim, George Adams, Cathy Carruthers, Mark Sheehan, and Susan Cochrane. I also thank Kerry Walter of the Center for Plant Conservation for providing printouts of data used to analyze the state distribution of rare plants.

REFERENCES

Adams, George, Texas Parks and Wildlife Department [Personal Conversation] February 1985.

Anon. Conservation of native plants. Desert plant life 1(1):2; May 1929.

Anon. The governor of Arizona declares for conservation. Desert Plant Life 4(4):46-47; 1932.

Anon. Native plants protected in Arizona by a new amendment. Desert plant life 5:40; 1933.

Anon. Nevada threatened and endangered plant workshop, Nov. 13-14, 1981, Reno, Nevada. Printed notes from the meeting on file at the Center for Plant Conservation.

Carruthers, Cathy, New Mexico Department of Natural Resources. [Telephone conversation]. 31 October 1986.

Chambers, Kenton L. The northwestern United States. In: Prance, Ghillian T. and Elias, Thomas S. eds. Extinction is forever. New York: The New York Botanical Garden; 1977:45-49.

Cochrane, Susan. California Department of Fish and Game. [Telephone conversation] 21 August 1986.

Fish and Wildlife Service. Endangered and threatened wildlife and plants; review of plant taxa for listing as endangered or threatened species; notice of review. Federal register 50(188):39526-39527 (plus 57 pages of lists); 27 September 1985.

Fitzgerald, Sarah Gates. The states of the states in plant protection. Garden 10(5):2-5,31-32; September/October 1986.

Geological survey, U.S. Department of the Interior. The National Atlas of the United States of America. Washington D.C.; 1970. 417 pp.

Howard, Alice Q. The legal position of rare plants today. Fremontia 5(4):17-21; 1978.

Johnston, Marshall C. The southwestern United States. In: Prance, Ghillian T. and Elias, Thomas S. eds. Extinction is forever. New York: The New York Botanical Garden; 1977:60-61.

Kartesz, John T.; Kartesz, Rosemarie. The biota of North America, part 1: vascular plants, volume I, rare plants. Pittsburgh: BONAC; 1977. 361 pp.

Manheim, Bruce. The Environmental Defense Fund, Summary of EDF efforts with state conservation programs under section 6 of the Endangered Species Act as of September 1986. On file at the Center for Plant Conservation.

McAvoy, Ester, Native Plant Society of Oregon, Corvallis, OR. [Telephone conversation]. 27 October 1986.

McMahan, Linda. Legal protection for rare plants. The American Univ. Law Rev. 29(3):515-569; Spring 1980.

McMahan, Linda. What is protection? The Tennessee Conservationist L(2):5-7; March/April 1984.

McMahan, Linda R. History of the cactus and succulent trade. In: Fuller, D. and Fitzgerald, S. eds. Conservation and commerce of cacti and other succulents. Washington, D.C.: World Wildlife Fund; In press.

Pinzl, Ann. Nevada's endangered plant program. Fremontia 7(1):21-22; 1979.

Reveal, James L. The western United States. In: Prance, Ghillian T. and Elias, Thomas S. eds. Extinction is forever. New York: The New York Botanical Garden; 1977:50-59.

Richards, Larry, Arizona Commission of Agriculture. [Telephone conversation]. 31 October 1986.

Schilling, F. A. Arizona calls for help. Desert Plant Life 3:100; 1932.

Sheehan, Mark. Washington Natural Heritage Program [Telephone Conversation]. 31 October 1986.

Stebbins, G. Ledyard. Why are there so many rare plants in California? I. environmental factors. Fremontia 5(4):6-10; January 1978a.

Stebbins, G. Ledyard. Why are there so many rare plants in California? II. Youth and age of species. Fremontia 6(1):17-20; April 1978b.

The Nature Conservancy. Preserving our natural heritage, volume I, federal activities. Washington, D.C.: U.S. Government Printing Office; 1977; 323 pp.

The Nature Conservancy. Preserving our natural heritage, volume II, state activities: Washington, D.C.: U.S. Government Printing Office; 1978. 671 pp.

The Nature Conservancy. Fact Sheet on Heritage Programs. 1986.

Endangered Plants and California State Laws

Susan A. Cochrane [1]

Abstract: California State laws to protect endangered native plants, and the California Department of Fish and Game's efforts to implement them are the subject of this paper. Discussions of the new California Endangered Species Act, its relationship to the original Native Plant Protection Act and the use of the California Environmental Quality Act in plant protection are presented. Recent additions to the lists and protection projects for listed species are highlighted.

THE NATIVE PLANT PROTECTION ACT

In 1977, as a result of the endeavors of many farsighted people, the California Native Plant Protection Act (NPPA) became law. The act, authored by Senator Nejedly, directed the California Department of Fish and Game (CDFG) to carry out the Legislature's intent to "preserve, protect and enhance endangered plants of this State". It gave the power to designate native plants as endangered or rare, and to require permits for collecting, transporting or selling such plants, to the Fish and Game Commission, a five-member Committee appointed by the Governor that establishes the policies by which the Department operates.

During this time, the Department created the Endangered Plant Project to coordinate and carry out listing and protection activities for plants. The number of Project staff has fluctuated and currently has a fulltime coordinator, a project assistant and some temporary student assistants.

The definitions of "endangered" and "rare" are found within the legislation itself (Section 1900, Chapter 10 of the Fish and Game Code):

> A native plant "is rare when, although not presently threatened with extinction, it is in such small numbers throughout its range that it may become endangered if its present environment worsens."

> A native plant "is endangered when its prospects of survival and reproduction are in immediate jeopardy from one or more causes."

The NPPA also instructed all State agencies to "utilize their authority in furtherance of the purposes" of the Act by carrying out programs for the conservation of listed species.

The legal protection afforded listed plants under the NPPA involves provisions that prohibit the taking of plants from the wild and a salvage requirement for landowners. Once they have been notified of the presence of a listed species on their property, landowners are required to tell the Department at least ten days in advance of any land use change. This allows for the salvaging of plants that would otherwise be destroyed. This provision obviously does not ensure the protection of plants in their native habitat, a situation that continues to be a weak link in legislative authority for plant protection, one not overcome by the more recent California Endangered Species Act.

Under the NPPA, 175 plants have been designated by the Fish and Game Commission (101 as endangered, 74 as rare).

THE CALIFORNIA ENDANGERED SPECIES ACT

In the fall of 1984 two Assembly bills, 3270 (Campbell) and 3309 (Costa), were signed into law. Together they are called the California Endangered Species Act (CESA). The major intent of this legislation was threefold: (1) to unite various sections of the Fish and Game Code dealing with endangered species issues into one congruous unit, now Sections 2050-2098 of the Code, and align State laws as closely as possible with Federal legislation; (2) to provide the public with a more formalized method of petitioning the Fish and Game Commission to add, delete or change the listing status of a species; and (3) to provide a

---

[1] Coordinator, Endangered Plant Project, California Department of Fish and Game, Sacramento, CA.

consultation process whereby potential impacts to species caused by projects subject to CEQA can be determined and dealt with in a timely and consistent manner. With CESA, the intent of the Legislature to protect species habitat as well as the species itself has been expressed for the first time:

> "The Legislature further finds and declares that it is the policy of the State to conserve, protect, restore and enhance any endangered species or any threatened species and its habitat and that it is the intent of the Legislature, consistent with conserving the species, to acquire lands for habitat for these species (Sec. 2052)."

For plants, this new law expands upon, but does not replace, the original NPPA. In aligning with Federal regulations, the CESA created the categories of "Threatened" and "Endangered" species. Endangered is defined the same as that in the NPPA. The definition of threatened is a native species, subspecies or variety "that, although not presently threatened with extinction, is likely to become an endangered species in the foreseeable future in the absence of the special protection and management efforts required by this Act". The CESA grandfathers all "Rare" animals into the Act as now being Threatened species. However, it did not grandfather the rare plants. Thus, we now have three categories for listing plants in California: Endangered, Threatened and Rare. Species in all three categories are protected from taking from the wild (Sec. 1908 and Sec. 2080, Fish and Game Code); however, the Rare taxa are not covered by the new consultation and five-year review procedures (that is, Rare taxa are regulated only under the NPPA).

The CESA also creates a "candidate" species category. A candidate is a taxon that has been officially noticed by the Commission as being under review by the Department for addition to the Threatened or Endangered list. Candidate species are also protected from taking.

Through permits or memorandums-of-understanding (MOU), the Department may authorize individuals, public agencies, universities, zoological gardens and scientific or educational institutions to import, export, take or possess any endangered species, threatened species or candidate species for scientific, educational or management purposes (Sec. 2081).

The Endangered Plant Project authorizes the collection of voucher specimens for newly discovered locations of listed plants by use of a letter permit. The letter permit stipulates that collections made will not impact the reproductive success of the population. The letter permit is not issued for collecting within already known populations. This situation is handled through creation of an MOU between the researcher and the Department.

An MOU outlines the procedures for studies or enhancement projects involving State listed taxa, including the amount of material to be collected or impacted and timelines for reports of study results. It is important that the Project be made aware of all projects or studies impacting or involving listed plants, since it is the Project's responsibility to direct protection efforts and conduct reviews of species status. Developing MOUs or requests for permits can be promptly handled by the Project. A format for information needed to create the MOU is available from the Project office or CDFG regional offices.

While research MOU requests are most often handled by Project staff, MOUs for mitigation projects (enhancement, restoration or protection agreements to mitigate unavoidable impacts caused by construction projects) can be handled by the local Fish and Game biologists or office reviewing the CEQA project. An important aspect of an MOU in these situations is the need to include a guarantee of completion of proposed mitigation actions. Adequate guarantees should be provided by the applicant, and required in the final permit by the permitting agency, to assure that the agreed upon work is completed. Such guarantees may include surety deposits or bonds. These guarantees should be in place prior to Department approval of the MOU.

The new law also establishes a petition process whereby individuals or organizations can submit a petition to the Fish and Game Commission requesting that a species, subspecies or variety of a plant or animal be added to, deleted from or changed in status on the lists of Threatened and Endangered species. A standard petition format has been devised and is available from the Commission Office at 1416 Ninth Street, Sacramento, CA 95814. For practical purposes, the Department will follow the petition format and process when it proposes to list plants, including Rare species. A petition must include sufficient information on species threats, abundance, distribution (including maps), habitat, suggested management, species description and information sources prior to being accepted for consideration.

Once accepted, the Commission refers the petition to the Department for review. the DFG has 90 days to return with a recommendation of whether or not the taxon warrants the requested action. If the requested action appears warranted, the Department has one year to prepare a formal response to the Commission to accept or reject the proposed action, although such a response can be made any time before a year is up. If the Department's recommendation is to proceed with the proposed action, the Commission announces its intention to propose a rule at a Commission meeting in a "Notice of Intent to Adopt a Proposed Regulation." The public then has 45 days to comment. The proposal is brought before the Commission for approval at the first meeting scheduled after the 45-day comment period. Public comment is also accepted at this meeting. If approved, a final rulemaking is filed with the Office of Administrative Law and then with the Secretary of State. The rule becomes effective 30 days later.

The Department may still submit its own proposals to the Commission. This was the case this fall when the Department promoted and the Commission accepted the listing of eleven taxa as Endangered and three as Threatened, the upgrading of five Rare plants to Endangered or Threatened status and the deletion of two taxa now taxonomically invalid. As of November 7, 1986, there are 187 species listed as Endangered (114), Threatened (5) and Rare (68) by the State of California. Given current staffing constraints, the Department now expects that most new listing suggestions will come from the interested public and not be formulated in-house. However, in situations of grave endangerment to a species, emergency listing is also possible under the CESA.

Other aspects of the CESA include a new five-year review of the status of listed plants and animals. The Department must provide the Commission with an analysis of the current status of each species and any need for its reclassification every five years after its initial designation. In addition, an annual summary of species status is prepared for all listed taxa.

The new State agency consultation procedures are a major addition to State laws on endangered species. This part, Article 4 of the CESA (Sections 2090-2098), encourages State agencies not to approve projects under CEQA that would "jeopardize" the continued existence of a listed species. It directs agencies to consult with the Department, that the Department determine whether or not jeopardy will occur and if so, that the Department determine "reasonable and prudent alternatives" to the project, and that the agency shall require such alternatives consistent with conserving the species. The CESA leaves agencies the option of determining overriding considerations approving the project even if jeopardy is found, much in the same way that CEQA does; however, agencies are prohibited from approving projects that would cause the extinction of a species. A more thorough explanation of the consultation process is presented in the paper written by Earle Cummings in these proceedings.

CALIFORNIA ENVIRONMENTAL QUALITY ACT

Because of the salvage aspect of the NPPA and the fact that it was carried over into the CESA, the protections provided under CEQA are actually as strong or stronger a tool for protecting native plants than the NPPA or CESA. A project under CEQA cannot have a significant impact upon the environment, without adequate mitigation or compensation. Notwithstanding the ability of permitting (lead) agencies to recognize "overriding considerations" of economic, social or other benefit that can nullify intended environmental protections, CEQA can be used to enforce habitat and species protections. It is often a matter of public interest that determines the outcome of projects that impact the environment -- a good reason for concerned individuals and organizations to keep abreast of project proposals.

In addition, CEQA can provide protection to species not yet listed by the Commission but deserving of such status. Section 15380 of the CEQA Guidelines states that a species not included on the Rare or Endangered list shall nevertheless be considered to be rare or endangered if the species can be shown to meet the criteria for State listing. In general, the Department recognizes that the CNPS Inventory List 1 contains plants that in a majority of cases would qualify for listing, and DFG requests their inclusion in EIRs as necessary.

DFG ENDANGERED PLANT PROJECT

The following is a short overview of the types of projects and activities the Department's Endangered Plant Project (EPP) is involved in to promote the protection of listed species. First, a short introduction to the Department's overall organization in relation to plant protection is in order.

The Environmental Services Division is responsible for reviewing all environmental impact reports that are sent through the State Clearinghouse to the Department. EIRs are routed by Headquarters Environmental Services staff to the appropriate DFG region (there are five regional offices in the State). Within the regions, Environmental Services staff and unit biologists review the documents and compile the Department's comments, which are then forwarded back to Headquarters.

The majority of environmental documents originate from local agencies or offices of State agencies. These are sent directly by the agency to the DFG regional office. The unit biolgist is the Department's front-line representative, dealing directly with lead agencies and project proponents to work out protection and mitigation requirements for projects. Regional staff use the Natural Diversity Data Base and information provided by EPP when making their recommendations. Unit biologists are also responsible for dealing with the public on wildlife issues within their area, usually one or two counties in size.

Throughout the environmental review process the Endangered Plant Project is not directly involved unless the Environmental Services or unit biologist staff requests assistance. However, the EPP is a source of information and guidance for the Department on endangered plant matters. The EPP promotes the Department's Guidelines for Assessing Effects of Proposed Developments on Rare and Endangered Plants and Plant Communities, adopted from those prepared by CNPS. These guidelines are given to all project proponents and lead agencies when they request DFG participation or information.

In addition, the EPP is in the process of updating the plant status reports originally written by CNPS. We are organizing handbooks for each of the unit biologists and each region as a whole that include all endangered plant laws and policies and general information on plant identification and protection. Each handbook also includes the status report, a line drawing and photographs of each listed plant found within the particular biologist's unit. The handbooks are designed to be a one-stop sourcebook for Department staff, many of whom have not had extensive botanical training.

Recent production of a slideshow on endangered plants in California, and the future production of a book on listed species are other educational projects to expand California's knowledge about their endangered plants.

To encourage appropriate protection activities for listed taxa, the EPP has developed a species management plan format to outline species needs and recovery activities. Most of these species management plans will be completed by researchers under contract to the Department. At this time, the EPP has two main sources of contract funds: the rare and endangered species income tax donations (Tax Check-off funds) and the Federal Endangered Species Act monies administered by the U.S. Fish and Wildlife Service (Section 6 funds). Tax Check-off funds have been used thus far to produce management plans for the Kaweah brodiaea and Alameda manzanita, to conduct surveys of the San Diego thornmint and to fence and protect the native stand and reintroduce Catalina Island mahogany to available habitat, to name a few. Section 6 funds are available for protection and recovery activities for Federally-listed plants in California, such as a survey of vernal pools in San Diego, National Park Service research on the Santa Barbara Island live-forever and taxonomic work and habitat investigation of the Truckee barberry. A large portion of EPP time is spent administering contracts.

The EPP is also involved in reviewing legislation relating to plants and commenting on Federal and other State management plans concerning listed species. As indicated in the previous discussions on plant laws, the project writes MOUs and permits, reviews petitions to list or delist taxa, writes annual status summaries, compiles five year reviews of listed plants and answers questions on endangered plants from the general public.

A citizens committee, the Native Plant Advisory Committee, exists as a liaison to the botanical community and provides opinions and suggestions to the Department concerning native plant issues. The Committee is appointed by the Director of the Department and meets on an as-needed basis.

To provide adequate protection for 187 taxa, educate the public as to their values and investigate new potential listings is a tall order for any organization, public or private. A recent workload analysis indicated a need for more than nine full-time staff, as well as a botanist in each of the five DFG regions. While this is not a political reality, steps are being taken to increase the awareness of Department staff as to the necessity for increased Department attention in plant issues. The CNPS can have a large influence in this realm, both Statewide and at the local level. The visibility of a constituency, such as the number of you attending this conference, is the first step toward having your needs met by your government. Working together, we can have a longlasting impact on the preservation of California's endangered flora.

Inquiries may be directed to me in care of the Endangered Plant Project, California Department of Fish and Game, 1416 Ninth Street, Sacramento, CA 95814 or (916) 324-3814 or to your local CDFG office.

A List Is a List . . . or Is It?

Richard P. York [1]

Abstract: In California the list of State-designated Endangered, Threatened, and Rare plants is maintained by the California Department of Fish and Game's Endangered Plant Project and the list of Federally-designated Endangered and Threatened plants is maintained by the Office of Endangered Species of the U. S. Fish and Wildlife Service. In addition, the California Natural Diversity Data Base, also of the Department of Fish and Game, assigns status ranks to the plants for which it has computerized information. Finally, the California Native Plant Society has, since 1974, published the Inventory of Rare and Endangered Vascular Plants of California. This extensive inventory includes not only the State and Federally-listed plants but also a much larger group of plants the California Native Plant Society feels may qualify for State and/or Federal listing. As a result of the interaction between these programs and their lists, there has been some confusion about the legal implications of each list. This paper will detail the differences and similarities of each list, their programs, and the laws that guide them.

Since California has been blessed with more than its fair share of rare, threatened, and endangered plants, and interest in tracking these taxa and their status is equally high, there has been some confusion when dealing with the list(s) on which they reside. After reading this paper I hope the reader will be more comfortable with the lists and the programs/laws in California that administer them. What follows is a brief description of each list and its categories, name and address of the responsible agency/organization, and a listing of the law(s) that support it.

FEDERAL LIST

Responsible agency: U. S. Fish and Wildlife Service, Department of Interior

Address:
U. S. Fish & Wildlife Service
Sacramento Endangered Species Office
2800 Cottage Way, Room E-1823
Sacramento, CA 95824

---

[1] Botany Research Assistant, California Natural Diversity Data Base, California Department of Fish and Game, Sacramento, CA.

Title of list: List is published as a Notice of Review in the Federal Register.

Law supporting list: Federal Endangered Species Act of 1973, as amended.

Notice of Review Status Categories:
    LE - Taxa listed as Endangered
    LT - Taxa listed as Threatened
    PE - Taxa proposed for listing as Endangered
    PT - Taxa proposed for listing as Threatened
    1 - Candidate taxa for which there is adequate information to support the biological appropriateness of proposing to list as Threatened or Endangered. A single asterisk (*) indicates a taxon that is possibly extinct. A double asterisk (**) indicates a taxon possibly extinct, but is known to exist in cultivation
    2 - Candidate taxa for which there is biological information that indicates that proposing to list the taxa as Threatened or Endangered is possibly appropriate, but for which substantial data on biological vulnerability and threat are not currently known or on file to support the immediate listing. Asterisks mean the same as in Category 1.

3 - Taxa that are no longer under consideration for listing. There are three subcategories, depending on reason(s) for removal from consideration:
    3A - Taxa believed extinct
    3B - Taxa with taxonomic problems that do not meet the Endangered Species Act definition of a "species."
    3C - Taxa that are too common or widespread and/or those not subject to any identifiable threat(s).

STATE LIST

Responsible agency: California Department of Fish and Game

Address:
California Department of Fish and Game
Endangered Plant Project
1416 9th Street, Room 1225
Sacramento, CA 95814

Laws supporting list: California Endangered Species Act (1984), Native Plant Protection Act (1977), and the California Environmental Quality Act.

State List Categories:
    Rare - Taxa that, although not currently Threatened or Endangered, are in such small numbers or restricted habitats that they may become Threatened or Endangered if present conditions worsen.
    Threatened - Taxa likely to become Endangered in the foreseeable future in the absence of protection action(s).
    Endangered - Taxa seriously in danger of becoming extinct.
    Candidate - Those taxa that have been accepted by the California Fish and Game Commission for review to add to the State list. These taxa are selected from the California Natural Diversity Data Base list (see next section) and Lists 1, 2, and 3 of the CNPS Inventory (see last section of this paper).

CALIFORNIA NATURAL DIVERSITY DATA BASE

Responsible agency: California Department of Fish and Game

Address:
California Department of Fish and Game
California Natural Diversity Data Base
1416 9th Street, Room 1225
Sacramento, CA 95814

Law supporting list: The California Natural Diversity Data Base list does not have any legal implications.

"NDDB Priority Codes": The "NDDB Priority Codes", found on the California Natural Diversity Data Base computer printouts, are assigned by the biological staff at the Data Base and are based primarily upon the rarity, degree of threat, and amount of protection for each taxon. These ranks are an "in house" method of prioritizing taxa to determine the order in which information is gathered and processed, as well as to determine priorities for protection activities by others. In order to fulfill its responsibilities and to direct its yearly work activities, the Data Base staff conducts a thorough analysis of the inventory once a year; assigning a "NDDB Priority Code" for each taxon is part of this analysis. A full explanation of these codes/ranks can be obtained from the Data Base.

CALIFORNIA NATIVE PLANT SOCIETY

Responsible organization: California Native Plant Society (CNPS)

Address:
California Native Plant Society
Rare Plant Program
909 12th Street, Suite 116
Sacramento, CA 95814

Title of list: Inventory of Rare and Endangered Vascular Plants of California

Law supporting list: Section 15380 of the California Environmental Quality Act (CEQA) Guidelines have a discussion regarding non-listed (State) taxa. This section of the CEQA Guidelines states that a plant must be treated as Rare or Endangered if it meets the State's definitions and criteria, even if it is not officially listed as such. If a person (or organization) provides information showing that a plant meets the State's definitions and criteria, then the plant should be treated in the environmental review process as if it were already listed. With regards to non-listed, but rare and endangered plants in California this is a very important section in California environmental law. Since there are many hundreds of plants in the CNPS Inventory that appear to meet the State's definitions and criteria, but are not yet listed by the State, there needs to be some way to handle the non-listed but equally rare and endangered plants. CEQA does this. It offers a certain amount of visibility to the non-listed Rare, Threatened, and Endangered plants of California that are published in the CNPS Inventory.

CNPS Ranking and Lists - In order to increase the refinement of assigning a plant to a list, CNPS has developed a scheme that involves rating each plant on three coordinate, related elements that are scored independently. These components are:

Rarity(R), which addresses the extent of the plant, both in terms of numbers of individuals and the nature and extent of distribution;
Endangerment (E), which embodies the extent of the plant being threatened with extinction, for whatever reason; and
Distribution (D), which focuses on the general range of the plant.

Together these form the R-E-D Code. Each element in the code is divided into three classes or degrees of concern, represented by the number 1, 2, or 3. In each case, the higher the number the more critical is the concern.

Each plant in the CNPS Inventory is first assigned an R-E-D Code which will help decide which list it will be on.

The CNPS Inventory lists are:

List 1 - Highest Priority Plants
    List 1A - Plants Presumed Extinct in California
    List 1B - Plants Rare or Endangered in California and Elsewhere
List 2 - Plants Rare or Endangered in California, More Common Elsewhere
List 3 - Plants For Which We Need More Information
List 4 - Plants of Limited Distribution (A Watch List)
Appendix 1 - Plants Considered, But Not Included

CONCLUSION

Since California has at least three (Federal, State, and CNPS) lists that deal with its rare, threatened, and endangered flora, those people who are in positions responsible for these plants must be comfortable with each list.

Spending a little time in an attempt to understand these different lists may keep you from personifying the old addage: "There's never enough time to do it right, but there's always enough time to do it over." One should properly document the rare, threatened, and endangered plants i.e. acknowledge the Federal/State category for each plant and what CNPS Inventory list it is on, etc. If not done properly or completely, depending on what you are doing, this ommission could cost a great deal of time and money to correct and it may even slow proposed work.

A good, overall reference is the CNPS Inventory. It has an extensive introduction section that not only explains how and what CNPS' Rare Plant Program is doing, but also how the Federal and State programs function. This is really the only document available that has attempted to combine all three aspects.

REFERENCES

Department of the Interior, Fish and Wildlife Service. Endangered and Threatened Wildlife and Plants; Review of Plant Taxa for listing as Endangered or Threatened; Notice of Review. 50 CFR Part 17. Volume 50, Number 188. September 27, 1985. Pages 39526 - 39584.

Smith, James P., Jr.; Richard P. York (editors). Inventory of Rare and Endangered Vascular Plants of California; California Native Plant Society, Special Publication Number 1, 3rd Edition. September 1984. 174 pages.

Using the California Endangered Species Act Consultation Provisions for Plant Conservation

Earl W. Cummings [1]

Abstract: The legal authorities for rare, threatened, and endangered species protection in California include a number of interrelated statutes. The most effective of these laws and regulations are described, and the process by which the public and government agencies use them to protect plants is explained.

The environmental laws available to conserve rare and endangered plants can be conceived of as part of a system, like bricks in a wall. The most usable bricks, as I see them, are the State's general planning law, the Subdivision Map Act, the California Environmental Quality Act, and capping the others, the California Endangered Species Act. The Native Plant Protection Act is, in my judgment, a liability and dilutes the effectiveness of the other laws. We would be better off if it were repealed. Let me describe the foundation of plant conservation using the related laws and I will try to show how a sound wall should be built.

GENERAL PLANNING LAW

The foundation of your protective structure is, or should be, the State's general planning law. This law requires every county and city to prepare and adopt a comprehensive, long-term general plan for the physical development of the land within its boundaries. The general plan and its mandated elements are required to be integrated, internally consistent, and express a compatible statement of policies.

The first action in plant conservation should be to examine the general plan for your local jurisdiction and find the mapping of plant resources (if any) and the expression of policies for plant conservation

There may be neither, in which case, the need for plant protection, and the inability of the General Plan to provide it, should be brought to the attention of the legislative body (the board of supervisors or city council) and to the local planning agency (usually the planning commission). You will need to demonstrate a substantial public interest, probably by means of multiple letters, phone calls and by appearing at hearings to make sure the local government recognizes there is a problem.

The local general plan is updated periodically. If you make it clear that there is some inadequacy (for example, no reference to rare or endangered plant species) or inconsistency (for example the conservation element calls for plant protection but the land use element, or zoning, permits unrestricted development of rare plant habitat) the local agency will work quickly to correct the situation. Local agencies have been forced by court orders to put a moratorium on <u>all</u> development because of an inadequate element in the general plan. Remember, the General Plan is the Constitution for development in an area. If the constitution is flawed, development based on it is flawed, and no valid permit based on it can be issued. Even if your plant conservation group is not willing to undertake a lawsuit, some other group, with some other cause, can use an inadequacy you have identified to invalidate a General Plan and force an update.

General Plan Elements

The General Plan elements which you should particularly examine are mandated by the State. The most commonly significant of these state-mandated elements for plant

---

[1] Associate Wildlife Biologist, California Department of Fish and Game. Environmental Services Division, Sacramento, CA.

protection are the conservation element, land use element, open-space element and possibly the safety element.[2]

You should also look closely at policy statements set out in the General Plan which relate to development. Usually these are platitudes, which are sufficiently vague to be subject to broad interpretation. They are not supposed to be vague and can be challenged directly for inadequacy as well as used to show inconsistency between the policy and one or more of the elements.

Your approach should be to first evaluate the local general plan for clear neglect of plants. Chances are you will not find such a gross inadequacy. The State of California has had a respectable contingent of environmental planners working to comply with the general planning law, and usually there will be at least some reference to plants in the policy statements, a reference to the CNPS <u>Inventory of Rare and Endangered Vascular Plants</u>, and probably some reference to plant species and community protection in the open-space element or conservation element.

If plants are not properly addressed, and your broaching of the issue leads to an update, local governments are required to provide opportunity for citizen involvement in the general plan development and amendment process. If you express explicit concern for inadequacies in the treatment of plants and offer to assist in planning process with special expertise in plant distribution or habitat requirements, the planning agency will usually be pleased to involve you in the process. If you are aware of federally-listed plant species, particularly those which may occur in wetlands, you should point out to local planners that they are obligated to involve the U.S. Fish and Wildlife Service and U.S. Army Corps of Engineers, who have jurisdictions which would be affected by the plans.

Usually general plan amendments are requested and paid for by development interests who expect to increase the value of their holdings by having them planned and re-zoned for a more lucrative use. You may have to piggy-back on such an amendment for some small parcels, but there is a schedule of major general plan updates, and you can learn it and organize your information to be used in conjunction with the regular process.

If you are concerned that a significant plant resource will be lost as a result of projects which would be wholly consistent with the existing general plan, you may have to challenge the adequacy of the plan or show the internal inconsistency through legal action.

<u>Inadequate or Inconsistent General Plans</u>

An alternative approach is to bring inconsistencies or inadequacies of a General Plan to the State Office of Planning and Research, 1400 Tenth Street. They may take action on behalf of the State. As a resident or property owner in the local agencies' jurisdiction, you may also bring action yourself to compel the local zoning ordinances to be consistent with the General Plan.[3]

Rezoning requires an EIR if the proposed enactment could have a significant effect on the environment.

A possible (even though somewhat remote) avenue to gain a powerful co-litigant is to bring the lack of General Plan protection for plant resources to the attention of the Department of Fish and Game (DFG). The Fish and Game Commission, which sets policy for the Department, has policies which direct the Department to participate in land use planning, and to protect threatened and endangered species. In the event the Department fails to act to your satisfaction on these Commission policies, you can bring the failure to the attention of the

---

[2] Refer to Section 65302 of the Government Code for the subjects to be covered in these elements.

[3] Refer to Government Code Section 65860(a) and (b).

Commission itself, and they will ask the DFG embarrassing questions about the lapse, or may undertake a suit in behalf of the State.[4]

Such challenges have been highly successful and even a reference to legal action may get a quick positive response. If a single project or subdivision is involved which would depart from the expressions of policy in the general plan, you may also make use of provisions of the next two building blocks I will describe, the Subdivision Map Act, and the California Environmental Quality Act CEQA).

SUBDIVISION MAP ACT

The Subdivision Map Act, up until 1985, was a significant, although generally unrecognized tool for environmental protection. It prohibited the approval of tentative parcel maps which would result in harm or damage to the environment.

During the development process, if a developer wishes to subdivide a parcel, he must file a tentative parcel map with the local planning agency. Approval of the tentative (not the final) map is a discretionary activity and can be denied if the division conflicts with existing zoning or provisions of the General Plan. The way local planning agencies usually cope with this conflict is to amend the zoning and general plan, using a negative declaration, under the provisions of the CEQA, which we'll talk a lot more about later.

Principles of administrative law require that local governments make written findings of facts, supported by substantial evidence in the record, that a proposed subdivision is consistent with the General Plan (and specific plan, if there is one for the area). The decision must be based on a finding (among others) that the project will not cause environmental damage (absent an EIR).

The Subdivision Map Act prohibits approval of a tentative parcel map if it could result in harm to the environment.[5]

The legislature became aware that the Subdivision Map Act was a major potential obstacle to development when it was pointed out that a local government might receive a subdivision proposal, recognize it would harm the environment, prepare an EIR, approve the project, damage and all, with findings of overriding considerations (more about that later) and then, when it came to the actual approval of the tentative parcel map, be prohibited from granting the approval. The Subdivision Map Act had to go, and it did, at least in part. Now, if the local government has prepared the EIR and made the necessary findings of overriding considerations, they can go ahead with the decision on the tentative parcel map, and approve it even if it is harmful.

The Subdivision Map Act remains in effect if no EIR is prepared, so if you are aware of a subdivision which can reasonably be argued to have an adverse effect on a rare or endangered species, you should point out that an EIR is required before approval can be granted. This may only delay the eventual approval, or it may result in the lead agency denying the project once the EIR discloses the significance of its impacts on the environment. At least it may buy you time to work out a conservation plan with the project sponsor, so that the adverse impacts can be avoided.

<u>The Significance of Delay</u>

Delay should never be dismissed as a trivial inconvenience when it comes to a development. A great deal of development is proposed on property for which a developer has obtained an option to purchase, or for which he has obtained a loan. His option may expire or the interest on the loan must be paid, and unless the development actually proceeds, the developer may lose a great deal of money. Delay is very expensive for the sponsor under these circumstances,

---

[4] Refer to the Fish and Game Commission Policy on Land Use Planning, Policy on Endangered and Threatened Species and the Policy on Implementation and Review of Policies.

[5] Refer to Government Code sections 66410 through 66499.37.

there is a great incentive for him or her to compromise and negotiate. If a reasonable modification of the project would allow the project to proceed and still preserve the resources you want protected, there is a real advantage for both the developer and the environmentally concerned to work out a satisfactory solution.

Once a satisfactory conservation plan is part of the project, the tentative parcel map can be approved without requiring an EIR. At least that's how it ought to work on small projects using just the Subdivision Map Act.

The local agency can address potential damage by using the policies of the land use, conservation, or open space General Plan elements it has adopted. For instance, if you and the developer have worked out an agreement using some of the techniques addressing in the General Plan, such as clustering of the development, with transfer of residential unit density from conserved open space to already developed ground, or dedication of significant habitat to a park district or an open space trust, the local agency can permit the project to proceed.

But with large scale projects, an EIR is probably being prepared anyway, and the developer probably has enough money and political support to roll over your proposed compromises or project alterations. Now it's time to address the potential of the CEQA for rare and endangered plant protection.

THE CALIFORNIA ENVIRONMENTAL QUALITY ACT (CEQA)

Let us look at some of the key provisions of CEQA which can help us protect rare and endangered plants. I will address some in special detail because the DFG has a unique role to play in the environmental review process. Although this avenue is not clearly open to the participation of conservation groups, it may be more open than you realize.

Your familiarization with CEQA should begin with being aware that CEQA is implemented through the Law, passed by the Legislature, and the Guidelines, adopted to implement the law. The law is referred to as statutes, the guidelines as regulations.

Endangered Species Provisions

Early consultation

Let me first discuss the significant provisions of the law which relate to protection of endangered species. Section 21080.5(a) of CEQA (the law) states that prior to determining whether to use a negative declaration or an EIR for a project, any lead agency shall consult with responsible (i.e. permit-issuing) agencies, and trustee agencies. This can be considered the preliminary review or initial study stage, or the earliest possible consultation.

Trustee Versus Responsible Agency Status

As an aside, trustee agencies are those, which like DFG, are responsible for the protection of those assets of the state which are held in trust for all of the people. Trust resources are fish, wildlife, navigable waters, air, the ocean and so on. In practice, the DFG is the only agency which has responsibility for trust resources but has no clear permit authority over activities which may affect those resources, with the exception of hunting and fishing. That lack of authority beyond the granting of fish and hunting licenses is worth discussing further.

An area of the law which has never been tried is whether the DFG has "jurisdiction by law" over endangered species. The "take" of endangered species is prohibited by Fish and Game Code Section 2081 without a permit from DFG, but it is not clear that destruction of the home or habitat of an endangered species is a take as defined by Section 86 of the Fish and Game Code.

The next significant section of CEQA is 21104.2, which was added as part of the California Endangered Species Act of 1984.[6]

---

[6] Chapter 1245, statutes of 1984.

This section of the law provides that state lead agencies (not local governments, just the state government) shall consult Department of Fish and Game as to impacts on endangered species when preparing an EIR, and obtain written findings.

These two preceding sections, then, say that any lead agency shall consult with DFG when deciding whether to prepare an EIR or negative declaration, while State lead agencies must continue to consult while preparing an EIR. That continued consultation is to be reflected in written findings from DFG, on whether or not the project will jeopardize listed species and setting forth alternatives or mitigation.

The provision of 21104.2 is virtually identical to Section 21153 which requires every local lead agency during EIR preparation to consult with and obtain comments from any agency which has jurisdiction by law with respect to the project. As indicated, it is not clear whether DFG is such an agency, but if you are involved in endangered species litigation, it is worth checking to see whether DFG and other agencies were consulted by the local lead agency. That would include federal agencies in many cases, because the U.S. Fish and Wildlife Service, for instance, has jurisdiction over all migratory birds, whether endangered or not, and most lead agencies will probably have neglected to provide them with the project documents. This observation may result in my friends at the Fish and Wildlife Service getting a lot of new business, but it really is an important and generally overlooked aspect of the law.

The substance of all these consultation requirements is that any lead agency, whether local or state-level, should be consulting with DFG, at the preliminary review and initial study stages, as well as later.

Exemptions

The preliminary review stage is where many projects are identified as exempt, because the local lead agency believes they can see with certainty that there is no possible way their project could have a significant effect on the environment. For example, flood control districts may decide they will clear a stream channel to prevent flooding. They figure that when the flood comes it will devastate the channel anyway, so if they do it, there will be no impact. As another example, local planning agencies may decide that their existing general plan calls for all the rural land to be divided into 5-acre parcels, so if they amend the plan to allow all the land to be divided into 7-acre parcels, there would be no impact, because 7-acre parcels are "less damaging" than 5-acre parcels. They forget that the parcel size now is 640 acres, and the real impact of adopting a new plan is the potential change from what is existing, rather than the paper change between plans.

A common mistake in preliminary reviews is to confuse the plan with reality or the map with the territory. Clearing a flood channel is a discretionary activity which has a reasonable likelihood of producing a significant effect. It doesn't matter if a storm might accomplish the same thing. Adopting a plan which could result in parcels being split substantially is a significant impact even if existing plans would have permitted much the same thing. Remember the distinction between paper plans and reality when you review an EIR or a notice of exemption. Many of the projects declared exempt really ought not be. Watch the County Clerk's office for local notices of exemption and subscribe to the State Clearinghouse Newsletter to keep tabs on state agencies. You must challenge such a notice within 30 days of the posting of notice to get them back on track to preparing an EIR.[7]

Funding of Mitigation

Most state agencies are reluctant to adopt environmental protection measures if they think they will have a to pay for them. However, CEQA Section 21106 requires that all state lead agencies include in their budget the funds necessary to protect the environment from problems cause by their activities. The preceding section, 21105, requires the state

---

[7] Refer to sections 21108. 21152, and 21167(b).

lead agency to include the EIR as part of the project report for the state budgetary process, and to make the report available to the Legislature. If you have a problem with a project, which appears not to have adequate funding for environmental protection, it may be worth asking your Legislator, or the appropriate legislative committee, or supervisor at the local level to review the EIR and add funds to the state or local lead agency's budget in a way which earmarks the funds for mitigation.

Unfortunately, as in other parts of CEQA, there are no penalties if an agency fails to comply with the provisions related to their funding and budgetary procedures. The law is intended to be self-enforcing by citizen lawsuits, but successful suits are usually based on procedural errors rather than substantive flaws, and a suit for insufficient mitigation funding would, in my opinion, most likely be unsuccessful.

Using the CEQA Guidelines

There are some provisions in the CEQA Guidelines which substantially improve the environmental protection called for in the statutes. Of particular value is the provision in Section 15065(a) of the Guidelines which set forth findings which force lead agencies to prepare an EIR. These are termed "mandatory findings of significance". In summary, the lead agencies must prepare an EIR if a project has the potential to: substantially reduce the habitat of a fish or wildlife population; to cause a population to drop below self-sustaining levels; to threaten to eliminate a plant or animal community; or to reduce the number or restrict the range of a rare or endangered plant. The preparation of an EIR is thus necessary for essentially all projects with the potential to eliminate a single individual rare plant or an increment of habitat. Lead agencies may not fully realize that they have this obligation, because it is not frequently brought to their attention.

As a conservationist, you should be familiar with this requirement. If a project is proposed in endangered plant habitat, or in habitat, such as wetland, or vernal pool areas, which are locally significant, as there are in most cities, you can bring up this obligation.

Procedural Opportunities

Two other provisions of the CEQA guidelines relate to this obligation to prepare EIRs and address rare, threatened, and endangered species in them. Section 15082(d) states that a lead agency must send a copy of the Notice of Preparation to the State Clearinghouse (SCH) when a trustee agency (such as DFG) would have a resource affected which it is supposed to protect. Since virtually every development has the potential to affect fish or wildlife, including plants, virtually every local lead agency is required by this provision to send notice to the SCH. Most don't. Or perhaps I should say most don't for many projects, even though an argument could be advanced that the project could affect a trust resource. Conservationists watching local projects could force local lead agencies to prepare EIRs by reciting this provision, and advising lead agency that the NOP to the SCH is obligatory. To be optimally effective, the conservationist may have to advise the DFG biologist reviewing the NOP that a significant effect is possible. I'm sorry, but let me be the first to inform you that the vast majority of DFG biologists are only rather dimly aware that plant resources exist and fall under their jurisdiction.

A similar provision of the CEQA Guidelines is 15206(b)(5) which directs a lead agency to determine that a proposed project is of regional or statewide significance if the project would substantially affect sensitive wildlife habitats including, but not limited to riparian lands, wetlands, bays, estuaries, marshes, and habitats for rare and endangered species. Environmental documents for such a project must be routed through the SCH. As the discussion in the Guidelines for this section notes, "The sensitive wildlife habitats are regarded as even more critical and subject to damage than the larger geographical areas identified by name in Subsection (b)(4) (Tahoe Region, Santa Monica Mountains, Coastal Zone, Wild and Scenic Rivers, Sacramento-San Joaquin Delta, Suisun Marsh, and San Francisco Bay.)

THE CALIFORNIA ENDANGERED SPECIES ACT

Historical Perspective

There are few people who recall that California pioneered in endangered species preservation, preceding the Federal Endangered Species Act by a year. In 1984, the California Endangered Species Act was amended to tie the preservation of endangered species into CEQA.

To appreciate how this was done, let me summarize the historical basis for the structure of the DFG, and how it addresses endangered species. The first conservation laws were passed to limit the duration of hunting season; later, licenses were required for fishing and hunting. Enforcement by a DFG warden force was relatively late in coming. During the gradual development of legislation to protect endangered species, the State Water Project had led to the creation of the Water Projects Branch of the DFG. One of the spinoffs from the DFG's review of the State Water Project was the establishment of elements of a staff with a background of environmental analysis. When the environmental decade arrived (1972 to 1982, let's say), there were DFG staffers with the appropriate background to assess the impacts of proposed projects in light of biological concerns and state legal requirements such as those established in the Porter-Cologne Act, the Burns-Porter Act and the Davis-Grunsky Act. These acts all established the DFG in an advisory role in environmental protection. That advisory role, as distinguished from that of a responsible agency having permit authority over a project, was continued, in part by CEQA, which was passed after the old Endangered Species Act.

The old California Endangered Species Act of 1972 stated that take of an endangered, or a rare species required a permit from the DFG and prescribed the circumstances under which a permit could be issued.

Let's examine what that requirement entailed. Essentially, if a project was approved by a lead agency, and an individual or an endangered species would be killed, the project sponsor would either have to obtain an permit from the Department for the take (with DFG under no obligation to issue one) or risk being cited for unlawful take (assuming a DFG warden was able to detect the take and issue the citation).

In practice, of course, many projects have been approved in endangered species habitat, with few, or no citations written for take. It is difficult to issue a citation and prosecute a case for take of a kangaroo rat, for example, because there is a serious problem obtaining the evidence. The major grading associated with a subdivision eliminates nearly all surface features, yet collapsing a burrow system would not be direct evidence that there were kangaroo rats in it when it was collapsed. This same problem of evidence collection applies for a host of animal species which are hard to find and not very abundant to being with, but fortunately many plants are detectable on the surface year-round.

I believe the most effective way for conservationists to use the California Endangered Species Act would be to ensure that the other environmental statutes force local lead agencies to seek DFG input when addressing protection of rare threatened or endangered plants. I want to point out that this discussion is largely theoretical, because there is very little history of Endangered Species Act use in CEQA situations.

The specific actions I recommend would be to have consultation adopted as General Plan policy whenever a project could affect a species which is listed or is rare in fact.[8] A second specific action would be to make sure maps or diagrams of known rare plant distributions are incorporated in the General Plan and all appropriate elements of it. This informational approach would trigger a finding of significance at the preliminary project review stage. It would be clear during the initial study that a reasonable argument exists that a significant impact would

---

[8] Refer to CEQA Guidelines Section 15380.

occur. At that point, the local lead agency and project sponsor would have an incentive to consult with DFG to see whether avoidance of impact was possible or whether a species mangement plan would be an option consistent with conservation of the species. If avoidance is possible, a negative declaration could be issued, which would save time and money for the sponsor. If impacts are such that mitigation measures could fully compensate for impacts, an EIR should be prepared using a DFG-approved habitat conservation plan which is circulated as part of the EIR. In the worst case, even with a habitat conservation plan, the project would lead to a reduction in the range or numbers of a species. The DFG might refuse to issue a permit for take under these circumstances because it would be bad policy to approve a project which would jeopardize a listed species. In that case, the lead agency would have to approve the EIR and follow up with findings of overriding considerations to explain why they had approved a project which still had significant adverse impacts. In this situation, the DFG might still cite the project developer or lead agency for take of endangered species if they attempted to carry out the project or an inadequate compensation plan.

There is an important cautionary note to sound at this point. Under the "formal" consultation provisions, DFG cannot require a state lead agency to provide greater protection for plants than are required by the Native Plant Protection Act (NPPA). That means state lead agencies may simply notify DFG to move the listed plants 10 days before the start of construction. This is rather unsatisfactory, and I'll address the problem further later. DFG's consultations with local lead agencies are not subject to that "move it or lose it" policy expressed in the NPPA, but are instead guided by the policies found in CEQA and the CEQA guidelines.

FUTURE DIRECTIONS

In my discussion, I have emphasized the interlocking nature of the environmental planning and protection laws. The NPPA, in my view is a weak link which needs to be eliminated or repaired. As it stands, state lead agencies, through formal consultation, can now virtually ignore the protective CEQA provision which they would otherwise have to address. Local lead agencies don't have this loophole, because the formal consultation provisions, which limit DFG input on plant protection to the requirements of the NPPA, are not available to them. The ironic truth is that the state lead agencies are held to lower standards of plant species preservation than local lead agencies.

The best protection for endangered plants is CEQA, and if the NPPA were eliminated, that protection would continue. There does not seem to be a downside risk if it were eliminated. The advantage of relying on CEQA alone is that the CEQA guidelines make it clear that reduction in the numbers or range of a species which is rare, even though unlisted, is a significant impact. That means an EIR, which means delay and expense, unless a resolution can be found that protects the plant and avoids or fully compensates for any harm. With the negotiating advantage that CEQA provides, conservationists can persuade lead agencies to change plans, adopt less damagiong alternatives or fund propagation efforts. With the NPPA, you may have to watch DFG carry out an emergency transplant effort, probably at the wrong time of year to be successful. I'm inclined to propose it be repealed or greatly modified to eliminate the objectionable provisions.

A second choice would be to eliminate the reference to the NPPA in Section 2091 of the Endangered Species Act. Then DFG could hold state lead agencies to the same standards as local agencies. The disadvantage is that the NPPA would still exist, and be a confusing and contradictory guide to plant protection.

The third choice would be to eliminate Section 1913 from the NPPA. Even though some of the provisions in this section may be tolerable for retention, they conflict with the CEQA guidelines and harm the prospects for effective plant conservation.

The State of California has some fine statutes and regulations which can be used to protect plants. The key is to learn them. I hope this paper helps make all of you more effective at plant conservation.

Conservation of Rare Plants on Public Lands in California

Edward L. Hastey [1]

Abstract: The Bureau of Land Management (BLM), an agency of the United States Department of the Interior, is responsible for the management of over 17 million acres of public lands in California. These public lands support populations of six federally listed endangered and threatened plants and more than 130 plants considered by BLM to be sensitive, by virtue of being either State listed or candidates for Federal listing. BLM's policy on the conservation of sensitive and listed plant species is clarified, using examples of management issues relating to these plants and actions taken by BLM on their behalf.

The Bureau of Land Management (BLM), an agency of the United States Department of the Interior, is charged with the administration of programs for conservation and development of public lands and resources. Nationwide, the agency manages 337 million acres of Federal lands. These lands are known collectively as the public lands and are managed consistent with the principles of multiple-use to produce a sustained yield of renewable resources, such as livestock forage, timber, wildlife, water, and recreational opportunity. The BLM is also responsible for other resources on the public lands, including oil, gas, coal, minerals, and archeological resources.

The BLM in California manages about 17.1 million acres of public lands, some in almost every one of the fifty-eight California counties. Another 1.5 million acres in northwestern Nevada fall under the jurisdiction of BLM's California State Office. Management responsibilities for these 18.6 million acres of public lands are divided among 4 BLM districts and 15 resource areas.

Rare plants occur in each of BLM's California districts and resource areas. These plants are managed in accordance with Federal laws and Bureau policies that operate to ensure their conservation.

---

[1] State Director, Bureau of Land Management, U.S. Department of the Interior, Sacramento, CA.

RELEVANT LAWS AND BUREAU POLICIES

The driving force behind the protection and conservation of rare plants on the public lands is the Endangered Species Act of 1973, as amended. That act provides for the listing of plant species as endangered or threatened and requires Federal agencies to take three major actions: 1) to conserve listed species; 2) to ensure that the continued existence of a listed species is not jeopardized; and 3) to ensure that the Critical Habitats of listed species are not destroyed or adversely modified. Further discussion of the Endangered Species Act and its implications for Federal agencies can be found in Bartel (1986) and Kobetich (1986).

The Federal Land Policy and Management Act (FLPMA) of 1976 is the principal law under which BLM operates. Although FLPMA does not directly deal with threatened or endangered species, it gives the scope of possible actions that the BLM can employ in managing such species on public lands. One important management tool authorized by FLPMA is the designation of Areas of Critical Environmental Concern. As we shall see this tool has been used in great degree to conserve rare plants on public lands in California.

In addition to these two major Federal laws and others (for example, the National Environmental Policy Act), the BLM in California has enacted a policy for the conservation of rare plants on public lands. Whereas the provisions of the Endangered Species Act afford ample protection for federally listed plant species, most of California's rare plants remain unlisted. The U.S. Fish and Wildlife Service maintains a list of "candidate" plant species. Candidate plants are those that appear to be in need of Federal listing (see FWS 1985 for the most recent list of candidate plants). Unless officially proposed for listing, these candidate plants enjoy none of the protection provided by the Endangered Species Act. Recognizing that these candidate plants may require the same level of conservation as federally listed plants, the BLM in California has established the following sensitive plant policy.

Pending formal listing all sensitive plant species are afforded the full protection of the Endangered Species Act unless the BLM State Director judges on a case-by-case basis that the evidence against listing a particular plant species is sufficient to allow a specific action. Federal candidate and proposed plants become sensitive species by definition. Other plants may be designated as sensitive by the State Director. Similar consideration is given to plants listed as endangered, threatened, or rare by the State of California.

RARE PLANTS ON PUBLIC LANDS IN CALIFORNIA

Six federally listed endangered and threatened plants occur on public lands managed by the California BLM (Table 1). A seventh species, spring-loving centaury (Centaurium namophilum), listed as threatened, is known historically from three sites in California. Two of these sites, one near Tecopa and the other near Resting Springs in the Mohave Desert east of Death Valley, are on or near public lands. To date, however, the species has not been relocated at either site, nor has it been found at the third historical site, Furnace Creek in Death Valley National Monument. Thus, as far as is currently known, spring-loving centaury is extant only in Ash Meadows, Nevada, where populations occupy private lands, Federal land managed by the Fish and Wildlife Service, and public lands under the jurisdiction of BLM's Nevada State Office.

Twenty-one plant species occurring on public lands in California are listed as endangered by the State; another 16 are designated rare species by the State.

Public lands under BLM's jurisdiction in California support populations of 131 BLM sensitive plants. Over 100 more species are suspected on public lands, but their occurrence has not yet been documented: if found on public lands they would be treated as sensitive species. Numerical distribution of known and suspected sensitive plants is given in Table 2.

In addition to federally listed, State-listed, and BLM sensitive plants, many other plants considered rare or of limited distribution by the California Native Plant Society (Smith and York 1984) are found on public lands managed by BLM in California. The large number of rare plant species found on California's public lands reflects the great diversity of habitats present on these lands and in California generally.

Table 1--Federally listed endangered and threatened plants on public lands managed by the Bureau of Land Management in California.

Scientific Name	Common Name	Status[1]	BLM District of Occurrence
Nitrophila mohavensis	Amargosa niterwort	E	California Desert
Grindelia fraxino-pratensis	Ash Meadows gumplant	T	California Desert
Oenothera avita ssp. eurekensis	Eureka Valley evening-primrose	E	California Desert
Swallenia alexandrae	Eureka Valley dunegrass	E	California Desert
Arabis mcdonaldiana	McDonald's rockcress	E	Ukiah
Camissonia benitensis	San Benito evening-primrose	T	Bakersfield

[1] Status: E=endangered; T=threatened.

Table 2--Number of plants by BLM district designated as sensitive species by the California State Director of the Bureau of Land Management.

BLM District	Number of Sensitive Plants		
	Known on Public Lands	Suspected on Public Lands	Total
Bakersfield	43	49	92
Susanville	7	5	12
Ukiah	18	45	63
Calif. Desert	66	12	78
Total[1]	134	111	245

[1] Actual state total is 234 plants, 131 of which are known to occur on public lands and 103 of which are suspected to occur on public lands. The higher totals shown in the table result from species reported in more than one BLM district as follows: 6 plants are known to occur on public lands in one district and are suspected in another; 3 plants are known to occur on public lands in two districts; and 2 plants are suspected to occur on public lands in two districts.

BLM'S EFFORTS TO CONSERVE RARE PLANTS IN CALIFORNIA

The BLM in California has approached the conservation of its rare plant resources from several directions. These are discussed in turn below.

Inventory

As pointed out in a previous paper (Hastey 1978), inventory is of primary importance: it is impossible to ensure the conservation of a resource you do not know you have. Inventory efforts for rare plants began in earnest in the mid-1970's and continue today. Extensive inventories were made of the 18 areas in California and northwestern Nevada for which environmental impact statements were prepared to assess the impact of BLM's livestock grazing management program. More intensive inventories have been made of many, mostly smaller areas, either because these areas were known to be "hot spots" for rare plants or because more detailed distributional information was necessary to prescribe management for the areas' resources. Such site-specific inventories have been conducted both by BLM personnel and by contract. Some of the areas intensively inventoried for rare plants include the Algodones (Imperial) Dunes in Imperial County (Westec 1977), the Red Hills in Tuolumne County (BioSystems Analysis 1984; Marcus 1979), Clear Creek and San Benito Mountain in San Benito County (Griffin 1978; Kiguchi 1983), Santa Ana River Wash in Riverside County (Bio-Tech 1985), Ash Valley in Lassen County, the Geysers Area in Lake and Sonoma Counties, and the Knoxville area of Lake and Napa Counties.

Inventory methodologies have varied depending on the size and nature of the area inventoried and the distribution of the area's rare plants. In the Red Hills Management Area of Tuolumne County, certain of that area's sensitive plants--though restricted to the serpentine soils found there--are rather widely distributed throughout the area. Such distributional patterns required the development of an innovative sampling methodology described in Davilla et. al. (1986).

In addition to the inventory efforts described above, site-specific inventories are conducted as part of the Bureau's environmental assessment process. All surface disturbing actions authorized by BLM require an assessment of the environmental consequences of such actions. The magnitude of projects can vary from large (e.g., the construction of large pipelines or transmission corridors running the width of California) to the small (e.g., development of a spring for use by wildlife and livestock). Site-specific inventories help BLM determine the effect of projects on sensitive plants and to develop project modifications to avoid impacting these species.

It is the policy of BLM in California to share the rare plant information gathered through its inventory efforts with the California Natural Diversity Data Base (CNDDB) maintained by the California Department of Fish and Game. California Native Plant Field Survey Forms are filled out and submitted to the CNDDB. The Bureau is a subscriber to the detailed periodic reports provided by the CNDDB and thus makes use of the additional rare plant data on file there.

Areas of Critical Environmental Concern and Research Natural Areas

One of the most important tools for the conservation of sensitive plants was provided by the Federal Land Policy and Management Act of 1976 (FLPMA), which authorized the establishment of Areas of Critical Environmental Concern. Areas of Critical Environmental Concern (ACEC), as defined by FLPMA, are "areas within the public lands where special management attention is required...to protect and prevent irreparable damage to important historic, cultural, or scenic values, fish and wildlife resources or other natural systems or processes...."

Designation of ACECs and/or of the pre-FLPMA (but still operable) Research Natural Areas (RNAs) has been employed to great degree in California to conserve sensitive plant species. Twelve ACECs and/or RNAs have been designated to date primarily because of the presence of rare plants. An additional 13 ACECs and/or RNAs have been designated in consideration of several resources, one of which is the presence of rare plants. An example of the latter is the Fish Slough ACEC in Mono County. In addition to 2 sensitive plant species, the nearly 36,000 acres of public lands that comprise the ACEC support a unique desert wetland, the federally listed endangered Owens pupfish, disjunct plant populations, an undescribed species of mollusc, and significant cultural and scenic resources. Table 3 gives a complete listing of California ACECs and RNAs harboring rare plants.

Upon designation of an ACEC or RNA a management plan is developed for the area. The primary objective of each plan is to prescribe management actions that will ensure the conservation of the sensitive resources present. Monitoring studies are designed to measure progress in meeting plan objectives. Sensitive plant monitoring is discussed in more detail below. Schoolcraft (1986) provides a description of BLM's ACEC and RNA designation process. Dawson (1986) and Farve (1986) discuss the development of site-specific management plans for sensitive plants.

In addition to BLM developed plans, the U.S. Fish and Wildlife Service develops recovery plans for federally listed species. To the extent these recovery plans involve public lands, BLM includes actions recommended in recovery plans in its own plans. See Knudsen (1986) for a discussion of the Fish and Wildlife Service's recovery planning process.

Monitoring

Monitoring to assess change over time is an integral part of BLM's program to conserve sensitive plants. Monitoring methodologies must be keyed to specific plant species and management situations. Monitoring intensity, timing, and frequency are also dependent upon the species to be monitored and the circumstances of a given area. Sensitive plant monitoring on public lands in California ranges from quick inspection of a species' habitat every few years to ensure no detrimental changes have occurred to intensive and frequent sampling of study plots to assess changes in population size and vigor. The former procedure is acceptable for stable populations of plants occurring in remote areas with little potential for disturbance. More intensive monitoring is necessary for other sensitive plants. For example, plants with unstable populations or habitat, plants in areas prone to disturbance, plants whose populations fluctuate widely, and plants for which the objective is to increase numbers may require intense and frequent monitoring.

A monitoring study was recently designed and baseline data collected for the sensitive plants of the Eureka Dunes, Inyo County (Bagley 1986). Monitoring will consist of the periodic reading of a series of permanent study plots to compare changes in densities and age classes of the sensitive plant species and changes in the overall vegetation of the study area. Similar monitoring studies are being conducted for other of BLM's sensitive plant species. Examples include monitoring of sensitive plants in the Ash Valley Research Natural Area, the Indian Valley Brodiaea ACEC and RNA, and the Clear Creek ACEC and San Benito Mountain Natural Area.

For some sensitive plants, it is more important to monitor changes to their habitat than changes in the plant populations themselves. The ACEC portion of the Red Hills Management Area, for example, is closed to off-road vehicle use. To ensure that violations of this closure are not occurring to the extent the sensitive plants' habitat is adversely affected, aerial photographs of the area are taken and examined every 3 years. Newly formed off-road vehicle tracks would be clearly visible; if present, a new management strategy might be needed.

Research and Special Studies

Often it is not enough to know just the extent of a species' distribution or whether its numbers are changing over time. In order to prescribe proper management it may be necessary to know why the species is restricted to certain habitats and the causes--be they natural or manmade--of population change over time. Sometimes, available scientific literature provides the answers to these questions. Because these plants are

Table 3--Bureau of Land Management (BLM) Areas of Critical Environmental Concern (ACECs) and Research Natural Areas harboring federally listed and BLM sensitive plants in California. Areas marked with an asterisk (*) were designated primarily because of the presence of rare plants. The remaining areas were designated for a variety of reasons, one of which was consideration for rare plants.

District	Area and Designation	County	Size of Area (Acres)	Plant(s) Scientific Name	Common Name	Status[1]
Bakersfield	Clear Creek ACEC and San Benito Mountain Natural Area*	San Benito	30,000	Camissonia benitensis	San Benito evening-primrose	T
				Fritillaria falcata	talus fritillary	S
				Layia discoidea	rayless tidytips	S
	El Dorado Manzanita ACEC*	Tuolumne	80	Arctostaphylos nissenana	El Dorado manzanita	S[2]
	Fish Slough ACEC	Mono	35,926	Astragalus lentiginosus var. piscinensis	Fish Slough milk-vetch	S
				Calochortus excavatus	Inyo mariposa	S
	Ione Manzanita ACEC*	Amador	120	Arctostaphylos uva-ursi ssp. myrtifolia	Ione manzanita	S
	Point Sal ACEC	Santa Barbara	50	Cirsium rhothophilum	surf thistle	S
	Red Hills ACEC*	Tuolumne	4,500	Allium sanbornii var. tuolumnense	Rawhide Hill onion	S
				Chlorogalum grandiflorum	Red Hills soaproot	S
				Lomatium congdonii	Congdon's lomatium	S
				Verbena californica	Red Hills vervain	S
	Soda Lake ACEC	San Luis Obispo	2,970	Atriplex vallicola	Lost Hills saltbush	S
Susanville	Ash Valley Research Natural Area*	Lassen	1,120	Astragalus tegetarioides	Deschutes milk-vetch	S
				Eriogonum procidum	prostrate milk-vetch	S[2]
				Ivesia paniculata	Ash Creek ivesia	S[2]
Ukiah	Indian Valley ACEC and Research Natural Area*	Lake	40	Brodiaea coronaria var. rosea	Indian Valley brodiaea	S
				Streptanthus morrisonii	Morrison's jewel-flower	S
	Red Mountain ACEC and Research Natural Area*	Mendocino	6,957	Arabis mcdonaldiana	McDonald's rock cress	E
				Eriogonum kelloggii	Red Mountain buckwheat	S
				Sedum laxum ssp. eastwoodiae	Red Mountain stonecrop	S
				Silene campanulata ssp. campanulata	Red Mountain campion	S
California Desert	Big Morongo Canyon ACEC	San Bernardino and Riverside	3,186	Monardella robisonii	Robison's monardella	S
	Big & Little Sand Spring ACEC*	Inyo	259	Astragalus lentiginosus var. sesquimetralis	Sodaville milk-vetch	S
	Cerro Gordo ACEC*	Inyo	9,990	Caulostraminea jaegeri	Jaeger's caulostraminea	S
				Eriogonum eremicola	Wild Rose Canyon buckwheat	S
				Eriogonum microthecum var. panamintense	Panamint Mountains buckwheat	S
				Perityle inyoensis	Inyo lamphamia	S
	Chuckwalla Bench ACEC	Riverside	52,749	Coryphantha vivipara var. alversonii	Alverson's pincushion cactus	S
				Opuntia munzii	Munz' cholla	S
	Clark Mountain ACEC	San Bernardino	17,826	Forsellesia pungens var. glabra	pungent forsellesia	S
				Sphaeralcea rusbyi ssp. eremicola	Rusby's desert mallow	S
	Corn Springs ACEC	Riverside	2,690	Coryphantha vivipara var. alversonii	Alverson's pincushion cactus	S
				Ditaxis californica	California ditaxis	S
	Eriophyllum Preserve ACEC*	San Bernardino	320	Eriophyllum mohavense	Barstow woolly-sunflower	S
	Eureka Valley Dunes ACEC*	Inyo	9,324	Astragalus lentiginosus var. micans	shiny milk-vetch	S
				Oenothera avita ssp. eurekensis	Eureka Valley evening-primrose	E
				Swallenia alexandrae	Eureka Valley dunegrass	E
	Grimshaw Lake ACEC	San Bernardino	960	Cordylanthus tecopensis	Tecopa bird's beak	S
				Centaurium namophilum[3]	spring-loving centaury	T
	Mohave Fishhook Cactus ACEC*	San Bernardino	320	Sclerocactus polyancistrus	Mohave fishhook cactus	S[2]
	New York Mountains ACEC	San Bernardino	54,750	Eriogonum ericifolium var. thornei	Thorne's buckwheat	S

Table 3--Continued.

District	Area and Designation	County	Size of Area (Acres)	Plant(s) Scientific Name	Common Name	Status[1]
California Desert	Salt Creek ACEC	Riverside	4,000	Salvia greatae	Orocopia sage	S
	Southern East Mesa ACEC	Imperial	40,712	Croton wigginsii	Wiggins' croton	S[4]
				Helianthus niveus ssp. tephrodes	desert sunflower	S
	Surprise Canyon ACEC	Inyo	13,168	Dudleya saxosa ssp. saxosa	Panamint live-forever	S
				Enceliopsis covillei	Panamint daisy	S
	Table Mountain ACEC	San Diego	3,960	Astragalus douglasii var. perstrictus	round-podded milk-vetch	S
				Lupinus excubitus var. medius	Mountain Springs bush lupine	S

[1] Status: E=federally listed endangered plant; T=federally listed threatened plant; S=BLM sensitive plant.
[2] Considered to be sensitive species at time of special area designation, these plants have since been removed from the sensitive species list, either partly or wholly because of management afforded by special area designation.
[3] Known historically from near Tecopa, in or very near the Grimshaw Lake ACEC, this species has apparently not been seen at this location since 1950.
[4] Considered to be sensitive by virtue of being listed by the State of California as rare, this species is not considered rare or endangered by either BLM or the U.S. Fish and Wildlife Service.

rare, however, it is more often the case that very little information on a species' ecology is on hand. Furthermore, what information does exist may be in error or not present an accurate picture of the species' habitat requirements. The information on herbarium specimen labels is often the only data available regarding habitat requirements. When only one or a few collections of a rare plant have been made the likelihood increases that such information is either in error or does not represent the more typical habitat of the species. Early collectors often did not make note of habitat features botanists consider very obvious today. For example, the restriction of many of California's rare plants to serpentine substrates is well known to today's botanists. As Kruckeberg (1984) points out, however, very few botanists working in California prior to the 1940's gave any indication of recognizing the close association with serpentine of many California endemic plants.

When faced with a dearth of information regarding a species' ecology, it becomes necessary to conduct research or special studies to collect data necessary to support decisions on the species' management. Examples of BLM funded studies are Pavlik's (1979) study of the ecology of the plants of the Eureka Valley Dunes; the study by Romspert and Burk (1979) of the sensitive plants of the Algodones Dunes; Taylor's (1979) ecological life history studies of localized calciphytes (plants restricted to limestone substrates) in the Mohave Desert; BioSystems Analysis' (1984) study of the sensitive plants of the Red Hills; and a study by Willoughby (1986) of the effects of livestock grazing on two sensitive plant species in the Red Hills.

A three year BLM-contracted study by Dr. Michael F. Baad of the ecology of McDonald's rockcress (Arabis mcdonaldiana) and other sensitive plants on Red Mountain, Mendocino County, is currently in its third year. A long-term study of the ecology of an extremely rare annual plant, San Benito evening-primrose (Camissonia benitensis), federally listed as threatened, is slated to begin in 1987.

A study with a somewhat different focus is underway in BLM's Ukiah District. A complex of populations in the genus Streptanthus (jewel-flowers) occurs in The Geysers area of Sonoma and Lake Counties. Two species have been named from this complex, Streptanthus brachiatus (Socrates Mine jewel-flower) and S. morrisonii (Morrison's jewel-flower), both of which are sensitive species. Because of the presence of several different, unnamed forms of these two named species, it became clear that the current body of knowledge on the taxonomy of the Streptanthus brachiatus-morrisonii complex was not adequate to assess rarity or assign significance to individual populations. Because The Geysers is an area of active development of geothermal energy, such knowledge was determined to be essential to prescribing proper management for these species. The Bureau therefore entered into a memorandum of understanding with several of the most important geothermal development companies of the area to conduct the necessary study. Funding is being provided jointly by BLM, Northern California Power Agency, Pacific Gas and Electric Company, Sacramento Municipal Utility District, Grace Geothermal Corporation, Union Oil Company of California, and Aminoil USA, Inc. The three year study, contracted to Tierra Madre Consultants, will be completed in 1987. In addition to addressing taxonomic questions involving the species complex, the study is focusing on its ecology and demography.

Habitat Protection and Enhancement

For rare plant species whose habitats are not threatened by natural processes or human activities, no habitat protection or enhancement measures are necessary. Management actions would likely consist of low-level monitoring efforts such as an occasional visit or interpretation of periodic aerial photographs.

Other plant species may be in need of more direct measures to protect and enhance their habitats. Following are examples of some of the types of actions BLM has taken to protect or enhance the habitat of some of California's rare plants.

Closure to Off-road Vehicles

The BLM has effected numerous off-road vehicle (ORV) closures to protect rare plants in California. One of the earliest such closures was of the Eureka Valley Dunes in Inyo County to protect federally listed and sensitive plant species. Although the closure posed early enforcement problems, perseverance by BLM rangers has greatly minimized problems to the point that ORVs are no longer considered a threat to these species. In other closed areas old ORV trails are being rehabilitated.

Enforcement of BLM Regulations

The BLM ranger force continues to ensure compliance with BLM's regulations dealing with protection of natural resources. The BLM in California has recently expanded its ranger force to include uniformed rangers in the Folsom, Hollister, and Arcata Resource Areas. Significant among these rangers' duties is protection of rare plant species. Other Bureau employees ensure compliance with the regulations governing mineral development, lands actions, livestock grazing, and timber management.

Construction of Management Facilities

Numerous management facilities have been constructed to protect and enhance the habitats of rare plants. Examples are:
1. Pipe barriers and fences built to protect populations of the San Benito evening-primrose.
2. A fence constructed to protect Menzies' wallflower (Erysimum menziesii) from ORV activities.
3. Vehicle barricades constructed to protect the rare plants of the Eureka Valley Dunes, Big Morongo Canyon, and Amargosa Canyon ACECs.
4. Exclosure fences built around populations of Sodaville milk-vetch (Astragalus lentiginosus var. sesquimetralis) and Barstow woolly sunflower (Eriophyllum mohavense) to prevent damage from livestock and burros.
5. Signs posted in many locations on public land to inform the public of vehicle or other use restrictions effected to protect rare plants.

Public Education

An important part of the Bureau's program to conserve rare plants is to educate the public on the importance of conserving California's rare plants. BLM personnel regularly make presentations at meetings of public interest groups and lead field tours of botanically important areas. Brochures have been developed for some of California's ACECs; these include discussions of the rare plants of the areas. Interpretive signs have been installed at several important rare plant sites.

Land Acquisition

Although land acquisition has not yet been used specifically to conserve rare plants, it has been proposed for one area. The management plan for the Ash Valley Research Natural Area proposes to acquire 120 acres of private lands supporting rare plants. Future plans will likely propose additional land acquisition.

Use of Volunteers to Supplement BLM'S Management Capability

The BLM in California has been the fortunate beneficiary of the help of many qualified volunteers, who have given freely of their time to help conserve rare plant species. Members of the California Native Plant Society have helped BLM in conducting an inventory of the Indian Valley brodiaea, in monitoring rare plant populations in the Red Hills, and in controlling invading Russian thistles (Salsola australis) at the Eureka Valley Dunes. They have offered suggestions on the management of many BLM areas supporting rare plants. Members of The Nature Conservancy have also been very helpful. Recently, volunteers from that organization assisted BLM in a survey for leafy reed grass (Calamagrostis foliosa). Their efforts resulted in the documentation of 27 new occurrences of that species.

Volunteers have gathered periodically on weekends in the Red Hills Management Area to assist BLM in clearing litter from this area, which supports 4 sensitive plant species. Other volunteers have helped BLM in many other ways. The Bureau is greatly indebted to these individuals.

FUTURE DIRECTIONS

Although BLM in California has accomplished a great deal in conserving the State's rare plants, there is still much to be done. Inventory and monitoring must continue. The Bureau's planning process must continue to recognize sensitive plants and their habitats and prescribe management to ensure their conservation. Implementation of BLM management plans and U.S. Fish and Wildlife Service recovery plans must continue.

A recent analysis of BLM's botanical capabilities in California has led to the conclusion that more botanists are needed. The California Desert District is taking action to add a botanist to its District Office staff. The Bakersfield District, given adequate funding in fiscal year 1987, will follow suit. These actions should serve to increase the Bureau's level of effort in rare plant conservation. It is important to note, however, that other BLM personnel--although they may not be classified as botanists--have demonstrated they have the knowledge and initiative necessary to manage California's rare plant resources. These individuals will continue to make important contributions to the conservation of rare plants.

The BLM will continue to depend upon volunteers to assist it in the various actions necessary to conserve rare plants. Organizations and individuals interested in rare plant conservation are encouraged to offer their assistance to BLM in managing rare plants. In addition to the types of actions discussed above, other arrangements are possible. We have entered into cooperative management agreements with The Nature Conservancy whereby that organization takes over much of the management responsibility for certain significant areas. Although to date these have been initiated primarily for conservation of significant wildlife habitat (examples are the Kern River Preserve in Kern County, Soda Lake in San Luis Obispo County, and Big Morongo Canyon in San Bernardino and Riverside Counties) the use of such agreements for the management of areas supporting rare plants is certainly an option to which BLM is receptive. This may be an effort that the California Native Plant Society may wish to consider.

REFERENCES

Bagley, Mark. Baseline data for a sensitive plant monitoring study on the Eureka Valley Dunes, Inyo County, California. Administrative report prepared for U.S. Department of the Interior, Bureau of Land Management. 1986 April. 104 p. On file at BLM California State Office.

Bartel, Jim A. The Federal listing of rare and endangered plants: What is involved and what does it mean? 1986 [These proceedings].

Bio-Tech/Environmental Planning Consultants. Rare plant survey--Santa Ana River Wash. Administrative report prepared for U.S. Department of the Interior, Bureau of Land Management. 1985. 13 p. On file at BLM California State Office.

BioSystems Analysis, Inc. Study of sensitive plant species on the BLM Red Hills Management Area, Tuolumne County, California. Administrative report prepared for U.S. Department of the Interior, Bureau of Land Management. 1984 December. 60 p. + appendices. On file at BLM California State Office.

Davilla, William B.; Stone, Doug R.; Taylor, Dean W.; Willoughby, John W. Techniques for determining population sizes and relative densities of rare but locally widespread plants: A case study. 1986 [These proceedings].

Dawson, Bruce. Management plan development for sensitive plant species. 1986 [These proceedings].

Farve, Reynaud. A management plan for rare plants in the Red Hills of Tuolumne County, California. 1986 [These proceedings].

FWS--Fish and Wildlife Service, U.S. Department of the Interior. Endangered and threatened wildlife and plants; review of plant taxa for listing as endangered or threatened species; notice of review. Federal Register 50(188): 39526-39584; 1985 September 27.

Griffin, James R. Survey of rare and endangered plants: Clear Creek Recreation Area. Administrative report prepared for U.S. Department of the Interior, Bureau of Land Management. 1978 September. 6 p. + appendices. On file at BLM California State Office.

Hastey, Edward L. BLM's plant preservation policies. Fremontia 5(4): 25-27; 1978 January.

Kiguchi, Laurie M. Sensitive plant survey: Clear Creek Recreation Area and San Benito Mountain Natural Area. Administrative report prepared for U.S. Department of the Interior, Bureau of Land Management. 1983 June. 5 p. + appendices. On file at BLM California State Office.

Knudsen, Monty D. Recovering endangered plants. 1986 [These proceedings].

Kobetich, Gail C. The "Incidental Take" concept in the Endangered Species Act of 1973. 1986 [These proceedings].

Kruckeberg, Arthur R. California serpentines: flora, vegetation, geology, soils, and management problems. Berkeley: University of California Press; 1984. 180 p.

Marcus, Diane. A status report of the rare and endangered plants of the Red Hills. Administrative report prepared for U.S. Department of the Interior, Bureau of Land Management. 1979 spring-summer. 10 p. On file at BLM California State Office.

Pavlik, Bruce M. The biology of endemic psammophytes, Eureka Valley, California, and its relation to off-road vehicle impact. Administrative report prepared for U.S. Department of the Interior, Bureau of Land Management. 1979 July. 110 p. On file at BLM California State Office.

Romspert, Alan P.; Burk, Jack H. Algodones Dunes sensitive plant project. Administrative report prepared for U.S. Department of the Interior, Bureau of Land Management. 1979. 56 p. On file at BLM California State Office.

Schoolcraft, Gary D. The designation process for a research natural area. 1986 [These proceedings].

Smith, James Payne, Jr.; York, Richard. Inventory of rare and endangered vascular plants of California. Special Publication No. 1 (3rd Edition). Berkeley, CA: California Native Plant Society; 1984; 174 p.

Taylor, Dean W. Ecological life history studies of localized calciphytes in the Mohave Desert of California. Administrative report prepared for U.S. Department of the Interior, Bureau of Land Management. 1979. On file at BLM California State Office.

Westec Services, Inc. Survey of sensitive plants of the Algodones Dunes. Administrative report prepared for U.S. Department of the Interior, Bureau of Land Management. 1977 August. 141 p. + appendices. On file at BLM California State Office.

Sensitive Plant Management on the National Forests in California

Zane G. Smith, Jr.[1]

Abstract: The Forest Service sensitive plant program develops and implements management practices to ensure that candidate plant species do not become threatened or endangered on the National Forests. Data is provided describing the policies and processes for plant conservation along with the criteria for plant taxa to be placed on the Forest Service Sensitive Plant List. The Forest Service continues to be a leader for plant conservation among federal agencies to ensure the long-term viability of candidate and sensitive plant taxa.

California has a total land area of 101.5 million acres. Of this total, approximately 20 million acres are National Forest System lands (NFS) administered by the U.S. Forest Service, Department of Agriculture. The Pacific Southwest Region (R-5) of the Forest Service comprises 19 National Forests (Figure 1).

Of all the National Forest Regions, R-5 contains the largest assembledge of sensitive plant species in comparison to its land base. This is due to the diversity of topography, geography, geology and soils, climate, and vegetation that occurs on NFS lands in California. This also accounts for the exceptionally high endemic flora for the State. Of the nearly 7,000 vascular plants occurring in California, well over half are known to occur on the National Forests in California.

WHAT IS A SENSITIVE PLANT SPECIES?

Sensitive plant species is a term used to designate those plants known or highly suspected to occur on NFS lands that are considered viable candidates for federal threatened or endangered classification under the Endangered Species Act of 1973 (as amended). The term "sensitive" removes the basic confusion of using terms such as 'rare', 'threatened' or 'endangered' since these categories have legal meanings under various federal and state laws as well as local useage for plants having either small geographical ranges and/or low population numbers.

---

[1] USDA-Forest Service, Pacific Southwest Region (R-5), 630 Sansome Street, San Francisco, CA. 94111.

WHY DOES THE FOREST SERVICE HAVE A SENSITIVE PLANT LIST?

With the passage of the federal Endangered Species Act by Congress, federal departments and agencies are to utilize their authorities by carrying out the programs for the conservation of listed endangered and threatened species. In addition, they are to take such action necessary to insure that actions authorized, funded, or carried out by them do not jeopardize the continued existence of such endangered and threatened species or result in the destruction or modification of habitat of species determined to be critical.

By early 1975, the Forest Service (R-5) issued a policy statement concerning endangered, threatened, and sensitive species. This policy developed into the current Sensitive Plant Program. Activities of the continuing plant program are (1) inventory and expand the initial knowledge base, (2) design and implement interim management to maintain viable populations throughout the species range, and (3) implement recovery management to remove the actual causes of endangerment and official listing under federal law.

Activities of the sensitive plant program include field verification of known or reported locations, preparation of individual population records, field reconnaissance of projects and input to Environmental Assessments and Environmental Statements, identifying basic research needs, monitoring key populations, and preparing individual species management guides.

HOW IS THE FOREST SERVICE (R-5) SENSITIVE PLANT LIST DEVELOPED?

The R-5 Sensitive Plant List has been developed from lists of plant species under review for federal listing by the U. S. Fish & Wildlife Service (USFWS) as outlined in the Federal Register. The list is also evaluated with the State of California Endangered Plant Project and the California Natural Diversity Data Base (CNDDB), both within the California Department of Fish & Game. In addition, plants recommended by the California Native Plant Society (CNPS) are also considered for inclusion on the sensitive plant list. It also reflects the professional knowledge of Forest Service personnel directly responsible for sensitive plant management on NFS lands in California (R-5).

Of the 272 taxa currently on the 1986 edition of the Sensitive Plant List for R-5, 100 are taxa endemic to NFS lands. Region 5, therefore, has the sole responsibility for the viability and long-term conservation of these species. Plants actually listed as threatened or endangered under federal law are placed on the R-5 list for convenience even though they are already "listed" plants rather than sensitive. At present, there are four federally listed plants and two proposed for listing on the National Forests in Region 5. The R-5 sensitive plant list also takes into account those taxa listed under state laws as either "endangered", "threatened" or "rare". Any State listed species which may need special management is also placed on the R-5 Sensitive Plant List.

The Sensitive Plant List includes only those taxa known, reported, or highly suspected to occur on <u>National Forest System</u> lands in Region 5. The list is subject to continued change (both additions and deletions) as new data is obtained, taxonomic problems clarified, or as revisions to the source documents are made. Many plants thought to be in jeopardy since 1980 have been proven to be either (1) more common than earlier believed, (2) they have been documented as not occurring on NFS lands, or (3) are not threatened or endangered. Most of these species are either on List 4 (Plants of Limited Distribution, A Watch List) or on Appendix 1 (Plants Considered, But Not Included) of the CNPS Rare Plant Inventory, 3rd edition, 1984.

WHAT IS THE FOREST SERVICE POLICY FOR SENSITIVE PLANTS?

In March 1975, the Forest Service, R-5 issued a policy statement regarding 'sensitive' plant species. From this policy, interim guidelines were provided and the sensitive plant program was developed. Region 5 of the Forest Service led the way for the eventual development of a national policy to be directed to all Forest Service regions. This policy direction is located in the Forest Service Manual (FSM). The FSM provides several specific and key objectives for sensitive plant management.

Implementation of the Region 5 Sensitive Plant Program is outlined in the 2670 section of the FSM titled Threatened, Endangered, and Sensitive Plants & Animals. The FSM is the working policy and framework for implementing all Forest Service programs. Key parts of the FSM 2670.22 concerning sensitive plants are:

(1) Develop & implement management practices to ensure that species do not become threatened or endangered because of Forest Service actions.

(2) Maintain viable populations of all native and desired nonnative wildlife, fish, and plant species in habitats distributed throughout their geographic range on NFS lands.

(3) Develop & implement management objectives for populations and/or habitat of sensitive species.

In addition, further policy for sensitive taxa is located in FSM 2670.32 which states:

(1) Assist states in achieving their goals for the conservation of endemic species.

(2) As part of the National Environmental Policy Act (NEPA) process, review programs and activities, through a biological evaluation, to determine their potential effect on sensitive species.

(3) Avoid or minimize impacts to species whose viability has been identified as a concern.

(4) If impacts cannot be avoided, analyze the significance of potential adverse efforts on the population or its habitat within the area of concern and on the

species as a whole (the line officer, with project approval authority, makes the decision to allow or disallow impact, but the decision must not result in loss of species viability or create significant trends toward federal listing).

(5) Establish management objectives in cooperation with the States when projects on National Forest System lands may have a significant effect on sensitive species population numbers or distributions. Establish objectives for federal candidate species in cooperation with FWS and the States.

The entire FSM 2670 section can be reviewed at any National Forest Supervisor or District Ranger Office.

Each National Forest has a 'Sensitive Plant Coordinator' responsible for the day to day implementation of the plant program at the forest level. Forests with high numbers of sensitive plants may also have a botanist or other highly trained biological persons working on sensitive plant issues on the forest.

The Endangered Species Act (ESA) and the National Forest Management Act (NFMA) provide additional framework for the sensitive plant program. Forest Service national goals strive to recover threatened and endangered species from the need for continued listing under the ESA, and to ensure that candidate and sensitive plant species never require federal listing. This is the policy and direction that is being implemented in the Forest Service, R5.

HOW ARE SENSITIVE PLANTS ACTUALLY MANAGED?

Distribution patterns, habitats, and ecological parameters differ for each of the 272 sensitive plants on the R-5 list. We have learned first-hand that to protect and conserve these taxa does not necessarily mean to keep all activities away from the plants.

In trying to figure out ecological requirements, opportunities, and constraints for species, past management activities and practices often provide important insights. Some species require frequent burning, others are early successional taxa, while others prefer a specific microenvironment to optimize population numbers and vigor. By trying to assess how to maintain viable populations of sensitive species in dynamic forest ecosystems throughout their range on NFS lands, we learn much more than by foolishly thinking 'fence them and leave them' is always the best prescription. The key objective for long-term sensitive species management is not how much forest management the species can take, but rather, what type of forest management does the species need to assure long-term conservation.

As the various forest inventories for sensitive plants reach completion, long-range species management guides are to be prepared. These guides are not intended to be exhaustive documents, but are designed as "work plans" outlying site-specific objectives, activities, and time tables for implementing the guide on the ground. They are also designed with monitoring along with periodic review to ensure that the guide is working. As new data becomes available, this information is also incorporated into the species management guide.

Unfortunately, most of the R-5 sensitive plant species lack the basic ecological data necessary to develop comprehensive species management guides. However, several guides are currently operational. As an example, the sensitive plant Shirley Meadows mariposa lily (Calochortus westonii Eastw.) currently has an approved management guide that utilizes various un-even timber harvesting practices to create a more park-like forest environment which the species favors. In addition, the area is closed to all activities (such as fuelwood gathering) when the plants are flowering and setting seed. After seed set, the area is opened to fuelwood gathering to reduce the amount of downed wood on the forest floor. This assists in creating the open park-like condition which the mariposa lily favors. Implementation of this relatively simple species management guide ensures the long-term conservation of this species and removes the need to list the plant under federal law.

I want to reinforce the point that not all sensitive plants can be managed the same. The key is developing what are the needs for the conservation of each sensitive plant and when required, design projects through forest management practices that provide for the species continued well-being. In the case of the Shirley Meadows mariposa lily outlined above, not to implement those selected projects identified in the species management guide would eventually impact and increase jeopardy to the species which we could not biologically justify or defend. Some sensitive plants need to be 'left alone', while others require prescribed management treatments to ensure their long-term conservation. Managing sensitive plants in R-5 is indeed a dynamic and challenging part of multiple resource conservation.

HOW IS R-5 SENSITIVE PLANT DATA HANDLED?

It is important that forest resource managers have the most up-to-date information for all of the sensitive plants on NFS lands. Each forest has developed a specific methodology for collecting sensitive plant data. The most common format is a 3-ring binder Sensitive Plant Handbook(s) which contain the cumulative data on each species. Generally field survey forms, topographical maps, color photographs, aerial photos, along with a status report form the basic data gathered on each species. Some forests have designed map overlays that show what areas of the forest have received various levels and intensity of inventory work for the presence or absence of sensitive plants or their essential habitats. The aid of detailed color aerial photos also greatly assists forest personnel in predicting the probability of locating populations of sensitive plants on any part of the forest. Region 5 has a close association with the Natural Diversity Data Base. All of the sensitive plant data generated by each National Forest is yearly forwarded to NDDB. This aids the state, FWS, CNPS, The Nature Conservancy, and other interested parties on the current range, population trends, condition and vigor for each sensitive species being inventoried and managed on NFS lands in California.

WHAT ARE THE R-5 FOREST SERVICE ACCOMPLISHMENTS REGARDING BOTANICAL CONSERVATION?

The Forest Service in R-5 has a long history of conserving rare and unique plants. Region 5 developed the first sensitive plant program in the Forest Service. One classic example of botanical conservation is the establishment of the Ancient Bristlecone Pine Forest. This botanical area contains 26,900 acres on the Inyo National Forest. Currently five botanical areas in R-5 have been formally established as outlined in the Special Interest Areas section 2360 of the FSM. Many more botanical areas (several containing sensitive plant species) are being recommended for establishment on National Forests in R-5 during the current development of Land and Resource Management Plans. Other sensitive plants are within established or proposed Research Natural Areas (RNA's) as outlined in section 4060 of the FSM. In addition to the above land designations, many endemic and sensitive plant species are located in the 3.9 million acres of National Forest Wilderness in California established by Congress since the creation of the Wilderness Act in 1964.

CONCLUSION

Sensitive plants are indeed a unique and scientifically valuable resource on the National Forests. Persons interested in sensitive plant management need to work closely with forest personnel at the local level. I personally encourage CNPS and other concerned groups and individuals dealing with sensitive plants to aid the Forest Service in our inventory efforts and gathering the necessary ecological data to prepare species management guides by volunteering your expertise to your favorite or local National Forest in California.

FIGURE 1. Map of the Pacific Southwest Region showing 19 National Forests.

Government Funding of Research, Protection and Management of Rare Plants in California

Stephen J. Nicola [1]

Abstract: This paper summarizes data on investment by state and federal agencies in California on management of native plants, with emphasis on the California Department of Fish and Game (DFG). Approximately $750,000 per year is spent by the DFG, U.S. Fish and Wildlife Service, U.S. Forest Service and Bureau of Land Management directly for the benefit of native plants. The agency with the greatest authority for native plants, the Department of Fish and Game, has increased its funding in recent years, but much more is needed. CNPS can (and should) have a role in influencing agency investment in native plant management.

The California Native Plant Society collectively, and its members, individually, know full well the importance of native plants, not only as sources of aesthetic and intellectual gratification, but also at least to some of us, as a source of income. Whether we actively study them or simply passively accept them as part of our physical and spiritual being, we depend on plants.

And they depend on us. Because of the ability of Homo sapiens to alter the environment, we realize that native plants may not always be available to enjoy. Today's Hibiscus californicus may be tomorrow's Amsinckia grandiflora. If we want native plants around for research and enjoyment tomorrow we must invest in their future today.

How exactly does one invest in the future of native plants? Your botanical heritage is a common property resource held in trust for you by me. Well, actually, I'm employed by the state government, which is the trustee of your property, and they have asked me and others, on your behalf, to see to it that your property is properly managed.

It is analogous to a bank holding your estate in trust for your children until they become old enough (and, presumably, wise enough) to manage it for themselves. So how are we doing, the state and federal "banks", the state and federal resource management agencies, at conserving your trust? Have we preserved your capital? Have we secured the future of your botanical heritage?

To be sure, over the years we have invested heavily in parks, wilderness areas, nature reserves and the like, but despite these investments some of your capital, as the bankers say, has eroded. Much of the loss occurred well before your time and long before plants were generally recognized as being part of the public trust. But you have a right, indeed an obligation, to hold us, the bank managers, accountable for our present stewardship of your public estate. One indication of the condition of your account and a reflection of the investment we are making on your behalf is the amount of money the trustees commit each year to management of the trust, as indicated in our yearly budgets.

GOVERNMENT FUNDING

Department of Fish and Game

Management of native plants began in earnest in California for the first time in July 1977, when the state Legislature appropriated $75,000 from the General Fund for the Department of Fish and Game to carry out the provisions of the Native Plant Protection Act of 1977. Since then, its budget for plants has increased nearly five-fold, to $355,700 (Table 1).

For eight of the last 10 years, including the current fiscal year, our budget has included funds received from the U.S. Fish and Wildlife Service under Section 6 of the Federal Endangered Species Act. From July 1978 through June 1983 these funds were the only monies our program was receiving. When Congressional appropriations ceased in 1981, the Department returned to the Legislature for General Funds, which have continued ever since. We continued to spend previously unencumbered Section 6 money in FY 1981-82; in FY 1984-85 appropriations resumed. Nineteen-eighty-four also marked the first year that the Department began spending money from the Endangered and Rare Fish, Wildlife and Plant Species Conservation and

---

[1] Natural Diversity Data Base Coordinator, California Department of Fish and Game, Sacramento, CA.

Table 1. Funding of Department of Fish and Game Programs and Activities Undertaken for the Direct Benefit of Native Plants[1]

FUND	Fiscal Year									
	1977-78	1978-79	1979-80	1980-81	1981-82	1982-83	1983-84	1984-85	1985-86	1986-87
General Fund (S)[2]	75,000	∅	∅	∅	∅	4,000	74,034	89,683	105,172	132,700
Section 6 (F)[3]		76,904	84,682	107,994	90,276	5,000	∅	70,000	88,000	33,000
Environmental License Plate (S)						83,513	∅	∅	∅	∅
Tax Check-off (S)								33,000	34,000	190,000
Total	75,000	76,904	84,682	107,994	90,276	92,513	74,034	192,683	227,172	355,700

1 Expended through the Department's Endangered Plant Project. Does not include capital outlay (for land acquisition).

2 F = Federal, S = State

3 Endangered Species Act grant-in-aid to states.

Enhancement Account, a fund derived from the voluntary contributions of individual California taxpayers. This "Tax Check-off Fund" accounts for over half of the money allocated this year for native plant management.

The above figures represent money expended through the DFG Endangered Plant Project. This is the only program in the DFG that expends staff time and money for the direct and primary benefit of native plants. It carries out not only the Native Plant Protection Act, but also the amended state Endangered Species Act of 1984 as it pertains to plants. It has the same mission and activities as our two other DFG endangered species programs, one for birds and mammals and the other for fishes, reptiles, amphibians, and invertebrates. In addition, there are also special projects for nongame birds and mammals, the condor and the sea otter. Together with more general nongame programs for such things as ecological reserve management, federal lands habitat restoration, and the Natural Diversity Data Base, they constitute the Department's total effort applied directly for the benefit of nongame and endangered species, a commitment in excess of $6.7 million, or some 6 percent of the Department's total budget (Table 2).

Federal Agencies

The Department of Fish and Game of course is not the only government agency that manages your public trust. Table 2 also shows approximate expenditures in California by three of the major federal agencies with authorities and responsibility for the management of native plants or their habitats. Expenditures for all nongame and endangered species, including plants, range from 10.8 to 47.7 percent of their total fish and wildlife expenditures in California. For plants alone, expenditures range from 1.5 to 6.7 percent. In contrast, DFG expenditures will be 6.3 percent for nongame and endangered species and 0.3 percent for plants.

However, what is significant is not so much the comparison between the DFG and the federal agencies, but the small proportion and relatively small amounts of agency funds spent on plants. Unlike the DFG total, the federal agency totals do not include administrative support costs, which can represent a significant expenditure. Were such costs included in the federal agency totals, the percentage of funding for plants by the federal agencies would have been proportionately less. Conversely, if the DFG total excluded administrative support, as well as marine fisheries expenditures, the proportion of its funding for plants by the DFG would have been slightly more (0.4 percent instead of 0.3 percent).

My purpose in this exercise is not to conduct a detailed analysis of agency funding, but simply to illustrate the relative commitments of your trustees to the conservation of plants. It reveals the relative level and order of magnitude of resources that your trustees directly invest each year to manage your public trust resource.

RETURN ON INVESTMENT

Importance of the Department of Fish & Game

As the principal constituent group representing the interests of society in the management of its public trust (plants) to the trustee agencies, you may (and should) well ask: Are we investing enough in the management of your trust to keep it intact for future generations?

Of course there are institutions who manage your trust other than the four I have singled out here, and, as I mentioned above, large amounts are reasonably secure in parks, wilderness areas, and on military lands. But, as you know, plants and the ecosystems they are a part of cannot just be put away in the bank and left alone. They need to be managed. Management, or stewardship, is necessary for two reasons.

First, man's presence in the environment has produced unnatural effects on natural successional processes which, if left unmanaged, can lead to local extirpations and extinctions. Second, and more importantly, all agencies except the DFG and USFWS exist for purposes other than native plant conservation. Usually they have missions involving resource extraction and uses that are in direct conflict with wildlife conservation needs in general, let alone those of plants.

Many state and federal agencies have biologists on their staffs who try to look after the needs of fish and wildlife. Some even have one or more botanists. Most spend their time trying to help their employers satisfy federal and state endangered species and environmental protection requirements, while trying to get the best deal they can for plants. It is usually the officially-listed endangered and threatened species that receive the most, if not all, of the attention.

Table 2. Approximate Recent Levels of Funding of the Department of Fish and Game for Wildlife Management Programs and Activities in California, Including Plants[1]
(Figures in parentheses are percent of total.)

Category	Agency			
	DFG[2]	USFWS[3]	USFS[4]	BLM[4]
TOTAL	$106,430,000	[5]$7,000,000	$5,277,000	$1,492,000
Nongame and Endangered[6]	6,729,090 (6.3)	[7]1,000,000 (14.3)	572,000 (10.8)	712,000 (47.7)
Native Plants Only	355,700 (0.3)	133,000 (1.9)	157,000 (3.0)	100,000 (6.7)

[1] Does not include capital outlay (e.g., land acquisition). Please note that the dollar figures for the federal agencies are not official. They were derived by the author after discussions with knowledgeable agency staff. Because expenditures are not always specifically identified in agency reports, they constitute educated "guestimates" on my part. Therefore, I bear sole responsibility for the accuracy of these amounts (SJN).

[2] FY 1986-87 appropriation

[3] FY 1984-85 expenditures

[4] FY 1985-86 expenditures, Fish and Wildlife budget only

[5] Does not include law enforcement

[6] Including plants

[7] Does not include Section 6 funds disbursed to state

Despite the seemingly impossible odds, I know for a fact that these agency biologists accomplish a lot. But in relation to the scope of the problem, is it realistic to expect that their agencies are doing all that is necessary to safeguard your botanical heritage? Those of us in government know intuitively that the answer is no.

When your mission is something other than the conservation of native plants, this is understandable. Therefore, if you are to rely on any agency to do the job, it should be the agency that has as the basis of its constitutional and legislative authority the conservation of all wildlife, including plants; the agency that has no conflicting and overriding mission of commodity production or resource use which subjugates wildlife conservation to a subordinate role. For native plants, I am referring to the California Department of Fish and Game.

The U.S. Fish and Wildlife Service also has legislative authorities to conserve wildlife, but these are restricted basically to migratory species and endangered and threatened species. Thus, the DFG has primary management responsibility for virtually all species of plants that are found in California.

Reality

This is a responsibility that should not be taken, nor given, lightly. We are holding in trust for you over 7,000 known species of vascular plants. In contrast, there are less than 1,000 species of vertebrates. Fully 1,000 or 14% of these plants are believed by DFG and CNPS experts to be rare, depleted or otherwise vulnerable to endangerment or extinction. One-hundred-eighty-seven have been officially recognized by the State and listed as endangered, threatened or rare. We believe that as many as 900 taxa have the potential to be on these lists.

Now I don't pretend that we will ever see a day when a single threatened plant receives as much money as the condor or the sea otter, but I have to believe that someday we will be investing more than we are now. The $355,700 budget of the Endangered Plant Project represents an average direct investment of only $1,900 per listed species. This can be a misleading statistic, however, since most listed species have received no direct management outlay for years.

How then is your trust conserved? At its present level of funding and staffing (three positions, one of which is a temporary help or seasonal aide position) the Endangered Plant Project can do little more than coordinate with others to implement or influence programs and activities under the control of others that may directly or indirectly benefit plants. Endangered Plant Project botanists must work through the DFG's own regional and headquarters staff, other state and federal agency botanists, and the private sector to carry out its goals. In the DFG, where plant management has potentially the greatest payoff, there are no field staff in the regional offices with exclusive responsibility for nongame species or plants. Plant protection and management is but one of many responsibilities of the Department's wildlife field biologists, and their level of involvement with plants is not under the control of the Endangered Plant Project.

Absent a direct link between the Endangered Plant Project and in-the-field management, plant conservation becomes heavily dependent upon what can be accomplished incidentally for plants. Activities such as enforcement of laws intended to protect specific habitats (for example, stream channels) and review of projects under CEQA and NEPA, have potentially large indirect benefits for native plants. If a listed species happens to be involved, then the benefits are more direct.

Also potentially important are the benefits that can accrue in the careful design and implementation of the Department's own activities and programs undertaken for the benefit of animals, both game and nongame. I say "potentially" in reference to benefits because the protection obtained, if any, depends on how informed are the staff undertaking the program or activity, their motivation and skill in obtaining protection and the extent to which they are held accountable for how well they do their jobs in relation to plants.

These same facts also apply in the case of other state and federal agencies and they depend in large part on how much the Endangered Plant Project can do in dissemminating information, training and support.

The Promise

The Department recently has initiated programs that will improve our ability to provide protection for plants. We have established the California Natural Diversity Data Base and a Lands and Natural

Areas Project. The Data Base maintains the most current information on the locations of rare and threatened native plants in the state. The information is provided to public and private sector users to aid in the planning, implementation and review of programs and projects for the purpose of enhancing, or avoiding adverse effects on native plants.

Our Lands and Natural Areas Project is a user of the Data Base. In addition to coordinating the acquisition of rare plant habitats, it coordinates with other state and federal land management agencies, as well as The Nature Conservancy, to achieve protection of "significant natural areas", including those containing rare and threatened plants and plant communities. This program also coordinates the expenditure of nearly $1 million a year appropriated by the Legislature since FY 1985-86 for management of DFG Ecological Reserves.

We also have undertaken some administrative measures to provide greater efficiency and accountability for nongame and endangered species management that will have benefits for native plants. The DFG has implemented a new cost accounting system that will enable us to more accurately identify where and how much time and effort is being spent department-wide on plants. Soon we hope to begin an annual work objective planning system that will enable us to more effectively direct that effort. Finally, the Department has recently centralized the statewide coordination of nongame and endangered species activities by creating the Nongame-Heritage Program, headquartered in Sacramento. The program includes the Natural Diversity Data Base and the Endangered Plant Project. It also includes the Lands and Natural Areas Project, which was formed by combining the Significant Natural Areas Program (established in 1981 along with the Data Base) with the Lands Program, formerly in the Wildlife Management Division.

The Need

While these measures will no doubt lead to increased benefits for native plants, they may not be sufficient for addressing the major protection needs that exist. For example, identifying and recognizing the status of a species by official designation as endangered, threatened or rare is only the first step in the protection and recovery of a taxon. The taxon needs to be monitored and steps need to be taken to restore the taxon to a secure status. Yet the resources have been lacking to adequately address these needs on a systematic basis. Fully one-third of the state-listed plants have been monitored so poorly or not at all that we don't know what has happened to them since they've been listed. Another one-third are assessed as being either declining or stable-to-declining in status. Less than 10% of state-listed species are believed to be increasing or stable-to-increasing.

The management effort required to bring about recovery of the listed taxa will be great. Yet recovery will be slow in coming because only a handful of recovery or management plans have been written. Furthermore, before recovery plans can be written, it is necessary to have status reports describing the threats and management needs of a taxon. However, fewer than half of the listed taxa have current status reports.

These are some of the major needs of state-listed native plant taxa. Yet there are as many as 700 or more plant taxa that may also qualify for official recognition, many of which may require the same level of protection and recovery activity. And remember, we have been talking only about vascular plants; we have yet to even begin thinking about the thousands of non-vascular taxa that some of you have asked us to be accountable for.

CONCLUSION

The significance of native plants to society as a source of aesthetic and intellectual gratification, even as a source of income to some, is readily apparent, especially to the members of the California Native Plant Society. The level of investment in this public trust resource by your government agency trustees is small in relation to the problems and needs of native plants in California. The California Department of Fish and Game, the agency with the principal authority to manage native plants in California, has made notable progress in recent years in increasing its investment in native plants. But much remains to be done.

Although there probably will never be a day when rare plant management in government agencies receives the same emphasis as commodity production or game animals, the future for native plants in California could well depend on how much of a say CNPS chooses to have in how government agencies invest in the management of this public trust heritage.

Rare and Endangered Species Management in the California State Park System

James Barry [1]

Abstract: The major objective in ecosystem management in the State Park System is the perpetuation of dynamic natural ecosystems in a pristine state. Rare and endangered species and their supporting ecosystems are given special protection through the Natural Preserve classification. Various management manipulations in natural preserves and areas that meet the criteria for natural preserve status, but have not yet been classified as such are summarized. Specific examples include the protection of Inglenook Fen and rare and endangered plants within MacKerricher State Park and alien species control in prairie ecosystems restoration projects at Pt. Lobos State Reserve and La Jolla Valley Natural Preserve. Dune stabilization techniques used to protect the fen ecosystem from sand encroachment are discussed, and rare plant niche enhancement and creation are also discussed. The effects of prescribed fire on rare plant niches and alien species in graminoid ecosystems is also discussed. Various techniques of rare plant niche enhancement and propagation are outlined. Niche enhancement includes hand removal of competing alien species. Propagation experiments for rare dune plants has been underway for a number of years.

INTRODUCTION

The California Department of Parks and Recreation has three primary missions:
1. Preserving California's Cultural Heritage
2. Preserving California's Natural Heritage
3. Providing Californians with Significant Recreation Opportunities.
The natural heritage mission is as follows: "The State Park System, in concert with other agencies and organizations, preserves and interprets representative examples of Californian's natural and scenic landscape and its ecosystems for public recreational, inspirational, educational, and scientific purposes. To accomplish this, the department:
1. Acquires outstanding complete ecological units that represent the natural features unique to each of the landscape provinces of California;
2. Acquires other outstanding natural areas as primary destination scenic landscape and its ecosystems for public recreational, inspirational, educational, and scientific purposes. To accomplish this, the department:
1. Acquires outstanding complete ecological units that represent the natural features unique to each of the landscape provinces of California;
2. Acquires other outstanding natural areas as primary destination scenic attractions or areas that possess natural features of statewide significance;
3. Manages the natural resources of each State Park System unit to promote and enhance the public's enjoyment of the unit in accordance with the stated purpose of the unit;
4 Provides interpretive and visitor orientation programs to enhance the enjoyment of visitors and to increase their appreciation of natural values and processes.
Most of the natural heritage lands preserved in the State Park System are in state parks, state reserves, state wildernesses, and natural preserves."
(Troy et. al., 1980).

Several regulations of the Department of Parks and Recreation are specific to rare and endangered species. According to the California Public Resources Code (Section 5019.71) "The purpose of natural preserves shall be to preserve such

---

[1] Sr. State Park Ecologist, Department of Parks and Recreation, Resources Agency, State of California, Sacramento, CA.

features as rare or endangered plant and animal species and their supporting ecosystems, representative examples of plant and animal communities existing in California prior to the impact of civilization,...Areas set aside as natural preserves shall be of sufficient size to allow, where possible, the natural dynamics of ecological interaction to continue without interference, and to provide in all cases, a practicable management unit. Habitat manipulation shall be permitted only in those areas found by scientific analysis to require manipulation to preserve the species or associations which constitute the basis for the establishment of the natural preserve."

Not all sensitive species (defined here to denote rare, endangered, threatened or narrow endemic native taxa) within the State Park System are protected by natural preserve status; disjunct and/or annual distribution patterns and small niches may make natural preserve designation impractical. However, sensitive species ecotopes are protected in all units of the State Park System by general or specific policies.

The California Park and Recreation Commission Policy No. 7 "Preservation of Vegetation Entities" States in part that: "It shall be the policy of this commission, in concert with other agencies and organizations, to acquire and preserve outstanding examples of native California species, and to acquire and perpetuate significant natural plant communities, associations, and examples of rare, endangered, endemic, or otherwise sensitive native California plants, as indicated on state or federal lists. Whenever possible, significant vegetative entities shall be acquired in natural ecological units so that their integrity may be better perpetuated." Policies for sensitive and special interest plants are formulated in the resource Element of the General Plan. General Plans are required by law for each unit of the State Park System. The policy statement for sensitive species might read as follows: Rare and endangered plants shall be protected and managed for their perpetuation in accordance with State law (PRC, Div. 2, Ch. 10, Sec. 1900 and 1911). Systematic surveys for sensitive species shall be made throughout the unit during the appropriate flowering season. For each species, populations, stands (and in some cases individuals) shall be mapped and niche management guidelines for its protection and perpetuation shall be formulated and implemented as part of the unit ecosystem restoration and management plan. This plan shall be based upon sound scientific analysis. Prior to any potentially deleterious activity including, but not limited to, campground development, facilities or trail construction or relocation, or prescribed burns, site-specific surveys of potential sensitive species ecotopes in impacted areas shall be conducted. Working drawings, or site specific plans shall be modified, when necessary, in order to minimize their impact on sensitive species.

Once the General Plan is adapted by the California Park and Recreation Commission, rare and endangered species surveys are normally budgeted for as part of the Major Capital Outlay Program. The autecological and synecological research necessary for development of the unit ecosystem restoration and management plan may be funded as part of the Major Capital Outlay Program as an agency retained item or it may be funded in the Statewide Resource Management Program. The implementation of the plan is usually funded through either the Statewide Resource Management Program and/or the Statewide Stewardship Program.

ECOSYSTEM RESTORATION AND MANAGEMENT

One of the Departments management objectives is to perpetuate natural ecosystems in as near a pristine state as possible. Ecosystem management is often separated into a number of tasks. Special consideration is given to archeological sites and niches of sensitive species. There are two general forms of ecosystem management practiced in the State Park System - passive and active. Passive management is to leave the ecosystem alone with observations only, including the establishment of quantitative baselines followed by long term monitoring. Distribution maps are drawn up using a combination of remote sensing and ground truthing techniques.

Protection through land acquisition, classification and special designations is included in this definition. The protection of sensitive species from potential adverse effects of human impact (such as off-road vehicles, grazing trespass, etc.) by field staff is also included in this definition. Active management includes altering of one or more environmental factors. Common examples include restoration of natural fire cycles, alien species control, and revegetation.

Passive Management

Where natural ecosystems have not been influenced by the activities of modern man, the best method of ecosystem management is to maintain natural conditions. Passive management should include ecological baseline establishment and periodic monitoring of baselines. Some time in the future, data from monitoring may indicate that a shift to active management is in order. An example of such a shift is alien species eradication in Red Rock tarweed (Hemizonia arida Keck) edaphotopes reported by Faull (1986).

Passive management of California terrestrial ecosystems often occurs in areas with desert, alpine and subalpine ecotopes. The let burn policy for lighting strike fires in designated zones is an example of this type of management. Passive management is the usual method in state wildernesses. For example, in Sinkyone Wilderness State Park, leafy reed-grass (Calamagrostis foliosa Kearny) dominates miles of Franciscan bluff and cliff faces from the splash zone to the bluff tops. Passive management, including proper trail alignment, appears to be all that will ever be necessary to protect its formidable niche.

Active Management

Active ecosystem management is often termed resource management, habitat manipulation or habitat inhancement. These popular terms all have incorrect elements, and will not be utilized or perpetuated by this author. Natural resource is defined by Webster (1971) as "industrial materials and capacities (as mineral deposits, waterpower) supplied by nature". Since we are not managing for some form of harvest, as do foresters and range managers, the term resource should not be used for natural ecosystem management. Habitat refers to the area where a given organism occurs. It includes the organisms environment or niche but, in addition, encompasses those external forces and substances which may not affect the organism directly (McNaughton and Wolf, 1973). Since for the most part, we are not manipulating external forces or substances (i.e. cloud seeding), the term "niche management" best describes the focused management objectives necessary for sensitive or special interest species. A given ecosystem may contain a number of niches all of which must be considered when making management decisions.

NICHE MANAGEMENT TECHNIQUES

Restoration of Natural Ecological Cycles

Pyric

Restoration of natural fire cycles is often difficult since around 80 years of fire suppression has caused unnatural buildups of fuels as well as unnatural plant successional patterns throughout much of the State. Many rare cypresses (Cupressus L. sp.) and some rare pines (Pinus L. sp.) however, the frequency and intensity of fire may be critical. If fire is too frequent, trees may not produce cones or the cones of these closed cone species will not mature enough to produce viable seed. An example is the rare Cuyamaca cypress (Cupressus stephensonii C. B. Wolf.) which forms a single stand population along and near the headwaters of King Creek on the southwest slope of Cuyamaca Peak. According to Vogl, et. al. (1977) one other population is reported from the Sierra Juarez, Baja California del Norte, Mexico. The Cuyamaca cypress is adapted to chaparral fires on a frequency greater than 30 years. The Boulder fire of 1970 was the last fire to burn the stand within Cuyamaca Rancho State Park. The current management strategy is to protect this population from fire until after the year 2000.

Similar management decisions have been made with Monterey cypress (Cupressus macrocarpa Hartw. ex Gord.) and Gowen cypress (C. goveniana Gord.) at Point Lobos State Reserve and with Mendocino cypress (C. pygmaea (Lemmon) Sarg.) at Salt Point, Van Damme, and Russian Gulch State Parks and Jughandle State Reserve. Small burn plots in, or adjacent to the niches of these rare conifers may be established in order to determine the fire frequencies and intensities necessary to perpetuate these species or to expand their niches.

At Torrey Pines State Reserve, Torrey pine (Pinus torreyana Parry ex Carr.) has shown very little regeneration over the past 70 years with an exception. In the area of the 1972 high intensity wildfire, I observed many young seedlings on sites missed by ryegrass seeding. However where ryegrass was present the pine seedlings could not compete. The specific policy for the perpetuation of the Torrey pine ecosystem includes the use of prescribed fire as a management tool to restore fire's role in this ecosystem. A long term Torrey pine monitoring program has also been established.

Hydrologic

Wetland drainage patterns have often been modified. The restoration of natural drainage systems is being investigated in montaine meadow ecosystems in Calaveras Big Trees State Park and the Lake Country Estates project in the Tahoe Basin. Similar restoration projects are underway in coastal wetland ecosystems at Pescadero

Marsh Natural Preserve and San Simion State Beach.

Alien Species Control

Prescribed Fire

In graminoid ecosystems, prescribed fire has been useful in controlling some alien plant species. However, it also inhances the competitive advantage of others. In coastal prairie management units prescribed fires have been conducted each autumn since 1980 with a dramatic increase in native bunch grasses (Barry, 1984). Large stands of field mustard (Brassica campestrus L.) were nearly illiminated after 5 years of burning. Alien annual grasses have decreased, however, alien perennial grasses have increased along with the native perennials in some plots. Three stands of Brodiaea versicolor (Hoover) Munz. occur in the coastal prairie ecosystem. The Mound Meadow stand has been burned and the release in competition is expected to increase the size of this population. On the other hand California Dichondra (Dichondra donelliana Thorp & Johnston), which is no longer considered sensitive, dropped out of the plot established within the stand after one control burn. This may be due to the competition for light brought on by a combination of release from domestic grazing followed by fire which stimulated lush gramminoid growth in the plot.

A native grassland restoration project has been underway since 1979 in the Santa Monica Mountains. This project is focused on the relic native grassland stands in La Jolla Valley Natural Preserve, Pt. Mugu State Park and Liberty Canyon Natural Preserve, Malibu Creek State Park. Permanant plots have been burned at various times of the year to determine which season is best at shifting the competitive advantage to native species. In the Santa Monica Mountains preliminary result indicate spring burning is best in these ecotopes. Permanant plots are being monitored annually for species compisition changes due to pyric factors; no sensitive species have been noted to date.

Herbicide Use

Where alien species cannot be effectively controlled by other means, the use of herbicides is necessary. Herbicides are currently being used at Asilamar State Beach to remove ice plant (Carpobrotus spp.) from dune edaphotopes with niches of Menzies' wallflower (Erysumum menziesii (Hook) Wettst.) and Tidestrom's lupine (Lupinus tidestromii Greene var. tidestromii).

The niches of many sensitive coastal dune plants have been drastically altered due to the widespread practice of planting European beachgrass (Ammophila arenaria (L.) Link.)for dune stabilization. This invasive alien crowds out native dune species where ever it occurs. One of the most critical areas effected by European beachgrass is the Oso Flaco Lake "Natural Area" within Pismo State Vehicular Recreation Area. In 1982, I proposed a dune revegetation and stalilization project which would eradicate the beachgrass, utilizing herbicides, and revegetate the effected dune edaphotopes with native shrub and forb communities, including propagation and planting of 15 sensitive species. Several phases of this project have been completed, including ecological studies of sensitive and common dune species. Fencing has protected the area from off-road vehicular enchroachment.

In MacKerricher State Park, the seaward side of the Menzies' wallflower ecotope is being invaded by European beachgrass which has spread down coast for several miles since my first observations in 1971. European beachgrass is to be eradicated from the unit using the only practical means, which is unfortunately, the use of herbicides.

Hand Removal

Hand removal of easily identified alien species is the most practical method of control where a sufficient labor force is available. An example is the removal of ice plant from the the Monterey pine (Pinus radiata D. Don.) - coastal bluff ecotone at Point Lobos State Reserve. Ice plant is directly competing with the dune erigonum (Eryogonum parvifolum Sm. in Rees. var. lucidum (J. T. Howell) Reveal). Ice plant has also been removed from the understory of Torrey and Monterey pines where it appears to compete with the pine for moisture, thus adding to moisture stress that weakens these pines during drought years.

Soil Improvement

Ammendments

Where the niches of sensitive species are edaphically controlled the addition of soil ammendments, incuding nutrients, may enhance the distribution of the species. In the Ten Mile Dunes, MacKerricher State Park Menzies' wallflower is often associated with the edges of kitchen midden sites. It appears that the shell leachate contains a micronutrient or forms a nutrient gradient which enhances the wallflower. Fertilizer field plots have been established and standard pot nutrient tests will soon be underway to determine if dune edaphotopes can be chemically modified to give Menzies' wallflower and Howell's spinechorizanthe (<u>Chorizanthe</u> <u>howellii</u> Goodm.) a competitive advantage in this harsh environment.

Stabilization

Soil stabilization techniques are often necessary to protect unique ecosystems and sensitive species. An example is Inglenook Fen; this unique wetland ecosystem contains the swamp harebell (<u>Campanula californica</u> (Kell.) Heller)(Barry and Schlinger 1977). Several mechanical stabilization technuques have been formulated to hault dune enchroachment into the fen. These methods include crimped straw, straw mulch with netting, plastic polymer spray coatings and sand fencing. These methods are used in combination with revegetation The success of these methods have not been fully evaluated.

<u>Revegetation</u>

Revegetation techniques utilized in the state park system are summarized by Barry (1984). Current community prescriptions for revegetation of a portion of Ten Mile Dunes include reestablishment of the beach sagewort (<u>Artemisia phycnocephyala</u> Nutt.) short open forb community of (Barry, 1985). Menzies' wallflower is associated with this plant community both at MacKerricher State Park and Asilamar State Beach. It will be plug planted into stabilized dune areas along with other associates in January 1987. Specific methods for enhancing Menzies' wallflower niches are discussed by Ferreira and Smith (1986).

REFERENCES

Barry, W. James. Ecosystem restoration in the California State Park System. In: Rieger, John P.; Steele, Bobbie A. ed. Proceedings of the native plant revegetation symposium; 1984 November 15; San Diego, CA: The Wildlife Society and the California Native Plant Society; 1984:22-33.

Barry, W. James. A hierachial vegetation classification system with emphasis on California plant communities. 1985. Unpublished draft.

Barry, W. James; Pismo Dunes State Vehicular Recreation Area, Oso Flaco Lake area resource management program. 1981. Unpublished draft.

Barry, W. James; Schlinger, Evert, I. ed. Inglenook fen, a study and plan. Sacramento,CA: California Department of Parks and Recreation. 1977. 212 p.

Faull, Mark R. Management of <u>Hemizonia arida</u> by the California Department of Parks and Recreation. 1986. (These Proceedings).

Ferreira, Jean E.; Smith, Suzanne K. Methods of increasing native populations of <u>Erysimum menziesii</u>. 1986. (These Proceedings).

McNaughtington, S. J.; Wolf, Larry L. General ecology. New York: Holt, Rinehart, and Winston, Inc.; 1973

Troy, Richard E.; Treece, Randall D.; Hallet, Harold E. Jr. California State Park System plan, 1980. Sacramento: California Dept. of Parks and Recreation; 1980. 239 p.

Vogl, Richard J.; Armstrong, Wayne P.; White, Keith L.; Cole, Kenneth L. The closed-cone pines and cypresses. In: Barbour, Michael G.; Major, Jack ed. Terrestrial vegetation of California. New York: John Wiley & Sons; 1977:295-358.

Webster, Merriam-. Webster's seventh new collegiate dictionary. Springfield, Massachusetts. G. & C. Merriam Company, Publishers; 1971. 1222 p.

Endangered Plants Along California Highways: Considerations for Right-of-Way Management

Craig Martz [1]

Abstract: Over 15,000 miles of roadway are maintained as part of California's State Highway System. This amounts to nearly 230,000 acres of right-of-way managed by the State. A wide variety of rare and endangered plant taxa can be found within these areas. Roadside management programs have only recently recognized the needs of sensitive plants. Most efforts to date have focused on preventing disturbance near sensitive plant locations. This "hands off" approach may not be appropriate in all situations. A more active management strategy is outlined using case studies as examples.

The California Department of Transportation (Caltrans) currently maintains over 15,000 miles of roads and associated rights-of-way as part of the State Highway System. These 15,000 miles represent nearly 230,000 acres of land managed primarily for highway purposes.

This network of highway lands provides abundant opportunities for the conservation of threatened and endangered plants. Only 10 percent of this network is covered by landscape plantings; these occur mostly in urban areas. The remaining 210,000 acres of land adjacent to State Highways provide existing and potential habitats for native vegetation. Due in part to the diversity of these roadside habitats, a wide variety of endangered plant taxa occur inside the right-of-way fence. At present, over 20 sensitive taxa[2] are known to occur along State Highways. The number and diversity of these plants is certain to increase as more of this extensive right-of-way is inventoried.

Endangered plants within the right-of-way present a new and special challenge for highway maintenance personnel, whose primary directive is to provide a safe and serviceable transportation facility. Highway maintenance operations routinely involve a host of activities that can affect endangered plant populations.

---

[1] Associate Environmental Planner, California Department of Transportation, Sacramento, CA.

[2] Sensitive plant taxa include those that are listed, proposed for listing, or candidates for listing by the U. S. Fish and Wildlife Service or the California Department of Fish and Game.

These include physical disturbances (eg. blading road shoulders, cleaning roadside ditches, repairing slides and slip-outs) and the direct modification of vegetation (eg. herbicide treatment of the shoulders, mowing to reduce fire hazard, removal of plants that obstruct sight distance). At the same time, maintenance policies also call for the protection of sensitive environmental resources within the right-of-way. Developing maintenance prescriptions which accomplish both of these goals is one of the greater challenges in right-of-way management.

AN ACTIVE APPROACH TO PLANT MANAGEMENT

Traditional approaches to rare plant management have been developed in the context of parks, preserves, or other protected areas where natural systems remain largely intact. These approaches rely on the preservation of natural habitat and the reduction or elimination of disturbance to protect rare species. Inherent in this approach is the assumption that natural processes will continue to support rare plants in the absence of human influence (Bratton and White, 1981).

In contrast, human activity has frequently been a pervasive and long-standing influence within the right-of-way environment. The role of human habitat modification (both past and on-going) thus warrants special consideration when planning for rare plants within this unique setting. Past highway maintenance activities need to be carefully evaluated to determine how they may have influenced the distribution and abundance of sensitive species within the right-of-way. Similarly, current programs need to be reviewed in light of the biological requirements of individual species to determine if changes are necessary to benefit roadside populations.

Conservation of rare plants in what is often a severely altered environment requires a more active management approach. The following discussion will be used to present a general overview of the kinds of rare plants that occur in these altered habitats, and to describe management techniques that are appear suitable in each case.

TYPES OF RARE PLANTS ALONG HIGHWAYS

Sensitive plants growing within highway rights-of-way exhibit a number of habits and strategies. As might be expected, seral species and opportunists that colonize disturbed sites are well represented. At the other end of the spectrum, taxa that are intolerant of disturbances such as grazing are also present. These relict taxa often benefit from the reduced herbivory afforded by the right-of-way fence. Still other taxa, innocent bystanders, occur within the right-of-way simply as accidents of highway route selection.

Artificial classification schemes can often be useful in understanding the causes and types of rarity in plants (Rabinowitz, 1981). Although necessarily oversimplified, the three groups discussed here provide a convenient framework for examining the kinds of rare plants that occupy roadside habitats. This does not imply that all rare plants within the right-of-way can be grouped according to this classification. Our knowledge of many species is too limited to allow any classification to be made. An example of such a species will be presented later under "problem taxa." Nontheless, these three groups can provide a useful focus for delineating types of rare plants and possible management strategies in a rather complex setting.

Opportunists

Highways and transportation networks in general have long been recognized as disturbance corridors playing a major role in the dispersal and establishment of ruderal species (Frenkel, 1970). Not surprisingly, rare species that colonize disturbed sites or occupy early successional stages are well represented within the right-of-way. These native "opportunists" are often legumes and frequently members of the genus Lupinus.

Highways provide habitat for opportunists in two basic ways: by creating environments which mimic the preferred habitats of local rare species, and by creating new areas of disturbance for colonization. An example of the former can be found along State Route 158 in Mono County. Here roadside accumulations of cinders from winter snow removal have been invaded by Mono Lake lupine (Lupinus duranii) and Mono milk-vetch (Astragalus monoensis). These two species are regional endemics that normally colonize barren pumice flats. The blanket of cinders apparently provides an environment that is analogous to their natural habitat.

A rare species that aggressively colonizes disturbed sites within the right-of-way is shaggy hair lupine (Lupinus spectabilis), a serpentine endemic from Mariposa and Tuolumne Counties. This annual lupine occupies outcrops of serpentine rock in a matrix of chaparral and open digger pine woodland. In this setting, Lupinus spectabilis occurs in widely scattered colonies of up to several hundred plants. Interestingly, the largest populations and highest plant densities are found on disturbed slopes along State Route 49. Here populations numbering several thousand individuals have become established on unweathered serpentine cut and fill slopes.

This distribution pattern suggests that Lupinus spectabilis is a disturbance follower that readily invades mineral soil or rock areas after natural (eg. landslides, rockfalls) or anthropogenic (eg. highway slopes, mine tailings) catastrophes. As succession progresses the species presumably will become increasingly restricted to natural rock outcrops which provide habitat between disturbance events.

Management Considerations

Seral species present some unusual management problems. Traditional approaches to rare plant conservation tend to focus on reduction or elimination of human disturbance, and are therefore of limited value. On the other hand, while some form of disturbance may be desirable, not all types of disturbance are equal. Types of disturbance and effective levels must be determined on an individual species basis.

In the case of Lupinus spectabilis, minor physical disturbance associated with blading shoulders, drainage improvement, or the repair and removal of slope failures may actually benefit the species by providing additional areas for colonization. Other forms of disturbance, such as the application of contact herbicides to control brush and reduce fire danger, are potentially damaging to plants growing within 8 to 10 feet of the pavement. While herbicide damage at this level does not pose a serious threat to Lupinus spectabilis, damage can be reduced or avoided entirely by delaying roadside spraying until after seed set --usually by late May. This spray schedule is being evaluated on a trial basis.

In addition to management actions at the population or species level, it is important to consider the effects of processes acting on a larger, ecosystem level. How are populations within the right-of-way likely to be affected by successional processes occurring on adjacent lands? Are local and regional disturbance regimes likely to insure a continued seed source for the right-of-way? Processes at this level typically operate on a scale that cannot be managed effectively within the limited area of the right-of-way. However, they often suggest a different emphasis for conservation efforts. In this instance, it may be desirable to maintain a balance between recently disturbed areas and natural serpentine outcrops within the right-of-way. Natural outcrops may prove to be important seed reservoirs for the establishment of future populations.

Relicts

Significant examples of native vegetation are occasionally preserved when lands are withdrawn for transportation corridors. In rapidly developing areas these "relict" stands within rights-of-way may become the sole representatives of the original flora.

The preservation of prairie relicts in the upper Midwest provides the best example of this phenomenon. In many parts of this region, railroad rights-of-way established prior to the development of intensive agriculture now provide the few remaining refuges for native prairie (Curtis, 1959; Bacone and Harty, 1981). The importance of these railroad relicts has been recognized for many years. Aldo Leopold (1949) referred to Wisconsin railroad lands as "linear reservations." More recently, these lands have been seen as valuable habitats for endangered plant species. Special management agreements on railroad rights-of-way are currently being used to preserve 15 plant taxa considered to be endangered, threatened or rare in Michigan (Kohring, 1981).

In California, railroad prairies were apparently extensive prior to 1918 when most were converted to a wartime wheat crop (Clements, 1934). Highway rights-of-way have yet to play such a major role in the preservation of relict vegetation. In part this is because the displacement of native vegetation in California has been less extreme than in the agricultural Midwest. Where vegetation loss has been most profound (eg. the Central Valley), development of a highway network occurred after the replacement of the native flora.

Nonetheless, a variety of rare plant species do occur within the right-of-way as individual relicts. These tend to be taxa that are intolerant of heavy or prolonged grazing. For these plants the right-of-way provides a refuge from grazing impacts on adjacent private lands. Species in the genera Fritillaria and Calochortus often occur as relicts inside the right-of-way fence. These include adobe lily (Fritillaria pluriflora) along State Route 20 in Colusa County and long-haired star-tulip (Calochortus longebarbatus var. longebarbatus) along State Route 139 in Modoc County.

While these taxa are by no means restricted to highway rights-of-way, roadside populations are often notably more vigorous than those on adjacent grazed lands. Jokerst (1983) observed dramatic differences between grazed and roadside populations of Calochortus longebarbatus var. longebarbatus. Populations within the right-of-way contained both larger numbers of plants and higher plant densities.

Perhaps the most extreme example of a grazing relict is provided by Roderick's fritillary (Fritillaria roderickii). The species is known from only two locations in Mendocino County. In Boonville, the plant occupies the older sections of a local cemetery where it has been protected from grazing since the 1880's. The remaining population is found along State Route 1 south of Point Arena. At this site the species occurs on a remnant coastal headland on the seaward side of the highway. Here too, the species is protected from grazing. The narrow strip of land between the highway and the sea cliff has remained unfenced and ungrazed at least since 1933, and possibly since the the turn of the century. In contrast, the pastures on the landward side of the highway are heavily disturbed by livestock grazing.

Management Considerations

By definition, relict species are those that persist in areas that offer protection from unfavorable environmental conditions. Those that survive along roadsides usually occupy the portion of the right-of-way between the highway slopes and the fence. These areas often require only a minimum level of maintenance, and are frequently less disturbed than either the immediate roadside or the adjoining private lands. In most cases the best management option is to continue this strategy of "benign neglect." When some form of vegetation control is needed, mowing after flowering and seed set is probably less damaging than chemical methods.

In the case of _Fritillaria roderickii_, maintenance crews have been informed of the plant's location and asked to review their program for potential conflicts. Because the low, wind-pruned vegetation on the coastal bluff provides little in the way of a traffic or fire hazard, no chemical or mechanical vegetation control is required along this highway segment. Ironically, the principal threat to the population stems from the very factor that has protected it thus far --its position at the edge of a sea cliff. Coastal bluff erosion has accelerated in recent years, and now threatens both the highway and _Fritillaria roderickii_. As a result, the highway was moved approximately 20-30 feet inland in 1985. Temporary fencing was used to protect the population during construction. While the plants are secure for the moment, their removal to a more stable site will be necessary in the near future.

Innocent Bystanders

The term "innocent bystander" is used here to describe a rather diverse group of roadside rare plants. These plants owe their occurrence within the right-of-way more to accidents of highway route selection than to factors associated with the roadside environment. Innocent bystanders most often result from near misses during highway construction. In this scenario, rare plants and their habitats become inadvertent additions to the right-of-way.

This admittedly heterogenous group includes taxa with large and relatively stable populations as well as others with extremely limited occurrences. Examples of the former include Cantelow's lewisia (_Lewisia_ _cantelowii_) and Feather River stonecrop (_Sedum_ _albomarginatum_) along State Route 70 in the Feather River Canyon. Rock outcrop habitats preferred by both plants are abundantly represented within the right-of-way. Both species occur here in expansive populations that extend well beyond the influence of the highway. In these instances routine maintenance activities are of little consequence to the long term survival of the populations.

In other situations, plants growing within the right-of-way can represent significant portions of a species' total range. Most notable of these is Merced clarkia (_Clarkia_ _lingulata_), which occurs along State Route 140 in the canyon of the Merced River. The entire known distribution of this clarkia consists of two populations within a 2-mile section of the canyon. Both populations occupy steep, north-facing slopes immediately adjacent to the highway.

Unlike many rare plants _Clarkia lingulata_ has received a fair amount of study. As a result we know a good deal more about its origin and biology than we do for many species. The taxon's extremely limited range and its close relation to _Clarkia_ _biloba_ subsp. _australis_, suggest that it is derived from the latter via rapid and relatively recent speciation (Lewis and Roberts, 1956). Electrophoretic analyses have confirmed this mode of origin (Gottlieb, 1974). Moreover, genetic differences between the two populations suggest that there is very little gene flow between colonies. Annual monitoring of the two populations indicates that the species depends on high annual recruitment to replenish soil seed reserves and maintain population size (Taylor, 1984). All of these factors-- limited range, lack of genetic exchange, and dependence on high annual success-- point to the extreme vulnerability of the species.

Management Considerations

Local maintenance forces were made aware of the two populations in 1981. At that time, herbicide application was identified as a potential threat to the species. An initial "no spray zone" was established to avoid accidental spraying impacts. The 2.5-mile zone was informally designated with the local spray crew. Because local crews were aware of the spray restriction, no signs were posted within the right-of-way.

This system worked well for 2 years. However spraying operations were subsequently centralized, and the spraying restrictions were apparently lost in the transfer. The populations were accidently herbicided in the spring of 1984. It is ironic that one of the reasons for centralization was to assure better control over spraying operations.

This accident underscores one of the more difficult aspects of roadside management: coordination between the many different units in a large organization. The incident has led to a refinement of the previous management strategy. To insure that spraying restrictions are not lost during personnel changes, paddles marked "no spray" have been posted at each end of the protection zone. This now appears to be an essential aspect of any special management zone within the right-of-way. In addition, the zone itself has been extended (to a total length of 5 miles) to provide a larger buffer on either side of the populations. Hopefully these two measures will provide more effective protection for the species in the future.

Problem Taxa

Taxa that are largely or wholly restricted to the right-of-way are frequently difficult to evaluate. The absence of extant "natural" habitat severely limits our understanding of the environmental requirements of these species. Identifying the factors which limit these species to the roadside environment is usually not possible without a substantial research effort. Ironically, these are the species that appear to depend most completely upon some aspect of past or current right-of-way management.

Milo-baker lupine (_Lupinus milo-bakeri_) provides the best example of this situation. This Mendocino County endemic grows almost exclusively within the right-of-way of State Route 162 in Round Valley. A single, disjunct population is found on along Highway 101 approximately 20 miles southwest of the main population center. Within Round Valley, a single population can be found outside the right-of-way in an abandoned, low-lying orchard.

Roadside populations occupy the immediate shoulder of the highway as well as ditches and cleared areas adjacent to guard rails and bridge abutments. The plants at the orchard site occupy open areas among invading riparian species such as valley oak and willows.

Management Considerations

This distribution indicates that some aspect of the roadside environment is favoring _Lupinus milo-bakeri_. Annual maintenance operations along this section of the highway have included a spraying program to keep ditches clear and to control blackberries (_Rubus_ spp.) for many years. This program utilizes Fall applications of a pre-emergent herbicide followed by spot treatments with a contact herbicide during the growing season. The road shoulders are also subject to annual mowing.

An experimental management approach has been developed for this section of the highway. Application of pre-emergent herbicides has been discontinued in the areas occupied by _Lupinus milo-bakeri_. While spot treatments with contact herbicide will continue, these will occur prior to seed germination or after seed set. In a similar manner, mowing will be delayed until after the lupine has flowered and set seed.

In addition to these measures, 4 test plantings were established from seed to provide additional information on the species' response to herbicides. Part of each planting was treated with both pre-emergent and contact herbicides at the time of seeding; the remainder of each planting was left untreated. Preliminary results suggest that the lupine has at least some degree of tolerance to Fall applications of pre-emergent herbicide. Poor establishment in areas with dense stands of annual grasses suggest that the species may benefit from reduced competition within the right-of-way. More study will be required to determine competitive interactions for this species. Reducing competition through carefully timed mowing or spraying may ultimately be useful in managing this species.

CONCLUSIONS

Highway rights-of-way provide a unique setting for the conservation of endangered plants. Human influence has been an important factor in the genesis and development of these environments. Historical disturbance and the need for on-going highway maintenance suggest that a greater degree of human intervention may be needed when managing sensitive plant populations in this setting.

A variety of management techniques can be used to benefit rare plants in this setting. Relict species and those with extremely limited populations usually benefit from protective measures such as temporary fencing and spraying or mowing restrictions. Delineation of these special management zones with signs or markers is necessary to warn maintenance personnel of sensitive resources within the right-of-way.

Seral species and opportunists require a more active management approach. It is often necessary to continue historical disturbance regimes to maintain suitable habitat for these taxa. The forms and levels of disturbance need to be determined on an individual basis.

Management plans for other roadside plants are hampered by a lack of information on the environmental requirements of individual rare species and the ecological effects of maintenance operations. It is hoped that future work in both areas will provide a basis for improved rare plant management in this unusual setting.

REFERENCES

Bacone, J. A.; Harty, Francis M. An inventory of railroad prairies in Illinois. In: Stuckey, Ronald L.; Reese, Karen J. eds. Proceedings of the sixth North American prairie conference; 1978 August 12-17; Columbus, OH; Ohio State Univ.; Ohio Biological Survey, Biological Notes No. 15; 1981; 278 p.

Bratton, Susan P.; White, Peter S. Rare and endangered plant species management: potential threats and practical problems in U. S. national parks and preserves. In: Synge, Hugh ed. The biological aspects of rare plant conservation; New York, NY; John Wiley and Sons, Ltd.; 1981; 459-474.

Clements, Frederic E. The relict method in dynamic ecology. Journal of Ecology 22:39-68; 1934.

Curtis, John T. The vegetation of Wisconsin. Madison, WI; Univ. of Wisconsin Press; 1959; 657 p.

Frenkel, Robert E. Ruderal vegetation along some California roadsides. Berkeley, CA; Univ. of California Press; Univ. of California Publ. in Geography Vol. 20; 1970; 163 p.

Gottlieb, L. D. Genetic confirmation of the origin of Clarkia lingulata. Evolution 28:244-250; 1974.

Jokerst, James D. The ecology and geography of Calochortus longebarbatus var. longebarbatus Watson with an updated view of its population status in California. Unpublished report prepared for Shasta-Trinity National Forest, Forest Service, U. S. Department of Agriculture; 1983 August.

Kohring, Margaret A. Saving Michigan's railroad strip prairies. In: Stuckey, Ronald L.; Reese, Karen J. eds. Proceedings of the sixth North American prairie conference; 1978 August 12-17; Columbus OH; Ohio State Univ.; Ohio Biological Survey, Biological Notes No. 15; 1981; 150-151.

Leopold, Aldo. A Sand County almanac. New York; Oxford University Press; 1949; 226 p.

Lewis, Harlan; Roberts, M. R. The origin of Clarkia lingulata. Evolution 10:126-138; 1956.

Rabinowitz, Deborah. Seven forms of rarity. In: Synge, Hugh ed. The biological aspects of rare plant conservation. New York NY; John Wiley and Sons, Ltd.; 1981; 205-217.

Taylor, Dean Wm. (Letter to Preston Kelley). 1984 August 28. 1 leaf. Located at: California Department of Transportation, Sacramento, CA.

The Designation Process for a Research Natural Area

Gary Schoolcraft [1]

Abstract: A presentation of a government agency's selection and official designation process for a research natural area, from the identification point through planning document and final designation. Major steps in the designation process along with possible alternative actions are discussed. The Ash Valley RNA in northeastern California is used as an example in the process, relating its specific attributes and problem areas in the designation process.

The Bureau of Land Management (BLM) is mandated to give priority to areas of critical environmental concern (ACEC) in the management of its 337 million acres of Federal lands. The identification, planning analysis, designation, and subsequent management of a special area are the major steps toward that goal.

The following describes the designation process used by the BLM. It is a long and sometimes complicated procedure, but properly applied ensures recognition and protection of the many unique areas located on public lands. Application of this designation process is directed to both agency personnel and the public in the pursuit of preserving those special areas.

WHAT ARE SPECIAL AREAS?

Special areas interpret into many different types, titles, and designations as different authorities for designation have developed over the past many years. Often these titles are confusing, definitions not clear, and relationships between each other totally unknown. There are research natural areas (RNA), outstanding natural areas (ONA), natural areas, areas of critical environmental concern (ACEC), critical habitat areas, essential habitat areas, scientific areas, and the list goes on too numerous to list and much more difficult to define. Each has or had a specific purpose and usually different authority from which it evolved. Although many have a clear definition and still useable purpose, the proliferation of these special area titles is confusing to the public and managers, especially when the intended purposes overlap.

Only two of these special area designation types, area of critical environmental concern (ACEC), and research natural area (RNA), will be defined here. These two special area types relate most directly to rare and endangered plants and will be used in this paper to explain the designation process.

Area of Critical Environmental Concern

ACEC is the most recent of the two terms and came directly from FLPMA (Federal Land Policy Management Act), also known as the Organic Act. This is a law passed in 1976 that gave a new management mandate to the federal lands under BLM jurisdiction.

FLPMA specifically stated that: "The Secretary shall prepare and maintain on a continuing basis an inventory of all public lands and their resources and other values (including, but not limited to, outdoor recreation and scenic values), giving priority to areas of critical environmental concern."

ACEC is defined in FLPMA as "...areas within the public lands where special management attention is required (when such areas are developed or used or where no development is required) to protect and prevent irreparable damage to important historic, cultural, or scenic values, fish and wildlife resources or other natural systems or processes or to protect life and safety from natural systems.". As the definition states, this term was also used to designate areas that are hazards to the public (i.e. open mine shafts).

---

[1] District Botanist, Bureau of Land Management, U.S. Department of the Interior, Susanville, CA.

Subsequent to passing of the law the BLM published planning regulations in the Code of Federal Regulations, 43 CFR Ch. II, Part 1600, defining two criteria, relevance and importance, which must be met in order for an area to become a potential ACEC.

Relevance - There shall be present a significant historic, cultural, or scenic value; a fish or wildlife resource or other natural system or process; or a natural hazard.

Importance - The above described value, resource, system, process, or hazard shall have substantial significance and values. This generally requires qualities of more than local significance and special worth, consequence, meaning, distinctiveness, or cause for concern. A natural hazard can be important if it is a significant threat to human life or property.

Research Natural Area

Research natural area (RNA) is widely used by both federal agencies and private organizations in setting aside areas. The use and purpose of the RNA designation, usually setting aside unique areas for research and education purposes, is similar among these groups.

The definition as published in the Code of Federal Regulations, 43 CFR Ch. II, Subpart 8223 is: "Research natural area" means an area that is established and maintained for the primary purpose of research and education because the land has one or more of the following characteristics: (1) a typical representation of a common plant or animal association; (2) an unusual plant or animal association; (3) a threatened or typical representation of common geologic, soil, or water features; or (5) outstanding or unusual geologic, soil, or water features.

These two designation types, ACEC and RNA, have overlapping definitions, with some areas, especially rare plant sites, falling into either category. A more appropriate process may be to designate an area under the ACEC authority but indicating the special purpose of the area in its name, such as research natural area.

The ACEC authority has advantages in that it has well defined criteria and designation process. Also, ACEC's have added protection from mining operations in that an approved plan of operations is required prior to commencing an activity other than casual use within a designated ACEC.

The BLM is presently circulating for review and comment a draft of proposed revisions to ACEC guidance. This should further refine the ACEC process and give BLM better guidance in the use of the ACEC designation process in planning. This draft guidance states that all areas which meet the identification criteria must be considered as potential ACEC's in the planning process.

IDENTIFICATION OF SPECIAL AREAS

Now that we sort of have an understanding of 2 types of special areas, what do we do if we know of an area that meets the special areas definition and feel that it should be designated?

Special area nominations can come from the public or agency staff at any time. These nominations are reviewed by an interdisciplinary team with the District Manager making final findings on which areas meet the criteria for ACEC, if that is the special area designation being considered.

The designation is considered through the planning process in the preparation of a resource management plan (RMP) or an amendment to an existing RMP. The RMP is usually done on a planning schedule and could be a few years aways. A plan amendment can be done at any time as needed. If an area is threatened, temporary management to protect the important resource values can be implemented until the planning process is complete.

When a nominated area is found not to meet the ACEC criteria, the analysis concluding that will be incorporated into the planning record.

PLANNING PROCESS

The identification and designation of special areas are separate processes. Once identified, designation of an area must be considered through the planning process. This includes public involvement and thorough analysis of several management options. This process contains 9 major steps which I'll try to explain briefly.

Identification of Issues

This action orients the planning process to the significant resource management problems and land use conflicts in the plan area. Other resources not identified in the planning issues are analyzed as appropriate so that all the public land resources are covered by the plan. A formal Notice of Intent (NOI) to prepare a plan is published in the Federal Register and includes the identified issues. This initiates public participation in the planning effort and helps the manager learn what the public perceives as management problems or issues in the area. A 30 day period is allowed to comment on the NOI.

Development of Planning Criteria

Planning criteria are the standards or rules developed by the manager and interdisciplinary team to focus the planning process on the issues and concerns. The planning criteria guide development of the plan and define appropriate standards or rules by which to make judgements about decision making, analysis, and data collection. Planning criteria are based on laws, executive orders, regulations, and other internal guidance by which a manager must abide by in management decisions.

Inventory and Data Collection

Baseline inventory data are collected on an ongoing basis in general support of resource management. Available data is organized and summarized to be fully used in resource management planning. New inventories are conducted during the planning process when necessary to fill critical information gaps. These available data bases provide the essential facts for making analysis, evaluations, and decisions. These inventories are the sources for internal recommendations for special area designations. Any special areas not already nominated would be revealed here if a thorough resource inventory has been done. This inventory information is used to consider potential resolutions of planning issues and the effects of various possible management options.

Analysis of the Management Situation

Inventory data and resource information are analyzed and interpreted to determine the ability of the public lands to respond to the planning issues and other management concerns. The analysis of the management situation shall provide, consistent with multiple use principles, the basis for formulating reasonable alternatives, including the types of resources for development or protection.

Although part of the process, this analysis is not part of the published plan and Environmental Impact Statement (EIS) document but is a key record of the planning process.

Formulation of Alternatives

Alternatives are developed and proposed through interdisciplinary discussion to portray a mix of multiple uses and management actions which could resolve the planning issues and address management concerns. They inform the decisionmakers and the public of different land and resource management options available and when analyzed provide a basis for comparing and making reasonable decisions. A set of alternatives is developed which represents a reasonable range of options. They should represent a practical range and include alternatives that favor resource protection and ones that are commodity and resource production oriented. One alternative will be the "no action alternative" which reflects the present management situation. The number of alternatives is kept at a manageable level capable of detailed analysis.

Estimation of the Effects of Alternatives

The consequences of the resource management alternatives are analyzed and documented in this action. This is the "Affected Environment" portion of the RMP/EIS document and presents the effects of each alternative on the environment and other resources. The presentation and analysis of each alternative allows the manager and the public to understand the effects, trade-offs, and changes associated with the alternatives and to visualize the relationships between alternatives. This action may help identify ways to avoid or mitigate adverse impacts or may suggest other alternatives. Thorough and accurate analysis of the effects of the alternatives is important since it is used to identify the preferred alternative and to select the proposed plan.

Selection of Preferred Alternative

A comparison of estimated effects and trade-offs associated with the various alternatives leads to development and selection of the preferred alternative. The preferred alternative is identified in the Draft RMP and shows interested parties which alternative the State Director believes, at this point, best meets the planning criteria. The preferred alternative may be one of the alternatives studied in detail or it may be developed from the components and subalternatives, if any, of several alternatives which were studied in detail. The preferred alternative is published in the draft RMP and EIS for public review and comment. A 90 day period is allowed for public comment on the draft RMP and EIS.

Selection of the Resource Management Plan

Public comments on the draft RMP and draft EIS and any new information received are evaluated by an interdisciplinary team. A proposed plan is developed by the Area Manager from an alternative or a combination of alternatives identified in the draft RMP and draft EIS. The proposed plan must utilize an alternative or combination of alternatives that were analyzed in detail in the draft plan and EIS. If the proposed plan is a new alternative not in the range of alternatives previously selected and analyzed in detail, it must be recycled through the process. A new draft plan and EIS is prepared and filed. The proposed plan and final EIS are published and filed with the Environmental Protection Agency. The proposed plan and final EIS contain comment letters received on the draft plan with analysis and Bureau response to all substantive comments. Publication of the proposed plan and the final EIS documents this planning action and triggers the opportunity for protests. A 30 day period is allowed for filing a protest. Changes resulting from a decision on a protest and response to the Governor's review completes preparation of the plan.

Monitoring and Evaluation

Monitoring and evaluation requirements and standards are considered throughout the planning process. They help a manager determine the plan's progress towards established goals and objectives. The results of monitoring and evaluation are used to determine if the plan needs amendment or revision. Monitoring can be used to reveal unanticipated and/or unpredictable effects or determine the adequacy of mitigation measures. Subsequent evaluation would determine if changes in resource commitments or uses are needed.

APPLYING THE DESIGNATION PROCESS

Now that we know what special areas are and that they must go through a rather complicated planning process to be designated, how do we best use this process?

The Ash Valley Research Natural Area, nominated as an RNA through this planning process and designated as such in December 1984, will be used as an example in following this process.

The Ash Valley RNA is an 1121 acre area of BLM lands in north central Lassen County, California designated to provide protection for 6 California Native Plant Society (CNPS) listed rare plants occurring on the area. The area is to be preserved for research and education purposes and the continued existence of the rare plants and their habitat. I will try to relate the special attributes and problem areas of the Ash Valley RNA as they relate to the designation process.

Thorough and accurate application of the designation process is important in lending credence to the special area system. This should start at the earliest stages, at the identification point, and continue through the planning process. Whether within the Bureau or from a public interest, individuals nominating a special area should make a thorough effort to insure that the specialness of an area is expressed so that management understands why the area is special. This can be submitted in short narrative form to the office having jurisdiction over the area.

Describe the resource values present, the location, and the specific aspects of this area that make it unique and special and worthy of designation. Relate the description specifically to the two ACEC criteria that the area must meet. A minimum size or boundary necessary to protect the resource should be indicated. Input and support from specialists in fields relating to the specific resource value in the area can be helpful. Identify the specific purpose for designation of the area, such as for research and education, recreation, or preservation. This will govern what special area designation type to recommend. Describe protective measures that would be necessary to protect and preserve the special area status. Protective measures such as mineral withdrawals, OHV closures, or grazing exclusion that conflict with or limit other resource development, must go through the planning process to be implemented. The recommendation to designate Ash Valley as an RNA came from within the BLM with support from outside groups. The uniqueness of this area was expressed verbally to management since it was convenient in this case but a narrative is still more desirable. The area had also been identified as "a unique botanical area" in the "Candidate or Potential

Natural Areas" program by the state of California in the mid 1970's.

Once an area has been identified as a potential ACEC or RNA, designation of the area is analyzed through the planning process. I will not attempt to explain that any farther than I already have but will try to relate to the process in general. If the number, size, public or management concern, or resource conflicts of special areas is significant, special areas would probably be identified as an issue at the issue identification stage. Otherwise, designation of special areas may not evolve until the formulation of alternatives stage. Ash Valley itself was not identified as an issue but "how to improve sensitive plant habitat" was identified as an issue. Alternatives developed in the plan should resolve the identified issues. RNA designation for Ash Valley plus necessary protective measures were actions to help resolve that issue.

The formulation of alternatives step pulls all the other steps together, hopefully resulting in a good array of alternatives. Here, many options are available to special areas, whether to designate, what to designate, size, restrictions, protective measures, and the list goes on. I guess that is why they are called alternatives. Whatever the resulting alternatives, they must respond to the identified issues and planning criteria.

Of the four alternatives analyzed in the RMP covering the Ash Valley RNA, two recommended designation as an RNA with various protective measures. The other two alternatives, one of which was the "No Action Alternative", recommended continued protection of the sensitive plants as required by BLM policy but with no special designation.

Ensuring that all restrictions and preservation measures necessary to protect the special areas resources are included in as many alternatives as possible is very important. This will be governed by each alternatives development criteria. Any action required to protect the special area that conflicts with other resources must be analyzed through the planning process to be implemented. The only exceptions to this are actions required by law or policy. Requirements under the Endangered Species Act is a good example of this but this is limited to official federally listed or proposed listed species.

Formulation of alternatives is an internal action but is guided by the issue identification step where public comment is initiated.

The effects of the alternatives guides the manager in the selection of the preferred alternative. The significance of each action in an alternative, its effects on other resources and actions, and degree to which the action solves issues and meets planning criteria govern the selection of a preferred alternative. As stated earlier, the preferred alternative can be a combination of various aspects of the other analyzed alternatives.

The Ash Valley designation and required protective measures presented in two of the alternatives had minimal affect on other actions or resources.

Use the Monitoring and Evaluation process to answer any questions concerning other activities. If the effects of another resource use on the special area are unknown, establish a monitoring program and evaluation standards to measure the effects. It is difficult to exclude other uses in an area if the detriment of that use cannot be shown. The monitoring and evaluation requirements can be established in the plan or subsequent to it in a monitoring plan or habitat management plan (HMP).

Once the preferred alternative is selected, the draft RMP and draft EIS are published presenting this preferred alternative. A 90 day period is allowed for public comment on the draft plan and EIS. Public comments and concerns guide the final selection of an alternative and are an important part of the planning process. The preferred alternative should be understood to assure that it meets minimum requirements to protect and preserve the special area. If it does not, then in a comment letter, address why the preferred alternative doesn't meet those requirements and what additional measures are needed.

Designation of Ash Valley as an RNA and necessary protective measures were included in the preferred alternative.

As mentioned in the Planning Process section, there is another public comment period on the Proposed Plan and Final EIS at which time protests can be filed. If there is concern over the effects the plan will have on a special area, definitely use this final chance to express those concerns.

After the comment period and any necessary decisions on protests, the special area is officially designated by publication in the Federal Register.

CONCLUSION

This concludes the process for designation of a special area, however long and laborious. I tried to present it such that both agency and public individuals could identify with the process and those steps critical to their input.

The use of identification and public comment portions of the process are the most important tools for the public. The concerns of the public can often be the deciding factor as to whether a special area does or does not get designated.

It is important that agency personnel dwell on the identification and formulation of alternatives section. Ideas must be presented in an alternative before they can be implemented. Alternative formulation can be sort of a bargaining step, especially as the degree of effect one resource has on another increases. Attempts are made to resolve some conflicts at this stage. A resource specialist may have to concede to some alternative actions because of management concerns or conflicts with alternative formulation criteria. Designation and preservation of the special area are the critical elements. Achieve this and subsequent actions can be pursued through plan amendments at a later date if they become critical to the areas preservation.

In selecting the type of special area designation to use and in the interest of eliminating confusion on the definition and actions required to designate an area, I would recommend using the ACEC designation and authority. It is the most recent and well defined designation process. Attach the special area purpose to the ACEC name. As example, the Ash Valley RNA-ACEC. My confusion over these two terms, their purpose, and questioned use of the dual designation and desire to establish the area for research and education purposes resulted in Ash Valley being designated an RNA. Oregon BLM uses this dual type of designation and developing California BLM policy on special areas recommends using the ACEC authority for all special areas, attaching it's special purpose to the name.

The ease with which a special area becomes designated depends on several things, with each case being different. Along with Ash Valley's very unique resource, the lack of any significant resource conflicts was probably most instrumental in the ease with which designation was attained. You may not have control over major resource conflicts but sometimes the degree of the conflict can be lessened during the formulation of alternatives - do some creative bargaining. If you feel your creative bargaining may have conceded to some actions whose effects to the special area are unknown, be sure that monitoring steps are included in the RMP or HMP that will resolve the questioned concern. The monitoring evaluation should conclude measures to take if monitoring reveals a detriment to the area. In any case, actions crucial to the preservation of the special areas should definitely be included in the alternatives, no matter what the degree of resource conflict. The estimation of the effects portions of the planning process serves the purpose of helping the manager make a decision on what actions are in the environment's and the public's best interest.

Hopefully you now know everything you ever wanted to know about designating special areas, or enough to get one designated anyway. But the process doesn't end there, hopefully, especially for the government agency involved. Designation alone doesn't ensure protection. Once designated, a habitat management plan (HMP) should be developed that guides the use and protection of the area in a manner that retains those values for which the area was established. The plan should identify a monitoring program, specific actions needed to protect the area, and a schedule for implementation of the plan.

The special area designation along with a completed management plan expresses management's concern over an area and will give the area priority in receiving budgeted funds to implement the plan.

As a closing thought, especially for agency individuals, share and implant your enthusiasm for the preservation of a special area to managers and fellow workers. They may have to be the ones to guide the continued implementation of the management plan and ensure the continued pursuit of the goals of the designation.

REFERENCES

Hastey, Edward L. Conservation of rare plants on public lands in California. 1986 [These proceedings].

U.S. Department of Interior. Final Alturas Resource Area Resource Management Plan and Environmental Impact Statement. Alturas, CA: Bureau of Land Management; 1983 October.

Plant Exploration in California, the Frontier Is Still Here

James Shevock,[1] Dean Wm. Taylor[2]

Prior to 1973, most botanical field work in California concentrated on making general plant collections for exchange between herbaria and focused on taxonomic matters such as monographic and floristic studies. Rarity was not an issue except that botanists enjoyed collecting the endemics and other localized and regional taxa. Conservation or preservation actions were rarely involved. The environmental movement of the 1970s to the present time evolved into a conservation/preservation mode for the state's rarest plants. In California, CNPS and The Nature Conservancy, as private non-profit organizations, played key roles in focusing botanical efforts towards rare plant conservation. The establishment of the California Natural Diversity Data Base (CNDDB) became the centralized repository for all rare plant data in the state.

Historically, most plant collecting in California was done by professional botanists with ties to the major scientific centers and educational institutions. Although these researchers at the major herbaria are still fundamental to our understanding of the California flora, a distinct shift in emphasis occurred shortly after the passage of the Endangered Species Act (ESA) of 1973, as amended. By this time, California Native Plant Society (CNPS) members were concerned with the conservation of the state's rarest plants. This identification process, determination of exactly which plants in the state were rare, became the first CNPS Inventory of Rare and Endangered Vascular Plants of California (Powell 1974). Another key factor is the interest toward rare plant inventories and conservation involved with land management issues. Both federal, state and local government agencies needed to know what plants could become listed by the U.S. Fish and Wildlife Service under the ESA, and what effects this might have on their programs. As early as 1975, the Forest Service developed their 'sensitive plant program' to address this issue on the National Forests. Other federal agencies soon followed with similar programs. Some of these agencies either hired botanists on their staffs or contracted for rare plant inventories on lands under their jurisdiction. Consequently, there was an immediate need to gather the current status of the distribution of rare plants, especially their actual rarity, jeopardy, threats and population data that were basically not part of the herbarium record. This data void created many jobs for field botanists.

[1] U.S. Forest Service, Region 5, San Francisco, CA.

[2] BioSystems Analysis Inc., 303 Potrero Suite 29-203, Santa Cruz, CA. 95060

Abstract: Published floras for California have been available since the early part of this century, yet the native flora is still far from completely documented. Remote areas of California have received only cursory field work, and the overwhelming majority of plant collections are adjacent to existing roads. Since the arrival of A California Flora in 1959, dozens of new rare and localized endemics have been discovered and published, with the majority of these new species from the southern Sierra Nevada and the Klamath mountains in the northwest corner of the state. Noteworthy range extensions are still frequently encountered, and the distributional limits of more widely distributed taxa are only generally established. With the rapid conversion of much native habitat to agricultural and urban uses, the need to know what taxa we may be impacting has never been greater.

As field botanists began specializing in 'rare plant surveys', various collections and species checklists were compiled as part of the documentation for environmental impact reports and statements. These data added greatly to the understanding of species distribution, especially in areas of the state that previously had not been surveyed botanically.

Today, need for rare plant conservation requires a review of the process by which botanists have uncovered and described those components of the flora unknown as recently as twenty years ago. Where might new species in California be found? Where should field work be concentrated? Our essay seeks to provide a look at these questions. We hope that such a review will provide impetus to increase the pace of floristic exploration of the California Floristic Province.

CURRENT TRENDS

The flora of the California Floristic Province (CFP, Howell 1957) is characterized by an unusually high rate of local endemism (Stebbins & Major 1965, Raven & Axelrod 1978). Even though comprehensive floristic manuals have been available for several decades, the flora is still far from completely documented. The new Jepson Manual Project is evidence of the need to update and expand the knowledge base since the publication of A California Flora (Munz & Keck 1959) and Supplement (Munz 1968).

Frequent descriptions of new taxa, many taxonomically and morphologically remote from congeners, is directly indicative of the magnitude in the gap of our knowledge regarding the California flora. Patterns of discovery and naming of new taxa of plants from California suggest that as yet undescribed species are subject to extinction.

Even though California is the most populous state in the nation, there are still millions of acres supporting relatively natural vegetation conditions. Due to the size of the California (411,014 km^2, or 101,563,520 acres) it is not surprising that remote areas have not been systematically surveyed for endemic species. However, lands in relatively unmodified condition are not located physiographic units of the CFP. A significant portion of the California flora is threatened with drastic distributional range reductions. Some taxa, along with complete native plant communities, are faced with the possibility of extinction due to population growth coupled with rapidly changing land use patterns.

The coastal counties in the state comprise the greatest urban growth. It is these counties where floras are generally available. Basic reasons for this is the fact that the major scientific centers and universities with botanical programs are located in the two largest metropolitan areas; the Los Angeles Basin and the San Francisco Bay region. Driving times of up to 10 hours are needed to reach parts of the state remote from urban centers. Comprehensive floristic inventories in remote areas require repeated collecting visits over a number of years -- even decades. By way of illustration of this point, the example of the flora of the White Mountains of Inyo and Mono counties is of interest. Lloyd and Mitchell (1973) considered their local flora 90 percent complete when published, but ongoing collection in the range has documented over 200 previously unreported taxa[3], including one new taxon (Taylor and Dedecker 1982, Morefield et al. 1983, 1986, Rollins 1982) -- a 25 percent increase in the known flora! Other reasons why the California flora is not completely documented is that the herbarium record is overwhelmingly based on collections adjacent to roads and that much of the field work prior to the current interest in rare and endemic plants dates prior to 1950. The biggest factor, however, in our opinion is that many new taxa have simply been overlooked due basically to the fact that plant collecting occurs in selected areas during the "peak" flowering season for a given geographic area. Those taxa that appear very early or quite late in the growing season are never or rarely encountered. This latter example has been clearly demonstrated by field work done by the senior author in the southern Sierra Nevada (Shevock & Constance 1979, Bartel & Shevock 1983, and Heckard & Shevock 1985). Some new taxa have been located during snowmelt and others do not appear until the hottest and driest time of year -- conditions which generally discourage most botanical investigations. Timing is critical in doing any floristic survey to assure that a taxon is not overlooked because the 'collecting period' was too short.

A relatively recent trend in new distributional knowledge and discoveries in the CFP are the results of localized floristic projects, many directed by masters students. These are basically intensive collecting projects over several seasons covering a relatively small geographical area. Several new taxa were described as a result of these types of studies (Shevock 1978, Messick 1982). On the other hand, new taxa are not readily recognized by university students not already familiar with a particular part of the state's flora. This is even more acute in remote areas where few collections are available for comparative study. Specimens obtained in these floristic projects can either be misidentified, or remain identified only at the generic level, filed in herbarium cabinets awaiting the monographic student. Although most small state university herbariums are not staffed to ship out herbarium material for loan purposes, the dedicated monographer should seek out these institutions and verify or annotate the material, especially since the great majority of student collections are unicates. We have found countless examples of undocumented rare plant locations from these smaller institutions, and occasionally an undescribed taxon.

Another reason why new taxa are overlooked is that several families and/or genera are perceived as being taxonomically "too difficult" and are therefore rarely collected. Good examples would include the Apiaceae, Poaceae, and the genera *Carex*, *Lupinus*, *Cryptantha*, *Galium*, etc. Also, plants can be easily overlooked or totally ignored if they are exceedingly small, not showy, or are too time consuming to collect. Annual species of *Juncus*, *Mimulus* and *Phacelia* appear to be good examples.

METHODS

Newly described taxa published during the 19 year period from 1968 to 1986 (inclusive) were studied. This interval corresponds to the period following the preparation of the <u>Supplement</u> to <u>A California Flora</u> (Munz 1968).

Data on salient historical and ecological attributes of newly described CFP taxa were collected. Information not provided in publications describing new taxa was assembled and evaluated by the junior author using herbaria surveys, geologic maps, and direct field inspection where possible. The following variables were studies: taxonomic level of the new taxon; year first collected and length of intervening period until valid publication; number of collections and collectors; occurrence in or on one or more vegetative types or substrates; median elevation of occurrences and elevational range; geographic range and floristic region or regions of occurrence; and rarity using "R" of the CNPS R-E-D code (Smith & York 1984) as an index.

RESULTS

During the 19 year period since the last revision of Munz's flora, at least 219 plant taxa have been validly published from the CFP: one new genus (*Dedeckera* in the Polygonaceae), 116 new species, and 103 infraspecific taxa (Appendix 1). We are also aware of at least an additional dozen taxa awaiting valid publication.

Patterns of Plant Discovery

History of discovery and naming new plant taxa from California is varied, reflecting both the distribution of unique habitats within the CFP, and probably also the collecting habits of botanists. Most new taxa are described from relatively few collections--almost half are known from fewer than 5 specimens when named. This is based primarily on the actual rarity of the taxon and a reflection of its extremely localized distribution. Interestingly, over 80 percent of all new taxa were collected independently by at least 2 botanists other than the author of the taxon. The interval between

---

[3]A list of additions to the White Mountain Flora is available from the junior author upon request.

when a taxon is first collected and its formal published description ranged from 1 to 121 years, averaging 41 years--not exactly prompt publication of new discoveries! This unbelievable long interval can be explained: A few old historical collections were often recognized as "new" to science, however, the specimen lacked essential parts to be properly described. Additionally, specimens often contained such scant location data that botanists had difficulty relocating the new taxon in the field. Several of these were collected independently by other botanists not realizing that they had relocated a plant that was recognized as being 'new'. The rare instance occrus where a single botanist collects and promptly describes and publishes a new taxon.

Of the nearly 220 newly described CFP plants since 1968, 70 percent were recognized as the result of a taxonomic study. The remaining plants were discovered and named in the general course of floristic exploration. Epithets commemorating persons accounted for exactly a third of all new names. Taxa recognizing G. L. Stebbins (5), Lincoln Constance (3), R. F. Hoover (3), and the senior author (2 plus 3 in press) top the list. In all, 50 persons were commemorated with taxa in their honor. Interestingly, names indicative of geographical origin and morphology equally shared the remaining epithets.

Rates of Discovery and Trends in Rarity

Rates of description of new taxa from the CFP have been high in general, and exhibit a notable decreasing trend in recent years (fig. 1). Although declining, the rate of description of new taxa is still substantial--between 5 and 10 taxa/year during the last decade. These data strongly indicate that the flora of the CFP is as yet imperfectly known. When one also considers the scrutiny new taxa receive today from reviewers prior to publication in most journals, botanists describing new taxa must be convinced that their new taxon is indeed distinct and worthy of recognition.

Part of the apparent trend of a decreasing rate of description of new taxa is due to the unusually large number of species of *Galium*, *Camissonia* and *Eriogonum* described in the early 1970s. Omitting these species from consideration, the rate is practically constant.

A similar non-static time-series trend is exhibited by the running average of rarity ("R" of CNPS R-E-D Code, Smith and York 1984), which is generally increasing (fig. 2). Mean (± Standard Error) rarity for taxa described during the post-Supplement period was 1.40 ± 0.08, significantly higher (Mann-Whitney U-Test, $p < 0.05$) than the mean rarity of 1.18 ± 0.14 for taxa named during the 1959-1967 period treated in the Supplement. No difference in rarity was exhibited by taxa described at the specific versus infraspecific level.

Geographic Origin of New California Taxa

Geographical distribution of newly described taxa within the CFP is decidedly non-uniform. Density of newly described taxa is mapped in Figure 2, using the floristic regions recognized by Stebbins & Major (1965). The Sierra Nevada exhibits the highest density, with most new Sierran taxa originating in the central and southern portion of the range. Several new taxa from the southern Sierra are currently in preparation for

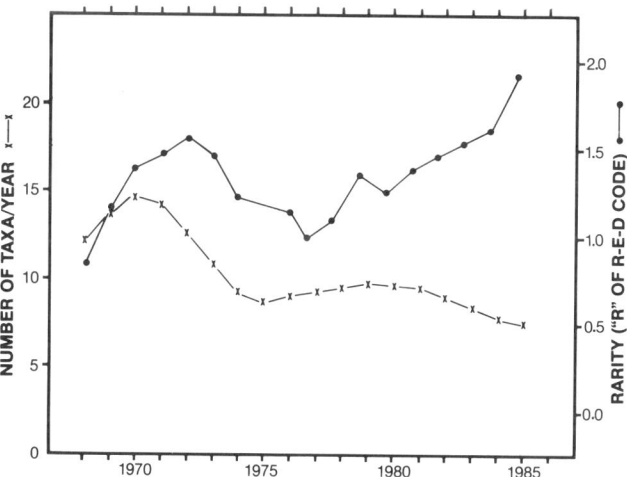

Figure 1. Five-year running means of rates of description of new species from the California Floristic Province (solid circles) and mean rarity (x's) for the period since publication of the *Supplement to A California Flora*. Rarity was determined by using "R" of the CNPS R-E-D Code as an index.

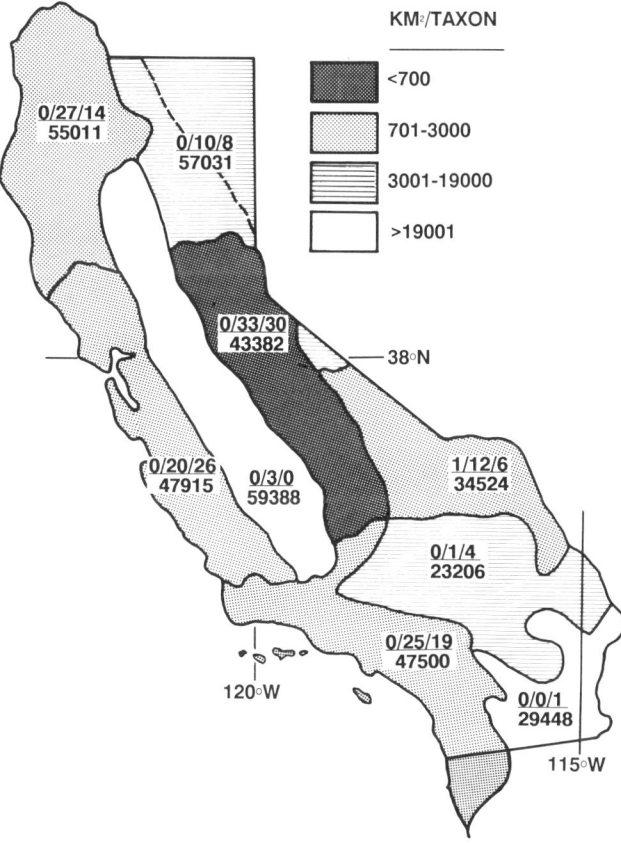

Figure 2. Map of the California Floristic Province showing density of newly described taxa by region. Numerator gives the number of new genera/species/infra-specific taxa occurring in each region, while the denominator gives the size of the region in km^2.

publication from field work of the senior author. The Klamath mountains region is the second geographic center contributing new taxa. Floristic regions along the coast exhibit moderate density of newly named taxa, as does the Inyo region. The transmontane desert regions of California and the Central Valley yield the fewest new taxa.

Edaphic Factors

Not surprisingly, nearly 55 percent of all newly described taxa can be considered substrate endemics (those restricted to a narrow range of unusual soil parent materials). Serpentine and other ultramafic rocks accounted for the largest portion of new taxa, not an unexpected pattern considering the importance of serpentine endemism in the CFP generally (Kruckeberg 1984). Perhaps the most surprising, volcanic substrates were the second most important contributors of newly described taxa, but this observation is likely a complex, indirect result of vegetation features of volcanic landscapes in California rather than strict substrate endemism.

Plant Community/Habitats

Major plant communities of the CFP differ substantially in their yield of new taxa. Most important community types with new taxa were chaparral (29 percent), coniferous forests (26 percent), desert scrub (20 percent), grassland and vernal pools (8 percent), and oak woodlands (7 percent). Relatively few new taxa were described from riparian, freshwater marsh, salt marsh, alkali sink and alpine communities. Many newly described taxa actually occur on azonal habitats, (e.g., rock outcrops) within the major communities listed above. Characteristics of median and range of elevation indicate that the majority of newly described taxa occur at altitudes below 6,000 feet and range through less than 1,500 feet. Relatively few of the newly named taxa occur at high altitudes or occur throughout a great range of altitude.

Life-Form Spectra

Newly described taxa are not distributed evenly among all plant life-forms: perennial herbs (34 percent), annual herbs (27 percent), evergreen shrubs (19 percent), and geophytic monocots (10 percent) are more frequent than other types. These proportions are roughly equivalent to the life-form composition of the flora as a whole.

Taxonomic Patterns

Particular plant families contributed a disproportionate share of newly discovered taxa. Rank order of the 10 most important families is (number of taxa in parentheses): Onagraceae (24), Ericaceae (24), Polygonaceae (21), Asteraceae (18), Rubiaceae (17), Fabaceae (13), Liliaceae (sensu lato, 13), Apiaceae (10), Brassicaceae (9), Polemoniaceae (8), and Campanulaceae (7). Compared to the rank order family composition of the California flora as a whole (Smith & Noldecke 1960), certain differences stand out. Onagraceae, Rubiaceae, and Polygonaceae are more common than in the flora as a whole, due in part to large numbers of new taxa of *Camissonia*, *Clarkia*, *Galium*, and *Eriogonum* described as the result of intensive biosystematic studies of these genera. All of the 24 newly described taxa of Ericaceae are *Arctostaphylos*, a genus that has yet defied nearly all attempts to erect a workable classification. Important families in the overall flora which yielded few or no new taxa are: Poaceae, Cyperaceae, Boraginaceae, Hydrophyllaceae, and Scrophulariaceae.

CONCLUSIONS

Two physiographic regions in the CFP clearly demonstrate the continued need for more intensive and systematic field work, these being the Sierra Nevada and the Klamath mountains region. These two areas are not only rich in species diversity, but they also contain the widest ranges in geology, soils, plant communities, relief, and climate, factors directly correlated with plant species diversity in California (Richerson & Lum 1980). The other factor that makes these areas so rich is that they are still relatively remote and rugged and only the most dedicated botanists are willing to do the field work necessary to document their floras. In addition, we suggest a that state-wide survey of serpentine habitats and other unusual substrates should be initiated.

There are still literally hundreds of important floristic studies to be done in California. We strongly encourage the development of floras in biology/botany programs, especially those based on physiographic parameters (e.g., watersheds, mountain ranges) along with properly prepared and labeled voucher herbarium specimens. These floristic projects are one of the best cumulative approaches necessary to complete the flora of the California Floristic Province.

Our review indicates that undescribed California taxa are probably in danger of extinction. Loss of species prior to their documentation is not just confined to lowland tropical rain-forest habitats, it could be happening in our own state. Critical, comprehensive floristic review is thus a much needed component of the environmental review process.

REFERENCES

Bartel, James A. and James R. Shevock. *Dudleya calcicola* (Crassulaceae), a new species from the southern Sierra Nevada. Madrono 30:210-216; 1983.

Heckard, Lawrence R. and James R. Shevock. *Mimulus norrisii* (Scrophulariaceae), a new species from the southern Sierra Nevada. Madrono 32:179-185; 1985.

Howell, John Thomas. The California flora and its province. Leaf. W. Bot. 8:133-138; 1957.

Kruckeberg, Arthur R. California Serpentines: flora, vegetation, geology, soils and management problems. Univ. Calif. Pubs. Bot. 78:1-180; 1984.

Lloyd, Robert M. and Richard S. Mitchell. A Flora of the White Mountains of California and Nevada. University of California Press, Berkeley; 1973. 202 p.

Messick, Tim. Flora and phytogeography of the Bodie Hills of Mono County, California and Mineral County, Nevada. M.S. Thesis, Humboldt State University, Arcata, CA; 1982. v + 167 p.

Morefield, James D., Timothy Spira, Ann Pinzl, Mary Dedecker and Dean Wm. Taylor. Additions to the flora of the White Mountains II. California Native Plant Society *Bristlecone Newsletter* 2(6):4-6; 1983.

Morefield, James D., Dean Wm. Taylor and Mary DeDecker. Additions to the flora of the White Mountains III. California Native Plant Society *Bristlecone Newsletter* 6(3):3-6; 1986.

Munz, Philip A. and David D. Keck. A California Flora. University of California Press, Berkeley; 1959. 1,681 p.

Munz, Philip A. Supplement to A California Flora. University of California Press, Berkeley; 1968. 224 p.

Powell, W. Robert. Inventory of Rare and Endangered Vascular Plants of California. California Native Plant Society, Special Pub. No. 1 [1st edition]; 1974. iii + 67 p.

Raven, Peter H. and Daniel I. Axelrod. Origin and relationships of the California Flora. Univ. Calif. Pubs. Bot. 72:1-134; 1978.

Richerson, Peter J. and Kwei-Lin Lum. Patterns of plant species diversity in California in relation to weather and topography. Amer. Natur. 116:504-536; 1980.

Rollins, Reed C. Studies on *Arabis* (Cruciferae) of western North America. J. Arnold Arboretum 64:491-510; 1982.

Shevock, James. R. Vascular flora of the Lloyd Meadows Basin, Sequoia National Forest, Tulare County, California. M.S. Thesis, California State University, Long Beach; 1978.

Shevock, James R. and Lincoln Constance. A new species of *Oreonana*, a genus of snow-adapted Umbelliferae. Madroño 26:128-134; 1979.

Smith, Gladys L. and Anita M. Noldecke. A statistical report on A California Flora. Leaf W. Bot. 9:117-132; 1960.

Smith, James P. and Rick York. Inventory of Rare and Endangered Vascular Plants of California. California Native Plant Society, Special Pub. No. 1 [3rd edition]; 1984.

Stebbins, G. Ledyard and Jack Major. Endemism and speciation in the California flora. Ecol. Monog. 35:1-35; 1965.

Taylor, Dean Wm. and Mary Dedecker. Additions to the flora of the White Mountains. California Native Plant Society, *Bristlecone Newsletter* 1(4):3-5; 1982.

APPENDIX 1.

Enumeration of CFP taxa described since the 10 December 1968 publication of Munz's **Supplement** to **A California Flora** listed by geographic regions (after Stebbins & Major 1965). Taxa occuring in more than one region are so listed. Nomenclatural authorities are listed for only the novel portion of a given epithet.

NORTH COAST RANGES:
Arabis serpenticola Rollins.
 Cont. Gray Herb. 204:149-154. 1973.
Arctostaphylos canescens ssp. *malloryi* W. Knight & R. Gankin. Four Seasons 7:22-24. 1981.
A. klamathensis S. Edwards, T. Keeler-Wolf & W. Knight. Four Seasons 6:17-21. 1983.
A. knightii R. Gankin & R. Hildreth.
 Four Seasons 3(3):23-24. 1970.
A. manzanita ssp. *roofii* (R. Gankin) Wells.
 Leaf. W. Bot. 10:329-331. 1966.
A. manzanita ssp. *wieslanderi* Wells.
 Madroño 19:193-224. 1968.
A. patula var. *coalescens* W. Knight.
 Four Seasons 7(1):20-21. 1984.
A. stanfordiana ssp. *raichei* W. Knight.
 Four Seasons 7(3):16-20. 1985.
Balsamorhiza sericia W. A. Weber.
 Phytologia 50:357-359. 1982.
Brodiaea elegans ssp. *hooveri* Neihaus.
 Univ. Calif. Pubs. Bot. 60:1-66. 1971.
Campanula shelteri Heckard. Madroño 20:231-235. 1969.
Eriogonum diclinum Reveal. Aliso 7:217-230. 1970.
E. libertinii Reveal. Madroño 28:163-166. 1981.
Eryngium constancei Sheikh. Madroño 30:93-102. 1983.
Eupatorium shastense D. W. Taylor & Stebbins.
 Madroño 25:218-220. 1978.
Galium grayanum ssp. *nanum* Dempster & Ehrendorfer.
 Brittonia 17:289-331. 1965.
G. porrigens Dempster. Madroño 22:312-313. 1974.
G. serpenticum ssp. *scotticum* Dempster & Ehrendorfer.
 Brittonia 17:289-331. 1965.
G. sparsiflorum ssp. *glabrius* Dempster & Stebbins.
 Univ. Calif. Pubs. Bot. 46:1-52. 1968.
Hastingsia atropurpurea Becking. Madroño 33:175-181. 1986.
Lathyrus biflorus T. Nelson & J. Nelson.
 Brittonia 35:180-183. 1983.
L. glandulosus Broich. Madroño 33:136-143. 1986.
Lewisia stebbinsii R. Gankin & W. Hildreth.
 Four Seasons 2(4):12-14. 1968.
Linanthus nuttallii ssp. *howellii* T. Nelson & R. Patterson.
 Madroño 32:102-105. 1985.
Lupinus constancei T. Nelson & J. Nelson.
 Brittonia 35:180-183. 1983.
Madia doris-nilesiae T. Nelson and J. Nelson.
 Brittonia 37:394-396. 1985.
M. stebbinsii T. Nelson & J. Nelson.
 Brittonia 32:323-325. 1980.
Monardella siskiyouensis Hardham.
 Leaf. W. Bot. 10:320-326. 1966.
Minuartia decumbens T. Nelson & J. Nelson.
 Brittonia 33:162-164. 1981.
Periderdia leptocarpa Chuang & Constance.
 Univ. Calif. Pubs. Bot. 55:1-74. 1974.
Phacelia cookei Constance & Heckard.
 Brittonia 22:25-30. 1970.
Phlox azurea G. Smith. Wasmann J. Biol. 43:43-45. 1985.
Sedum laxum ssp. *flavidum* Denton.
 Brittonia 30:233-238. 1978.
S. obtusatum ssp. *paradisum* Denton. Ibid.
Sisyrinchium hitchcockii D. Henderson.
 Brittonia 28:149-176. 1976.
Smilax jamesii G. Wallace. Brittonia 31:416-421. 1979.
Streptanthus drepanoides Kruckeberg & Morrison.
 Madroño 30:230-244. 1983.
Trillium albidum G. Freeman. Brittonia 27:1-62. 1975.
T. kurabayashii G. Freeman. Ibid.

APPENDIX 1 (Continued)

T. ovatum ssp. *oettingeri* Munz & Thorne.
  Aliso 8:15-17. 1973.
Triteleia ixioides var. *unifolia* Lenz.
  Aliso 8:221-258. 1975.

CENTRAL VALLEY:
Orthocarpus brevistylus Hoover.
  Four Seasons 2(4):14-15. 1968.
Paronychia ahartii B. Ertter. Madrono 32:87-90. 1985.
Lilaeopsis masonii Mathias & Constance.
  Madrono 24: 78-83. 1977.

CENTRAL COAST RANGES:
Allium serra McNeal & Ownbey. Madrono 24:24-29. 1977.
Arctostaphylos benitoensis Roof.
  Four Seasons 5(4):2-18. 1978.
A. bowermaniae Roof. Ibid.
A. chaloneorum Roof. Ibid.
A. hookeri ssp. *ravenii* Wells. Madrono 19:192-210. 1969.
A. pilosula ssp. *pismoensis* Wells. Ibid.
A. pseudopungens Roof. Four Seasons 5(4):2-18. 1978.
A. purissima Wells. Madrono 19:193-224. 1968.
A. serpenticola Roof. Four Seasons 5(4):2-18. 1978.
A. stanfordiana var. *repens* Roof.
  Four Seasons 4(2):16-17. 1972.
A. tomentosa ssp. *eastwoodiana* Wells.
  Madrono 19:193-224. 1968.
A. uva-ursi var. *leobreweri* Roof.
  Changing Seasons 1(2). 1980.
A. uva-ursi var. *marinensis* Roof. Ibid.
A. uva-ursi var. *suborbiculata* W. Knight.
  Four Seasons 7(2):31-32. 1984.
Berberis nervosa var. *mendocinensis* Roof.
  Four Seasons 3:7-10. 1969.
Calochortus tiburonensis Hill. Madrono 22:100-104. 1973.
Calystegia collina ssp. *oxyphylla* Brummitt.
  Kew Bulletin 35:327-334. 1980.
C. collina ssp. *venusta* Brummitt. Ibid.
C. subacaulis ssp. *episcopalis* Brummitt. Ibid.
Camissonia benitensis Raven.
  Cont. U.S. Nat. Herb. 37:161-387. 1969.
C. campestris ssp. *obispoensis* Raven. Ibid.
C. confusa Raven. Ibid.
C. hardhamiae Raven. Ibid.
C. intermedia Raven. Ibid.
C. luciae Raven. Ibid.
C. lacustris Raven. Ibid.
Campanula sharsmithiae Morin. Madrono 27:163-194. 1980.
Clarkia jolonensis Parnell. Madrono 20:322. 1970.
Eriastrum densifolium var. *patens* Hoover.
  Vasc. Pl. San Luis Obispo Co.: 230. 1970.
Eryngium aristulatum var. *hooveri* Sheikh.
  Madrono 30:98-101. 1983.
Galium andrewsii ssp. *intermedia* Dempster & Stebbins
  Univ. Calif. Pubs. Bot. 46:1-52. 1968.
G. porrigens Dempster. Madrono 22:312-313. 1974.
Githopsis diffusa ssp. *robusta* N. Morin.
  Syst. Bot. 8:436-468. 1983.
Hemizonia paniculata ssp. *cruzensis* Hoover.
  Vasc. Pl. San Luis Obispo Co.:288. 1970.
H. paniculata ssp. *foliosa* Hoover. Ibid.
Limnanthes vinculans Ornduff. Brittonia 21:11-14. 1969.
Loeflingia squarrosa ssp. *artemisiarum*. Barneby & Twisselmann. Madrono 20:398-408. 1970.
Lupinus nanus var. *maritimus* Hoover.
  Vasc. Pl. San Luis Obispo Co.:169-170. 1970.
Navarretia miticarpa var. *villosa* Hoover. Ibid.
Orobanche californica ssp. *condensa* Heckard.
  Madrono 22:41-70. 1973.
O. californica ssp. *grandis* Heckard. Ibid.
O. valida ssp. *howellii* Heckard & Collins.
  Madrono 29:95-100. 1982.
Orthocarpus brevistylus Hoover.
  Four Seasons 2(4):14-15. 1968.
Pentachaeta exilis ssp. *aeolica* Van Horn & Ornduff.
  Univ. Calif. Pubs. Bot. 65: 1-41. 1973.
Pogogyne clareana J. T. Howell. Four Seasons 4(3):22. 1974.
Streptanthus insignis ssp. *lyonii* Kruckeberg & Morrison.
  Madrono 30:230-244. 1983.

SOUTHERN CALIFORNIA
(INCLUDING CFP PORTION OF BAJA CALIFORNIA):
Arctostaphylos catalinae Wells. Madrono 19:193-210. 1968.
A. peninsularis Wells. Madrono 21:268-273. 1972.
A. tomentosa ssp. *insulicola* Wells.
  Madrono 19:193-210. 1968.
Baccharis vanessae Beauchamp. Phytologia 46:216-222. 1980.
Berberis claireae Moran. Phytologia 52:221-226. 1982.
Calystegia macrostegia ssp. *amplissima* Brummitt.
  Kew Bulletin 35:327-334. 1980.
Camissonia confusa Raven.
  Cont. U.S. Nat. Herb. 37:161-387. 1969.
C. intermedia Raven. Ibid.
C. lewisii Raven. Ibid.
C. proavita Raven. Ibid.
C. luciae Raven. Ibid.
C. robusta Raven. Ibid.
Castilleja montigena Heckard, Morris & Chuang.
  Syst. Bot. 5:71-85. 1980.
Cordylanthus rigidus ssp. *setigerus* Chaung & Heckard.
  Syst. Bot. Monog. 10:1-105; 1986.
Delphinium kinkinense Munz. Aliso 7:65-71. 1970.
D. variegatum ssp. *thornei* Munz. Ibid.
Ericameria cuneata var. *macrocephala* Urbatsch.
  Madrono 23:338-345. 1976.
Eriogonum grande var. *duncklei* Reveal.
  Brittonia 33:441-448. 1981.
E. grande var. *timorum* Reveal. Aliso 7:217-230. 1970.
E. microthecium var. *corymbosum* Reveal.
  Brigham Young Univ. Sci. Bull. 13:1-44. 1971.
E. microthecium var. *johnstonii* Reveal. Ibid.
E. umbellatum var. *munzii* Reveal. Aliso 7:217-230. 1970.
Erysimum moranii Rollins.
  Cont. Gray Herb. 200:190-195. 1970.
Galium andrewsii ssp. *intermedia* Dempster & Stebbins.
  Univ. Calif. Pubs. Bot. 46:1-52. 1968.
G. angustifolium ssp. *jacinticum* Dempster & Stebbins.
  Madrono 21:70-94. 1971.
G. angustifolium ssp. *nudicaule* Dempster & Stebbins. Ibid.
G. porrigens Dempster. Madrono 22:312-313. 1974.
G. californicum ssp. *prinum* Dempster & Stebbins.
  Univ. Calif. Pubs. Bot. 40:1-50. 1968.
G. hilendiae Dempster & Ehrendorfer.
  Brittonia 17:289-331. 1965.
Githopsis diffusa var. *guadalupensis* N. Morin.
  Syst. Bot. 8:436-468. 1983.
Hazardia enormidens (Moran) Clark.
  Phytologia 34:371-374. 1976.
H. odontolepis (Moran) Clark.
  Trans. San Diego Nat. Hist. Mus. 15:150-164. 1969.
H. rosarica (Moran) Clark. Ibid.
  see also Madrono 26:105-127.

APPENDIX 1 (Continued)

SOUTHERN CALIFORNIA (Concluded)
Hemizonia increscens ssp. *villosa* Tanowitz.
  Syst. Bot. 7:314-339. 1982.
Hulsea vestita ssp. *gabrielense* Wilken.
  Madrono 24:48-55. 1977.
Hymenoclea platyspina Seaman. Madrono 23:111-113. 1975.
Lotus crassifolius var. *otayensis* Moran ex Isley.
  Brittonia 30:466-472. 1978.
Linanthus jamavensis Moran. Madrono 24:141-159. 1977.
L. floribundus ssp. *glabrus* R. Patterson.
  Madrono 24:36-47. 1977.
Machaeranthera canescens ssp. *ziegleri* Munz.
  Aliso 7:65-71. 1969.
Navarretia fossalis Moran. Madrono 24:155-159. 1977.
Orobanche parishii ssp. *brachyloba* Heckard.
  Madrono 22:41-70. 1973.
Pinus juarezensis Lanner. Southw. Nat. 19:75-95. 1974.
Quercus cornelius-mulleri Nixon & Steele.
  Madrono 28:210-219. 1981.
Stephanomeria diegensis Gottlieb. Madrono 21:463-482. 1972.
Suaeda esteroa Ferren & Whitmore.
  Madrono 30:181-190. 1983.
Trifolium wigginsii Gillett. Madrono 23:334-337. 1976.
Triteleia guadalupensis Lenz. Aliso 7:145-148. 1970.

CASCADE RANGE AND GREAT BASIN (MODOC PLATEAU AND NORTHERN MONO COUNTY):
Arabis bodiensis Rollins.
  Cont. Gray Herb. 212:103-111. 1982.
Astragalus oophorus ssp. *lavinii* Barneby.
  Brittonia 36:167-173. 1984.
Camissonia pusilla Raven.
  Cont. U.S. Nat. Herb. 37:161-387. 1969.
C. tanacetifolia ssp. *quadriperforata* Raven. Ibid.
Centaurium namophilum var. *nevadense* Broome.
  Great Basin Nat. 41:192-197. 1981.
Eriogonum beatleyae Reveal. Aliso 7:415-419. 1972.
E. nutans var. *glabrum* Reveal.
E. procidiuum Reveal. Aliso 7:217-230. 1970.
E. rupinum Reveal. Ibid.
Eryngium mathiasiae Sheikh. Madrono 30:93-102. 1983.
Galium glabrescens ssp. *modocense* Dempster & Ehrendorfer.
  Brittonia 17:289-331. 1965.
G. serpenticum ssp. *warnerense* Dempster & Ehrendorfer.
  Ibid.
Ivesia paniculata T. Nelson & J. Nelson.
  Brittonia 33:165-167. 1981.
Linanthus nuttallii ssp. *pubescens* R. Patterson.
  Madrono 24:36-47. 1977.
Polygonum triandrous Coolidge. Madrono 20:266-269. 1970.
Phacelia monoensis Halse. Madrono 28:121-131. 1981.
Scutellaria holmgreniorum Cronquist.
  Brittonia 33:449-450. 1981.
Trifolium andersonii ssp. *beatleyae* Gillett.
  Can. J. Bot. 50:1975-2007. 1972.

SIERRA NEVADA:
Allium lacunosum var. *kernensis* McNeal.
  Madrono 29:79-87. 1982.
A. obtusum ssp. *conspicuum* Mortola & McNeal.
  Aliso 11:27-35. 1985.
Angelica callii Mathias & Constance.
  Madrono 24:78-83. 1977.
Arabis constancei Rollins.
  Cont. Gray Herb. 201:4-6. 1977.
A. rigidissima var. *demota* Rollins.
  J. Arnold Arb. 64:491-510. 1983.
A. tiehmii Rollins. Ibid.
Arctostaphylos manzanita ssp. *wieslanderi* Wells.
  Madrono 19:193-224. 1968.
A. truei W. Knight & J. T. Howell.
  Four Seasons 3(1):19-20. 1969.
A. uva-ursi var. *monoensis* Roof.
  Changing Seasons 1(2). 1980.
Astragalus shevockii Barneby. Brittonia 29:376-381. 1977.
Calycadenia hooveri G. Carr. Brittonia 27:136-141. 1976.
Calystegia atriplifolia ssp. *buttensis* Brummitt.
  Kew Bulletin 35:327-334. 1980.
C. stebbinsii Brummitt. Kew Bulletin 29:499-502. 1974.
Camissonia integrifolia Raven.
  Cont. U.S. Nat. Herb. 37:160-387. 1969.
C. lacustris Raven. Ibid.
C. sierrae Raven. Ibid.
C. sierrae ssp. *alticola* Raven. Ibid.
Castilleja praeterita Heckard & Bacigalupi.
  Madrono 20:209-213. 1970.
Ceanothus roderickii W. Knight.
  Four Seasons 2(4):23-24. 1968.
Clarkia australis E. Small.
  Can. J. Bot. 49:1211-1217. 1971.
C. borealis E. Small. Ibid.
C. borealis ssp. *arida* E. Small. Ibid.
C. calientensis Vasek. Syst. Bot. 2:251-279. 1977.
C. cylindrica ssp. *clavicarpa* W.S. Davis.
  Brittonia 22:270-284. 1970.
C. mosquinii E. Small.
  Can. J. Bot. 49:1211-1217. 1971.
C. mosquinii ssp. *xerophila* E. Small. Ibid.
C. rostrata W.S. Davis. Brittonia 22:270-284. 1970.
Cordylanthus tenuis ssp. *barbatus* Chaung & Heckard.
  Syst. Bot. Monog. 10:1-105. 1986.
C. eremicus ssp. *kernensis* Chaung and Heckard.
  Ibid.
Dichelostemma lacuna-vernalis Lenz. Aliso 8:129-131. 1974.
Dudleya calcicola Bartell & Shevock.
  Madrono 30:210-216. 1983.
Eriogonum apricum var. *prostratum* Myatt.
  Madrono 20:320-321. 1970.
E. breedlovei var. *shevockii* J. T. Howell.
  Mentzelia 1:19-21. 1975.
Eriogonum kennedyi var. *pinicola* Reveal.
  Supplement to A Calif. Flora:68; 1968.
E. microthecium var. *alpinum* Reveal.
  Brigham Young Univ. Sci. Bull. 13:1-44. 1971.
E. nudum var. *murinum* Reveal. Aliso 7:217-230. 1970.
Fritillaria eastwoodiae MacFarlane.
  Madrono 25:93-100. 1978.
Galium andrewsii ssp. *intermedia* Dempster & Stebbins.
  Univ. Calif. Pubs. Bot. 46:1-52.
G. californicum ssp. *sierrae* Dempster & Stebbins. Ibid.
G. hypotrichium ssp. *ebbettsense* Dempster & Ehrendorfer.
  Brittonia 17:289-331. 1965.
G. hypotrichium ssp. *inyoense* Dempster & Ehrendorfer.
  Ibid.
G. porrigens Dempster. Madrono 22:312-313. 1974.
Githopsis diffusa ssp. *robusta* N. Morin.
  Syst. Bot. 8:436-468. 1983.
G. pulchella ssp. *campestris* N. Morin. Ibid.
G. pulchella ssp. *serpenticola* N. Morin. Ibid.
G. tenella N. Morin. Ibid.

APPENDIX 1 (Concluded)

SIERRA NEVADA (Concluded)
G. pulchella ssp. *serpenticola* N. Morin. Ibid.
G. tenella N. Morin. Ibid.
Lewisia serrata Heckard & Stebbins. Brittonia 26:305. 1974.
Linanthus nuttallii ssp. *pubescens* R. Patterson.
 Madrono 24:36-47. 1977.
L. pachyphyllus R. Patterson. Ibid.
Limnanthes floccosa ssp. *californica* Arroyo.
 Brittonia 25:177-191. 1973.
Lotus stipularis var. *ottleyi* Isley.
 Brittonia 30:466-472. 1978.
Mimulus norrisii Heckard & Shevock.
 Madrono 32:179-185. 1985.
Oreonana purpurascens Shevock & Constance.
 Madrono 26:128-134. 1979.
Perideridia bacigalupii Chuang & Constance.
 Univ. Calif. Pubs. Bot. 55:1-74. 1973.
P. bolanderi ssp. *involucrata* Chuang & Constance. Ibid.
Phacelia stebbinsii Constance & Heckard.
 Brittonia 22:25-30. 1970.
Pinus balfouriana
 ssp. *austrina* R. Mastroguiseppi & J. Mastroguiseppi.
 Syst. Bot. 5:86-104. 1980.
Poa sierrae J. T. Howell. Wassmann J. Biol. 37:18-20. 1979.
Sidalcea stipularis J. T. Howell & G. True.
 Four Seasons 4(4):22-24. 1974.
Stephanomeria exigua ssp. *macrocarpa* Gottlieb.
 Madrono 21:463-482. 1972.
Trillium albidum G. Freeman. Brittonia 27:1-62. 1975.
T. kurabayashii G. Freeman. Ibid.
Triteleia ixioides var. *unifolia* Lenz.
 Aliso 8:221-258. 1975.

INYO:
Arabis pinzlae Rollins.
 Cont. Gray Herb. 212:103-114. 1982.
Astragalus lentiginosus var. *piscinensis* Barneby.
 Brittonia 29:376-381. 1977.
Camissonia pusilla Raven.
 Cont. U.S. Nat. Herb. 37:161-387. 1969.

Centaurium namophilum Reveal, Broome & Beatley.
 Bull. Torrey Bot. Club 100:353-356. 1973.
Cryptantha alpicola Cronquist.
 Intermountain Flora 4:248. 1984.
Dedeckera eurekensis Reveal & J. T. Howell.
 Brittonia 28:245-251. 1976.
Eriogonum bifurcatum Reveal. Aliso 7:357-360. 1971.
E. contiguum Reveal. Aliso 7:217-230. 1970.
E. microthecium var. *lapidicola* Reveal.
 Brigham Young Univ. Sci. Bull. 13:1-44. 1971.
E. rupinum Reveal. Aliso 7:217-230. 1970.
Euphorbia ocellata var. *kirbyi* J. T. Howell.
 Mentzelia 1:7-8. 1975.
Galium argense Dempster & Ehrendorfer.
 Brittonia 17:289-331. 1965.
G. hilendiae Dempster & Ehrendorfer. Ibid.
Githopsis diffusa ssp. *robusta* N. Morin.
 Syst. Bot. 8:436-468. 1983.
Grindelia fraxino-pratensis Reveal & Beatley.
 Bull. Torrey Bot. Club 98:332-335. 1971.
Lathyrus hitchcockianus Barneby & Reveal
 Aliso 7:361-364. 1971.
Linanthus nuttallii ssp. *pubescens* R. Patterson.
 Madrono 24:36-47. 1977.
Perityle megacephala var. *oligophylla* Powell.
 Sida 5:61-128. 1973.
Trifolium dedeckerae Gillett. Madrono 21:451-455. 1972.

MOJAVE DESERT:
Camissonia pusilla Raven.
 Cont. U.S. Nat. Herb. 37:161-387. 1969.
Echinocereus engelmannii var. *howei* Benson.
 Cactus Succ. J. 46:80. 1974.
Eriogonum ericifolium var. *thornei* Reveal & Henrickson.
 Madrono 23:205-209. 1975.
Galium angustifolium ssp. *gracillimum* Dempster &
 Stebbins. Madrono 21:70-94. 1971.
Lotus argyraeus var. *notitius* Isley.
 Brittonia 30:466-472. 1978.

COLORADO DESERT:
Galium angustifolium ssp. *borregoense* Dempster &
 Stebbins. Madrono 21:70-95. 1971.

Research Needs for Rare Plant Conservation in California

Timothy C. Messick [1]

Abstract: Types of research needed to clarify conservation needs and promote implementation of conservation measures are reviewed for California rare plants. Types of research described include taxonomic studies, status surveys, several kinds of ecological studies, biotic inventories, chemical screening, and reviews of past and ongoing research. Examples are given of specific projects that would benefit rare plants in California. Graduate students, professional researchers and others are encouraged to give priority to these or similar projects when selecting research topics.

California's remarkably diverse native flora is steadily becoming less diverse as a result of habitat destruction, population depletion, and competition from introduced nonnative species. This creates a need for much information about the biology of species and communities we would like to protect. The most urgent needs are for information that will help us 1) clarify conservation needs, 2) set priorities for conservation efforts, 3) develop methods for protecting, restoring and managing threatened species and their ecological support systems, and 4) implement specific conservation measures.

This paper reviews the types of research that will most effectively meet the above needs and provides examples of specific projects that would contribute to conservation of rare plants in California. It is intended to stimulate research with direct applications in plant conservation by university students, botanic gardens, government agencies and private researchers. The material presented here is a synthesis of ideas from recent publications in plant conservation and conservation biology, and suggestions received from botanists throughout California and elsewhere.

TYPES OF RESEARCH FOR RARE PLANT CONSERVATION

Taxonomic Studies

Taxonomic systems can provide stable and widely accepted definitions of species, unambiguous means of identification, and practical frameworks for management activity, ecological research, and legal action. Unfortunately, in many groups of plants, the available taxonomy achieves few or none of these goals. Problems include confused nomenclatural history, descriptions based on inadequate sampling, overly narrow geographical perspectives, uncertain phylogenetic affinities, lack of observations on populations to support those on individuals, and/or difficulties in applying species concepts in groups with incomplete reproductive isolation. The rarity of many California taxa cannot be determined until they are more clearly defined in ways that distinguish them from closely related taxa. A number of California's rare plants, including some now protected by the state and federal Endangered Species Acts, are of questionable taxonomic validity.

Biosystematic studies in these groups could help to identify the genetic and morphological entities deserving protection and encourage appropriate legal recognition. Two types of plants have high priorities for taxonomic work. One type is plants that do not occur on lands under federal or state government jurisdiction, and therefore are less likely to receive management consideration. Another is plants for which protection has or could cause economic hardship to proponents of development projects because of unresolved taxonomic status. The Appendix at the end of this paper lists several possibilities for such research.

Status Surveys

Status surveys summarize existing data on taxonomy, identification, legal status, habitat, distribution, life history, ecology, degree and types of threat, and identify management constraints and opportunities. In addition, such surveys often include new field work or other studies to fill selected gaps in the existing data.

Status surveys are presented in a variety of formats. Most are no more than a few pages long. Examples are the "Status Reports" of the California Native Plant Society and the California Department of Fish and Game's Natural Diversity

---

[1] Botanist, Jones & Stokes Associates, Sacramento, CA.

Data Base and Endangered Plant Project, the "Element Abstracts" of The Nature Conservancy, and the "Red Data Sheets" of the International Union for Conservation of Nature and Natural Resources. Henifin et al. (1981) present an outline and an example of the much more extensive type of status report needed to support proposals to list species under the federal Endangered Species Act.

Two topics receiving insufficient attention in most status surveys are type of rarity and causes of rarity. An understanding of both the type and causes of rarity in a species is important for making decisions about management and protection, monitoring methods, and impact assessment.

Rabinowitz et al. (1986) recognized 7 forms of rarity in plants based on geographic distribution (wide or narrow), habitat specificity (broad or restricted), and local population size (somewhere large or everywhere small). Cody (1986) described 3 types of species rarity, linking them to 3 components of community diversity. Types of rarity can be determined by analyzing distributional records, observing habitat characteristics and species demography, and interpreting knowledge of impacts and evolutionary history.

Causes of rarity are usually complex. Changes in the environment and interactions with other organisms combine with various qualities of the species or population to create rarity and vulnerability to extinction. Usually several such interactions are operating at once, and may exert their influences differently at different times of the year or of the plant's life cycle. Soule (1983) illustrated a method of tabulating these factors for the purpose of "extinction vulnerability analysis." This method could help in analyzing how particular environmental impacts could affect individual populations or the entire species.

Status reports can be extremely valuable tools for rare plant conservation and management if the information they contain is relatively current. They are used by people who manage preserves and public lands, conduct environmental impact assessments, administer regulations for government agencies, and produce educational materials promoting conservation. They also provide valuable points of departure for the more focused ecological studies discussed below.

Status reports have been prepared for about 450 of the 638 plants listed by Smith and York (1984) as being "rare and endangered in California and elsewhere," or "extinct in California." Many date to the late 1970s, however, and are in need of major revision or expansion. Reports are available for only a dozen of the 114 taxa they list as "plants about which more information is needed" to properly assess their status. Status reports have been prepared for only 32 of the 499 "watch list" taxa that are of limited distribution. The Appendix lists some of the California species for which status surveys would be useful at this time.

Habitat and Life History Studies

Habitat requirements are so poorly known for many of California's rare plants that we have only such brief descriptions as "occuring on serpentine," "in vernal pools," or "with saltgrass and sometimes iodine bush." Similarly, our knowledge of life history is often limited to generalities based on observations that they are biennial herbs, perennial shrubs, or grow in abundance after a fire.

This level of knowledge is not sufficient for effective population management, preserve planning, impact assessment, or for proposals to list endangered species. Details should be known on seed production and viability, conditions promoting germination, habitat requirements for seedling establishment (not necessarily the same as requirements for survival of the mature plant), needs for seasonal or diurnal changes in conditions, seral stage preferences, survivorship patterns, phenology, growth rates, water use efficiency, stomatal physiology, nutrient cycling, symbionts and parasites, responses to disturbance, and longevity. Standard methods of population biology and ecophysiology can be used in answering such questions.

Habitat and life history studies of individual species can be used to establish a framework for more holistic, comparative studies. Greater insight can be obtained by studying all taxa within a group containing one or more rare species, or groups of unrelated common and rare species that compete for resources at the same site.

Population Size and Density Studies

When populations become too small, inbred, or widely dispersed, random forces that are nonadaptive begin to prevail over deterministic forces that are adaptive (Soule 1986). Nonadaptive phenomena include genetic drift (random deleterious changes in allele frequencies), inbreeding depression (loss of selectable variation), and outbreeding depression (loss of "internal harmony") (Gilpin and Soule 1986, Ledig 1986, Beardmore 1983).

Several questions about population biology are therefore of vital interest to people wanting to preserve and manage a rare species: 1) what is the minimum size of a viable, self-sustaining population? 2) how much larger than minimum viable size is best for effective management? 3) what are the minimum and optimum densities of stable populations? 4) what is the optimum level of relatedness between outbreeding individuals?

Unfortunately, there are no straightforward answers to these questions, and no clear procedures for making quantitative estimates. A major research need is to determine the kinds of data and the methods of analysis that are needed to obtain satisfactory answers to these questions. At present, several kinds of data can be gathered that enable us to make qualitative estimates. These include electrophoretic studies to determine the degree of variability within and between populations, and breeding studies to determine the compatability of populations and the fitness of their offspring (Chambers and Bayless 1983). Any of the ecological studies discussed in this paper would also help in finding qualitative answers to the above questions.

Pollination and Dispersal Studies

These studies are undertaken to 1) identify pollinators and seed dispersal vectors of plant species, 2) determine the degree of dependence of a plant on specific animal pollinators or dispersal vectors, and 3) describe the factors that increase or decrease pollination and dispersal efficiency. Such studies utilize a variety of field, laboratory and greenhouse techniques.

Pollination and dispersal processes are important to consider in designing and managing preserves for plants, and in assessing the impacts of habitat disturbance and land management near rare plants. Some rare plants may lack adequate protection if the pollinators or dispersal vectors upon which they are dependent are not protected in reserves or if impacts to their habitats are not mitigated. Such plants could be adversely affected by habitat disturbance, introduction of insect predators, and use of insecticides away from the plant populations, if the insects on which they depend are extirpated by such actions (Tepedino 1979). Habitat fragmentation can lead to reproductive isolation of plant populations once linked through dispersal of pollen and seeds.

These aspects of ecology have been studied in few of California's rare plants. The Appendix lists several possible subjects for pollination and dispersal studies.

Propagation Studies and Preservation in Gardens

Species that have been reduced to a small number of individuals in the wild or survive only in cultivation should have their numbers increased artificially through propagation in botanic gardens, arboreta, or preserves. Objectives of such work are to prevent extinction caused by stochastic events such as fires, landslides and vandalism, and to maximize the amount and genetic variability of material available for possible future reintroductions to the wild.

Admittedly, most such species have entered genetic bottlenecks and are likely to suffer from genetic load and inbreeding depression (Clegg and Brown 1983), but such species should not be abandoned to extinction while there is hope of at least partial recovery. A few examples of species recently benefiting from propagation include the St. Helena olive (_Nesiota elliptica_), the palmiste boucle (_Tectifiala ferox_) of Mauritius, _Hakea crassinerva_ of Australia, and numerous plants of the eastern Atlantic islands (Goodenough 1984, Wrigley 1985, Woods and Miller 1983). Many of California's rarest plants would also benefit from this kind of work.

Often, however, little is known of treatments required to germinate seeds, root cuttings, or culture tissues for micropropagation. The Appendix lists some California plants for which propagation research is needed.

Habitat Restoration and Population Reestablishment Studies

In principle, it is better to prevent habitat loss than to seek a cure after it has happened, and to focus on the causes of endangerment rather than its effects (Talbot 1984); but such choices are not always available. Many rare California plants have already suffered such widespread loss or degradation of habitat that restoration of habitat and/or reestablishment of extirpated populations may be necessary to ensure their long-term survival.

Habitat restoration has not been attempted in the majority of habitats supporting rare plants in California, but useful methods and experience can be gleaned from several areas. Creation and restoration of coastal wetland communities has been successful in some situations (U.S. Army 1978, Anonymous 1978, Josselyn 1982). Planting methods for erosion control are also well developed (Amimoto 1981, Gray and Leiser 1982) and can be incorporated into most restoration projects. Areas devastated by surface mining in the Rocky Mountains and elsewhere have been recontoured, the soil reconstructed, and the indigenous vegetation reestablished (Hutnik and Davis 1973, Wright 1978, Cairns 1980, 1986). Research is needed into methods for restoring natural communities and the rare plants they support in many of California's more specialized habitats. These include vernal pools, coastal dunes, native grasslands, serpentine soils, and a variety of other unusual and stressful soils. Some site-specific examples are listed in the Appendix.

More controversial and less predictable in outcome is the establishment of new populations in the wild at sites with seemingly suitable habitat, but no documented history of occupancy by the rare species. Potential hazards are "pollution" of the rare plant's gene pool through introgression with a closely related taxon in the new location, outbreeding depression from crossing of distant relatives in the same taxon, and legal or economic complications if the site is later proposed for development and the plant has gained legal protection. Research into this approach would be valuable, but should be planned with careful consideration of possible future complications.

Monitoring Effects of Mitigation

Regulatory agencies frequently require mitigation of past, planned, or potential impacts to rare plant populations at sites of development projects. General types of mitigation (in order of decreasing desirability) include avoiding impacts, minimizing impacts, reducing impacts by spreading them over time, restoring affected populations or habitats, and compensating for impacts through protection or enhancement of the taxon at another site. Monitoring is not in itself a form of mitigation, but it may be used to provide feedback and quality control in any mitigation program.

Too often, however, agencies and consultants make site-specific mitigation recommendations with little or no knowledge of how effective similar measures have been in previous instances. At other times, no mitigation is recommended and projects are stopped, delayed or modified, because the probability of successful mitigation is considered too low.

Monitoring basic parameters of population biology and habitat quality after implementation of mitigation measures would help us learn what measures are feasible for more kinds of impacts, and help make recommendations more effective. Specific monitoring needs can be identified by asking federal, state and county regulatory agencies where mitigation has recently been implemented for impacts to rare plants.

Botanical Inventories

California's flora is fairly well known. Yet it is sufficiently rich, and some areas are sufficiently remote, that range extensions and new taxa are continually being discovered. Floristic studies in selected parts of the state would expand our knowledge of rare species distributions, provide valuable specimens of rarely collected species, and call attention to previously unknown taxa. A few examples follow.

High Plateau, in Six Rivers National Forest, is an isolated serpentine area with a variety of habitats, numerous regionally endemic species, and possibly undescribed taxa. There may be threats in the future from mining and ore processing in this area.

The Warner Mountains in Modoc County have yet to be subjected to a complete and accurate floristic study. Northeastern California contains many rare plants, and it is likely that additional populations would be found with intensive surveys in the Warners. Several other mountain ranges in far northern California have rarely been visited by botanists because of their remoteness from universities and major routes of travel.

Several new and rare species have been discovered in recent years in remote portions of the southern Sierra Nevada in Kern, Tulare and Inyo counties. Further exploration in this area is likely to produce additional discoveries.

Military reservations in several parts of the state contain large areas of relatively undisturbed and unexplored vegetation. Notable among these are Fort

Hunter Liggett, Fort Irwin and the China Lake Naval Weapons Station. Floristic studies in any of these areas would probably lead to discoveries of undocumented populations of rare plants. Many relatively natural areas within military reservations are threatened with degradation from expanded training activities and facilities construction. Limitations on access would, however, make ordinary field work difficult in most of these areas.

Local inventories and checklists could contribute more directly to plant conservation by including locations of rare species occurrences (or stating that this information has been sent to the California Natural Diversity Data Base), descriptions of their habitats, and suggestions regarding actions and sizes of buffer areas needed to protect them.

Reviews of Management Experience, Biological Resarch, and Conservation Status

The literature reporting studies of the sort described above is increasing rapidly, but is widely scattered. There is a growing need to synthesize this literature, supplement it with the unpublished knowledge of reserve managers and field botanists, and derive recommendations for future conservation action and research. Especially important, but not easily done, is the translation of biological information into options for land use or management action, and criteria for deciding which options to select.

Such reviews could focus on plants of a particular habitat, taxonomic group, or geographical area, or on plants that are exposed to particular environmental impacts. Reviews of topics with a limited geographic focus may benefit from the findings of researchers and managers outside that geographic region.

Possibilities for such studies in California include restoration of coastal dune habitats, assessment and mitigation of impacts to vernal pools, optimum fire management in grassland and chaparral with rare plants, and establishment methods for rare hemiparasites (e.g. Cordylanthus spp.).

Chemical Screening

The uses and importance of plants in supplying chemicals for pharmaceutical, agricultural, and industrial uses have been reviewed by Meyers (1983). These many valuable compounds have been derived from only a small fraction of all species, and some of these species are now rare and threatened in the wild (King 1984). Most species and genera in California have never been examined for potentially useful compounds. Botanists and chemists could collaborate in screening such groups for biologically active compounds before rare species are lost. The presence of useful compounds in a rare species would provide incentive for its preservation in the wild and in cultivation.

Basic Research

Basic research in plant physiology, reproduction, morphology and other fields is most often carried out on common or weedy species. This may be done as a matter of convenience to obtain large amounts of seed, known high germination rates, or genetic variability with relative speed and ease. It may also be done when a weed is of economic importance and there is financial support for research that may improve weed control.

More basic research should be conducted on rare species. Many of the attributes that facilitate good basic research can be found in a variety of rare plants. Minor additional effort may be required at the outset to identify suitable species, determine where material may be obtained, and learn how to avoid significant impacts to populations.

Information obtained from studying these plants would contribute not only to basic knowledge of plant biology, but also to knowledge of how these species may best be managed for their protection and the perpetuation of natural diversity. Any of the taxa listed in this article may serve as examples; those included in List 1b of Smith and York (1984) ("rare and endangered in California and elsewhere") would benefit most.

Conservation Incentives

Much has been written on the reasons why we should preserve threatened species and their habitats (IUCN 1980, Erlich and Erlich 1981, Meyers 1979, and King 1984, to cite just a few). While most agree that the most fundamental and compelling reasons for species preservation are moral (Gunn 1980, Devall and Sessions 1985, Naess 1986), much recent emphasis has been placed on economic arguements (e.g. Meyers 1983).

New and persuasive arguements for species preservation need to be developed. These could relate to the social and economic values of rare plant resources, respect for the integrity of ecosystems, or perpetuating a conservation ethic in times of social and economic stress. One very neglected area with great potential benefits is building support within the religious community for species preservation and sustainable resource use.

CONCLUSIONS

It is hoped that this paper and others in this volume will encourage researchers -- especially prospective graduate students -- to select projects that will clarify conservation needs or promote conservation action for California's rare plants and their habitats. Conservation and scientific organizations providing financial support for biological conservation and research should be encouraged to solicit proposals and award grants for projects with the greatest potential for making such contributions. Contributions to plant conservation can be made not only by field-oriented botanists, but by laboratory botanists, entomologists, soil scientists, chemists, and others.

One final "research" need is to continue the task begun in this paper of publicizing research needs for various aspects of conservation. This paper has focused on, but not exhausted the topic of research needs for rare plant conservation in California. More articles and notes should be published on research needs for conservation of threatened natural communities, plants and animals in California and in other areas. These should be printed in journals and newsletters widely read by large numbers of undergraduate and graduate students, as well as professional biologists. This would be one of the most valuable services that any conservation, scientific or educational organization could provide.

The kinds of research discussed in this paper are needed and important in California, but for proper perspective it should be noted that many areas of the world are more urgently in need of such work than our own. Tropical forests especially, have levels of diversity, concentrations of endemics, and rates of biotic depletion orders of magnitude greater than in California. Compilations of research needs for living resource conservation would be most useful in many of the lesser-developed countries. People who develop skills for species conservation research in this country could do no better, if they wish to continue their work, than to undertake similar projects in the tropics.

Acknowledgements: I wish to thank the following individuals for generously sharing their knowledge of rare plants and conservation research needs: Dennis Anderson, Linda Barker, Jim Bartel, Roxanne Bittman, Norden (Dan) Cheatham, Susan Cochrane, Charli Danielsen, Mary DeDecker, Dave Diaz, Steve Edwards, Linnea Hanson, Larry Heckard, Vernon Heywood, Jim Hickman, Robert Holland, David Imper, David Isle, Subodh Jain, Deborah Jensen, Jim Jokerst, Monty Knudsen, Tim Krantz, Gren Lucas, Craig Martz, Joe McBride, Jim Nelson, Larry Norris, Robert Ornduff, Peter Raven, Cyndi Roye, Teresa Sholars, Gary Schoolcraft, Jim Shevock, Francis Thibodeau, John Tonnesen, Barbara Williams, Rick York, and Jana Zantovska.

Valuable suggestions for improving the manuscript were made by Ted Beedy, Jim Jokerst, Jordan Lang and Rick York. Office services were provided by Jones & Stokes Associates.

REFERENCES

Amimoto, Perry Y. Erosion and sediment control handbook. Sacramento, CA: Calif. Dept. of Conservation; 1981. 197 p.

Anonymous. Handbook for terrestrial wildlife habitat development on dredged material. Wilmington, NC: Coastal Zone Resources Div., Ocean Data Systems, Inc.; 1978. 353 p. + appendices.

Beardmore, John A. Extinction, survival, and genetic variation. In: Schonewald-Cox, Christine M.; Chambers, Steven M.; MacBryde, Bruce; Thomas, W. Lawrence. eds. Genetics and conservation. Menlo Park, CA: Benjamin/Cummings; 1983. 125-151.

Cairns, John, Jr. ed. The recovery process in damaged ecosystems. Ann Arbor, MI: Ann Arbor Science; 1980. 167 p.

Cairns, John, Jr. Restoration, reclamation and regeneration of degraded or destroyed ecosystems. In: Soule, Michael E., ed. Conservation biology: the science of scarcity and diversity. Sunderland, MS: Sinauer Associates; 1986. 465-484.

Chambers, Steven M.; Bayless, Jonathan W. Systematics, conservation, and the measurement of genetic diversity. In: Schonewald-Cox, Christine M.; Chambers, Steven M.; MacBryde, Bruce; Thomas, W. Lawrence. eds. Genetics and conservation. Menlo Park, CA: Benjamin/Cummings; 1983. 335-348.

Clegg, Michael T.; Brown, A. H. D. The founding of plant populations. In: Schonewald-Cox, Christine M.; Chambers, Steven M.; MacBryde, Bruce; Thomas, W. Lawrence. eds. Genetics and conservation. Menlo Park, CA: Benjamin/Cummings; 1983. 216-228.

Cody, Martin L. Diversity, rarity, and conservation in Mediterranean-climate regions. In: Soule, Michael E., ed. Conservation biology: the science of scarcity and diversity. Sunderland, MS: Sinauer Associates; 1986. 123-152.

Devall, B.; Sessions, G. Deep ecology: living as if nature mattered. Layton, UT: Peregrine Smith; 1985.

Ehrlich, Paul; Ehrlich, Anne. Extinction: the causes and consequences of the disappearance of species. New York: Random House; 1981.

Gilpin, Michael E.; Soule, Michael E. Minimum viable populations: processes of species extinctions. In: Soule, Michael E., ed. Conservation biology: the science of scarcity and diversity. Sunderland, MS: Sinauer Associates; 1986. 19-34.

Goodenough, Simon. St. Helena: so far so good. Threatened Plants Newsletter No. 13:9-10; 1984, August.

Gray, Donald H.; Leiser, Andrew T. Biotechnical slope protection and erosion control. New York, NY: Van Nostrand Reinhold; 1982. 271 p.

Gunn, Alastair S. Why should we care about rare species? Environ. Ethics 2:17-37; 1980, Spring.

Henifin, Mary Sue; Morse, Larry E.; Reveal, James L.; MacBryde, Bruce; Lawyer, Jane I. Guidelines for the preparation of status reports on rare or endangered plant species. In: Morse, Larry E.; Henifin, Mary Sue. eds. Rare plant conservation: geographical data organization. Bronx, NY: New York Botanical Garden; 1981. 261-282.

Hutnik, Russel J.; Davis, Grant. eds. Ecology and reclamation of devastated land. 2 vols. New York: Gordon and Breach; 1973. 583+504 p.

IUCN. World Conservation Strategy. Gland, Switzerland: International Union for Conservation of Nature and Natural Resources; 1980. 41 p.

Jain, S. K.; Olivieri, A. M.; Fernandez-Martinez, J. Serpentine sunflower, _Helianthus exilis_, as a genetic resource. Crop Sci. 17:477-479; 1977.

King, F. Wayne. Preservation of genetic diversity. In: Thibodeau, Francis R.; Field, Hermann H. eds. Sustaining tomorrow: a strategy for world conservation and development. Hanover, NH: Univ. Press of New England; 1984. 41-55.

Ledig, F. Thomas. Heterozygosity, heterosis, and fitness in outbreeding plants. In: Soule, Michael E., ed. Conservation biology: the science of scarcity and diversity. Sunderland, MS: Sinauer Associates; 1986. 77-104.

Lucas, Gren; Synge, Hugh. compilers. The IUCN plant red data book. Morges, Switzerland: International Union for Conservation of Nature and Natural Resources; 1978. 540 p.

Meyers, Norman. The sinking ark. New York, NY: Permagon Press; 1979. 307 p.

Meyers, Norman. A wealth of wild species. Boulder, CO: Westview Press; 1983. 272 p.

Naess, Arne. Intrinsic value: will the defenders of nature please rise? In: Soule, Michael E., ed. Conservation biology: the science of scarcity and diversity. Sunderland, MS: Sinauer Associates; 1986. 504-515.

National Research Council. Conservation of germplasm resources: an imperative. Washington, DC: National Academy Press; 1978. 118 p.

Rabinowitz, Deborah; Cairns, Sara; Dillon, Theresa. Seven forms of rarity and their frequency in the flora of the British Isles. In: Soule, Michael E., ed. Conservation biology: the science of scarcity and diversity. Sunderland, MS: Sinauer Associates; 1986. 182-204.

Smith, James P., Jr.; York, Rick. Inventory of rare and endangered vascular plants of California. Special Publication No. 1. 3rd ed. Sacramento: Calif. Native Plant Soc.; 1984. 174 p.

Soule, Michael E. What do we really know about extinction? In: Schonewald-Cox, Christine M.; Chambers, Steven M.; MacBryde, Bruce; Thomas, W. Lawrence. eds. Genetics and conservation. Menlo Park, CA: Benjamin/Cummings; 1983. 111-124.

Soule, Michael E., ed. Conservation biology: the science of scarcity and diversity. Sunderland, MS: Sinauer Associates; 1986. 584 p.

Talbot, Lee M. The World Conservation Strategy. In: Thibodeau, Francis R.; Field, Hermann H. eds. Sustaining tomorrow: a strategy for world conservation and development. Hanover, NH: Univ. Press of New England; 1984. 3-15.

Tepedino, V. J. The importance of bees and other insect pollinators in maintaining floral species composition. Great Basin Natur. Mem. 3: 139-150; 1979.

Woods, Anne; Miller, Kathyrin. Kew propagation news. Threatened Plants Newsletter No. 12:7; 1983, November.

Wright, Robert A. ed. The reclamation of disturbed arid lands. Albuquerque, NM: Univ. of New Mexico Press; 1978. 196 p.

Wrigley, J. W. Refound: at Burrendong. Threatened Plants Newsletter No. 15:21; 1985, November.

APPENDIX

Taxonomic Studies

Astragalus lentigenosus Dougl.: Two varieties, _piscinensis_ Barneby and _sesquimetralis_ (Rydb.) Barneby, might be treated as separate species. Both are desert taxa of wet saline soils.

Calycadenia fremontii Gray: Long presumed extinct, but now known from Butte, Shasta and Tehama counties. With the availability of new material, validity of the taxon is now questioned. If taxonomic study supports current treatment, field surveys should be conducted to assess overall rarity.

Cordylanthus rigidus (Benth.) Jeps. ssp. *littoralis* (Ferris) Chuang & Heckard: Populations in Santa Barbara and Monterey counties may not be the same taxon. Collections do not adequately represent the range of variability in these plants.

Echinocereus engelmanii (Parry) Ruempler var. *munzii* Pierce & Fosb.: May warrant treatment as species; relationship to *E. mojavensis* (Engelm. & Bigel.) Ruempler needs clarification.

Eriogonum beatleyae Reveal: Mono County material may be only ecotypically different from *E. rosense* Nels. & Kenn. of the Sierra Nevada. With numerous populations of *E. beatleyae* now known in Nevada, its relationship to other species in the complex should be reassessed.

Eriogonum nudum Dougl. ex Benth. var. *murinum* Reveal: May not be distinct from the common var. *auriculatum* (Benth.) Tracy ex Jeps. of the Coast Ranges. If not, special management by Sequoia National Park may not be needed and candidate listing status not warranted.

Fritillaria ojaiensis A. Davids.: Populations in San Luis Obispo Co. may actually be *F. viridea* Kell. More thorough comparison of these taxa in San Luis Obispo and Ventura counties needed.

Fritillaria roderickii Knight: Occurs in 2 widely separated populations which differ ecologically and morphologically. Taxonomy and nomenclature need clarification.

Helianthemum suffrutescens Schreib.: Has been lumped with *H. scoparium* Nutt., but there is not much agreement with this. Additional collection and study of *Helianthemum* taxa in the Sierra Nevada foothills could clarify the situation.

Helianthus exilis Gray: Shows promise as a genetic resource in breeding sunflowers because of its high linoleic acid content and germination polymorphism (Jain et al. 1977), but taxonomic relationship to *H. bolanderi* Gray is unclear, and identification is difficult.

Lewisia cotyledon (Wats.) Rob. in Gray var. *howellii* (Wats.) Jeps.: Rarity uncertain because of difficulties in field identification of this and other varieties. Taxonomy has been studied, but may need refinement for use in field.

Lilium vollmeri Eastw. and *L. wigginsii* Beane & Vollmer: Extent of hybridization and reproductive isolation needs clarification. See also under ecological studies.

Mahonia nervosa (Pursh) Nutt. var. *mendocinensis* (Roof) Roof: Very difficult to distinguish from the common *M. n.* var. *nervosa*. Clarification of taxonomy and a functional key are needed before populations can be identified and managed.

Scrophularia atrata Penn.: Appears to hybridize or intergrade with *S. californica* Chan & Schlecht. Taxonomic study needed where these occur together in Santa Barbara and San Luis Obispo counties so that rarity of *S. atrata* can be determined.

Silene hookeri Nutt. ex T. & G. ssp. *pulverulenta* (M. E. Jones) C. L. Hitchc. & Maguire: Relationships to other taxa in the *S. hookeri* complex are unclear, thus distribution and rarity are poorly known; plants ascribed to this taxon in the Gasquet area appear to be undescribed.

Streptanthus morrisonii F. W. Hoffm.: Complex needs application of numerical and chemical methods to clarify relationships and stabilize nomenclature.

Status Surveys

Allium hickmanii Eastw.: Distribution is poorly documented because plants are easily overlooked. Habitat is being reduced rapidly by development.

Arctostaphylos hookeri D. Don ssp. *hookeri*: Locally abundant in the Monterey region, but its overall distribution very limited. Development is reducing its numbers, and field surveys to clarify limits of distribution would be useful.

Atriplex patula L. ssp. *spicata* (Wats.) Hall & Clem.: Most records are very old and many collections are of material too young for positive identification. Taxonomic validity is also questioned. Surveys are needed to clarify its present range, rarity and endangerment.

Camissonia tanacetifolia (Torr. & Gray) Raven ssp. *quadriperforata* Raven: Documented only from Sierra Valley, but believed to be more widespread. Field surveys and documentation needed.

Castilleja latifolia Hook. & Arn. ssp. *mendocinensis* Eastw.: Threatened with habitat loss from development and disturbance from recreation. Status survey needed to determine distribution of the plant and its habitat and to support management guidelines.

Chorizanthe parryi Wats. var. *fernandina* (Wats.) Jeps.: Not seen since 1940. Surveys of this south coast plant needed to relocate populations and determine present status.

Cordylanthus tenuis Gray ssp. *pallescens* (Penn.) Chuang & Heckard: Status survey of this Siskiyou Co. endemic needed to clarify range, threats, ecology, reasons for observed decline, and options for protection.

Delphinium californicum Torr. & Gray ssp. *interius* (Eastw.) Ewan: Few documented populations. Field surveys needed throughout its range in Santa Clara, Alameda and Contra Costa counties.

Dirca occidentalis Gray: Only California member of Thymelaeaceae and endemic to the San Francisco Bay area. Appears to be rare and endangered, but locations and threats are not adequately known.

Epilobium oreganum Greene: Often misidentified and its distribution not well understood. Field surveys would be useful. See also under ecological studies.

Ribes amarum McCalt var. *hoffmanii* Munz: Few documented locations. Field surveys of this Santa Barbara County endemic are needed.

Silene invisa C. L. Hitchc. & Maguire: Has been thought to occur only in red fir forests, but recent observations indicate it may also occur in more open vegetation. Report of this Sierran species in the Trinity Alps needs verification. Field surveys needed to identify habitat preferences and develop management guidelines for National Forests.

Thlaspi montanum L. var. *californicum* (Wats.) P. Holmgren: Known only from Kneeland Prairie and Brannan Mountain in Humboldt County. More populations should be sought and ecology should be studied for protective management.

Trifolium amoenum Greene: Recorded from Santa Clara to Mendocino counties, but no plants seen since 1969. May now be extinct, but seems a likely candidate for rediscovery. Field surveys are needed to visit locations of all previously recorded occurrences and clarify present status. If found, requirements for protection and suitability for artificial propagation and dispersal should be assessed.

Ecological Studies

Astragalus johannis-howellii Barneby: Does not occupy seemingly suitable habitats within and between the three known population areas. Research needed to identify these unknown limiting factors and to determine effects of grazing on population vigor.

Bensoniella oregona (Abrams & Backig.) Morton: Appears to reproduce only asexually. Study needed to determine reproductive modes and requirements in Humboldt Co. and Oregon for National Forests to implement protective management.

Dedeckera eurekensis Reveal & J. T. Howell: Does not occur at some localities where soil and vegetation suggest that it could. Autecological, dispersal and field planting studies would help to clarify habitat needs and constraints and causes of rarity.

Epilobium oreganum Greene: Study needed to determine ecological requirements and tolerance to livestock grazing on Six Rivers National Forest. See also under status surveys.

Hemizonia conjugens Keck: Needs research on viable population sizes, reproductive ecology, and dispersal for management of small remaining populations. Comparative study of the several rare southern Californian *Hemizonia* species would be valuable.

Ivesia paniculata T. W. Nelson & J. P. Nelson: Occurs in Ash Valley Research Natural Area with *Astragalus tegetarioides* M. E. Jones, *Eriogonum procidum* Reveal, and 3 other locally rare plants. Would benefit from studies of habitat, population dynamics, pollination, and dispersal, for development of management guidelines.

Lilium vollmeri Eastw. and *L. wigginsii* Beane & Vollmer: Need study of minimum population sizes for management on National Forests. See also under taxonomic studies.

Opuntia basilaris Engelm. & Bigel. var. *treleasei* (Coult.) Toumey: Populations appear to be reproducing poorly and loosing vigor. Soft tissues may be adversely affected by acid deposition or ozone. Study of possible air pollution effects needed.

Penstemon personatus Keck: Needs more detailed study of habitat requirements, viable population sizes and responses to disturbance. Other species on Plumas National Forest with these needs include *Lupinus dalesiae* Eastw. and *Vaccinium coccinium* Piper.

Pinus longaeva D. K. Bailey: The bristlecone and other pines of the White Mountains appear to be adversely affected by dry deposition of alkali dust from Owens Lake; similar impacts from Mono Lake dust are possible. Visible injury and tree growth parameters should be monitored to assess the extent and significance of alkali dust impacts on bristlecone pines.

Ribes tularense (Cov.) Fedde: Appears to be pollinated by beetles. Would be good subject for pollination and dispersal study in Sequoia area.

Silene marmorensis Kruckeberg: Limited in both distribution (Siskiyou Co.) and reproductive capacity. Study of reproductive requirements and effects of timber harvesting needed.

Propagation, Restoration and Recovery Studies

Amsinckia grandiflora Kleeb. ex Gray: Should be propagated to increase dwindling population size. Experimental management studies needed to identify the best means of maximizing seed production and maintaining populations.

Arctostaphylos densiflora M. S. Baker: Continues to suffer disturbance and loss of individuals despite partial protection. Propagation and protection needed on-site; should be cultivated off-site.

Arctostaphylos myrtifolia Parry: Dominant shrub in Ione chaparral in Amador County. Research needed of methods to counteract severe dieoff that has destroyed many acres of the largest population and threatens much more. Research also needed of methods to restore Ione Chaparral to sites cleared by clay and sand mining. Associated rare taxa that would also benefit are *Eriogonum apricum* J. T. Howell (2 vars.) and *Helianthemum suffrutescens*.

Arctostaphylos hookeri D. Don ssp. *ravenii* P. V. Wells: Reduced to a single plant in the wild and a few in cultivation. Propagation needed in gardens and for possible establishment of new wild populations.

Calochortus tiburonensis Hill: Not seriously endangered, but a narrow endemic and very attractive. Micropropagation and development of suitable cultural methods could make this serpentine plant available for horticultural use.

Carpenteria californica Torr.: Widely cultivated from cuttings, but rarely if ever grows from seed. The dust-like seeds are unusual in a chaparral plant. Methods are needed to grow it from seed and for planting in wild.

Cordylanthus palmatus (Ferris) Macbr.: Should be propagated to increase declining and vandalized populations. One new population has been established at Mendota State Wildlife Management Area, but it remains small. Natural hosts of this hemiparasite should be identified.

Eriastrum densifolium (Benth.) Mason ssp. *sanctorum* (Mlkn.) Mason: Extirpated at most recorded sites, but may be useful in reclamation of aggregate quarries. Study of seedling ecology and garden populations for source of seed are needed.

Erythronium tuolumnense Applegate: Excellent potential horticultural subject. Could benefit from establishment of new populations in the wildand in gardens. Needs application of suitable micropropagation methods.

California's Most Endangered Plants

Richard P. York [1]

Abstract: The International Union for the Conservation of Nature and Natural Resources (IUCN), a worldwide conservation organization of which CNPS is a new member, recently (1984) publicized its list of the world's most endangered species. Unfortunately no California endangered plants were mentioned, even though the California flora has one of the longest lists of endangered plants in the world. This paper presents a brief description of the plight of these California species submitted to the IUCN.

In November 1984 the International Union for the Conservation of Nature and Natural Resources (IUCN) publicized it choices of the endangered species that they felt needed to be given top priority for conservation action. The results were 66 candidates, 34 animals and 32 plants. From this list a dozen animals and a dozen plants were choosen as the taxa needing immediate attention. Unfortunately, or fortunately, depending on your point of view, there were no taxa from California.

The California Native Plant Society (CNPS) is a member of IUCN and our representative, Tim Messick, felt that CNPS needed to choose and publicize California's most endangered plants in conjunction with this conference.

There are two purposes for choosing such a list. First, it is a way to alert IUCN about the endangered plants of California. And second, it is a publicity tool that can be use right here in California to publicize the need for rare plant conservation.

HOW PLANTS WERE CHOOSEN

In 1984 Martyn Murray and Sara Oldfield were asked by IUCN to devise the criteria and then choose the endangered species that need to be given top priority for conservation actions (Murray and Oldfield, 1984). The criteria they devised had two major considerations: conservation value and operational considerations. Under conservation value Murray and Oldfield assigned scores depending upon urgency, prominence (attractiveness, crisis appeal, usefulness to mankind, and symbolic or figurehead appeal), and biological value (monotypic genera, conservation linked to other endangered species). Under operational considerations scores were given depending upon need for international support, cost, and liklihood of success (possibilities of using a variety of conservation measures, government support possibilities, local support availability, IUCN/World Wildlife Fund involvment).

For those plants choosen to represent the most endangered plants of California, a similar, but different, set of criteria were evaluated. First, a list of candidates needed to be choosen.

Since CNPS has a computerized inventory of California's endangered flora (Smith and York, 1984), I decided to have our computer select our candidate list.

Each plant in the CNPS <u>Inventory of Rare and Endangered Vascular Plants of California</u> is assigned to a specific list depending upon the plant's <u>R</u>arity, <u>E</u>ndangerment, and <u>D</u>istribution. Together these form the R-E-D Code. Each element in the code is divided into three classes or degrees of concern, represented by the numbers 1, 2, or 3. In each case, the higher the number, the more critical the concern. The system is summarized as follows:

<u>Rarity</u> (R)

1 - Rare, but found in sufficient numbers and distributed widely enough that the potential for extinction or extirpation is low at this time

2 - occurrences confined to several populations or to one extended population

---

[1] Botany Research Assistant, California Natural Diversity Data Base, California Department of Fish and Game, Sacramento, California.

3 - occurrence limited to one or a few highly restricted populations, or present in such small numbers that it is seldom reported

Endangerment (E)

1 - not endangered

2 - endangered in a portion of it range

3 - endangered throughout its range

Distribution (D)

1 - more or less widespread outside California

2 - rare outside California

3 - endemic to California

An R-E-D Code of 3-3-3 indicates that the plant is limited to one population or a few restricted ones, is endangered throughout its range, and is endemic to California.

The computer was asked to create a list of plants that had an R-E-D Code of either 3-3-3 or 2-3-3, keeping in mind that we wanted our candidate list to be those plants that are endangered throughout their range and endemic to California. The resulting list contained 132 taxa.

After receiving such a large list of candidates to choose from, the Rare Plant Scientific Advisory Committee (RPSAC) of CNPS was asked to help develop the criteria to use to pick the most endangered plants of California. The committee suggested that each candidate be evaluated on its showiness, taxonomic status, potential for agricultural use (horticultural uses included), whether or not it represented a large group in the California flora, possibilities of extinction, and whether it is monotypic or not. Once the most endangered plants were choosen it was hoped that they would be showy plus represent a variety of families, threats, habitats, habits, and areas. It was also suggested that at least one of the choosen few be a California island endemic.

The reader must keep in mind that the following taxa do not, indeed can not, pretend to represent all cases under the greatest risk of extinction. These 12 plants have been choosen to represent, on behalf of a much larger number of endangered California endemics, the range of threats and their effects on the California flora. The plants choosen are not necessarily the most endangered, although several are on the brink of extinction. These plants have been choosen since they are all excellent examples of the plight of the rare, threatened, and endangered flora of California.

CALIFORNIA'S MOST ENDANGERED PLANTS

ACANTHOMINTHA OBOVATA Jeps. ssp. DUTTONII Abrams. (See Figure #1, Map #1)
Vernacular name: San Mateo thorn mint
Family name: Mint family (Lamiaceae)
Plant description: The San Mateo thorn mint is an aromatic annual, 1-2 dm high with small white flowers tinged lavender at the tips of the corolla.
CNPS status: List 1B (Highest Priority)
State status: Endangered
Federal status: Endangered
Habitat: This annual can be found on serpentine soils on the edge of chaparral and grassland.
Distribution: The San Mateo thorn mint is known only from a single occurrence at Edgewood Park in San Mateo County on land owned and managed by the San Mateo County Parks and Recreation Department.
Rarity: There are 4 historic occurrences, but 3 have been extirpated by development.
Threats: Development and off-road-vehicles are major threats, but the single extant occurrence is on land being considered for a golf course.
Protection: Supposedly the current golf course design will not affect the San Mateo thorn mint, but adjacent residential develoment (above the plant's habitat) may change the hydrologic patterns, adversely impacting the only occurrence.

ARCTOSTAPHYLOS DENSIFLORA M. S. Baker (See Figure #2, Map #2)
Vernacular name: Vine Hill manzanita
Family name: Heath family (Ericaceae)
Plant description: The Vine Hill manzanita is a low, spreading, shrub with numerous slender crooked and blackish branches. Flowers are rose to white, numerous, and about 4-5 mm long. This handsome shrub is available commercially and can be found under the name Arctostaphylos densiflora "Howard McMinn".
CNPS status: List 1B (Highest Priority)
State status: Endangered
Federal status: Category 1 (Federal Candidate)

Habitat: This shrub is historically known from roadside banks and adjacent areas.
Distribution: The Vine Hill manzanita is known from the Northcoast Range in the vicinity of Vine Hill in Sonoma County.
Rarity: 3 of the 4 historic occurrences have been extirpated.
Threats: Roadside maintenance is a major threat, but the 20-30 remaining shrubs are also threatened by a fungal disease and are experiencing dieback.
Protection: The single extant occurrence of the Vine Hill manzanita occurs on land owned and managed by the California Native Plant Society.

CARPENTERIA CALIFORNICA Torr. (See Figure #3, Map #3)
Vernacular name: tree-anemone or carpenteria
Family name: Hydrangea family (Hydrangeaceae)
Plant description: The tree-anemone is an erect perennial shrub 1-3 m tall with pale shredding bark. Its large white flowers, up to 1 dm broad, are very fragrant. This very handsome shrub is very popular horticulturally, but is best propagated by cuttings since propagation by seed is extremely difficult.
CNPS status: List 1B (Highest Priority)
State status: Not State-listed
Federal Status: Category 1 (Federal Candidate)
Habitat: The tree-anemone is known from dry granitic ridges and slopes in the chaparral and foothill woodland.
Distribution: The tree-anemone is endemic to the foothills of the Sierra Nevada Mountains between the San Joaquin River and Kings River in Fresno County.
Rarity: There are less than 10 native occurrences known to exist.
Threats: The tree-anemone does not appear to be reproducing in the wild. Since it is a component of the chaparral plant community fire may be beneficial to the species.
Protection: 1 occurrence is protected in the Carpenteria Botanic Area managed by the Sierra National Forest, but it is managed in an attempt to exclude fire which may be beneficial to the species. All other occurrences are not receiving any protection.

CAULANTHUS CALIFORNICUS (Wats.) Pays. (See Figure #4, Map #4)
Vernacular name: California caulanthus
Family name: Mustard family (Brassicaceae)
Plant description: The California caulanthus is an erect 2-5 dm high glabrous annual. Its handsome flowers have unequal, purple-tipped sepals and narrow, whitish, waxy petals that are slightly longer than the sepals.
CNPS status: List 3 (Plants Needing More Information)
State status: Endangered
Federal status: Category 2 (Federal Candidate)
Habitat: The California caulanthus occurs in the valley and foothill grassland plant communities.
Distribution: The California caulanthus is known from the Upper San Joaquin Valley in Kings, Fresno, Tulare and Kern counties. It has also been found in eastern San Luis Obispo and adjacent Santa Barbara counties.
Rarity: A 1986 survey of all 38 historic occurrences resulted in the discovery of only 2 occurrences.
Threats: Much of the habitat once occupied by the California caulanthus has been converted to irrigated agriculture. In addition, a great deal of its habitat has been significantly altered by intensive grazing. Intensive grazing has caused the vegetation to be converted from shrubs to grasses.
Protection: 1 of the 2 extant occurrences is on The Nature Conservancy's Paul Paine Wildflower Preserve, but it is a transplant. The only native, extant occurrence is on private land in Santa Barbara County and has no protection.

CORDYLANTHUS PALMATUS (Ferris) Macbr. (See Figure #5, Map #5)
Vernacular name: palmate-bracted bird's-beak or Ferris' bird's-beak
Family name: Figwort family (Scrophulariaceae)
Plant description: The palmate-bracted bird's-beak is a low, 1-2 dm high, many-branched, hemi-parasitic annual. Flowers are inconspicuous, nearly hidden within the bracts, usually white or dull yellow, slightly tinged purple. Plants are covered with salt droplets.
CNPS status: List 1B (Highest Priority)
State status: Endangered
Federal status: Endangered
Habitat: The palmate-bracted bird's-beak is restricted to saline-alkaline soil in alkaline meadows and freshwater seeps.
Distribution: Historic occurrences range from Fresno County to Alameda County in the San Joaquin Valley, and to Yolo County in the northwestern portion of the Sacramento Valley.

Rarity: Of 10 historic occurrences only 3 are extant, but 1 is a transplant from an extirpated occurrence. The remaining 2 native occurrences have been vandalized by private landowners in an attempt to eradicate the species.

Threats: The 2 remaining, native occurrences are threatened by urbanization, vandalism, waste water treatment facilities, and agriculture.

Protection: The transplanted occurrence is located on the Mendota Wildlife Area managed by the California Department of Fish and Game; this area is managed for its wildlife value, not for this particular endangered species, but the management staff is aware of the plant's existence. One of the two native, extant occurrence is located in the Livermore Valley in Alameda County. This, the largest occurrence, is threatened by residential development, but a mitigation plan is in early stages of development. The other native occurrence is on land owned by the City of Woodland. It too may be saved by agreements drawn up by the City of Woodland, the California Department of Fish and Game, the U. S. Fish and Wildlife Service, The Nature Conservancy, the California Native Plant Society, and the Corp of Engineers.

ERIASTRUM DENSIFOLIUM (Benth.) Mason ssp. SANCTORUM (Mikn.) Mason. (See Figure #6, Map #6)

Vernacular name: Santa Ana River woolly-star

Family name: Phlox family (Polemoniaceae)

Plant description: The Santa Ana River woolly-star is an erect perennial, much branched from the woody base, with many blue flowers clustered at the ends of the branches.

CNPS status: List 1B (Highest Priority)

State status: Endangered

Federal status: Category 1 (Federal Candidate)

Habitat: This plant occurs in coastal scrub areas with gravelly to sandy soil in the Riversidian Alluvial Fan Sage Scrub plant community.

Distribution: The Santa Ana River woolly-star is historically known from the Santa Ana River drainage of Orange, Riverside, and San Bernardino counties. It is thought to be extirpated from Orange County.

Rarity: It has been estimated that 80-90% of the habitat for this plant is gone, and there are only a few extant occurrences.

Threats: Many activities affect the remaining occurrences of the Santa Ana River woolly-star. Among these are flood control work, construction/ maintenance of groundwater recharge facilities, sand and gravel mining, grazing, off-road-vehicle activities, highway construction/ maintenance, and urbanization. Loss of habitat to non-native, weedy grasses may also be a threat. Several historic occurrences have been extirpated and there is little evidence of the remaining occurrences expanding or recovering.

Protection: There are no protected occurrences of the Santa Ana River woolly-star.

ERYSIMUM MENZIESII (Hook.) Wettst. (See Figure #7, Map #7)

Vernacular name: Menzies' wallflower

Family name: Mustard family (Brassicaceae)

Plant description: Menzies' wallflower is a biennial or short-lived perennial from a long tap root. It has several short flowering stems and many bright yellow four-petaled flowers.

CNPS status: List 1B (Highest Priority)

State status: Endangered

Federal status: Category 1 (Federal Candidate)

Habitat: Menzies' wallflower can be found on northern coastal foredunes.

Distribution: Menzies' wallflower can be found on coastal foredunes north of Monterey (Monterey County), at MacKerricher State Beach (Mendocino County), and along the Samoa Peninsula of Humboldt Bay (Humboldt County).

Rarity: There are approximately 25 total occurrences in the 3 main areas where this plant occurs.

Threats: Menzies' wallflower is seriously threatened by industrial and residential development, off-road-vehicle activities, and loss of habitat to weedy, non-native plants.

Protection: Most occurrences are not protected, however several occurrences are on land owned and managed by the California Department of Parks and Recreation at MacKerricher State Beach. This park has a dune management/revegetation program that is attempting to stabilize degraded dune habitat. Around Humboldt Bay Menzies' wallflower occurrences are on land owned by the Bureau of Land Management, but protection is questionable. Other Humboldt Bay occurrences are managed by The Nature Conservancy's Lanphere-Christensen Dunes Preserve.

LAVATERA ASSURGENTIFLORA Kell. ssp. GLABRA Philbrick. (See Figure #8, Map #8)
Vernacular name: southern island mallow
Family name: Mallow family (Malvaceae)
Plant description: Southern island mallow is an erect shrub, 1-4 m tall with showy rose to deep red flowers that have a yellow-green center. These flowers usually have purple stripes/veins. L. assurgentiflora is a popular horticultural plant and is widely planted on the mainland.
CNPS status: List 1B (Highest Priority)
State status: Not State listed
Federal status: Category 2 (Federal Candidate)
Habitat: Southern island mallow is found near the coast on sandy flats, grasslands, and rocky slopes.
Distribution: Southern island mallow is known from Santa Catalina Island and San Clemente Island, Los Angeles County.
Rarity: This plant was once common on these two islands, but the introduction of non-native herbivores, and subsequent erosion, have reduced this plant to only a small fragment of its once more widespread range.
Threats: The main threat continues to be non-native herbivores. Most of the remaining occurrences are very small in size with only a few plants at each occurrence.
Protection: There are no protected occurrences of the southern island mallow.

LILIUM OCCIDENTALE Purdy. (See Figure #9, Map #9)
Vernacular name: western lily
Family name: Lily family (Liliaceae)
Plant description: The western lily arises from a rhizomatous bulb and has simple and slender stems, 6-8 (-25) dm tall. Its flowers are nodding, crimson with a green center, and dotted with maroon spots. Tepals are recurved on upper half.
CNPS status: List 1B (Highest Priority)
State status: Endangered
Federal status: Category 1 (Federal Candidate)
Habitat: The western lily is found in the northern coastal scrub plant community in and adjacent to moist meadows and forests.
Distribution: The western lily is known only from the Table Bluff area at the southern end of Humboldt Bay, Humboldt County.
Rarity: There are only 4 extant occurrences out of 10 historic occurrences, and all are from the same general area.
Threats: Grazing and plant collectors threaten this extremely showy lily.
Protection: Of the four extant occurrences, two have been registered by The Nature Conservancy's Landowner Contact Program. This involves private landowners voluntarily agreeing to protect the plants. One other occurrence is on land owned and managed by the California Department of Fish and Game.

ORCUTTIA INAEQUALIS Hoover. (See Figure #10, Map #10)
Vernacular name: San Joaquin Valley Orcutt grass
Family name: Grass family (Poaceae)
Plant description: The San Joaquin Valley Orcutt grass is a short, pilose, grayish-green, tufted annual grass, 0.5-1.5 dm tall. Its foliage and inflorescences are covered by a sticky, aromatic, bitter-tasting secretion characteristic of two other genera, Neostapfia, and Tuctoria.
CNPS status: List 1B (Highest Priority)
State status: Endangered
Federal status: Category 1 (Federal Candidate)
Habitat: The San Joaquin Valley Orcutt grass can be found in dried vernal pools in the San Joaquin Valley.
Distribution: The San Joaquin Valley Orcutt grass is known from Fresno, Madera, Merced, Stanislaus, and Tulare counties in the southern half of California's Central Valley.
Rarity: There are 38 documented occurrences of the San Joaquin Valley Orcutt grass, but many are extirpated.
Threats: Well over half of the 38 historic occurrences have been extirpated or damaged by agricultural conversion, grazing, and alteration of hydrologic regimes. As a result, it is thought to be extirpated from Fresno and Stanislaus counties.
Protection: The only occurrences receiving protection are those on the Flying M Ranch in Merced County. This area is part of The Nature Conservancy's Landowner Contact Program. All other occurrences are unprotected.

POGOGYNE ABRAMSII J. T. Howell. (See Figure #11, Map #11)
Vernacular name: San Diego mesa mint
Family name: Mint family (Lamiaceae)
Plant description: The San Diego mesa mint is an erect, aromatic annual that has ascending branches from the base and stands 1-3 dm tall. Flowers are lavender, 11-14 mm long, and arranged in whorls.

CNPS status: List 1B (Highest Priority)
State status: Endangered
Federal status: Endangered
Habitat: The San Diego mesa mint is restricted to vernal pools on the mesa tops in the vicinity of San Diego.
Distribution: This aromatic annual can only be found on mesa tops north of San Diego, San Diego County.
Rarity: Nearly two-thirds of the occurrences of this plant have been either extirpated or are damaged and declining.
Threats: Urbanization is the major threat to the continued existence of the San Diego mesa mint. The metropolitan San Diego area is rapidly developing and the mesa tops are perfect for development.
Protection: Some of the best remaining occurrences are on lands administered by the Department of the Navy's Miramar Naval Air Station, but there is no protection or management plans for these occurrences. In addition, there are no protection strategies for privately owned occurrences.

SIDALCEA PEDATA Gray. (See Figure #12, Map #12)
Vernacular name: pedate checker mallow or bird-footed checker mallow
Family name: Mallow family (Malvaceae)
Plant description: The pedate checker mallow is a perennial herb, 1-3 dm tall, with few to several reddish stems arising from a rootcrown. The inflorescence has many rose-purple flowers.

CNPS status: List 1B (Highest Priority)
State status: Endangered
Federal status: Endangered
Habitat: The pedate checker mallow is known from meadows and seeps in the pebble plains plant community.
Distribution: The pedate checker mallow is known only from the vicinity of Big Bear Lake/Baldwin Lake area of the San Bernardino Mountains in San Bernardino County.
Rarity: There are only 16 historic occurrences, but 4 have already been extirpated.
Threats: Primary threats include off-road-vehicle activities, road maintenance, urbanization, herbicides, raising of the lake level, grazing, and vandalism.
Protection: The Nature Conservancy, the San Bernardino National Forest, and the California Department of Fish and Game are working together to preserve what remains of this plant and its habitat.

REFERENCES

Data on file, California Natural Diversity Data Base, California Department of Fish and Game, Sacramento, California.
Murray, Martyn; Oldfield, Sara. Choosing a top ten. IUCN Bulletin 15(7-9): 79-82; July-September 1984.
Smith, James P., Jr.; York, Richard P. Inventory of rare and endangered vascular plants of California. California Native Plant Society Special Publication Number 1, 3rd Edition; 1984. 174 p.

Figure 1--<u>Acanthomintha obovata</u> ssp. <u>duttonii</u>.

Figure 2--<u>Arctostaphylos densiflora</u>.

Map 1--Distribution of <u>Acanthomintha obovata</u> ssp. <u>duttonii</u>.

Map 2--Distribution of <u>Arctostaphylos densiflora</u>.

Figure 3--Carpenteria californica.

Figure 4--Caulanthus californicus.

Map 3--Distribution of Carpenteria californica.

Map 4--Distribution of Caulanthus californicus.

Figure 5--Cordylanthus palmatus.

Figure 6--Eriastrum densifolium ssp. sanctorum.

Map 5--Distribution of Cordylanthus palmatus.

Map 6--Distribution of Eriastrum densifolium ssp. sanctorum.

Figure 7--Erysimum menziesii.

Figure 8--Lavatera assurgentiflora ssp. glabra.

Map 7--Distribution of Erysimum menziesii.

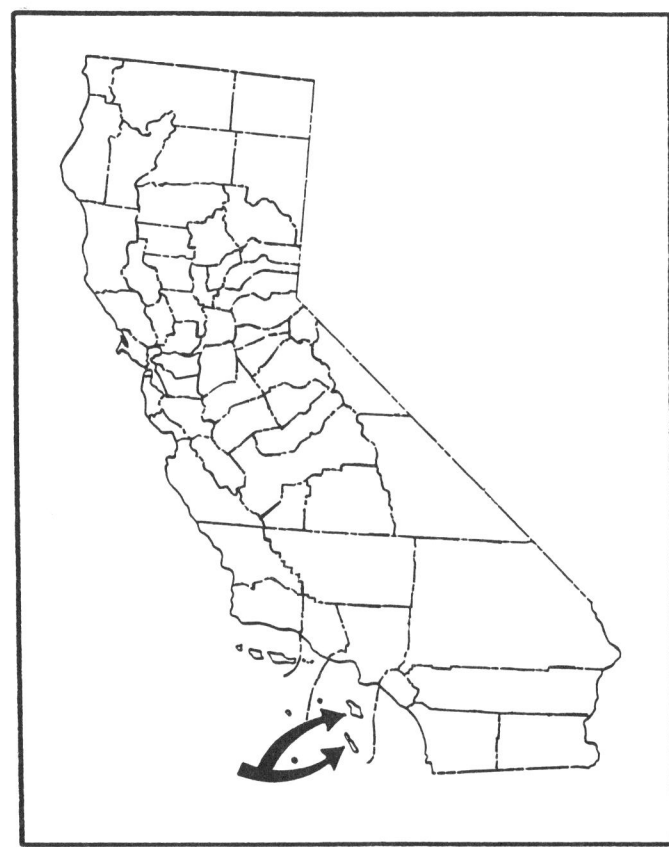

Map 8--Distribution of Lavatera assurgentiflora ssp. glabra.

Figure 9--Lilium occidentale.

Figure 10--Orcuttia inaequalis.

Map 9--Distribution of Lilium occidentale.

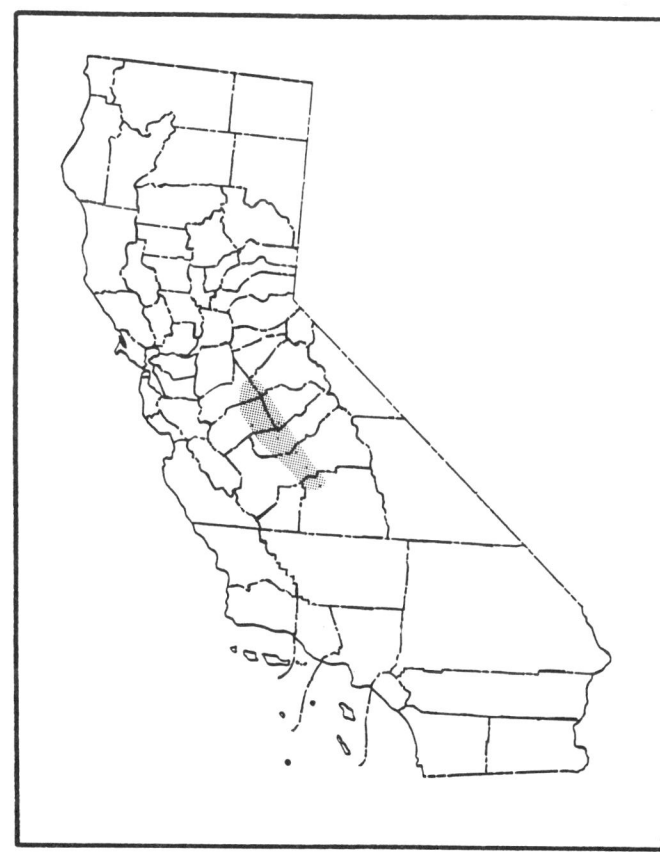
Map 10--Distribution of Orcuttia inaequalis.

Figure 11--Pogogyne abramsii.

Figure 12--Sidalcea pedata.

Map 11--Distribution of Pogogyne abramsii.

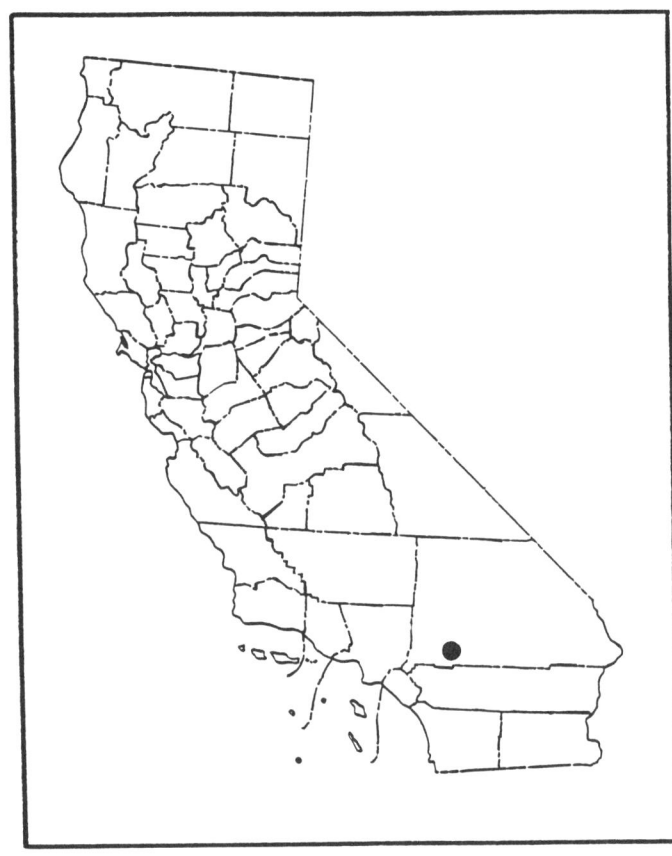
Map 12--Distribution of Sidalcea pedata.

Serpentine Endemism and Rarity

Arthur K. Kruckeberg[1]

Abstract: Plants on California serpentines are (1) narrow endemics (215 taxa); (2) indicator and indifferent species; and (3) they have an unmistakable physiognomy: sparse vegetation cover. Soils derived from serpentinite have properties that exclude many native species. Low Ca, high Mg and metal toxicity (high nickel), combine with low NPK, aridity and slope instability to create the serpentine syndrome. Yet a novel flora has emerged on serpentines in the Coast Ranges and Sierra foothills. The causes of rarity of serpentine endemics can be put in neo-Darwinian terms: genetic tolerance, population size, and isolation. Species of the crucifer, Streptanthus, illustrate the possible stages in the evolution of narrow serpentine restriction.

Our images of rarity and endangerment are strongly linked to specialized habitats. And when unique habitats are arrayed discontinuously in space, the prospect for detecting rarity escalates. Plants on soils derived from serpentinite and other ultramafic rocks portray in dramatic fashion this model for rarity. In California, as in few other places in the world, the widespread and often discontinuous display of serpentine soils has had a marked effect on the flora. Substantial endemism, tell-tale indicator species, and singular vegetation types are the botanical hallmarks of serpentine habitats. The most commanding attribute of serpentine landscapes, though, are their total appearance; the "look" of a serpentine barren, the scenes of sharp contrast with adjacent nonserpentine vegetations - these are the unmistakeable signs of ultramafic geology making its mark on plant life. David Rains Wallace, in his book The Klamath Knot, devotes a whole chapter to the "Red-rock Forest". In it, he captures the essence of a serpentine landscape: "The red-rock forest may seem hellish to us, but it is a refuge to its flora...It is the obdurate physical adversity of things such as peridotite bedrock which often drives life to its most surprising transformations." (Wallace 1983).

I first give an account of serpentine endemism - its geologic and botanical features in the Californian Floristic Province (CFP).[2] Then, I examine the linkages between endemics, rarity and endangerment. In a third section, I explore the possible causes of endemism on serpentine soils. The final section is devoted to the present status and need for protection of serpentine endemics and their associated unique vegetation types.

For more extended, technical accounts of these topics, I suggest the following recent publications: Fiedler 1986, Kruckeberg 1984a, b, c, Kruckeberg and Rabinowitz 1985, Kruckeberg 1986, and Kruckeberg (in press).

PLANT LIFE ON SERPENTINES IN THE CFP

Geology and Soils

The term "serpentine" has been loosely applied to rock, mineral and soil, as well as to flora and vegetation associated with these substrates. While the word serpentine is so engrained in ecological literature and its loose usage certain to persist, it is well to provide the current vocabulary for components of what Hans Jenny (1980) calls the "serpentine syndrome". Various rock types that botanists have called serpentine, are named members of a large family of rocks called ultramafics (ma = magnesium, fic = Fe or iron). All contain some form of iron-magnesium silicate minerals. In California, the several kinds of ultramafic rocks occur either as igneous outcrops (such as peridotite or dunite), or more commonly as metamorphic (hydrothermally transformed) rock types, mainly serpentinite. These two classes of ultramafic

---

[1] Professor of Botany, University of Washington, Seattle, WA 98195.

[2] As defined by Raven and Axelrod (1978), the CFP is all of cismontane California west of the Sierra Nevada crest and north to southwestern Oregon.

rocks were formed from deep-seated magma of the earth's mantle. They have intruded and surfaced onto the earth's crust, mainly through plate tectonics - the collision of oceanic plates with continental plates. The ultramafics of California north to Alaska usually have this mode of origin (Coleman & Irwin 1977).

The events leading to the present day distribution and exposure of ultramafics in both the Coast Ranges and in the Sierra Nevada are presumed to have begun ca. 150 million years ago (middle Mesozoic), though later intrusions undoubtedly have occurred.

The Coast Range occurrences of ultramafic rocks extends from Santa Barbara County north to the Klamath-Siskiyou country of northwestern California and southwestern Oregon. Every Coast Range county from the south to Del Norte County has ultramafics, often in massive displays (e.g. in San Luis Obispo, San Benito, Santa Clara and all Bay Area counties; then north into Sonoma, Napa, Lake Colusa, Trinity, Siskiyou and Del Norte counties). Serpentinite and other ultramafic rocks in the Sierra Nevada are confined to the lower western slopes, beginning in the south with Tulare County, and with substantial outcrops in Fresno County, then continuously from Mariposa County north to Plumas County. The serpentinites of the Feather River country are fine samples of the Sierra Nevada occurrences. Approximately 1 percent (2860 km^2) of the total land area of the CFP (285,000 km^2) is of ultramafic rocks.

Soils derived from ultramafic rocks have long been known to be infertile for agriculture and in extreme sites, even to be barren of plant life. Yet native flora, in fascinating ways and significant variety, does grow on ultramafics. Therein lies the crux of the mystery. How can plants cope with such an inhospitable habitat? I examine this question a bit later.

Infertility of serpentine soils is compounded of many factors. Not only does the parent ultramafic rock play a part, but other physical and biological factors influence the quality of the serpentine habitat. The grand old man of California soil science, Hans Jenny, perceived this complex interaction of factors in coining the term "serpentine syndrome". (Jenny 1980). Jenny's serpentine syndrome acknowledges the totality of factors that yield a serpentine flora and its landscape.

Chemical analyses of soils derived from ultramafic rocks have some common attributes: High levels of magnesium, low levels of calcium, nitrogen and phosphorous, often high levels of nickel, a toxic element, are present. On some soils, molybdenum, an essential element for plants, may be in short supply (Walker 1948). The other environmental factors that contribute to the degree of severity of serpentine sites include steepness of slope, exposure (north- or south-facing, etc.), moisture availability, plant cover, etc. Indeed, Jenny's designation, the serpentine syndrome, is most apt for the combination of operational factors that yield a particular serpentine site.

Plant Life

There are two ways to view the remarkable plant life of ultramafics in the CFP. One is vegetational - What kinds of associations of plant species or lifeforms are present? The other is floristic, yielding an inventory of the kinds of plants (species, subspecies and varieties) that can live on serpentines. The vegetational approach is, in fact, the one that we take initially when observing a serpentine barren or when we see an abrupt discontinuity between plant cover on serpentine in contact with vegetation on normal, nonserpentine soils. Inevitably a sharp, often spectacular, break in the regional plant cover results when ultramafic rocks intervene in an area's normal lithology. Dense forest gives way to sparse woodland or hard chaparral, and grassland of introduced annual species, yields to a unique serpentine grassland of native grasses and forbs. In many instances, surrounding vegetation on nonserpentine soils gives way to the extreme barren landscapes of serpentine outcrops. The most common vegetation types on ultramafics in the CFP are montane woodland, serpentine chaparral, and serpentine grassland (Barbour and Major 1977, Kruckeberg 1984a). But it is the remarkable flora on CFP serpentines that is most germane to our theme of endemism and rarity. Approximately 215 vascular plant taxa (species and intraspecific variants) appear to be wholly or largely restricted to ultramafics in California. No one knows what the tally for non-vascular plants (bryophytes, lichens, algae and fungi) might be. Besides endemics, other vascular plants have varying degrees of fidelity to serpentines, from local or regional indicator species, and taxa with exceptional range extensions (geographical and altitudinal), to indifferent species found on both serpentine and nonserpentine sites. A fourth category consists of those taxa that avoid ultramafics (Kruckeberg 1984a).

In the CFP, rare plants on serpentine outcrops are nearly always narrow endemics. The concept of endemism (Kruckeberg and Rabinowitz 1985) has been used by botanists for over a century to denote some degree of geographic restriction of a taxon (species, genus or even family). Thus, Sequoia sempervirens, Douglas fir, Streptanthus callistus and the Silk Tassel Family (Garryaceae) are all endemic to western North America, but with varying degrees of restriction. Only one of these, S. callistus, is a narrow endemic in the sense of very local restriction... one or a very few localities (Mason 1946a,b). Further, endemism - and rarity - are often the consequences of close tracking of a particular environment by the rare taxon. I have asserted (Kruckeberg 1986) that geoedaphic environments, compounded of rock types, soils, and their topographic settings, are primary causes of this fastidious nature of narrow endemics. Serpentine occurrences in California are unparalleled examples of this geoedaphically induced narrow endemism.

Of the 215 serpentine endemics in the CFP, a considerable number qualify as narrow endemics. Good examples include Calochortus tiburonensis, Streptanthus niger, S. batrachopus, Phacelia dalesiana and Veronica copelandii. Each is known only from a very local distribution and occurs exclusively on serpentine soils. Other serpentine endemics have intermediate to extensive ranges in California. Thus all the woody serpentine endemics are widespread: Cupressus macnabiana, C. sargentii, Ceanothus jepsonii, Garrya congdonii and Quercus durata. Why are there no narrow, spatially restricted endemics among the woody life-forms on serpentine? We examine this curious question a bit later. Herbaceous lifeforms (annuals, biennials and perennials) can show all degrees of restriction to serpentine - from narrow occupancy of a single or a few sites to those that occur nearly the full latitudinal extent of serpentines in the CFP.

The number of serpentine endemics is unequally distributed in the CFP. Many more (192) are in the Coast Ranges than in the Sierra Nevada (13). Further, the number of endemics in the Coast Ranges is unevenly distributed from south to north: The South Coast Ranges with 40 taxa; the Bay Area with 19, Napa, Sonoma and Lake counties with 27, the North Coast Ranges with 14, and the Klamath-Siskiyou country with 19 (Kruckeberg 1984a). Besides the bias towards the herbaceous life-form, serpentine endemics crop up in particular genera and families more than others. At the genus level, Clarkia, Eriogonum, Linum, Lomatium, Phacelia and Streptanthus have several to many serpentine endemics. At the family level, Liliaceae, Compositae and Cruciferae are well represented on serpentine. Thus in the Liliaceae, Allium, Calochortus, Erythronium, Fritillaria and Lilium have several endemic taxa on serpentines. Such taxonomic bias inevitably provokes questions such as: Why are some taxonomic groups well represented on serpentine? And, why are other genera and families poorly represented or not present at all? These questions compel us to consider now the possible causes of restriction - narrow or otherwise - to soils derived from ultramafic rocks.

CAUSES OF RARITY ON ULTRAMAFIC SOILS

Causes of Rarity in General

The great deluge of literature on rare plants in the last decade has been turned on by the concern for their preservation. A logical outcome of this heightened concern should be inquiries into how plants become rare, apart from human causes. In a nutshell, what are the biological bases for narrow endemism and rarity? This question is an evolutionary one and can be rephrased to ask: How do narrow endemics come into being? Unfortunately, plant scientists have not provided us with a simple set of answers. Apart from serendipitous theorizing, very little is known. No one has traced the origin and establishment of a rare species. Gottlieb's (1973) experience with the rare Stephanomeria malheurensis may be our only convincing case-history.

Two recent articles summarize what is known about the mystery of origins for rare species; both acknowledge that much is yet to be learned (Fiedler 1986, Kruckeberg and Rabinowitz 1985). Both papers emphasize that the answers will be idiosyncratic; each case of rarity will have its own profile of possible causes for its rarity. Fiedler (1986, Table I) summarizes the various factors involved in accounting for rarity of a plant taxon. These include age of the taxon, its genetic or hereditary resources, its evolutionary history, its ecology and population biology (including its reproductive biology), as well as the history of environmental impacts (land uses and other human interferences). Crediting Stebbins (1980), these two reviews of rarity cited above recognize that a "synthetic approach" is needed to evaluate the orgins, vitality and endangerment of rare plants. Such a synthesis calls for examining three major aspects of a rare plant's biology: its unique and local environment, its genetic endowment, and its past (evolutionary) history (Fiedler 1986). When applied to the problem of narrow endemism on serpentine, this synthetic approach can have rewarding results.

The geologic setting of a region or a local habitat can be a potent selective force in promoting or inhibiting the occurrence of plants with restricted distribution. I have called this arbiter of diversity the geoedaphic factor, a critical determinant of plant distribution and diversity in a region (Kruckeberg 1986). Within a given climatic regime, geology can multiply habitats by variables in chemical, physical and topographic attributes. Further, particular geoedaphic displays are often arrayed discontinuously across terrains. The gaps, for instance, in distribution of ultramafics in California afford the crucial isolation to organisms, a necessary prelude to diversification (read speciation!). Ultramafics in the CFP have all the ingredients - chemical and physical properties of rocks and soils arrayed on varying topographies - and usually with discontinuous pattern - to create a strong set of selective forces acting on the plant life that ventures there. The evolutionary consequence has been the genesis of a series of geoedaphic endemics, many of which are rare just because of the discontinuity in this demanding environment.

Possible Origins of Rare Taxa on Serpentines

Two critical questions arise when trying to account for the genesis of rarity on serpentines - and indeed, rarity in general. One is: Are there any unique processes or phenomena connected with the origins of rare plants that are not found with other kinds of evolutionary diversification? After all, any new lineage starts out as rare; it either stays rare or becomes common. The second question asks: Is there one favored sequence of events and processes leading to rare taxa, or are there several possible scenarios? Given Stebbins' (1980) caution that a synthetic approach is required, one can give an unequivocal answer to these questions. The causes of rarity are not rooted in some unique mechanism; the rich variety of models as coined by evolutionary biologists can be fitted to the rarity syndrome. This answer suggests still another general premise - that more than one mechanism or sequence of stages is necessary to account for the various kinds of rarity, both in general, and for the rare plants of serpentines.

Any model or hypothesis that attempts to account for the origin of rare species or higher taxa must trace the origins through several stages. First there has to be a fortuitous preparedness in the hereditary resources of the lineage about to embark on a new and localized adventure (read new environment!). This is called by the evolutionist, genetic preadaptation, the presence in the gene pool of the progenitor species, particular genetic resources, as yet untested and not purposefully attained, for the new habitat. The preadaptation will be fortuitous. The second stage is the inital exploitation by the preadapted genotypes (suitable genetic combinations) that permit a progenitor gene pool to contribute to the invasion of a new habitat (serpentine outcrops in our context). Since such new habitats, when colonized, are functionally and spatially isolated from the ancestral environment, crucial isolation of a new gene pool is initiated. The third stage is simply the intensification of the initial isolation, so that the isolate become even more uniquely fitted genetically to the serpentine substrate. At this stage, the taxonomist might recognize the isolate as a new variety or subspecies. Continued isolation in a local, specialized habitat may then also involve the genetic events of reproductive isolation; the serpentine endemic is no longer able to exchange genes with its nonserpentine ancestor. If this reproductive isolation is associated with other traits unique to the isolate, the taxonomist has no difficulty in recognizing the serpentine entity as a full-fledged species. I have sketched out this sequence of stages in figure 1. The evidence for this pathway to rare (or narrow) serpentine endemic species is largely circumstantial. The early stages are best paraphrased from the examples for evolved tolerance to heavy metals (copper, zinc, lead, nickel, etc.) worked out on mine tailings in Great Britain by Bradshaw and his associates (Antonovics, et al 1971; Bradshaw and MacNeilly 1981).

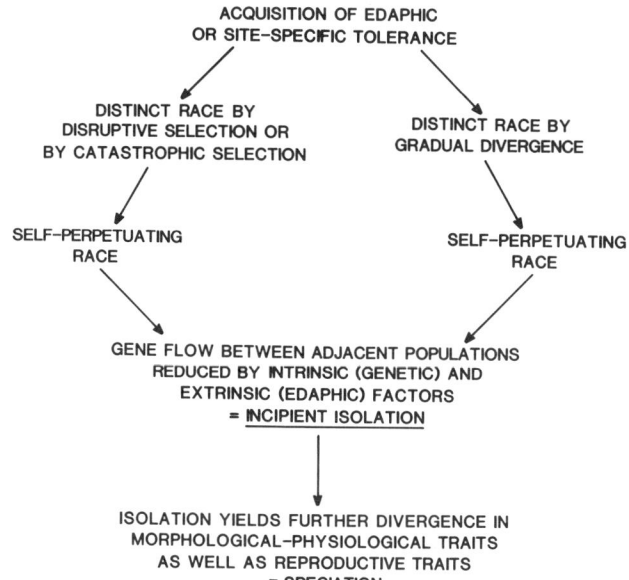

Fig. 1 Scenario for stages in origin of serpentine endemics

Yet there is some parallel evidence from California species with serpentine addiction. The Section Euclisia of the cruciferous genus Streptanthus contains 16 species, 14 of which are in varying degrees associated with serpentine soils. One species, S. glandulosus, appears to have reached only the early stages of serpentine accommodation. Certain of its subspecies (e.g., S. glandulosus subsp. glandulosus and S. glandulosus subsp. secundus) are found both on and off serpentine. I demonstrated (Kruckeberg 1951, 1954) that serpentine tolerance in these variants was genetically fixed. Streptanthus niger, that remarkable serpentine endemic of Tiburon Peninsula, is convincingly placed near S. glandulosus, but has attained reproductive isolation (Kruckeberg 1957) and narrow restriction. It is now a very rare species, cut off from S. glandulosus spatially and genetically. Other species of Streptanthus are either local or regional serpentine endemics (S. batrachopus, S. brachiatus and S. hesperidis). They appear to be later stages in the evolution of local, rare taxa. Two other Streptanthus species, S. breweri and S. polygaloides, both restricted to serpentine have wider distribution. S. polygaloides is so remarkably distinct that it has been put in its own genus, Microsemia (Greene 1904). Recent evidence that this species is the only serpentine endemic in the genus to take up excessive amounts of nickel lends support to its singular taxonomic status (Reeves, et al. 1981).

The scenario just traced applies best to what evolutionists call neoendemics. These are species that have come to occupy unique and often narrowly confined niches rapidly and in recent geologic history, so recent that their ancestry with common progenitor species is still clearly traceable. However, some rare plants are clearly hangers-on from some past events or environments. These so-called paleoendemics may well have examples among the serpentine endemics of California. The two serpentine cypresses, Cupressus sargentii and C. macnabiana may be paleoendemics. These and other types of endemics have been treated in a now classic paper by Stebbins and Major (1965).

The hypothetical (and circumstantial) sequence of events described above for creating serpentine endemics is only one possible model. One other route to narrow serpentine endemism may be the only model unique to these stressful habitats where geology and soils act as primary selective agents. This model for rapid speciation is called saltational speciation by catastrophic selection (Lewis 1962); it has been applied to the serpentine case by Raven (1964). Evolutionary theory is rich with yet other scenarios to account for new species from old. I have reviewed these models as they apply to narrow endemics of serpentines and other exceptional substrates (Kruckeberg 1984a, 1986). From all this we can draw a significant inference. Discontinuities like serpentine outcrops, created by geological processes, set the stage for diversification of a flora. In California, as in other parts of the world where a dazzling variety of geologic displays occur, one can be assured that plant life will respond. We need a new aphorism! "Geologic diversity begets plant diversity".

CONSERVATION OF SERPENTINE RARITIES

The California Native Plant Society is the best thing that ever happened to the preservation of California's serpentine flora. Each of the several revisions of the CNPS Inventory of Rare, Threatened and Endangered Species has included a large number of serpentine endemics having a restricted distribution. A bit later I sample some of these to illustrate the kinds of problems encountered in taking the step beyond inventory: the preservation of serpentine rarities. However, the task of converting the CNPS inventories into a secure protection for rare plants is far from completed. The several agencies responsible for watchdogging these plants include the California Data Base, and the several state and federal agencies that manage lands with serpentine outcrops. But without the CNPS inventory and the continued surveillance by its members, I doubt that the land managers would worry too much about rarities growing on the barren, semi-lunar ultramafic landscapes. A saving grace for serpentine endemics, though, is the very barrenness of their habitats. Serpentine vegetation is marginal for any uses other than livestock grazing. Much is thus "protected" by neglect, benign or unintentional. To be sure, some major disturbances of serpentine outcrops have occurred in the past, and are still occurring. But many miles of serpentine barren are simply left alone. Apart from livestock, little or no agriculture is possible on serpentine slopes. Some grapes have been tried on them, but with little success. Where serpentine alluvium accumulates in valleys and meadows downslope from the outcrops, attempts to grow crops have largely failed; the cost of correcting nutrient deficiencies with fertilizers is too great. Some timber harvest occurs on serpentine woodland; cutting this oldgrowth is a one-time-only venture, for reforestation of serpentines is barely feasible.

Off and on, mining has made major inroads on serpentine. Mercury, nickel, chromium, asbestos and magnesite, not to mention geothermal power, all have been exploited with consequent disturbance of plant life on serpentines. The disturbances continue. Witness the threatened or on-going mining activities near Gasquet (nickel), near Knoxville (gold) and geothermal power (the Geysers area of the Mayacamas Mountains).

Serpentine vegetation occurs on land with a variety of ownerships, from private and local government to state and federal jurisdiction. Hence the matter of preservation is subject to the vagaries of each type of custodianship. For each kind of ownership, there is both good news and bad for the protection of serpentine rarities. Some private owners have deliberately or inadvertently prevented any development of their serpentine holdings. Where private ownership involves the independent sector of our society, protection is more secure. The Nature Conservancy, a leader in land preservation, has helped California with preserving some serpentine sites, notably on Tiburon Peninsula (The Howell Wildflower Garden with Streptanthus niger as the centerpiece, and Ring Mountain Preserve with Calochortus tiburonensis and Castilleja neglecta). Local governments have inadvertently protected serpentine flora in the context of parks and watersheds. The Crystal Springs reservoir area in San Mateo County and the Carson Ridge area of Mt. Tamalpais (Marin County), as watersheds, each has given protection to serpentine endemics (e.g., Cirsium fontinale and Streptanthus batrachopus). Only one serpentine preserve, the Jasper Ridge site, is preserved by a University (Stanford).

State lands, either as state parks (Mt. Tamalpais, Mt. Diablo and Robert Louis Stevenson) include serpentine flora with a de facto preservation. A variety of federal lands in the state have major samples of serpentine habitats. The largest areas are under U.S. Forest Service management, mostly as multiple use domains. Only one site, Frenzel Creek, is designated as a Research Natural Area (the Little Stony Creek drainage in Colusa County). De facto protection of serpentine biota is assured in Forest Service wilderness areas (examples in the Yolla Bolly, Snow Mountain, Marble Mountains, and Trinity Alps wilderness areas). The Bureau of Land Management's (BLM) disposition of its serpentine holdings is still uncertain. The Red Hills of the Sierra Nevada and New Idria in the South Coast Ranges, both with spectacular serpentine landscapes and supporting several rare taxa, await a more secure protection.

The impetus to preserve rare serpentine species can take on a political flavor. A current case is the fate of members of the Streptanthus brachiatus - morrisonii complex in the geothermal belt of Sonoma, Napa and Lake counties. In order to determine if these taxa are narrow endemics with taxonomic standing, the BLM has sponsored sophisticated taxonomic research on the group. The fate of these local populations in the face of geothermal power development apparently rests with the taxonomic decisions forthcoming. Another kind of sociopolitical conflict between a serpentine endemic and the public "good" exists at New Idria, San Benito County. The rare taxa on serpentine here, including Layia discoidea, now under intensive study at University of California at Davis, are threatened by off-road vehicle (ORV) activity. Even BLM's admonitory warnings that ORV travel here may be injurious to one's health (due to asbestos in the serpentine dust) has not reduced this conflict between preservation and misuse of the landscape.

It would seem from the above, then, that preservation of rare serpentine taxa is mostly a byproduct of other reasons for leaving these lands alone. By chance some rare species are in the right watershed, wilderness or state park and thus escape major disturbance. The number of specific serpentine sites preserved intentionally for their botanical rarities is very low.

Future Needs.

The focus on preservation of rare taxa is most laudable. One of its defects, though, is its bias towards particular rare plants. The concept of rarity should also embrace rare or unusual environments. To be sure, preservation of a serpentine endemic in its wild state includes the preservation of its habitat. But, with the emphasis on securing habitat for an endemic taxon, some unique habitats without rare species may be lost.

It is a moot question as to how many serpentine rarities on the official endangered or threatened listings should be, or will be, eventually preserved. Since some rarities are safe through inadvertent protection, conservation efforts should focus on areas where threats are known and imminent. This is in fact being done in cases I know about: the mining threats in Del Norte County and the Knoxville area of Napa County. With all the genuinely well-intentioned efforts, though, very few serpentine endemics in jeopardy have been given secure protection.

Serpentine flora offers unlimited challenge for research. Especially germane to this Symposium is the opportunity presented by the serpentine syndrome (its physical presence and its biological responses) to expand our knowledge of rarity - its origins and fates. A beginning has been made with the recent studies on Calochortus (Fiedler, 1985) and Streptanthus (Kruckeberg 1984a, Kruckeberg and Morrison 1983). But many more mysteries about rarity remain to be solved. Serpentine endemics are choice subjects for this important biological research.

REFERENCES

Antonovics, J.; Bradshaw, A.D.; Turner, R.G. Heavy metal tolerance in plants. In: Advances in Ecological Research 7: 1-85; 1971.

Barbour, M.G.; Major, Jack. Terrestrial Vegetation of California. New York: John Wiley and Sons; 1977; 1002 p.

Bradshaw, A.D.; McNeilly, T. Evolution and Pollution. Studies in Biology No. 130. London: Edw. Arnold Ltd.; 1981; 76 p.

Coleman, R.G.; Irwin, W.P. North American Ophiolites. Bulletin 95. Portland Oregon: Oregon Dept. of Geology and Mineral Industries; 1977; 183 p.

Fiedler, Peggy Lee. Heavy metal accumulation and the nature of edaphic endemism in the genus Calochortus (Liliaceae). Amer. J. Botany 72(11): 1712-1718; 1985.

Fiedler, Peggy Lee. Concepts of rarity in vascular plant species, with special reference to the genus Calochortus Pursh (Liliaceae). Taxon 35(3): 502-518; 1986 August.

Gottlieb, L.D. Genetic differentiation, sympatric speciation and the origin of a diploid species of Stephanomeria. Amer. J. Bot. 60: 545-553; 1973.

Greene, Edward Lee. Certain west American Cruciferae. Leaflets of Botanical Observation and Criticism No. 1:81-90; 1904.

Jenny, Hans. The Soil Resource: Origin and Behavior. Berlin and New York: Springer-Verlag; 1980; 377 p.

Kruckeberg, A.R. Intraspecific variability in the response of certain native plant species to serpentine soil. Amer. J. Bot. 38: 408-419; 1951.

Kruckeberg, A.R. The ecology of serpentine soils: A symposium. III. Plant species in relation to serpentine soils. Eology 35: 267-274; 1954.

Kruckeberg, Arthur R. Variation in fertility of hybrids between isolated populations of the serpentine species Streptanthus glandulosus Hook. Evolution 11:185:211; 1957.

Kruckeberg, Arthur R. California Serpentines: Flora, Vegetation, Geology, Soils, and Management Problems. Univ. of California Publs. in Botany 78: 1-180; 1984a December.

Kruckeberg, Art. California's serpentine. Part I. Fremontia 11(4): 11-17; 1984b.

Kruckeberg, Art. The Flora on California's serpentine. Part II. Fremontia 11(5): 3-10; 1984c.

Kruckeberg, Arthur R. An essay: The stimulus of unusual geologies for plant speciation. Systematic Bot. 11(3): 455-463; 1986.

Kruckeberg, Arthur R. Plant life of western North American serpentinized ultramafics; Chapt. III. In: The Ecology of Areas with Serpentinized Rocks, A World View. Dordrecht, The Netherlands: Dr. W. Junk Publ.; 1987 (in press).

Kruckeberg, A.R.; J.L. Morrison. New *Streptanthus* taxa (Cruciferae) from California. Madrono 30: 230-244; 1983.

Kruckeberg, Arthur R.; Deborah Rabinowitz. Biological aspects of endemism in higher plants. In: Ann. Rev. Ecol. Syst. 16: 447-79; 1985.

Lewis, H. Catastrophic selection as a factor in speciation. Evolution 16: 257-271; 1962.

Mason, H.L. The edaphic factor in narrow endemism. I. The nature of environmental influences. Madrono 8: 209-226; 1946a.

Mason, H.L. The edaphic factor in narrow endemism. II. The geographic occurrence of plants of highly restricted patterns of distribution. Madrono 8: 241-257; 1946b.

Raven, P.H. Catastrophic selection and edaphic endemism. Evolution 18: 336-338; 1964.

Raven, P.H.; D.I. Axelrod. Origin and relationships of the California flora. Univ. of Calif. Publs. in Botany 72: 1-134; 1981.

Reeves, R.D.; R.R. Brooks; R.M. Macfarlane. Nickel uptake by Californian *Streptanthus* and *Caulanthus* with particular reference to the hyperaccumulator *S. polygaloides* Gray (Brassicaceae). Amer. Journ. Bot. 68: 708-712; 1981.

Stebbins, G.L. Rarity of plant species: A synthetic viewpoint. Rhodora 82: 77-86; 1980.

Stebbins, G.L., Jr.; Jack Major. Endemism and speciation in the California flora. Ecol. Monogr. 35: 1-35; 1965.

Walker, R.B. Molybdenum deficiency in serpentine barren soils. Science 108: 473-475; 1948.

Wallace, David R. The Klamath Knot: Explorations of Myth and Evolution. San Francisco: Sierra Club Books; 1983; 149 p.

Is *Quercus lobata* a Rare Plant? Approaches to Conservation of Rare Plant Communities That Lack Rare Plant Species

Robert F. Holland [1]

Abstract: California is richly endowed with rare and endangered plants for which species-oriented conservation actions are necessary. But California also has whole plant communities which do not harbor many sensitive plants. Over the past 5 years, the Natural Diversity Data Base has developed a classification of the state's "natural communities" in order to identify those rare communities dominated by not-so-rare species. Riparian forests dominated by Quercus lobata (valley oak) are one example. Brief descriptions have been prepared for each of the communities in this classification, both common and rare, in order to guide conservation efforts for the roughly 85 percent of California's native flora that is too common to justify species-oriented conservation efforts. The Data Base solicits information and opinion on community definitions as well as data on occurrences of about 125 communities identified in the classification.

Most of the papers presented in this conference concern one or another aspect of the conservation of some particular rare species or closely related group of species. Many conference participants have contributed to the body of knowledge about this rarest elite of California's flora by conducting research on these taxa or by contributing data on the location and condition of populations of these plants to the California Native Plant Society's rare plant project or to the California Natural Diversity Data Base. These two programs coordinate and share this data to assure that the most accurate and current information is available to guide rare plant conservation. The current edition of the CNPS Inventory (Smith and York 1984) provides information on 1449 taxa. The Natural Diversity Data Base has processed available data on the 702 rarest of these taxa in its computerized inventory. Shevock and Hennessy (these proceedings) provide details about this data base.

The Natural Diversity Data Base is patterned after the "heritage methodology" devised by The Nature Conservancy (Jenkins 1976). This method of monitoring locations of significant biological resources has been evolving for more than a decade. Similar programs have been established in over 40 states and in several Latin American countries,

so the method appears capable of accommodating a broad range of biological diversity.

Heritage methodology inventories the location and condition of so-called "elements of diversity" through a two-pronged approach that has as its major objective the identification and preservation of the best, most defensible example of each of these components of biological diversity. The first of these prongs is the "fine filter." The fine filter is supposed to catch those last, however mangled examples of biological diversity (both animal and plant species) before they slip into extinction. This fine filter approach represents the main focus of this conference: species-oriented conservation. In the parlance of heritage methodology, the fine filter is supposed to catch "the last of the least."

But heritage methodology recognizes that even if we lived in an ideal world and could secure the long-term survival prospects of all 1449 species in the CNPS Inventory, there still would be a lot of the state's biological diversity for which no examples enjoyed protection. Plainly it would be impractical and prohibitively expensive to secure protection for each of the more than 5000 plant species known in California. What is needed, then, is a "coarse filter" to catch the best of the rest of California's biotic diversity. This coarse filter is the second prong of the heritage methodology.

---

[1]. Vegetation Ecologist, Natural Diversity Data Base, California Department of Fish and Game, 1416 Ninth St., Rm. 1225, Sacramento, CA 95814

Where species provide the grist for the fine filter, "natural communities" are the focus of the coarse filter. Natural communities are recurring combinations of species that reflect parallel responses to similar combinations of environmental conditions. Like species, natural communities are tangible units that can be counted, protected, and managed. As such, they provide a convenient means of packaging together into a manageable number of categories the roughly 85 percent of California's flora that is plainly too common to justify species-oriented conservation.

For example, valley oak (_Quercus lobata_ Nee) is a familiar tree in many parts of California. It is a common sight in parks and along roads from Mendocino to Los Angeles County. Hundreds of thousands of acres in Monterey, San Luis Obispo, and Kern counties still support upland valley oak forests or woodlands (Mayer 1986), although there is scant evidence of adequate recruitment of young trees into these stands.

In preagricultural California valley oak also dominated hundreds of thousands of acres of bottomland forests along most of the larger rivers of the Great Valley, but these forests have been decimated by flood control and agricultural development. Recent estimates suggest that only about 15 percent of the original riparian acreage in the Central Valley still is extant, and that nearly half of this surviving area is in damaged or declining condition (Warner and Hendrix 1985). These figures combine willow-, cottonwood-, and oak-dominated types. There do not appear to be any estimates of the proportional losses endured by these subdivisions of riparian habitat. Presumably valley oak riparian forests have suffered disproportionately in this loss, given their preference for outer floodplains that are less frequently and less severely flooded during spring high water. These outer floodplains were cleared for agriculture and fuelwood long before the cottonwood- and willow-dominated forests that flourished closer to the river (Thompson 1961).

In spite of these losses, _Quercus lobata_ is hardly a rare plant in the sense of this conference. Programs that focus on conservation of California's rarest species would not even consider valley oak. Although the species is not rare, riparian forests dominated by it are rare and declining today. These forests are a good example of an uncommon plant community dominated by common plants.

There are a number of interesting parallels between species and natural communities. There are a lot of plant communities, like plant species, that are very common today. Examples include creosote bush scrub and chamise chaparral. There are a lot of communities that used to be common, but now are rare due to habitat loss. Familiar Californian examples in addition to valley oak riparian forest include freshwater marsh, vernal pools, coastal sage scrub, and the shrublands of the southern San Joaquin Valley. There are other communities that never were extensive in California, but somehow have managed to persist. These frequently occur on economically marginal sites such as the pygmy conifers on the Blacklock soils of Mendocino and Sonoma counties (Jenny et al 1969). There are still other communities whose distributions just barely reach into California from adjoining states where they may be much more common. Examples of this last group include the maritime succulent scrubs of coastal San Diego County (Westman 1983) and the Arizonan woodland that occurs sparingly in the Whipple Mountains of southeastern San Bernardino County (Shreve 1951).

Heritage methodology uses identical procedures for both coarse and fine filter approaches. Central to such an undertaking is deciding which elements are "rare enough" to warrant inventory. For plants, we have used the substantial efforts of the CNPS rare plant project to help with this decision.

The concept is the same for the coarse filter: make and refine a list of the California plant communities that warrant focused conservation action. Implicit in this suggestion is that somewhere there is a list of California's natural communities (just as floras list the species known from an area) and that all that remains is to work out which communities really are rare or unprotected.

But ecologists do not have the same universally accepted protocol as taxonomists. Other than parks, refuges, and preserves, there are no vegetaria full of specimens or type stands. There is, however, a vast and diffuse literature that has accumulated over the decades. This literature represents hundreds of studies of varying geographic scope and disciplinary bias: some studies examine variation within a selected community over its range, others treat all the communities found in some study area, while still others reject the plant community concept altogether, preferring to relate responses of individual species to environmental gradients. Two studies, one in Mendocino and the other in Ventura County, may use the same name for a community (say, "north slope chaparral") while the constituent species and their relative abundances may be quite different. Or 2 studies may use different labels to describe what is essentially the same community (eg. "creosote bush scrub" vs. "Larrea divaricata - Franseria dumosa").

All of these kinds of problems have exacerbated deciding which communities should be included in the natural community inventory. Several lists of California's communities have been developed since the Natural Diversity Data Base was established in 1979. At one point, the list included some 2600 named entities (Holstein 1980). This proved too unwieldy and in 1982 was replaced by a scheme developed by Cheatham and Haller (1976). Their scheme divided the California bioscape into about 250 types. Since then several more communities have been recognized and added to the list, bringing the current count to near 375.

Unfortunately, Cheatham and Haller's classification and accompanying descriptions never got the wide circulation it deserved. Adding more communities to their list only made matters worse. By 1985 there were dozens of communities in the Data Base classification for which no concise description was available. It had become increasingly difficult and frustrating to understand the current classification and to interpret the results that users received from Data Base enquiries.

Recognizing this need, I set myself the task of preparing a conspectus of the current classification. This includes a brief description of the overall aspect of each community, the abiotic factors typically found on a site, a short list of characteristic species found in typical stands, the geographic range of the community, and one or more citations to literature. In many cases I was satisfied with the descriptions found in Cheatham and Haller: I have borrowed these verbatim, choosing only to add a few taxa to their species list or to add a few literature citations.

The other descriptions were prepared primarily from literature and from discussions with biologists knowledgeable about particular areas or habitats. Only in a few areas did I have the luxury of extensive field work. The current list and descriptions represent my distillation of the available literature and opinion on classification of California's vegetation. I have every expectation that the classification and descriptions will profit from scrutiny by California's larger biological community. To this end I solicit constructive criticism of both the classification and the descriptions.

The descriptions are not intended as a definitive discourse on California's vegetation, but as a draft patterned after the early lists of plants of limited distribution within California that ultimately lead to the first edition of the CNPS Inventory (Powell 1974).

Just as the early lists of California's rare plants were seen as dynamic, so too are this classification and descriptions. I have every expectation that I have missed some important communities, and that I have flagged some communities in this classification that really are too common or adequately protected to justify immediate action. So I am asking the biological community to point out errors and omissions and to provide data on the location, composition, and condition of good examples of those communities that have been marked by an asterisk, just like you have been doing for rare plants for more than a decade. I hope that biologists who take issue with some aspect of the classification or descriptions will communicate these points to me. Improving this scheme depends on this kind of constructive criticism. If you don't like the classification, descriptions, or approach, please let me know how they can be improved.

In short, the Data Base communities program is today where the rare plant program was in the early seventies: trying to improve the list of species most needing inventory and protection.

The aim of the coarse filter is to catch "the best of the rest," before we have to be content with the last of the least. It is my hope that this list and descriptions can be scrutinized and improved while there still is time to protect whole forests dominated by valley oaks...it would be terrible if we lost these forests and had to resort to saving the trees.

REFERENCES

Cheatham, N.H., and J.R. Haller. An annotated list of California habitat types. California, University of California, Natural Land and Water Reserves System, Berkeley. 77 pp. Mimeo. 1975.

Holstein, G. California vegetation cover types. California Department of Fish and Game, Natural Diversity Data Base, Sacramento. Pages various. Mimeo. 1980.

Jenkins, R. Maintenance of natural diversity: approach and recommendations. Transactions of the 41st North American Wildlife and Natural Resources Conference. Wildlife Management Institute, Washington, DC. pp 441-451. 1976.

Jenny, H., R.J. Arkley, and A.M. Schultz. The pygmy forest-podsol ecosystem and its dune associates of the Mendocino coast. Madrono 20: 60-74. 1969.

Powell, W.R. (ed.) Inventory of rare and endangered vascular plants of California. California Native Plant Society, Special Publication Number 1. First edition. 56 pp. 1974.

Shevock, J.A., and L. Hennessy. The California Natural Diversity Data Base -- A common denominator. These proceedings.

Shreve, F. Vegetation of the Sonoran Desert. Carnegie Institution of Washington Publ. 591. xii + 192 pp. 1951.

Smith, J.P., and R. York. (eds.) Inventory of rare and endangered vascular plants of California. California Native Plant Society, Special Publication Number 1. Third edition. 174 pp. 1984.

Thompson, K. Riparian forests of the Sacramento Valley, California. Annals Assoc. of American Geographers 51:294-315. 1961.

Westman, W.E. Xeric mediterranean-type shrubland associations of Alta and Baja California and the community/continuum debate. Vegetatio 52:3-19. 1983.

Implications of Ecological Theory for Rare Plant Conservation in Coastal Sage Scrub

Walter E. Westman [1]

Abstract: Coastal sage scrub is an endangered California habitat, with as little as 10-15% of its former extent remaining. Approximately half the plant species are of rare occurrence within the type. The rare species are mostly herbs which appear to be part of a regional seed rain over coastal shrublands. Many can survive only in the first few years after fire in hard chaparral, but can survive in mature coastal sage scrub, to which they are disseminated slowly from other shrubland patches. Although few California endemics within the habitat are formally listed as endangered, recent ecological evidence suggests that, at least in the Venturan association of coastal sage, certain dominant species may be acting as keystone species. The decline or removal of these dominants could result in the loss of many associated rarer species. The modular structure of the community argues against the endangered species approach to conservation in this situation, and for habitat conservation per se.

Coastal sage scrub is a drought-deciduous, soft-leaved shrubland found in the lowlands and Coast Ranges from San Francisco south to El Rosario in Baja California (Kirkpatrick & Hutchinson 1977; Westman 1981a, 1983a). Although analogues of the vegetation type are found in similar Mediterranean-type climates along the central coast of Chile and in the Mediterranean proper (Westman 1981a), virtually the only species held in common between the three analogues are herbaceous exotic weeds.

Coastal sage scrub, or "soft chaparral", is dominated by shallow-rooted shrubs, typically 0.5-2.0 m tall, that produce relatively large, mesophyllous leaves shortly after the onset of the first winter rains. These main axis or "dolichoblast" leaves wither and fall acropetally as the dry season progresses. In their place, smaller leaves on axillary shoots ("brachyblast" leaves) develop (Westman 1981b). These side-shoot leaves have higher levels of stomatal resistance to water loss than do dolichoblast leaves on the same plant (Westman et al. 1985). In addition to reducing foliar mass and water conductance rates, leaves of several sage shrub species are capable of nastic movement to reduce exposure of leaf surfaces to direct rays of the sun (e.g. Gill & Mahall 1981). Because of these drought adaptations, coastal sage species are capable of permanently occupying drier sites than hard chaparral, although sage species may also occupy some chaparral sites temporarily after fire.

Work by Cooper (1922) established the floristic distinctiveness of coastal sage scrub from hard chaparral, but early ecologists tended to portray coastal sage scrub only as successional to chaparral. In the last decade, more extensive field work has established the climax status of coastal sage scrub throughout a large region (Kirkpatrick & Hutchinson 1977; Axelrod 1978; Bradbury 1978; Westman 1981a,1983a). Furthermore, a series of growth form and ecological characteristics distinguish coastal sage scrub from chaparral, with significant implications for conservation and management of the two types (Westman 1981c, 1982; Malanson 1985). Nevertheless, the historical perception of coastal sage scrub as merely a transitory variant of chaparral, in addition to the frequent proximity and superficial resemblance between the two, has meant that these quite different community types have often been treated as one for preservation and management purposes.

Unlike chaparral, the foliage of coastal sage scrub is soft, moist, and unarmed with prickles; these characteristics, plus its original occurrence on coastal plains and shallow slopes, made it an early target for grazing both on the mainland and on the California Islands (Westman 1983b). In addition, its extensive occurrence on

---

[1] National Research Council Research Associate, NASA Ames Research Center, M.S. 242-4, Moffett Field, CA 94035

relatively fertile lowlands in southern California led to clearing for agriculture and urbanization. As a result, coastal sage scrub is now one of the most endangered habitat types in the nation (Klopatek et al. 1979). Estimates of the extent of the former vegetation which has been cleared range from 36 to 85 percent for coastal sage (Klopatek et al. 1979; Westman 1981a) compared to 12 percent for chaparral (Klopatek et al. 1979). Since coastal sage scrub occupied probably less than 5 percent of the land in chaparral in California, the more extensive clearing of coastal sage scrub has had an outsized effect on both the habitat type and its component species. In this article I will discuss two recently-discovered features of the ecological structure of coastal sage communities that argue strongly for a rare plant conservation strategy centered on preserving the community type, rather than endangered species alone.

DISTRIBUTION OF FLORISTIC ASSOCIATIONS

Based on a survey of 99 0.063 ha plots of mature coastal sage scrub throughout its range, the community type has been classified into four floristic associations (fig. 1) (Westman 1983a). This classification evolved from, and is largely consistent with, the earlier classifications of several authors (Kirkpatrick & Hutchinson 1977; Axelrod 1978; Westman 1981a,1982). In addition to the Diablan, Venturan, Riversidian and Diegan associations of coastal sage scrub, figure 1 shows two floristic associations (Martirian, Vizcainan) of a separate formation, the coastal succulent scrub of northern Baja California and California Islands. Coastal succulent scrub differs from coastal sage scrub in its dominance by stem and leaf succulents, the somewhat increased abundance of a deciduous small tree element (present to a small extent in the Diegan association as well), and the reduced abundance of seasonally-dimorphic shrubs that dominate the coastal sage (Westman 1983a). Threats to the conservation of plant species in coastal succulent scrub have been recently reviewed (Westman 1987).

Two distinct floristic subassociations occur within the Venturan type (Kirkpatrick & Hutchinson 1977; Westman 1981b, 1983a,b). Venturan I is dominated by Salvia Mellifera, with Encelia californica as a frequent codominant; Venturan II is dominated by Salvia leucophylla. Venturan I tends to be found on equator-ward, coarse-textured

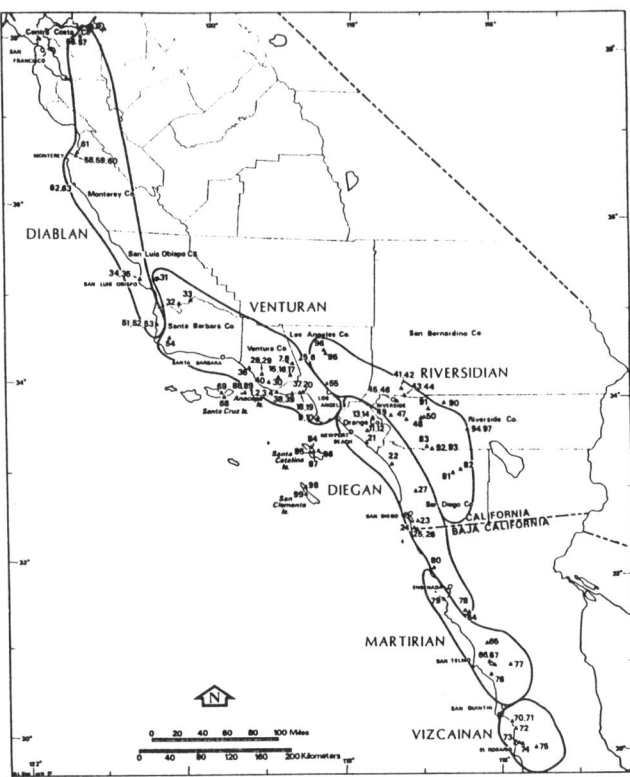

Figure 1--The four floristic associations of coastal sage scrub in California, and the two associations of coastal succulent scrub in Baja California. Numbered triangles are locations of the 99 study sites upon which the TWINSPAN classification was based. Reprinted from Westman (1983a) with permission of Dr. W. Junk, The Hague.

slopes, Venturan II on poleward, finer-textured ones. Despite the lack of obvious habitat discontinuities on certain hillsides, the two subassociations can meet at relatively sharp boundaries, with at least 45 herb species occurring in only one or the other subassociation (Westman 1983a). The boundary persists following fire (Malanson 1984;Westman, pers. observation).

PATTERNS OF DIVERSITY

Geographic patterns of variation in species richness in coastal sage scrub have been mapped, based on a study of 67 0.063 ha plots (Westman 1981a). Site richness was found to vary primarily with the abundance of herb species. The percentage of the flora composed of herb species gradually diminishes from north to south, with 80 percent of the Diablan sage flora as herbs, 66-67 percent in Venturan and Riversidian, and 57 percent in Diegan sage (Westman 1983a). Because the Riversidian association is itself the richest in species (198 vs. 172-173 in Diablan and Venturan, 138 in Diegan), it has a herb flora comparable in size to the Diablan (132 vs. 139 in Diablan)(Westman 1983a).

In a seminal paper on the distribution of rare and common species in a biota, Preston (1948; see also Preston 1962) noted that when an entire census of species of a particular taxon and region is considered, the typical form of a species-abundance curve is lognormal. That is, the number of species represented by a few individuals ("rare"), and the number of species represented by a very large number of individuals ("common") is low compared to the number of moderately abundant species, and rare and common species make up the tails of a normal distribution when number of species in each abundance class is plotted on the ordinate, and $\log_2$ abundance is plotted on the abscissa.

When such a curve is constructed from the species in the 67 sage and succulent scrub sites noted above, using percent occurrence in the 67 sites as a measure of commonness, it is seen that the number of rare species rises exponentially relative to the common species (fig. 2; Westman 1981a). Sixty-four percent of the 375 species encountered in the 67 sites occurred on only one or two sites. At least two hypotheses exist to explain this observation. The first is that the 67 sites were an inadequate sample of the scrub flora: the apparently "rare" species are actually moderately abundant, and with increased sampling, the truly rare species would be encountered. In Preston's terminology, an invisible "veil line" hides the mode and right tail of the normal curve in figure 2; additional sampling should move the veil line to the left. When an additional 32 sites of coastal sage and succulent scrub (also 0.063 ha) were added to the sample (Westman 1983a), the species-abundance curve increased in the number of moderately abundant and "rare" species, leaving the curve shape largely unchanged. Now 41 percent of the 549 species were encountered only once, 60 percent only once or twice.

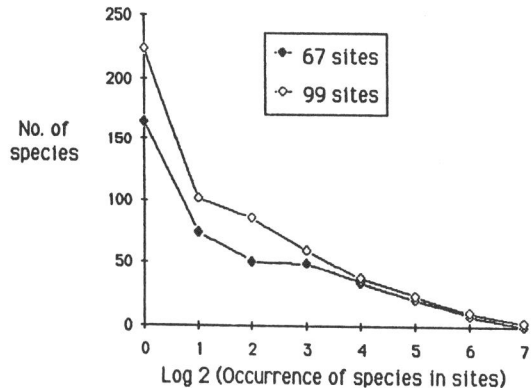

Figure 2--Number of species found one or more times in 67 or 99 0.063 ha sites of coastal sage scrub. Abscissa shows frequency of occurrence by classes, $\log_2$ scale; ordinate shows number of species in each class. Data for 67 sites from Westman (1981a); for 99 sites, unpublished data derived from the study described in Westman (1983a).

Problems with this test include the fact that the 32 new sites did extend the geographic area of the sample somewhat (to the south and to the islands); further, species rarity is being measured by percent occurrence within the samples (a geographic measure of "rarity", with more localized species being more "rare"), whereas perhaps a measure of local abundance would provide different results. In figure 3, these problems are addressed by dividing the samples into associations so that the island and succulent scrub samples to the south are separated from the mainland sage samples; further, the average foliar cover of the species within the samples of the association is used as the measure of abundance. All associations continue to show an exponential rise in rare species, with the Diegan also showing a slight increase in moderately abundant species. Figure 3 suggests that the high number of rare species in the sage flora is not an artifact of inadequate sample size.

A second hypothesis to explain the observation is that the large number of species of low abundance and local distribution arise from some ecological features of sage scrub dynamics. We can rule out the hypothesis that the "rare" species are mere transitory fire-followers, since all 99 sites above

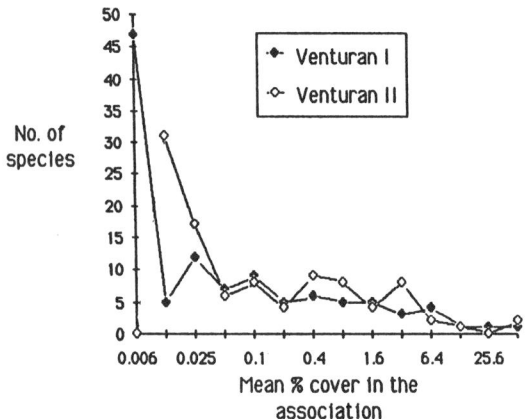
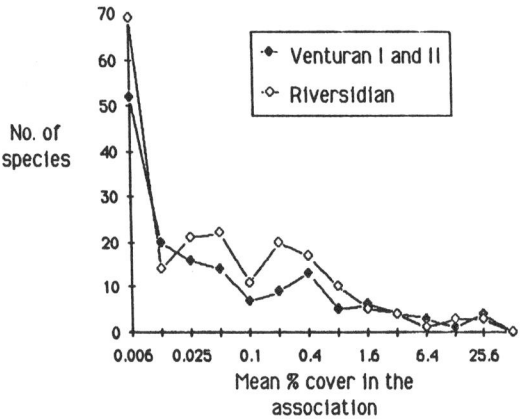
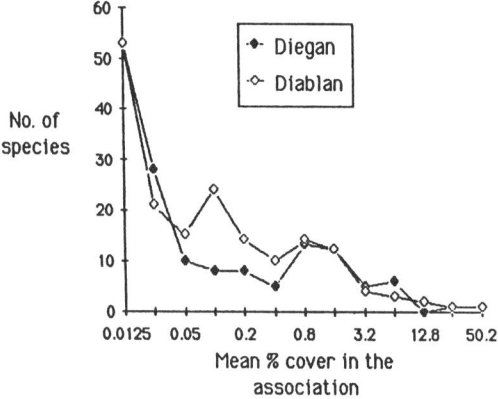
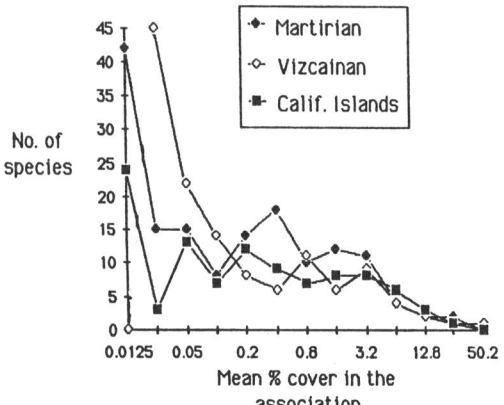

had not burned in at least seven years. If the rare species are part of the regional seed rain, and disperse to the sites by chance over time, one would expect a rise in species richness with age. In a series of matched sites of Venturan sage of different ages since fire, Westman (1981a) observed a rise in species richness from 7 to 21 yr following fire. The main source of the rise was an increase in herbaceous annuals, 70 percent of which were different from the annual herbs which appeared immediately after fire. Since shrub cover also increased during this period (from 58 to 72 percent), increased light penetration cannot explain the rise. Rather, the data seem to support the hypothesis that herb species immigrated to the site over the period. While the same herb species may disperse to chaparral sites, they normally do not survive under the higher levels of shade (Gray 1983; Westman 1982) in chaparral. Allelopathic substances may also inhibit herb germination in chaparral (e.g. Christensen and Muller 1978), as may the lack of charrate or other fire-induced cue (Keeley et al. 1985).

Fifty-eight percent of the herb species found in mature coastal sage scrub are found in recently burned chaparral sites (Westman 1979). This observation is consistent with the hypothesis that recently burned chaparral sites may serve as one seed source for sage scrub herbs, and that the sage scrub understory may indeed serve as a repository for some of the post-fire herbs in chaparral communities (Westman 1979). Species which die out under increased shade or species-specific allelopathics in chaparral, but do not require charrate to germinate, could be among those surviving in mature sage scrub stands. At the same time, a small number of herb species also appear in the first 1-2 years after fire in sage scrub and disappear thereafter (O'Leary and Westman 1986).

An explication of the second hypothesis, then, is that herb species capable of growing both in mature sage scrub canopies and in recently burned sage and chaparral sites form part of a

Figure 3--Number of species found in each foliar cover class for sites classified into coastal sage scrub and coastal succulent scrub associations. Abscissa shows cover classes, $\log_2$ scale. Unpublished data derived from the study described in Westman (1983a).

regional seed rain, dispersed by strong winds and/or animals. Because conditions under mature sage canopies are favorable to the survival of these species while those under mature chaparral are generally not, one can observe a gradual accumulation of herb richness in sage communities over time, unless the canopy becomes so thick with live and dead branches that shading ultimately becomes limiting. These many herb species are scarce both in regional occurrence and in local abundance, and hence swell the ranks of rare species in coastal sage scrub communities.

If this scenario is accurate, it implies that the preservation of rare species in coastal sage scrub requires the maintenance of a large mosaic of sage and chaparral shrublands, with fire as a part of the natural processes. Since the rare species are also localized, establishment of preserves within each of the separate sage associations, and within the two Venturan subassociations, would also appear necessary to capture the variation in the regional flora. A strategy in which a small, local preserve is set aside, and fire suppressed, in an attempt to preserve an "endangered species" would ultimately work counter to the preservation of the larger number of rare and threatened species in the sage flora. This is not to say that the preservation of the endangered species itself is not necessary or desirable, but that if efforts are focused exclusively in this way, sage habitat will continue to be cleared for development, and the sources of maintenance of the whole suite of rare species could be lost.

MODULAR STRUCTURE AND KEYSTONE SPECIES

As a result of studies of intertidal communities, Paine (1980) has proposed that "modules" of strongly interacting species may exist within a community. Species that depend on a common pool of resources, and disappear with the removal of a strongly interacting species, or appear with its addition, are said to belong to a module (Paine 1980). The strongly interacting species, whose addition or removal causes marked changes in community structure and function, is called a "keystone species". Terborgh (1986) has described the functioning of some keystone plant species in relation to frugivores in the neotropics, and Westman (1985a, pp.336-349) has reviewed the literature on keystone species more generally.

Although there have been no detailed studies on whether some plant species may be acting as keystone species for other plant species in a module, some suggestive evidence exists for the presence of keystone species within the Venturan sage scrub. Westman (1983a) has reviewed the evidence that 45 or more herb species may be dependent for their presence or absence on the occurrence of the dominant shrubs (Salvia mellifera, S. leucophylla) in the Venturan I and II subassociations. While the dominants themselves may be segregating in the landscape by habitat features affecting moisture availability, these habitat discontinuities cannot fully explain the segregation of the associated herb species in several respects. First, there is a suppression of species richness and equitability in Venturan sites relative to sites containing other associations, suggesting that the potential flora of the region is being partitioned into the two subassociations, rather than evenly distributed throughout the habitat range. Second, this sharp species segregation by dominants occurs only in the Venturan association, and not in the other coastal sage associations, suggesting that this floristic segregation is a phenomenon linked to biotic factors in the Venturan association. Third, the two subassociations can abut at relatively sharp boundaries at a local scale, yet cooccur throughout the Venturan range; habitat factors may or may not change dramatically at the boundaries between the two associations, nor is the boundary associated with a past fire border (Westman 1983a; Malanson 1984). A slight difference in moisture availability between sites may be sufficient to select for one Salvia species over the other; once established, the Salvias, and Encelia californica in Venturan I, may act to influence the associated flora through allelopathic effects, partitioning of herbivores, or alteration of microhabitat conditions (Westman 1983a).

Clearly further study is needed to establish the causal basis for the existence of the two Venturan subassociations. To the extent that the biotic-control hypothesis holds, it implies the existence of a modular structure within the Venturan sage scrub, with a subset of herb species being dependent on keystone shrub species. This modular structure in turn would support the earlier conclusion that to preserve rare herb species, at least in the Venturan sage scrub, conservation efforts should be directed toward preserving samples of the entire community type, rather than toward preserving the physical habitat for an endangered herb species without regard to its more common coassociates.

ENDANGERMENT STATUS AND FUTURE THREATS

Some of the rare plant species occurring in Californian coastal sage scrub that do not occur with greater abundance outside California are *Hemizonia conjugens*, *Dudleya parva* and *Castilleja mollis*. As emphasized earlier, however, the future threats to these species and other rare species in the sage scrub flora lie with factors that threaten entire parcels of sage scrub, and associated chaparral. The main factors threatening the sage scrub in future are changes in fire frequency, urbanization, air pollution, and grazing.

Prescribed burning in coastal sage scrub began in southern California in 1982, and has since increased in extent from a few hundred to a few thousand hectares per year. Malanson (1985) studied the long-term effect of prescribed burning on coastal sage dominants using a simulation model and concluded that under the shortened fire intervals occurring under prescribed burning, *Artemisia californica* and *Salvia mellifera* are most at risk because of their weak resprouting potential. The prescribed burning program has not been in operation long enough to affect fire intervals. From the point of view of species preservation, it would be desirable if return intervals were varied between 10 and 40 years among sage parcels to permit the more vulnerable species to maintain adequate population sizes on some parcels.

Clearing of coastal sage scrub habitat for urbanization has already been a major factor in the loss of sage scrub in California. Nevertheless, clearing continues today under pressure for new home development in southern California. The rate or extent of loss has not been quantified. While the Santa Monica Mountains National Recreation Area and associated State and City parks represent an important public preserve of Venturan sage scrub, representatives of the other types are less well preserved. The largest contiguous repositories are on military lands, where preservation is not always the highest priority use of the land, and some efforts at "restoration" have involved the planting of non-indigenous tree species on sage scrub lands (La Rosa 1982). A large amount of sage scrub is in private holdings; commonly, such parcels are periodically cleared to reduce fire hazard, or grazed.

The reductions in growth of coastal sage scrub from air pollution have been studied for ozone and sulfur dioxide, and the topic recently reviewed by Preston (1986), Westman (1985b, 1987b) and Westman et al. (1985). Current evidence suggests that the growth of sage scrub dominants are being adversely affected by air pollutants (probably ozone) at the eastern and northern margins of the Santa Monica Mountains, and in the Riverside-San Bernardino basin. Two of the shrub species most vulnerable to the interaction of air pollution and fire are *Artemisia californica* and *Salvia mellifera* (Westman 1987b). Since the latter may be a keystone species for the Venturan I subassociation, severe growth reductions in *S. mellifera* can be expected to affect the associated herb species. Preston (1980) has documented just such an effect downwind of a point source of sulfur dioxide on the central coast of California at Nipomo Mesa. A common effect of the reduction in shrub foliage is an increase in abundance of the exotic grass species, *Bromus rubens*, which can further usurp resources formerly occupied by the indigenous herb species (Westman 1987b).

Grazing has similarly caused a reduction in native perennial grass species in the coastal sage, with replacement by exotic annuals (Westman and O'Leary 1986; O'Leary and Westman 1986). More severe grazing, of course, has a significant effect on the entire community structure. While the most extreme effects of retrogression under grazing can be observed on the California Channel Islands, significant grazing effects can be seen on the mainland. Currently, grazing activity is most extensive in Riversidian sage scrub, where truck-transported sheep are having an extensive impact on sage scrub understories.

Preservation of rare plant species in Californian coastal sage scrub will require more widespread recognition of the distinctive nature of the community type, and acquisition of further parcels of land which can be kept free of grazing or clearing, and in which fire management policies aimed at species preservation can be pursued. A hopeful note is that areas of coastal sage which have been bulldozed, irrigated, fertilized, sprayed with herbicides and planted with exotic species can return to a semblance of native sage scrub within 1 - 2 decades if such disturbances cease and the area is surrounded by sage parcels within a few kilometers (Westman 1976).

ACKNOWLEDGEMENTS

This article was written while the author held a National Research Council Research Associateship at NASA Ames Research Center.

REFERENCES

Axelrod, D. The origin of coastal sage vegetation, Alta and Baja California. Amer. J. Bot. 65:1117-1131; 1978.

Bradbury, D.E. The evolution and persistence of a local sage/chamise community pattern in southern California. Yearbook of the Assoc. Pacific Coast Geographers 40:39-56; 1978.

Cooper, W.S. The broad sclerophyll vegetation of California. Publ. 319. District of Columbia: Carnegie Institute of Washington; 1922.

Gill, D.S.; Mahall, B.E. Leaf curling and recovery with reference to water relations in Salvia mellifera, a mediterranean-climate shrub. Bull. Ecological Soc. America 62: 66; 1981.

Gray, J.T. Competition for light and a dynamic boundary between chaparral and coastal sage scrub. Madrono 30:43-49; 1983.

Keeley, J.E.; Morton, B.A.; Pedrosa, A.; Trotter, P. Role of allelopathy, heat and charred wood in the germination of chaparral herbs and suffrutescents. J. Ecology 73:445-458; 1985.

Kirkpatrick, J.B.; Hutchinson, C.F. The community composition of Californian coastal sage scrub. Vegetatio 35:21-33; 1977.

Klopatek, J.M.; Olson, R.J.; Emerson, C.J.; Joness, J.L. Land-use conflicts with natural vegetation in the United States. Environ. Conserv. 6:191-199; 1979.

LaRosa, R. Coastal sage environmental conservation -- the Navy's experience at Point Loma. In: Proceedings of the Intl. Symp. on Dynamics and Management of Mediterranean-type Ecosystems; 1981 June 22-26; San Diego, CA. Gen. Tech. Rep. PSW-58. Berkeley, CA: Pacific Southwest For. and Range Exp. Stn., U.S. Dept. of Agriculture; 1982; p. 614.

Malanson, G.P. Fire history and patterns of Venturan subassociations of Californian coastal sage scrub. Vegetatio 57:121-128; 1984.

Malanson, G.P. Fire management in coastal sage-scrub, southern California, USA. Environ. Conserv. 12:141-146; 1985.

O'Leary, J.F.; Westman, W.E. Disturbance effects on regional patterns of postfire herb succession in coastal sage scrub. 1986. Unpublished draft.

Paine, R.T. Food webs: linkage interaction strength and community infrastructure. J. Animal Ecology 49:667-685; 1980.

Preston, F.W. The commonness, and rarity, of species. Ecology 29:254-283; 1948.

Preston, F.W. The canonical distribution of commonness and rarity. Part I. Ecology 43: 185-215; 1962.

Preston, K.P. Effects of sulfur dioxide pollution on coastal sage scrub. Los Angeles, CA: Univ. of California; 1980. M.A. thesis.

Preston, K.P. Effects of sulfur dioxide and ozone on the growth of coastal sage scrub. Los Angeles, CA: Univ. of California; 1986. Dissertation.

Terborgh, J. Keystone plant resources in the tropical forest. In: Soule, M.E., ed. Conservation Biology. The Science of Scarcity and Diversity. Sunderland, MA: Sinauer Assoc. Inc.; 1986; Pp. 330-34.

Westman, W.E. Vegetation conversion for fire control in Los Angeles. Urban Ecology 2:119-137; 1976.

Westman, W.E. A potential role of coastal sage scrub understories in the recovery of chaparral after fire. Madrono 26:64-68; 1979.

Westman, W.E. Diversity relations and succession in Californian coastal sage scrub. Ecology 62:170-184; 1981a.

Westman, W.E. Seasonal dimorphism of foliage in Californian coastal sage scrub. Oecologia 51:385-388; 1981b.

Westman, W.E. Factors influencing the distribution of species of Californian coastal sage scrub. Ecology 62:439-455; 1981c.

Westman, W.E. Coastal sage scrub succession. In: Proceedings of the Intl. Symp. on Dynamics and Management of Mediterranean-type Ecosystems; 1981 June 22-26; San Diego, CA; Gen. Tech. Rep. PSW-58; Berkeley, CA: Pacific Southwest For. and Range Exp. Stn., U.S. Dept. of Agriculture; 1982; pp. 91-99.

Westman, W.E. Xeric Mediterranean-type shrubland associations of Alta and Baja California and the community-continuum debate. Vegetatio 52:3-19; 1983a.

Westman, W.E. Island biogeography: studies on the xeric shrublands of the inner Channel Islands, California. J. Biogeography 10:97-118; 1983b.

coastal sage scrub. In: Proceedings of an Intl. Symp., 1986 October 20-22; Woods Hole, MA.; G.M. Woodwell, ed. Biotic Impoverishment: Changes in the Structure and Function of Natural Communities under Chronic Disturbance. Cambridge, England: Cambridge Univ. Press; 1987b. In press.

Westman, W.E.; O'Leary, J.F. Measures of resilience: the response of coastal sage scrub to fire. Vegetatio 65:179-189; 1986.

Westman, W.E.; Preston, K.P.; Weeks, L.B. Sulfur dioxide effects on the growth of native plants. In: W.E. Winner, H.A. Mooney, R.A. Goldstein, eds. Sulfur Dioxide and Vegetation -- Physiology, Ecology, and Policy Issues. Stanford, CA: Stanford Univ. Press; 1985. Pp. 264-280.

Westman, W.E. Ecology, Impact Assessment, and Environmental Planning. New York: Wiley-Interscience.; 1985a. 535 pp.

Westman, W.E. Air pollution injury to coastal sage scrub in the Santa Monica Mountains, southern California. Water, Air, and Soil Pollution 26:19-41; 1985b.

Westman, W.E. Pacific coastal shrublands of the U.S. - Mexico borderlands: characteristics and conservation challenges. In: Proceedings of the Intl. Symp. on Bioresources and Environmental Hazards of the U.S.-Mexico Borderlands. 1983 September 11-14; Los Angeles, CA; Los Angeles, CA: Univ. of California Latin American Center. 1987a. In press.

Westman, W.E. Detecting early signs of regional air pollution injury to

Rare Plants in the Arroyo de la Cruz Endemic Area, San Luis Obispo County, California

David J. Keil, Malcolm G. McLeod [1]

Abstract: The Arroyo de la Cruz Endemic Area, located on a coastal lowland strip in NW San Luis Obispo County, California, comprises ca. 7 square miles with elevations ranging from sea level to ca. 610 ft. The study area is geologically complex, dissected with faults that have juxtaposed chemically diverse parent materials. The climate is dominated by marine influences. The vascular flora comprises over 520 species. Of these, 6 taxa are endemic to the study area and 3 more are endemic to the county. The C.N.P.S. lists 12 taxa as rare and/or endangered and an additional 6 taxa are on the Watch List. The endemics occur mostly in grassland and maritime chaparral communities situated on Pleistocene marine terraces or on soils derived from highly weathered ultrabasic parent materials.

The windswept coastal hills around Arroyo de la Cruz in northwestern San Luis Obispo County, California, have diverse vegetation characterized by the presence and local dominance of several endemic taxa. The botanical uniqueness of the area was first noted in the mid-1940's by the late Dr. Robert Hoover, who repeatedly visited the area. Dr. Hoover discovered and named several of the taxa found in the area. In addition to the endemics, the Arroyo de la Cruz area is a haven for other rare species.

Our studies of the Arroyo de la Cruz area began in the mid-1970's and have continued to the present. The research has included a floristic inventory of the region, a survey of the vegetation and a detailed study of the distribution of rare and endangered plants. We have been particularly interested in assessing the interactions of historical and ecological factors that may have contributed to the diversity of the area's vegetation, the presence of endemic taxa and the persistence of other rare taxa.

CHARACTERISTICS OF THE STUDY AREA

The Arroyo de la Cruz endemic area is located in the northwestern corner of San Luis Obispo County, California, about 6 miles northwest of the village of San Simeon. The area studied in our research (fig. 1) extends from about 2 miles north of Arroyo de la Cruz along California Highway 1 to about 1.5 miles south of the Arroyo. It extends inland to the base of the higher ridges of the Santa Lucia Mountains to a maximum of about 2.5 miles from the ocean. The study area comprises about 7 square miles. With the exception of the narrow strip of right-of-way that parallels California Highway 1, the entire study area is located on the Hearst Ranch.

The topography of the study area ranges from essentially flat coastal terraces to gently sloping and rounded hills dissected by steep-walled canyons. Elevations rise from sea level to about 610 ft. Directly to the east the principal western ridge of the Santa Lucia Mountains rises to 2636 ft. on Pine Top Mountain and 3594 ft. on Pine Mountain.

The study area is geologically complex. Several NW trending strike-slip faults have juxtaposed parent materials ranging from ultrabasic metamorphics to shales, conglomerates and intrusive igneous formations. Movement along the San Simeon Fault has offset the course of Arroyo de la Cruz by about 1.5 miles. Changes in shoreline profiles during the Pleistocene have produced a graduated series of old marine terraces that extend inland in some areas about 2 miles. Soils on these terraces are mostly very fine-grained, highly weathered clays and clay-loams. The clay soils become saturated and sticky following winter rains but bake hard and crack in summer. Erosion on steep slopes, particularly in canyon areas has exposed younger, less weathered soils and bedrock. Immediately to the north of Arroyo de la Cruz at Point Sierra Nevada is a well-stabilized dunefield perched atop the marine terrace. Sea stacks and steep cliffs mark the boundary between land and sea. The intertidal zone is narrow and ranges from narrow sandy or cobbly beaches to rocky intertidal areas.

---

[1] Professor of Botany and Professor of Botany, California Polytechnic State University, San Luis Obispo, CA

Arroyo de la Cruz is the largest of several seasonal to semipermanent streams that arise as steep, narrow-walled canyons that cut downward through the various parent materials. Other streams of note within the study area include Arroyo de los Chinos and Arroyo Hondo (both north of Arroyo de la Cruz) and Arroyo del Oso and Arroyo del Corral (both to the south). Our study area does not include the steep upper canyons of Arroyo de la Cruz and the two streams to the north. It does, however, include the headwaters of the streams to the south.

During winter storms floodwaters sweep through the channels, but by summer most of the flow is subsurface. The lower channel of Arroyo de la Cruz is braided and has a well-developed flood plain with deep, interbedded stream sediments. Cutoff meanders support marshes and grasslands (some now in agriculture). The mouth of the Arroyo is blocked by a sand bar during times of low stream flow and a brackish lagoon forms in the lee of the bar. A small area of salt marsh occurs around the fringes of the lagoon.

Oceanic influences dominate the climate. Prevailing winds from the northwest carry moisture and salt spray well inland. Vegetation on windward slopes is often markedly different from that in sites sheltered from the wind. Summer fog is common, maintaining a moderate climate. Frost is infrequent in winter. Precipitation averages about 25 inches per year, concentrated from November to April. The higher ridges of the Santa Lucia Mountains receive 2 to 3 times as much rainfall, and this increases the erosive powers of the coastal streams.

VEGETATION PATTERNS

The diverse vegetation in the Arroyo de la Cruz area reflects the topographic, geologic and climatic variability of the region. The vegetation has been modified in portions of the study area by human influences. Plant communities represented in the study area are described below. Community nomenclature follow Holland and Keil (1986).

Grasslands

Grassland communities dominate most of the flat to gently sloping marine terrace formations. The dominant plants comprise a mixture of native perennial bunchgrasses and introduced annuals. Perennials that are well-represented include California oatgrass (Danthonia californica), western hairgrass (Deschampsia holciformis) and purple needlegrass (Stipa pulchra). Annual grasses include species of wild oats (Avena), bromes (Bromus), barleys (Hordeum), ryegrass (Lolium) and annual fescues (Vulpia) as well as members of several other genera. The grasslands on the coastal terraces have the characteristics of northern coastal grasslands with dominance of perennials. Some grassland sites inland from the coast near Arroyo de los Chinos are entirely annual-dominated and resemble the valley grasslands of interior and southern California.

In addition to the grasses there are numerous introduced and native wildflowers. Particularly well represented are perennial herbaceous species including numerous bulb-forming monocots. These include four of the rare taxa present in the study area: Hickman's onion (Allium hickmanii), dwarf goldenstar (Bloomeria humilis), Arroyo de la Cruz mariposa lily (Calochortus clavatus ssp. recurvifolius) and Cook's triteleia (Triteleia ixioides ssp. cookii). Other rare taxa are also present. Gairdner's yampah (Perideridia gairdneri ssp. gairdneri) is a deep-rooted perennial dicot. In some areas, maritime ceanothus (Ceanothus maritimus), a prostrate shrub endemic to the area, grows as a common understory plant among the grasses. Large clumps of San Luis sedge (Carex obispoensis) occur in some sites. Local seepage areas support small populations of adobe sanicle (Sanicula maritima). Saint's daisy (Erigeron sanctarum) is very localized in one grassland site.

The grasslands of the Arroyo de la Cruz area are used by the Hearst corporation primarily as grazing land for cattle. The grazing pressure has been comparatively light during the years we have been studying the area. With the exception of some slopes near Arroyo de

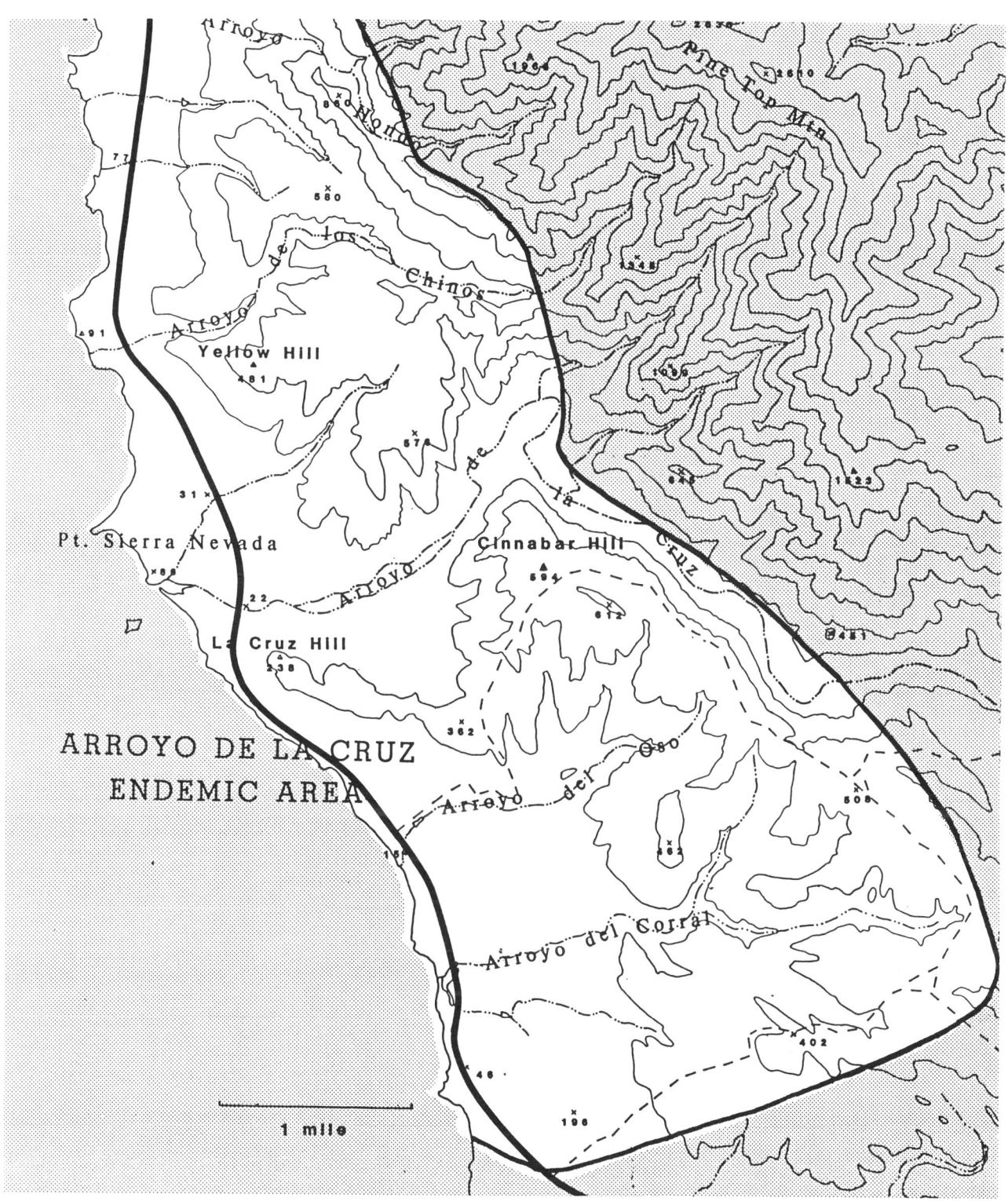

Figure 1--The Arroyo de la Cruz Endemic Area. Only the shaded area was included in our study. Redrawn from U.S.G.S. 15' Quadrangles: Piedras Blancas (1959) and San Simeon (1958). Elevations are in feet; contour intervals are 200 feet.

los Chinos, the grasslands of the study area have apparently never been plowed. This has undoubtedly contributed to the diversity and abundance of perennial herbaceous species. One slope was burned during the period of our study. Recovery of the herbaceous vegetation was rapid with apparent increase in stature of some of the bulb-forming monocots.

Coastal Shrub Communities

Communities dominated by soft-stemmed shrubs occur in several areas. These intergrade to some extent but are separated here into four community types.

Near the ocean, grasslands intergrade with and are ultimately replaced by assemblages of succulents, low subshrubs and perennial herbs. These seabluff scrub communities form a narrow discontinuous strip along the shore. The best development is on Point Sierra Nevada where the scrubby vegetation forms a low continuous cover. Dominants include tree lupine (Lupinus arboreus), coastal goldenbush (Isocoma veneta), dwarf coyote-bush (Baccharis pilularis var. pilularis), coastal golden-yarrow (Eriophyllum staechadifolium), coastal buckwheat (Eriogonum parvifolium), dudleya (Dudleya caespitosa) and seaside daisy (Eriogonum glaucus). One rare taxon occurs in the immediate coastal zone as a component of grasslands, seabluff scrub and dune scrub communities. Compact cobweb thistle (Cirsium occidentale var. compactum) forms low mounds, mostly to the west of Highway 1.

The dune field north of Arroyo de la Cruz supports a dune scrub community typical of central California. Dominants include sand-bur (Ambrosia chamissonis), purple sand-verbena (Abronia umbellata), yellow sand-verbena (A. latifolia), poison-oak (Toxicodendron diversilobum), Eriophyllum staechadifolium, Lupinus arboreus and ice plant (Carpobrotus chilensis). Most of the dunes are well-stabilized and much less disturbed than the more accessible dunes along the south coast of San Luis Obispo County.

Inland from the immediate coast two different coastal scrub communities are largely separated by a combination of edaphic conditions and slope aspect. Steep south-facing slopes with shallow soils tend to have a cover typical of the coastal scrub of southern California. Dominants include black sage (Salvia mellifera), coyote bush (Baccharis pilularis ssp. consanguinea), sticky monkeyflower (Mimulus aurantiacus), California sagebrush (Artemisia californica), and Eriogonum parvifolium. There is little understory development and often a bare-zone ecotone with adjoining grasslands. Two rare taxa occur in association with this community. San Simeon Creek baccharis (Baccharis plummerae ssp. glabrata) occasionally grows in coastal sage scrub and Hoffmann's sanicle (Sanicle hoffmannii) is locally common in the ecotone between the scrub and grasslands.

On north-facing slopes that are protected from the strong prevailing winds, coastal scrub communities more typical of northern California occur. Northern coastal scrub has a taller canopy, greater species diversity and more herbaceous cover. Dominants include bluebrush (Ceanothus thyrsiflorus), Baccharis pilularis var. consanguinea, Artemisia californica, Toxicodendron diversilobum, figwort (Scrophularia californica), mugwort (Artemisia douglasiana), blackberry (Rubus ursinus) and pearly everlasting (Anaphalis margaritacea). No rare plants have been recorded from these communities.

Chaparral Communities

Chaparral at Arroyo de la Cruz is a peculiar maritime form of this widespread formation. On windward slopes and windswept ridgetops the chaparral is often severely dwarfed. Coast live oak (Quercus agrifolia), a plant that under ordinary conditions is a tree, grows as a prostrate shrub, sometimes only a few inches tall. Chaparral shrubs such as chamise (Adenostoma fasciculatum), coffeeberry (Rhamnus californica) and toyon (Heteromeles arbutifolia), are similarly dwarfed. Often small individuals of Salvia mellifera occur in these communities as well. Associated with the wind-dwarfed shrubs are several endemic, genetically dwarfed shrubs. These include Hearst's manzanita (Arctostaphylos hookeri ssp. hearstiorum), Arroyo de la Cruz manzanita (A. cruzensis), Ceanothus maritimus and Hearst's ceanothus (C. hearstiorum). In some chaparral stands, these endemic dwarf shrubs are dominant.

The canopy of the maritime chaparral may be only 2-18 inches tall. Often it is associated with large clumps of Carex obispoensis. Herb cover is sparse and includes species of Sanicula, including the rare S. hoffmannii, bedstraw (Galium) and the rare Dudley's lousewort (Pedicularis dudleyi). Along the ecotone with grasslands, mats of Ceanothus maritimus, C. hearstiorum and Arctostaphylos hookeri ssp. hearstiorum extend into the grass-dominated vegetation. In sheltered sites, taller shrubs including Ceanothus thyrsiflorus, shaggy-bark manzanita (Arctostaphylos tomentosa) and normal-sized Adenostoma fasciculatum and Heteromeles arbutifolia are often dominant.

Some steep windswept slopes support a peculiar herb-rich dwarf chaparral with Ceanothus maritimus as the dominant shrub. The soils are typically clay-loams that are very moist in winter and early spring. Bunchgrasses, clumps of Carex obispoensis, ferns, subshrubs such as golden-yarrow (Eriophyllum confertiflorum) and Bentham's deerweed (Lotus benthamii), dwarfed individuals of Rhamnus californica, redberry (Rhamnus crocea), Toxicodendron diversilobum, and various other shrubs, along with a diversity of wildflowers complete the association. The stature of most plants is no taller than that of the grasses, but there is a significant woody component in the vegetation. Baccharis plummerae ssp. glabrata and Calochortus clavatus var. recurvifolius have been found in some such areas.

Parent material apparently plays a major role in determining whether a dwarf chaparral or a coastal scrub community occupies a particular site. In the vicinity of Cinnabar Hill, faulting has juxtaposed a Tertiary conglomerate formation and a Jurassic ultrabasic formation. Weathering of the two parent materials yields very different soils. The soils derived from the conglomerate lose moisture quickly and support a coastal scrub community with little or no herbaceous cover. The serpentinite ultrabasic rock, on the other hand, yields a clay-rich soil that holds moisture well into the spring. These soils are occupied by maritime chaparral dominated by endemic Ceanothus and Arctostaphylos species. The chaparral extends to a limited extent onto the overlying Pleistocene marine terrace as well.

In an ecotonal fringe between maritime chaparral and grassland communities near Cinnabar Hill, a dwarf colonial form of Brewer's oak (Quercus garryana var. breweri) has been located. This is apparently the southernmost coastal outpost for this species (John Tucker, pers. comm.) and is a very unusual growth form. Near the oak colonies are patches of the endemic dwarf shrubs.

Coastal Live Oak Woodlands

Quercus agrifolia is widely distributed in the Arroyo de la Cruz area. In canyons and on north-facing slopes that are protected from the prevailing winds, it attains its typical tree stature. The understory varies greatly from site to site. Grassland species predominate under some oak stands, particularly where the oaks are scattered. In denser stands, particularly on north-facing slopes the understory is dominated by Toxicodendron diversilobum, Rubus ursinus, hedge-nettle (Stachys bullata), bracken (Pteridium aquilinum), and other shade-tolerant herbs and shrubs. In moist protected sites, madrone (Arbutus menziesii), California bay-laurel (Umbellularia californica) and (Acer macrophyllum) occasionally grow with the oaks. No rare species are known to occur in the oak woodlands.

Riparian Communities

The stream channels of Arroyo de la Cruz and of smaller streams support a rich riparian woodland association. Because it has the best-developed floodplain and greatest water flow, Arroyo de la Cruz, itself, has the best-developed riparian vegetation. It is dominated by black cottonwood (Populus trichocarpa), willows (Salix spp.), sycamores (Platanus racemosa), alders (Alnus rhombifolia), etc. Where best developed, this vegetation ranges from a dense shaded gallery forest to an open discontinuous canopy. Willows, in particular, form dense stands by their vegetative propagation. Some of the best-developed riparian vegetation near the Highway 1 bridge was cleared for agriculture during the autumn of 1983.

In portions of the flood plain and channel of Arroyo de la Cruz, thickets of willows, mulefat (Baccharis salicifolia), bricklebush (Brickellia californica) and the introduced Spanish broom (Spartium junceum) cover the alluvial soils. Higher and drier deposits of coarse alluvium support an open scrubby vegetation dominated by California buckwheat (Eriogonum fasciculatum), Baccharis pilularis var. consanguinea, buckbrush (Ceanothus cuneatus), yucca (Yucca whipplei) and other drought-tolerant shrubs.

The main channel of Arroyo de la Cruz is generally swept clear of most vegetation during winter storms. As stream-flow subsides, a temporary stream vegetation composed of a mixture of seedlings, moisture-tolerant herbs, such as monkeyflowers (Mimulus spp.), dock (Rumex spp.), rabbitfoot grass (Polypogon spp.), etc., and waif individuals of otherwise dryland species, such as lupines (Lupinus spp.), deervetch (Lotus spp.), clover (Trifolium spp.), develops. Various spring wildflowers persist well into summer in the damp sands and gravels of the channel.

Tributary canyons and small coastal streams tht lack the broad alluvial deposits of Arroyo de la Cruz generally have a narrower, more discontinous riparian corridor. Quercus agrifolia, Platanus racemosa, arroyo willow (Salix lasiolepis), Umbellularia californica, Heteromeles arbutifolia and occasionally big-leaf maple (Acer macrophyllum) predominate, generally with an understory of assorted herbs and shrubs. No rare species have been documented from any of the riparian areas.

Freshwater Marshes

Cutoff stream meanders and the fringes of the lagoon at the mouth of Arroyo de la Cruz support (or until recently supported) freshwater marsh vegetation. The dominants include sedges (Scirpus spp., Carex spp., Eleocharis spp.), rushes (Juncus spp.), cattails (Typha spp.), docks (Rumex spp.), water-parsley (Oenanthe sarmentosa), common monkeyflower (Mimulus guttatus), coastal silverweed (Potentilla egedii) and assorted other species. Some of the marshes have been degraded in various ways by draining, cattle-grazing and clearing for agriculture. No rare species have been located in the marshes.

Coastal Salt Marsh

Salt marsh vegetation is poorly developed at Arroyo de la Cruz. Around the lagoon at the mouth of the Arroyo, saltgrass (Distichlis spicata), arrowgrass (Triglochin striata), and a few salt-tolerant sedges and rushes form a transitional band between the brackish water of the lagoon and the adjacent freshwater marsh.

Vernal Pools

Seasonal marshes develop in the lee of the dunefields north of Arroyo de la Cruz during exceptionally wet seasons. These marshes have some characteristics of the larger, more permanent marshes, but fewer tall, perennial dominants. They have some characteristics of vernal pools with species such as water starwort (Callitriche heterophylla), coyote-thistle (Eryngium armatum), water pygmy-weed (Tillaea aquatica), Douglas' pogogyne (Pogogyne douglasii), woolyheads (Psilocarphus tenellus), allocarya (Plagiobothrys spp.) and slender lasthenia (Lasthenia glaberrima). Other winter-wet depressions, some situated on ocean terraces well away from the shoreline, support a mixture of vernal pool species and grassland plants. About 1.8 miles north of Arroyo de la Cruz a depression on the seabluff contains perennial goldfields (Lasthenia macrantha var. macrantha) as a locally common species. None of the vernal pool species are considered to be rare and endangered although several are at or near the limits of their ranges at Arroyo de la Cruz.

Ruderal Communities

Disturbance of the natural vegetation of the Arroyo de la Cruz vegetation has taken several forms. Natural landslides, stream erosion and fires have occasionally modified the existing vegetative cover, allowing secondary succession to take place. The pattern of natural succession in the area has been modified by the introduction of alien plant species and disturbance factors. In grassland areas and some riparian areas the introduced species have become thoroughly integrated into the vegetation. Species such as English plaintain (Plantago lanceolata), bur-clover (Medicago polymorpha), windmill pink (Silene gallica) and various annual grasses are components of the grassland vegetation throughout the Arroyo de la Cruz region. Spartium junceum, apparently introduced to the area during the construction of the Hearst Castle, is well established in the riparian corridor.

Heavily disturbed areas, however, are in some cases completely dominated by introduced plants, to the exclusion or near exclusion of the native vegetation. Typically these areas are the subject of long-term patterns of disturbance, such as heavy grazing around water tanks and the disturbance along Highway 1. Just south of the highway bridge over Arroyo de la Cruz is a highway maintenance yard used by the California Department of Transportation to store gravel and other supplies. The near-continuous disturbance associated with this site has served as a focus for the introduction of weedy species. Road construction and maintenance activities have the potential of damaging or destroying some localized populations or individuals of certain of the rare species found in the study area.

Ruderal communities in the study area are dominated mostly by rank-growing, often spiny, poisonous or foul-smelling herbs. The most common of these are milk thistle (Silybum marianum), Italian thistle (Cardus pycnocephalus), sow thistles (Sonchus asper and S. oleraceus), wild radish (Raphanus sativus), mustards

(Brassica spp.), fennel (Foeniculum vulgare), poison hemlock (Conium maculatum) and stinging nettle (Urtica holosericea). All but the last of these are Eurasian species. Fortunately at present, the areas occupied by these species are small and these plants do not appear to be threatening any of the rare species of the region.

RARE AND ENDANGERED PLANTS OF THE ARROYO DE LA CRUZ ENDEMIC AREA

Of the 520+ taxa found in the Arroyo de la Cruz endemic area, 12 are currently placed in List 1B of the Inventory of Rare and Endangered Vascular Plants of California (Smith and York, 1984) (table 1). These are plants considered to be rare and endangered in California and elsewhere. Plants of this list exist in low total numbers and/or are of limited distribution. We are proposing that an additional taxon from the Arroyo de la Cruz area, Baccharis plummerae ssp. glabrata (San Simeon Creek baccharis), be placed in List 1B. In addition to the plants from List 1B of the C.N.P.S. Inventory, several taxa from the study area are included on List 4. These are also included in table 1. List 4 is a "watch list" of plants of limited distribution. At present, they exist in large enough numbers or are widespread enough that their current vulnerability or susceptibility to threat is low.

Generalized Distribution of Rare Plants that Occur in the Vicinity of Arroyo de la Cruz

Rare and endangered plants of Arroyo de la Cruz have distributions that could be placed in several categories. They are discussed starting with taxa having the widest distribution and gradually narrowing to those endemic to the study area.

Sanicula maritima must be considered separately because of the great changes that have occurred in its distribution. It was once known from Oakland, Alameda and San Francisco (Constance, 1977). However, it has not been seen in those areas since before 1900. It was also found within Camp Roberts (interior northern San Luis Obispo County) in 1950, but has not been confirmed for that area since. Hoover (1970) reported S. maritima from Los Osos Valley and from Cerro Romauldo both in the San Luis Obispo area (central San Luis Obispo County). It has apparently been extirpated from both locations. The former is now a heavily grazed pasture and the latter coincides exactly with the location of a house. There are at present two centers of distribution for S. maritima, one on the ridge south of Cerro Romauldo and the other in the vicinity of Arroyo de la Cruz. We have heard reports of the recent discovery of a small population in southern coastal Monterey County (V. Yadon, pers. comm.).

A second category includes those taxa found in the Monterey area and at Arroyo de la Cruz. Two species fit this category, Allium hickmanii and Pedicularis dudleyi. Allium hickmanii is found between Monterey and Pacific Grove and perhaps a few other locations in that area (Niehaus, 1977a). Pedicularis dudleyi was known only in San Mateo and Santa Cruz counties until 1966 (Niehaus, 1977b). At that time, it was discovered along the Little Sur River in Monterey County. In spite of the fact that the Arroyo de la Cruz endemic area had fascinated botanists for many years, Pedicularis dudleyi was not discovered there until 1981 (Riggins, 1983), a range extension of 50 miles.

A third distributional category includes plants that are found in the general area of San Luis Obispo and at Arroyo de la Cruz. This would include the present distribution of Sanicula maritima and two additional taxa, Carex obispoensis and Arctostaphylos cruzensis, both endemic to San Luis Obispo County. In addition to its occurrence at Arroyo de la Cruz, Carex obispoensis grows under the Sargent cypresses at Cuesta Ridge West, in Reservoir Canyon just east of San Luis Obispo and in the vicinity of the Rinconada Mine near Santa Margarita Lake.

Arctostaphylos cruzensis, contrary to its common name, is not limited to the Arroyo de la Cruz area. It is also found to the southeast near Morro Bay on the volcanic peaks between the Chorro and Los Osos valleys. There are, in fact, some relatively large populations on or near Hollister Peak. Its southernmost known distribution is within the community of Los Osos, at the southern end of Morro Bay.

Two of the rare taxa are limited to the coastal strip that includes the Arroyo de la Cruz endemic area but extend southward to near the town of Cambria. Cirsium occidentale var. compactum is found along the immediate coast from near the San Luis Obispo County - Monterey County line to as far south as the Monterey pine groves at Cambria. Baccharis plummerae ssp. glabrata has a similar distribution to that of C. occidentale var. compactum, but grows a bit farther inland. It was named from a

Table 1. Rare and Endangered Plants of Arroyo de la Cruz Endemic Area[1]

TAXON	R E D CODE[2]
PLANTS FROM LIST 1B	
1. *Allium hickmanii* Eastw. - Hickman's onion	2 2 3
2. *Arctostaphylos cruzensis* Roof - Arroyo de la Cruz manzanita	2 2 3
3. *Arctostaphylo hookeri* D. Don ssp. *hearstiorum* (Hoover & Roof) P. V. Wells - Hearst's manzanita	3 2 3
4. *Bloomeria humilis* Hoover - dwarf goldenstar	3 2 3
5. *Calochortus clavatus* Wats. ssp. *recurvifolius* (Hoover) Munz - Arroyo de la Cruz mariposa lily	3 2 3
6. *Carex obipoensis* Stacy - San Luis sedge	2 1 3
7. *Ceanothus hearstiorum* Hoover & Roof - Hearst's ceanothus	3 2 3
8. *Ceanothus maritimus* Hoover - maritime ceanothus	3 2 3
9. *Cirsium occidentale* (Nutt.) Jeps. var. *compactum* Hoover - compact cobweb thistle	2 1 3
10. *Pedicularis dudleyi* Elmer - Dudley's lousewort	2 1 3
11. *Perideridia gairdneri* (H. & A.) Math. ssp. *gairdneri* - Gairdner's yampah[3]	1 2 3
12. *Sanicula maritima* Kell. ex Wats. - adobe sanicle	3 3 3
PLANTS FROM LIST 4	
13. *Baccharis plummerae* Gray[4] - Plummer's baccharis	1 1 3
14. *Corethrogyne leucophylla* Jeps. - branching beach-aster	1 1 3
15. *Eriogeron sanctarum* Wats. - Saint's daisy	1 1 3
16. *Lomatium parvifolium* (H. & A.) Jeps. - small-leafed lomatium	1 2 3
17. *Sanicula hoffmannii* (Munz) C. R. Bell - Hoffmann's sanicle	1 1 3
18. *Tritelia ixioides* (Ait. f.) Greene ssp. *cookii* (Hoover) Lenz - Cook's triteleia	1 1 3
19. *Ribes divaricatum* Dougl. var. *pubiflorum* Koehne[5] - swamp gooseberry	? ? ?

[1] Excerpted from Smith and York (1984).
[2] Numbers indicate rarity, endangerment and distribution. 3 = most rare, most endangered, most limited in distribution, etc.
[3] York and Smith (1986) indicate that this plant is sufficiently common that it is to be transferred to list 4 in the forthcoming edition of the C.N.P.S. Inventory. For this reason, it is not discussed in detail.
[4] ssp. *glabrata* Hoover - San Simeon Creek baccharis was not recognized in the 1984 Inventory but is to be placed on List 1B. (R. York, pers. comm.).
[5] This taxon is to be added to List 4 (R. York, pers. comm.). Its status is discussed by Sinnott, 1985.

---

collection made along San Simeon Creek east of Cambria (Hoover, 1970). Keil has discovered several populations within the Arroyo de la Cruz endemic area.

The remaining 5 taxa are all endemic to the Arroyo de la Cruz area: *Arctostaphylos hookeri* ssp. *hearstiorum*, *Bloomeria humilis*, *Ceanothus hearstiorum*, *Ceanothus maritimus* and *Calochortus clavatus* var. *recurvifolius*. One of these taxa, *A. hookeri* ssp. *hearstiorum*, could be grouped with the taxa showing ties with the Monterey area. It is closely related to *A. hookeri* ssp. *hookeri*, which occurs in the Monterey Bay area.

Distribution of Rare Plants within the Arroyo de la Cruz Endemic Area

All 12 taxa considered here have distinct independent distributional patterns within the endemic area (figs 2-4). A discussion of each of these follows.

Cirsium occidentale var. *compactum* is, as has been stated, a coastal plant (fig. 2A). It is very often found in sand or sandy soils, particularly in the dunes at Point Sierra Nevada. It is also found on seabluffs both north and south of Arroyo de la Cruz and along highway fence lines. Inland there are plants which tend

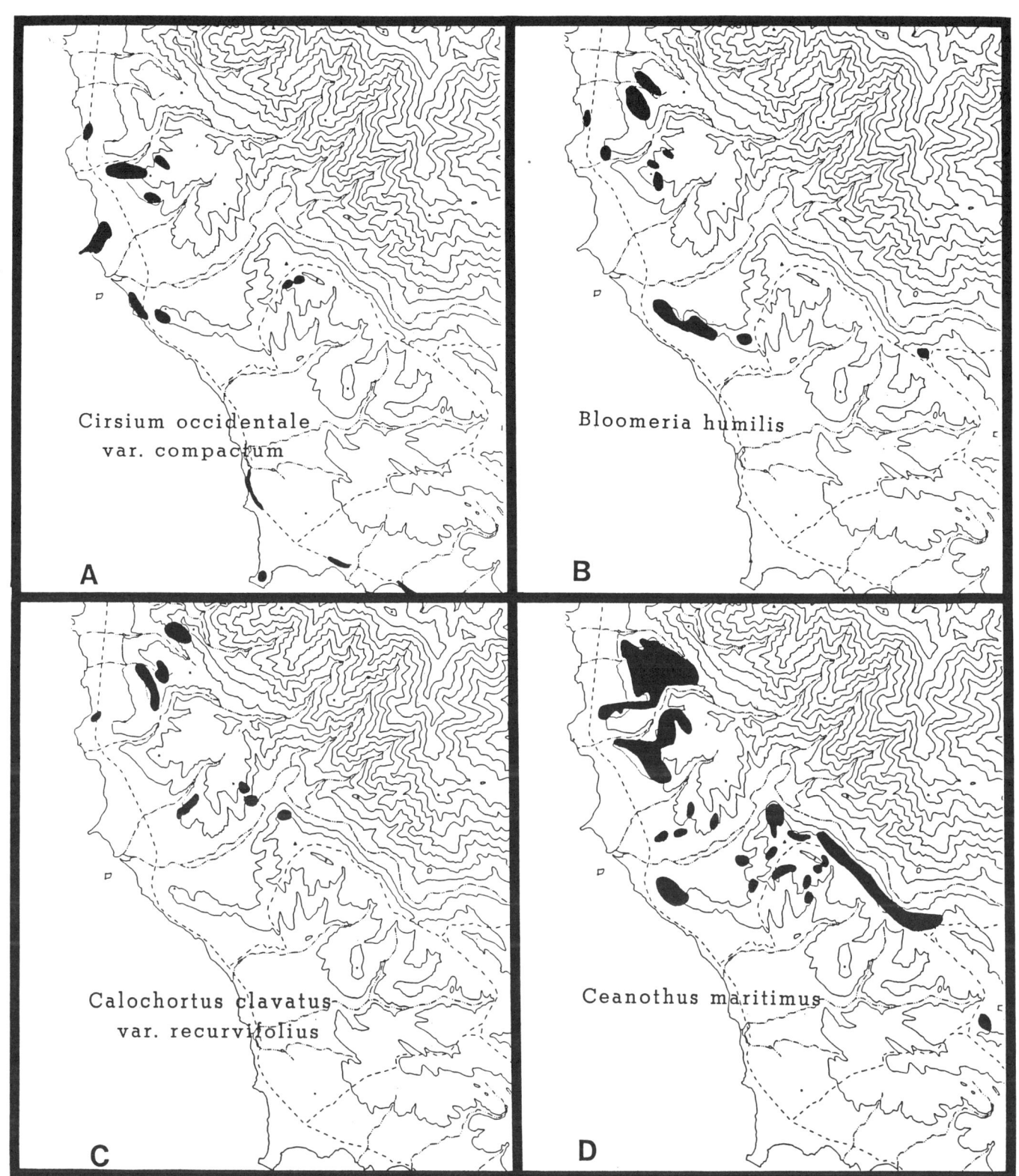

Figure 2--Distributions of rare plants within the Arroyo de la Cruz Endemic Area. A. *Cirsium occidentale* var. *compactum*; B. *Bloomeria humilis*; C. *Calochortus clavatus* ssp. *recurvifolius*; D. *Ceanothus maritimus*.

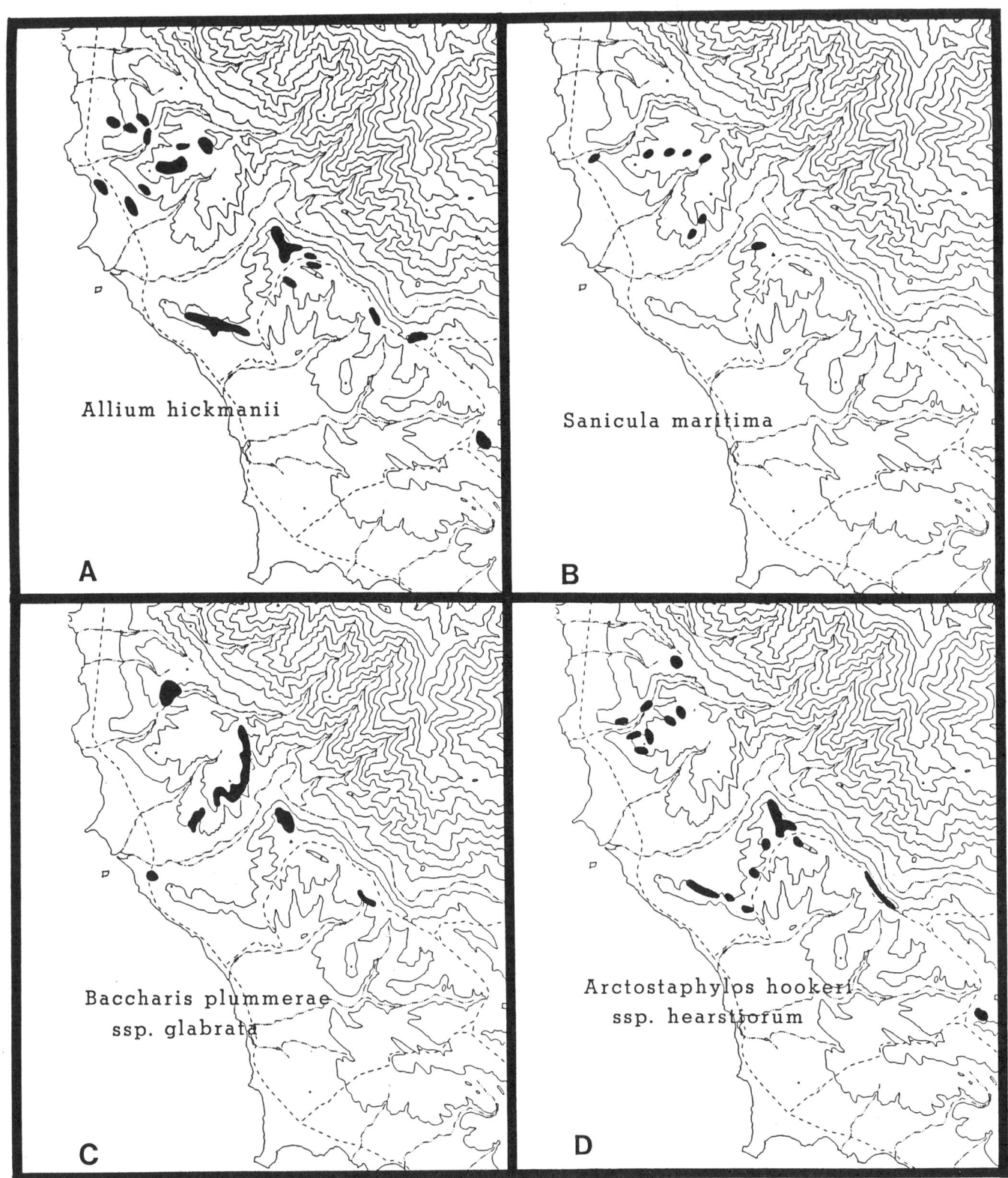

Figure 3—Distributions of rare plants within the Arroyo de la Cruz Endemic Area. A. *Allium hickmanii*; B. *Sanicula maritima*; C. *Baccharis plummerae* ssp. *glabrata*; D. *Arctostaphylos hookeri* ssp. *hearstiorum*.

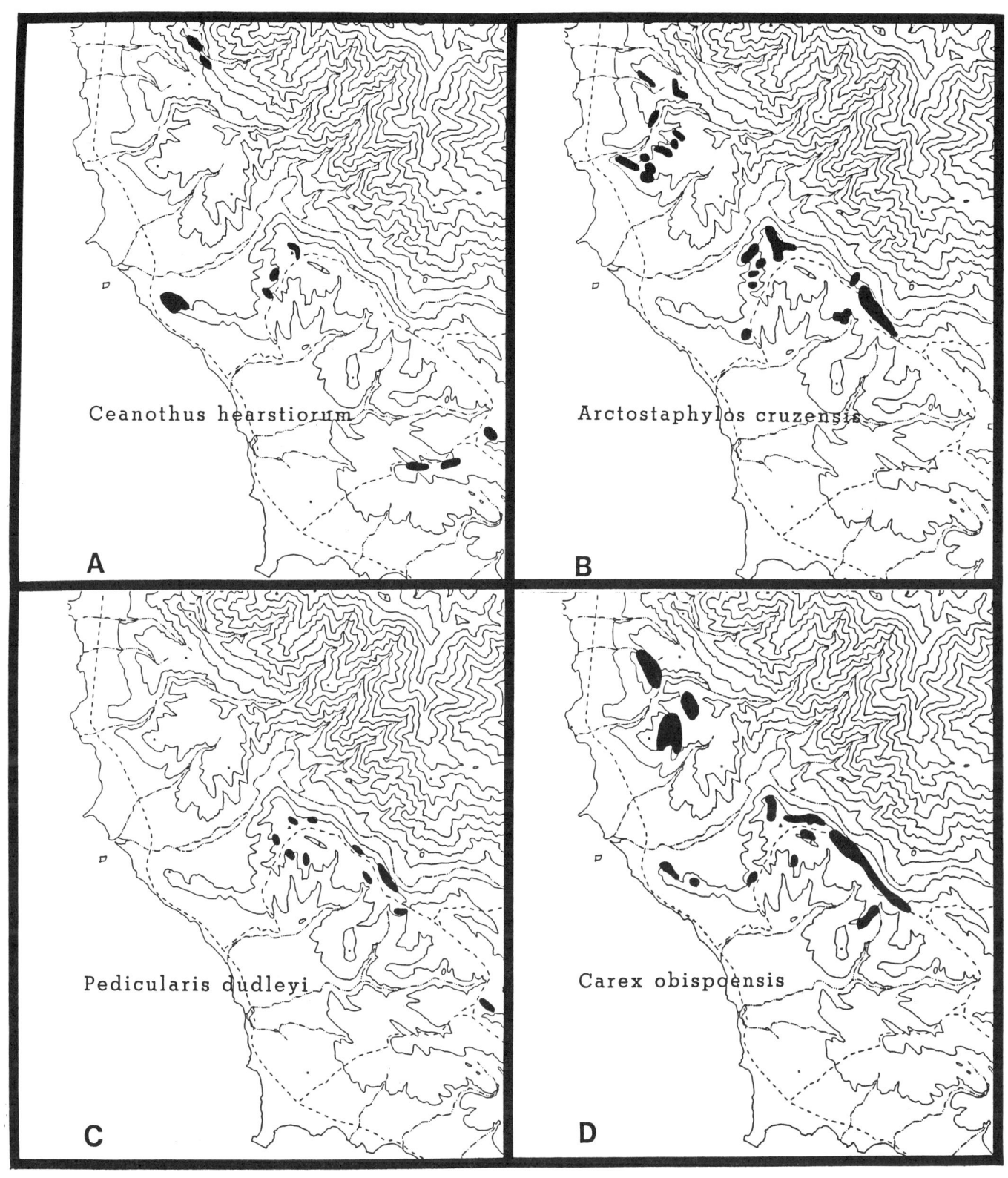

Figure 4--Distributions of rare plants within the Arroyo de la Cruz Endemic Area.
A. Ceanothus hearstiorum;
B. Arctostaphylos cruzensis;
C. Pedicularis dudleyi; D. Carex obispoensis.

toward intermediacy with typical cobweb thistle (*Cirsium occidentale* var. *occidentale*).

Bloomeria humilis was first discovered on the maritime terraces north of Arroyo de los Chinos. It is also found on grassy hillsides and ridges in various other sites essentially throughout the endemic area (fig. 2B). It is apparently restricted to deep clay soils. The common goldenstar (*Bloomeria crocea*) has also been found in the area, but is considerably less common than the dwarf goldenstar. The two taxa are closest on the ridge south of Arroyo de la Cruz where their populations are separated by several hundred meters. No intermediates have been located.

Calochortus clavatus var. *recurvifolius* was described as a dwarfed form of its species with recurved leaves. It was originally found on the marine terrace north of Arroyo de los Chinos. We have found that it is rather widespread in the endemic area (fig. 2C). Delimitation of this taxon from *Calochortus clavatus* var. *clavatus* is difficult. We have noted dwarfing in other species of *Calochortus* in the Arroyo de la Cruz area, and we believe that further taxonomic study is needed.

Ceanothus maritimus is also found on the marine terraces where locally it is the only shrubby plant. It is, however, ubiquitous and often locally dominant in the endemic area (fig. 2D). Northeast of Yellow Hill it is a codominant in chaparral with *Salvia mellifera*. The only place it is not found in the area is on the ridge above Arroyo Hondo. As mentioned above, its distribution is determined to some extent by edaphic conditions. It is very low-growing and does not survive in the shade of taller plants.

Allium hickmanii is found in swales or grassy places that are wet in winter and early spring. This species tends to occur in fairly large colonies in deep clay soil. We have located populations on several sites both to the north and to the south of Arroyo de la Cruz (fig. 3A).

Sanicula maritima also occurs in seasonally moist clay soils of the old marine terraces. It is considerably less common than is Hickman's onion and forms smaller populations (fig. 3B). Although the two species occur in similar habitats we have not found them growing together.

Baccharis plummerae ssp. *glabrata* is found along the ridges north and south of Arroyo de la Cruz and north of Arroyo de los Chinos (fig. 3C). It is found at the interface between the grassland and the coastal sage scrub below. It often extends down into the scrub. This species also has been located on steep slopes in dwarf chaparral dominated by maritime ceanothus.

The remaining taxa are either associated with, or are part of the chaparral. They are particularly evident on windswept ridges. *Arctostaphylos hookeri* ssp. *hearstiorum* (fig. 3D) is a prostrate plant which grows around the margins of chaparral patches. It is often concealed by bunch grasses. It is usually found in small populations which are fairly widespread in the area. Often *A. hookeri* ssp. *hearstiorum* forms a low ground cover that grades into a taller chaparral dominated by *A. cruzensis*. This, in turn, may grade into still taller shrubs.

Ceanothus hearstiorum is another prostrate plant with a similar distribution to that of *A. hookeri* ssp. *hearstiorum*, but is much less common (fig. 4A). An interesting point is that it occurs on the ridge above Arroyo Hondo. The largest known population is at the southern end of the endemic area. At that location, it has come in after a fire. It is also recovering vigorously from a fire that swept over a portion of the ridge just south of Arroyo de la Cruz.

Arctostaphylos cruzensis is a mounding or spreading shrub. It is often found associated with other chaparral species including both the taller shaggy-barked manzanita (*A. tomentosa*) and the prostrate *A. hookeri* ssp. *hearstiorum* (fig. 4B). Suspected hybrids with *A. tomentosa* have been noted. On north-facing slopes that are protected from direct wind, chaparral dominated by *A. cruzensis* often grades into that dominated by taller chaparral species. In a few places it is seen in almost pure stands. It often occurs with dwarfed forms of *Adenostoma fasciculatum*.

Pedicularis dudleyi is found in open spaces in the chaparral or growing up through the branches of the prostrate shrubs. It has been observed only at Cinnabar Hill and southeastward in scattered small populations near the southern extreme of the endemic area (fig. 4C). It tends to occur in association with either *Adenostoma fasciculatum* or *Arctostaphylo hookeri* ssp. *hearstiorum*. Most species of *Pedicularis* are hemiparasitic. Perhaps these two shrubs are the hosts in such a relationship.

Carex obispoensis is a tall (to more than 1 meter) clump-forming plant that is rather widespread on the ridge systems both north and south of Arroyo de la Cruz (fig. 4D). There it occurs in association with grasslands and with dwarf chaparral stands where it often towers over the shrubs. It occurs most commonly in clay soils or in seasonally moist soils derived from ultrabasic parent materials. It extends from near the shore on marine terraces to the eastern extreme of the endemic area. In places it is the dominant plant.

DISCUSSION

The maritime chaparral of Arroyo de la Cruz has much in common with that described by Griffin (1978) from the Monterey area. In both areas, the chaparral is characterized by dominance of endemic taxa of Arctostaphylos and Ceanothus growing in association with Adenostoma fasciculatum. There are close floristic ties between the two areas. Each area has a race of Arctostaphylos hookeri: var. hookeri at Monterey and var. hearstiorum at Arroyo de la Cruz. Monterey ceanothus (C. rigidus) and maritime ceanothus (C. maritimus) are apparently closely related, as are dwarf ceanothus (C. dentatus) and Hearst's ceanothus (C. hearstiorum). The two areas share various other species or species pairs as well. The maritime chaparral communities of the two areas are developed on different parent materials: sandstone or old dune sands are the predominant parent materials at Monterey.

Griffin (1978) also noted similarities of the Monterey maritime chaparral with that in southern San Luis Obispo County near Morro Bay and on the Nipomo Mesa, and that in northern Santa Barbara County at Point Sal, at Orcutt and on the Burton Mesa. All of these areas have similar climates. Species connections among these areas suggest that they share a common history. We agree with Griffin that a program of intensive floristic and vegetational comparison of these now separated maritime chaparral communities needs to be instituted while intact samples of the communities remain.

The future of the Arroyo de la Cruz area is dependent upon various factors. The Hearst Corporation controls all but the roadside along Highway 1. Proposals for development in the San Simeon area have been raised in the past and some have been successful. Wells have been drilled into the aquifer of the Arroyo to supply water for some of these developments. To the best of our knowledge there are no active development plans for the Arroyo de la Cruz area itself at present. Economic and political pressures could change this situation. Detailed knowledge of the botanical resources of the area will be valuable if any development is proposed.

To date, the Hearst Corporation has managed the land fairly well. Grazing pressure has been maintained at a low level. The lack of plowing of most of the marine terraces has been a major factor that has allowed many of the perennial grasses, bulb-forming monocots and other native species to persist. In areas where plowing has apparently occurred, the flora consists mostly of annual Mediterranean grasses.

A potential threat to some of the rare and endangered plants in the study area is the practice of converting "brush" to rangeland. We have noted instances where heavy machinery has been used to remove the original vegetative cover from chaparral or coastal scrub dominated sites. In some cases this has affected rare species. Such practices apparently have a long history at Arroyo de la Cruz. Hoover (1970, p. 90) describes the impact of such "range improvement" practices on the then southernmost known population of large-flowered star-tulip (Calochortus uniflorus). Although these activities have impacted rare species, to date the impacts have been minor.

Tight control of access to the property by the Hearst Corporation has prevented much of the wanton destruction that has occurred in other areas (e.g., the Nipomo Dunes) as a result of off-road vehicular activities. In a few sites along the seabluffs south of Arroyo de la Cruz vehicular and foot traffic have degraded the vegetation, but some of these areas are now blocked to access.

ACKNOWLEDGEMENTS

We thank Mr. A. J. Cooke of the Hearst Corporation and Mr. and Mrs. Harlan Brown, Ranch Supervisors at the Hearst Ranch, for allowing access to the ranch for these studies. We thank the various lay and professional botanists who participated in field trips and assisted in the inventory of data on rare species.

REFERENCES

Constance, Lincoln. Sanicula maritima Kellogg ex S. Watson, adobe sanicle. Rare Plant Status Report. California Native Plant Society. 1977.
Griffin, J. Maritime chaparral and endemic shrubs of the Monterey Bay region, California. Madroño 25:65-81; 1978 April.

Holland, V. L.; Keil, David J. California Vegetation. El Corral Bookstore, California Polytechnic State Univ. 1986. 292 p.

Hoover, Robert F. Vascular plants of San Luis Obispo County, California. Univ. California Press; 1970. 350 p.

Niehaus, Theodore. *Allium hickmanii* Eastw., Hickman's onion, Rare Plant Status Report. California Native Plant Society; 1977a. 3 p.

_____. *Pedicularis dudleyi* Elmer, Dudley's lousewort, Rare Plant Status Report. California Native Plant Society; 1977b. 3 p.

Riggins, Rhonda. Noteworthy collections: *Pedicularis dudleyi* Elmer (Scrophulariaceae). Madroño 30(1):63; January.

Sinnott, Q. P. A revision of *Ribes* L. subg. *Grossularia* (Mill.) Pers. sect. *Grossularia* (Mill.) Nutt. (Grossulariaceae) in North America. Rhodora 87:189-286; 1985, April.

Smith, James P.; York, Richard. Inventory of rare and endangered vascular plants of California. Spec. Publ. #1 ed. 3, California Native Plant Society; 1984. xviii + 174 p.

Tucker, John, Professor of Botany, Univ. California, Davis, CA. [Letter to David Keil]. October, 1983.

Yadon, Vernal, Director, Museum of Natural History, Pacific Grove, CA. [Conversation]. Spring 1984.

York, R.; Smith, J. CNPS rare plant program inventory notes 86/1; September, 1986. 15 p.

The Problem of the Salmon Mountain

J. O. Sawyer [1]

Abstract: The 17 conifer species occurring in one square mile of the Salmon mountains is a unique situation in the Klamath Mountains of northern California. These conifers are not restricted to a single community-type, but instead occur in stands within three forest zones. Comparable habitats in the Marble Mountains and the Trinity Alps have similar conifer composition, but with only some of the Salmon Mountain species. The conifers in these stands are not rare, yet together they represent an important aspect of California's vegetation. Herein lies the problem: How do we treat this singular assemblage of individually common plants?

In the late 1960's and early 1970's there was much excitement among the conifer enthusiasts over finding of subalpine fir in California. The known range of this Rocky Mountain species was extended south from Oregon (Sawyer et al. 1971). At the same time unusual mixtures of conifers were noted in the same area, the drainages of Sugar, Duck and Horse Range Creeks of the Salmon Mountains, one of many ranges which are collectively referred to as the Klamath Mountains. Surveys of the area showed mixtures of up to 10 species in a single stand. Also found were 17 species growing in a section (square mile) area of Sugar Creek (table 1). This area was hailed as supporting the richest assemblages of conifers in California, if not in the world (Sawyer and Smith 1973). In the excitement it seemed appropriate to name this new kind of vegetation, and so the name "enriched mixed conifer" was applied to species-rich stands at mid-elevations. Stands like the one in Horse Range Creek seemed to be Sierran mixed conifer forests enriched with high-elevation species of the Sierra and Cascades, and by Klamath endemics. The name has been used since then but in some rather different ways, the most stressing being in reference to the forests of the Klamath Region as a whole (Axelrod, 1977). Subsequent work has demonstrated that subalpine fir is found elsewhere in California, but that mixture of 17 species is not duplicated. Here I will try to put the Salmon Mountain forests in to perspective.

---

[1] Professor of Botany, Humboldt State University, Arcata, CA.

FLORA AND VEGETATION OF THE KLAMATH MOUNTAINS

Flora

The area has long been known for its high floristic diversity (Stebbins and Major 1965). The Klamath Mountains and North Coast Ranges of California support over 3500 taxa of vascular plants (Smith and Sawyer 1986). The traditional explanation for rich flora is that the area supports a mixture of California and northern plants growing in a geological province of ancient rocks and diverse landforms (Whittaker 1961). Great topographic and parent material variability support many habitats in a moderated climate (Whittaker 1960, Richardson and Lum 1980). The mountains are viewed as a refugium of temperate Tertiary plants mixed with those of Mexican origin (Axelrod 1977, Wolfe 1969). Events of the Pleistocene and hypsithermal allowed species from north, Great Basin and central California to become established in the area as well.

The Salmon Mountain conifers are an interesting element of the flora. Brewer spruce, which now only grows in the Klamath Mountains, is known from Miocene fossils in Oregon and Nevada (Wolfe 1969). Subalpine fir is seen as a later Pleistocene introduction (Cope 1983). Montane glaciation in the Klamath Mountains was for the most part restricted to individual drainages. Today the Salmon Mountain conifer mixtures grow on glaciated granite bedrock, till and moraines.

Vegetation

Existing forests are controlled primarily by differences in parent material, and secondarily by elevation and soil moisture as it relates to topography (Whittaker 1960, Waring 1969). Unlike the flora the vegetation pattern in general is rather predictable. Mature, climax forests growing on deep soils are elevationally zoned. Over much of the region the low elevations are characterized by Douglas-fir/hardwood forests (Sawyer et al. 1977). Montane forests are recognized by the common occurrence of white fir on mesic sites. At higher montane elevations Shasta red fir dominates mesic locations. At subalpine elevations mountain hemlock is the dominant tree (Sawyer and Thornburgh 1977). Within each zone, forests rich in herbs and shrubs along streams give way to simple ones all but barren of understories on dry slopes. This straight forward-pattern is complicated, though, by a confusing variety of seral stages due to variable fire history.

SUBALPINE FIR

Since 1969 several additional populations of subalpine fir have been found. Critchfield and Griffin (1972) detail two areas in the Marbles. Sawyer and Cope (1982) describe another location in the southern Marble Mountains. This summer Don Hemphill, of the Pacific Union College, found the second largest population in California between Virginia Lake and Marvis Lake in the Scott Mountains of the Trinity Alps Wilderness. Populations grow in several different kinds of habitats. Granite is the parent material of preference, and the trees are inclined to grow on northeast-facing aspects at montane or subalpine elevations. But exceptions exist. In some cases a single tree is seen near a ridge; other times large populations are found restricted to lakesides and meadows.

ENRICHED MIXED CONIFER

No other stands of "enriched mixed conifer" have been found in my wanderings in the Klamath Mountains. Some stands in the Trinity Alps are diverse, but the Salmon Mountain composition is not duplicated. In the Siskiyou Mountains enriched stands of different composition are found (table 2). Noble fir, Alaska-yellow-cedar and Port-Orford-cedar occur there; subalpine fir and Engelmann spruce do not. Silver fir, another other rare conifer in the Klamath Mountains, is found not in species-rich stands, but instead only with shasta red fir, mountain hemlock and western white pine. Large areas of the Trinity Alps lack lodgepole pine, a component of the enriched mixed conifer stands of the Salmon Mountains. Since conifer-rich stands do not have the same composition throughout the Klamath Mountains, it is hard to argue for the existence of such a vegetation type.

Even in the Salmon Mountains the 17 species did not occur in a single stand. At mid-elevations the five mixed conifer species, ponderosa pine, sugar pine, Douglas-fir, white fir and incense-cedar, are enriched with shasta fir, logdgepole pine, western white pine, Brewer spruce, and Jeffrey pine. Other mixes are found along the creeks with Engelmann spruce and mountain hemlock replacing Jeffrey pine. At higher elevations ponderosa pine, incense-cedar, and sugar pine are supplanted by foxtail pine, lodgepole pine, whitebark pine and Juniperus communis. At lakes and meadows all mixed conifers are gone leaving a less assorted mix of mountain hemlock, shasta red fir, western white pine, subalpine fir, Engelmann spruce and Brewer spruce.

In common among these areas are open forests with little interaction among individual trees. White fir and Douglas-fir grow next to whitebark pine and foxtail pine at 2200 m elevation, for example. Eclectic stands occur on moraines, rocky ridges, and glaciated bedrock not only in the Salmon Mountains but also in the Marbles, Siskiyous, and the Trinity Alps. Defining a vegetation-type, such as enriched mixed conifer, is inappropriate. Instead these unique stands should be recognized within the context of regionally reoccurring stands. The repeating pattern should be classified. When this classification is done, then the unique stands can be fully appreciated.

Table 1. The conifers in one square mile of the montane and subalpine zones of the Salmon Mountains, Siskiyou County CA. MAR = also in the Marble Mountains. SIS = also in the Siskiyou Mountains. TRI = also in the Trinity Alps and associated ranges in Trinity Co.

Abies concolor (Gord. ex Loud.) ex Hildebr. var. lowiana Lemmon WHITE FIR [MAR, SIS, TRI]
A. lasiocarpa (Hook.) Nutt. var. lasiocarpa SUBALPINE FIR [MAR, TRI]
A. magnifica A. Murr. var. shastensis Lemmon SHASTA RED FIR [MAR, SIS, TRI]
Juniperus communis L. var. montana Ait. [MAR, SIS, TRI]
Calocedrus decurrens (Torr.) Florin INCENSE-CEDAR [MAR, SIS, TRI]
Picea breweriana Wats. BREWER SPRUCE [MAR, SIS, TRI]
P. engelmannii Parry ex Engelm. ENGELMANN SPRUCE
Pinus albicaulus Engelm. WHITEBARK PINE [MAR, SIS, TRI]
P. balfouriana Grev. & Balf. in A. Murr. var. balfouriana FOXTAIL PINE [MAR, TRI]
P. contorta Dougl. ex Loud. var. murrayana (Grev. & Balf.) Engelm. LODGEPOLE PINE [MAR, SIS, TRI]
P. jeffreyi Grev. & Balf. in A. Murr. JEFFREY PINE [MAR, SIS, TRI]
P. lamberiana Dougl. SUGAR PINE [MAR, SIS, TRI]
P. monticola Dougl. WESTERN PINE [MAR, SIS, TRI]
P. ponderosa Dougl. ex P. & C. Lawson var. ponderosa PINE [MAR, SIS, TRI]
Pseudostuga menziesii (Mirb.) Franco var. menziesii DOUGLAS-FIR [MAR, SIS, TRI]
Taxus brevifolia Nutt. PACIFIC YEW [MAR, SIS, TRI]
Tsuga mertensiana (Bong.) Carr. MOUNTAIN HEMLOCK [MAR, SIS, TRI]

Table 2. Other species in the montane and subalpine zones of the Klamath Mountains of northwestern California and southwestern Oregon. MAR = in Marble Mountains. SIS = in the Siskiyou Mountains. TRI = Trinity Alps and other ranges in Trinity Co.

Chamaecyparis lawsoniana (A. Murr.) Parl. [SIS, TRI]
Chamaecyparis nootkatensis (D. Don) Spach [SIS]
Cupressus bakeri Jeps. ssp. mathewsii C. B Wolf [SIS]
Abies procera Rehd. [SIS, MAR, TRI]

LITERATURE CITED

Axelrod, D. A. Outline history of California vegetation. In: Barbour, M. G.; Major, J. eds. Terrestrial vegetation of California. New York: Wiley-Interscience; 1977: 140-193.

Cope, E. A. Chemosystematic affinities of a California population of Abies lasiocarpa. Madrono 30:102-115; 1983.

Critchfield, W. B.; Griffin, J. R. The distribution of forest trees in California. Res. Paper PSW-82. Berkeley, CA: Pacific Southwest Forest and Range Experiment Station, Forest Service, U. S. Department of Agriculture; 1972. 114p.

Richardson, P. J.; Lum, K. K. Patterns of plant species diversity in California: relation to weather and topography. Amer. Nat. 116:504-536; 1980.

Sawyer, J. O.; Cope, E. A. Noteworthy collection, California; Abies lasiocarpa. Madrono 29:218; 1982.

Sawyer, J. O.; Thornburgh, D. A.; Bowman, W. F. Extension of the range of Abies lasiocarpa in California. Madrono 20:413-415; 1070.

Sawyer, J. O.; Smith, J. P. The Klamath Region. California Native Plant Society Newsletter 8:3-6; 1973.

Sawyer, J. O.; Thornburgh, D. A. Montane and subalpine vegetation of the Klamath Mountains. In: Barbour, M. G.; Major, J. eds. Terrestrial vegetation of California. New York: Wiley-Interscience; 1977: 699-732.

Sawyer, J. O.; Thornburgh, D. A; Griffin, J. R. Mixed evergreen forest. In: Barbour, M. G.; Major, J. eds. Terrestrial vegetation of California. New York: Wiley-Interscience; 1977: 359-382.

Smith J. P.; Sawyer, J. O. A checklist of vascular plants of northwest California. 9th edition. Miscellaneous Publication No. 2. Humboldt State University Herbarium; 1986.

Stebbins, G. L.; Major, J. Endemism and speciation in the California flora. Ecol. Monogr. 35:1-35.

Waring, R. H. Forest plants of the eastern Siskiyous: their environmental and vegetational distribution. Northwest Sci. 43:1-17.

Whittaker, R. H. Vegetation of the Siskiyou Mountains, Oregon and California. Ecol. Monogr. 30:279-338.

Whittaker, R. H. Vegetation history of the Pacific Coast States and the "central" significance of the Klamath Region. Madrono 16:5-23.

Wolfe, J. A. Neogene floristic and vegetational history of the Pacific northwest. Madrono 20(3):83-110; 1969.

Rare Plant Surveys: Techniques for Impact Assessment

James R. Nelson[1]

Abstract: Rare plant surveys are used to locate rare and endangered plants and natural communities. Surveys provide the basis for identifying adverse effects and the design of mitigation measures. In order for efforts to be productive, the methods must be well planned. Suggestions are made for the entire survey process including consideration of goals, selecting a competent investigator, planning surveys, conducting field work, and reporting the results.

Passage of environmental quality legislation in the early 1970's and later passage of endangered species legislation, produced a need for reliable information about the effect of proposed projects on rare and endangered plants. Rare plant surveys are used to identify rare plant populations that are near proposed development projects. Information on the occurrence of rare plants is used along with knowledge of the proposed project to assess the potential for adverse effects and ultimately to design mitigation measures, should it become necessary to do so.

Over the past decade, many rare plant surveys have been conducted. Approaches to surveys have varied considerably; for some agencies a written certification from an acknowledged botanist stating his opinion about the presence of rare plants has been considered to be sufficient proof of the occurrence of rare plants. This type of certification has often been given without any field examination, or may have used field examination techniques that were not likely to locate rare species even when they were present.

Most agencies in California currently require field surveys when rare species are known to occur in the immediate vicinity of pa project. Still, many field searches may not locate all of the rare plants on a particular parcel, because they target a specific group of species that are expected to occur based on historic collection records rather than taking a purely objective approach. Depending on what flowering season and must completely cover species are actually searched for, targeted surveys might take place at a time of year when other rare plants on the site are not recognizable.

A few agencies still accept quantitative vegetation analysis techniques for rare plant surveys. Goff et al. (1982) correctly point out that quantitative vegetation analysis techniques are inappropriate for rare plant searches due to their inherent bias toward the dominant species on a site rather than rare ones.

Perhaps the reason for the variety of approaches to survey techniques has been the lack of standardized field procedures. In an attempt to address this problem, the California Native Plant Society has presented guidelines for rare plant surveys (Nelson, 1984). These were subsequently adopted by the California Department of Fish and Game in an attempt to standardize assessment procedures and review standards.

The purpose of this article is to review the major components of rare plant surveys. It is important that project proponents and agency personnel understand the process involved in conducting a rare plant survey to allow for sufficient time to find qualified investigators and properly conduct the survey. Furthermore, it is essential that consultants and staff biologists insist on using the best techniques to locate rare species.

Floristic surveys are required to discover all of the rare plants of a given parcel. Floristic surveys require that an attempt be made to examine all taxa in the study area, and that every plant discovered be identified to a taxonomic level that allows the investigator to determine its rarity. In order to be complete, floristic surveys must be conducted periodically through at least one areas that will be affected by the proposed project. Documentation of methods, procedures, and results is critical for reviewers to determine the adequacy of the study effort.

GOALS OF RARE PLANT SURVEYS

A rare plant survey is the process by which the spatial distribution of rare plants is characterized. When used as the basis of impact identification, the

---

[1] Staff botanist, California Energy Commission, Sacramento, California 95814

purpose of a rare plant survey is to locate all rare plant species at one location.

An investigator may also be asked to identify plant communities that require protection because of values to wildlife, water quality, or other natural features, or to identify other vegetational characteristics that may influence a proposed project (e.g., fire potential, erosion control, timber values, etc.). These purposes can usually be accommodated during a rare plant survey.

When To Conduct A Rare Plant Survey

A rare plant survey is needed for any project where the existing information is insufficient to show that no rare plants occur in areas that could be affected by the project. When the proposed project has the potential to adversely affect plants, there needs to be enough factual information on hand to indicate that no rare plants are present (or at least that rare plants that are present will not be adversely affected).

There are often clues which strongly indicate the need for a rare plant survey. Records of previous sitings, or the presence of habitat that is suspected or known to support rare plants are examples of information that clearly indicate the need to look closer. The lack of such clues is not, however, sufficient reason to assume that rare plants do not occur! The fact that rare plants have not been reported from a site may merely be an indication of no previous field work in the area. The way to determine if rare plants are present is to conduct a field survey.

Qualifications Of Investigators

Few agencies employ qualified botanists on a full-time basis. When a proposed project requires additional information on the occurrence of rare plants, it is common practice to contract with a consultant for a rare plant field survey and subsequent impact analysis.

Deciding if a person has the qualifications to conduct a botanical survey can be difficult. Unfortunately discerning between the skilled and the incompetent is often a matter of experience. The skills required to design and conduct rare plant surveys are not clearly connected to any college degree, license, or other certificate, and there are both qualified and incompetent practitioners conducting botanical field work. With this warning in mind, the following characteristics are offered as an indication of proper qualifications (whether a person uses his full capability may be an entirely different matter).

A qualified botanist should have: 1) experience as a botanical field investigator, including experience in field sampling design and field methods; 2) knowledge of the local flora; 3) taxonomic experience and a knowledge of plant ecology (while rare exceptions exist, college coursework in these areas should usually be required); 4) familiarity with state and federal laws and agency policies and regulations which pertain to rare plant protection and environmental quality; 5) a demonstrated ability to prepare detailed technical reports; and 6) enthusiasm for field studies and the physical capability to conduct strenuous field work.

PLANNING RARE PLANT SURVEYS

Once the need for a study has been established and a competent botanist has been found, the planning begins. The plan for rare plant surveys must take into account the proposed project, habitat types on the site, the phenological and physical characteristics of plants in the area, and other characteristics of the site. To ensure a complete and accurate study, it is essential that a study plan be developed prior to conducting field work.

Review Project Proposal

In order to conduct an adequate survey for purposes of impact evaluation, an investigator must have a clear understanding of the activities of the proposed project. The types of disturbance, the location of facilities, and the potential for effects after construction may influence the emphasis of the survey, the location of the study area and the intensity of field study. The project proposal must be evaluated for potential effects from operation as well as construction.

The project proponent should provide the following items to the field investigator to aid in planning and reporting the survey:

- A clear project proposal.
- A base map of project site.
- Engineering drawings showing the location of all facilities.
- Aerial photographs of the project area.
- Information on the post-construction operation of the facility.

These are essential to understanding the proposal, designing field search techniques, and ultimately to preparing an adequate report.

Review Existing Rare Plant Information

Data should be collected on rare and endangered plants suspected to occur in the region. Species known from near the site, or reported in similar habitat (even though not known to occur locally) may occur on the study site. Information collected on these species prior to conducting the field survey should include 1) a taxonomic description and illustration or photograph; 2) information on habitat and associated species; 3) phenological and ecological data; 4) endangerment assessment; and 5) data on known locations.

Information sources include floras and other published literature (taxonomic monographs, ecological studies), environmental impact reports and previously completed rare plant survey reports, informal reports (status reports prepared by agency personnel, local checklists, etc.), herbarium specimen labels and rare plant field reports, knowledgable persons, and for many regions computer data bases, e.g., state heritage programs sponsored by the state government and The Nature Conservancy (Barkley, 1981; Crovello, 1981).

Existing information generally is not a substitute for field searches. Information in the literature is almost always incomplete and may be confounded by inaccuracies, lack of space to publish pertinent data, and in some cases data overload (Crovello, 1981). Herbarium specimen labels and rare plant field data forms may be subject to problems with nomenclature, identification, and imprecise locality information (Barkley, 1981). While these limitations should be kept in mind, it remains critical to examine any pertinent data sources before begining field searches for rare plants.

This information should be obtained prior to conducting field work to increase the investigator's familiarity with the species and ultimately result in a more successful survey. In addition to collecting these data, it is important to become personally familiar with the morphology and ecology of these species by examining herbarium specimens or, better yet, visiting extant populations prior to the field search. All members of a field search crew should have a clear search image of the rare plants that are suspected to be in the area prior to initiating field searches.

Identify The Study Area

The study area must reflect the goals of the survey and the characteristics of the proposed project. For the purpose of impact identification, the study area should include 1) areas that will be disturbed during construction; 2) a substantial buffer area; and 3) areas that will be disturbed by project operation. In addition, examination of neighboring areas may be necessary when rare plants are found.

The study area should be large enough to allow the developer adequate design flexibility. Because rare plant surveys are often conducted early in the project planning process, changes in initial plans must be expected. Thus it is important to select a study area which is large enough to accomodate unforeseen changes in development plans. It is good practice to examine the areas to be affected and a significant buffer zone.

The study area should be designed to consider both construction and operation of the project. For projects that have the potential to affect vegetation beyond the boundaries of disturbance from construction it is necessary to survey larger areas. For example, the construction of a campground may actually disturb very little ground. Yet a rare plant population located near the campground on hiking trails may be affected by users of the campground. Industrial facilities may have distinct boundaries to the disturbance from construction activities, yet produce pollutants that affect surrounding vegetation.

The field botanist must be prepared to expand the survey area if rare plants are found. I have on several occasions found small populations many miles from the nearest known population; further examination showed them to be the tip of a range-extension "iceberg". When a rare plant population is found, the investigation should assess its significance on local and regional scales, as well as with respect to the overall distribution.

Describe plant communities

The description of habitats should include a map of major habitat types and a written description. The map should accurately show the boundaries of different habitat types. Aerial photograph are the best data source for mapping vegetation. Aerial photos are available for public use at many government agencies and universities. Transfer of information from aerial photos can be accomplished without expensive and complex equipment. The use of aerial photos is essential for delineating plant community boundaries accurately, but cannot be considered adequate for identifying many plant communities without ground verification.

A written description of the natural

communities should be based on field observations. Nomenclature should be based on major references on the subject. In order to standardize community nomenclature, the classification system used by the local heritage program is generally recommended.

Predicting Rare Plant Occurrence

For some species, correlation of the geographic distribution of habitat features can suggest the location of potentially suitable habitat and can be extremely useful for locating new populations of a rare species (Nelson, 1979). Predicting the occurrence of a plant is a geographical problem that involves correlating the geographic overlap of the habitat features that appear to limit the distribution of the plant. An experienced field investigator does this through a subjective and intuitive evaluation of the appearance of a particular site. A planner would overlay maps of different habitat features to see where all habitat features overlap.

There are serious limitations to use of predictive approaches (whether intuitive or based on map overlays) for impact analyses where all rare plants should be identified. The problems include: 1) the inaccuracy of prediction for some species and 2) the "surprise" occurrence of unexpected, unrecorded, and uncooperatively disjunct species. Thus, while the investigation of species that are known to be in a region can be assisted by predicting habitat distributions, there remains no suitable substitute for floristic field investigations for impact analysis.

Timing field work

Rare plant surveys must be conducted at the right time of year to ensure that plants in the field are both evident and identifiable. Many plants are more or less invisible except during periods when flowers cause them to stand out from surrounding plants. Because of this, and the fact that most identification requires floral parts, it is important to attempt to locate plants during flowering periods.

In California, it is nearly impossible to identify all of the plants in one area during a single visit. Because of differing flowering periods, it is important to plan botanical surveys in advance and allow for several visits during the entire flowering season. It is helpful to construct a calendar of flowering periods to help establish the proper time to conduct field work. Such a calendar should be based on the phenology of the common plants of the area using taxa which represent the spectrum of blooming periods in the area.

The best time to locate most plants is while they are flowering, but it is not always possible to identify plants from the flowers alone. For some taxa (e.g. Apiaceae, Brassicaceae, Boraginaceae, Fabaceae, etc.) return visits are often necessary to collect post-flowering plant parts (fruits or seeds) to confirm an identification.

There are times when even the best field survey would not reveal a rare plant that exists on a site. The relative abundance of any species can vary annually. Some species, particularly those in deserts, have the ability to withstand stresses, such as drought, by storing seed for extended periods. Thus in unfavorable years, some rare species may not be apparent at all. A search for these species may require more than one season to locate populations. Because of these uncertainties, it is fair to say that a rare plant survey cannot deny a species' existence, it can only confirm it.

Conflicts may arise between the scheduling of a plant survey and the desired project schedule, or legal time frames. It is up to the project proponent to provide the agency with sufficient information to properly process and evaluate its application. Where the presence of rare plants is unresolved, the lead agency should delay processing the application until sufficient information is submitted.

CONDUCTING FIELD SURVEYS

The purpose of field surveys is to locate and document all rare plant populations within the study area. This requires that 1) every species encountered be identified to the point that its rarity can be confirmed, and 2) the entire study area be covered completely (although the intensity of coverage may vary based on study goals and site characteristics).

The Floristic Survey

While rare plants can be abundant in a particular study area, it is prudent to expect that rare plants will make up only a very small percentage of the total plant cover or species present. The field investigator may have to cover much ground and identify many species before locating a rare plant population. Floristic approaches to rare plant investigations ensure the most complete examination possible. Floristic studies require the investigator to identify every species found. By contrast, targeted searches focus on species whose presence is expected based on previous records. When surveys are targeted to a few species, the investigator is not encouraged to locate and identify rare plants that are not expected or not previously recorded in the area.

The amount of time required for a floristic survey depends on the diversity of the area being studied. The more species, the greater the time required. By their nature, floristic surveys proceed slowly at first (as many "new" species are encountered) but speed-up as investigators learn the species and reduce the time required for plant identification. An increase of new species can be expected as the investigator crosses into different habitat types. The time required for a floristic survey will generally be more than that required for species-targeted surveys, but it remains the only method of ensuring that a rare plant will be identified if encountered during a field survey.

Search Patterns

Investigators must select approaches that provide the greatest confidence of completely examining the study area with the least overlap (thus keeping time and costs to a minimum). Many investigators use a random meander (Figure 6). The investigator searches areas that appear good based on professional judgement and intuition. The problem with this method is that it is often very difficult to keep track of what has and what has not been covered. When a random meander is used, some areas may be covered twice (or more times) while others may never be covered.

Systematic methods that divide the study area into manageable units is more likely to cover an area completely with the least possible duplication. If the study area is larger than can be easily divided, the use of transects is especially helpful. Transects are used for systematically sampling populations in the field with the greatest assurance of complete coverage (Anderson et al., 1976). For rare plant searches, however, transects serve only as a guide. They should not be confused with transect sampling methods for quantitative vegetation sampling. Transects do not need to be delimited with stakes or other markers, although this may be helpful.

Some conditions may not allow the use of transects, and other divisions of the study area should be considered. Goff et al. (1982) used a random, timed meander of field units to examine homogeneous vegetation types at two utility sites in Michigan. They used a "species/effort curve" (number of species/time) to define the sampling

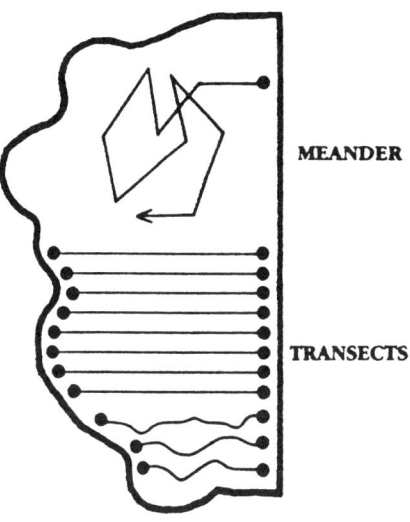

Figure 6. Two search approaches: random meandering and systematic transects. Transects serve to aid the investigator in completely covering the study area.

duration required for adequate floristic representation of each vegetation type. This approach may be less desirable than a thorough examination of an entire project area, yet is far more defensible than targeted rare plant searches in that it is still floristic in nature.

Survey Intensity

Intensity should reflect the circumstances of the study site. It is not essential that all areas be surveyed with the same intensity nor that all areas be examined. There are several factors to consider when deciding survey intensity including development plans, habitat conditions, vegetation density, terrain, physiognomy, size of the area, and the expected visibility of rare plants in the area. Table 1 gives examples of conditions that indicate appropriate survey intensity.

The intensity of the search will determine the amount of time required to cover the study area. Sometimes in an attempt to reduce costs of a rare plant survey, the intensity of the search is diluted. The intensity of a search should be determined by the size of the plants, and the density of the vegetation; as these control the effort required to locate a single species.

Documenting Rare Plant Populations

If a rare plant population is located, it needs to be properly documented. This should include the identity of the species, the number of plants, the precise location, the area covered by the population, and the habitat characteristics of the population. Additional information may include phenology, and ecological observations including any evidence of predation, competition, or pollination activities. These data are important for evaluating the importance and sensitivity of a population and may be useful in a larger sense toward a better understanding of the species.

When a plant is suspected to be rare, clear documentation of the identity is called for. The identification of each species should be made to a level that allows the investigator to determine the species' rarity status. Correct identification in the field may be extremely difficult. Some taxa require examination by taxonomic experts for confirmation. A voucher specimen should be collected whenever possible, but only when 1) population levels allow, 2) the investigator knows of no other collections from that location, and 3) that an appropriate collecting permit has been obtained by the investigator.

Plant collections must follow accepted methods (e.g. see Herbarium, University of California, 1975) and the specimen should be deposited in a recognized public herbarium for future reference. In addition, if there is any question about the identity of the specimen, the appropriate taxonomic expert should be contacted for confirmation. Correspondance on the identity of a specimen should be attached to written reports.

Populations may be too small to allow any collecting. In such cases, careful notes and photography must suffice. Notes should be taken on the taxonomic methods used to identify the plant (how many flowers were examined, what were the measurements of the parts, etc.). Photos should be taken of the plant, its habitat, and close-ups of morphological features used to identity the plant.

Proper identification of rare species is obviously important. When legal conflicts involve the question of proper identification, it may be important to produce physical evidence of the identity of a particular plant or population. Even where legal questions never arise, misidentification of specimens could be detrimental to a developer who implements unnecessary mitigation measures. Such events can erode the credibility of the investigator and the entire effort to preserve rare species.

Counting the number of plants can be a formidable task if the population is large, the plant is very small, or if the plant produces many off-shoots vegetatively. Where possible it is best to count the entire population. Where this is not feasible, the population should be sampled and the numbers and area estimated. If the data are to be used as a baseline for future monitoring it is important to develop a practical and repeatable methodology that will accurately chacterize the population. For most situations, the precise population size it not critical and order-of-magnitude estimates may suffice.

For impact assessment, the precise location of the rare plant population (i.e., habitat that is occupied by the plant) is most important. Boundaries of populations should be accurately delimited using measurements from fixed land marks, aerial photographs, or by a professional surveyor. Surveyed population boundaries are particularly important where there is a possibility of creating an easement or dedicating the land for mitigation purposes, in which cases a legal description would need to be developed.

Ecological requirements of the plant should be kept in mind while mapping the boundaries of the population. Often, plant populations are limited for environmental reasons (e.g., soils, exposure, moisture, etc). An attempt should be made to discover the reason for population boundaries whenever possible. If the population is dependent upon land features (e.g., springs, drainage patterns, etc.) that do not occur within the population itself, these should be noted also. Where buffer zones are included in the mapping, they should be clearly marked and the investigator should explain their necessity.

Often rare plant surveys are conducted in areas that have not been examined before. When rare species are found during the search, it may indicate the presence of other populations in the area. In order to accurately put into perspective the anticipated loss of a population, it may be necessary to determine other occurrences in neighboring areas. Roadside spot-checks may have to suffice when access is limited.

REPORTING SURVEY RESULTS

One of the problems with many rare plant surveys is the quality of reporting. Many reports are written in such a fashion that there is no way to determine how the results were obtained.

In general, the survey report must tell exactly what was done, why it was done, and any uncertainties involved. Without this information, it is impossible to determine if the field work has been detailed enough to eliminate the possibility that additional rare plants might occur within the study area. Agency personnel should reject reports that fail to use or document methods that would be successful in locating rare plants.

A rare plant survey report should include:

1. A description of the project. This should include maps of major facilities that will cause ground disturbance, and a discussion of construction and operation of the project.

2. A detailed description of the methods employed in collecting background information and conducting the field work. This should include a discussion of the methods that were employed in the field to search for rare plants in sufficient detail to permit the reader to understand the method used and appreciate the reasons for using them. At the very minimum, an accurate description of what areas were covered, the methods to cover these, and the dates of the field work need to be included.

3. A discussion of the survey results. Included should be a description of the biological setting with a clear vegetation map where more than one plant community exists. Description of what was found (include detailed maps, and description), and the characteristics of the population and its habitat. Standardized data forms (e.g, those used by the local heritage program) should be attached for all rare species found. A list of all species identified should be attached.

4. References used in preparing the survey report. References cited, persons contacted, herbaria visited, and the location of voucher specimens should be included.

Summary Reports Within Impact Reports

Many environmental impact reports face space limitations and do not include full details of every supporting study. Where space is a problem, the major points of the survey report should be briefly summarized. The summary within the environmental report should include a statement that a floristic survey was conducted (if this is the case), the dates of field work, the methods employed, and the results of the survey. Environmental reports must also include a discussion of potential impacts and mitigation measures.

The full report should be cited and its location given to enable reviewers to examine the report (since such reports are not otherwise available). The full report should be made available to appropriate institutions. For example, in California, the Natural Diversity Data Base (within the Department of Fish and Game) maintains records of the occurrence of rare and endangered species, and willingly accepts rare plant survey reports. Other repositories might include the lead agency that review the environmental report, universities and herbaria in the region of the proposed project, and public libraries.

SUMMARY

Rare plant surveys range from a process of expert certification to floristic searches. The steps required for a rare plant survey are singly simple but collectively complex. It is important to use a systematic approach in order for a survey to provide complete and accurate information. Only where a systematic approach is taken, can there be any assurance that survey conclusions truely reflect the factual occurrence or absence of rare plant species.

It is important to select qualified persons to conduct this work. "[T]he complexity of the floristic examination process, with the ecological knowledge that it demands and the taxonomic and identification issues that it inevitably raises, requires a relatively high level of expertise... for the site examination to yield information that is of value in guiding the development process, it must be conducted by qualified personnel utilizing systematic procedures that assure a reasonable intensity of investigation with adequate seasonal and geographic coverage" (Goff et al., 1982).

It is hoped that governmental agencies will work to improve the quality of rare plant investigations by adopting a stricter standard of evaluation that requires rare plant information to be derived from a systematic approach.

Acknowledgements: I wish to thank Jim Bartel, Ken Berg, Dan Cheatham, Susan Cochrane, Alice Howard, Jim Jokerst, Barbara Malloch, Craig Martz, and Rick York for their thoughts, comments, and criticisms.

REFERENCES

Anderson, D. R., J. L. Laake, B. R. Crain, and K. P. Burnham. Guidelines for Line Transect Sampling of Biological Populations. Western Energy and Land Use

Team, Fish and Wildlife Service, Fort Collins, Colorado; 1976. 28 p.

Barkley, T. M. Use and abuse of specimen labels in distribution mapping. In: L.E. Morse, M. S. Henifin eds. Rare Plant Conservation: Geographic Data Organization, New Botanical Garden, New York; 1981. p. 79-82.

Crovello, T. J. The literature as a rare plant information resource. In: L.E. Morse, M. S. Henifin eds. Rare Plant Conservation: Geographic Data Organization, New Botanical Garden, New York; 1981. p. 83-93.

Goff, F. G., G. A. Dawson, and J. J. Rochow. Site examination for threatened and endangered plant species. Environmental Management 6:307-316. 1982.

Herbarium, University of California. Selecting and Preparing Flowering Plant Specimens. Division of Agricultural Sciences, University of California, Berkeley; Leaflet 2787. 1975. 5 p.

Nelson, J. R. The Assessment and Protection of Rare and Endangered Plants of Butte County, California. Masters Thesis. California State University, Chico; 1979. 119 p.

Nelson, J.R. Rare plant field survey guidelines. In: J. P. Smith and R. York. Inventory of Rare and Endangered Vascular Plants of California. 3rd ed. California Native Plant Society, Berkeley; 1984. 174 p.

Determining Population Sizes of Narrowly Endemic but Locally Common Plants in the Red Hills, California

William B. DaVilla,[1] Dean Wm. Taylor,[2] R. Douglas Stone,[1] John W. Willoughby[4]

Abstract: Population sizes for most rare plants can be determined by direct census techniques. For species distributed throughout restricted habitats, population estimation is difficult, particularly when plants are locally common. A study of two such rare plants, *Chlorogalum grandiflorum* and *Lomatium congdonii*, was conducted for the Bureau of Land Management (BLM) to aid in developing a land use plan for public lands in the Red Hills, Tuolumne County, a center of significant serpentine endemism in the Sierra Nevada foothills. The major product of the inventory was a map showing the distributions of the two species in five density classes. Sampling techniques developed to provide this information are explained and the results of the study reviewed.

Serpentine endemism is a major theme exemplifying the California flora (Kruckeberg 1984). The Red Hills serpentine area is an ecological 'island' supporting a number of endemic and rare taxa. Several species that are essentially restricted to the Red Hills area include *Verbena californica* (Moldenke 1942), *Senecio clevelandii* var. *heterophyllus* (Hoover 1938), *Brodiaea pallida* (Hoover 1938), *Chlorogalum grandiflorum* (Hoover 1940), *Allium sanbornii* var. *tuolumnense* Ownbey and Aase, and *Lomatium congdonii* (Coulter & Rose 1900). Additionally, several restricted Sierran serpentine endemics considered rare by the California Native Plant Society (Smith and York 1984), including *Senecio layneae* Greene, *Lupinus spectabilis* (Hoover 1938), *Githopsis pulchella* ssp. *serpenticola* (Morin 1983), *Cryptantha mariposae* I. M. Johnston, and *Asclepias giffordii* Eastwood (cf. Gilmartin 1980) occur in the Red Hills.

The Bureau of Land Management (BLM) required detailed inventories of these rare taxa so that land management planning decisions could be developed that provide protection and conservation for these species and their habitats (cf. Reynaud Farve this conference, U.S.D.I. 1984).

Three species were directly considered in our study (BioSystems Analysis, Inc. 1984): *Allium sanbornii* var. *tuolumnense*, *Lomatium congdonii* and *Chlorogalum grandiflorum*.

The major objective of this study was to collect data 1) on the distribution of each sensitive plant species on public lands of the Red Hills Management Area; 2) to determine their absolute density, and 3) to characterize their habitat preference.

STUDY AREA

The Red Hills are located in the Sierra Nevada foothills of western Tuolumne County, California (latitude 37°51'N, longitude 120°27'W; fig. 1).

---

[1]Principal, BioSystems Analysis, Inc., 303 Potrero St. Suite 29-203, Santa Cruz, CA.

[1]Senior Botanist, BioSystems Analysis, Inc.

[3]Botanist, BioSystems Analysis, Inc.

[4]Range Conservationist, U.S. Dept. of Interior, Bureau of Land Management, Sacramento, CA.

The BLM administers approximately 2873 ha (7100 acres) of public lands in the Red Hills region. Elevations within the study area range from below 250 m (800 feet) at the shore of Don Pedro Reservoir to nearly 500 m (1700 feet) at the top of Taylor Hill.

The Red Hills region is characterized by a mediterranean-type climate typical of lowland California (Major 1977). Winters are moist and mild, and summers are hot and rainless. The elevation of the area is low enough to experience only very ephemeral snow, but is concomitantly high enough to avoid prolonged foggy periods typical of the Central Valley during winter months.

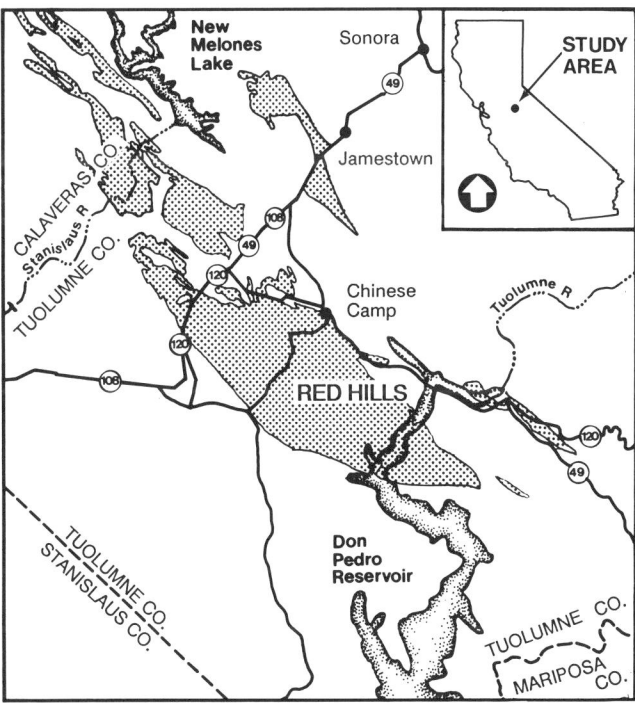

Figure 1. Location of the Red Hills study area on the western slope of the Sierra Nevada, California. Shaded area indicates distribution of serpentine or other ultramafic substrates (Rogers 1966).

The Red Hills appear as a rolling, maturely eroded landscape. The reddish cast of the sparsely vegetated, iron-rich soils give the Red Hills their name. Bedrock of the Red Hills region is principally dunitic serpentine of Mesozoic age (Clarke 1960). The serpentine soils of the area have been mapped in two soil series, Delpiedra and Henneke (Stone et al. 1977).

Vegetation characteristics of the study area are strongly correlated with soil conditions. The primary vegetation type on the Delpiedra soils is a woodland/shrubland complex composed of digger pine (*Pinus sabiniana*) and buckbrush (*Ceanothus cuneatus*) which combine to form a sparse to open woodland with an open shrub understory. The shrub interspaces are characterized by a diverse assemblage of annual and perennial grasses and herbaceous species.

METHODS

Distribution of Sensitive Plant Species

The overall distribution and extent of sensitive plant occurrences within the Red Hills Management Area was initially derived by systematic searches of the area. A topographic base map of the study area was divided into 185 16.6-ha (40 acres) quadrants. Searches were then conducted in the majority of these quadrants for occurrences of each of the target species. Results of this reconnaissance indicated that two of these species, *Chlorogalum grandiflorum* and *Lomatium congdonii*, were diffusely distributed throughout the region, and could not be directly censused. A sampling program was then designed to quantify their density patterns.

Absolute Density of Sensitive Plant Species

Quadrat sampling was undertaken to determine the absolute density of *Chlorogalum grandiflorum* and *Lomatium congdonii*. A stratified, random (Kearshaw 1973) selection system was used to select study sites.

Selection of transect sites was governed by subdivision of the study area into eight physiographic site classes:

1. Ridges
2. Upper south-facing slopes
3. Middle south-facing slopes
4. Lower south-facing slopes
5. Upper north-facing slopes
6. Middle north-facing slopes
7. Lower north-facing slopes
8. Valley bottoms

Transect locations were chosen by dividing each 265-ha (640-acre) Section of the Township grid in the study area into a 67 x 67 coordinate grid system (using USGS 1:24,000 scale topographic maps). A pair of random numbers corresponding to X- and Y-coordinates were chosen so as to locate a random point within each physiographic site class within the study area.

Once one of these randomly selected sample sites was approximately located in the field, the origin of the transect was determined by a quasi-random procedure (i.e., the toss of a hat). On slopes the transect line was oriented parallel to the slope contours and on ridges the transect was oriented along the ridgeline. On valley bottom sites both the transect origin and direction were randomly selected. Transect sites were inspected for vegetation and site homogeneity prior to sampling. Any transects which were visually judged to be heterogeneous were rejected, and another was randomly selected. Quantitative estimates of density were obtained by sampling in $1m^2$ quadrats placed at alternating 1-meter intervals along a 25-meter transect for a total of 25 quadrats per transect. Individuals of each target plant species were tallied only if rooted within the quadrat. Density was calculated per hectare by extrapolation.

Habitat Preference of Sensitive Plant Species

General observations on ecological conditions were made in conjunction with the reconnaissance-level inventory of the geographic distribution of each of the target species. Inferences concerning the habitat requirements of the species were made using these observations, and by analysis of data collected during the density sampling. Site variables recorded at each density transect site include: elevation, slope steepness, slope exposure, percent cover of bedrock, percent cover of loose surface rock, percent total herb cover, percent total shrub cover, and percent total tree cover.

Data Analysis

Plots of variance of density as a function of cumulative sample number of randomly ordered samples were used to evaluate the degree to which the quadrat sampling data represented the true mean density (Sokal and Rohlf 1981). A leveling off of such a variance plot indicates that sufficient sample size has been obtained to adequately represent the variation in density. Univariate and bivariate statistical comparisons employed standard parametric tests (Sokal and Rohlf 1981). Values reported herein are ± one standard error about the mean.

RESULTS AND DISCUSSION

Absolute Density of Sensitive Plant Species

Quadrat density data for *Chlorogalum grandiflorum* and *Lomatium congdonii* were collected from 26 May through 3 June 1984. One hundred and fifteen transect sites were sampled within the Red Hills Management Area (BioSystems Analysis, Inc. 1984).

Field observations indicated a clumped (non-random) distribution of *Chlorogalum grandiflorum* and *Lomatium congdonii* on a localized scale, which would have required an exhaustive sampling effort to map and describe using qualitative methods. *Chlorogalum* occurred on 51 (44 percent) of the 115 transects sampled while *Lomatium* occurred on 36 (31 percent) of the transects. Figure 2 illustrates a plot of variance in *Chlorogalum* and *Lomatium* density as a function of cumulative number of samples. The leveling off of the graph with increasing sample size indicates that sufficient sample size has been obtained to adequately represent the range of variability in density within the study area populations. A frequency distribution of observed densities for *Chlorogalum grandiflorum* and *Lomatium congdonii* showed a preponderance of zero and near-zero density values suggesting the data was not normally distributed.

Table 1 gives the estimated mean density of *Chlorogalum grandiflorum* and *Lomatium congdonii* for each physiographic site type within the study area. The highest density of *Chlorogalum* within the sites sampled occurred on ridges: 3200 ± 980 plants per hectare. Upper south-facing slopes were next in importance, with an average density of 1600 ± 620 plants per hectare. Density of *Chlorogalum grandiflorum* on other site types was comparably low, between 100 and 800 plants per hectare.

Table 1. Mean density of *Chlorogalum grandiflorum* (CHGR) and *Lomatium congdonii* (LOCO) by physiographic site type in the Red Hills Management Area.

Site Type	Density (plants per hectare)	
	CHGR	LOCO
Ridges	3200	700
Upper north-facing slopes	100	6600
Middle north-facing slopes	100	4700
Lower north-facing slopes	600	600
Upper south-facing slopes	1600	100
Middle south-facing slopes	800	1400
Lower south-facing slopes	600	100
Valley bottoms	200	100

Concomitantly, the density of *Lomatium congdonii* was found to be greatest on upper and middle north-facing slopes, with densities of 6566 ± 4767 and 4700 ± 3348 plants per hectare, respectively. Density of this species on other site types ranged from 1366 ± 1366 plants per hectare on middle south-facing slopes to a very low density of ca. 100 plants per hectare on upper south-facing slopes and valley bottom sites. The higher density on middle south-facing slopes was skewed by a single transect in this site type with extremely high *Lomatium* density. Reconnaissance observations suggest that the actual density for this topographic position is lower.

The Student-Newman-Keuls test (Sokal and Rohlf 1981) was used to test for significant differences between means of *Chlorogalum* and *Lomatium* density as a function of physiographic site type (topographic position). The only significant result obtained in this test was that *Chlorogalum* density was significantly higher on ridges as compared to all other site types ($p = 0.05$) and *Lomatium* density was significantly higher on upper and middle north-facing slopes as compared to other physiographic site types ($p = 0.05$).

Five *Chlorogalum grandiflorum* and *Lomatium congdonii* density classes were recognized for mapping purposes (table 2). The boundaries of these density classes were determined by successive standard error increments on either side of the mean density value for all samples.

The mean *Chlorogalum* and *Lomatium* density for each physiographic site type (table 1) was then assigned to the appropriate density mapping class. The final density map was modified to reflect only those portions of the study area in which *Chlorogalum grandiflorum* and *Lomatium congdonii* was actually observed during extensive, reconnaissance-level surveys. A combined density and known distribution map for *Chlorogalum*

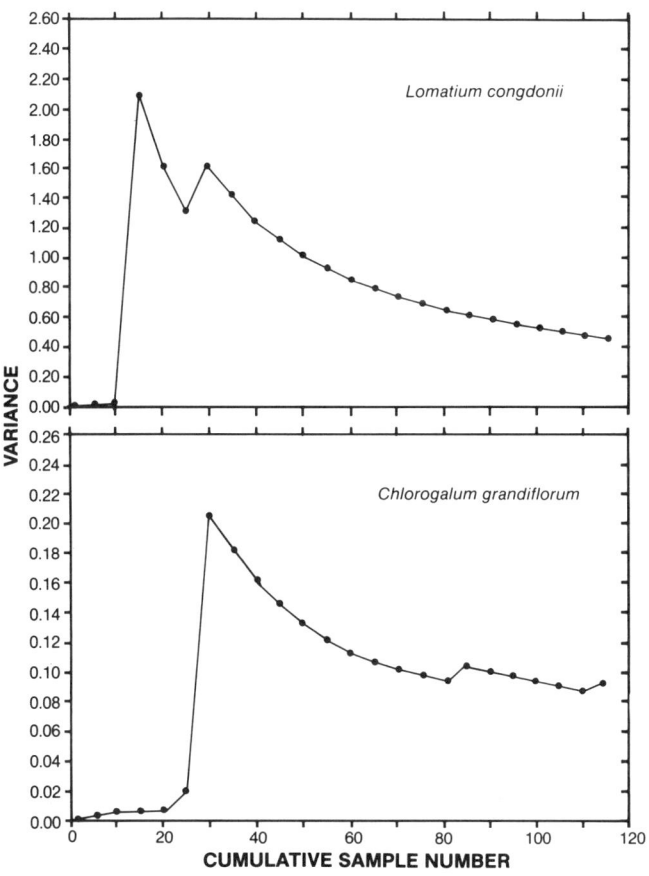

Figure 2. Plot of variance versus cumulative number of randomly ordered samples for *Chlorogalum grandiflorum* and *Lomatium congdonii* density data.

Table 2. Density ranges for *Chlorogalum grandiflorum* (CHLO) and *Lomatium congdonii* (LOCO) by physiographic site class.

Class	Density (density in plants per hectare)	
	CHGR	LOCO
1	Absent	Absent
2	≤ 375	≤ 334
3	376 - 1511	335 - 971
4	1512 - 2079	972 - 2248
5	≥ 2080	≥ 2249

grandiflorum is shown in figure 3. Note that the species is widely distributed throughout the study area, with relatively high estimated density on the major ridgelines. *Lomatium congdonii* was of similarly widely distributed (BioSystems Analysis, Inc. 1984).

Habitat Preference of Sensitive Plant Species

Distribution of these two sensitive plant species is relatively habitat and site specific within the Red Hills Management Area. Each species has an 'optimal' habitat in which population density is greatest. The species differ in the degree to which they can exploit 'marginal' habitat (sensu Brown 1984). Both *Lomatium congdonii* and *Chlorogalum grandiflorum* occur at relatively low densities on public lands throughout most of the Red Hills Management Area. However, they reach their highest densities in specific physiographic sites--ridges and upper south-facing slopes for *Chlorogalum* and upper and middle north-facing slopes for *Lomatium*. The ranges of density show a similar trend where the importance of optimal sites are an order of magnitude greater than marginal sites.

Covariance between density for the two species is non-significant, indicating that they are distributed independently with respect to one another. Each species, therefore, reaches its highest density in a unique site type unrelated to that occupied by the other species.

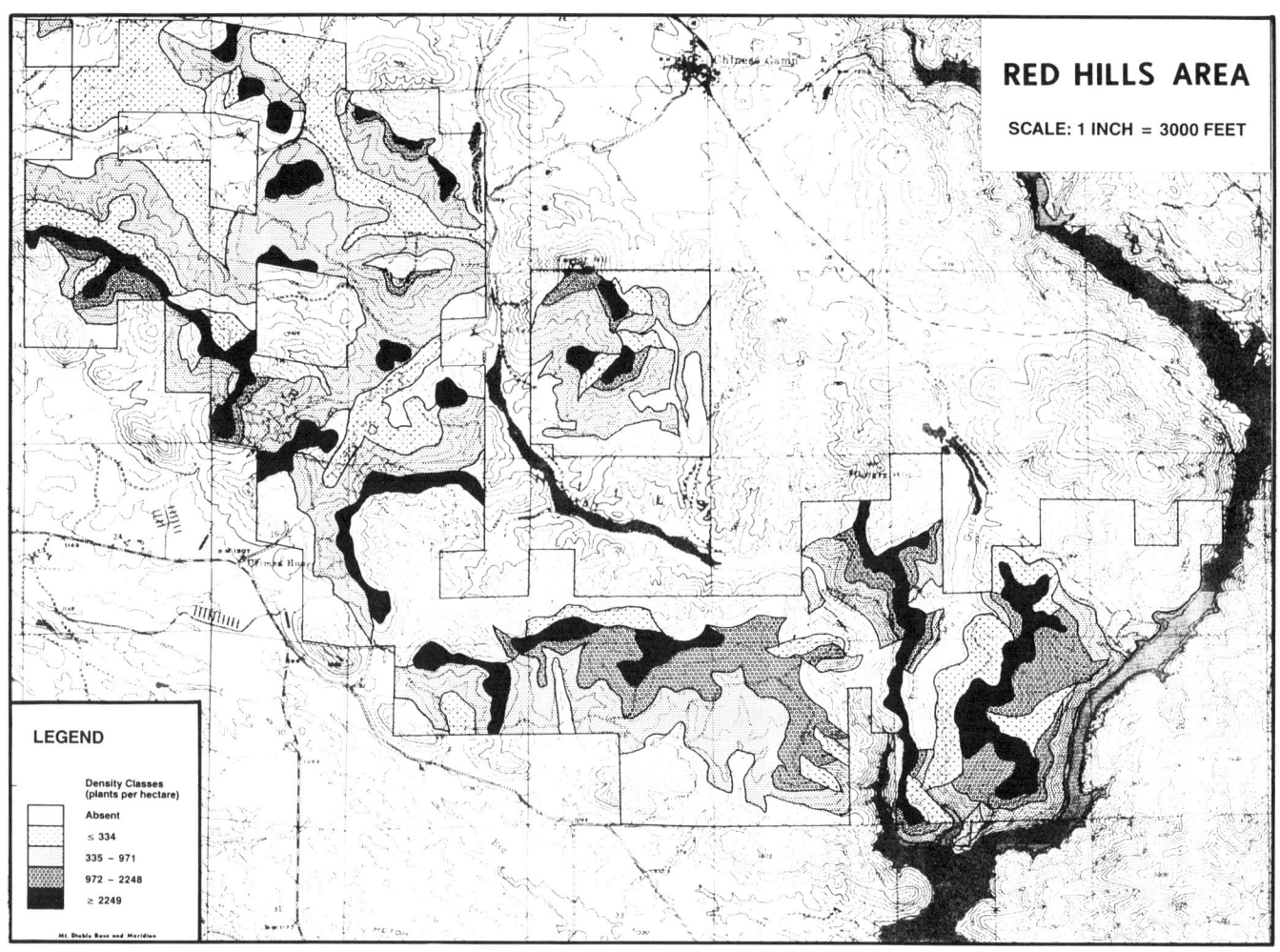

Figure 3. Density and known distribution map for *Chlorogalum grandiflorum* in the Red Hills Management Area.

For the 115 transects sampled, *Chlorogalum* density was negatively correlated with steepness of slope (Pearson r = -0.25, p > 0.05), indicating that *Chlorogalum* occurred at higher density on slopes of low relief (i.e., ridges). *Chlorogalum* density was positively correlated with surface exposure of bedrock (r = 0.24, p > 0.05). Herb cover and surface bedrock cover within the study area were negatively correlated (r = -0.36, p > 0.01).

The results of our data analysis verified our field observations that the distribution of *Chlorogalum grandiflorum* in the Red Hills area is strongly associated with ridges and upper south-facing slopes, where soil erosion has formed localized patches of exposed bedrock characterized by reduced herb cover. The observed high density of *Chlorogalum* on these microsites may reflect a peculiar adaptation to rocky substrates. *Chlorogalum* is a geophyte (bulb-plant). Its large bulb is more deeply rooted than the rooting depth of most of the annual herbs with which it grows. We hypothesize that *Chlorogalum* may be responding to the increased soil moisture resulting from an increase in runoff channelization due to the presence of surface rock. Interstices in surface rocks may provide ideal germination and growth sites for *Chlorogalum*, with its rather large seeds and deeply rooted bulb (Jernstedt 1979). The numbers of competing herbs may be reduced due to lack of suitable germination sites.

An alternative hypothesis for the positive correlation of *Chlorogalum* density with surface bedrock involves the potential effects of competitive exclusion on more favorable sites by herbaceous species, particularly introduced annual grasses. Hoover (1940) cultivated large numbers of individuals of several *Chlorogalum* species over a period of several years. He noted that although vegetative reproduction (in the form of longitudinal splitting of the bulbs) was frequently seen in *Chlorogalum pomeridianum*, it is unusual in the other *Chlorogalum* species where reproduction was accomplished almost entirely by seeds. While mature *Chlorogalum* plants may be relatively insensitive to competition from annual herbs, the same cannot be said about *Chlorogalum* seedlings, which must face severe competition from annual grasses with similar canopy architecture.

Lomatium density was found to be a function of slope aspect (r = 049, p = 0.05, Batschelet 1981) independent of slope position, which is consistent with our field observations that this species is most frequent and achieves its highest density on middle and upper north-facing slopes. Although primarily found on slopes, this species also occurred in rocky, ephemeral drainages (particularly on southerly exposures). These observations tend to support the hypothesis that this taxa prefers sites with favorable moisture regimes.

SUMMARY AND CONCLUSIONS

Extensive reconnaissance surveys of the study area found *Chlorogalum grandiflorum* and *Lomatium congdonii* to be generally frequent and widespread throughout the study area on Delpiedra soils. Field observations indicated that both *Chlorogalum* and *Lomatium* are characterized by a patchy (non-random) distribution pattern on a localized scale, which would have required an exhaustive sampling to describe and map using qualitative methods. By combining the method of detailed reconnaissance survey with stratified random sampling of quadrats we were able to accurately define the distribution and density pattern of these widespread endemic species in the Red Hills Management Area.

LITERATURE CITED

Batschelet, E. 1981. Circular statistics in biology. Academic Press, New York.

BioSystems Analysis, Inc. 1984. Study of sensitive plant species of the BLM Red Hills Management Area, Tuolumne County, California. Unpublished report to the Bureau of Land Management, California State office, Sacramento. v + 60 p. + appendices.

Brown, J.H. 1984. On the relation between abundance and distribution of species. American Naturalist 124:255-279.

Clarke, L. 1960. Foothill fault system, western Sierra Nevada, California. Bulletin Geological Society of America 71:483-496.

Coulter, John M. and Joseph N. Rose. 1900. Monograph of the North American Umbelliferae. Cont. U.S. Nat. Herb. 7:1-256.

Gilmartin, Amy J. 1980. Numerical phenetic determination of the taxonomic status of *Asclepias giffordii*. Bull. Torrey Bot. Club 107:496-505.

Hoover, Robert F. 1938. New California plants. Leaf. W. Bot. 2:128-133.

Hoover, Robert F. 1940. A monograph of the genus *Chlorogalum*. Madroño 5:137-176.

Jernstedt, J.A. 1979. Studies of the anatomy, morphology, and taxonomy of *Chlorogalum* (Liliaceae). Ph.D. Dissertation, University of California, Davis.

Kershaw, Kenneth A. 1973. Quantitative and dynamic plant ecology (2nd Ed.). Elsevier Publ., Inc., New York. 308 p.

Kruckeberg, Arthur R. 1984. California serpentines: Flora, vegetation, geology, soils and management problems. University of California Press, Berkeley. 180 p.

Major, Jack. 1977. California climate in relation to vegetation. pp. 11-74 in Michael G. Barbour and Jack Major [Eds.], Terrestrial Vegetation of California. Wiley, New York.

Moldenke, Harold L. 1942. The known geographic distribution of the members of the Verbenaceae and Aviccenniaceae. Privately published [1st edition].

Morin, Nancy. 1983. Systematics of *Githopsis* (Campanulaceae). Syst. Bot. 8:436-468.

Rogers, Thomas H. 1966. Geologic Map of California: San Jose sheet. 1:250,000. California Division of Mines and Geology.

Smith, J.P., Jr. and R. York (eds.). 1984. Inventory of rare and endangered vascular plants of California, 3rd ed. Special Publication No. 1, California Native Plant Society, Berkeley. 174 p.

Sokal, R.R. and F.J. Rohlf. 1969. Biometry (2nd edition). Freeman, San Francisco.

Stone, C.O., B.H. Wickman, and W.R. Powell. 1977. Soil-vegetation map, southwest quarter of the Sonora quadrangle, Tuolumne County, California. U.S. Dept. of Agriculture, Forest Service, Pacific Southwest Forest and Range Experiment Station, Berkeley.

U.S. Dept. of the Interior, Bureau of Land Management. 1984. Red Hills Management Plan and Environmental Assessment Draft). Bakersfield District Office, California.

Predicting the Habitat Geography of Sensitive Plants and Community Types

Mona M. Myatt [1]

Abstract: The physical and hydrological components of the Southern California Edison Geographic Information System will be used with data from the California Natural Diversity Data Base linked to a new data system called the Vegetation Habitat Relationship System. The products will be predictive models displayed as maps which rank habitats for their potential to support rare, threatened, and endangered plants. These results will be validated and used to 1) determine sensitive areas to avoid, 2) locate areas of high potential species occurrence, 3) delimit clusters of habitats with great diversity, 4) show areas with good potential for the introduction of endangered plants, and 5) display areas where protection or elimination of multiple resource utilization is the best option.

Why is the second largest investor-owned electric utility in the United States interested in predicting the location of sensitive habitats and plants? There are two basic answers. First, because of a service territory of about 50,000 square miles and numerous facilities and activities that interface with an even larger geographic area, effects on the environment are ongoing, increasing and significant. Secondly, that environment, if not properly considered in the siting, construction, operation, and maintenance of facilities, can have a large negative effect on the economics of providing reliable electricity at a reasonable cost to Southern California Edison's 3.5 million customers who used 65 billion kilowatt hours of electricity in 1985. The goals of the research discussed in this paper, therefore, are: 1) the improvement of good land stewardship in the interest of the public good and 2) the reduction of land management costs.

Without the proper tools, however, avoiding or minimizing environmental impact while considering the cost of this action is not possible. To achieve these goals, the Environmental Research organization at Edison has developed a Land Rehabilitation Techniques project as part of its California Public Utilities Commission-approved Natural Resources Management Program. The research and techniques development plan were designed to help meet the land stewardship, regulatory, and cost needs imposed by active and varied land use effects. This program will develop and recommend land use patterns and land rehabilitation techniques to avoid negative impacts, if possible, or minimize impact effects and their repercussions where avoidance is not possible.

Impact avoidance is the method of choice. Improved siting by early consideration of siting limitations and long-term effects is first; however, the push to build new facilities is decreasing. Current building plans include the completion of already sited projects or the upgrading of existing structures. Also, the increasing reliance on alternative and renewable energy types has meant that siting is highly restricted by the availability of the "fuel" being used, e.g., capable geothermal fields or areas with high average wind speeds. Unless the affected resource is a federally protected species with very high public visibility and emotional appeal, these sites will be used as energy capacity need and economics dictate, even if environmental effects cannot be minimized on those sites. The public has shown very little awareness of the negative impacts of many alternative and renewable technologies; licensing is relatively less restrictive than for other technologies.

The second choice is management or mitigation of the impact. In some cases,

---

[1] Senior Research Scientist, System Planning and Research Department, Southern California Edison Company, Rosemead, CA.

neither avoidance nor management is possible. The third possibility is offsite species population or habitat improvement. This paper will emphasis how the prediction of habitat geography can improve siting, increase land management success at reduced cost, and locate offsite impact mitigation potential.

If a land user does not understand the relationship of species to their environment and cannot predict their location, there is a very low probability that the land user will be able to predict or manage the effects of using a particular parcel of land. If there is little understanding of the effects of land use at one site, no basis exists for quantifying or managing indirect, rippling or cumulative effects. Unfortunately, what knowledge exists in this area is both incomplete and unorganized. The research proposed will have the added benefit of systematically organizing habitat information which will, by clarifying what additional information and tools are needed, help direct further research efforts.

The first objective of impact avoidance has been considered in Edison's research plans since 1976. The pilot study of a program to develop an Edison service territory-wide geographic information system was initiated. This database was designed to include all regional variables that should be considered in the siting of any type of electric utility facility. Since that beginning, information has been mapped and computerized for 26,000 square miles of Southern California and Nevada. This system is known as the Southern California Edison Geographic Information System (SCE-GIS); it stores the data needed to focus the engineering, environmental, social and cost criteria that should be considered and optimized for a utility project (Myatt, 1984).

Because such variables as slope, aspect, elevation, geology, soils, geomorphology, vegetation community type, land use, and many other characteristics used to define habitat types were mapped over a very large region, the first tool to support habitat location prediction is in place. The concept used to map these factors is that of the "terrain unit" (see top half of table 1). A map of terrain units (fig. 1) shows the boundaries of homogeneous areas on the earth's surface. Each polygon corresponds to an area visible on an aerial photo with homogeneous color, pattern and texture. These resultant polygons are habitats classified to the

TABLE 1

INTEGRATED TERRAIN UNIT MAP VARIABLES
(Boundaries for the following integrated information; also see figure 1)

Slope
Surface Configuration
Surface Modifier
Landform
Geology (Geologic Age, Rock Type, Geologic Formation)
Soil (Survey, Family/Association, Series, Phase)
Land Use
Vegetation (Stature, Density, Cover Type, Special Note)
Field Validation Type

Other available data layers which might be useful in species/habitat/rehabilitation technique modeling are:

HYDROLOGY
SPECIAL PHYSICAL FEATURES
SPECIAL RESERVED AREAS
INFRASTRUCTURE
ADMINISTRATIVE UNITS

level of detail and for the types of variables which show up on the aerial photographs (usually stereo pairs). Other sources of information are used to supplement the photo interpretation and classify various characteristics of the units. Satellite sensors have been used in the same manner to define areas of the same energy reflectance or emission. These units are currently of less resolution and definability when compared to the terrain units resulting from aerial photo interpretation. Once habitats have been mapped over a region, prediction of what species occur in the habitat may be attempted.

While much is known about the relationship of species to microhabitat characteristics, understanding the fidelity of species to macrohabitat parameters, as mappable with the resolution available through a regional geographic information system, is often primitive. There are also many confounding variables which a geographic information system cannot consider. Even if more detailed habitat characteristics could be mapped, the cost would be prohibitive. Several other tools are available or could be developed to improve the probability of accurately predicting the species found in habitats mapped on a regional basis.

Figure 1

Terrain Unit Map for the Lanfair Valley, CA. U.S.G.S. Topographic Quadrangle. Each polygon bounds a relatively homogeneous area described for slope, surface configuration and texture, landform, geology, soil, land use, and vegetation. Each polygon is an area of equivalent response.

Use of the habitat maps can be greatly improved by overlaying information from maps showing the actual location of species or special habitats. The most complete and accepted source of this mapped data is the California Natural Diversity Data Base (CNDDB). Once known locations are correlated with habitat characteristics of the known location, habitats with the same characteristics can be quickly located throughout the area mapped with the SCE-GIS. Using these two tools together would produce rough predictions of which habitats could support selected sensitive species; however, unrecorded locations might mean that many habitats capable of supporting sensitive species would not be included in those selected by the model. Of course, occurrence of a species as located in the CNDDB and coincidently located within a terrain unit/habitat of the SCE-GIS only means that the microhabitat supporting that species occurred at least once in the terrain unit. The same microhabitat characteristics might not occur in other terrain units with the same description; these identically described terrain units could even be outside the species natural distributional range.

Other tools must be linked to the SCE-GIS and the CNDDB to make that combination more reliable. Two other tools are required. First vegetation or plant species habitat/community requirements or "preferences" need to be codified. There is much progress in this type of database as developed by the California State-Federal Interagency Committee for Resource Information and Classification Systems' Interagency Wildlife Task Group for all wildlife in the state. A second system known as the Southern California Wildlife Habitat Relationship Database is almost complete. These databases codify the species needs for general and special habitat characteristics and include species distribution maps within California. No similar system yet exists for plant species although much of the information is known. Preparing Vegetation Habitat Relationship Database (VHR) distribution maps used to limit the outer boundaries of all the terrain units to be considered by a predictive model is a large task.

Due to the length of time needed to develop a VHR and the possibility that much of the information it contains will never really be of a quantitative nature, a knowledge system may be developed to substitute for much of the VHR. A knowledge or "expert" system would contain heuristic knowledge about selection from the various alternatives as presented by varying terrain unit parameters. Other components are the inference mechanisms that could embody one or more problem solving strategies, an interface between the expert and the system to enter species specific knowledge, an explanation to track how the logic of a predictive model was applied, and a link with the databases on which predictions results are applied then displayed.

The interaction of these components, their interfaces and products is shown in figure 2. The results of developing and linking these tools only partially meet the goals of Edison's Land Rehabilitation Techniques research. The _potential_ location of sensitive habitats or species has been predicted. This information might be used to: 1) avoid siting through a habitat, if species occurrence was confirmed; 2) provide input to field sample planning, if locating sensitive species is a goal of that field effort; 3) quantify the amount of habitat of varying types; 4) relate habitat and species occurrence to development plans then display, for example, a disturbance or risk scenario affecting the future viability of a species or habibat; 5) locate high diversity areas to initiate protection measures; and 6) provide a basis for developing habitat-specific rehabilitation or revegetation plans.

Habitat-specific management has been practiced for some time; but a high percentage of the efforts have not been properly monitored to see if the methods used were successful over along time period. Often emphasis is placed only on an individual population of a sensitive species or a human-valued habitat. Consideration of the regional context of site management is only superficially addressed. More common habitats are often grouped in one or a few general types; little attempt is made to vary rehabilitation techniques or revegetation species composition even when examination of the habitats might show marked variation in the physical environment and associated species. A good example of this oversimplification is the usual treatment of creosote-dominated desert lands as being "all the same". In fact, due to their current disturbance recovery time, these habitats may be at a higher long term risk than many others currently protected. It is also important to be able to understand the significance of environmental interface. Currently held values and beliefs about the threat to species or

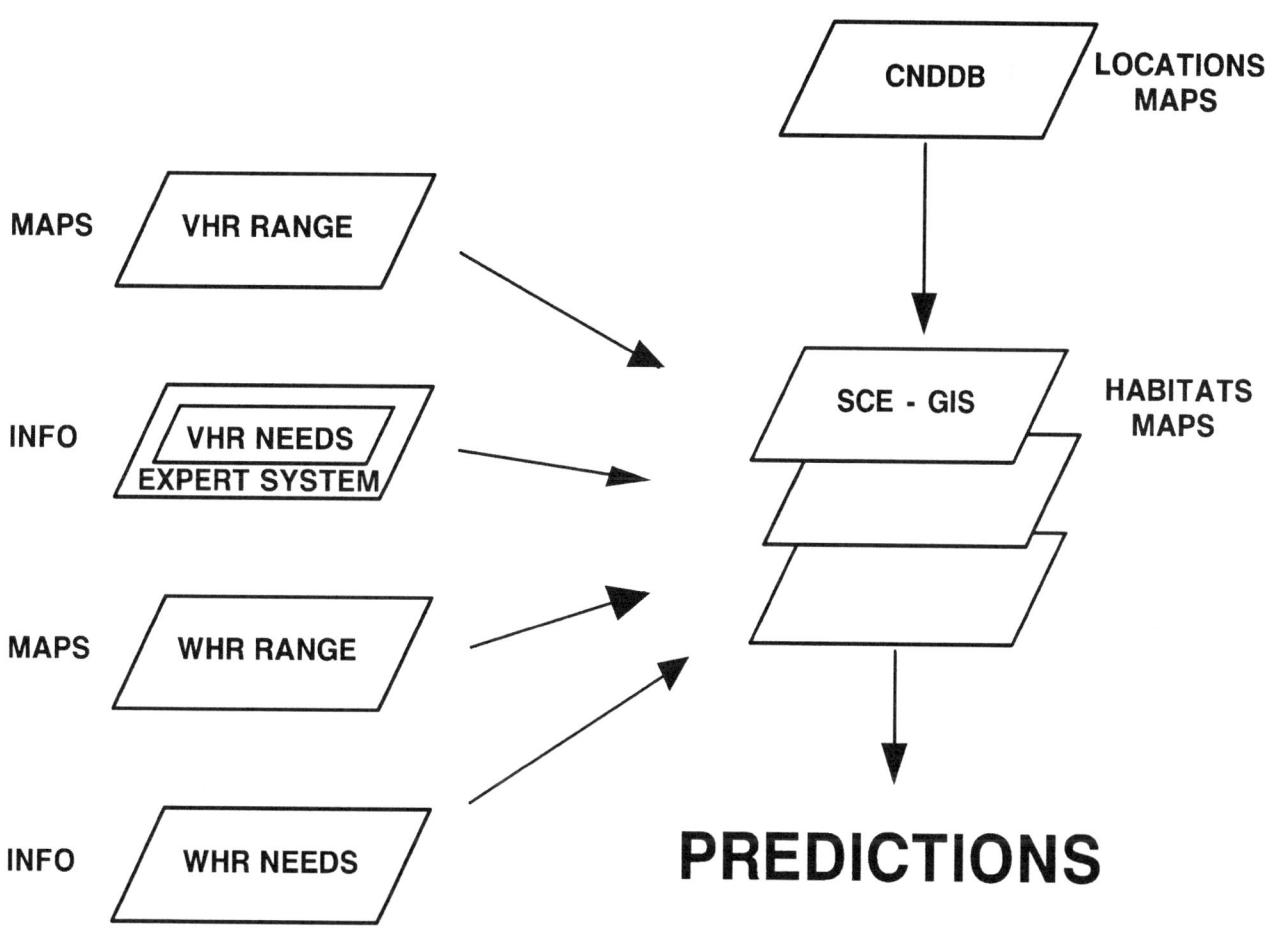

Figure 2

Flow Chart for All Linked Databases Used to Predict the Location of Sensitive Species and Habitats.

habitats may be revised if the impact patterns could be seen for a large area.

By using a set of tools that clarify the geographic relationships and extent of habitats and predict species occurrence over large land areas, a much more realistic quantification of ecosystem trends is available. If impact avoidance is not possible, rehabilitation can then be customized by habitat or management goal. The objectives of this step in the research design are to: 1) make land management plans meet legal obligations; 2) improve the success rate of techniques; 3) minimize need for land rehabilitation by reducing mechanical land disturbance; 4) use techniques that will not require ongoing maintenance; 5) prepare substrate to control erosion and encourage natural revegetation, 6) use native species; 7) introduce or expand populations of sensitive species to suitable habitat, especially if that area is protected or unlikely to be developed; and 8) coordinate efforts with resource management agencies.

The techniques are available, but they need to be matched to specific situations and management needs. Finally, these techniques and when/where to use them must be transferred to personnel responsible for implementation. Often these personnel are located in a properties management group or the operations groups. One way to transfer this information is shown in figure 3. This map of the Landfair Valley U.S. Geological Survey 15 minute quadrangle (1 inch = 62,500 feet) is a simple model of the data depicted in figure 1. The shadings represent different recommended land management techniques if a 220 kV transmission line were routed across this area. The black shading also suggests that these areas should be spanned by the line and may require the additional expense of culverted or bridged access roads. Not only is reduction of impact on the environment planned on this map, but also reduction of impact on the facility by the environment is addressed. With a good description of the techniques to be used, this format is one that is clear to operational personnel.

When impact avoidance or management are not possible, offset mitigation might be a viable alternative. This might mean enhancing habitats or populations in already protected areas or setting aside groups of habitats to be enhanced and protected. Again species and habitat occurrence models displayed in a map format are a very useful tool for suggesting appropriate locations for offsite mitigation. Much more effort is needed, however, in developing the legal framework for this type of mitigation. There is also a tendency to use offsite mitigation when onsite is possible but more expensive.

This tool will be years in development although certain components can be accessed now. The potential benefits are numerous, not only to Southern California Edison, but also to any developer or land manager in Southern California. A cooperative effort is desirable so that these tools and techniques can be developed in a timely, cost effective manner and widely subscribed to and supported by the user community. Better land stewardship for the public good would be the best possible result of such cooperation in development, use and support.

REFERENCES

Myatt, Mona M. Utility Siting Decisions Using a Geographic Information System. In: Proceedings of the Facility Siting and Routing 1984 Energy and Environment Symposium, Volume 1; 1984 April 15-18; Banff, Alberta, Canada. Ottawa, Ontario Canada: Publications Section, Environmental Protection Service, Environment Canada; 1984; 305-319.

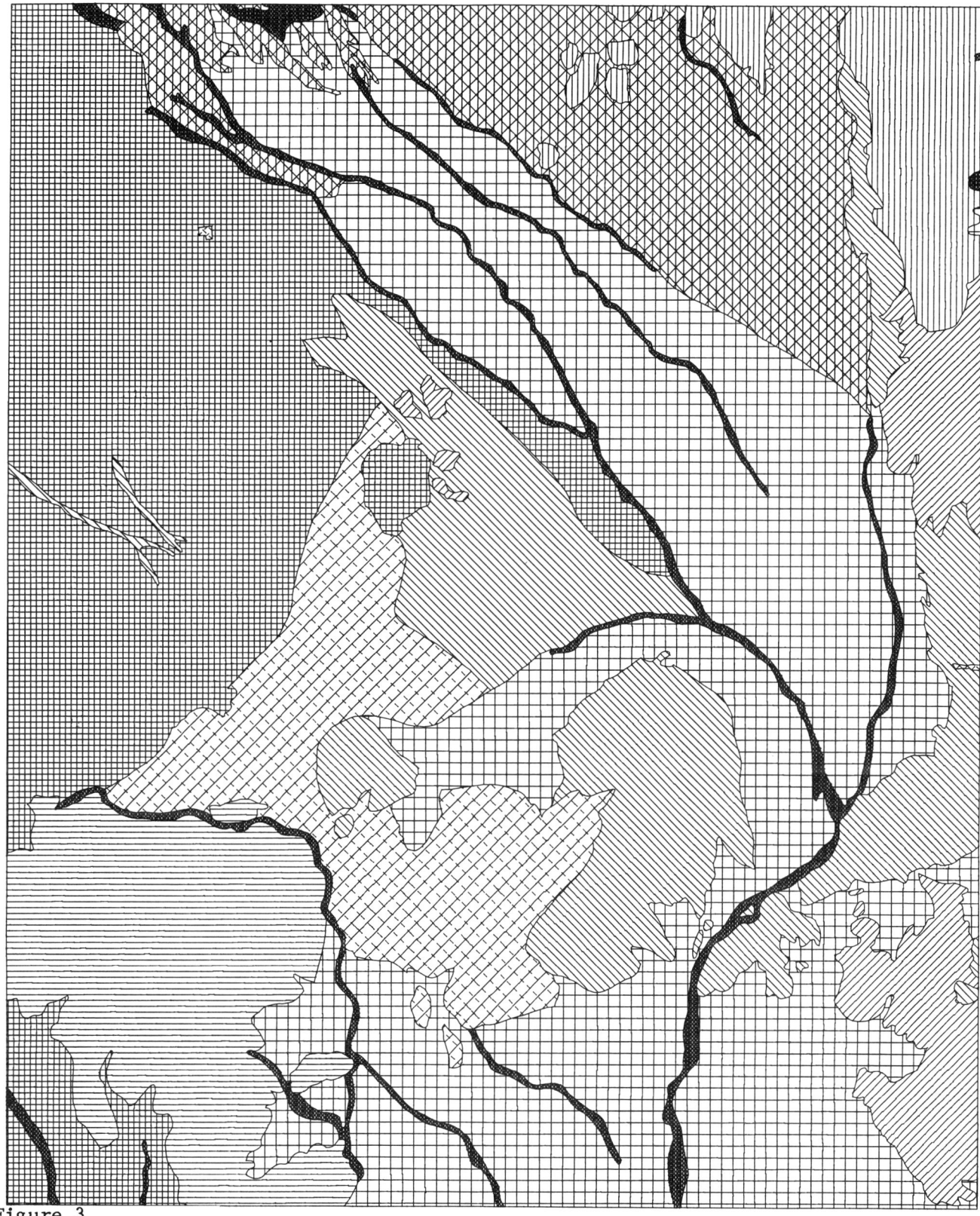

Figure 3

Map of Suggested Types of Rehabilitation Techniques for Lanfair Valley, CA. This model was developed only on the data presented in Figure 1. Other data from the SCE-GIS, listed on the bottom half of Table 1, and information from CNDDB, VHR, and WHR should also be used to develop this type of model as shown in Figure 2.

The California Natural Diversity Data Base— A Common Denominator

James R. Shevock,[1] *Linda L. Hennessy* [2]

Abstract: The California Natural Diversity Data Base (CNDDB) is a statewide manual and computerized inventory of locational information on rare and endangered species. CNDDB is the best centralized source for locational data on plants, animals, and natural communities in the state thereby eliminating the need for each agency or institution to establish and maintain separate information systems. Having all of the known locations for rare and endangered species in CNDDB provides the best opportunities for long-term conservation. Recognizing the rapid environmental change in California, it becomes essential that individuals concerned with species and habitat protection seek out new locations, update the status of known locations and see that these data get sent to CNDDB in a timely manner.

Individuals and various agencies involved in land-use planning and resource management have long desired to have a statewide system for documenting rare and endangered plant data. The CNDDB is a statewide manual and computerized inventory of locational information on rare elements (plants, animals, and natural biotic communities) of natural diversity. The basic unit of information is the documented location (=occurrence) of an element, or the "element occurrence." The species inventoried include officially listed (state and federal) endangered and threatened taxa, state listed rare plants, sensitive species and candidates (both state and federal), plus those species considered by the scientific community so limited in their distribution as to warrant inclusion in the inventory.

The CNDDB was initially established in 1979 with the signing of an agreement between the State of California, Department of Fish and Game and The Nature Conservancy. Since the inception of CNDDB more than 9,000 element occurrence records for approximately 700 special plant species have been entered into the computerized inventory. The CNDDB is staffed by botanists, biologists, ecologists, data managers and technicians who collect data on statewide distribution, occurrence condition, and known protection or conservation activities for these elements.

CNDDB is the best centralized repository for locational data on rare plants, animals, and natural communities in the state of California, thereby eliminating the need for other groups and agencies to fund, establish, and maintain similar information systems. While other organizations and individuals may excel in the collection of information on the population biology, ecology, and evolutionary biology (disciplines which are surely requisites for the recovery and management of endangered and threatened species), CNDDB is the best clearing house for the information which:

--provides knowledge of the conditions and quality of individual locations of rare species and

--provides, as a result of the mapping process on topographical maps, the ability to determine the spatial relationships between various element locations in order to identify and select areas containing groups of rare elements that may require priority for conservation action.

---

[1] Nongame Heritage Program, California Department of Fish and Game, 1416 Ninth St. Room 1225, Sacramento, CA. 95814. Currently with USDA-Forest Service, Fisheries and Wildlife Management, 630 Sansome St., San Francisco, CA. 94111.

[2] Nongame Heritage Program (address as above), currently with the California Department of Health Services, Toxic Substances Control Div., 4250 Power Inn Road, Sacramento, CA. 95826.

FUNCTIONS OF CNDDB

Information on rare plants comes to CNDDB through a variety of sources including the 7,000+ member California Native Plant Society, state and federal agency biologists, utility district biologists, environmental consultants, amateur botanists, university faculty and students, and interviews with botanical specialists. Actual plant occurrence data also comes to CNDDB in numerous forms. The most desirable format is a completely filled out 'California Native Species Field Survey Form' (Fig. 1). Other sources of locational information are obtained through phone conversations and written correspondence, maps, theses, herbarium specimens, and environmental impact reports and statements. These data are updated regularly as new information arrives at the CNDDB. The botany staff at CNDDB strives to keep all of the incoming data processed as it arrives either into the manual or computerized portion of the data base system depending on the rarity of the element, current threats and jeopardy to the species, and if it is currently listed as endangered or threatened under state and/or federal law.

Computer products available from CNDDB include textual reports and map overlays (showing the locations of elements) which can be generated at any map scale. The California legislation authorizing CNDDB requires that the data be available to users on a cost-reimbursement basis; that is, the data is free, and only the minimal cost of data retrieval is charger to the user. CNDDB products are available by either yearly subscription or on an as-needed basis. Most agencies and environmental consulting firms find the yearly subscription as the most cost-effective approach. Each subscription is tailored to the specific needs of the user. A detailed program booklet is available which further describes the various costs and products, and is free on request by writing to CNDDB, California Department of Fish and Game, 1416 Ninth St., Room 1225, Sacramento, CA. 95814 or call (916) 322-2493.

CNDDB METHODOLOGY

The methodology used by CNDDB was developed by The Nature Conservancy (TNC), a national non-profit organization whose primary function is the protection of natural diversity. Similar inventories based on TNC methodology are currently operating in 42 other states in the country. These programs are called 'Heritage Programs' and they basically utilize standard terminology, file structures, and information management methods to determine the total range and abundance of elements of natural diversity being inventoried. This methodology is centered around an 'element-based' inventory.

Site identification for conservation is based on an analysis of the priority ranks of elements and quality of their occurrences. The key to the CNDDB system is that it is designed to evaluate and compare between different elements of natural diversity regardless if they are plants, animals, or natural communities. This results in an objective biological assessment, so that site identification and resource conservation recommendations are based on the analysis of similar biological 'entities' rather than attempting to compare 'sites' having different attributes. Elements are 'ranked' (=prioritized) primarily on the number of occurrences, along with the geographic range, viability, jeopardy, and their taxonomic status. Sites which support highly ranked elements or where numerous elements occur are referred to as 'ensembles.' Such information is very valuable for various conservation organizations who utilize CNDDB records to locate the most significant areas of natural diversity that might require protection action. Ranking elements also ensures that subjectivity which may accompany the analysis and comparison of sites is kept to a minimum; that is, sites are identified based on BIOLOGICAL criteria rather than subjective SCENIC qualities.

USE OF CNDDB FOR SPECIES CONSERVATION

Agencies and individuals involved in land and resource planning use the inventory to identify species and natural areas which may be affected by proposed projects and land-use policy decisions. Federal agencies such as the U. S. Fish and Wildlife Service, U. S. Forest Service, Bureau of Land Management, National Park Service, and the Army Corps of Engineers use locational information on the state's rarest plants to identify and designate Special Interest Areas, Botanical Areas, Areas of Critical Environmental Concern (ACEC) etc. The inventory is also utilized in the preparation and review of environmental impact statements, highway plans, proposed land exchanges, section 404 wetland permits, national forest plans, and a host of other planning documents.

CALIFORNIA NATIVE SPECIES FIELD SURVEY FORM

OFFICE USE ONLY

Document Code _____ Quad Code _____
Index Code _____ Occurrence # _____
Copy Sent To _____

PLEASE ENTER ALL INFORMATION AVAILABLE TO YOU. USE THE BACK FOR COMMENTS IF NECESSARY. *PLEASE ATTACH OR DRAW A MAP ON BACK.*

Scientific name (no codes): _____

Reporter: _____ Phone: ( ) _____

Address: _____

Date of Field Work: ___ ___ –19___ County: _____ Collection? If yes, # _____ Mus./Herb _____
               day mo. yr.

Location: _____

Quad Name: _____ T ___ R ___ ¼ of ___ ¼ Sec ___
___ 7½' ___ 15' Elevation: _____ ft(m) T ___ R ___ ¼ of ___ ¼ Sec ___

Landowner/Manager _____

Species found? ___ Yes ___ No If not, reason: _____

Is this a new location record? ___ Yes ___ No ___ Unknown

Total # of Individuals = ___ Is this a subsequent visit? ___ Yes ___ No Compared to your last visit: ___ more ___ same ___ fewer

Phenology (plants): _____ # vegetative _____ # flowering _____ # fruiting

Population Age Structure (animals): _____ # adults _____ # juveniles _____ # others

Site Function for Species (animals): ___ breeding ___ foraging ___ wintering ___ roosting ___ denning ___ other

Habitat Description: (plant communities, dominants, associates, other rare spp., substrate/soils, aspect/slope)

Current Land Use/Visible Disturbances/Possible Threats

Overall Site Quality: ___ Excellent ___ Good ___ Fair ___ Poor
Comments:

Should/Could this site be protected? How?

Other comments:

DETERMINATION (Check one or more, fill in blanks)
___ Keyed in a site reference:
___ Compared with specimen housed at: _____
___ Compared with photo/drawing in: _____
___ By another person (name): _____
___ Other

OTHER KNOWLEDGEABLE INDIVIDUALS (Name/Address/Phone)

PHOTOGRAPHS (Check one or more)
Subject   Type
___ Plant/Animal   ___ Slide
___ Habitat   ___ Print
___ Diagnostic Feature
___ Other
May we obtain duplicates **at our cost?**
___ Yes ___ No

MAIL TO: NATURAL DIVERSITY DATA BASE, CALIFORNIA DEPARTMENT OF FISH AND GAME, 1416 NINTH ST., SACRAMENTO, CA 95814

California state agencies using the CNDDB inventory include the Department of Fish and Game (DFG), Department of Parks and Recreation, Department of Transportation, Department of Water Resources, and Energy Commission. The data from CNDDB is specifically used by DFG to identify those plants most in need of state listing as threatened or endangered, and to locate potential ecological reserves for these taxa.

Private conservation groups, developers, and local government entities also rely on CNDDB for the most up-to-date information available. The Nature Conservancy utilizes CNDDB for selection and design of their preserve system and to prioritize identified elements requiring more detailed field studies. Private developers use CNDDB on a daily basis for project analysis and planning. County and city governments and utility districts are using CNDDB data to plan zoning and activities within their respective jurisdictions. Frequent use of CNDDB products and data provides all parties with the same data set of information, and hopefully the most biologically sensitive areas in California can be accordingly conserved.

CONCLUSION

The average number of occurrences for each of California's special plants inventoried by CNDDB is phenomenally low (approximately 13 occurrences per taxon). Over 80 percent of the plant elements inventoried by CNDDB are endemic to California. Long-term conservation for these elements present one of the most complex land management issues requiring resolution. Recognizing the rapid environmental changes occurring in California, it is essential that organizations and individuals concerned with species conservation and protection not only become aware of the existence of CNDDB, but also use the bank of information which CNDDB provides. Since CNDDB is a dynamic and expanding data base inventory, it DEPENDS on your continued contributions of information so that the best and most up-to-date knowledge on the distribution, abundance, current jeopardy, threats, and conservation actions for these plant taxa can be made available to all persons working in natural resource conservation and land-use planning.

The Displacement of Native Plants by Exotics

Elizabeth McClintock [1]

Abstract: As agriculture and civilization developed man has selected many plants for his uses. At the same time nature plant areas have been greatly reduced, native plants displaced and the natural landscape changed. Because of these changes we now have, in addition to the native flora, 3 man-made aggregations of plants: agricultural, weedy and ornamental, each occupying its particular man-created habitat. Of the many useful plants introduced into California some have escaped from cultivation to become weeds. These fall into 3 groups depending on their degree of naturalization: urban, ruderal and weeds established in areas of native vegetation.

The flora of the earth was once made up only of native plants that have evolved around the world through millions of years of geological time. Today in many regions or counties of the world plants have been studied and accounts of them published as floras of those regions. But today if we want to use a local flora where do we find a region's native plants? Depending on where we live we may have to travel some distance to find them. The obvious reason for this is that large parts of the earth's surface have been converted to agricultural uses and developed into cities. Therefore, in place of only one group of plants, the original natives, we find that man has changed the plant cover or vegetation pattern in many parts of the earth and filled them with introduced, mostly exotic or alien plants that he has transported around the world, and that can be cultivated under the changes brought about by agriculture and urbanization. Thus in addition to its original native plants, any area may have also three man-selected aggregations of plants, two of which have been transported intentionally by man and are cultivated. First are the agricultural plants grown for food and other uses, and second are the ornamental plants grown to make urban areas more attractive. The third are the weeds that grow without cultivation in disturbed areas, in and around both agricultural lands and cities but always where they are not wanted; in addition they are disseminated through the many and varied activities of man, either intentionally or unintentionally.

Looking back thousands of years before agriculture and cities came into existence, when there were only native plants on earth, people were nomadic. They lived in simple structures and mostly moved with the seasons in search of food by hunting and gathering. But these simple ways of life changed with the beginnings of agriculture about 10,000 years ago. As time passed permanent settlements were established, civilizations evolved and through people's activities plants were taken from place to place, eventually from continent to continent. Inevitably populations increased and more and more land had to be used for agriculture and cities; therefore, the land occupied by native plants decreased. At the same time more and more plants were found to be economically useful. With this came the selection, development and establishment of the three aggregations of plants mentioned above: agricultural, weedy and ornamental. It should be emphasized that these man-selected plants are all native to some part of the world but as man takes them to a different area they displace the original native plants of that area. The introduction and establishment of large numbers of plants into a new area results in a change in the area's vegetation pattern from its original pattern to one modified by man.

In California the change from the original to the present day vegetation pattern, modified by man, began with the arrival of Father Junipero Serra in San Diego, May 1769, followed by the building of the chain of Spanish missions. During the mission period, 1769-1824, mission settlements covered only limited local areas and were widely scattered. About 16 exotic plant species were established during this period. During the following Mexican period, 1825-1848, another 63 were added and during the American pioneer settlement, 1849-1869, 55 more, making a total of 134. By 1925 this figure had increased to 292 according to Jepson in his manual of California plants.

---

[1] Research Associate, Department of Botany, University of California, Berkeley, CA.

Jepson's manual, the first complete flora of California, described 4,019 species. The figure of 292 introductions indicates that 7 percent of the flora was introduced. These introductions, which Jepson called alien immigrants and exotics, came from all continents but chiefly from the Mediterranean region. Some aliens proved to be very aggressive and produced countless numbers of individuals that according to their dominance or persistence have had an impact on native species in many cases displacing them. In some areas, according to Jepson, aliens constitute 50 to 75 percent of the total plant population. Jepson included in his flora only aliens that "are really established... and truly competitive." In other words those that are naturalized and capable of surviving in the natural conditions including lack of summer water. He did not include cultivated plants that are "transiently spontaneous or may persist only in a protected spot."

In 1959 Munz' flora of California was published, it was followed by a supplement in 1968. In both the flora and the supplement Munz described 6002 species including 975 introductions. According to these figures 16 percent of the flora is introduced, indicating that during the 40 years between the Jepson and Munz floras the percentage of introductions had more than doubled (from 7 to 16 percent). Certainly during those years the number of introductions would have increased, however, the number in the Munz flora appears to represent an "exaggerated increase" according to Howell in 1972. Munz, unlike Jepson, did not explain his criteria for the introductions that he included. Examination of the information that he gives for most of his introductions shows that some are not naturalized in the strict sense of the word. Many of these are plants that have been cultivated in gardens or as minor agricultural crops. They have moved from their original sites in urban areas but not completely away from the benefits that they derive from cultivation and civilization. Examples: Lentil (_Lens culinaris_), "an occasional escape...Ventura and San Francisco counties." Horseshoe geranium (_Pelargonium zonale_) "reported from Oceanside, Monterey, San Francisco." Such casual escapes are not naturalized and as such (at least by some) would not be considered part of the flora.

Raven in 1977 also commented on the large number of introductions included in the Munz flora. Raven calculated the introduced, and presumably naturalized, flora to consist of about 650 introductions, instead of the 975 included by Munz.

I believe that including casual introductions such as the lentil and pelargonium mentioned adds to the interest of the flora and accounts for plants that will be found. While some may be ephemeral, we should remember that the "waifs of today may become the weeds of tomorrow" (Howell 1972). Criteria should be defined, however, for placing introductions in the flora. They might be grouped into categories according to what I call--for lack of a better term--their degree of naturalization. This would indicate the impact that each has had on the native flora and those that are actually displacing native plants.

Using the distributional and other information given by Munz together with that in several local floras from different parts of the state, I selected about 300 introductions that originated as ornamentals and have escaped from their cultivated habitats to become what the California Native Plant Society (CNPS) has called escaped exotics. These 300, which show varying degrees of naturalization, I have divided into 3 groups. The first 2 groups include most of the 300, leaving a much smaller number for group 3. Groups similar to these might be used for all weedy introductions.

Group 1--Introductions persisting only locally within urban areas where they derive benefits from cultivation such as summer water. As garden weeds, many would not survive if separated from their cultivated situations. Not all, therefore, are actually naturalized, nor do they have an impact on native vegetation. Most do not increase greatly in numbers and do not cause problems in their urban areas. Examples:
English daisy (_Bellis perennis_) in lawns
Garden nasturtium (_Tropaeolum majus_)
Creeping buttercup (_Ranunculus repens_)

Group 2--Introductions that occupy disturbed habitats such as vacant lots, roadsides, areas around former habitations, old fields, pasturelands and other waste places or ruderal areas. These habitats I consider to be intermediate between the urban habitats of Group 1 and native plant areas of Group 3. Native plants were displaced by the original disturbances of the habitat areas into which these introductions have moved. In time some may make inroads into adjacent areas of native vegetation, however, for the most part they remain within their particular disturbed sites.
Examples:

Calla (*Zantedeschia aethiopica*)
Tree tobacco (*Nicotiana glauca*)
Ox-eye daisy (*Chrysanthemum leucanthemum*)
Feverfew (*Chrysanthemum parthenium*)

Group 3--Introductions that have moved farther afield than the above, invading areas of native vegetation where they have displaced native plants. California has more than a dozen aggressively invading escaped exotics. Each occurs in its particular kind of area in different parts of the state. Examples:
Tree of heaven (*Ailanthus altissima*)
Beach grass (*Ammophila arenaria*)
Ice plant (*Carpobrotus edulis*)
Giant reed grass (*Arundo donax*)
Andean pampas grass (*Cortederia jubata*)
French broom (*Cytisus monspessulanus*)
Scotch broom (*Cytisus scoparius*)
German ivy (*Senecio mikanioides*)
Salt cedar (*Tamarix ramosissima*)
Gorse (*Ulex europaeus*)
Purple periwinkle (*Vinca major*)

Because the escaped exotics listed in group 3 have invaded areas of native vegetation mostly adjacent or close to urban regions they are readily observed by many people. Their generally colorful flowers make them showy and attractive. For this reason the many people who observe them do not realize their invasive weedy nature. But those who have traveled up and down California during recent years have seen how greatly some of these have expanded their territories. Several years ago the California Native Plant Society realized that a number of escaped exotics were becoming a threat to the native flora. In order to better understand the impact of this group of introductions on native plants the society established the Escaped Exotics Committee in 1977. At this time the committee was charged with the preparation of a list of the ten most invasive and damaging escaped exotics. Several years later the committee was asked to extend its charge to include research and recommendations on control. The committee has considered the problems of control and possible eradication of these plants but solution of these problems is complicated. The use of biological control, chemical control and even control by mechanical means have been discussed. Each plant presents its particular problems that need further investigation before recommendations can be made.

One question sometimes asked is whether the State Department of Food and Agriculture could aid in the control of escaped exotics that invade native plant areas. According to Barbe (1985) this department is mandated by the legislature to "promote and protect the agricultural industry in the state." One threat to agriculture includes "noxious weeds." Weeds in California are evaluated and rated according to the damage they cause to agriculture. Non-agricultural weeds, including escaped exotics, are among those not damaging to agriculture. Therefore, the Department of Food and Agriculture is not responsible for controlling them. The Food and Agriculture Code, however, was recently amended by the legislature to include "plants in native stands...as part of the agricultural industry for the purpose of any law that provides for protection of the agricultural industry from pests." While this amendment gives the Food and Agriculture Department statutory authority to protect native plants from invasive weeds, funds are not likely to be available for this without allocations from the legislature for this purpose. The Escaped Exotic Committee, however, will continue to consider ways and means of control and eradication of these invasive weedy plants.

The displacement of native plants by escaped exotics is far less than that caused by the earlier introductions of annual grasses into California from the Mediterranean Region. These persistent weedy grasses have displaced native, largely perennial, grasses in the grasslands that comprise one of the largest areas of the state's natural vegetation. California grasslands occupy the Central Valley, valleys of the inner Coast Ranges, the north Coast Ranges and the southern California valleys. Several perennial bunchgrasses, once predominant in the original grasslands before European man arrived include:
California oatgrass (*Danthonia californica*)
Prairie Junegrass (*Koeleria cristata*)
Pine bluegrass (*Poa scabrella*)
California melic (*Melica californica*)
Purple stipa (*Stipa pulchra*)

Perennial bunchgrasses were largely displaced through agricultural practices during the last century. Not a single factor but several interacting factors contributed to this change in the composition of the state's grasslands. These included grazing by cattle and sheep, intensified by fluctuating weather cycles, disturbances of the land for various agricultural crops, and the greater competitive ability of the introduced annual grasses compared with native perennial grasses under these varying conditions.

Several introduced annual grasses include:
Wild oats (*Avena fatua*)
Ripgut brome (*Bromus mollis*)
Soft brome (*Bromus mollis*)
Medusa head (*Elymus caput-medusae*)
Wild barley (*Hordeum leporinum*)
Italian ryegrass (*Lolium multiflorum*)

In summary I want to say that California's large and diverse flora has approximately 6,000 species, according to Munz. Included in the flora are 975 introduced alien plants. These introductions, which have been distributed around the state during the 200 years of European and American settlement, have greatly changed both the landscape and the vegetation patterns. The areas most changed are the lowlands west of the high mountains. Throughout this north to south region of the state are areas of grassland, chaparral and brushland. With the development of agriculture and the building of cities in a large part of this region, native plants have been displaced by those plants introduced by man for his use from other parts of the temperate world. These extensive changes brought about by man's activities make it apparent that man has come to be the great distributor of plants in California and around the world as well.

REFERENCES

Barbe, Doug. The role of the California Department of Food and Agriculture. Fremontia 13 (2): 13-14; 1985 July.

Howell, John Thomas. A statistical estimate of Munz' Supplement to A California flora. Wasman J. Biol. 30 (1 & 2): 93-96; 1972 Spring and Fall.

Jepson, W. L. A manual of the flowering plants of California. Berkeley: Associated Students Store, University of California; 1925. 1238p.

Munz, P. A. A California flora. Berkeley: University of California Press; 1959 1681p. Supplement 1968. 224p.

Raven, P. H. The California flora. In: M. G. Barbour; Jack Major. Terrestrial Vegetation of California. New York: John Wiley & Sons; 1977: 109-137.

Feral Hog Management at Golden Gate National Recreation Area

Alison G. Willy [1]

Abstract: The Golden Gate National Recreation Area is working with Audubon Canyon Ranch and Point Reyes National Seashore on a plan to remove feral hogs (Sus scrofa) from southern and western Marin County, CA. Damage to resources is monitored photographically and by line transect surveys. Future plans include fencing off units of the region and continuing an intensive control effort over the next several years. The management goal is total eradication of the hogs from all park and reserve lands.

Marin County, CA, supports a rich diversity of habitats and scenic areas which have been set aside under the auspices of various land managing agencies. The county contains two national parks, a national monument, five state parks, several county open space areas, extensive watershed lands, and one private reserve. The agencies overseeing these lands share a complex alignment of boundaries and a host of resource management problems that are not contained by those boundaries.

The recent introduction of feral hogs (Sus scrofa) into southern Marin County has compounded the resource problems of the Marin County land managers. Feral hogs have been shown to have significant impacts on native flora (Bratton 1974, Bratton 1975), fauna (Graves 1984), and soils (Howe and Bratton 1976, Singer et al. 1984) in the eastern United States and there is a growing concern that they will have a similar impact on native systems in California.

A factor which makes feral hogs a difficult problem to control is the reproductive biology of the animal which allows them to reproduce at a remarkable rate. A handful of animals can turn into hundreds within just a few years, if the conditions are right in the environment. This makes the sheer presence of hogs a continual threat to the plant communities of Marin County and to locally rare species such as the calypso orchid (Calypso bulbosa).

The National Park Service has had feral hog problems historically in several park areas (Singer, 1981), where the hogs are degrading habitats that the parks were established to protect. Often the act of extirpating hogs from park lands requires a complex balance of research, politics, and funding.

The Golden Gate National Recreation Area (GGNRA), in southern Marin County has developed a plan using three techniques: trapping, hunting, and fencing. When used concurrently these techniques have proved effective in eliminating hogs from park lands. The plan dovetails with the objectives of Audubon Canyon Ranch[2] and a similar plan developed by Point Reyes National Seashore. Other agencies in Marin County are looking to GGNRA as a model to assess the effectiveness of an eradication plan as compared to one of control.

METHODS

Trapping

Several trap designs have been used in Marin County, but for ease of assembly and multicapture ability, corral traps have been selected for use at GGNRA. These traps are enclosures three to five meters in diameter and are made of lightweight, commercial livestock panels attached to steel posts. The advantages of these traps are that they are species specific, mobile, inexpensive, and effective. They are also more humane than poison or snares, which are not species specific

Terrain and accessability can add complications to trapping. Fox (1972) found that "The lack of hog activity in areas accessible to live trapping was one of the most limiting factors to live trapping success." Fox also found that the traps placed near recent hog activity were more successful than those placed

---

[1] Park Ranger, National Park Service, U. S. Department of Interior.

[2] A private reserve, within GGNRA.

near areas of older activity. Hone and O'Grady (1980) emphasized the importance of prebaiting a trap site and leaving the trap open for a few days to allow the hogs to feed in the trap without actually setting it. They recommended setting the trap after hogs have taken the bait from within and moving the trap if the hogs are not taking the bait. This method will be adopted at GGNRA as it is more likely to catch the wary individuals that would not enter a trap unless they had established a routine of feeding in it.

Not all feral hogs can be trapped. Trapping success depends on a resource being in limited supply. In areas where water is the limiting factor water traps can be built, but in Marin County year-round water supplies are abundant in the form of springs, creeks, and reservoirs. Abundant seasonal food of acorn mast in the fall and grasses in the spring restrict trapping as a viable form of control to the summer drought and the early winter.

Hunting

Feral hogs are a popular game animal, and land managers in Marin County continue to get requests from private hunters and hunting interest groups to come onto park lands to hunt. This apparently simple and economical solution has drawbacks; unsupervised hunting would conflict with park use by park visitors and endanger several susceptible nontarget species.

To insure an effective eradication program, GGNRA has hired a professional feral hog eradicator to hunt on park lands. This contract hunter has a Park Ranger, acting in the capacity of a California Department of Fish and Game Warden, in attendance during hunts.

GGNRA has had a hunting program since July, 1985, and thirty-eight hogs have been removed from approximately two thousand acres in the Bolinas Ridge area near Stinson Beach, which includes Audubon Canyon Ranch. In the spring of 1985 over one hundred acres of hog rooting were mapped by volunteers working in the Bolinas Ridge area. The following spring, less than five acres of rooting were recorded.

Two hunting styles have been used at GGNRA, both require the use of dogs that have been trained to hunt hogs exclusively. The early method used was with dogs that worked close to the hunter, had "hot" noses (i.e. able to detect a fresh trail), and caught the hog for the hunter to kill. As the population declined, there became a need to detect the farther ranging individuals and to eliminate the hogs that had learned to run for miles when they were pursued by dogs. At that time the method was changed and dogs were used that had "cold" noses (i.e. similar to bloodhounds, able to detect a cold trail). These dogs chased the hogs until they quit running and then waited for the hunter to catch up. As the dogs range farther, this method requires that they be equipped with radio transmitters so the hunter knows where they are at all times. In both hunting styles the dogs are trained not to bark and alert the hogs of their presence.

As soon as the first hog was taken at GGNRA, the "law of diminishing returns" went into effect. The first hogs caught cost the park thirty dollars per hog and the hunter could catch one or two in a day. The hogs were increasingly difficult to catch, and the last hog caught in the park cost over fifteen thousand dollars and took nine weeks to catch. These stunning figures have an element of artificiality that should be noted: Legal restrictions kept the hunter from hunting throughout the park, causing him to place a large amount of effort in a relatively small area.

One legal difficulty faced was how to deal with the hunting dogs from one agency when they crossed onto the property of another agency. The solution came in the form of a memorandum of understanding (a written agreement) that allows hunters from each agency to follow hogs onto the lands of neighboring agencies, if their dogs are in hot pursuit and provided the regulations of each agency are adhered to. The signing of this memorandum makes it possible for GGNRA to hunt the full extent of their lands.

Fencing

Fencing is the only known method of preventing an ingression of feral hogs once they have been extirpated from an area. The type of fence to be used at GGNRA is modelled after the one in use at Hawaii Volcanos National Park, where fences have been used to successfully keep feral hogs out of cleared areas for several years.

GGNRA lies in three separate portions which will comprise the individual fenced units: The Marin Headlands, Muir Woods National Monument, and the Bolinas Ridge area. Muir Woods National Monument has been chosen for the first installment of fence due to the ecological sensitivity of the area. After Muir Woods, the Bolinas Ridge area will be fenced and the Marin Headlands will follow.

It has been determined at GGNRA that the fenced units are of a manageable size. The Marin Headlands may be an exception to this and if so, the unit can be divided into two smaller units. Once there is an understanding of the size constraints of the fenced units locally, other managers in the county or state with similar habitat types can use that information in their own fencing programs.

The proposed fence will be thirty-two inches high, made of an eleven gauge woven hog-wire with nine gauge top and bottom for added strength and support. To prevent the hogs from rooting under the fence, a taught strand of barbed-wire will be run along the bottom of the fence and staked down between the fence posts. The reduced height of the fence will allow for easy crossing by both hikers and wildlife.

Building a fence in GGNRA has not been without its controversies. Visual impacts must be considered in sensitive areas like Muir Woods National Monument, which receives over one and a half million visitors every year. Preferred alignment places the fence in ecotonal areas and away from trails, where vegetation and distance will obscure it. Much of the preferred alignment will place the fence on Mount Tamalpias State Park property, above Muir Woods. GGNRA is working closely with the California Department of Parks and Recreation to allow for the preferred alignment.

Monitoring

To determine the effectiveness of the feral hog eradication program, monitoring will be done to detect the presence or absence of the hogs within each fenced unit. Monitoring will also demonstrate the magnitude of feral hog damage and the ecological recovery, or lack of recovery.

Belt transects have been placed within the proposed fenced units at GGNRA to determine the percent of the area that has been rooted and to establish the presence or absence of hog sign. Data from these transects will be collected periodically to plot the reduction of damage as the hogs are being removed and detect presence of any hogs left.

The Marin Headlands are a popular area for viewing spring wildflowers. Barrett (1978) found that brodiaea (Brodiaea spp.) bulbs are susceptible to feral hogs as they are a preferred food item. Two species of brodiaea (B pulchella and B. laxa) make notable displays in the Marin Headlands and will be monitored by photographs and line transects to establish base-line data on visual effects and species density.

Permanent quadrats have been established in each unit to determine species composition and vegetative response to rooting. Photo points will monitor visual changes as hog presence increases or decreases within the fenced units.

SUMMARY

GGNRA has developed a feral hog eradication plan which involves fencing three separate units and hunting and trapping within those units. The plan will be adopted by Point Reyes National Seashore and will include Audubon Canyon Ranch, a private reserve. GGNRA is working closely with other land managing agencies in Marin County, CA, to insure the effectiveness of their program.

REFERENCES

Barrett, Reginald H. The feral hog at Dye Creek Ranch, California. Hilgardia 46(9):282-355; 1978 December.

Bratton, Susan Power. The effect of the European Wild Boar (Sus scrofa) on the high-elevation vernal flora in Great Smoky Mountains National Park. Bull. Torrey Bot. Club. 101(4):198-206; 1974 July-August.

Bratton, Susan Power. The effect of the European wild boar, Sus scrofa, on gray beech forest in the Great Smoky Mountains. Ecology 56(6):1356-1366; Autumn 1975.

Fox, James Ronald. An evaluation of control techniques for the European wild boar (Sus scrofa) in the Great Smoky Mountains National Park of Tennessee. The University of Tennessee; 1972. 75 p. Thesis.

Graves, H. B. Behavior and ecology of the wild and feral swine (Sus scrofa). J. Anim. Sci. 58(2):482-492; 1984.

Hone, Jim; O'Grady, Jim. Feral pigs and their control. Division of Animal Production Bulletin A4.1.1. New South Wales Department of Agriculture. 1980.

Howe, Thomas D.; Bratton, Susan Power. Winter rooting activity of the European wild boar in the Great Smoky Mountains National Park. Castanea 41:256-264; 1976.

Singer, Francis J. Wild pig populations in the National Parks. Envt. Manage. 5(3):263-270; 1980.

Singer, Francis J.; Swank, Wayne T.; Clebsch, Edward E. C. Effects of wild pig rooting in a deciduous forest. J. Wildl. Manage. 48(2):464-473; 1984.

Management of Feral Pigs at Pinnacles National Monument: Why and How

Steven H. DeBenedetti [1]

Abstract: Feral pigs have inflicted acute and systemic impacts to ecosystems of several National Parks and now threaten the ecological integrity of Pinnacles National Monument. As mankind's influences upon the earth become more pervasive, the importance of protecting the scientific value of our National Parks and Monuments increases. Existing conditions and constraints at Pinnacles, and Park Service policy have dictated a management strategy dependent on fencing and localized, periodic hunting for control of feral pigs.

Pinnacles National Monument was established in 1908 for the protection of the scientific "curiosities" [values] of its rocks and caves (Proclamation No.796, January 16, 1908 {35. stat. 2197}). In 1916 the Organic act of the National Park Service (16 U.S.C. 1 et seq) drew together a National Park System and directed the Service in a mandate common to all units of the system, to conserve the scenery, objects, and wildlife therein. Simultaneously, the National Park Service was directed to provide for the use and enjoyment of each unit such that Park resources remain unimpaired for future generations. On October 20, 1976 Congress designated 13,270 acres at Pinnacles as Wilderness (Public Law 94-567 [90 stat. 2692]).

These directives have been augmented as scientific and ecological knowledge has progressed and been incorporated into park management philosophy. In its present form, wildland and wilderness parks and monuments seek to provide a setting where people can observe environmental processes interacting to shape ecosystems in dynamic fashion; uninfluenced, unencumbered and unenhanced by modern man's inputs. Today, the scientific value of Pinnacle National Monument remains a principal reason for her protection. The relatively unaltered ecosystems of the Monument provide a laboratory for recognizing and monitoring in environmental conditions. Such changes may be derived environmental or anthropogenic sources and their origins may be external of the Monument. The benefits of early detection of these changes may be of incalculable value to our economy and quality of life. Thus, as the earths natural areas become fewer and mankind's influence upon them more pervasive, protecting the scientific values of the nation's system of Parks and Monuments becomes increasingly important.

The colonization of park areas by non-native (exotic) plants and animals is clearly incongruent with the National Park Service goal of perpetuating naturally functioning ecosystems. Executive Order 11987 states that "Executive agencies shall, to the extent permitted by law, restrict the introduction of exotic species into the natural ecosystems on lands and waters which they own, lease, or hold for the purposes of administration; and, shall encourage the States, local governments, and private citizens to prevent the introduction of exotic species into natural ecosystems of the United States". The National Park Service recognizes that Pinnacles National Monument is not an entirely natural ecosystem (exotic plants dominate herbaceous vegetation; fire regimes have been altered by fire suppression; and adjacent lands have been domesticated). However, it is expressed goal to rectify these conditions to the fullest extent possible and protect the Monument from further deviation from this goal.

Consistent with this goal, we are developing a fire management program that will allow for the types of fires Monument ecosystems evolved with. We are beginning to learn how to facilitate the re-establishment of a number of native plant species. We are encouraged that native grass species may again become dominant. Feral pigs are a nonnative species inflicting widespread influences in the Monument (Thompson, 1984). These influences may complicate efforts to maintain and restore naturally functioning ecosystems as mandated by law.

---

[1] Resource Management Specialist, National Park Service, U.S. Department of the Interior, Pinnacles National Monument, Paicines, CA.

Feral pigs and their impacts, though relatively new to Pinnacles (sightings were incidental prior to 1975), have confronted other National Park Service natural areas for many years. Much of the following summary is taken from Bratton (1982). Bratton (1974, 1975) found that plant species diversity was reduced by at least 50 percent and total herbaceous cover diminished by as much as 98 percent in grey beech forest heavily utilized by feral pigs in Great Smoky Mountains National Park. Altering vegetation, either temporarily or permanently, has secondary impacts on the distribution of small mammal and amphibian species dependent on the vegetation for food and cover. Singer (1981), also working in Great Smoky Mountains, found that salamander, vole, and shrew population levels and distribution patterns were affected by rooting. He found that rooting reduced the amount of leaf litter on the ground by about 1/3 and increased its rate of decomposition. Singer also found that soil chemistry was affected by concentrated rooting (P, Mg, Mn, and Cu levels were reduced in all soil horizons). Feral pigs have been judged to compete with native wildlife species, such as deer, for fall mast crops. This competition may be critical in years of mast failure (Wood and Barrett, 1979).

Feral pigs have contributed to the extinction of flightless birds and endangering other ground nesting species in Hawaii (Baker, 1976). Pigs are also suspected to have contributed to the spread of avian diseases by creating aquatic habitats for non-native mosquito vectors in Hawaii and to the spread of root fungi which may be the cause for loss of native trees there (Baker, 1976). These examples illustrate the pig's potential for acute and systemic impacts to native ecosystems. It is our goal to minimize the potential for such influences at Pinnacles.

IMPACTS OF FERAL PIGS AT PINNACLES

The impacts of feral pigs upon the resources and facilities at Pinnacles are readily observable. Among the most common are:

1. Soil Disturbance

The coarse gravely and sandy loam soils common to Pinnacles (Laniger and Sheridan Soil Series) combine with steep slopes to form extremely erodable conditions (USDA, 1969). Disturbance of the soil by pigs causes rill formation which predisposes the soil to significant losses in the event of heavy rain. Soil disturbance has been observed in all major plant associations and is concentrated in riparian and oak-savannah vegetation (Thompson, 1984). Soil disturbance may also have secondary effects on water quality and aquatic habitats. These have not been quantified at Pinnacles.

2. Disturbance and Consumption of Native Plant Species

Many of the plants disturbed by rooting or that have their roots, rhizomes, or tubers consumed by pigs are native species. Among the notable plants being rooted are several native grass species (Stipa lepida, S. pulchra, Melica torreyana) and the acorns (and possibly seedlings) of the Valley Oak (Quercus lobata). The Valley Oak, though not officially listed as a threatened or endangered species, is subject to considerable attention in California. Its' range has shrunk from an estimated 775,000 acres in 1850 to less than 20,000 acres at present (Dutzi, 1979). Pinnacles possesses one of only two populations given National Park Service protection.

3. Competition With Native Wildlife

Fall mast, especially acorns, has been shown to be an important component of pig diets in the Pinnacles area (Pine and Gerdes, 1973; Barrett and Pine, 1980) as in other parts of California (Barrett, 1978). The availability of mast may be critical to the nutritional condition of deer during breeding and gestation, and to other acorn dependent species such as squirrels and black bear. It is very likely that competition from pigs has adverse impacts upon deer and other acorn dependent species in years of acorn shortages (Wood and Barrett,1979).

Feral pigs may prey on the eggs and young of ground nesting birds and opportunistically feed on wildlife species such as salamanders, frogs and turtles. Though unobserved, these influences are undoubtedly occurring.

4. Vectoring Disease

Feral pigs vector a number of diseases that can be transmitted to wildlife, domestic livestock, and to man. These include brucellosis, plague, leptospirosis, hog cholera, trichinosis, foot and mouth disease, African swine fever, and pseudorabies. In xeric areas such as Pinnacles, the probability of direct and indirect contact between feral pigs and native wildlife around water holes is substantial.

5. Path Formation

Pigs that regularly frequent specific areas create paths and trails. Where these routes intersect maintained Monument trails, they often do direct damage to the trail and lead visitors astray. When pig routes form between switchbacks, serious trail damage occurs.

6. Damage to Drainage Structures

Waterbars, trailside drainways, and roadside culverts are frequently excavated and clogged by rooting pigs. Damage to these structures may lead to serious and costly resource degradation.

Summarily, the presence of feral pigs in Pinnacles National Monument is incongruent with legal mandates and National Park Service management directives; and is resulting in measurable and potentially systemic impacts to Monument resources. The National Park Service must take all feasible steps to minimize the influence of pigs at Pinnacles.

THE MANAGEMENT STRATEGY

Any strategy employed to minimize the influence of feral pigs at Pinnacles must possess the following features:

1. A respect for the general management objectives and traditional values of the Monument.

2. A reasonable potential for success.

3. Employ a cost-effective method of achieving success.

4. Be protective of all or nearly all Monument land.

5. A monitoring system to evaluate the effectiveness of the program.

6. Opportunities for involvement by adjacent landowners and administrators, state agencies, and local governments.

7. Regular public information and interpretive efforts by the Park Service.

Existing conditions that define the scope of the feral pig management challenge at Pinnacles; present constraints upon the upon the management strategy employed; and assertions implicit in the final strategy are identified:

1. A portion of the boundary has been fenced to exclude trespass cattle. The Monument has long planned to extend this fence to its' entire perimeter.

2. Feral pigs are present inside and outside the Monument. Those outside serve as a constant repopulation reservoir.

3. While pigs are present in the Monument year-around, they are much more abundant in the fall. The Monument is not a year-around candy store.

4. Pig sign has been observed throughout the Monument.

5. Blacktail deer fawns and offspring of a limited number of other species may have difficulty crossing hog wire fences during their first few weeks of life. This is not viewed as a significant problem, as few would be abandoned in this situation. The fence may aid predators in their pursuit of young animals. Most age groups will have no problem passing through or jumping the fence. The small negative impact the fence may have on wildlife is more than balanced by its role in controlling the influence of pigs on Monument ecosystems.

6. Hog wire is utilized throughout Monterey and San Benito Counties in sheep and barley operations and is present on many cattle ranches.

7. The Monument's boundary is defined by section lines and possesses no topographic continuity.

8. Approximately 11.5 miles of the Monument's legal perimeter is bounded by public land administered by the Bureau of Land Management.

9. Approximately 12 miles of the Monument's legal perimeter is bound by private land.

10. Localized and periodic (rather than continuous and dispersed) hunting to remove pigs within the fence will be publicly acceptable and is consistent with National Park Service resource protection policy.

THE MANAGEMENT PROGRAM

The feral pig management program at Pinnacles is comprised of three concurrent activities: 1) providing a barrier to unencumbered access, 2) systematic removal, and 3) monitoring and evaluation. Each is detailed below.

1. <u>Reduce Access of Feral Pigs to the Monument.</u>

The National Park Service is establishing a barrier to the unimpaired entry of feral pigs by upgrading the Monument's long planned cattle fence to a pig deterrent fence. The pig fence consists of a 26 inch tall span of woven hog wire stretched between posts and securely anchored to the ground. Two strands of barbed wire are strung above the hog wire panel to exclude cattle and prevent them from crushing the hog panel. Upgrading the cattle fence is perceived to be an efficient and cost-effective action. For an expenditure about 25 percent greater than that of a cattle fence, a key element in a program to eliminate the influence of pigs on Monument resources can be erected. It is recognized that the fence will not be impervious to pigs. However, the number and location of entry points will be reduced to an essentially predictable array. This creates the opportunity for successful employment of secondary removal efforts such as fence traps, free standing traps, and localized direct reduction.

The fence will be erected along much or all of the Monument's legal or "negotiated" boundary in stages spanning four or five years. The Monument's legal boundary is defined by section lines that have no respect for topographic continuity or ecological units. Most are located midslope along steep gradients and in heavy brush. A fence is very difficult to build, maintain, and protect under these conditions and by bisecting small watersheds and ecological units, increases the probability of interfering with local ecological processes (soil stability, wildlife movements). A fence that deviates substantially within the Monument's legal boundary to take advantage of topography, does not allow for full protection of lands designated as Wilderness.

Whenever possible, a negotiated topographically coherent, ecologically sensitive, cost efficient, and effectively maintainable fence location is preferred. The Park Service strongly supports locating the fence on the perimeter of a 2,200 acre portion of a BLM wilderness study area where this land is contiguous to the Monument (NPS, 1984). A number of additional benefits will also result from this location. Firebreaks and tractor lines are present along much of this proposed boundary, making access for construction and maintenance easier and reducing the amount of clearing that needs to be done. By locating the fence on ridgelines defining the 2,200 acre area, impacts to the movement of wildlife will be minimized.

Adjacent private land the Monument's legal boundary will guide the fenceline. However, minor adjustments inward of the boundary will occur to take advantage of topographic features. Likewise, and subject to formal agreements or land exchanges, minor deviations onto private land may be negotiated.

2. <u>Systematic Removal of Pigs</u>

The fence will not completely eliminate pigs from the Monument. Pigs will enter through temporary breaks and in areas where effective fence maintenance is difficult (ephemeral stream channels). A number of pigs will be trapped inside the Monument as the fence is closed. However, as designed, the fence will significantly reduce pig movement (Hone and Atkinson, 1983).

An effective removal program is critical to achieving the basic objective. The presence of a fence that excludes hogs along all but a few predictable portions of its length, makes possible a manageable and affordable removal program that does not require wholesale compromise of traditional Monument values and visitor expectations. Given the prevailing dry summer conditions, the scarcity of water, a limited number of access points, and the fall mast period, pigs are concentrated into a small number of areas in the late summer and early fall. This occurrence is condusive to several removal techniques:

A. Trapping with disposal of live animals to California Department of Fish and Game or to other public land management agencies with any carcasses being donated to charitable organizations.

B. Localized hunting. This will probably be done by employee or contract hunters using dogs.

A combination of these and other techniques will be employed. Together, a fence and an annual removal program can reduce the impact of feral pigs at Pinnacles to marginal levels without seriously eroding traditional values.

3. <u>Monitoring and Maintenance</u>

It is essential that systematic monitoring and maintenance programs are developed to complement fence construction. Objectives of these programs include:

A. Regular inspection and repair of the fence.

B. Indentification of pig entry points.

C. Censusing pigs within the fence.

D. Determining the distribution of pigs within the fence.

This information will be utilized to formulate specific removal strategies.

CONCLUSION

Evidence demonstrates that the influences of feral pigs threaten the long term integrity of Monument ecosystems. It is clear that legal mandate and National Park Service policy direct managers to take action to eliminate this exotic species. The destructive influences of feral pigs can be reduced to minimal levels by constructing a perimeter fence and employing an annual removal program. Costs include a 25 percent surcharge to the cost of erecting a fence to eliminate trespass cattle; cyclic replacement; an estimated 1.0 person year in salary for maintenance and pig removal; and minor and largely mitigable increases to black-tail deer mortality. This latter cost may be offset by increased fawn to doe ratios and survival rates in the absence of competition from pigs for mast during critical years.

The principal benefit derived from the program is the opportunity to preserve for future generations, a setting where environmental processes continue to shape Pinnacles' ecosystems without the destructive influences of feral pigs. In preserving this opportunity, the value of Pinnacles as an indicator of subtle and pervasive ecological change resulting from external sources will be enhanced.

ACKNOWLEDGMENTS

I would like to thank Regionald Barrett, University of California, Berkeley; Charles van Riper III, David Graber, and Francis Jacot, National Park Service, United States Department of the Interior for their comments on an earlier version of the paper and Debbie Shields for her help in preparation of the manuscript.

REFERENCES CITED

Baker, J. K. The feral pig in Hawaii Volcanoes National Park. In: Linn, R. M., editor. Proceedings of the first conference on scientific research in the national parks, vol. 1; 1976 November 9-12; New Orleans, LA. National Park Service Transactions and Proceedings Series Number 5. Washington, D. C.: U. S. Department of the Interior; 1979; 365-367.

Barrett, R.H. The feral hog on Dye Creek Ranch, California. Hilgardia 46: 283-355; 1978

Barrett, R.H.; Pine, D.S. History and status of wild pigs, Sus scrofa, in San Benito County, California. California Fish and Game 67(2): 105-117; 1980.

Bratton, S.P. The effects of exotic species in nature preserves. Natural Areas Journal 3: 3-13; 1982.

Bratton, S.P. The effect of the European Wild Boar (Sus scrofa) on grey beech forest in the Great Smoky Mountains National Park. Ecol. 56: 1356-1366; 1975.

Bratton, S.P. The effect of the European Wild Boar (Sus scofra) on high-elevation vernal flora in the Great Smoky Mountain National Park. Bull. Torrey Bot. Club 101: 198-206; 1974.

Dutzi, E.J. Reduction of valley oak (Quercus lobata) range in the Sacramento Valley, California. Davis, CA: Univ. of California; 1979. Masters Thesis.

Griffin, J.R. Oak woodland. In: Barbour, M.G. and Major, J. eds. Terrestrial vegetation of California. New York: Wiley-Interscience; 1977: 385-415.

Hone, J.; Atkinson, B. Evaluation of fencing to control feral pig movement. Aust. Wildl. Res. 10: 499-505; 1983.

National Park Service. Resource Assessment. Bureau of Land Management Wilderness Study Areas. San Francisco, CA. National Park Service, Department of the Interior. 1984. On file, Pinnacles National Monument, Paicines, CA.

Pine, D.S.; Gerdes, G.L. Wild pigs in Monterey County, California. California Fish and Game 59(2): 126-137; 1973.

Singer, F.J. Wild pig populations in the National Parks. Environ. Manage. 5: 263-270; 1981.

Thompson, L. Wild pig rooting in Pinnacles National Monument. Unpublished draft supplied by author. 1984. On file, Pinnacles National Monument, Paicines, CA.

United States Department of Agriculture. Soil Survey San Benito County. Washington, D.C.: U.S. Government Printing Office; 1969: 111 p.

Wood, G.W.; Barrett, R.H. Status of wild pigs in the United States. The Wilderness Society Bulletin 7(4): 237-246; 1979.

Effects of Livestock Grazing on Two Rare Plant Species in the Red Hills, Tuolumne County, California

John W. Willoughby [1]

Abstract: The effects of grazing by domestic livestock on two rare perennial plant species were measured by means of paired transects in grazed and ungrazed areas. Populations of both species on public lands managed by the Bureau of Land Management in the Red Hills, Tuolumne County, California, have been adversely affected by grazing. Leaf lengths and leaf areas of Chlorogalum grandiflorum were much smaller in the grazed area. Herbivore utilization on this species ranged from 42 to 63 percent in the grazed area, compared to only 1 to 3 percent in the ungrazed area. Plants of Lomatium congdonii were much smaller, both in height and canopy cover, in the grazed area, and seed production was practically nonexistent under grazing. Vigor of established individuals, even when ungrazed in the year of measurement, was much lower in the grazed area. Alternatives to reduce or eliminate grazing impacts to the two rare plants are discussed, as is the need to closely monitor rare plant populations subjected to livestock grazing.

Multiple use land management agencies are often faced with the problem of balancing sometimes conflicting uses of public lands. Domestic livestock grazing is an authorized use on many millions of acres of public lands administered by the Bureau of Land Management (BLM) in the 16 Western States.

The BLM is charged with the responsibility of ensuring that authorized livestock grazing is managed in a manner consistent with land-use plans, multiple use, sustained yield, environmental values, economic, and other objectives (43 Code of Federal Regulations 4100.0-2, 1985). To properly manage livestock grazing within a grazing allotment (an area of land designated and managed for livestock grazing), the land manager must determine the number of livestock the allotment will support, the kind of livestock that may be grazed, and the period of the year such grazing use can be made. In making these determinations inventory and monitoring studies typically focus on the key forage plant species in the allotment. These key plant species are the most important forage species on the allotment and provide the bulk of the forage (Stoddart et al. 1975). On perennial rangelands, utilization (the percentage of the annual production of forage removed by animals throughout a grazing period) is measured on these key species to determine if proper use is being made or if the use is too heavy or light to meet management objectives (BLM 1984).

In the annual grasslands of the Central Valley and foothills of California, utilization is determined by measuring the amount of the current year's forage crop that remains at the time the next year's crop starts growth (Sampson et al. 1951). This residual, dead forage, often called mulch, can greatly influence the species composition and production the following year (Heady 1977; Bartolome et al. 1980). Again, however, the focus of studies is on the bulk of the forage available.

In grazing allotments supporting rare plant species it may be necessary to depart from the above approaches to ensure the rare plants are not adversely impacted by livestock grazing. It may be necessary to monitor the grazing use made on the rare plants instead of studying the use made on key species or on the plant biomass as a whole.

---

[1] Range Conservationist, Bureau of Land Management, U.S. Department of the Interior, Sacramento, CA.

The Red Hills, Tuolumne County, California, support populations of at least five rare plants (BioSystems Analysis 1984; Davilla et al. 1986; Farve 1986). Two of these plants, *Chlorogalum grandiflorum* Hoover (Red Hills soaproot) and *Lomatium congdonii* Coulter and Rose (Congdon's lomatium), though restricted to the serpentine-derived soils of the Red Hills, are rather widely distributed throughout the area. Part of their distribution in the Red Hills lies within a grazing allotment.

During the course of an earlier study (BioSystems Analysis 1984) it became apparent that the portions of the two species' populations within the allotment were being impacted by grazing. Grazed leaves of *Chlorogalum grandiflorum* appeared to be much more prevalent in grazed areas than in ungrazed areas. Grazing on *Lomatium congdonii* individuals was evident within the grazing allotment and plants seemed to be stunted in the grazed areas when compared to those in ungrazed areas. Also, reproductive structures of the latter species seemed to be much less common in grazed than in ungrazed areas. The study reported herein was initiated to verify and quantify these observations and draw conclusions relative to the management of livestock grazing in the Red Hills.

STUDY AREA

The Red Hills are located in western Tuolumne County, California, about 16 km southwest of Sonora and 1.6 km southwest of Chinese Camp (see Davilla et al. 1986, these proceedings, for a map of the Red Hills). The Bureau of Land Management administers 2873 hectares (7100 acres) of public lands in the Red Hills. About 1821 hectares (4500 acres) of public lands in the southeastern part of the Red Hills have been designated an Area of Critical Environmental Concern (ACEC) to protect rare plant resources, including *Chlorogalum grandiflorum* and *Lomatium congdonii* (BLM 1985b; Farve 1986). The management plan for the Red Hills (BLM 1985a) restricts cumulative surface disturbance in the ACEC to no more than 5 percent and closes the area to off-road vehicle activity.

A grazing allotment comprising 477 hectares (1178 acres) of public lands exists in the eastern portion of the ACEC. Cattle grazing within the allotment has been authorized since 1957. Although actual livestock use records are not available, grazing has likely occurred annually since that time. The present livestock forage allocation is 73 animal unit months (an animal unit month is the forage required to sustain one cow or its equivalent for a period of 1 month). The BLM grazing lease specifies no particular season of use (i.e., cattle grazing can occur at anytime during the year), but grazing normally occurs between April 1 and May 30 at the discretion of the livestock operator. The public lands in the allotment are currently unfenced from adjacent private lands, which are owned by the grazing lessee, but the BLM is in the process of building a fence to enclose the allotment's public lands.

The substrate of most of the Red Hills is serpentine. Two serpentine-derived soil series have been mapped in the Red Hills, the most important by far being the Delpiedra series (Stone et al. 1977). The Delpiedra series is predominant within and adjacent to the Red Hills grazing allotment.

The two rare plants that are the subject of this study are confined to the Delpiedra soil series. Both are perennial herbs whose above ground parts die following seed set. *Chlorogalum grandiflorum* is a bulbous lily with linear, strap-shaped leaves up to 45 cm in length and 2.2 cm in width. It produces an almost leafless, paniculate inflorescence up to 60 cm tall. Flowering takes place in May and June. *Lomatium congdonii*, a member of the carrot family, is an acaulescent plant growing from a tap root. It grows to a height of up to 35 cm including the leafless inflorescence, which may extend up to twice the height of the leaves. It flowers in late April and May.

Elevations where sample plots were located range from 350 m to 400 m. Vegetation consists of a woodland/shrubland complex composed almost entirely of *Pinus sabiniana* Douglas (digger pine) and *Ceanothus cuneatus* (Hooker) Nuttall (buck brush), forming a sparse to open woodland with an open shrub understory. The shrub interspaces are characterized by a diverse assemblage of annual and perennial grasses and forbs (BioSystems Analysis 1984).

Climate in the area is Mediterranean, with moist, mild winters and hot, rainless summers. Average rainfall for the study area is about 76 cm per year, with 85 to 90 percent falling between November and April. Winter temperatures average 8.3°C and range from -10.0°C to 27.8°C. Summer temperatures average 23.3°C and range from 1.7°C to 42.8°C.

The elevation of the study area supports only very ephemeral snow but is sufficient to avoid prolonged foggy periods typical of the Central Valley during winter months (BioSystems Analysis 1984).

METHODS

Effects of grazing on the two rare plants were measured by means of paired transects placed in and outside the Red Hills grazing allotment. A separate pair of transects was used for each of the rare plants. Transects were randomly located within areas predetermined to support the rare species in question. Chlorogalum grandiflorum occurs in highest densities on ridges (BioSystems Analysis 1984) so the paired transects were located on ridges inside and outside the allotment. Highest densities of Lomatium congdonii are on upper and middle north-facing slopes (ibid). Accordingly, paired transects were located on middle to upper north-facing slopes. Attempts were made to duplicate, insofar as possible, habitat attributes of the grazed and ungrazed sampling sites and to locate these sites as close to one another as possible and at similar elevations. The elevation of both Chlorogalum grandiflorum transects is 400 m; the ungrazed transect is 1.6 km west of the grazed transect. The elevation of the grazed Lomatium congdonii transect is 320 m; elevation of the ungrazed transect, located 1.3 km to the west, is 350 m.

Starting points and directions of the transects were randomly determined. Plant measurements were made in quadrats placed at alternating 1 m intervals on each side of the transects. Habitat attributes were estimated in square 0.25 m^2 quadrats. All other measurements were made using square 1 m^2 quadrats. The side of the transect on which the first quadrat was placed (and which then determined the placement of all succeeding quadrats in that transect) was determined randomly.

Beginning and ending points of all transects were marked permanently with rebar stakes. Measurements were first made on May 16 and 17, 1985. Those measurements determined to be valuable to the purposes of this study were repeated on May 21 and 22, 1986. Quadrat placement along the transects in 1986 duplicated that of 1985.

Three of the four transects were 15 m long. The ungrazed Lomatium congdonii transect was extended to 25 m because too few plants of that species were encountered in the first 15 m of the transect. Addition of the ten 1 m^2 quadrats added sufficient Lomatium congdonii individuals to obtain a relatively large sample size in determining per plant means. Comparison of per quadrat mean values on the first 15 m of the transect with those on the entire 25 m showed no significant differences. Thus, addition of the extra 10 m did not introduce bias into the study.

The following habitat attributes were measured (in 1985 only) for all transects: canopy cover of annual herbs, Pinus sabiniana, and Ceanothus cuneatus; and cover of bedrock, loose rock, bare ground, and litter. Percent cover was estimated using the Daubenmire cover scale (Daubenmire 1968). Cover classes were then converted to their midpoint percentages for analysis.

Rare plant variables measured varied by plant species. Variables measured and analyzed are listed below by species and year measured. Where necessary, method and scale of measurement are also given for each.

Chlorogalum grandiflorum

Number of plants/quadrat (1985 and 1986).
Number of grazed plants/quadrat (1985 and 1986). Includes all plants showing any evidence of grazing.
Number of leaves/quadrat (1985 and 1986).
Number of grazed leaves/quadrat (1985 and 1986).
Leaf length of all leaves encountered in transect (1985 and 1986). Measured to the nearest cm.
Leaf length of all ungrazed leaves in transect (1985 and 1986). Measured to the nearest cm.
Leaf width of all leaves in transect (1985). Widest part of leaf measured to the nearest 0.1 cm.
Leaf area of all leaves in transect (1985). Calculated by multiplying leaf length by leaf width.

Lomatium congdonii

Number of plants/quadrat (1985 and 1986).
Number of grazed plants/quadrat (1986). Includes all plants showing evidence of grazing.
Number of leaves/quadrat (1985).
Height including inflorescence of all plants in transect (1985 and 1986). Measured to the nearest cm.

Height excluding inflorescence of all plants in transect (1985 and 1986). Height to top of tallest leaf measured to the nearest cm, without manipulating leaves.

Canopy cover of all plants in transect (1985 and 1986). Total width of each plant to the nearest cm. Two diameters measured parallel to the two perpendicular quadrat lines and multiplied to derive area covered.

Number of plants with viable reproductive structures/transect.

Number of plants with no or aborted reproductive structures/transect.

Analysis of the measurements described above result in parameters of two types: 1) mean values/m^2 where the sample is comprised of the total quadrats in each transect; and 2) mean values per plant where the sample is comprised of the total plants in each transect. In the case of Lomatium congdonii the number of reproductive and nonreproductive individuals were tallied for each transect. The sample in this case is composed of the total plants in each transect; no mean values were derived but the resulting distribution can be tested against expected values.

In addition to the measurements described above, other variables were measured at the outset of the study but were dropped because it was soon obvious they would serve no use in this study. For example, the original study design called for several variables involving the reproductive structures of both species to be measured. Because of the almost complete absence of reproductive structures on grazed Lomatium congdonii individuals and the small number of reproductive Chlorogalum grandiflorum individuals on both grazed and ungrazed plots (especially on the former) these measurements were abandoned.

RESULTS

Chlorogalum grandiflorum

The grazed site differed significantly from the ungrazed site in four of the seven habitat attributes measured (Table 1). The grazed site had higher canopy cover of Pinus sabiniana, less exposed bedrock, more bare ground, and more litter. One of these differences, exposed bedrock, may influence the densities of Chlorogalum grandiflorum plants and leaves. BioSystems Analysis (1984) found a positive correlation between the amount of exposed bedrock and the density of the species. Densities of plants and

Table 1--Chlorogalum grandiflorum habitat attributes. Mean (X) percent cover and standard error (SE) of grazed and ungrazed areas in the Red Hills. Values for vegetation parameters represent percent canopy cover.

Parameter	G[1] (n=15)		UG[1] (n=15)		p[2]
	X	SE	X	SE	
Annual herbs	23.4	4.0	31.9	5.3	.250
Pinus sabiniana	12.5	5.3	0.0		.001*
Ceanothus cuneatus	4.6	4.1	13.1	6.6	.217
Bedrock	14.6	6.5	28.8	8.6	.042*
Loose rock	7.2	3.2	9.2	3.2	.200
Bare ground	13.1	3.5	5.5	2.5	.021*
Litter	35.0	4.5	14.8	2.8	.001*

[1] G=grazed; UG=ungrazed.
[2] From Mann-Whitney U tests comparing grazed and ungrazed transects. Significant differences indicated by *.

leaves, therefore, might be expected to be higher in the ungrazed site because of the greater bedrock. However, as shown in Table 2, there were no significant differences between the sites in plants/m^2, grazed plants/m^2, leaves/m^2, or grazed leaves/m^2.

Leaves of Chlorogalum grandiflorum plants were significantly shorter in the grazed area in both 1985 and 1986 (Table 3). When only ungrazed leaves are considered, lengths were significantly shorter in the grazed area only in 1986; only 10 leaves could be found in that year which had not been grazed to some extent. Leaf width in 1985 showed remarkable similarity in both grazed and ungrazed areas. For this reason it was not remeasured in 1986. Leaf area, calculated by multiplying mean leaf length by leaf width, was significantly smaller in the grazed area. Because leaf width was measured only in 1985 it was possible to calculate leaf area only for 1985.

Leaf lengths in the ungrazed area were significantly longer in 1986 than in 1985. Conversely, leaf lengths in the grazed area were shorter in 1986 than in 1985. Precipitation in the 1984-1985 growing season was 83 percent of normal (as measured at the Sonora Ranger Station, about 16 km to the north at an elevation of 526 m, just slightly higher than the elevations of the study area). Precipitation in the 1985-1986 growing season was 128 percent of normal. Longer leaf lengths in 1986 in the ungrazed area were likely the result of the greater

Table 2--*Chlorogalum grandiflorum* per quadrat means (X) and standard errors (SE) for each of four parameters in grazed and ungrazed areas in the Red Hills. All values based on n=15.

Year	Treatment[1]	Plants/m^2 X	SE	P[2]	Grazed plants/m^2 X	SE	P[2]	Leaves/m^2 X	SE	P[2]	Grazed leaves/m^2 X	SE	P[2]
1985	G	1.7	0.5		1.3	0.4		7.6	2.2		4.8	1.5	
	UG	1.9	1.0	.574	0.5	0.2	.065	10.3	5.6	.797	1.5	0.7	.051
1986	G	1.4	0.6		1.4	0.6		5.2	2.0		4.5	1.7	
	UG	2.5	1.0	.282	0.4	0.3	.159	11.5	4.5	.255	0.7	0.5	.119
P[2] between years													
G			.423			.656			.412			.492	
UG			.463			.674			.536			.557	

[1] G=grazed; UG=ungrazed.
[2] From Mann-Whitney U tests comparing grazed and ungrazed transects. Significant differences indicated by *.

Table 3--*Chlorogalum grandiflorum* per transect means (X) and standard errors (SE) for each of four parameters in grazed and ungrazed areas in the Red Hills.

Year	Treatment[1]	Leaf length (cm) X	SE	N[2]	P[3]	Leaf length (cm) ungrazed leaves only X	SE	N[2]	P[3]	Leaf width (cm) X	SE	N[2]	P[3]	Leaf area (cm^2) X	SE	N[2]	P[3]
1985	G	11.8	0.8	114		20.3	1.1	43		0.76	0.02	114		9.6	0.8	113	
	UG	21.7	0.5	155	<.001*	22.0	0.5	133	.282	0.75	0.02	155	.740	21.2	1.6	153	<.001*
1986	G	8.3	0.8	82		22.3	2.0	10		No data				No data			
	UG	28.7	0.8	171	<.001*	29.7	0.8	160	.022*	No data				No data			
P[3] between years																	
G			.006*				.480				----				----		
UG			<.001*				<.001*				----				----		

[1] G=grazed; UG=ungrazed.
[2] Sample size (number of leaves).
[3] From Mann-Whitney U tests comparing grazed and ungrazed transects. Significant differences indicated by *.

precipitation in the growing season preceding measurement. The shorter 1986 leaf lengths in the grazed area, however, are attributable to heavier grazing pressure, as borne out by data given below.

When confining analysis to ungrazed leaves only, leaf lengths in the grazed area are slightly longer in 1986, but this difference is not statistically significant. It is likely, however, that a larger sample size of ungrazed leaves (only 10 were encountered in 1986 in the ungrazed area) would have conformed to the pattern shown in the ungrazed area.

If one assumes that mean leaf area of ungrazed leaves in the grazed area reflects total annual production in the absence of grazing by herbivores, it is possible to calculate the utilization on *Chlorogalum grandiflorum* that had taken place by the time of each year's measurements. Leaf length can be used as a good substitute for leaf area because leaf widths are very uniform in the grazed and ungrazed areas. Therefore, comparison of leaf lengths alone will give a valid estimate of the amount of leaf area utilized. The formula for calculating utilization is:

$$\text{Utilization} = \frac{\left[\text{mean leaf length of ungrazed leaves}\right] - \left[\text{mean leaf length of all leaves}\right]}{\text{mean leaf length of ungrazed leaves}} \times 100\%$$

Utilization on <u>Chlorogalum grandiflorum</u> within the grazed area was 42 percent in 1985 and 63 percent in 1986. In the ungrazed area utilization was 1 percent in 1985 and 3 percent in 1986. Utilization values calculated in this manner will be conservative because additional grazing, by cattle and/or native herbivores, likely occurs after the time the measurements were taken. Actual utilization values, therefore, may be somewhat higher than those given here.

<u>Lomatium congdonii</u>

The grazed site differed significantly from the ungrazed site in three of the seven habitat attributes measured (Table 4). The grazed site had lower canopy cover of annual herbs and <u>Pinus sabiniana</u> and less exposed bedrock. The lower annual herb canopy cover at the grazed site was probably the result of heavier grazing pressure. Except for slope exposition, BioSystems Analysis (1984) did not find any correlation between site variables and variation in density of <u>Lomatium congdonii</u>. Thus, the habitat differences between the grazed and ungrazed sites would not appear to affect <u>Lomatium congdonii</u> densities. Any differences in densities are more likely the result of differential grazing pressure between the two sites.

Table 4--<u>Lomatium congdonii</u> habitat attributes. Mean ($\overline{X}$) percent cover and standard error (SE) of grazed and ungrazed areas in the Red Hills. Values for vegetation parameters represent percent canopy cover.

Parameter	G[1] (n=15)		UG[1] (n=25)		p[2]
	X	SE	X	SE	
Annual herbs	4.6	1.1	20.4	3.5	<.001*
<u>Pinus sabiniana</u>	1.0	0.4	0.0		.002*
<u>Ceanothus cuneatus</u>	2.4	1.3	12.6	4.7	.292
Bedrock	6.2	1.4	21.3	3.5	.001*
Loose rock	5.4	1.3	10.1	2.0	.109
Bare ground	32.8	5.9	24.2	3.7	.274
Litter	14.7	3.4	12.0	1.9	.678

[1] G=grazed; UG=ungrazed.
[2] From Mann-Whitney U tests comparing grazed and ungrazed transects. Significant differences indicated by *.

The grazed site differed significantly from the ungrazed site in all parameters relative to density of <u>Lomatium congdonii</u> (Table 5). The number of grazed plants/m^2 averaged 2.2/m^2 at the grazed site compared to 0/m^2 at the ungrazed site in 1986. Conversely, the total numbers of plants/m^2 and leaves/m^2 in both 1985 and 1986 were significantly higher at the grazed site.

Table 5--<u>Lomatium congdonii</u> per quadrat means (X) and standard errors (SE) for each of three parameters in grazed and ungrazed areas in the Red Hills.

Year	Treatment[1]	Plants/m^2				Grazed plants/m^2				Leaves/m^2			
		X	SE	N[2]	p[3]	X	SE	N[2]	p[3]	X	SE	N[2]	p[3]
1985	G	5.6	0.9	15		No data				18.2	3.4	15	
	UG	2.2	0.7	25	.001*	No data				8.0	2.7	25	.003*
1986	G	4.5	0.9	15		2.2	0.5	15		No data			
	UG	2.2	0.7	25	.012*	0.0			<.001*	No data			
p[3] between years													
	G		.404			----				----			
	UG		.876			----				----			

[1] G=grazed; UG=ungrazed.
[2] Sample size (number of 1m^2 quadrats).
[3] From Mann-Whitney U tests comparing grazed and ungrazed transects. Significant differences indicated by *.

Table 6--*Lomatium congdonii* per transect means (X) and standard errors (SE) for each of four parameters in grazed and ungrazed areas in the Red Hills.

Year	Treatment[1]	Height (cm)				Height (cm) excluding inflorescence				Height (cm) ungrazed plants only				Canopy cover (cm^2)			
		X	SE	N[2]	P[3]	X	SE	N[2]	P[3]	X	SE	N[2]	P[3]	X	SE	N[2]	P[3]
1985	G	5.2	0.2	84		5.2	0.2	84		No data				14.4	1.4	84	
	UG	16.4	0.8	56	<.001*	11.0	0.4	56	<.001*	No data				72.3	6.9	54	<.001*
1986	G	6.5	0.4	68		6.0	0.3	68		7.6	0.6	35		11.9	1.5	68	
	UG	19.9	1.1	56	<.001*	12.3	0.4	56	<.001*	19.9	1.1	56	<.001*	48.5	5.3	56	<.001*
P[3] between years																	
G		.032*				.052*				----				.036*			
UG		.031*				.024*				----				.003*			

[1] G=grazed; UG=ungrazed.
[2] Sample size (number of individuals).
[3] From Mann-Whitney U tests comparing grazed and ungrazed transects. Significant differences indicated by *.

Although densities of *Lomatium congdonii* were higher at the grazed site, the plants there were much smaller than those at the ungrazed site (Table 6). Height, height excluding inflorescence, height of ungrazed plants only, and canopy cover were all significantly greater at the ungrazed site for both years of measurement.

There were significant differences between years for most of the parameters measured. Plants were taller in 1986 at both grazed and ungrazed sites. Height excluding the inflorescence was greater in 1986 at the ungrazed site (means for the grazed site are very close to being significantly different at the 95 percent confidence level). Just as for *Chlorogalum grandiflorum*, the greater heights in 1986 are satisfactorily explained by the higher precipitation preceding the 1986 measurements. Not so easily explained are the differences in canopy cover between years. Whereas height increased in 1986, canopy cover decreased. Reasons for this are unclear but may be the result of plants responding to the greater precipitation by growing up more than out.

The number of reproductive individuals at grazed and ungrazed sites was significantly different for both years of measurement, as shown in Table 7. Reproductive *Lomatium congdonii* individuals were practically nonexistent at the grazed site in both years of measurement (0 and 3, respectively, for 1985 and 1986).

Table 7--Number of *Lomatium congdonii* individuals in either of two reproductive classes at grazed and ungrazed sites in the Red Hills.

Year	Treatment[1]	Number of individuals		P[2]
		Reproductive	Nonreproductive	
1985	G	0	84	
	UG	37	19	<.001*
1986	G	3	65	
	UG	31	25	<.001*

[1] G=grazed; UG=ungrazed.
[2] From chi-square analysis, with the Yates correction for continuity, of contingency table data. Significant differences from expected distributions are indicated by *.

Utilization on *Lomatium congdonii* cannot be satisfactorily calculated based on the data collected in this study. Because canopy cover was not separately measured for grazed and ungrazed plants, no determination of utilization based on this parameter is possible. Although the heights of ungrazed plants were recorded (in 1986 only), these heights include the inflorescences. In utilization studies the focus is normally on the quantity of green, photosynthetic tissue removed (Stoddart et al. 1975). Although peduncles doubtless contribute to photosynthesis, their contribution is not nearly as great as the leaves. Basing utilization on differences between the total heights of grazed and ungrazed plants would therefore not be valid, since the peduncles can contribute up to half of the total heights of the plants.

It is tempting to calculate utilization based on the differences between mean canopy cover of plants in the ungrazed and grazed areas. If the mean canopy cover of Lomatium congdonii in the ungrazed area is considered to represent the total production in the absence of grazing, comparison with the mean canopy cover of plants in the grazed area would yield a utilization value. For the grazed site utilization values of 75 and 80 percent, respectively, for 1985 and 1986 result from such a comparison.

As this study's data show, however, there is a major problem in calculating utilization in this way. Ungrazed plants are significantly shorter at the grazed site than plants at the ungrazed site. The same is undoubtedly true for canopy cover. Thus, it cannot be assumed that the canopy cover values for the ungrazed site would be attainable at the grazed site in the absence of grazing, at least--and this is critical--not in the same growing season. The reason this is true is probably related to reduced vigor of Lomatium congdonii brought about by repeated, heavy grazing pressure over a number of years.

What can be said, however, is that canopy cover of Lomatium congdonii at the grazed site was less than 25 percent of that at the ungrazed site for both years of measurement (19.9 percent and 24.5 percent, respectively, for 1985 and 1986). This difference is most probably the result of grazing, but site differences other than grazing may also play a role.

DISCUSSION

Grazing animals can affect plants in several ways. Defoliation can result in: 1) decreased aboveground biomass; 2) fewer stems; 3) less seed; 4) reduced height of leaves and stems; 5) decreased root biomass; 6) reduced root length; 7) decreased carbohydrate reserves; and 8) reduced vigor (Heady 1975). Such effects and their degree of severity is dependent upon the intensity, timing, and frequency of defoliation (Heady 1975; Stoddart et al. 1975). Grazing animals may determine the relative abundance of different species in a habitat because of preference for certain species over others (Harper 1977).

In addition to defoliation, grazing animals can affect plants, either directly or indirectly, in other ways. Trampling and deposition of feces, for example, can exert effects either on plants themselves or on soil properties, which in turn influence the growth of plants (Heady 1975).

The physiological ability of a plant to withstand grazing varies by species (Stoddart et al. 1975). Management objectives for key forage species typically call for utilization of no more than 50 percent (see Sampson 1952). These key species, however, are most often grasses. Grasses as a whole are more tolerant of grazing than are forbs, particularly in the seedling stage (Harper 1977). Thus, where a perennial forb is the key species being monitored, proper utilization might be less than 50 percent.

For rare plant species management objectives should call for utilization levels of much less than 50 percent and, depending on the degree of rarity and response to grazing, might prescribe no utilization, at least by livestock (utilization by native animals is much more difficult to control).

As this study has shown, utilization on Chlorogalum grandiflorum ranged from 42 percent in 1985 to 63 percent in 1986. No grazing induced differences in densities of individuals or leaves of this species were detected. In 1986 mean leaf length of ungrazed leaves was significantly smaller at the grazed site than at the ungrazed site suggesting that the vigor of Chlorogalum grandiflorum plants is reduced by these levels of utilization. No similar difference, however, was detected in 1985.

For Lomatium congdonii the effects of grazing are much more apparent. Plants at the grazed site are much smaller both in height and canopy cover. Of particular note is the fact that the mean height of ungrazed plants is significantly less at the grazed site. This strongly suggests greatly decreased vigor of Lomatium congdonii individuals from past, repeated heavy grazing.

The density of Lomatium congdonii is greater in the grazed area, but the plants are much smaller. This result is difficult to explain, particularly in light of the finding that practically no individuals in the grazed area are producing seed. Quite likely there is not a good correlation between size and age; the small plants in the grazed area may therefore be as old or older than much larger plants in the ungrazed area. Establishment may have taken place during a year in which livestock grazing pressure was less or nonexistent. The absence of actual livestock use records makes this impossible to assess.

It is clear that livestock grazing is adversely affecting Chlorogalum grandiflorum and Lomatium congdonii in the Red Hills. Grazing effects appear to be more severe on the latter species. This fact is important in prescribing proper management since Lomatium congdonii is also more rare, at least as far as distributional limits are concerned (see BioSystems Analysis 1984). Changes in livestock management are necessary. Alternatives include: 1) complete elimination of livestock grazing; 2) reduction in the amount of livestock use; 3) change in the season of livestock use; or 4) a combination of 2 and 3. If alternatives 2, 3, or 4 are implemented, temporary exclusion of livestock grazing for two or more years should first take place. This will enable existing plants to improve their vigor and allow the establishment of seedlings. It will also permit further study to determine the role of site factors other than grazing in the observed differences between parameters of grazed and ungrazed sites. More accurate measurements of potential production of the two rare plants within the grazing allotment should also be possible following several years of rest from grazing.

If grazing is to continue it will be necessary to establish a season of use, as opposed to the yearlong authorization now in force. To minimize grazing impacts on the two rare species the season of use should be earlier than the April-May use period currently practiced by the livestock operator. Annual grasses and forbs in the Red Hills begin drying about the end of April. Being perennials, the two rare plants remain green longer. It is likely, therefore, that livestock show a greater preference for the rare plants in May than in April. Thus, earlier grazing in March and April may reduce the grazing pressure on the rare plants. This, of course, remains to be demonstrated. It is vital, therefore, that any decision to continue grazing in the Red Hills be followed by intensive monitoring studies to answer such questions.

Resumption of grazing would also require careful monitoring of utilization on the rare plants. Because of its greater sensitivity to grazing, Lomatium congdonii should be treated as the key species. A management objective relative to the amount of allowable utilization on this key species would have to be established. Because of the rarity of the species allowable utilization should be low, perhaps 10 percent. Utilization could be determined by comparing canopy cover or volume (canopy cover multiplied by height without inflorescence) of plants protected from grazing by cages to that of plants subjected to grazing.

ACKNOWLEDGMENTS

I thank David M. Moore, Reynaud M. Farve, and Timothy J. Burke, all of the Bureau of Land Management, U.S. Department of the Interior, for contributing data and assisting in field measurements.

REFERENCES

Bartolome, James W.; Stroud, Michael C.; Heady, Harold F. Influence of natural mulch on forage production on differing California annual range sites. J. Range Management 33(1): 4-8, 1980 January.

BioSystems Analysis, Inc. Study of sensitive plant species on the BLM Red Hills Management Area, Tuolumne County, California. Administrative report prepared for U.S. Department of the Interior, Bureau of Land Management. 1984 December. 60 p. + appendices. On file at BLM California State Office.

BLM--Bureau of Land Management, U.S. Department of the Interior. Rangeland monitoring--utilization studies. Technical Reference 4400-3; 1984. 105 p.

BLM--Bureau of Land Management, U.S. Department of the Interior. Final Red Hills management plan and environmental assessment. BLM Bakersfield District, CA; 1985a February 12. 148 p. + appendix.

BLM--Bureau of Land Management, U.S. Department of the Interior. Designation of the Red Hills Area of Critical Environmental Concern, Bakersfield District, CA. Federal Register 50(138): 29276; 1985b July 18.

Daubenmire, Rexford F. Plant communities: A textbook of plant synecology. New York: Harper & Row; 1968. 300 p.

Davilla, William B.; Taylor, Dean W.; Stone, Doug R.; Willoughby, John W. Determining population sizes of narrowly endemic but locally common plants in the Red Hills, California. 1986 [These proceedings].

Farve, Reynaud. A management plan for rare plants in the Red Hills of Tuolumne County, California. 1986 [These proceedings].

Harper, John L. Population biology of plants. New York: Academic Press; 1977. 892 p.

Heady, Harold F. Rangeland management. New York: McGraw-Hill Book Co.; 1975. 460 p.

Heady, Harold F. Valley grassland. In: Barbour, Michael G.; Major, Jack. Terrestrial vegetation of California. New York: Wiley Interscience; 1977: 491-514.

Sampson, Arthur W. Range management: Principles and practices. New York: John Wiley & Sons; 1952. 570 p.

Sampson, Arthur W.; Chase, Agnes; Hendrick, Donald W. California grasslands and range forage grasses. CA Agricultural Exp. Stn. Bulletin 724; 1951. 130 p.

Stoddart, Laurence A.; Smith, Arthur D.; Box, Thadis A. Range management. 3d ed. New York: McGraw-Hill Book Co.; 1975. 532 p.

Stone, C.O.; Wickman, B.H.; Powell, W.R. Soil-vegetation map, southwest quarter of the Sonora quadrangle, Tuolumne County, California. Berkeley, CA: Pacific Southwest Forest and Range Experiment Station, Forest Service, U.S. Department of Agriculture; 1977.

Threats to San Diego Vernal Pools and a Case Study in Altered Pool Hydrology

Ellen T. Bauder [1]

Abstract: Three categories of threats to San Diego vernal pools are described: 1) clear threats with known impacts; 2) suspected threats with evidence of adverse impacts; and 3) possible threats with unknown, potentially catastrophic long term impacts. Data were collected in 1986 during a county-wide survey of remaining pools. One threat- altered pool hydrology- is discussed in detail. Research on year-to-year changes in micro distributions of vernal pool species gives evidence of higher frequencies of exotics in pools with low water holding capacity. Some pool species are favored by at least 2 weeks of standing water which eliminates exotics intolerant of inundation. Others require long periods of standing water to flourish.

Vernal pools are small temporary ponds which form above a hardpan or claypan layer with the winter rains and drain completely by spring. Within these pools a unique flora has developed, with species and even genera which occur nowhere else. Pools are found to the west of the Sierra Nevada in an area extending from southern Oregon through California and into northern Baja California. In San Diego County they are mostly on the coastal terraces, with a few patches of pools in small inland valleys.

Because they are situated on level mesa tops in a region dominated by mountains, hills, and canyons, most pools have been eliminated by construction related to the growing urbanization of San Diego County. Those not destroyed outright by construction face numerous threats.

These can be placed in three general groups: 1) clear threats with known impacts; 2) suspected threats with evidence of adverse impacts; and 3) possible threats with unknown- but potentially catastrophic- long term impacts.

THREATS

In the first category of threats are construction, vehicles, cattle grazing, dumping, and deep plowing. Secondly are altered hydrology (damming, draining), introduced species, and habitat fragmentation (edge effects).

The third category includes loss of genetic diversity and locally adapted genotypes, air and water pollution, changes in nutrient availability, habitat fragmentation with disruption of dispersal (whole organisms and genes) and changes in species' interactions (herbivory, competition, pollination), and altered nutrient cycling.

Clear Threats

A 1979 survey for the California Department of Fish and Game (Beauchamp 1979) estimated there once had been 28,595 acres of vernal pool habitat in San Diego County. Based on that figure only 8.7 per cent of the original habitat remained in March of 1979. In the spring of 1986 pools mapped in 1979 were resurveyed (Bauder 1986). The remaining habitat had dropped to 7.2 per cent of the original. Between summer of 1978 and spring of 1986, 27 per cent of the remaining San Diego County vernal pools were lost to construction projects, and within the next four years this will jump to well over 30 per cent. Of privately owned pools, 62 per cent were lost between 1978 and 1986, and 7 per cent of the publicly-owned pools were lost. Most of the pools lost were privately owned pools on the north central mesas between Miramar Road and the community of Penasquitos.

Beyond construction the greatest threat with known effects on vernal pools is vehicle damage. No pool grouping is exempt from their impact. Some vehicle damage is sheer vandalism; other results from ignorance and is inflicted in the course of legitimate activities including fire fighting, security patrols, military manoeuvers, and children´s play. In small groups on finger mesas all pools in the group may be vulnerable to vehicles using the dirt road crossing the mesa. Vehicles cause deep ruts, compact soil, bury seeds, crush plants, and alter pool hydrology. In

---

[1] PhD Candidate, San Diego State University/University of California, Davis, San Diego, CA.

many cases all but a few weedy species have been eliminated from pools repeatedly assaulted by vehicles. Hand in hand with vehicle damage is dumping. Trash buries or shades plants in addition to its unsightly appearance. Cattle may be thought of as biotic vehicles with impacts similar to their motorized counterparts. Deep plowing disrupts the hardpan and claypan soil layers so that water no longer ponds in the winter.

Suspected threats

Suspected threats include changes in pool hydrology, the introduction of exotic species, and edge effects. These threats are often interrelated. Pools normally hold water for three months or less and are totally dry at least five months of the year. Endemic pool species are adapted to this seasonal pattern of alternating drought and standing water. If the period of standing water is either reduced or increased, the invasion of exotic species is promoted. The percentage of the vegetation which is non-native is closely tied to length of inundation. In a year when pools fill to capacity one-third of the species just outside pools is non-native and less than 10 per cent of species are non-native in pool areas with over two months' inundation (fig. 1).

Hydrology can be altered in a variety of ways. If there is an abrupt grade change, erosion may allow water to spill out of pools. Cuts near pools cause water to flow out of the subsoil more quickly than it would otherwise. Plowing ruptures the hardpan or claypan layer reducing the water-holding capacity of the pools. Exotic herbs and grasses invade pools with reduced periods of standing water.

Water holding capacity of pools is often increased by the damming effect of roadways, runways, or earth moving and by soil compaction from vehicles. This can eliminate many pool species such as the mesa mint (Pogogyne abramsii J. T. Howell) which tolerate 2-3 months of inundation but have sharply increased mortality with longer inundation.[2] It also favors invasion by marsh and aquatic genera such as Typha (cattails) and Scirpus (bulrushes). A similar situation occurs with irrigation or sprinkler runoff which not only increase the amount of water, but eliminate the drought period to which vernal pool species are adapted.

Altered pool hydrology favors pool invasion by exotics. However, some introduced species have requirements similar to vernal pool plants. Two such species are brass buttons (Cotula coronopifolia L.) and beard grass (Polypogon monspeliensis Desf.). Once introduced to a pool, they spread rapidly and take up space which would otherwise be occupied by native vernal pool plants.

Fragmentation has resulted in many extremely small, isolated parcels. With small parcels, nearly all pools are edge pools. Edge pools are more vulnerable to disturbance by vehicles, dumping, altered hydrology, and invasion by exotics.

Possible Threats

Possible threats pose a real difficulty for land use planners and managers. Since these threats could destroy pools just as surely as construction, it is important to keep them in the forefront of discussions. Yet, evidence on fragmentation, genetics, and pollution is limited, and when available the information is often not generalizable to more than one ecosystem.

CASE STUDY IN ALTERED HYDROLOGY

A group of pools on the Miramar NAS offers insight into the effects of one important threat- altered pool hydrology. Cultivation in the 1940's disturbed some of these pools (the W series pools). Brush was removed from the surrounding area, mounds between pools leveled, and the land disced and planted to celery (Beauchamp pers. comm.). Along with less disturbed pools nearby (U and AA series), these pools have been part of a study begun in 1979 (Zedler et al.) and continued by the author up to the present. Data is presented from 2 of the highly disturbed pools and 10

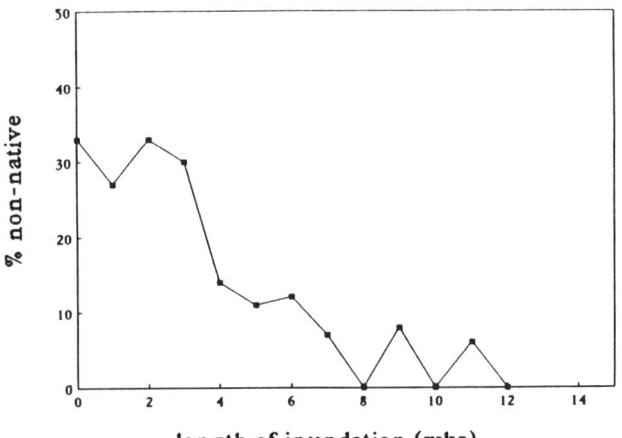

Figure 1. Mean per cent non-native species as a function of length of inundation in 1983 (n= 12 pools).

---
[2] Data on file, Ellen T. Bauder, San Diego State University, San Diego, CA.

relatively undisturbed pools which represent a wide range of depths and water holding capacities. Six years of presence and absence data have been collected for all vascular plant species in dm^2 quadrats along transects bisecting pools. Only quadrats below the overflow elevation, that is all quadrats which would be inundated when the pool is filled to capacity, are considered here.

Compared to less disturbed pools, the highly disturbed pools in any rainfall season hold water for fewer days total and for shorter periods at a time than do all but 2 of the relatively undisturbed pools.

Water depth measurements taken throughout five rainfall years indicate that in years when pools fill to maximum capacity the disturbed pools' water holding capacity is within the range of less disturbed pools but generally 2 to 6 weeks less. In drier than average years they have no standing water at all.

Whether disturbed or relatively undisturbed, pools with limited water-holding capacity have a higher percentage of quadrats with exotic herbs and grasses, particularly in years of low rainfall. If the 12 study pools are divided into two groups, those which did and did not hold water in 1984 (a record-setting dry year), the percentage of quadrats with cat's ear (_Hypochoeris glabra_ L.) is much higher in the 3 pools which held no water compared to the other 9 pools (fig. 2). The frequency of quadrats with cat's ear had a greater range in the pools with low water holding capacity than in the pools that hold some water even in dry years. In wet years the difference between the two groups is much less than in dry ones. This results from the low tolerance of exotic herbs to inundation. In a controlled experiment filaree (_Erodium botrys_ Bertol.) and cat's ear had substantial mortality after two weeks' inundation and total mortality after two months' inundation (table 1). Thus in wet years exotic herbs are excluded from most pools by their intolerance of inundation.

Typical vernal pool species also behave differently in pools with low water holding capacity compared to pools with longer periods of standing water. By looking at the average per cent frequency of 3 pool species over 6 years, it can be seen that the two disturbed pools are at the low end of the range of frequencies for the 12 pools studied (fig. 3). Pool species vary in their responses. In pools with a higher maximum period of inundation, _Downingia cuspidata_ has a higher average per cent frequency both in drier (1983-4) and wetter (1982-3) than average rainfall years (fig. 4). The regression equation is significant at p 0.01 (df 9, r^2=0.76 and 0.61, respectively) in both years. Myers (1975) found that germination of _Downingia_

cuspidata was favored by osmotic tension in the range of 0 to 1 bars. The soil in pools with low water holding capacity may not be saturated long enough for _Downingia cuspidata_ to germinate. Pools with a longer maximum period of inundation would have more habitat with saturated soil or standing water than pools with shorter maxima. Per cent frequency of mesa mint (fig. 5) and woolly marbles (_Psilocarphus brevissimus_ Nutt.) was not significantly correlated with maximum period of inundation.

These two species are sensitive to the per cent frequency of exotics. If the average per cent frequency of mesa mint over 6 years in each of 10 pools is plotted against the average per cent frequency of cat's ear, there is a negative correlation (fig. 6) with the regression line significant at p .05 (df= 9, r^2 =0.42). Results of experiments growing mesa mint in pots indicate that its survivorship and final dry weight are reduced when it is grown at high densities alone or with exotic herbs.[3] Exotic herbs and grasses typically grow at very high densities, except where water stands for two weeks or longer.

---

[3] Data on file, Ellen T. Bauder, San Diego State University, San Diego, CA.

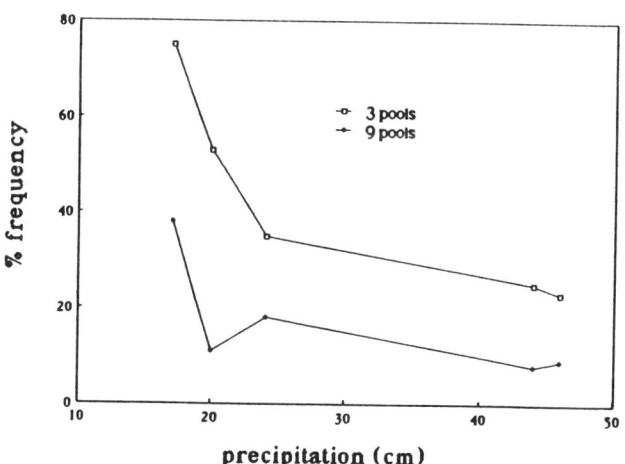

Figure 2. Mean per cent frequency of _Hypochoeris glabra_ as a function of yearly precipitation in 3 pools with low water holding capacity and 9 pools with higher water holding capacity.

Table 1. Survivorship (proportion of initial number) of 2 exotic species grown under different moisture conditions.

Species	Saturated Soil	Short Inundation[1]	Long Inundation[2]
Erodium botrys	.708	.208	.000
Hypochoeris glabra	.739	.281	.000

[1] Inundated at 10 cm depth for 3 weeks.

[2] Inundated at 10 cm depth for 8 weeks.

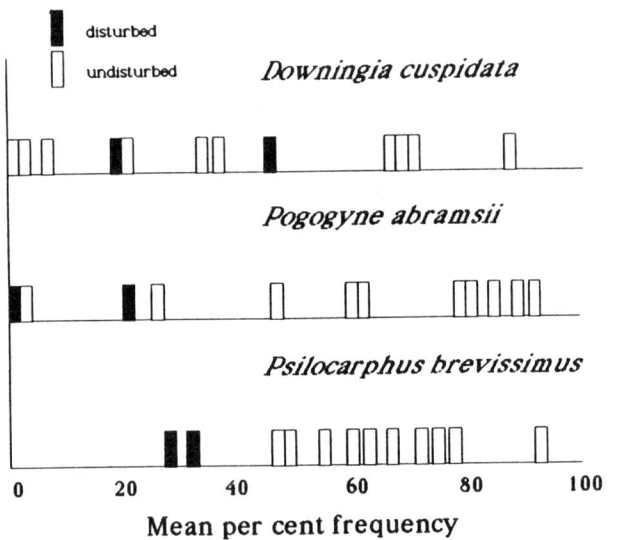

Figure 3. Range of mean per cent frequency occurrence of 3 pool species in 12 pools over 6 years.

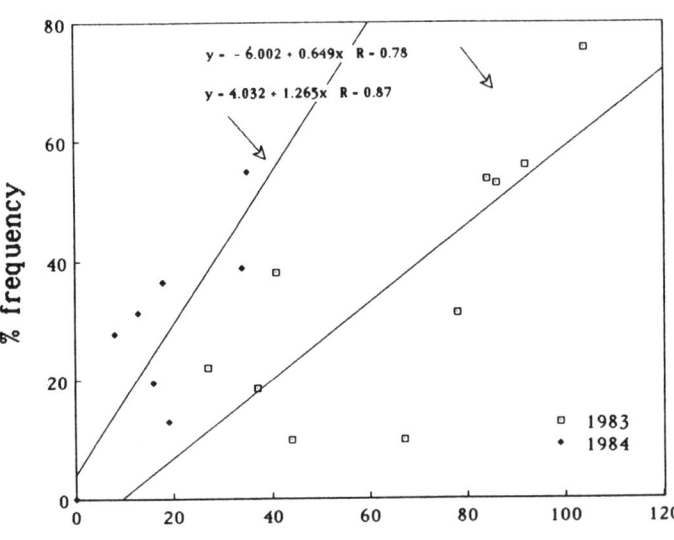

Figure 4. Mean per cent frequency of Downingia cuspidata versus maximum period of inundation in 10 pools during 1983 and 1984.

CONCLUSIONS

Over 90 per cent of estimated vernal pool habitat in San Diego County has been destroyed, primarily by construction. Other threats to San Diego vernal pools include a variety of disturbances and the many effects of habitat fragmentation. Disturbance and habitat fragmentation often result in altered pool hydrology.

Vernal pools with low water holding capacity have a higher percentage of quadrats with herbaceous exotic species than do pools with longer periods of standing water. This is most evident in dry years because the exotic species cannot tolerate two weeks or more of inundation. Endemic pool species are at higher frequencies in pools with longer inundation periods. Species such as Downingia cuspidata appear to require a lengthy period with saturated soil to germinate. Other pool species like Psilocarphus brevissimus and Pogogyne abramsii are more common in pools which simply hold water long enough to exclude exotics.

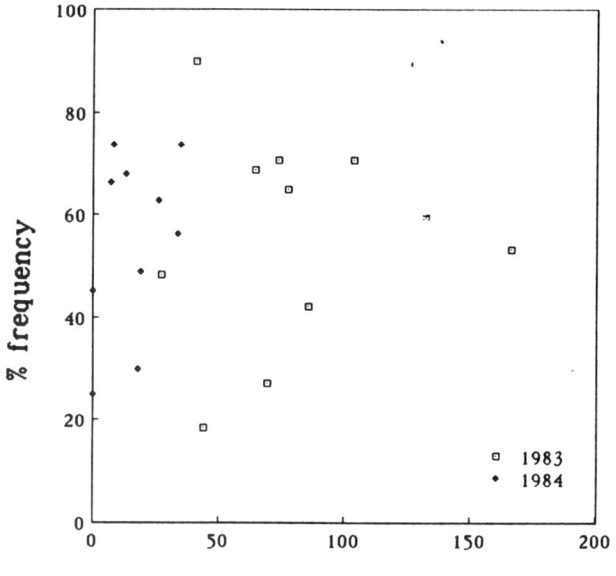

Figure 5. Mean per cent frequency of Pogogyne abramsii versus maximum period of inundation in 10 pools during 1983 and 1984. Correlation not significant and the slope of the regression line not significantly different from 0.

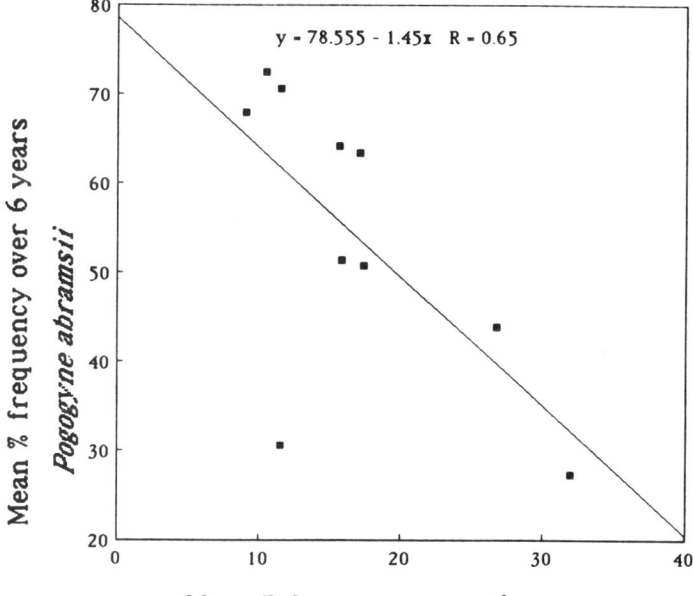

Figure 6. Mean per cent frequency of Pogogyne abramsii versus mean per cent frequency of Hypochoeris glabra in 10 pools over 6 years.

ACKNOWLEDGMENTS

I thank D. Clinton Bauder, University of California, San Diego, for assistance in field work and with graphics; Susan Cochrane, California Department of Fish and Game; and Paul H. Zedler, San Diego State University. The county-wide survey of vernal pools was supported by the Endangered Plant Project of the California Department of Fish and Game under Interagency Agreement No. C-1483. Research on vernal pools was supported by the Joint Doctoral Program in Ecology, San Diego State University/University of California, Davis.

REFERENCES

Bauder, Ellen T. San Diego vernal pools: recent and projected losses; their condition; and threats to their existence, 1979-1990. California Department of Fish and Game, Sacramento, CA; 1986.

Beauchamp, R. Mitchel. San Diego regional vernal pool survey. California Department of Fish and Game, Sacramento, CA; 1979.

Beauchamp, R. Mitchel, Pacific Southwest Biological Services, National City, CA. Telephone conversation. October 1986.

Myers, Ernest Linwood III. Seed germination of two vernal pool species: Downingia cuspidata and Plagiobothrys leptocladus. San Diego, CA: San Diego State University; 1975. 76 pp. M.S. Thesis.

Zedler, P. H., T. A. Ebert, M. L. Balko, M. L. Beauchamp. A survey of the vernal pools of Kearny Mesa, San Diego County. California Department of Transportation; 1979. 152 pp.

Cactus Collection Factors of Interest to Resource Managers

Peter S. Bennett, R. Roy Johnson, Michael R. Kunzmann [1]

Abstract: Theft of native plants is a growing problem for managers of public lands in the desert Southwest, often creating a serious threat to populations of rare species. Observations show that cactus removal is positively correlated with the time of flowering, growth form, proximity to vehicular access, and seclusion from observation. Detection of illegal plant collection can be enhanced by understanding the most popular kinds of plants and the most vulnerable sites. Botanists can assist the manager in planning for the prevention of cactus theft opportunities in populations of rare plants.

At a recent meeting of the Arizona Plant Recovery Team the status of the cactus, Neolloydia erectocentra var. acunensis was discussed. Since at least one known population is protected by inclusion within a national monument, several team members wanted to temporarily defer consideration of this cactus. The protection offered under a panoply of federal agencies and laws was mentioned. Federal preservation, limited to a relatively small number of species is shared principally by five agencies: Fish and Wildlife Service (FWS), National Marine Fisheries Service, U.S. Forest Service (USFS), Bureau of Land Management (BLM), and the National Park Service (NPS). At the meeting several team members discussed the NPS which has the strongest congressional mandate to "preserve and protect." However, congressional mandates are not enough to guarantee the protection of any species. For example, years ago at Organ Pipe Cactus National Monument a road was built through a small population of Neolloydia erectocentra. Bennett pointed out that in 1968 this population of rare cacti was mentioned in a visitor's guide book. As an aid to finding them, rings of white rock had been placed around several plants. Each ring of rocks was found to be empty. The rings aided in identifying the cactus locations, but they also aided in their subsequent removal by interested visitors. One team member had found it impossible to keep a display specimen of Echinocereus beside a nature trail in Grand Canyon National Park. The visitor removal of this cactus, even in daylight, was so frequent that the effort had to be abandoned.

---

[1] Research Scientist, Unit Leader, and Research Biologist, respectively, Cooperative Park Studies Unit/University of Arizona, National Park Service, U.S. Department of Interior, Tucson, AZ.

These examples raise several questions concerning cacti. How safe are cactus plants in National Park areas? Can any land managing agency really prevent removal of collectable species from its lands? What are some factors that contribute to cactus theft?

A grim picture of widespread theft was presented at a meeting in November, 1981. Persons from various land managing agencies, universities, conservation organizations, commercial growers and botanists, met in Tucson. Even then, the cactus and succulent business was a multi-million dollar industry. There was also a brisk illegal cactus trade. Today in Tucson alone, 20 out of 56 (36 percent) of the retail nurseries advertise a specialty in cactus sales and there are 3 large wholesale growers. These legitimate businesses feel they are being harmed by operations that illegally collect cacti from public lands in the United States and Mexico (Scannell, 1986). Illegally collected plants sell to hobyists for $5 to $500 each (Palermo, 1986). In addition, private citizens are known to collect cacti for their own use, often aided by cactus and succulent clubs which publish explicit directions for finding rare/endangered plant localities.

Catching and successfully prosecuting illegal plant collectors (both amateur and professional) is difficult. The Arizona Commission of Agriculture and Horticulture reports that it was able to issue only 20 citations in the course of 139 investigations while driving 71,770 miles. The courts usually regard cactus theft as a petty matter, and fines, if imposed at all, do not greatly exceed the cost of a commercially obtained plant.

Our paper presents the results of a feasibility survey which examines some of the factors that influence cactus theft. This study is designed to assist in protection, detection and enforcement by characterizing sites that are at great risk.

METHODS

Eight areas were selected for preliminary examination (Table 1). These lands are administered by the Bureau of Land Management, National Park Service, U.S. Fish and Wildlife Service, U.S. Forest Service, and the Maricopa County Parks and Recreation Department. In addition, areas near Pto. Peñasco, Sonora, Mexico and private land in the vicinity of the Chiricahua Mts. were examined. These sites represent a variety of vegetation types managed by widely differing methods. These lands hold in common the characteristic of having cacti that are freely accessible to the public in normal physical condition.

TABLE 1.
STUDY SITE DATA
(Vegetation according to Brown, 1982)

Site Name/Location	# Plots	Vegetation Association
Bureau of Land Management, (BLM)*, Harquahala Valley on west pediment of Big Horn Mountains	7	Ambrosia deltoidea - Cercidium microphyllum - Mixed Scrub Association (154.121)
Maricopa County, Cave Creek County Park, Cave Creek, Arizona (County Park)	8	Simmondsia chinensis - Mixed Scrub Association (154.123)
U.S. Fish and Wildlife Service (FWS)	5	Ambrosia deltoidea - Cereus gigantea - Mixed Scrub Association (154.122)
Black Mountain, 5 km north of Cholla Bay, Sonora, Mexico (Sonora)	4	Larrea divaricata - Mixed Scrub Association (154.125)
National Park Service: Organ Pipe Cactus National Monument at a, b) Quitobaquito, a) Pozo Nuevo, a) Alamo Canyon, a) Senita Basin, a) Puerto Blanco Mountains (NPS)	21	a) Paloverde - Mixed Cacti Series (154.12) and b) Saltbush Series (154.17)
Grand Canyon National Park (NPS)	3 24 total	Pinus edulis Association (122.412)
Private Land, Bernardino, Arizona (Private)	3	Mixed Grass - Mixed Scrub Association (142.221)
U.S. Forest Service (USFS) Chiricahua National Forest, Tex Canyon	3	Mixed Quercus - Association (123.311)

* Acronyms in parentheses are names used in the text to describe samples stratified by land ownership.

Plot selection for this study was not random and no claim is made that our findings are representative of the overall conditions prevailing on the lands where they are located. This unfunded study consisted of sites near work being done on other funded studies or places handy to the authors' vacation sites or where they had a few moments of free time. Sites were selected because of a combination of factors: (a) easy visibility from well traveled roads, (b) seclusion, (c) evidence of cactus digging, or (d) an abundance of cacti attractive to the public.

Within a plot, one or more 10 m square quadrats were laid out. Since destruction of quadrat corners by vandals is a concern, quadrats are oriented parallel to magnetic cardinal directions, ie. N-S, E-W. In heavily visited areas the location of the corners were determined by distances and bearings from fixed features such as large rocks. In seldom visited areas the corners were marked by bridge spikes. In either case plot corners could be accurately relocated.

Quadrats were gridded with string into 1 m squares to facilitate the drawing of a map which would indicate the location of all perennial plants. Each cactus was marked on this map and its species noted. Cacti with multiple heads (_Mammilaria thornberi_, _Echinocactus polycephalus_, etc.) were recorded according to the number of heads on the plant in addition to species and location. When plots were reread it was a simple matter to relocate the cacti by their spatial relationship to nearby perennial vegetation. Special attention was given to signs that might indicate the mode of removal. Where the heel (bottom of the stem) remained, the plant was judged to have been removed by rodents or lagomorphs and was not counted as poached. If the plant had been entirely removed, with appropriate surface indicators, it was counted as poached. The quadrats were reread annually during various months of the year. The flowering or fruiting condition of each species was noted when the quadrats were read.

The distance from the center of each plot to the nearest frequented route (usually roads but in some cases trails) was measured. This distance in meters became the "access" variable. A low access number indicates close proximity to a route. A high number indicates that the site is more remote.

RESULTS

The number of cacti originally present, the number remaining, the percentage removed, the access (m) and the seclusion (coded 1 to 3) measurements were analysed by Tukey's Honest Significant Difference (HSD) with the plots stratified by land ownership. Because the number of plots measured were not equal in the stratified samples, analysis of variance was tested by Bartlett's Chi-square test. Tukey's HSD was calculated using the harmonic mean with the level of confidence set at 95 percent (Sokal & Rolf, 1981).

The mean number of cacti per plot are not significantly different among the samples stratified by land ownership (Bartlett's Chi-square p=0.138) and the variance within the plots is relatively high. These data suggest that the mean number of cacti originally present are distributed in a continuum between the stratified samples and that inferences drawn about the number or percentages of cacti removed can have statistical significance. Similarly, seclusion is not significantly different among stratified samples (Bartlett's Chi-square p=0.934).

Unfortunately, access (the number of meters from a traveled visitor access route) shows significant differences when the data are stratified by land ownership (Bartlett's Chi-square = 0.001). This relict of casual sample design prevents comparison of data stratified by land ownership if access data is considered. This is so because all of the plots stratified by ownership do not have access data whose differences are due to chance alone as is the case with the number of cacti originally present and with site seclusion.

Each site was assigned a seclusion score. Sites were called highly secluded when situated so that a poacher would have 45 sec. or more warning of the approach of another person and are scored with a value 3. Sites with medium seclusion were those where 20 to 10 sec. warning are possible and are scored with a value of 2. Sites with poor seclusion are those were less than 10 seconds warning , making it difficult to escape detection and are scored 1. Seclusion is coded 1 to 3 with 1 being sites with the least warning and 3 the most.

The balance of stratified measurements taken (number of cacti removed and percentage of cacti removed) are significantly different when analysed by Bartlett's Chi-square and Tukey's tests with samples stratified by ownership. Since the number of cacti removed and the percentage of cacti removed are self correlating, (r=0.909) the percentage variable will be used in this paper.

Percentage removed means are significantly different when stratified by land ownership (Chi-squarred p=0.002). Tukey's test divides the data into two groups. The first group (BLM, County Park, FWS, Sonora, Private, and USFS) have low means. The second group (Sonora, NPS, and USFS) have high means. The Sonora and USFS means are part of both groups and are intermediate (Figure 1). The NPS mean is the only one that is a member of the second group but not the first and is, therefore, significantly different. Mean percent cacti removed on NPS land (23.8 percent) compared by Student's t test with the mean for all other agencies pooled (6.4 percent) shows a difference that is highly significant (t=4.045, d.f.=52, p=0.00009). That is, the percentage of cacti stolen from National Parks and Monuments is significantly greater than from other land managing agencies.

Pooled statistics for 5 variables on all 54 plots representing all land ownerships show poor correlations with the exception of the number of cacti and the percentage of cacti removed (R = 0.717 overall).

Correlation Matrix
All Variables On All Plots

	Pct-Rem.	Acc.	Secl.	N-Rem.
No. Orig.	-0.086	-0.271	0.080	-0.239
Pct-Removed		-0.530	0.668	0.909
Access			-0.516	-0.554
Seclusion				0.660

Figure 1--Percentage of Cacti Removed From Plots; Data Stratified by Land Ownership. The data have been analysed by Tuckey's Honest Significant Difference (HSD). Private, FWS, BLM, County Park, Sonora and USFS ownerships form a group with low percentages of theft. Sonora, USFS, and NPS form a group with higher percentages of removal. NPS thefts are significantly greater than those for other agencies.

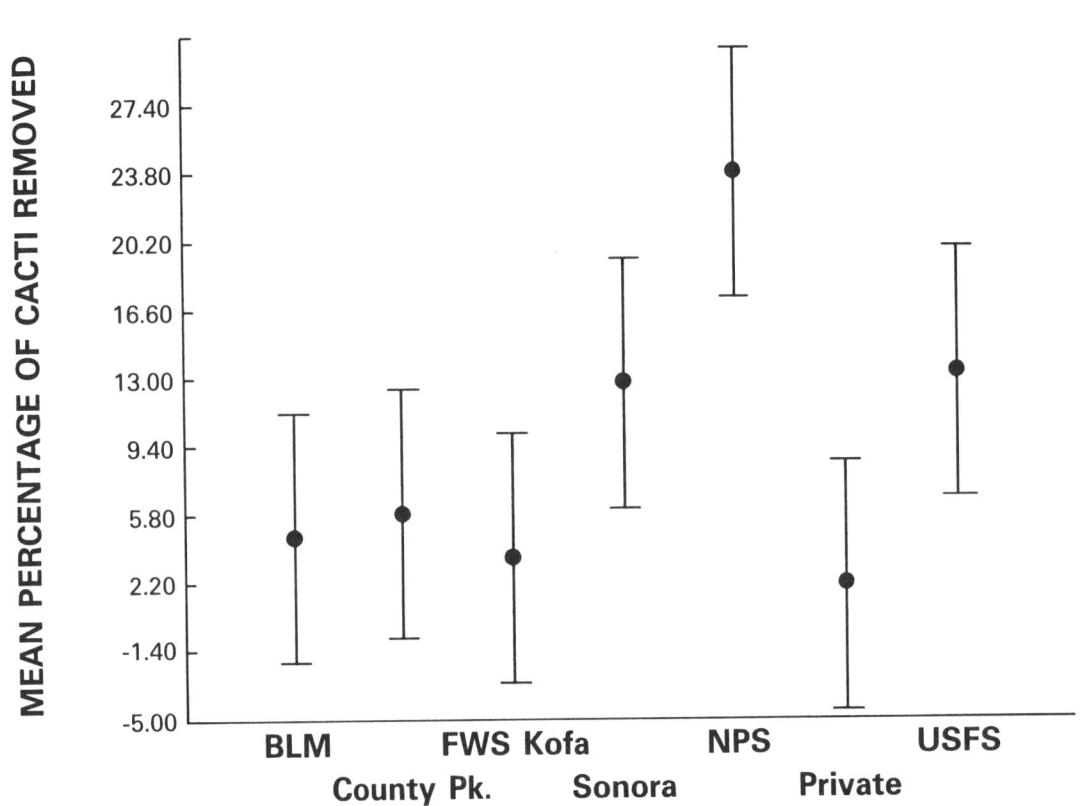

If the "percentage removed" variable is included and the "number removed" variable is excluded (to eliminate autocorrelation) the resulting coefficient of correlation remains essentially the same (R = 0.731) and the resulting correlation matrix then looks like this:

CORRELATION MATRIX

	Access	Seclusion	Pct-Removed
N-Orig.	-0.271	0.080	-0.086
Access (m)		-0.516	-0.530
Seclusion			0.668

However, if the data are partitioned by land ownership, and statistically treated in a similar manner (using Pct-Removed, Access, and Seclusion as variables), correlations are improved:

Overall Correlation from Linear Regression

Ownership	R
Private	0.999
USFS	0.999
Sonora	0.992
BLM	0.966
County Park	0.925
FWS	0.906
NPS	0.869
All Ownerships	0.706

This significant improvement in correlation when the sample is stratified by land ownership indicates that different ownerships have different factors controlling correlation.

Figure 2 presents a three dimensional graphic that summarizes the relationship between the "seclusion," "access," and "percent removed" statistics for these data on all plots pooled.

The species of cacti removed, the numbers originally present and the number removed, are listed in Table 2. Each is classified by its growth form as columnar, cholla-like (cylindropuntia), pricklypear-like (platyopuntia), or globular. Each of these classes are further subdivided by size as small (<0.1m high), medium (>0.1m -<0.3m tall), and large (>0.3m tall). These data appear graphically in Figure 3 and Figure 4 and are presented in Table 3. Large columnar cacti and cylindropuntias are rarely removed while small and medium

Figure 2--Three Dimensional Plot of Seclusion, Access, and Percentage of Plants Removed. Data pooled from all plots shows that seclusion is positively correllated with removal while access is negatively correlated.

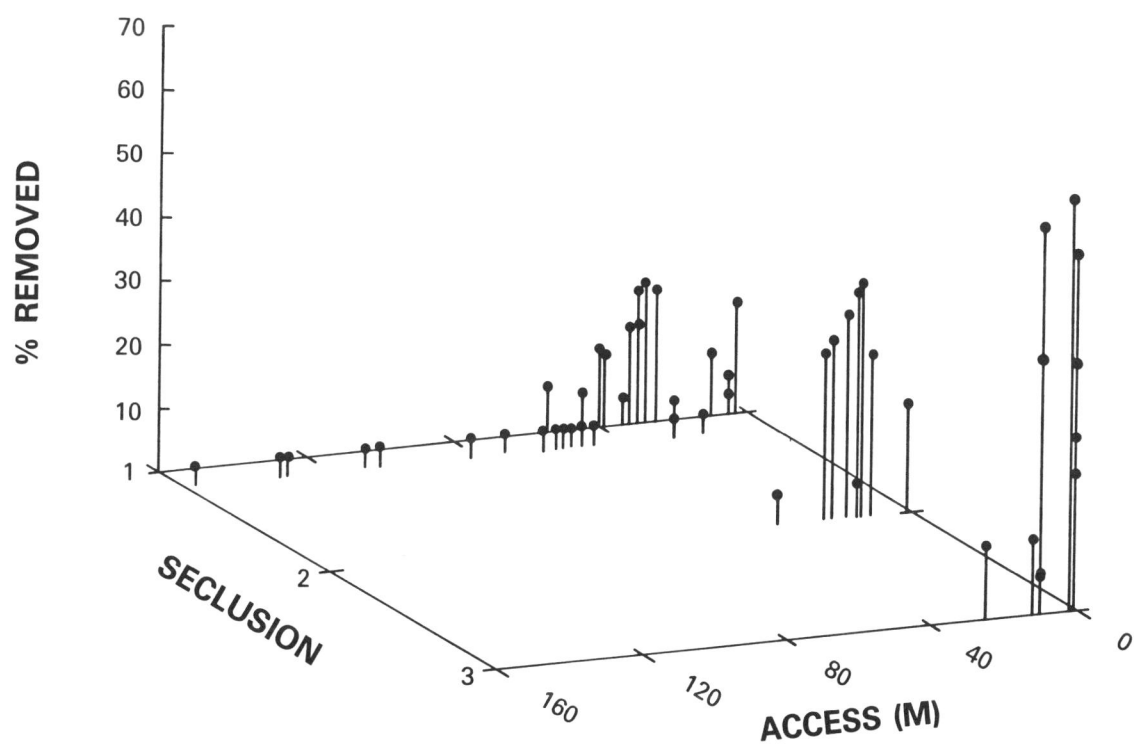

CACTUS PLOTS

TABLE 2.
STATISTICS FOR CACTUS SPECIES REMOVED

SPECIES	SHAPE*	SIZE^	NUMBER ORIGINAL	PERCENT+ ORIGINAL	NUMBER REMOVED	PERCENT+ REMOVED
Cereus greggii	col	m	3	0.21	0	0.00
C. schottii	col	l	16	1.11	0	0.00
C. thurberi	col	l	21	1.46	1	4.76
Coryphantha aggregata	gl	s	2	0.14	0	0.00
Echinocactus polycephalus	gl	m	8	0.55	2	25.0
Echinocereus engelmannii	col	s	135	9.39	13	9.63
E. mojavensis	col	s	14	0.97	2	14.3
E. pectinatus	gl	s	4	0.28	1	25.0
E. triglochid.	col	s	19	1.32	8	42.1
Ferocactus acanthocarpa	gl	l	39	2.70	6	15.4
F. covellei	gl	m	42	2.91	29	69.0
F. wislizenii	gl	l	55	3.81	11	20.0
Mammilaria microcarpa	gl	s	324	22.4	101	31.2
M. olivae	gl	s	25	1.04	8	53.3
M. thornberi	gl	s	9	0.62	4	44.4
Neoloydia erectocentra	gl	s	5	0.35	0	0.00
Opuntia acanthocarpa	co	l	39	12.6	0	0.00
O. basilaris	po	l	30	2.08	9	30.0
O. bigelovii	co	l	99	6.86	0	0.00
O. fulgida	co	l	216	15.0	0	0.00
O. kleiniae	co	s	23	1.59	0	0.00
O. leptocaulis	co	s	19	1.32	1	5.26
O. phaecantha	po	l	52	3.6	0	0.00
O. versicolor	co	l	62	4.30	1	1.61
O. whipplei	co	s	49	3.40	0	0.00
Totals			1443		197	

* Shape: co = cylindopuntia; col = columnar; gl = globular, barrel-like; po = platyopuntia.
^ Size: s = <0.1 m high; m = >0.1 <0.3 m high ; l = >0.3 m high.
+ Percentages given are by plot and are not pooled statistics.

TABLE 3.

PERCENTAGE OF CACTI REMOVED AS RELATED TO SHAPE AND SIZE

	Pct-Original	Pct-Removed
Columnar	14.41	12.18
Cylindropuntia	45.04	1.02
Platyopuntia	5.68	4.57
Globular	34.86	82.23
Large	53.52	14.21
Medium	3.67	15.73
Small	42.83	70.05

CACTUS MORPHOLOGY RELATED TO REMOVAL
Based on Percent of All Cacti Removed

	Large	Medium	Small
Columnar	2.70	0	13.7
Cylindropuntia	0.18	0	1.10
Platyopuntia	11.0	0	0
Globular	18.1	62.0	31.8

size globular cacti are popular. Small columnar cacti and large globulars are intermediate. The number of globular species removed far exceeds the number of all other forms.

During the flowering season, cacti are significantly more likely to be removed. Figure 5 shows the plot of percentage of cactus species in flower and the percent of cacti removed. The coefficient of correlation (0.88) shows a moderately strong relationship between flowering and theft. Note that the most cacti are removed in the summer, but theft is also appreciable in the fall and winter months when no cacti are flowering. This reflects a positive correlation between winter visitation in southern Arizona and cacti collected. This effect is most notable in late winter (March and early April, before the onset of cactus blooming) when many people visit natural areas to see the wildflower displays.

SHAPE VS. THEFT

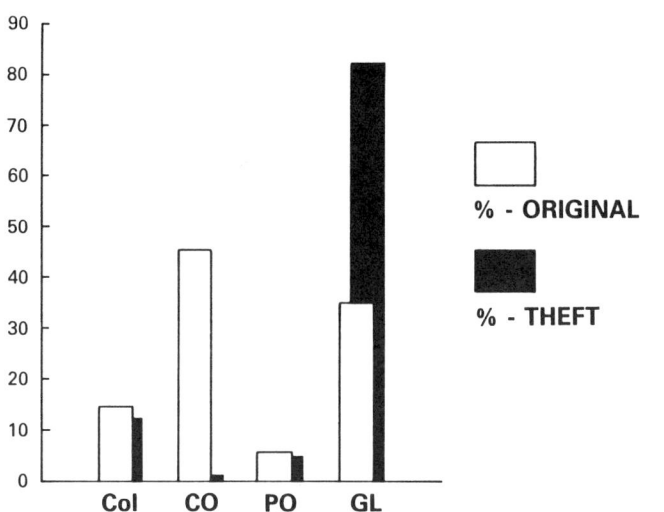

Figure 3--Influence of Cactus Shape on Percentage of Removal. Percentage of theft is based on the number of cacti taken, not on number originally present. The theft of globular shaped cacti far exceeds that for any other form. COL = columinar shape; CO = cylindropuntia shape; PO = platyopuntia shape; GL = globular shape.

SIZE VS. THEFT

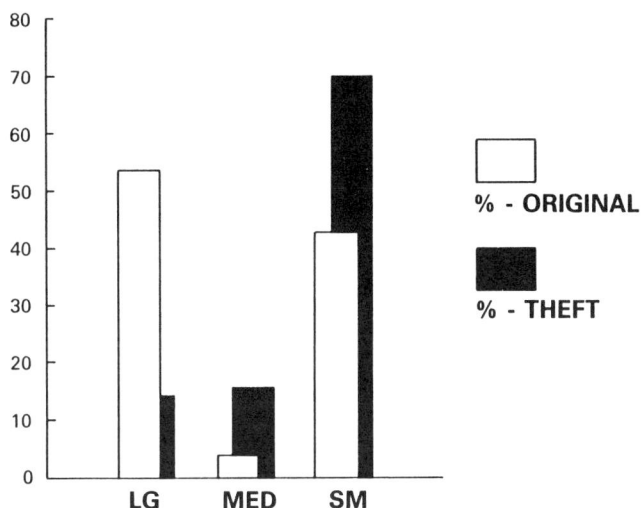

Figure 4--The Influence of Cactus Size on Percentage of Removal. Small plants are much more likely to be taken than large ones. LG = plants > 0.3 m tall; MED = plants <0.29 m and > 0.1m tall; SM = plants <0.09 m tall.

DISCUSSION

Since this project is a feasibility study intended to determine the severity of cactus theft in Arizona, and what obvious and measurable factors might relate to removal, the sampling design is experimental. The most prominent problem with this design is the significant difference of the "access" variable between the plots on lands of different ownership. Also of concern are generally small number of plots included in the study. This is especially critical when the sample is stratified by ownership. If and when a larger study is implemented, these difficulties can be overcome by appropriate sample design.

To answer the original question that generated this feasibility study, namely: does inclusion within a National Park Service area provide special protection for cacti, the answer must be no. This is visibly obvious in Figure 1. When the data from BLM, County Park, BSF, Sonora, Private, and USFS are pooled and compared by Student's t distribution with the National Park Service data, the difference in the means is found to be highly significant (6.44 percent for the pooled data vs. 23.82 percent for NPS with a t probability of 0.00002, d.f.= 52). In spite of sampling difficulties, this difference is so great that there is high probability that it is real. Persons interested in or responsible for the preservation of cacti found on lands administered by the NPS cannot assume that cacti are safe automatically. On the contrary, our study indicates these cacti are in the greatest danger for any of the lands we examined.

This project was not designed to test why cacti seem to be at higher than expected risk on National Park Service lands. But the authors' many years of informal observation of park visitors may permit legitimate speculation. Visitor management policies (high use density campgrounds, concentrating concessioner facilities, development of scenic drives, etc.) of the NPS tend to concentrate people and their impact in some areas. Where such places are in the vicinity of cactus populations, our results may be biased and the results do not reflect impact throughout the park.

Our typical park visitor differs from the average 'person on the street' in that they have a greater than usual interest in the out of doors and natural

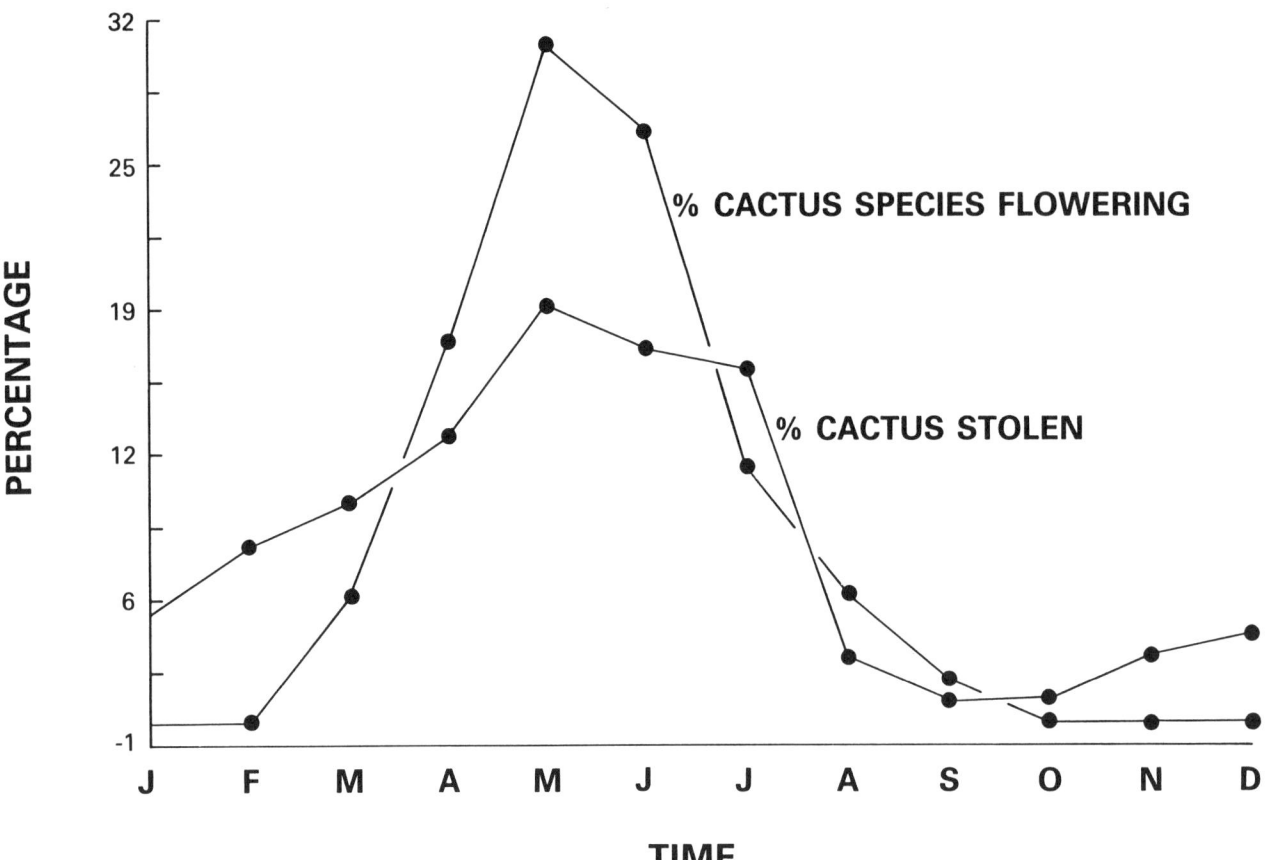

Figure 5--Influence of Cactus Bloom on Theft, Percentage of Removal Plotted Against Month. Percentage of cactus flowering is calculated by species present. Percentage stolen reaches its peak in May when the most species of cacti are in flower. In Arizona, the peak visitor season is in the winter months and not when most cacti flower. Winter theft relates to high visitation but summer theft does not. Summer theft apparently reflects the desirabilty of cacti in flower and perhaps in fruit too.

history. The Park Service thinks so, at any rate, since it devotes much time and money to construction and maintenance of nature trails and natural history exhibits for these people. Curio shops in and around National Parks often sell commercially raised cactus plants and other natural history objects to commemorate the visit. This trade in outdoor trophies is sometimes brisk. Most visitors are willing to satisfy this need through purchase, but a small percentage are not. Since park areas concentrate people, they also concentrate persons willing to take illegal souvenirs. In short, National Parks concentrate persons who will take cacti.

Cacti within Arizona are protected by state law, regardless of who manages the land. Most federal agencies protect state listed native plants, even where they have sole jurisdiction, regarding the state law as policy. Many visitors know that cactus removal is "wrong." Therefore, many persons removing cacti do so furtively. Small cacti that are growing close to roads, especially near turnouts, and where seclusion is high, are found to be at special risk. These factors minimize risk and permit a quick getaway. Our data (Figure 2) shows seclusion to be positively related and access negatively related to removal.

The negative correlation between theft and "access" has at least two components: ease of getaway and ease of observation. The "access" and "seclusion" variables may interact since high seclusion and high access may provide a situation where cacti are not easily detected from the route of travel. The small species favored for removal are not easily seen unless they are close to the road or trail or unless they are in flower. This is especially true of the smaller globular forms. These cacti are readily overlooked because they often blend in with their background and are effectively screened by bushes. This study did not provide for discrimination between ease of access and visibility.

The high correlation ($R = 0.88$) between the number of species flowering and the percentage of cacti stolen would seem to be a matter of aesthetics. Nurseries report that their best sales are for flowering plants. Cacti in flower are well known to be favorite photographic subjects for visitors. Our National Park areas receive many calls every year from persons wondering when the heroic cacti, such as saguaros and organ pipes, are in flower, etc.

In these times of fiscal constraint, land managing agencies must limit law enforcement patrols for apprehension of cactus thieves. The general unwillingness of the judicial system to view cactus theft as a serious matter gives the public the idea that cactus theft is a minor offense. Understanding the factors that contribute to cactus theft can allow for more cost effective patrols and management. Roadside pullouts, rest stops, campgrounds, and other facilities that concentrate people should be eliminated in areas with large cactus populations. Patrols should concentrate on secluded areas where there is easy access with the maximum patrol effort taking place during the cactus flowering (and probably the fruiting) season.

LITERATURE CITED

Brown D. [ed.]. 1982. Biotic communities of the American Southwest - United States and Mexico. Desert Plants 4(1-4):1-342.

Palermo, D. 1986. "Cactus Thefts: A Prickly Problem." Los Angeles Times, March 23, 1986.

Scannell, C. 1986. Personnel communication. Owner of Tanque Verde Greenhouses, Tucson.

Sokal RR and Rohlf FJ. 1981[c]. Biometry; The Principles and Practice of Statistics in Biological Research. WH Freeman, New York.

Endangerment Status of *Collomia rawsoniana* (Polemoniaceae), Western Sierra Nevada, California

Dean Wm. Taylor,[1] John C. Stebbins,[2] William B. DaVilla[3]

Abstract: Populations of Rawson's Flaming Trumpet (*Collomia rawsoniana* Greene), a distributionally restricted paleoendemic riparian herb, were surveyed in 1984. Threats to the species arise from stream diversions for hydroelectricity. Transect sampling quantified the location of *Collomia* colonies with respect to riparian zonation: highest abundance is within 3 to 6 m of the streambank, and less than 1.5 m vertically above the thalweg (deepest part of stream channel). Adjacent to streams, plants occur in microsites varying from open to deep shade, whereas plants far from streams are limited to shaded microsites. Data suggest a high water requirement for the species, and indicate stream diversions could reduce vigor of *Collomia* populations. The existing level of hydroelectric development within its range has not significantly affected populations of *Collomia*, but future small-hydro projects could result in increased endangerment.

Collomia rawsoniana (Greene 1881) is a narrowly endemic perennial herb (fig. 1) restricted to riparian habitats of mid-elevation coniferous forest streams in the central Sierra Nevada, California. Recently, construction of numerous small hydroelectric facilities has been proposed for headwater streams throughout the Sierra (FERC 1985, 1986). Diversion of streamflow from streams supporting *C. rawsoniana* populations could influence the endangerment status of the species.

We undertook studies of the ecology and distribution of *C. rawsoniana* in response to the need for information to assess existing and potential impacts of hydroelectric facilities (Taylor et al. 1985).

Two specific objectives of our studies were: 1) determine if *C. rawsoniana* was of limited enough distribution to be potentially impacted by streamflow diversions, and 2) determine if its distribution within the riparian zone suggest a strong dependence upon streamflow for its water requirements.

SPECIES BIOLOGY

Taxonomic Relationships

Grant (1959) placed *C. rawsoniana* in Section Collomiastrum, comprised of four perennial species: two of these, *C. larsenii* (Gray) Payson and *C. debilis* (S. Watson) Greene (considered but two extremes of a polymorphic complex, cf. Kartesz and Kartesz 1980) are alpine cushion plants of the northern Rocky Mountains and Cascade Range.

The closest relative of *C. rawsoniana* is *C. mazama* Coville (Wilken et al. 1982), also a narrow endemic of mesic sites, occurring in the southern Oregon Cascades (vicinity of Crater Lake).

Distribution and History

C. rawsoniana is essentially restricted to the westernmost portion of the upper San Joaquin River watershed (fig. 2), being known outside this drainage only from a single tributary of the adjacent Fresno River watershed (Nelder Creek).

The geographic distribution of *C. rawsoniana* is restricted, while its habitat (coniferous forest streams) is not, suggesting paleoendemism (Stebbins and Major 1965). Consistent with a paleoendemic history is its primitive taxonomic status within the genus Collomia.

Contraction and fragmentation of moist forest habitats occurred over much of western North America during and after the Pliocene (Axelrod 1975).

In pre-Pliocene times, the common ancestor of *C. rawsoniana* and *C. mazama* was probably more widely distributed. Disjunction and differentiation of the two taxa occurred as the result of increasing aridity (Grant 1959), generally restricting the geographic extent of mesic forest taxa. Endemism of *C. rawsoniana* in the central Sierra is similar in historical pattern to that of *Sequoiadendron giganteum*.

Figure 1. Rawson's Flaming Trumpet (*Collomia rawsoniana*). Line drawing by Kathleen A. Teare.

---

[1] Senior Botanist, BioSystems Analysis, Inc., 303 Potrero, Suite 29-203, Santa Cruz CA 95060.

[2] Biology Department, California State University, Fresno, CA 93740.

[3] Principal, BioSystems Analysis, Inc.

Life-History Characteristics

Collomia rawsoniana is a herbaceous perennial with an extensive rhizome system (fig 2). Field observations indicate that reproduction is often clonal. A rhizomatous growth habit may allow clones to obtain resources from spatially separate microsites: water from nearby streams and light from canopy gaps. Such a habit may also be adaptive in a habitat experiencing frequent flooding, as rhizome segments would be easily transported during high-flow events.

Floral morphology of *C. rawsoniana* suggests an outcrossing breeding system. The large, red, tubular flowers (3-4 cm long) fit the typical hummingbird pollination syndrome (Grant and Grant 1965).

METHODS

Population Inventories

Distributional records for *C. rawsoniana* in CNDDB files (Cochrane and Jensen 1984) and U.S. Forest Service, Sierra National Forest records indicated known populations only in riparian sites with road access. We thus conducted a systematic distributional survey of the region of known occurrence in order to obtain a picture of its abundance unbiased by proximity to roads.

Streams within the Willow Creek and Chiquito Creek watersheds were surveyed. Field observations were allocated proportional to stream length for 1st-order through 4th-order streams in a stratified-random sampling design (Taylor and Davila 1985). In total, nearly 50 percent of all stream length in the two watersheds was observed (Taylor et al. 1985).

Collomia rawsoniana populations were inventoried by downstream traverses of stream sections. Two botanists walked on opposite banks of the stream, beginning data collection at their first encounter with the species, and at 6 m (20 ft) altitude intervals thereafter. Data on clone size, cover of *Collomia* within each clone and proportion of flowering stems was estimated. Data on site characteristics, including vegetation composition, substrate, and canopy cover were recorded using methods given by Taylor and Davila (1985).

Position in Riparian Zonation

Transect sampling of selected populations was undertaken to quantify gradient position of *C. rawsoniana* within the riparian zone.

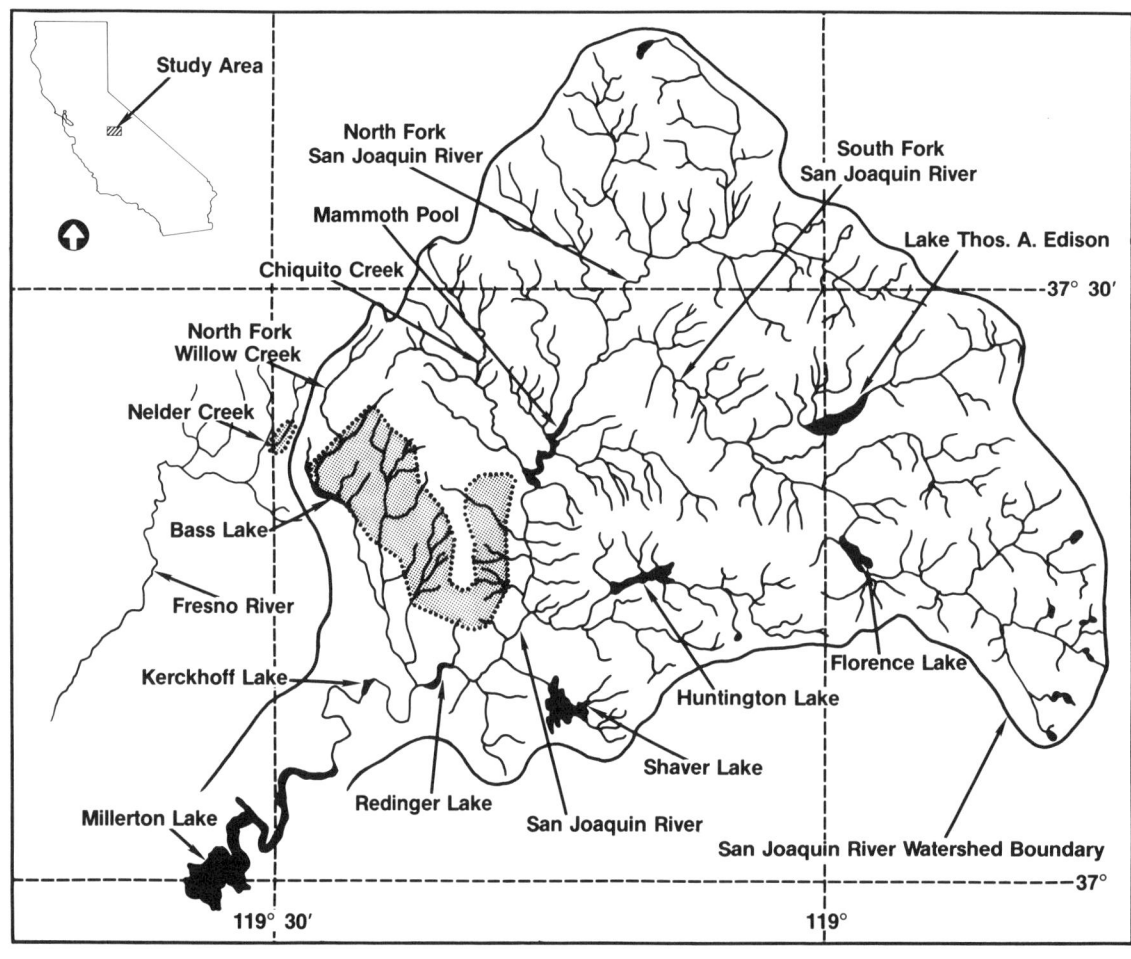

Figure 2. Map of drainage network of the upper San Joaquin River basin, California, showing the distribution of *Collomia rawsoniana* (shaded area).

Systematic quadrat sampling (Mueller-Dombois and Ellenberg 1974) was conducted to study habitat selection and utilization patterns within the riparian zone. Three streams were sampled within the Willow Creek watershed: Whisky Creek, Chilkoot Creek, and an unnamed tributary to Chilkoot Creek. Along each stream, a sample reach was selected. A random point was chosen upstream from the lower reach end. From this point, 25-m long transects were established at 5-m intervals upstream, each transect perpendicular to the stream and extending uphill from the streambank. A series of $0.10 m^2$ quadrats, 0.2 by 0.5 m, was placed at 0.5 m intervals along each transect. Quadrats were oriented with their long axis parallel to the stream channel. The elevation of each quadrat above the thalweg (deepest part of the channel) was determined using a surveyor's level.

The number of *C. rawsoniana* stems rooted within each quadrat was recorded, as was the number of flowering stems. Canopy cover over each quadrat was determined using a spherical densiometer (Lemmon 1956). Sampling continued until a total of 100 quadrats containing *C. rawsoniana* were encountered or until a stream section 300 m long had been sampled.

RESULTS
Stream Survey Results

Previously unknown populations of *C. rawsoniana* were documented from a number of localities, primarily from 2nd-order streams in the vicinity of Bass Lake in the Willow Creek watershed.

Elevational Trends

Survey along the entire length of several streams, beginning at their headwaters, provided an indication of the elevational distribution of the species (Table 1). Field observations suggest that the median elevational extent, 1480 m (4850 feet) is close to optimum for populations of *C. rawsoniana*.

Figure 3. Illustration of growth habit of *Collomia rawsoniana*, showing its extensive rhizome system. Line drawing by Kathleen A. Teare

Table 1. Known upper and lower elevational limits of *Collomia rawsoniana* populations (sources: Taylor et al. 1985, Hamon 1982, Smith 1983, USFWS 1983).

Stream	Elevation Limit			
	Upper		Lower	
	meters	feet	meters	feet
Rock Creek				
Main Stem	1,730	(5,675)	1,260	(4,150)
Tributary	1,840	(6,050)	-	-
Gordon Cr.	1,770	(5,800)	-	-
Whisky Creek				
Main Stem	1,800	(5,900)	1,060	(3,480)
Owl Creek	1,750	(5,750)	-	-
North Fork Willow Creek				
Main Stem	1,395	(4,580)*	1,005	(3,300)
Chilkoot Cr.	1,870	(6,125)	-	-
Tributary	2,148	(7,050)	-	-
Browns Cr.	1,875	(6,150)	1,225	(4,018)
Sand Cr.	1,925	(6,325)	-	-
Peckinpah Cr.	1,510	(4,950)	1,225	(4,018)
Salter Cr.	1,675	(5,500)	1,100	(3,600)
S. Fork Willow Cr.	-	-	890	(2,920)
MEANS ± S.D.	1,808 ± 160 (5,931 ± 525)		1,146 ± 105 (3,761 ± 347)	

* not included in mean calculation

Figure 4 provides a histogram showing frequency of occurrence in randomly selected locations. Again, the elevational distribution of the species indicates a strong concentration of occurrences in the 1370 m to 2250 m (4500 to 6000 ft) range.

An elevational trend in clone density was noted: distance between clones was negatively correlated with elevation (Spearman r = -0.31, p>0.01). Often, at their lower elevational extent, *Collomia* clones are up to 200 m apart. Size of clones was correlated with elevation (r = 0.35, p >0.01), although this relation is best characterized as curvilinear. The largest clones of *Collomia* occurred between 1400 m and 1800 m (4600 and 5900 ft), with notably smaller mean clone size at elevations above or below this range.

The proportion of stems flowering increases with elevation (r = 0.48, p > 0.01), and larger clones tend to have a significantly greater proportion of flowering stems (r = 0.48, p > 0.01).

Habitat Characteristics

Vegetation composition and structure was noted at 100 sites supporting *Collomia rawsoniana* populations. Table 2 provides a summary of floristic composition for these stands. *Alnus rhombifolia* and *Calocedrus decurrens* were the trees most often dominant, while *Rhododendron occidentale* and *Rubus parviflorus* were important shrubs. Overstory cover of stands supporting *Collomia* populations averaged 44 percent, and shrub cover averaged 20 percent. Herbaceous diversity and cover were often very high, as compared to other riparian community types in these watersheds (Taylor and Davilla 1985). Herb cover in stands supporting *Collomia* averaged nearly 50 percent, with *Boykinia major*, *Senecio triangularis* and *Peltiphyllum peltatum* the more important associates.

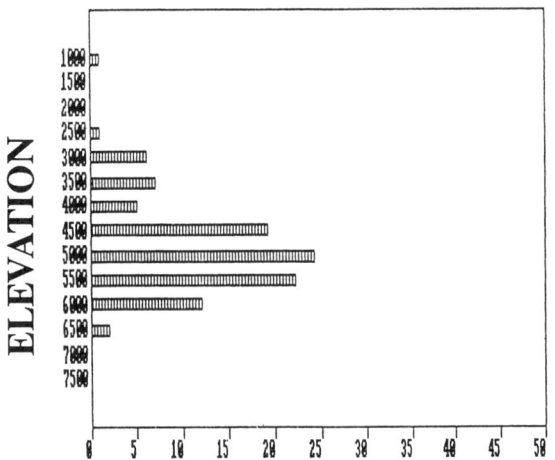

Figure 4. Histogram of elevation distribution for 100 observations of *Collomia rawsoniana* populations, taken from randomly sampled sites within the Willow Creek watershed.

Table 2.

Summary cover, constancy and Importance Value tabulation of vegetation composition for *Collomia rawsoniana* populations (n=100). Constancy is the percentage of sites in which a species occurred; cover is the mean cover over only the stands in which a species occurred; I.V. is an Importance Value index (sum of constancy and cover). Species (those occurring in greater than 10 percent of sampled stands) are listed in descending order by I.V.

Taxon[1]	Constancy	Cover	I.V.
Collomia rawsoniana	100.00	4.58	104.58
Rhododendron occidentale	87.88	4.35	102.23
Calocedrus decurrens	89.90	8.09	97.99
Alnus rhombifolia	60.61	26.27	86.87
Boykinia major	78.79	3.45	82.24
Abies concolor	74.75	6.16	80.91
Athyrium felix-femina	76.77	2.94	79.70
Rubus parviflorus	60.61	3.26	63.86
Senecio triangularis	61.62	1.64	63.25
Pteridium aquilinum	59.60	1.29	60.88
Peltiphyllum peltatum	50.51	6.81	57.32
Ribes nevadense	50.51	2.38	52.88
Viola glabella	46.47	0.79	47.26
Galium triflorum	42.42	0.22	42.64
Mimulus moschatus	38.38	0.21	38.59
Aquilegia formosa	35.35	0.57	35.93
Carex amplifolia	34.34	0.32	34.67
Cornus nuttallii	30.30	2.81	33.11
Mimulus cardinalis	32.32	0.58	32.90
Prunella vulgaris	32.32	0.15	32.48
Cornus stolonifera	28.28	1.47	29.75
Adenocaulon bicolor	29.29	0.41	29.71
Corylus cornuta	26.26	2.69	28.95
Pinus lambertiana	28.28	0.64	28.93
Lotus oblongifolius	28.28	0.62	28.90
Alnus tenuifolia	19.19	9.50	28.69
Lilium pardalinum	27.27	0.82	28.09
Circaea alpina	27.27	0.77	28.04
Carex nervina	27.27	0.32	27.59
Stachys albens	27.27	0.18	27.45
Osmorhiza chilensis	27.27	0.16	27.44
Deschampsia elongata	27.27	0.13	27.40
Glyceria elata	26.26	0.10	26.37
Pinus ponderosa	23.23	2.00	25.23
Potentilla glandulosa	24.24	0.07	24.31
Elymus triticoides	23.23	0.30	23.53
Mimulus guttatus	21.21	0.35	21.57
Epilobium glaberrimum	21.21	0.05	21.26
Quercus chrysolepis	19.19	1.22	20.41
Hypericum anagallioides	20.20	0.10	20.30
Epilobium ciliatum	19.19	0.20	19.40
Equisetum arvense	18.18	0.26	18.44
Glyceria striata	18.18	0.13	18.31
Quercus kelloggii	16.16	0.54	16.70
Lupinus latifolius	16.16	0.09	16.25
Veronica americana	16.16	0.05	16.22
Carex jonesii	16.16	0.04	16.20
Agrostis filicumis	16.16	0.02	16.18
Heracleum lanatum	15.15	0.22	15.37

Table 2 (Concluded).

Taxon[1]	Constancy	Cover	I.V.
Oxypolis occidentalis	15.15	0.16	15.31
Lilium kelleyanum	15.15	0.07	15.22
Juncus nevadensis	15.15	0.04	15.20
Salix lasiolepsis	14.14	0.91	15.05
Artemisia douglasiana	13.13	0.84	13.97
Ribes roezelii	13.13	0.18	13.32
Juncus effusus	13.13	0.07	13.20
Rumex angiocarpus	12.12	0.08	12.20
Epilobium angustifolium	12.12	0.07	12.19

[1] Nomenclature follows Kartesz and Kartesz (1980).

Transect Sampling Results
Stem Density

Density of stems in stream sections sampled by quadrat methods is summarized in Table 3. Stem density data obtained by the U.S. Fish and Wildlife Service (1983) is comparable to the values observed in our study. Given the data in Table 3, no clear relationship is evident between stream size and density. Whisky Creek, which exhibits the highest *Collomia* density, is a 3rd-order stream at the location sampled. Density along Rock Creek (a 3rd-order stream) and Chilkoot Creek tributary (a 1st-order stream) are equivalent.

Riparian Gradient Position

Position of *Collomia* within the riparian zone (fig. 3) indicates a non-uniform distribution with respect to proximity to the streambanks. The mean distance of quadrats with *Collomia* was 6.5 m (21 ft) from the stream thalweg, and 50 percent of the occurrences were found closer to the stream than the mean distance (fig. 3a). Few quadrats within the border of the active stream channel supported *Collomia*, presumably due to high incidence of inundation. Using transects, we measured *C. rawsoniana* up to 22 m (72 ft) away from the study streams, and casual observations of clones up to 40 m (130 ft) from stream banks have been made (Hamon 1982). Height of quadrats with *Collomia* above the thalweg (fig. 3b) indicate that the species does not frequently grow more than 2 m (6 ft) above the deepest part of the channel.

Our data indicate an interesting trend of *Collomia* occurrence in relation to canopy cover and distance from the stream (fig. 4). In locations nearby streams, quadrats with *Collomia* are equally likely to be located under dense overstory cover as under canopy gaps. Away from streams, however, *Collomia* only occurs in shaded microsites, and is apparently unable to grow in open microsites except next to streams.

DISCUSSION

Data on height above and distance from the stream channel indicate that *Collomia rawsoniana* occurrences are strongly concentrated close to streams. These data are consistent with the hypothesis that *Collomia* is dependent on streamflow for its water requirements. The differential occurrence of *Collomia* in relation to canopy closure indicates that it is unsuccessful at growing away from streams except in dense shade, where transpirational demands would be lower than in sun. We often observed mid-day wilting of *Collomia* clones located in sites not adjacent to streambanks, affirming this hypothesis.

The available data indicate that *C. rawsoniana* is a mesophytic herb that is dependent on cool, moist riparian conditions for its growth and reproduction.

Development of hydroelectric facilities would thus have the potential to degrade *C. rawsoniana* habitat if diversions result in lower moisture availability within the riparian zone.

By fortuitous juxtaposition, the present level of hydroelectric development in the vicinity of Bass Lake is limited to elevations generally below known or historical *Collomia* occurrences (Taylor et al. 1985), thus limiting impacts on the species. However, pending proposals for new hydroelectric facilities would divert smaller, higher-elevation headwater streams which support the majority of *Collomia* populations. Botanical reports conducted for proponents of new diversions have generally ignored the potential indirect impacts of stream dewatering on *Collomia rawsoniana* populations (Hamon 1982, Smith 1983, WESCO 1984, Jokerst 1984), preferring to gauge impacts only on the basis of direct losses related to construction disturbance. Our studies indicate that dewatering effects require evaluation.

Table 3.

Density of *Collomia rawsoniana* at streams from which quantitative data are available.

Site (Source)	Density (stems/m^2)	Stream Order
Whisky Creek (Taylor et al. 1985)	26.2	3rd
Chilkoot Creek Tributary (Ibid)	12.9	1st
Chilkoot Creek (Ibid)	0.96	2nd
Whisky Creek (U.S.F.W.S. 1983)	31.8	3rd
Rock Creek (Ibid)	12.8	3rd

Hydroelectric diversions are not the only potential threat to status of *Collomia rawsoniana* populations. Our data suggest that logging within the riparian zone, resulting in lowered canopy cover, could influence population structure and vigor by changing the mosaic of sun and shade in peripheral riparian areas.

Our study suggests that *Collomia rawsoniana* is an obligate riparian herb, depending on the high moisture availability adjacent to streams for its water requirements.

This would indicate that the species may respond to reductions in streamflow, and that hydroelectric diversions could influence populations of this unique paleoendemic herb.

ACKNOWLEDGEMENTS

Funding for our studies was provided by Pacific Gas and Electric Company, Department of Engineering Research. We thank Sheila Byrne and Roland Risser for their critical review of our data. Field work for this project was aided by the able assistance of Glenn Clifton and Doug Stone. Jim Bartel of the U.S. Fish and Wildlife Service provided information and data from previous studies.

REFERENCES

Axelrod, Daniel I. History of the coniferous forests, California and Nevada. Univ. Calif. Pubs. Bot. 70:1-62; 1975.

Cochrane, Susan and Deborah Jensen. The Natural Diversity Data Base. pp. ix in: James P. Smith and Rick York [Eds.], Inventory of Rare and Endangered Vascular Plants of California. California Native Plant Society, Special Publication No. 1 [3rd edition]; 1984.

F.E.R.C. Final environmental impact analysis of small-scale hydroelectric development in selected watersheds in the Upper San Joaquin river basin, California. Federal Energy Regulatory Commission, Office of Hydropower Licensing, FERC/EIA-0001; 1985.

F.E.R.C. Draft Environmental Impact Statement. Owens River Basin: seven hydroelectric projects, California. Federal Energy Regulatory Commission, Office of Hydropower Licensing, FERC/DEIS-0041; 1986.

Grant, Vern. Natural History of the Phlox Family. Martinus Nijhoff, The Hague; 1959. x + 280 p.

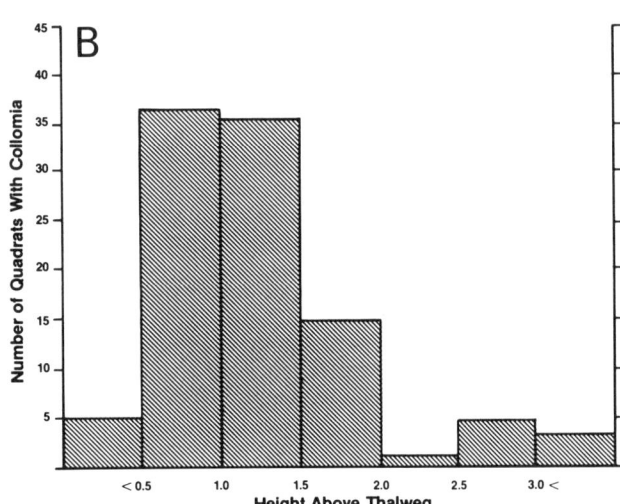

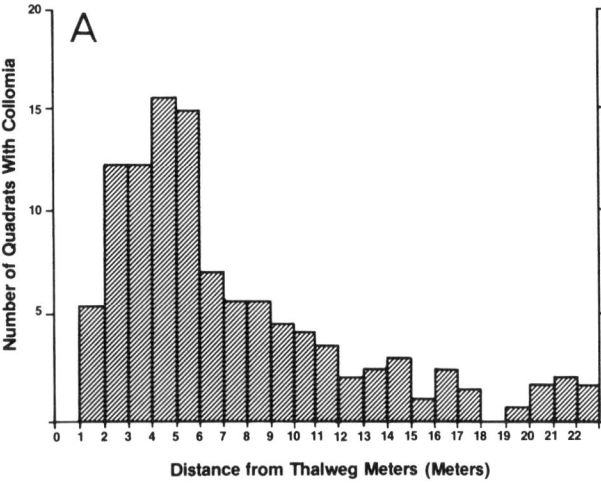

Figure 5. Histograms depicting riparian gradient position of *Collomia rawsoniana* occurrences: 5a. distance (in meters) from thalweg (deepest portion of stream channel); 5b. elevation (in meters) above thalweg.

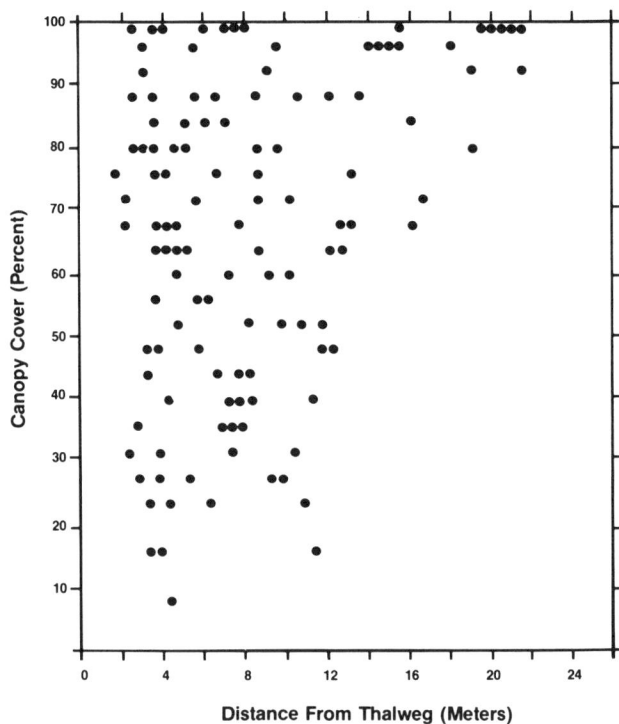

Figure 6. Scattergram depicting location of *Collomia rawsoniana* occurrences as a function of canopy cover (measured with a spherical densiometer) and distance (in meters) from the thalweg. *Collomia* does not occur in open sites away from streams.

Grant, Vern and Karen L. Grant. Flower pollination in the phlox family. Columbia University Press, New York; 1965. 180 p.

Greene, Edward L. New and noteworthy plants. Pittonia 1:221; 1888.

Hamon, Dan. *Collomia rawsoniana* botanical survey, Whisky Creek hydroelectric Projects Nos. 1 & 2. Unpublished report to West Slope Power Company, Sacramento, CA.; 1982. 9 p.+ attachments.

Jokerst, James D. A botanical survey and rare plant inventory of the proposed Nelder Creek small hydroelectric project. Unpublished report prepared

Lemmon, Paul. A spherical densiometer for estimating forest overstory density. For. Sci. 2:314-320; 1956.

Mueller-Dombois, Dieter and Heinz Ellenberg. Aims and Methods of Vegetation Ecology. John Wiley & Sons, New York; 1974. xi + 547 p.

Smith, Peggy. *Collomia rawsoniana* botanical survey, Rock Creek Power Project, Sierra National Forest. Unpublished report to Megahydro, Inc., Redding, CA.; 1983. 10 p.

Stebbins, G. Ledyard and Jack Major. Endemism and speciation in the California Flora. Ecological Monographs 35:1-35; 1965.

Taylor, Dean Wm., William B. Davilla and John Stebbins. Distribution, ecology and status of *Collomia rawsoniana* within the Crane Valley Project vicinity, Madera County, California. Unpublished report prepared for Pacific Gas and Electric Company, Department of Engineering Research, San Ramon, CA.; 1985. 81 p.

Taylor, Dean Wm. and William B. Davilla. Riparian vegetation in the Crane Valley Project, Madera County, California. Unpublished report prepared for Pacific Gas and Electric Company, Department of Engineering Research, San Ramon, CA.; 1985. 109 p.

U.S. Fish and Wildlife Service. Field survey of Flaming Trumpet, *Collomia rawsoniana*, and effect of small hydro and logging on the species. Unpublished memorandum, Sacramento Endangered Species Office; 1983. 3 p. + appendix.

WESCO, Inc. Riparian vegetation impact for Sand Creek. Unpublished report prepared for West Slope Power Company, Sacramento, CA.; 1984. 11 p.

Wilken, Dieter H., Dale M. Smith, Jeffrey B. Harborne and C. William Glennie. Flavinoid and anthocyanin patterns and the systematic relationships of *Collomia*. Biocm. Syst. and Ecol. 10:239-243; 1982.

Effects of Wet-Season Management Burns on Chaparral Vegetation: Implications for Rare Species

V. Thomas Parker [1]

Abstract: Many chaparral species depend upon soil seed banks for recovery after fire, including most rare and endangered chaparral species. Prescribed burns in Marin County on both sandstone and serpentine have been followed for the last three growing seasons. Field and experimental data indicate decreased germination for shrubs and herbaceous post-fire species following burns during winter. Prescribed burns during the moist conditions of winter should be carefully considered with respect to species regeneration.

The reproductive cycles of many chaparral species depend on the frequency of fire. Following wildfire, chaparral regenerates rather quickly with many fire successional species appearing for a few years before the woody shrubs dominate the site again. Prescribed burning, as a consequence, has been adopted as a common and generally well-accepted management treatment because its application mimics nature while achieving other objectives, for example reducing fuel-loads.

Reliable management techniques are critical, however, when maintenance of plant diversity is an objective. Managing the vegetation from a "fuel" perspective, relatively accurate predictions can be made about fire frequency or intensity of a fire, but managing chaparral as a dynamic association of many different species must be considered experimental. While considerable information exists regarding chaparral, present knowledge is still rather fragmentary.

Because of the need for control, prescribed burns usually occur under moist, cool conditions from late fall to spring, especially in the beginning stages of a long-term prescribed burn program. These conditions are probably not historically typical of fires to which chaparral evolved and adapted. As a consequence, many species that could otherwise survive wildfires may have difficulty recovering from prescribed burns.

Wet-season fires can have a number of effects on vegetation response. Seed germination and establishment is a critical stage of regeneration for many chaparral species, especially among those considered rare or endangered. Because many prescribed burns occur after the first fall rains, soil is commonly moist at the time of the fire. I will examine in this paper the influence of moisture on the viability of seeds stored in the soil at the time of a fire.

VARIATION IN REPRODUCTION IN CHAPARRAL SPECIES

Three different life history reproductive patterns are associated with chaparral response to fire. One pattern is that of sprouting from parts that survive a fire, for example perennial bulbs in Zigadenis or the base of the stem in Quercus. Other species resprout after a fire, but also have a dormant seed bank that is stimulated by a fire. This is the pattern in chamise, Adenostoma fasciculatum, and in many Arctostaphylos and Ceanothus species. A third pattern can be found among species that only survive fire as seed. These species are completely dependent on the germination of dormant seed to reestablish their populations. Most species within both Arctostaphylos and Ceanothus follow this pattern as do many of the herbaceous species that appear in the first year after a fire.

Almost all of the rare and endangered chaparral species fall into this last category. Many currently listed species are non-sprouting woody species of the genera Arctostaphylos and Ceanothus (Table 1). Among the herbaceous species that appear after fire are those that have been or are being considered for rare or endangered status. Evaluation is more difficult for these species because they are normally present at a site only as dormant seed making it difficult to evaluate their locations, size of

---

[1] Associate Professor of Biology, San Francisco State University, San Francisco, CA.

Table 1--Taxa of Arctostaphylos and Ceanothus that are considered on various rare and endangered species lists within California.

	Arcto	Ceano
State and Federally listed R & E	8	4
CNPS-Rare and Endangered (List 1)	30	10
CNPS-Rare only in Calif. (List 2)	1	1
CNPS-Need more inform. on (List 3)	6	0
CNPS-Of limited distr. (List 4)	11	5
CNPS-Considered, not incl. (Appen.)	14	8

populations and viability of the populations. Such herbaceous species will increasingly become rare or endangered because of loss of habitat and human manipulation or management. For all of these species, woody and herbaceous, the soil seed bank represents their only opportunity to regenerate a new population following fire.

Formerly, only heat was thought to be required to break dormancy but chaparral species turn out to differ in which conditions will break seed dormancy and stimulate germination. Seeds of Adenostoma fasciculatum and of species of Arctostaphylos can be stimulated to germinate by compounds leached from charred wood with no other treatment, while seeds of Ceanothus require something like heat to break their thick seed coats (Table 2, 3).

Herbaceous species present a large variety of responses, many of which are not known. One large group of fire-response species are also readily stimulated by chemicals extracted from charred wood (Wicklow 1977, Keeley et al. 1985). Another group of herbaceous species have

Table 2. Germination from soil seed banks of two dominant shrubs, Adenostoma fasciculatum and Ceanothus ramulosus. Treatments included 100 C for 1 hr, aqueous leachate of charred wood, and no treatment (control). Data are expressed as numbers per m².

Seed Bank Source	Control	100 C	Charred Wood
A. fasciculatum	3.0	1.5	22.0
C. ramulosus	0	13.0	0

Table 3. Germination of Arctostaphylos canescens seeds in laboratory trials. Treatments include various combinations of aqueous leachate of charred wood (char), a plant hormone, gibberillic acid (GA), high temperature (120 C), and no treatment (ctrl). Seeds were of two types, "old seeds" collected from soil seed banks and fresh seed from field collections.

Seed	Ctrl	Char	Char/GA	120	120/Char	120/Char/GA
Old	0	14	9	1	1	0
Fresh	0	0	14	0	0	0

rather thick seed coats and rely on the heat pulse from the fire to break open those seed coats (Sweeney 1956). These two groups might be expected to respond differently to prescribed fires under moist soil conditions, particularly if the species responding to chemicals produced in the fire readily absorb moisture.

Within the dormant seed bank of a single species there also can be a variety of responses. For example, within Arctostaphylos canescens, the age of the seed also can influence the response. Seeds long dormant in the soil are more easily stimulated to germinate than those freshly produced (Table 3), thus there can be variability of response within the same population of seeds.

GERMINATION OF SEEDS IN RELATION TO WET-SEASON BURNS

Seed banks are a significant component of chaparral and important in recovery from fire. Dormant seed banks are formed by a variety of species and by rare and endangered species in particular, as well as more common species. Few chaparral areas are not dominated by some combination of seed bank forming species of Adenostoma, Arctostaphylos, and Ceanothus; any post-fire annual species will be present only as seed in the soil. What effect will prescribed burning have on the soil seed bank? Prescribed fires will heat the soil and cause chemical changes similar to wildfires, but one major difference can be higher soil moisture under prescribed burn conditions. The influence of moisture on soil seed banks during prescribed burns, therefore, must be considered for successful vegetation management.

I have followed the germination response of chaparral species to prescribed burns for the past three years. These burns have occurred in the watershed of the Marin Municipal Water District. This agency has been experimenting with chaparral fires in cooperation with the Marin County Fire Department and the California Department of Forestry to determine if burning can be incorporated into their management policies. These fires have been conducted from October to April and generally under cool conditions with moist soil.

Shrub response

The germination from seed banks by dominant shrubs following these fires has been rather poor (Kelly and Parker 1984, Parker 1986a, Parker 1986b). The highest density observed for Adenostoma fasciculatum only was 16 seedlings per m^2. In response to an April burn, no seedlings germinated at all the first year. This compares poorly with responses to wildfires in other parts of the state where seedling establishment can reach well over 100 seedlings per m^2. While considerable mortality of seedlings during the first several years is common, three years after a single fire that occurred in January, almost two-thirds of the total burn area had less than one surviving seedling per m^2; thirty percent of the burn area had no surviving seedlings.

Similarly, Arctostaphylos canescens, A. montana, Ceanothus jepsonii, and C. ramulosus all demonstrated poor germination after these prescribed burns; typically less than 1 per m^2 were found and no areas with over 8.4 per m^2. Similar to Adenostoma, no seedlings appeared the first spring following an April burn but did a year later. The rates of seedling establishment for these species on any site would not result in general in a one-to-one replacement of the preburn adult population. Seedling response in these non-sprouting species to previous wildfires in the same locations has been described as "hosts of seedlings" (Brandegee 1891), "carpets", "flourishing", or "abundantly " established (Howell 1946, 1947), a marked contrast to these prescribed burns (see also Riggan et al. 1986).

Herbaceous response

The response of herbaceous species after these wet-season fires has also been poor (Kelly and Parker 1984). One burn on sandstone substrates on Pine Mountain showed a good herbaceous cover following a January 1983 fire with Phacelia divaricata, Calandrinia breweri, and Calystegia occidentalis as the common species. All of the other burns, and those on serpentine in particular, have had few species and little cover by herbaceous species. Previous reports of herbaceous response to wildfires in these Marin County locations have described annuals covering the slopes and listed large numbers of species, few of which appeared after these recent prescribed fires (Brandegee 1891, Howell 1946, 1947).

SEED TOLERANCE TO HEAT UNDER MOIST CONDITIONS IN LABORATORY TESTS

To test these ideas with seeds of species specific to chaparral areas, soil seed banks of dominant shrubs and seeds of post-fire annuals were collected for experiments. When soil seed banks were moistened prior to heating, the germination response of shrubs were inhibited (Table 4). In this particular example, the heat was provided by burning a light cover of wood shavings (excelsior). The heat was variable within each heat treatment and differed somewhat between the moist and dry treatment; the dry treatment experienced a higher range of temperatures. In additional laboratory experiments with the heat applied using controlled ovens, the difference between moist and dry treatments was dramatic using soil from beneath either Adenostoma fasciculatum or Ceanothus jepsonii. In these experiments, no seeds germinated from the soil that was moist before experiencing either 80 C or 100 C for one hour. In the dry soil treatment, seedling numbers averaged from 30-125 per m^2 regardless of the temperature treatment.

Of the herbaceous species I collected, some absorbed moisture and the percent moisture uptake ranged between 28-45% of the seed dry weight (e.g., Emmenanthe

Table 4. Average number of Arctostaphylos seedlings $\pm$ S.D. in moist (44% & 48%) and dry seed banks experimentally heated by burning excelsior on top of them. Temperature ranges were 31 ± 3 - 190 ± 85 C (moist soil, subsurface to near surface) and 36 ± 6 - 260 ± 76 C (dry soil, subsurface to near surface).

Source of Soil	No Heat	Excelsior Fire Moist Soil	Excelsior Fire Dry Soil
A. canescens	0.8+1.1	11.8+4.3	29.6+11.0
A. glandulosa	0.4+0.5	1.6+1.6	6.0+5.5

penduliflora). The seeds of species requiring heat scarification (e.g., Calystegia macrostegia) absorbed less than 4% of their dry weight in water. Seeds of each species were either presoaked or left dry and subsequently heated to various temperatures for 10-20 minutes depending upon the particular experiment. The response of Emmenanthe penduliflora and Calystegia macrostegia illustrate the two types of responses encountered (Fig. 1).

The upper graph of figure 1 shows the response of Emmenanthe penduliflora and is indicative of the other species whose seeds absorb moisture. When moistened prior to heating, the seeds can tolerate temperatures below 70 C but all are killed above 80 C. Under dry conditions these seeds can tolerate temperatures well over 100 C. On the other hand, there is no difference in the response of Calystegia macrostegia seeds to temperature between dry or premoistened treatments.

CONCLUSIONS

These experiments illustrate a probable cause for the lack of shrub and herbaceous seedling response observed throughout the Marin watershed on areas burned by prescription under cool, moist conditions. The seeds of most of these species become particularly sensitive to heat when moist. Consequently higher mortality occurs with prescribed burns of this type, even though the fires are of generally lower intensity.

Gradually knowledge of the dynamics of chaparral seed banks is increasing. Soil seed banks of chaparral plants survive wildfires to some extent and the wildfires create appropriate conditions for seed germination. Species that make up chaparral respond to a variety of germination stimuli; there is no uniform response. Rare and endangered chaparral species are predominantly those that depend upon dormant seed banks for regeneration of their populations following fire.

Prescribed burns, if under moist soil conditions, do not duplicate the natural conditions that has maintained a great diversity of chaparral species. Prescribed burning under moist conditions will differentially affect these species by influencing seed bank mortality. This can create serious regeneration problems for annuals or shrubs with dormant seed, reducing their populations or in some cases perhaps eliminating them altogether. The loss or depletion of species can disrupt the species balance and perhaps allow invasion by new species, e.g., french broom.

The recovery of vegetation must be of prime consideration if long-term successful management is the goal. Thus the soil seed bank and its condition at the time of a fire must be integrated into management plans. Any management action will differentially favor certain species, even no action. Management plans, therefore, need to consider each species affected and their types of responses. Responses of the same species can differ within the same fire due to changes in soil type or a number of

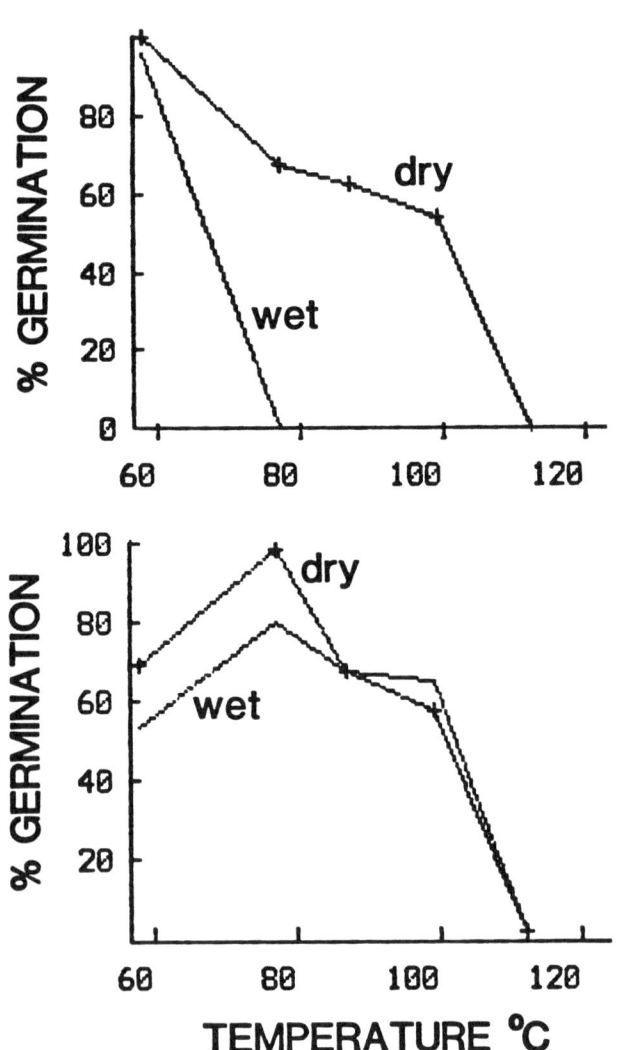

Figure 1--Top: Percent germination of Emmenanthe penduliflora. Bottom: Percent germination of Calystegia macrostegia. In both cases, seeds were dry or presoaked prior to brief heating treatments.

other conditions. Thus every site should be considered unique, and any burn program as experimental for any particular location and combination of species.

Acknowledgments: I thank Vicky Kelly, Chris Rogers, and Sam Hammer for their invaluable help in the field collection of data, laboratory experiments and discussions. R. W. Patterson helped with the manuscript. This work was supported by grants from the Marin Municipal Water District and the California Department of Fish and Game, Rare Plants program.

REFERENCES

Brandegee, T. S. The vegetation of "burns". Zoe 2:118-122; 1891.

Howell, J. T. Carbonated landscape. Sierra Club Bull. 37(7):18-23; 1946.

Howell, J. T. Marin County miscellany - IV. Leaflets Western Bot. 5:41-56; 1947.

Keeley, J. E., B. A. Morton, A. Pedrosa, and P. Trotter. Role of allelopathy, heat, and charred wood in the germination of chaparral herbs and suffrutescents. J. Ecol. 73:445-458; 1985.

Kelly, V. R. and V. T. Parker. The effects of wet season fires on chaparral vegetation in Marin County, California. Technical report submitted to the Marin Municipal Water District, Corte Madera, CA; 1984.

Parker, V. T. Vegetation response to prescribed burning under moist conditions. Technical report submitted to the Marin Municipal Water District, Corte Madera, CA; 1986a.

Parker, V. T. Evaluation of the effect of off-season prescribed burning on chaparral in the Marin Municipal Water District Watershed. Technical report submitted to the Marin Municipal Water District, Corte Madera, CA; 1986b.

Riggan, P. J., S. Franklin, and J. A. Brass. Fire and chaparral management at the chaparral/urban interface. Fremontia 14(3):28-30; 1986.

Sweeney, J. R. Response of vegetation to fire: a study of the herbaceous vegetation following fires. Univ. Calif. Publ. Bot. 28:143-250; 1956.

Wicklow, D. T. Germination response in Emmenanthe penduliflora. Ecology 58:201-205; 1977.

Endangerment Status of the Grass Tribe Orcuttieae and *Chamaesyce hooveri* (Euphorbiaceae) in the Central Valley of California

R. Douglas Stone[1], Glenn L. Clifton[2], William B. DaVilla[3], John C. Stebbins[4], Dean Wm. Taylor[5]

Abstract: A progress report is presented on a two-year study assessing the endangerment status of the vernal pool annuals *Neostapfia colusana*, *Orcuttia inaequalis*, *O. pilosa*, *O. tenuis*, *O. viscida*, *Tuctoria greenei*, and *Chamaesyce hooveri*. Extensive field studies were conducted in historic and potential habitat areas to determine population status and identify population threats. A total of 42 previously undocumented populations of these taxa were located during 1986 field research. Conversion to irrigated agriculture and irrigated pasture is the major cause of extirpation among historic populations. Except for *T. greenei*, all of the species exhibit some degree of tolerance to cattle grazing.

The genera *Neostapfia*, *Orcuttia*, and *Tuctoria*, comprising the tribe Orcuttieae, are among the rarest and most unusual of California's native grasses. Reeder (1965) studied the systematic isolation of this distinctive group of grasses, which led him to establish a special tribe to accomodate them. Ecologically, these late spring and summer-flowering annuals are narrowly restricted to vernal pools and similar habitats, and all but two of the tribe's nine species are essentially endemic to the Central Valley of California.

Vernal pools at one time were a common and widespread habitat type in California's Central Valley. However, continuing agricultural development and urbanization have eliminated an estimated 90 percent of the valley's vernal pool environments (Holland 1978a,b). Consequently, the grasses *Neostapfia*, *Orcuttia*, and *Tuctoria* have all suffered population losses through conversion of vernal pool habitat.

Several authors, including Hoover (1941), Crampton (1959,1976), Griggs (1980), Reeder (1982), and Griggs and Jain (1983), have expressed concern over the loss of populations of these distinctive grasses. Holland (1978a,b) has used soils data and aerial photography to conduct a mapping survey and physiographic classification of Central Valley vernal pools. In spite of these and other previous studies, the current endangerment status of the Orcuttieae in the Central Valley remains unclear.

[1] Associate Botanist, BioSystems Analysis, Inc., Santa Cruz, CA and Environmental Planning, Department of Landscape Architecture, University of California, Berkeley.

[2] Associate Botanist, BioSystems Analysis, Inc.

[3] Principal, BioSystems Analysis, Inc.

[4] Curator of the Herbarium, California State University, Fresno, CA.

[5] Senior Botanist, BioSystems Analysis, Inc.

The paucity of current and comprehensive data on the status of the Central Valley Orcuttieae led the U.S. Fish and Wildlife Service (FWS) to authorize a status survey of these grasses and *Chamaesyce* (née *Euphorbia*) *hooveri*, an associated summer-flowering vernal pool annual in the Central Valley of California. The information gained during the survey will be used by the FWS to determine whether any or all of these taxa meet the criteria for listing under the federal Endangered Species Act.[6] This paper presents some tentative findings based on the first year of progress on this two-year study.

APPROACH AND STUDY AREA COVERAGE

The need for a comprehensive status survey of the Central Valley Orcuttieae and *Chamaesyce hooveri* required an extensive study approach. Sites to be visited in the field were identified through herbarium surveys, literature and data base review, personal communications, and aerial photograph analysis. In addition, aerial reconnaissance of vernal pool habitat was conducted from a light aircraft over portions of the Sacramento and San Joaquin valleys.

Field surveys were conducted in areas of historic and potential habitat to document current population status and identify population threats. The field survey period extended from 21 May through 1 September 1986. An estimate of the completeness of our field effort may be made by calculating the ratio of the number of known occurrence areas visited in 1986 for all species (210) versus the total number of known occurrences, including both sites visited and sites not visited in 1986 (261). By this comparison our field effort is about 80 percent complete. This probably represents an underestimate, however, since a number of the historic sites that went unsurveyed in 1986 are known extirpated based on reliable secondary data.

[6] *Tuctoria mucronata*, which is endemic to two vernal lakes south of Dixon in Solano County and is undoubtedly the rarest member of the Central Valley Orcuttieae, became a federally listed endangered species in 1978 (43 Federal Register 44812).

RESULTS OF 1986 FIELD STUDIES

Assessment of Climatic and Phenological Conditions

The 1986 field season was generally a successful one for surveying the Orcuttieae and *Chamaesyce hooveri* in the Central Valley. The valley experienced heavy winter rains during the period from November 1985 through March 1986. For example, the weather station at Sacramento recorded 27.24 inches of rainfall during this period, the second highest seasonal total ever recorded at this station and 12.63 inches above "normal". The unusually high winter and early spring rainfall caused the valley's vernal pools to become fully charged with runoff. This was followed by a period of below-average rainfall and relatively warm temperatures from April through May 1986, resulting in relatively rapid dry-down of the valley's pools when compared with more favorable years. However, this early-drying trend was somewhat mitigated by cooler-than-average temperatures in the Central Valley during July and August of 1986 (U.S. Department of Commerce 1985-1986).

The unequable distribution of rainfall over the winter and spring and the relatively warm spring temperatures may have negatively affected our 1986 survey results at some locations. Crampton (1959), Griggs (1976, 1980, 1981), and Griggs and Jain (1983) have documented the extreme year-to-year fluctuations in abundance and morphological development for Orcuttieae populations in relation to climatic variables. At several historical occurrence areas we visited, the habitat was in reasonably good condition (i.e., not severely degraded), and yet the species of concern could not be found. Similarly, at some historical localities where two (or more) of the species of concern are reported to occur sympatrically, not all of the reported species were present. The possible effect of climatic conditions on species presence and abundance (or lack thereof) made it difficult at times to evaluate the effect of population threats such as grazing and hydrological alteration.

Extant Populations

Based primarily on 1986 field survey results, the total number of populations known or presumed extant was estimated for each species (Figure 1). Our data show that *Orcuttia tenuis* possesses the greatest number of extant populations (39) among the species studied. *Neostapfia* has the second largest number of extant populations (38). *Chamaesyce hooveri*, with only 19 extant populations, has the highest proportion of extant populations (95 percent) remaining among known populations (Figure 2). *Orcuttia tenuis* has the second highest proportion of extant populations among those known (89 percent).

Orcuttia viscida comprises the lowest number of extant populations (10) among the species studied. However, this species ranks rather high in terms of the proportion of extant populations among known populations (77 percent). *O. viscida* is followed closely by *O. inaequalis* with only 13 populations extant and *Tuctoria greenei* with 18; however, these species have

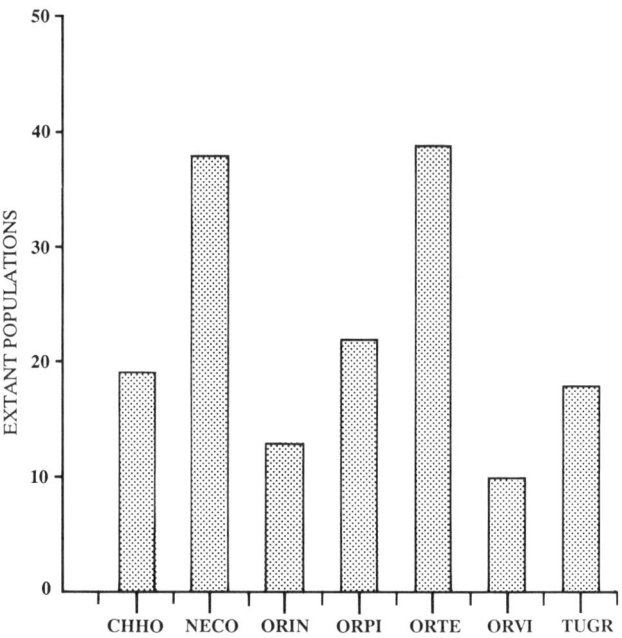

Figure 1. Number of extant populations for each species under study. **CHHO** = *Chamaesyce hooveri*; **NECO** = *Neostapfia colusana*; **ORIN** = *Orcuttia inaequalis*; **ORPI** = *Orcuttia pilosa*; **ORTE** = *Orcuttia tenuis*; **ORVI** = *Orcuttia viscida*; **TUGR** = *Tuctoria greenei*

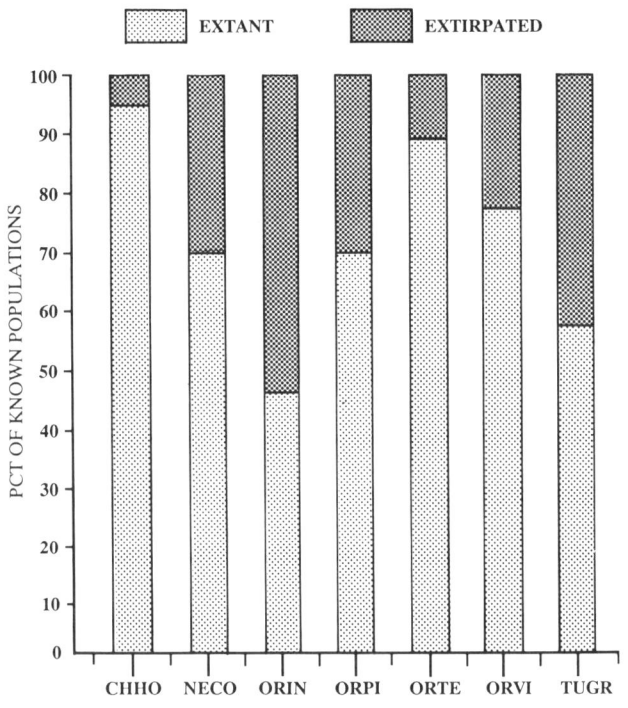

Figure 2. Extant and extirpated populations as a proportion of the total known populations for each species.

the lowest proportion of extant populations among known populations (45 percent for *O. inaequalis*; 56 percent for *T. greenei*).

Previously undocumented or "new" populations form a subset of our data on total extant populations. At least one previously undocumented population was found for each species under study (Figure 3). For example, one new population of the rare *Orcuttia viscida* was found at Rancho Seco in southern Sacramento County. Although this represents the lowest number of new populations found for any of the species studied, the *O. viscida* discovery is significant because before this only nine pools were known to support the species.

Orcuttia tenuis has the largest number of new populations discovered (16). Our discoveries raise the total number of known populations for this species to 39, an increase of 41 percent. Nine of these new *O. tenuis* populations were found on a single parcel, the Inks Creek Ranch northeast of Red Bluff in Tehama County.

Extirpated Populations

For each species an estimate was also made of the total number of populations known or possibly extirpated (Figure 4).[7] According to our data, *Neostapfia* has the greatest number of extirpated populations (17) of the species under study. *Orcuttia inaequalis* follows closely with 16 extirpated populations and ranks highest in terms of the proportion of populations extirpated (55 percent) among known populations

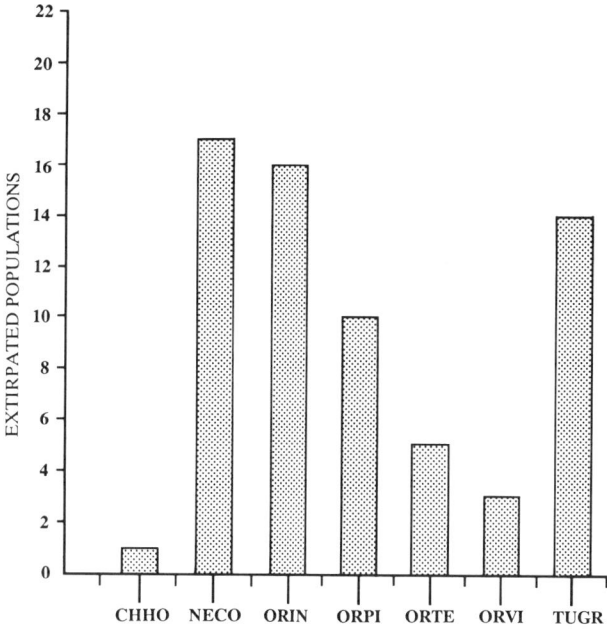

Figure 4. Number of populations extirpated for each species studied.

(Figure 2). Second in proportion of populations extirpated is *Tuctoria greenei* (44 percent). The species with the least number of extirpated populations are *Chamaesyce hooveri* (1) and *O. viscida* (3). *Chamaesyce* also has the lowest proportion of populations extirpated among known populations (5 percent). *O. tenuis* is second lowest in terms of proportion of known populations extirpated (11 percent).

Using land-use data, we analyzed for causes of extirpation among populations known extirpated or possibly extirpated for each species (Table 1). From these data the cumulative impacts to each species might begin to be addressed. Of the 17 extirpated populations of *Neostapfia colusana*, a total of nine result from conversion to irrigated agriculture. Compared with other types of impacts, population losses to irrigated agriculture also are proportionately largest for the other Orcuttieae species occurring in the San Joaquin Valley: *Orcuttia inaequalis*, *O. pilosa*, and *Tuctoria greenei*. Conversion of dry-farmed grainfields and dry pasture into irrigated pasture has been another significant cause of population losses in this region.

In the Sacramento Valley, a different land-use pattern has caused the loss of several *Orcuttia tenuis* populations. Of a total of five extirpated populations,

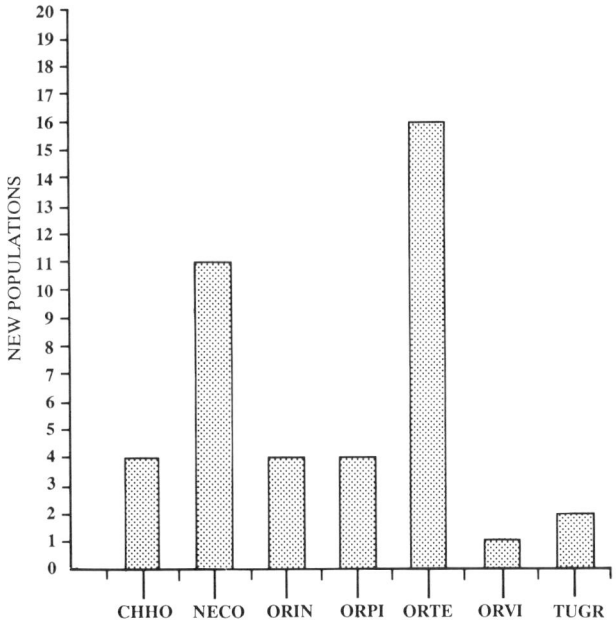

Figure 3. Number of previously undocumented populations of each species located during the 1986 field season.

---

[7] Note that the data presented in the figure are only for populations known through herbarium specimen data, literature sources, and the like. Assuming that some unknown populations also have been lost, our data underestimate the actual number of extirpated populations of each species.

Table 1. Land-use changes[1] causing extirpation among known populations (data are number of populations affected).

Sp.	IA	IP	D	HA	HG	WC	CN	U	Un
CHHO	1	-	-	-	-	-	-	1	-
NECO	9	3	1	1	5	1	1	-	-
ORIN	9	3	1	-	-	-	-	1	4
ORPI	8	1	-	1	2	-	-	-	-
ORTE	-	-	-	1	-	-	-	4	-
ORVI	-	1	-	1	-	-	-	1	-
TUGR	5	3	1	1	3	2	-	2	-

[1] IA = Irrigated agriculture; IP = Irrigated pasture; D = Disced; HA = Hydrologic alteration; HG = Heavy grazing; WC = Weed competition; CN = Competition with native species; U = Urbanization; Un = Unknown

four are the result of urbanization and residential development. These populations were located on the Stillwater Plains of Shasta County, an area where urban expansion on the fringe of the city of Redding has been the primary cause of vernal pool habitat loss.

Impacts to Extant Populations

Based on site-specific observations of population impacts, we have constructed a typology of population threats allowing us to address the cumulative impacts to the remaining extant populations of each species (Table 2). The following sections describe the nature and degree of some of these population impacts in more detail.

Livestock Grazing

The majority of the remaining extant populations for the species of concern are located on private cattle ranches. Therefore, it is not surprising to find that some level of cattle grazing was the most frequently observed impact to extant populations. One conclusion that can be reached in evaluating these data is that the species of concern have a greater resistance to grazing impacts than to other, more intensive land uses such as irrigated agriculture or irrigated pasture. This is not unexpected since the Orcuttieae and *Chamaesyce hooveri* complete their life cycle mostly during the late spring and summer, largely a time of year when cattle have been moved from dry pasture to irrigated pasture, feed lots, or greener pastures in the mountains. To analyze the effects of different grazing regimes on each species, we compared the observed level of grazing intensity with the corresponding population vigor at each site (Table 3).

Chamaesyce hooveri appears to be resistant to light-to-moderate grazing, since all populations under light and moderate grazing were ranked as stable or thriving. This makes sense in terms of the prostrate habit of this plant, which may have adaptive value in providing resistance to both grazing and trampling. However, all populations of this species under heavy grazing regimes were ranked as damaged or declining, suggesting that heavy grazing is detrimental to this species.

Other species showing similar resistance to light-to-moderate grazing in our study include *Neostapfia colusana*, *Orcuttia inaequalis*, *O. pilosa*, and *O. viscida*. In the San Joaquin Valley of Stanislaus County, *Neostapfia* apparently is the most resistant to grazing of the Orcuttieae species studied, having persisted in vernal pools in which *Orcuttia* or *Tuctoria* species have since vanished due to grazing. This fact may result from: (1) the greater size, robustness, moisture content, and probably greater vigor of individual *Neostapfia* plants; (2) their strong ability to continue tillering after grazing and trampling; and (3) their high levels of the characteristic viscid, acrid exudate produced to some extent by all members of the Orcuttieae, which has a putative ecological role in deterring herbivores (Hoover 1941; Griggs 1974, 1980; Reeder 1982).

Tuctoria greenei apparently is the most susceptible to grazing impacts of all the species studied. We observed that some *T. greenei* populations were damaged or declining even under conditions of light-to-moderate grazing. Additionally, at every historic occurrence area we visited for this species where heavy grazing was observed, the species was not found and the population was presumed extirpated. *T. greenei* seems to be most susceptible to grazing due to

Table 2. Observed threats[1] to extant populations (data are number of populations affected).

Sp.	HA	D	VA	CG	WC	CN	GH	HT	NO	Un
CHHO	2	-	-	16	10	-	-	-	1	-
NECO	4	-	-	14	7	1	2	-	1	-
ORIN	1	1	-	12	10	-	2	-	-	-
ORPI	4	4	1	15	14	-	3	-	-	-
ORTE	1	-	7	27	4	8	2	-	2	3
ORVI	1	-	-	7	-	2	-	1	1	-
TUGR	1	-	-	14	8	1	8	-	-	2

[1] HA = Hydrologic alteration; D = Discing; VA = Vehicle activity; CG = Cattle grazing; WC = Weed competition; CN = Competition with native species; GH = Grasshopper damage; HT = Human trampling; NO = None observed; Un = Unknown

Table 3. Population vigor for each species under different grazing intensities (data are number of extant populations).

Sp.	Light Grazing		Moderate Grazing		Heavy Grazing		
	Stable or Thriving	Damaged or Declining	Stable or Thriving	Damaged or Declining	Stable or Thriving	Damaged or Declining	Approaching Extirpation
CHHO	3	-	9	-	-	4	-
NECO	6	5	5	5	1	7	3
ORIN	6	3	2	-	1	-	-
ORPI	1	-	8	2	-	4	-
ORTE	1	1	16	3	3	2	-
ORVI	6	1	-	-	-	-	-
TUGR	3	2	2	3	-	-	-

its observed preference for marginal sites in vernal pools and vernal swales. This micro-habitat preference is remarkably different from that of the other species of Central Valley Orcuttieae. The apparent preference for marginal sites imparts a greater likelihood of trampling damage earlier in the season when cattle are still present on the range, and also makes *T. greenei* relatively susceptible to competition from introduced grasses such as *Lolium* and *Hordeum*, which colonize the margins of heavily grazed vernal pool habitats.

Orcuttia tenuis may possess the greatest resistance to grazing of all the species studied. The majority of extant populations were found to be stable or thriving, even under moderate-to-heavy grazing pressure. Griggs (1980) compared demographic characteristics among the species of *Orcuttia* and *Tuctoria* and found that *O. tenuis* typically occurs in the highest densities. His quantitative measurements were verified by our 1986 field observations. At a number of sites this species occurred uniformly and densely over the vernal pool bed to form a kind of sod, and in these instances the mass of culms and matting of roots may provide some physical resistance to damage from trampling by cattle. Also, this high density of individuals may reduce the ability of weedy plant species to colonize and compete in the vernal pool habitat, even under moderate-to-heavy grazing pressure. In this manner the strong tolerance to grazing shown by *O. tenuis* may be a result of the tendency for this species to occur at higher densities.

Competition from Weedy Species

Competition from weeds, if not the most significant population impact observed at most sites, was second only to grazing in overall frequency among extant populations of the species of concern. Holland and Jain (1984) found that the frequency and abundance of upland grass species in vernal pools was increased during drought years. Our data further suggest that the frequency and severity of weed problems among extant Orcuttieae and *Chamaesyce hooveri* populations is correlated with other types of impacts such as grazing and discing, which cause soil disturbance on the pool bed, thereby introducing colonization sites for weedy upland plants. In addition, invasion of vernal pool habitat by introduced species adapted to conditions of permanent moisture was observed at sites that have been hydrologically altered to retain standing water through most or all of the growing season.

Sites characterized by significant cover or dominance of weedy taxa were relatively few in number (17) among extant populations of the species studied (14 percent of the remaining extant populations). In the Sacramento Valley, potentially significant weed problems were observed at several sites on the Vina Plains in southern Tehama County, involving *Xanthium strumarium*, *Convolvulus arvensis*, *Proboscidea louisianica*, and *Asclepias fascicularis* in large vernal pools (habitat for *Orcuttia pilosa* and *Chamaesyce hooveri*). The introduced perennial grass, *Lolium multiflorum*, was a problem in one of the smaller, swalelike pools on the Vina Plains (*Tuctoria greenei* habitat). A similar problem was found at the *Tuctoria greenei* site at the Richvale vernal pools in southern Butte County. There *Lolium* and *Phalaris paradoxa*, along with the native perennials *Eleocharis palustris* and *Eryngium vaseyi*, dominated the majority of the pool bed.

At Olcott Lake in Solano County, we observed the introduced malvaceous herb, *Sida hederacea*, to be widespread and abundant over extensive portions of the lake bed. Although *Neostapfia colusana* was also widely distributed here, *Sida* was present mostly in rather pure stands which appeared to effectively exclude *Neostapfia* from occupying some portions of the pool.

In the San Joaquin Valley, we observed significant weed competition at the series of five "Hickman pools", which represent the largest remaining populations of *Neostapfia*, *Orcuttia pilosa*, and *Chamaesyce hooveri* in Stanislaus County. A nearly pure stand of *Xanthium strumarium* densely covered an extensive area in the largest pool, which is several hundred acres in area. *Sida hederacea*, *Crypsis miliacea*, and *Bergia texana* were also abundant weeds in other portions of this vast pool. Two vernal pools in dry pasture near Planada and Le Grand in eastern Merced County, both supporting extant populations of *Tuctoria greenei*, had a weedy vegetation component characterized by the non-native grasses *Lolium multiflorum*, *Phalaris paradoxa*, *Hordeum geniculatum*, and *Polypogon monspeliensis*, probably related to overgrazing.

Competition from Native Species

In addition to competition from weeds, we also observed that competition from native plant species may be limiting the distribution and abundance of the Orcuttieae and *Chamaesyce hooveri* at some sites. Crampton (1959) found that "the best stands of either *Orcuttia* or *Neostapfia* occur mostly in the absence of other vegetation . . . . The presence of the ubiquitous vernal pool [perennials] *Eryngium vaseyi* and the sedge, *Eleocharis palustris*, restricts the density of *Orcuttia* and *Neostapfia*." Our field observations seem to confirm the preference for relatively barren areas of low competition on the part of all the species studied, especially *Chamaesyce hooveri*.

Generally, our data show that *Eryngium* dominates only near the margins of the larger, deeper vernal pools frequented by the Orcuttieae and *Chamaesyce hooveri*. Dominance by *Eryngium* over the entire pool bed was seen only in the smaller-type, early-drying vernal pools where the Orcuttieae and *Chamaesyce* were more frequently absent. These observations suggest that, at least in some localities, it is not moisture relations directly but rather competition with more marginal vernal pool species such as *Eryngium* and *Plagiobothrys* that is limiting the distribution and abundance of the species studied on the drier sites along the vernal pool topographic and moisture gradient.

Pools dominated by *Eleocharis* were recognized by Crampton (1959) in the vicinity of the Redding municipal airport on the Stillwater Plains of Shasta County. Our 1986 field studies also found *Eleocharis* dominant at some sites, generally in the deeper portions of the larger vernal pools which retain some standing water all year or late into the season. Four of the five remaining extant populations of *Orcuttia tenuis* on the Stillwater Plains are in pools with *Eleocharis* dominant over the majority of the pool bed, and *Eleocharis* competition along with hydrological modification may have caused the loss of one *Orcuttia* population west of the Redding airport.

Eleocharis dominance was observed in one natural pool supporting *Orcuttia tenuis* on the volcanic tablelands northeast of Red Bluff in Tehama County. On the Inks Creek Ranch located in this region, the margins of six artificial cattle ponds and reservoirs also were broadly and densely covered by *Eleocharis*. At these sites, *O. tenuis* and other typical vernal pool species occurred above the *Eleocharis* zone, in a narrow band occupying the ecological transition into the surrounding upland introduced grassland. Our observations at these artificial ponds suggest that, at least in some localities, it is competition with marsh species such as *Eleocharis* rather than moisture conditions that is directly limiting the distribution of *O. tenuis* and some other members of the Orcuttieae in the lower portions of the vernal pool bed.

In the vernal pool containing the "new" population of *Orcuttia viscida* at Rancho Seco in Sacramento County, the main portion of the pool bed is covered by a dense stand of *Eleocharis* with minor *Eryngium*, and the only suitable habitat for *Orcuttia* is in a small, relatively barren area at the pool inlet. A fenceline straddles the main portion of this pool, and south of the fence the pool bed is heavily grazed, with *Eleocharis* density significantly reduced. This observation suggests that a grazing regime of controlled periodicity and intensity may have a role in managing the habitat of this and other species of Central Valley Orcuttieae.

In the San Joaquin Valley, we observed negative impacts to *Neostapfia colusana* resulting from *Eleocharis* competition at one site south of Modesto Reservoir in eastern Stanislaus County. This pool is a remnant of what once was a much larger vernal lake, which was bisected by an unpaved road (Dienstag Road). The grade of this road has deepened the pool and reduced its surface area, thereby increasing the inundation time during the growing season. In this manner the shift to *Eleocharis* dominance in this pool remnant may result from hydrological alteration.

Grasshopper Predation

During our 1986 field studies in the San Joaquin Valley, a large concentration of grasshoppers was observed on the Flying M Ranches in eastern Merced County. Damage due to grasshopper predation was observed in a few populations of *Neostapfia* and *Orcuttia inaequalis* in this area. In the Sacramento Valley, two populations of *Orcuttia tenuis* northeast of Red Bluff (Tehama County) sustained impacts from grasshopper predation. Grasshopper damage was particularly prevalent in seven *Tuctoria greenei* populations on the Vina Plains of southern Tehama County and in the Pentz Road population of this species in southern Butte County; *Orcuttia pilosa* populations in the Vina Plains region were also attacked but to a lesser extent. Grasshopper damage was not observed in any populations of *Orcuttia viscida* or *Chamaesyce hooveri*.

Griggs (1980) also noticed extensive grasshopper damage to the Sacramento Valley populations of *Tuctoria greenei* during field work conducted in 1978. The preference of grasshoppers for *T. greenei* may be correlated with the near absence in this species of the viscid, acidic exudate found in the other members of the Orcuttieae (Hoover 1941; Griggs 1974, 1980). We also observed that grasshoppers seem to attack Orcuttieae populations during the period of senescence at the end of the growing season. This fact may reflect a preference on the part of grasshoppers for dried plant tissues (Scott 1986), but might also be attributable to lower levels of viscid Orcuttieae exudate in the dried plants or an increase in the grasshoppers' biochemical tolerance to this exudate.

Grasshopper populations are known to fluctuate from year to year in relation to climatic factors, and their impact on Orcuttieae populations will vary correspondingly. According to Scott (1986), above-average spring temperatures and below-average precipitation during the same period are correlated with large grasshopper populations during the summer months. Karban (1986) reports that 1986 was a much greater "grasshopper year" when compared with the last several years.

Land Ownership and Protection Efforts

Populations of all seven species studied now enjoy some degree of protection within ecological preserves or through conservation easements, largely due to the activities of the California Field Office of The Nature Conservancy (TNC). The number of protected populations of each species can be summarized as follows: 5 populations of *Chamaesyce hooveri* (26 percent of the remaining extant populations); 5 populations of *Neostapfia* (13 percent); 4 populations of *Orcuttia inaequalis* (31 percent); 5 populations of *O. pilosa* (23 percent); 2 populations of *O. tenuis* (5 percent); 1 population of *O. viscida* (10 percent); and 3 populations of *Tuctoria greenei* (17 percent).

At the TNC Vina Plains Preserve in the Sacramento Valley of southern Tehama County, there are no less than eight vernal pools supporting 5 populations of *Orcuttia pilosa*, 5 populations of *Chamaesyce hooveri*, 3 populations of *Tuctoria greenei*, and 1 population of *Orcuttia tenuis*. However, we observed that cattle from an adjoining ranch were somehow able to find their way onto the Vina Plains Preserve in 1986, where they caused evident damage to some populations of the species of concern, particularly in the three large pools at the southern end of the Preserve.

Another large population of *O. tenuis* is protected at the TNC Boggs Lake Preserve in the North Coast Ranges of Lake County. However, direct vehicular impacts to the *Orcuttia* population were observed in one area along the lake's eastern margin.

Neostapfia colusana is protected at Olcott Lake on the TNC Jepson Prairie Preserve in Solano County, which is administered through the University of California, Davis. This huge, alkali vernal lake is also the type locality for the federally listed *Tuctoria mucronata* (Crampton 1959, Reeder 1982). Olcott Lake is bisected by Cook Lane, with *Neostapfia* abundant in the portion east of the road but almost entirely absent from the larger western half. This phenomenon may be due to the hydrologic alteration of the habitat caused by construction of the road. The southeastern quadrant of Olcott Lake remains in private ownership, and there the *Neostapfia* habitat is grazed by sheep in the earlier part of the growing season, without apparent detriment to *Neostapfia*.

The rare *Orcuttia viscida*, which is endemic to 10 vernal pools in Sacramento County, receives explicit protection only at one site: a small ecological preserve owned by the California Department of Fish and Game east of Phoenix airfield in Fair Oaks. Although surrounded on three sides by suburban residential development, the site is bordered by a tall chain-link fence which seems to deter pedestrians and vehicles adequately. However, long-term decline of the population as a result of hydrological changes within the pool drainage area remains a question.

In the San Joaquin Valley, TNC retains a conservation easement on 2400 acres of the 15,000-acre Flying M Ranches in eastern Merced County (Johnson 1986). According to our data, this easement protects 4 populations of *Orcuttia inaequalis* and 4 populations of *Neostapfia colusana* distributed among seven pools. Several other populations of *Neostapfia* and *O. inaequalis* occur on this large parcel and are not currently protected by any easement. However, the ranch generally experiences only light cattle grazing, and so grazing impacts to Orcuttieae populations were found to be minimal.

Despite the above-mentioned protection efforts, the vast majority of the remaining extant populations of Central Valley Orcuttieae and *Chamaesyce hooveri* occur on private rangeland. Consequently, any attempts to protect and manage these populations will be difficult at best. Fortunately, there exist some exceptions to this generalization which may provide opportunities for future protection.

For example, our data show that 5 of the 39 remaining extant populations of *Orcuttia tenuis* are on public land administered by the federal Bureau of Land Management (BLM) and managed under private grazing leases. Three of these *O. tenuis* populations occur on the volcanic table-lands northeast of Red Bluff in Tehama County, and the other two are on the Stillwater Plains in Shasta County. These populations are protected to some degree under official BLM policy concerning sensitive species. A newly discovered population of *Orcuttia inaequalis*, on Table Mountain east of Millerton Lake in Fresno County, is also partly on BLM land (Hansen 1986). Similarly, one of the two populations of *O. tenuis* remaining in Goose Valley (northeastern Shasta County) is on the Lassen National Forest, and therefore should be protected under U.S. Forest Service sensitive species policy.

Orcuttia viscida is unusual among the species studied in that all but one of the remaining extant populations are located on lands owned by state and local governments. In addition to the CDFG preserve at Phoenix airfield, *O. viscida* occurs in Phoenix Park (City of Fair Oaks Recreation and Parks District), at the county dump site (County of Sacramento), and near Rancho Seco nuclear power plant (Sacramento Municipal Utility

District). Whether conservation opportunities at these sites can be fully realized remains to be seen.

On the Stillwater Plains of Shasta County, two extant populations of *Orcuttia tenuis* remain on land owned by the Redding Municipal Airport. Being located on airport property, these populations have received *de facto* protection while several neighboring pools supporting the *Orcuttia* have been destroyed by activities related to airport and urban expansion. Perhaps a management agreement or conservation easement could be negotiated to provide explicit protection for the remaining *O. tenuis* populations at the airport.

CONCLUSIONS

The results presented here indicate that the Central Valley species of the Orcuttieae and *Chamaesyce hooveri* have been and are now threatened by a variety of human-caused impacts, especially on-going conversion of the remaining vernal pool habitats for these species to irrigated agriculture and irrigated pasture. *Neostapfia colusana* and *Orcuttia tenuis* possess the largest number of extant populations remaining and presently appear to be the least threatened of the seven species studied. The above two species and *Chamaesyce hooveri* also seem to possess the greatest resistance to livestock grazing, which was the most frequently observed impact among extant populations of the species studied.

Orcuttia viscida comprises the smallest number of extant populations remaining and may be considered the rarest member of the Central Valley Orcuttieae, aside from the federally listed *Tuctoria mucronata*. However, *Orcuttia inaequalis* has a similarly low number of extant populations remaining and has undergone the most dramatic loss of populations among the seven species studied, with greater than 50 percent of the known populations extirpated. *Tuctoria greenei* also has experienced a drastic reduction in numbers, and furthermore this species seems to be particularly sensitive to grazing impacts when compared with the other species under study.

Griggs and Jain (1983) studied the genetics and demography of *Orcuttia* populations in California and recommended that the optimal conservation strategy for these species would be one which maximizes genetic diversity. Without arguing the soundness of this approach on the basis of species biology, it should be realized that existing patterns of land ownership and land use, as well as the type and degree of associated impacts, provide a set of constraints and opportunities to land and resource managers and conservation organizations interested in protecting these species and their fragile habitats. As an example, consider that 6 of the remaining 10 populations of *Orcuttia viscida* occur at the dump site for Sacramento County. Similarly, 8 of the 13 extant populations remaining for *Orcuttia inaequalis* occur on the Flying M Ranches in eastern Merced County. There are only three known extant populations of *Tuctoria greenei* remaining in the San Joaquin Valley. These types of information need to be considered as well in decision-making toward effective species protection and management.

Our study observed a variety of threat factors to extant Orcuttieae and *Chamaesyce hooveri* populations. Most of these populations have been negatively affected, but positive impacts to the species of concern were also observed, as in the series of artificial ponds and reservoirs on the Inks Creek Ranch in Tehama County, which have been colonized by *Orcuttia tenuis*. Although the majority of remaining extant populations occur on private grazing land, all of the species studied, with the exception of *Tuctoria greenei*, displayed at least some tolerance to grazing. Furthermore, livestock grazing may have a beneficial role in management of the species studied at sites where native vernal pool perennials such as *Eleocharis palustris* are outcompeting the species of concern on the pool bed. More research is needed to model the importance of various factors influencing the phenology and demography of the species of concern at specific sites. These factors should include the effects of seasonal rainfall patterns, ambient temperature and wind conditions, pool size (surface area and depth), soil conditions on the pool bed, and pool drainage area. Greater understanding of these factors may lead to more effective, site-specific protection and management of Orcuttieae and *Chamaesyce hooveri* populations.

ACKNOWLEDGMENTS

This two-year study was funded in part under U.S. Fish and Wildlife Service Contract No. 14-16-0001-85115(NR). We thank Monty Knudsen and the staff of the USFWS Sacramento Endangered Species Office for reviewing this document and releasing it for presentation. Also, thanks to Bob Holland of the California Department of Fish and Game, who has made a number of helpful comments and suggestions during the course of this project.

REFERENCES

Climatological data, California. Asheville, NC: Environmental Data and Information Service. U.S. Department of Commerce, National Oceanic and Atmospheric Administration; 1985-1986.

Crampton, Beecher. The grass genera *Orcuttia* and *Neostapfia*: a study in habitat and morphological specialization. Madrono 15:97-110; 1959.

Crampton, Beecher. Rare grasses in a vanishing habitat. Fremontia 4(3):22-23; 1976.

Griggs, F. Thomas. Systematics and ecology of the genus *Orcuttia* (Gramineae). Chico, CA: California State University, Chico; 1974. 69 p. M.A. thesis.

Griggs, F. Thomas. Life history strategies of the genus *Orcuttia* (Gramineae). In: Vernal pools--their ecology and conservation. Publication No. 9. Davis, CA: Institute of Ecology, University of California, Davis; 1976:57-63. Proceedings.

Griggs, F. Thomas. Population studies in the genus *Orcuttia* (Poaceae). Davis, CA: University of California, Davis; 1980. 98 p. Dissertation.

Griggs, F. Thomas. Life histories of vernal pool annual grasses. Fremontia 9(1):14-17; 1981.

Griggs, F. Thomas.; Jain, Subodh K. Conservation of vernal pool plants in California, II. Population biology of a rare and unique grass genus *Orcuttia*. Biological Conservation 27:171-193; 1983.

Hansen, Rob (Letter to Steve McCormick). 1986 June 20. 2 leaves + enclosures. Located at: California Field Office, The Nature Conservancy, San Francisco, CA.

Holland, Robert F. Biogeography and ecology of vernal pools in California. Davis, CA: University of California, Davis; 1978. Dissertation.

Holland, Robert F. The geographic and edaphic distribution of vernal pools in the Great Central Valley, California. Special Publication No. 4. Sacramento, CA: California Native Plant Society; 1978. 12 p. + maps.

Holland, Robert F.; Jain, Subodh K. Spatial and temporal variation in plant species diversity of vernal pools. Publication No. 28. Davis, CA: Institute of Ecology, University of California, Davis; 1984:198-209. Proceedings.

Hoover, Robert F. The genus *Orcuttia*. Bull. Torrey Bot. Club 68:149-156; 1936.

Johnson, Stephen. Director of Science and Stewardship, California Field Office, The Nature Conservancy, San Francisco, CA. [Telephone conversation with R. Douglas Stone]. 23 October 1986.

Karban, Richard, Assistant Professor of Entomology, University of California, Davis, CA. [Telephone conversation with R. Douglas Stone]. 28 October 1986.

Reeder, John R. The tribe Orcuttieae and the subtribes of the Pappophoreae (Gramineae). Madroño 18:18-28; 1965.

Reeder, John R. Systematics of the tribe Orcuttieae (Gramineae) and the description of a new segregate genus, *Tuctoria*. Amer. J. Bot. 69(7):1082-1095; 1982.

Scott, Susan. Doctoral candidate in Entomology, University of California, Davis, CA. [Telephone conversation with R. Douglas Stone]. 30 October 1986.

Electrophoretic Analysis of Variation in Native Monterey Cypress (*Cupressus macrocarpa* Hartw.)

M. Thompson Conkle[1]

Abstract: One of California's rarest endemic conifers, Monterey cypress, was sampled by collecting seeds from 142 native trees; 75 trees from Cypress Point and 67 from Point Lobos State Reserve. Genotypes were determined by electrophoretic analysis of gametophyte tissue from 6 seeds of each tree. A total of 28 genes were analyzed; 17 of the total (61 percent) had two or more allelic variants. Heterozygosity averaged for all genes equalled .18. The allele frequencies for Cypress Point and Point Lobos populations differed for several genes. Patterns of enzyme variation indicated that the northern stands at Cypress Point differed from the southern and the western stands at Point Lobos differed from the eastern.

Monterey cypress is a valuable and picturesque tree with one of the smallest natural ranges of any conifer. Knowledge about the amount and distribution of natural variation is requisite for effective gene conservation and efficient sampling for growth trials and improvement programs. This report provides genetic information about levels and patterns of variation based on biochemical markers that are products of nuclear genes.

The native cypresses grow within 400 meters of the ocean in two small populations flanking Carmel Bay (fig. 1). The northern population, which is referred to here as the Cypress Point population, extends about 3 kilometers along the Seventeen Mile Drive from Cypress Point to Pescadero Point. 4.5 kilometers to the south, the Point Lobos population occupies rocky north-facing promontories wholly within the Point Lobos State Reserve.

Genetic analyses of enzymes provide valuable information about variation in natural populations. One measure of variation is heterozygosity, the proportion of individuals with two different forms of a gene (heterozygotes), or alternatively, the proportion of heterozygous loci in an individual. Analyses of enzyme variants indicate that conifers have high heterozygosity values in comparison with other plant taxa (Hamrick et al. 1979), and that high values are related to various life history traits of conifers: widespread geographic ranges, wind pollination,

---

[1] Geneticist, Institute of Forest Genetics, Pacific Southwest Forest and Range Experiment Station, U.S. Department of Agriculture--Forest Service, Box 245, Berkeley, CA 94701

primarily outcrossed mating systems, high fecundity, and later stages of ecological succession.

Among California conifers, species with high average heterozygosities (between .24 and .30) are Douglas-fir (<u>Pseudotsuga menziesii</u> (Mirb.) Franco), sugar pine (<u>Pinus lambertiana</u> Dougl.), and Jeffrey pine (<u>Pinus jeffreyi</u> Grev. & Balf.). Many others in California have mid-range values from .12 through .22: ponderosa pine (<u>Pinus ponderosa</u> Dougl. ex Laws.), lodgepole pine (<u>Pinus contorta</u> Dougl. ex Loud.), incense-cedar (<u>Libocedrus decurrens</u> Torr.), white fir (<u>Abies concolor</u> (Gord. & Glend.) Lindl. ex Hildebr.), and California red fir (<u>Abies magnifica</u> A. Murr.) are near .20; giant sequoia (<u>Sequoiadendron giganteum</u> (Lindl.) Buchholz), Coulter pine (<u>Pinus coulteri</u> D. Don), and Monterey pine (<u>Pinus radiata</u> D. Don) are near .15; bishop (<u>Pinus muricata</u> D. Don), knobcone (<u>Pinus attenuata</u> Lemm.), and Digger pines (<u>Pinus sabiniana</u> Dougl.) are near .12. The endemics with very narrow ranges, bristlecone fir (<u>Abies bracteata</u> D. Don ex Poiteau) and Torrey pine (<u>Pinus torreyana</u> Parry ex Carr.) have low values: bristlecone fir is .05 and Torrey pine is devoid of enzyme variation; heterozygosity for 59 genes equals 0.0 (Ledig and Conkle 1983).

The explanation proposed for Torrey pine's lack of variation relates to evolutionary events that must have driven the species to conditions near extinction. Ledig and Conkle hypothesized that effective population sizes probably reached dangerously low numbers during increasingly arid conditions imposed by the Xerothermic period 8,500 to 3,000 years ago. Large and unpredictable shifts in allele frequencies imposed by the closed breeding system eventually led to the loss of variation within the two surviving populations.

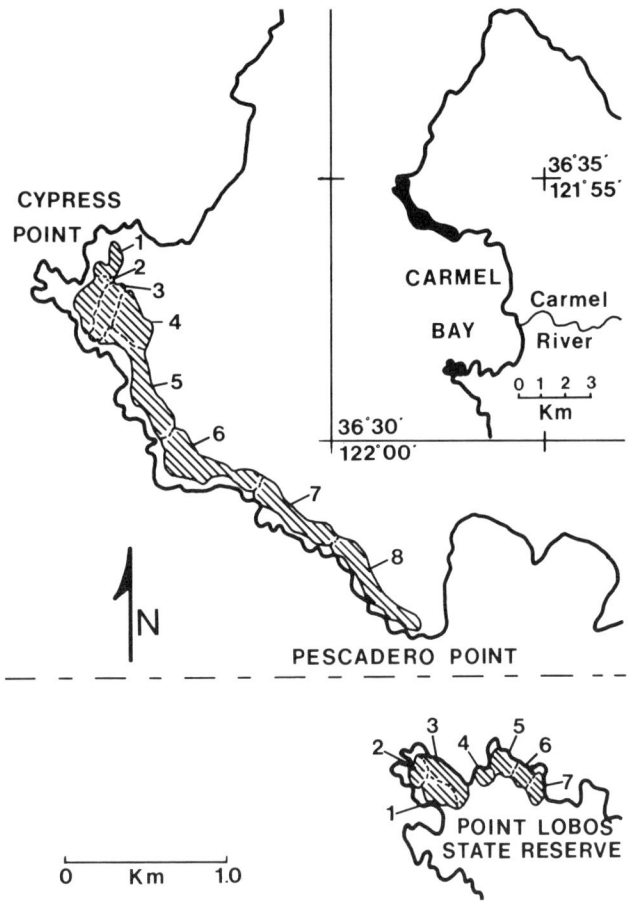

Figure 1--Diagrammatic map of Monterey cypress distribution in central coastal California (adapted from Griffin and Critchfield 1972). The shaded areas indicate the natural occurrence of cypresses and numbers identify the stands sampled at Cypress Point and Point Lobos State Reserve (Kafton 1976).

The loss of diversity means that Torrey pine is ill-equipped to adapt to future environmental change.

Monterey cypress resembles Torrey pine in its growing conditions and possible evolutionary history. The cypresses are restricted to Mesozoic granitic headlands in a narrow ecological zone between the ocean's edge and a Monterey pine forest. Only two cypress populations remain, and both encounter pines along their inland edges: there, the more aggressive pine appears to limit cypress reproduction. The cypresses probably number near 10,000, a number similar to the estimates for native Torrey pines.

The cypress's close association with Monterey pine suggests parallel evolution. The maritime California closed-cone pines probably originated in western Mexico, and fossils of Monterey pines are known from collections as far north as Drakes Bay (Axelrod 1980). Increasing aridity caused local extinctions and the eventual restriction of Monterey pines to populations of modest size at three locations on the central California coast and on two islands off Baja California (Axelrod 1980). But unlike Torrey pine, Monterey pines have mid-range genetic diversity values suggesting that their populations have always remained sufficiently large to maintain significant levels of variation.

The fossil record of Monterey cypress is scant but also provides evidence of a more wide-spread distribution. Cones, seeds, branches, and wood dating from 30,000 years ago were found at Rancho La Brea in Los Angeles (Warter 1976 cited in Axelrod 1983).

With a goal of gaining knowledge important for gene conservation, David L. Kafton undertook a study of diversity in Monterey cypress as a dissertation project at the University of California, Berkeley (Kafton 1976). Two of Dr. Kafton's goals were to evaluate the amount and the geographic distribution of variation in the native cypress populations. He subdivided the native populations into stands and then collected cones from individual trees well scattered throughout each stand. Enzyme analyses were done in the Forest Service laboratory at Berkeley. Using starch gel electrophoresis of haploid seed tissues, he determined the genotypes of individual trees for two enzyme genes.

The remaining seeds were stored in freezers. Subsequent improvements in laboratory techniques greatly increased the number of genes that could be analyzed, and Kafton made his stored seed collections available for additional analyses.

MONTEREY CYPRESS SAMPLES

Kafton (1976) subdivided the two native populations into stands by noting natural associations (fig. 1). He identified 8 stands within the Cypress Point population. In this report, the most northern is numbered 1: stands 2 and 3 occupy the same headlands. The Crocker Grove, bounded by Portola Road on the east and the Seventeen Mile Drive on the west, is stand 4. Stand 5 includes trees west of the Seventeen Mile Drive near the Crocker Grove. Stands 6, 7, and 8 are each about .6 km in length and extend along the coastal side of the Seventeen Mile Drive to Pescadero Point. Stand 6 includes Sunset Point: the Lone Cypress Tree is near its southern border. Trees near Midway Point are in Stand 7. The southernmost stand consists of the cypresses on Pescadero Point.

The seven stands identified at Point Lobos conform to the natural ridges and depressions on these rocky headlands. The trees are in two groups separated by deep, wave-cut Cypress Cove. The westernmost stands, here called Point Lobos 1, 2, and 3, are on a rocky promontory. Stands 4, 5, 6, and 7 are to the east on promontories between Cypress and Bluefish Coves.

Genetic analyses were performed using the haploid tissues from 6 seeds per tree to infer each tree's multilocus genotype. An average of about 10 trees per stand were genotyped, a total of 75 from Cypress Point and 67 from Point Lobos.

Laboratory procedures for performing electrophoresis are described in Conkle et al. (1982): the genetic interpretations and gene notations are similar to those described in Strauss and Conkle (1986). Different forms of enzymes for each gene are identified by noting their migration distances relative to the most common one: for example, an allele designated 1.20 identifies a band that migrates 20 percent further than the common band (the 1.00 allele). Analyses were calculated with the BIOSYS computer program (Swofford and Selander 1981). The subdivision of diversity into contributions from different levels of nested sampling (two populations in the total, genetically similar areas within each population, stands within the areas, and variation within stands) followed Chakraborty's procedures (Appendix 1, Beckwitt and Chakraborty 1980).

VARIATION IN NATIVE STANDS

This analysis provides information on 28 genes in Monterey cypress. Of this total, 17 genes (61 percent) had two or more alleles. Allele frequencies for the variable genes are listed by stands in table 1. The genes and their alleles are coded down the left column of the table.

The first gene listed is Aco (aconitase). Cypress Point stands 1, 2, and 3 had similar Aco frequencies: near .60 for the 1.05 allele and .40 for the 1.00. Cypress Point stands 4 through 8 had lower frequencies of the 1.05 allele: their combined frequencies equaled about .4 for the 1.05 and .6 for the 1.00 alleles. The frequencies for Point Lobos stands 1, 2, and 3 were about .25 for the 1.05 allele and .75 for the 1.00; while stands 4, 5, 6, and 7 had nearly equal frequencies of the two alleles. An Aco allele with .95 mobility was rare; it was only found in Point Lobos stand 1.

Each additional gene yields some information on the amount and geographic distribution of variation in Monterey cypress. There was a moderate concentration of an acid phosphatase allele, Acph(.91), in Point Lobos stands 1, 2, and 3; frequencies were .23, .23, and .35, respectively; the allele was absent or at lower frequencies in other stands.

A gene for alcohol dehydrogenase had 5 alleles. The Adh(1.00) allele was common to all stands and its frequency always exceeded .50. The 1.18 allele was scattered throughout populations at relatively low frequencies. One noteworthy allele, Adh(.92), was in the Point Lobos population where its frequency equaled .10; the allele was absent from all Cypress Point samples. Another allele, Adh(.68), was absent from the four northernmost stands, Cypress Point stands 1, 2, 3, and 4. The fifth allele, Adh(.52), was found only once, in a heterozygote from Point Lobos stand 1.

Alap, Est, Flest, and Gdh were genes with two alleles; their alleles all had intermediate frequencies; both alleles of each gene occurred throughout all stands and geographic variation appeared random.

A glucose-6-phosphate dehydrogenase gene had three alleles. The second most common, allele G6pd(1.08), had moderate frequencies in Cypress Point stands 1, 2, and 3 and Point Lobos stands 1, 2, and 3. The allele was less frequent in the five southern stands at Cypress Point and in the four eastern stands at Point Lobos.

One of two variable glutamate oxaloacetate transaminase genes had an allele that was only present in the Point Lobos population. Got1(1.06) was absent from all Cypress Point stand samples. The second Got gene had a low-frequency allele that was distributed throughout most stands.

A gene for leucine amonopeptidase had three alleles; one was common throughout all stands; one, Lap(.94), was more frequent in the three western stands on Point Lobos than elsewhere; and the last Lap(.89) was rare and was only found in Point Lobos stand 1.

Table 1--Allele frequencies for 17 genes listed by their occurrence in 8 stands at Cypress Point and 7 at Point Lobos. Eleven additional genes lacked mobility variants (Ald1, 2, and 3; Cat; Got2; Idh; Mdh1, 2, and 3; Pgi1; Pgm).

Locus Allele	Cypress Point Populations								Point Lobos Populations						
	(Northern)			:	(Southern)				(Western)			:	(Eastern)		
	1	2	3	: 4	5	6	7	8	1	2	3	: 4	5	6	7
Aco															
1.05	.62	.58	.60	: .50	.43	.33	.46	.44	.17	.27	.30	: .63	.57	.50	.40
1.00	.38	.42	.40	: .50	.57	.67	.54	.56	.76	.73	.70	: .37	.43	.50	.60
.95				:					.07			:			
Acph															
1.00	.88	.92	.95	: .94	.97	1.0	.82	.88	.77	.77	.65	: 1.0	1.0	.94	.90
.91	.12	.08	.05	: .06	.03		.18	.12	.23	.23	.35	:		.06	.10
Adh															
1.18	.06	.08		:	.07	.06		.12	.10	.08		:			.20
1.00	.94	.92	1.0	: 1.0	.83	.88	.86	.63	.70	.54	.70	: 1.0	.64	.88	.80
.92				:					.14	.15	.05	:	.22	.06	
.68				:	.10	.06	.14	.25	.03	.23	.25	:	.14	.06	
.52				:					.03			:			
Alap															
1.00	.69	.75	.70	: .88	.80	.44	.86	.81	.87	.69	.75	: .50	.86	.69	.65
1.03	.31	.25	.30	: .12	.20	.56	.14	.19	.13	.31	.25	: .50	.14	.31	.35
Est															
1.54	.31	.08	.35	: .19	.13	.11	.05	.06	.23		.10	: .25	.07	.06	.20
1.00	.69	.92	.65	: .81	.87	.89	.95	.94	.77	1.0	.90	: .75	.93	.94	.80
Flest															
1.00	.31	.58	.50	: .56	.53	.22	.59	.44	.40	.88	.80	: .38	.86	.75	.75
1.16	.69	.42	.50	: .44	.47	.78	.41	.56	.60	.12	.20	: .62	.14	.25	.25
Gdh															
1.00	.81	.67	.75	: .44	.63	.79	.77	.88	.80	.85	.75	: .63	.79	.75	.80
.91	.19	.33	.25	: .56	.37	.22	.23	.12	.20	.15	.25	: .37	.21	.25	.20
G6pd															
1.08	.50	.17	.35	: .06	.07	.06			.10	.27	.20	:	.14	.12	.05
1.00	.50	.83	.65	: .94	.90	.94	.95	1.0	.83	.73	.80	: 1.0	.86	.88	.95
.92				:	.03		.05		.07			:			
Got1															
1.06				:					.03	.08	.15	:	.07	.12	
1.00	1.0	1.0	1.0	: 1.0	1.0	1.0	1.0	1.0	.97	.92	.85	: 1.0	.93	.88	1.0
Got3															
1.47			.15	: .19	.07	.06	.14	.12	.10	.15	.05	:	.07		.05
1.00	1.0	1.0	.85	: .81	.93	.94	.86	.88	.90	.85	.95	: 1.0	.93	1.0	.95
Lap															
1.00	.94	.83	.90	: 1.0	1.0	.83	.96	.94	.63	.81	.80	: .88	.79	.88	1.0
.94	.06	.17	.10	:		.17	.04	.06	.30	.19	.20	: .12	.21	.12	
.89				:					.07			:			
Per															
1.00	.88	.92	.95	: .75	.60	.89	.73	.88	.87	.50	.95	: 1.0	1.0	1.0	.80
1.45	.12	.08	.05	: .25	.40	.11	.27	.12	.13	.50	.05	:			.20
6Pgd1															
1.06	.31		.10	: .12	.07	.11			.23	.12	.10	:		.06	
1.00	.69	1.0	.90	: .88	.93	.89	1.0	1.0	.77	.88	.90	: 1.0	1.0	.94	1.0
6Pgd2															
1.20	.06		.10	: .12	.10				.20	.12	.20	:	.21		
1.00	.94	1.0	.90	: .88	.90	1.0	1.0	1.0	.80	.88	.80	: 1.0	.79	1.0	1.0
Pgi2															
1.60		.08		:	.07		.05		.03	.12	.35	:	.07	.06	
1.00	.63	.58	.70	: .81	.56	.67	.54	.81	.57	.54	.35	: .75	.22	.44	.30
.56	.12			: .13	.37	.33	.41	.19	.17	.15		: .13			
.28	.25	.34	.30	: .06					.23	.19	.30	: .12	.71	.50	.70
Skdh															
1.15				:		.06		.06				: .12			
1.07	.19	.08	.15	:	.16	.44	.45			.08	.05	:	.50	.06	.20
1.00	.81	.92	.85	: .88	.77	.50	.50	.81	.97	.88	.95	: .50	.50	.63	.80
.93				: .12	.07		.05	.13	.03	.04		: .38		.31	
Tzo															
1.00	1.0	1.0	1.0	: .94	.93	.94	.86	.63	.93	.85	.95	: 1.0	.79	.69	1.0
.82				: .06	.07	.06	.14	.37	.07	.15	.05	:	.21	.31	

A peroxidase allele, Per(1.45), was found in comparatively low frequency in the four easternmost stands at Point Lobos. Two loci for 6-phosphogluconic dehydrogenase had nearly identical variation. The rarer of two alleles for both loci were consistently represented in Point Lobos stands 1, 2, and 3. Elsewhere their frequencies fluctuated from modest values to zero.

Four alleles of phosphoglucose isomerase had interesting patterns of variation. Pgi2(1.60) which had a low frequency overall, reached moderate frequencies in the three western stands on Pont Lobos. The common allele (1.00) was found in about .70 frequency at Cypress Point, but was in less than .50 frequency at Point Lobos. Pgi2(.56) was an allele with relatively high frequencies in the 5 southern stands at Cypress Point. The fourth allele, Pgi2(.28), had high frequencies in the three easternmost stands at Point Lobos where it equaled or exceeded .50; the frequency in Cypress Point stands 1, 2, and 3 and Point Lobos stands 1, 2, and 3 equaled about .25; and the allele was absent from the 4 southernmost stands at Cypress Point.

A shikimate dehydrogenase gene had 4 alleles with frequencies that varied from stand to stand. The 1.15 allele was rare, about .02 frequency for the species, but was found in samples from both Cypress Point and Point Lobos. Skdh(1.07) was present throughout all areas but Skdh(.93) was notably absent from the three northern stands at Cypress Point.

The final variable gene, tetrazolium oxidase, had two alleles. The lower frequency allele, Tzo(.82), was absent from the three northern stands at Cypress Point.

Some genes (Adh, Flest, Got1, Lap, Pgi2) showed minor but consistent differences between the Cypress Point and the Point Lobos populations and others (Aco, Acph, Adh, G6pd, Per, 6Pgd1, 6Pgd2, Pgi2, Skdh) showed minor but consistent differences between the northern and southern stands at Cypress Point or the western and eastern stands at Point Lobos.

The data from all genes was combined to estimate the genetic distances among stands (Nei 1978). Stands with very similar frequency profiles have genetic distances near 0.0. As frequency differences increase among stands, their corresponding genetic distances increase. The maximum value is 1.0; the case where two taxonomic units have no alleles in common.

A matrix of genetic distances for all combinations of stands was used to construct a cluster diagram (fig. 2). First, stands with near 0.0 distances were placed on the same branch: Cypress Point 1 and 3, Cypress Point 2 and Point Lobos 4, Cypress Point 4 and 5, Point Lobos 2 and 3, and Point Lobos 5 and 6. Frequencies for each pair were then averaged and a new matrix of values was computed. Stands with the shortest distances were then added to the appropriate branches. This process with unweighted pair-group averaging was continued until all branches were joined.

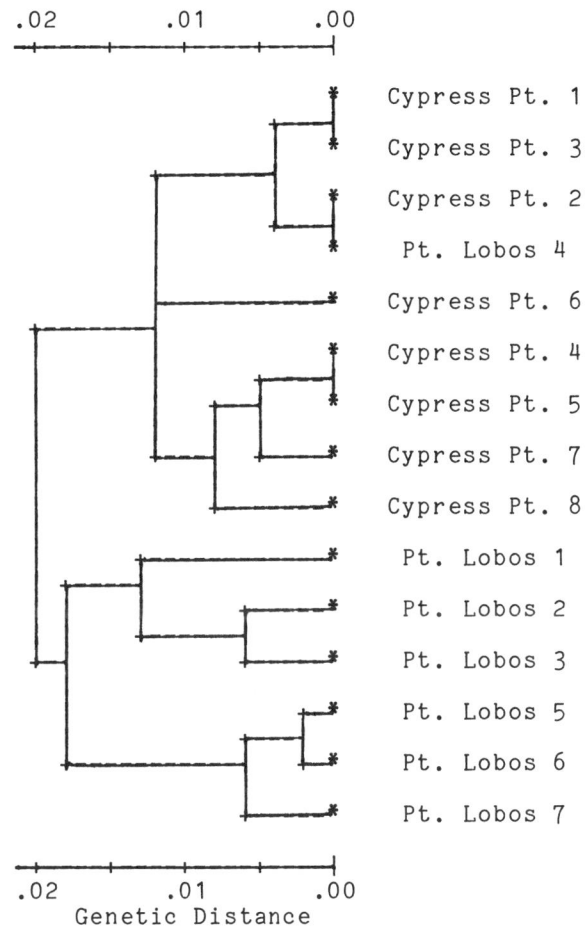

Figure 2--Phenogram representing the genetic similarities among Monterey cypress stands.

The Cypress Point stands occupy one primary branch, Point Lobos stands occupy the other, with only one exception. The exception was Point Lobos stand 4: it was the stand with the smallest sample size, only 4 trees, owing to failures in seed germination. I judge this sample to be too small to accurately place the stand within the cluster diagram. Note that Cypress Point stands 1, 2, and 3 cluster on one sub-branch and stands 4, 5, 7, and 8 cluster on another. There were also 2 sub-clusters at Point Lobos: one consists of stands 1, 2, and 3 and the other with 5, 6, and 7.

These genetic associations closely correspond to geographic associations. The main populations differed and each, in turn, had genetic sub-structure. The three northern stands at Cypress Point form one group, the five southern stands another; the three western stands at Point Lobos form one group, and the four eastern stands another. The minor decisions about group relationships required adding Cypress Point stand 6 to its appropriate geographic cluster, and I reasoned that small sample size contributed random variation to frequencies for Point Lobos stand 4: comparisons with frequencies for Point Lobos stands 3 and 5 provided evidence that it may be added to the eastern group.

Allele frequencies were useful for evaluating amounts of variation: table 2 contains expected heterozygosities averaged over all genes, including those with no allelic variation, for three levels of the nested hierarchy.

Table 2--Sample sizes and expected heterozygosity values for various levels of hierarchical sampling of Monterey cypress.

Population	Number of trees in sample	Expected heterozygosity and (S.E.)
Cypress Point		
Northern	24	.162 (.036)
Southern	51	.164 (.035)
Total	75	.167 (.035)
Point Lobos		
Western	38	.203 (.038)
Eastern	29	.161 (.036)
Total	67	.190 (.036)
Species Total	142	.177 (.035)

Heterozygosity values obtained by direct counts were virtually identical to Hardy-Weinberg expected values when the comparisons were made among the groups in populations. Correspondence between the observed and expected heterozygosity estimates was evidence that each of the four groups consists of trees in genetic equilibrium: tree genotype frequencies were those expected with random pollination and random survival within each group.

The western group of stands at Point Lobos had higher heterozygosity (equal to about .20) than the other three groups: northern and southern Cypress Point and eastern Point Lobos had values near .16. The Point Lobos population had slightly higher heterozygosity than the Cypress Point population (about .19 versus .17) when data were pooled. Averaged over all genes and disregarding any genetic or geographic structure, the species heterozygosity was .177.

To estimate the variation associated with the genetic structure of populations, the heterozygosity value for each gene was partitioned into the sources of variation associated with different levels of the nested hierarchy (Appendix 1, Beckwitt and Chakraborty 1980). Then the values were averaged for all loci and the percent of variation associated with each level was computed (table 3).

Table 3--Partition of expected heterozygosity into sources of variation associated with various levels of hierarchical sampling in Monterey cypress.

Source of variation	Partition of expected mean heterozygosity	
	Value(S.E.)	Pct.
Between Cypress Pt. and Pt. Lobos	.003 (.002)	2
Between the two areas within Cypress Pt. and within Pt. Lobos	.006 (.002)	3
Between stands within areas	.012 (.004)	7
Within stands	.156 (.039)	88
Total	.177 (.045)	

The total species heterozygosity of .177 consisted of a small proportion between the two main populations (2 percent) and slightly more (3 percent) between the two areas within each population (table 3). Thus, about 5 percent of the total variation was associated with these two levels of population structure. Variation among stands within areas accounted for 7 percent of the variation. As with many conifers, most of the variation within Monterey cypress (88 percent) was associated with genetic differences among trees within the stands.

CONCLUSIONS

Genetic variation in this very narrowly restricted species equaled that of much more geographically and ecologically diverse California conifers: Monterey cypress's average heterozygosity, which is here estimated to equal .18, is similar to those of lodgepole and ponderosa pines, incense-cedar, and white and California red firs. It exceeds the average heterozygosities for the California closed-cone pines which are between .12 and .14. But its greatest contrast is with Torrey pine, which is devoid of enzyme variation.

The high average heterozygosity in Monterey cypress is a result of a high proportion of heterozygous genes, alleles having intermediate frequencies, and genes with up to five alternative forms.

Monterey cypress's heterozygosity is a puzzle in light of Torrey pine and bristlecone fir's low values. The cypress must have avoided genetic bottlenecks caused by low numbers of founding colonists or fluctuating population sizes that occasionally reached very small numbers.

A likely explanation of high heterozygosity in the cypress is that the extant populations are remnants of a once widespread progenitor species. The occurrence of Monterey cypress fossils in the Los Angeles area supports this conclusion. A parallel hypothesis has been proposed to explain high heterozygosity in eastern Great Basin bristlecone pine (Hiebert and Hamrick 1983). Populations of bristlecone pine, which were once widespread at low to mid-elevations, became fragmented as climates became warmer and drier. The pines are now restricted to high altitudes, near tree line, on a few mountains in eastern Nevada and western Utah. The present distribution of Monterey cypress may mark its nadir. It is a relict of a species that has become extinct in all locations except the relatively cool and moist refugium adjacent to Carmel Bay.

Several of Monterey Cypress's reproductive (Johnson 1974, Kafton 1976) and growth traits favor the maintenance of genetic variation in its populations: many trees have abundant yearly pollen and seed cone production; seed cones are serotinous and the seed maintains high viability for up to four years on the trees; seed cone and pollen production often begins in trees younger than 10 years and continues throughout their life-spans; many trees favor outcrossing by offsetting periods of pollen shed and seed cone receptivity; and some trees, and the populations overall, have exceptionally long periods of pollen shed and seed cone receptivity, a feature that promotes panmixia. The serotinous cones of cypresses may be an adaptation to regeneration after fire but the native stands appear to have trees with over-lapping age classes. Individual trees may have longevity approaching 200 years (Sudworth 1908, Green 1929), but in park plantings in San Francisco, they grow rapidly during early ages and are over-mature by about 70 years of age; many trees of that age have stem and root rot, excessive lean, large dead branches, and only a small proportion of live crown (McBride and Froehlich 1984).

Knowledge of the geographic distribution of genetic variation is helpful for gene conservation, whether the goals are to maintain the extant variation in native stands, collect a wide sample of the natural variation for growth trials in new locations, or develop a genetically variable base population preparatory to a directed breeding program. This study indicates that trees in stands are the main source of variation but from the viewpoints of preservation and sampling, there are significant differences between the Cypress Point and Point Lobos populations and likewise, between two groups of stands within each population. These new results are very similar to and extend previous findings that were based on two genes (Adh and Lap, Kafton 1976). Kafton found differences between the two populations and the same two groups of stands within each.

Enzyme differentiation over such short geographic distances is unusual in forest trees, but another example in California is bishop pine (Millar 1983). Near Sea Ranch, one Got allele abruptly replaces another and that steep cline in allele frequencies coencides with the abrupt change between the blue and green morphological forms.

Monterey cypresses must have minimal gene migration to maintain differentiation over short distances. Its heavy, angular seeds with only rudimentary wings fall near the seed trees (Sudworth 1908) and pollination may mostly occur among near neighbors owing to a combination of wind direction, spatial relationships, and flowering times (Kafton 1976).

There were a total of 44 different alleles for the variable genes listed in table 1 of this paper. If vegetative cuttings were taken from the sample trees of the northern three stands at Cypress Point, only 34 of those 44 alleles would be included. Sampling from the 5 southern

Cypress Point stands would omit 5 alleles and collecting from the eastern Point Lobos trees would miss 4. The most variable group of trees are the three western stands at Pont Lobos: samples from those stands would miss only one allele, Skdh(1.15).

One final observation to note is the occurrence of rare alleles in one of the Point Lobos stands. Western stand 1 had alleles of three different genes, Aco(.95), Adh(.52), and Lap(.89) that were not found in any of the other 14 stands sampled. This unusual cluster of rare alleles calls particular attention to the stand and underlines the importance of the cypresses on the western promontory at Point Lobos. Those trees should receive special consideration for gene conservation and long-term germ plasm preservation.

REFERENCES

Axelrod, Daniel I. History of the maritime closed-cone pines, Alta and Baja California. Univ. CA Pub. Geol. Sci. 120; 1980; 143 p.

Axelrod, Daniel I. New Pleistocene conifer records, coastal California. Univ. CA Pub. Geol. Sci. 127; 1983; 108 p.

Beckwitt, Richard; Chakraborty, Ranajit. Genetic structure of Pileolaria pseudomilitaris (Polychaeta: spirorbidae). Genetics 96:711-726; 1980 November.

Conkle, M. Thompson; Hodgskiss, Paul D.; Nunnally, Lucy B.; Hunter, Serena C. Starch gel electrophoresis of conifer seeds: a laboratory manual. Gen. Tech. Rep. PSW-64. Berekley, CA: Pacific Southwest Forest and Range Experiment Station, Forest Service, U. S. Department of Agriculture; 1982. 18 p.

Green, Harry Ashland. Historical note on the Monterey Cypress at Cypress Point. Madroño 1:197-198; 1929.

Griffin, James R.; Critchfield, William B. The distribution of forest trees in California. U. S. Department of Agriculture, Forest Service Research Paper, PSW-82; 1972; 114 p.

Hamrick, J. L.; Linhart, Y. B.; Mitton, J. B. Relationships between life history characteristics and electrophoretically detectable genetic variation in plants. Ann. Rev. Ecol. Syst. 10:173-200; 1979.

Hiebert, Ronald D.; Hamrick, J. L. Patterns and levels of genetic variation in Great Basin bristlecone pine, Pinus Longaeva. Evolution 37(2):302-310; 1983.

Johnson, LeRoy C. Cupressus L. Cypress. In: Schopmeyer, C. S., Tech. Coordinator. Seeds of woody plants in the United States. U. S. Dep. of Agric. Handb. 450. Washington, DC; 1974; 363-369.

Kafton, David Lewis. Isozyme variability and reproductive phenology of Monterey cypress. Berkeley, CA: Univ. of California; 1976. 196 p. Dissertation.

Ledig, F. Thomas. Heterozygosity, heterosis, and fitness in outbreeding plants. In: Soulé, Michael E., ed. Conservation biology: the science of scarcity and diversity. Sinauer Associates, Sunderland MA; 1986:77-104.

Ledig, F. Thomas; Conkle, M. Thompson. Gene diversity and genetic structure in a narrow endemic, Torrey pine (Pinus torreyana Parry ex Carr.). Evolution 37(1):79-85; 1983.

Millar, Constance I. A steep cline in Pinus muricata. Evolution 37(2):311-319; 1983.

McBride, Joe R.; Froehlich, Denice. Structure and condition of older stands in parks and open space areas of San Francisco, California. Urban Ecol. 8:165-178; 1984.

Nei, Masatoshi. Estimation of average heterozygosity and genetic distance from a small number of individuals. Genetics 89:583-590; 1978.

Strauss, S. H.; Conkle, M. T. Segregation, linkage, and diversity of allozymes in knobcone pine. Theor. Appl. Genet. 72:483-493; 1986.

Sudworth, George B. Forest Trees of the Pacific Slope. Dover Pub., Inc.; NY; 1967; p. 158-161. Reprinting of USDA For. Serv., Gov. Printing Office, Washington, DC. 159 p.; 1908.

Swofford, David L.; Selander, Richard B. BIOSYS-1: A fortran program for the comprehensive analysis of electrophoretic data in population genetics and systematics. J. Hered. 72:281-283; 1981.

Bureau of Land Management's Efforts to Conserve *Pediocactus peeblesianus* var. *peeblesianus* (Cactaceae)

Mary Butterwick [1]

Abstract: The Peebles Navajo Cactus habitat management plan outlines nine planned actions, including monitoring, that when implemented will assist in the recovery of Pediocactus peeblesianus var. peeblesianus. Data from a population that has been monitored since 1980 show a total reduction in number of plants of 44 percent, an overall recruitment survivorship of 57 percent, and variable rates of fruit production. It has not been determined whether the changes observed represent a cyclic event or a continuing trend in the population. The 1986 population exhibited a wide range of size classes indicating at least a minimum level of maintenance.

Peebles Navajo Cactus (Pediocactus peeblesianus (Croizat) L. Benson var. peeblesianus) is one of the first Arizona plant taxa to receive endangered status under the Endangered Species Act of 1973, as amended. Populations of the variety occur on land administered by the Bureau of Land Management (BLM) and, consequently, the BLM has been involved in efforts to conserve Peebles Navajo Cactus.

Morphology--the genus Pediocactus, as circumscribed by Benson (1982), consists of nine species many of which are obscure plants that are geographically restricted to a particular habitat type. P. peeblesianus can be distinguished from other members of the genus by the spongy-fibrous texture of the spines. Two varieties of P. peeblesianus are currently recognized. The typical variety will be addressed here and can be distinguished from P. peeblesianus var. fickeiseniae L. Benson by the smaller, unbranched stem, the absence of a central spine, and fewer radial spines.

Peebles Navajo Cactus is a very inconspicuous plant. During much of the year only the apex of the depressed-globose stem is emergent. The mature stems are 1.5-3.5 centimeters in diameter and produce 1-4 yellow flowers that often obscure the stem at anthesis. The brown fruit is dry at maturity and dehisces along a dorsal slit and along a rim around the circumscissile apex. The seed is black to dark gray with a papillate surface.

Phenology--flowering occurs over an approximately two week period from late April to early May. Flowers begin opening at 9:00 A.M. and remain open until late afternoon. Anthesis was observed to last for at least three days. By mid-May fruit development is evident. Dehiscence of the mature fruit occurs from the end of May (approximately one month after anthesis) until mid-June. The seed and/or the dried fruit containing one or more seed can function as the unit of dispersal.

Distribution And Habitat--Peebles Navajo Cactus is a narrow endemic, the known populations occurring within a 11 X 1.6 kilometer area in northeastern Arizona. The total number of individuals is estimated at 1000 (Phillips et al., 1984). The cactus grows in shallow soils derived from the Shinarump Member of the Chinle Formation. The Shinarump Conglomerate consists of quartz, quartzite, and chert pebbles held together by a fine- to coarse-grained friable sandstone (Stewart et al., 1972). The plants occur on gently sloping to flat mesa tops at 1700-1750 meters elevation.

The local vegetation is open and sparse and Peebles Navajo Cactus typically occurs in the exposed sites providing full sunlight. The biotic community is the Plains and Great Basin Grassland near the ecotone with Great Basin Desertscrub (Brown et al., 1980). Important associates are Atriplex confertifolia, Eriogonum corymbosum, Artemisia bigelovii, Hilaria jamesii, and Gutierrezia sarothrae.

Threats--within the historic range, much suitable habitat has been destroyed by highway construction and gravel pit operations. The habitat is subject to additional disturbances from off-road vehicle use and trampling by livestock. Evidence of predation, presumably by rodents and/or rabbits, has been observed.

---

[1] Field Associate, California Academy of Sciences, San Francisco, CA.

The removal of this cactus and/or its seed by both private collectors and commercial suppliers is considered a major threat to the species. Because of the low numbers of plants and the threats to known populations, the U. S. Fish and Wildlife Service (USFWS) listed Peebles Navajo Cactus as an endangered species in 1979.

Habitat Management

In 1984 the USFWS finalized the recovery plan for Peebles Navajo Cactus and the following year the BLM Phoenix District Office approved a habitat management plan (HMP) for the variety. The objective of the plan is to assist in the recovery of Peebles Navajo Cactus through habitat protection and the maintenance of viable populations occurring on BLM administered land. The plan calls for the construction of a fence to exclude livestock, maintenance of existing fences, a mineral withdrawal, aerial surveillance of the habitat, an off-road vehicle designation, fecal analysis of lagomorph and rodent samples, possible acquisition of state and/or private lands supporting populations of Peebles Navajo Cactus, inventory, and monitoring of the populations on BLM land for at least 10 years.

The HMP area is grazed and livestock tracks have been observed in the immediate vicinity of established plants. The Peebles Navajo Cactus is particularly vulnerable to the effects of trampling when the soils are moist and the cactus is emergent. In 1985 a 40-acre exclosure was completed that includes the major concentrations of this cactus and also closes off an unauthorized road.

The Shinarump Conglomerate contributes most of the sand and gravel used commercially in the general area. A portion of the HMP area has been destroyed, presumably by the extraction of sand and gravel. The HMP area is currently covered by an oil and gas lease. Pending a complete mineral withdrawal, the removal of saleable minerals such as sand and gravel and surface occupancy for the development of leasable minerals such as oil and gas will not be allowed.

---

[2] Data on file, Phoenix District Office, USDI Bureau of Land Management, Phoenix, Arizona.

Aerial surveillance of the general area to detect the theft of petrified wood and archeological artifacts is currently being funded by the Arizona State Land Department, Petrified Forest National Park, and BLM. A BLM archeologist is also providing surveillance of Peebles Navajo Cactus habitat in an effort to document human activity within the HMP area. The monitoring is a continuation of an on-going project. The remaining actions have not yet been implemented.

Monitoring

Methods--a permanent monitoring plot was established in 1980 within one of the two known concentrations of Peebles Navajo Cactus on land administered by BLM.[2] The objective was to map the population so that individual plants could be relocated and measured.

The boundaries of the population were delineated and a baseline transect bisecting the population was established and permanently located at each end by means of steel reinforcing rods. The location of each plant intercepted along the course of the baseline tape was noted. Additional plants were mapped using a series of plots established by line transects run on either side of and perpendicular to the baseline tape. The perpendicular transects vary in length and terminate near one or more plants. A five-inch nail was driven into the ground to mark the end of each transect. The location of individual plants was recorded using distance and direction from the nail.

The plot has been read annually from 1980 to 1986. In 1985 ten observations of the population between April 23 and June 13 recorded data on flowering, fruit set, seed production, and insect visitation.

Results--seven readings of the plot have recorded 166 plants. The population is situated along the edge of a mesa within a 50 X 20 meter area. The plants are not evenly distributed throughout the population. The clumped distribution pattern may be the result of limited seed dispersal. The reproductive plants may also provide 'safe sites' for the establishment of new individuals. Over half of the seedlings and young juvenile plants are situated in the immediate vicinity of reproductive plants.

Stem diameters ranging from 1 to 35 millimeters have been recorded. Growth

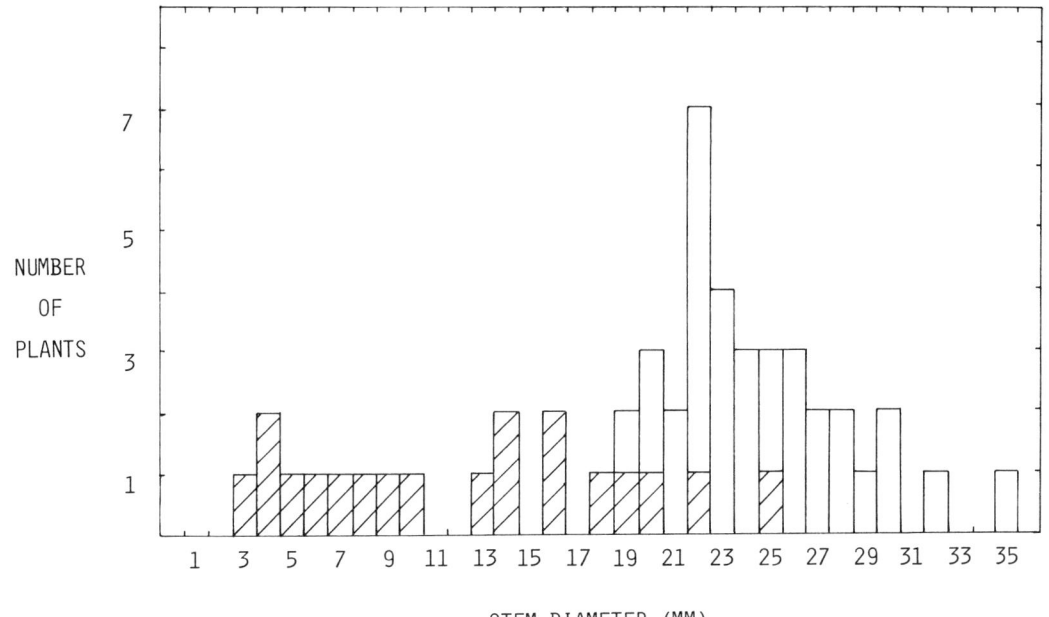

Figure 1--Size structure of the observed 1980 population. Hatched bars represent nonreproductive plants; clear bars are reproductive plants.

rates and the exact age of the plants have not been determined. Stem diameters do provide a general indication of the age structure of the population. The size structure of the observed 1980 population is shown in figure 1. A variety of size classes were represented with stem diameters ranging from 3 to 35 millimeters. Of the 51 plants recorded, 32 plants, or 63 percent, were reproductive and produced a total of 60 flowers. Subsequent readings of the plot documented 115 additional plants of varying sizes, including 46 recruits or very young juveniles, that is, plants 5 millimeters or less in diameter. In 1986 89 plants were recorded with stem diameters ranging from 2 to 27 millimeters (fig. 2). Thirty-three plants, or 37 percent, were reproductive and produced a total of 47 flowers.

Since 1980 the removal of 77 plants, or 44 percent, from the population has also been noted. The population depletion curve (fig. 3) shows a significant reduction in numbers of plants, particularly between 1980 and 1982. Only 6 plants, or 12 percent, of the 51 plants observed in 1980 are present in 1986. The size distribution of extirpated plants includes a wide range of size classes (fig. 4). Mortality risks are greatest in the 2-5 millimeter and 21-27 millimeter size classes. The cause(s) of these losses is not completely known. No recent human disturbance was noted although trampling by livestock was apparent prior to construction of the exclosure. Predation apparently accounts for a portion of the observed mortality. In 1981 10 mature plants were partially eaten by rabbits or rodents; these plants were missing the following year.

Flowering periodicity was determined for 19 reproductive plants that have been observed for at least a four year period. Of these, 10 plants flowered consistently every year. Interruptions in flowering of either a one or two year duration occurred with the remaining 9 plants and in every case the lapse in flowering took place during 1984.

In 1985 three open flowers on two plants were observed for a four hour period to record and collect insect visitors. Throughout this period several, as yet unidentified, thrips (Thysanoptera) were observed moving among the perianth, stamens, and style. Additional visitors included two individuals of an ant (Hymenoptera, Formicidae, Iridomyrmex pruinosus) and a single bee (Hymenoptera, Halictidae, Lassioglossum sp.).

Reproductive effectiveness in terms of fruit and seed production and recruitment survivorship are important factors because the maintenance of Peebles Navajo Cactus populations depends exclusively on establishment from seed. Initial indica-

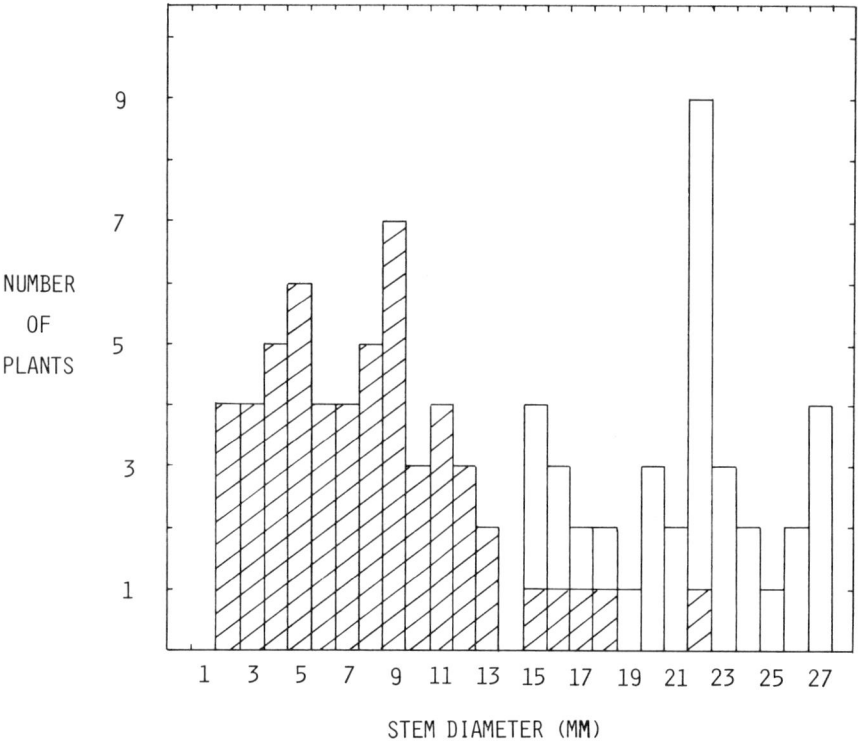

Figure 2-- Size structure of the observed 1986 population. Hatched bars represent nonreproductive plants; clear bars are reproductive plants.

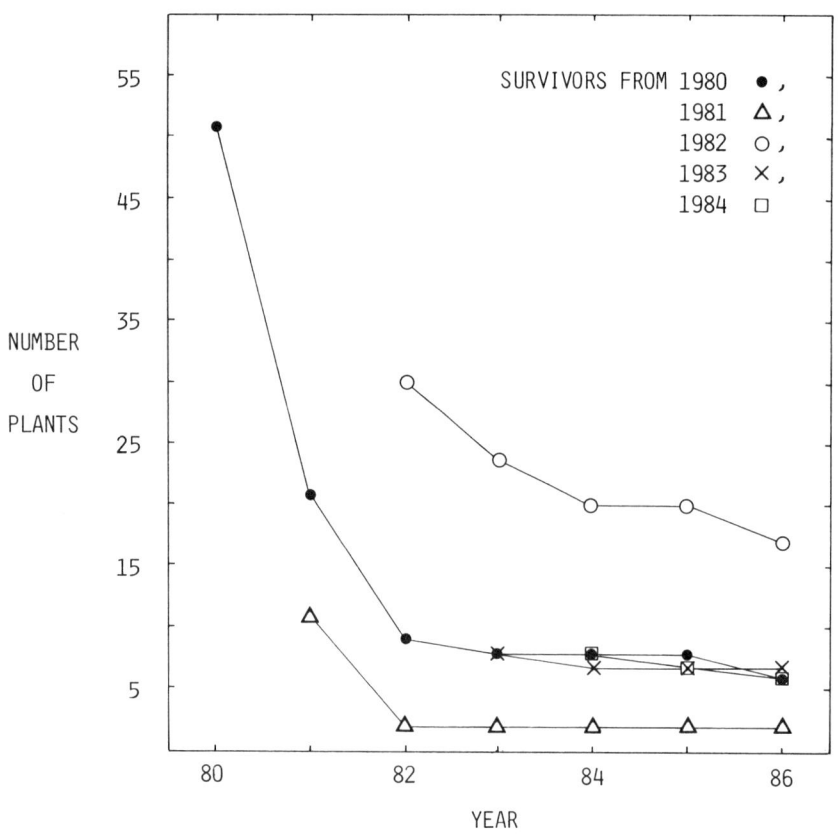

Figure 3--Population depletion curves. The separate curves indicate plants first observed each year between 1980 and 1984.

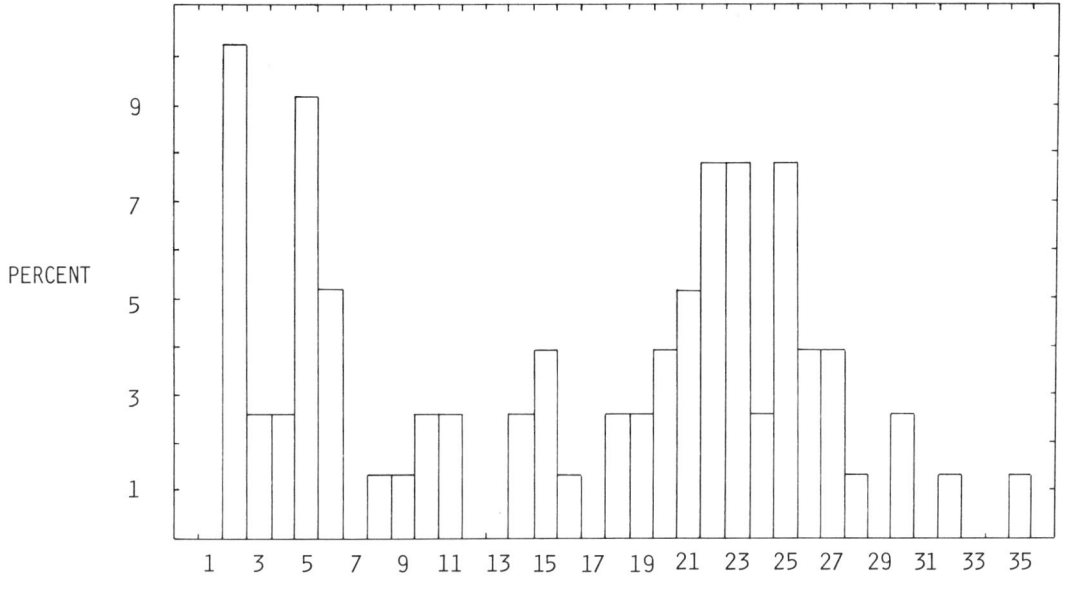

Figure 4--Size distribution of the plants extirpated between 1980 and 1986. The frequency of each size class is shown as a percentage of the 77 extirpated plants.

tions are that the plant's reproductive effectiveness can vary considerably from year to year. For instance, the number of flowers setting fruit varied from 18, or 32 percent, in 1985 to 38, or 81 percent, in 1986. In 1985 a major storm system entered the northeastern part of the state in late April bringing snow, rain, and extreme winds. For three days the flowers did not open and no insect activity was observed. The unfavorable weather conditions during the peak flowering period may account for the low rate of fruit set. In 1985 seed production was determined for 13 fruits. The number of seed per fruit varied from 1 to 27 for a total of 148 seed. Recruitment survivorship during the first years of monitoring appears to be low (fig. 5). Of the 44 recruits recorded between 1980 and 1985, 25 plants, or 57 percent, remained in 1986.

A second concentration of Peebles Navajo Cactus is situated about 70 meters northwest of the monitored plot. Within this population exclosure cages covered with 0.3 millimeter nylon screening were placed over 10 plants just prior to anthesis to determine if Peebles Navajo Cactus is capable of self-pollination. One of the cages was blown away in a storm. None of the flowers on the remaining 9 caged plants, including the one flower that was artificially selfed, set fruit. Of the 10 uncaged control plants, 5 set fruit, a rate comparable to that observed in the population as a whole.

Conclusions

Perhaps the most significant change noted within the monitored population is the level of extirpation between 1980 and 1982. Given the limited distribution and population size of this variety, the loss of 77 plants over a 6-year period is a matter of concern. Over the past three years mortality rates have stabilized and the earlier rates of depletion may have been a cyclic event rather than a continuing trend in the population. In 1986 a wide range of size classes was represented by one or more individuals indicating at least a minimum level of maintenance. Fruit production was relatively low in 1985. Peebles Navajo Cactus apparently requires an insect vector for pollination and poor weather conditions during anthesis may have been a limiting factor.

Many of the life history attributes of Peebles Navajo Cactus, particularly those relating to pollination, dispersal, and establishment processes remain unknown. As part of the recovery effort for this cactus, USFWS contracted to have additional population studies conducted (Phillips et al., 1985). Permanent monitoring plots were established in 1985 within two more populations. A comparison

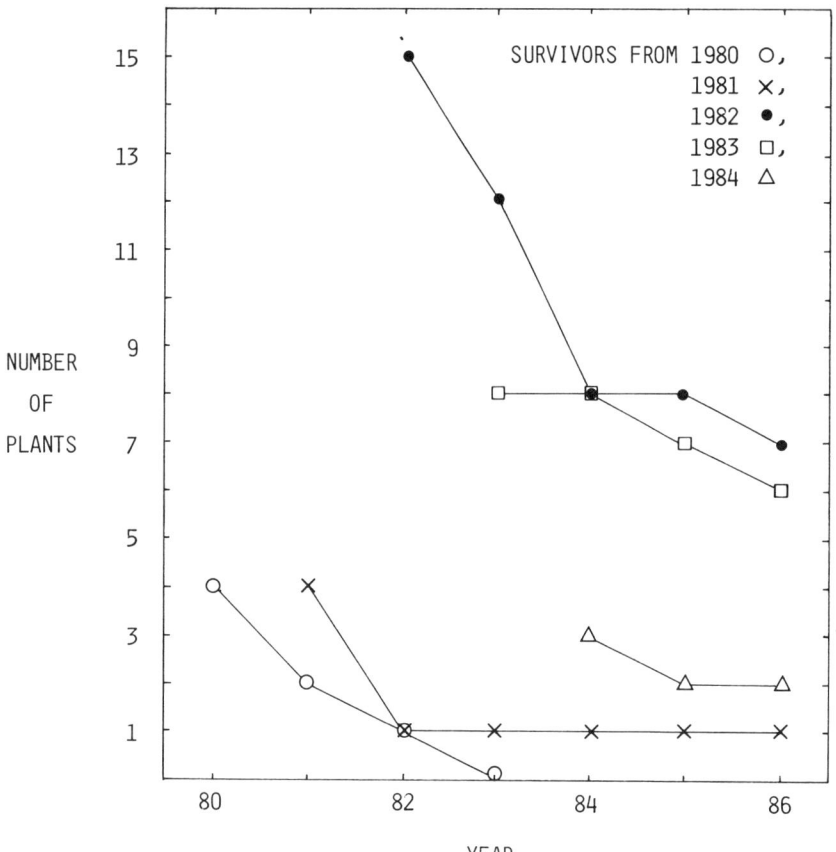

Figure 5--Recruitment survivorship. The separate curves indicate 1-5 mm plants first observed each year between 1980 and 1984.

of data from these populations will eventually provide a more thorough assessment of the status of Peebles Navajo Cactus. Should changes in the populations prove to be long-term downward trends, more active management on the part of BLM may be required in order to conserve this endangered taxon.

ACKNOWLEDGEMENTS

I thank David Anderson, Don Ducote, Deborah Hillyard, Janet Milne, Peggy Olwell, Arthur Phillips, Barbara Phillips, and Marilyn Schmidt for their assistance in reading the monitoring plot. Jud May and Bill Frank of the Arizona Agriculture and Horticulture Commission provided the insect determinations. I am grateful to Colleen Sudekum for producing prints of the illustrations and to Tom Daniel for reviewing the manuscript. This study was supported by the Bureau of Land Management, U. S. Department of Interior.

REFERENCES

Benson, Lyman. The cacti of the United States and Canada. Stanford, CA: Stanford University Press; 1982. 1044 p.

Brown, David E., Charles H. Lowe, and Charles P. Pase. A digitized systematic classification for ecosystems with an illustrated summary of the natural vegetation of North America. Gen. Tech. Rep. RM-73. Fort Collins, CO: Rocky Mountain Forest and Range Exp. Stn., Forest Service, U. S. Department of Agriculture; 1980. 93 p.

Phillips, Barbara G., Arthur M. Phillips, and Mary Butterwick. Peebles Navajo Cactus Pediocactus peeblesianus (Croizat) L. Benson var. peeblesianus Recovery Plan. Albuquerque, NM: Fish and Wildlife Service, U. S. Department of Interior; 1984. 58 p.

Phillips, Barbara G., Arthur M. Phillips, and Ann Wildman. Population biology, inventory and monitoring studies of Pediocactus peeblesianus var. peeblesianus. Albuquerque, NM: Fish and Wildlife Service, U. S. Department of Interior; 1985. 38 p.

Stewart, John H., Forrest G. Poole, and Richard F. Wilson. Stratigraphy and origin of the Chinle Formation and related Upper Triassic Strata in the Colorado Plateau region. Geological Survey Professional Paper 690. Washington, D.C.: Geological Survey, U. S. Department of Interior; 1972. 336 p.

The Ecology and Management of Three Rare Salt Marsh Species of Humboldt Bay

Gail A. Newton [1]

Abstract: Humboldt Bay salt marshes contain three rare and endangered species, Humboldt Bay owl's clover (Orthocarpus castillejoides var. humboldtiensis), Point Reyes bird's beak (Cordylanthus maritimus ssp. palustris), and Humboldt Bay gumplant (Grindelia stricta ssp. blakei). These three species occur in high elevation salt marshes, which are the most heavily impacted of all salt marshes on Humboldt Bay. While the species do tolerate some disturbance, coastal development continues to decrease the total available habitat of the species. Restoration and enhancement programs need to take into account the habitat requirements of the three rare species by using manual revegetation and by building elevational and floristic diversity into the design.

Wetland restoration and enhancement are becoming increasingly common in California, mostly as the result of mitigation for coastal development. Areas near bays are important for agricultural and urban development, which often involve the destruction or degradation of wetland habitat.

In Humboldt Bay nearly 90% of the original salt marshes have been either diked or filled for agricultural and urban purposes. Only 700 acres of the estimated 7,000 acres of salt marshes remain, with the largest contiguous areas of salt marsh occurring on the low elevation islands in the middle of the bay.

In 1976 the California Coastal Act gave the California Coastal Commission the power to require mitigation work in conjunction with development of the coastal habitats. Since then, marsh restoration and enhancement projects have become more numerous. However, marsh restoration is still very new on Humboldt Bay; the oldest project now only in its seventh year.

Humboldt Bay is located approximately 220 nautical miles north of San Francisco and 180 nautical miles south of Coos Bay, Oregon. It is the only area of appreciable acreages of salt marshes between San Francisco Bay and Coos Bay and links the two floristically. Like San Francisco Bay, Humboldt Bay has pickleweed (Salicornia virginica) salt marshes, and like Coos Bay, Lyngby's sedge (Carex lyngbyei) and tufted hairgrass (Deschampsia caespitosa) salt marshes. Unique to Humboldt Bay are the large areas which are dominated by an exotic cordgrass (Spartina densiflora).

In addition to the different plant associations represented in Humboldt Bay, there are three rare salt marsh plant species, which are on List 1B of the CNPS Inventory as rare and endangered throughout their range. These three species are Humboldt Bay owls' clover (Orthocarpus castillejoides var. humboldtiensis Keck), Point Reyes bird's beak (Cordylanthus maritimus ssp. palustris (Behr) Chuang & Heckard), and Humboldt Bay gumplant (Grindelia stricta ssp. blakei (Steyerm.) Keck). The owl's clover and the gumplant are endemic to the Humboldt Bay area.

Populations of the three rare species on Humboldt Bay are centered around the high elevation salt marshes. These marshes are currently decreasing in total acreage and are not being recreated in most marsh restoration plans. This paper will review what is currently known about the ecology of the three species and address the impacts that current mitigation policies have on them.

RARE SPECIES

Humboldt Bay Owl's Clover

Humboldt Bay owl's clover (Orthocarpus castillejoides var. humboldtiensis) is an annual member of the Scrophulariaceae, the snapdragon family. It is distinguished by its two-celled anthers, purple bracts, and bright pink flowers on a large showy spike. This species is only known to occur in the Humboldt Bay area. A white form has been reported from only two locations on Humboldt Bay, Jacoby Slough and Second Slough (A. Eicher pers. comm. and Newton

---

[1] Gail Newton and Assoc., Biological Consultants, Arcata, CA.

pers. obs.).

Many species of owl's clover have been found to employ haustorial connections. While Humboldt Bay owl's clover has not been studied in detail, it is possible that it also forms haustoria. However, it can grow in large patches fairly far removed from other species (pers. obs.). If it does form haustorial connections, they may not be necessary for survival.

This species has been collected from the mid to high elevation salt marshes with the large populations usually centered around the high elevation salt marshes. The two main plant associations of these high elevation salt marshes have been described as the pickleweed-jaumea association and the pickleweed-salt grass association (Koplin et al 1984; Newton 1985a, 1985b, 1986; A. Eicher per. comm.). These salt marsh associations are diverse, as salt marshes go. They usually include dodder (Cuscuta salina), sickle grass (Parapholis incurva and P. strigosa), sea plantain (Plantago maritima ssp. juncoides), and arrow grass (Triglochin concinnum), as well as the three rare salt marsh species.

Populations of Humboldt Bay owl's clover which have been monitored over a number of years have been found to fluctuate widely between years (Koplin et al 1984, J.O. Sawyer pers comm). Though no one has investigated such fluctuations, possible causes include a seasonal lack of adequate germination and/or survival conditions, low seed production, lack of adequate number of pollinators, and man-made disturbance.

The role that disturbance plays in the distribution of this species is not clear. Open habitat within the proper part of the salt marsh tends to favor germination and growth. Therefore, disturbance, such as light trampling, that decreases the cover of pickleweed while not destroying the marsh will encourage the growth of owl's clover. It has been suggested that the more use an area receives, for example by birders and students, the more plants appear the following year (M. Boyd pers. comm.).

Point Reyes Bird's Beak

The second species is Point Reyes bird's beak (Cordylanthus maritimus ssp. palustris). The taxonomy of this subspecies is currently in question. It was separated based on geography from the southern California ssp. maritimus by Chuang and Heckard (1973), but recently Dunn (in prep) has decided that the two subspecies are not distinct.

Bird's beak is also an annual species of the snapdragon family and is distinguished by the oblong shape of its leaves and bracts, and the purple flower. The distribution of subspecies palustris is from Morro Bay, San Luis Obispo County, California, to Coos Bay, Oregon. If ssp. palustris is not a distinct subspecies, but is determined to be ssp. maritimus, its distribution would include southern California as well.

Bird's beak is a hemiparasitic plant that has been observed to vary both spatially and temporally. On Humboldt Bay it occurs within approximately the same elevational range, to slightly higher, as the owl's clover.

Humboldt Bay Gumplant

Humboldt Bay gumplant (Grindelia stricta ssp.blakei), the third rare species of Humboldt Bay salt marshes, is a member of the Asteraceae, the daisy family. It is distinguished by recurved phyllaries and reddish erect stems. This species occurs at mid to high elevation salt marshes, with its population centered around Humboldt Bay.

Gumplant has wider habitat requirements and is much more tolerant of disturbance than the other two rare species. It can be found interspersed with cordgrass tufts in mid elevation salt marshes, in pickleweed stands in high elevation salt marshes, and along berms and dikes adjacent to salt marshes.

The taxonomy of one outlying population that closely resembles Humboldt Bay gumplant is in question. The population is located at approximately 1500 feet on what is locally known as the Mattole Road and is currently not treated as the Humboldt Bay gumplant. If it is determined to be the Humboldt Bay gumplant, then the habitat restrictions of this species will have to be reexamined.

MANAGEMENT OF THE RARE SPECIES

All three of these rare salt marsh species are most often found in high elevation salt marsh associations. Such associations have been the most heavily impacted of all salt marsh associations on Humboldt Bay because they are located nearest the dikes, fills, and developments.

For many locations, it is debatable whether the disturbance or the rare plant population came first. Openings in the salt marsh canopy do favor germination and growth of all three species, and robust populations can be found along footpaths within salt marshes. But is disturbance increasing the population numbers or is the disturbance occurring within already existing populations? The answer is probably yes to both questions.

Soil samples taken from areas where the rare species grow showed significantly higher bulk densities than samples from neighboring areas devoid of rare plants, indicating some sort of compaction by disturbance.[2] The rare species can also be found in sandy soils that support marginal pickleweed marshes. It would seem that soil conditions that decrease the overall growth of pickleweed, jaumea, and salt grass, favor the growth of the rare species.

Therefore, I believe that the species do tolerate some disturbance. Disturbances that decrease the growth of the dominant species but that do not destroy the salt marsh habitat will open up the canopy and favor the growth of the rare species. The three rare species were probably originally concentrated in the narrow band of upper elevation salt marshes but have taken advantage of disturbance to spread from their diminishing natural habitat to the edges of dikes and footpaths.

The scarcity of habitat results from historical wetland destruction and the relative newness of the science of salt marsh restoration. Early attempts to create salt marshes on Humboldt Bay merely reintroduced tidal circulation to an area and then allowed the area to revegetate naturally. While this technique is successful at creating a "wet land", it allows little to no control over the plant associations that develop.

The laws that govern mitigation for destroyed habitat do not require creation of anything more specific than a salt marsh; the associations that develop in a mitigation site are determined by invading species and existing elevations. Rarely is the elevation or topography manipulated and, if so, it is without regard to desired plant associations. Therefore, restoration attempts seldom take into account the higher elevation habitat requirements of the rare salt marsh species. While impacts to higher elevation salt marshes are being mitigated politically, they are not being mitigated ecologically.

This oversight is due in part to the general belief that "a salt marsh is a salt marsh", and in part to the lack of exact formulas or techniques that can be enforced by agencies during restoration attempts. Restoration of the correct habitat for these rare species is further complicated by the lack of detailed information on the specific habitat requirements of the three species on Humboldt Bay. (Elevational studies are currently being conducted by A. Eicher, pers. comm.)

To further compound the question of high elevation salt marsh restoration, Humboldt Bay has been invaded by an exotic cordgrass (Spartina densiflora), from Chile, which is able to germinate from seed (Spicher 1984). The presence of this cordgrass, whose elevational range overlaps with pickleweed's, presents only a slight problem to the perennial gumplant; however, the annual owl's clover and bird's beak do not occur in cordgrass marshes.

While the high rate of pickleweed germination has been used as evidence for the lack of necessity for manual revegetation in pickleweed marshes (Josselyn and Buchholz 1984), I believe that manual revegetation of pickleweed may be necessary on most restoration projects in Humboldt Bay. The exotic species of cordgrass is able to out compete pickleweed where the cordgrass is not limited by tidal circulation (Newby 1980). Therefore, in restoration of mid to high elevations on Humboldt Bay, manual reintroduction of the pickleweed gives it a competitive edge over the exotic cordgrass.

CONCLUSION

Salt marsh restoration rarely takes into account the need for elevational and floristic diversity. This need is especially pertinent considering that the three rare salt marsh species of Humboldt Bay (Humboldt Bay owl's clover, Humboldt Bay gumplant, and Point Reyes bird's beak) occur mainly in the high elevation salt marshes. In order to ensure the future survival of the three species in their native habitat, future projects on Humboldt Bay must build topographical diversity into restoration designs and evaluate the need for manual revegetation to ensure the development of native plant associations.

REFERENCES

Boyd, M. Professor of Biology, Humboldt State University, Arcata, CA. [Conversation with G.A. Newton] June 1985.

Chuang, T.I.; Heckard L.R. Taxonomy of Cordylanthus subgenus hemistegia (Scrophulariaceae). Brittonia 25(2):135-158; 1973.

---

[2] Data on file, Gail Newton and Associates, Arcata, CA.

Eicher, A. M.A. Student at Humboldt State University, Arcata, CA. [Telephone conversation with G.A. Newton] November 1986.

Josselyn, Michael N.; Buchholz, James W. Marsh Restoration in San Francisco Bay: A Guide to Design and Planning. Technical Report #3 Tiburon Center for Environmental Studies, San Francisco State University. 1984; 104pp.

Koplin, J.R.; Franklin, A; Newton, G.A. Elk River Wildlife Area Monitoring Project, Final Report. 1984. Unpublished summary report available from the City of Eureka, CA.

Newby, L.C. Impact of Salt Marsh Chemistry on *Spartina*, *Salicornia*, and *Distichlis*, Indian Island, Humboldt Bay, CA. PhD dissertation, University of California, Los Angeles, CA. 1980.

Newton, G.A. Botanical Survey of the Proposed Wetland Mitigation Sites: Belcher, Ford, and Lambert. 1985a. Unpublished report available from the Natural Resources Division of Humboldt County Public Works, Eureka, CA.

Newton, G.A. Botanical Review and Mitigation Plan for the Second and Third Slough Sewer Line Project. 1985b. Unpublished report available from the City of Eureka, CA.

Newton, G.A. Botanical Review and Recommendations for the Palco Marsh Enhancement Program. 1986. Unpublished report available from the City of Eureka, CA.

Sawyer, J.O. Professor of Botany, Humboldt State University, Arcata, CA. [Conversation with G.A. Newton] September 1983.

Spicher, D.P. The ecology of a caespitose cordgrass (*Spartina* sp.) introduced to San Francisco Bay. M.S. thesis. San Francisco State University, San Francisco, CA 81pp; 1984.

The Endangered Sandhills Plant Communities of Santa Cruz County

Michael S. Marangio, Randall Morgan [1]

Abstract: Sandy soils of the Zayante series are inland marine sand deposits that support two unique plant communities in the coast range mountains of Santa Cruz County, California. This report describes these plant communities, one dominated by ponderosa pine (Pinus ponderosa), the other dominated by silverleaf manzanita (Arctostaphylos silvicola). Approximately 90 species of plants, many that are sandhills endemics, coastal relics, locally rare, or undescribed ecotypes and subspecies can be described as "sandhills specialty" plants. Sand quarrying and residential development have destroyed much of these sandhill plant communities. Preservation of the best examples of what remains of these plant communities is critical for their protection.

The inland sandhills of Santa Cruz County, California are located within the coastal Santa Cruz mountains. These areas support a unique flora that includes sandhill endemics, coastal ecotypes or subspecies, and populations at the limits of their distributional range. Disjunct populations of ponderosa pine (Pinus ponderosa) along with the endemic silverleaf manzanita (Arctostaphylos silvicola) are the dominant species and are the principal indicators of several plant communities that are found within the Santa Cruz County sandhills. These species, and approximately 88 other plants, are local indicators of the sands of the Zayante series. The combination of deep, coarse-textured and poorly developed soil under a relatively humid coastal climate is rare in California, and is probably the basis for the unique flora found there. In addition to the plants, a number of unique animal species are found in this habitat.

Because of the distinct nature of the biotic communities found on this sand substrate, they can be characterized as "biological islands," contrasting sharply with adjacent mixed evergreen and redwood forests that are more typical of the Santa Cruz Mountains region.

The sandhills vegetation existing today is a remnant of a previously more extensive habitat. Residential development, agriculture, and sand quarrying operations have destroyed or disturbed much of this habitat. Although the unique nature of the sandhills has been noted for some time (Griffin 1952, 1964), little has been done to protect the unique plant communities found there.

Since 1981, the California Department of Fish and Game Natural Diversity Data Base (CNDDB) has placed "Coastal Ponderosa Pine Forest Community" (their descriptive term for the sandhills vegetation discussed in the present report) on Priority List One, their list of plant communities of greatest concern for protection.

LOCATION OF SANDHILLS PLANT COMMUNITIES

Santa Cruz County is a small coastal county located in central California (Inset map, Figure 1). The largest and best-known sandhills areas within the Santa Cruz Mountains are located in central Santa Cruz County, from just north of the City of Santa Cruz, north to the Scotts Valley and Felton areas, and northwest through Olympia to Ben Lomond. An isolated

---

[1] Associate, Environmental Science Associates, 760 Harrison Street, San Francisco, CA 94107; 3500 N. Main Street, Soquel, CA 95073

area of sandhills is also located further west near the town of Bonny Doon (Figure 1).

Sandhills vegetation is found almost exclusively on the Zayante soils series. These soils are light colored, coarse, deep, well-drained, and erodible. They cover over 8,000 acres (three percent of Santa Cruz County's 281,000 acres) (USDA 1980). The Zayante soils are derived from loosely consolidated Miocene marine sand deposits called the Santa Margarita formation.

VEGETATION

The Zayante series soils (as defined and mapped by the Soil Conservation Service (USDA 1980) support a range of vegetation types – some unique, others more commonly distributed throughout the Santa Cruz Mountains (e.g., mixed evergreen forest). The unique vegetation types under discussion include what has been termed "Coast Range Ponderosa Pine Forest" (Cheatham and Haller 1975) and "Silverleaf Manzanita Mixed Chaparral" (after Davilla 1978).

Coast Range Ponderosa Pine Forest

This forest habitat type, as classified by Cheatham and Haller (1975), in addition to being found in Santa Cruz County, also occurs in isolated areas in other parts of California. The Santa Cruz County populations are unique in being found on deep, coarse-textured, poorly-developed soil in a relatively humid coastal climate where the average rainfall may range from 40 to 56 inches per year. Ponderosa pine forest in Santa Cruz County has been termed an "edaphic complex" (Griffin 1964). Presumably P. ponderosa is excluded from adjacent soils due to competition from the species of plants found there. The

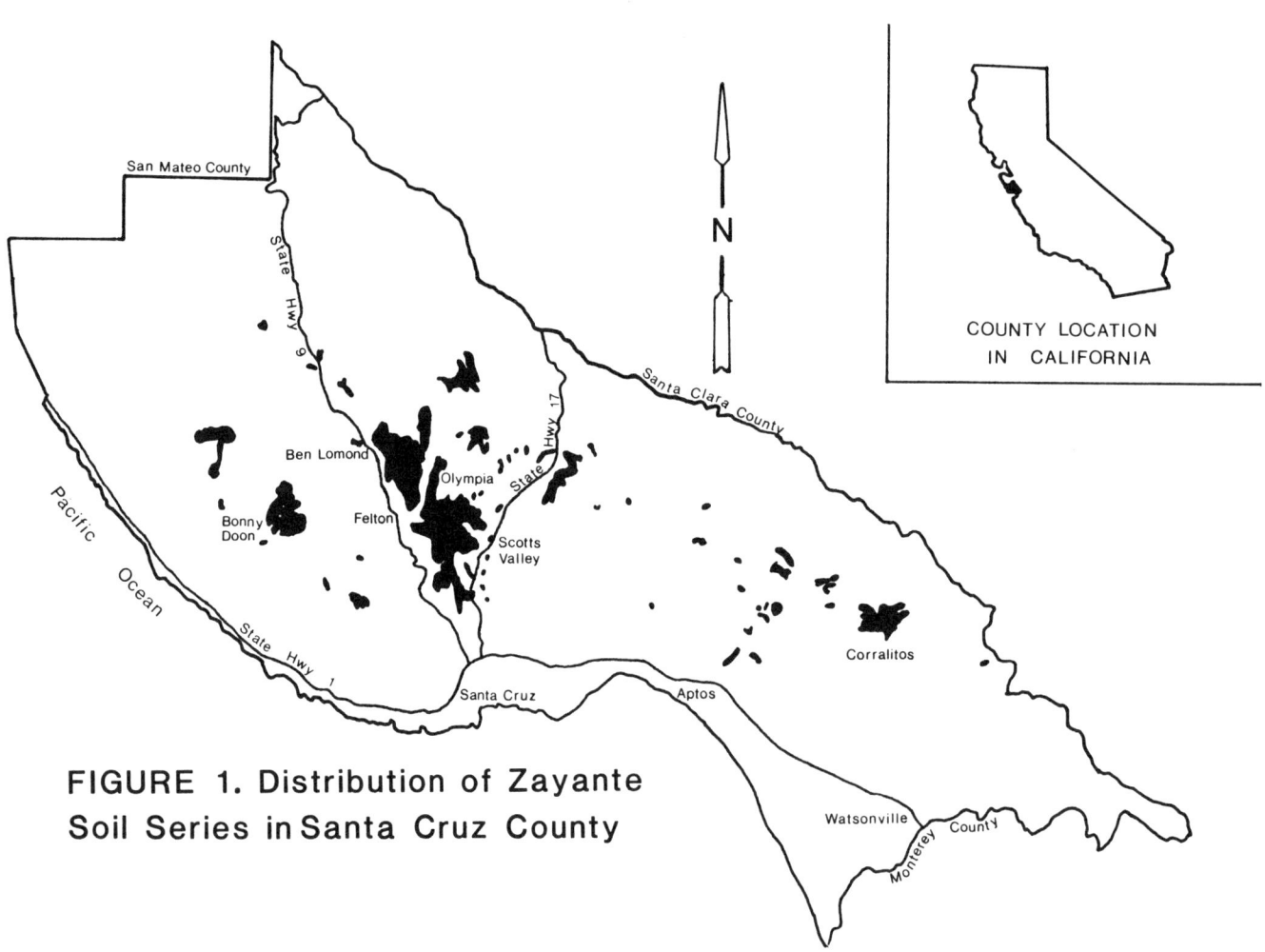

FIGURE 1. Distribution of Zayante Soil Series in Santa Cruz County

well-drained Zayante soils limit plant species to those that are well-adapted to drought.

The isolated populations of ponderosa pine in Santa Cruz County had been previously described as *Pinus benthamiana*, and there is some evidence that the sandhills population is morphologically sufficiently distinct to deserve at least subspecies status (McCully 1984).

Although the ponderosa pine trees are disjunct and possibly genetically distinct, they are not the primary feature of the ponderosa pine sandhills community. Where these pines occur in open stands, they often grow in association with an understory of small ephemeral, isolated populations of herbaceous species, generally with no shrub understory. This more specific type of ponderosa pine forest, "Ponderosa Pine Sand Parkland" (henceforth referred to in this report as "Parkland"), is typically restricted to the tops and upper slopes of the highest hills and ridges of the sandhills, although it is occasionally found in small pockets at lower elevations. The ponderosa pines are widely spaced, with only occasional oaks and manzanitas encroaching from adjacent habitat (Morgan 1983a).

Except under trees, the herbaceous layer is a diverse assortment of small annual and perennial flowering herbs with an irregular distribution of four species of semi-woody (suffrutescent) perennials (*Eriogonum nudum*, *Lupinus albifrons*, *Lotus scoparius*, and *Corethrogyne filaginifolia*). Grass is very sparse and sometimes absent. Total plant cover is so sparse that the sandy soil often looks nearly bare, except on northfacing slopes where the ground may be covered by a thin crust of mosses and lichens (Morgan 1983a).

Ninety species of plants deserve status as "sandhill specialty" plants in Santa Cruz County (see Appendix A). The criteria for inclusion in this list are: plants that are designated "Endangered," "Threatened," or "Rare" (federal, state), on California Native Plant Society lists (Smith and York 1984); plants designated "Locally Unique" by Santa Cruz County (1980); plants endemic to the Zayante sands, including taxonomically undescribed ecotypes that are definitely or possibly distinct from other populations (Morgan 1983a, b); disjunct populations (isolated by at least 50 miles) (Thomas 1961); coastal relict species (Thomas 1961); or species that are more evident or frequent in sandhills than in other local plant communities (Morgan 1983a, b). Most of these species are herbaceous plants most closely associated with Parkland sites.

Ponderosa pines also grow in fairly dense, mature stands with a tree and shrub understory which can be called "Ponderosa Pine Forest" (after Morgan 1983a). These pine stands appear to be in a late successional stage of the sandhills plant community.

Silverleaf Manzanita Mixed Chaparral

This plant association is characterized by generally dense stands of woody shrubs, primarily silverleaf manzanita (*Arctostaphylos silvicola*), a plant designated "rare" by the California Native Plant Society (Smith and York 1984). The community name was used by Davilla (1978), where he designated this type of chaparral as a subdivision of "Californian Mixed Chaparral" of Cheatham and Haller's (1975) classification system.

Silverleaf Manzanita Mixed Chaparral (henceforth to be referred to as "Silverleaf Manzanita Chaparral"), except for the dominance of its namesake, varies in its composition of associated plants. This plant community is fairly common in the Santa Cruz sandhills, and is not particularly threatened although like the Parkland community, it has been significantly reduced and altered. Other associated shrub species include *Ceanothus* (*C. cuneatus* and/or *C. ramulosus*), *Salvia mellifera*, *Eriodictyon californicum*, and *Diplacus aurantiacus*. In some areas, knobcone pine is a notable component of this type of chaparral.

Community Mosaics/Succession

Generally, boundaries of the previously described plant communities are difficult to define. Typically, the ponderosa pine and chaparral communities interdigitate and intergrade into each other. In addition, other plant communities, such as mixed evergreen forest of chamise chaparral, may gradually mix into the sandhill communities.

The variable composition of the sandhill plant communities and their unclear gradation from one to another has much to do with successional trends that are little understood for these associations. Based on historical aerial photos, many of the Parkland sites appear quite stable, with no evidence of replacement of the herbaceous plants by shrub species. As for the relationship between Silverleaf Manzanita Chaparral and Parkland, McMinn (1939) suggested that silverleaf manzanita "develop into nearly pure stands of chaparral as a fire type replacement of Pinus ponderosa." Griffin (1964) noted that "chaparral coverage seems to have expanded with the cutting and burning of the original forest. Several large chaparral stands still contain remains of pine stumps." He also noted that knobcane pine "probably also is increasing in dominance as a result of frequent fires in recent times" (p. 411, Griffin 1964).

At present, fire may be less frequent than in previous times. Along Graham Hill Road, Hihn Road, and in Bonny Doon, the encroachment of mixed evergreen forest into Ponderosa Pine Forest is evident. In these areas, large ponderosa pine grow within a dense understory of coast live oak, madrone, and other species typical of mixed evergreen forest. Historically, fire may have prevented the invasion of these mixed evergreen species which are not as well-adapted to fire survival.

WILDLIFE

Several species of unique animals inhabit the sandhills. The only known populations of the Western whip-tailed lizard (Cnemidophorus tigris) in Santa Cruz County are known from the vicinity of the Santa Cruz Aggregates quarry. The Coast Horned lizard (Phrynosoma coronatum) is becoming less commonly observed in coastal California, but was also seen in this area. These two species are considered "locally rare" by the Santa Cruz County Planning Department (County of Santa Cruz 1980).

The Roadrunner (Geococcyx californicus) was once an inhabitant of the Mount Hermon, Quail Hollow, and Bonny Doon areas. However, only one observation has been reported since 1955. Quarrying and residential development may already have led to the local extinction of this unique sandhills bird (Singer 1979).

The Santa Cruz kangaroo rat (Dipodomys venustus) is a unique nocturnal rodent that is closely associated with, but not limited to, the loose sandhills soils. It is a little-known species that only recently has once again been found in the sandhills (Roest 1984).

THREATS TO THE SANDHILLS PLANT COMMUNITIES

Sand quarrying, and housing development are the primary activities that have destroyed much of the sandhills plant communities. Of roughly 5,000 acres of sandhills plant communities, about one-tenth or 500 acres consisted of Parkland sites containing the most diverse habitat. Only about 250 acres of this Parkland habitat remains. Most Parkland is scattered over about 20 sites, but about half of the area is located around the active Santa Cruz Aggregates quarry near Olympia. Most of this remaining area is proposed for sand quarrying. A recent study (Marangio 1985) evaluated the primary sandhills habitat areas that remain. Four preserve units were proposed that are composed of sandhill habitat remnants, quarries, and buffer areas. Particular sites were given high priority for protection based primarily on diversity of species and on threats of habitat loss.

State and local environmental regulations ostensibly protect the sandhills plant communities. California Environmental Quality Act (CEQA) regulations have required environmental impact reports for most subdivisions and sand quarry expansion permits in the sandhills. However, the importance of some of the sites for populations of unique species was insufficiently known at the time of these studies. As a result, several quarries now have permits allowing for expansion into high quality sandhills habitat.

Santa Cruz County has a Sensitive Habitat Protection Ordinance that designates most of the sandhills plant communities as "Indigenous Ponderosa Pine Forest." Conditions that reduce site disturbance and housing density apply in these areas. Environmental impacts to the area are reduced, but the integrity of the plant communities is disrupted by houses and ranchettes that are allowed.

RECOMMENDATIONS

Although state and local regulations act to reduce impacts on the sandhills plant communities, they cannot alone prevent the loss of integrity of these habitat islands. Additional protection will be necessary through preservation techniques and management by private and public organizations. Preservation of the most diverse and most threatened sites deserve priority for conservation organizations and relevant state agencies. Consolidation of property to protect larger units will also be important. Additional study of the components of the sandhills communities is critical to determine the level of distinctiveness of the many unusual plant forms found there. Dissemination of information concerning the values and the unique nature of the sandhills is the final recommendation. A constituency of "sandhills appreciators" must be developed in order to promote preservation efforts. It is hoped that this report will assist in that aim.

REFERENCES

Cheatham, N.H. and J.R. Haller. An annotated list of California habitat types. unpublished manuscript, 1975.

Davilla, W. Vegetation Analysis. In Draft Environmental Impact Report, Quail Hollow Quarry, Santa Cruz Aggregates Company. Timothy Downey Associates, prepared for the County of Santa Cruz, Community Resources Agency, 1978.

Griffin, J.R. A study of the distribution of Pinus ponderosa Laws. and Pinus attenuata Lemm. on sandy soils in Santa Cruz County, California. Unpublished Master's thesis, University of California, Berkeley, California, 1952. 40 pp.

_____. Isolated Pinus ponderosa forests on sandy soils near Santa Cruz, California. Ecology 45 (1964): 410-412.

Hall, B.C. The occurrences of rare or endangered plants in Santa Cruz County. Unpublished Senior thesis. University of California, Santa Cruz, California, 1952. 40 pp.

Marangio, M.S. Preservation Study: Sandhills Biotic Communities of Santa Cruz County, California. Professional Project, Dept. Landscape Architecture, University of California, Berkeley, 1985. 71 pp.

McCully, H. Letter to Adrienne Libby, 1984.

McMinn, H.E. An illustrated manual of California shrubs. University of California Press, Berkeley, California, 1939. 663 pp.

Moldenke, A. R. A biological assessment of Kincaid's Colletes Solitary Bee. In Appendix F of "A Biotic Assessment of the Bonny Doon Rance." Unpublished report by W. Davilla, submitted to the County of Santa Cruz Planning Department, 1980.

Morgan, R. Endemic plant communities of the Santa Margarita parkland vegetation at Lone Star Industries' Olympia Quarry, and the potential for reestablishing the sand parkland vegetation and other options." Harvey and Stanley Associates. Unpublished report, 1983a.

_____. Letter to California Natural Diversity Data Base, Sacramento, California, 1983b.

Roest, M. A study of the Santa Cruz Kangaroo Rat. Senior thesis. University of California, Santa Cruz, California, 1984. 41 pp.

Santa Cruz, County of. General Plan, Santa Cruz County Planning Department, Santa Cruz, California, 1980.

Singer, S. W. San Lorenzo River Waterbed Management Plan. Vegetation and Wildlife Section. County of Santa Cruz Community Resources Agency. 1979

Smith, J.P. and R. York. Inventory of rare and endangered vascular plants of California. Special Publication No. 1 (3rd ed.), California Native Plant Society, Berkeley, California. 1984

Thomas, J.H. Flora of the Santa Cruz Mountains of California. Stanford University Press, Stanford, California, 1961.

U.S. Department of Agriculture. Soil Survey of Santa Cruz County, California. USDA Soil Conservation Services, 1980.

APPENDIX A
Sand Specialty Plants of Santa Cruz County

Scientific Name	Status*	Endemism/Distrib.**
Achillea borealis		2
Antirrhinum multiflorum		5
Arctostaphylos silvicola	C2,L1	1,5
Arenaria californica		2,3,5
A. douglasii		5?
Armeria maritima		2,4
Artemisia pycnocephala		1',4
Brodiaea pulchella		5?
Calochortus venustus		3,5
Calyptridium umbellatum		2,3,5
Campanula angustiflora		5
Cardionema ramosissima		3,4
Carex globosa		2
Castilleja affinis		3
Ceanothus cuneatus dubius		2,5
Chorizanthe diffusa		5
C. pungens hartwegii		2,5
Chrysopsis villosa camphorata		2,5
Clarkia purpurea ssp.		5
C. rubicunda	SC	5
C. unguiculata		2,5
Collinsia bartsiaefolia hirsuta		2,3,5
Corethrogyne filaginifolia virgata		2,5
Cryptantha hispidissima		
C. micromeres		
C. muricata jonesii		5
Cupressus abramsiana	CE,C1,L1	
Delphinium parryi seditosum		2,3,5
Dudleya caespitosa		1'
Eriogonum nudum ssp.		1',5
Eriophylum confertiflorum		2,5
Erysimum teretifolium	CE,C1,L1	1,5
Eschscholzia californica ssp.		1',5
Festuca confusa		5
F. octoflora		5
F. o. hirtella		5
F. pacifica		2
F. rubra		4
Filago californica		5
Gilia tenuiflora		2,3,5
Gnaphalium beneolens		5
Gnaphalium ssp.		2
Haplopappus ericoides blakei		4,5
Helianthemum scoparium		5
Hesperomecon linearis var. pulchella		2,3?,5
Heterotheca grandiflora		5
Horkelia cuneata		2,4,5
Koeleria cristata		2,5
Lasthenia (Baeria) chrysostoma		2
Layia platygloss ssp.		1'
Linanthus parviflorus		2,5
Linaria texana		5
Loeflingia squarrosa		2,5
Lotus scoparius		5
L. strigosus		5
Lupinus albifrons		2,5

APPENDIX A - (continued)
Sand Specialty Plants of Santa Cruz County

Scientific Name	Status*	Endemism/Distrib.**
L. arboreus		2,4
L. bicolor ssp.		2,5
Luzula multiflora		5
Malacothrix floccifera var.		2,5
Mimulus androsaceus		2,3,5
M. rattanii decurtatus	L4,SC	2,5
Monardella undulata	L4,SC	2,3,5
M. villosa ssp.		2,5
Muilla maritima		2,5
Navarretia atractyloides		5
N. hamata		2,5
Nemophila humifusa		2,5
Oenothera contorta strigulosa		2,5
O. micrantha		2,5
Orthocarpus purpurascens		2,5
Pectocarya penicillata		2,3,5
Pellaea mucronata		5
Phacelia distans		5
P. douglasii		2,3,5
P. ramosissima		2,5
Pinus ponderosa (benthamiana)		2,3,5
P. sabiniana		2
Plagiobothrys tenellus		2,5
Plantago erecta		2
Poa scabrella		
Sagina occidentalis		
Salvia mellifera		2
Saxifraga californica		
Scutellaria tuberosa		5
Silene verecunda platyota		2,3,5
Stephanomeria virgata		2
Stylocline gnaphalioides		3?,5
Thysanocarpus curvipes		2
Tillaea erecta		5

* CE = State Listed, endangered
  C1 = Enough data are on file to support federal listing
  C2 = Threat and/or distribution data are insufficient to support federal listing
  L1 = California Native Plant Society (1984) List 1 (Plants of Highest Priority)
  L4 = California Native Plant Society (1984) List 4 (Plants of Limited Distribution)
  SC = "Locally unique" (Santa Cruz County General Plan, 1980)

** 1 = Endemic to the Zayante Sands
   1' = Endemic form not yet described as taxonomically distinct
   2 = Sandhills population deserving critical taxonomic study to determine whether distinct from other populations (and thus endemic)

(continued)

(continued)

3 = Disjunct (i.e., isolated from other populations by considerable distance--at least 50 miles)
4 = Coastal relict population (i.e., isolated inland population of a coastal species)
5 = More evident or frequent in sandhills than in other plant communities of Santa Cruz County

Rare and Endangered Plant Successes in San Luis Obispo County

Malcolm G. McLeod [1]

Abstract: San Luis Obispo county has a great diversity of microclimate and substrate with a resultant diverse flora. 46 of these taxa are limited in numbers and/or distribution and are considered rare and endangered. The San Luis Obispo county chapter of the California Native Plant Society has been involved in the program from its inception. The rare and endangered plant committee has worked for several agencies gathering data concerning condition and extent of populations. Several taxa have also been rediscovered. The Nipomo lupine and the Camatta Canyon amole have been protected at least in part, and we are hopeful about a project concerning the San Luis lupine.

San Luis Obispo County is located about halfway between Los Angeles and San Francisco. It extends from San Miguel on the north to the Santa Maria river on the south. From the ocean on the west it extends across the Santa Lucia (outer coast) range to the Temblor (inner coast) range. It covers a total area of 8615 square kilometers (3326 square miles) (Donley, et. al., 1979). The county ranges in altitude from sea level at the coast to 1556 meters (5106 feet) elevation at Caliente Mountain near Cuyama valley. There are a number of small mountain ranges, altogether forming a very rugged countryside. There is a strong marine influence on the coastal side of the Santa Lucias, with greater aridity and range in temperature eastward.

There is also great range in substrate within the county. Wells (1962) indicates that no other point in the outer coast ranges has greater substratal diversity than the San Luis Obispo area. Certain substrates have significance because there are high levels of endemism associated with them. This is particularly true of the ultramafic rock with serpentine and derived clay soils of Hoover's (1970) Obispoan pocket of endemism (in the area of San Luis Obispo). It is also true to a lesser extent for unconsolidated sand, sandstone including the Pismo formation, and siliceous shale of the Monterey formation. Eastward there are what have been termed Miocene redbeds. There are also playas with no outlet which have become quite alkaline. In many cases the narrow endemics of these substrates have also proven to be rare and endangered.

Some endangered plants are found in northern San Luis Obispo county and northward into Monterey county. There are several taxa which are found in the dunes of southern San Luis Obispo county that continue southward into Santa Barbara county. The adobe sanicle (*Sanicula maritima*) once grew in the San Francisco Bay area where it has long been extirpated. It is now found in a few populations in San Luis Obispo and southern Monterey counties. Such plants as the Pt. Reyes bird's beak (*Cordylanthus maritimus* ssp. *palustris*) and the beach spectaclepod (*Dithyrea maritima*) are still widespread but impacted in other areas of the coast.

Hoover (1970) lists 1287 native species for San Luis Obispo county and Keil, et. al. (1985) have added a few more. In the Inventory of Rare and Endangered Vascular Plants of California (Smith & York, 1984), 46 San Luis Obispo county taxa have been placed in list 1B - plants rare and endangered in California and elsewhere; 6 in list 3 - plants about which we need more information; and 58 in list 4 - plants of limited distribution. This indicates that a total of 110 county taxa, or about 8.4 percent, are at least of limited distribution and of concern to the rare plant committee. We have emphasized those of list 1B (Table 1) but have also tried to collect information concerning the others, particularly those of list 3. Eight taxa are officially

---

[1] Professor of Botany, California Polytechnic State University, San Luis Obispo, CA; Rare Plant Coordinator, San Luis Obispo County Chapter California Native Plant Society.

Table 1 --- Rare and endangered plants of San Luis Obispo county[1]

1. _Allium hickmanii_ Eastw., Hickman's onion
2. _Amsinckia furcata_ Suksd., forked fiddleneck
3. _Arctostaphylos cruzensis_ Roof, Arroyo de la Cruz manzanita
4. _Arctostaphylos hookeri_ D. Don ssp. _hearstiorum_ (Hoover & Roof) P.V. Wells, Hearst's manzanita. CE[2]
5. _Arctostaphylos luciana_ Wells, Santa Lucia manzanita
6. _Arctostaphylos montereyensis_ Hoover, Toro manzanita
7. _Arctostaphylos morroensis_ Wies. & Schreib., Morro manzanita
8. _Arctostaphylos pilosula_ Jeps. & Wies. ssp. _pilosula_, Santa Margarita manzanita
9. _Arenaria paludicola_ B. L. Robins, swamp sandwort
10. _Atriplex vallicola_ Hoover, Lost Hills saltbush
11. _Bloomeria humilis_ Hoover, dwarf goldenstar. CR[3]
12. _Calochortus clavatus_ Wats. ssp. _recurvifolius_ (Hoover) Munz, Arroyo de la Cruz mariposa lily
13. _Calochortus obispoensis_ Lemmon, San Luis Mariposa lily
14. _Camissonia hardhamiae_ Raven, Hardham's evening primrose
15. _Carex obispoensis_ Stacey, San Luis sedge
16. _Castilleja mollis_ Penn., soft leaved paintbrush
17. _Ceanothus hearstiorum_ Hoover & Roof, Hearst's ceanothus. CR
18. _Ceanothus maritimus_, Hoover, maritime ceanothus. CR
19. _Chlorogalum purpureum_ Bdg. var. _reductum_ Hoover, Camatta canyon amole. CR
20. _Chorizanthe breweri_ Wats., Brewer's spineflower
21. _Chorizanthe pungens_ Benth. var. _pungens_, Monterey spineflower
22. _Chorizanthe rectispina_ Goodm., one awned spineflower
23. _Cirsium fontinale_ (Greene) Jeps. var. _obispoense_ J. T. Howell, Chorro creek bog thistle
24. _Cirsium loncholepis_ Petrak, La Graciosa thistle
25. _Cirsium occidentale_ (Nutt.) Jeps. var. _compactum_ Hoover, compact cobweb thistle
26. _Cirsium rhothophilum_ Blake, surf thistle
27. _Clarkia speciosa_ Lewis & Lewis ssp. _immaculata_ Lewis & Lewis, Pismo clarkia. CR
28. _Cordylanthus maritimus_ Nutt. ssp. _palustris_ (Behr) Chuang & Heckard, Pt. Reyes bird's beak
29. _Dithyrea maritima_ A. Davidson, Beach spectaclepod
30. _Dudleya bettinae_ Hoover, San Luis serpentine dudleya
31. _Eremalche kernensis_ C. B. Wolf, Kern mallow
32. _Eriodictyon altissimum_ P. V. Wells, Indian Knob mountain balm. CE
33. _Erysimum insulare_ Greene, island wallflower
34. _Eschscholzia rhombipetala_ Greene, diamond petaled California poppy
35. _Fritillaria ojaiensis_ A. Davids., Ojai fritillary
36. _Fritillaria viridea_ Kell., San Benito fritillary
37. _Galium hardhamiae_ Dempster, Hardham's bedstraw
38. _Layia jonesii_ Gray, Jones' layia
39. _Lupinus ludovicianus_ Greene, San Luis lupine
40. _Lupinus nipomensis_ Eastw., Nipomo lupine
41. _Malacothamnus palmeri_ (Wats.) Greene var. _involucratus_ (Rob.) Kearn., Carmel Valley bushmallow
42. _Monardella crispa_ Elmer, crisp monardella
43. _Monardella undulata_ Benth., var. _frutescens_ Hoover, San Luis Obispo monardella
44. _Pedicularis dudleyi_ Elmer, Dudley's lousewort. CR
45. _Perideridia gairdneri_ (H. & A.) Math. ssp. _gairdneri_, Gairdner's yampah
46. _Sanicula maritima_ Kell. ex. Wats., adobe sanicle. CR
47. _Sidalcea hickmanii_ Greene ssp. _anomala_ C. L. Hitchc., Cuesta Pass checker mallow. CR

[1] Excerpted from Smith & York (1984) list 1B
[2] CE listed California endangered
[3] CR listed California rare

listed by the state of California as rare, two as endangered. None are federally listed but there are several candidates.

The San Luis Obispo county chapter of the California Native Plant Society (C.N.P.S. S.L.O.) has been involved with the rare and endangered plant program from it's inception. Dirk Walters and I attended the 1974 map-in. We have established a rare plant committee with individuals interested in particular parts of the county such as north coast, Morro Bay area, Atascadero-Paso Robles and south county. The several taxonomists at Cal Poly and elsewhere in the county have been considered ex officio members of the committee and have proven invaluable in the field. The conservation committee has implemented preservation projects.

We have attempted to establish a data file for each of the 46 list 1B taxa (Table 1). We have obtained data from several sources including floras, field notes, herbarium labels, the data base, personal discussions and field work. We have acquired a complete set of 7.5 minute USGS topographical maps for Monterey, San Luis Obispo and Santa Barbara counties and the necessary 1^0 by 2^0 USGS maps for use with overlays furnished by the data base. The photographers on the rare plant committee have assembled a set of slides which includes pictures of almost all of the 46 taxa.

We have done field surveys for the California Natural Diversity Data Base in such diverse locations as Arroyo de la Cruz, Cuesta West and Navajo road. We also have done searches for a number of taxa for the Nature Conservancy Element Preservation program. These have taken us to Vandenberg AFB, Carizzo Plain and many places in between. We did a thorough study for the California Department of Fish and Game Endangered Plant program at Arroyo de la Cruz. This required nine field trips spread over a 3 year period. We have also furnished information to the Federal Endangered Species program and the California Department of Parks and Recreation.

REDISCOVERING TAXA

Field notes are often sketchy or otherwise unclear. Where this is the case, careful research and field work is necessary. Hoover states on herbarium labels that the Camatta Canyon amole (_Chlorogalum_ _purpureum_ var. _reductum_) was found on "hard red soil" 18 miles east of Creston. In the original mapping it was placed near Shell Creek. It was also difficult to visualize a plant which no one in the area had seen in nature. We set the odometer at Creston and proceeded 18 miles eastward. As we approached that distance we began to see the "hard red soil". The next consideration was to find the plant in flower. It proved to be as diminutive as the name "reductum" indicates. It is five miles away from our original hypothetical location.

The La Panza population of the diamond petaled California poppy (_Eschscholzia_ _rhombipetala_) is one of only two thought to be extant in San Luis Obispo county. The only collection from this population was made in 1950 with La Panza district as the location. The herbarium label did give an indication as to substrate and of course, collection date. From that it was a matter of going to the area and looking. Our 1984 trip was successful. We are now watching this population carefully.

A particularly significant event was the rediscovery of the Santa Lucia mint (_Pogogyne_ _clareana_) which is found only in a very narrow area on Fort Hunter Liggett in southern Monterey county. We undertook this project at the request of the Database and the Nature Conservancy and in cooperation with the Monterey chapter of the California Native Plant Society. Trips were required in two consecutive years before it was located. On the second trip the original collector (and namesake), Clare Hardham, accompanied us. It was found along Los Bueyas creek rather than Los Burros creek as we had originally thought. It had not been seen since the original collection was made in 1960.

PROTECTING IMPACTED TAXA

The rare and endangered plants in our area (as elsewhere) are impacted in a number of ways. The largest population of the very rare Nipomo lupine (_Lupinus_ _nipomensis_) was found to be located at the Callendar Switching Station of Pacific Gas and Electric (P.G. & E.) on Nipomo Mesa. Activities at and near the switching station heavily impacted the Nipomo lupine population.

Conversations were begun with P.G. & E. as early as 1976 at the urging of Leslie Hood, but direct negotiations were not undertaken until 1982. Local lawyers were very helpful and a number of C.N.P.S. S.L.O. members worked long hours to hammer out the details of the Conservation Management Agreement. The result was that P.G. & E. agreed to allow C.N.P.S. S.L.O. to furnish the materials and construct a fence on the P.G. & E. property outside the switching station compound. The fence presently limits access to the area on three sides of the switching station where lupines are found. It was not possible to save the lupines inside the compound.

With rediscovery of the population of the Camatta Canyon amole we became aware of another problem. This is the only known population of the taxon. The largest part of it proved to be in the middle of an off-road-vehicle (ORV) staging area. It was distressing to see motorhomes parked on top of the plants with three-wheelers circling them. Since it was Forest Service land we contacted the chief ranger in Santa Maria.

This time there was no formal agreement. It was decided that C.N.P.S. S.L.O. would furnish most of the materials and labor. The Forest Service would furnish expertise and help in the construction of the fence. At one session the chief ranger's mother helped.

We fenced about halfway across the mesa where the plant grows along Navajo Road. There is still need for more fence, but we have excluded vehicles from the most important areas. We checked the area last spring and it is recovering from the ORV damage.

A third project was initiated after the Las Pilitas fire last year. ORVs had worn a track across a population of the San Luis lupine (Lupinus ludovicianus) off Pozo road. Bulldozing during the fire gave the vehicles access to the center of the population. We are presently negotiating through the district ranger with the ranch foreman to protect the population. The proposal is for C.N.P.S. S.L.O. to furnish fencing materials and have the fence constructed by the California Conservation Corp. This would protect the plants and apparently benefit the rancher.

FUTURE PROSPECTS

The surveys we have done for the Nature Conservancy Element Preservation program have pinpointed places where action will soon be necessary. A port is proposed for the coast between Oso Flaco creek and the Santa Maria river. There are at least 6 list 1B taxa present in that area. Thwarting this development will be the biggest challenge yet. We will furnish information to the environmental groups involved.

The work done for the California Department of Fish and Game Endangered Plant Program will eventually result in actions designed to protect more endangered plants. We are also in the process of writing a status report for the Federal Endangered Species Program in hopes of getting the Nipomo lupine federally listed. We are keeping the lines of communication open and furnishing data upon request.

The full effect of development has not yet reached our area. Now is the time to delimit the areas to be protected. We are keeping that in mind as we continue to gather information. We hope to preserve all the endangered taxa of the county.

REFERENCES

Donley, Michael W.; Allan, Stuart; Caro, Patricia; Patton, Clyde P. 1979; Atlas of California. Pacific Book Center, Culver City, CA. v + 191 p.

Hoover, Robert F. 1970; The vascular plants of San Luis Obispo County. U.C. Press. 350 p.

Keil, David J.; Allen, Robert L.; Nishida, Joy H.; Wise, Eric A. 1985. Addenda to the vascular flora of San Luis Obispo County, California. Madroño 32(4):214-224.

Smith, James Payne ed. and Richard York. 1984. Inventory of rare and endangered vascular plants of California. California Native Plant Society Spec. Pub. no. 1, ed. 3. xviii + 174 p.

Wells, Philip V. 1962; Vegetation in relation to geological substratum and fire in the San Luis Obispo quadrangle, California. Ecological Monographs 32(1):79-103.

Status of Five Rare Plant Species in Sequoia and Kings Canyon National Parks

Larry L. Norris [1]

Abstract: Twenty-six rare plant species are known to occur in Sequoia and Kings Canyon National Parks. Of these, 5 have been recommended for additional study or for management actions to mitigate threats to one or more of their populations. Short reports on the research needs for Astragalus ravenii, Ribes tularense, and Streptanthus fenestratus are discussed and management concerns and actions for populations of Eriogonum nudum var. murinum and Oreonana purpurascens are presented. Pertinent information on inventory skills, concepts of rarity, mitigation techniques, and the ecology of these southern Sierran endemics are discussed as appropriate.

During the summers of 1980 and 1981 field work in Sequoia and Kings Canyon National Parks surveyed 158 populations of 24 rare plants species (Norris and Brennan 1982). A 1984 update of the inventory added 2 more species of concern and 40 more populations, bringing the total inventoried populations to 198 (Norris 1984). As a result of the Parks' inventory and the 3 inventories done on the surrounding national forests (Sierra, Inyo, and Sequoia) many of the taxa in the southern Sierra that were once considered rare are now known to be more common and have been dropped from federal consideration. The resulting list of Sequoia and Kings Canyon National Parks is much more precise and allows for a prioritization of research needs for the 14 remaining rare species, 6 of which are candidate species for threatened status in the U.S. Fish and Wildlife Service endangered species list (USFWS 1985).

Sequoia and Kings Canyon National Parks have an obligation under the Endangered Species Act and the U.S. National Park Service Management Policies (USNPS 1978) to monitor the various populations of the 6 candidate species for threatened status to ensure that the populations are not subject to any severe threats. Four of these 6 species are in remote wilderness habitats seldom visited by park users or park personnel. Of the 4 "wilderness" species, only Purple Mountain Parsley (Oreonana purpurascens Shevock & Constance), in the Hockett Meadow population, is known to have been impacted, and this was by stock rolling during the summers of 1980 and 1984. The Midget Milk-vetch (Astragalus ravenii Barneby) is so rare that further searches of its wilderness habitat are required to determine the true status and distribution of the species within the Parks, and in the southern Sierra as a whole. The 2 remaining candidate species are in the lower elevation foothills. Both are endemic to marble outcrops in the Kaweah River drainage. One, the Mouse Buckwheat (Eriogonum nudum Dougl. ex Benth. Var. murinum Reveal) is threatened by proposed road widening in its 3 populations along the Generals Highway in Sequoia National Park.

Management considerations are also extended to those 8 sensitive plant species that are not on the federal list, but qualify for special attention under National Park Service Management Policies. These policies direct park managers to consider the occurrences of species that have unique distributions within park boundaries. Of these 8 species none face any serious threats, but some require additional study to determine what effects wildfire has on their numbers, distribution, and vigor. Sequoia Gooseberry (Ribes tularense (Cov.) Fedde.) and Kings Canyon Jewel Flower (Streptanthus fenestratus (Greene) J.T. Howell) are in special need of such study since most of their known range is within the boundaries of Sequoia and Kings Canyon National Parks, in areas that will eventually be prescribed burned.

SPECIES ACCOUNTS

Midget Milk-vetch

Midget Milk-vetch is a restricted southern Sierran endemic that is known from only 2 populations on the Sierran crest in Fresno and Inyo counties. The population near Taboose Pass in the Inyo National Forest is estimated to contain between 200 - 300 individuals, and the population on Sawmill Pass, in Kings Canyon National Park, is estimated at

---

[1] Naturalist, Sequoia and Kings Canyon National Parks, National Park Service, Department of the Interior, Three Rivers CA 93271

"several thousand (5000?)" plants (Norris and Brennan 1982). A total of less than 6000 individuals are known to exist. The species is listed in Category 2 on the U.S. Fish and Wildlife Service list of threatened and endangered species, but has not been listed by the state of California. Midget Milk-vetch grows on gravel flats between 3355m (11,000') and 3445m (11,300') in elevation. These flats are open with sparse herb and grass cover. They are exposed to full sunlight throughout the day. The species is absent on talus slopes. Trails pass through or by each population and this probably accounts for their discoveries.

The research need identified for this species is to conduct searches in likely habitat along the Sierran crest. It is difficult to believe that only 2 populations exist, and that both of them happen to be along the only 2 trails that cross the crest in that section of the Sierra. Two uninventoried localities have been identified on the crest that could support populations of Midget Milk-vetch. One area is the moderate southwest-facing slope of Colosseum Mountain; the other is located in the low saddle north of Split Mountain. Searches in these and similar areas should be conducted during late July when the species is at peak bloom. Although no threats are documented for this species it is incumbent upon the National Park Service to make an extra effort to determine the true numbers and distribution of this rare species. The species may prove to be more common then previously considered and no longer qualify as a candidate for threatened status.

Purple Mountain Parsley

Purple Mountain Parsley is a Tulare County endemic known to occur in 14 populations, 6 of which are within Sequoia National Park. The sum of estimated individuals in these 14 populations is 41,500; 11,500 of that total occurring in the Park. The remaining 30,000 individuals are on the Sequoia National Forest. This species is listed as a candidate for threatened status on the federal list and is not listed by the state of California. Purple Mountain Parsley occurs between 2520m (8260') and 2915m (9550') in Sequoia National Park. It grows on coarse, sandy to gravelly soils on either granitic or metamorphic substrates in red fir, lodge-pole pine, and mixed coniferous forests. These sites are mostly on gentle slopes and ridgetops of varied aspect. Two Hockett Plateau populations are atypical in that they are found on glacial drift and streamside gravel bar deposits. The parsley is absent from very bouldery areas and areas with dense vegetation cover, preferring full sunlight exposure and bare soils.

During the sensitive plant species inventory of the Hockett Meadow population in July 1980 it was noted that severe damage to the population was occurring by pack and saddle stock rolling on the dry, glacial drift at the upper end of the meadow. Some of the areas disturbed by stock rolling was about 1dm deep, exposing the storage roots of these rare mountain parsleys. Each winter the ground freezes and the subsequent movement of the top few centimeters of soil erases evidence of the past summer's damage to the plants, except, of course, for areas where the plant has been totally removed by stock rolling.

Monitoring during the 3 successive summers showed a downward trend in population numbers. By the 1984 season a nearby stock camp had been closed to use and rehabilitated. The local packer was advised to unpack his stock in a camp further away from the population so the animals would roll in other less sensitive areas. Also, photo points had been established to annually monitor the population. Following a low of "several hundred" individuals in 1983, a population count in July 1986 showed a total of 4500 individuals, very close to that originally estimated in 1980. The credit for the success of this recovery effort belongs to the wilderness rangers who have been stationed at Hockett Meadow over the last 6 years. Their diligence in keeping stock from rolling on the rare plants and their careful advise to stock parties that use the area has helped protect this population better than any fences ever could.

Mouse Buckwheat

Mouse Buckwheat is endemic to the Kaweah River drainage in the western, low elevation portions of Sequoia National Park. Nine populations are known to exist, 7 inside the park and 2 outside, but near the boundary. In part, due to the rugged cliffsides upon which most populations are found, only a total of 7500 individuals can be estimated to exist from the 9 population reports. The actual number may be less. This species is a federal candidate for threatened status on the U.S. Fish and Wildlife Service list. It is not listed by the state of California.

Mouse Buckwheat occurs on marble outcrops in the foothill woodland between 295m (960') and 1220m (4000') in elevation. Soil pockets, cracks, and fractures in the marble rock provide rootholds for this woody buckwheat. Slopes are steep with aspects generally facing south, exposed to full sun throughout the day. Since this subspecies is lithospecific to marble it was easy to locate potential populations on geologic maps or during field surveys. Getting to those outcrops was often difficult because of thick brush and steep terrain. The Mouse Buckwheat is a vigorous species that colonizes disturbed slopes that have ample runoff. This ability has allowed it to reestablish on marble outcrops disturbed by road construction. Three populations along the Generals Highway in Sequoia National Park, are, for the most part, made up of the plants that colonized these roadcuts.

While no threats exist for this subspecies in most of its populations, the 3 populations along the Generals Highway are in peril. The Federal Highway Commission intends to widen the roadbed of the Generals Highway by 1 meter (3 feet). This will probably necessitate bin-walls in 2 of the 3 populations, causing the removal of up to 1000 plants, nearly one seventh of the world's population! At present plans are being developed for the road widening and the Mouse Buckwheat has been included as an element of concern that must be addressed.

The construction project offers 2 research/resource management opportunities. One is to determine if the species can be successfully transplanted or seeded, or if seeds from the roadside plants need to be brought to germination and successfully grown before transplanting. Secondly, and perhaps more challenging, is the need for real mitigation proposals that would protect the major portions of these populations on the downslope side of the road. The present management proposal will likely leave the plants above the road alone, while the plants below the road will be buried. Reseeding from upslope plants would likely occur sometime after construction had been completed. Of course the success of this would depend on what habitat was left on the downslope side of the road. Since the Mouse Buckwheat is lithospecific to marble or other calcareous substrates it will probably not do well on steel bin-walls or imported fill. Some serious decisions must be made before road construction begins.

One population of Mouse Buckwheat was entirely consumed in a wildfire in August 1984. I discovered the population of 21 plants in April 1985 as they were beginning to grow back from partially burned rootcrowns and seeds (?). A modest monitoring effort to document the recovery of this population would provide valuable data on this rare subspecies' response to wildfire. Nature rarely gives us opportunities to monitor recovery from the very start; usually we must create the opportunities, as we must in the following 2 species.

Sequoia Gooseberry

Probably only 14,000 individuals exist in 8 populations of the Sequoia Gooseberry. Six populations are in Sequoia National Park and 2 are on Bureau of Land Management property just west of the Park. The plant has a prostrate habit and vegetatively reproduces by means of rooting stolons. This causes a great deal of difficulty when trying to count individuals in a population. The species is a Tulare County endemic in a restricted habitat, geographically and numerically rare, but remains unlisted on both the state and federal levels.

The Sequoia Gooseberry only grows on the westernmost forested peaks of the mixed coniferous forest between 1635m (5360') and 2149m (7040') in elevation. I refer to these areas as "pine islands" as they are almost always isolated "hilltop" stands of conifers that rise just above the foothill woodland or chaparral covered slopes. Sequoia Gooseberry is found on sandy loams or clayey loams on granitic, calcareous, and metamorphic substrates. What is unique about this species' habitat preference is that it is almost always found in partial sun or open shade of natural forest openings, or along abandoned roadbeds, or on roadcuts and banks. The species is generally sparse or absent from very dense mixed coniferous forest and from streamside banks.

Since the Sequoia Gooseberry occurs most often in natural or manmade forest openings what effect has natural fire had on the distribution of this species in the past? And, more importantly, what effects will current fire management practices have on the survival of the species? Research is needed to determine if the plant is, indeed, being made rare by loss of habitat due to fire exclusion over the last 60+ years. Research is also needed on the pollination ecology of this species. Since the flowers hang close to the ground and are shaded by the leaves is appears that the species is beetle pollinated. Does fire play a significant role in the life cycle of the pollinator as well? Further field searches are also needed to complete the inventory of likely "pine island" habitat, specifically on Conifer and Dennison ridges within the optimal elevation range.

Kings Canyon Jewel Flower

Another species in need of fire ecology research is the Kings Canyon Jewel Flower. Only 8 populations exist in the Kings River drainage: 7 in Kings Canyon National Park and 1 nearby in the Sierra National Forest. The total number of individuals is estimated at 51,000 from the population reports, but the abundance of this little annual fluctuates widely from year to year in response to vagaries in the weather. In Tehipite Valley, at 1266m (4150') in elevation, four 10 meter square plots yielded actual individual counts of 305, 500, 596, and 1,971 plants! Enough data were gathered on this species to remove it from candidate threatened status.

The Kings Canyon Jewel Flower occurs in a narrow elevational range of less than 610 vertical meters (2000 vertical feet). The lowest population is on the sandy, flat floor of Tehipite Valley at 1266m where it grows by the thousands. The highest population occurs along the Copper Creek trail on the north wall of Kings Canyon at 1830m (6000') elevation. It grows in openings within forest and brush. All population sites are hot, dry, southfacing slopes of granitic sands and gravels with full sunlight exposure. Given the narrow elevational range of known Kings Canyon Jewel Flower populations in the Kings River drainage, this species will probably never be found over extensive areas. However, much potential habitat within this drainage has not been inventoried, mainly due to the rugged terrain and the time constraints of the original inventory. Additional Kings Canyon Jewel Flower populations may exist in these uninventoried areas.

A dense population of the Kings Canyon Jewel Flower occurs within the site of a 1972 wildfire in Tehipite Valley. This fire may have created the open habitat required by the species. The response of this species to fire-created openings needs to be determined. Small prescribed burns adjacent to populations of Kings Canyon Jewel Flower should be conducted, and the burned areas monitored for invasion of the jewel flower.

CONCLUSIONS

Within Sequoia and Kings Canyon National Parks, management for rare plant species is a relatively easy task, due to the remote locations of most populations and lack of any serious anthropogenic threats. However, in 4 species real management problems exist, either in the form of direct physical threats as with Purple Mountain Parsley and Mouse Buckwheat, or by threats caused by current management practices as with Sequoia Gooseberry and Kings Canyon Jewel Flower and their probable reduction of habitat due to fire supression. On some species we simply need more information. A good example of this need is the almost total lack of data on Midget Milk-vetch, currently recognized as a very rare plant. Many rare plant research needs and opportunities exist in Sequoia and Kings Canyon National Parks. The five species discussed above do indeed represent just a few of the questions for which park managers are in need of answers.

Acknowledgements: I thank Dr. David J. Parsons, Research Scientist, Sequoia and Kings Canyon National Parks for support during the field inventories and for reviewing the draft of this paper.

REFERENCES

Norris, Larry L.; Brennan, David A. Sensitive plant species of Sequoia and Kings Canyon National Parks. Technical Report No. 8. Cooperative National Park Resources Studies Unit, Univ. of California, Davis. CA: 1982; 120p.

Norris, Larry L. Sensitive plant species of Sequoia and Kings Canyon National Parks. Technical Report No. 17, update to Technical Report No. 8. Cooperative National Park Resources Studies Unit, Univ. of California, Davis, CA; 1984;15p

U.S. Fish and Wildlife Service. Endangered and threatened wildlife and plants: status of review of plant taxa for listing. Federal Register 50:188; 1985.

U.S. National Park Service. Management Policies. U.S. Department of the Interior, Washington, D.C. 4-78 edition; 1978.

Rare Plant Conservation in the Southwestern Cape

E. L. Gawith[1], N.J. Schmeidler III[2]

Abstract: The Cape Floristic Kingdom in the South-Western Cape is one of the six plant Kingdoms in the world. This Kingdom has the highest concentration of threatened plants of any temperate region. Thirteen hundred and twenty-six of the estimated 6500 species are threatened with extinction. Conservation activities at present involve locating and documenting the status of these plants in order to establish priorities for conservation. <u>Witsenia maura</u> Thung., a monotypic genus, is an endemic member of the Iridaceae. As a result of a survey conducted on the species, it was suggested that measures be taken to conserve <u>W. maura ex situ</u>.

The South-Western Cape Province lies within that region of southern Africa experiencing a mediterranean-type climate. Winters are cool and wet, while summers are hot and dry. The annual precipitation, which falls predominantly in winter, ranges from 300 mm to 900 mm, although exceptionally high rainfalls are recorded in certain mountains, for example, Jonkershoek (3000 mm per year). Average annual temperatures range between 16° and 18° C. The geology of the area is dominated by the Cape Folded Belt comprised mainly of sandstone and to a lesser extent shale. This formation gives rise to the mountains while much of the lowlands are comprised of shales, granites and aeolian sands.

The vegetation of the South-Western Cape, characterized by small sclerophyllous-leaved plants, is known locally as the Fynbos. Typical forms of the Fynbos have been designated by Acocks (1953) as veld types 69 Macchia and 70 False Macchia (now generally grouped together as Mountain Fynbos), and 47 False Macchia (Coastal Fynbos). The Mountain Fynbos is found predominantly on quartzite mountain ranges and on those upland plains and valleys of the Cape Folded Belt where soils are acid, nutrient-poor and highly leached. The Coastal Fynbos is mainly restricted to recent drift sands, limestones and coastal plain soils.

The Fynbos occurs south from Vanrynsdorp to the Cape Peninsula, a distance of 250 km, and east 800 km to scattered patches near Grahamstown, in a broken belt 40 km to 150 km wide . Although it covers such a small area (originally 4.6 million hectares, or 0.04 percent of the world's land area), the Fynbos is recognised as one of the six floristic Kingdoms of the world, namely, the Cape Floristic Kingdom, due to the unique nature of the vegetation. Seven plant families, approximately 20 percent of the genera, and about 70 percent of the estimated 6000 species found in the Fynbos are endemic.

The Cape Floristic Kingdom probably represents the most species-rich flora in the world, comprising approximately 10 percent of the world's flowering plant flora (Edwards, 1976). Using the method of comparison employed by Cailleux (1953, in Hall, 1978), a species-richness figure of about 1300 species per 10000 km was obtained. This is considerably higher than that of an area in Central America which Cailleux reports to contain the second richest flora in the world, with 420 species per 10000 km (Hall, 1978). It is generally believed that this high concentration of species is the result of climatic changes that have occurred since the evolution of the Fynbos. These changes have resulted in the subsequent expansion and contraction of its distribution range. At present, the Fynbos is confined to a considerably smaller area than the area it occupied during the glacial periods, in part explaining the very high concentration of species.

Despite its scientific uniqueness, the Fynbos has been considerably reduced by land-use activities such as urbaniza-

---

[1] Graduate student, University of Cape Town, Rondebosch, South Africa.
  Graduate student, Wichita State University, Wichita, Kansas.

[2] Present address: University of Colorado Boulder, Colorado 80309.

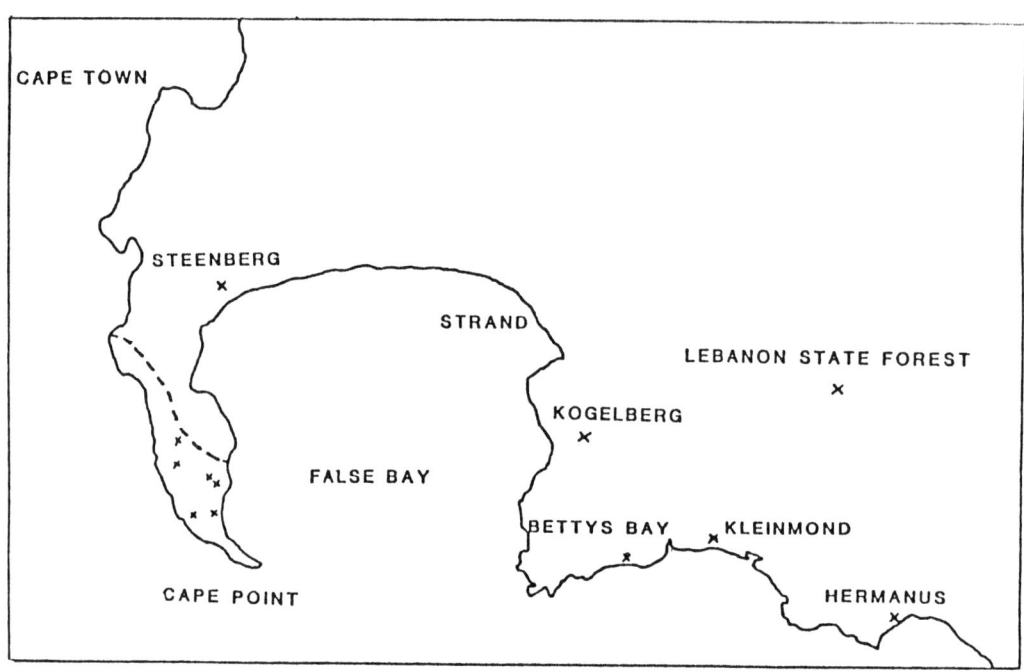

Figure 1. Location of Witsenia maura in the Southwestern Cape.

tion and agriculture. Formerly covering an area of 4.6 million hectares, the Fynbos has been reduced by 61 percent and now only covers 1.8 million hectares, confined chiefly to narrow mountain corridors (Hall, 1978). Twenty-four percent of the remaining 39 percent is severely infested by alien vegetation. This habitat destruction has resulted in 11 percent of the flora being presently threatened with extinction. To date there are 1621 plant species known to be rare or threatened, while 26 species are already known to be extinct (Hall and Veldhuis, 1985). One explanation for the large number of threatened plants is that many species have very restricted distribution ranges. Fifty-seven species are endemic to the Cape Peninsula, a small area of 471 square kilometers (Axelrod and Raven, 1978).

CASE STUDY: WITSENIA MAURA THUNB.

W. maura is one of these threatened plants. It is confined to seven populations on the Cape Peninsula, and five populations on the opposite side of False Bay between Steenbraskop and Hermanus (Fig. 1), in perenially marshy areas of the Mountain Fynbos.

Morphology

W. maura is a woody member of the Iridaceae. The following morphological information about this species was obtained from herbarium records, University of Cape Town, Thiselton-Dyer (1897), Marloth (1915), Pole Evans (1922), Adamson (1926), Adamson and Salter (1950) and Levyns (1966). Adult plants range from 0.5 to 2 meters tall. Stems are erect, flattened and can be simple or branched. The leaves are closely two-ranked, equitant, rigid and erect. The bare portion of the stem below the leaves has prominent leaf scars which become obliterated in the older portions. The basal portion of the stem is considerably wider than the upper portion. Roots are adventitious.

Inflorescences are terminal and flower clusters crowded. Flowers are borne in pairs of four to six oblong, green-yellow bracts. The inner bract is 25 to 40 mm long and contains a shorter acute or acumate brown spathe, 1.4 to 3.3 cm long, firm, folded, in each axil. Each spathe subtends a single flower. Flowers are 50 to 70 mm in length. The perianth tube is long, cylindrical, widening slightly towards the top. The perianth segments are shorter than the perianth tube, and are closed. Flowers are green-yellow at the base, becoming blue-black. The blue-black zone ranges from 10 to 20 mm wide. Between the blue-black zone and the top of the flower, there is a narrow belt, green to green-yellow in color, 1 to 3 mm wide. The uppermost 10 to 16 mm are bright yellow. The outer three segments are pilose on the exterior, while the three inner segments are only pilose at the tips (Fig. 2).

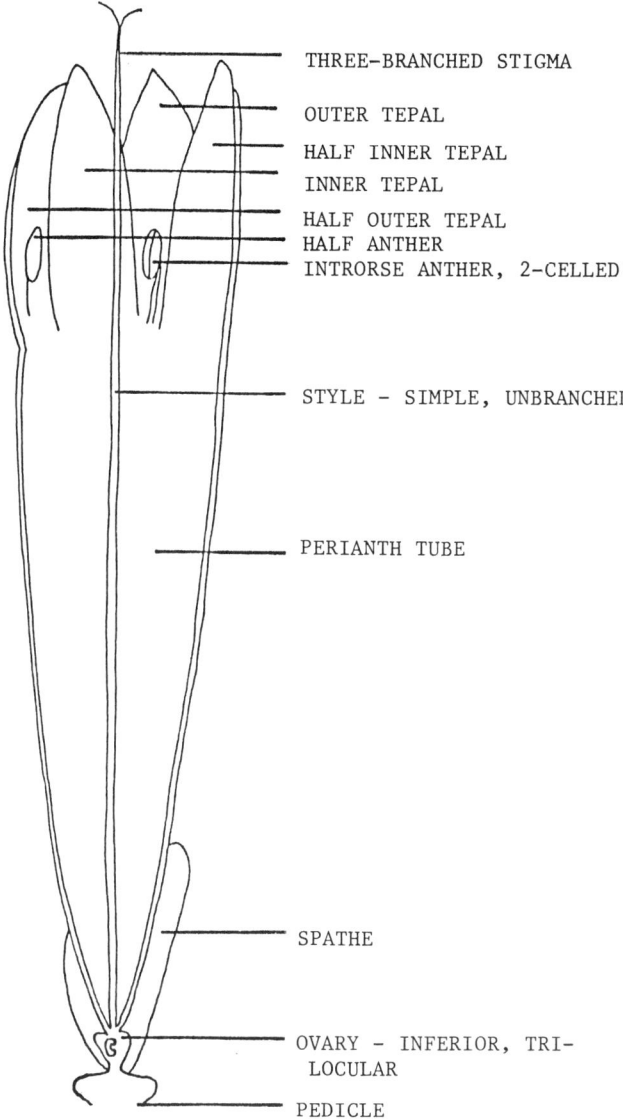

Figure 2: Half-flower diagram of Witsenia maura.

There are three introse stamens attached to the top of the perianth tube. The filaments are short and flat, and the anthers small (4 mm long). The style is 7 cm long and simple. The stigma is filiform. Only the stigma and 1 to 2 mm of the style is exserted. The fruit of W. maura is a tri-locular capsule 10 to 12 mm long. Each locule contains 1 to 2 seeds. Seeds are two-grooved and pale brown, with a thin, rugose seed coat. Seeds range between 6.0 x 2.5 mm and 8.0 x 3.5 mm in size. At the tip of the seed is an aril 1.0 to 1.5 mm long, which can be easily removed.

Methodology

Each of the 12 naturally occurring populations of W. maura was surveyed. At each site, abiotic parameters, namely altitude, slope, exposure and edaphic factors of soil moisture and soil type were noted. Associated plants were identified. The area covered by the population was measured, and the number of individuals estimated. The most recent form of disturbance experienced by each population was recorded, in addition to the type of reproduction subsequent to the disturbance (i.e. resprouting and/or reseeding) and the age of aerial growth. The range in plant height was measured, the flowering and fruiting time and the percent seed set noted. The vigor of each population was assessed as the proportion of adult plants to seedlings. Existing and potential threats to each population were noted to assist in evaluating their conservation potential.

Pollination

Floral morphology of W. maura suggests cross-pollination. The perianth segments are personate with a small opening through which the stigma and upper portion of the style is exserted. Self-pollination is unlikely to occur since the stigma is exserted before the anthers have ripened. Wind pollination in W. maura is not possible since the petals never open to expose the anthers. Thus pollination is believed to be conducted by birds and insects. Since the perianth tube is approximately 5 cm long, pollination is restricted to those birds that have long bills and protrusive tongues. Two species of sunbird were observed on the flowers, the malachite sunbird (Nectarinia famosa famosa) and the orange-breasted sunbird (Anthobaphes violacea) (pers. obs.). The chances of pollen of a rare species such as W. maura being transported over distances of between 5 and 80 km to other isolated populations would be greater if sunbirds were specialist pollinators. However, sunbirds are generalist pollinators. Therefore, the 12 populations comprising this species probably experience geographical, and subsequent genetic, isolation. This has important implications in the conservation of the species.

Seed dispersal

Seed dispersal is believed to occur through the abiotic vector, water, and the biotic vector, ants. There are a number of advantages to both these types of dispersal. The Fynbos is a highly heterogeneous vegetation located on soils of low nutrient status. A major limiting nutrient in seed production is phosphorous (Westoby et al, in Bond and Slingsby, 1983). Consequently, local plant species tend to accumulate large quantities of this nutrient in the seeds to facilitate their germination (Mitchell, pers. comm.). Thus short-distance dispersal may be advantageous in that it would both reduce the chance of seed landing in unfavorable habitat and the loss of phosphorous-rich seed from the habitat. In this species, neither water nor ants cause long-distance seed dispersal.

DISCUSSION

The conservation of rare plants may be achieved in situ, ex situ, or a combination thereof (IUCN, 1980). In situ conservation is obviously preferable since the transferral of plants to a different habitat may result in the collapse of the population. In a vegetation type such as the Fynbos, which contains an exceptionally large number of rare and threatened species, in situ conservation cannot be implemented in all instances. Thus, priority should be given to species endangered throughout their ranges and those that are the sole representatives of their family or genus (IUCN, 1980). The uniqueness of W. maura justifies the in situ conservation of this species. At the time of the survey (1983), only 4 populations were in protected areas, the remaining 8 in areas soon to be developed.

Plants that comprise the Fynbos are adapted to fire, as is evidenced by the presence of serotiny in some members of the Proteaceae, and fire-stimulated germination. However, the optimum fire regime(s) for the Cape Floristic Kingdom have not yet been determined, because of the wide variability in optimum fire cycles for species.

If rare species are to be conserved in situ, the effects of fire should be monitored to establish the optimum regime for the species. The absence of any population of W. maura older than six years makes it impossible to state what happens to this species if not burned for a long period of time. It is generally believed, however, that W. maura is a fire-adapted species. The reasons for this are as follows:

1. Plants resprout and seed germinate 2 to 3 months after a fire (D. Clarke, pers. comm.)

2. Plants occur in firebreaks which are burned every 4 to 6 years

3. Seeds subjected to temperatures of 60° C had a 37 percent germination success while seed in the control treatments had a 27 to 47 percent germination success

4. Temperatures of 100° C for 30 seconds did not kill all the seeds; there was a 3 percent germination success.

Individuals that resprout following a fire generally start flowering 2 years after a fire although some flowers are produced in the first year. The age at which seedlings reach reproductive maturity is unknown. This needs to be researched in order to establish a fire regime that will ensure sexual reproduction. Although the species will survive more frequent fires because of its ability to reproduce vegetatively, this form of reproduction does not increase genetic variation and will therefore not benefit the species evolutionarily when the pressures of natural selection change.

Ex situ conservation should be introduced as a backup to in situ conservation, should any of the remaining 4 viable populations experience a disaster. Ex situ conservation offers a number of alternatives such as introduction to horticulture, establishment in botanic gardens or storage in seed banks. The specific habitat requirements of W. maura make the introduction of this species into horticulture unlikely. Thus, ex situ conservation is likely to be restricted to botanic gardens and private reserves (Frankel and Soule, 1981). Botanic gardens can assist conservation in many fields, among them the cultivation of species and establishment of seedbanks (Simmons et al., 1976; Frankel and Soule, 1981).

The probable isolation that the 12 populations have been subjected for the past 10000 years suggests that they may have diverged genetically. Therefore, the artificial 'mixing' of gene pools is not recommended until the genetic constitution of the populations has been examined. The production of maladapted genomed could result in further decline of the species.

This case study examined one of the many threatened plants in the Cape Floristic Kingdom. Management of this vegetation-type is difficult because of the many species differing requirements. This results in the need for a highly heterogeneous and pristine environment.

Acknowledgements: We would like to thank the following people who offered assistance in the preparation of this paper: Prof. A.V. Hall, Dr. I.J.M. Williams, the staff of the Cape of Good Hope Nature Reserve. Thanks also go to Dr. J. Bock, and Dr. Y. Linhart for reading earlier drafts of the manuscript. This research was supported by a CSIR post-graduate award.

REFERENCES

Acocks, J.P.H. Veld types of South Africa. Memoires of the botanical survey of South Africa. Pretoria, 28, 1953.

Adamson, R.S. On the anatomy of some shrubby Iridaceae. Trans. Roy. Soc. S.A. 13(2): 175-195, 1926.

Adamson, R.S. and Salter, T.M. eds. Flora of the cape peninsula. Juta, Cape Town, 887 pp. 1950.

Axelrod, D.I. and Raven, P.H. Late cretaceous and tertiary vegetation history of Africa. pp 79-130. In Werger, M.J.A. ed. Biogeography and ecology of southern Africa. Volume 1. Junk, the Hague, 1978.

Bond, W.J. and Slingsby, P. Seed dispersal by ants in shrublands of the cape peninsula and its evolutionary implications. S.A. J. of Science, 79: 231-233, 1983.

Edwards, D. Resources of southern Africa. pp. 154-160. In Baker, G. ed. Resources of southern Africa - today and tomorrow. Assoc. Sci. and Tech. Soc. of S.A., JHB. 403 pp., 1976

Frankel, O.H. and Soule, M.E. Conservation and evolution. Cambridge University Press, London, 327 pp., 1981.

Hall, A.V. Endangered species in a rising tide of population growth. Trans. Roy. Soc. S.A., 43: 37-49, 1978.

Hall, A.V. and Veldhuis, H.A. South African red data book: plants - fynbos and karoo biomes. S.A. Nat. Sci. Prog. Rep. no. 117: 1-160, 1985.

IUCN. World conservation strategy. International union for the conservation of nature and natural resources. Gland, Switzerland, 1980.

Levyns, M.R. A guide to the flora of the cape peninsula. 2nd ed. Juta, Wynberg, S.A. 310 pp., 1966.

Marloth, R. The flora of South Africa. Vol. 4 monocotyledones. Darter Bros. and Co., Cape Town, 208 pp., 1915.

Moll, E.J. and Bossi, L. Assessment of the extent of the natural vegetation of the fynbos biome of South Africa. S.A. J. of Sci. 80(8): 355-358, 1984.

Pole Evans, I.B. The flowering plants of South Africa. Vol 14., Perskor, JHB, S.A., 1922.

Thieselton-Dyer, W.T. ed. Flora capensis. Vol. 6. Reeve and Co., London, 563 pp., 1897.

Point Loma Lichens— Now and Then

Charis C. Bratt [1]

Abstract: The lichen flora of Pt. Loma (Cabrillo National Monument) was surveyed. The historical record was researched both for literature references and for actual specimens at various herbaria. Unpublished collections from 1966 were also used. These were then compared to recent collections and the changes in the flora were noted. Most of the fruticose lichens can no longer be found. The foliose lichens seem to be reduced in size.

There is no inventory of the rare and endangered species of lichens in California. It was not until 1979 that a catalog of California lichens was published. That catalog lists the lichen species mentioned in literature up to that time, but does not give distributions or abundance. Anyone working with lichens soon becomes aware that there are many lichens no longer found in great quantity, if at all. Documenting changes in lichen vegetation can be a difficult and frustrating process. The lichens of Point Loma provide a case history.

Lichen collectors from the 1800's and early 1900's were notoriously lax when labeling their collections. "Coastal California" or even just "California" are too often the only locations listed. Fortunately, people who took the trouble to make their way from San Diego out to Point Loma often labelled their collections "Point Loma," so there is a scattered record of collectors and collections. Some of these are mentioned in literature, but others are unpublished. In no way is this report to be considered complete - quite the contrary. Collections from Point Loma will probably come to light for a long time yet. Nor can the present day collecting be called complete. A different collector with a different eye will inevitably see different things.

Point Loma forms the western arm of San Diego Bay. In 1854 the first lighthouse was built on Point Loma. The road to the lighthouse provided an access and it soon became a popular excursion site. In 1891 a new lighthouse was built farther out on the point and much closer to the water level. In 1913 the old lighthouse was designated a National Monument. Today Cabrillo National Monument encompasses 144 acres near the tip of Point Loma.

The rest of Point Loma is under the jurisdiction of various branches of the military. Parts of this are intensely developed. Within the National Monument are the remains of fortifications built during the World Wars.

The native vegetation is classified as Maritime Succulent Scrub, a coastal sage scrub with many succulents. This vegetation is best developed in Baja California. The Torrey Pines area marks its northernmost continental extension. The lichen flora consists of species endemic to Maritime Succulent Scrub, species from the California coastal bluffs lichen community, as well as lichen species of widespread distribution.

A summary of the lichen collections known to the author is set forth in Table 1. The lichen species are listed alphabetically in groups; foliose, fruticose and crustose. Currently accepted nomenclature for historic records is shown in parentheses. Historic collection were all from the period of 1880 to 1910. Weber and Santesson collected the area briefly in 1966 and the authors collections are all from the 1980's.

The foliose lichens are notable for their scarcity. Historically only one, <u>Physcia erinacea</u> (now <u>Heterodermia</u>) was collected. It is a sub-fruticose species and may be sensitive to air pollution as many of the fruticose species are. Although it was re-collected in 1966 by Weber and

---

[1] Research Associate, Santa Barbara Museum of Natural History, Santa Barbara, CA.

LICHENS OF POINT LOMA

Pre 1910	1960's	1980's
FOLIOSE LICHENS		
Physcia erinacea (Heterodermia)	Anaptychia erinacea (Heterodermia)	Parmotrema hypoleucinum
Physcia callosa
		Pseudoparmelia caperata
Xanthoparmelia mexicana
FRUTICOSE LICHENS		Cladonia chlorophaea
Cladonia furcata
Cladonia sp.
Evernia prunastri		Leprocaulon microscopicum
Ramalina crinata (Trichoramalina)
Ramalina evernioides
Ramalina homalea (Niebla)
Roccella fuciformis (babingtonii)
Roccella leucophaea (Dendrographa)
Sterocaulon albicans
Teloschistes villosus	Ramalina homalea	Niebla homalea

LICHENS OF POINT LOMA

Pre 1910	1960's	1980's
CRUSTOSE LICHENS		
Acarospora schleicheri	Acarospora schleicheri	Acarospora scheicheri
		Acarospora obpallens
Buellia halonia		Acarospora smaragdula
	Buellia oidalea	Buellia oidalea
		Buellia stellulata
Blastenia luteominia (Caloplaca)	Caloplaca bolacina	Caloplaca cf. fraudans
		Caloplaca luteominia
		Dimelaena radiata
		Diploicia canescens
		Diploschistes scruposus
		Lecania brunonis
	Lecania fructigena	Lecania fructigena
	Lecania sp.	
	Lecanora atra	
		Lecanora caseiorubella ssp. merrillii
Lecidea enteroleuca (Lecidella)		Lecidella subincongrua var. elaeochromoides
Lecidea glebulosa		
Pertusaria flavicunda		Pertusaria flavicunda
*Pertusaria leioplaca (pustulata)		
		Pertusaria santamonicae
Placodium aurantiacum (Caloplaca)		
		Polysporina simplex
Rinodina turfacea	Rinodina angelica	
Sclerophyton californicum		Schismatomma californicum
	Siphula sp.	Siphula sp.
		Thelomma mommosum
Toninia massata	Toninia sp.	

291

Santesson, the author was unable to find any. However, four other foliose species were collected, three of them from the bases of shrubs or trees and one from soil. None of the foliose species collected could be termed abundant or common on Point Loma, but they are abundant and common in other locations. Perhaps that explains why they were not collected historically.

The fruticose species present a different story. Of the eight species collected historically, only one has been recollected. *Ramalina homalea* (now *Niebla*) is the most commonly collected *Niebla*. Its coastal bluff habitat outside of parklands has all but disappeared.

Ramalina crinita (now Trichoramalina) and *Teloschistes villosus* are lichens whose North American distributions are limited to coastal areas along Baja California and extending north to Torrey Pines for *Trichoramlina crinita* and Santa Cruz Island for *Teloschistes villosus*. *Trichoramalina crinita* is presumed extinct within our boundaries. *Teloschistes villosus* has not been recollected at Point Loma or on Santa Cruz Island. It was collected on Santa Barbara Island in 1985 by the author. It certainly could be classified as rare.

Roccella fuciformis is the name put on specimens collected by W.G. Farlow when he visited Point Loma in 1885. The catalog of California lichens lists this as a probable misidentification, as Point Loma is not within the known distribution pattern. The specimen of Farlow that is at the Smithsonian Institution has been annotated to *R. phycopsis* and later to *R. babingtonii*. Along with *R. leucophaea* (now Dendrographa) these species are a part of the coastal bluff lichen community whose habitat is disappearing.

While *Ramalina evernioides* and *Evernia prunastri* have not been recollected on Point Loma, they can be found in other localities.

Stereocaulon albicans is a puzzle that won't be solved until the specimen is found. This is most likely a misidentification. Its description as "not rare on ground under bushes" could refer to the *Leprocaulon microscopicum* collected by the author.

The three species of Cladonia collected by the author were probably overlooked by earlier collectors as being common elsewhere. In certain places they form extensive mats over the soil. Their role as soil consolidators is very evident along the Bayside Trail.

The crustose lichens show even different results. It is to be expected that an attempt to do a thorough collection would result in a greater number of crustose species collected. Weber and Santesson spent less than an hour on their hurried collection trip to Point Loma. Of the nine crustose lichens they collected, only one was a recollection of an historic collection. The author's more thorough collections yielded 20 crustose species but only four were recollections. There is a rich variety of crusts on rocks, soils and plants. It is this area especially that different collectors see different things. Perhaps another collector would be able to find more of the historic species.

Acarospora schleicheri, a bright yellow crust lichen common on rocks, was the only crust lichen in all three collections. *Pertusaria flavicunda*, which was collected historically and again by the author, is part of the coastal lichen community. Its light yellow-green color makes it readily identifiable in the field. *Blastenia luteominea* (now *Caloplaca*) is another recollected species. With *Lecania brunonis* and *Polysporina simplex*, this lichen fulfills a valuable function of binding soils and preventing erosion. *Lecidea enteroleuca* is now known as *Lecidella subincongrua* var. *elaeochromoides* and is the fourth of the crustose recollections as well as being another soil consolidator.

The *Siphula* species collected by Weber and Santesson and by the author is probably the most common soil lichen in southern California. When collected in 1966 Santesson remarked that it resembled a *Siphula* that he had collected in Chile. Weber distributed it under this name in his Exsiccati. No one has ever followed up on this and determined whether or not this is the proper genus for this lichen or given it a species name. It seems strange that so widespread a species should remain so little known.

It is unfortunate that the early collectors never made a thorough collection of the area. Without that information, it is not possible to know for certain what crusts were present historically on Point Loma. What we know of crust lichens at that time in the greater San Diego area would indicate that many more were probably present that are recorded here.

In summary we find that the fruticose lichen species have declined drastically. Whether this is due to air pollution is not known. This could be tested by doing some lichen transplants using common lichens such as *Evernia prunastri* and monitoring them over a period of time to see how they fare. The foliose lichens are mostly small and hard to find. It will be interesting to check again in a few years to see how they are surviving. Further work on the crust lichens will provide an even better record to use for comparison in future years.

It was 50 years ago that Dr. A.W. Herre published in Madrono an impassioned plea to botanists to save our vanishing lichen flora. He lamented the destruction of habitat in the previous 25 years and feared what would happen in the future. What would he think today? Development, air pollution, acid rain and the ever increasing impact of man have taken their toll.

Hopefully some day, the same level of caring and effort put into rare and endangered vascular plants will be extended to the lichens.

Acknowledgments: Thanks are due Dr. William A. Weber and Dr. Bruce McCune for help in identifying specimens, to the Smithsonian Institution, the Farlow Herbarium of Harvard University and the Herbarium of the University of Colorado for loan of specimens. The cooperation of the staff of the Cabrillo National Monument is greatly appreciated.

References:

Hasse, Hermann E. The Lichen Flora of Southern California. Contributions from the United States National Herbarium, volume 17, part 1. 1913.

Herre, Albert W. Our Vanishing Lichen Flora. Madrono 3:193-199. 1936.

Rundel, Philip W. and Peter A. Bowler. The lichen genus *Trichoramalina*, Bryologist 77:188-194. 1974.

Tucker, Shirley E. and William P. Jordan. A Catalog of California Lichens. The Wasmann Journal of Biology 36 (1 and 2). 1979.

Evolutionary Relationships of *Holocarpha macradenia*

Rexford Palmer [1]

Abstract: Intrapopulational crosses in Holocarpha macradenia (Compositae, Madiinae), the Santa Cruz Tarplant, yielded F 1's with full fertility and normal chromosome pairing at meiosis. Chromosome pairing configurations in artificial hybrids from H. macradenia X H. virgata indicate that H. macradenia differs from H. virgata by two chromosome translocations. H. macradenia shows continuous variation with H. virgata in most morphological characters. H. macradenia evolved through juvenilization of characters in a common ancestor similar to H. virgata that invaded the central coast region of California during a recent xerothermic.

Holocarpha macradenia (Figure 1) is now one of the rarest of the eighty-five or so species of the Madiinae or "Tarplant" or "Tarweed" subtribe of the Compositae. In pristine times Holocarpha macradenia occurred abundantly in coastal grassland bordering San Francisco and Monterey Bays, but because of extensive agricultural and urban development in these areas during the last century, its populations have been vastly reduced. Now, Holocarpha macradenia may be nearing extinction.

Because of the tenuous existence of the remaining populations of Holocarpha macradenia, and the importance of H. macradenia to understanding the phylogeny of the entire genus Holocarpha, the present study was undertaken to document ecological, morphological, cytological, reproductive, and genetic relationships among a significant portion of the remaining populations and to examine aspects of the relationship between Holocarpha macradenia and populations of the Holocarpha virgata complex in the interior of California.

In their pioneering biosystematic work on the Madiinae, Clausen, Keck and Heisey studied Holocarpha in detail. They concluded that Holocarpha, as is the case in other groups in the Madiinae (see Clausen 1951), consists of two pairs of species, H. virgata and H. macradenia with four pairs of chromosomes, and H. heermannii and H. obconica with six pairs of chromosomes. Furthermore, they found, as a result of crossing experiments, that there was a complex geographic pattern of interfertility relationships among populations of the interior species complex. In many cases, barriers to crossing exist even between neighboring populations of the same species (Clausen 1951). Many populations, however, crossed easily with Holocarpha macradenia, leading Clausen (1951) to conclude that H. macradenia and the interior species complex were interconnected "as maritime and inland races of one species before the coast ranges arose in the early Quaternary period."

Clausen (1951) reported that much of the sterility of artificial hybrids in Holocarpha is a result of the extensive chromosome repatterning that has taken place, both on the interpopulational and interspecific levels. Little was known about Holocarpha macradenia when Clausen, et al. did their work. It was not known if chromosome repatterning exists among populations of Holocarpha macradenia in the manner described by Clausen, Keck, and Heisey for H. virgata. The nature of the chromosomal differences between Holocarpha macradenia and Holocarpha virgata were also not fully described by Clausen, et al.

Holocarpha virgata, clearly the nearest relative of Holocarpha macradenia (Clausen 1951), covers literally hundreds of square miles in the coast ranges and great central valley; whereas, Holocarpha macradenia is restricted to a handful of sites along a limited portion of the central California coast. Does Holocarpha macradenia represent the "maritime end" of a cline of variation as Clausen (1950) hypothesized, or does it represent an ancestral relect -- formerly more widespread during more favorable recent

---

[1] Department of Botany, University of California, Davis. Present address: Rt. 2 Box 660, Dixon, CA 95620

Figure 1. <u>Holocarpha macradenia</u> (DC) Greene the Santa Cruz Tarweed (from Abrams and Ferris 1960).

climates, but now confined to equable climates on the coast, as is the case with numerous relect perennials (Raven and Axelrod 1980, Stebbins and Major 1964). Alternatively, perhaps both <u>Holocarpha macradenia</u> and the interior species complex represent derivatives of some madrean tarweed stock that speciated as it spread northward in response to changing climate (Axelrod 1981).

METHODS

Seven extant <u>Holocarpha macradenia</u> populations were investigated cytologically and in terms of crossing relationships. Six populations are(were) in the Monterey Bay area (Figure 2). Another population is(was) located near Pinole in Contra Costa County and has now mostly been extirpated. This population has been the subject of recovery efforts (see Havlik, this vol.).

Achenes were collected from plants in the field, germinated on moist filter paper, and transplanted to pots in the U. C. Davis Botany Department greenhouse facilities. It was found that ray achenes were not easily germinable by this method, but dormancy could be overcome by dissection of the embryos from the pericarp, integuments, and nucellus. Disk achenes germinated readily with no treatment.

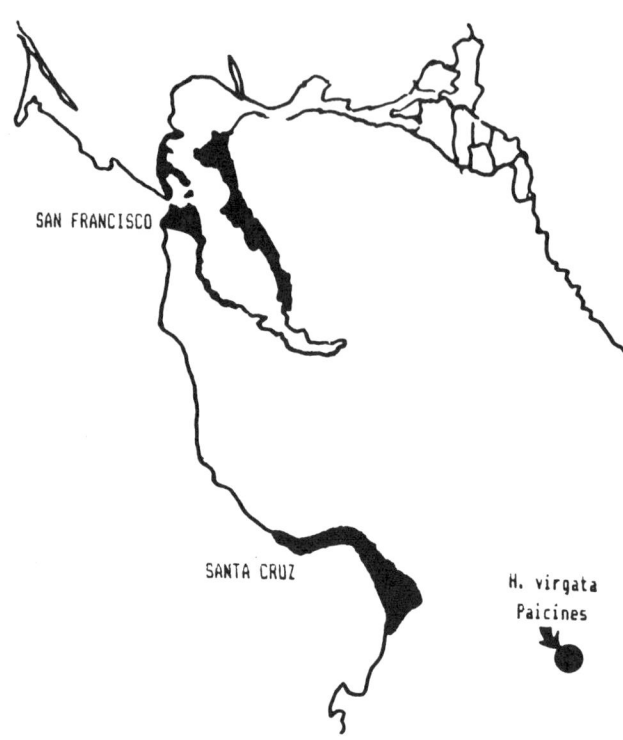

Figure 2. Total distribution of <u>Holocarpha macradenia</u> (shaded). Also shown: <u>H. virgata</u> Paicines population.

Artificial hybridizations among plants from <u>Holocarpha</u> populations were made in the greenhouse by rubbing flowering heads together. Because the plants are self-incompatible, emasculation of the flowers was not necessary. Upon maturation of the achenes, heads were harvested and seed set was scored as normal, reduced, or zero.

For analysis of chromosome pairing configurations, hybrids were grown out in the greenhouse and buds fixed in modified Carnoy's fluid. Anthers were macerated in Acetocarmine stain and squashed in the standard manner. Slides were made semi-permanent following Beek's (1955) method. Chromosomes were photographed on a Zeis Phase Contrast Microscope. Pollen fertility was determined by observation of number of grains stainable in cotton blue in lactophenol; at least 500 grains were observed for each individual.

Data were gathered on 33 morphological characters. These are enumerated in Table II. Six populations were studied morphologically, three of Holocarpha macradenia representing the range of the species, two of H. virgata, one from the northern part of the range, and one from the central part, and one population of Holocarpha virgata ssp. elongata from San Diego County. Cluster analysis and principal components analysis were performed using the methods of Dixon (1979). The nomogram (Figure 4) follows Bailey (1964).

RESULTS

Taxonomy

Holocarpha macradenia was first described by DeCandolle from collections sent to him by David Douglas in the early 1800's. In his Prodromus (1836) DeCandolle placed "Hemizonia macradenia" in a separate section of Hemizonia that he called "Olocarphae". In 1859 Asa Gray described a tarplant from the interior of California "probably on the Sacramento" from collections made by Fremont, as a new species in Hemizonia, H. virgata. In 1882 E. L. Greene described another species of Hemizonia, H. heermannii, from collections at Tehachapi Pass, Kern County. In his Flora Franciscana (1897), Greene broke up DeCandolle's genus Hemizonia and raised the section Olocarpha to the level of genus which he called Holocarpha. DeCandolle retained the only other species in "Olocarphae", H. luzulaefolia, in Hemizonia, leaving Holocarpha monotypic. Greene placed H. virgata and H. heermannii and three other species of Hemizonia in the genus Dienandra.

Jepson (1925) recognized Holocarpha macradenia as monotypic but submerged Greene's genus Dienandra in Hemizonia. In 1935, Clausen and Keck concluded that "...four other species are phylogenetically associated with Hemizonia macradenia DC. and should be included in this (Olocarpha) section; namely, H. virgata Gray, H. heermannii Greene, and the two following new species:...(Hemizonia obconica and Hemizonia vernalis)." They distinguished H. heermannii and H. obconica from H. virgata on the basis of chromosome number. H. heermannii and H. obconica each have six pairs of chromosomes, while H. virgata has four pairs, as does H. macradenia. Both H. obconica and H. heermannii have yellow anthers, while H. virgata and H. macradenia have black anthers.

After Clausen, Keck, and Heisey had concluded their biosystematic studies on Holocarpha and Hemizonia, Keck (1958) removed all of the interior taxa, that is, H. virgata, H. heermannii, and H. obconica, from Hemizonia and placed them all with Holocarpha macradenia in Holocarpha. Keck also recognized H. virgata ssp. elongata as the taxon for four-paired plants from San Diego County and H. obconica ssp. autumnalis as designating an unusual form of H. obconica on the northeastern slopes of Mt. Diablo.

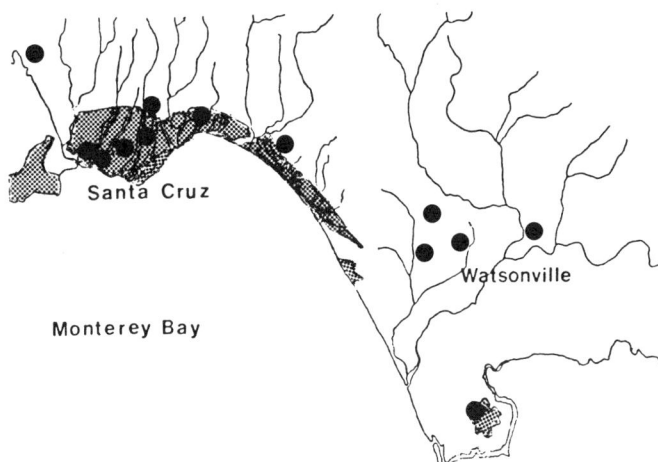

Figure 3. Marine terraces around Monterey Bay as mapped by Alexander (1953). H. macradenia populations studied are also shown.

Substrate

The coastline of the northern half of Monterey Bay comprises a marine terrace which continues north at least to Ano Nuevo Point (Bradley and Addicott 1968). The terrace is actually a series of terraces of progressively higher elevation and presumably greater age as one proceeds inland (Alexander 1953, Bowman, et al. 1980). These terraces are dissected by streams flowing westward out of the Santa Cruz Mountains and the Gabalin Range into a series of gently sloping terrace platforms separated by steep-seded "gulches" such as Rodeo Gulch or Arana Gulch. It is on the tops of these terrace platforms that most populations of H. macradenia occurred (Figure 3). A few populations occur further inland on remants of older terraces. In the vicinity of Watsonville the dissection of the marine terraces becomes complex, and some populations in this area occur on alluvium derived from terrace deposits.

The *Holocarpha macradenia* populations in the San Francisco Bay area also occurred on marine alluvial deposits (Holmes 1917, Lawson 1915, Page 1966). These alluvial deposits are gradually subsiding (Axelrod 1981, Christensen 1966, Howard 1979).

Climate

Holocarpha macradenia occupies sites along the central California coast where the influence of the Pacific Ocean dampens temperature fluctuations. Climate data for Watsonville, for example, show an annual mean temperature of 55.7 deg. F., with an annual range of temperature of only 13.7 deg. F. The interior species complex, *H. virgata*, *H. heermannii*, and *H. obconica*, occurs where temperatures are more extreme than on the coast. The nomogram (Figure 4) shows that the interior species complex occurs in areas of greater annual temperature and greater annual range of temperature than *Holocarpha macradenia*. The stations at Martinez Livermore represent sites on the western edge of the distribtion of *H. virgata*.

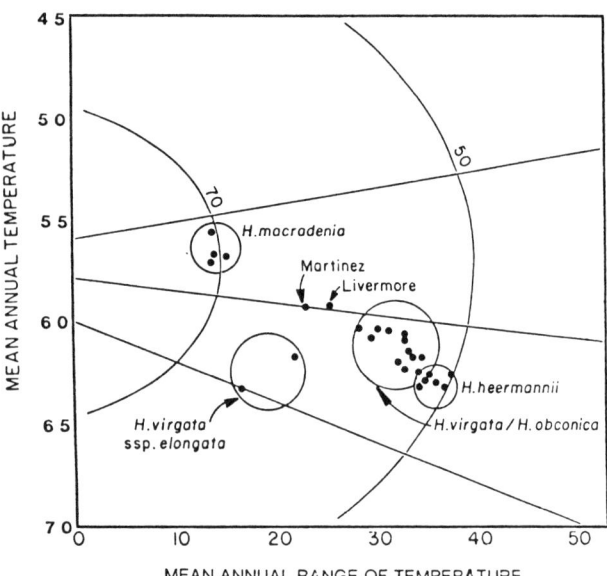

Figure 4. Thermal regime at *Holocarpha* locations (after Bailey 1964).

Morphology

Table II summarizes thirty-three morphological characters used in comparing populations of *H. macradenia* and *H. virgata* (Palmer 1982). Figure 5 shows the plotted values for four charachters for six *Holocarpha* populations (3 of *H.*

Table I. Morphological characters used in comparing populations of *Holocarpha*.

1. Plant height.
2. Diameter of main stem at base.
3. Number of nodes on lowest 5 cm of main stem.
4. Number of primary laterals greater than 3 cm long.
5. Mean length of uppermost lateral branches.
6. Mean number of heads per lateral branch.
7. Mean angle of departure of lateral branches.
8. Terminal head present, absent, rudiment.
9. Cauline leaves persistent vs. withering.
10. Peduncular bracts appressed, erect, intermediate.
11. Peduncular bracts isolateral, revolute, cylindrical.
12. Mean length of peduncle from base containing 5 bracts.
13. Mean length of peduncular bracts.
14. Mean length of leaf subtending peduncle.
15. Mean peduncle length.
16. Anther color (yellow, brown, black)
17. Mean head diameter.
18. Mean phyllary length.
19. Mean phyllary width.
20. Mean number of glands per phyllary.
21. Pubescence: puberulent/glandular, hirsute/pilose, glabrous.
22. Mean length of ray achenes.
23. Mean width at top of ray achenes.
24. Mean thickness at top of ray achenes.
25. Mean beak length of ray achenes.
26. Mean number of rays per head.
27. Presence or absence of medial ridge on ray achenes.
28. Presence or absence of lateral ridge on ray achenes.
29. Mean number of fertile disk achenes per head.
30. Mean length of disk achenes.
31. Mean width at top of disk achenes.
32. Mean thickness at top of disk achenes.
33. Disk corollas pubescent, glandular, or glabrous.

macradenia and 3 of *H. virgata*) in which the analysis of variance gave an F value significant at $P < .01$. The remaining characters show variation within populations as great or greater than the variation between populations.

All populations studied were highly variable and showed overlapping frequency distributions in vegetative characters such as mean number of laterals, and mean angle of departure of lateral branches. Achene characteristics, including ray achene thickness and ray achene width, show little within-population variation and little difference among species in *Holocarpha*.

Figure 6 illustrates a cluster analysis (Dixon 1979) of the three *H. macradenia* and three *H. virgata* populations used as examples in Figure 5. The analysis used the full set of characters in Table I. The diagram indicates greater

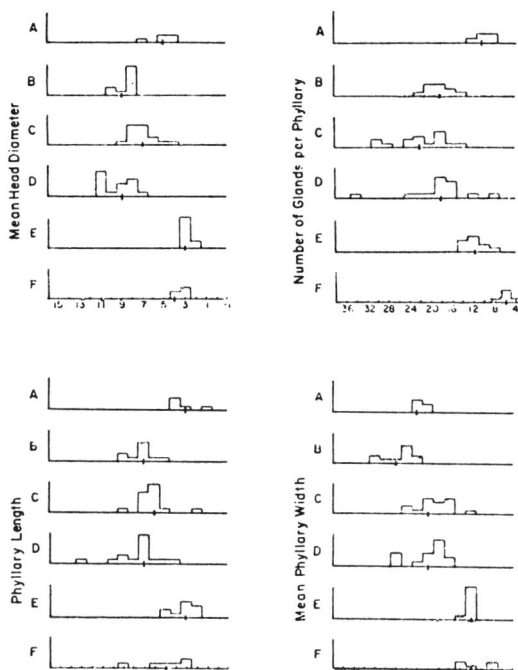

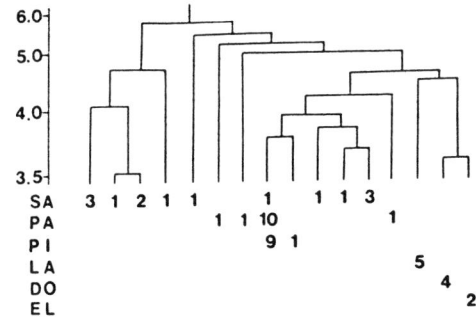

Figure 6. Cluster diagram showing results of cluster analysis of individuals from 3 populations of H. macradenia and 3 of H. virgata.

Figure 5. Characters showing a significant difference between H. macradenia and H. virgata

A, E: H. virgata; F: H. virgata ssp. elongata; B, C, D: H. macradenia.

The factor loadings for component two are greatest for mean lateral departure angle, number of laterals, and length of laterals. In H. macradenia the lateral branches do not elongate as in H. virgata, nor are as many produced. The angle of departure of the laterals in H. macradenia is also greater than in H. virgata.

morphological similarity between the Pinole and Pajaro H. macradenia populations than between either and the Santa Cruz H. macradenia population. The H. virgata populations separate from the H. macradenia populations and cluster together.

Figure 7 shows the results of a principal components analysis of the same six populations. Table II gives factor loadings for the first six factors as principal components. The table indicates that for the first component, the most significant loadings are on characters that relate to the size of the capitulae or on closely related characters. The size of the heads, both in terms of diameter of the capitulum and number of ray achenes per head, and number of glands per phyllary are traditional taxonomic characters used to separate H. macradenia and H. virgata. The significant loading on peduncular bract length is understandable because H. macradenia does not develop the highly modified, reduced unifacial bracts found in H. virgata.

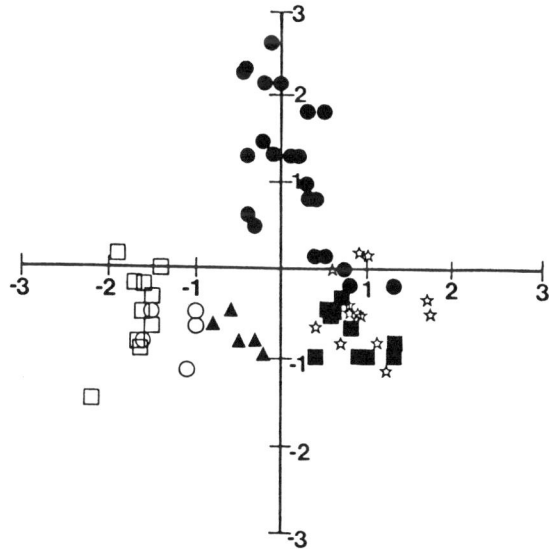

Figure 7. PCA ordination of the Holocarpha populations in fig. 6.

299

Table II. Factor loadings for variables used in principal components analysis of H. macradenia and H. virgata populations.

Character Number from Table I	Factor 1	Factor 2	Factor 3	Factor 4	Factor 5	Factor 6
7	0.134	0.512	-0.237	-0.322	0.132	-0.327
12	0.469	0.438	0.273	0.504	0.010	0.001
13	0.853	0.148	-0.138	0.066	0.106	0.005
14	0.453	0.335	0.319	-0.219	-0.263	-0.049
15	-0.023	0.300	0.291	0.712	-0.214	-0.012
16	-0.368	0.095	-0.341	0.209	0.650	0.246
17	0.867	0.170	-0.310	-0.068	-0.001	0.175
19	0.428	0.181	0.474	-0.279	0.049	0.046
20	0.726	-0.201	0.260	0.040	0.111	-0.101
22	-0.278	0.164	0.568	-0.259	0.277	-0.015
23	0.068	0.125	0.161	-0.305	-0.178	0.843
24	-0.136	0.333	0.479	-0.485	0.059	-0.088
25	0.470	0.145	0.302	-0.036	0.665	-0.020
26	0.650	0.100	-0.438	-0.289	-0.139	-0.195
4/1	-0.167	0.692	0.266	0.057	-0.220	0.048
6/1	-0.491	0.424	0.092	-0.044	-0.134	-0.209
5/1	0.173	0.759	-0.058	0.365	0.107	0.073
18/17	-0.888	0.030	0.312	0.010	0.105	-0.055
3/1	0.271	-0.780	0.420	0.126	-0.003	-0.027
2/1	0.456	-0.458	0.554	0.173	-0.028	-0.073

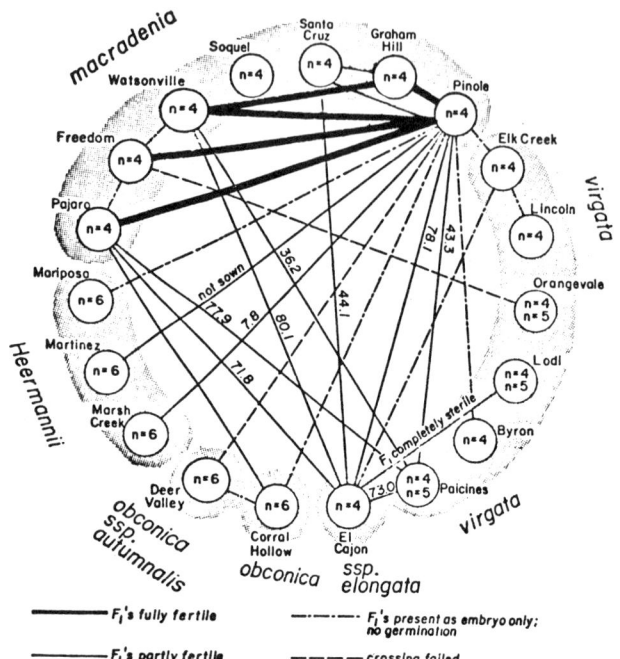

Figure 8. Crossing relationships and results of artificial hybridizations in Holocarpha.

Clausen (1951) presented a crossing diagram (p. 103) illustrating the results of artificial hybridizations among populations of Holocarpha. Clausen gave no information, however, on crossing relationships among populations of H. macradenia. Figure 8 is a similar diagram showing the results of artificial hybridizations carried out by the author among populations of Holocarpha, especially H. macradenia. The Pinole H. macradenia population was used as a standard. All H. macradenia crosses to Pinole resulted in normal seed set, with the exception of one cross, Pinole X Santa Cruz, which produced plants with significantly reduce pollen fertility. As discussed below, this lowered fertility may be associated with chromosomal rearrangements between the Santa Cruz H. macradenia population and the other H. macradenia populations studied.

The pattern of crossing relationships obtained in this study is similar to that obtained by Clausen, Keck and Heisey (Clausen 1951). In H. virgata, Clausen, et al. found that local populations are unable to cross and form fertile hybrids. Many interspecific crosses involving H. macradenia show zero or reduced seed set. Other crosses in H. virgata produce Fl's with reduced fertility, while others produce weak achenes that either will not germinate or die soon after germination. This is apparently typical of Holocarpha populations (Clausen 1951).

Cytology of Artificial Hybrids

Table III summarizes pollen fertilities and chromosome associations in Fl progeny of artificial hybridizations. Crosses of the Pajaro, Freedom Watsonville, and Graham Hill H. macradenia populations to the Pinole standard population yielded Fl's that were of normal fertility and showed a maximum meiotic configuration of four pairs of chromosomes. An exception was the cross between the Pinole population and the Santa Cruz population. Santa Cruz X Pinole Fl's have a mean pollen fertility of 38.6%. The reduced fertility is correlated with a modal chromosome pairing configuration of a chain of four and two pairs present at a frequency of about 56%. One Fl individual from this cross showed a maximum configuration of a chain of six.

Plants from the Graham Hill H. macradenia population, which form fully fertile hybrids with plants from the Pinole population, were crossed with plants from Santa Cruz. Preliminary data indicate pollen fertility of about 75% and a chromosome pairing configuration of a chain of four and two pairs (Palmer 1982).

Although a complete understanding of

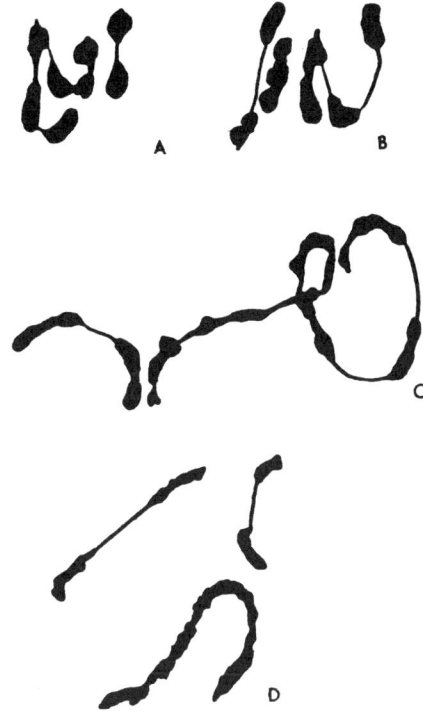

Figure 9. Chromosomes of Holocarpha. A - H. virgata Paicines X H. macradenia Pajaro, chain of 6. B - H. virgata Paicines X H. macradenia Pinole. C - H. virgata Paicines X H. macradenia Pajaro, chain of 6 at earlier phase. D - H. virgata ssp. elongata El Cajon X H. macradenia Pajaro.

the cytological behavior of the Santa Cruz H. macradenia population must await further study, it is apparent that the observed pairing configurations in the hybrids are the result of different chromosome arm arrangements in the Santa Cruz population with respect to the other H. macradenia populations studied (Palmer 1982).

Table III summarizes pollen fertilities and modal and maximum chromosome pairing configurations in crosses between H. macradenia populations and populations of species in the interior species complex of Holocarpha. Both the Pinole H. macradenia population and the Pajaro H. macradenia population were crossed to a population of H. virgata from Paicines, about 25 miles east of Pajaro. When the F1's from this cross were examined cytologically, most of the progeny were found to exhibit a modal chromosome pairing configuration of a chain of four and two pairs, and a maximum configuration of a ring of four, indicating a single chromosome translocation difference between the two species.

Some unusual progeny, however, showed a chain of six (Figure 9), indicating the presence of another translocation, probably involving a short segment of chromosome arm. In one cell the chain of six appeared as a closed ring. This cross shows a higher than expected fertility, possibly due to alternate segregation of multivalents (Palmer 1982).

The F1 progeny of the cross Pinole H. macradenia X Paicines H. virgata showed a maximum of a chain of five and three univalents, again indicating the presence of two translocations. The mean pollen fertility of 43% (Var=6.6) was significantly below that of the Pajaro X Paicines cross. Crosses of H. macradenia to four other H. virgata populations failed. In some, no seed was set; in others, embryos were produced but would not germinate; in others seedlings died soon after greening of the cotyledons.

Table III. Summary of pollen fertilities and modal and maximum meiotic chromososme pairing configurations in synthetic Holocarpha hybrids.

Cross	Pollen Stainability (%)	Modal Chromosome Association	Maximum observed Chromosome Association
H. macradenia, Pinole / H. macradenia, Graham Hill	98.9	4_{II}	4_{II}
H. macradenia, Pinole / H. macradenia, Santa Cruz Harbor	38.6	$Ch_4 + 2_{II}$	$Ring_4 + 2_{II}$; $Ch_6 + 1_{II}$
H. macradenia, Pinole / H. macradenia, Watsonville	98.0	4_{II}	4_{II}
H. macradenia, Pinole / H. macradenia, Grainfield west of Fairgrounds	99.0	4_{II}	4_{II}
H. macradenia, Pinole / H. macradenia, Pajaro	97.5	4_{II}	4_{II}
H. macradenia, Pinole / H. virgata ssp elongata, El Cajon	78.1	$Ch_4 + 2_{II}$	$Ch_4 + 2_{II}$
H. macradenia, Pajaro / H. virgata, Paicines	77.9	$Ch_4 + 2_{II}$	$Ring_4 + 2_{II}$; $Ch_6 + 1_{II}$
H. macradenia, Pajaro / H. virgata ssp elongata, El Cajon	71.8	$Ch_4 + 2_{II}$	$Ring_4 + 2_{II}$
H. macradenia, Graham Hill / H. macradenia, Santa Cruz	74.9	4_{II}	$Ch_4 + 2_{II}$
H. macradenia, Pinole / H. virgata, Paicines	43.3	$Ch_3 + 1_I + 2_{II}$	$Ch_5 + 3_I$
H. virgata, Paicines / H. virgata ssp elongata, El Cajon	73.0	4_{II}	4_{II}

Four H. macradenia populations, Pajaro, Watsonville, Santa Cruz, and Pinole, were crossed to H. virgata ssp. elongata from El Cajon in San Diego County. The results are summarized in Table III and Figure 8. The Pinole X El Cajon Fl's show a mean pollen fertility of 78.1% and a modal and maximum chromosome pairing configuration of a chain of four and two pairs. The Pajaro X El Cajon Fl's show a modal chain of four, a maximum ring of four, and a mean pollen fertility of 71.8%.

Table III also gives the results of selected crosses within the interior species complex. The cross between H. virgata ssp. virgata at Paicines and H. virgata ssp. elongata at El Cajon gives hybrid progeny with a mean pollen fertility of 73%. The maximum chromosome pairing obsered in this cross is four bivalents. Most intraspecific crosses in H. virgata fail (Clausen 1951).

DISCUSSION

H. macradenia shows little of the interpopulational reproductive isolation found in H. virgata. With the exception of the Santa Cruz population, crosses to the Pinole standard population resulted in fully fertile Fl's that showed normal pairing at meiosis (Palmer 1982). In contrast, in H. virgata many crosses fail to even produce Fl's or often only Fl's as weak, inviable embryos. In its ease of crossability, H. macradenia, therefore shows a pattern similar to that reported by Clausen (1951) for H. obconica.

The same factors resulting in the interpopulational isolation of populations of H. virgata may not be operating in H. macradenia, or it may be that H. macradenia has evolved so recently that different biotypes have not had time to develop. Axelrod (1981), in discussing Holocene climatic change in the present San Francisco Bay area has shown that during a Xerothermic period about 7000 years BP, mesic taxa in the region became restricted in distribution, while xeric taxa from the interior and southern Coast Ranges were able to invade the area. Climatically the xerothermic period would have favored the spread of Holocarpha populations from the interior into the coastal area. More recent cooling then would have resulted in selection and adaptation of these Holocarpha populations.

The chromosome translocations that differentiate H. macradenia and H. virgata indicate that the genomes of the two species are very similar. The observed chromosomal differences may have arisen as a reproductive isolation mechanism in H. macradenia, or these translocations may have been selected for because of their effects on morphology or other adaptive features.

In terms of most of the morphological characters studied here, H. macradenia and H. virgata show overlapping distributions. The characters showing significant differences (Figure 5) are the traditional taxonomic characters used to separate the two species. The factor loadings in Table II indicate that most of the variance on the principal component axes (Figure 7) is the result of variance in characters related to capitulum size. For component one, the greatest loadings are on head diameter, ray achenes per head, closely correlated with head diameter, and ratio 6, phyllary length divided by head diameter (see Table I). Mean length of peduncular bracts also shows a significant loading for component one, an expected result, since the peduncular bracts in H. macradenia remain bifacial and never achieve the reduced cylindrical form found in H. virgata.

For component two, the greatest factor loadings are on characters related to length and number lateral branches. In H. macradenia the lateral branches do not elongate to the same extent as in H. virgata, resulting in shorter branches with aggregated glomerules of catpitulae in H. macradenia, and longer "virgate" branches with many small capitulae in H. virgata. Most of the morphological differences between the species are therefore reducible to differences among these variables. In terms of the remaining morphological characters, there is little real difference between H. macradenia and H. virgata.

Three different explanations may be advanced to explain the existence of H. macradenia: (1) H. macradenia is a relict ancestor of H. virgata and perhaps other parts of the interior species complex as well. This concept is supported by the traditional taxonomic interpretation that views the morphology of H. macradenia as primitive, and by the ease of crossability of H. macradenia with other populations of Holocarpha in the interior of California. The lack of interpopulational reproductive isolation in H. macradenia under this hypothesis is explained as biotype depauperization, and the extant populations are seen as relicts that are persistinfg in the equable climate of the central coast area. (2) H. macradenia is the maritime end of a cline of variation and represents a coastal ecotype of H. virgata that was separated from H. virgata populations in the interior by uplift of the Coast Ranges in the early Quaternary (Clausen 1951). This hypothesis implies greater age for H. macradenia than the uplift which occurred about two million years BP (Christensen 1966, Howard 1979, Taliaferro 1951). (3) H. macradenia represents a recent derivative of H. virgata, or some similar ancestor, that invaded the central coast area during a xerothermic period and developed into H. macradenia as more mesic conditions returned.

As shown in the crossing polygon in Figure 8, H. virgata ssp. elongata in San Diego County, H. macradenia populations, and H. virgata at Paicines, are all able to cross and form relatively fertile Fl's. The cladistic relationships of these three taxa are not entirely clear, but the speculation has been advanced (Palmer 1982, and in prep.) that the relationship between H. virgata ssp. elongata and H. virgata may be an ancestral-descendant one. The Southern California and adjacent northern Baja California region is a center of tertiary relicts (Raven and Axelrod 1979). Several taxa in the Madiinae often regarded as primitive, e.g., Hemizonia minthornii, Adenothamnus occur in the area. The high diversity in the Madiinae in Southern California and adjacent Baja California supports the notion that the area is the center of origin of the entire group (Axelrod 1958).

H. macradenia is a valid species, it is geographically isolated and morphologically distinct. But, Holocarpha macradenia is a recent derivative of the more widespread interior species complex. The small number of differences in the chromosomes between H. macradenia and H. virgata, the relative lack of chromosome differentiation among populations of H. macradenia, the overlapping morphological variation, and the spread of other xeric taxa into the coastal area during the xerothermic (Axelrod 1981), indicate a recent origin for Holocarpha macradenia. If intermediate forms occurred they are no longer extant. In pristine times nearly continuous expanses of grassland connected H. macradenia and H. virgata sites. Agriculture and urban development has obliterated the Holocarpha habitat between Paicines and Pajaro, and similar development has obscured the connections of that area with the grasslands bordering San Francisco Bay.

When the recent origin of H. macradenia is considered, the critical need for preserving at least some populations of the species becomes apparent. Plant species that have recently evolved provide a unique scientific resource for the study of mechanisms of genetic change (Gottlieb 1979). If H. macradenia has indeed appeared since the xerothermic of a few thousand years ago, its lifetime as a species may prove to be exceedingly short.

ACKNOWLEDGEMENTS

The following people provided comments, help, and guidance: D. W. Kyhos, D. I. Axelrod, G. L. Webster, Jack Major, G. Carr, D. W. Taylor, and W. Davilla. Field assistance was provided by Biosystems Analysis, Santa Cruz. Portions of this paper are from a dissertation submitted in partial fullfillment of the requirements for the Ph.D. degree in Botany, University of California Davis.

REFERENCES

Alexander, C. S. 1953. The marine and stream terraces of the Capitola-Watsonville area. University of California Publications in Geography, vol. 10, number 1.

Axelrod, D. I. 1958. Evolution of the Madro-Tertiary Geoflora. Bot. Rev. 24:433-509.

Axelrod, D. I. 1981. Holocene climatic changes in relation to vegetation disjunction and speiciation. Amer. Nat. 117:847-870.

Bailey, H. P. 1964. Toward a unified concept of the temperate climate. Geogr. Rev. 54:516-545.

Bowman, R. H., et al. 1980. Soil Survey of Santa Cruz County, California. USDA Soil Conservation Service.

Bradley, W. C. and W. O. Addicott. 1968. Age of first marine terrace near Santa Cruz, California. Geol. Soc. Amer. Bull. 79:1203-1210.

Carlquist, S. 1959. Studies on Madiinae: Anatomy, cytology, and evolutionary relationships. Aliso 4:171-236.

Carlquist, S. 1959. Glandular structures of Holocarpha and their ontogeny. Amer. J. Bot. 46:300-308.

Clausen, J. 1951. Stages in the Evolution of Plant Species. 206 pp. Cornell University Press, Ithaca.

Clausen, J. and D. D. Keck. 1935. Studies upon the taxonomy of the Madiinae. Madrono 3:4-18.

DeCandolle, A. P. 1936. Prodromus systematis naturalis regni vegetailis. Paris.

Dixon, W. J. 1979. Biomedical computer programs. P-series. University of California, Los Angeles, Health Science computing facility.

Gottleib, L. D. 1979. The Origin of Phenotype in a Recently Evolved Species. In: Solbrig, O. T., Subodh Jain, G. B. Johnson, and P. H. Raven (eds.) Topics in Plant Population Biology. Columbia U. Press, New York.

Gray, A. 1859. In: Torrey, J. Botany Mexican Bound. p. 100.

Greene, E. L. 1882. New species of Compositae chiefly California. Bull. Torrey Club 9:15.

Greene, E. L. 1897. Flora Franciscana.

Holmes, L. C., et al. 1917. Reconnaisance soil survey of the San Francisco Bay region, California. USDA Bureau of Soils.

Howard, A. D. 1979. Geologic History of Middle California. California Natural History Buide 43. Univ. of Calif. Press, Berkeley.

Jepson, W. L. 1925. A manual of the flowering plants of California. Univ. of California Press, Berkeley.

Keck, D. D. 1958. Taxonomic notes on the California flora. Aliso 4:101-114.

Lawson, A. C. 1915. Description of the San Francisco district: Tamalpaias, San Francisco, Concord, San Mateo, and Hayward quadrangles. U. S. Geological Survey. Geological Atlas, San Francisco Folio (No. 193).

Leppik, E. E. 1977. The evolution of capitulum types of the Compositae in the light of insect-flower interaction. Ch. 4. in Heywood, V. H., J. B. Harborne and B. L. Turner (eds.). The Biology and Chemistry of the Compositae. Academic Press.

Moldenke, A. R. 1976. California pollination ecology and vegetation types. Phytologia 34:305-361.

Page, B. M. 1966. Geology of the Coast Ranges of California. In: Bailey, E. H. 1966. Geology of Northern California. Bull. 190. California Division of Mines and Geology.

Palmer, R. 1982. Ecological and Evolutionary Patterns in Holocarpha (Compositae: Madiinae). Ph.D. Dis., Botany Dept., Univ. Calif. Davis.

Palmer, R. (in prep). Cytology of artificial hybrids in Holocarpha.

Raven, P. H. and D. I. Axelrod. 1978. Origin and Relationships of the California Flora. Univ. of Calif. Pub. in Botany. Vol. 72.

Stebbins, G. L. and J. Major. 1968. Endemism and speciation in the California flora. Ecological Monographs 35:1-35.

Taliaferro, N. L. 1951. Geology of the San Francisco Bay counties. Calif. Div. of Mines and Geology Bull. 154:117-150.

Agave arizonica:
An Endangered Species, A Hybrid, or Does it Matter?

Rick DeLamater, Wendy Hodgson [1]

Abstract: Agave arizonica Gentry and Weber was federally listed as endangered in 1984. Little is known about this agave which appears to be a continually occurring hybrid. It is not known if this species can maintain population numbers through sexual reproduction. Fruit development is rare as cattle, grazing on lands administered by the U.S. Forest Service, destroy its emerging flower stalks, as well as those of their putative parents. Studies on its breeding, distribution, pollination, and chromosomes are being conducted. Because agaves use hybridity, polyploidy, and vegetative reproduction as their evolutionary strategies, the question of legal status for the protection of such species becomes apparent.

Since its discovery in 1959, Agave arizonica Gentry & Weber has proven to be one of the rarest and most beautiful agaves in Arizona. This agave is characterized by attractive rosettes of bright green leaves with dark mahogany margins. Field surveys in the early 1960's by the plant's discoverer, John H. Weber, resulted in the discovery of 10 plant clones, each clone consisting of 1 to several rosettes. These plants were found scattered in a 20 square mile area in the New River Mountains in central Arizona. Plants were removed from each of several clones for propagation and research. One of these plants flowered in the Desert Botanical Garden in 1968 and the plant was described by H.S. Gentry and J.H. Weber in 1970. Continuing research revealed but a few new clones and in 1974 A. arizonica was nominated for endangered species status.

Rick DeLamater began field study on A. arizonica in January 1983. Although 2 new clones had been found, the population was thought to have dwindled to just a few plants. The discovery of 3 new clones prompted a field trip into the New River Mountains with the authors of the species. This trip was made in order that they might see this agave in habitat and evaluate its need for protection.
Recommendations for protection was made shortly thereafter, and in May 1984 A. arizonica was listed as an endangered species.

By March 1984 10 new clones were known from the New River Mountains. Only 1 of J.H. Weber's original clones still existed. All of these new discoveries occurred as randomly scattered individual plant clones of 2 to 5 rosettes, all within sympatric populations of two other endemic agaves, A. toumeyana Trel. ssp. bella (Breitung) Gentry and A. chrysantha Peebles. The former is a member of the subgenus Littaea with a spicate inflorescence. This small compact agave with filiferous light green leaves, produces many offsets and forms dense clones via vegetative reproduction. An abundant amount of seed is also produced. These clones may include over 50 plants and reach an age of over 100 years. Agave chrysantha, on the other hand, is a member of the subgenus Agave with a candleabra-like inflorescence with flowers in large umbellate clusters on lateral peduncles. Unlike A. toumeyana ssp. bella, this comparatively large gray-green agave rarely offsets. But like A. toumeyana ssp. bella it has the potential to produce abundant seed.

A comparison of morphological characters shows A. arizonica to be intermediate to these agaves (Table 1). Its intermediacy, its occurence with sympatric populations of the aforementioned agaves, the scarcity of clones, and the lack of any real populations seemed to indicate that A. arizonica is of recent hybrid origin.

---

[1] Research Associate and Herbarium Curator, respectively; Desert Botanical Garden, Phoenix, AZ.

CHARACTER	A. toumeyana ssp. bella	A. arizonica	A. chrysantha
Leaf Length	9-20 cm	17-24 cm	40-75 cm
Flower Length	18-25 mm	25-32 mm	40-55 mm
Ovulary Length	10-15 mm	12-15 mm	22-30 mm
Flower Tube	2-4 mm	3.5-8 mm	8-13 mm
Filament Length	13-17 mm	25-37 mm	35-48 mm
Anther Length	9-10 mm	9-11 mm	16-20 mm
Capsule Length	8-12 mm	15-20 mm	35-50 mm
Capsule Width	8-10 mm	8-9 mm	13-15 mm
Seeds	2x3 mm	3x2 mm	6-7x4.5-5 mm
Corolla Color	Green w/whitish tepals	Pale yellow	Yellow
Panicle Height	1.5-2.5 m	3-4 m	4-7 m
Panicle Width	Spicate	Very narrow	Narrow
Panicle Branch Arrangement	Densely flowered spike on upper 1/3 shaft	35-50 short branches on upper 1/4-1/3 shaft	8-18 branches on upper 1/4-1/3 shaft

Table 1. Character Comparison (based on Gentry 1982).

Based on this suspicion, other sympatric populations of A. toumeyana ssp. bella and A. chyrsantha were surveyed.

Three new clones were discovered in the Camp Creek drainage 10 miles east of the New River Mountains. Field investigations at the type locality of A. toumeyana ssp. bella in the Sierra Ancha Mountains (where A. chrysantha is also present) resulted in the discovery of 2 new clones, 100 miles disjunct from the population as previously known.

Many species of agave are of hybrid origin such as A. glomeruliflora, A. peacockii, A. pumila, and varieties of A. scabra. Pinkava and Baker (1985) conclude that agaves apparently combine hybridity, polyploidy, and vegetative reproduction as their evolutionary strategy. Agave arizonica is the product of just such strategies. The putative parents are each among the more highly advanced groups in their respective subgenera. Gentry concludes that A. chrysantha "may be a geologically young species which has not yet reached a stable or isolated condition...It appears to be mixing genes with its neighbors and may even have had its own origins through introgression...Some of the taxa [in the Ditepalae] appear to be adapting frontier plants, naturally generating new forms and species; A. chrysantha among them".[2] Agave toumeyana ssp. bella itself, appears to indicate distinction from the typical species. By freely cloning and seeding it ensures a long sexual generation, and hence, unlimited gene combinations that will favor its ability to colonize new environments.

According to Granick (1944) polyploid populations are more likely to be found in the more advanced groups. Over 50 percent of those species of Agave whose chromosome numbers are known are polyploids (Pinkava and Baker 1985). In the subgenus Littaea, 8 of 20 taxa are polyploid while in the more advanced subgenus Agave, 18 of 28 taxa are known to be polyploid. Pinkava and Baker (1985) determined A. toumeyana ssp. bella to be diploid (based on 1 chromosome count) but Cave (1964) found A. toumeyana to be a polyploid. Four chromosome counts of A. chrysantha were done from collections made in the vicinity of its type locality, 75 miles from the New River Mountains. All were determined to be diploid. Agave arizonica was also determined to be a diploid, again based on only 1 count. A large number of chromosome counts are required to determine the ploidy levels within any given species. More counts are needed, particularly from the New River Mountains. Part of our research program has involved the collection of vouchered bud material from as many individuals representing the 3 taxa as possible. Thus far, counts have not been determined.

Diploid populations are more common in stable habitats of permanent

---
[2] Gentry 1982; pp. 430 - 431.

or climax communities, while recent polyploids are often found in liable or successional biotas (Ehrendorfer 1980). Both A. chrysantha's and A. toumeyana ssp. bella's northwestern limit of distribution is in the New River Mountains, where polyploidy may very well be a factor in their evolutionary strategies. This becomes important in light of the fact that there occurs a tendency of polyploids to occupy newly available habitats (Stebbins 1950). Hybridization and polyploidy is 1 means enabling a species to increase its ecological tolerances and hence, its geographic range.

DeLamater performed a breeding experiment with 1 A. toumeyana ssp. bella and 1 A. chrysantha in 1983. Agave chrysantha pollen was used to fertilize Agave toumeyana ssp. bella flowers, and vice versa. The former cross produced 35 seeds while the latter produced none. Of the 35 seeds, 32 germinated. The experiment was repeated in 1984 with 10 A. toumeyana ssp. bella plants and 3 A. chrysantha plants. Only the pollen of Agave chrysantha was used to fertilize A. toumeyana ssp. bella flowers as it was doubtful the pollen tube of A. toumeyana ssp. bella could reach the ovulary of an A. chrysantha flower. We have since learned that the pollen tube in certain members of the Orchidaceae receive nutrients from the receptive stigma in interspecific crosses enabling continued growth (Koopowitz 1986). We will continue to attempt crosses both ways. In the 1984 breeding experiment only 3 A. toumeyana ssp. bella plants set seed, each receiving pollen from a different A. chrysantha. Seedlings resulting from these crosses are just beginning to show the characteristic leaf margins of A. arizonica.

These findings strongly suggest that A. arizonica is a continually occurring hybrid between A. chrysantha and A. toumeyana ssp. bella. As field investigations over the last several years have shown, A. arizonica occurs in greater numbers than previously thought. It is a difficult plant to find due, in part, to the ruggedness of its habitat. Yet, since 1983 we know of 42 more clones consisting of 1 to 26 plants per clone. Also, 37 of these clones occur within a 20 square mile area in the New River Mountains. Two clones suggest a backcross with A. toumeyana ssp. bella.

We have been unable to determine if A. arizonica can reproduce itself sexually because of the apparent scarcity of clones in close proximity to one another and the infrequency of mature flowering stalks. At the Desert Botanical Garden A. arizonica has produced viable seed from 2 different plants in different years. Whether or not these plants may have been self-pollinated is unknown.

Pressures identified as exerting a negative impact on agave populations in the New River Mountains include damage by cattle and to a lesser extent, by insects and deer. Agave flower stalks provide an irresistable food for cattle. All of the New River Mountains, including what we thought to be the most inaccessible areas, show severe degradation by overgrazing. In the many areas visited the majority of flowering stalks of all 3 taxa never reach maturity. Transects run on A. toumeyana ssp. bella and A. chrysantha populations show that 0 to 33 percent of the stalks reach fruition (Tables 2 and 3). Out of 38 A. arizonica plants known to have reached maturity, only 10 flowering stalks were undamaged. As we can see, chances of successful development of flowers and fruit by A. arizonica is unlikely. But this is not the only factor to be considered. If A. arizonica is indeed a hybrid the drastically reduced number of flowering stalks on the putative parents inhibits any population increase. The sexual reproductive success of A. toumeyana ssp. bella and especially the rarely cloning A. chrysantha is significantly reduced. Of no less concern is the decrease in the genetic variability conferred by the larger gene pool.

PLOT	I	II	III	IV	V
NUMBER OF CLONES	12	9	9	10	12
NUMBER OF INFLORESCENCES	4	7	5	8	9
NUMBER OF MATURE INFLORESCENCES	0	1	1	3	2

Table 2. Agave chrysantha. A comparison of stalks produced and those that mature.

PLOT	I	II	III	IV	V
NUMBER OF CLONES	19	17	64	18	22
NUMBER OF INFLORESCENCES	14	27	85	34	37
NUMBER OF MATURE INFLORESCENCES	0	0	0	11	2

Table 3. Agave toumeyana ssp. bella. A comparison of stalks produced and those that mature.

Another threat to A. arizonica and other agaves in the New River Mountains is insect damage. Agave snout weevil (Scyphophorus acupunctatus Gyll.) a member of the family Curculionidae, as been observed to damage A. chrysantha and 1 clone of A. arizonica. The longhorn beetle, a member of the family Cerambisidae, attacks agave leaves, flowers, and fruits of all 3 taxa. Agave flowering stalks can be felled by this beetle's feeding behavior.

Collection of this very attractive agave is not considered a threat as it is extremely difficult to find in its rugged habitat.

Much remains to be learned about A. arizonica. Field surveys continue to locate additional clones. During a recent 5 day trip into the southern end of the New River Mountains, 8 additional clones of A. arizonica were found. Three of these clones show signs of flowering next year. Resources are now being directed toward fencing clones against livestock and wildlife damage. Of the 10 known undamaged flower stalks of A. arizonica 3 were protected, one by a barbed-wire fence constructed in 1985 and 2 by densely growing junipers. Fencing clones will enable us to collect bud material and pollen for chromosome and pollen stainability studies. The deposition of fencing materials and construction of the enclosures is extremely difficult due to the rugged topography. The use of a helicopter has enabled us to drop 48 T-posts and 4 rolls of heavy gauge barbed wire near 12 clones. The continued use of a helicopter will also transport us to areas otherwise inaccessible.

The collection of pollen will allow us to crossbreed different clones of A. arizonica to determine if sexual reproduction is possible. Chromosome studies in conjunction with a breeding program will help to answer questions about hybridization and polyploid agave populations as well as provide information about A. arizonica, A. chrysantha, and A. toumeyana ssp. bella. Crossbreeding plants of known ploidy levels will provide valuable insights into the effects of polyploidy on morphological characters.

Pollination studies to determine the important pollinators of each taxa is crucial to our understanding of the reproductive biology of the New River agaves. Bats, primarily of the genus Leptonycteris, are thought to be important pollinators of members of the group Ditepalae (Gentry 1982). It is known that the pollination success of A. palmeri Engelmann is strongly dependent on these nectar-feeding bats (Howell and Roth 1981). (It should be noted that A. chrysantha was once published as a variety of A. palmeri.) Agave toumeyana ssp. bella, on the other hand, is pollinated by carpenter bees and bumble bees (Schaffer and Schaffer 1977). Studies to determine the agaves' most important pollinators as well as their visitors will be conducted during the next flowering season.

In 1985, the U.S. Forest Service attempted to delist A. arizonica as an endangered species citing low reproductive potential, the inability to maintain itself in discrete populations in nature, and its uselessness as an easily created plant through artificial propagation (Fletcher 1985). The possibility of A. arizonica as an evolving species was overlooked. Their request was denied and A. arizonica remains on the list of endangered species. But an important question has been raised. How do we legally deal with the status of species such as A. arizonica, A. murpheyi Gibs., Helianthus paradoxus Heiser, H. neglectus Heiser, Phaseolus supinus Wigg. & Roll, and Opuntia imbricata Haw. that appear to be of recent hybrid origin? History is showing us that we must protect these plants until we know enough to base our decision on fact, not politics. From a botanist's point of view, any plant has an intrinsic right to exist, but given the present climate of land management practices we must search for reasons to justify their existence. As history has shown us, the possible values to mankind are too easily lost before they are even discovered.

CONCLUSION

In conclusion, *A. arizonica* appears to be a continually occurring hybrid between *A. chrysantha* and *A. toumeyana* ssp. *bella*. This agave may well be a case of species development in the early stage before its generative patterns have become fixed into a more survivable genotype and population (Gentry 1982). Cattle, overgrazing on lands administered by the U.S. Forest Service, are cited as the major threat to its continued survival as well as to the population dynamics of *A. toumeyana* ssp. *bella* and particularly, *A. chrysantha* in the New River Mountains. A long term study has begun to determine the distribution, taxonomic status, and reproductive biology of *A. arizonica*. It is hoped that our studies will shed more light on agave speciation in general. Protection of *A. arizonica* clones is necessary to enable such research. With such a long sexual generation this, like any breeding study of agave, promises to be a long one.

ACKNOWLEDGMENTS

Acknowledgments: We thank Peggy Olwell, U.S. Fish and Wildlife Service, Office of Rare and Endangered Species, Albuquerque, Dr. Robert Bruenig, Dr. Gary Nabhan, Dr. H. S. Gentry, Victor Gass, Jane Cole, and Linda Trawick of the Desert Botanical Garden, Phoenix.

This study is supported in part by funding from the Desert Botanical Garden, US Fish and Wildlife Service, Office of Rare and Endangered Species, and the Center for Plant Conservation, Cambridge, Massachusetts.

REFERENCES

Ehrendorfer, F. Polyploidy and distribution. In: Polypoidy, biological relevance. W.H. Lewis, ed. New York: Plenum Press; pp. 45-60; 1980.

Fletcher, R. 1985. *Agave arizonica* status report supplement. Region 3, USDA-FS; 7 pp; March 1985.

Gentry, H. S. Agaves of continental North America. Tucson: University of Arizona Press; 670 pp; 1982.

Gentry, H. S.; personal communication, 1986.

Granick, E. B. A karyosystematic study of the genus *Agave*. Am. J. Bot. 31(5):283-298; 1944.

Howell, D; Roth, B. Sexual reproduction in agaves: the benefits of bats; the cost of semelparous advertising. Ecology 62(1)1-7; 1981.

Koopowitz, H; personal communication; 1986.

Pinkava, D.; Baker, M. Chromosome and hybridization studies of agaves. Desert Plants 7(2):93-100; 1985.

Schaffer, W.; Schaffer, M. The reproductive biology of Agavaceae. Southw. Nat. 22:157-167; 1977.

Stebbins, G. Variation and evolution in plants. New York: Columbia University Press; 643 pp. 1950.

Attributes of Plant Populations and Their Management Implications

Bruce M. Pavlik [1]

Demographic studies of plants indicate that each species population can possess unique attributes that ultimately determine local abundance and/or persistence through time (Harper 1977). A thorough analysis of these attributes is of primary importance in the management of endangered populations simply because abundance and persistence are at the center of all recovery efforts. Such efforts are usually undertaken once the threat of human disturbance has been minimized (preservation by land-use restriction). This is because preserve management requires a knowledge of the population's status (whether it is declining, stable or growing) under the most "natural" of conditions. This determination can be made by selecting a few, relevant population attributes and conducting a demographic monitoring program (Pavlik 1987). The purpose of this paper is to illustrate the use of survivorship, seed production, seed bank and temporal establishment data for determining the post-preservation status of the endemic populations at Eureka Dunes, Inyo County, California. The Eureka populations comprise the entire known distribution of Swallenia alexandrae[2] (Soderstrom and Decker), Oenothera avita ssp. eurekensis W. Klein and Astragalus lentiginosis var. micans Barneby. All three taxa are perennial, suffrutescent herbs restricted to deep, windblown accumulations of sand (Pavlik 1979a).

---

[1] Bruce M. Pavlik, Assistant Professor of Biology, Mills College, Oakland, CA 94613

[2] All three endemic taxa are herein referred to by their generic epithet

Abstract: Plant survivorship, seed production, seed bank dynamics and frequency of establishment can be used to determine if endangered plant populations are declining (thus requiring intensive monitoring and recovery efforts) or stable and/or growing when protected from human disturbance. A two year study of the perennial endemics Swallenia alexandrae, Oenothera avita ssp. eurekensis and Astragalus lentiginosus var. micans was conducted at Eureka Dunes, Inyo County, California. Based on analyses of survivorship it was concluded that the populations are at least stable (even short-lived Oenothera cohorts survive long enough to reproduce) or growing (the number of established Swallenia and Astragalus plants doubled during the study). The high mortality and short life span of Oenothera and Astragalus populations were offset by copious seed production, long-lived seeds, low to moderate seed predation, and frequent establishment. The low and variable seed production, high seed predation and infrequent establishment of Swallenia populations were counterbalanced by a low mortality of recruits and established plants, a long reproductive life and long-lived seeds. It is possible, therefore, to conclude that the factors endangering these endemic populations are mostly extrinsic. No additional manipulations are warranted if adequate protection from human disturbance is maintained. Occasional monitoring in the future is necessary in order to verify these conclusions.

METHODS AND MATERIALS

Plant Survivorship

In February 1985 three sites were established on the northwest flank of the main dune in an area that has been extensively studied in the past (Henry 1976, Pavlik 1979a, 1979b, 1980, Pavlik and Barbour 1985). The sites were chosen so that each represented one of the study species according to the following criteria; 1) the species population was composed of at least 150 individuals from all age/size classes, 2) the population was located in a dune habitat typical of the species (e.g. steeper, less stable slopes for Swallenia and lower, more stabilized slopes for Oenothera and Astragalus (DeDecker 1976, Pavlik 1979a)), 3) germinule and seedling densities were similar to those observed in other parts of the dune system and 4) the site was a great distance from footpaths taken by dune visitors.

At each site a large plot was randomly located with its lower boundary oriented along a 60° compass bearing. Plot size varied among the three species and reflected differences in the size and density of individual plants. The upper plot contained the Swallenia subpopulation and was 50 m X 50 m (2500 m^{-2}). The Oenothera plot was placed approximately 100 m downslope (north) from the Swallenia plot and was 50m X 10m (500 m^{-2}). Approximately 10 m north of the Oenothera plot was the 30 X 25 m (750 m^{-2}) Astragalus plot. The corners of the plots were marked with 5 cm diameter stainless steel rods that were threaded over their entire length and had a 8 cm diameter hook on one end. These rods could be screwed into the sand for a distance of about 30 cm leaving the hooked end exposed. They were used to attach sampling tapes during subsequent visits and insure that the relocation of sub- plots could be accurately achieved. The markers remained in place after the 1986 field season.

On five occasions during 1985 (2/15-16, 3/21-22, 4/26, 5/31-6/1 and 8/11-12) and three during 1986 (3/22-23, 5/29 and 10/4-5) the demographic plots were sampled for the number of live individuals and notes were made regarding their vigor, growth, life history stage and phenological state. Life history stages (see below) for the study plants were developed from observations made on laboratory and field-grown plants (Pavlik 1979b, Pavlik and Barbour 1985). Swallenia and Oenothera plots were subsampled using 10 or 15 randomly-placed subplots, respectively. The Astragalus plot was sampled in its entirety. Each time the census was taken, a scaled map of each subplot was generated by marking the location of live and dead individuals rooted within the subplot. This allowed the fates of individual plants to be accurately monitored throughout the study. Attempts were made to tag all plants in addition to mapping, but this effort was defeated when wind storms removed the 28 cm wire stakes that held the tags.

Plots of time (days since the February 1985 census) versus the number of living individuals were made using the 1985-86 census data. These plots represented true survivorship curves for young plants of Swallenia, Oenothera and Astragalus (germinules, seedlings and juveniles) that were established as a single cohort after the fall 1984 germination event. Plots for older, established plants of the three species represented population depletion curves because these individuals may have been from different cohorts of various ages (Harper 1977). It was then possible to calculate mortality and half-lives (the time in which a population decreases by 50%) for the population as a whole or for subpopulations at different life history stages (Harper 1977, Hutchings 1986). These stages included established plants (mature (M) or senescent (St)) and recruits (germinule (G), seedling (S), juvenile (J) or in the case of Swallenia, hummock-forming juvenile (Ⓙ)). Details of these methods may be found in Pavlik and Barbour (1986).

Seed Production

At least 15 individuals of each taxon were selected prior to flowering for making estimates of seed production during the springs of 1985 and 1986. All individuals were located very near or in the survivorship plots of their respective species. Plants varied in terms of canopy volume (Vc) as calculated from measurements of plant length, width and height.

An enumeration model was used for each species in order to estimate the actual seed output per plant having a given Vc at the time of maximum flower and fruit production (March-April for Astragalus, May-June for Swallenia and Oenothera). During March, April, May and July these plants were surveyed for Vc, the number of inflorescences per plant and the number of developed fruits, aborted fruits, flowers and flower buds per infrutescence (from a subsample of 5 infrutescences). During peak fruit production, 20-44 infrutescences per taxon were examined in the laboratory to determine the mean number of seed-containing fruits per infrutescence. In the case of Swallenia it was possible to estimate the mean number of caryopses (herein referred to as seeds) per infrutescence directly since each caryopsis contains one seed.) This mean value compared favorably with field estimates of the same parameter and so it was used to calculate the mean number of seed-containing fruits per individual from other field measurements mentioned above. This was converted to the mean number of filled, undamaged seeds per individual of Oenothera and Astragalus by counting the number of filled seeds in 30 fruits of each taxon and determining the mean. Details of this method are found in Pavlik and Barbour (1985).

In order to estimate the seed rain (seed output of a stand of plants on a habitat area basis) the survivorship data (number of live, mature plants per square meter of the stand of size Vc) were combined with regressions of seed production on plant size for each taxon. This method takes into account differences in mortality and reproductive output among individuals in the population and, therefore, represents a partial life table analysis (Hutchings 1986).

Seed Bank Dynamics

In March, May and October of 1986, estimates of the seed bank within survivorship plots of Swallenia, Oenothera and Astragalus were made by pressing 1 liter plastic containers into the dune and trapping the sand in the container with a plastic lid. These containers sampled 0.178 m^2 of dune surface near and between mature plants. Their placement was random but spread throughout 100 m^2 of each plot. Owing to the patchy vegetation cover found in the Swallenia stand, 50 of these samples were required, whereas 8 were used for Oenothera and Astragalus stands on each date. Seeds of Swallenia and Astragalus could be separated from the sand with medium coarse soil sieves. Oenothera samples, however, required sieving with fine-mesh screens and immersion of the throughfall (very fine sand + seeds) in tubs containing a saturated salt solution. The small seeds floated on the salt solution more than 90% of the time as determined by spiking studies.

Seed longevity was tested by germinating seeds from the 1978 and 1985 crops. These had been stored dry and at room temperature. They were germinated under optimal light, temperature and moisture conditions according to the results of Pavlik (1979a). Three replicate dishes of 50 seeds each were used for Swallenia and Oenothera and 25 scarified seeds for Astragalus. In addition, tetrazolium tests were run on all ungerminated seeds at the end of the 10 trials to determine if they were dormant or dead.

On two nights in October 1986, seed selection experiments were run at Eureka Dunes by placing 10 naked Swallenia seeds, 10 Swallenia seeds in their floral bracts, 10 Oenothera seeds, 1 ripe Oenothera capsule (containing numerous seeds), 10 Astragalus seeds and 10 Astragalus pods (with seeds) in a shallow glass or plastic dish. A total of 27 dishes were sunken below the sand surface (9 in each species plot). Some were placed next to the canopies of established plants and some up to 3 m away. Seeds could not be easily blown from the dishes (the two nights were perfectly still anyway) and footprints in the surrounding sand revealed if seeds were missing due to nocturnal, mammalian predators. Foraging ants, however, could not escape from the dishes once they had fallen in. This allowed some assessment of ant vs. mammal seed predation.

Frequency of Establishment

Estimates of fall seedling density of Swallenia were available for most years between 1972 and 1986 (Henry 1976, Pavlik 1979, Pavlik and Barbour 1986). The records for Oenothera and Astragalus were not as long-term or complete and came only from the author's field notes. These could, however, provide information on the frequency of germination over the same time period.

RESULTS AND DISCUSSION

Survivorship

Survivorship and depletion curves for the three endemic taxa are shown in figures 1-3. Changes in the total Swallenia population (□) are the result of mortality in the fall 1984 cohort of germinules, seedlings and juveniles (■). After nearly two years 24 percent of this cohort had survived and grown into hummock-forming juveniles whereas 97 percent of the mature and senescent plants (▲) were still alive. The total population was more than twice its original size two years after cohort emergence. This contrasts with Oenothera which produced cohorts of seedlings in both years. Only 4% of the winter 1984-85 cohort survived until the next year (thus, the truely perennial population was very small), but nearly 75 percent had produced seed during that time. The winter 1985-86 cohort had higher survivorship (41 percent) a lower percentage of reproductive individuals (48) and was comprised of smaller mature plants (mean Vc = 12 dm^3) than the 1984-85 cohort (mean Vc = 60 dm^3). This pattern was also observed for Astragalus, except that none of the winter 84-85 cohort survived or reproduced. Seedling survivorship was much higher in 1986 (54%) but none of these had reproduced within the year. Like Swallenia,

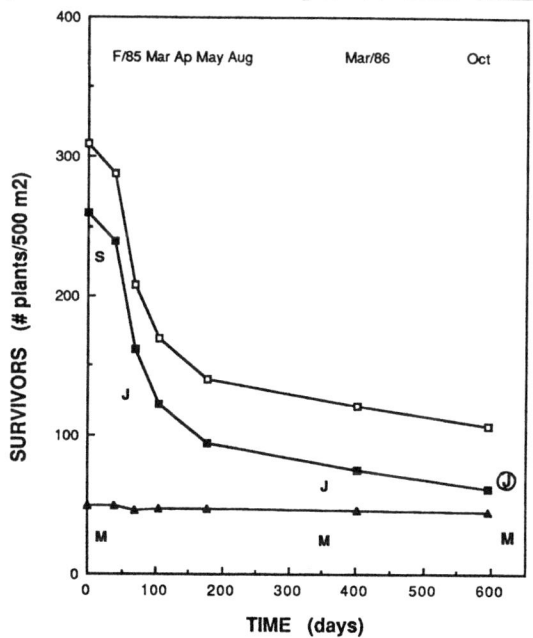

Figure 1. Survivorship of the 1984 cohort (■), and depletion of the total (□) and established (▲) populations of Swallenia 1985-1986. Letters refer to life history stages (see text).

survivorship of mature Astragalus plants was high (69 percent) thereby making a rather large population of perennial plants. If even half of the 1986 cohort survives another year (likely in that they already survived the first summer), then the established Astragalus population will more than double in size.

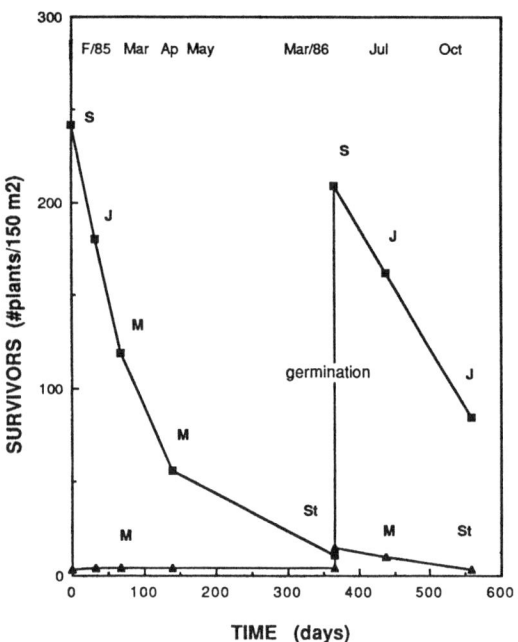

Figure 2. Survivorship of the 1984 and 1985 cohorts (■) and depletion of the established population (▲) of Oenothera, 1985-86. Letters refer to life history.

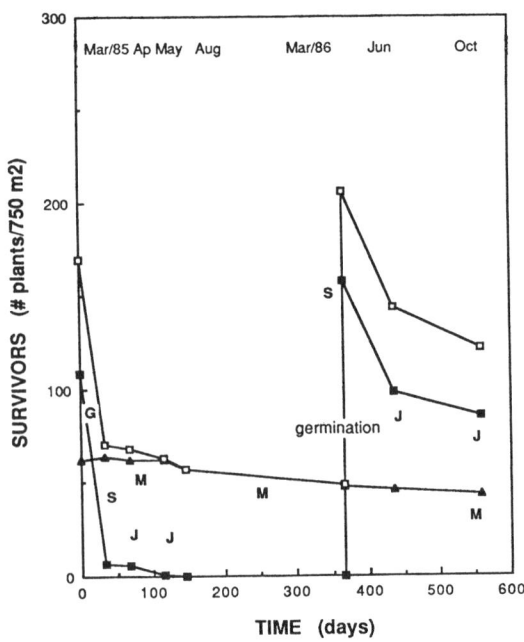

Figure 3. Survivorship of the 1984 and 1985 cohorts (■) and depletion of the total (□) and established (▲) populations of Astragalus, 1985-86. Letters refer to life history stages.

Survivorship data are re-interpreted in figure 4 as the mean mortality (1985-86) experienced by each life history stage. Mortality was generally low (< 25 percent) and constant for Swallenia, high (25-80 percent) and increasing with age for Oenothera and extremely variable (15-95 percent) and perhaps declining with age for Astragalus.

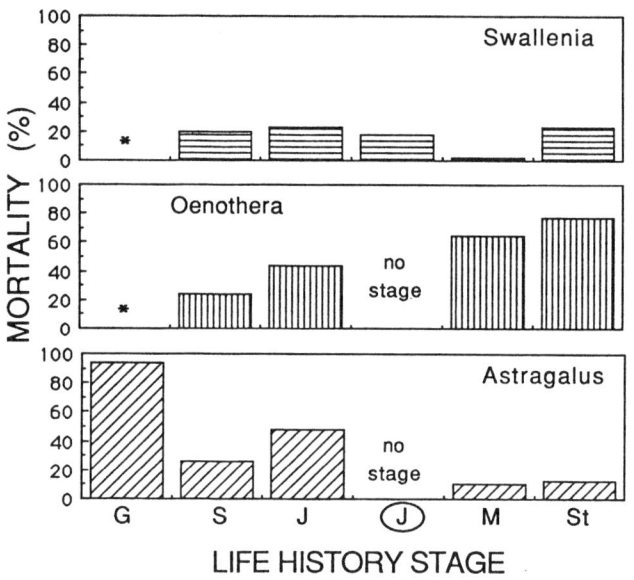

* insufficient data

Figure 4. Average mortality during each stage of the life cycle, 1985-1986.

Half-lives for recruits, established (adult) plants and the total population were derived from survivorship data (table 1). The values for Oenothera and Astragalus were similar and about half those of Swallenia. Swallenia half-lives compare favorably with those of non-endangered perennial grasses from arid environments (0.5-4.5 years, Williams 1970, West et al. 1979). Those of Oenthera and Astragalus, however, are on the low end of the spectrum for non-endangered herbaceous perennials (0.5- >50 years, Harper 1977). Extrapolating until the time of population extinction (potentially erroneous but nevertheless valuable for comparative purposes), established Swallenia populations might persist for as long as 88 years in the absence of recruitment while Oenothera and Astragalus might persist from 3 to 16 years. Based on survivorship data alone, Oenothera is the most endangered of the three taxa (high mortality and short half-life of recruits and adults), Astragalus the next (high mortality and short half-life of recruits but high adult survivorship) and Swallenia the least (lowest mortality, longest half-life of all stages).

Table 1. Half-lives (in years) of Eureka Dune endemics averaged during the 1985-86 study period.

	recruits (G+S+J)	established (J+M+St)	total (G+S+J+J+M+St)
Swallenia	0.5	15.9	0.8
Oenothera	0.3	*	0.4
Astragalus	0.3	2.7	0.4

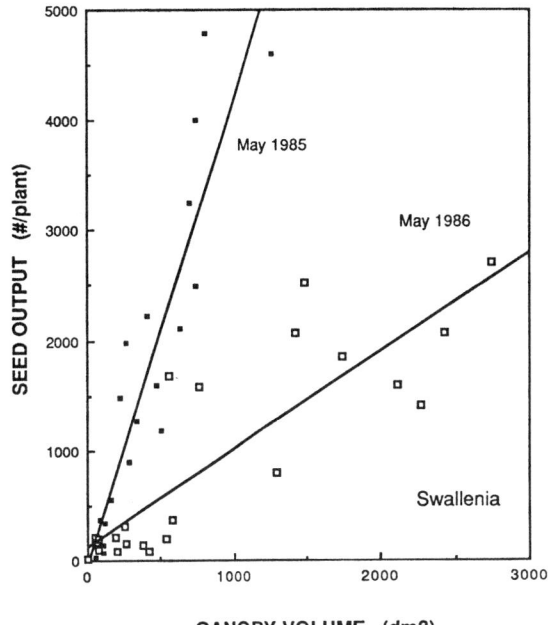

Figure 5. Seed production as a function of plant size for Swallenia, 1985 and 1986.

Seed Production

The relationship between canopy volume and seed output during 1985 and 1986 is shown in figures 5-7. Swallenia seed production was a linear function of canopy volume ($r > 0.90$) and varied significantly between 1985 and 1986. The output for an averaged sized Swallenia was low (3,100 seeds/plant/year, $V_c = 750$ dm^3) compared to non-endangered perennial grasses from arid environments (16,000-200,000 seeds/plant/year, Stevens 1932, Huiskes 1979, Davy 1980). Annual seed production by Oenothera and Astragalus was a logarithmic function of canopy volume ($r > 0.85$) and fairly constant from year to year. Average size individuals of Oenothera (60 dm^3) produced 36,000 seeds in 1985 and those in 1986 (12 dm^3) produced 7000. Average size individuals of Astragalus (200 dm^3) produced 10,000 seeds in 1985 and those in 1986 (190 dm^3) nearly 12,000). These estimates of annual seed output per plant compare favorably with those presented for other non-endangered members of the genera Oenothera and Astragalus (Stevens 1932).

Based on seed production data alone, it would appear that Swallenia is the most endangered of the three taxa and Oenothera the least. When the survivorship data are taken into consideration, however, it is obvious that the high mortality and short half-life observed in the Oenothera population are to some extent ameliorated by copious and consistent seed production from year to year. On the other hand, Swallenia is a poor seed producer but its recruits and adults experience lower mortality and greater longevity.

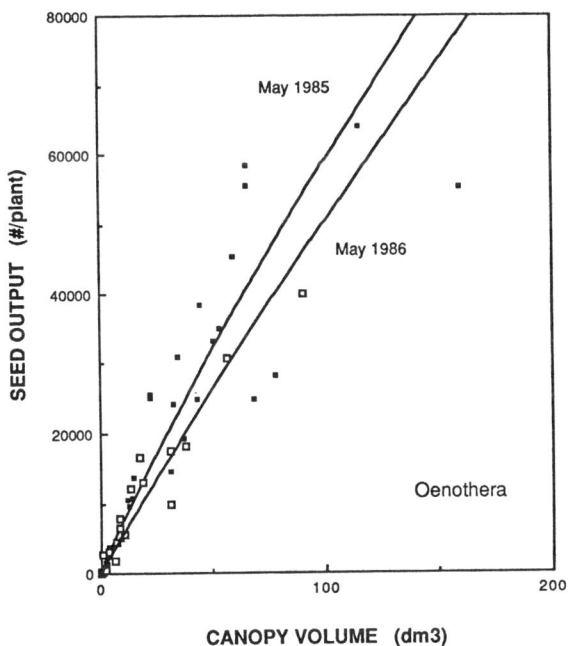

Figure 6. Seed production as a function of plant size for Oenothera, 1985 and 1986.

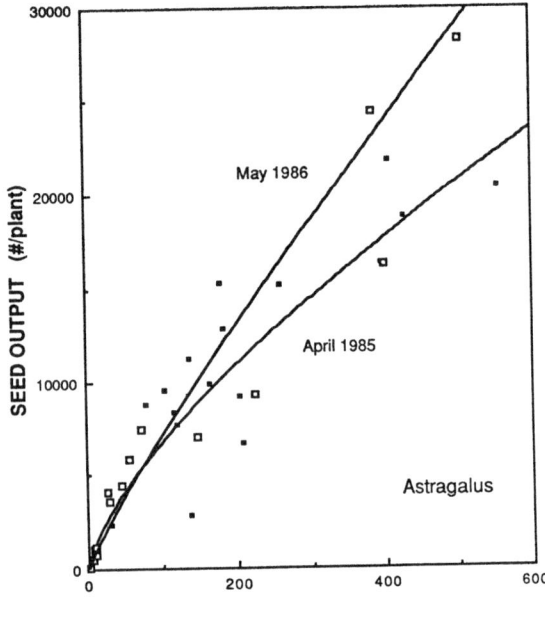

Figure 7. Seed production as a function of plant size for <u>Astragalus</u>, 1985 and 1986.

Seed Bank Dynamics

The densities of <u>Swallenia</u> and <u>Astragalus</u> seeds in the seed bank corresponded with the magnitude and timing of seed rain during 1986 (fig.8a and 8c and table 2). Increases in seed density were on the order of 8 to 35 fold as seed output and dispersal peaked during the April-May period. The seed bank of <u>Oenothera</u>, however, did not peak during the period of maximum seed production, but declined from March to May (fig. 8b). There are at least two factors contributing to this pattern; 1) the large 1985 and small 1986 seed rains (i.e. the dune sand contained a large number of 1985 seeds and was not enriched during 1986) and 2) dispersal of the extremely mobile seeds during spring wind storms. Regarding the latter, Pavlik and Barbour (1985) compared the small, lightweight <u>Oenothera</u> seeds to those of <u>Swallenia</u> and <u>Astragalus</u> and found they were the fastest dispersers at any wind velocity (and, therefore, most likely to leave the habitat). This dispersal ability allows <u>Oenothera</u> to maintain the largest geographic range of all three dune endemics.

Considerable variation in the seed rain was observed during the two years of study (table 2), but the cause of the variation differed for each taxon. <u>Swallenia</u> seed rain was more than halved due to an intrinsic decline of seed output per plant (fig. 5). <u>Oenothera</u> seed rain declined by more than 75 percent because each plant was on the average 80 percent smaller (see above). Most of the 30 percent decline in <u>Astragalus</u> seed rain was due to the death of mature plants after 1985, resulting in a lower density of reproductive individuals.

Table 2. Plant density and seed rain for populations at Eureka Dunes, 1985-86.

	1985		1986	
	density (#/m^2)	seed rain (#/m^2/yr)	density (#/m^2)	seed rain (#/m^2/yr)
Swallenia	0.084	63	0.082	25
Oenothera	0.600	21,317	0.510	3568
Astragalus	0.081	693	0.063	491

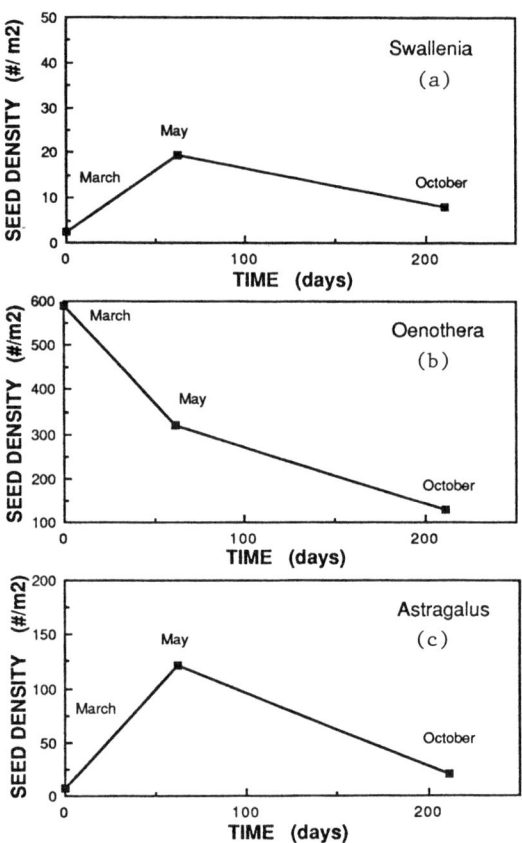

Figure 8. Seed density in the seed bank, 1986. Note the different scales on the y axes.

All three taxa had much smaller seed banks in October. In unstable sand dune habitats there are five possible fates of these seeds; 1) aging, death and decay, 2) predation, 3) germination, 4) deep burial by moving substrate, and 5) dispersal out of the stand as substrate is moved by high wind.

Table 3 shows that seeds of all three taxa remained viable and germinated after 8 years. It seems unlikely that seeds in situ would age, die and decay after five months.

Seed predation, however, must significantly contribute to decreasing the seed reserves of Swallenia and Astragalus. Over a single night period, 14 percent of all naked Swallenia seeds and 9 percent of all naked Astragalus seeds were collected (principly by the kangaroo rat Dipodomys, as judged from tracks). Swallenia disseminules were also taken (6 percent). In three dishes there were several ants observed carrying Swallenia seeds, suggesting that if they could leave the dish they would take the seeds with them. Of all seeds and disseminules removed, those of Swallenia

Table 3. Laboratory germination and viability of seeds from the 1978 and 1985 crops. Differences between 1978 and 1985 germination are significant (ANOVA, P<0.01) for Swallenia and Oenothera.

	1978		1985	
	germination (pct)	viability (pct)	germination (pct)	viability (pct)
Swallenia	5.0 ± 5.0	100	81.2 ± 5.4	100
Oenothera	40.8 ± 15.0	60	74.9 ± 2.9	80
Astragalus	76.6 ± 15.0	60	100.0 ± 0.0	100

were more likely to be selected by rodents and ants (table 4). There was no evidence that Oenothera seeds or fruits experienced any predation by nocturnal rodents or ants.

Germinule emergence was not observed during the May to October period and so it seems unlikely that seed bank decline is a result of germination. The possibility of subsurface germination and death is remote owing to the fact that 1) the upper 30 cm of dune sand was dry and significant rain did not occur over the summer and early fall, 2) dead germinules were never found in seed bank samples and 3) summer sand temperatures (35-55 C) completely inhibit germination of the three taxa even if supplied with ample moisture (Pavlik 1979a).

Table 4. Relative nocturnal predation on seeds and disseminules (seeds with fruit wall or floral bracts), October 1986. Mean values from nine dishes per taxon. Differences in seed predation between species are statistically significant (ANOVA, P<0.05).

	seeds removed (pct)	disseminules removed (pct)	
Swallenia[1]	61.3 ± 9.0	100.0 ± 0.0	(+bracts)
Oenothera	0.0 ± 0.0	0.0 ± 0.0	(capsules)
Astragalus	38.7 ± 9.0	0.0 ± 0.0	(legumes)

[1] seed = caryopsis

Casual observations made in all three populations indicate that less than 10 cm (mostly less than 4 cm) of sand accumulated in portions of the study plots over the summer. In this case the seed bank samples would not have been greatly affected by the deposition of small amounts of seedless substrate (the most biasing case). Sand accumulation can vary greatly with position on the dune and time of the year (Pavlik 1979a) and it is entirely possible that many seeds become deeply buried for long periods of time. The size and dynamics of this "quiescent" seed bank remain unknown.

The last possible fate of seeds in the dune seed bank is dispersal out of the stand. This cannot be excluded for any of the taxa since all three are capable dispersers (Pavlik and Barbour 1985). Dispersal and predation both contribute to the summer-fall decline of Swallenia and Astragalus seed banks but only dispersal affects the Oenothera seed bank. It could be argued that since seeds might be transported in as well as out of the seed bank by substrate movement, only predation significantly affects these seed banks. This argument is extreme and does not recognize the very patchy and sparse cover by endemics on the dune and the great volume of lifeless, shifting sand.

Frequency of Establishment

Finally, the available evidence suggests that significant germination and establishment of Swallenia many occur infrequently, perhaps once every 8-10 years (fig. 9). Apparently this phenomenon is associated with sporadic occurrences of unusually large amounts of late summer-early fall precipitation. This agrees with other studies of desert perennials (Brum 1973, Jordan and Nobel 1981). If the population of mature Swallenia individuals can persist for 16 years (its half-life, a conservative estimate) to 90 years (the time of population extinction, a very rough approximation), then 2-9 establishment events could occur. <u>Oenothera</u> and <u>Astragalus</u> can germinate more frequently (perhaps annually as in figures 2 and 3), although successful establishment and reproduction may be less common (every 2-4 years according to field notes).

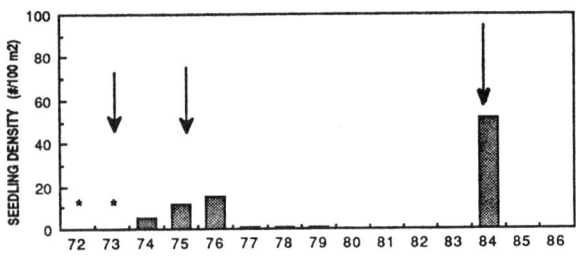

Figure 9. Density of <u>Swallenia</u> seedlings in the fall or winter of each year, 1972-1986. Arrows indicate years of exceptional fall precipitation. Astrisks indicate incomplete data, but little evidence of establishment. Data from Henry (1976) and Pavlik (unpublished field notes).

CONCLUSIONS

The data clearly indicate that the endemic populations of <u>Swallenia</u>, <u>Oenothera</u> and <u>Astragalus</u> at Eureka Dunes are not declining. Based on analyses of survivorship they are at least stable (even short-lived <u>Oenothera</u> cohorts survive long enough to reproduce) or growing (the number of established <u>Swallenia</u> and <u>Astragalus</u> plants more than doubled during the study period). As might be predicted from the r-K selection hypothesis, the high mortality and short life of <u>Oenothera</u> and <u>Astragalus</u> populations were offset by copious seed production, long-lived seeds, low to moderate seed predation, and frequent establishment. <u>Oenothera</u> even has the ability to clone in order to increase population half-life (data not included). The low and variable seed production, high seed predation and infrequent establishment observed in <u>Swallenia</u> populations is counterbalanced by a low mortality of recruits and established plants, a long reproductive life and long-lived seeds. At this time it seems possible to conclude that the factors endangering the endemic populations at Eureka Dunes are mostly extrinsic. These extrinsic factors include the status of <u>Oenothera</u> and <u>Astragalus</u> pollinators (Pavlik and Barbour 1985), the watershed management practices affecting dune hydrology (Pavlik and Barbour 1986), and human disturbance (Pavlik 1979b). The latter two can be minimized by regional planning, management and enforcement. No additional manipulations of the Eureka Dune populations are warranted **if adequate protection from human disturbance is maintained.** Occasional monitoring in the future is necessary in order to verify these conclusions. Although we can never turn our backs on endangered but stable populations, we can for the moment turn our attention to other, more critically threatened taxa.

ACKNOWLEDGEMENTS

I gratefully acknowledge the field assistance of Lauren Krieger, Eileen Manning, Monty Knudsen, Bob Pavlik, Lynn Suer and Derham Giuliani. This research was made possible by grants from California Department of Fish and Game, Endangered Species Office, the University of California at Davis, and Mills College. The support of Susan Cochrane of California Fish and Game, Office of Endangered Species is especially appreciated.

LITERATURE CITED

Brum, G.D. Ecology of the Saquaro (<u>Carnegia gigantea</u>): phenology and establishment in marginal populations. Madrono 22: 195-204; 1973.

Davy, A.J. Biological flora of the British Isles. <u>Deschampsia caespitosa</u> (L.) Beauv. J. Ecol. 68: 1075-1096; 1980.

DeDecker, M. The Eureka Dunes. Fremontia 3(4): 17-20; 1976.

Harper, J. Population biology of plants. London: Academic Press; 1977.

Henry, M.A. A living fossil -- <u>Swallenia alexandrae</u> (Eureka Dune Grass). Paper presented at Southern California Academy of Sciences, Santa Barbara, CA 8 May, 1976. Available from M.A. Henry, 609 Saratoga, China Lake, CA. 93555.

Huiskes, A.H.L. Biological flora of the British Isles. <u>Ammophila arenaria</u> (L.) Link. J. Ecol. 67: 363-382; 1979.

Hutchings, M.J. Plant population biology. In: Moore, P.D.; Chapman, S.B. eds. Methods in plant ecology. Oxford: Blackwell Scientific Publications; 1986. Chapter 8.

Jordan, P.W.; Nobel, P.S. Seedling establishment of Ferocactus acanthodes in relation to drought. Ecology 62: 901-906; 1981.

Pavlik, B.M. A synthetic approach to the plant ecology of desert sand dunes, Eureka Valley, California. M.S. thesis, University of California at Davis. 1979a. 136 p.

Pavlik, B.M. The biology of endemic psammophytes, Eureka Valley, California and its relation to off-road vehicle impact. BLM contract CA-060-CT8-00049, California Desert Plan; 1979b. 110 p. Available from Riverside Office of the Bureau of Land Management.

Pavlik, B.M. Patterns of water potential and photosynthesis of desert sand dune plants, Eureka Valley, California. Oecologia 46: 147-154.

Pavlik, B.M. Autecological monitoring of endangered species. 1987 [These proceedings].

Pavlik, B.M.; Barbour, M.G. Demography of endemic psammophytes, Eureka Valley, California I. Seed production, dispersal and herbivory. State of California, Department of Fish and Game, Office of Endangered Species, Sacramento, CA. 77 p.; 1985.

Pavlik, B.M.; Barbour, M.G. Demography of endemic psammophytes, Eureka Valley, California II. Survivorship, seed bank dynamics and climatology of establishment. State of California, Department of Fish and Game, Office of Endangered Species, Sacramento, CA. (in prep.); 1986.

Stevens, O.A. The number and weight of seeds produced by weeds. Amer. J. Bot. 19: 784-793; 1932.

West, N.E.; Rea, K.H.; Harniss, R.O. Plant demographic studies in sagebrush-grass communities of southeastern Idaho. Ecology 60: 376-388; 1979.

Williams, O.B. Population dynamics of two perennial grasses in Australian semi-arid grassland. J. Ecol. 58: 869-875; 1970.

Ecology and Endangerment Status of *Silene invisa* Populations in the Central Sierra Nevada, California

Dean Wm. Taylor[1], Rexford E. Palmer[2]

Abstract: Populations of Camouflaged Campion (*Silene invisa* Hitchcock and Maguire) were studied on the Eldorado National Forest, California. Two-hundred and fifty montane sites were surveyed for populations of the species. Data on vegetation and environmental features was recorded at each site. Detailed reproductive data were collected from study populations in 1983, 1985 and 1986. Typical habitat is old-growth red fir (*Abies magnifica*) forest - meadow ecotones on north-facing slopes at 7000-8500 feet elevation on volcanic substrates. Fecundity was higher in fir than in lodgepole pine (*Pinus contorta*) habitats, but was highly variable both within populations and years. Long-term monitoring is recommended to assess the significance of fecundity variability on population fate.

Silene invisa (Hitchcock and Maguire 1947) is an inconspicuous herb of upper montane and subalpine forest sites in the northern Sierra Nevada and southern Cascade Range of California. In 1983, we conducted a survey on the Eldorado National Forest to evaluate the endangerment status of *S. invisa* populations (Taylor and Palmer 1983). During that survey, 25 previously undocumented populations were located. At that time, we noted that although there were a large number of widely scattered populations, many consisted of less than 300 flowering individuals.

The habitat favored by *S. invisa*, mostly undisturbed forest, is undergoing rapid conversion from a naturally regulated community to a silvicultural system (Barbour 1984). Old-growth red fir (*Abies magnifica*) forests in the Sierra are increasingly being converted to plantations. On many California National Forest lands, *A. magnifica* stands will provide most of the production of wood products during the remainder of this century and early into the next.

The objective of our studies are two: 1) to conduct long-term monitoring of pertinent demographic variables of *S. invisa* populations, and 2) to correlate long-term success (measured in units of fecundity) with ecological variables. In the present paper, we provide a characterization of habitat selection of *S. invisa* populations, and summarize initial findings of our demographic monitoring in relation to habitat characteristics. A more comprehensive paper treating trends and variability in reproductive statistics will be published elsewhere.

SPECIES BIOLOGY
Taxonomic Relationships

The relationships among North American taxa of *Silene* is uncertain. In their comprehensive monograph of the genus, Hitchcock and Maguire (1947) placed *Silene invisa* in Subgenus Melandryum - a variable group comprising some 40 species. Within this subgenus, the affinities of *S. invisa* to *S. aperta* Greene were noted, and to *S. antirrhina* L. (of Subgenus Eusilene), but without implication of common ancestry. Hitchcock and Maguire described *S. invisa* having seen only six specimens, so it is not surprising they were uncertain of its classification.

Recently, Tiehm (1985) has described a closely related taxon, *Silene nachlingerae*, from calcareous subalpine habitats in central Nevada. Tiehm noted the close relationship between *S. invisa*, *S. aperta* and *S. nachlingerae*, but he considered *S. invisa* and *S. nachlingerae* to differ "strikingly" in a suite of vegetative characters. In our opinion, Tiehm's impression of the vegetative habit of *S. invisa*, based on herbarium specimens, underestimates the degree of variability in vegetative characters, and, in fact, *S. invisa* and *S. nachlingerae* differ morphologically by only quantitative degrees.

Silene invisa, *S. aperta* and *S. nachlingerae* form a complex of taxa sharing close common ancestry, differing mainly in ways consistent with evolutionary divergence following isolation. In our view, the three taxa were isolated geographically during disintegration of Pleistocene conifer woodland and steppe vegetation (Wells 1983), and have evolved as separate taxa in isolation: *S. aperta* in the very southern Sierra, *S. invisa* in the very northern Sierra, and *S. nachlingerae* in central Nevada.

Growth-Form

Silene invisa has a relatively simple, modular growth form (fig. 1). The leaves are basal, borne on caudices. Inflorescences are simply configured, with flowers at nodes. Most inflorescences consist of a single terminal flower. In undamaged inflorescences, the terminal flower is largest. Subordinate flowers are usually borne singly at one to three inflorescence nodes.

Breeding System

Taxa of *Silene* have morphologically complex, chasmogamous flowers. Many species have strongly dissected petals and petal appendages; floral traits suggestive of highly evolved pollination systems. Breeding systems of *Silene* taxa are, in general, obligate outcrossing systems (including dioecy, Gross and Soule 1981, Kruckeberg 1961, Brockman and Bocquet 1978).

Our observations of *S. invisa* suggest that the species is self-compatible and mostly autogamous for two reasons. First, its small, undifferentiated petals are suggestive of such a breeding system. The anthers of *S. invisa* produce small amounts of pollen, indicating a pollen/ovule ratio characteristic of autogamy (Cruden 1977). Second, we have observed seed production in inflorescences buried under forest debris, and thus lacking access to pollen vectors, suggesting autogamy.

---

[1]Senior Botanist, BioSystems Analysis, Inc., 303 Potrero, Suite 29-203, Santa Cruz, CA 95060.

[2]Rt. 2, Box 660, Dixon, CA 95620

Geographic Distribution

Silene invisa exhibits a relatively wide distribution in the northern Sierra Nevada (fig. 2), with one disjunct record in the Trinity Alps (Kruckeberg 1961). Populations at the northern end of its range occur at lower elevations (1800 m to 2100 m) than at the southern end of its distribution (2070 m to 2700 m). This trend reflects a shift in elevation zone of habitats appropriate for *S. invisa* populations, which occur at increasingly higher elevation to the south.

Most reported populations from areas to the north of the our study area consist of relatively few individuals -- generally less than 100 plants (according to CNPS/Data Base records).

METHODS

Vegetation Sampling and Analysis

Populations of *Silene invisa* on the Eldorado National Forest were studied (Taylor and Palmer 1983). At each site, a stand-survey of vegetation composition and structure was conducted: all species within a homogeneous area were identified, and their cover estimated visually (Mueller-Dombois and Ellenberg 1974). Salient environmental variables, including site moisture, soil depth and development, and snow cover depth and duration, were rated using scalar indices. Canopy cover was estimated using a spherical densiometer. Forest stand age was estimated by one of three methods: ring counts of stumps (where available); increment cores (for *Pinus contorta* ssp. *murrayana*); regression from stem diameter (for *Abies magnifica*, Barbour and Woodward 1985).

Nearly 250 sites were searched for *Silene invisa* populations on the Eldorado National Forest, providing a sufficient sample size for characterization of its habitat requirements. Locations of sites searched are given in Taylor and Palmer (1983).

Vegetation data was analyzed using multivariate methods (Gauch 1982). Populations were classified into habitat groups using Two-way Indicator Species Analysis (TWINSPAN, Hill et al. 1975, Hill 1979a). Relationships between vegetation and ecological site characteristics were analyzed using Detrended Correspondence Analysis (DCA) ordination (Hill and Gauch 1980, Hill 1979b).

Demographic Sampling

For small populations (fewer than about 200 plants) no subsampling was conducted, as data was taken from all individuals. In larger populations, data was collected from all individuals in subjectively chosen, spatially defined subpopulations consisting of about 200 or more plants. These sample sizes are sufficient to meet the requirements given by Croy and Dix (1984). Sampling was conducted at the period of maximum capsule ripening.

Variables measured were: plant height, number of flowering stems, number of flowers per stem, and capsule length. Randomly chosen subsamples (n=40) of capsules from all sampled populations were pooled, and their seeds counted.

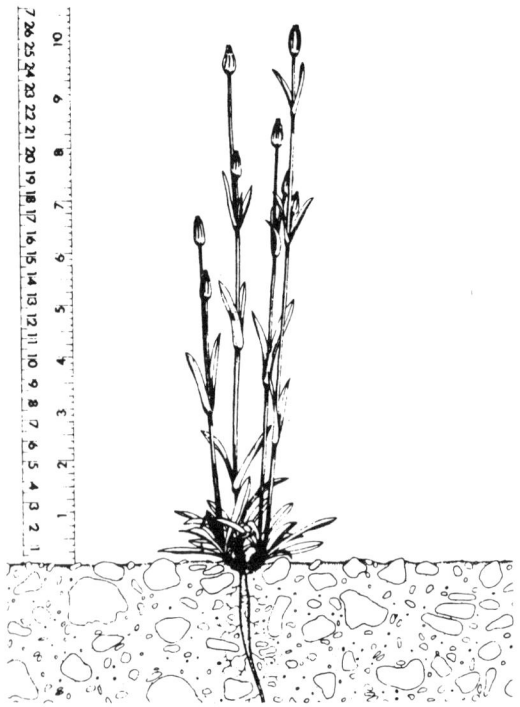

Figure 1. Illustration of *Silene invisa* (Source: Charly Price, Eldorado National Forest).

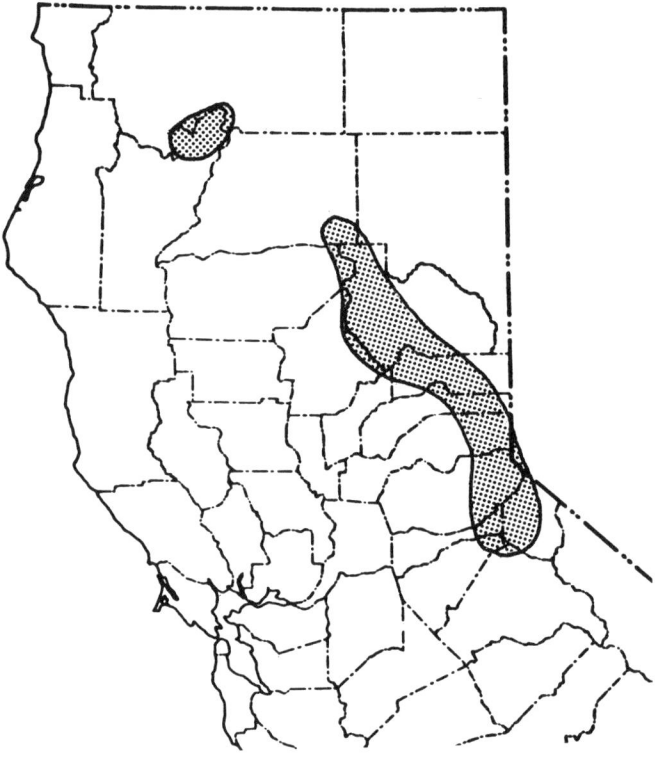

Figure 2. Map of northern California showing the distribution of *Silene invisa* (shaded area). County boundaries are outlined.

RESULTS

Relationships between Morphological Fecundity Variables

Covariance between a number of growth-form attributes and seed production were identified. Plant height and number of flowers per plant were correlated (Pearson r = 0.49, p > 0.01). Length of the capsule in upper-most flowers was also correlated with plant height (r = 0.34, p > 0.01). Number of flowering axes per plant was uncorrelated with plant height.

Figure 3 plots the relationship between capsule size and number of seeds. The two variables are significantly correlated (r = 0.75 p > .001). Capsule size was determined by multiple regression of capsule length, width and volume against number of seeds. The resultant index for capsule size is (measurements in mm):

Capsule Size Index = (length x 0.517) x width

Estimation of number of seeds per capsule is given by the regression equation (which accounts for 55 percent of the variance in seeds per capsule):

No. Seeds = 3.548 + (2.40 x Capsule Size Index)

Variation in number of seeds per capsule is for the most part a function of capsule size, suggesting that there is little variation in seed weight. The exception is two populations with noticeably smaller seeds than all the others (the two smaller capsules shown in Figure 3). The mean number of seeds/capsule was 60.9, with a Coefficient of Variation of ± 26 percent.

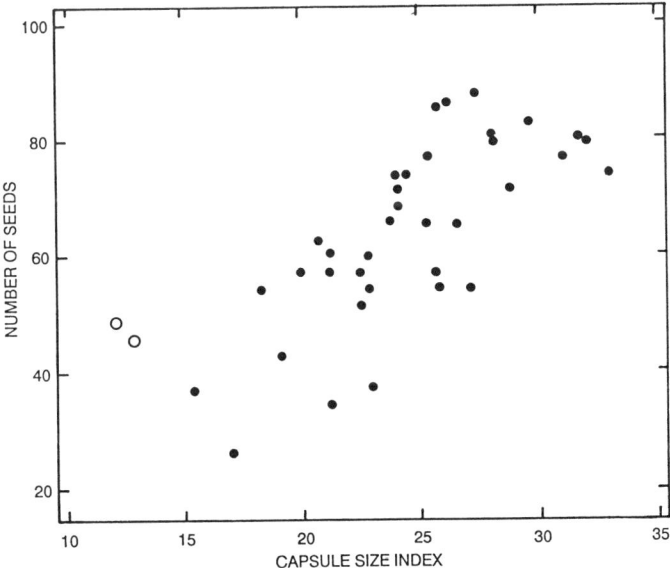

Figure 3. Scattergram showing relationship between Capsule Size Index and number of seeds per capsule for *Silene invisa*. Two outliers (open circles) exhibit smaller seeds than other populations.

The relationship between capsule size and fecundity can be used to study the reproductive characteristics of *S. invisa* populations using a single attribute (capsule length) easily measured in the field.

Habitat Selection

Vegetation

TWINSPAN analysis of vegetation data from 36 *S. invisa* populations identified four distinct community-types:

Abies concolor/Poa bolanderi
Abies magnifica/Erigeron peregrinus
Abies magnifica/Poa nervosa
Pinus contorta murrayana/Carex rossii

Table 1 compares the floristic composition of these four communities. Each community type is characterized by differing site factors and vegetation composition.

The *Abies concolor/Poa bolanderi* community is an old-growth, closed canopy fir forest. Shrub understory cover is low (averaging <1 percent), and herb cover and diversity is also low (about 5 percent, with about 5 species). This vegetation typically develops on north-facing, moderately inclined slopes on sites below ridges capped by barren volcanic flows (mud-flow breccia, Bateman and Warhaftig 1966).

The *Abies magnifica/Erigeron peregrinus* community is a moderately dense, old-growth fir forest with a diverse and lush herbaceous understory. Shrub cover can be moderately high (ca. 20 percent) and patchy. Herb cover averages about 30 to 50 percent in this type, with around 20 to 30 frequent species. This forest is typical of mesic sites: deep soils, north facing slopes, meadow margins are usual locations of its development. This community is a moist-phase of typical *Abies magnifica* forest (cf. Oosting and Billings 1943).

The *Abies magnifica/Poa nervosa* community is a moderately dense, relatively young fir forest. Shrub understory cover is variable, reaching as high as 30 percent in some stands. Herb cover is high, usually between 30 percent and 50 percent, and is moderately diverse (with between 15 to 20 common species). This forest type occurs on similar kinds of sites as the previous type, and probably represents an earlier successional stage than the *A. magnifica/E. peregrinus* community.

The *Pinus contorta* ssp. *murrayana/Carex rossii* type is typically a young, open pine forest. Understory shrub cover is usually minimal. Herbaceous understory cover is moderate (between 5 percent and 20 percent), and characterized by dominance by graminoids. Configuration of this community suggests it is an early-successional forest type. It is most typical of soils derived from granitic rocks. This forest type is a relatively xeric phase of typical Sierran lodgepole pine forests (cf. Taylor 1976, 1984).

DCA ordination of vegetation data from 36 *Silene invisa* populations identified two principal structuring gradients: canopy cover and elevation. Figure 4 gives the ordination diagram resulting from this analysis. The first DCA axis is correlated with degree of canopy cover (r = - 0.36, p > 0.05). The *Abies concolor/Poa bolanderi* and the *Abies magnifica/Erigeron peregrinus* communities, which ordinate at low values on the first axis, have greater canopy closure than do the *Abies magnifica/Poa nervosa* and the *Pinus contorta/Carex rossii* communities, which ordinate at high values on the first axis. The second DCA axis is correlated with elevation (r = -0.33, p > 0.05), indicating a response to climate. The *Abies concolor/Poa bolanderi* community, which ordinates at high values on the second DCA axis, is typical of a warmer, dryer climate (i.e., lower elevations) than the *Abies magnifica/Erigeron peregrinus* community, which ordinates at low first DCA axis values.

Ranges of important site characteristics for *S. invisa* populations at the southern end of its range were identified by our studies.

Table 1.

Comparison of vegetation composition of the four community types supporting *Silene invisa* populations in the southern Sierra Nevada. Characteristic cover (mean cover for only stands of occurrence) is given. Species listed in the table are those occurring in the highest proportion of stands of each type. ABCO = *Abies concolor*, ABMA = *Abies magnifica*, PICOM = *Pinus contorta* ssp. *murrayana*, POBO = *Poa bolanderi*, ERPE = *Erigeron peregrinus*, CARO = *Carex rossii*.

	VEGETATION TYPE			
SPECIES[1]	ABCO/ POBO	ABMA/ ERPE	ABMA/ PONE	PICOM/ CARO
TREES:				
Abies concolor	23.3	8.0	.	.
Abies magnifica	36.6	41.2	25.3	2.2
Pinus contorta	.	3.9	14.3	44.6
Pinus monticola	.	2.9	3.9	.
Tsuga mertensiana	.	.	7.5	.
SHRUBS:				
Lonicera conjugialis	.	0.3	0.3	.
Ribes viscosissimum	.	.	1.0	.
Ribes roezelii	.	0.4	.	.
FORBS:				
Erigeron peregrinus	.	8.0	12.3	1.7
Senecio integerrimus	0.2	3.3	2.1	0.5
Viola purpurea	0.2	0.8	0.2	0.4
Collinsia torreyi	3.3	1.1	1.0	.
Ligusticum grayi	.	2.7	3.0	0.2
GRAMINOIDS:				
Carex rossii	.	0.6	1.7	11.2
Carex raynoldsii	.	2.0	0.3	.
Festuca viridula	.	0.1	1.1	4.9
Poa bolanderi	0.5	1.8	2.5	2.4
Poa nervosa	.	0.3	4.8	8.6
Allium campanulatum	3.6	1.8	0.6	.
Stipa lemmonii	.	1.0	0.2	0.1

[1]Nomenclature follows Munz and Keck (1959).

Exposure - Nearly all *S. invisa* populations on the Eldorado National Forest occur on north facing slopes. Mean exposure for the study populations (using Batschelet 1981) was NNE (033°N). No populations were located on slopes with western, southern or eastern exposures.

Slope Steepness - Figure 5a shows a frequency distribution of slope steepness for the study populations. A strong tendency is exhibited because most populations are located on moderately sloping sites (20 to 40 percent), with relatively few populations located on level terrain or on very steep slopes.

Elevation - Mean elevation for the study populations was 2350 ± 156 m (7715 ± 512 ft), but the majority (80 percent) of the observations fall between 2255 and 2560 m (7400 and 8400 ft).

Canopy Cover - The majority of *Silene invisa* populations occur on sites with moderately dense canopy cover (fig 5b). The relatively few occurrences in sites with open canopies can be attributed to the xeric nature of such habitats. The absence of *S. invisa* populations from very dense forests is probably a function of poor growing conditions, since few herbs can grow in the dense shade of *Abies magnifica* forests (Barbour and Woodward 1985).

Substrate - Nearly 80 percent of the known *S. invisa* populations occur on sites underlain by volcanic substrates. This observation is probably not related to soil nutrient characteristics of granitic versus volcanic soils, since soils derived from these parent materials differ little in elemental composition (Taylor 1976). Rather, this restriction is due to the nature of habitat distribution on volcanic terrain, where meadow margin and other moist sites suitable for *S. invisa* are common.

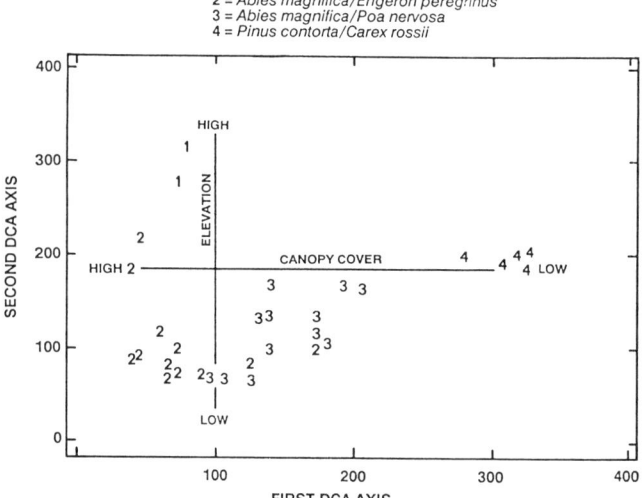

Figure 4. Detrended Correspondence Analysis (DCA) ordination for stands of vegetation at *Silene invisa* populations. The first DCA axis is correlated with canopy cover, and the second DCA axis is correlated with elevation. Hypothetical structuring gradients are indicated. Stands are shown according to TWINSPAN community-type.

Stand Age - Figure 6 shows a frequency distribution of stand age for populations of *S. invisa*. Most occurrences are in relatively old *Abies magnifica* stands, usually >150 years since the last stand regeneration event. Only a single population was located in a relatively young (i.e., less than 100 years) stand of *Pinus contorta* ssp. *murrayana*. Other populations in *P. contorta* habitats were in stands that exhibited characteristics of successional change to increased *Abies magnifica* dominance.

Relationships between habitat and reproductive characteristics

Table 2 summarizes reproductive characteristics of *S. invisa* populations by habitat-type. A number of reproductive variables differ with respect to habitat. The number of flowering axes per plant and number of flowers per axis were highest in the *Abies concolor* sites and lowest in the *Pinus contorta* sites. Variation in reproductive attributes within habitats was relatively constant (Table 2), except that populations in *Pinus contorta* habitats had less variation in number of axes per plant in addition to having the lowest mean. Variation between populations and years was greater than among habitats.

DISCUSSION

Ten years ago, *Silene invisa* was known from fewer than a dozen herbarium specimens, mostly unicates, scattered in an equal number of herbaria. Our survey resulted in the identification of those habitat factors favorable to *Silene invisa* populations. As a result, we were able to locate many previously undocumented occurrences. Today, records indicate nearly 60 known populations. This increase in the number of known stations is a direct function of intensity of field searches. Casual collectors tend to overlook *S. invisa* because the plant is easily camouflaged in the lush grass-herb understory in which it typically grows. Its abundance is consequently not reflected by the few herbarium records.

Silene invisa populations predominately occur in old-growth red fir forest stands. A common habitat for *S. invisa* is the margin of moist openings, such as alder thickets, in *Abies magnifica* dominated forest. *S. invisa* populations occurring in *Pinus contorta* forests are generally on steep rocky, slopes.

Silene invisa populations in *Abies concolor* or *Abies magnifica* dominated sites are more fecund than populations on *Pinus contorta* dominated sites. Populations occurring in *Abies magnifica* forests are generally larger and more fecund than those on *Abies concolor* habitats. One might speculate that the *A. magnifica* forest populations of *S. invisa* are growing in a more favorable habitat than the populations in *Pinus contorta* forest. Such speculation requires the assumption that long-term population variability is minimal or trivial. We have noted significant within

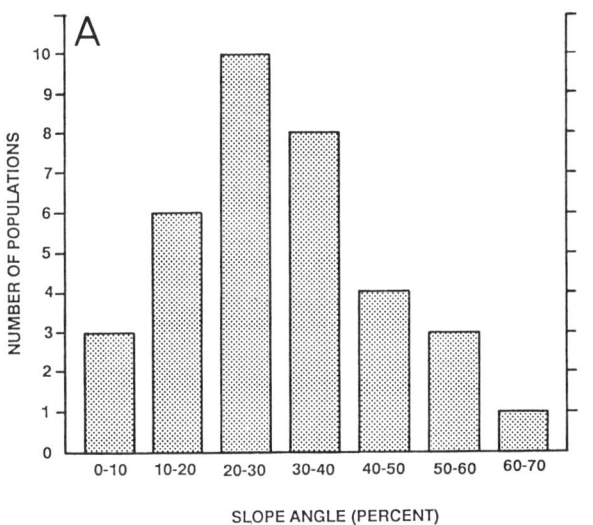

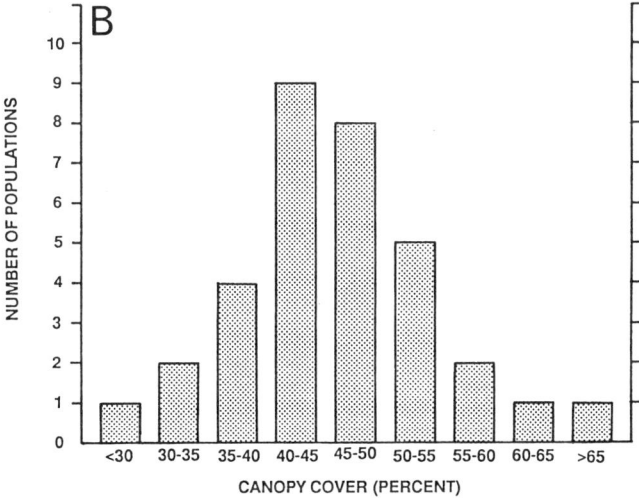

Figure 5. Histograms showing frequency of *Silene invisa* occurrences by ecological factors: 5a; slope angle, 5b: canopy cover.

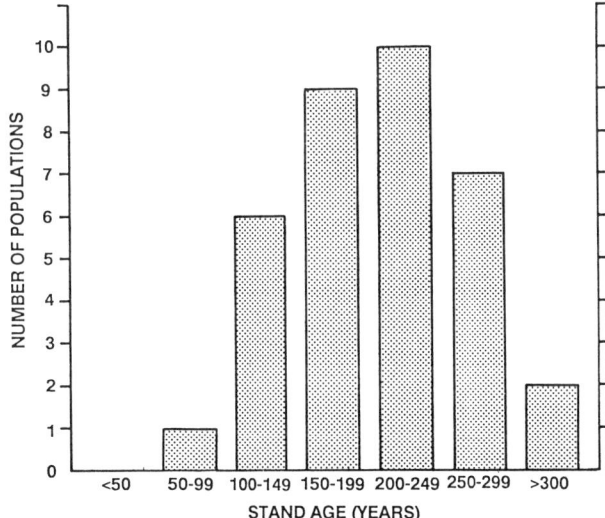

Figure 6. Histogram showing frequency of *Silene invisa* occurrences by forest stand-age class.

population variability of reproductive attributes, but long-term reproductive data will be required to determine the significance of these trends in relation to the fitness of individuals or populations.

Silene invisa sites are places where snow drifts accumulate and persist until late in the season. We believe it is probable that the modular growth form and suspected autogamous breeding system of *S. invisa* represents an adaptation to variations in the length of the snow-free period. Seed output is directly related to capsule size. Plasticity in capsule size, number of capsules, and number of flowering axes allows herbaceous perennials like *S. invisa* to adjust their growth and hence reproductive output to the conditions of a particular season (Wilson 1983). Our data from 1983, with one of the heaviest snow packs on record for the Sierra Nevada, indicates that *S. invisa* populations produced less seed that year than in any subsequent year of observation. Nearly all study populations increased their reproductive output in years following 1983 (all years which have had lower snowfall). Since then, reproductive output has varied, but has not fallen to the levels observed in 1983.

Annual variation in reproductive output could have profound effects on the dynamics of *S. invisa* populations. Although to date our data do not reveal all the reasons for variation in *S. invisa* reproductive output, they emphasize the necessity for continued, long-term population monitoring in order to generate a data set sufficient to make predictions about future population fate. As Likens (1983) has pointed out, many ecological phenomena take place on a time scale of many years or decades, and can only be detected by long term study. For plants, population fluctuations are probably the rule rather than the exception (Harper 1977). The implications of this fact for rare plant management should not be overlooked.

Rare plants like *S. invisa* provide an opportunity to study the population dynamics of an entire species. Sampling a large proportion of the populations of a widespread plant is not practical. Rare plants, however, provide tractable situations in which population behavior can be studied on an evolutionary scale.

An endemic plant with a characteristically small population size occurring in a habitat under increasing threat of disturbance requires monitoring. Red fir forests in the Sierra Nevada will come under intensive forestry practices in the coming decades. Information of the type presented here is necessary to manage *S. invisa* populations in a manner compatible with multiple uses.

ACKNOWLEDGEMENTS

Funding for a portion of this research was provided by the U.S. Forest Service, Eldorado National Forest. We thank Zoe Tyler, Forest Botanist, for her facilitation of our studies. Information on undocumented populations identified in PGandE surveys was provided by John Stebbins and Mike Fry.

REFERENCES

Bateman, P. C. and C. Warhaftig. 1966. Geology of the Sierra Nevada, pp. 107-172 in: E. H. Bailey [Ed.], Geology of Northern California. California Division of Mines and Geology, Bulletin 190.

Barbour, M. G. 1984. Can A Red Fir Forest Be Restored. Fremontia 11(4):18-19.

Barbour, M. G. and R. A. Woodward. 1985. The red fir forest of California. Can. J. For. 15:570-576.

Batschelet, E. 1981. Circular statistics in Biology. Academic Press, London.

Brockman, I. and G. Bocquet. 1978. Ecological influences on the distribution of sexes in *Silene vulgaris* (Moench) Garcke (Caryophyllaceae). Ber. Deutch. Botan. Gessel. 91:217-230.

Croy, C. D. and R. L. Dix. 1984. Notes on sample size requirements in morphological plant ecology. Ecology 65:662-666.

Table 2.

Summary of reproductive statistics for *Silene invisa* populations by habitat type; ABMA = *Abies magnifica*, ABCO = *Abies concolor*, PICOM = *Pinus contorta* ssp. *murrayana*, POBO = *Poa bolanderi*, ERPE = *Erigeron peregrinus*, CARO = *Carex rossii*, Coef. Var. = Coefficient of Variation. Data represent means for 1986 observations only. Variables with less than n = 100 are omitted from the tabulation.

Reproductive Attribute	VEGETATION TYPE			
	ABCO/ POBO	ABMA/ ERPE	ABMA/	PICOM/ CARO
AXES/PLANT	1.67	1.59	1.42	1.16
Coef. Var.	63pct	65pct	67pct	43pct
Sample Size	392	952	1195	140
FLOWERS/AXIS	1.86	1.84	1.57	1.60
Coef. Var.	47pct	54pct	50pct	55pct
Sample Size	403	1136	1221	162
CAPSULE LENGTH				
UPPER FLW.	11.5	11.8	12.2	-
Coef. Var.	13pct	13pct	15pct	-
Sample Size	120	239	325	-
SECOND FLW.	-	10.8	11.0	-
Coef. Var.	-	16pct	21pct	-
Sample Size	-	101	142	-
THIRD FLW.	-	11.0	10.4	-
Coef. Var.	-	16pct	17pct	-
Sample Size	-	135	147	-

Cruden, R. W. 1977. Pollen/ovule ratios: A conservative indicator of breeding systems in flowering plants. Evol. 31:32-46.

Gauch, H. G. 1982. Multivariate analysis in community ecology. Cambridge University Press, Cambridge.

Gross, K. L. and J. D. Soule. 1981. Differences in biomass allocation to reproductive and vegetative structures of male and female plants of a dioecious, perennial herb, *Silene alba* (Miller) Krause. Am. J. Bot. 68:801-807.

Harper, J. L. 1977. Population Biology of Plants. Academic Press, London.

Hill, M. O. 1979a. TWINSPAN, a FORTRAN program for arranging multivariate data in an Ordered two-way table by classification of the individuals and attributes. Cornell University, Ithaca, New York.

Hill, M. O. 1979b. DECORANA, a FORTRAN program for Detrended Correspondence Analysis ordination. Cornell University, Ithaca, New York.

Hill, M. O., R. G. Bunce and M. W. Shaw. 1975. Indicator species analysis, a divisive polythetic method of classification, and its application to a survey of native pinewoods in Scotland. Journal of Ecology 63:597-613.

Hill, M. O. and H. G. Gauch. 1980. Detrended correspondence analysis: an improved ordination technique. Vegetatio 42:47-58.

Hitchcock, C. L. and B. Maguire. 1947. A revision of the North American species of *Silene*. University of Washington Publications in Biological Science, Vol. 13:1-72.

Kruckeberg, A. 1961. Artificial crosses of western North American Silenes. Brittonia 13:305-333.

Likens, G. E. 1983. A priority for ecological research. Bull. Ecol. Soc. Am. 64:234-243.

Mueller-Dombois, D. and H. Ellenberg. 1974. Aims and methods of vegetation ecology. John Wiley & Sons, New York.

Oosting, H. J. and W. D. Billings. 1943. *Abietum magnificae*, Red Fir forests of the Sierra Nevada. Ecol. Monog. 13:259-274.

Taylor, D. Wm. 1976. Ecology of timberline vegetation at Carson Pass, Central Sierra Nevada, California. Ph.D. Dissertation, University of California, Davis.

Taylor, D. Wm. 1984. Vegetation of the Harvey Monroe Hall Research Natural Area, Inyo National Forest, California. U.S. Forest Service, Pacific Southwest Forest and Range Experiment Station, Berkeley, CA.

Taylor, D. Wm. and R. E. Palmer. 1983. Endangerment status of *Silene invisa* on the Eldorado National Forest, California. Unpublished report to the U.S. Forest Service, Eldorado National Forest, Placerville, CA.

Tiehm, A. 1985. A new species and a new combination in western North American *Silene* (Caryophyllaceae). Brittonia 37:344-346.

Wilson, M. F. 1983. Plant Reproductive Ecology. John Wiley & Sons, New York.

What Constitutes a Good Year for an Annual Plant? Two Examples from the Orcuttieae

Robert F. Holland [1]

Abstract: Annual plant populations fluctuate widely from year to year. Traditional wisdom attributes these fluctuations to annual vagaries in climatic conditions. This traditional wisdom is evaluated in relation to: 1) annual population estimates of a population of Orcuttia viscida between 1973 and 1986, and 2) annual population estimates of a population of Tuctoria mucronata between 1958 and 1988. These 2 closely related and narrowly distributed vernal pool grasses exhibit divergent responses to parallel shifts in annual weather: a good year for one species is not necessarily a good year for the other.

Annual plant population sizes vary widely from year to year. Traditional wisdom attributes this variation to the vagaries of annual weather, a familiar example being the colorful displays of desert wildflowers following particularly rainy winters. Rare annuals also experience wide population fluctuations, a condition that exacerbates survey work. A poor year may result in very low (or even non-existent) population sizes, leading to an incorrect conclusion that no rare plants would be impacted by a proposed project.

Trees, shrubs, and perennial herbs also experience "poor" years, where "poor" is defined as limited growth or reproductive output. "Good" years for perennials imply considerable growth or reproductive output -- for example the occasional bumper acorn crops that were so important to the California Indians (Gifford 1936). But the perennial habit reduces the premium on reproductive output, especially in comparison to annuals. Local extinctions of annual species could occur after even a single bad year if the species did not have some means of seed carry over or an efficient means of redispersing into the area.

This study examines the relationship between annual rainfall and population sizes of 2 rare annuals, Sacramento sticky Orcutt grass (Orcuttia viscida (Hoover) Reeder) and Solano grass (Tuctoria mucronata (Crampton) Reeder). Both of these grasses have been designated Endangered by the California Fish and Game Commission. T. mucronata additionally has been designated Endangered by the US Fish and Wildlife Service.

[1] Vegetation Ecologist, Natural Diversity Data Base, California Department of Fish and Game, Sacramento, CA.

These plants are closely related both taxonomically and ecologically. They both are members of the grass tribe Orcuttieae. Until recently they were considered congeneric (Reeder 1982). Both taxa occupy the summer beds of large vernal pools, a habitat that has endured considerable loss to agricultural development, urban expansion, and other causes (Holland 1978).

Orcuttia viscida is known to germinate in spring, as the water in the pools begins to warm following the cessation of winter rains. The seedlings produce long. slender leaves that float on the water surface, presumably providing photosynthate to the developing root system because the leafy rosette does not grow much while inundated. The plants do not begin to tiller and flower until the water has receded and the pool bed has dried for the summer. Seed set occurs during the hottest parts of June and July, after which the plants die. Most dead plants remain standing untill shattered by early fall rain.

Tuctoria mucronata currently is known from only 2 vernal pools in central Solano County. These pools differ from the 8 Sacramento County pools known to support O. viscida: they are somewhat alkaline and so turbid from suspended clays that apparently no one has ever observed the aquatic stage in T. mucronata's life cycle. Available specimens do not have the slender juvenile leaves, although several O. viscida specimens also lack these structures. The terrestrial phase of T. mucronata's life cycle is similar to that of O. viscida: flowering occurs in June, with seed ripe by early to mid-July. These life cycle descriptions are taken from Griggs (1974), Griggs and Jain (1983), and personal observation.

Crampton (1959) recognized that populations of Orcuttieae have good and bad years, and provided an anecdotal comparison of a population of Neostapfia colusana in 1957 (a dry year) and 1958 (a wet one). In the dry year it was difficult to find any individuals, while in the wet year the plants were very abundant.

METHODS

This study examines this relationship between precipitation and population size in more detail. I have compiled population estimates for both species from as many sources as I could find. These sources include specimen labels, interviews with botanists who had seen or collected either species, and my own observations and counts. In addition, I and several others have sought and counted T. mucronata in Olcott Lake each year since 1975. Griggs and Jain (1983) provide order-of-magnitude population estimates for O. viscida between 1973 and 1979. Each year since 1980 I have estimated O. viscida population sizes at the Phoenix Field Ecological Reserve by counting all individuals in 720 quadrats (each 10x10 cm) along an established series of transects, then multiplying the resultant mean density per square decimeter by the known area of the pool in order to estimate the total population size. The data from all these sources are summarized in Tables 1 and 2.

Table 1. Population observations of Tuctoria mucronata at Olcott Pool, and rainfall gathered at Fairfield during the preceeding rainfall year.

Year	Abundance	Observer	Rain, cm
1958	Estimated 100-150 plants in 4 patches each about 3-8 m in diameter	Crampton	84.45
1959	"Abundance as the previous year"	Crampton	34.29
1960	"Overall abundance greater than the previous two years"	Crampton	42.49
1961	"More common in area 3, but smaller area of 1 and 2	Crampton	32.51
1962	"...fewer but larger specimens overall..."	Crampton	44.02
1963	"...rather poor stand in areas 1 and 2, areas 3 and 4 not visited..."	Crampton	71.63
1964	Plant not sought		29.87
1965	Plant not sought		50.29
1966	Plant not sought		40.69
1967	Plant not sought		79.78
1968	Plant not sought		36.98
1969	"Population of less than one dozen plants"	Crampton	76.20
1970	Plant not sought		61.62
1971	Plant not sought		46.86
1972	No plants found	Reeder	27.48
1973	"...about 2 dozen plants"	Griggs	86.82
1974	"...15 to 20 plants..."	Reeder	63.91
1975	Two plants	Holland and Taylor	54.94
1976	No plants found	Griggs and Holland	23.01
1977	No plants found	Griggs and Holland	24.64
1978	No plants found	Griggs and Holland	88.06
1979	No plants found	Griggs and Holland	50.44
1980	No plants found	Griggs and Holland	92.13
1981	Three plants	Malloch-Leitner	34.93
1982	53 plants	Malloch-Leitner	92.35
1983	26 plants	Malloch-Leitner	101.40
1984	241 plants	Lozier	47.96
1985	221 plants	Wooley	42.88
1986	186 plants	Wooley	78.69

Table 2. Population observations of Orcuttia viscida at the Phoenix Field Ecological Reserve, and rainfall at Folsom Dam in the preceeding rainfall year.

Year	Abundance	Source	Rain, cm
1973	10-100 plants	Griggs and Jain 1983	79.22
1974	Over 10000 plants	Griggs and Jain 1983	83.92
1975	10-100 plants	Griggs and Jain 1983	55.63
1976	No plants found	Griggs and Jain 1983	25.10
1977	No plants found	Griggs and Jain 1983	24.03
1978	Over 10000 plants	Griggs and Jain 1983	87.60
1979	Over 10000 plants	Griggs and Jain 1983	58.04
1980	Estimated 59000 plants	Holland	77.93
1981	Estimated 30000 plants	Holland	50.22
1982	Estimated 154000 plants	Holland	102.59
1983	Estimated 57000 plants	Holland	126.49
1984	Estimated 146000 plants	Holland	62.48
1985	Estimated 46000 plants	Holland	45.62
1986	Estimated 215000 plants	Holland	88.47

Rainfall data are available from nearby stations at Folsom Dam (for O. viscida) and at Fairfield Fire Station (for T. mucronata). These data also are summarized in tables 1 and 2. Both stations were within 16 km and 30 vertical meters of the study sites. No major topographic barriers exist between the study areas and the reporting stations, so the data should be fairly reliable.

Because of the wide range in precision of population estimates (from 20 year old recollections to actual counts), I converted these population and rainfall data to ranks, then used Spearman's rank order correlation coefficient to evaluate the following null hypotheses:

1. There is no relation between a species' abundance in a particular year and the rainfall received during that growing season. (Do larger populations occur in rainyer years?)

2. There is no relation between the population sizes of the 2 species in any particular year. (Is a good year for one species a good year for the other?)

RESULTS

Results of the correlation analysis appear in Table 3. O. viscida showed a very strong positive rank correlation between population size and rainfall over the 14 years for which observations were available. There appears to be ample basis for rejecting the null hypothesis concerning O. viscida's response to variations in rainfall.

Tuctoria mucronata's response to rainfall was substantially more obscure in the 22 years for which I could find population estimates. Table 3 indicates very little basis for rejecting the null hypothesis: the rainyest years had no larger populations than the driest years.

But there is a very strong positive rank correlation between the population sizes of the 2 taxa within years: a good year for 1 species apparently was a good year for the other.

Table 3. Spearman's rank order correlations between:

	Abundance and precipitation for populations of		O. viscida and T. mucronata populations in each year
	O. viscida	T. mucronata	
r	.602	.046	.647
t	2.610	.207	2.941
df	12	20	12
p	.02	.84	.01

DISCUSSION

These statistical manipulations suggest that O. viscida does better in wetter years, while T. mucronata does not. The same statistics also make the counterintuitive suggestion that even though the 2 taxa respond so differently to variations in rainfall, they both enjoy large populations in the same years. How can the 2 species have good years the same years when they respond so differently to rainfall?

One possible explanation is that the two areas experienced different rainfall regimes. This does not appear to be the case, however, as the within-years correlation between rainfall data for the 2 sites is very strong ($r=0.908$, $t=7.49$, $df=12$, p lt $.0001$).

Biological rather than statistical thinking can help to solve this apparent dilemma. With only 2 exceptions, populations of O. viscida exceeded 10,000 plants if 40 or more cm of rain fell at Folsom Dam. The 2 exceptions occurred in years (1973, 1975) in which the plant's habitat was ravaged by trespass ORV use.

There were 3 years in which the populations exceeded 100,000 plants. One of these years had over half again as much rain as the other (102.6 vs 62.5 cm). Several other years had rainfalls between these values but smaller populations developed in these intermediate years. Thus, O. viscida appears to have a threshold response: populations are large given adequate precipitation, but the actual amount of rain seems to have little importance as long as this threshold is surpassed.

Careful examination of plots of monthly precipitation antecedent to each census suggested that the 2 years with over 100,000 plants (presumably the best years) had longer than usual rainy seasons. These were the only 2 years in which heavy rains began in November (all others began in December) and lasted longer into the spring (heavy rains extending into late April or even May, rather than tapering off in March). This suggests that length of inundation (Zedler 1981) may be more important than depth of inundation in determining population sizes in O. viscida.

Tuctoria mucronata did not have a comparable threshold response. Instead, this species had larger populations in those years with 45-60 cm of rain. Smaller populations occurred in drier and in wetter years. The timing of initiation and termination of precipitation had no clear relation to population sizes in T. mucronata.

These results indicate divergent responses in the 2 species in relation to rainfall variation. This is reassuring since these are 2 species in different (although closely related) genera. Arguments invoking limiting similarity and niche partitioning tell us that the two taxa should evolve different adaptive responses to the same environmental gradient.

PROSPECT

It is quite common when developing strategies for management of rare, incompletely understood taxa to borrow what is known about closely related but better understood species. Often this is the best available hint. The takehome message from this study is that, while this is a viable strategy, it is one fraught with potential pitfalls.

This is well illustrated in the recovery plan for Tuctoria mucronata (US Fish and Wildlife Service 1985). The plan includes provisions for modifications to the drainage of Olcott Lake "to retain water at a higher level for a longer period of time. An increased inundation time may aid Solano grass population sizes in drought years." (ibid, p. 46). To base such an intervention on a "more water is better" philosophy may be misguided given this study's finding that at least populations of Tuctoria mucronata do not directly reflect the amount of rainfall received. Both O. viscida and T. mucronata failed to produce plants during the droughts of 1976 and 1977, a pattern observed in several other populations of Orcuttieae throughout California (Griggs and Jain, 1983). But all these populations eventually recovered, apparently from seed stored in the soil column.

Presumably the conclusion that more water is not necessarily better also applies to other amphibious annual plants. Experimental evaluation of alternative hypotheses under controlled conditions will be required in order to corroborate these correlations.

ACKNOWLEDGEMENTS

I thank B. Crampton, T. Griggs, L. Lozier, B. Malloch-Leitner, J. Reeder, and G. Wooley for sharing their unpublished population observations.

REFERENCES

Crampton, B. The grass genera Orcuttia and Neostapfia: a study in habitat and morphological specialization. Madrono 15: 97-110. 1959.

Gifford, E.W. Californian balanophagy. In: Essays in anthropology presented to A.L. Kroeber. Berkeley, Univ. Calif. Press. pp. 87-98. 1936.

Griggs, F.T. Systematics and ecology of the genus Orcuttia (Gramineae). Chico, CA: California State Univ. Thesis.

Griggs, F.T.; Jain, S.K. Conservation of vernal pool plants in California, II: population biology of a rare and unique grass genus Orcuttia. Biol. Conservation 27: 171-193. 1983.

Holland, R.F. Geographic and edaphic distribution of vernal pools in the Great Central Valley, California. Berkeley, CA: California Native Plant Society, Special Publication No. 4. 1978.

Reeder, J.R. Systematics of the tribe Orcuttieae (Gramineae) and the description of a new segregate genus, Tuctoria. Amer. J. Bot. 69: 1082-1095. 1982.

US Fish and Wildlife Service. Delta green ground beetle and Solano grass recovery plan. Portland, OR: Fish and Wildlife Service, US Department of Interior. 68 pp. 1985.

Zedler, P. Micro-distribution of vernal pool plants of Kearny Mesa, San Diego County. In: Proceedings of the symposium on vernal pools and intermittent streams; May 9-10, 1981; Davis CA. Davis, CA; Univ. Calif. Institute of Ecology Publication No. 28. pp. 185-197. 1981.

Ecology of the Serpentine Vegetation in the San Francisco Bay Region

Niall F. McCarten [1]

Abstract: A comparison is made of soil chemistry and other microhabitat characteristics for several serpentine plant communities and their associated rare plants in the San Francisco Bay Region. Multiple soil factors are found to produce a series of complex and hetergeneous microhabitats. The variation in habitats associated with serpentine soils has resulted in the evolution of many rare plant species and generally a high plant species diversity. The observed distribution of plant species through the serpentine habitat offers important information for the design of preserves and their management.

The high diversity of California plant species on serpentine soils, noted by Mason (1946), has generated considerable interest among botanists. Ecological studies have mostly been directed toward the unusual chemistry of serpentines in terms of nutrient imbalances and high heavy metal concentrations. Studies on the soil chemistry (Fiedler 1985, Kruckeberg 1954, Turitzin 1982, Willett and Batey 1977) in relation to plant tolerance and adaptation have produced contrasting results and interpretations. In discussing the causes of the serpentine barrens syndrome Kruckeberg (1984, p. 83) states that "the single-factor explanation is abandoned here in favor of a multiple-factor one" and continues to suggest the potential for involvement of other environmental factors. Few studies have attempted to describe patterns of high species diversity on serpentines with regard to microhabitat characteristics as well as edaphic factors. Studies that have discussed diversity and edaphic factors (Kruckeberg 1984) cover broader geographic areas. Clearly, the stage has been set for studies that compare and contrast the plant communities and species composition and distribution within those communities at the regional level.

SAN FRANCISCO BAY REGION

At least six serpentine plant communities are found in the San Francisco Bay Region due to the variation of local climatic conditions, topography and soil factors. Plant communities containing predominantly shrub or small tree species occur in areas having a rocky substrate with relatively steep slopes and, therefore, little soil development. Grassland and annual forb communities grow in areas with more level topography, or gradual slopes where soil development may exceed one meter in depth. The plant communities most commonly encountered in this region are: Serpentine Bunchgrass Grassland, Serpentine Wildflower Field, Franciscan Serpentine Coastal Scrub, Mixed Serpentine Chaparral, Sargent Cypress Woodlands and Serpentine Barrens (Jensen and Holstein 1983, plus additions).

Serpentine Locations

The serpentine plant communities occur in over twelve areas spread through six counties of the San Francisco Bay Region (figure 1). Marin County includes Carson Ridge, which has a recently burned Mixed Serpentine Chaparral; Mt. Tamalpais State Park which has Mixed Serpentine Chaparral, Sargent Cypress Woodland and Serpentine Barrens; the Tiburon Peninsula where the Nature Conservancy's Ring Mountain Preserve and St. Hilary's Preserve support Serpentine Bunchgrass Grassland. San Francisco County has the Presidio area, which includes the U.S. Army Presidio and neighboring Golden Gate National Recreation Area which supports Serpentine Bunchgrass Grassland and Franciscan Serpentine Coastal Scrub. San Mateo County includes Edgewood County Park, the "Triangle", a State Fish and Game Preserve, Crystal Springs Reservoir, Pulgas Ridge and Stanford Universitys' Jasper Ridge Preserve; these areas support Serpentine Bunchgrass Grassland, Serpentine Wildflower Field, Mixed Serpentine Chaparral and Serpentine Barrens. Santa Clara County, in the vicinity of Coyote, supports Serpentine Bunchgrass Grassland. Alameda County includes Redwood Regional Park which supports a Serpentine Bunchgrass Grassland. Contra Costa County includes Mt. Diablo State Park which supports a Mixed Serpentine Chaparral that burned in 1976.

Author Niall F. McCarten
Department of Biology, San Francisco State University

Serpentine Soils

Serpentine soils in the San Francisco Bay Region are derived from intrusive igneous rocks associated with the Mesozoic age Franciscan formation. Serpentine outcrops in this region are related to extensive faulting. Specifically, the serpentines along the west side of San Francisco Bay are associated with the San Andreas fault, while serpentines of the east side of the Bay are associated with the Hayward fault. The name serpentine is at best a generic term referring to a complex of ferromagnesium-silicates. Ultrabasic and ultramafic are alternative terms that include numerous mineral types (see Kruckeberg 1984).

Characteristic of serpentine soils is the low calcium-magnesium exchangeable cation ratio. In serpentine soils calcium concentrations are very low. Calcium is essential for plant cell membrane development and stability and enzyme activation (Fitter and Hay 1983). Further, high magnesium concentrations in these soils compete with calcium such that calcium ions must work against a magnesium gradient. Calcium-magnesium ratios can be used to determine the Mg^{++} gradient or simply the severity of the serpentine nutrient imbalance. Well balanced soils have a Ca^{++}/Mg^{++} greater than two. A Ca^{++}/Mg^{++} of less that 0.2 is considered extreme. The ratios in the San Francisco Bay Region range from 0.7 to 0.04 (McCarten 1986).

Another, more highly variable, component of serpentine soils is the presence of heavy metals such as nickel, iron, manganese and chromium. These heavy metals can be extremely toxic to plants. However, the toxicity of metals such as nickel is dependent on soil pH with slightly acidic soils enhancing metal toxicity. Accumulation of heavy metals in some serpentine endemic plant species has raised many questions about the evolution and adaptations of these plants. Some serpentine endemic plant species have been found to accumulate heavy metals in very high concentrations (Kruckeberg 1984, p. 83). However, other studies have found little correlation with heavy metal accumulation and the occurrence of species on versus off serpentines (Fiedler 1985). Analysis of twenty-four soil samples (McCarten 1986) throughout the San Francisco Bay Region found that many serpentine sites do not have abnormally high heavy metal concentrations. Leaf tissue analysis on four species of Arctostaphylos does not indicate heavy metal accumulation in these plants. However, Acanthomintha obovata ssp. duttonii (San Mateo thornmint) had a relatively high concentration of iron (500 ppm) in the stems, but no other unusually high concentrations of other metals. While heavy metal concentrations are generally low throughout the Bay Region serpentines, the areas that have high concentrations of those metals are very localized. The highest concentrations of nickel and manganese were found less than 100 meters from soils that had no detectable heavy metals.

Particular sites in the Bay region have other soil components such as phosphorus and potassium in such low concentrations as to render these soils nearly infertile. Carbon and nitrogen concentration also varied considerably from site to site. The remarkable variation in the serpentine soil chemistry within this region suggests that few generalizations can be made. Rather, the local soil chemistry must be considered a unique character that contributes to the many other environmental factors.

Species Diversity

Floristic analysis has found that California serpentine plant species represent nearly 10% of the endemic State flora (Kruckeberg 1984, p. 53). Further, this diversity is to be found associated with serpentine soils, which represent only 1% of California's landmass. In the San Francisco Bay Region local species diversity is proportioanlly higher. The table below enumerates floristic values for the serpentine areas:

TOTAL TAXA	CALIFORNIA NATIVES	RARE TAXA
463	323	35

The total number of taxa are those thus far known to grow on serpentine soils in the region. Of the total number of taxa, forty-two are non-natives. The thirty-five rare taxa alone make up nearly 11% of the California endemics growing on serpentine in this region. Comparison with the flora of the region, including non-serpentine areas, cannot be made as it would require an arbitrary dilineation of this region. It is noteworthy that all these endemics and rare taxa are found in an area covering approximately five square kilometers (2000 acres).

Community Species Diversity and Rare Taxa

The amount of plant species diversity can vary considerably between plant communities and this is especially true for those growing on serpentine soils.

Sargent Cypress Woodland--this is one of the least diverse communities and is often a monoculture of Cupressus sargentii. The soils on which the Sargent cypress grow are the most nutrient poor serpentines in the Bay Region.

Serpentine Barrens--this community may also have a single taxon such as Allium falcifolium or Streptanthus species, but the barrens can have a sparse vegetation of several species. It is not been determined why the Serpentine Barren "syndrome" occurs in the Bay Region, but high heavy metal concentration have been suggested for other areas (Kruckeberg 1984).

Mixed Serpentine Chaparral--this community is a rather heterogeneous mix of Arctostaphylos species, Quercus durata, Garrya congdonii, Ceanothus jepsonii var. albiflora, Heteromeles arbutifolia, Rhamnus californica and occassionally Adenostoma fasciculata. The general structure of the Serpentine Chaparral can range from "patches" of Quercus durata or an Arctostaphylos species to a mixture of several shrub species that can include an understory of bunchgrass (e.g. Calamogrostis ophitidis). The diversity in the chaparral of Mt. Diablo and Carson Ridge is presently high due to past fires. Many native bunchgrass and annual forb species are present in the openings created by these fires.

Serpentine Bunchgrass Grasslands-- this community is similar to the Mixed Serpentine Chaparral community in having a mosaic or series of patches of species. These patches may extend for some distance and contain a single bunchgrass species or a highly diverse mix of species. For instance Stipa pulchra or Sitanion jubatum or Koeleria macrantha may form dense hummocks that exclude other species. More often, however, a number of bunchgrass species will grow together and include as many as ten different taxa. Among the "mixed" bunchgrasses annual grasses often grow along with perennial and annual non-grass herbaceous species. The relative diversity in Serpentine Bunchgrass Grassland can be related, in part, to disturbance. The serpentine grasslands in Santa Clara County near Coyote are cattle grazed to the extent that Stipa pulchra is the dominant bunchgrass species. Sites in that area excluded from grazing have up to five bunchgrass species in equal abundance. The Nature Conservancy's Ring Mountain Preserve and Redwood Regional Park, neither of which are grazed, have as many as twelve native bunchghrass species, most of which are evenly mixed throughout the grassland. Disturbance mostly from non-grazing activites appears to have caused a mixing of serpentine soils creating a more homogeneous environment. However, naturally occurring, i.e. undisturbed, areas having patches of a single bunchgrass species do exist. The areas that have a patchy distribution of bunchgrass species are often encountered in San Mateo County. Edgewood Park, Pulgas Ridge, Crystal Springs Reservoir and the "Triangle" have distinct areas dominated by a single bunchgrass species that form a dense hummock. These single species patches are separated by areas that can have up to eight bunchgrass species or by other plant communities such as Serpentine Wildflower Fields. Soils analysis suggests that soil water relations such as high field capacity and permanant wilting point maybe the critical factors creating these microhabitat conditions.

Serpentine Wildflower Fields--this community is associated with the serpentine grasslands, but can form extensive areas that are devoid of perennial bunchgrass species. Annual herbaceous species diversity can be very high in some areas such as Edgewood Park and the "Triangle." As many as thirty-three plant taxa per meter squared have been measured in these areas (McCarten in prep). However, not all Serpentine Wildflower Fields are equally diverse. Of special interest are some of the areas where a single species is dominant and in very high densities. These local situations often represent sites where the dominant species is a rare taxon.

Rare Plants--The high diversity of the Serpentine Wildflower Fields and Serpentine Bunchgrass Grasslands includes a higher proportion of rare plants than in the chaparral or woodland communities. Twenty-three of the thirty-five rare taxa in this region are associated with the grassland and wildflower field plant communities. In many respects very little is known about most of these rare taxa other than their geographic distributions. Nearly all the rare serpentine species in the region are restricted to local microhabitats. One taxon, Acanthomintha obovata ssp. duttonii, a Federally Endangered species, has a particular microhabitat requirement that differs from other serpentine species and forms a good basis from which to discuss rare serpentine plants. Acanthomintha obovata ssp. duttonii is restricted to deep (over one meter) serpentine clays that have developed in local fracture faults. The clays have an exceedingly high moisture retention, in fact higher than in the bunchgrass grassland, and an extreme serpentine condition (Ca^{++}/Mg^{++} less than 0.09) and very high cation exchange capacity relative to other serpentines. These clays are the deepest serpentine soils so far found in the region.

Other rare plant habitats, such as those for Pentachaeta bellidiflora and

Hesperolinon congestum, that grow in the vicinity of Acanthomintha obovata ssp. duttonii have relatively low percent soil moisture, different cation ratios and exchange capacities and the soils are shallow (5-10 cm). Yet other rare taxa, such as Cirsium fontinale, grow directly in seeps. The main point to understand is that within a serpentine area, such as Edgewood Park, very local microhabitats exists. Factors such as soil chemistry, texture water holding capacity and water availability, for example, create unique microhabitats. Such factors control the density and species composition of a particular site. We readily recognize major site differences when comparing different plant communities such as Serpentine Chaparral or Serpentine Bunchgrass Grasslands. However, similar recognition is needed in understanding how these broadly defined communities are structured in terms of their species composition.

THE DESIGN OF SERPENTINE PLANT PRESERVES

The Nature Conservancy's Ring Mountain Preserve, Marin County Water District's Carson Ridge Ecological Preserve and the Jasper Ridge Preserve in the San Francisco Bay Region are, at present the only areas specifically set aside in the San Francisco Bay Region, to protect serpentine vegetation. Areas such as Mt. Diablo and Mt. Tamalpais State Parks, do provide general protection. Other areas, even though they may be owned by a government agency, have no guarantee of protection.

Several problems exist for the present and future viability of the San Francisco Bay Region serpentines. Immediate problems concern the survival of the serpentine habitat. Housing developments and highways have reduced the amount of serpentine habitat in this region by nearly 20% in the last two decades. Housing developments are no longer a threat due to foundation destabilization serpentine soils. However, golf courses and county sanitation landfill areas are the new popular urban projects. Direct habitat loss is of course a major concern. However, proposals to mitigate this loss by setting aside very small areas containing rare species do not consider the impacts from surrounding land use. The importation of different soils and the use of fertilizers would not only change local soil conditions, but the new soil components would bleed into the neighboring serpentine. Increases in water run-off and erosion will further change the soil chemistry, water retention and depth. Local hydrological conditions, such as those created by fault blocks in San Mateo County, are very much a part of the microhabitat parameters that support local patches of species. Therefore, changes in soil moisture in one area could change ground water levels elsewhere. Species such as Acanthomintha obovata ssp. duttonii and the seep plant Cirsium fontinale would be the first species to be disturbed from changes in soil water relations. Further, the structure of the plant community in the area to be set aside for mitigation would change, since the local microhabitat conditions that control species occurrences and their densities would be changed.

While the number of rare species is extremely high in the San Francisco Bay Region, the setting aside of small areas for each rare plant would not necessarily preserve them or the large species diversity that exists. As mentioned previously, many of the rare plant species grow in specific microhabitats. In these localized situations the rare plant may be the dominant species and associated with but a few other taxa. Therefore preserving only the rare plant habitat does not preserve the extremely high species diversity outside this habitat. The very diverse Serpentine Wildflower Field community should be recognized as unique in its level of diversity and species composition. It is by far one of the rarer plant communities in the State. The Serpentine Bunchgrass Grassland, like all native bunchgrass grassland communities in California, is also a very rare plant community by any standards. Preservation of the diversity of this community so that it will include the mosaic of microhabitats requires protecting areas not within existing preserves.

Even if sufficient land is preserved and neighboring land use does not impact the serpentines, the future of the serpentine vegetation is still in question. Invasion from non-native species is having a serious impact. Major impacts are resulting from invasion of eucalyptus trees. Eucalyptus create unnatural shade, but more important, the leaves change the soil chemistry by adding allelochemicals and increasing nutrient levels. Plant species that occur under eucalyptus trees are mostly non-native. The use of non-native plant species to "revegetate" disturbed serpentine habitat may be providing a pool of species that could displace not only rare taxa, but entire communities. The general affects of non-natives on the diverse serpentine flora requires further study. Monitoring of the serpentine plant communities will be critical in evaluating what management, if any, is needed.

The San Francisco Bay Region serpentines provide a great opportunity to protect a large number of endemic and rare plant species and very diverse natural communities. However, one must seriously consider the complexities of the habitat in designing preserves for serpentine plants and communities.

ACKNOWLEDEMENTS: I wish to thank Suzanne Sommers and Toni Corelli, Department of Biology, San Jose State University; Neil Havlick, East Bay Regional Parks; Roxanne Bittman, The Nature Conservancy; Jim Birtenshaw and Paul Zinke, Department of Forestry, University of California, Berkeley. This study was supported by a grant from the Endangered Plant Program, California Department of Fish and Game.

REFERENCES

Fiedler, P. L. Heavy Metal Accumulation and the Nature of Edaphic Endemism in the Genus Calachortus (Liliaceae). Amer. J. Bot. 72(11):1712-1718. 1985 November.

Fitter, A. H.; Hay, R. K. M. Environmental Physiology of Plants. London: Academic Press; 1983. 355 p.

Jensen, D. B.; Holstein, G. Natural Communities. Natural Diversity Data Base, California Department of Fish and Game. 1983. 10 p.

Kruckeberg, A. R. The Ecology of Serpentine Soils. Ecology 35(2):267-264; 1954 April.

Kruckeberg, A. R. California Serpentines: Flora, Vegetation, Geology, Soils, and Management Problems. Berkeley: University of California Press; 1984. 180 p.

Mason, H. L. The Edaphic Factor in Narrow Endemism. II. The Geographic Occurrence of Plants of Highly Restricted Patterns of Distribution. Madroño 8:241-257; 1946.

McCarten, N. F. Soil Nutrient and Heavy Metal Chemistry from Serpentine Areas in the San Francisco Bay Region. Report submitted to the Endangered Plant Program, California Department of Fish and Game. 1986. 7 p.

Turitzin, S. N. Nutrient Limitations to Plant Growth in a California Serpentine Grassland. The American Midland Naturalist 107(1):95-99; 1982.

Willett, I. R.; Batey, T. The Effects of Metal Ions on the Root Surface Phosphatase Activity of Grasses differing in Tolerance to Serpentine Soil. Plant and Soil 48:213-221. 1977.

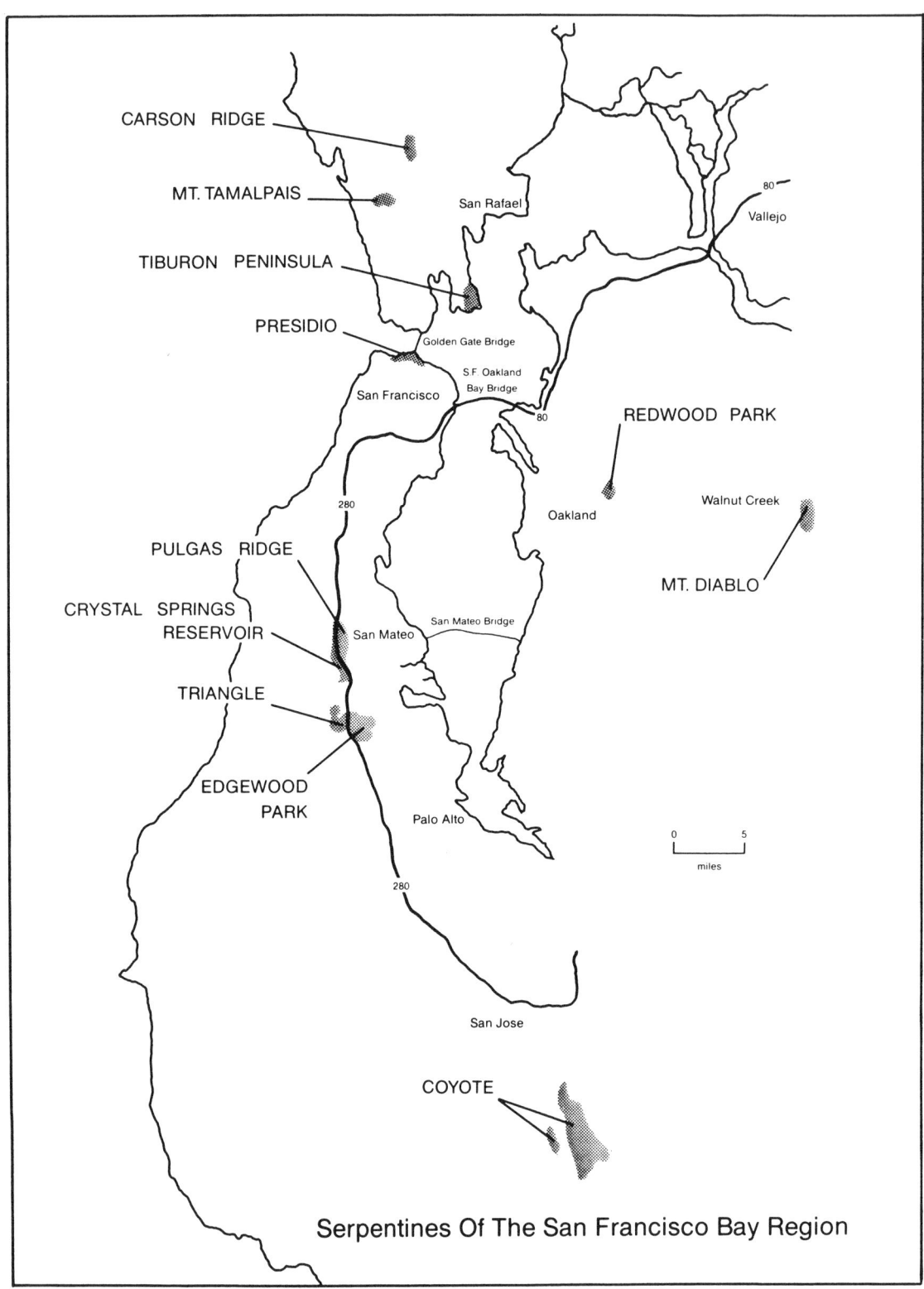

Figure 1. Serpentine Areas in the San Francisco Bay Region.

Ecology and Distribution of *Poa marcida* Hitchc. in Northwestern Oregon

Rexford Palmer, Ronald Vanbianchi, Larry Schofield, Susan Nugent [1]

Abstract: Results of Bureau of Land Management research on Poa marcida, Weak Stem Bluegrass, in the northwestern Oregon Coast Range are reported. Poa marcida populations occur on volcanic substrates in sites with strong marine climatic influence. Reproduction from seed contributes significantly to the persistence of colonies, and high seedling mortality occurs during the winter snow season and during summer drought. Poa marcida is rooted in the upper layers of litter, and events that disturb this layer have detrimental effects on the species. Mild disturbance benefits Poa marcida by reducing competition. A correlation of Poa marcida distribution on a local scale with elk bedding areas and trails and other wildlife activity was documented.

The peaks of the Coast Range mountains of northwestern Oregon are of great floristic interest because of the occurrence of plant species there disjunct from the Olympic Mountains of Washington, the Cascade Mountains, and the high Coast Range peaks to the south. Poa marcida, or "weak stem bluegrass," is one such plant species. In Oregon the plant reaches its southern limit in the northwestern Coast Ranges. The distribution and ecology of Poa marcida is illustrative of the environmental features of this region and the complex of factors that result in the area's unique floristic relationships.

The botanical significance of northwestern Oregon has been documented by Chambers (1973), who described the flora of Onion Peak and other areas in Clatsop County, and Detling (1954), who examined the floristic relationships of Saddle Mountain. The area also is rich in endemic plant species (Aldrich 1972, Hammond and Chambers 1985, Meinke 1981, Johnson 1980, Siddal, et al. 1979, Soper, et al. 1985).

Poa marcida is distributed from British Columbia to Central Oregon (fig. 1). In northwestern Oregon Poa marcida has historically been known from sites on the immediate coast and, in the same region, inland on the highest Coast Range ridge systems. Peck (1961) describes the habitat of Poa marcida as "bogs in the coastal mountains." Hitchcock, et al. (1973) describes the habitat of Poa marcida as "moist areas in the coastal mountains." The exact southern limit of Poa marcida in Oregon is not known with certainty, but it may extend as far south as the Alsea area (Scofield 1985).

Poa marcida (fig. 2) is a rare plant in Oregon. At major population sites the plant may form dense colonies covering many square meters, but only a small number of such sites exist in Oregon. The species is presently listed by the U.S. Fish and Wildlife Service as a category 3C species. USFWS has indicated that if populations of Poa marcida continue to be lost, the listing status of the plant may be raised. The Oregon State Land Board lists Poa marcida as a sensitive species.

Botanists with the Bureau of Land Management (BLM) have studied the distribution of Poa marcida in Tillamook, Yamhill, and Lincoln Counties (Scofield et al. 1978-1985). These studies have concentrated on timber sales, and preliminary work has shown that normal clearcut logging practices result in the elimination of most Poa marcida from clearcut units. The Bureau of Land Management has set aside populations of Poa marcida for protection and has initiated a study on the effects of logging on the species.

The present paper summarizes existing and historical distributional information on Poa marcida and the results of new field surveys carried out

---

[1] Palmer and Vanbianchi: Holton Associates, Berkeley, CA 94710; Scofield and Nugent: Bureau of Land Management, Salem, OR.

Figure 1--Distribution of *Poa marcida* in the Pacific Northwest.

Figure 2. *Poa marcida* (from Hitchcock and Chase 1950)

by the authors. We also present some results of ecological and life-history observations that explain, at least in part, the distribution pattern in Oregon of this rare grass.

METHODS

During 1985 and 1986 the authors searched for *Poa marcida* populations in the area of Northwestern Oregon shown in figure 3. In addition we visited many populations known from historical and herbarium records. Information sources for known locations included herbaria, scientific literature, the Oregon Natural Heritage Data Base, the Bureau of Land Management, the U.S. Fish and Wildlife Service, the Oregon Native Plant Society, and knowledgeable individuals.

Field surveys were conducted to determine the distribution of *Poa marcida* in the study area. First, known populations were visited. At each known population, we compiled data on the habitat of *Poa marcida*. From these data we developed a predictive model for the occurrence of the species following the methods of Nelson (1984, 1986). Habitat variables scored for each population are given in table 1. Precipitation data is summarized in figure 3d.

Table I. *Poa marcida* habitat variables.

Cover of associated species
Tree cover
Stand age/diameter class
Tree density
Elevation
Slope
Aspect
Topographic position
Geological formation
Substrate structure
Litter characteristics
Disturbance gradient

For analysis of plant community attributes associated with *Poa marcida* populations, lists of associated species and their cover values were compiled from

1 m. sq. plots located randomly throughout Poa marcida populations. We also sampled circular plots 50 meters in diameter for attributes of the forest overstory at Poa marcida sites. Data from these forest overstory plots included tree density and basal area by species. Ages of forest trees at Poa marcida sites were determined by increment borings.

Species presence/cover data was subjected to a two-way indicator species analysis using the TWINSPAN program (Cornell Ecology Programs). These data were also examined for variations correlated with environmental gradients by means of detrended correspondence analysis (DCA). Results are presented in Palmer and Vanbianchi (1986).

Life history attributes of Poa marcida were studied in 120 permanent plots at the BLM Sheridan Peak Area of Critical Environmental Concern (ACEC). One-meter square plots were staked. In 20 plots standard wire-flags were used to mark all the plants in the plot, including seedlings. Each plant was given a unique number and data on plant size, number of parts, number of seeds, and number of flowering stems was recorded. Plots were resampled at monthly intervals during the growing season, and approximately bimonthly during the winter. New seedlings were marked as they appeared.

RESULTS

Distribution

Poa marcida is a species endemic to the Pacific Northwest, distributed from the northern portion of Vancouver Island through Washington in the Olympic and Cascade mountains and into Oregon in the Coast Range and Cascades (fig. 1). The geographic limits of its known distribution are the Tsitika River Valley on Vancouver Island to the north, Lindsey Ridge in the Lincoln County portion of Oregon's Coast Range to the south, the west slope of the Cascade range, and the Pacific Ocean.

In Oregon Poa marcida is distributed in scattered locations along the immediate coast (fig. 3) including Tillamook Head, Cascade Head, and Cape Lookout. It is also found on ridges and peaks inland from the coast, including Lindsey Ridge in northern Lincoln County, on High Peak and along Moon Creek on the ridge system between Grindstone Mountain and Hardscrabble Peak in Tillamook County, and on the ridge system running southwest from Sheridan Peak in western Yamhill County to Rye Mountain in eastern Tillamook County. To the north, Poa marcida is known from Saddle Mountain and Onion Peak in Clatsop County (Chambers 1973).

The earliest collections of Poa marcida were made in Oregon during the late 1800's, and the species was described from a 1927 collection at Sol Duc Hot Springs in Washington's Olympic Mountains. The type locality is a low elevation moist forest, as are all of the early collections. Later collections throughout its range are primarily from inland montane areas, and habitat descriptions in floras, such as Hitchcock (1973) cited above, reflect this.

Recent work by Bureau of Land Management researchers in northwest Oregon has located Poa marcida populations scattered throughout the Coast and Cascade Ranges on public lands (fig. 3a). The largest concentration of populations is in southeast Tillamook and adjacent parts of Yamhill Counties. BLM botanists first discovered Poa marcida in this area in 1978 while doing pre-harvest surveys on BLM timber lands, and have continued to discover new sites up to the present (Scofield 1982-1986). The highest peaks in this area, all supporting Poa marcida colonies, include Bald Mountain (elevation 3057 ft.), Sheridan Peak (3200 ft.), Trask Mountain (3424 ft.), Dovre Peak (2844 ft.), Bell Mountain (2602 ft.), Rye Mountain (2400 ft.), and High Peak (2800 ft.). Associated ridges, peaks, sideslopes and drainages also support Poa marcida populations. This area is referred to as the "Bald Mountain Complex" in what follows.

Poa marcida is apparently disjunct between the coastal sites and the sites on the inland ridge systems. Although Poa marcida occurs on the coast, it has not been found in lowland inland areas away from the coast. Poa marcida populations in the interior are only known from above 2000 feet. The coastal Poa marcida populations are on mountains that end precipitously at the ocean, for example Cascade Head or Tillamook Head.

Poa marcida was first reported from the Cascade Range in Oregon in 1982 by researchers working in the Mount Hood National Forest, and was discovered on adjacent BLM land in 1986 during a

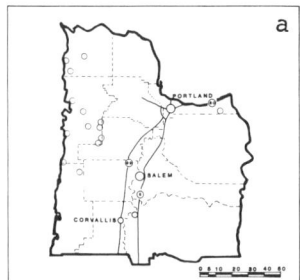
Known locations

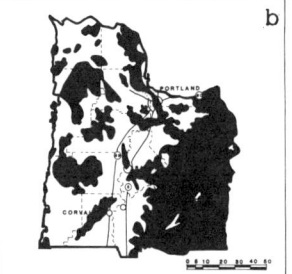
Geologic association (volcanics)

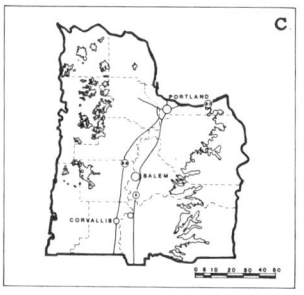
Lower elevation limit (2,000 ft.)

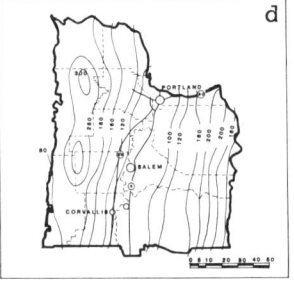
Precipitation (cm.)

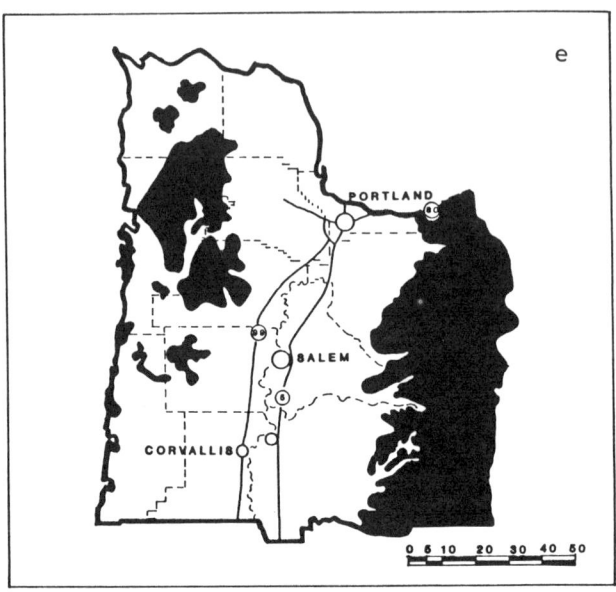
Predicted occurrence of Poa marcida.

Figure 3. Factors used to predict Poa marcida occurrence.

BLM land in 1986 during a pre-sale survey by BLM botanists. The Cascade range population is relatively small, and thus far the Bald Mountain complex of populations represents Oregon's largest and most diverse area of Poa marcida habitat.

Two sites within the Bald Mountain complex, High Peak and Sheridan Peak (including Bald Mountain), have been designated "Areas of Critical Environmental Concern" by the BLM and are managed in part to preserve habitat for Poa marcida. Of the remaining Oregon colonies, the Tillamook Head, Cascade Head, and Saddle Mountain populations are within the boundaries of State Parks or Research Natural Areas and are protected, but the rest are not, and a recent survey (Cooney 1979) of the historical locations at Garibaldi and Sand Lake reported no Poa marcida and noted disturbance from clearcutting and construction.

On the local scale of a mountain summit, Poa marcida may be common. It sometimes forms dense colonies but most often is scattered throughout a species-rich herbaceous understory as small patches of one to several hundred individual clumps. At major population sites Poa marcida can be found along game trails and in dense stands in old disturbances like skid roads.

A typical Poa marcida local distribution pattern, which occurs for example on Bald Mountain and Trask Mountain, is a high density of Poa marcida colonies just within the cover of the forest surrounding an opening or meadow. Many of the summits in the region are treeless or have a natural opening or grassland on the summit (Aldrich, 1972). Poa marcida occurs in greatest abundance in the forest immediately surrounding these summit grassy areas but is not found in the open areas themselves.

Climate

Greater amounts of precipitation fall on the ridges and peaks of the northwestern Oregon Coast Ranges than are recorded at nearby climate stations at lower elevations. Annual precipitation averages over 200 centimeters on the ridge systems where Poa marcida occurs (fig. 3d). Maximum July temperatures are normally less than 24.5 C.

A characteristic climatic feature of all the sites where Poa marcida is known to occur is a strong marine influence. This is obviously the case for coastal populations, but the climate of the ridgetop sites further inland is strikingly similar to that of the immediate coast. The ridges where Poa marcida grows are the first Coast Range peaks above 2000 feet east of the coast, and marine air, laden with moisture in the form of fog and rain, bathes the summits. Even during dry summer months, the ridges where Poa marcida grows are often foggy. This not only lowers temperatures; the fog also condenses on the forest trees, which drip water onto the understory plants, including Poa marcida.

Substrate

The upland ridge system sites where Poa marcida occurs are composed in part of intrusive Miocene basalt breccias that penetrate the surrounding Tertiary sediments (Schlicker et al. 1972). Some of the volcanics in the area represent seafloor basalt of Eocene age (Alt and Hyndman 1978). The coastal Poa marcida populations also occur on large blocks of volcanic rock separated from other such areas by many miles of sedimentary rocks (Beauleu 1971, Peck 1961). Figure 3b shows the distribution of volcanic rocks in northwestern Oregon.

Plant Communities

Herbaceous understory vegetation associated with Poa marcida populations is a rich mixture of mesic forest herbs (table II). Typically, sites are dominated by one or two herbaceous species, usually Oxalis oregana and Smilicina stellata, with as many as 50 additional herbs present in minor amounts. Grasses other than Poa marcida occurred at only low density in our plots. Two grasses showed very high constancy, Trisetum cernuum and Melica subulata. Another rare Poa, Poa laxiflora, also occurs sympatrically with Poa marcida at a limited number of sites. Cover values for dominant herbs often sum to greater than 100 percent, reflecting micro-differentiation of the understory into distinct layers (Palmer and Vanbianchi 1986).

The species that compose the understory vegetation of Poa marcida sites are characteristic of the "Tsuga/Polystichum-Oxalis stratum" of the Tsuga heterophylla vegetation zone as defined by Franklin and Dyrness (1973). For Poa marcida sites in the coastal Picea sitchensis forest zone, no substantial differences in understory occur. Coastal Poa marcida locations have essentially the same assemblage of herbs as inland ridge sites.

Table II. Plant species commonly associated with Poa marcida.

Abies procera	Linnea borealis
Acer circinatum	Listera cordata
Achlys triphylla	Lupinus latifolius
Adenocaulon bicolor	Luzula campestris
Agoseris grandiflora	Luzula parviflora
Alnus rubra	Lysichitum americanum
Anaphalis margaritacea	Maianthemum dilatatum
Anemone deltoidea	Montia siberica
Anemone lyallii	Oplopanax horridum
Arenaria macrophylla	Osmorhiza chilensis
Asarum caudatum	Oxalis oregana
Athyrium felix-femina	Petasites frigida
Berberis nervosa	Polystichum munitum
Blechnum spicant	Pseudotsuga menziesii
Bromus sitchensis	Prunella vulgaris
Calypso bulbosa	Pteridium aquilinum
Campanula scouleri	Rhododendron macrophyllum
Carex mertensii	Rosa gymnocarpa
Chimaphila menziesii	Rubus parviflora
Circaea alpina	Rubus spectabilis
Clintonia uniflora	Rubus ursinus
Collinsia parviflora	Rumex acetosella
Coptis laciniata	Smilacina stellata
Cornus canadensis	Symphoricarpos albus
Corylus cornuta	Synthris reniformis
Cynoglossum grande	Thuja plicata
Dicentra formosa	Tiarella trifoliata
Disporum hookeri	Trientalis latifolius
Disporum smithii	Trillium ovatum
Fragaria vesca	Trisetum cernuum
Galium oreganum	Tsuga heterophylla
Galium triflorum	Vaccinium membranaceum
Gaultheria shallon	Vaccinium parviflorum
Hieracium albidiflorum	Vancouveria hexandra
Iris tenax	Viola glabella
Lilium washingtonianum	Viola sempervirens

Cover of Poa marcida is negatively correlated with cover of associated herbaceous species. The most dense Poa marcida colonies form almost a turf with only a few associates. Other colonies may consist of only scattered Poa marcida and dense growth of associates. Most commonly, Poa marcida averages about 50 percent cover and a rich mixture of associated species is present (Palmer and Vanbianchi 1986).

Forest overstory characteristics for the Poa marcida population on Bald Mountain are given in table III. Cover is high, ranging from 50-100 percent. Trees on this site averaged about 75-110 years in age, determined from increment borings. Most stands with Poa marcida date from the period of the Tillamook burn or series of burns between 1875 and 1945. Note that Noble Fir is a common component at Poa marcida populations.

A characteristic feature of these rapidly growing forests is a significant amount of litterfall, which decays quickly but continually buries the understory herbs beneath a layer of mulch. Many perennials simply die back to underground parts each year and resprout through the new layers of litter. Poa marcida, however, remains as above-ground clumps while its associates

Table III. Characteristics of forest overstory at a Poa marcida site.

Species	Density (trees/ha)	DBH (m2/ha)
Abies procera	15.3	9.5
Pseudotsuga menziesii	224.2	101.1
Tsuga heterophylla	5.1	0.2

disappear for the winter. Mature clumps of Poa marcida are able to grow new tillers from under small sticks and branches that fall on them, but seedlings may be killed by larger pieces of litter. Clumps of Poa marcida, excavated from a unit to be clearcut, were rooted almost entirely in the litter layer, apparently constantly growing over the unceasing rain of branches, twigs, and leaves. Evidence (Swanson, et al. 1982) indicates litterfall in these forests is seasonal, coming mostly in fall and winter.

Population Biology

Dissection of excavated Poa marcida revealed that small size class plants in the Poa marcida populations were not vegetative offshoots of mature individuals but rather juvenile individuals and seedlings. We found only a few weak rhizomes from the clumps of Poa marcida. This meant that unlike many grasses it was possible to distinguish individual Poa marcida plants, at least in colonies of average density, and follow their fate.

Preliminary observations on the behavior of Poa marcida populations indicate that a "reverse J-shaped" (Barbour et al. 1980) size-class distribution is characteristic of these populations. Figure 4 is an example of this distribution from a plot at the Bald Mountain Poa marcida population. A majority of individuals are in the smallest size classes (Palmer and Vanbianchi 1986). Preliminary data indicate that Poa marcida individuals add an average of one to two new tillers per year (Palmer and Vanbianchi 1986).

In figure 4 the number of tillers represents the number of leafy stems or structural units per plant. Five sample periods for each size-class are shown from left to right: September 1985, March 1986, May 1986, June 1986, and July 1986. The first size-class, plants with just one tiller, includes both seedlings and juveniles that may have germinated previously but have not so far grown additional structural units. In practice, newly germinated Poa marcida seedlings are readily identified, but once growing seedlings are only arbitrarily separated from juveniles with a single tiller.

Flowering occurs in late summer, and seed are ripened and shed rapidly. Seed production varies widely from site to site but averages about 1000 seeds per square meter (Palmer and Vanbianchi 1986).

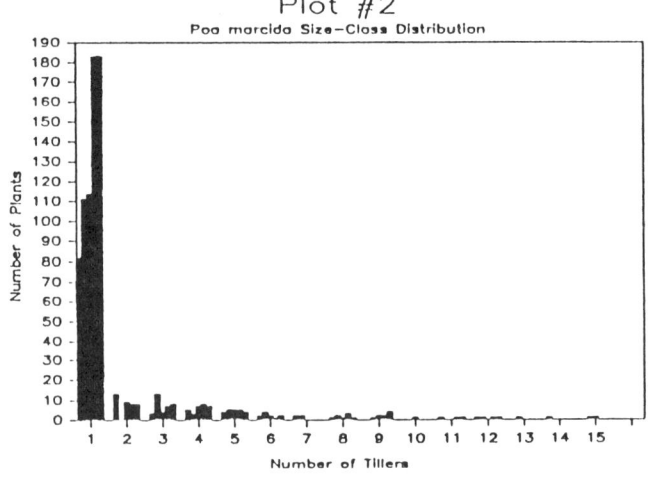

Figure 4. Poa marcida size-class distribution at Bald Mountain

Some fall germination may occur, but the most important period of seed germination begins in spring and peaks in early summer (Palmer and Vanbianchi 1986). Some seedling mortality occurs, probably from drought, during late summer; however, the majority of seedlings that are lost die during the winter. The major cause of death of seedlings during the winter is crushing by tree litter brought down by winter snows, and by mechanical injury from the snow itself. Low temperature by itself is probably not a major cause of death since *Poa marcida* clumps regularly survive burial by snow unaffected (Palmer and Vanbianchi 1986).

Disturbance and Dispersal

Perhaps the most difficult attribute of *Poa marcida* to quantify is its apparent ability to colonize disturbances in the herb community in which it grows. Past workers have noted a relationship between *Poa marcida* and disturbance (Bieley 1980, Cooney 1979). In all *Poa marcida* populations examined by the present authors there was evidence of some kind of disturbance of the understory herb layer. The most commonly observed disturbances at *Poa marcida* populations were game trails resulting from elk and deer activity; areas where, judging from droppings, animals grazed or congregated; *Aplodontia* denning and foraging areas; and human disturbances from past thinning and logging activities.

Poa marcida is able to take advantage of a reduction in competition caused by disturbance. We found numerous sites where *Poa marcida* grows very densely in a game trail, but occurs only as scattered individuals in the surrounding herbaceous understory community. Sites around tree stumps left from pre-commercial thinning in *Poa marcida* populations were often observed to support dense stands of *Poa*. Likewise, old skid roads and logging trails are favored sites for *Poa marcida*.

Elk populations in the vicinity of *Poa marcida* populations in the Oregon Coast Ranges are large enough to have a visible impact on the landscape. We have found in some populations large numbers of *Poa marcida* clumps that have been bitten off together with clear sign of elk in the same site. We have also found grass seedlings germinating on elk droppings. We collected some of this material and grew out the seedlings and they were not *Poa marcida*. However, it is probable that given a large amount of mammal activity in *Poa marcida* populations, the animals are dispersing the plant. We also have found *Poa marcida* in *Aplodontia* food caches.

DISCUSSION

Known *Poa marcida* populations are on ridge tops where moisture-laden marine air and cool temperatures maintain a high moisture, low water stress environment. Clouds moving inland southeast from Tillamook Bay are forced into a giant "bowl" formed from the high ridges that extend in an arc to the east from Tillamook Head and Saddle Mountain on the north to Cougar Mountain and Lindsey Ridge on the south. As the clouds move eastward, they run into the ridges, releasing much of their moisture. These peaks and ridges support *Poa marcida*.

The coastal *Poa marcida* locations, while lower in elevation than the inland ridge system populations, are nevertheless mountains directly on the coast, like Cascade Head. *Poa marcida* does not grow in the coastal strand, and has never been found at low elevation between the inland ridge system sites and the coastal sites. It may be that *Poa marcida* has simply not been collected in these areas, although this is probably unlikely given significant numbers of botanical surveys on timber sales in the region.

The rocks composing the ridge systems that support *Poa marcida* populations are volcanic. Nearly all *Poa marcida* in Oregon occur on volcanics. Conclusions probably can not be drawn regarding any substrate specificity of *Poa marcida*, however. The correlation could occur because the ridge systems with the appropriate elevation and climate are volcanic rocks.

Whether or not substrate is limiting *Poa marcida*, the species is still adapted to the soils on which it grows. These volcanic soils, while extremely productive forest soils (Franklin and Dyrness 1971), are generally considered nutrient-poor for plants other than forest trees, in part because the heavy rainfall leaches mobile nutrients away (Alt and Hyndman, 1978). *Poa marcida* is apparently able to grow under conditions of at least slight deficiency. *Poa marcida* leaves normally appear yellow-green in the field. When found at elk urination sites, or beneath large *Alnus rubra* (a nitrogen fixer), *Poa marcida* is typically much larger than usual and deep green, an obvious response to nitrogen supplementation (Palmer and Vanbianchi 1986).

The herb community of which *Poa marcida* is a part represents the wet end of a gradient of understory community types in the Tsuga heterophylla forest zone (Franklin and Dyrness 1973). The forest at Poa marcida populations is douglas fir (Pseudotsuga menziesii (Mirbel) Franco) with noble fir (Abies procera Rehder) common and occasionally dominant. It has a park-like aspect, with relatively few shrubs and large areas dominated by Oxalis oregana and Smilicina stellata, intermixed with patches of Polystichum munitum (Table II). Although a vegetation mosaic actually occurs, at lower elevations the Oxalis/Smilicina dominated understory gives way to an understory dominated by Acer circinatum, Vaccinium spp., Gaultheria shallon, and Rubus spp. Poa marcida does not occur under this dense shrub cover.

Poa marcida populations in the Coast Ranges are in plant communities characterizing cool wet sites and are similar in composition to the Abies procera/Achlys triphylla or Abies procera/Clintonia uniflora community types defined by Zobel et al (1976) from the H. J. Andrews Experimental Forest. The Polystichum/Oxalis community type of Franklin and Dyrness (1973) also corresponds to the herb community at Poa marcida populations (Palmer and Vanbianchi 1986).

Competitive interactions and natural herb community gap phase dynamics are poorly known in the forests of northwestern Oregon. Evidence (Palmer and Vanbianchi 1986, Cooney 1979, Bieley 1980) that disturbance is correlated with increased cover of Poa marcida indicates that competitive interactions may be important in the dynamics of these herb communities. Animal disturbance is clearly important in Poa marcida populations, but the interaction of animal disturbance with other forms of disturbance is not yet understood. In general, the relationship of understory herb community development to gaps, disturbances, and interspecific interactions is not fully known for most herb communities (Bierzychudek 1982, Collins, et al 1985, Thompson 1980, Harper 1980).

Tree thinning operations carried out at some Poa marcida populations duplicate in some ways the disturbances caused by large grazing animals. The forest canopy remains but a gap is created in the herb community. These open sites are readily colonized by Poa marcida (Palmer and Vanbianchi 1986).

Poa marcida apparently disappears from clearcut areas, due to a combination of factors. Slash burning consumes litter and slash and exposes mineral soil, a requirement for good conifer regeneration. Unfortunately, because Poa marcida is rooted in the upper litter layers, it is destroyed by slash burning. We have found Poa marcida growing in recent clearcuts on High Peak in sites that were not burned, whereas no Poa marcida could be found in adjacent burned units (Palmer and Vanbianchi 1986). Poa marcida colonies are also destroyed by being uprooted as logs are dragged over them during yarding operations, or by other ground disturbing activities associated with logging.

Environmental characteristics of Poa marcida sites change drastically following clearcutting. The change in light and temperature regimes resulting from removal of overstory trees, and a tremendous increase in sun-loving species, makes survival in a clearcut of any Poa marcida that escapes slash burning unlikely. In unburned clearcuts where we have found Poa marcida, it has always been in the shade of logs, slashpiles, or shrubs.

Poa marcida was also found in a regenerated clearcut under trees approximately 25 years of age. The site is on a game trail within .2 miles of an existing Poa marcida population. Apparently Poa marcida can recolonize clearcut and burned areas under appropriate conditions once sufficient forest development has taken place.

Poa marcida may be able to take advantage of disturbances in the forest by its ability to produce large numbers of seedlings. The age/size-class distribution shown for the Poa marcida plot in Figure 4 indicates that many seedlings and young plants are present. This "reverse J-shaped" distribution is expected in plant populations that are capable of colonizing disturbed sites (Barbour, et al 1980). The size-class distribution expressed by Poa marcida in Figure 4 shows the same form as the age structure of many other perennial herb populations (Harper 1977, Sarukhan 1974).

Age-structure can be misleading, however, and plants need to be followed through time (Harper 1977). Tamm's (1956) classic study of plant populations in Swedish forests showed, among other things, that seed germination and seedling recruitment in many plants varies considerably from year to year. Monitoring of Poa marcida populations by BLM biologists now in progress will provide data on annual variations in seedling recruitment and population structure (Palmer and Vanbianchi 1986).

Clausen, et al. (1949) studied the genus Poa in terms of its breeding behavior. It was found that in many species of Poa agamospermous reproduction accounts for 10-90 percent of the reproductive output. It is not known if Poa marcida is agamospermous.

At the present time, extant Poa marcida populations in northwestern Oregon are persisting and possibly increasing in size as they move into fairly recent disturbances. Populations continue to be clearcut, however. Key management issues are how to maintain viable Poa marcida populations, and how to encourage or assist recolonization of clearcut sites. The danger faced by many rare plants, including Poa marcida, is that they will be protected in only a tiny fraction of their range, resulting in fragmentation and loss of gene flow among populations, followed by a decline in genetic variability and eventual extinction (Hamrick 1983).

Nothing is known at the present time about gene flow among populations of Poa marcida. We may speculate that the populations in northwestern Oregon are experiencing some degree of interpopulational gene flow because they all occur on an interconnected system of ridges and peaks over which large herbivores freely migrate. The future effects on Poa marcida of the inevitable fragmentation of this interconnected system of populations remain to be seen.

ACKNOWLEDGEMENTS

We thank Jack Maze, University of British Columbia; Robert Ogilvie, British Columbia Provincial Museum; Richard Brown, Mount Hood National Forest; and the Washington Natural Heritage Program, for contributing data. This study is supported by a research contract from the Bureau of Land Management, U.S. Department of the Interior.

REFERENCES

Aldrich, F. T. 1972. A chorological analysis of the grass balds in the Oregon Coast Range. Ph.D. Thesis, Oregon State University, Corvallis.

Alt, D. D. and D. W. Hyndman. 1978. Roadside Geology of Oregon. Mountain Press, Missoula.

Barbour, M. G., J. H. Burk, and W. D. Pitts. 1980. Terrestrial Plant Ecology. Benjamin Cummings Publ. Co.

Beauleu, J. D. 1971. Geologic formations of western Oregon: Oregon Dept. Geology and Mineral Industries Bull. 70.

Bieley, P. 1980. Poa marcida 1980 field survey. Bureau of Land Management, Salem District.

Bierzychudek, P. 1982. Life histories and demography of shade-tolerant temperate forest herbs: a review. New Phytologist 90:757-776.

Chambers, K. L. 1973. Floristic relationships of Onion Peak with Saddle Mountain, Clatsop County, Oregon. Madrono 22(3):105-114.

Clausen, J., D. D. Keck, W. M. Hiesey, and P. Grun. 1949. Experimental taxonomy. Carnegie Inst. Washington Yearbook 48:95-106.

Collins, B. S., K. P. Dunne, and S. T. A. Pickett. 1985. Responses of forest herbs to canopy gaps. In: S. T. A. Pickett and P. S. White (eds.). The ecology of natural disturbance and patch dynamics. Academic Press, New York.

Cooney, C. M. 1979. Poa marcida A. S. Hitchcock 1979 field survey and status review. Bureau of Land Management, Salem District.

Detling, L. E. 1954. Significant features of the flora of Saddle Mountain, Clatsop County, Oregon. Northwest Sci. 28:52-60.

Franklin, J. F. and C. T. Dyrness. 1973. Natural Vegetation of Oregon and Wahsington. U. S. D. A. Forest Service General Technical Report PNW-8.

Hammond, P. C. and K. L. Chambers. 1985. A new species of Erythronium (Liliaceae) from the Coast Range of Oregon. Madrono 32:49-56.

Hamrick, J. L. 1983. The distribution of genetic variation within and among natural plant populations. In: Schonewald-Cox, C. M., S. M. Chambers, Bruce Macbryde, and W. L. Thomas (eds.). Genetics and Conservation, a Reference for Managing Wild Animal and Plant Populations. Benjamin Cummings Publ. Co. Harper, J. L. 1977. Population Biology of Plants. Academic Press, London.

Hitchcock, A. S. and Agnes Chase. 1950. Manual of the grasses of the United

States. U. S. D. A. Miscellaneous Publication No. 200.

Hitchcock, C. L. and A. Cronquist. 1973. Flora of the Pacific Northwest. University of Washington Press, Seattle.

Johnson, J. M. 1980. Handbook of uncommon plants in the Salem BLM district. Bureau of Land Management, Salem District.

Meinke, R. J. 1981. Threatened and Endangered Vascular Plants of Oregon: An Illustrated Guide. U. S. Fish and Wildlife Service, Office of Endangered Species. Region 1, Portland, Oregon.

Nelson, J. R. 1984. Rare plant surveys: techniques for impact assessment. Fremontia 12(3):19-23.

Nelson, J. R. 1986. Rare plant surveys: techniques for impact assessment. Natural Areas Journal 5(3):18-30.

Palmer, Rexford and Ronald Vanbianchi. 1986. Poa marcida project: Annual Report 1986. Bureau of Land Management, Salem District.

Peck, D. L. 1961. Geologic map of Oregon west of the 121st meridian; U. S. Geological Survey, Misc. Geol. Invest. Map I-325.

Peck, M. E. 1961. A manual of the higher plants of Oregon. Oregon State University Press.

Sarukhan, J. 1974. Studies on plant demography: Ranunculus repens L., R. bulbosus L., and R. acris L. II. Reproductive strategies and seed population dynamics. J. Ecol. 62:151-177.

Schlicker, H. G., et al. 1972. Environmental geology of the coastal region of Clatsop and Tillamook Counties. Oregon State Dept. Geol. and Mineral Resources Bull. 74.

Scofield, L. 1978-1985. Botanical studies annual reports. Bureau of Land Management, Salem District.

Siddal, J. L., K. L. Chambers, and D. H. Wagner. 1979. Rare, threatened and endangered vascular plants in Oregon. Oregon Rare and Endangered Plant Species Task Force.

Soper, K., et al. 1985. Rare, Threatened, and Endangered Plants and Animals of Oregon. Oregon Natural Heritage Program Data Base.

Swanson, F. J., R. L. Fredriksen, and F. M. McCorison. 1982. Material transfer in a western Oregon forested watershed. In: Edmonds, R. L. (ed.). 1982. Analysis of coniferous forest ecosystems in the western United States. US/IBP Synthesis Series 14.

Tamm, C. O. 1956. Further observations on the survival and flowering of some perennial herbs. Oikos 7:274-292.

Thompson, J. N. 1980. Treefalls and colonization patterns of temperate forest herbs. Am Midl. Nat. 104:176-184.

Zobel, D. B., A. McKee, and G.M. Hawk. 1976. Relationships of environment to composition, structure, and diversity of forest communities of the central western Cascades of Oregon. Ecol. Monogr. 46(2):135-156.

Population Dynamics of *Erysimum menziesii*, a Facultative Biennial Mustard

Ken S. Berg [1]

Abstract: Menzies' wallflower, (*Erysimum menziesii* (Hook.) Wetts.), is an endangered mustard endemic to California coastal dunes. Demographic characteristics can help explain the endangerment of populations. Size-specific survivorship, flowering and fecundity rates allow populations to be studied with non-destructive field techniques. High natural mortality in juvenile phases underscores the vulnerability of populations to human impacts.

Understanding the population dynamics of rare plants is essential for their long-term conservation. Population studies can identify vulnerable life-stages or environmental factors causing endangerment. Demographic information should be used in the assessment of potential impacts to rare plant populations and serve as a basis for developing mitigation and recovery programs. Few rare species have been the subject of population studies, so conservation and management decisions are often made without necessary information (MacBride 1979, Massey and Whitson 1980, Davy and Jeffries 1981).

This paper examines life-history characteristics to explain the endangerment of populations of a facultative biennial mustard. The non-destructive sampling methods used should be useful for studying other rare plants with similar life-histories.

Biennial Plants

Biennial plants are rare, overall. They comprise less than 2 pct of the North American flora (Hart 1977). Some families, such as cruciferae and umbelliferae, have a relatively high proportion of biennial species. Biennial plants are relatively more common in open habitats subject to intermittent disturbance or unproductive sites with sparse vegetation cover (Grime 1979, During, et. al. 1985).

Studies have shown that true biennial plants rarely occur in the wild.

Most putative biennials delay reproduction until their 3rd or 4th year in the wild. Studies on weedy facultative biennial plants have shown that size-specific survivorship, flowering and fecundity rates allow population demographics to be assessed from size and life-stage information (Werner 1975). This allows rare plant populations to be studied with non-destructive methods.

Life-history information for California rare plants is limited (Messick 1986). Examination of available taxonomic and floristic literature reveals that approximately 10 rare or endangered California plant species (Smith and York 1984) may be facultative biennials or short-lived monocarpic perennials (appendix).

Menzies' wallflower

Menzies' wallflower, (*Erysimum menziesii* (Hook.) Wetts.), is endemic to California coastal dunes. Populations of the typical form are known only from the Monterey Peninsula in Monterey County, the Ten Mile River dunes in Mendocino County, and the Samoa Peninsula in Humboldt County (Price 1986). Coastal developments and recreational impacts have eliminated and altered dune habitats throughout the species range. The species is listed as endangered by the California Department of Fish and Game and is a candidate for listing by the U. S. Fish and Wildlife Service under the Endangered Species Act (Smith and York 1984).

Menzies' wallflower is generally restricted to semi-stabilized dunes that are sparsely vegetated with native mat-forming perennial herbs and subshrubs. Low soil nutrient levels and summer drought are the primary agents that maintain sparse coastal dune vegetation (Willis and Yemm 1961). Within the dune mosaic, these sparsely vegetated areas

---

[1] Herbarium Botanist, Humboldt State University, Arcata, CA. Currently: Botanist, California Native Plant Society, 909 12th St. Suite 116, Sacramento, CA.

occur interspersed with dune hollow wetlands, barren moving dunes, stabilized shrublands and forests.

Study Site

I studied a population on the Samoa Peninsula of Humboldt Bay, near Eureka, CA (Lat. 49° 48', Long. 124° 10'). This dune system is the largest that supports Menzies' wallflower, extending 22 km from the mouth of the Mad River to the entrance of Humboldt Bay. The largest wallflower occurrences locally, are on the 6 km of dunes south of Samoa. There, native dune vegetation persists amid developments and non-native vegetation planted for stabilization.

The study population was located in a patch of native dune vegetation between the Eureka city airport and the town of Samoa. The area was selected because it appeared to be representative of other areas where Menzies' wallflower occurs and it was away from popular off-road vehicle recreation areas. Associated native perennial plants included Ambrosia chamissonis, Artemisia pycnocephala, Eriogonum latifolium, and Solidago spathulata.

METHODS

Population Monitoring

Survivorship and Flowering

In late October 1984, I located and marked 159 plants. Since seed germination occurs during December and January, all these plants were entering at least their second year of growth.

For each plant, I measured the rosette diameter and counted the number of emerged leaves. From these two measurements, I calculated a rosette size index (size index = number of leaves X rosette radius in mm). I made monthly visits for one year, to examine the condition and measure the size of each plant.

Fecundity

In July 1985, I made additional measurements on 52 reproductive plants. For each plant, I counted the number of fruits present and measured the length of each fruit. For a sample of 50 fruits, I measured the fruit length and counted the number of developed seeds present. To determine average seed weight, I weighed 5 samples of 100 seeds each.

Rosette Establishment

To examine the establishment rate of rosettes, I planted locally collected seeds into permanent field plots. In November 1984, I planted 400 seeds in 2 plots at an average density of 200 seeds/m^2. Each seed was placed in a depression approximately 5 mm deep and covered with sand. In November 1985, I examined the plots to determine establishment success.

Rosette Size and Plant Weight

To determine how rosette size relates to plant weight, I propagated a sample population of wallflowers from seed. After ten months, I harvested and cleaned the plants. For each plant, I calculated the rosette size index and obtained the green weight.

RESULTS

Rosette Size and Plant Weight

For the cultivated plants, the rosette size index was highly correlated with plant weight ($r=0.95$, $p<0.001$; $n=52$).

Survivorship and Flowering

In the wild plants, an individual's fate was related to its rosette size index in the previous fall. As rosette size increased, so did the probability that an individual would survive or bolt (figs. 1-2).

There appeared to be a critical size for reproduction. No plants less than 152 size units, and all plants greater than 352 size units in November, bolted the following January.

Once a wallflower reaches reproductive size, the probability that it will survive is very high. Ninety-one pct of the plants larger than the November reproductive size survived, compared to 67 pct for smaller plants. Ninety pct of the flowering plants survived to set seed. All fruiting plants died after setting seed.

Fecundity

Total fruit set per plant was correlated with rosette size in the previous spring (fig. 3). Average fruit set was 25 (range=5-135; S.E.=3). Seed

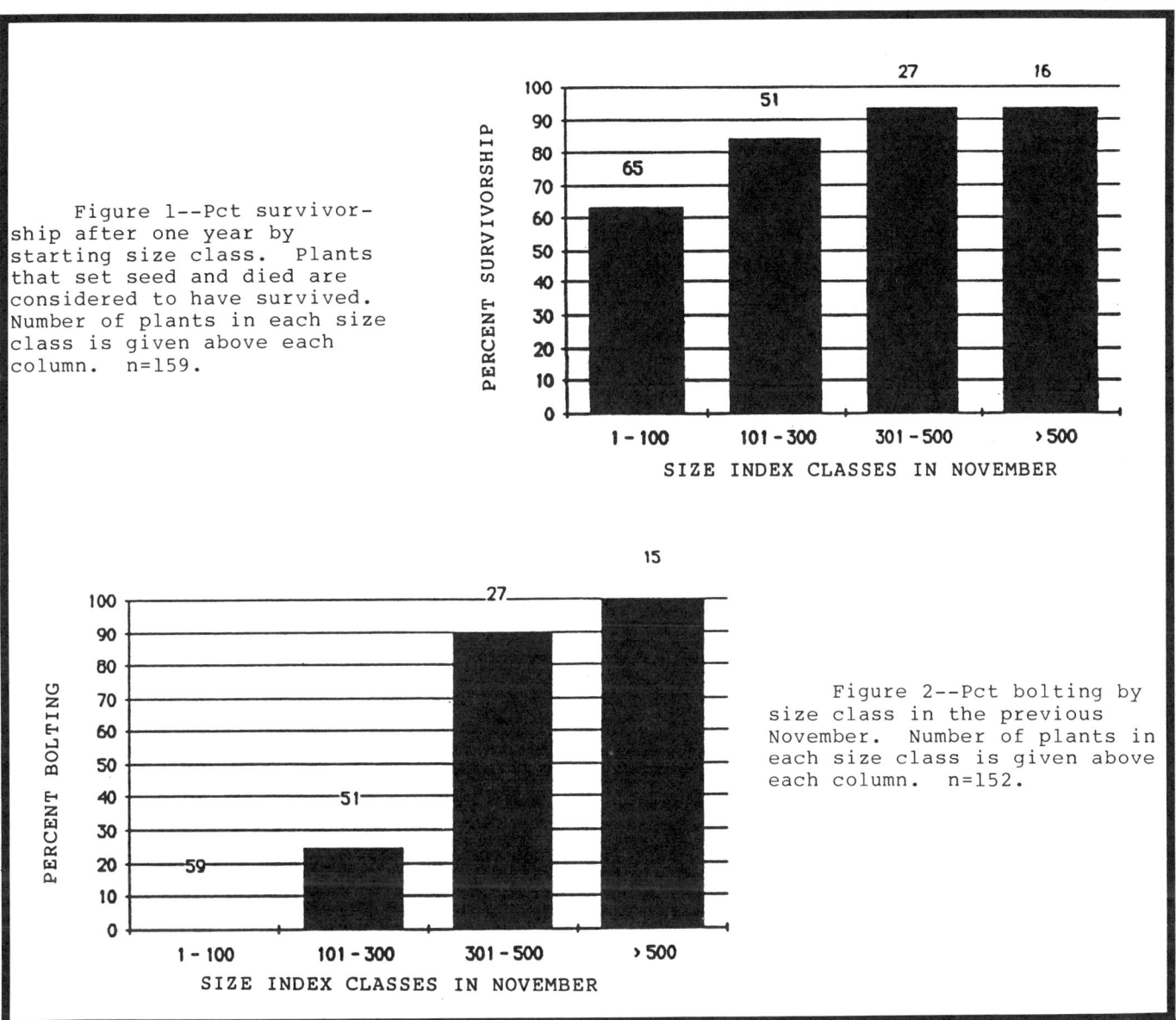

Figure 1—Pct survivorship after one year by starting size class. Plants that set seed and died are considered to have survived. Number of plants in each size class is given above each column. n=159.

Figure 2—Pct bolting by size class in the previous November. Number of plants in each size class is given above each column. n=152.

number was highly correlated with fruit length (fig. 4). Average estimated seed production per plant was 787 (range=63-2973; S.E.=79). Total estimated fecundity for the the population in 1985 was 44,076 seeds. Average seed weight was 0.57 mg.

Population Dynamics

Rosette Depletion

Only 48 pct of the original population of established rosettes remained after one year. Twenty-two pct died prematurely, while 29 pct fruited and died.

Delayed Reproduction

Many plants exhibited little growth during the study. Sixty-one pct of the surviving rosettes ended the study in the same size class that they began in. Thirty-three pct of the original population remained below reproductive size at the end of the study. Extrapolating from the 1984-85 pattern, these plants would not flower until at least their 4th year, if they survived.

Seasonal Patterns

Seasonal growth and mortality patterns appeared related to rainfall. Rosette size increased during the wet season, from November to March and from

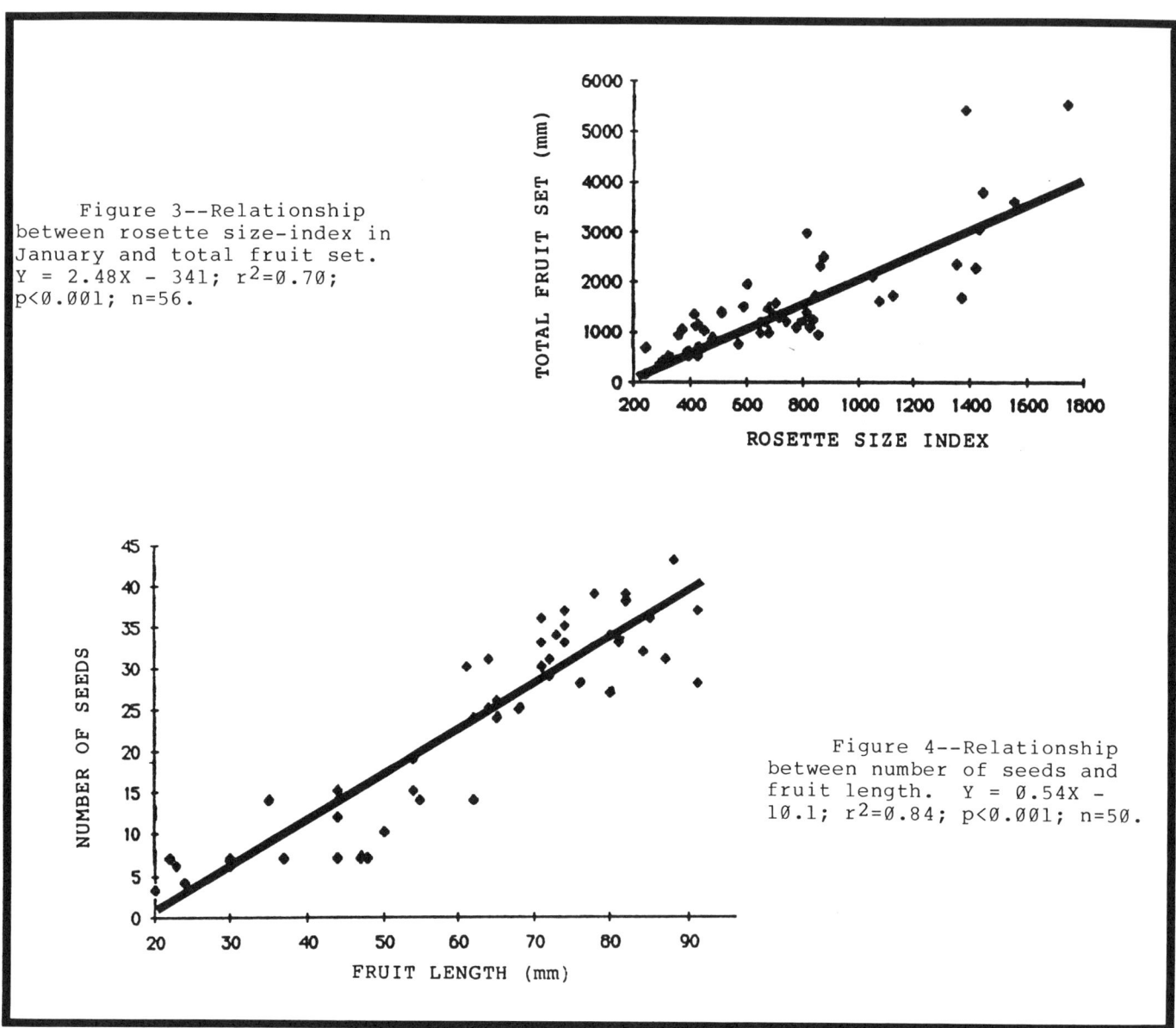

Figure 3--Relationship between rosette size-index in January and total fruit set. $Y = 2.48X - 341$; $r^2=0.70$; $p<0.001$; $n=56$.

Figure 4--Relationship between number of seeds and fruit length. $Y = 0.54X - 10.1$; $r^2=0.84$; $p<0.001$; $n=50$.

September to October. During the dry period, from April through August, rosette size decreased because many of the longer lower leaves withered. Peak mortality for all size classes occurred during the season of lowest rainfall, from June through August.

Mortality Factors

It was difficult to determine specific causes of mortality for individual plants due to the infrequency of observations. Recreational use was light, and only one plant appeared to die from trampling. Most plants appeared to die from drought, predation, or erosional effects.

Juvenile Stages

Seed germination and seedling survival exceeded 90 pct in cultivation. Field establishment of rosettes from seed was only 3 pct, after one year. All one-year-old rosettes were below reproductive size.

DISCUSSION

Size-specific Fate

The fate of an individual Menzies' wallflower is related to its size. This relationship probably occurs because rosette size is directly related to plant weight, which presumably reflects the amount of energy an individual has available for growth, maintenance and reproduction.

The size-specific values found for this study population, may not apply to other populations. Survivorship and fecundity rates may vary among populations of facultative biennials, or from year to year within populations, because of genetic or environmental variation (Klemow and Raynal 1981 and 1983, Lee and Hamrick 1983). Size-specific predictions of fate may be impossible in populations dominated by stochastic influences.

Delayed Reproduction

On sparsely vegetated dunes, reproduction is delayed because wallflowers grow slowly. A reproductive age of 2.5 or more years, is comparable with other facultative biennials from unproductive habitats (Baskin and Baskin 1979a, Evans 1982, Klemow and Raynal 1985, Kachi and Hirose 1985).

Wallflower populations are maintained by slow growing rosettes. The high mortality of small plants and death of fruiting plants prevent this rosette bank from persisting through long periods without establishment. Rosettes that remain supressed below reproductive size for several years probably have little chance of surviving to reproduce.

Critical Size and Fecundity

The critical size for flowering may be a mechanism to ensure that plants have enough energy available for both reproductive growth and adequate seed production. Once a wallflower reaches the critical size, the probability of it surviving another year is relatively high, so natural selection might favor delayed reproduction to increase fecundity (Schaffer and Gadgil 1975). Greater seed production may compensate for the higher cumulative mortality resulting from slow growth in nutrient poor habitats (Hirose and Kachi 1982).

The average estimated seed set for wallflowers is comparable to the fecundity reported for two species of facultative biennials from unproductive sites (Klemow and Raynal 1985). The large variation in wallflower seed set indicates that some plants have the potential to contribute disproportionately to the next generation. I have observed some plants which I estimated to have set 10,000 or more seeds.

Juvenile Stages

The stages between seed set and rosette establishment are critical to the overall dynamics of plant populations (Harper 1977). This study provides information which indicates that rosette establishment may be a vulnerable life stage for wild Menzies' wallflowers. Research on the dynamics of seed populations is needed.

In sparsely vegetated dunes, wallflower establishment may be controlled by rainfall. Rainfall influences germination and establishment of other facultative biennial plants in unproductive sites (Baskin and Baskin 1979, Klemow and Raynal 1985). The ability of populations to expand during favorable years is characteristic of many biennial plants (Grime 1979).

Menzies' wallflower may be generally restricted to semi-stable dunes because of a limited ability to colonize vegetated areas. Other small-seeded biennial species require bare ground for seedling establishment (Gross and Werner 1982).

Human Impacts

Humans eliminate sparse dune vegetation, and affect the dynamics of Menzies' wallflower populations, by overstabilizing some dunes with non-native plants and by destabilizing others through recreational use.

Dune Stabilization

Dune stabilization with non-native plants results in dense vegetation cover without open sand. The most commonly used plants locally are European beachgrass (_Ammophila arenaria_), yellow bush lupine (_Lupinus arboreus_) and iceplant (_Carpobrotus edulis_). Yellow bush lupine is a particularly effective dune stabilizer because it fixes atmospheric nitrogen (Holton 1980). Increased soil nutrients accelerate dune stabilization and encourage invasion by non-native plants which exclude less vigorous species (Boorman 1977).

The dense vegetation and litter cover of completely stabilized dunes may inhibit establishment of wallflowers, by reducing light needed for germination. Rosettes that become established in dense vegetation are probably slow growing, because of interspecific competition and shading, and may be prevented from reproduction if mortality is high. Other facultative biennial plants have shown these responses to growth in dense vegetation cover (Werner 1975, Rheinhartz 1984).

Trampling

Trampling, by people, livestock, horses, or off-road vehicles, is a severe threat to coastal dune vegetation around the world (Boorman 1977, Gilbertson 1983). Sparsely vegetated dunes are especially vulnerable to trampling because their openness attracts visitors and their low productivity makes recovery slow (Liddle 1975, Boorman 1975).

Coupled with the high natural mortality of small plants, trampling can greatly reduce wallflower populations. Trampling can reduce populations of dune plants by killing individuals, damaging flower stalks and reducing seed set, and by burying seed crops and lowering establishment rates (Bradshaw and Doody 1978, Maun and Lapierre 1985).

The increasing popularity of off-road vehicles is a severe threat to Menzies' wallflower populations. Off-road vehicle use on dunes reduces plant cover and species diversity, accelerates erosion, and leads to the spread of more resistant alien plants (Gilbertson 1983).

Delayed reproduction prolongs the period that individual wallflowers are exposed to trampling. A plant that delays flowering until its 3rd year (seed set at 29 months of age), must survive over 120 weekends of potentially heavy recreational impacts.

CONCLUSIONS

This study indicates that wallflower populations have the potential to sustain themselves if protected from human impacts. Fecundity is high, so if environmental conditions periodically allow high establishment, rosette populations can build up to levels that can withstand depletion from natural mortality of juvenile and fruiting plants. However, the naturally high mortality in juvenile stages underscores the need to protect populations from human impacts, especially trampling.

REFERENCES

Baskin, J. M.; Baskin, C. C. Studies on the autecology and population biology of the monocarpic perennial *Grindelia lanceolata*. Am. Midl. Nat. 102:290-99; 1979.

Berg, K. S. Population ecology of Menzies' wallflower, *Erysimum menziesii* (Hook.) Wetts., an endangered California mustard. Arcata, CA: Humboldt State University; 1986. 53 p. Thesis.

Boorman, L. A. Sand-dunes. In: Barnes, R. K., ed. The coastline. London: John Wiley; 1977.

Bradshaw, M. E.; Doody, J. P. Plant population studies and their relevance to nature conservation. Biol. Conserv. 14:223-42; 1978.

Davy, A. J.; Jeffries, R. L. Approaches to the monitoring of rare plant populations. In: Synge, H., ed. The biological aspects of rare plant conservation. Chichester: John Wiley; 1981.

During, H. J.; Schenkeveld, A. J.; Verkaar, H. J.; Willems, J. H. Demography of short-lived forbs in chalk grassland in relation to vegetation structure. In: White, J., ed. The population structure of vegetation. Dordrecht: Junk; 1985.

Gilbertson, D. The impacts of off-road vehicles in the Coorong dune and lake complex of South Australia. In: Webb, R. H.; Wilshire, H. G., eds. Environmental effects of off-road vehicles: impacts and managmenent in arid regions. New York: Springer-Verlag. 1983.

Gross, K. L. Predictions of fate from rosette size in four "biennial" plant species: *Verbascum thapsus*, *Oenothera biennis*, *Daucus carota*, and *Tragopogon dubius*. Oecologia (Berl.) 48:209-13. 1981.

Gross, K. L.; Werner, P. A. Colonizing abilities of "biennial" plant species in relation to ground cover: implications for their distribution in a successional sere. Ecology 63:921-31. 1982.

Gross, R. S.; Werner, P. A. Probabilities of survival and reproduction relative to rosette size in the common burdock (*Arctium minus*: Compositae). Am. Midl. Nat. 109:184-93.

Harper, J. L. The population biology of plants. London: Academic Press. 1977.

Hart, R. Why are biennials so few? Am. Nat. 111:792-99.

Holton, B., Jr. Some aspects of the nitrogen cycling in a northern California dune-beach ecosystem, with emphasis on *Cakile maritima*. Davis, CA: University of California; 1980. 128 p. Dissertation.

Klemow, K. M.; Raynal, D. J. Demography of two facultative biennial plant species in an unproductive habitat. J. Ecol. 73:147-67. 1985.

Liddle, M. J. A theoretical relationship between the primary productivity of vegetation and its ability to tolerate trampling. Biol. Cons. 8:251-55. 1975.

MacBryde, B. Information needed to use the Endangered Species Act for plant conservation. In: Morse, L. E.; Henefin, M. S., eds. Geographical data organization for rare plant conservation. Bronx, NY: New York Botanical Garden. 1979.

Massey, J. R.; Whitson, P. D. Species biology, the key to plant preservation. Rhodora 82:97-103. 1980.

Maun, M. A.; Lapierre, J. Effects of burial by sand on seed germination and seedling emergence of four dune species. Amer. J. Bot. 73:450-55. 1986.

Messick, T. C. Research needs for rare plant conservation in California. 1986 [These proceedings].

Munz, P. A. A California flora. Berkeley, CA: Univ. of CA Press. 1959.

Price, Robert. Doctoral Candidate, University of California, Berkeley, CA. [Letter to the author]. June 1986.

Reinhartz, J. A. Life history variation of common mullein (Verbascum thapsus) III. Differences among sequential cohorts. J. Ecol. 72:927-36. 1984.

Silvertown, J. W. Death of the elusive biennial. Nature 310:271. 1984.

Smith, James P. Jr.; York, Richard. Inventory of Rare and Endangered Vacular Plants of California. Special publication No. 1; 3rd edition. Berkeley, CA: California Native Plant Society. 1984.

Werner, P. A. Predictions of fate from rosette size in teasel (Dipsacus fullonum L.) Oecologia (Berl.) 20:197-201. 1975.

Willis, A. J.; Yemm, E. M. Braunton burrows: mineral nutrient status of the dune soils. J. Ecol. 49:377-90. 1961.

APPENDIX

Rare or Endangered Putative Biennial or Monocarpic Perennial Plants

Draba aureola
Erysimum menziesii
E. capitatum var. angustatum
E. teretifolium
Frasera umpquaensis
Sanicula maritima
S. saxatilis
S. tracyi
Streptanthus brachiatus
S. morrisonii
Thelypodium stenopetalum

Studies of the Population Biology of Prairie Bush-Clover (*Lespedeza leptostachya*)

Welby R. Smith [1]

INTRODUCTION

Lespedeza leptostachya is a declining prairie legume that is currently known to survive at approximately 30 locations in Minnesota, Iowa, Wisconsin and Illinois. Loss of habitat is the major reason for the decline, which has prompted the U.S. Fish and Wildlife Service to list the species as federally threatened (Federal Register, 1985). Several of the known populations are quite small, and consist of fewer than 100 plants [2]. Such depleted populations may require intensive management to prevent their extinction.

Before active management can commence, several difficult questions must be answered about the basic biology and life history of the species. Without such information it is not possible to prescribe a prudent management regime or even monitor the results of management. Unfortunately, the published literature (Clewell, 1966a, 1966b) (Isely, 1955) provides very little information of this type, so the impetus for the present study was a practical need for basic information. The study was designed to answer such questions as: how long do individual plants live? How quickly do they reach reproductive maturity? Do the same plants produce flowers year after year? Do individuals habitually remain dormant some years in response to environmental or biological stimuli? What, if any, population parameters are density dependent? Can the structure of a population be easily determined, and can structural dynamics be interpreted to reveal trends? It was determined that the solution to these questions would

---

[1] Minnesota Natural Heritage Program, MN Dept. of Natural Resources, Box 7, 500 Lafayette Road, St. Paul, MN 55155-4007

[2] Endangered Species Information System, U.S. Fish and Wildlife Service, Washington, D.C.

Abstract: A population of a federally threatened species, *Lespedeza leptostachya*, is described in terms of size, area and structure. Changes in these parameters over a 4 year period are summarized, and trends are analyzed. Certain aspects of life history and phenology are also summarized. Methods include annual census and mapping as well as detailed demographic sampling. Permanent plots were established to follow the fate of individuals and measure recruitment. A designed experiment involving prescribed fire was initiated to determine the response to potential management regimes. The population showed dramatic increases in nearly all population parameters as well as a distinct shift in structure toward younger age classes.

---

require long-term monitoring of a demographic nature employing permanent plots and marked individuals. An annual census was also deemed desirable because knowing the precise location and number of plants would be important for purposes of future management.

The Study Area

The study area is a prairie remnant in Jackson County, located in the southwestern corner of Minnesota. The plants occur on a north-facing slope in clay-loam soil derived from Wisconsin-age glacial till. The site has a long history of cattle grazing commencing soon after settlement in the 1880's and continuing intermittently until 1952 when the site was acquired as an addition to Kilen Woods State Park. Once grazing ceased, weeds were perceived as an increasing problem and the site was sprayed repeatedly with the herbicides 2,4,D and 2,4,5,T. In 1978, general spraying was replaced by spot spraying, but all spraying was curtailed in 1981. Beginning in 1976, management for control of weeds was supplemented by prescribed burns conducted during the dormant season and early in the growing season. In 1978, *L. leptostachya* was discovered at the site by the park manager, and in 1983 the site was designated a State Scientific and Natural Area. A management plan was prepared in 1983 that resulted in fire management being curtailed pending an evaluation of the effects of fire on the population. Since 1983, weed control has been effected by hand pulling.

The Species

Lespedeza leptostachya is an herbaceous perennial which may reach one meter in height. It has numerous small trifoliate leaves covered with a dense pubescence. Plants usually produce a single unbranched stem, but occasionally a plant will produce 2 or even 3 stems which may branch near the middle. Mature plants may produce both chasmogamous and cleistogamous flowers in slender axillary spikes. Flowers appear in mid-summer and by fall produce legumes bearing one seed.

METHODS

In August, 1982, the population of *L. leptostachya* at Kilen Woods State Park was crudely mapped and censused. It became evident that the plants were somewhat scattered, but with two discrete concentrations about 150 meters apart. The larger concentration occurred near the top of a small knoll, and was separated from the smaller concentration by two small ravines. There were no plants found in the intervening area. Each concentration was presumed to function as an independent population, although the actual degree of reproductive isolation is not known. The current study area was delineated to encompass the boundaries of the larger concentration or "population". The area measured 26 x 30 meters, and was subdivided into a grid of 780 plots, each one square meter in size.

Census

Beginning in 1983, and continuing through 1986, the site was visited annually in late August (at the peak of seed production and vegetative growth) for data collection. During the course of each visit, the entire study area was censused, and the number of plants present in each plot was recorded. This constituted the annual census.

Demographics

Demographic data were recorded along an east-west transect through the center of the study area. The transect consisted of 30 contiguous plots, thereby forming a belt transect 30 meters long and 1 meter wide. The transect included the densest portion of the population as well as the sparsely occupied edges. There were also unoccupied areas along the transect.

Within the demographic transect, each individual plant was located and assigned a unique set of map coordinates based on an x, y grid system. This was accomplished using a 1 square meter collapsible frame with a cross-bar graduated in 1 centimeter increments (Appendix). The frame was assembled in succession over each of the 30 plots in the transect and data were recorded. Data included the height of each stem, as well as the height of the inflorescence and the number of inflorescence branches (for reproductive individuals). In each successive year during late August, the individual plants were relocated and comparable data were recorded.

When an individual plant was not relocated at its previously mapped coordinates it was recorded as "not seen". Rarely could actual mortality be determined because of the possibility of biologically induced dormancy. There was also the possibility that non-fatal herbivory had removed the stem, but left the root to resprout the following year. However, if an individual was not found at its assigned coordinates for two or more consecutive year, mortality was presumed.

Individuals appearing where no plant was previously mapped were considered recruits. Since *L. leptostachya* does not normally reproduce vegetatively, these recruits were invariably seedlings, and were designated as such if they conformed to the gross morphological parameters of a seedling. Each recruit was assigned map coordinates and added to the data base.

On April 22, 1986, a designed experiment was incorporated into the ongoing research. Prescribed dormant-season fire was introduced as a potential management tool for the purpose of maintaining the vigor of the population as well as the structure of the associated plant community. Three plots along the demographic transect were randomly chosen to receive the burn treatment and 3 plots were randomly chosen to receive no treatment. Each burned and unburned plot included a buffer area of at least one meter in each direction to minimize edge effect. The burn was conducted using a back fire ignited with a drip torch. Control was accomplished using a wet-line layed down with the use of a pump truck. For practical purposes, the entire prairie was burned except for the control plots and their buffer.

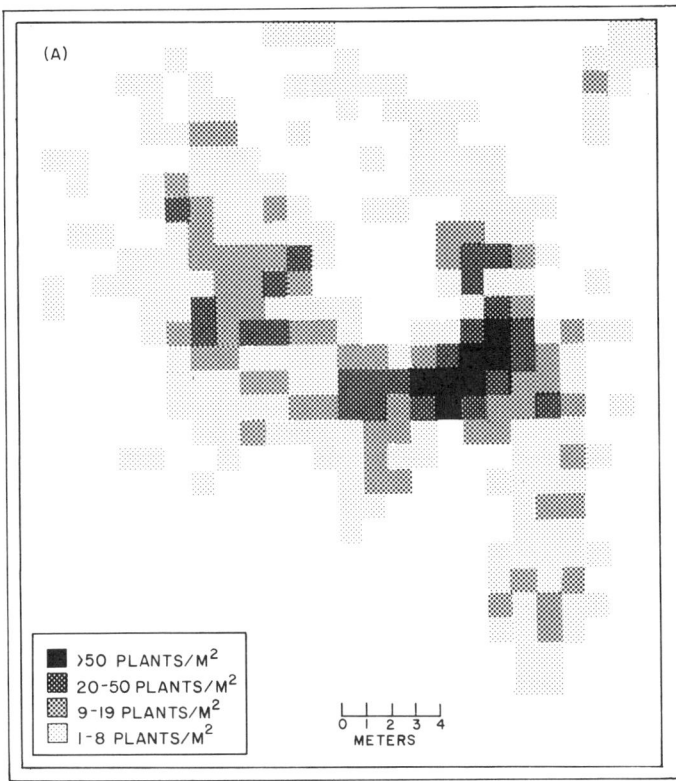
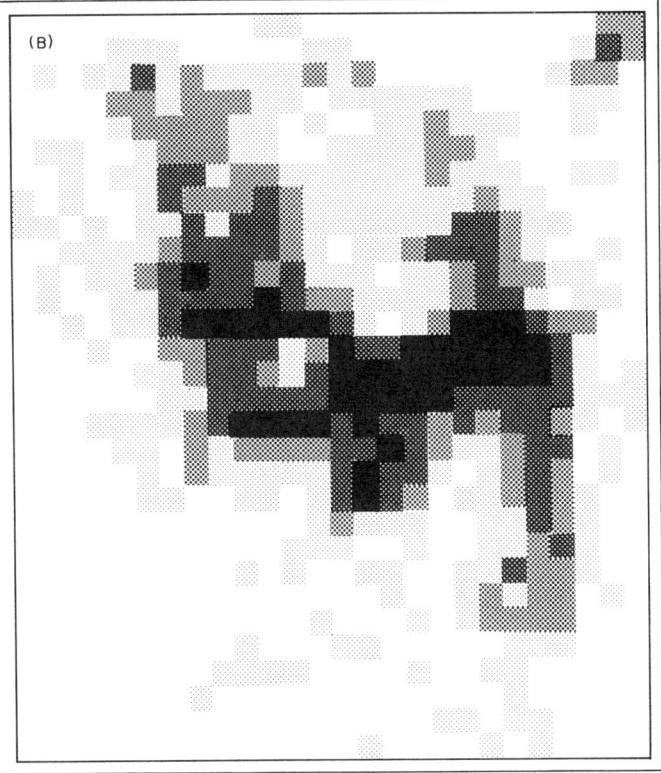

Figure 1. Density and areal extent of L. leptostachya in study area: (A) 1983, (B) 1986.

RESULTS

Census

The annual census revealed a rapidly expanding population (fig. 1) with large annual increases in the number of individuals:

Year:	No. of individuals	Pct. increase
1983	2,514	-
1984	3,318	32 percent
1985	5,999	40 percent
1986	7,246	21 percent

The number of plots occupied by the plants also increased each year:

Year:	No. of plots occupied	Pct. increase
1983	261	-
1984	291	11 percent
1985	411	40 percent
1986	413	1 percent

Actually, the increases were somewhat greater than the figures indicate because after the first year the population expanded beyond the study area. The plants that appeared outside the study area were not counted annually, or included in the census, but were estimated to number approximately 700 by 1986. The population density within the study area also increased, with the average density rising from 9.6 plants/m^2 in 1983 to 17.5 plants/m^2 in 1986. Actually, the final figure would be somewhat lower if the expansion outside the study area was considered. The maximum density recorded in any single plot in 1983 was 98 plants. The number had risen to 152 plants by 1986 and does not appear to have leveled off.

Observations indicate that newly occupied plots are typically adjacent to plots with one or more reproductive age plants. This pattern of increase in the spatial distribution indicates that the seeds are not widely dispersed, but fall to the ground and germinate in the immediate vicinity of the parent plant. This is also attested to by the remarkably high densities seen near the center of the population where the number of reproductive plants is greatest.

Demographic

Four years of demographic data are now available, but additional data is needed before analysis would be useful. However, the available data can be summarized to reveal some interesting

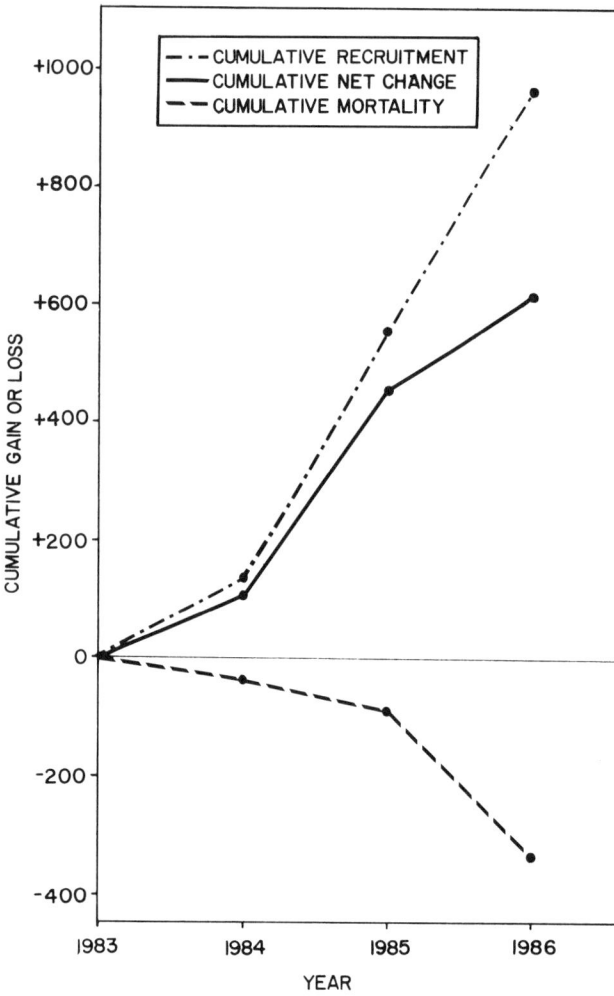

Figure 2. Population dynamics of L. leptostachya in demographic transect.

trends. The total number of plants in the demographic transect has increased from 305 in 1983 to 834 in 1986, a 273 percent increase. This correlates closely with the 288 percent increase in the population as a whole. The dynamics of the increase are indicated by figure 2, which shows the overall net change measured against cumulative recruitment and mortality.

Individual seedlings that germinated and died between annual sampling dates were, of course, never observed and are therefore not represented in either recruitment or mortality statistics. Therefore, recruitment refers only to those seedlings that survived their first growing season. Likewise, mortality refers only to those individuals that died after surviving their first growing season.

The phantom group of seedlings that are too short-lived to be recorded by an annual sampling regime present an interesting data gap. The dynamics of their activity can only be measured by resorting to a shorter sampling interval of perhaps 1-2 weeks. Such a study is now underway by the author, but results are not yet available.

Knowing the changes in the population structure is also important to understanding the significance of the population increase. In this regard, a breakdown by age class would be desirable. But the only plants that could be positively aged are those that appeared as seedlings during one of the four sampling years. However, all of the plants, even those whose age is unknown, can be assigned to one of four general classes similar to the "life states" described by Harper (1977). In the case of L. leptostachya, the life states may correspond more closely to size and reproductive classes than age classes. I have termed these life states seedling, juvenile, sub-adult and flowering. Although this classification is somewhat artificial, it provides a useful index by which to measure changes in the population structure.

Seedling Life State

Seedlings are individuals that arise from seeds and have lived no more than one season. Individual specimens of L. leptostachya can be positively identified as seedlings only by the distinctive cotyledonous leaves which are often retained through August (fig. 3). Seedlings which have lost their cotyledonous leaves can usually, but not always, be identified by their short stems (usually 2-8 cm in height) few leaves (typically 3-5), undeveloped root system (not easily seen without sacrificing the plant) and thin, wire-like stem.

Juvenile Life State

Individuals in their second growing season have entered the juvenile life state, and may remain in this state for 2 or more years (fig. 4). Plants in this state do not posses cotyledonous leaves, but in other respects may appear similar to well developed seedlings. However, juvenile plants are typically taller (6-12 cm), have more leaves (usually 4-8), better developed root systems and thicker stems.

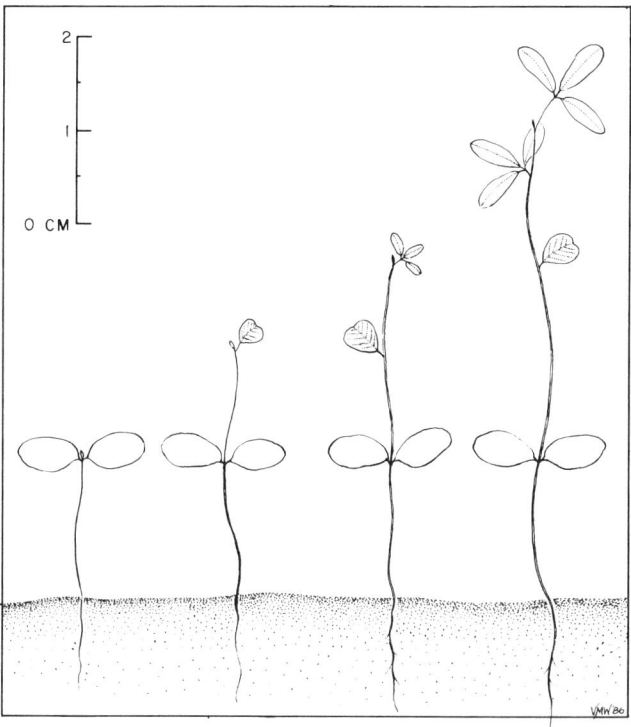

Figure 3. Various stages in the development of 4 seedlings of L. leptostachya.

Figure 4. Examples of the three post-seedling life states of L. leptostachya: (A) juvenile, (B) sub-adult, (C) flowering.

Sub-Adult Life State

Sub-adult plants may be morphologically similar to robust juveniles, but have taller stems (13-20+cm), more leaves (usually 7-12) and greater general development (fig. 4). However, by definition sub-adults lack an inflorescence and therefore have no reproductive potential. This is the life state from which flowering plants are recruited. Rarely a sub-adult plant will produce 2 stems (both unbranched) that arise from opposite sides of the root crown. Sub-adult plants may, on occasion, revert to the juvenile state for 1 or rarely 2 years.

Flowering Life State

All plants possessing an inflorescence are considered to be in the flowering life state. However, plants first recruited into this state may produce only a few flowers which may not develop into mature seeds. Older individuals may produce up to 3 stems with 200-400 flowers per stem. Individuals can be relatively large (20-100 cm tall) with numerous leaves (20 or more per stem) (fig. 4). On occasion, a flowering state plant will revert to a non-flowering sub-adult state for 1 or 2 years. But typically a flowering state plant will produce flowers (and seeds) year after year, with older plants generally producing more seeds and taller stems than do younger plants. There were no observed cases of plants habitually "resting" or becoming dormant the year after producing a large seed crop. On the contrary, the occasional reverting to a lower life state is believed to be a response to some unperceived stress, such as root damage or pathogen, possibly in combination with an environmental stimuli such as drought, frost, etc. This would presumably reduce the vigor of the affected individual resulting in a diminished capacity for vegetative and floral production. Likewise, there was no indication of any synchronous or cyclical pattern to flowering except for normal seasonality. However, continued observation may reveal otherwise. There was no case of individual plants progressing from the seedling state to the flowering state during the 4 years of the study. It therefore appears that plants in this population require at least 5 years to reach reproductive maturity, and possibly much longer.

By using these four life states to define the population structure, a comparison has been made of annual changes (fig. 5).

As the population grew, every life state increased in number, but the rate of increase in the seedling and juvenile life states was greater than the sub-adult and flowering states. This resulted in a distinct shift in the population structure toward earlier, and presumably younger, life states. However, it appears that the declining proportion of flowering plants is still adequate to maintain a high proportion of seedlings in the population, provided mortality rates remain constant. Furthermore, a continued influx of seedlings should, in time, fuel recruitment into each life state and maintain a healthy population.

Another interesting comparison is the survival rate for each life state (fig. 6). This rate can be expressed in terms of "half-life". For example, of all the seedlings present at the end of the 1983 growing season, one-half survived until 1986, resulting in a half-life of 3 years. The juvenile life stage has a projected half-life of 5.5 years, the sub-adult 6.5 years, and the flowering state 7.0 years. However, the half-life projections for the non-seedling states are based on mixed groups of cohorts, and as such are not directly comparable.

The results of the prescribed burn experiment are incomplete. Data must be gathered for one additional season before analysis or summation will be meaningful.

Observer impact was a serious concern from the beginning of the study, especially considering the threatened status of the species. If the impact of conducting the study were to cause more damage than the value received from the data, then the purpose of the study would be defeated. As it turned out, soil compaction and direct physical damage to the plants were the greatest impact of our presence, but the actual effects appeared to be minimal. Significant soil compaction occurred only in a small area downslope of the demographic transect where the observer would stand while recording data. Likewise, physical

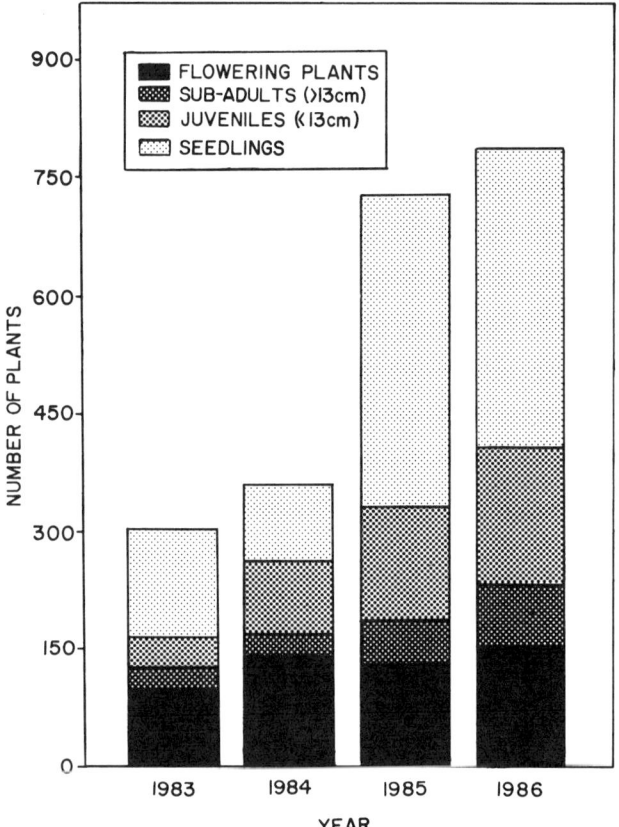

Figure 5. Population structure of L. leptostachya for a 4 year period.

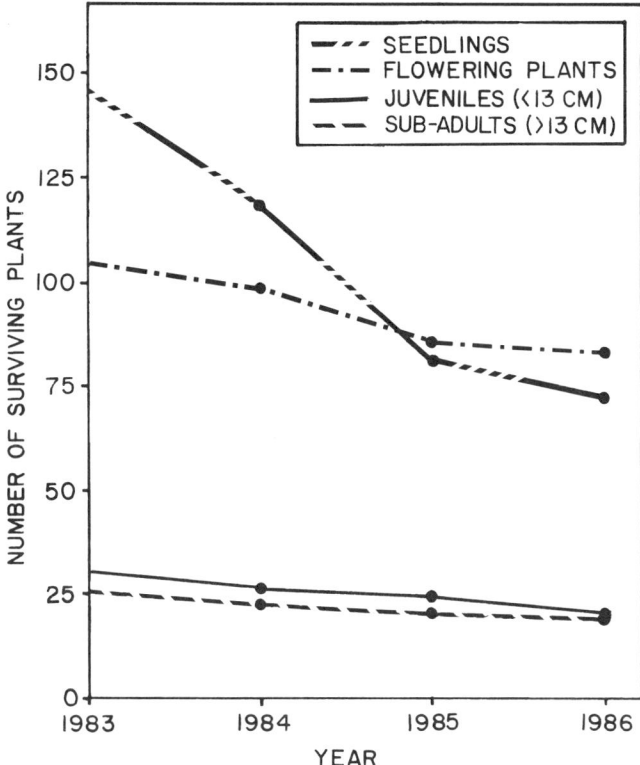

Figure 6. Survivorship curve and depletion curves for 4 life states in demographic transect through population of L. leptostachya. Based on a total of 306 plants present in 1983.

damage to the plants was not great because the plants proved remarkably resilient. Even if stepped upon, the stems would rarely break. Also, sampling was conducted near the end of the growing season when the roots had ample food reserves and the stems were no longer needed to support photosynthesis.

DISCUSSION

The stated goals of this research have proven to be reachable with the methods employed, but additional data are clearly needed before many conclusions can be reached. However, some very basic life history traits and population characteristics have been revealed, and will become even clearer with the completion of this study in 3 years. Other questions concerning seedling dynamics and the response of the population to fire will, hopefully, be answered as well.

Management implications are already apparent. But the fact that the population increased so dramatically following the cessation of fire probably raises more questions than it answers, given that the species is endemic to a fire-maintained habitat. However, additional data may reveal that fire does, in fact, play an important role in maintaining the population, although the effects may be selective and not readily apparent.

Where interpretation of the data is concerned, the frame of reference does not extend beyond this population because of the lack of off-site replicates. And yet it is difficult to avoid the conclusion that for a threatened species, L. leptostachya has a remarkable capacity for rapid and sustained population increases. This is especially encouraging to all of those who are working so hard for the recovery of this species.

ACKNOWLEDGEMENTS

I would like to acknowledge the assistance of the following individuals: Joyce Bender, Carmen Converse, Alexis Duxbury, John Erickson, Lowell Jaeger, Blair Joselyn, Wendi Pennings, Nancy Sather, Ed Valentine, Vera Wong.

REFERENCES

Bradshaw, M. E. 1980. Monitoring grassland plants in Upper Teesdale, England. In: The Biological Aspects of Rare Plant Conservation, Ed: H Synge. John Wiley and Sons, New York.

Clewell, A. F. 1966a. Native North American species of Lespedeza. Rhodora 68:359-405.

Clewell, A. F. 1966b. Natural history, cytology, and isolating mechanisms of the native North American Lespedezas. Tall Timbers Research Station Bulletin, No. 6, Tallahassee, Florida; 30pp.

Federal Register 50 (235):49967. December 6, 1985

Harper, J. L. 1977. Population Biology of Plants. Academic Press, New York. 892pp.

Isely, D. 1955. The leguminosae of the North Central United States. V. II. Hedysareae. Iowa State College Journal of Science 30:94-95.

APPENDIX

The need to periodically relocate individual plants within a specific area requires that each plant be permanently

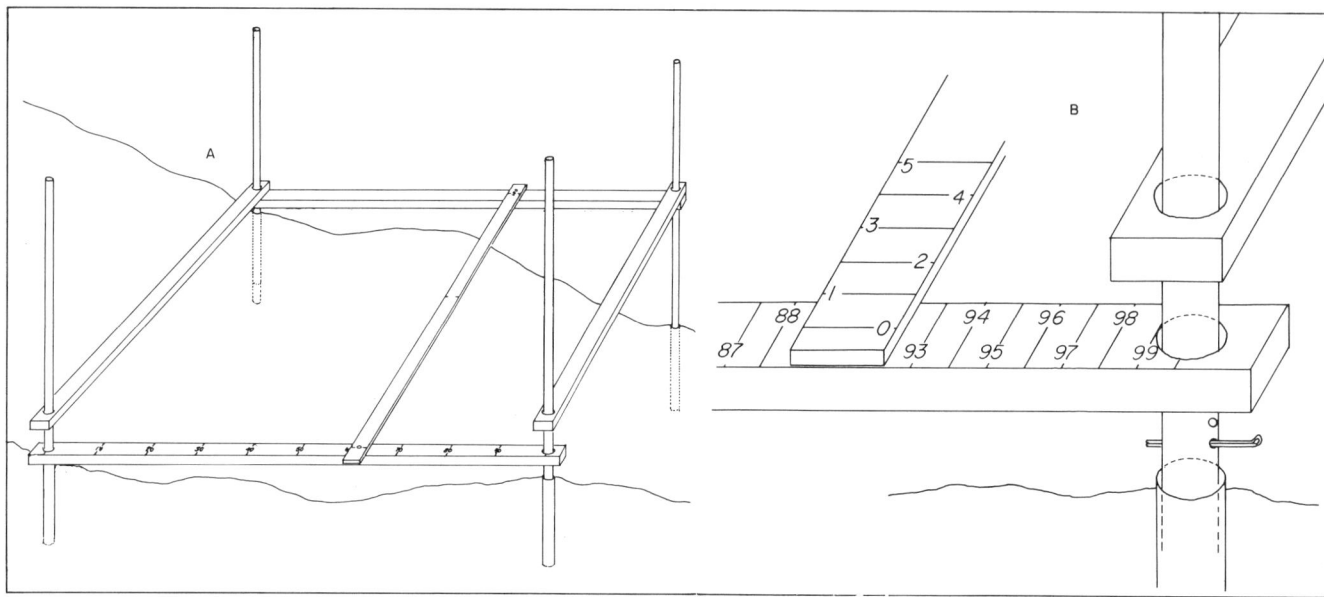

Figure 7. Bi-coordinate sampling apparatus used to locate positions of individual plants: (A) Frame fully assembled as it appears in actual use. (B) Detail of corner construction.

marked, labeled or otherwise identified. In the case of L. leptostachya, there is no perennating above ground part to tag, and markers placed in the ground at the base of the plants would risk damaging the roots, considering the high density of the population.

To solve these problems, a bi-coordinate mapping system was employed to describe the points at which each stem emerges from the ground. This eliminates the need to physically mark the plants. To accomplish this task, each square meter plot was subdivided into square centimeter subplots, which were each assigned unique map coordinates on an x, y grid. The grid was not physically placed over the plot, but was represented on a large scale map. This required only 4 permanent reference points to be established at the corners of each plot. This method proved very satisfactory largely because the annual shoot of L. leptostachya emerges from essentially the same point each year. Identification was more than 95 percent reliable.

The apparatus used to determine the coordinates of each plant was loosely adapted from Bradshaw (1980), and is illustrated in figure 7. It consists of a square meter frame made from 1 x 3 inch lumber. A 5/8 inch diameter hole was drilled near the end of each side, one meter apart (center to center). This allowed 1/2 inch diameter metal poles (electrical conduit works well) to pass vertically through the holes and thereby connect each corner. When the frame was in use, the connecting poles were fitted into 3/4 inch diameter poles (cut to 10 inch lengths) which had been sunk flush with the ground. In this manner, the frame was re-assembled in precisely the same position each year to guarantee reproduceable results. The base stakes were put in using a plumb to assure that the plots were truely level and not following contours of the terrain. A compass was used to assure squareness, but a large carpenters square would work well. When the frame is being assembled over each plot, cotter pins are inserted into pre-drilled holes in the connecting poles to level the frame. A square, level frame allows the final data to be accurately displayed on a plane map.

The north and south margins of the frame represent the x axis, and are graduated into centimeter increments. A moveable cross-bar represents the y axis when lined up perpendicular to the north and south margins. The cross-bar is also graduated into centimeters (any commercially available meter stick can be used as the cross bar). The coordinates of each plant within the frame is then determined by moving the cross-bar to a position directly above the base of the plant (a plumb can be used for added precision). The x coordinate is the point at which the plant (or a vertical line extending from the base of the plant) intersects the cross-bar. The y coordinate is the point at which the cross-bar intersects the frame.

Population Dynamics of the Tecate Cypress

Anthony T. Dunn [1]

Abstract: Research conducted in San Diego County revealed an inverse relationship between fire frequency and the distribution and density of Cupressus guadalupensis var. forbesii. The Tecate Cypress is an obligate seeding species, dependent upon fire to release seeds stored in its cones. Analysis of cone production and seedling mortality rates indicated that the cypress does not reach full reproductive maturity until 35-40 years of age. An abrupt reduction, and in some cases, elimination of cypress occurred in areas experiencing fires of a higher frequency.

Though there is no doubt that fire has been an integral part of the California landscape for millions of years (Hanes 1971, Raven and Axelrod 1978), there has been much speculation as to its exact role in the pre-European chaparral environment (Aschmann 1959, Dodge 1975, Lewis 1973, Minnich 1983). Still, virtually no one has looked to the ecology of the chaparral plants themselves as a guide to understanding the natural, pre-human fire environment. Though this project was undertaken primarily with the intent of studying the population dynamics of the Tecate cypress itself, it also sheds considerable light on the nature of the pre-historic fire environment and the changes that have taken place since European settlement--changes that may threaten the cypress's survival.

DESCRIPTION AND RANGE

The Tecate cypress (Cupressus guadalupensis var. forbesii [Jeps.] Beauchamp) is a small, attractive coniferous tree generally less than 10 meters tall. It displays the eglandular foliage characteristic of the coastal cypresses and the exfoliating, cherry red bark of its close relative, the Guadalupe cypress (C. guadalupensis Jeps.). Like many of the other species of Cupressus in California, the Tecate cypress is not common within the limits of its range, but occurs in widely scattered and isolated "floristic islands" in the chaparral of southern California and Baja California Norte. The Tecate cypress ranges from an isolated stand east of San Quintin, Mexico to the extreme northern end of the Santa Ana Mountains of Orange County, ranging in elevation from near sea level to over 1300 meters on Cerro El Cipres, east of San Vicente, Mexico. Between the northernmost and southernmost stations there are about 15 known populations (fig. 1), and it is possible that there are populations in Baja California yet to be discovered. In California, the Tecate cypress is found only on Guatay Mountain, Otay Mountain and Tecate Peak in San Diego County, and Sierra Peak in Orange County.

Figure 1--Distribution of the Tecate Cypress.

---

[1] San Luis Obispo, CA

FLORISTIC ASSOCIATIONS

Considering that the sites studied in this report are at the northern end of the cypress's range, the floristic associations studied may be somewhat atypical for the species as a whole. Armstrong (1966) lists Rhus integrifolia (Nutt.) Benth. & Hook., Populus fremontii Wats., Trichostema lanatum Benth., Ceanothus cuneatus (Hook.) Nutt. ex T. & G., Rhamnus crocea var. insularis Sarg., Heteromeles arbutifolia (Ait.) M. Roem. and Cneoridium dumosum (Nutt.) Hook. as the principal species associated with the southernmost Tecate cypress stand near Rancho El Cipres. In Canon de Pinitos, about 45 km south of Ensenada, Arctostaphlos pungens H.B.K., Adenostoma fasciculatum H. & A., Xylococcus bicolor Nutt., Quercus dumosa Nutt. and Pinus muricata D. Don. are listed as occurring in association with the Tecate cypress (Epling and Robison 1940).

In southern California, the Tecate cypress is found with a wide variety of chaparral species, many of which are of extremely limited range, having evolved in floristic isolation with the cypress. The chaparral species associated with the Tecate cypress in southern California can be generally divided into four groups: 1) truly wide-spread species, including Adenostema fasciculatum, Arctostaphlos glandulosa Eastw., Heteromeles arbutifolia, Cercocarpus betuloides Nutt. ex T. & G., Dendromecon rigida Benth., Quercus dumosa, and Malosma laurina Nutt. ex Abrams; 2) wide-spread species with regional varieties, including Ceanothus tomentosus Parry ssp. olivaceous (Jeps.) Munz, C. greggii Gray ssp. perplexans (Trel.) Beauchamp and Pickeringia montana Nutt. ssp. tomentosa Abrams; 3) regional or "southern" species, including Cercocarpus minutiflorus Abrams, Cneoridium dumosum, Chamaebatia australis (Bdg.) Abrams, and Xylococcus bicolor; and 4) endemic or rare species, including Lepechinia cardiophylla Epl. and Astragalus brauntonii Parish on Sierra Peak, Fremontodendron mexicanum A. Davids, Arctostaphlos otayensis Wies. & Schreib., Ceanothus otayensis McMinn, Lepechinia ganderi Epl., Lotus crassifolius (Benth.) Greene var. otayensis Moran and Calochortus dunnii Purdy on Otay Mt., and Solanum tenuilobatum Parish, Calochortus dunnii and Lathyrus splendens Kell. on Tecate Peak (Dunn 1984, Dunn 1985).

REPRODUCTIVE ECOLOGY

Methods

One of the objectives of this study was to sample as many different cypress age groups as possible, and as a result, some sites were subjected to more extensive sampling than others. Field work on Guatay Mountain was carried out in July of 1983, while sampling on Tecate Peak and Otay Mountain was conducted in July and August of 1984. Sampling consisted of plots run adjacent to a 15 meter line intercept transect, placed parallel to elevation contours. Plot size was determined by the density of the vegetation and varied from four 1 m^2 plots per transect on dense regeneration to 31 m^2 rectangular plots on less dense, mature sites. The 31 m^2 plots were also used for measuring the standing dead stems on recently burned sites. All vegetation within each plot was tabulated as to species, height, cover, and in the case of mature cypress, stem diameter at 10 cm above ground.

Fire Adapted Morphology

Mutch (1970) discusses some of the morphological, physiological and life history characteristics that can be used to indicate the relative fire dependency of a species or ecosystem, suggesting that flammability may be directly related to dependence on recurrent fires. The Tecate cypress and its associated community exhibit a number of distinct adaptations that indicate a strict dependence on not merely recurrent fires, but fires of a particular frequency.

First of all, the Tecate cypress itself exhibits a number of morphological characteristics that encourage flammability. The foliage of the cypress is highly resinous and is extremely flammable when dry. The bark of the tree is at all ages very thin, leaving the cambium unprotected (Vogl and others 1977), virtually insuring the death of the tree when burned, even if it is not consumed by the fire.

The mixed chaparral habitat of the cypress insures the presence of a fuel ladder into the cypress canopy when the trees are at their reproductive peak (age 40+ years). Before this age, the biomass of the community is lower, and there is considerably less dead material in and under the canopy. At about age 40 years, the cypress begin completely overtopping the shrub species, limiting the availability of light to the shrubs and causing what I refer to as "exclusion

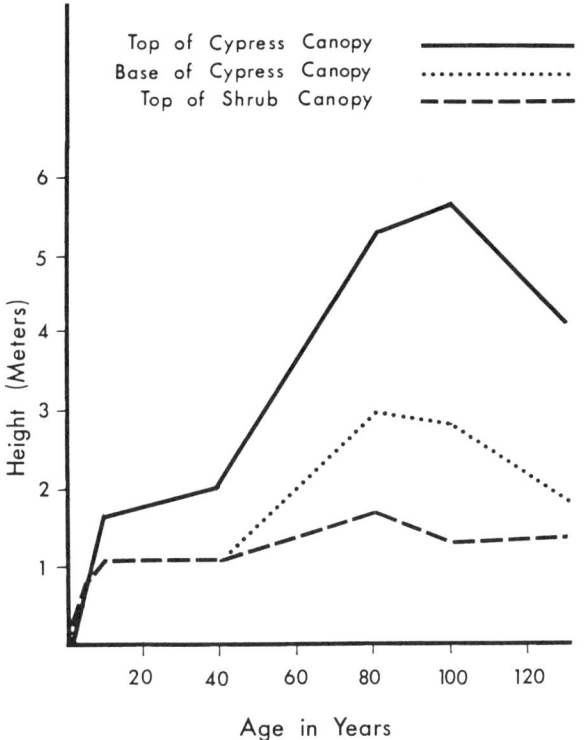

Figure 2--Mean heights of the cypress and shrub canopies by age.

mortality." This period, when the base of the cypress canopy is at about the same level as the top of the shrub canopy (fig. 2), is the time of greatest flammability in the stand. Exclusion mortality produces a considerable amount of highly flammable standing dead fuels that, along with the still living brush, is capable of carrying fire into the cypress canopy. From about 80 years onward, however, the flammability of cypress stands may decline somewhat as exclusion mortality produces an essentially single species "climax" almost completely devoid of understory. Fires occurring under non-extreme conditions may fail to carry into the cypress, as appears to be the case on Guatay Mountain where 135 year old trees are surrounded by brush that is only about 40 years old.

Closed-Cone Habit

The Tecate cypress belongs to the class of chaparral species referred to as obligate seeders, unable to stump sprout after fire and relying entirely on seed for reproduction. Like the "fire pines" and the other cypress species in California, the Tecate cypress has evolved serotinous cones that remain unopened on the tree for many years, until the occurrence of fire forces them to open. Typically, a fire passing through a stand of cypress consumes the entire canopy. Upon exposure to flame, the resin contained in the cones boils and ignites. Within minutes, the entire outer surface of the cone chars and ceases to burn (Armstrong 1977), insulating the seeds within from the extreme heat of the fire. This heat, however, serves to break the resinous seal between the scales of the cone, causing them to separate. The cones continue to open after the fire has passed and begin depositing seed on the bare mineral soil, ideal for cypress germination. Cone production begins at about 5-7 years of age, but is sporatic until the trees reach about 30 years of age.

Reproductive Capacity

In order to determine the relative reproduction of the Tecate cypress, two recently burned stands (1979 and 1982) were sampled on Otay Mountain in 1984. However, since there were no other recently burned stands in San Diego County, data collected by Zedler (1977) and Armstrong (1966) has been incorporated into this report in order to fill out the reproductive curve for the species (fig. 3, and table 1).

The observed reproduction rate at maturity of 1400 percent of pre-fire density (as shown in fig. 3) would cause immense crowding in the stands without a high juvenile mortality rate to compensate for the overabundant regeneration. Preliminary data from Otay Mountain indicates a mortality rate as shown in figure 4 (Dunn 1984). Initial mortality rates are very high, characteristic of many obligate seeding species, and gradually taper off to virtually zero after about 50 years. Data collected by Zedler [2] indicates a similar pattern. Before intraspecific competition reaches its peak at about 40-60 years of age, the major factors (beside weather) controlling the success or failure of reproduction are tree density and age.

---

[2] Zedler, Paul H. Population studies in a fire-adapted species of *Cupressus*. Unpublished transcript of a paper presented at AIBS Meeting, August 29, 1972; [Location unknown].

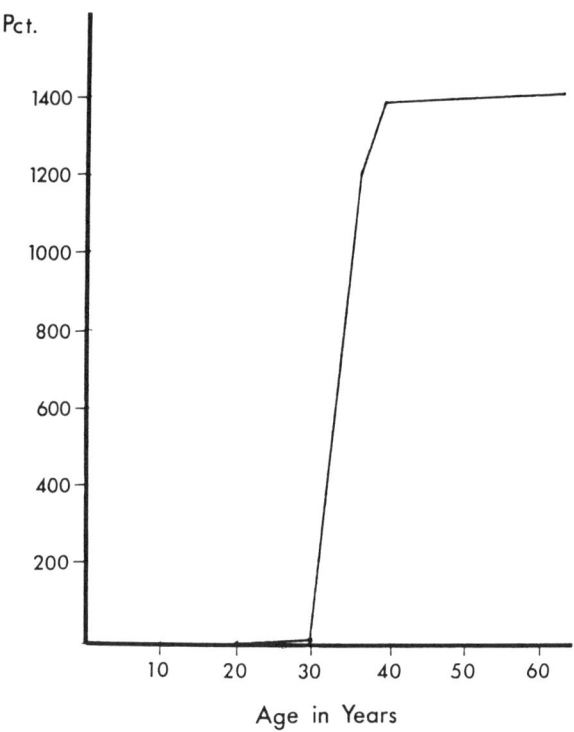

Figure 3--Relative reproduction of the Tecate cypress at various ages, in precent of pre-fire density.

Until the point where the trees begin to suppress each other, greater age and stem density will mean greater reproductive potential due to the greater number of cones per area of cover. With these factors in mind, it was possible to construct a tentative reproductive scale for Tecate cypress stands of any age using the simple equation:

$$dr = D$$

where d equals the pre-burn stem density in numbers per square meter; r equals the reproductive capacity in percent divided by 100 (as taken from figure 3); and D equals the first year post-fire seedling density in numbers per square meter. For example, a 35 year-old stand will generate about 7 times as many seedlings as there are mature trees under "nonextreme" conditions. If the stand has a pre-burn density of 1.5 stems/m^2, it will reproduce with a density of about 10.5 seedlings/m^2 in the first year following a fire.

Table 1--Sources used in the preparation of figure 3, showing relative reproduction of Cupressus at various ages. From Dunn (1984).

STAND AGE (YRS)	REPRODUCTION (PERCENT)	SOURCE
10	neg.	Zedler (1977)
19	0.1	Armstrong (1966)
20	2.9	Zedler (1977)
20	26.5	Armstrong (1966)
30	15.7	Zedler (1977)
36	1206.5	Dunn (1984)
39	1387.3	Dunn (1984)
63	1400.0+	Zedler (1977)

Incorporating the data on mortality, it is possible to construct a relative reestablishment scale, using the equation:

$$Sr = R$$

where S equals survivorship in percent of first year post-fire density (fig. 4); r equals the reproductive capacity in percent divided by 100 (from figure 3); and R equals the reestablishment index in percent of pre-fire density at the same age. Though this may seem complex, all that this formula states is that a reestablishment index of greater than 100 percent indicates that stand population and density are increasing and that a reestablishment index of less than 100 percent indicates that stand population and density are decreasing.

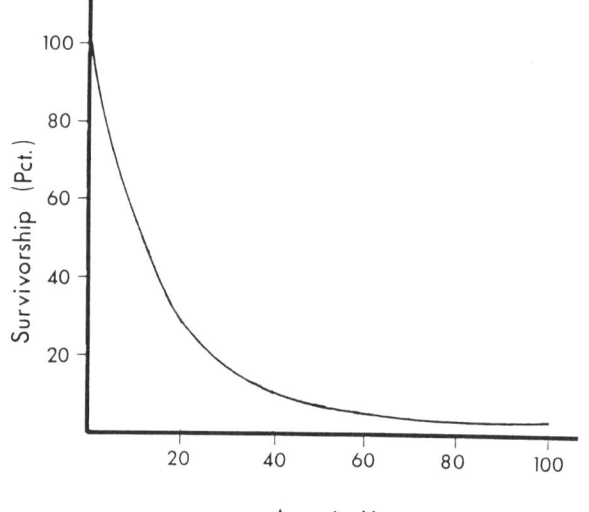

Figure 4--Tecate cypress survivorship in percent of first year's seedlings.

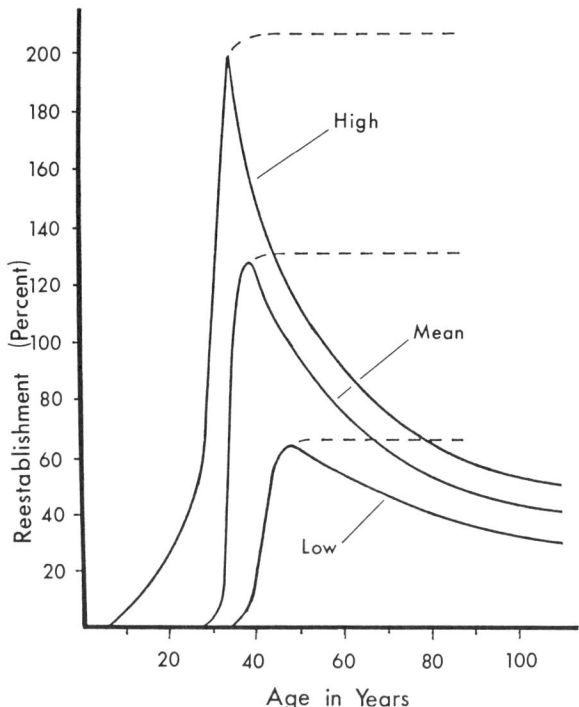

Figure 5--Reestablishment index for the Tecate cypress, in percent of pre-fire density at the same age.

In the above example, using the mortality rate in figure 4, we can see that 35 years after the fire, the stand's density will have dropped to about 12.5 percent of the first year density, or 1.3 stems/m^2. This is only 87 percent of the stand's original density, so this population of cypress is actually declining. Using the formula $Sr = R$ it was possible to generate a reestablishment index curve (fig. 5) for the Tecate cypress. Arbitrary high and low limits were set for inputs to indicate the effects of unusually favorable or unfavorable conditions affecting reproduction--they are meant to be illustrative, not rigorous.

As can be seen in figure 5, a stand of cypress reaches 100 percent reestablishment at about 36 years under "non-extreme" conditions and peaks at 40 years. In years that favor high reproduction, the stand may reach reestablishment capability as early as 30 years of age, and peak at around 200 percent reestablishment; a situation that could give rise to extremely dense thickets of dwarf cypress that never fully mature (Armstrong 1966). In extremely unfavorable years, however, reproduction may be negligible until the stand is over 40 years old and may never reach 100 percent reestablishment.

Table 2--Stem densities compared to cone densities in numbers per square meter. As stem densities decrease, the number of cones per tree increases and cones per square meter remains about the same.

AGE OF TREES	STEM DENSITY	CONES PER TREE	CONES/m^2
40	1.2	18	21
80	0.5	53	25
100	0.4	78	29

However, there is a problem associated with such a simple model of cypress reproductive behavior. According to the proposed model, mortality becomes the dominant factor in the species' reproduction after the reproductive peak has been reached, causing reestablishment rates to decline as the stand ages. However, there is no indication that mortality has much effect on a stand's reproductive capability after a "saturation level" of about 20-25 cones per square meter is reached at about 35-40 years. All mature stands sampled had cone densities near or above this level and it appears that this level is reached virtually independently of stem density, since a stand with a low stem density will have significantly more cones per tree than a stand with a high stem density (table 2). After full maturity is reached, there is no reason that this "saturation level" cannot be maintained indefinitely if the trees are healthy. The dashed line in figure 5 indicates this reproductive stasis. Since the environmental conditions following a burn can never be accurately predicted, and certainly not by the trees themselves, the species would necessarily have evolved toward optimum reproduction under the worst likely conditions. As the model indicates, poor environmental conditions (primarily drought) reduce the ability of younger stands to replace themselves. Since drought is a relatively common occurrence in California, it becomes clear that the cypress must have evolved in an environment where fires were no more frequent than once every 35-40 years at a minimum. Fires of a greater frequency would have greater likelihood of severely reducing stand density. This is clearly shown in the curve in figure 5, as replacement jumps from virtually nil at 30 years to over 100 percent at 40 years.

Water Availability

The availability of water in the first years following a fire is probably the major single external factor in determining cypress seedling establishment and survival, and is affected primarily by rainfall, soils and slope aspect.

Rainfall

Paula Jacks (1984) study of the responses of Adenostema and Ceanothus to drought conditions in the early post-fire years clearly shows that dramatic changes can occur in a community under such extreme conditions. In her study, Ceanothus seedlings proved to be much more drought tolerant than the Adenostema's and were able to gain dominance in the stand. Though no similar study has been done for the Tecate cypress community, it is clear that extreme drought years following a fire would be detrimental to a species, such as the cypress, which is virtually limited to the more mesic north-facing slopes and canyons within the chaparral community. In the case of young stands, where the reproductive capability of the tree is low, drought conditions could mean the nearly complete failure of regeneration.

Soils

Though a number of cypress species in California have definite soil relationships or edaphic restrictions, the Tecate cypress shows no such definite restrictions, occurring on soils derived from gabbro, granite and metavolcanic rock in San Diego County, and various sedimentary substrates in Orange County (Sottlemeyer 1980). Still, soils do have an effect on the distribution of the cypress. Popenoe's (1974) study of the south slope vegetation of Otay Mountain indicated that the cypress there were virtually confined to the deeper soils occurring on joints and bedding planes, while chamise dominated the shallower "off-band" soils on the slopes. The "on-band" soils on which the cypress occurred were generally higher in nutrients and had three times the organic matter than the associated "off-band" soils. These deeper soils also had more available water later in the year than did the "off-band" soils, and therefore encouraged the establishment and survival of the cypress.

Slope Aspect

The Tecate cypress is usually limited to north-facing slopes (with the rare exception of deep-soiled south-facing slopes), very likely due to the effect of decreased evapotranspiration. In order to test the effects of slope aspect on cypress regeneration, five plots were set up in a recently burned stand on Otay Mountain with aspects between 250° and 340°. Densities of cypress seedlings, shrub and sub-shrub species were measured in each plot along with the burned cypress stems. Figure 6 summarizes the relative densities of the three categories in descending order of cypress density. Plot 293°-1 shows higher relative cypress densities than plots 314°-1 and 314°-2 primarily because it was located on a turn in the slope and was less exposed than any of the other plots. Though this sample is too small to be definitive, it is clear that the cypress prefers the more northerly facing slopes, while chaparral shrubs are most abundant on the intermediate sites, and the sub-shrubs and herbaceous species dominate on the driest, south-western facing slopes.

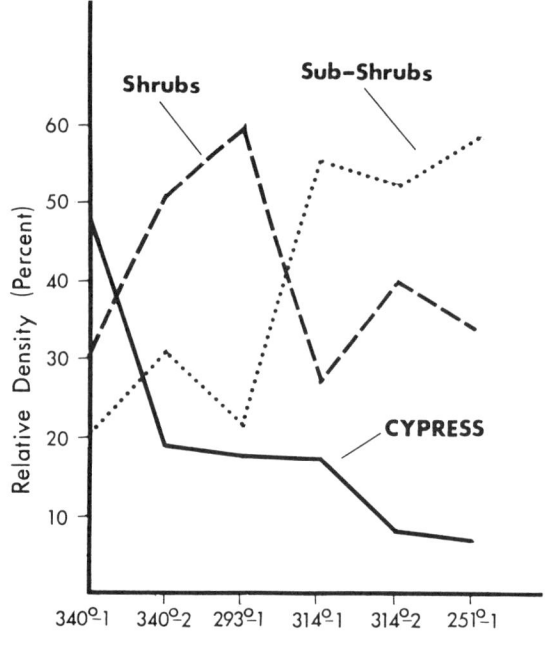

Figure 6--Relative densities of Tecate cypress, shrubs and sub-shrubs in a 2-year old stand on Otay Mountain. Organized by decreasing cypress density. Plot numbers reflect slope aspect.

EFFECTS OF FIRE FREQUENCY ON VEGETATION PATTERNS

It is clear the the reproductive capability of the Tecate cypress changes greatly with age, and it will perhaps be useful for management purposes to simplify the life history of the species with respect to effects of fire frequency on vegetation patterns and reproduction.

High Fire Frequency (1-25 years)

Zedler and others (1983) have shown that fires occurring at intervals of 1-5 years have dramatic and relatively permanent effects on the scrub vegetation of southern California; reducing the density of all species and eliminating, at least locally, obligate seeding species by destroying their seedlings. Vegetation after such a short fire interval is reduced to primarily herbaceous species, with only the most hardy resprouting shrub species surviving. A greater fire frequency, in the 6-25 year range, would maintain a chaparral type of vegetation. Because of the extended period of time necessary for the cypress to reach 100 percent replacement capacity, few, if any, cypress seedlings will become established after a set of fires within this frequency range, and unless a few mature trees manage to survive the first fire, the cypress would be more or less permanently eliminated from the community.

Moderate Fire Frequency (26-39 years)

Fires of this frequency would cause highly variable reproduction of the cypress, depending primarily on other variables, such as the actual age of the trees, post-fire rainfall and site quality. As figure 3 shows, the reproductive capability of the cypress undergoes material changes every year during this sensitive period. During the first part of this period, relatively good reproduction may occur under only the most favorable conditions. Later in this period, cypress reproduction would be reasonably good except under the most extreme conditions. Because of the frequency of severe drought in southern California it is very unlikely that the Tecate cypress would be able to maintain its present range over an extended period of time with a fire frequency in this range.

Low Fire Frequency (40+ years)

According to the data presented in figures 3 and 5, the Tecate cypress reaches maximum reproductive capability at approximately 40 years of age. With a fire frequency of 40 years or longer, there is no reason to suspect that cypress populations could not be maintained at their present levels. All management proposals for Tecate cypress populations should be geared toward maintaining fire frequencies within this range.

STATUS AND FUTURE IN CALIFORNIA

The three Tecate cypress populations studied are quite distinct in character and display unique fire histories. A discussion of each site will not only describe their present status, but will also serve as an illustration of the species' response to different fire regimes.

Sierra Peak

The Sierra Peak stands of Tecate cypress were not studied as part of the research project. However, examination of fire records for the area indicate that the fire frequency in the area of Sierra Peak's 400 hectares (1000 acres) of cypress has risen dramatically this century. Fires burned much or all of the stand in 1948 and again in 1967. Apparently the stand reproduced reasonably well after the second fire, though there is no way of knowing to what extent, if any, the stand was reduced. The western two-thirds of the stand burned again in 1982, and though the following winter was extremely wet, it is probable the reproduction was very poor, if not virtually non-existent.

Guatay Mountain

Of the four Tecate cypress stands in California, the Guatay Mountain stand is far and away the smallest, covering an area of less than 16 hectares (40 acres), about half of which was set aside last year as a Research Natural Area by the U.S. Forest Service. It is also the only Tecate cypress stand in the state that lacks a documented fire history. Ages of the trees on Guatay Mountain were determined by taking core samples with an increment borer. The bulk of the trees date from a circa 1850 fire and are now approximately 135 years old. About a quarter of the stand also burned between

1890 and 1895. There are also indications that the fire previous to the circa 1850 fire occurred in about 1750. If so, most of the Guatay Mountain stand would have burned only twice in the past 230 years, certainly one of the lowest fire frequencies in the California chaparral. With such a low fire frequency the stand seems safe from immediate threat, though its small size makes it vulnerable to localized events.

Otay Mountain

In direct contrast to Guatay Mountain, Otay Mountain supports the largest population of Tecate Cypress in California. The cypress occupies about 2400 hectares (5900 acres) on Otay Mountain, over 80 percent of which is within the boundaries of extensive federal land holdings (Dunn 1984). The Otay Mountain cypress stands occur primarily on north-facing slopes, but in virtually every conceivable environment, from 220 meters to 1040 meters elevation, from streambed to ridgetop, from seedlings to 100+ year old patriarchs. However, the majority of cypress on Otay Mountain are just over 40 years old, having burned during World War II.

At the present time, with the bulk of Otay Mountain's cypress just reaching full maturity, a fire would do little damage to the community. However, as San Diego and its suburbs continue to grow, there is an increasing threat of development and its effects on fire frequency in the area. Otay Mesa, just west of the mountain, is developing rapidly. In 1984 the federal government completed and opened the Otay Mesa border crossing a few miles from the foot of Otay Mountain. Last year, construction began on a state prison near the mountain, and a Formula I raceway is planned. During the summer of 1984, the San Diego County Department of Planning and Land Use proposed a 1000 acre ORV park for the southwestern base of the mountain. This park would immediately impact 200-300 acres of cypress and indirectly threaten perhaps one third of Otay Mountain's cypress by increasing the potential of fire. Still, this population appears to be very healthy at this time, and there is no reason that it can't be maintained if developments are controlled at the mountain's base.

Tecate Peak

Of all the Tecate cypress bearing mountains in California, the fire history of Tecate Peak has been the most complex and has had the greatest impact on the cypress that grow there. Because of this it deserves the most attention as it throws light on the ecology and future of the Tecate cypress.

No fire records were kept in San Diego County before 1910, but there is good evidence that a fire occurred on the mountain in about 1880. However, the circa 1880 fire probably did not burn the entire mountain as Saunders (1916) notes the state of the chaparral at the mountain's peak before a fire that occurred only 30 years after the 1880 fire, in 1911. He states that "formerly [before 1911] the brush cover must have been much heavier, as I noticed charred stumps of manzanita half a foot through burned even with the ground..." He also quotes from a letter from a Mr. Stevens, who visited a now extinct stand of cypress on the summit of Tecate Peak in 1903. Stevens states that "they were large old trees--not erect, but as might be expected on a wind-swept summit, spreading, low-branched and gnarled. I feel sure that some were two feet in diameter of trunk near the ground." These statements indicate both that the summit escaped the 1880 fire and that an extremely long period of time had elapsed since the previous fire there.

In 1911, part of the mountain, including the grove described by Stevens, burned. Tree ring samples taken from cypress on the west side of the mountain indicate another fire in about 1919. However, since there is no record of this fire, its extent remains unknown. In September of 1928, a fire swept the east slope of Tecate Peak. The extent of this fire was confirmed using aerial photos taken in 1929.[3]

These photos also allowed a detailed mapping of the extent of the cypress on Tecate Peak at this time, as shown in figure 7. The 1928 fire probably eliminated the cypress on the summit and may have burned some of the cypress in Mexico. In 1945, the Tecate Peak fire burned almost the entire population of cypress on Tecate Peak.

---

[3] Aerial photos on file, San Diego County Dept. of Public Works, Survey Records Division.

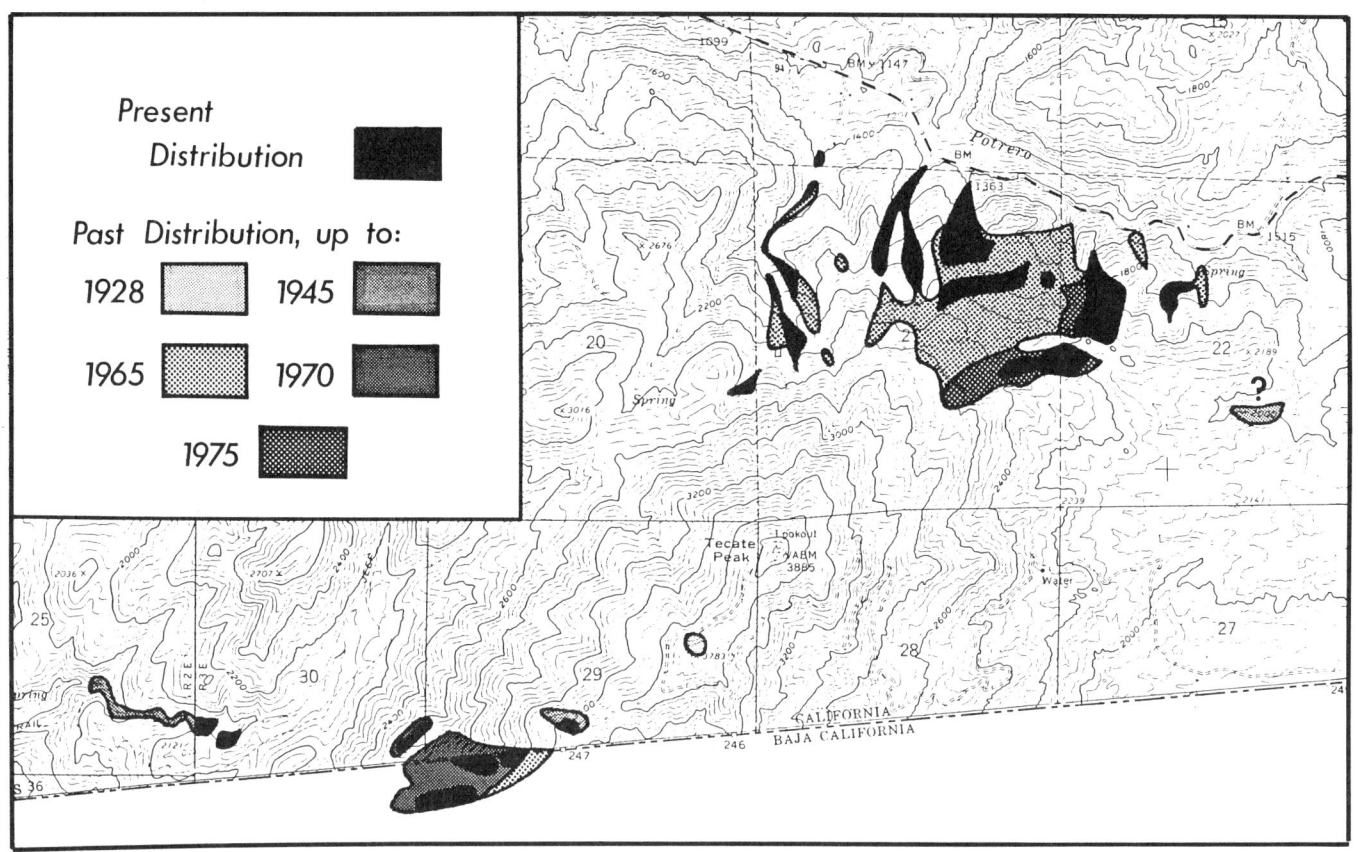

Figure 7--Historical distribution of Tecate cypress on Tecate Peak since 1920. shaded areas indicate the last year in which the cypress was present in that location.

Up to this point in time, only very little of the cypress population on Tecate Peak had been reduced due to fire. This situation changed 20 years later, in 1965, when a fire again swept much of the same area as in 1945. the 19 year old trees had not had sufficient time to develop enough cones to reproduce successfully after such a short return period and, as a consequence, the extent of the cypress groves was reduced by half (fig. 7). In 1970, another fire reburned much of the area burned in 1928, including most of the cypress in Mexico. The exact fire history of the stand in Mexico is unclear, but the fires there have severely reduced the extent of the stand. Most of the trees that remain there date from 1970. There are also a few mature trees dating from an earlier fire, probably either 1911 or 1919.

Another severe blow struck the Tecate Peak cypress in September 1975 when virtually all of the northern groves burned once again. Most of this area had sustained fires in 1945 and 1965, and with this fire, the extent of the cypress was once again almost cut in half.

The fire frequency on Tecate Peak has, in the past 67 years, gone from one fire every 40+ years to, in some areas, one fire every 15 years (Dunn 1984). In the same period, the extent of the cypress has dropped from 105 hectares (260 acres) to 31 hectares (74 acres). There is perhaps 1 hectare (3 acres) of mature cypress on Tecate Peak, and it will be until about the year 2015 before the rest of the population reaches maturity (Dunn 1985). If the cypress are to mature and reestablish themselves, a very strict fire exclusion policy must be pursued on Tecate Peak. Unfortunately, fire protection on these steep slopes is nearly impossible, and the mountain's location near the Mexican city of Tecate and State Highway 94 is a dual curse that will most likely thwart any plans to protect the trees. The problem is further complicated by the fact that nearly all of the cypress are found on a multiplicity of private land. In the final analysis, if things continue as is, it is unlikely that most of the cypress on Tecate Peak will see the 21st century.

SUMMARY

The Tecate cypress has long been a member of the flora of southern California and Mexico, adapted to burning once every 40 or more years. Yet today it is rapidly declining on Tecate Peak and probably Sierra Peak also. Will this decline spread to other cypress areas? Is this a local phenomenon or part of a larger picture? Unfortunately, its decline appears to be symptomatic of the widespread and pervasive changes in the fire regime of California that have occurred since European settlement, particularly in this century (Dunn 1986). The arrival of a highly mobile, technological society has created a situation where the potential for wildfire, previously limited to periods of extreme conditions, now exists year round. Even our highly trained fire suppression forces have not been able to keep up with the dramatic increase in the number of fires. Where once lightning fires accounted for virtually all fires on the landscape, today they account for only 5 percent. Unless major changes in our attitudes toward the chaparral environment occur soon, species such as the Tecate cypress, that are not able to adapt to the present unnatural manmade fire environment, will be threatened with their very existence.

REFERENCES

Aschmann, Homer. The evolution of a wild landscape, and it persistence in southern California. Annals, Association of American Geographers. 49 (3) Part 2: 34-56. 1959.

Armstrong, Wayne P. Ecological and taxonomic relationships of *Cupressus* in southern California. Los Angeles: California State University; 1966. 124 p. M.A. Thesis.

Dodge, J. Marvin. Vegetational changes associated with land use and fire history in San Diego County. Riverside: University of California; 1975. 216 p. Ph.D. Dissertaion.

Dunn, Anthony T. A preliminary report on the ecology and management of the Tecate cypress in San Diego County., On file, Descanso District Office, Cleveland National Forest, Forest Service, U.S. Department of Agriculture, Alpine, CA; 1984. 157 p.

Dunn, Anthony T. The Tecate cypress. Fremontia. 13 (3):3-7; 1985.

Dunn, Anthony T. Fire history in San Diego County. Fremontia. 14 (3): 24-27; 1986.

Epling, Carl; Robison, William. *Pinus muricata* and *Cupressus forbesii* in Baja California. Madrono. 5(8):248-250; 1940.

Hanes, Ted L. Succession after fire in the chaparral of southern California. Ecological Monographs. 41:27-50; 1971.

Jacks, Paula Mary. The drought tolerance of *Adenostema fasciculatum* and *Ceanothus crassifolius* seedlings and vegetation change in the San Gabriel chaparral. San Diego, CA: San Diego State University; 1984. M.S. Thesis.

Lewis, Henry T. Patterns of Indian burning in California: ecology and ethnohistory. Ramona, CA: Ballena Press; 1973: 101p.

Minnich, Richard A. Fire mosaics in southern California and northern Baja California. Science. 219:1287-1294; 1983.

Mutch, Robert. W,. Wildland fires and ecosystems--a hypothesis. Ecology. 51:1046-1051; 1970.

Parish, S.B. The Tecate cypress. Bulletin of the Southern California Academy of Science. 13:11-13; 1914.

Popenoe, James H. Vegetation patterns on Otay Mountain, California. San Diego, CA: San Diego State University; 1974. 94 p. M.S. Thesis.

Raven, Peter H.; Axelrod, Daniel I. Origin and relationships of the California flora. Berkeley, CA: University of California Press; 1978: 134 p.

Saunders, Charles F. The Tecate cypress. Bulletin of the Southern California Academy of Sciences. 15: 18-21; 1916.

Stottlemeyer, David E. Relationship of Tecate cypress distribution to soil types. Loma Linda, CA: Loma Linda University; 1980. M.S. Thesis.

Vogl. R. J.; Armstrong, W.P.; White, K.L.; Cole, K.L. The closed-cone pines and cypress, In: Barbour, M. and Majors, J., eds. Terrestrial vegetation of California. New York; London; Sydney; Toronto: John Wiley & Sons; 1977:295-358.

Zedler, Paul H. Life history attributes of plants and the fire cycle: A case study in chaparral dominated by *Cupressus forbesii*. In: Mooney, H.A.; Conrad. C.E., eds. Proceedings of the symposium on the environmental consequences of fire and fuel management in Mediterranean ecosystems. Gen. Tech. Rep. WO-3. Washington, DC: Forest Service, U.S. Department of Agriculture; 1977:451-458.

Zedler, Paul H.; Gautier, Clayton R., McMaster, Gregory S. Vegetation change in response to extreme events: the effects of a short interval between fires in California chaparral and coastal scrub. Ecology. 64 (4):809-818; 1983.

Nurse Plant Ecology of Threatened Desert Plants

Gary P. Nabhan [1]

Abstract: Numerous desert plants depend upon protective overstory species for survival. By comparing line and belt transect data from sites where the same threatened species occurs, one may evaluate: 1) dependence of a threatened species on particular nurse plants; 2) possible differential dispersal to the nurse plants' canopies; and 3) increased plant survival through buffering from temperature extremes; mycorrhizal transfer; reduced trampling and predation under nurses. Species examined include: wild chiles (Capsicum annuum L. var. glabriusculum (Dunal) Heiser and Pickersgill; Thornber's fishhook cactus (Mammillaria thornberi Orcutt); and grama grass cactus (Toumeya papyracantha (Engelm.) Britton and Rose. Management of nurses may be key to conserving these threatened species.

The nurse plant ecology of common desert plants has been the subject of numerous investigations, but the same phenomenon has been less-studied with regard to rare or threatened species ranging into arid zones. Nevertheless, it is reasonable to assume that some of the same functions of protective overstory or camouflaging vegetation may affect the dispersal, establishment and survival of rare desert plants. Knowledge of such functional relationships between threatened plants and their associated species is important in assessing the status of these plants, and managing them for persistance in their natural habitat.

A review of the potential effects of nurse plants on their associated "underlings" is therefore pertinent to endangered species conservation. First, seeds may be differentially dispersed beneath the canopies of certain nurse trees and shrubs which are used by avian seed vectors as feeding or nesting sites. For instance, saguaros (Carnegiea gigantea (Engelm.) Britton and Rose) are differentially dispersed to mesquites (Prosopis spp.) and palo verdes (Cercidium spp.) by mourning doves which intensively utilize these trees for nesting (Olin and Alcorn 1985). Second, once seeds are dispersed beneath this overstory vegetation, the microclimate there may be more suitable for germination, establishment and survival (Turner et al. 1966). This may be particularly true for species of neotropical origin which reach their northernmost ranges in deserts that are subject to periodic frosts. Nobel (1980) has determined that various columnar cacti have, in effect, their ranges extended 100 or more kilometers northward by the protection from freezing afforded them by nurse plants.

---

[1] Assistant Director, Desert Botanical Garden, Phoenix, AZ.

Third, nurses may host certain endomycorrhizae critical to the establishment of root systems of these underlying plants. After analyzing field-collected mycorrhizae from desert plant associations, Bloss (1985) suggests that barren desert soils may lack the inocula required by certain cacti for establishment and growth, but that the root zones of desert shrubs maintain these very strains. He recently determined that Mammillaria thornberi specimens which we provided to him have the same symbiotic fungi as the creosote bush, (Larrea tridentata (D.C) Coville) a predominant nurse in the same desert valley (Nabhan, Gass and Quirk 1986).

Fourth, certain spiney nurse plants, may serve as prey refugia, protecting palatable and easily trampled seedlings (McAuliffe 1984). Also, vulnerable mimics may hide in unpalatable "models" to avoid predation (Wiens 1978), as in the case of the grama grass cactus (Toumeya papyracantha (Engelm.) Britton and Rose) which is camouflaged within fairy rings of several grasses.

Given that there are many potentially functional relationships that threatened species may have with putative nurses, the first step of inquiry must be establishing the degree of fidelity that the species has with other associates in the vegetation. Is the threatened plant non-randomly distributed in relation to other species in its natural habitat?

To answer such a question for two infrequent but non-threatened desert cacti, McAuliffe (1984) utilized line transect enumerative data on vegetative cover to compare with belt transect data on the frequencies with which these cacti were associated with various canopy plant species. He compared the two data sets by computing chi-square statistics to see if there were any differences between the expected percent cover of canopy plants on the line transect, and the observed percent association with the understory cacti found in the intensively-searched belt transect. In the following examples, I have attempted to adapt this methodology to fit the population densities of selected threatened plants, and to evaluate its usefulness in studying their ecological relationships with nurse plants.

MATERIALS AND METHODS

Three desert species of plants were investigated with respect to the possibility that one or more species in their environment were serving as nurses, and functioning in at least one of the manners described above. The actual field techniques and sample sizes were slightly varied to fit the conditions, available time and materials at hand. For each species, however, techniques were identical. Table 1 summarizes the study site locations and sampling techniques used.

The wild chile, (Capsicum annuum L. var. glabriusculum (Dunal) Heiser and Pickersgill), is also referred to as var. minimum (Miller) Heiser or var. aviculare Dierbach in various reports (Heiser and Pickersgill 1975). Though not endangered as a species or variety, the few island-like populations in Arizona at the northern extreme of its range are threatened as gene pools (Baker 1984). This variety was once on the Arizona Natural Heritage Program special plant list, and such status should be reconsidered in Arizona and New Mexico. It is a frost-sensitive, scandent shrub associated with riparian and thornscrub vegetation (Nabhan 1985).

Thornber's fishhook cactus (Mammillaria thornberi Orcutt) is listed as proposed threatened (PT) in the last Federal Register review of plants (Department of Interior 1985). It is a small-statured, multi-headed cactus of desert plains and valleys, known only from south-central Arizona and adjacent Sonora (Nabhan, Gass and Quirk 1986).

Grama grass cactus, (Toumeya papyracantha (Engelm.) Britton and Rose) is often placed in the genus Pediocactus. As such, it is listed as a status 2 plant in the Federal Register (Department of Interior, 1985), suggesting that federal protection may be appropriate in the future. It is already protected by CITES and by New Mexico and Arizona. This small cactus grows in grassland, semi-arid woodland and desert scrub vegetation.

TABLE 1: Location and size of nurse plant sample sites.

Species	Locality	Line Transect	Belt Transect
C. annuum	Tumacacori, AZ	2 50 m., 1 hit/m.	1/20 ha., 10 m. wide
C. annuum	Onavas, SON, MEX	2 50 m., 1 hit/m.	1/20 ha., 10 m. wide
C. annuum	Onavas, SON, MEX	2 50 m., 1 hit/m.	1/20 ha. 10 m. wide
M. thornberi	Avra Valley, AZ	2 500 ft., continuous	1/10 ha., 20 ft. wide
M. thornberi	Avra Valley, AZ	2 500 ft., continuous	1/10 ha., 20 ft. wide
T. papyracantha	Navajo Co., AZ	1 300 ft. 1 200 ft., 1 hit/3 ft.	1/20 ha., 10 ft. wide
T. papyracantha	Navajo Co., AZ	1 300 ft., 1 200 ft., 1 hit/3 ft.	1/20 ha., 10 ft. wide

Upon arrival at a site where the presence of these species was known or suspected, a preliminary search was done for an appropriate baseline. One or more line transects were then layed out perpendicular to this baseline, parallel to one another. These transects were read either every one meter, every three feet, or continuously, as noted in table 1. Plants overlapping at the same point were each tallied separately, so that conceivably, total frequency of vegetative cover could tally greater than 100 percent of the ground.

Belt transects, established adjacent to these line transects, were used to slowly and intensively search for every visible seedling or mature plant of the target species. When an individual of the target species was found, all overlying or shadowing plant species above it were recorded and then divided into those with trunks 2 meters or less away, and those with main trunks 2 meters or more away. For these purposes, only the former are considered true nurses, affording both climatic buffering and possible physical protection from trampling.

Enumerative data from these samples were then analyzed by computing chi-square statistics to test the null hypothesis that there is no difference between the frequency of the nurses in the overall vegetative cover (line transect) versus in association with the target species (belt transect). I compared enumerative data from separate samples (Duncan, Knapp and Miller 1977) using binomial chi-square tests on these data. Several variations were devised, depending upon the frequency of the target species and its putative nurses. These area explained in the following results and discussion.

RESULTS AND DISCUSSION

Wild chiles

In the case of the population islands of wild chiles at the northern edge of their range, it is hypothesized that three factors may encourage their need for nurse plants: 1) escape from catastrophic freezes; 2) refuge from trampling and grazing; and 3) differential dispersal to canopies of red-fruited trees by cardinaline finches (Nabhan 1985). The latter hypothesis is based on the suggestion that the red fruits of chiles mimic fruits of roughly the same size and color (red through purple-black) that are produced on more common components of the vegetation. By doing so, they are eaten by frugivorous birds that are attracted primariliy by the overstory plant, which adventitously disperse them to other feeding sites. Such a hypothesis fits with data on red, black and blue fruits in areas seasonally low in frugivorous birds (Willson and Thompson 1982). It does not preclude the protective advantages that may accrue to chiles that are dispersed beneath a shrub or tree.

Therefore, to test the fruit mimicry hypothesis, the line transect frequency values of small, dark-fruited shrubs and trees were compared with the frequency with which these same species served as putative nurses for wild chiles. These putative nurses vary from site to site, but include certain small-fruited, non-toxic species in the following genera: hackberry (Celtis); graythorn (Zizyphus); nightshade (Solanum); sumac (Rhus); and wolfberry (Lycium).

The northernmost population of this species occurs at Tumacacori, Arizona where the putative nurses are represented by four fruiting shrub species which make up less than 5 percent of the vegetative cover of the area, where a total of 28 vascular plant species were recorded. Table 2 summarizes the test of null hypothesis for cumulative data on these four species.

The test suggests that the frequency of association between the wild chiles and three of the four shrubs with somewhat similar fruits is greater than what would be expected if the chiles were randomly dispersed in the vegetation. These shrubs are Celtis pallida Torrey; Rhus choriophylla Woot. and Standl.; and Zizyphus obtusifolia (Hook. ex T. & G.) A. Gray; although on the site, Lycium was not abundant enough to confirm or deny its role as a nurse. As a rule of thumb, I project that chiles are about seven times more frequently associated with these bird-attracting shrubs than would be expected if randomly-dispersed among the plant cover. It is worth noting that other thorny shrubs, such as mesquite and palo verde, are on the site, but do not show such a high association with the chiles, even though they may offer just as much protection. The nurse plant phenomena for chiles appears to involve more factors than simple protection, as interpretation of data from other sites suggests in the following discussion.

TABLE 2: Nurse plant relations within the Tumacacori chile population.

Type of ground cover	Frequency in cover (line transect) Observed	Expected	Association with chiles (belt) Observed	Expected
Shrubs with bird-dispersed fruits (4 spp.)	4	(8.26)	6	(1.73)
Other plants (24 spp.)	96	(92)	15	(19)

$\chi^2 = 7.879$, d.f.=1, $P<0.005$

The same methodology was used at two sites in the municipio of Onavas, Sonora, Mexico, which is virtually free of annual killing frosts. If nurse plants served only for protecting underlings from temperature extremes, one might hypothesize that the chiles would not be as tightly-associated with them. Table 3 presents the data from the Rio Mayo floodplain teraces near Onavas, where nurse plants remain highly-associated with chiles.

Instead of being less-tightly associated with the wild chiles, red-fruited, bird-dispersed nurse shrubs such as Celtis, Lycium and Solanum are ten times more frequently found in association with chiles than would be expected if the chiles were randomly-dispersed. Similarly, at the other site near Onavas, red-fruited shrubs were found at a frequency of less than 1 percent in the vegetation, but 26 percent of the chiles were found under them.

Although there is no obligate association between chiles and these shrubs, it is remarkable how frequently with which red chiltepines can be found in the canopy of red fruited shrubs with the same fruit size. To conserve wild chile genetic resources in situ, shrubs attracting frugivorous birds should be maintained.

Thornber's fishhook cactus

Data regarding Mammillaria thornberi populations were collected during the Desert Botanical Garden's participation in two plant salvages along Reach Four of the Central Arizona Project right-of-way clearing in Pima County, Arizona. The Garden staff was interested in determining whether this cactus was found in any particular microenvironment, so that salvaged plants could be transplanted into similar settings on the Garden grounds.

TABLE 3: Nurse plant relations within Onavas chile population.

Type of ground cover	Frequency in cover (line transect) Observed	Expected	Association with chiles (belt) Observed	Expected
Shrubs with bird-dispersed fruits (4 spp.)	6	(15.8)	13	(3.2)
Other plants	92	(82.3)	7	(16.8)

$\chi^2 = 38.7$, d.f.=1, $P<0.005$

In this case, I have combined the two sets of line transect data taken on either side of the salvaged area. Table 4 indicates that the creosote bush (Larrea) plays a highly significant but not exclusive role as a nurse plant for fishhook cacti.

nurse for this species supercedes both the dominant cover species, triangle-leaved bursage, and the cholla cacti that offered prey refugia to other small cacti in McAuliffe's (1984) nurse plant studies nearby.

TABLE 4: Nurse plant relations with a Thornber's fishhook cactus.

Type of ground cover	Frequency in cover (line transect) Observed Expected	Association with Thornber's fishhook cactus (belt) Observed Expected
Creosote bush	8 (11.7)	6 (2.1)
Other plants (11 spp.)	70 (66.3)	8 (11.9)

$\chi^2 = 7.49$, d.f.=1, $P < 0.01$

It is possible to reject the null hypothesis--- that creosote bush is no more frequently associated with this cactus in belt transects than it is represented in line transect samples of frequency of cover. Although 42 percent of the fishhook cactus clumps found on the belt transects were found under creosote canopies, this shrub makes a small contribution to the overall vegetative cover relative to that of the dominant shrub, triangle-leaved bursage, Ambrosia deltoidea (Torr.) Payne. For further discussion, see Nabhan, Gass and Quirk (1986).

Because the 14 plant sample of this cactus within the belt transects was so meager, I have also tallied data on 51 plants which we salvaged from the area bracketed by the transects. None of these fishhook cactus clumps grew on open ground. They were overlain by 72 nurse plants representing 7 species of other cacti and of shrubs. Of these 51 fishhook plant clusters, 33 percent of them utilized creosote bush as their only nurse, while 25 percent used bursage as their only nurse.

Of the 847 cactus heads found within these 51 clumps, 57 percent of them were under creosote bushes. Thus, Thornber's fishhook cactus appears completely dependent upon nurse plants for survival in the wild, and creosote bush serves as its nurse to an extent that has been overlooked until recently (Nabhan, Gass and Quirk 1986). Creosote's role as a

Grama grass cactus

In the literature on grama grass cactus, the dependence upon particular sod and bunchgrasses has long been referred to anecdotally (Wiens 1978). However, at the Arizona sites where I attempted to study this cactus, no strong association could be empirically confirmed although it may indeed exist. Despite 5 hours of transect measurements and another 20-30 hours of intensive ground search, I found too small a sample of these cacti to confirm or deny any nurse plant relationship.

In the northwestern, marginal portion of its range, the grama grass cactus exists in densities of less than 50 per hectare. Also, muhly and grama grass so dominate the vegetative cover at these sites that it would be unlikely that one would find a greater-than-random association of these species with the cactus.

Instead, two indicators of grass cover condition can be derived from these sampling techniques: 1) percent vegetative cover (or lack of it) on the ground; and 2) the ratio of (grama and muhly) grass cover to overall vegetative cover. At one site where grazing is intensive, these grasses make up only half of the vegetative cover, in part because of the presence of unpalatable shrubs such as snakeweed (Gutierrezia sarothrae (Pursh) Britt. & Rusby). Barren ground was hit 60 percent of the time, in part because of unsuccessful juniper chaining having disturbed the entire vegetative cover. It appears that there has been a recent loss of grama grass cactus from this site. At the other site, perennial grasses made up 95 percent of the plant cover, and barren ground was hit only 40 percent of the time. Heavy trampling and disruption of the grama grass sod was not evident, even though the site was lightly to moderately grazed. The grama grass cactus was still hidden by Bouteloua grass cover (fig. 1). In future studies, I will be comparing these two sites with ones in New Mexico where grama grass cacti are reputed to be more abundant.

CONCLUSIONS

The combination of line transects and belt transects to study the desert habitats of threatened species appears useful in some instances. Vegetative cover and condition can be rapidly assessed from analysis of line transect data. There are two advantages of belt transects for which 100 percent of the ground is intensively searched for target species: 1) population densities per unit area can be obtained; and 2) nurse plant associations of target species can be recorded, then analyzed in relation to line transect data.

The average size of the target species' individuals, the size of transects, and population densities all affect the utility of these methods. Whereas wild chile and fishhook cactus densities were in the range of 100-400 per hectares, grama grass cactus densities were too low for many individuals to be "hit" by small samples. Even when a threatened species may have a strong dependence upon a particular nurse plant, this relationship will likely remain obscure for small plants which are widely dispersed if these are the only sampling methods used.

The potential importance of nurse plants to the survival of threatened desert species should not be overlooked. These nurses may function in the dispersal of seed to safe sites, plant establishment, and protection of both seedlings and reproductively mature individuals. If habitats are not managed to perpetuate these protective nurse plants, the threatened plant populations themselves are likely to be depleted.

Figure 1. Grama grass cactus camouflaged in grass ring (arrow shows cactus).

ACKNOWLEDGEMENTS

I thank Peggy Olwell, U.S. Fish and Wildlife Service; Wendy Hodgson, Victor Gass, Tom Ahlstrom, Patrick Quirk, Jane Cole, Linda Trawick and Steve Jones of the Desert Botanical Garden for their assistance with data collection and manuscript preparation; Joe McAuliffe of the University of Arizona for discussion of methods; and Amadeo Rea, David Shaul, Laura Merrick, and Cindy Baker for assistance in data collection in Mexico. Parts of this study have been funded by the Desert Botanical Garden, the U.S. Fish and Wildlife Service Office of Endangered Species, the Wenner-Grenn Foundation, and Native Seeds/SEARCH.

REFERENCES

Baker, Cindy. In hot pursuit of wild chiles. The Seedhead News 8: 1-3; 1984 Winter Solstice.

Bloss, H. E. Studies of symbiotic microflora and their role in the ecology of desert plants. Desert Plants 7(3): 119-127.

Department of Interior. Endangered and threatened wildlife and plants; review of plant taxa for listing as threatened or endangered species; notice of review. Federal Register 50(188): 39526-00057. 1985 September 27.

Duncan, Robert C., Knapp, Rebecca G., Miller, M. Clinton. Introductory biostatistics for the health sciences. New York: John Wiley and Sons; 1977; 163

Heiser, Charles H.; Pickersgill, Barbara. Names for bird peppers (Capsicum-Solanaceae). Baileya 19: 151-156; 1975.

McAuliffe, Joseph R. Prey refugia and the distributions of two Sonoran Desert cacti. Oecol. 65: 82-85; 1984.

Nobel, Park S. 1980. Influences of minimum stem temperature on ranges of cacti in southwestern United States and central chile. Oecol. 47: 10-15; 1980.

Nabhan, Gary P. For the birds: the red-hot mother of chiles. In: Gathering the Desert. Tucson: University of Arizona Press; 1985: 123-136.

Nabhan, Gary P.; Gass, Victor; Quirk, Patrick. Thornber's fishhook cactus: conserving a declining species. Agave 2(2): 4-8; 1986 Fall.

Olin, George; Alcorn, Stan M. Distribution of viable saguaro seeds by white-winged doves (Zenaida asiatica). 1985 draft for submission to Desert Plants; in preparation.

Turner, R. M.; Alcorn, S. M.; Olin, G.; Booth, J. A. The influence of shade, soil and water on saguaro seedling establishment. Bot. Gaz. 127: 95-102; 1966.

Wiens, Delbert. Mimicry in plants. Evol. Biol. 11: 365-403; 1978.

Willson, Mary F.; Thompson, John N. Phenology and ecology of color in bird-dispersed fruits, or why some fruits are red when they are "green." Can. J. Bot. 60: 701-713;; 1982.

Autecological Monitoring of Endangered Plants

Bruce M. Pavlik [1]

Abstract: The management of endangered plant populations requires quantitative, autecological data that can readily be generated from field monitoring programs. Of primary concern in a Type I program are relatively long-term demographic studies that document population trends. These must emphasize descriptive and small-scale manipulative approaches to survivorship and seed production over other possible parameters. This information is used to determine the net reproductive rate within the population and/or other measures of population status (e.g. half-lives, reproductive limitations). The Type I program should be considered a standard feature of population management regardless of the degree of endangerment. A Type II program, emphasizing physiological ecology, is best applied to the most precarious of populations where the survival, reproduction, and establishment of additional plants is the immediate goal of the manager. This goal is met by identifying patterns of resource use, characterizing physiological responses in relation to recovery treatment and developing schedules of manipulation to maximize performance of the target species. The available techniques and instrumentation allow for *in situ*, non-destructive measurements of water status, stomatal conductance, photosynthesis and whole plant growth. Both Type I and Type II monitoring programs can easily be incorporated into existing procedures for recovering endangered plant taxa.

Over the last fifteen years, rare plant research has concentrated on providing information on the distribution and synecological relationships of endangered populations. Such research has greatly benefitted from the standardization of survey and documentation techniques (Barkley 1981, Goff et al. 1982, Nelson 1984), thereby allowing the development of reliable data bases for identifying and protecting the most threatened taxa. In some cases the result has been the establishment of rare plant preserves in one form or another (e.g. "areas of critical environmental concern" such as Eureka Dunes in Inyo County, CA, "wildlife refuges" such as Ash Meadows National Wildlife refuge in Nye County, NV, and "botanical areas" like Cuesta Ridge in San Luis Obispo County, CA).

Although these preserves and other forms of land-use restriction are absolutely essential, they do not, in and of themselves, ensure the recovery and persistence of endangered populations. It has become increasingly apparent that once protected from human disturbance, these populations must be managed to some extent in order to slow and eventually reverse their decline. Endangered species management requires quantitative, autecological data that can readily be generated from field monitoring programs. The purpose of this paper is to suggest a framework for standardizing monitoring programs and incorporating them into the management and recovery plans for endangered plant taxa. These programs are based on two fields of autecological investigation, demography and physiological ecology, and are designated Type I and Type II programs, respectively.

---

[1] Bruce M. Pavlik, Assistant Professor of Biology, Mills College, Oakland, CA 94613

TYPE I MONITORING PROGRAM

Of primary concern in a Type I monitoring program are relatively long-term demographic studies that document population trends (stability, growth or decline) at a specific site. Practically speaking, "long-term" may mean two or three years of intensive study. Depending on the taxon and the year-to-year environmental variablity associated with its habitat, these studies may have to be extended beyond three years in order to provide meaningful data. With long-lived perennials this extension can be accomplished by utilizing relationships between canopy size or basal area and the age of an individual. These relationships permit the analysis of population age structure and the frequency of establishment over time (Barbour et al. 1977, Barker 1979).

There are many potential attributes of populations that can be studied in a Type I program (table 1). Survivorship and seed production (and/or vegetative segmentation) should be considered the primary elements of any demographic monitoring because of their obvious relation to rare plant preservation.

These data also have potential utility in constructing life tables (Begon and Mortimer 1981, Hutchings 1986) and estimating net reproductive rate (R_O);

$$R_O = \Sigma\ l_x m_x$$

where l_x is the probability of an individual surviving from day x to day x' and m_x is the average number of progeny (seeds) produced per individual during the interval x'-x

Table 1. Population attributes for managing endangered plants.

---

survivorship/mortality
seed production/vegetative segmentation
age structure
genetic structure
spatial distribution/nearest neighbors
seed dispersal
seed bank composition/dynamics
temporal patterns of establishment

(Harper 1977, Hutchison 1986). The product of these variables is calculated for each time interval during the life of a cohort (or for each stage in the life cycle, such as seed, seedling, juvenile, etc.) and summed. The result, R_O, is an estimate of the number of new individuals each plant will produce under the environmental conditions found within the population. If R_O is greater than 1.0, then the population is growing, if it is less than 1.0 the population is declining. Despite the potential utility of this measure in rare plant monitoring, it is seldom employed because of problems associated with determining survivorship within seed cohorts between dispersal and germination. Efforts are being made to develop techniques that circumvent these difficulties (Pavlik and Barbour 1986).

If it is not possible to construct life tables for a particular taxon, survivorship and seed production data can still be analyzed to predict population trends and to identify the factors that contribute to population instability or decline (Pavlik and Barbour 1986). These analyses take can take advantage of a variety of quantitative expressions that can be generated from the data. For example, by following survivorship in a cohort or depletion in several cohorts, population half-lives (the time required for half of the individuals to die) can be calculated. Half-lives from different populations can be directly compared (Pavlik and Barbour 1986). They also allow statistical evaluation of management practices (resource supplementation, weed control, grazing exclosure). Another useful index for summarizing demographic trends is cohort survivorship at reproductive maturity. Seed production data can be used to examine the reproductive output of individual plants (e.g. on a canopy volume basis) or whole populations (on a habitat area basis). The latter provides an estimate of seed rain for comparison to the number of seeds in the seed bank. These measures allow direct comparison of endangered and non-endangered taxa as well as assessment of experimental treatments. Pavlik and Barbour (1985) have also used seed production data to examine the limitations imposed on seed output by pollination, fertilization and pre-dispersal predation.

The selection of other, secondary attributes is governed by the life form of the taxon (annual, herbaceous perennial, shrub, etc.), the particular circumstances surrounding that taxon (e.g. the disturbance factors that contributed to its predicament, nature of the habitat and its land-use status), and the practical limitations that are often imposed on these kinds of studies (time, money, available labor). In some cases, these attributes can be condensed (e.g. seed dispersal, predation, and mortality into seed bank dynamics) or even ignored until the results of the survivorship/seed production studies are known.

The Type I monitoring program should be considered a standard feature of population management regardless of the degree of endangerment. If the taxon under study is particularly rare or comprised of small, unstable populations, then basic demographic monitoring (survivorship and seed production) would be built into all efforts that attempt to enhance the populations. Those efforts would be immediately suspended if greater mortality (e.g. significantly decreased half-lives) or decreased seed output were detected in experimental populations relative to unmanipulated controls.

TYPE II MONITORING

The essential features of a Type II monitoring program are its ecophysiological basis and short-term time framework. It is best applied to the most precarious of populations, those in immediate danger of extinction. In this case, the physiological status and reproductive performance of each established individual becomes the primary focus of the recovery efforts. Type II monitoring uses _in situ_, non-destructive measurements to determine if favorable conditions for growth and reproduction exist at the moment (i.e. are the plants stressed?). If these measurements are made on plants under natural conditions, then they could suggest what kinds of small-scale manipulations (resource supplementation, competitor control) would relieve the stress. If the measurements are made on manipulated plants, then they can indicate if the manipulation has been effectively applied (in terms of amount, timing and duration) or if alternative manipulations should be implemented.

Resource abundance in the habitat will determine the kind of measurements to be made in a Type II program (table 2). Soil moisture and plant water status are relevant measures for drought-prone communities in western North America. Related to, and perhaps more important than plant water status is stomatal conductance to water vapor. Conductance is sensitive to the water status of leaves and its maximum values reflect the photosynthetic capacity of the leaf mesophyll (Farquhar and Sharkey 1982).

Table 2. Ecophysiological measurements that could be used in a Type II monitoring program.

---

plant water status (xylem water potential)
stomatal conductance to water vapor
leaf temperature-air temperature differential
whole leaf photosynthesis
rates of leaf area development
leaf nutrient status
whole plant growth

Therefore, the absolute magnitude and temporal patterns of stomatal conductance can indicate the potential for photosynthetic carbon gain, whole plant growth and reproduction. This allows stomatal conductance to be used as an instantaneous index of plant performance and as a tool for evaluating many types of experimental manipulations (water and nutrient supplementation, weed control, overstory thinning, etc.). Other types of physiological measurements may also be included depending on the characteristics of the taxon and its habitat (e.g. nitrogen and calcium levels in the leaves of serpentine endemics).

The justification for using ecophysiological techniques in endangered species monitoring lies in the relationship between short-term physiological processes and long-term demographic trends observed in populations (fig. 1). As plant water status (Ψ) declines in the absence of precipitation or moisture supplementation, the stomates will close and create a high resistance (R_s) to water vapor loss (fig. 1a). (It is easier to speak of stomatal resistance in the context of figure 1 rather than its inverse, stomatal conductance, as discussed above.) As stomatal resistance increases, CO_2 uptake is impeded and photosynthesis declines (fig. 1b). The relationship between total plant photosynthesis integrated over time and whole plant growth is approximately exponential in the absence of stress (fig. 1c). Finally, as plant size increases so does reproductive output (fig. 1d). Greater reproductive output results in more seeds in the seed bank or more ramets established so that the probability of population growth is increased.

The principle advantage of implementing a Type II monitoring program is that the status of individual plants can be continuously assessed. If the population continues to decline despite intensive monitoring and small-scale manipulation, emergency greenhouse propagation may be necessary. If the population is stable or growing, it may then be possible to enter into a Type I monitoring program and begin larger-scale enhancement efforts. This would depend on the absolute size of the population(s) and the probability that additional individuals will establish and reproduce in the immediate future.

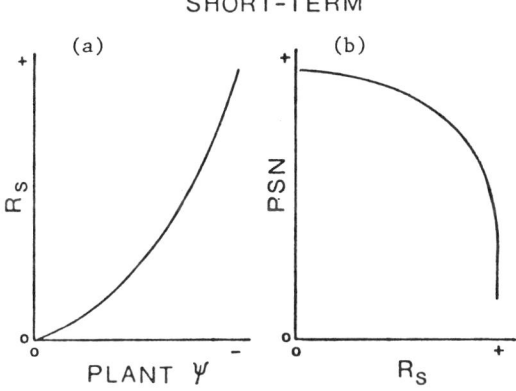

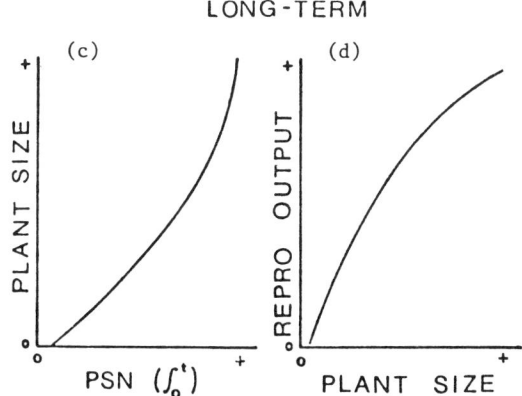

Figure 1. Relationships between short-term physiological measurements (Type I) and long-term demographic measurements (Type II). See text for explanation.

INCORPORATION INTO RECOVERY PLANS

Both Type I and Type II monitoring can easily be incorporated into the existing procedures for recovering endangered plant taxa. Two examples, one general and one specific, will be used to illustrate the possible relationships between the two programs and between monitoring and the recovery effort as a whole. In should be emphasized, however, that these flow diagrams do not represent the only possible configurations and that each taxon will probably require its own, uniquely tailored flow diagram.

In all but the most endangered populations Type I monitoring would precede Type II (fig. 2). After discouraging change in the habitat due to human disturbance (by closing roads, regulating access, etc.), a Type I monitoring program would be used to assess the initial status of the population. If positive, then the population could be subjected to large-scale manipulation for purposes of increasing the number of individuals. A Type II monitoring program could be used to follow the manipulation on a short-term basis and insure continued population stability or growth. If the results of Type I monitoring indicate population decline, another evaluation is made regarding the urgency of the situation. Unless the population is in immediate danger of extinction, the Type I phase is re-entered after an evaluation of monitoring and management methods. If extinction is a possibility, emergency small-scale manipulations and Type II monitoring are warranted until the population shows signs of recovery.

Figure 3 illustrates a flow diagram for the recovery of the Large-flowered Fiddleneck (*Amsinkia grandiflora* (Gray) Kleeb. ex Greene) that was used to re-organize the tasks suggested in the draft recovery plan (U.S.F.W.S. 1986). The results of the Type I monitoring program could be used to coordinate the activities of researchers and to determine if the suggested population enhancements at the only known site (site 300) would be beneficial. If the manipulations resulted in greater mortality, these activities would be suspended and small-scale manipulations used to insure seed set in the treated plots. Otherwise, additional research and recovery efforts could be implemented.

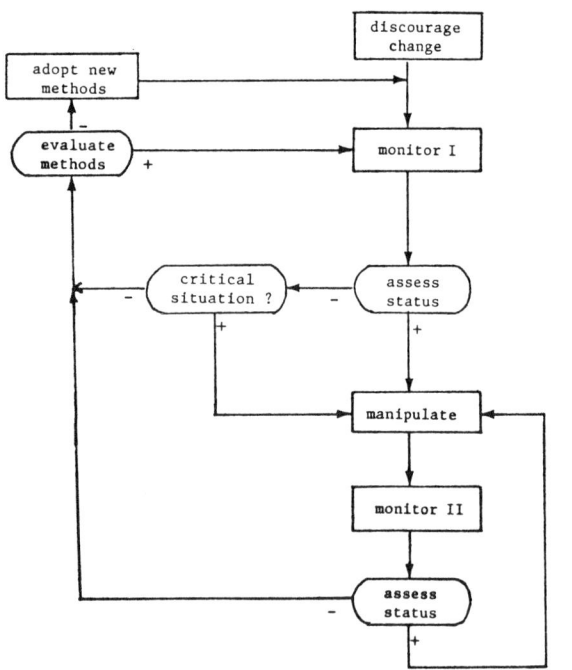

Figure 2. Generalized flow chart for incorporating Types I and II monitoring into the recovery plan of an endangered population.

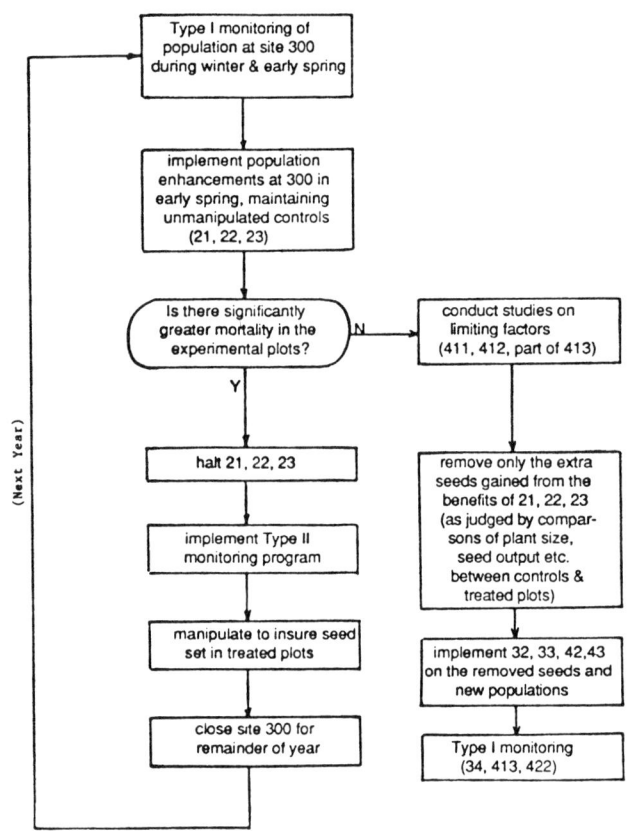

Figure 3. One possible flow diagram for the recovery of *Amsinkia grandiflora* using both types of monitoring programs. Numbers refer to tasks in the draft recovery plan (U.S.F.W.S. 1986).

This general organization also can used to develop a logical distribution of tasks between teams of investigators (fig. 4). In this example, Team A is the principle monitoring and manipulating group at site 300. They would be responsible for conducting the initial enhancements (tasks 21, 22, 23 in the draft recovery plan) and knowing exactly how those manipulations are affecting the population at all times. Until they are able to make a decision as to the treatment effects, teams B and C are "on hold". Team B is the group primarily concerned with investigating other relevant aspects of fiddleneck biology that limit population expansion (tasks 411, 412, 413). Using the additional seed provided by team A manipulations and the knowledge of limiting factors obtained by team B, team C can proceed to propagate and eventually establish colonists for the new populations.

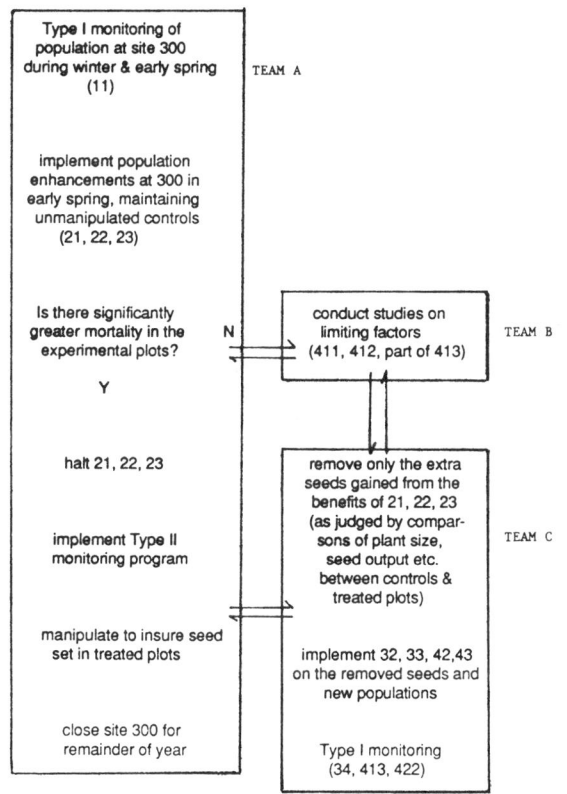

Figure 4. Same flow diagram as in figure 3 showing the distribution of tasks among three research teams, A, B and C. Arrows indicate interfacing.

CONCLUSIONS

These two types of monitoring, when used together, take advantage of the important relationship that exists between short-term ecophysiological processes and long-term demographic trends within populations.

Therefore, it should be possible to infer long-term success of endangered species conservation from a detailed series of short-term, ecophysiological measurements, such as plant water status and stomatal conductance. Long-term demographic measurements should always emphasize survivorship and seed production with secondary attributes chosen according to the specific situation under study. Combining these types of autecological monitoring into a cohesive recovery program can reduce the probability of extinction within natural populations and increase the probability that efforts to establish additional populations will be successful.

ACKNOWLEDGEMENTS

I gratefully acknowledge the support of Susan Cochrane, California Fish and Game and Monty Knudsen, United States Fish and Wildlife Service during this and other studies of endangered plants.

REFERENCES

Barbour, M.G.; Cunningham, G.; Oechel, W.C.; Bamberg, S.A. Growth and Development. In: Mabry, J.H.; Hunziker, J.H. eds. Larrea and its role in desert ecosystems. Stroudsberg, Pa: Dowden, Hutchison and Ross; 1977: Chapter 4.

Barker, S. Shrub population dynamics under grazing - with paddock studies. In: Graetz, R.D.; Howes, K.M.W.; Studies of the Australian arid zone IV. Chenopod shrublands. CSIRO, Division of Land Resources Management, Austrailia; 1979. p 93-106.

Barkley, T.M. Use and abuse of specimen design in distribution mapping. In: Morse, L.E.; Henifin, M.S. eds. Rare plant conservation; Geographic Data Organization. New York: New York Botanical Garden; 1981; 79-82.

Begon, M.; Mortimer, M. Population ecology: A unified study of animals and plants. Oxford: Blackwell Scientific Publications; 1981.

Farquhar, G.D.; Sharkey T.D. Stomatal conductance and photosynthesis. Ann. Rev. Plant Physiol. 33:317-345; 1982.

Goff, F.G.; Dawson, G.A.; Rochow, J.J. Site examination for threatened and endangered plant species. Environmental Management 6: 307-316; 1982.

Harper, J. Population biology of plants. London; Academic Press; 1977.

Hutchings, M.J. Plant population biology. In: Moore, P.D.; Chapman, S.B. eds. Methods in plant ecology. Oxford: Blackwell Scientific Publications; 1986. Chapter 8.

Nelson, J.R. Rare plant surveys: Techniques for impact assessment. Fremontia 12(3): 19-23; 1984.

Pavlik, B.M.; Barbour, M.G. Demography of endemic psammophytes, Eureka Valley, California I. Seed production, dispersal and herbivory. State of California, Department of Fish and Game, Office of Endangered Species, Sacramento, California. 77 p.; 1985.

Pavlik, B.M.; Barbour, M.G. Demography of endemic psammophytes, Eureka Valley, California II. Survivorship, seed bank dynamics and climatology of establishment. State of California, Department of Fish and Game, Office of Endangered Species, Sacramento, California. (in prep.); 1986.

U.S. Fish and Wildlife Service. Draft recovery plan for the large-flowered fiddleneck (Amsinkia grandiflora). U.S. Department of the Interior, Sacramento Endangered Species Office, Sacramento, California. June, 1986. 48p.

Monitoring the Geysers' Panicum (*Dichanthelium lanuginosum* var. *thermale*) at the Little Geysers, Sonoma County, California

Barbara Malloch Leitner, Sally deBecker [1]

Abstract: The Geysers' panicum (<u>Dichanthelium lanuginosum</u> var. <u>thermale</u>), a state-listed endangered perennial grass, grows in association with active surface geothermal features near geothermal energy development in Sonoma County, California. Data have been collected there annually to monitor population viability. Cover and frequency are recorded in permanent plots. Demographic data are collected by mapping individuals, recording age and reproductive data from marked individuals, and following seedling survival. Data collected during 1983-86 indicate a strong decline in plant vigor from 1984 to 1985, and little change in other years. No link to geothermal development is evident, but a connection is postulated between plant vigor in a given year and precipitation in the current and preceding year.

The Geysers' panicum (<u>Dichanthelium lanuginosum</u> (Ell.) Gould var. <u>thermale</u> (Bol.) Spellenberg is restricted to hydrothermally altered soils found in areas of hot springs and fumaroles in the Big Sulphur Creek watershed of Sonoma County, California. It is listed as rare and endangered by the California Native Plant Society (Smith and York 1984) and as endangered by the California Department of Fish and Game (CDFG 1984). The plant occurs entirely within The Geysers Known Geothermal Resource Area (KGRA), a highly productive commercial geothermal electric development. Earliest geothermal development was concentrated in areas having surface geothermal features; as a result, habitat for this rare grass species has been lost.

The Little Geysers is a 12 ha (30 ac) area of mud pots, fumaroles and hot springs that supports the second-largest population of The Geysers' panicum. It is a natural area of statewide significance (California Natural Areas Coordinating Council 1985) and is protected by the geothermal developers in the region, Unocal (Union Oil of California), Geothermal Division, and Pacific Gas and Electric Company (PGandE).

PGandE and Unocal have initiated monitoring studies to determine whether nearby geothermal development has an effect on the population of The Geysers' panicum in the Little Geysers. Unocal supplies steam for PGandE power plant units; PGandE Geysers units 18 and 20 are located 0.5 km and 0.3 km distant, respectively. Geysers Unit 18 began operation in February 1983, and Unit 20 began operation in October, 1985. This paper describes some of the methods employed by PGandE and Unocal to monitor The Geysers' panicum, compares results obtained to date, and makes a preliminary evaluation of the effect of geothermal development on the plant.

NATURAL HISTORY OF THE GEYSERS' PANICUM

The Geysers' panicum occupies four microhabitats in the Little Geysers. Along the thermal streams, it occupies a monotypic band in the permanently moist zone. In xeric areas where the substrate is most strongly altered by natural geothermal effluents, the plant occupies three microhabitats: steep slopes, many of which show evidence of erosion; flat microhabitat where sediment is deposited; and level areas with little erosion or deposition.

The Geysers' panicum has two distinct growth forms. It often has a compact appearance, with short, erect stems. This form is common along unshaded streams and on steep slopes where erosion has created pedestals. On more gentle slopes away from the streams and on shaded streambanks, The Geysers' panicum has a decumbent growth form with long, spreading stems.

Although described as a short-lived perennial, our observations indicate that tussocks can persist over at least five years, and probably much longer. Large tussocks contain several hundred stems, with multiple panicles per stem. Whether

---

[1] Consultant, Oakland, CA; and Biologist, Department of Engineering Research, Pacific Gas and Electric Company, San Ramon, CA.

the tussocks are single large individuals, genetic clones, or clusters of separate plants was not tested in our studies.

Like other members of the genus Dichanthelium, The Geysers' panicum has a C4 photosynthetic pathway. As is typical for C4 plants, this plant grows well in high temperature. Thompson (1984) found that under greenhouse conditions, the most rapid stem elongation took place in July and August, and significant growth ceased only with onset of cool weather, in early October.

METHODS

Physical parameters

Several methods have been employed to measure physical parameters that might affect the growth or vigor of The Geysers' panicum. The location, level of flow, and temperature of the geothermal features were monitored quarterly. Because boron carried in cooling tower drift was implicated as a cause of vegetation damage near operating Geysers power plant units (Malloch et al. 1979), three pre-operational and operational boron measurements were taken. Soil boron concentration was measured in September 1982 and 1985 in two plots in the Little Geysers. Aerosol deposition was collected at a single location and its boron content measured annually for two years, in September 1984 and 1985. Foliage boron content of The Geysers' panicum was sampled from two plots annually, in September 1982 through 1985 (Jones and Stokes 1986). Precipitation was measured at PGandE Geysers Unit 13, about 1.7 km distant.

Frequency of The Geysers' panicum

In 1982, Unocal established five permanent plots to measure the frequency of The Geysers' panicum. The plots were subjectively chosen to encompass a variety of site conditions and ranged in size from 3 by 10 meters to 10 by 10 meters. Presence or absence of the plant was recorded along 10 cm intervals on transects spaced 10 cm apart. The plots were sampled once annually in 1982 through 1986. Between-year comparisons were made using the chi-square analysis.

Demographic studies

PGandE in 1984 and Unocal in 1985 initiated demographic studies of The Geysers' panicum. The methods used by PGandE and Unocal were similar, permitting pooling of some data.

Plants were individually marked and monitored annually to determine longevity and annual survival and growth. Marked plants were located in clusters subjectively placed to represent the four micro-habitats of the Little Geysers. In 1984, 87 plants were marked, and 42 were added in 1985 to increase sample size and to replace plants that had died. After the assumed end of the growing season in each year, the status (alive or dead) of each plant was recorded.

In 1985, 11 seedling survival plots were established to determine season of germination, the first-year seedling survival rate, and annual variation in this rate. The size and location of plots was subjectively chosen to represent all micro-habitats. Monthly data on seedling mortality and germination were recorded.

Percent cover

From 1983 to 1986, PGandE measured cover from vertical photographs of ten 1.5 by 1.5 meter, subjectively chosen permanent quadrats. The photographs were taken at the assumed end of the growing season, using a camera suspended from a boom tripod (de Becker and Mahler 1986). Percent cover was determined by projecting a 100 cell grid onto each photograph and counting each cell having more than 50 percent cover.

RESULTS

Physical parameters

Qualitative monitoring of the surface geothermal features showed that flows increased and temperature decreased during the winter storm season. This suggests that the water supplying the geothermal features is largely local and meteoric in origin. Surface geothermal features showed little spatial movement over the two-year study period (Mills, unpubl. data)[2].

Jones and Stokes (1986) found maximum soil concentrations of 0.24 mg/l of boron in 1982, and 0.30 mg/l in 1985; they considered the increase biologically unimportant. Both values were lower than the 1.0 mg/l level considered safe for agricultural crops (Keren and Bingham 1985, cited in Jones and Stokes 1986), though they were higher than samples taken at comparable distance from cooling towers but located on soils unaltered by natural geothermal fluids.

---

[2]Mills, Jim, engineer, Unocal Geothermal Division, Santa Rosa.

Aerosol boron deposition decreased from 1983-84 to 1984-85. Higher boron levels were found at other sampling stations closer to cooling towers, but the Little Geysers values were still higher than were predicted from a PGandE model of cooling tower drift deposition. This was attributed to the natural boron emission from mudpots and fumaroles (Jones and Stokes 1986).

Foliage boron in all years was within the range expected for vegtation growing at sites unaffected by cooling tower drift (Jones and Stokes 1984, 1986). The 1985 concentration, <40 ug/g, was lower than in previous years.

Precipitation recorded in the 1982-83 season was 63% above average; the 1983-84 season was average; the 1984-85 season was 40% below average; and the 1985-86 season was 13% above average for precipitation (figure 1).

Highly significant increases also were measured between 1982, 1983, and 1984 (Leitner 1985); however, these comparisons appeared to be due in part to measurements that were taken in June and July, respectively, while maximum annual growth is attained later in the year. In 1984 and

Table 1. Comparison of frequency of The Geysers' panicum, Dichanthelium lanuginosum var. thermale, at the Little Geysers, 1984-86.

Quadrat	Comparison 1984-1985	1985-1986
1(n=10,000)	-31 pct.*	-10 pct.*
2(n=7,500)	-26 pct.*	-2 pct.
3(n=3,300)	0 pct.	+1 pct.
4(n=4,800)	+2 pct.	-7 pct.*
5(n=8,000)	+1 pct.	0 pct.

*significant between-year difference (p<0.05)

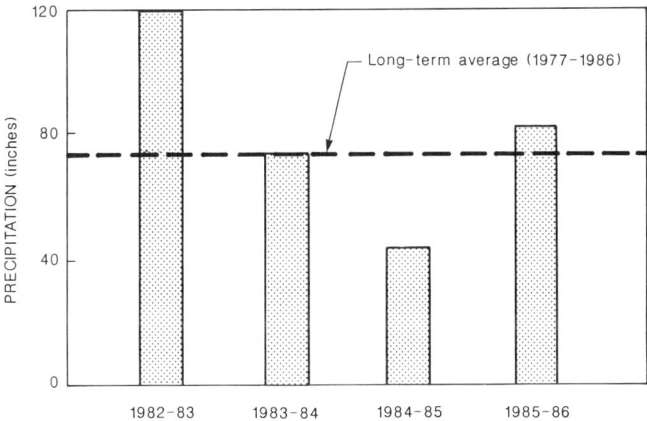

Figure 1. Annual and long-term average precipitation near the Little Geysers (measured at Pacific Gas and Electric Company's Geysers Power Plant Unit 13).

subsequent years, frequency measurements were taken in August, when maximum potential growth appeared to be balanced against mortality and grazing.

It appears that The Geysers' panicum growing on slopes varies more in frequency from year to year than do plants growing in flat sites; that is, plant vigor is less variable in plants growing on level sites. To test the null hypothesis that no significant difference in variability existed between sloping and level sites, pairs of square meter segments taken from sloping and level areas were matched by frequency values. The Wilcoxon signed-rank test was used to determine whether slope was a significant factor in between-year variation. In 2 out of 3 comparisons, areas having slope of more than 10 degrees were more variable than areas having slope of less than 10 degrees (p<0.1).

Demographic studies

Mortality

Of 62 mature plants (those with panicles) marked in summer 1984, 45 (72.5 percent) survived until summer 1985. Thirty-seven (59.7 percent of the original) were still alive in summer 1986. Mortality for immature plants was higher; of 25 marked in 1984, only 13 (52.0 percent) survived one year.

Annual mortality rates of mature plants in the four microhabitats differed greatly (table 2) between years. Consistent with the results of the frequency measurements, flat habitat appeared to favor

Frequency measurements

Table 1 presents the comparisons between frequency plots in the 1984, 1985 and 1986 seasons. Plots 1 and 2, two of the largest plots, had large and significant declines in frequency between 1984 and 1985. Plots 1 and 4 had significant, though smaller, declines between 1985 and 1986. All other plots showed no significant change. The declines in frequency were correlated with a general reduction in plant vigor observed over the three sampling seasons and throughout the Little Geysers.

longevity and a stable population. An exception was depositional areas, which had high mortality. However, depositional areas may support densities of mature plants equal to other areas, because the depositional environment appears to permit rapid growth, and flowering in the first year.

Table 2. Annual mortality of mature The Geysers' panicum, Dichanthelium lanuginosum var. thermale, by microhabitat, at the Little Geysers, 1985-86.

Microhabitat	Mortality (pct.) 1985	1986
Steep	33 (n=18)	23 (n=39)
Depositional	83 (n=6)	69 (n=16)
Level	0 (n=31)	14 (n=43)
Streamside	14 (n=7)	21 (n=19)

Mortality results showed that a substantial proportion of mature plants survived at least two years. Additional years of data on these plants, combined with data from newer cohorts, are needed to determine average life spans.

Seedling Germination and Survival

Germination occurred in every quarter from spring 1985 through summer 1986 (fig. 2). Germination in the spring, fall and winter quarters was about equal. The summer quarter appeared least favorable for seedlings; germination was low, mortality was high, and only in the summer quarter did mortality exceed germination and survivorship.

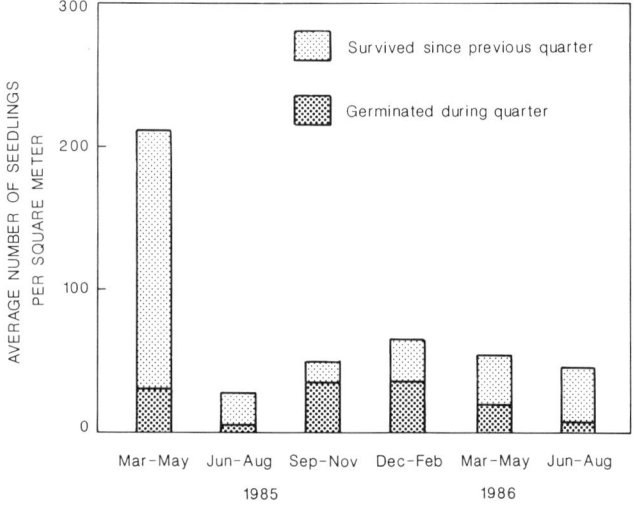

Figure 2. Quarterly seedling germination and survival of The Geysers' panicum.

Percent cover

Results from measurements of percent cover over four years (table 3) show less cover in 1986 than in 1983 on all plots combined. There was little change from 1983 to 1984, a sharp decline from 1984 to 1985, and little change from 1985 to 1986. The pattern is generally consistent regardless of microhabitat.

The annual photography revealed possible competition from another perennial grass, Andropogon virginicus. One plot had three small A. virginicus plants and 43 percent cover by The Geysers' panicum in 1983 and dropped to 17 percent cover in two years while the A. virginicus plants grew larger.

Table 3. Percent cover of The Geysers panicum, Dichanthelium lanuginosum var. thermale, by microhabitat, 1983-86.

Microhabitat	Average cover (pct.)			
	1983	1984	1985	1986
Steep (n=5)	55.0	56.0	39.2	40.6
Level (n=3)	57.0	64.0	48.0	53.0
Streamside (n=2)	65.0	49.5	40.5	39.5

CONCLUSIONS

Causes of trends in The Geysers' panicum vigor

Both frequency and cover showed overall declines from 1984 to 1985, although some sample plots did not change significantly. The two methods differed in their comparison between 1985 and 1986 results: while frequency data showed a smaller decline in some plots, cover had no change. More years of data are needed to separate the effects of sampling methodology, site characteristics, and annual variation. However, the general agreement in the trends evidenced by both methods permits a discussion of possible causes of change, both natural and human-caused.

The only known significant adverse effect of geothermal power plant operation on vegetation is boron toxicity. But preoperational and operational monitoring of aerosol boron, soil boron and geothermal features at the Little Geysers show no trends likely to adversely affect The Geysers' panicum.

The potential relation between steam extraction and the observed trends in The Geysers' panicum is not supported by the physical data. The surface geothermal features remained constant in location and seasonally-adjusted temperature during the sampling period; moreover, most of the population grows in xeric microhabitats at some distance from thermal features. Thus, operational impact seems an unlikely source of change in plant vigor at this time. Measurements of physical parameters should be continued, though, as they provide the direct link between geothermal development and potential impact to this rare plant.

A second human-caused factor that may deserve further attention is the potential effect of intensive surveying carried out in a relatively small area of steep slopes and loose, poor soil. Localized physical disturbance may have caused damage to this plant in some areas.

The most significant natural variable is precipitation. Patterns of precipitation generally follow annual patterns of vigor in The Geysers' panicum. However, observation of weather data suggest that plant response has more closely followed precipitation levels in both the current and preceding year. Under this model of response to two years' precipitation, the relatively high vigor values seen in 1984 resulted from high precipitation in the previous year, coupled with average precipitation during the current year; the low vigor values in 1985 resulted from two years of average or below-average precipitation. A single-year model might have predicted a marked increase in 1986 vigor over the 1985 results; however, the stable vigor observed may be the response to a slightly above-average year preceded by an unusually low precipitation year in 1984. This model suggests that the high vigor observed in 1983 was the result of two consecutive years of above-normal precipitation; we examined the 1981-82 records from the same station and found that precipitation was 25% percent above normal during that season, a finding which supports this model. As a further prediction based on this model, we suggest that an average or above average precipitation in 1986-87 will result in significant increase in The Geysers' panicum vigor; only far-below average precipitation would be likely to result in decreased frequency and cover.

Limitations of the methods and results

As with all non-randomly selected permanent plot measurements, the results obtained may not apply to the entire population of The Geysers' panicum at the Little Geysers. Random samples were attempted during earlier studies, but with the highly aggregated distribution characteristic of the species, sampling time was prohibitively high (de Becker 1984).

The difficulty we encountered in determining an optimum sampling date underscores the need to plan a sampling effort in light of the biology of the taxon, even if information is available only at the generic level. The growth pattern of a C4 photosynthetic pathway species differs from most spring-growing California plants.

Recommendations

Continuing the data collection reported here will provide more extensive understanding of the annual variations in germination rates and locations, longevity of individuals, and reproduction. Sample sizes of most of these measurements have already been increased to provide greater representation of the population. Additional vigor and growth data not reported here will be useful indications of annual variation among mature plants and of possible interspecific competition.
Continuing measurements of frequency and cover will permit assessment of the contribution of physical factors to annual change in the vigor of The Geysers' panicum, including precipitation, slope, and erosion.

Study plots vary in soil moisture, temperature, and chemistry. These parameters should be measured, because they might further define microhabitat and might explain germination and establishment patterns based on plot location.

REFERENCES

California Department of Fish and Game. List of endangered or threatened plants. Sacramento, CA: California Department of Fish and Game; 1984. 4 pp.
California Natural Areas Coordinating Council. Inventory of California natural areas. Sonoma, CA: California Natural Areas Coordinating Council; 1985. 12 vols.
de Becker, Sally. Geysers panicum monitoring study, 1983 report. San Ramon, CA: Pacific Gas and Electric Company Department of Engineering Research, DER Report 417-84.19; 1984. 43 pp.
_____ and D. Mahler. Photographing quadrats to measure percent cover. Natural Areas J. 6:67-69; 1986.
Jones and Stokes Associates. The Geysers vegetation stress and monitoring study--1983 annual report. San Ramon, CA: Pacific Gas and Electric Company; 1984. 240 pp.

_____. Draft, The Geysers vegetation stress monitoring study--1986 annual report. San Ramon, CA: Pacific Gas and Electric Company; 1986.

Keren, R., and F.T. Bingham. Boron in water, soils, and plants. Adv. in Soil Science. 1:229-276; 1985.

Leitner, Barbara Malloch. Little Geysers vegetation monitoring study, third year report, 1984. Prepared for Unocal Geothermal Division, Santa Rosa, CA; 1985. 70 pp.

Malloch, B.S., M.K. Eaton, and N.L. Crane. Assessment of vegetation stress and damage near The Geysers power plant units. San Ramon, CA: Pacific Gas and Electric Company Department of Engineering Research Report, DER Report 420-79.3; 1979. 88 pp.

Smith, James Payne, Jr., and Richard P. York. Inventory of rare and endangered vascular plants of California. Sacramento, CA: California Native Plant Society, CNPS Special Publication No. 1 (Third Edition); 1984. 174 pp.

Thompson, R.J. Progress report on Geyser's panicum horticultural study. San Francisco, CA: Pacific Gas and Electric Company Civil Engineering Department; 1984. 20 pp.

Monitoring Rare Plant Populations in the Knoxville Area of California

Glen Clifton, Joe Callizo [1]

Abstract: Monitoring of 102 rare plant populations at 39 sites has been initiated in the Knoxville area of Napa, Lake, and Yolo Counties of California. All are located proximal to gold mining activities now being conducted by Homestake Mining Company. Population numbers and endangerment are to be determined at least biennially. In addition, a special study is being made annually on 4 of the populations.

In 1983 and 1984 vegetation surveys made by one of us, G. C., located over 400 populations of 26 rare plant species in the Knoxville region of Napa, Lake, and Yolo Counties of California (appendix 1). They occur in the Knoxville and Jericho Valley Quadrangles in an area of 9650 acres roughly bounded by Knoxville, Hunting Creek, the north end of Morgan Valley, and Davis Creek.[2]

A gold mining plan for this region proposed by Homestake Mining Company would have extirpated 126 rare plant populations. Therefore, suggestions were made for a number of modifications, e.g., relocations of facilities, shiftings of roads, and movements of pipelines. An amended plan, subsequently adopted, resulted in the extirpation of only 80 rare plant populations. In some cases one population was sacrificed in exchange for saving or fencing another. Fencing was recommended for several sites in order to exclude cattle grazing and construction equipment. Consequently, the Company fenced 3 populations of Adobe Lily (Fritillaria pluriflora Torr. ex Benth.); the only population of Thelypodium, thought to be species brachycarpum Torr.; and 23 other rare plant populations at 10 sites.

---

[1] Plant Taxonomist, Biosystems Analysis, Inc.; and Naturalist, California Native Plant Society.

[2] D'Appolonia, 1982.

ONGOING MONITORING

During the construction phase of the mining plan, many peripheral populations of rare plants were flagged and frequently monitored by one of us, G. C., working for Biosystems Analysis, Inc. This insured that populations which were not to be extirpated, would not be disturbed by laborers or construction equipment.

A Periodic Plant Watch conducted by members of the Napa Valley Chapter of the California Native Plant Society has become part of the annual monitoring program conducted by Biosystems Analysis, Inc., for Homestake Mining Company. Thirty-nine sites and 126 populations of rare plants immediately peripheral to the gold mining activities are being monitored in mid-May. In 1985 most of these populations were located and visually assessed for signs of endangerment. Although no new, major disturbances were observed, the Company's attention was called to a few minor threats. These, they subsequently alleviated. In 1986 we began direct and estimated counts of population numbers and continued assessments of endangerment. Once again, no new, major disturbances were noticed. Several new populations of rare plants were discovered, however, in areas of earlier disturbance. These were of species, like Four-petaled Calyptridium (Calyptridium quadripetalum Wats.), Serpentine Sunflower (Helianthus exilis Gray), and Serpentine Collomia (Collomia diversifolia Greene), that are known pioneers. They thrive on disturbance. The plant monitoring in this area is to be repeated annually for the next 35 years or so, i.e., for the duration of the gold mining. We have found that 2 of us working together can visit over ½ of the sites and survey over ½ of the populations in 1 day's time. The purpose of this monitoring program is to determine any significant changes in population numbers that could be attributed to the mining work. The assessments of endangerment could help avert unfavorable impacts from external sources.

Table 1. Results of the 1985 and 1986 inventory of 4 _Fritillaria pluriflora_ populations in the Homestake Mining Company's McLaughlin Mine Project Area.[1]

Site No.	Year	No. of plants w flowers	No. of plants w capsules	No. of plants vegetative	No. of 1st.-yr. rosettes	Mean Ht. plants w. 1 capsule	Mean Hght. plants w. 2 capsules	Total No. of plants
No. 32 (Unfenced)	1985	321	182	190	154	4.9"(N=117)	6.0"(N=65)	847
	1986	543	239	304	474	5.6"(N=178)	6.8"(N=61)	1560
No 41A (Fenced)	1985	162	62	139	17	7.0"(N=54)	8.4"(N=8)	380
	1986	272	153	119	75	7.0"(N=122)	8.4"(N=31)	619
No. 41B (Fenced)	1985	132	60	136	8	5.5"(N=56)	7.8"(N=4)	336
	1986	114	49	65	49	6.4"(N=46)	7.7"(N=3)	277
No. 44 (Fenced)	1985	82	15	178	60	5.4"(N=13)	7.5"(N=2)	335
	1986	107	19	88	124	5.8"(N=18)	5.0"(N=1)	338

[1] from Davilla, Bill. "Sensitive Plant Monitoring Program" 1986; 9p.

ONGOING RESEARCH

One of us, J. C., and Richard Smith, a graduate student at the University of California at Davis, have separately and successfully grown the Thelypodium from seed collected from the Knoxville population. Some of these plants, along with a few from the extant population, have been transplanted to several other sites. Many of them have flowered and some have fruited, but establishment has not been achieved. Two new sites have been identified recently which appear to be more appropriate than any used so far. They are located in the NE¼ of the NE¼ of Section 34 and in the NW¼ of the SE¼ of Section 29, Township 12 North, Range 5 West. Transplants are planned there in the near future.

A special study has been initiated on 4 populations of Adobe Lily. Three are fenced to exclude cattle grazing; 1 is not. For each of these populations, annually in the month of June, an attempt is made to count every plant and to categorize each according to its stage of growth. The categories used are as follows: first-year rosettes, older vegetative, flowered but not fruited, fruited with one capsule, and fruited with two or more capsules. In addition, the heights of all plants that have fruited are measured and tabulated. The results from 2 years of observation are shown in table 1. The total number of plants increased markedly in 2 of the populations, 1 fenced and 1 not, and decreased somewhat in 1 fenced population. It is unclear as yet if the presence or absence of direct grazing, or an increase or decrease in grass cover, are significant causitive factors. The increase in mean heights of the fruiting plants of some of the populations and the increases in numbers of the first-year rosettes could be attributed to the increase in rainfall during the winter of 1985-86 over that of 1984-85. Hopefully, the data of future years will clarify these interpretations.

CONCLUSIONS

The rare plant monitoring program in the vicinity of Knoxville should contribute to the protection and survival of the many rare plant populations peripheral to the gold mining activity. An increase in our understanding of the population dynamics of Adobe Lily will come from the research on the 4 populations of that species. The propagation of the Thelypodium could result in the establishment of replacement populations should the 1 existing population be destroyed. All in all, the plant work in the vicinity of Knoxville has been and is proceeding with the cooperation of private enterprise (Homestake Mining Company), environmental consultants (Biosystems Analysis, Inc.), governing agencies (Bureau of Land Management, California Department of Fish and Game), academic institutions (University of California, Pacific Union College), non-profit organizations (California Native Plant Society), and many concerned individuals.

Appendix 1. Rare plant populations discovered in the Knoxville Area of California.

Plant Species		Regulatory Status		Number of Populations			
Scientific Name	Common Name	USFS[1] Candidate List No.	CNPS[2] LIST	Total	Fenced	Extirpated	Being monitored
Antirrhinum virga Gray	Tall Snapdragon		4	1		1	
Arabis spp.	Rock-cress			7			
Asclepias solanoana Woods	Prostrate Milkweed		4	9			
Astragalus breweri Gray	Brewer's Milkvetch		4	5	2	2	1
Astragalus clevelandii Greene	Cleveland's Milk-vetch		4	26		7	9
Calyptridium quadripetalum Wats.	Four-petaled Calyptridium		4	9			5
Collomia diversifolia Greene	Serpentine Collomia		4	19		4	6
Cryptantha hispidula Greene ex Brand	Napa Cryptantha		4	*			5
Delphinium uliginosum Curran	Swamp Larkspur		4	48	3	13	22
Eriogonum nervulosum (Stokes) Reveal	Snow Mt. Buckwheat	2	1B	7			
Fritillaria pluriflora Torr. ex Benth.	Adobe Lily	2	4	9	3	1	4
Fritillaria purdyi Eastw.	Purdy's Fritillary		4	40	4	6	9
Helianthus exilis Gray	Serpentine Sunflower	2	3	64	2	13	13
Hesperolinon drymarioides (Curran) Small	Drymaria-like Dwarf Flax	2	1B	4			
Juglans hindsii Jeps. ex Smith	Northern Calif. Black Walnut	1	1B	1			
Lepidium latipes Hook	Dwarf Peppergrass		4	3			2
Lomatium ciliolatum var. hooveri (Jeps.) Math. & Const.	Hoover's Wild Parsnip		4	14	2	4	7
Madia hallii Keck	Hall's Mountain Tarweed		4			1	

*widely distributed.

Appendix 1 continued.

Plant Species		Regulatory Status		Number of Populations			
Scientific Name	Common Name	USFS[1] Candidate List No.	CNPS[2] List	Total	Fenced	Extirpated	Being monitored
Malacothamnus fremontii (Torr. ex Gray) Greene	Heller's Shrub Mallow		4	1			
Mimulus nudatus Curran ex Greene	Bare Monkey Flower		4	34	2	7	20
Navarretia jepsonii Bailey ex Jeps.	Jepson's Navarretia		4	22	7	10	12
Orobanche valida var. howellii Heckard & Collins	Howell's Broomrape	1	4	3			
Pogogyne douglasii ssp. parviflora (Benth.) Howell	Douglas' Pogogyne	2	4	1			
Senecio clevelandii Greene	Cleveland's Butterweed		4	46	1	11	14
Streptanthus morrisonii Hoffman	Morrison's Jewel Flower	1	3	33			
Thelypodium brachycarpum Torr.	Short-padded Thelypodium	2	4	1	1		1
			Grand totals:	410	27	80	126

ACKNOWLEDGEMENTS

Major contributive efforts have been made by Ray Krauss (Homestake Mining Company), Bill Davilla (Biosystems Analysis, Inc.), Ivana Roland (Bureau of Land Management), Stephen Raye (California Department of Fish and Game), Richard Smith (University of California, Davis), Gilbert Muth (Pacific Union College, Angwin, California), and several members of the California Native Plant Society.

REFERENCES

D'Appolonia. McLaughlin Project Environmental Report, volume 1; 1982: section 9.0, 31-37.

[1] USFWS Federal Register Vol. 45, No. 242.

[2] Smith, Payne S.; York, Richard. Inventory of Rare and Endangered Vascular Plants of California, Special Publication No. 1, 3rd. Edition, California Native Plant Society; 1984; 174p.

Innovative Programmatic Approaches to Resource Conservation

Peter Grenell [1]

Abstract: Most conventional resource planning falls short of successful implementation. Conservation through isolated projects may have specific on-site value and occasionally some demonstration effects, but does not adequately address the magnitude and complexity of resource conservation needs and issues. Several innovative approaches based on broad program applications are discussed, drawing upon the ten year experience of the California State Coastal Conservancy in Coastal resource conservation. Topics presented include use of transfer of development credits (TDCs), mitigation banking, watershed management, wetland enhancement and restoration programming, "creative development", nonprofit stewardship, and use of dispute resolution and multiple-use problem-solving techniques.

The State Coastal Conservancy was created by the California Legislature in 1976. It was organized to implement programs of agricultural land preservation, to provide public access to the coast, renovation of poorly planned development, open space preservation, wetland and other habitat enhancement, and urban waterfront restoration. The Conservancy has jurisdiction in the coastal zone, an area stretching from Mexico to Oregon, ranging in width from a few city blocks to as much as five miles inland.

The Conservancy's principal objective is to resolve resource-based land-use disputes not capable of resolution through traditional regulatory processes like those used by the Coastal Commission. The Commission was established in 1972 by the people of California with the passage of the controversial ballot initiative Proposition 20. The Commission was given development permit jurisdiction in the coastal zone and the task of preparing an overall coastal plan for the zone by 1975. The Coastal Act of 1976 extended the Commission's life and extablished a local coastal planning process for all jurisdictions in the zone. The Coastal Conservancy attempts to find solution to intractable resource issues identified in the coastal plan, and to help the coastal communities carry out their plans once they are completed.

In fulfilling it's objective, the Conservancy has pioneered along the way, the use of innovative conservation and development methods, and has extended and adapted the use of others into new areas. The following paragraphs briefly describe the most interesting and potentially applicable approaches used by the Conservancy in some of its program areas.

WETLAND AND WATERSHED PROGRAMS

Wetland Restoration and Enhancement

One of the top priorities stated in the Coastal Act is the preservation, restoration, and enhancement of the state's rapidly vanishing coastal wetlands. Over ninety percent of the state's wetlands have disappeared to date, and the situation seems nowhere near reversing itself. The Conservancy has adopted an affirmative action approach to this critical issue. One of its earliest projects, in the north coast city of Arcata, sought to transform an abandoned dumpsite into a functioning series of salt, brackish, and freshwater marshes. Designed to increase public access and provide a variety of habitat areas, the project has since attracted national attention for its creative design and active citizen and local government participation.

This approach has been applied throughout the coastal zone in the Conservancy's wetlands program. Its priorities now include Humboldt, San Francisco, Morro and San Diego Bays, the Tijuana Estuary, and San Diego County's coastal lagoons. The program funds individual projects in these locations, but each project is considered an important part of the entire coastal ecosystem. The value of these wetlands for the Pacific flyway, for marine species propagation, for public education and recreation, and potentially for recycling treated urban effluent is incalculable.

The need to treat wetland ecosystems comprehensively is illustrated by the range of Coastal Conservancy-funded activities in the Tijuana River Estuarine Sanctuary on the Mexican border. There,

---
[1] Executive Officer, California State Coastal Conservancy

the conservancy has funded land acquisitions, wetland enhancement and protection, public access and interpretive facilities. Most recently, in an exploration into alternatives of dealing with the untreated sewage problem in the estuary, the Conservancy also funded an innovative low cost wastewater treatment plan whose preliminary testings have shown to be successful.

Watershed Management

As the Conservancy's programs evolved, watershed management emerged as a major priority to assure that the benefits created in coastal wetlands are not negated by uncontrolled impacts generated upstream. Working with multiple interests and jurisdictions to negotiate agreements on flood control approaches, sediment basins, tougher grading ordinances, and funding distribution is difficult, time-consuming work; but it is necessary if coastal watersheds are to be preserved, and it can be done. The Conservancy is now working with ranchers in northern California counties to arrive at equitable means of sharing the public and private responsibilities for the protection of riparian corridors. These efforts, should they prove successful, could become significant precedents and serve as models for other organizations.

Mitigation Banking

The concept of mitigation banking is receiving attention as a new means of coping with continued development pressures on wetland habitats. Mitigation "banks" are wetland sites created or restored in advance of a proposed development. The costs of restoration and maintenance would be paid for by the development on the basis of a determination of comparable habitat values to be mitigated for. Mitigation banks are being examined for their potential usefulness in assuring mitigation of several small and scattered developments which may not be capable of successful mitigation individually. They may also provide known costs of mitigation requirements and this could expedite permitting processes where mitigation is deemed acceptable. Finally, they hold the potential for providing greater assurance that wetland values and functions which are to be lost because of overriding development needs can be recovered if not on-site than off-site.

Numerous problems exist with the concept of mitigation, which as not as yet proven successful. The Conservancy has been involved in several mitigation projects on what can only be considered as an experimental basis, given the scant knowledge of how wetland systems really work. Should regulatory agencies continue to consider mitigation as an acceptable alternative under certain conditions, it should be done within the context of broader regional wetland policies and goals.

INNOVATIVE LAND MANAGEMENT METHODS

Cluster Design, Easements and Mixed Use Development

Open space, habitat and public recreation issues come in various forms in different parts of the coast. For example, small lot or "antiquated" subdivisions characterize several different regions in California. If developed, these subdivisions would destroy open space and upland habitat areas, block scenic coastal vistas, and eliminate areas that would have been more suitable for public use. When public funds are inadequate to acquire such areas, other approaches must be used. The redesign of a development project to a cluster design in non-sensitive portions of the property and placing conservation or similar easements over the remainder, or the use of life estates, and planning for mixed use development, can all generate needed funds for financing conservation while preserving environmentally sensitive areas. The Conservancy has successfully employed these methods to resolve land management issues.

A broad program such as that of the Coastal Conservancy with a consistent overall approach can provide a series of models for replication or adaption by others. More importantly, a regional, programmatic approach can result in a greater impact with respect to organizing more cost-effective projects, local commitment, understanding, support, and direct beneficial impact on resources. Organizations such as the New Jersey Pinelands Commission, and recent thinking in the State of Florida, appear to demonstrate that this vein of thinking is being supported.

Transfer of Development Credits (TDCs)

Another approach used to resolve land-use conflicts which is receiving increasing attention involves the transfer of development credits (also known as development rights or TDRs) to other off-site locations more suitable for development. Once again, this is an alternative to fee acquisitions when shortage of finance is a constraint. Though the TDC approach can take different forms and use a variety of value determinations, the basic idea is as follows: the local county government determines a limit on development; a parcel's development value is then determined on the basis of a formula; it is then used either by the owner or sold to someone else, at another location called a "receiver" site. The cost of public acquisition of the development right (if this occurs) is, if necessary, recovered at the receiver site, where the development right can be sold by the public acquiring agency to a private developer. These methods can also be directly employed by the private sector.

The Conservancy's experience thus far with TDC programs has been that on the one hand, local governments have requested assistance to get such programs underway; and on the other hand, the private sector has desired greater assurance that TDCs can be sold or purchased when the need or desire exists. The Coastal Conservancy is now developing in the Santa Monica Mountains of Los Angeles County, Big Sur in Monterey County, San Luis Obispo County and Sonoma County, with other possible locations on the horizon. Interestingly enough, the New Jersey Pineland Commission currently operates a seven county TDC program, in which TDCs can be transferred across county lines.

TECHNIQUES FOR RESOLVING MULTIPLE USE CONFLICTS

Mediation Alternatives

In contrast to conventional environmental mediation techniques, the Coastal Conservancy has evolved more informal methods based on several principles: Accepting the commitment to work through to arrive at a mutually satisfactory solution; involve all relevant parties and identify all real interests in the conflict; include consideration of economic and financial factors as an integral part of the dialogue to provide a realistic basis for resolution; and encourage expansion of the scope of the discussion to enable the broadest consideration of alternative solutions.

In the Cascade Ranch project in San Mateo County, the Conservancy found itself working with several non-profit organizations, local farming interests, the County and State Department of Parks and Recreation and the Coastal Commission to arrive at an acceptable resolution. The project, located on a very scenic 4,000 acre coastal ranch, began as a conflict between a proposed residential development and the need for public recreation and overnight accommodations on this well-visited part of the coast. The conflict evolved into one between advocates of a state park expansion on the ranch and the continuation of farming. A grueling series of meetings, discussions, and negotiations went on for over eighteen months before agreement was finally reached on use distributions, site designs, buffers, water rights, and financing. In the process, a wide range of alternatives were considered in a manner not characteristic of more formal mediation arrangements.

A similar approach is now being used to help resolve the long-standing controversy over preservation of old-growth redwoods and retention of jobs and revenues in Mendocino County's Sinkyone Wilderness. Where emotions run high, more informal analysis and discussion with individual parties has often shown to be more productive than conventional larger meetings.

Community Design Workshops

In certain settings, especially urban ones, modified public workshops have proven successful in resolving tense local use disputes. The Conservancy adapted such methods to enable citizen-designed plans to be presented and subsequently approved by initially hesitant local governments in Seal Beach, Oceanside, Santa Monica, and other small coastal cities. The approved plans were then implemented to restore deteriorated and under-used urban waterfronts.

CONCLUSION

A coherent, programmatic approach to resource conservation, whether carried out by a single agency such as the Coastal Conservancy or several organizations, provides a strong base for establishing conservation policy implementation. Identification and use of innovative techniques, demonstration methods, and developing local capacity for stewardship are priority elements for success. The Conservancy experiences briefly described, have all involved collaboration with a wide range of local, regional, or national nonprofit organizations. These groups provide a strong base, and often the cutting edge, for efforts to develop an informed, committed and active population willing to share the burdens of resource stewardship. The combined result of such a concerted effort is of greater value than that of a single project carried out in isolation. A broad resource conservation program is critical to dealing effectively with the scale of resource issues facing us today.

Is Bonding Any Guarantee in Ecological Management?

Deborah Hillyard [1]

Abstract: Performance bonds are used to guarantee that specific tasks are completed; this is a commonly accepted practice in general contracting. Applications of similar methods to guarantee a good faith effort in rare plant mitigation, and the pros and cons of using this practice in mitigation, are discussed with regard to the dynamic nature of biological systems. Use of these techniques is most successful when a surety deposit is secured, tight specifications are developed beforehand, and the results are monitored.

Bonds, surety deposits, and in some cases memoranda of understanding between agencies, all fall into a general category of techniques that are available to guarantee a good faith effort. They can be used to insure compliance with various project and permit conditions that relate to mitigation efforts and similar types of resource protection and restoration projects. This paper outlines these procedures, and some potential pitfalls of using the method in resource situations; then presents some guidelines to help make this method more usable, and more enforceable, for resource oriented projects.

The use of performance bonds has long been accepted in the construction industry to guarantee that all specified work is accomplished; this generally involves the contractor posting a bond with a bonding company under the stipulation that if specific tasks are not accomplished, a pre-determined amount of money will be paid by the bonding company for completion of the necessary work.

Less commonly used, but preferred, is an actual certificate of deposit or letter of credit filed by the contractor. This method is preferred because collecting from bonding companies can be quite difficult; they, of course, can't pay up on too many claims and expect to stay in the black. By demanding a surety deposit, rather than a bond, the money is available immediately, without the middleman. An MOU between agencies can function in the same manner--the project proponent agrees to meet specified costs under specified conditions. No money is deposited, but the understanding is that they're good for it.

It must be pointed out that the use of bonds in construction is a standard, accepted practice only because there are standard, accepted ways in which to construct a facility--whether it is a road, a building, or a dam. Various regulations are compulsively explicit, and there are multitudes of trained building inspectors willing to point out any and all departures from the accepted methodology. There is also a definite finished product that you get at the end of a project; no waiting for things to grow.

In the context of developing in resource sensitive situations, the developer (or project proponent) can be anyone from an individual wishing to grade a new driveway, to a government agency wishing to inundate hundreds of thousands of acres. As long as the development is going in on private property subject to permitting, or on public lands, a guarantee of good faith effort can be used. The use of bonds or surety deposits is usually required by the permitting agency; but it can be required by any agency (or individual for that matter) initiating any type of work to be done under contract, to insure that their own objectives are met.

Various guarantees of good faith can be effectively used in projects that impact natural systems in two different, but related, situations: protection and restoration. First, where protection is an issue, and sensitive areas are to be avoided, a guarantee of good faith can be used to maintain a population of rare plants, or avoid habitat disturbance for rare vertebrate or invertebrate animal species, or protect sensitive or protected habitats such as wetlands. Any

---

[1] Associate State Park Resource Ecologist, California Department of Parks and Recreation, Sacramento, CA

disturbance or damage to the protected resource can then result in release of a predetermined amount of the surety deposit.

Secondly, where restoration is the task at hand, a guarantee of good faith can be used to insure that disturbed areas are restored to a specific condition. Failure to meet those conditions within a specified time period results in relinquishment of that portion of the surety deposit sufficient to cover the cost of completing the job. Unfortunately, the two situations are sometimes related: the failure of a developer to meet criteria for protection results in a new responsibility for meeting conditions for restoration.

Determination of the actual dollar amount depends on the type of guarantees needed. In terms of protection, this could simply boil down to the cost for replacement, although we can also include various punative damages as a penalty for destruction of valued resources. In terms of restoration, usually the dollar amount is calculated on the basis of cost to complete work to restore the site should the original restoration effort fail, and can include costs for any additional mitigation necessitated by non-compliance.

Additionally, and more importantly, there's the matter of under what conditions the bond is terminated, either with or without award of money to the party demanding a guarantee of good faith. These conditions must be predetermined and explicit. In the case where protection is the goal, action is taken as soon as damage, or lack thereof, is verified. For restoration projects, it's as soon as time limits and conditions are met or violated. An incremental schedule of release from bonding is often more acceptable to the project proponent; a portion of the original amount can be refunded according to specified task completion. It is up to the agency requiring the deposit to specify how any unrefunded portion of the money is to be spent. It's preferable that this, too, be done in advance, particularly if punative damages or additional mitigation are involved.

The preceding covers the basic logistics of the various guarantees of good faith; however, there are numerous potential problems with using them in natural resource work. The assignment of arbitrary dollar values to resources is dangerous; the actual cost for replacement does not account for the non-consumptive, virtually non-quantifiable values intrinsic in every ecosystem, particularly for limited resources such as rare plants or sensitive habitats. Non-compliance becomes merely a "cost of doing business" rather than a responsibility that must be met before receiving project benefits. Also, we are dealing here with biological systems that are dynamic in nature. We quite frankly don't have the body of knowledge comparable to that available in engineering and construction, and no building code for ecosystems that allows us to enforce compliance with a set of standards.

The issues we face in trying to quantify, or even qualify, conditions of compliance include:

1. What is "damaged" or "affected"? The loss of how much of a tree limb, or how many seed pods, is considered an impact? How do we assign a dollar value to stress of a plant vs. death of a plant?

2. What is a reasonable time limit for damage to manifest itself? For example, in cases where changes in ground water foster a shift in species composition, or root-zone disturbance results in a decline in the health of a particular plant.

3. What is considered "restored"?

    ◦ Are we asking for pre-project conditions, including age-class structure?

    ◦ Will we settle for "pre" pre-project conditions, with a much younger age-class distribution that we hope is predictive of what we want in 7 or 18 years?

    ◦ What is appropriate species diversity?

    ◦ Do we measure success by cover or density? Especially for rare plants, this can be critical.

    ◦ What about genetic considerations? Do we want the same genetic material as the disturbed or destroyed population? Did we specify a reproducing population?

It's a complex task, considering what we don't know, to be able to use the various methods of guarantee in this type of work. There are, however, a few necessary ingredients for establishing enforceable criteria for mitigation of projects impacting sensitive resources.

A fundamental need is a sympathetic political climate, a willingness on the part of the permitting agency to protect important resources. Without this, there will be no bonding requirements, or no enforcement of the specific conditions.

Equally as important are iron-clad specifications, upfront, and the pettier, the better. They must define what constitutes damage or destruction, what the penalties are, and when something is restored. Without these, there are no enforcement capabilities, no matter what amount of money is retained as a guarantee. The task of monitoring the project must be included, so that we can determine compliance or non-compliance with the bonding criteria, and equally as important, to develop a body of knowledge to assist us in writing criteria for future projects. These types of projects can only become more numerous and complex.

Finally, a little imagination won't hurt. We don't yet have standard language and procedures for dealing with these problems, or for setting a value on non-commercial resources. For example, be creative in assessing the dollar value of living things. Recent estimates conclude that an average tree living 50 years would contribute to the environment $31,250 in oxygen; $62,500 in pollution control; $31,250 in soil fertility; and $35,500 in recycling water as a humidifier (Moll, 1985).

The concept of punitive damages, the so-called "pain and suffering" aspect of personal injury cases, can be utilized for protection of valued resources. This can be determined on a geometric progression: for the first few plants damaged, say 5, the penalty is $50 for each plant; from 5 to 25, the penalty is $100 per plant; from 25-50, $200 per plant. The cost for wanton destruction then becomes much more prohibitive than that for incidental damage.

Denial of any benefits from the project, such as occupation of buildings or use of a roadway, until mitigative obligations are met may be the most effective method of assuring compliance. This directly affects the project proponent, in more than just the pocketbook, and provides the motivation to comply in a timely manner.

We can use the various devices of guarantee to our advantage by securing a deposit; by having tight specifications of conditions and penalties, set up beforehand; by monitoring the results. The operational maxim is: the more prohibitive the penalty for destruction of valued resources, and the more explicit the specifications for enforcement purposes, the less likely that the project proponent will walk out without compliance.

Acknowledgments: For information used in putting together this article, I wish to thank Dawn Lawson, Camp Pendleton Marine Corps Base; David Showers, California Department of Fish and Game; Roman Gankin, San Mateo County Planning Division; Craig Martz, California Department of Transportation; and Mary Ann Scott and Marta Machacek, County of Santa Barbara.

References

Moll, Gary. How valuable are your trees? Am. For. 91(4); 14-16. April 1985.

Strategies for Protecting Rare Plants from Oil Developments: A Santa Barbara County Perspective

Ann M. Howald [1]

Abstract: Santa Barbara County is currently experiencing an oil boom that will result in the construction of up to 40 new offshore platforms, several hundred miles of pipelines and four major processing facilities. These projects could adversely affect more than 35 rare plant species. During the review process required by state and federal laws, the County Energy Division, local botanists and environmental consultants have worked with the oil companies to minimize rare plant losses and protect sensitive plant communities. Several conservation strategies have been used, including onsite and offsite techniques such as revegetation and creation of new preserves. Preliminary findings on their effectiveness indicate that development of site-specific plans, monitoring of mitigation efforts, and making results available are all important factors for success.

Santa Barbara County's current oil boom has resulted in the potential for adverse impacts to more than 35 rare plant species, and has mobilized a search for effective mitigations to eliminate or reduce the severity of these impacts. The fact that Santa Barbara County's population and most of its elected officials know about and care about the County's natural resources has contributed greatly to successful rare plant mitigation.

Onshore and offshore oil development has been on-going in Santa Barbara County since about 1900. However, in recent years, enormous new offshore oil and gas reserves have been discovered. No one knows exactly how much oil and gas lie offshore, but it's estimated that pumping it out will take 20 to 30 years, using current technology. When peak production is reached in 1993, about 600,000 barrels of oil will be produced each day. Impacts to rare plants result from this activity because, even though the oil will be pumped from offshore platforms, facilities that will treat it, and pipelines that will carry it to destinations as distant as Texas, are located onshore.

Impacts to Rare Plants

Most oil development-related rare plant impacts are the direct result of habitat loss from vegetation clearing. The areas affected are large. Unocal's dehydration plant, currently under construction just north of Lompoc, has resulted in the clearing of about 25 acres. Chevron's new facility west of Santa Barbara, is about 50 acres in size. Pipeline construction generally requires clearing of a 100-foot wide right-of-way, which translates into more than 2000 acres of cleared land for the 200 miles of pipelines that have been proposed within the County. These pipelines pass through almost every vegetation type present in the County, including widespread types like grassland, coastal scrub, and oak woodland, as well as restricted types such as coastal dune scrub, Burton Mesa chaparral, Bishop Pine forest and riparian woodland. To date, oil projects proposed in the County have threatened more than 35 rare plant species of these communities.

Construction activities also can result in additional habitat losses from accidental fires caused by welding sparks or other sources, and from accelerated erosion. Construction also generates large quantities of fugitive dust, which coats plant leaves and can result in decreased rates of photosynthesis. In addition to habitat losses from construction of oil facilities, additional losses result from construction of new housing, stores, and roads that are needed when population growth results from new jobs created by growth of the oil industry. All these have the potential of adversely affecting rare plants, as well as more common species.

The operation of oil and gas facilities can result in other rare plant impacts. Although offshore spills are more often publicized, onshore spills from pipeline leaks or tank failures can affect rare plants. Offshore spills that hit the coastline can potentially

---

[1] Ann M. Howald, Consulting Biologist
Arthur D. Little, Inc., Santa Barbara, CA
phone (805) 964-8807.

enter estuaries such as the Carpinteria Estero, threatening species such as the federally endangered Saltmarsh Bird's-beak (_Cordylanthus maritimus_ ssp. _maritimus_). Oil and gas treating facilities produce air pollutants, and although next to nothing is known about the species-specific effects of increased levels of ozone, SO_2 and NO_2 on rare plants, data from studies of commercially valuable species suggest that some rare plants could be adversely affected if subjected to worst-case fumigations.

Rare Plant Mitigation Strategies

Both on-site and off-site mitigations have been proposed to reduce these impacts. On-site mitigations are those that involve modifications to the project itself, such as (1) relocation of facilities, (2) rerouting of pipelines, (3) addition of erosion control structures, (4) revegetation of temporarily disturbed areas, and (5) use of specially designed technology to contain oil spills and control air pollution.

For example, several relocations of the Unocal pipeline were made as a result of the environmental review process. The landfall site (place where the pipeline comes ashore), which crosses the dunes in northern Santa Barbara County, was selected to avoid the habitat of local rare species such as _Cirsium rhothophilum_ and _Castilleja mollis_. Further inland, the Unocal pipeline was moved from Burton Mesa chaparral into a firebreak, reducing from 50 to 30 acres the amount of Burton Mesa chaparral habitat lost, and avoiding impacts to _Ceanothus impressus_, _Arctostaphylos rudis_ and _A. purissima_, and other rare plants of this community.

Exxon's Lompoc pipeline was found to pass through several populations of _Cordylanthus rigidus_ ssp. _littoralis_, the state-listed Seaside Bird's-beak, as well as sandy sites containing _Monardella undulata_ var. _undulata_, a rare variety of _Erysimum suffrutescens_, and several acres of Burton Mesa chaparral containing rare shrubs and herbs. The solution here was to realign a major section of the route to the south. This realignment was developed with the cooperation of the Exxon pipeline engineer. The survey of the Exxon pipeline route also turned up a new species previously unknown in Santa Barbara County, _Quercus dunnii_, or Holly-leaved Oak. The pipeline would have eliminated the one clone of this species that was found. A major realignment was impossible because of the need to protect nearby archaeological sites, so mitigation involved marking the plant and narrowing the construction right-of-way so that the major portion of the clone will be preserved.

Unocal pipeline construction will result in the removal of many individuals of _Scrophularia atrata_, the Black-flowered Figwort, a species whose taxonomic status and rarity is being investigated by the U.S. Fish and Wildlife Service. Mitigation for this herbaceous perennial involved collecting seeds in late summer, which will be sown in areas of the pipeline corridor that are being revegetated. Construction of the Celeron pipeline, which will carry Santa Barbara County oil to refineries in Texas, resulted in the removal of _Solanum xantii_ var. _hoffmannii_, or Hoffmann's Nightshade, a CNPS List 4 species. Cuttings of the nightshade were made from plants that would be removed during construction. These have been maintained in the greenhouse of the University of California, and will be replanted during the restoration and revegetation phase of construction. The success of these methods will be determined during a monitoring program that is part of the overall mitigation plan. The lengthy periods needed for environmental review and development of permit conditions provide the lead time that is required to carry through mitigations such as these.

Restoration of native backdune scrub, which supports rare and endemic species such as _Erigeron foliosus_ var. _blochmaniae_, or Blochman's Leafy Daisy, _Monardella undulata_ var. _frutescens_, _Delphinium parryi_ ssp. _blochmaniae_, or Blochman's Larkspur, and other rare plants, is the goal of an on-site revegetation effort currently underway at Unocal's Santa Maria Refinery. The revegetation plan called for the separate removal and storage of the upper 10 inches of soil, to which was added chipped twigs from cleared shrubs. Existing iceplant was removed and disposed of offsite. The conserved topsoil was spread over the surface of the recontoured disturbed sites and jute netting was applied in areas subject to wind and water erosion. Although an irrigation system was installed, all water has been provided by natural rainfall. Construction was scheduled so that restoration was completed just before the beginning of the rainy season. Monitoring of the first year's growth has revealed that most dominant shrubs and some rare plants of the native community have become established in the revegetated areas. Some _Lupinus chamissonis_ plants grown from seed have reached 2 1/2 feet in height during the first year. _Haplopappus ericoides_ seedlings also are present in large numbers, but are smaller in size. Native annuals such as _Eschscholzia_, _Amsinckia_, _Chaenactis_, and _Orthocarpus_ were common, especially in moister sites. _Prunus punctata_, or Sand Almond, and _Senecio blochmaniae_, or Blochman's Groundsel, both CNPS List 4 species, are growing back in the disturbed areas from root sprouts and seeds.

A surprising result of this revegetation program is that Lupinus nipomensis, or Nipomo Mesa lupine, a CNPS List 1B species previously known from only two small populations nearby, has appeared in low density, scattered throughout the revegetated area, without having been planted or seeded. This suggests that its dormant seeds may be far more widespread than its known distribution indicates, and that it depends on semi-disturbed conditions to perpetuate itself over the long term.

In addition to mitigations like these, which are focussed on the project site, protection and restoration of off-site habitats have been successfully implemented as mitigations in Santa Barbara Couinty. One of the conditions of the Unocal project was the setting up of a 200-acre preserve for Burton Mesa chaparral, a restricted community that supports about 20 species of endemic and rare plants. The establishment of this preserve was a cooperative effort involving local botanists, County Energy Division staff, and Unocal personnel. Off-site mitigation efforts in Santa Barbara County will be discussed in greater detail by Dr. MaryAnn Scott of the Santa Barbara County Energy Division.

In conclusion, recent experiences in Santa Barbara County suggest that the components of successful rare plant mitigation include (1) education of the public, agencies, and corporations as a means of fostering appreciate for natural resources, including rare plants, (2) striving for cooperation between biologists, agency representatives, and oil company personnel, (3) developing specific plans and procedures that address individual problems in creative ways, (4) monitoring of ongoing programs such as protection strategies and revegetation plans, and modifying such efforts as needed, and (5) publicizing the results of mitigation efforts, so that all who are concerned with protecting California's rare plants can learn from each other's successes and failures.

REFERENCES

Arthur D. Little, Inc. 1985. Technical Appendix F: Terrestrial and Freshwater Biology. Union Oil Project/Exxon Project Shamrock and Central Santa Maria Basin Area Study EIS/EIR. Prepared for County of Santa Barbara, U.S. Minerals Management Service, California State Lands Commission, California Coastal Commission, California Office of Offshore Development. SBC #84-EIR-17.

Arthur D. Little, Inc. 1986. Exxon Lompoc Pipeline Project Supplemental EIR. Technical Appendix B: Terrestrial and Freshwater Biology. Prepared for the County of Santa Barbara. SBC-86-2.

URS Corporation. 1986. Revegetation and soil stabilization plan. permit Condition H-1. Union Oil Company of California. OCS Tract P-0441: Platform Irene Project. Prepared for Union Oil Company of California, Orcutt, and Santa Barbara County Resource Management Department, Energy Division.

Celeron Pipeline Company of California. 1986. Final Development Plan. Restoration, erosion control, and revegetation plan. Environment Quality Assurance Program. Permit Condition H-1. Prepared for Santa Barbara County Resource Management Department, Energy Division.

Transplantation of Sensitive Plants as Mitigation for Environmental Impacts

Lauren A. Hall [1]

Abstract- Fifteen cases of transplantation of sensitive plants as a viable form of mitigation are reviewed here. Each is measured against a matrix of five criterion for success. The resulting scores are juxtaposed against their success rates and the results analyzed. The data shows that there is some correlation between low scores and project failure. It was found that monitoring is the variable most often neglected in the transplantation process. Peer review, bond requirements and longer maintenance and monitoring times are recommended.

One of the basic purposes of the California Environmental Quality Act (CEQA) is to provide for the mitigation of adverse impacts to the environment caused by development such as loss of habitat for or populations of plants. CEQA says "... when an EIR (Environmental Impact Report) shows that a project would cause substantial adverse changes in the environment, the (responsible) governmental agency must respond to the information by one of the following methods... (1) Changing the proposed project; (2) Imposing conditions on the approval of the project." CEQA's definition of mitigation is "Rectifying the impact by repairing, rehabilitating, or restoring the impacted environment" and "Reducing or eliminating the impact over time by preservation and maintenance operations during the life of the action" (CEQA, 1984).

Restoration and rehabilitation are mitigation techniques which are becoming more common and refined. Much work has been done on large scale projects such as restoration of strip mines and overgrazed range and rehabilitation of impacted prairie and riparian ecosystems (Liegel, 1981; Anderson and Ohmart, 1979).

Another means of the mitigation for impacts to sensitive plants specified by CEQA is transplantation to alternate sites. This paper will review some of the transplantation projects that have been attempted in San Diego County. Fifteen case histories and their success rates will be examined.

There are numerous factors involved in the successful reestablishment of a population of sensitive plants. Five of the most important are used as a matrix to help correlate success with transplantation conditions. These are: appropriateness of the planting technique and the integrity of its execution; site or habitat selection; completeness of documentation; adequacy of maintenance; and the presense and length of a monitoring period. These are not the only factors which are important but were selected because they varied widely from case to case and had much bearing on each. For example, adequate population size is not considered here as it was a given in each case.

For the purposes of this paper, transplantation may be defined as the removal of any propagable part of a plant from its original occurrence site with the intention of reestablishing it in the same or a new location. Transplantation sites include tracts of land set aside specifically as open space easements and public parks and gardens.

METHODS

Documentation of several notable cases of transplantation for mitigation was done by contacting the environmental consulting firms and lead agencies involved in each of the projects. The San Diego County Department of Planning and Land Use made available records which involved the target species of this study, as did the City of San Marcos, Oceanside, and Chula Vista. These records were often not complete, and in many cases the actual EIR was the only comprehensive document available. A number of private environmental consulting firms also made available their records. Questionnaires and personal interviews were employed to fill in the gaps in project records. These questionnaires were completed either by the researcher through the course of phone interviews or by the respondents themselves.

---

[1] San Diego State University
San Diego, CA 92182

Results

Of the 26 land use planning departments and environmental consulting firms contacted, 20 had substantial amounts of information on a total of 15 transplantation projects. The most common technique was the rootball transplantation of adult plants taken from the ground with a majority of their root tissue intact and placed. Post-transplantation care and site preparation varied from pre-soaking and fertilizing to no preparation or maintenance at all. Some of the study species were propagated in nurseries to augment their numbers or improve their overall fitness. Seeds were harvested in three cases and sown on adjacent suitable sites. One sensitive plant producing bulbs was dug up individually and the bulbs placed in a preserve to augment the population in the mitigation area. All of these techniques show varying degrees of success, depending upon attendant conditions.

The following is brief narrative account of the results.

Case 1. *Acanthomintha ilicifolia* was transplanted through the removal of portions of the indigenous soil which was built up into a small mesa and seeded. The project was completed in 1983. Although the consultant agreed to monitor and maintain this planting for up to 5 years, the records of both the lead agency and the consultant have been lost. The property has since changed hands and the new owner claims no responsibility for the project in the absense of paperwork. The project has since been destroyed through trash dumping and dirt bike riding (Mitchel Beauchamp, pers. comm.).

Case	Species	Common Name
1.	*Acanthomintha ilicifolia*	San Diego Thornmint
2.	*Acanthomintha ilicifolia*	
3.	*Acanthomintha ilicifolia*	
4.	*Ambrosia pumila*	San Diego Ambrosia
5.	*Dudleya attenuata* ssp. *orcuttii*	Orcutt's Dudleya
6.	*Brodiaea filifolia*	Thread-leaved Brodiaea
7.	*Brodiaea filifolia*	
8.	*Baccharis vanessae*	Encinitas Baccharis
9.	*Baccharis vanessae*	
10.	*Archtostaphylos glandulosa* ssp. *crassifolia*	Del Mar Manzanita
11.	*Monardella linoides* ssp. *viminea*	Willowy Monardella
12.	*Monardella linoides* ssp. *viminea*	
13.	*Ferocactus viridescens*	Coast Barrel Cactus
14.	*Opuntia parryi* var. *serpentina*	Snake Cholla
15.	*Hemizonia conjugens*	Otay Tarweed

Case 2. A second planting from this same project but to a slightly different location was also done. Again, indigenous soil was removed and area seeded. This project was also fenced. The consultant has checked this area in October of 1986 and found the plants to be coming up well after an early fall rain. The plant is present in numbers typical to its usual occurrence in the sage-scrub and mixed grassland community. The consultant's continuing care of this project includes elimination of competitors by cutting them off at the ground to lessen soil disturbance. (Mitchel Beauchamp, per. comm.).

Case 3. Seeds of the San Diego Thornmint were collected and sown on the proper soil type on a west facing slope. The same consultant performed this mitigation as in Case 1 and 2 and is using the same techique for eliminating competitors. The plants are coming up well to this date. Maintenance and monitoring of this project is planned for at least another year and the prognosis is good.

Case 4. A threatened population of San Diego Ambrosia (a member of the ragweed family) received some unfavorable press concerning the delay of a 1981 airport expansion project. Consequently, funding for transplantation was denied. The work was then performed by volunteers under less than ideal conditions before bulldozing commenced. Although the ground around each plant was soaked before removal, the temperature on the day of transplantation was in the upper 90's and many of the plants wilted before they could be placed back into the ground. Late in 1982, a volunteer checking the site found no plants at all. The only provision for maintenance was an informal agreement with the airport to occasionally water the area by tank truck. Whether this was done is not known. A thick mat of perrenial grasses covered the area where the Ambrosias were planted may have excluded them (Harold Wier, pers. comm.).

Case 5. In 1976, California Native Plant Society members noted that grading for the renovation of Border Field State park nearly buried a portion of the only known U.S. population of _Dudleya attenuata_ ssp. _orcuttii_. They collected salvagable plants and propagated them vegetatively for reestablishment within the park. In June of 1977, over 200 specimens in excellent health were planted. The slope which had originally been chosen as acceptor site had suffered erosion and was unstable so the dudleyas were placed on an adjacent flat. A site check 2 years later and found no plants in evidence. This volunteer speculates that a combination of foot traffic, improper season of planting and herbivory by rabbits all contributed to the project's failure. There had been no agreements with the State Park for either maintenance or monitoring (James Dice, pers. comm).

Case 6. A transplantation project involving _Brodiaea filifolia_ was done with bulb removal just after the flowering season. These were divided into two portions. One was planted within an open space easement within the development. The other site involved the removal of the indigenous soil to a nearby community park. The bulbs were then planted in the park and surrounded by a white picket fence. By 1984, records for this project had been lost. Currently, there is no sign of either the on-site preserve or the picket fence in the park. The planner familiar with the project suggested that irrigation from the park's sprinkler system may have destroyed the park population but had no knowledge about the absent fence or the location of the on-site mitigation area (Jack Larimer, pers. comm.). There had been no provisions for maintenance or monitoring.

Case 7. A second transplantation involving _B. filifolia_ was performed in 1984 in the city of Carlsbad. An area of open space on the development site was enclosed with chain link fencing. This area contained some Thread-leaved Brodiaea already and the population was augmented with bulbs transplanted by hand from the impacted area. Monitoring is performed occasionally by the consultant who says that project is successful so far and has not required maintenance (Mitchel Beauchamp, pers. comm.).

Case 8. A population of the newly described and uncommon _Baccharis vanessae_. In 1978, 90 specimens were removed for preservation off-site. The specimens were divided between two locations; Quail Botanical Gardens and a utility easement. Six went to the gardens and the remainder to the easement. Ninety-seven plants were removed by rootball and placed into 15 gallon containers. During a 9 month storage period water and rooting hormone were applied to the ones slated for the easement. At the end of 6 months, 21 plants were dead, 7 of which were destroyed by vandalism. Forty-eight of the remaining plants appeared in good health at the time of planting in August of 1980. No maintenance was done. At the end of the one year monitoring period, 13 B. vanessae were alive. The last site check by the project biologist revealed 4 plants in poor condition with signs of disturbance in the area due to road building (Steve Lacy, pers. comm.). Of the 6 plants taken to Quail Botanical Gardens, one is alive and doing well (Gil Voss, pers. comm.).

Case 9. A previous attempt to transplant B. vanessae produced similar results. Thirty plants were containerized by rootball and an additional 4 were propagated from cuttings. These were transplanted to a county park where they received irrigation and rooting hormone. These plants were maintained and monitored for a period of one year. They were watered every few weeks for the the first 3 months and rooting hormone applied as needed. Watering was discontinued during the winter months and resumed in the summer. A bond of $5,000.00 was returned to the developer at the end of the monitoring period. At that time, 15 plants were alive. Since that time, the horticulturists at Quail Botanical Gardens reports that all are dead (Gil Voss, pers. comm.).

Case 10. A rare manzanita, Arctostaphylos glandulosa ssp. crassifolia was found at the same site as the Baccaris in Case 9. No provisions for salvation were required of the developer so horticulturists at Quail Botanical Gardens salvaged a number of plants. From 35 specimens propagated from cuttings in 4 inch peat pots came 75 offspring which were planted in a back lot. They were watered over the hot summer months in the first year. The next 2 years saw unusually heavy rainfall and no further care was given. There was a mortality of approximately 50 percent over this period leaving 37 maturing plants in 1983. At the end of 1984, an additional 14 had died during a 10 month dry spell. The head horticulturist at the gardens reported that as of October 1986, there were 17 plants in good health (Gil Voss, pers. comm.).

Case 11. In early 1983, the California Department of Transportation (Caltrans) discovered a population of Monardella linoides ssp. viminea which would be destroyed by freeway expansion. Fifty-five specimens were dug up by rootball, placed in canvas and transplanted to a city park a few miles away. They were placed close to an annual stream and watered at that time only. A check in May of 1984 showed that 4 of the plants were left. It appeared to Caltrans biologists that the plants had been planted to close to the water's edge and had become water-logged (John Rieger, pers. comm.).

Case 12. A second population of M. l. viminea consisting of 20 specimens was discovered by Caltrans at a later freeway expansion in early 1984. Twenty "parent" plants were removed and provided stock to produce 800 specimens from cuttings. These are being propagated and maintained at a native plant nursery. This represents a population augmentation potential of 4000 percent. Transplanting into the acceptor site is scheduled for January of 1987. The plants will be watered if necessary and planted with time release fertilizer. A 50 percent success rate is hoped for. Monitoring for 1 year is planned and there will be no maintenance performed (John Rieger, pers. comm.).

Case 13. A second sensitive species Feroctaus viridescens occurred at the freeway expansion site in Case 12 as well. These were removed by rootball and placed bare root on a pallet for storage in nursery. Two hundred of these were eventually sold or given away to interested parties. The rest have been replanted on the cut and stabilized slope from which they were taken. This was done in 1984 and so far shows a 90 percent success rate. No provisions for maintenance or monitoring were made (John Rieger, pers. comm.).

Case 14. Road building in southern San Diego county threatened another rare cactus, Opuntia parryi var. serpentina. 20 adult plants were removed by rootball, planted in containers and stored in a nursery for 6 months. They were then placed on a grade, south facing slope. No post-transplantation watering was done as the consultant felt that this would not benefit a drought resistant species. Erosion and exposure have impacted this project and only 10 percent of the specimens were alive at the last 1986 check by the consultant. A $10,000 bond was required of the developer which was refunded upon the completion of the transplantation. There was no contractual agreement for maintenance or monitoring (Mitchel Beauchamp, pers. comm.).

Case 15. Hemizonia conjugens was transplanted through soil removal and reseeding. Indigenous soil was scooped up by bulldozer and deposited in an adjacent open space easement. After the plants in situ had bloomed, the seeds were collected by hand, fumigated and sown in the prepared area. The following year, the plants came up in reasonable numbers. However, since there were no provisions for care and monitoring of this project in writing, a maintenance man unfamiliar with the situation mowed the area before the plants had the chance to set seed and the whole project was lost. There have been no further efforts to replant at this site (Steve Lacy, pers. comm.).

Although each transplantation project studied here was unique from the others in numerous ways, there are some common variables which are useful in analysing the data. Table 2 lists and scores each case in relation to the five criterion considered in this study.

I. Technique/execution; was the method of transplantation used appropriate for the species of plant being moved and were the plans executed in the most efficacious manner?

II. Environment; did the habitat meet all of the biological needs of the plant? This includes variables such as planting season, soil, slope angle and aspect, competition, and moisture.

III. Documentation; were complete and accurate records of the project maintained from the beginning of the project to the anticipated end and are these records still assessible?

IV. Maintenance; was appropriate post-transplantation care given whether it be on-going, preventative or remedial?

Table 1

Criterion

Case	I	II	III	IV	V	Total
1	1	1	0	0	0	2
2	1	1	1	1	1	5
3	1	1	1	1	1	5
4	0	0	1	0	0	1
5	1	0	0	0	0	1
6	1	0	0	0	0	1
7	1	1	0	1	1	4
8	1	0	1	0	1	3
9	1	1	1	1	1	5
10	1	1	1	1	0	4
11	1	0	1	0	0	2
12	1	1	1	0	1	4
13	1	1	1	0	1	4
14	0	0	1	0	0	1
15	1	1	0	0	0	2

V. Monitoring; How frequently was the plantation checked and were there any provisions for feedback in the event of a problem?

These criterion formed the matrix for evaluation of each project. Table 1 is a breakdown of the scores by individual criteria. Projects fulfilling the criterion's requirements satisfactorily rated a 1. Projects displaying a deficiency to the point that it adversly impacted the outcome of the project were assigned a value of 0. This binary system of scoring reflects the author's subjective attempt to draw some general conclusions out of circumstances involving a large number of possible variables. A more finely tuned approach would require that a horticulturist study each case in greater depth than treatment in this paper will accomodate.

Table 2 illustrates the relationship between project ratings and their overall success rate.

Table 2

Case Number	Percent Success	Rating
1	0	2
2	100	5
3	100	5
4	0	1
5	0	1
6	0	1
7	100	4
8	10	3
9	10	5
10	50	4
11	10	2
12	50	4
13	100	4
14	0	1
15	0	2

It can be seen cursorily that there is a correlation between rating score and success rate. Seven transplantation projects rated a 4 or higher. Of these, 4 achieved a 100% success rate. Of the 7 projects rating a 2 or less, 6 of these had a zero success rate. Success greater than 30 percent was achieved on a little better than one third of the projects studied.

DISCUSSION

Review of the projects covered in this study show a pattern of less than optimal success. There appear to be several reasons for this. Some of these include lack of knowledge about habitat requirements (Case 11); lack of appropriate preparation and funding (Case 4); poorly timed or hasty transplanting (also Case 11 and 4); poor choice of transplantation site (Case 5, 6, 11); lack of maintenance throughout the establishment period (Cases 4, 6, 8, 9); and lack of monitoring (Cases 1, 4, 5, 6, 11, 14, 15). Maintenance and monitoring are the criterion most often figuring in the failure of a project. The data suggests that these are frequently the most important and most neglected variables in the transplantation process.

Speaking on the related topic of restoration of plant communities, Liegel (1981) has outlined some cogent points which should be considered in the execution of most revegetation projects. Among these are 1) site analysis; an understanding of the biotic and physical requirements; 2) site preparation; the elimination of existing unwanted species or the formulation of a strategy for their suppression, and the creation of an environment favorable for the desired species; 3) species placement; consideration of distribution patterns and associations; 4) short and long term management, provisions for periodic review and evaluation. Liegel's steps are analagous to the criterion for transplantation outlined in this study.

Criterion I (Technique and execution) may have been a factor in the failure of the San Diego Ambrosia of Case 4 to take hold. As Liegel has suggested site preparation is an important part of technique. Competing species should be controlled. The grasses among which the Ambrosia were planted may have choked them out. Elimination of competition in Case 7 is being done as post-transplantation maintenance. Another factor to be considered is the necessity of transplanting any attendant or host species necessary to the survival of the sensitive species. For instance, both Encinitas Baccharis and Willowy Monardella seem to grow better in the presense of a shade and support host. Planting of the target species has been conscientiously executed in the majority of cases and only lack of knowledge about the plants biology may have contributed to planting errors.

Site analysis is a function of Criterion II which appears to have had some bearing on the success or failure of some of the transplantations. Case 5 and 11 appear to have suffered as a direct result of the site chosen for them.

Criteria 3, 4 and 5 are inclusive in Liegel's Step 6. This is the part of the process most consistently neglected by consultants and lead agencies alike. Accurate and complete documentation, and appropriate maintenance and monitoring should be considered crucial factors in any management policy dealing with transplantation. Some or all of these factors were insufficient in 11 of the 15 cases studied.

Powell (1983), in a thesis on the use of open space easements as mitigation in San Diego County states "...post-development field checks of the biological species of habitat protected by an easement should be an ongoing activity by the lead agency to ensure adequate protection of the resources...Presently, no monitoring by the County occurs, and due to lack of county funds, this recommendation may not be implemented in the foreseeable future." Powell also noted a decided lack of cohesive documentation as to the status of open space easements throughout the county. The agencies responsible for the supervision of the projects often had very few records documenting the status of easements, especially for the older projects. The result of this was the use of the land by many local landowners, to the detriment of the species being protected. This proved to be the case as well for many transplantation projects. Although in all cases helpful, city and county personnel were frequently unable to provide information as to the procedures which had been or were being used to accomplish mitigation. Technical reports on the exact numbers of plants transplanted, the exact area, the seasonal conditions, quarterly updates and so forth are necessary for staff to accurately assess the ongoing progress of re-establishment of the species mitigated. This frequently had not been done. With few exceptions, there were no provisions made for feedback to the local regulating body on the status of the plant.

One means of facilitating the work of biological consultants in these transplantation endeavors is to place more responsibility for the successful reproduction of the species mitigated on the developer. This can and has been done through the use of bonds which are returnable upon the satisafactory completion of the project. There are two points to consider here. One is that the bond be of great enough amount that it is more cost effective for the developer to see the project through to completion than to perform a token effort and risk the loss of the bond. In most cases in this study, the cost of the project approximated the cost of the bond. This may tempt some developers, especially those pressing a deadline, to forfeit the bond in the interest of expediency. I recommend that the bond be at least twice the anticipated cost of the mitigation or $10,000, which ever is greater. Another point to consider is that of the definition of success of the project. In case 14, which was a complete failure, a bond of $10,000 was refunded to the developer immediately upon the mechanical completion of the project. A period of time appropriate to the phenology of the individual species mitigated should be allowed to pass and the project signed off by both the lead agency and the consultant at the time of completion.

The lack of information on various and unforeseen facets of transplantation has caused problems in more than one case. This could be lessened or circumvented by the process of peer review. This is common practice among the academic community and an argument can be made that this idea has merit for all forms of mitigation. A review of the project prior to execution by a panel of impartial experts may serve to bring to light previously unconsidered alternatives or techniques which will enhance the viability of the effort. It is usually difficult for the lead agency to devote the time required to become intimate with all aspects of the project. Peer review could ammeliorate this by making available other expertise from the community. A panel of qualified professionals can be asked to review and give opinions on the efficacy of the proposed plan. Such a panel might consist of a representative from the lead agency, an academician, and another professional in the field of biological consultation. In this way the burden of total comprehension of the technical aspects of the proposed mitigation may be lightened for lead agency staff. These staff members should retain the option of attending any review meetings in person.

Another practice which evinces merit and is espoused by a southern California native plant nursery operator is the ace in the hole method. This involves the transplantation of extant populations while concurrently collecting seeds and cuttings for nursery propagation. Then if the initial reestablishment is unsuccessful, there is a backup source of specimens to use when the problem has been discovered and solved.

CONCLUSION

It seems that transplantation has not been a panacea for botanical resource conservation. The majority of the cases studied indicate that further work needs to be down in the area of transplantation before it can truely be considered a reliable form of mitigation. Although there are many possible variables which may be brought to bear on this subject, the factors which stand out most in this study are lack of sufficient post-transplantation maintenance and monitoring. The results of this study suggest that some plants need to be tended for a much greater length of time than the standard 3 months to 1 year which is currently in practice. Other species, if properly transplanted and cared for initially, stand a good chance of survival with a minimum of care. For those plants needing a longer period of maintenance, arrangements should be specified by contract between the developer, the consultant and the lead agency. These arrangements should be enforced by a bond of appropriate amount, refundable at the time of successful completion of the project, however long that may take. This will insure that the the transplantation will be a conscientious effort to save the botanical resource. If maintenance cannot be guaranteed, preservation and protection in situ is the only logical preservation alternative. However, diligent attention to the details involved in transplantation will make it a more viable means of mitigation in times to come.

REFERENCES

Anderson, B.; Ohmart, R. Riparian revegetation: an approach to mitigating for a disappearing habitat in the southwest. In: Mitigation symposium: a national workshop on mitigating losses of fish and wildlife habitats, 1979 July 16-22; Fort Collins, CO. Colorado State University

Beauchamp, R. M. Biological consultant, Pacific Southwest Biological Services, San Diego, CA. [Telephone conversation] 24 October 1986.

Dice, J. Botanist, San Diego State University, San Diego CA. [Telephone conversation] 30 August 1984

Lacy, S. Biologist, Westec Services, San Diego, CA. [Telephone conversation] 27 October 1986

Larimer, J. Planner, City of Vista, Vista CA. [Telephone conversation] 27 August 1984

Liegel, K. Restoring american prairie. Oryx 16(2):171-77 1981 Oct.

Powell, D. Biological resource protection through the use of open space easements. San Diego, CA: San Diego State Univ; 1983 108 p. Thesis

Rieger, J. Biologist, Caltrans. [Telephone conversation] 24 October 1986

Voss, G. Horticulturist at Quail Botanical Gardens [Telephone conversation] 24 October 1986.

Wier, H. Biologist, Wier Biological Services, San Diego, CA. [Personal interview] 17 August 1984.

The 1986 Santa Cruz Tarweed Relocation Project

Neil A. Havlik [1]

Abstract: The Santa Cruz tarweed (Holocarpha macradenia) has been the subject of a local preservation project since 1982. In 1983, as part of that project, a previously unknown population of the tarweed was found near the Hilltop Shopping Center in Richmond, CA. In late 1985 the site of this population was granted approval for development of an apartment complex. As a result, effort was made this year to effect preservation of seed stock for transplanting to suitable locations nearby. This has included preserving parts of the site until seed could mature, and transplanting of small clumps of plants to a temporary site, both in winter and in summer, to also effect preservation of seed stock. These efforts are evaluated, and recommendations made to assist future projects of this type.

The Santa Cruz tarweed, (Holocarpha macradenia), is an aestival annual herb of the tarweed tribe (Madiinae) within the composite family (Compositae), native to the counties of Marin, Contra Costa, Alameda, Santa Cruz, and Monterey, in central coastal California. Described by Jepson (1911) as "abundant" in areas such as West Berkeley or Oakland, this species has lost much habitat to urbanization, and was considered by Munz (1959) to be extinct. In recent years, however, new populations of the species have been reported from Pinole and Richmond in Contra Costa County, and from near Watsonville in Santa Cruz and Monterey Counties.

For several years, the author has been the principal investigator of a Fish and Game Department sponsored "local preservation project" for the Santa Cruz tarweed. In the project, seed was collected annually from sites where the plant existed but was threatened by, or being destroyed by, development. That seed was sowed into areas considered to be suitable for successful germination and establishment where there was no threat of further habitat destruction. This meant public park or watershed lands. Seed was primarily collected from the Pinole site which was being developed into a shopping center, but minor amounts of seed were also collected from the Hilltop site after its discovery in 1983. The seed was sowed into areas of soils, exposure and grazing pressure similar to that which occurred in the areas from which the seed was collected. These sites were in the nearby Wildcat Canyon Regional Park, and San Pablo Reservoir watershed, both publicly owned properties.

By 1985 this effort had resulted in the establishment of an estimated 7,500 plants in 14 separate stands, and the project was proceeding in a systematic way; however, in January 1986 the author learned that the Hilltop site had been approved for development as a major apartment complex, apparently without the occurrence of the Santa Cruz tarweed on the site being known to the Contra Costa County Planning staff. Commencement of site grading was scheduled for February 1986, and it appeared that the tarweed population was doomed. However, through the efforts of the San Francisco Bay Chapter of the California Native Plant Society, the Contra Costa County Board of Supervisors, and the Nylen Company of Stockton, CA. (developers of the site), a compromise was reached resulting in the relocation project, subject of the present report.

METHODS OF PRESERVING SEED STOCK

Postponement of Grading Activities

The development plan for the Hilltop site called for complete grading of the entire 14 acres in a cut/fill

---

[1] Range Ecologist, East Bay Regional Park District, Oakland, CA.

balance; that is, no material would be taken off-site. Thus grading was very critical to the project. Indeed, it appeared at one point in discussion that there was no way to avoid a confrontation over this matter. Finally, however, engineers for Nylen found that an area containing perhaps two thirds of the Santa Cruz tarweed on the site could be protected from grading until after the seed had matured and been collected. This was the key point of agreement, since earlier efforts at transplanting of seed had proven successful. Thus a so-called "preservation area" was fenced off from grading activites, and seed was collected from the mature plants in September 1986. This seed was sown into the same general park and watershed areas where the earlier transplanting efforts had been undertaken.

Winter Transplanting

Not all areas where the tarweed grew could be protected from grading. Thus, an effort was made to transplant clumps of tarweed to a temporary "holding site" on the edge of the property where, if the plants survived the transplanting, they could mature and set seed which could also be used in the relocation project. The method used to accomplish this was to use a truck-mounted tree spade, to dig up a large volume of earth (approximately 3 feet in diameter and 3-4 feet deep), and place that earth in a hole prepared for it. The transplanted earth was then left alone until seed matured. Twelve such clumps of earth were transplanted in this manner.

This effort was a complete success. The wet soil was rather elastic, and was easily worked by the machinery. Heavy rains after the transplanting (done in February 1986) ensured protection against drying of the small plants. In September 1986 seed was gathered from nearly 1,000 winter-transplanted tarweeds.

Summer transplanting

After the winter transplanting and fencing off of the preservation area, the grading of the site began in earnest. Within a few days, virtually the entire site was stripped of its cover and mass grading, in some cases involving cuts or fills of 15 feet or more, was completed. During building construction an oversight in plans was found, which necessitated a minor encroachment into the preservation area for water line installation. The excavation necessary for the water line would go through a small area of tarweed. (The tarweed did not occur everywhere within the preservation area.) Thus it was agreed to attempt to transplant soil clumps containing the tarweed to another "holding area" where they could hopefully continue to mature.

This effort, undertaken in July 1986, was essentially a failure. As the clay soil dried out, it lost its earlier elastic qualities and become very hard and brittle. Thus, when the pipeline trench was dug, the soil tended to break apart. The roots of only a few plants remained even minimally intact, and of these, only two or three reached maturity.

CONCLUSIONS

Preserving the Santa Cruz Tarweed

The 1986 Santa Cruz tarweed project was an eleventh-hour effort. Application to develop the property had gone through an environmental review process by the local jurisdiction (without finding the reported occurrence of the tarweed on the property), and site grading was ready to proceed. Through cooperative efforts of all involved parties, an agreement was reached which permitted a viable and sizeable remnant of the site's tarweed population to mature and seed to be gathered from that population. The seed was then sown into suitable nearby areas where such seeding has been successfully done in previous years.

Earlier study by the author (Havlik, unpublished) has demonstrated that such seeding can be used to apparently create new, introduced populations of Santa Cruz tarweed. Such populations have persisted for five years at certain sites, including one drought year. Thus the 1986 project had as its goal the assurance that a seed crop would be available to harvest and sow elsewhere. The "preservation area" concept was the keystone of this effort; however, both the winter and summer transplanting efforts were intended to provide information on the suitability of those respective methods to allow temporary (or permanent) moving of soils containing plants to obtain their continued survival. The results of the present effort indicate that winter transplanting can be done relatively easily, but summer transplanting is very difficult to accomplish successfully. Care must be taken to ensure that areas intended to be left alone for a specified time period are indeed able to be so protected.

Seed gathering and sowing into new areas has been shown to be a viable method of preservation of the Santa Cruz tarweed where other alternatives are not available. Furthermore, it has been demonstrated that at certain times of the year soil masses can be dug up and moved to new locations successfully.

Implications for other Endangered Species

The author has found the Santa Cruz tarweed local preservation project to be an extremely satisfying effort, which has resulted in the apparently successful retention of the species in the East Bay flora. He has no illusions, however, about the appropriateness of this method of preservation for other species. The Santa Cruz tarweed is a species which was fairly common, though of rather limited distribution, and which has become rare through conversion of its habitat to new land uses, generally urban in nature. It is not particularly restricted in its occurrence or historical range to unusual or extreme soil types, or other narrow environmental constraints. Thus, an effort to carry out seed introduction in new sites can be reasonably argued.

This cannot be said of very many other rare or endangered species. The moving of seed or whole plants to new sites must be considered a last resort in preservation efforts. The true value of the Santa Cruz tarweed projects is in showing that seed transplanting can be successful, and that when we are faced with no on-site preservation alternative, there are still opportunities.

REFERENCES

Havlik, Neil. The Santa Cruz Tarweed Local Preservation Project. 1986. In: Transactions of the Western Section of the Wildlife Society. (In press.)

Jepson, W. L. A Flora of Western Middle California. San Francisco: Cunningham, Curtiss & Welch; 1911. 515 p.

Munz, P. A. A California Flora. Berkeley and Los Angeles: University of California Press; 1959. 1681 p.

A Management Plan for Rare Plants in the Red Hills of Tuolumne County, California

Reynaud M. Farve [1]

Abstract: The Bureau of Land Management's Red Hills Management Area consist of 7100 acres of public land 9 miles southwest of Sonora, CA. The area is used extensively by Off-Highway Vehicle users, rare plant enthusiasts, plinkers (shooters), and other recreationists. The Bureau developed a Management Plan, which was finalized in February 1985, to protect 5 endemic rare plant species. The most unique feature of the Management Plan is that it establishes a limit to the amount of surface disturbance allowable and the number of rare plants that may be impacted.

The public land that makes up the Red Hills Management Area is located in western Tuolumne County in the Sierra Nevada foothills, approximately 9 miles south of Sonora and 45 miles east of Modesto, CA (fig. 1). This area is one of several serpentine formations found in the foothills from Quincy to Mariposa (fig. 2). The 7100 acre Management Area is moderately sloped, rolling foothills of intermediate elevation (750' - 1750'). Rainfall is approximately 25-30 inches per year. Winter temperatures average 47 degrees F.; summer temperatures average 74 degrees F.

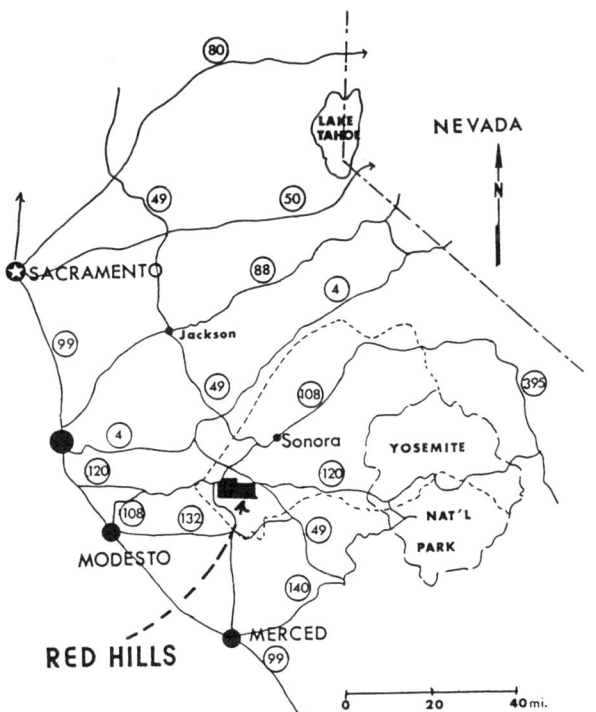

Figure 1--General location of the Red Hills Management Area.

---

[1] Wildlife Biologist, Bureau of Land Management, U.S. Department of Interior, Folsom, CA.

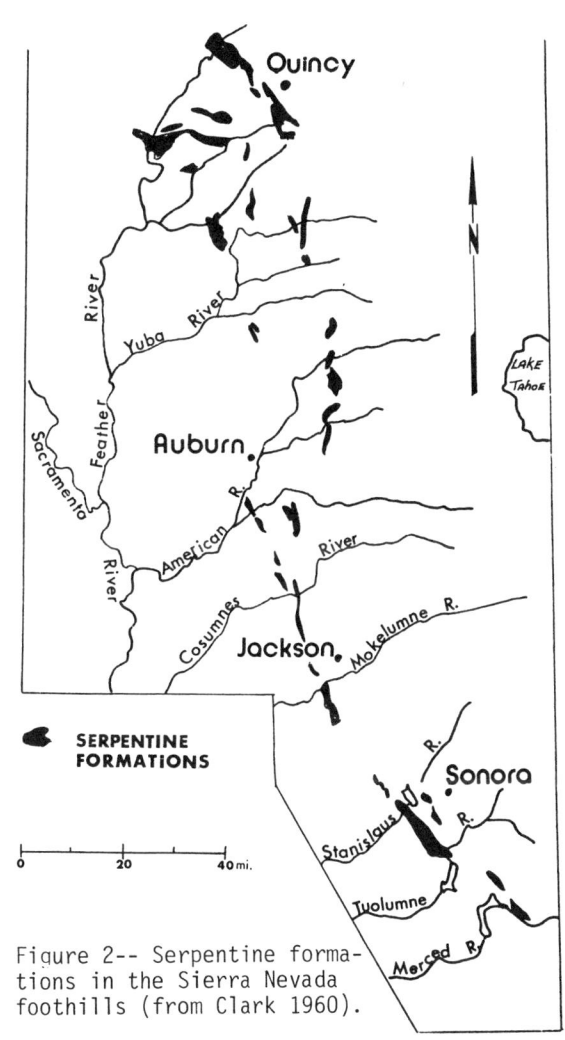

Figure 2-- Serpentine formations in the Sierra Nevada foothills (from Clark 1960).

The soils are entirely of the serpentine derived Delpiedra and Henneke series (Stone et al. 1977). Both types are shallow and low in fertility. Vegetation on the Delpiedra soils (which comprises 90 percent of the Management Area) is buckbrush (Ceanothus cuneatus) and digger pine (Pinus sabiniana) in a savannah type arrangement. Henneke soils support manzanita (Arctostaphylos manzanita and A. viscida), chamise (Adenostoma fasciculatum) and toyon (Heteromeles arbutifolia).

The Management Area is also habitat for 5 endemic plants: Chloragallum grandiflora (Red Hills soap plant), Verbena californica (California verbena), Lomatium congdonii (Congdon's lomatium), Allium sandbornii var. tuolumnense (Rawhide Hill onion), and Senecio laynae. All are U.S. Fish and Wildlife Service candidate/Bureau of Land Management sensitive species.

IMPACTS

The Red Hills, surprisingly, get tremendous usage for a place that can get well over 100 degrees in the summer with the only shade being an occasional shaggy digger pine. The area receives moderate to heavy usage by Off-Highway Vehicles (OHVs), plinkers, horseback riders, gold panners, as well as, rare plant enthusiasts.

Between 1979 to 1982 we received 3 major proposals for land usage in the Management Area. The first proposal was from the Red Hills Investment Company, which owns 860 acres adjacent to the northwest portion of the Management Area. Their proposal called for an industrial park which would bring 2500 people into the area by the year 2000. Because the county has refused to rezone the area for an industrial park, they are currently petitioning the county to allow subdivisions into twenty-two 40 acre parcels. The second proposal was from the California Gold Project (since taken over by the Sonora Gold Project). This project proposed to use 100 acres of public land as a tailings pond. This proposal was dropped when Sonora Gold took over. Finally, the Red Hills Sportsman Association (an ad hoc group composed of several rifle clubs from the central valley) approached us with a proposal to build a complex shooting range which would utilize some 1300 acres in the Management Area.

Along with these pending proposals, public usage of the area began to increase dramatically. The corridor along Red Hills Road was a favorite place for plinkers. On weekends the corridor would be alive with people shooting bottles, beer cans, trees, mannequins, and you name it- in every available nook and cranny. Of course no one policed their bullet riddled targets when departing. This tended to give the entire corridor a trashy appearance. Also since the area was technically open to OHVs, they could and would travel indiscriminately throughout the area. Existing OHV trails began to broaden and new trails began appearing. It soon became obvious that case-by-case management of the area was no longer feasible - a management plan was definitely needed.

DEVELOPMENT OF MANAGEMENT PLAN

In August 1983 our Resource Area held a public meeting in Sonora to solicit input on issues to consider in the development of a management plan. This meeting and several one-on-one meetings with user groups convinced us that the major objectives would be: 1) to provide protection for the sensitive plant populations, and 2) to provide for recreational opportunities.

A draft management plan and environmental assessment was prepared and distributed to the public for review in March of 1984. We received 65 comment letters on the draft, which is more than we have received for some of our environmental impact statements. Some of the more constructive comments and the results of a sensitive plant study (Davilla et al. 1986) contracted for the area were incorporated in the final management plan, which was distributed to the public in March 1985.

Planned Actions

Probably the most significant and unique aspect of the Management Plan is that it sets limits to the amount of discretionary[2] surface disturbance and the number of rare plants that may be impacted. The fact that a manager agreed to such a constraint is no small event!

The plan divides the Management Area into 2 use zones: a Restricted Use Zone (RUZ) and an Intensive Use Zone (IUZ) (fig. 3). The RUZ consists of 4500 acres. Surface disturbance is restricted to less than 5 percent. Ninety-five percent of populations[3] of Lomatium congdonii and Chloragallum grandiflora are protected from impacts. Ninety-eight percent of the population of Allium sandbornii is protected.

---

[2] Some actions on public land are beyond the discretion of the Area Manager's ability to approve or disapprove. This is especially true of some activities relative to hard rock mining authorized by the Mining Law of 1872.

[3] The population estimate will be based on the study by BioSystems Analysis (Davilla et al. 1986).

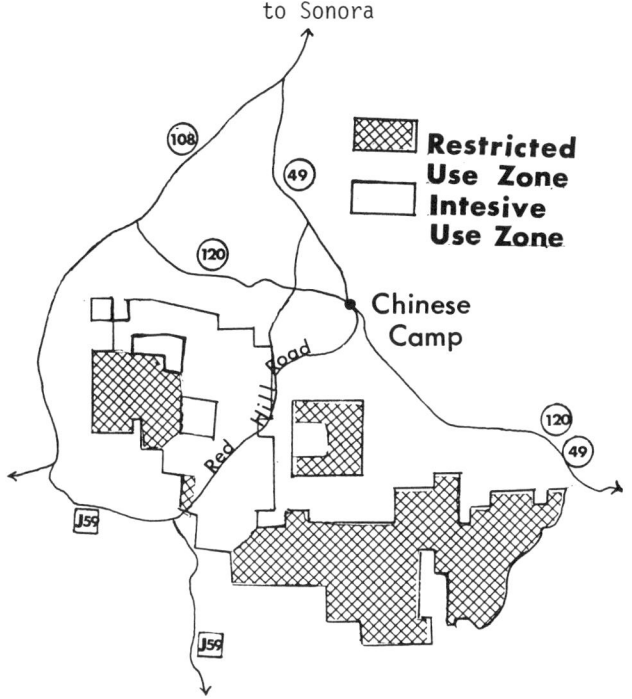

Figure 3-- Use zones in the Red Hills Management Area.

The IUZ consists of 2600 acres. Surface disturbance is restricted to less than 20 percent. Ninety percent of the populations of <u>Lomatium congdonii</u> and <u>Chloragallum grandiflora</u> is protected from impacts. Ninety-five percent of the population of <u>Allium sandbornii</u> is protected. These constraints, we feel, are a realistic attempt to protect the habitat and populations of rare plants while providing for multiple use.

Implemented Actions

Our intent for the Red Hills Management Plan is for it to be anything but a "paper tiger." We have already begun to aggressively implement several aspects of the plan. Indiscriminate shooting along Red Hills road is now restricted to a designated shooting area. An OHV staging area was fenced to prevent increased encroachment onto sensitive plant habitat. A low level aerial photo contract was completed and provides an up-to-date means to monitor additional OHV impacts and surface disturbance. A wildflower viewing zone was established in the Red Hills road canyon and is protected from discretionary surface disturbance. The RUZ was designated as an Area of Critical Environmental Concern (ACEC) on July 1985; this gives the area additional protection relative to the mining laws. Our newly acquired Ranger periodically patrols the area to enforce regulations.

Actions to be Implemented

Many trails have yet to be adequately signed as opened or closed to OHVs. A modified fire suppression plan to curb excessive surface disturbance associated with fire suppression is currently being negotiated with the California Department of Forestry. We are currently surveying the boundary in the eastern part of the ACEC to construct a fence and restrict grazing in the area.

There remains much to be done in the Red Hills. Vandalism is still, and probably will always be, a significant problem. Discarded targets accumulate in the designated shooting area, making it an eye-sore. Preventing new OHV trails from becoming established will be an ongoing battle.

Yet, in general, support from the various users has been positive and encouraging. We have had three clean-ups to date in the area and have always enjoyed a good turnout. We are optimistic that the area can continue to support the various uses and its unique resources.

REFERENCES

Clarke, L. Foothill fault system, western Sierra Nevada, California. Bulletin Geological Society of America 71:483-496; 1960.

DaVilla, William B.; Stone, Doug B.; Taylor, Dean W.; and Willoughby, John W. Techniques for determining population sizes and relative densities of rare but locally widespread plants: a case study. 1986. (These proceedings).

Stone, C.O.; Wickman, B.H. and Powell, W.R. Soil-Vegetation map, southwest quarter of the Sonora quadrangle, Tuolumne County, California. U.S. Department of Agriculture, Forest Service, Pacific Southwest Forest and Range Experiment Station, Berkeley. 1977.

Management of *Hemizonia arida* (Asteraceae) by the California Department of Parks and Recreation

Mark R. Faull [1]

Abstract: Hemizonia arida has prospered under the protective actions established by the California Department of Parks and Recreation which include natural preserve status, control of vehicle use, permanent staffing, signing, rock barriers, tamarisk control programs and habitat expansion. An apparent preference of H. arida for erosional remnants of specified geologic strata was identified. Herbivory that increases in summer was observed. Field work identified possible H. arida X H. Kelloggii hybrids and possible vernal and autumnal seasonal variation within H. arida. Insect pollinators from the Coleoptera were collected, with one named to genus. Discussion of evolution and potential for species survival is addressed.

Hemizonia is a genus within the family Asteraceae, tribe Heliantheae, subtribe Madiinae. Commonly known as tarweeds, its members are confined in their distribution largely to California including the coastal islands and neighboring Baja California. The subject of this dissertation, the Red Rock Tarweed, Hemizonia arida, first collected by David D. Keck and Palmer Stockwell (#3279) on May 11, 1935 from the mouth of Red Rock Canyon, Kern County, Cailifornia, was later published in 1958 as a distinct species (Keck). Known only from a limited range in the western end of the El Paso Mountains, H. arida was classified by the California Fish and Game Commission as "rare" (July 4, 1982) and is considered a "category 1" candidate for endangered and threatened status by the U.S. Fish and Wildlife Service. All of the known populations except one (Last Chance Canyon in the El Paso Range) occur within the lands managed by the State of California's Department of Parks and Recreation.

Hemizonia arida is a lightly glandular and mildly odorous annual with intricately branched alternated foliage 20 to 80 cm tall (n = 12). Leaves are not spine tipped with toothed basal and entire stem leaves. The herbage is hispid-hirsute. Flowers are numerous with 8 to 10 (preferring 8) fertile yellow ray flowers and 18 to 25 mostly sterile disk flowers (both with yellow anthers). The outer disk flowers are subtended by a row of bracts partially united into a cup, while the remaining disk flowers lack bracts. Ray flower ligules are 5 to 6 mm long, deep yellow and three lobed. This species is distinguished taxonomically by the lacking or vestigial pappus. Flowers are present from late April to November.

MANAGEMENT

Historical Endurance of Human Interference

The first inhabitants of European ancestry settled Red Rock Canyon beginning around 1868. Populations of settlers, mostly in search of gold, sputtered and varied for a century, until the State of California began the purchase of private lands in 1969 to create what is now Red Rock Canyon State Park. During the intervening years of private ownership and occupation Hemizonia arida populations endured heavy sheep grazing and disruption by off-highway vehicle (OHV) use.

Mary Austin (1906) describes the thousands of sheep and cattle driven through Red Rock Canyon on an annual basis from the San Joaquin Valley to the Bishop region before truck transportation became available. She writes of her personal account, "In the spring of '94 they were driven north in such numbers that the stage road between Mojave and Red Rock was trodden indistinguishable into the dust. ...All trails run together through Red Rock, the gorge by which the stage road climbs to the mesa. There is a water hole half way up its wind sculptured walls...". She continues describing the crowded sheep and cattle waiting four hours for a turn at the watering hole. It is unknown what short

---

[1] State Park Ranger, Red Rock Canyon State Park, California Department of Parks and Recreation, Cantil, CA. 93519

term effect sheep drives had upon our rare plant population. The depicted watering hole is most likely the type locality for H. arida. In the long term, however, the plant survived and potentially repopulated any lost habitat.

During the 1960s OHV use increased sharply in Red Rock Canyon. Twisselman (1967) describes his observations: "The recent increase in recreational use of the Red Rock region presents new hazards. ...[OHVs] spin wheels while making sharp turns in the sandy wash, which has become a favorite play area for motorcyclists, jeepsters, and other mechanized vandals who completely destroyed the plants [Hemizonia arida] that grew in 1965. If such activities are continued, Red Rock tarweed's future may be bleak."

As the features of the canyon in general began to diminish under this unsupervised recreation a grass roots citizens movement in Kern County convinced the State of California to establish Red Rock Canyon as a unit of the State Park System.

Management by the California Department of Parks and Recreation

Since the creation of this state park system unit protection has been extended to the populations and habitat of Hemizonia arida. OHV use has been restricted to planned designated routes of operation. Previously unrestricted camping has been limited to designated camping facilities. Delineating rock barriers have been constructed and maintained to assist in such management. Corrective and informational signing has been installed and maintained to properly orient and guide park visitor use.

The most significant management tool in protection of the Hemizonia arida populations has been the establishment of two natural preserves within Red Rock Canyon State Park (Hagen Canyon Natural Preserve and Red Cliffs Preserve). These natural preserves have been established in accordance with the California Public Resources code, division 5, chapter 1, article 1, section 5019.71 which reads in part ... "Natural preserves consist of distinct areas of outstanding natural or scientific significance established with in the boundaries of other state park system units. The purpose of natural preserves shall be to preserve such features as rare or endangered plant and animal species and their supporting ecosystems, ... Areas set aside as natural preserves shall be of sufficient size to allow, where possible, the natural dynamics of ecological interaction to continue without interference, and to provide ,in all cases, a practicable management unit ...".

The State Park and Recreation Commission first established the two natural preserves for Red Rock Canyon in 1973, expanding the acreage in September of 1981. The Red Rock Canyon State Park General Plan (1982) specifies that protection for rare plant populations was a consideration in establishing the preserves. On the state "owned" lands managed within this unit over 95 percent of the H. arida population is protected within the natural preserve system, which allows human entry only by foot. Delineating rock barriers and signing distinctly outline the boundary of the preserves.

A park staff of two permanent Rangers enforce park regulations which provide protection for H. arida populations, while monitoring these same populations as time permits. Occasional OHV variances from park regulations may damage individual H. arida plants or habitat. OHV use is currently listed as the major threat to this endemic's survival.

Memorandum of Understanding

In August of 1985 the California Department of Parks and Recreation acquired additional Hemizonia arida management responsibilities when a Memorandum of Understanding (MOU) was signed with the federal government's Bureau of Land Management (BLM). Under this agreement 2,164 acres of BLM property adjacent to Red Rock Canyon State Park, in the vicinity of Scenic Canyon and Nightmare Gulch, is operated by the state park in accordance with provisions established in the MOU. In the first year of our management previously unsupervised vehicular use has been restricted to designated routes of travel. A combination of rock barriers and signing have been implemented, as on the state owned land, to delineate the boundary between vehicular roads and those lands where such use is prohibited.

Uncommon plant species, Chorizanthe spinosa and Pholisma arenarium, have been confirmed as returning to MOU property previously damaged by concentrated vehicular use. H. arida populations should display similar improvement in time.

Under the provisions of the MOU a single road through Nightmare Gulch was designated as open to vehicular use one half of every month (the 16th to the end of each month). Scattered H. arida plants form a loose population within the steep walled canyon of Nightmare Gulch proper. The park staff has plotted individual H. arida specimens within the gulch in an attempt to monitor adverse vehicular influence.

The California Department of Parks and Recreation stated in the 1982 General Plan for Red Rock Canyon State Park that should the lands discussed above be successfully acquired for permanent inclusion within Red Rock Canyon State Park, natural preserve status is recommended for Scenic Canyon and Nightmare Gulch.

Non-native Tamarisk Control

A survey to determine the extent and influence of non-native Tamarix spp. occurence within Red Rock Canyon was undertaken by park staff in the autumn of 1985. The results in particular found that Tamarix parviflora was invading moist habitat within Tarweed Creek, the type locality for Hemizonia arida. Undesirable competition that eventually would displace H. arida would ensue without corrective action. A program to control tamarisk at Red Rock Canyon was approved within months. Funding for the removal of tamarisk was initiated in the 1986/87 fiscal year and on site removal of Tamarix parviflora invading H. arida habitat in Tarweed Creek will occur in the autumn of 1986.

Red Cliffs Habitat

During 1986 an evaluation of potential Hemizonia arida habitat enhancement was undertaken. Special attention was paid to land parcels which could potentially support H. arida, but upon which concentrated recreation currently exists. One particular site analysed at Red Cliffs Day Use parking lot appears to provide the highest potential for successful habitat enhancement.

The Red Cliffs vicinity was heavily used by OHV enthusiasts. Unrestricted camping and vehicle use prior to state park ownership resulted in devegetated hillsides. Under state ownership use has been restricted to a large parking area outlined by a rock perimeter. Following the establishment of controlled use, habitat has regenerated and a large population of H. arida has become established at the northeastern corner of the cliff. In 1986 a colony of H. arida extended from the cliff base population via a shallow wash south toward the parking lot perimeter. The colony ended abruptly at the rock barrier delineating the boundary of parking, despite the continuation of the shallow wash through the parking area. H. arida seeds obviously existed within the wash extension entering the parking lot, but were unable to germinate as a result of constant soil disruption by vehicle use.

To increase H. arida habitat the south end of the Red Cliffs parking lot was decreased by approximately 25,000 square feet, placing most of the wash outside the disruptive influence of vehicular use. Positive reclaimation should follow.

Last Chance Canyon Population

One known population of Hemizonia arida exists in the Last Chance Canyon drainage outside and adjacent to the lands managed under Red Rock Canyon State Park. This additional population, which exists on BLM property, was discovered by the Red Rock Canyon staff in 1973 and 1974. The author relocated this population in June 1986. This H. arida population was found to be susceptible to increasing Tamarix competition and vehicular use.

In lieu of H. arida's status as a U.S. Fish and Wildlife Service category 1 candidate for federal endangered or threatened status, the BLM attempts to protect known populations from possible damage. However, the BLM does not have funding for monitoring, management or distribution studies. The Red Rock Canyon State Park staff will share distribution, habitat and life cycle information, as it becomes available, to assist the BLM with its management of H. arida.

FACTORS EFFECTING MANAGEMENT

Prolonged management of rare species requires detailed understanding of the vital processes by which the species reproduce and survive within their habitat. Current protection of Hemizonia arida by the Dept. of Parks and Recreation must be supplemented by an increased familiarity with the species life cycle. H. arida is potentially a study in edaphic endemism. The pursuit of life cycle understanding is necessitated by the need to prevent accidental alteration of the limited factors which potentially bind this species with survival.

A general distribution survey was accomplished in May 1986 to examine the status, vitality, habitat and volume of the limited populations of H. arida.

This initial effort was supplemented by limited soil sampling, field observations, a search of the available literature and by personal contacts with scholars investigating the genus Hemizonia. The combined results obtained from this undertaking are categorized below. It is certain that continued investigations will reveal futher productive results. As is the tendency of investigation, in many instances the pursuit of knowledge has raised more questions than have been resolved.

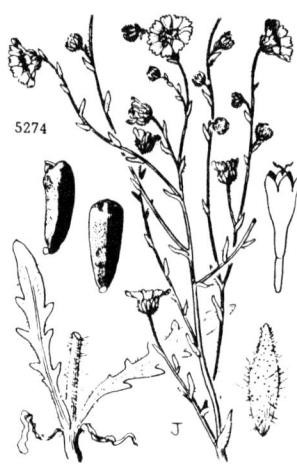

Figure 1--Hemizonia arida reprinted from Abrams and Ferris, An Illustrated Flora of the Pacific States, Volume 4, with permission of the publishers, Stanford University Press.

Habitat Preference

The habitat occupied by Hemizonia arida has been described by several individuals. The original description by Keck (1958) stated the tarweed as "from the mouth of Red Rock Canyon ... in hard-baked alkali-sand mix in wash". Abrams and Ferris (1960) characterized the habitat as a "dry sandy canyon-bottom, Lower Sonoran Zone". Twisselmann (1967) expanded the description to include "A very restricted endemic that grows along the short subalkaline seep in Red Rock Canyon about 300 yards above the freeway bridge. In years with wet winters, the colony extends along the ephemeral streamlet and moist subsurface sand for perhaps a quarter mile, in dry years for as little as 20 yards". Critchfield (1979) mimicked this description by expressing the habitat as "washes along ephemeral seeps and streams and on adjacent sand flats in moist, subalkaline gravelly sand. In wetter years, HEAR 1 [H. arida] also grows at the base and on the lower slopes of ridges and cliffs". Munz (1973) simply lists the plant community as "Creosote Bush Scrub".

Surveys by the author in 1986 found that H. arida habitat varies and can be best summarized by four somewhat overlapping descriptions: (1) Sandy to gravelly ephemeral alluvial washes, sometimes exhibiting surface platey structure; (2) Moist alkaline fringes of seeps and springs along alluvial flats and washes; (3) relatively shallow, dry, sandy alluvial and colluvial slopes at the base of ridges and cliffs and associated erosional ravines; and (4) ledges of dry colluvium suspended on steep cliff slopes up to 160 feet above the valley floor by ribs of resistant bedrock. In a May 1986 distribution survey elevation varied from 2230 to 2820 feet above sea level.

In its moister locations H. arida is found to associate with Mimmulus guttatus and M. palmeri. Both Mimmulus species normally bloom in Red Rock Canyon in surface moist ground from February to early May along seeps and springs. H. arida blooms along the fringes of these same intermittent seeps and springs as they become surface dry. When these fringes exhibit dry surfaces the Mimmulus species conclude their annual bloom. Thus, in some instances, H. arida is successional to M. guttatus and M. palmeri.

Observed Geologic Preference

As the May 1986 distribution of Hemizonia arida was plotted, the correlation between the plant's distribution and the occurrence of specific geological units became noticeable (Fig. 2). The geology of Red Rock Canyon consists of Cretaceous Granophyre (Dibblee 1952), Miocene Ricardo Group (Loomis 1984) and Quaternary alluvium. H. arida occurs solely within the latter two, seemingly preferring specific erosional remnants of the Ricardo Group.

The Ricardo Group consists of two formations, the Cudahy Camp Formation and the Dove Springs Formation, which are separated by an unconformity. Both formations are non-marine sedimentary depositions interspersed with episodic volcanism which collected in an ancient depression known as the El Paso Basin. North of Red Rock Canyon evidence exists within the strata to suggest a freshwater lake. Ricardo sedimentary deposition within Red Rock Canyon State Park is suggestive of stream deposited sands and gravels, probably enroute to the northern lake. H. arida is not normally located within lands occupied by the Cudahy Camp Formation. Within the Dove Spring Formation a striking correlation exists between the erosional remnants of Loomis' member 2 (Dibblee 1952 Ricardo Formation members 3 and 4) and the distribution of H. arida.

Within the Red Rock Canyon watershed member 2 of the Dove Spring Formation consists of pale red to light gray poorly sorted volcanic-plutonic pebble conglomerate, massive to crossbedded, coarse poorly sorted lithic sandstone, and tuff breccia. These iron oxidized red strata provide Red Rock Canyon with its title.

The close correlation between erosional byproducts of member 2 and H. arida distribution vary widely only in the vicinity of Last Chance Canyon where populations exist along a wash adjacent to Loomis' member 1 of the Dove Spring Formation. Analysis (Dibblee 1952, Whistler 1969 and Loomis 1984) of the Miocene stream sediments within the Ricardo Group indicate in general that fossil stream clast size diminished as these ancient waterways approached and fed into the freshwater lake. This gradation and reduction in clast size is generally observable as Loomis' member 2 approaches the present day land marks of upper Nightmare Gulch within the Red Rock Canyon watershed and the upper slopes of a previously unnamed Last Chance Canyon tributary which flows eastward to merge with the main Last Chance Canyon wash at Cudahy Camp. This transition also marks the departure of H. arida from Loomis' member 2 and it initiates its occurrence on Loomis' member 1 along the lower banks of the unnamed Last Chance Canyon tributary, now given the title Cudahy Creek.

Although sufficient field work to confirm has not been performed, H. arida might prefer member 1 in Last Chance Canyon because in this terrain member 1 displays a coarser clast than member 2. In the Red Rock Canyon watershed member 1 consists of coarse conglomerates with clasts approaching 1 meter. In this same watershed member 2 rarely exhibits clasts over 15 to 20 cm. It is possible that the reduction of stream gradient to the north has caused member 1 clast size in Last Chance Canyon to mimic member 2 clast size in Red Rock Canyon. It is also possible that the H. arida occurrence on member 2 within Last Chance Canyon is larger than discovered in 1986.

A second state classified rare tarweed also displays a strong geologic preference. Hemizonia minthornii, a perennial known from only 3 locations, appears restricted to arkose Upper Cretaceous sandstones (Tanowitz and Gordon 1980). This parallels the observed H. arida preference for coarse erosional remnants of Dove Spring Formation member 2. Whistler (personal commun. 1986) confirmed that much of member 2 of the Dove Spring Formation could be classified within the rather broad category arkose sandstone.

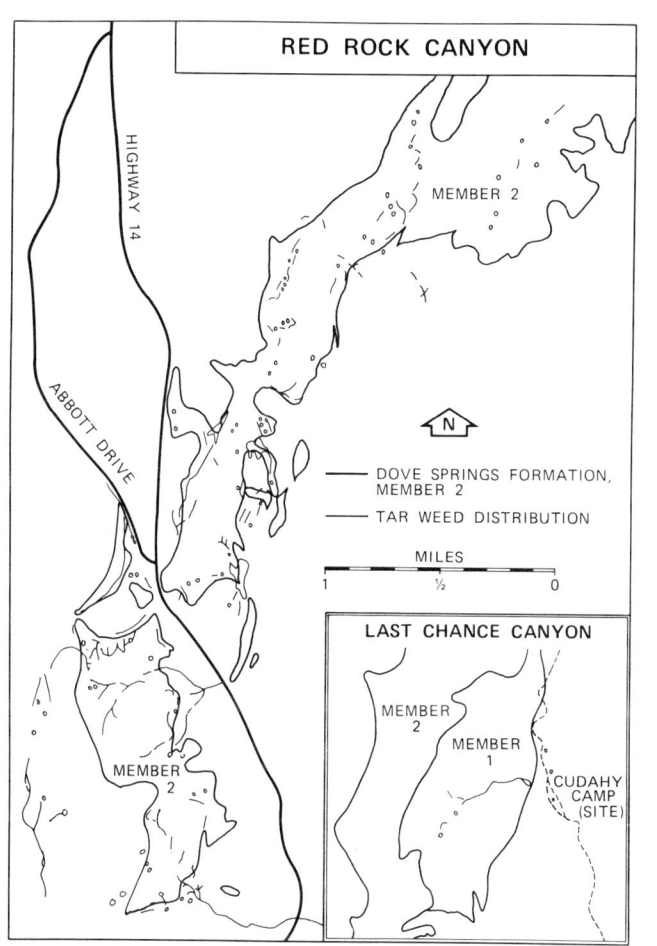

Figure 2--Correlation between 1986 Hemizonia arida distribution and Loomis' 1984 Ricardo Group - Dove Spring Formation - Member 2.

Soils

Soils upon which H. arida germinate and bloom were investigated in September 1986 in a preliminary manner. Four soil samples were analysed utilizing a field test kit. A LaMotte field test kit provided crude pH values.

Analysed soil textures varied from sandy to loamy sand, some of which were skeletal. Soil depth varied from paralithic contacts at 20 cm on slopes to depths in excess of 105 cm on alluvial flats. Soil pH was alkaline ranging from 8.0 to 9.0.

Future soil testing is required to analyse and contrast soils on which H. arida specimens are not found in Red Rock Canyon. Such research might provide illumination to the apparent correlation between H. arida distribution and member 2 of the Dove Spring Formation.

Herbivory

Field observations discovered physical damage to individual Hemizonia arida plants consistent with herbivory. The act of herbivory was not observed. A search of the available literature revealed several published instances of tarweed herbivory. Symbiotic insect herbivory is covered under the section on pollenation. Tree crickets [Oecanthus quadripunctatus (dwarf specimen) and O. argentinus, both from the Orthoptera: Gryllidae] have been documented to utilize Hemizonia spp. (H. lutescens named) as a host (Walker 1967). O. quadripunctatus (dwarf) was found abundantly only on tarweed.

A study of the California Ground Squirrel, Citellus beecheyi (now Spermophilus beecheyi), found that Hemizonia virgata and H. wrightii were both documented food sources (Fitch 1948). H. virgata was stated to be an important food plant for the squirrels, especially during the dry summer months when the succulent leaves may be a vital factor in providing necessary amounts of moisture. Usually in August or September H. virgata seeds are heavily utilized comprising the majority of the squirrels diet. Members of the Sciuridae who reside within Red Rock Canyon include the Antelope Ground Squirrel (Ammospermophilus leucurus) and the rare Mohave Ground Squirrel (Spermophilus mohavensis). Their interaction with Hemizonia arida is unknown.

The majority of herbivory damage observed in H. arida populations consisted of the abrupt truncation of the main stem and major auxillary branches. While no tarweed was measured prior to and immediately after truncation it is estimated (based upon the thickness of the truncated stems) that as much as 55 to 65 percent (20 cm) of the original plant height may have been removed in such a fashion. A survey of one large colony of tarweed within Red Cliffs Preserve, in September 1986, found that 201 of 266 H. arida specimens (75 percent) displayed truncation. The average thickness of truncated stems and the discovery of scat within the browsed population are consistent with herbivory by Lagomorphs. Two species of Lagomorphs (the Blacktailed Jackrabbit, Lepus californicus, and the Audubon Cottontail, Sylvilagus audubonii) are known to populate Red Rock Canyon. The observed scat indicate that both species have been present at browsed H. arida sites.

Similiar to ground squirrel herbivory of H. virgata, truncation of H. arida specimens is more common in the dry summer and autumn season. The succulent nature of H. arida may provide the browser with both necessary foliage and moisture to assist in arid survival.

While not herbivory in the true sense it must be noted that a few individual specimens were observed to disappear entirely, leaving small craters in their former locations. Physical evidence indicated uprooting through pulling of the stems. This combined with the proximity of these locations to public parking lots would lead one to speculate human interference.

Pollination

Individual tarweeds were reported to be self sterile, so that every fertile seed was the result of the crossing of two plants (Babcock 1924). However, Hemizonia arida appears to be the only self compatible species in the genus (Tanowitz 1982).

The achenes of the disk flowers of H. arida were originally listed as sterile (Keck 1958). Carlquist (1959) reports that sterility of disk flowers has resulted in the partial or entire loss of stigmatic hairs and the diminution in size of the style as a whole. He reports that this applies to Hemizonia section Dienandra [now Madiomeris (Nutt.)] with the exception of some disk flowers in H. paniculata and H. floribunda. H. arida belongs to this Hemizonia section. Tanowitz (1982) reports that H. arida disk florets rarely produce achenes with a sparse pubescence of bicellular hairs.

Hemizonia species are known to be pollinated by insects. Research confirmed H. congesta as an insect pollinated species with observed visits from flies and moths (Babcock and Hall 1924). Honey bees, syrphid flies, tachnid flies and halictid bees have all been observed to visit Hemizonia flower heads (Tanowitz personal commun. 1986).

A variety of insects were discovered utilizing H. arida during the authors 1986 observations. Honey bees were observed visiting H. arida flower heads. Small beetles of the order Coleoptera were observed actively entering and emerging the corolla tubes of H. arida disk and ray flowers from May through September 1986. Specimens of these suspected pollinators were collected by the author in September 1986. Dr. Charles L. Hogue[2] identified the most common, of possibly four species captured, as a member of the family Melandryidae, the genus Pentaria.

Other insects not necessarily involved in H. arida pollination were collected and analysed at the same time. Multiple deceased insects were collected from an extremely resinous and densely vegetated autumnal plant. Becoming adhered to the resinous exterior of these plants, the visiting insects were unable to detach. Of these specimens, Roy R. Snelling[3] identified a honey bee (Apis mellisera), a halictid bee (Augochlorella pomoniella) and a wasp from the family Sphecidae (Steniolia duplicata); all from the order Hymenoptera. Two members of the order Lepidoptera; a skipper butterfly from the family Hesperiidae (Pholisora libya) and a burrowing webworm moth from the family Acrolophidae (Acrolophus spp.) were identified by Julian P. Donahue[4] Adhered members of the order Neuroptera were identified to family by Dr. Charles L. Hogue (family Myrmeliontidae - antlion; family Chrysophidae - common lacewing; family Hemerobidae - brown lacewing). Dr. Hogue also identified a plant wasp from the family Tenthredinidae of the order Hymenoptera and a plant or leaf bug from the family Miridae of the order Hemiptera.

The exact relationship between H. arida and these identified insects is not well understood. All apparently displayed enough interest to approach the plant closely. Most of the specimens were retrieved from slightly inside the plant exterior indicating more than a casual passage. As mentioned previously, both honey bees and halictid bees are known tarweed pollenators.

---

[2] Curator of Entomology, Los Angeles County Museum of Natural History

[3] Curatorial Assistant for Entomology, Los Angeles County Museum of Natural History

[4] Assistant Curator of Entomology, Los Angeles County Museum of Natural History

Hybridization

Natural hybrids occur in the Madiinae, although strong external and internal reproduction isolating mechanisms operate among most members of this subtribe (Tanowitz 1985). Ecological and distributional factors operate as strong reproductive isolating mechanisms (Tanowitz written commun. 1986)

Although the current frequency of hybridization in the genus Hemizonia appears to be low, it may have been more common in the earlier stages of divergence of the genus (Tanowitz 1977). At a previous point in the evolution of Hemizonia, intra- and inter- sectional hybrids appear to have been reasonable sources for speciation, possibly involving aneuploid reduction through chromosomal repatterning (Tanowitz 1977, 1985 and written commun. 1986).

Red Rock Canyon has been known to harbor a second species of the genus Hemizonia. Munz (1974) and Critchfield (1979) both reported the existence of Hemizonia Kelloggii within Red Rock Canyon. During the 1986 field population survey, scattered individual specimens of H. Kelloggii were present intermixed amidst populations of H. arida on dry hillside localities. Their coexistence creates the potential of hybridization.

The genus Hemizonia has been taxonomically divided into four sections or sub-genera. Both H. arida and H. Kelloggii have been relocated to the section Madiomeris within the genus Hemizonia (Tanowitz 1982). Hemizonia species in a separate section, Centromadia, have been shown to form a natural group within the genus which are closely related to one and other evolutionary (Venkatesh 1958). These intrasectional species display a high degree of chromosome homology which enables hybridization. A few intersectional hybrids of Hemizonia have been reported (Clausen 1951, Tanowitz 1977 and 1985) the majority of which are sterile.

Since H. arida and H. Kelloggii are intrasectionally related and display definate overlap of habitat preference within the Red Rock Canyon vicinity, it could be anticipated that hybridization between the two species exist. During 1986 individual plants that displayed intermediate floral morphology were observed, but remained unstudied. Laboratory hybrids of H. fasciculata X H. minthornii and H. fasciculata X H. clementina display floral intermediacy (indicating lack of dominance), while vegetative traits varied towards one parent or the other

(Tanowitz 1985). This may prove true in H. arida X H. Kelloggii as further information is gathered.

It is worthy of mention that H. Kelloggii were found in bloom in Red Rock Canyon from May Through October in 1986, much longer than the April to July limit indicated by most California floral keys (Munz 1973, 1974; Abrams and Ferris 1960). This extends the possible hybrid interference with H. arida reproduction through out almost the entire H. arida reproductive season.

Clausen (1951) indicates the first generation hybrid offspring of H. arida and H. Kelloggii are completely sterile. What remains uncertain is the extent to which arida and Kelloggii hybridize in the wild and the effect to which the production of sterile hybrid young dillutes through misdirection successful arida reproduction.

The occurence of H. Kelloggii in Red Rock Canyon is not well published. A study of this colony is of scientific interest to determine if isolation of this population has resulted in variance from the norm of H. Kelloggii. It is also of interest to determine if H. arida and H. Kelloggii have evolved together in isolation (or is H. Kelloggii a recent introduction by way of the historic sheep drives through Red Rock Canyon).

Evolution

Based upon crossbreeding experiments Hemizonia arida's closest relative appears to be H. pallida known from the head of the southern San Joaquin Valley. When crossed these two species while producing mostly sterile offspring, produced limited first and second generation fertile hybrids (Clausen 1951). The Red Rock Canyon colony of H. arida was similiar enough in character to be originally considered as a population of H. pallida (Keck 1935) until later formally revised (Keck 1958). H. arida has not been shown to produce anything but sterile first generation offspring in attempted crossbreeding experiments with other intra- and inter- sectional species of Hemizonia.

As noted previously H. arida is listed within the Hemizonia section Madiomeris. Prior to recent work by Tanowitz (1982), section Madiomeris (Nutt.) was instead referred to by the not formally circumscribed title Dienandra (Keck unpublished). Clausen (1951) indicated that section Dienandra could be further bisected into natural groups, each of which consisted of a series of relatively closely related species that covered geographically different territory. Clausen listed H. Kelloggii, H. pallida, H. augustifolia, H. Halliana and the possibly extinct H. mohavensis within a natural group containing H. arida.

Both Twisselman (1967) and Clausen (1951) have speculated that H. arida was once of greater distribution. Twisselman stated: "It is possible that both species [H. arida and H. pallida] evolved from a common ancestor after separation and isolation by uplift of the Tehachapi Mountains. Hemizonia arida may have been widespread in the Mohavean woodland of Pliocene time. Drying of what is now the desert would have eliminated favorable habitats, resulting in the near extinction of the species." Similarly, Clausen indicated that H. arida may have originated as an ecological race of wider distribution becoming stranded in an unhospitable habitat far from close relatives.

Both of these speculations express the opinion that the H. arida population has suffered a demise rather than placing Red Rock Canyon as the home of an isolated ecological population which has undergone speciation. Tanowitz (personal commun. 1986) suspects the later indicating H. arida might be a recently derived relic.

The evolutionary derivation of H. arida may provide clues to its potential for survival. If H. arida was once significantly larger in distribution, the species may be best adapted to a vanished ecological environment. Under these conditions its potential for long range survival may depend upon its present ability to evolve to fit its current environment. Conversely, if Red Rock Canyon is the site of speciation, H. arida may currently possess specific evolutionary adaptations to the Red Rock Canyon environment, thus strenghtening its chance for survival.

Seasonal Variation in Tarweed

Various tarweeds possess seasonal ecological races (Babcock and Hall 1924). Some species of the Madiinae have succeeded in evolving races that have very different seasonal periodicities in the same locality (Clausen 1951). Several Hemizonia species originally listed as distinct were later identified as vernal and autumnal blooming variations of the same species. One such instance involved the spring flowering

Hemizonia luzulifolia and its late summer to fall flowering subspecies rudis (originally H. rudis Benth.). Morse (written commun. 1986) observed that both races germinate with the fall rains, yet reproduce under very different moisture regimes. The late blooming subspecies rudis, unlike the vernal race, was able to lose substantial amounts of water without detrimental changes in water status.

Elsewhere, H. luzulifolia ssp rudis was reported to produce a basal rosette in winter, a central stock in May, followed by the decline of leaf area during the summer as basal leaves senesced and were replaced by diminutive leaves on aerial stems (Gulman, et al. 1983). By August the basal rosette was completely senesced, leaving only aerial leaves.

Morse (personal commun. 1986) informed the author that H. luzulifolia ssp. rudis, with photoperiodically triggered growth, at the apex of its bloom grew taller than the vernal form H. luzulifolia.

In general early spring leaves of Hemizonia species are typically large soft and mesic, while leaves developed later become reduced, glandular and xeric (Clausen and Hiesey 1958).

Hemizonia arida displays seasonal variance to an undetermined extent. Vernal individuals are generally larger, open, airy specimens which contrast with autumnal lower growing, compacted and extremely glandular specimens. Some autumnal specimens were so densely foliated and glandular that tens of insects became adhered to their exterior.

The duration of the life cycle of individual plants is unknown. The H. arida population reaches its peak in late May to early June each year. Individuals, however, were observed that did not exist in any substantial state until late August or September. Unresolved is whether spring basal rosettes predated the discovery of individual plants displaying new autumnal stems. As concerns the entire population, the varied seasonal morphological characteristics observed could result from alteration of vernal flowering plants with each progressive season or possibly represents distinct seasonal races within the species. It remains unlikely, but remotely possible, that multiple germinations occur during widely divergent soil moisture conditions producing varied plant morphology. While autumnal H. arida are shorter in stature than vernal forms, the very dense compacted foliage may still represent increased vegetative production.

A series of 2 m square field plots are planned for 1987 to document germination periods, plant morphology and duration of life cycle through recorded observation.

Water Stress and Tarweed

Specimens of Hemizonia arida were found in bloom through out the harshest and driest months of the desert year. Summer and autumn blooming tarweeds, such as H. arida, must compensate for water decline through their growth season.

Research has found that xeric tarweeds (particularly H. luzulifolia ssp. rudis) contain extracellar polysaccharides which serve as an apoplasmic store of water buffering living cells from rapid and detrimental changes in water status (Morse 1986). The ability of tarweeds to store water is an important mechanism for maintaining a positive water balance and such storage of water by tarweeds increases as the availability of water in a habitat decreases (Morse written commun. 1986).

Carlquist (1959) reported another possible water retention property in tarweeds. Sclerenchyma cylinders of the stem appear to be indurate structures which not only aid in supporting tall, slender plant bodies of many annual tarweeds, but which may also have a relation to their resistance to desiccation during the dry months of summer and fall. A typical tarweed, such as Hemizonia fasciculata, exhibits, even before flowering, a collapse of cortical tissue, so that only withered papery sheets cover the sclerenchyma cylinder. Thus, the fiber cylinder may be capable of restricting transpiration in the same way that a layer of cork serves in other plants.

In a study of Hemizonia luzulifolia ssp. rudis taproots were recovered from depths as great as 0.50 m and it was concluded this species can root below the soil layer into a non-nutritive substrate through fissures in decomposed rock to obtain the water necessary for survival (Gulmon, et al. 1983). These authors further observed that in H. luzulifolia as water stress increases leaf area decreases and the species depends on storage and photosynthesis by stems. In Addition, the authors indicated that this late blooming species shows evidence of moderate to significant water stress before reproduction (flowering period July to October).

SUMMARY

The species *Hemizonia arida* was found to be vital, active and stable within its range during a 1986 field survey. The prospect for continued survival of the species under State of California management, protection and habitat restoration are extremely favorable. This paper attempts to collect life cycle information vital to longterm species management and identifies areas for future study. Hybridization, seasonal variation within the species and its apparent restrictive preference for certain erosional remnants of specific geological units are strong candidates for clarification research in the near future.

Acknowledgments: I would like to thank Susan Edinger, a graduate student at U.C. Riverside, for her contribution to field soil testing; Dr. Barry D. Tanowitz, professor, Biological Sciences Dept. at U.C. Santa Barbara, for his contribution of much verbal and written information regarding the genus *Hemizonia*; Suzanne R. Morse, a graduate student at U.C. Berkeley, for her information regarding tarweeds and water stress and direction to further helpful articles; Dr. Charles L. Hogue, Roy R. Snelling and Julian P. Donahue of the Los Angeles County Museum of Natural History for entomological identifications; and John and Dianne Zellmer of Ridgecrest, CA. for their assistance with the preparation of figure 2.

LITERATURE CITED

Abrams, Leroy; Ferris, Roxana S. Illustrated Flora of the Pacific States, Volume 4. Stanford, CA: Stanford University Press; 1960.

Austin, Mary (Hunter). The Flock. Boston, MA: Houghton, Mifflin and Company; 1906. p.74-77.

Babcock, Ernest B. Remarkable Variation in Tarweeds. Journal of Heridity. 15(3): 133 - 144; 1924.

Babcock, Ernest Brown; Hall, Harvey Monroe. *Hemizonia congesta*: A Genetic, Ecologic, and Taxonomic Study of the Hay-field Tarweeds. University of California Publications in Botany 13(2): 15-100. 1924.

Carlquist, Sherwin. Studies on Madinae: Anatomy, Cytology, and Evolutionary Relationships. Aliso 4(2): 171-236. 1959.

Clausen, Jens. Stages in the Evolution of Plant Species. Ithaca, New York: Cornell University Press. 1951.

Clausen, Jens; Hiesey, William M. Experimental Studies on the Nature of the Species, Volume IV. Genetic Structure of Ecological Races. Washington, D.C.: Carnegie Institution of Washington Publication 615. 1958.

Critchfield, W. B. Rare Plant Status Report: HEAR 1. California Native Plant Society. May 1979.

Dibblee, T. W., Jr. Geology of the Saltdale Quadrangle, California. San Francisco, CA: California Division of Mines, Bulletin 160. Sept. 1952.

Fitch, Henry S. Ecology of the California Ground Squirrel on Grazing Lands. The American Midland Naturalist 39(3): 513-595. 1948.

Gulmon, S. L.; Chiariello, N. R.; Mooney, H. A.; Chu, C. C. Phenology and Resource Use in Three Co-occuring Grassland Annuals. Oecologia (Berlin) 58: 33-42. 1983.

Keck, David D. Studies Upon the Taxonomy of the Madinae. Madrono 3: 4-18. 1935.

Keck, David D. Taxomonic Notes on the California Flora. Aliso 4(1): 101-114. 1958.

Loomis, Dana Paul. Miocene Stratigraphic and Tectonic Evolution of the El Paso Basin, California. Masters Thesis submitted to the University of North Carolina at Chapel Hill. 1984.

Morse, S. R. The Role of Extracellular Polysaccharides in the Water Balance of Annual Tarweeds. Abstract from Proceedings of the IV International Congress of Ecology / 71st Annual Meeting of the Ecological Society of America. Syracuse, N.Y. August 10-16, 1986.

Munz, Philip A.; Keck, Daivd D. A California Flora (and supplement). Berkeley, CA.: University of California Press. 1973.

Munz, Philip A. A Flora of Southern California. Berkeley, CA.: University of California Press. 1974.

Tanowitz, Barry D. An Intersectional Hybrid in *Hemizonia* (Compositae: Madiinae). Madrono 24(1): 55-61. 1977.

Tanowitz, Barry D.; Gordon, Patricia J. *Hemizonia minthornii* (Asteraceae: Madiinae). Madrono 27: 176-177. 1980.

Tanowitz, Barry D. Taxonomy of *Hemizonia* Section *Madiomeris* (Asteraceae: Madiinae). Systematic Botany 7(3): 314-339. 1982.

Tanowitz, Barry D. Systematic Studies in *Hemizonia* (Asteraceae: Madiinae): Hybridization of *H. fasciculata* with *H. clementina* and *H. minthornii*. Systematic Botany 10(1): 110-118. 1985.

Twisselmann, Ernest C. A Flora of Kern County, California. Wasmann Journal of Biology 25: 365-366. 1967.

Venkatesh, C. S. A Cyto-genetic and Evolutionary Study of *Hemizonia*, Section *Centromadia*. American Journal of Botany 45(2): 77-84. 1958.

Walker, T. J.; Rentz, D. C. Host and Calling Song of Dwarf *Oecanthus quadripunctatus* Beutenmuller. Pan-pacific Entomologist 43(4): 326-327. 1967.

Whistler, David P. Stratigraphy and Small Fossil Vertebrates of the Ricardo Formation, Kern County, California. Ph.D. Thesis submitted to the University of California at Berkeley. 1969.

Endangered Species Management in Southern California Coastal Salt Marshes: A Conflict or an Opportunity

Patrick V. Dunn [1]

Abstract: Single species management inherently results in a choice, whether to manage for one species or another. And when two or more endangered species, including an endangered plant, are involved, the endangered plant usually gets the least amount of attention. This is what has occurred in the coastal salt marshes of southern California. Single species management for two endangered birds, the light-footed clapper and California least tern, has caused problems for an endangered plant, the salt marsh bird's beak. Analysis of case studies shows that single species management for the endangered birds has resulted in the elimination or degradation of potential and actual habitat of the salt marsh bird's beak. In addition, if the habitat requirements of the endangered species are examined, it is evident that continued single species management will further intensify the conflicts between the species. It is, therefore, suggested that the management goals for these species be shifted from species specific goals to whole system goals. Whole system management will result in healthy coastal salt marsh systems, hopefully able to harbor stable populations of these three endangered species, as well as keeping other species from becoming endangered with extinction.

The federal endangered species Act of 1973 protects all species in danger of extinction, including plants. Yet the single-species management for two endangered birds, the light-footed clapper rail, Rallus longirostris levipes, and the California least tern, Sterna albifrons brownii, has resulted in the loss of both potential and actual habitat for an endangered plant, the salt marsh bird's beak, Cordylanthus maritimus ssp. maritimus. All three of these species occur in the coastal wetlands of southern California, although each species utilizes different portions of the wetlands. This partitioning of the habitat and the single species management practices currently in use often, result in a conflict between the species. When one species is preferentially managed for, then the other species lose habitat. And when managers choose a species, endangered plants seems to always lose to an endangered bird.

Several restorations in southern California show the problems inherent in single species management, particularly the negative effects on the salt marsh bird's beak. Each of the three cases to be discussed are major restoration projects and were reviewed by the regulatory agencies, and sometimes the academic community, prior to implementation. All of the restorations focus on one of the two endangered birds and create habitat suitable for only that species. The result are systems that do not function as a complete wetland system and, thereby, limit the usefulness of the systems.

Some of the causes, and possible cures, of the single species management syndrome are discussed including the structure of recovery plans for endangered species, the ease with which single species management can be quantified and the general ignorance of the values of the habitats in which the endangered species exist.

HABITAT REQUIREMENTS

The three federally endangered species which utilize California's coastal wetlands as their primary habitat include the salt marsh bird's beak, the light-footed clapper rail and the California least tern. Each of these species is in danger of extinction due to man impacting their habitat. Active management, including the establishment of new populations or colonies through restoration or creation of wetlands, is an integral part of delisting these taxa. Management

---

1. Graduate Researcher. California State University, Los Angeles, Los Angeles, CA.

decisions are an on-going process for each of the three.

A short description of each endangered species follows, and illustrates how each species utilize different portion of the marsh (fig. 1).

Bird's Beak Habitat Requirements

The salt marsh bird's beak is the only endangered plant occurring in the coastal wetlands of southern California. It is a small herbaceous annual which inhabits a narrow zone in the extreme high inter-tidal areas of salt marshes. It is known from only six sites ranging geographically from Bahia de San Quintin, Baja California, Mexico north to Carpinteria Marsh, just south of Santa Barbara, California. Populations of the plant were once more numerous (USFWS, 1984) and probably larger (Purer, 1942), but the destruction and alteration of habitat by man has resulted in its endangered status.

Bird's beak is a hemi-parasite its roots obtaining water and other resources from near by plants (Chuang and Heckard 1971). The potential host of bird's beak are many since the high marsh is composed of a matrix of up to eleven species (Vogl, 1966, Zedler, 1977, 1982, and Dunn, in prep.). This high marsh is also noted for a wide annual fluctuation in soil salinity. Brackish soil salinities occur in the early winter and climb to hypersaline values during the winter. The phenology of bird's beak conforms to the salinity regime with germination occurring before salinity levels reach 16 ppt and senescence probably occurring when high salinities and drought conditions result in too high of a negative water potential (Dunn, in prep.). Bird's beak seems to extremely fine tuned to, or barely tolerant of, this habitat and it occurs only in a narrow elevational range in the marsh between 6 to 7 ft. MLLW.

The recovery plan for bird's beak calls for the establishment and persistence of twelve populations prior to delisting the species to a threatened status. To this end, a population of bird's beak, with 50 to 150 individuals has been established at Upper Anaheim Bay (Massey, unpubl.) and the U.S. Fish and Wildlife has issued a contract for the Manipulative Management of Bird's Beak in southern California.

Clapper Rail Habitat Requirements

The light-footed clapper rail is one of three sub-species of clapper rail. Like bird's beak, it occurs in the coastal wetlands of northern Baja California and southern California. Clapper rails prefer marshes with good tidal inundation and vigorous marsh vegetation. The rails utilize the low elevation, *Spartina foliosa* dominated marsh escaping to the higher portions of the marsh only to avoid inundating tides. The nests of clapper rails are made of *Spartina* and are designed to float up and down with each tidal inundation and include a *Spartina* 'umbrella' which may shield the nest from avian predators. One to eight eggs, with an average of five, are laid during the nesting season, which occurs from April to late July (Jorgensen 1975, Massey and Zembal, 1979). Actual recruitment to the population is unknown. Clapper rails mainly forage in the low marsh and consume a wide range of food items, including crabs, insects, spiders, isopods and snails (Massey and Zembal, 1979). The clapper rail is limited by the occurrence of nesting habitat and the high quality marsh that is required (Zembal and Massey, 1981). Restorations for the clapper rail have emphasized the enhancement or creation of *Spartina* dominated low marsh.

Least Tern Habitat Requirements

The California least tern is the most cosmopolitan of these three endangered species, not only migrating to Central America during the winter, but nesting from Baja California, Mexico north to San Francisco Bay. The least tern originally nested on the beaches of California, usually near an estuary, lagoon or bay. Now the opportunistic tern nests on almost any type of flat level surface, including construction projects, airport runways and salt flats, near the food source contained in the bays, estuaries and near-shore waters. Although a variety of predators attack the nests and fledglings of least terns, it is undoubtably the loss of its primary nesting sites along the beaches of California, to the ocean loving Californians and their houses, which has lead to the decline of the least tern. Restorations for the least tern have emphasized the need for nesting sites and have recently been creating least tern nesting islands in the bays and lagoons of southern California.

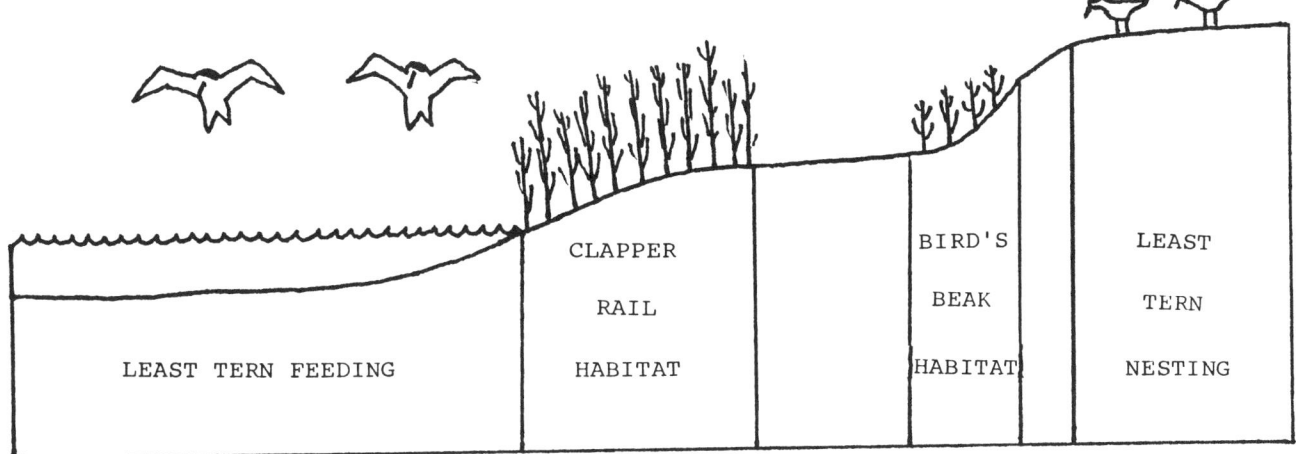

Figure 1-- Representational diagram of the habitat requirements of three endangered species in the coastal wetlands of southern California. Species are the light-footed clapper rail, California least tern and salt marsh bird's beak. See text for description of habitats.

As can be seen by the differing habitat requirements of the these three endangered species, single species management will necessarily result in conflicts for habitat on the simplist levels. Management for the clapper rail and the low elevational marsh precludes the upper marsh necessary for bird's beak and the open water needed as a feeding area for the least tern. Likewise creation of exclusive high marsh leads to the exclusion of habitat necessary for the clapper rail and least tern.

CASE STUDIES

Not only does single species management lead to conflicts between the species it also results in patchy unnatural habitats. Each of the case studies below illustrates how the creation of large single species habitat, results in new problems.

San Dieguito Lagoon

San Dieguito Lagoon is located in San Diego County and had to be restored due to catastrophic sedimentation from Crest Canyon, just above the wetland. A large open water basin was formed with fringing marsh vegetation and a large least tern nesting island. This island occurs at an elevation just above the high water level establishing an upland environment in the midst of the wetland. Although the island was planned to remain free of vegetation and allow least tern nesting, environmental conditions have been suitable for the invasion and establishment of upland plants. The island is now overrun with weedy plant species, with few wetland plants present. The island has become biologically deserted of wetland characteristics. The habitat that was created has been naturally altered to one which mirrors the conditions present.

This restoration not only illustrates the problems that arise when a new habitat is created without environmental conditions that favor the new habitat, but also underscores the possibilities of whole systems management. San Dieguito Lagoon is suitable not only for least terns, but also for bird's beak and clapper rails. In fact, a more holistic approach was attempted with the final plans for the restoration, which included areas designated for the management of clapper rails and bird's beak, (PRC Toups Corp., 1984). Yet funding for the establishment of the vegetation necessary for these areas was not included in the original allocation, and the whole system approach has seemingly been forgotten.

Yet, San Dieguito Lagoon still holds possibilities for whole-system management, including establishing a least tern colony on the natural beach near the mouth of the lagoon, reclaiming filled areas for further areas of marsh vegetation, linking seasonal wetlands to the main wetland area and establishing bird's beak along the eastern edge of the Lagoon.

Upper Newport Bay

The Upper Newport Bay Ecological Reserve contains the largest populations of clapper rails and bird's beak. It also harbors a least tern colony and this population was the focus of a recent large restoration. A large basin was excavated in the eastern end of the bay and two tern nesting islands constructed in the basin. These bare substrate islands again create an upland environment in the middle of the wetland and attempt to entice the terns to nest in an area other than their preferred beach habitat.

Unfortunately, the restoration is again single species in concept. Several minor additions to the project could have been added to benefit all wildlife in the Reserve, including bird's beak and clapper rails. The creation along the edges of the basin of gentle slopes over a large elevational range and the establishment of marsh vegetation on these slopes could have created habitat suitable for both bird's beak and clapper rails. The rails would have also benefited from the fresh water input, and the possible fresh water marsh, of San Diego Creek. Mudflats for shorebirds could have also been added with minor changes. All of these would have enhanced the value of the restoration for all wildlife in the Reserve, including salt marsh bird's beak.

Paradise Creek/Sweetwater River Marsh

This marsh complex is located adjacent San Diego Bay and has been recently impacted by a cooperative project of the Army Corps of Engineers and the California Department of Transportation. The mitigation for this flood control/highway improvement project includes the restoration and creation of 32 acres of wetlands (U.S. Army Corps of Engineers, 1982). The mitigation is planned for completion in 1990, and so far wetland has been created specifically to increase the population of clapper rails in the marsh (CA Dept. of Transportation, 1981). The design has emphasized low _Spartina_ dominated marsh with higher areas to allow the rails to escape inundation. The project is based on an island motif which is designed to reduce predation on the rails.

This emphasis on creating clapper rail habitat is in spite of the local extinction of salt marsh bird's beak and a history of low clapper rail usage in the marsh. Salt marsh bird's beak at the Sweetwater Marsh is known from herbarium collections and a field observation of the plant in 1981, (U.S. Fish and Wildlife Service, 1984). But surveys of the marsh since that time have failed to locate any bird's beak plants (Dunn, inprep.). Clapper rails have not been plentiful at the Sweetwater Marsh in recent times, with a maximum of four pairs nesting throughout the complex in a single year. The restoration focuses on this species, since it was the only endangered species which was known to inhabit the portion of the marsh which was directly impacted by the construction.

So far the restoration has been professionally undertaken and the results mirror the planned design. Yet field surveys of the restoration site show that the clapper rail habitat receives only limited use from other wetland birds, including the least tern[2]. In addition the islands are designed with steep unnatural slopes which has already resulted in minor difficulties with the sloughing or eroding of these slopes. Plans for the remainder of the restoration have not considered bird's beak, or to practice whole-system management. The bits and pieces which the restoration adds to the system are important, but the possible additions to the marsh via a whole system approach could have far surpassed the current restoration, including the re-establishment of an endangered plant species.

CAUSES AND CURES OF SINGLE SPECIES MANAGEMENT

Single species management has hurt the salt marsh bird's beak in southern California and seems to be the predominant management practice when an endangered species is involved. Four basic causes can be recognized for the single species management of endangered species, 1) the form of the Endangered Species Act, 2) the structure of the recovery program including recovery plans, 3) the ease with which the goals of single species management can be

---

2. Unpublished data of the author

quantified, and 4) an ignorance of the values of habitats with the consequence of an over reliance on endangered species to give value to the habitat. Each of these causes are discussed below along with some possible cures.

1. The Endangered Species Act itself is a cause of single species management. The Act recognizes endangered taxa and not the habitat upon which they are dependent. This is rightfully so, and this law gives us much more power to protect sensitive species than it causes problems.

2. The implementation of the Endangered Species Act via the recovery plan system is a major cause of a single species outlook. The plans focus on single endangered taxa and are not integrated with entire system goals. Even when the biologists which frame these plans are aware of whole system management, the plans are still not integrated with the other wildlife and values of the habitat, let alone other endangered species which might be affected by the plan. For example, the salt marsh bird's beak recovery plan mentions clapper rails and least terns in only two locations. Integration between the recovery plans and recovery teams is minimal to non-existent, and this integration is the first step of a whole system management approach for the endangered species.

3. The goals of single species management are easily formulated and quantified. Counting individuals of an endangered species is easy; recognizing a healthy system is not. Of course, endangered species may be good indicators of a healthy system, but once we begin to engineer habitat solely for an endangered species the value of the indicator is greatly diminished. Before we can identify whole system goals we should be familiar with the characteristics and values of the habitat, which leads to the final cause.

4. There is a general ignorance of the values of wildlife habitats, and therefore the presence or possible presence of an endangered species becomes over emphasized as a value of the area. The value of habitats is not easily conveyed, especially if those values are not known. Further research into the value of habitats is needed as well as the communication of the values already known.

CONCLUSION

Whole system management is not a new concept; it's importance has been discussed by ecologists and wildlife biologists for decades. Yet it seems that these discussions have been forgotten and our habitats and the species which utilize them have been impacted because of it. Let us hope that the conflict between the endangered species of southern California salt marshes will soon end and that a whole system approach will allow an opportunity for all species to flourish.

Literature Cited

CA Department of Transportation. Biological assessment for endangered species consultation on the Sweetwater flood control channel and freeway interchange combined project. CA. Deptartment of Transportation, District 11. 1981. 85 pp.

Dunn, Patrick V. The taxonomy and autecology of an endangered plant, the salt marsh bird's beak, Cordylanthus maritimus. Los Angeles, CA. CA State Univ., Los Angeles. In preparation. Masters Thesis.

Jorgenson, Paul D. Habitat preference of the Light-footed Clapper Rail in Tijuana Marsh, California. San Diego, CA. San Diego State Univ. Masters Thesis, 1975. 115 pp.

Massey, Barbara W. Salt marsh bird's beak. Unpublished report. 1985. 14 pp.

Massey Barbara W. and Richard Zembal. A comparative study of the light-footed clapper rail, Rallus longirostris levipes in Anaheim Bay and Upper Newport Bay, Orange County, California. U.S. Fish and Wildlife Service Endangered Species Office, Sacramento, CA. 1979.

PRC Toups Corp. Final Plans for the Resotration of San Dieguito Lagoon and Crest Canyon. PRC Toups Corp. San Diego, CA. 1984. 12 pp.

United States Army Corps of Engineers. Sweetwater River Final Environmental Impact Statement. U.S. Army Corps of Engineers, Los Angeles District. 1982. 242 pp.

United States Fish and Wildlife Service. Recovery Plan for the Salt Marsh Bird's Beak. Agency Review Draft. 1984. 85 pp.

Vogl, Richard. Salt-marsh vegetation of Upper Newport Bay, California. Ecology 47:80-87. 1966.

Zedler, Joy B. Salt marsh community structure in the Tijuana Estuary, California. Estuarine and Coastal Marine Science 5:39-53. 1977.

Zedler, Joy B. The ecology of southern California coastal salt marshes: a community profile. U.S. Fish and Wildlife Service, Biological Services Program, Washington, D.C. FWS/OBS-81/54. 1982.

Zembal, Richard L. and Barbara W. Massey. Continuation study of the light-footed clapper rail _Rallus longirostris levipes_, 1981. Final Report. Calif. Dept. of Fish and Game, Sacramento, Calif. 1981.

Assessment and Management of *Arctostaphylos pallida* Eastwood

David Amme, Neil Havlik [1]

Abstract: The Alameda manzanita is an officially designated rare and endangered shrub known to occur only in two isolated stands, with minor outliers, in Alameda and Contra Costa Counties. This fire-adapted non-sprouting chaparral shrub has narrow environmental tolerances limited to sterile mineral soil in areas of summer coastal fog. The manzanita habitat is showing signs of senescence with increased dead to live fuel ratio. The prime objective of the management plan is to determine and implement management activities which will improve the biological condition of the declining populations and help in the ultimate recovery of the species.

The Alameda or pallid manzanita (Arctostaphylos pallida Eastw.) is officially designated by the State of California as a rare and endangered shrub known to occur only in two isolated stands, with minor outliers, in Alameda and Contra Costa counties, California (Smith and York 1984). The East Bay Regional Park District (EBRPD) recently acquired one of these stands, that on Sobrante Ridge, and for some years has been the landowner of the other, Hucklebery Preserve. Thus the District now manages most of the range of this species. Following the drought of the late 1970's and the heavy rains of the early 1980's, the Alameda manzanita exhibited dieback that was noted by Park workers, homeowners and members of the California Native Plant Society (Johnson 1983). This dieback has been attributed to a root fungus and has gone into remission in the last two years. Recently the Park District and the California Department of Fish and Game agreed to conduct a study of this species, to be known as the Alameda Manzanita Recovery Program. A detailed distribution and assessment study was completed in November 1985. In future phases of the Recovery Program management activities will be planned and tested for improving the general condition of the species and ultimately helping to ensure its survival.

---

[1] Open Space Management Specialist, Berkeley, CA; and Senior Range Ecologist, East Bay Regional Park District, Oakland, CA.

TAXONOMY

For the purposes of this report, Alameda manzanita will be referred to as Arctostaphylos pallida even though not all taxonomists agree with its hierarchial taxonomic status. A. pallida is an upright, non-burl-forming manzanita with closely imbricated, cordate and glabrous leaves. It attains heights of up to 6 meters. The epithet "pallida" refers to the pale glaucous bloom which occurs on the young leaves. The Alameda manzanita is a member of the A. andersonii Gray complex, and is considered by some to be A. andersonii var. pallida Adams ex McMinn (Munz 1968). The A. andersonii complex includes as many as fourteen taxa, including several species of probably hybrid origin, all of which occur in central coastal California (Jepson 1983, Davis 1972). The distinguishing features of this complex are the sessile or very short-petioled, heart-shaped leaves that clasp or nearly clasp the branches.

The species of the A. andersonii complex with the exception of A. auriculata and A. luciana, are coastal and experience coastal fog (stratus). These manzanitas inhabit sterile acid substrates (lithosols) including sandstone, shale, old sand dunes and granite (Wells 1962, Roof 1967, Griffin 1978, Stratford and Edwards 1984). Both large and low plants have been described for many of the species (Jepson 1939). The taller plants except for A. viridissima and A. pechoensis are usually woodland inhabitants and shorter plants occur on exposed barrens or in chaparral habitats.

RANGE AND HABITAT

A. pallida was originally described as occurring in the "East Oakland Hills," "the hills back of Piedmont" (Eastwood 1934), and on "Moraga Ridge" (Adams 1940). Eastwood and Adams both described the Alameda manzanita as being small in stature--from 1 to 1.5 meters high. Today the Alameda manzanita averages between 2 to 3 meters in height. Presently in the East Bay Hills, the Alameda manzanita occurs in one main location on Huckleberry Ridge with several scattered satellite locations near Skyline Boulevard on private property, on East Bay Municipal Utility District property near Pinehurst Road, and in Joaquin Miller Park between 430 and 485 meters elevation. The Moraga Ridge site has been thought by many investigators to be the Flicker Ridge chaparral that overlooks Moraga Valley but extensive searching on Flicker Ridge and reviewing of the literature and old maps indicates that the name "Moraga Ridge" must refer to what is now known as Huckleberry Ridge. The second largest population of the Alameda manzanita and the northernmost location of the A. andersonii complex is in Contra Costa County on Sobrante Ridge between 200 and 235 meters elevation.

There are two naturalized stands of the Alameda manzanita in the East Bay Hills. One stand of several Alameda manzanita exists along Skyline Boulevard adjacent to the Arbor Day Reforestation Project of Joaquin Miller Park. This population was transported there in the early 1970's via road-cut material from Huckleberry Ridge which contained seed of both A. pallida and A. crustacea and is now known as Manzanita Flat. The other naturalized stand consists of several dozen Alameda manzanita plants that were planted by the former Regional Parks Botanic Garden director, James Roof. These plants line Shasta Road, Golf Course Drive, and Wildcat Canyon Road in Tilden Park near the Regional Botanic Garden. They are now mature, healthy specimens (fig. 1).

A. pallida has narrow environmental tolerances. It is limited to bare, sterile, siliceous mineral soil in areas of summer fog. The mean annual precipitation for the Alameda manzanita sites is between 550 and 660 mm (Rantz 1971). The presence of summer fog (stratus or high fog) greatly influences the Alameda Manzanita habitat. Stratus raises the relative humidity, lowers the temperature, reduces the solar exposure and may add up to 250 mm of accumulated

Figure 1--Large 5.7 meter tall specimen of A. pallida adjacent to Regional Parks Botanic Garden on Wildcat Canyon Road.

precipitation via fog drip on Huckleberry Ridge (Patton 1956, Gilliam 1962). Only 20-40 percent of impinging solar energy penetrates through fog to warm the air and ground (Meyers 1968). Associated with moisture condensation on the leaves of plants is a lowering of evapotranspiration rates. The result is less stress for many plants in summer (Stone et al 1950).

The two largest populations of the Alameda manzanita grow on Middle Miocene shales of the Monterey Group. The Rodeo Shale of Sobrante Ridge is light siliceous shale, while the Claremont Formation on Huckleberry Ridge consists of interbedded chert and shale (Lawson 1984, Radbruch 1969, Dibblee 1980). The satellite populations of the Alameda manzanita along Skyline Boulevard exist on Pinehurt Shale and Joaquin Miller Formation (Radbruch 1969). Both substrates are mixtures of shale, sandstone, and minor conglomerate. At both the Sobrante Ridge and Huckleberry Ridge sites the Alameda manzanita dominates in the central locations where there is little or no soil development. On these "barrens" sites A. pallida is the only vascular plant (fig. 2).

Figure 2--Exposed barren lithosols on Sobrante Ridge with A. pallida chapparal. Open grassland on top of hill related to abrupt soil change.

ECOLOGY

The most outstanding feature of the ecology of the Alameda manzanita is that it is a chaparral fire-adapted shrub. Fire is a significant and effective regeneration factor in the management and recovery of decadent chapparal (Hanes 1977). Fire partially recycles limiting nutrients, consumes allelopathic litter, scarifies seed for germination, opens up the canopy providing light and space for seedling establishment, and reduces the number and types of pests and pathogens that attack weakened plants (Jepson 1939, Sampson 1944, Cooper 1922, Detling 1961, Gankin and Major 1964, Wells 1969, Mirov and Kraebel 1939). Seedling establishment for the burl-forming manzanitas is not critical for stand regeneration; however, the obligate-seeding manzanitas like the Alameda manzanita need to regenerate from seed following fire or other disturbance (Keeley and Zedler 1978, Wells 1969).

The understory of the Alameda manzanita stands is generally free of herbs or other establishing shrubs and trees. This is due to the allelopathic effect of phytotoxins produced by roots, fallen fruit, leaf litter and exfoliating bark of the manzanitas (Chou and Muller 1972). It is generally believed that toxin removal by fire accounts for the subsequent flush of seedling germination of herbs and shrubs including the manzanitas. Manzanitas older than fifty years can begin to decline in vigor, accompanied by accumulating dead and downed wood and debris, contributing to a growing fuel load (Philpot 1977). Observations of the main Alameda manzanita populations indicate that the stands have not been burned in 80 to 100 years. The fuel load is high. The Alameda manzanitas exhibit signs of great age with many plants up to 75 percent dead. Seedling establishment has only been observed on recently cut slopes or disturbed sites associated with road grading and house building.

Within the two major "barrens" populations of Huckleberry Ridge and Sobrante Ridge, the main method of regeneration and recruitment is rooted branches (layering). The A. pallida populations within these barrens are stable; however, the Huckleberry Ridge manzanita population has the disadvantage of competing for branch rooting space with huckleberry (Vaccinium ovatum) and chinquapin (Castanopsis chrysophylla var. minor), which by their fairly large spread and size can shade the manzanita branches. The Alameda manzanita does root beneath its own canopy, and invasion of this space by other species is limited by the allelopathic properties of the manzanita litter. Shading is a major factor only at the edge of, or outside of the barrens populations because tree species fail to become large enough to shade out the Alameda manzanita within these areas.

Another conspicuous characteristic of the Alameda manzanita is the development of dead or decorticated areas on the branches and trucks (Davis 1973). This condition is called bark striping (fig. 3) and was first described by Adams (1934) in individuals of A. myrtifolia and A. viscida. Bark Striping is most common with the older individual plants. Adams indicated that it has a pathological origin but Davis disagrees and suggests that striping is a "positive adaptation to the Mediterranean climate". His hypothesis is that in areas protected from fire, the shade-intolerant manzanitas attain sizes that strain the plant's ability to maintain live tissue. In a sense, the plant shuts down portions of its mass in order to continue meristem growth. The Alameda manzanita has the ability to maintain healthy growing branches even when it has lost major portions of the crown and live cambium. Plants that are over 75 percent dead since the fungus attack of 1983 show dramatic signs of recovery utilizing their ability to develop striped cambium.

Figure 3--Bark striping on large specimen of A. pallida on Sobrante Ridge. Diameter of large stem on left is 25 centimeters.

ENDANGERMENT FACTORS

The Sobrante Ridge manzanita population has the least human impact of all the Alameda manzanita populations. There is no residential housing inside or on the edge of the chapparal and there are no planted exotic trees or shrubs. Effects of the root fungus disease were not observed on Sobrante Ridge. While the status and vigor of the Sobrante Ridge manzanita population can be described as good, much of the population exhibits great age and is approaching senescence.

There is significant direct and indirect human impact on the Huckleberry Ridge manzanita population where residential housing is built among the Alameda manzanitas on Manzanita Drive on the ridge top. Up to 50 percent of the original Alameda manzanita population has housing development or is privately owned. Associated with the housing is the presence of planted and escaped exotic trees, shrubs, and groundcovers. Several eucalyptus groves are present. A small grove of silver wattle (Acacia baileyana) is present as well as several Monterey pine groves. French broom (Cytisus monspessulanus) dominates along Manzanita Drive where the Reserve borders the road. Just below one of these sites is a large population of periwinkle (Vinca major) and a large area covered with German ivy (Senecia mikanioides). Extensive stands of French broom associated with eucalyptus are located at both the north and south entrances to the Reserve.

The shading of A. pallida plants by planted and naturalized Monterey pines and cypresses is perhaps the most outstanding endangerment factor upon the smaller outlying Alameda manzanita populations. The recent spraying and future spraying of herbicides along Skyline Boulevard has had and will have a deleterious impact upon roadside regeneration of the Alameda manzanita.

Over half of the A. pallida plants on Huckleberry Ridge and along Skyline Boulevard showed recent signs of branch and stem dieback due to the root fungus. This dieback has ceased within the last year and most of the dead branches and plants are one to two years old. The leaves turn a reddish color the first year and take on a skeleton white-grey color the following year. Only a few plants exhibited recent dieback initiation during the survey. Despite the dead and dying branches, the remaining healthy branches and meristems exhibited good vigor and had flowered and produced a large crop of seed in 1986. Root fungus thrives in the soil with high moisture levels coupled with poor drainage. Weakened plants are more susceptible to attack by this fungus. The observed dieback is the response to the branches not receiving moisture from the root system. Generally the status and vigor of the Alameda manzanita on Huckleberry Ridge is poor.

A subtle, perhaps significant, impact of human development upon the Alameda manzanita population is the introduction into local landscapes of "exotic" Manzanitas. A. densiflora is planted in several landscapes on Manzanita Way including the East Bay Municipal Utility District water tank landscape. These plants flower in

December, the same month the Alameda manzanita begins flowering. Two A. Uva-ursi cultivars and two A. hookeri cultivars are planted in other landscapes. The possibility of genetic introgression into the A. pallida population is great, assuming that the ease of hybridization of other members of the A. andersonii complex applies to the Alameda manzanita (Roof 1967, pers. com. Steve Edwards, Walter Knight, Roman Gankin).

MANAGEMENT IMPLICATIONS

Up to the present time there has been no conservation management activities or programs to improve the Alameda manzanita habitat. Based upon the findings of this survey it is concluded that the management and recovery of the Alameda manzanita should encourage the establishment of new plants and the enhancement of the health of the older plants. This must involve baring new sites on shale or sandstone, scarifying seed, consuming or removing allelopathic litter, planting new plants, and cutting and managing the overstory. In addition, more information is needed on the nature of the root fungus that most recently decimated the Huckleberry Ridge and Oakland hills manzanita populations.

Much can be learned from a prescribed fire in the Alameda manzanita habitat. The Sobrante Ridge population is a relatively safe area for a prescribed fire of a portion of this location. The Huckleberry Ridge population is problematic in terms of fire management. Residential housing at the top of the steep slopes with a high fuel load seriously limits fire management abilities (fig. 4). Alternative methods that mimic the effects of fire need to be developed on Huckleberry Ridge. The homeowners need to be made aware that their homes exist in a high fire hazard area that will suffer serious damage if (when) a catastrophic fire occurs. A fuel management plan must be designed that will reduce the fire hazard yet leave room for the growth and establishment of the Alameda manzanita.

One of the greatest threats to the Alameda manzanita is competition and shading from planted native and exotic trees. Exotic shrubs and groundcovers are also making significant inroads into the habitat. Eucalyptus, Monterey pines and cypresses, and colonies of French broom, German ivy and English ivy must be removed or appropriately pruned within the Alameda manzanita habitat.

Figure 4--This home on Huckleberry Ridge surrounded by senescent chaparral illustrates the extreme fire hazard.

Within and near the Alameda manzanita habitat are several areas on shale and sandstone that offer good sites for the establishment of new individual and satellite populations. These sites include roadcuts along Skyline Boulevard, areas where exotic competition has been removed, and new sites on adjacent parks and public agency lands.

The probability of genetic introgression needs to be carefully considered. Wells (1969) pointed out that each generation of the non-sprouter manzanitas is attended by rigorous selection and the intensity of natural selection is greater with the non-sprouting, obligate-seeding strategy in chaparral vegatation. Coupled with a high possibility of genetic introgression via bee pollination from the local exotic manzanitas, regeneration after a fire or disturbance may result in the beginning of a manzanita hybrid swarm that will portend the end of the purity of the A. pallida populations. The planting of exotic manzanitas on Manzanita Drive by the property owners was most likely done in the spirit of appropriate drought tolerant natives for the home landscape. An education program should be implemented that encourages property owners to replace their exotic manzanitas with the Alameda manzanita or appropriate non-invasive exotic groundcovers.

CONCLUSION

The prime objective of the management plan is to determine and implement management activities which will improve the biological condition of declining Alameda Manzanita populations and help in ultimate recovery of the species. An Alameda Manzanita Advisory Committee was formed to oversee and review the developing management plan. The Advisory Committee consisted of local experts who have intimate knowledge of the Alameda Manzanita's ecology and history. The members were: Neil Havlik, senior range ecologist of the East Bay Regional Park District (chairman), Steven Edwards, Director of the Regional Parks Botanic Garden, Walter Knight, manzanita expert and native plant taxonomist, Robert Martin, U.C. Berkeley fire ecologist, Marian Reeve, California Native Plant Society representative, and David Amme, open space management specialist and management plant coordinator.

Six primary goals were developed by the Advisory Committee.

1. Competition--To remove or appropriately prune all exotic and selected native trees and shrubs that pose direct shading and competition dangers to the Alameda manzanita. This goal includes pruning and removal, long-range plan for complete control, guidelines for restoration practices, land acquisition needs, and seeding and planting the Alameda manzanita.

2. Gene Pool--To protect the Alameda manzanita gene pool from genetic introgression from introduced exotic manzanitas. This goal primarily involves an inventory followed by public education program.

3. Ecology--To investigate the ecology and required habitat of Alameda manzanita to aid in development of a management plan. Included in this goal is a prescribed fire, seed germination investigations, and scarification/disturbance (fireless) experiments. In addition, there are research opportunities that need investigation including the nature of the root fungus and seed germination experiments.

4. New Manzanita Establishment--To establish new satellite populations as well as new plants within existing populations by direct seeding and container planting.

5. Stewardship Cooperation--To involve the private homeowners and public land holding agencies in the development and implementation of a management plan that will both protect the homes and the manzanita habitat. This goal particularly applies to Huckleberry Ridge along Manzanita Drive where there is an extreme fire hazard. Homes are built among the senescent chaparral with many exotic trees and shrubs contributing to the growing fuel load.

6. Outreach--To compile an educational pamphlet. The original purpose of the pamphlet was to educate the neighboring landowners on Huckleberry Ridge about the Alameda manzanita and how it can be used and cared for in home landscaping. The Advisory Committee developed additional ideas that should be included in the pamphlet including removing exotic manzanitas, listing non-invasive landscape plants, providing factual information concernig the acute fire hazard, and informing the homeowners on techniques to control the weedy exotics. It was the consensus of the Advisory Committee that the pamphlet be produced early in the planning process. The distribution of the pamphlet will be the first step in enacting the Alameda Recovery Plan.

Acknowledgments: We thank Steve Edwards, Director of the Regional Park Botanic Garden; and Susan Cochrane and Ann Marshall-Ross, of the Endangered Plant Project of the California Department of Fish and Game. This work was funded with monies from the Endangered-Species Tax Check-off Program.

LITERATURE CITED

Adams, J.E. Some observations on two species of Arctostaphylos. Madrono 2:147-152; 1934.

Adams, J.E. A systematic study of the genus Arctostaphylos Adans. Elisha Mitchell Sci. Soc. 56(1):1-62; 1940.

Chou, C.H. and C.H. Muller. Allelopathic mechanisms of Arctostaphylos glandulosa var. zacaensis. The Am. Midland Nat. 88(2):324-347; 1972.

Cooper, W.S. The broad-sclerophyll vegetation of California. Carnegie Inst. Wash. Publ. 319; 1922.

Davis, C.B. Comparative ecology of six members of A. andersonii complex PhD Dis., U.C. Davis; 1972.

Davis, C.B. "Bark striping" in Arctostaphylos (Ericaceae). Madrono 22:145-149; 1973.

Detling, L.E. The chaparral formation of southeastern Oregon with consideration of its post-glacial history. Ecology 42:348-357; 1961.

Dibblee, T.W. Preliminary geological map of the Richmond quadrangle, Alameda and Contra Costa Counties. USGS; 1980.

Eastwood, A. A revision of Arctostaphylos with key and descriptions. Leafl. West. Bot. 1(11): 105-127; 1934.

Gankin, R. and J. Major. Arctostaphylos myrtifolia, its biology and relationship to the problem of endenism. Ecology 45:792-808; 1964.

Gilliam, H. Weather of the San Francisco Bay Region, U.C. Press, Berkeley, CA; 1962; 72 p.

Griffin, J. Maritime chaparral and endemic shrubs of the Monterey Bay Region, California. Madrono. 25(2):65-81; 1978.

Hanes, T.L. Chaparral. From Terrestrial Vegetation of California. Ed. Barbour, M.G. and J. Majors. John Wiley & Sons, New York; 1977:417-469.

Jepson, W.L. A Flora of California. ASUC. University of California, Berkeley; 1939:18-50.

Johnson, B. Waterlogged and drenched. The Bay Leaf. CNPS Newsletter of the San Francisco Bay Chapter; 1983.

Keeley, J.E. and P.H. Zedler. Reproduction of chaparral shrubs after fire: a comparison of sprouting and seeding strategies. The Am. Midland Nat. 99(1):142-161; 1978.

Lawson, A.C. Geologic atlas of the U.S. San Francisco Folia. USGA Dept. of Int.; 1914.

Meyers, J.N. Fog. Scientific American 219(6):74-84; 1968.

Mirov, N.T. and C.J. Kraebel. Collecting and handling seeds of wild plants. Calif. For. and Rg. Exp. Sta. USDA. For. Pub. #5; 1939; 42 p.

Munz, P.A. A California Flora and Supplement. U.C. Press Berkeley, California; 1968; 1905 p.

Patton, C.P. Climatology of summer fog in the San Francisco Bay Area. U.C. Pub. in Geo. 10(3):113-200; 1956.

Philpot, C.W. Vegetation features as determinants of fire frequency and intensity. Pg. 12-17 In Symposium on the environmental consequences of fire and fuel management in Mediterranean ecosystems. Mooney and Conrad, Tec. Coordinators. Palo Alto, CA USDA For. Ser. GTR-WO-3; August 1-5, 1977:498 p.

Radbruch, D. Aerial and engineering geology of the Oakland east quadrangle. USGS; 1969.

Rantz, S.E. Mean Annual Precipitation and Precipitation Depth-Duration-Frequency Data for the San Francisco Bay Region, California. U.S. Geological Survey, Menlo Park, CA; 1971; 23 p.

Roof, J.B. Arctostaphylos montarensis, a new species of manzanita from San Mateo County, California. The Four Seasons. 2(3):6-16; 1967.

Sampson, A.W. Plant succession on burned chaparral lands in northern California, U.C. Berkeley. Ag. Exp. Sta. Bull. 685; 1944; 144 p.

Smith, J.P. and R. York. Inventory of rare and endangered vascular plants of California. CNPS Spec. Pub. #1, 3rd Edition. California Native Plant Society, Berkeley, CA; 1984.

Stone, E.C., F.W. Went, and C.L. Young. Water absorption from the atmosphere by plants growing in dry soil. Science 111(2890):546-548; 1950.

Stratford, J. and S. Edwards. The Huckleberry Preserve plantlist. The Four Seasons. 7(2):23-28; 1984.

Wells, P.V. Vegetation in relation to geological substratum and fire in the San Luis Obispo quadrangle, California Eco. Mon. 32(1):79-103; 1962.

Wells, P.V. The Relation Between Mode of Reproduction and Extent of Speciation in Woody Genera of the California Chaparral. Evolution 23:264-267; 1969.

Development of Management Plans for Sensitive Plant Species

Bruce E. Dawson [1]

Abstract: Activity plans for the management of sensitive plants are more than a logical progression from the location and identification of rare plant populations. Natural resource management agencies have routinely written planning documents for the management of such resources as wildlife and livestock grazing. Developing plans for the management requirements of sensitive plants, however, is often a new endeavor for public agencies. It presents the opportunity to manage rare plants as a viable resource unto itself and not simply as the subject of project mitigation.

This discussion centers on the development of sensitive plant[2] management plans from the perspective of a public land management agency, the Bureau of Land Management (BLM). The idea for this paper came out of the trials, tribulations and frustration in writing an activity plan for the management and protection of the Indian Valley Brodiaea (Brodiaea coronaria (Salisb.) Engler ssp. rosea (Greene) Niehaus).

Activity plans for the management of rare[3] plants are more than just the next progressive step after the identification of rare plant populations. Actions proposed within these plans have the potential to take resource management from the reactive phase to one that can be viewed as affirmative conservation. This is quite a quantum leap if you consider that a list of Federally recognized Threatened and Endangered plant species has only been in existence for roughly a decade. The concept of actively managing rare plant populations on public lands with more than just a fence and a "Keep Out" sign is coming of age.

BACKGROUND

To entertain a discussion of rare plant management, as set forth in a formal planning framework, one must really gain an historical perspective of where public land management has come in the last 50 years. In BLM's formative years (1934-1946), natural resource managers of the vacant public domain had one basic piece of guiding legislation, the Taylor Grazing Act of 1934. Though it was one of the first laws directing the nation towards conservation, protection of rare plants via statute or policy was still 40 years away. The mission of BLM and its precursors was livestock grazing, timber harvest and ultimately land disposal. To reiterate the obvious, the issues, public interest and agency focus were very different in 1934 than today.

It is, of course, difficult to pinpoint exactly when our focus relative to rare plants changed, when we began to recognize botanical values as a bona fide public land resource. However, January 1, 1970, is noteworthy; on this day the National Environmental Policy Act of 1969 (NEPA) went into effect. The way we were to do business

---

[1] Range Conservationist, Bureau of Land Management, U. S. Department of the Interior, Ukiah, CA.

[2] Sensitive plants, as defined here, are those that have been officially proposed or identified as candidates for inclusion into the Federal list of plants threatened or endangered of extinction.

[3] The terms rare and sensitive are used interchangably throughout the body of the text.

was forever changed. NEPA directed us to assess the environmental consequences of our proposed actions and alternatives on the affected environment, which included extant flora. Mitigation, now, was more than a good idea, it was a mandate. For all intent and purposes, implementation of NEPA can be considered the rudimentary beginnings of rare plant management on Federal lands.

Two additional pieces of legislation facilitated BLM's efforts toward rare plant conservation. First and foremost, of course, would be the Endangered Species Act of 1973, which extended protection to plants deemed Threatened or Endangered and directed the Federal government to prepare a list of such plants. This list of Category 1, 2 and 3 plants that the US Fish and Wildlife Service eventually published in the <u>Federal Register</u> in 1978 was important because it gave public land managers something concrete to work with. It not only provided them with a list of the taxa protected but also those that were under consideration as proposed or identified as candidates for listing.

The second law of major consequence, the Federal Land Policy and Management Act of 1976 (FLPMA), directed BLM to manage public lands under the auspices of multiple use in a manner that would protect the quality of many resources, including scientific, ecological and environmental values. This legislation also directed BLM to periodically inventory the public lands and to promptly develop plans and regulations for Areas of Critical Environmental Concern (ACEC). Perhaps of most significance was the charter given to BLM for land retention rather than land disposal.

MANAGEMENT PLAN DEVELOPMENT

Historically, natural resource management agencies have routinely written planning documents for the management of resources such as wildlife and domestic livestock grazing. Typically these plans have laid out a strategy for management that contains overall land management objectives and constraints common to the affected resources (e.g., continuation of a prescribed burning program underway in the area); specific management problems (e.g., critical watershed problems due to sheep grazing, road construction and unstable geologic conditions); and specific (quantifiable) objectives with supporting rationale (e.g., 750 kilograms/hectare residual mulch on slopes 25-40 percent; this prescription will ensure adequate watershed protection).

The planning document concludes with the planned action section, which in conjunction with the specific objectives is the driving force of the plan. Included in this section is a description of the system of use, proposed projects for resource improvement or habitat enhancement, mitigation for resources adversely impacted (e.g., cultural resources), and a component identifying inventory and monitoring strategies.

These types of traditional activity plans have become common place over the last 20 years, becoming the standard operating procedure for BLM. Developing such plans for the highly specialized management requirements of rare plants, however, is very often a new and unprecedented endeavor for public land management agencies. Frequently, the prototypes for sensitive plant management plans, in the context of multiple use management, are yet to be established or are in their formative stages.

Plans identifying the need for rare plant protection as part of an existing suite of values in certain sensitive areas have existed for some time. However, plans that seek to examine the single species or habitat as a primary focus, with proposals to actively manage for status improvement and not status quo are often a novel undertaking. Proposals to enhance habitat and to conscientiously inventory and monitor a rare entity solely for its inherent values and not simply as a project mitigation requirement are anything but common place.

For the natural resource specialist rare plant management plan development is largely an unchartered course. It is an exacting challenge to manage sensitive plants as a viable and legitimate public land resource unto itself and not simply as the subject stop-gap mitigation. Development of plans for rare plant management can be a tremendous opportunity. These documents present us with the chance not only to increase public awareness, but agency awareness as well.

Often botanical responsibilities are an ancillary inclusion to existing workloads. It is thus not surprising that at times management of a rare plant program is eschewed as an unwanted chore, as an impediment to proposed projects for other resource values (e.g., geothermal develoment, timber harvest, wildlife habitat improvement). It is, therefore, all the more incumbent upon us to approach sensitive species management as a rewarding challenge and as an opportunity to mentally stretch. It is imperative that the development of management plans not be a perfunctory exercise, that it not be just another task in the annual work schedule.

UNIQUE REQUIREMENTS OF RARE PLANT MANAGEMENT PLANS

How are the requirements of rare plant management different from more common forms of vegetation management found on public lands? A number of things come to mind: urgency for action, degree of endangerment, habitat management strategy, and inventory and monitoring methodology, to name a few. Let us take a look at some of these individually.

The degree of urgency required for sensitive species management is quite often different from that of other natural resource values. The species may not be in immediate jeopardy, but a subtle form of endangerment may be present. In the case of the Indian Valley Brodiaea (BRCOR), the most obvious threat is that of the possibility of increased water storage levels within the reservoir which would result from an episodic storm event of 100 year magnitude. Of less obvious threat, but still of serious concern, is the effect of controlling wildfires. BRCOR is shade intolerant (Niehaus 1977) and is suspected of poor root competition. Such conditions are the result of encroachment by brush species. Thus, it is important that all threats to a species continued existence be identified and evaluated in management plans.

Effective habitat management may be just protecting known populations from disturbance (e.g., prohibiting recreational pursuits and livestock grazing), or it may mean more active management practices like brush control or abating substrate erosion.

It may also mean identifying the need for specific research (e.g., pollination mechanisms, predator-plant relationships, soil chemistry requirements) or further study in general. Memoranda-of-Understanding (MOU) with research organizations are an effective means to secure such research needs.

One of the first and most basic questions that must be asked in designing an approach to rare plant management is how many are there? An analysis of species abundance must begin with data on samples or an actual count of the known statistical universe. The strategy we use to inventory and monitor rare plants is one of the primary and more complex items of consideration. We must take precaution not to violate basic statistical assumptions that apply to all population sampling when seeking measures of central tendency and dispersion.

Developing appropriate methodology for sampling sensitive plant populations is intrinsically more difficult than data collection on more common vegetation, although potential approaches to population monitoring for conservation are essentially the same as those to plant population biology in general (Davy and Jefferies 1981). Extrapolation of rare plant sample data to areas not sampled as an estimate of the total individuals in a population requires critical thought and planning. Unfortunately, formal guidance frequently is not readily available.

It has been suggested (Davy and Jefferies 1981) that a monitoring approach that is integrated contributes most significantly to a comprehensive understanding of rare species biology and is thus of the most utility for conservation management. The lack of permanent reference points appears to be the single greatest hinderance to assessing change in species populations (White and Bratton 1981).

One may obtain samples from populations in a number of ways; however, to reach valid conclusions about populations by inductive reasoning from samples, statistical approaches must assume the samples are randomly obtained (Zar 1974). We must also assume that the stand sampled is homogeneous (Daubenmire 1968). Heterogeneity needs to be eliminated as much as possible. Stratifying the vegetation association under study into discrete units which reflect maximum homogeneity will accomplish this end. Meeting these assumptions is not so straight-forward as it might seem at first. For example, rare plant populations do not necessarily occur randomly, and sampling near ecotones can present a serious problem in terms of community homogeneity.

Land management agencies have traditionally sampled vegetation for the purpose of resource allocation and appraisal. We might sample to determine the number of board feet on a given tract of land or to determine the percent of forage utilized by domestic livestock on a grazing lease. Typically, natural resource specialists have sampled plant communities for a host of parameters (e.g., plant density, frequency, foliar cover, weight estimates, ecological condition, trend, or forestry site index). We have gone to great lengths to ensure that these assumptions of homogeneity and randomness are met (and valid) in our data collection methodologies. The same assumptions must be met for the inventory and monitoring of rare plant populations.

A CASE IN POINT
(INDIAN VALLEY BRODIAEA)

In 1971, the level of awareness concerning rare botanical resources on public lands within the administrative jurisdiction of BLM's Ukiah District was generally low amongst the staff. This was no reflection on the talents and capabilities of incumbent personnel but rather a function of the task at hand (i.e., commodity production with a conservation ethic). As an agency, we were still adjusting to the passage of NEPA, and the Endangered Species Act of 1973 was only on the horizon. Botanical concerns and conflicts, as a part of the larger environmental movement, were only beginning to be heard.

It was in that same year that the first rare plant issue surfaced in Ukiah District. A proposal to inundate the Indian Valley area of Lake County was being brought forward. It was brought to our attention by a special interest group, the California Native Plant Society (CNPS) that the creation of the proposed Indian Valley Reservoir would pose a serious threat to a small member of the Amaryllidaceae, the Indian Valley Brodiaea, which appeared to have a very limited distribution.

This was indeed a perplexing problem. The District had no botanists or plant ecologists, per se, at that time; basically, it was staffed with foresters, range conservationists and engineers. The concern raised as a result of the suspected demise of the Indian Valley brodiaea was the genesis of our botany program and the impetus for our first sensitive plant inventory.

Thus the foundation was laid for the 40 acres of public land containing habitat for the brodiaea to be recommended for designation as an Area of Critical Environmental Concern (ACEC) in the Clearlake Management Framework Plan (MFP). Such a designation requires the development of an activity plan (i.e., management plan) to manage those values deemed of critical concern. The Indian Valley Area of Critical Environmental Concern and Research Natural Area Management Plan was developed in 1985 and the first inventory as a result of the plan was conducted in 1986 by BLM and a group of CNPS volunteers. Active management of a species that Ukiah District had been only remotely aware of 15 years before was underway.

CONCLUSION

The management of rare plants on public lands over the last 50 years has gone from little or no knowledge of existing values, to initial identification of populations, to project mitigation, to inventory of the public lands, and finally to where we are today.

The message here is a simple one: the time has come to manage. This does not merely mean designating an area (e.g., Research Natural Area) and deferring active management. We are at the point in resource management where populations of rare floral communities on Federal lands have been identified, usually with at least a cursory inventory. The time has come for us to take existing information, plug it into our central data clearinghouse (California Natural Diversity Data Base), acknowledge the rare values through special designation, develop activity plans, and, most importantly, to implement the recommendations set forth.

In the end, the responsibility for meaningful rare plant management does not lie with the upper echelon of management (i.e., BLM District Manager or

Forest Supervisor), but with the natural resource specialist. The success or failure of a rare plant program it is a direct function of the resident specialist's interest and desire.

It must be the purpose of the sensitive plant management plan to acknowledge that the lands therein described require special management attention. Furthermore, it must be our intent to implement this plan to manage, protect and prevent irreparable damage to the extant biological values so that future generations may enjoy this unique resource.

REFERENCES

Clearlake Resource Area transition management framework plan. Ukiah, CA: Ukiah District. Bureau of Land Management, U. S. Department of the Interior. 1984. 110 p.

Daubenmire, R. Plant communities. New York: Harper and Row, Publishers. 1968. 300 p.

Davy, A. J.; Jefferies, R. L. Approach to the monitoring of rare plant populations. In Synge, H. ed. The biological aspects of rare plants. New York: John Wiley and Sons, Ltd. 1981: 219-232.

Goff, F. G.; Dawson, G. A.; and Rochow, J. J. Site examination for threatened and endangered plant species. Environmental Management. 6(4): 307-316. 1982 July.

Indian Valley Area of Critical Environmental Concern management plan. Ukiah, CA: Ukiah District. Bureau of Land Management, U. S. Department of the Interior. 1985. 15 p.

Niehaus, T. F. *Brodiaea coronaria* ssp. *rosea*, rare plant status report. California Native Plant Society. 1977. 4 p.

White, P. S.; Bratton S. P. Monitoring vegetation and rare plant populations in U. S. national parks and preserves. In Synge, H. ed. The biological aspects of rare plants. New York: John Wiley and Sons, Ltd. 1981: 219- 232.

Zar, J. H. Biostatistical analysis. Englewood Cliffs, NJ: Printice-Hall. 1974. 620 p.

Recovery of Endangered and Threatened Plants in California: The Federal Role

Monty D. Knudsen 1

ABSTRACT: The requirements of the Endangered Species Act of 1973, as amended, are discussed in relation to recovery planning and implementation. Information is presented on developing recovery plan goals and objectives, and various recovery strategies. Several recovery plans and recovery actions are examined as well as the legal aspects and constraints of the Service recovery program for plants in California.

The Endangered Species Act of 1973 (Public Law 93-205), as amended (the Act), directs the Secretaries of Interior and Commerce to develop and implement recovery plans for the conservation and survival of Federally-listed endangered or threatened species. These plans serve as management guides to the U.S. Fish and Wildlife Service (Service), cooperating agencies, organizations, and individuals to direct, justify, and schedule recovery tasks and/or actions to restore, enhance, and secure endangered and threatened species as self-sustaining components of the ecosystems in which they exist.

The primary emphasis of the Service's recovery program is to maintain and enhance wild populations of endangered and threatened species and prevent degradation of the ecosystems upon which they depend. The ultimate objective of each recovery plan is to restore listed species to a condition where the measures provided by the Act are no longer necessary [Section 1532(3)] and deregulate the species by removal from the list of endangered and threatened species (delist). The Service recognizes, however, that for some species, delisting may never be possible because of severe population (genetic) depletion, irreversible destruction or alteration of significant portions of a species' range and/or reductions in or loss of the functional integrity of the ecosystem upon which the species depends.

RECOVERY PLANNING

Without clearly defined objectives and careful planning, cost-effective solutions to complex resource conservation problems are virtually impossible to achieve (Ripley 1969, Morrisey 1976). Consequently, the Service's endangered species program relies heavily on tactical planning (Phenicie and Lyons 1973, U.S. Fish and Wildlife Service 1973) and a framework of recovery plans to help guide management and budgeting for endangered and threatened species recovery. Tactical recovery planning involves establishing a series of tasks sequentially ordered to achieve an explicitly identified prime objective. Problems and/or limiting factors and methods for resolving them are listed in a step-by-step outline (step-down) of tasks or management actions (fig. 1). When all tasks or management actions have been completed or resolved, theoretically so has the recovery plan prime objective. At that point the species should be recovered and delisted.

Prime Objective: Ensure the continued health of the one remaining wild plant on U.S. Army property, augment the "population" at that site with at least 20 plants propagated from the remaining plant [or preferably pure stock from other sites (if found)], establish and/or locate at least 4 additional self-sustaining populations, each with 20 or more individuals, at secure sites within the presumed historic range, and consider reclassifying the species to threatened status. Following reclassification to threatened status evaluate the possibility of delisting the species.

1. Preserve, protect, and enhance the remaining Raven's manzanita plant and its habitat.
   11. Provide protection for the one Raven's manzanita plant on U.S. Army property.
      111. Secure immediate cooperation of the Army to monitor and protect the general condition of the existing plant.
      112. Develop a long-term agreement with U.S. Army to protect the plant and undertake necessary recovery actions.
   12. Manage habitat to reduce competition, maintain vigor, and encourage natural regeneration.

Figure 1. Example of a step-down outline (in part) from the Presidio (=Raven's) Manzanita Recovery Plan.

---

[1] Fish and Wildlife Biologist, U.S. Fish and Wildlife Service, Department of the Interior, Sacramento, California

Recovery Plans

Development of all recovery plans involves critical reviews by recognized technical (species) experts inside and outside the government (technical review), followed by reviews from the agencies that are responsible for plan implementation (agency review). After comments from these reviews have been incorporated, the draft final plan is sent to the Director or regional director (depending on the scope and magnitude of the plan), for final approval and printing. Updates and revisions occur as the need arises.

Service recovery plans typically consist of three parts, an introduction, the recovery plan, and an implementation schedule. The introduction provides background information on each species, summarizing what is known about habitat requirements, population limiting factors, past and current distribution, threats and conservation efforts. Lengthy taxonomic discussions are avoided, except in unusual circumstances.

The second part, entitled "Recovery", states the primary objective of the plan quantified, as much as possible, for the eventual delisting of the species. The "Recovery" section also outlines all the steps or tasks necessary to achieve the primary objective in a step-down format. The outline is intended to be comprehensive to the extent that it will be followed throughout the recovery process. A narrative following the step-down outline explains, describes, and justifies each step or task.

Because the step-down outline attempts to include everything necessary for full recovery of the species, it must include all the short- and long-term tasks and goals necessary for the protection of adequate habitat and population levels. Consequently, the detail and specificity of each task depends upon available knowledge of the species, its habitat requirements, and management methods to alleviate threats and limiting factors. Thus, some tasks may be very detailed while others provide only general guidance.

Despite the intent, changes in recovery goals and tasks often occur in subsequent revisions of the original plan. As plans are implemented and new information becomes available, goals and task details are expected to become more specific, focused, and definitive. Thus, recovery plans are considered dynamic documents, subject to change, resulting from new research findings, changes in the status of the species, and completion of the tasks in the plan. And, although deregulation or delisting is always the ultimate goal of each recovery plan, in many cases the immediate objective may be to prevent extinction or halt an ongoing decline in the species' population and/or habitat. Moreover, as stated previously, some species may be so depleted in habitat and population levels that delisting may not be possible in the forseeable future or ever.

The third part of each recovery plan, the implementation schedule, is, in many ways, the most important part of each plan. The implemention schedule prioritizes all recovery tasks, provides budget estimates for completing each task along with a time schedule for implementation, and identifies the agencies responsible for task implementation.

Task priorities are based on the criteria listed in table 1. Service funding for recovery tasks is keyed in large part to the recovery plan implementation schedule. Of course, agency appropriations from year-to-year also determine recovery funding. Figure 2 provides an example of an implementation schedule.

Table 1. Criteria for setting recovery task priorities.

task priority	criterion
1	any action that must be taken to prevent extinction or prevent the species from declining irreversibly
2	any action that must be taken to prevent a significant decline in species population/habitat quality, or some other significant negative impact short of extinction
3	all other actions necessary to provide for full recovery of the species

Although recovery plan details vary for different species as a result of differing biologies, threats, levels of knowledge, and other factors (biological and political), all recovery plans must resolve two basic tasks: 1) identification of limiting and/or threatening factors, and 2) elimination or reduction of those limiting factors to enhance survival. Accomplishing these two basic tasks requires that they be broken down into more detailed segments of problems and solutions specific to the species of concern. Table 2 lists some of the threats common to endangered and threatened plants.

Although there are presently 24 Federally-listed plants in California, only 15 have approved recovery plans. Table 3 lists the status of recovery plans for these California plants.

RECOVERY PLAN IMPLEMENTATION

In a large sense, the recovery of species begins upon listing as a consequence of the substantial protections provided under the 14 sections of the Act. Nonetheless, certain sections of the Act contribute more directly to recovery than others, the most direct being the required commitment on the part of the Federal Government, pursuant to Section 7 (a)(2), to avoid funding, permitting or authorizing any activities that are likely to jeopardize the continued existence and recovery of Federally-listed species. Beyond this requirement, however, the remaining provisions largely advise and admonish Federal agencies to "use their authorities in furtherance of the purposes of the Act", but do not explicitly require implementation of recovery actions, even when the responsible agencies are specifically identified in approved recovery plans. Consequently, each plan includes a disclaimer stating that obtaining the goals and objectives is contingent upon funding, priorities, and other budgetary constraints. Thus, the most active and successful recovery programs often are those with enthusiastic constituencies that effectively motivate the responsible agencies to provide adequate staffing and funding for recovery implementation.

Table 2. An outline of some conceptual threat factors considered in developing recovery plans for endangered or threatened plants.

A. Environmental influences
   1. Physical
      a. Habitat conversion or destruction (past or present)
      b. Pollution or environmental contaminants
      c. Human caused changes in habitat dynamics (eg. fire, erosion, soil nutrients, hydrology)
      d. Natural events that reduced or eliminated populations
   2. Biological
      a. Competitive displacement or interference
      b. Introgressive hybridation
      c. Genetic depletion
      d. Pollinator loss/poor reproduction
      e. Predation/herbivory
      f. Disease
B. Other influences
   1. Economic- overutilization for commercial, horticultural, medicinal, or scientific purposes
   2. Lack of adequate regulatory or legal protection
   3. Lack of adequate agency emphasis

GENERAL CATEGORY	PLAN TASK	TASK NO.	PRIORITY NO.	TASK DURATION	RESPONSIBLE/AGENCY FWS REGION	RESPONSIBLE/AGENCY FWS PROGRAM	OTHER	FISCAL YEAR COSTS $1,000's FY'84	FISCAL YEAR COSTS $1,000's FY'85	(EST.) FY'86	COMMENTS/NOTES
Protect Antioch Dunes Ecosystem											
A 6	Acquire Sardis property	1111	1		1	Realty*		Completed			Purchases completed in FY'80, $2.2 million
A 6	Acquire Stamm-Starr property	1112	1			Realty*		Completed			Purchase completed in FY'80 within above acquisition
A 4	Develop Management Plan	1113	1	Ongoing	1	Refuges*		2			FY'82, '83 PA Obj. 06, 5c(2)b
M 7	Manage refuge lands	1114	1	Ongoing	1	Refuges*		10	10	10	Ongoing AWR PA Obj.
A 3	PG&E MOU	1121	2	1 year	1	SE*		1			
A 3	Domtar MOU	1122	2	1 year	1	SE*		1			
A 3	McCullough MOU	1123	2	1 year	1	SE*		1			

Figure 2. Example of an Implementation Schedule (in part) from the Antioch Dunes Recovery plan.

Table 3. Status of recovery plan development for Federally-listed plants in California.

Species	date listed	plan printed	date plan approved	draft plan
San Mateo thornmint	(18 Sep 85)	no	n/a	no
large-flowered fiddleneck	(8 May 85)	no	n/a	T*
McDonald's rock-cress	(24 Apr 79)	no	(28 Feb 84)	n/a
Presidio (=Raven's) manzanita	(26 Oct 79)	yes	(10 Jul 84)	n/a
Truckee barberry	(6 Nov 79)	yes	(20 Jun 84)	n/a
San Benito evening-primrose	(12 Feb 85)	no	n/a	no
San Clemente Is. Indian paintbrush	(11 Aug 77)	yes[1]	(26 Jan 84)	n/a
spring-loving centaury	(20 May 85)	no	n/a	A[2]
salt marsh bird's-beak	(28 Sep 78)	yes	(6 Dec 85)	n/a
palmate-bracted bird's-beak	(1 Jul 86)	no	n/a	no
San Clemente Is. larkspur	(11 Aug 77)	yes[1]	(26 Jan 85)	n/a
Santa Barbara Is. liveforever	(26 Apr 78)	yes	(27 Jun 85)	n/a
Contra Costa wallflower	(26 Apr 78)	yes[3]	(25 Apr 84)	n/a
Loch Lomond coyote-thistle[4]	(26 Mar 86)	no	n/a	no
Ash meadows gumplant	(20 May 85)	no	n/a	A[2]
San Clemente Is. broom	(11 Aug 77)	yes[1]	(26 Jan 84)	n/a
San Clemente Is. bushmallow	(11 Aug 77)	yes[1]	(26 Jan 84)	n/a
Amargosa niterwort	(20 May 85)	no	n/a	A[2]
Eureka Dunes evening-primrose	(26 Apr 78)	yes[5]	(13 Dec 82)	n/a
Antioch Dunes evening-primrose	(26 Apr 78)	yes[4]	(25 Apr 84)	n/a
San Diego mesa mint	(28 Sep 78)	no	(16 Jul 84)	n/a
pedate checkerbloom	(31 Aug 84)	no	n/a	no
Eureka dunegrass	(26 Apr 78)	yes[5]	(13 Dec 82)	n/a
slender petaled thelypodium	(31 Aug 84)	no	n/a	no
Solano grass	(28 Sep 78)	yes[6]	(11 Sep 85)	n/a

[1] Included in Channel Islands Recovery Plan
[2] Included in Ash Meadows Recovery Plan
[3] Included in Antioch Dunes Recovery Plan
[4] Species emergency listed
[5] Included in Eureka Dunes Recovery Plan
[6] Plan includes the Delta green ground beetle

*T = Technical Review draft
A = Agency Review draft

Recovery Strategies

By and large the most common reason plants become endangered or threatened is human caused destruction of populations and their habitats. Consequently, the most common recovery plan task is to protect existing populations and habitat.

Land Acquisition

The most direct means of protecting habitat is through protective ownership via a conservation agency, organization or, in rare instances, sympathetic private individuals. While direct acquisition may be the most expedient and, to some, the most desirable means of obtaining protective ownership, Federal land acquisition in California for the purpose of conserving endangered and threatened plants has been virtually non-existent.

The most recent Fish and Wildlife Service land acquisition in California that secured habitat for Federally listed plants was the 1980 purchase of two parcels (55 acres) at the Antioch Dunes, Contra Costa County, at a cost of 2.2 million dollars. The purchase, funded through the Federal Land and Water Conservation Fund pursuant to Section 5 of the Act, became part of the San Francisco Bay National Wildlife Refuge. Interestingly, the acquisition specifically emphasized protection of the Lange's metalmark butterfly (Apodemia mormo langei), not the two endangered plants; Contra Costa wallflower (Erysimum capitatum var. angustatum) and Antioch Dunes evening-primrose (Oenothera deltoides subsp. howellii).

More recently, Federal acquisition of habitat for endangered and threatened animals (California condor and Coachella Valley fringe-toed lizard) required special congressional appropriations despite the clear authorities in the Act to use the Federal Land and Water Conservation Fund. This indicates the deemphasis on Federal land acquisition for conservation purposes.

Formal Protection Agreements

Protecting habitat through formal conservation easements or agreements with landowners (public and private) has been relatively successful on several occasions. Two signed agreements with the U.S. Forest Service help insure protection for two candidate plants, the Rawson's flaming-trumpet (Collomia rawsoniana) and Shirley Meadows mariposa (Calochortus coeruleus var. westonii) on the Sierra and Sequoia National Forests, respectively. At present a cooperative agreement is being developed among the U.S. Army, National Park Service, California Department of Fish and Game and the Fish and Wildlife Service to implement recovery actions for the Presidio manzanita (Arctostaphylos pungens var. ravenii) and other sensitive serpentine plant species. Tentative discussions recently initiated with Lawrence Livermore Laboratories seek a conservation agreement that would assist with implementation of recovery actions for the large-flowered fiddleneck (Amsinckia grandiflora). Although other agreements for habitat protection are anticipated, clearly, their development and successful implementation depend upon adequate agency staffing and funding. Existing Service botanical staffing and funding in California permit perhaps one, or at most two, such plans to be developed per year, but implementation and monitoring cannot be assured.

Interagency Consultation

Functionally, the most effective means of protecting species and habitats under the Endangered Species Act is via the Section 7 requirement for Federal Agencies to insure that any actions funded, authorized or carried out by them are not likely to jeopardize the continued existence of any Federally listed endangered or threatened species. For a detailed discussion of the process see Federal Register 51:19925-19963 (3 June 1986). Bean (1983) provides a detailed legal analysis of the Section 7 provision and Bartel and Knudsen (1984) discuss the application to vernal pools in California.

Although 24 California plants enjoy full protection under Section 7 of the Act at present, threats to these species frequently stem from non-federal activities that are not subject to the provisions of the Act, specifically formal consultation. Thus, although formal consultations for plants in California are not a frequent occurrence, in part because so few plants are listed, considerable informal consultation effort is still necessary to protect them. Informal consultation and technical assistance efforts at the State and local level for listed and candidate species can help prevent significant losses. In addition to the listed plants, the nearly 600 candidates stimulate seemingly constant requests for technical assistance from Federal, State and local government agencies. Via these technical informal exchanges the Service stresses to these agencies and private individuals, avoidance of impacts to help avert the need for federal listing. Table 4 shows the Service consultation effort for plants over the past three years.

Table 4. Service consultations involving listed, proposed, and candidate plants in California during Federal fiscal years 1984 to 1986.

Consultation category	FY86	pct tot	FY85	pct tot	FY84	pct tot
Species List Requests	144	(93)	178	(78)	153	(78)
Technical Assistance	128	(59)	76	(62)	34	(97)
Informal Consultation	51	(44)	37	(47)	50	(74)
Conference	0	(00)	2	(50)	0	(00)
Formal Consultation	1	(.02)	2	(.07)	3	(17)
Totals	324		295		241	

In those instances where a federal agency cannot avoid adverse impacts to a listed plant, the resultant consultation frequently involves mitigation, compensation or other measures to insure protection of the species. For example, during the past four years, Caltrans (San Diego), has purchased approximately 90 acres of vernal pool habitat supporting the endangered San Diego mesa mint (Pogogyne abramsii) as compensation for habitat destroyed by highway construction. The acquisitions resulted from several

Section 7 consultations among the Service, the Federal Highway Administration and Caltrans. Interestingly, Caltrans has been unable to transfer ownership of the acquired vernal pool properties to an appropriate conservation agency or organization, including the Service.

Cooperation with the State

One of the more active and successful areas of recovery implementation in California involves the cooperative effort between the Service and the California Department of Fish and Game (Department) pursuant to Section 6 of the Act, (see Bartel 1986, this symposium, for a brief description of this provision). Since 1979, when the Cooperative Agreement for plant conservation in California was consummated between the Service and the California Department of Fish and Game, slightly more than $335,000 dollars of federal funds have been made available to the Department for plant conservation purposes.

During the past three years, over $175,000 dollars of Section 6 funds have been made available for plant recovery activities in California. In 1987, the Department proposes to undertake 5 plant recovery actions totaling $54,000 dollars. These, and all other California proposals for endangered and threatened species are reviewed yearly by the Service's Regional Office in Portland, Oregon, for funding. Of course ultimately, funding is contingent upon Federal budget appropriations to the Service for the Section 6 program. Table 5 lists the cooperative plant recovery actions approved and funded by the Service to the California Department of Fish and Game from 1984 to 1986, as well as those proposed by the Department for 1987.

Service Recovery Actions

All funding for Service recovery actions comes through the federal budget process. In recent years budget cuts and increased fiscal restraint have resulted in a deemphasis on direct funding for most recovery actions and increased emphasis on legally mandated, largely administrative, Section 7 activities, established captive breeding programs, and some listing. In addition, the lack of field personnel, especially botanists, further limits the Service's ability to implement even the most routine recovery activities such as simple site monitoring or frequent coordination. In years when recovery money is available, the Service relies almost entirely on non-Service contractors to implement virtually all recovery activities. Table 6 lists those recovery action categories identified in the eight printed plant recovery plans scheduled for or needing implementation in FY87. If the funding needs and tasks for all listed species were included the amount would more than douable. Clearly, with existing staff and funding, only a few of these actions are likely to be implemented.

Table 5. Cooperative plant recovery actions approved and funded by the Service to the California Department of Fish and Game from 1984 to 1986 and those proposed by the Department for 1987.

Species	Recovery action	Funding ($1000)
FY84 (funded)[1]		
Truckee barberry	Habitat survey	10.0
Presidio manzanita & San Mateo thornmint	Serpentine study & survey	10.0
FY85 (funded)		
Truckee barberry	Taxonomic study	4.9
San Diego mesa mint	Habitat monitoring	27.7
Presidio manzanita	Habitat study	20.3
Santa Barbara Is. liveforever	Ecol. study	9.3
Eureka Dunes	Demographic study	10.0
FY86 (funded)		
Loch Lomond coyote thistle	Fencing	21.0
large-flowered fiddleneck	Habitat survey	12.0
FY87 (proposed)		
large-flowered fiddleneck	Reproductive study	9.0
Antioch Dunes	Demographic study	12.0
palmate-bracted bird's-beak	Habitat survey	6.0
Santa Barbara Is. liveforever	Reintroduction	9.0
San Diego mesa mint	Develop habitat mgmt. plan	18.0

[1]Four more studies were approved and funded in FY84, but staffing limitations in the Department's Endangered plant program prevented the funds from being expended.

Table 6. Estimated funding needs and recovery action categories identified in the eight printed plant recovery plans that should be undertaken in FY87.

Management Action	Funding ($1000)	no. tasks
A. Habitat		
1. legal protection		
a. Law enforcement habitat protection (ESA, NEPA, CEQA)	30.0	14
b. Obtain access to habitat (easements, coop. agreements, acquisition)	9.2	5
c. Promulgate new laws or regulations	0.0	0
2. Manage habitat		
a. Identify occupied habitat (surveys)	10.2	7
b. Habitat studies (synecological)	16.0	9
c. Mgmt plans	795.0	17
B. Species/population		
1. Law enforcement		
a. Prevent over-collection	.3	1
b. Promulgate new laws or regulations	0.0	0
2. Management, enhancement		
a. propagation (ex situ & in situ)	9.0	5
b. transplantation/reintroduction	7.0	4
c. develop new habitat	10.0	1
d. disease & herbivore control	3.0	2
e. reduce competition	2.0	3
3. Monitoring		
a. short-term (general conditions)	8.5	8
b. long-term (demographic)	6.5	6
4. Autecological research		
a. habitat requirements	5.0	3
b. life history	31.0	13
c. competition/interference	11.5	3
d. taxonomic	.5	1
C. Public awareness	3.7	4
Total	1,641.2	106

QUESTIONS AND PROBLEMS FOR PLANT RECOVERY PLANNING

Critical Population Levels

The delisting objective of the Act raises some difficult questions and management problems because formal quantitative guidelines for species conservation in the wild are still in the early developmental stages (Soule' and Wilcox 1980, Frankel and Soule' 1981, Schonewald-Cox et al. 1983, Verner et al. 1986). Most of the available models or criteria for species conservation in the wild have been developed for vertebrate animals with little or no consideration of the diverse reproductive and life history characteristics of plants (and invertebrates). The reasons for this largely relate to the general lack of basic demographic and life history data for most wild plants.

Attempts at setting critical population goals for plants could follow the recommendations of Frankel (1983) to minimize genetic losses through inbreeding by maintaining effective populations of at least 500 individuals in each subpopulation, colony, occurrence, or deme of a species. However, is this minimum number reasonable for all plants? What about those plants that are widely dispersed and occur naturally in low numbers? What about natural inbreeders? How can we tell when inbreeding is a problem? How do we determine effective populations for plants? Answers to these questions are needed not only to provide management guidance to conservation agency personnel for management of endangered plants on public lands, but they can be used as legal tools in land use decisions where decision-makers are required by law to give adequate consideration to environmental quality and rare, sensitive or endangered species.

Stochasticity and Patch Dynamics

Although genetic considerations are very important, extrinsic factors such as ecosystem patch dynamics (e.g. landslides, weather patterns, fires, floods, etc.), may present greater, more imminent threats to wild populations of plants and animals, even those with populations above the genetic critical number. Thus, we may need to increase critical numbers by at least an order of magnitude to further minimize the likelihood of stochastic extirpation. Of course, whether each site will be able to support a subpopulation of that size consistently over time without adverse impacts to the habitat or ecosystem as a whole will depend upon many factors, not the least of which are 1) the size and successional or ecological condition of each habitat or biotope, 2) the genetic condition of the species being managed and its life history and distributional characteristics, and 3) other extrinsic biological and political factors, including, but not limited to, a) the presence of other endangered, rare or sensitive species or habitats and b) the availability of each site for recovery management.

Environmental stochasticity also bears upon the number of subpopulations required to fully recover a species. We may think of species survival and extinction as a habitat-patch dynamic phenomenon (Levin 1976, Pickett and Thompson 1978, Zedler 1982). Under this concept, landscapes can be thought of as a mosaic or patchwork of suitable and unsuitable habitats of varying sizes and shapes, distributed over the range of a species. These habitat patches change over time (created and destroyed) as a consequence of the biotic and environmental processes within the ecosystem. These processes also vary according to the type of ecosystem (e.g. riparian, forest, grassland, sand dune, etc.), and magnitude of human modification. The extinction (or survival) probability of a species relates then, to the species' life history characteristics or strategies (Grime 1979, Grubb 1980), and the patch dynamics of the ecosystem in which it resides. The critical determinants are the number, size and dispersion of suitable habitat patches within the range of the species over time, and the life history features of the species (including, but not limited to, dispersal abilities, production of seed or offspring, germination and seedling establishment requirements, and environmental tolerance within the various life history stages). Of course, preventing human alteration of each ecosystem's natural patch dynamics is a major (perhaps impossible) task.

CONCLUSIONS

The Act primarily attempts to prevent or retard human activities that alter ecosystems of listed plants and animals. Thus management goals for the recovery of endangered and threatened species can be viewed as a continuum, where at one end (an ideal) the goal is to maintain or reestablish the ecosystem's natural (unmanaged) patch dynamics that insure the long term survival of its component native species (level 9 of Schonewald-Cox et al. 1983), and at the other end, the much less desirable and costly, maintenance of individual species in artificial habitats, captivity, or botanical gardens. Unfortunately, because of inadequate funding and personnel, most recovery programs operate closer to the latter.

In the absence of quantitative data on life history, habitat requirements and patch dynamics (synecological data) only tentative conceptual guidelines for plant and animal conservation are available. Thus, Service recovery plans provide tentative "best guess" recovery goals with further requirements to undertake additional life history and ecological studies to determine "appropriate" recovery goals. Fortunately, as stated previously, recovery plan goals and objectives can be modified as new information becomes available to ensure that they indeed provide for the recovery and survival of each species. In addition, because the federal regulatory process for downlisting and delisting requires the same public review process as listing, the public is given the opportunity to review and comment on any proposed change in status.

REFERENCES

Bartel, J. A. The Federal listing of rare and endangered plants: what is involved and what does it mean? Symposium proceedings 1986.

Bartel, J. A. The federal program. In: Smith, James Payne, Jr., editor; York, Richard, data entry and management. Inventory of rare and endangered vascular plants of California. Berkeley: California Native Plant Society; 1984:xii-xiii.

Bartel, Jim A.; Knudsen, Monty D. Federal laws and vernal pools. In: Jain, Subodh; Moyle, Peter. Proceedings, vernal pools and intermittent streams symposium; 1981 May 8-9; Davis, CA. Inst. Ecology Publ. 28; Univ. Calif. Davis, CA 1984 263-268.

Bean, Michael J. The evolution of national wildlife law. New York: Praeger Publishers; 1983. 449p.

Frankel, O. H. Chapter 1, The place of management in conservation. In: Schonewald-Cox, Christine M.; Chambers, Steven M.; MacBryde, Bruce; Thomas, Larry, editors. Genetics and Conservation: a reference for managing wild animal and plant populations. Menlo Park: Calif.; 1983:1-14.

Frankel, O. H.; Soule', Michael E. Conservation and Evolution. Cambridge, England: Cambridge University Press. 1981. 327p.

Grime, John P. Plant strategies and vegetation processes. Chichester, England: John Wiley and Sons. 1979. 222p.

Grubb, P. J. The maintenance of species richness in plant communities: the importance of the regeneration niche. Biol. Rev. 52:107-145; 1980.

Levin, S. A. Population dynamic models in heterogenous environments. Ann. Rev. Ecol. & Syst. 7:287-310; 1976.

Morrisey, George L. Management by objectives and results in the public sector. Menlo Park: Addison-Wesley Publishing Co.; 1976. 278p.

Phenicie, Charles K.; Lyons, John R. Tactical planning in fish and wildlife management and research. Wash. D.C.: Fish and Wildlife Service, U.S. Department of Interior; 1973; 19p.

Pickett, S. T. A.; Thompson, J. N. Patch dynamics and the design of nature reserves. Biol. Conserv. 13:27-37; 1978.

Ripley, Thomas H. Chapter 2, Planning wildlife management investigations and projects. In: Giles, Robert H., Jr., editor. Wildlife management techniques. 3d ed. Washington, D.C.: The Wildlife Society; 1971:5-12.

Schonewald-Cox, Christine M.; Chambers, Steven M.; MacBryde, Bruce; Thomas, Larry. Genetics and conservation: a reference for managing wild animal and plant populations. Menlo Park, CA: The Benjamin/Cummings Publishing Co., Inc.; 1983. 722p.

Soule', Michael E.; Wilcox, Bruce A. Chapter 1, Conservation biology: its scope and its challenge. In: Soule', Michael E.; Wilcox, Bruce A., editors. Conservation biology: an evolutionary-ecological perspective. Sunderland, MA: Sinauer Associates, Inc. 1980:1-8.

Verner, Jared; Morrison, Michael L.; Ralph, C. John. Introduction to Wildlife 2000: modeling habitat relationships of terrestrial vertebrates. In: Verner, Jared; Morrison, Michael L.; Ralph, C. John, editors. Wildlife 2000: modeling habitat relationships of terrestrial vertebrates. Based on an International Symposium held at Stanford Sierra Camp, Fallen Leaf Lake, California 7-11 October 1984. Madison, WI: Univ. Wisconsin Press; 1986:xi-xv.

U.S. Fish and Wildlife Service. Handbook on research and surveys: Federal aid in fish and wildlife restoration. Wash. D.C.: Fish and Wildlife Service, U.S. Department of Interior; 1983; 19p.

Zedler, Paul A. Plant demography and chaparral management in Southern California. In: Conrad, C. Eugene; Oechel, Walter C. tech. coord. Proceedings of the symposium on dynamics and management of Mediterranean-type ecosystems; 22-26 June 1981; San Diego, CA. Gen. Tech. Rep. PSW-58. Berkeley, CA: Pacific Southwest Forest and Range Experiment Station, Forest Service, U.S. Department of Agriculture; 1982; 123-127.

Approach to Rare Plant Management at Golden Gate National Recreation Area

Terri Thomas [1]

Abstract: Rare plant management in an urban park requires the participation of all personnel working in the vicinity of rare plants. Field staff not only need to know where the plants are, but also need to be committed to saving these plants. Golden Gate National Recreation Area (GGNRA) approached the management of rare plants in following manner: (1) A thorough literature review and herbarium search of each species. (2) Field reconnaissance of designated sites and possible habitat noting habitat features, endangerment factors and management needs. (3) Compilation of all information, photographs, line drawings, maps, endangerment factors and management recommendations into a usable field guide. (4) Assembly of an effective slide presentation to instill dedication toward rare plant protection. This program included information on the importance of rare plants, the use of the field guide and individual participation in management recommendations. The program was presented to park staff and they were urged to note rare plant areas, keep a watchful eye out for new endangerment factors and new populations and take an active role in active management needs.

Aldo Leopold remarked that the first rule in intelligent tinkering is to save all the cogs and wheels (Raven, 1983): The importance of this statement to the preservation of species was illustrated in a statement at hearings on the Endangered Species Act in 1982 (Raven, 1983); If we ignore the individual importance of a species, we may consider it dispensable and ignore it to act on demands of the moment. We could lose the cogs and wheels which might prove to be of the greatest interest and importance to our descendants.

Rare plant information needs to be in the hands of people who are responsible for the area and who can watch the population. The success of rare plant management depends upon the knowledge and commitment of individuals who are responsible for that management. At GGNRA this spread of rare plant information is critical due to the intense visitation and urban encroachment that threatens the plants.

Each park district in GGNRA is responsible for day to day operations in their area. The protection of the rare plants in this park is greatly enhanced if the district staff is dedicated to protecting the plants and actively begin participating in the management of these plants.

A usable field guide was introduced to the districts with a slide program. Personnel who would not normally seek out the guide, were informed about the plants and their importance. The purpose of the slide program was to instill a personal commitment of the employees to the importance of these plants and their management.

This paper describes: (1) the method used to gain information on each plant, (2) the information included in the field guide and (3) the type of script and program necessary to instill a personal commitment from staff members.

Several tid-bits of information that can be used to encourage understanding of the rare plant problems are included. Too often natural resources managers forget the importance of adequate public relations and communication to field staff. This can result in misunderstandings and eventually to the decline of the species.

---

[1] Plant Ecologist, Golden Gate National Recreation Area, San Francisco, CA.

METHODS

Methods used to gain information on each plant include: (1) Finding known plant locations and gathering all off site information about the plant and its management (2) Gather all on site information about each plant population, its habitat and management needs (3) Searching for new sites.

Plant Locations

Several sources were used to determine what rare plants exist in a certain area. Local botanists at universities, herbariums, local plant societies, government agencies and consulting firms were contacted. The California Natural Diversity Data Base and the California Native Plant Society were excellent resources.

Superb herbarium facilities in the bay area made it easy to learn more about each plant and where it might be found. All information from herbarium sheets were noted and filed by the plant name. Any references to literature were searched, found, copied and filed. Libraries were used to search for more information on each plant. The local floras were helpful and all information in them were also copied and filed.

The Field Survey

Each survey documented as much information about the population and the surrounding area as possible. The field survey form developed by the California Natural Diversity Database was used to note the information.

The habitat was described in detail. Included in this description was the geologic parent material to the soil and the type of soil on which the plants grow. The plant communities present were noted and any indicator plants associated with the species. Habitat description also contained the elevation of the sight, the slope, aspect, the amount of light available to the site and the moisture available to the plant. This information helped in locating new populations.

The location of the population was mapped at a scale which would facilitate easy relocation. The number of plants and the approximate size of the area was noted.

Endangerment factors and management recommendations were thoroughly researched. Any disturbances that alter the habitat were included as well as any possible future threats.

New Sites

Field survey information was used to locate areas of similar habitat. Geologic, soil and topographic maps were used to identify potential population sites. These sites were then visited and searched.

RESULTS AND DISCUSSION

Rare Plants

Eighteen rare plants were located in Golden Gate N. R. A. and the Presidio of San Francisco. These include:

Coast rock cress (Arabis blepharophylla)
Tamalpais manzanita (Arctostaphylos montana)
Raven's manzanita (Arctostaphylos hookeri ssp. ravenii
Bolinas manzanita (Arctostaphylos virgata)
Bolinas ceanothus (Ceanothus masonii)
Franciscan thistle (Circium andrewsii)
Presidio clarkia (Clarkia franciscana)
Western leatherwood (Dirca occidentalis)
Elymus californica
San Francisco wallflower (Erysimum franciscanum var. franciscanum
San Francisco gum plant (Grindelia maritima)
Marin dwarf flax (Hesperolinon congestum)
San Francisco lessingia (Lessingia germanorum var. germanorum
Santa Cruz microseris (Microseris decipiens)
San Francisco owls clover (Orthocarpus floribundus)
Dolores campion (Silene verecunda ssp. verecunda
Tamalpais jewel flower (Streptanthus glandulosus ssp. pulchellus
San Francisco dune tansy (Tanacetum camphoratum

Four plants are known to have occurred in the area and were searched for but not found in the park boundaries. These are:

Tiburon buckwheat (Eriogonum caninum)
Salt marsh bird's beak (Cordylanthus maritimus)
Showy indian clover (Trifolium amoenum)
San Francisco popcorn flower (Plagiobothrys diffuses)

The last two of these may be extinct.

Many of the rare plants at GGNRA have federal or state status and are considered of interest by the California Native Plant Society. The Raven's manzanita is listed as endangered at the state and federal level. The Presidio clarkia is considered endangered by the state and is a category one candidate species at the federal level. The Bolinas manzanita is state listed as rare and is a category 2 candidate at the federal level and the San Francisco popcorn flower is endangered at the state level and a category 2 candidate at the federal level. Remaining are one category 1 candidate, eleven category 2 candidates, two category 3 non- candidates, two that are proposed to be "watched" by the California Native Plant Society and one, the San Francisco dune tansy which is rare in the eyes of the park and needs genetic research.

Field Guide

A usable field guide was compiled from the information gathered. All information necessary for finding the plants in the field and initiating management were included in the field guide. The document is meant to be dynamic and updated frequently with any new information.

Two tables help area managers quickly find which plants to seek. Listing the rare plants by field area allows each district or area unit to quickly see which plants are of interest to them. The second is a table of blooming periods for each plant. This is useful in two ways (1) to note which plants can be easily found in a certain season or month (2) to tell which months to avoid activity that could affect seed production.

The field guide contains abstracts for each plant and information necessary for management. Included are: (1) the plant status as a federal and/or state listed plant and any other status it may have, (2) plant distribution within the management area and its general distribution along with a detailed map, (3) plant description, a photo and line drawing, (4) habitat description, (5) existing endangerment factors, (6) management recommendations, and (7) a list of information available in the natural resource files.

The plant is described in lay terms so that individuals can easily distinguish it from any nearby look-alike. A color photo and a line drawing are included. The photo shows the general look of the plant and also encourages the staff to look through the field guide. The line drawing shows detail that is often necessary in the identification. Plants that could be confused with the rare plant are mentioned and described so that they can be distinguished from the rare plant.

The habitat for the plant is described to help park personnel find the sites. This information also allows park staff to identify similar habitats and perhaps find new populations.

Endangerment factors vary for each population. Common threats are lack of fire, trampling, exotic species encroachment, routine maintenance activities and shading.

Management recommendations then respond to these threats: (1) Ways to remove exotic invaders emphasize non- chemical methods, mainly digging and pulling. (2) The careful introduction of prescribed fire is recommended in chaparral communities. (3) Ways to decrease trampling include fencing, signing, realigning trails, and placing barrier plants in strategic locations. (4) Tree removal is recommended in some cases, to decrease shading. (5) Changes in routine maintenance include restriction of mowing and trimming, and definition of areas around which staff should be careful.

Finally all information in the natural resource file is listed for each plant. All survey forms, herbarium information, articles, floras and database information are in these files.

Slide Program

Many causes are made or broken by what publicity they recieve and the amount of public and/or park backing. The importance of plant diversity and saving rare species, must be instilled in the hearts and minds of the park staff and the public if these fragile resources are to be saved in an urban park. Natural reource managers or interpreters must seek out public programs and speak on the issue.

The slide program developed by GGNRA did not take much money or time. It was designed by the natural resources staff with the intent to inform staff about the rare plant guidelines and to instill the dedication of park employees to rare plant management in an urban area.

To accomplish this, information that shows the affect of rare plant loss on personal life is introduced. Ecological dogma does not always obtain the internal conviction that results in action. Examples of information that help succeed in this endeavor are (1) the importance of wild plants in pharmaceuticals, (2) in foods, and (3) in ecological diversity and (4) the ethical question of eliminating a species from the earth forever.

Pharmaceuticals

Norman Meyers (1984) explains how important plants are in the pharmaceutical industry. Plant products are used to facilitate analgesics, antibiotics, heart drugs, enzymes, hormones, diuretics, anti- parasite compounds, ulcer treatments, dentifrices, laxatives, dysentery treatments and anti-coagulants. Modern medicine uses several thousands plant- derived products. An example is in leukemia victims. In 1960, a child with leukemia faced a 1 in 5 chance of remission and now enjoys a 4 in 5 chance thanks to an alkaloid derived from periwinkle (Vinca sp.).

Many extracts from plants have been synthesized for medicines and can be reproduced chemically at little cost. Aspirin is one such example. It was initially an extract from willow leaves. There are many important extracts that scientists have not been able to synthesize. In fact, of 76 drug compounds that the plant kingdom supplies, only 7 can be commercially produced through chemical synthesis from start to finish. An example is diosgenin which is the extract from a mexican yam. Ninty-five percent of all steroidal drugs on the market today are derived from diosgenin (Meyers, 1984). Oral contraceptives, cortisone, hydrocortisone, progesterone, estrogens and androgens are all the result of this extract. These compounds are used against rheumatoid arthritis, rheumatic fever, Addison's disease, allergies, sciatica and a number of skin diseases. For years chemists have tried to find a synthetic way to produce diosgenin but to no avail. All these drugs still use chemicals directly extracted from the plant. (Meyers, 1984).

Ecological Diversity

Great diversity in plant communities result in diverse food and cover relationships with animals. Plants are the first level in the food chain and a major element of all food webs. Ecological communities are intricate and interdependent systems and the loss of one plant species leaves the community somewhat impaired.

Diversity is also often related to community stability. Diseases, droughts, and other disasters will rarely destroy a diverse plant community where they will destroy a monoculture or a community of only several species.

Food

Little persuasion is needed to convince the public of the importance of plants as a food source, but what of the wild plants, those that are not cultivated, why are they important?

The diversity and stability principal also applies to the genetics of plants. In Ireland, the 1845 potato famine was caused by a disease that killed virtually all the potatoes, and more than a million people died of starvation (Southwick, 1972). This blight was finally controlled in the United States by crossbreeding with wild potatoes. Wild plants enable us to maintain genetic diversity in our barley, rice, oranges, spinach and all other agricultural plants.

Wild sources of corn were thought lost forever, and as a result the genetic diversity limited only to corn that had been inbred for generations. Recently, a wild, perennial relative of corn was discovered in Mexico. The population consists of a few thousand plants on a hillside. It is interfertile with the corn grown on over 70 million acres in the United States. This wild plant gained immediate interest and is very significant. Its loss would have clearly been detrimental to human interests (Raven, 1983).

Ethical Question

The ethical question is one by which everyone is touched. We have the power to eliminate a species but do we have the right? Are we conquerors or respectable citizens with respect for all members? Final biological extinction has become a significant threat to our resources. Once a species is gone, it is gone and can never make any scientific or humanistic contributions.

CONCLUSION

Golden Gate N.R.A. uses all its staff members to watch over its many threatened rare plants. The staff has necessary rare plant information at their finger tips. This encourages active management from area staff including: (1) Locating new populations (2) Watching for new endangerment factors and (3) Acting on the management recommendations for each population. This involvement will greatly help protect this threatened resource as San Francisco and Marin County continue to expand.

REFERENCES

Meyers, Norman. The primary source. New York. W.W. Norton and Company, Inc. 1984. 399p.

Raven, Peter H. The importance of preserving species. California. Fremontia 11 (1); 1983; 9-12.

Southwick, Charles H. Ecology and the quality of our environment. New York. D. Van Nostrand Company. 1972. 319

The Ring Mountain Restoration Plan

Jan Strahan, Gregory J. Wolley [1]

Abstract: The Ring Mountain Preserve features a serpentine bunchgrass community which includes 5 rare plant species. The Nature Conservancy plans to restore 12 acres of the Preserve's highest peak which was levelled and terraced for military use in the 1950's. The restoration plan outlines the reconstruction of the original topography and the development of special habitats for the rare species. The revegetation and maintenance strategy will be refined through two years of experimental testing. Seed will be collected on-site for seeding and planting a mix of native species resembling the former community. Weed management is critical for successful establishment of the native species. Guidelines were developed for community involvement in the project and for public access and visitor interpretation.

The Ring Mountain Preserve is one of The Nature Conservancy's (TNC) most popular Preserves. Located in Marin County, on the Tiburon Peninsula, the 377 acre Preserve offers sweeping views of the San Francisco Bay area. The Preserve is a unique geological and biological resource. Several plant communities occur within the Preserve: freshwater seep, serpentine bunchgrass, non-native annual grassland, mixed evergreen forest and northern coyote bush scrub. Serpentine, California's state mineral, outcrops on the steeper portions of the site. The serpentine weathers to a reddish clay soil which supports the serpentine bunchgrass community. This community is on the California Natural Diversity Data Base list of ranked elements.

This native grassland is dominated by California's state grass, purple needle grass (Stipa pulchra) and California oatgrass (Danthonia californica), another common native bunchgrass. Five rare serpentine endemics are found within the Preserve boundaries. The best known of these is the Tiburon mariposa lily (Calochortus tiburonensis), endemic to Ring Mountain. The other rare species are: Calamagrostis ophitides, Castilleja neglecta, Eriogonum caninum, and Hesperolinon congestum. Over 30 other species of native grasses and wildflowers are found within the bunchgrass community.

The site reflects a grazing history similar to many other northern California coastal grasslands. The native species persisted on the serpentine soils but gave way to non-native annual grasses on these lower grasslands overlying sandstone parent material. The property has not been grazed since acquisition by TNC in 1981. Efforts have been made to reduce noxious species such as purple star thistle (Centaurea calcitrapa) and fennel (Foeniculum vulgare).

The Army developed an anti-aircraft installation on the Preserve's highest peak in the 1950's. A large level pad was constructed on the summit of the eastern knoll and the side slopes were graded into a series of terraces. Exposed scraped subsoil, severe compaction and invasion by exotic annual grasses has limited the recovery of native species on approximately 12 acres of the knoll.

As part of its management program for the Preserve, TNC has decided to restore this knoll to its original condition. The first step in this process has been to develop a restoration plan. Unlike many recovery plans which focus on a single species, this project will restore the habitat of several rare species as part of the process of restoring the entire native bunchgrass community. TNC designated three goals for the plan:

* restoration of the site's original topography
* revegetation with a mix of native species approximating the native composition before disturbance
* development of a trail plan for access to the area

---

[1] Ring Mountain Restoration Plan Project Coordinator, Design Associates Working with Nature, Berkeley, CA and Ring Mountain Preserve Manager, The Nature Conservancy, Corte Madera, CA.

This paper summarizes the restoration plan developed by DAWN (Design Associates Working with Nature). DAWN, a non-profit organization dedicated to the restoration and management of California's native plant communities, was assisted by consultants with expertise in geology, soils, landscape architecture and rare plant ecology. The intent of the plan is to establish a bunchgrass community which will eventually become reproducing and stable without requiring an intensive long-term maintenance program. Thus, the plan represents a balance between "original" conditions and those practices necessary to successfully establish a native bunchgrass community.

The planning process began with a site analysis of the geology, soils and vegetation of the study area. Next, a number of alternative approaches to topographic reconstruction and revegetation were formulated. These alternatives were presented to TNC to select a feasible approach. Implementation guidelines for each task were also specified. The plan thus represents a combination of optimum revegetation techniques, cost effectiveness and technically feasible operations.

EXISTING SITE CONDITIONS

Geotechnical Evaluation

Remnants of the original ground surface are preserved in the rocky outcrops. The side slopes were graded into a series of terraces, in which level benches were cut into the hillside. At present, the site has side slopes which vary from about 2.5:1 on some of the excavated cut slopes to nearly level in graded portions of the ridgetop. There is little evidence of substantial grading further west of the summit. However, excavated native soils and rock were placed as berms 3-4 feet high for anti-aircraft emplacements throughout this area.

The type and distribution of fill materials and the location of excavations were mapped during a site reconnaissance. The fill consists of either the locally derived native soil-serpentinite mixture or imported chert. Most of the native material was placed on the downslope portions of the terraces, apparently to increase the usable size of the terraces. This material is generally a mix of surface soils and bedrock fragments ranging up to boulder size. The chert was used as a base rock to improve roadways, parking and building areas. Most of the chert fills range in thickness from a few inches to about 1 foot. An estimated total volume of 1600 cubic yards (CY) of chert was placed as fill within the site.

Soils

Physical and chemical properties of the soils were sampled at various sites within and surrounding the restoration area. The entire soil profile was sampled in non-disturbed areas at uniform depth increments. Surface variability samples were collected at five sites typifying the different categories of grading disturbance: serpentine soil piles, chert soil piles, scraped serpentine and scraped chert or chert covered surfaces. Laboratory tests of both physical and chemical properties were conducted.

The soils within the study area appear to be of the Montara series (Zinke, pers. comm.), a common soil series for serpentine bunchgrass areas. When rated against other serpentine soils in the state (Zinke and Stangenberger 1978), the non-disturbed soils typical of the restoration site are high in nitrogen, have low carbon/nitrogen ratios (typical of grassland soils), have high water-soluble phosphorus contents, high cation exchange capacities with below average calcium, above average magnesium and average sodium and manganese contents.

The serpentine soil stockpiles have almost the same characteristics as the control soils, except for very high phosphorus and potassium contents. The chert stockpile material differs greatly from the serpentine soils. The piles and scraped areas of chert both are light textured (sandy) and are low in pH, carbon, nitrogen, phosphorus, magnesium and calcium but high in manganese.

Soils of the scraped areas were removed to the previous C horizon (i.e., the parent material). They thus resemble the material at the bottom of the control soil profiles. These scraped areas are very low in organic carbon and nitrogen content, low in calcium, high in magnesium, low in manganese content and have a low water holding capacity.

Vegetation

The vegetation within the study area is a complex mix of native and non-native vegetation types. Several environmental factors influence the vegetation: wind and soil properties pose the major revegetation constraints. The following vegetation types were mapped:

* barrens: areas with little or no vegetative cover, occurring either naturally or formed by grading
* non-native grassland:
  -- _Avena_ phase
  -- _Lolium_ phase

* serpentine bunchgrass:
  -- <u>Stipa</u>/<u>Avena</u> phase
  -- <u>Stipa</u>/<u>Lolium</u> or
     <u>Stipa</u>/<u>Lolium</u>/<u>Danthonia</u> phase
* northern coyote bush scrub
* mixed evergreen forest (Bay phase)

Both the non-disturbed and disturbed grasslands contains a mix of native and exotic species. Annual ryegrass (<u>Lolium multiflorum</u>) is most dense and lush in moist areas while wild oats (<u>Avena</u> spp.) dominate the areas with drier soils. Both species cover the serpentine stockpiles. The shallow soils on rocky outcrops are generally dominated by natives. Purple needle grass (<u>Stipa pulchra</u>) is dominant in the drier, more exposed slopes, becoming less abundant in the rocky outcrops with very shallow soils where Melic grass (<u>Melica</u> spp.) and broad-leaved forbs are common. Oatgrass (<u>Danthonia californica</u>) grows in many conditions but is the most common native grass on the moister northern slope. The flora of some of the scraped areas is similar to the naturally-occurring exposed bedrock "barrens". For a short period during the spring, these "barrens" are covered by a profusion of native annuals, primarily goldfields (<u>Lasthenia californica</u>) and tidytips (<u>Layia platyglossa</u>). The moderately compacted chert has a mix of natives dominated by blue-eyed grass (<u>Sisyrinchium bellum</u>) and oatgrass. The roadsides are colonized by a strip of weedy vegetation, including wild oats, annual rye, fennel and purple star thistle.

Three of the five rare plants on the Preserve occur within the project site. Remnants of the <u>Calochortus tiburonensis</u> and <u>Calamagrostis ophitides</u> populationns occur in rocky habitats on the eastern half of the project area. <u>Hesperolinon congestum</u> occurs on barren areas across the entire site. There is no historical record of either <u>Castilleja neglecta</u> or <u>Eriogonum caninum</u> growing on this knoll (Fiedler, pers. comm.).

The military grading operation altered the range of the rare plant populations. The scraping during terrace construction increased the <u>Hesperolinon congestum</u> population: this tiny annual is prolific on the scraped serpentine exposures. A portion of the habitat for the rare perennial species, <u>Calochortus tiburonensis</u> and <u>Calamagrostis ophitides</u>, was destroyed by the grading.

TOPOGRAPHIC RECONSTRUCTION

This section summarizes the plan for the topographic reconstruction. The feasibility of reconstructing the original topography is followed by a summary of grading alternatives and the selected approach. Specific techniques for each phase of grading are then reviewed.

The Original Topography

Cross-sections of the estimated original topography were produced. These and the pre-grading aerial photographs indicate that the eastern knoll had a gently rounded shape similar to the other knolls of the Preserve. The excavation for the level pad in the summit area was probably relatively shallow, in the range of 3-4 feet. The side slopes were also excavated about 3-5 feet in depth. The grading plan for the reconstruction was produced at 5 foot contour intervals to reflect these estimates. The pre-grading aerials indicated a shallow swale on the eastern portion of the site which is also depicted on the grading plan.

The military's grading operations were relatively minor. Mapping and subsequent calculations indicate a fairly close agreement between volumes of cut-and-fill on the site (7200 vs. 7100 CY). Sufficient native soil and rock material are thus present on-site to restore the original topography. Because the natural ground surface developed on serpentinite bedrock is somewhat irregular, an exact reconstruction of the pre-grading conditions cannot be achieved. However, restoration of the general form and elevations appear geotechnically feasible by conventional grading practices.

The topography could easily be restored to an approximation of the original landform by merely moving the fills back into place. Such a mix of surface soil and excavated bedrock would not result in the highest establishment rates nor facilitate maintenance. Therefore, a three phased grading process was developed. The sub-grade reconstruction will be completed using conventional grading practices, with the initial grading and finish grading practices designed to prepare and develop a suitable "seedbed" and habitats for revegetation.

Alternative Grading Approaches

Several alternatives were developed for each of the three grading phases and for scheduling the grading. The initial grading alternatives formed a range of options that can be undertaken to prepare a suitable seedbed, reduce later maintenance efforts and create a naturally-appearing site. The sub-grade alternatives address the means of disposal of the chert to prevent it from deleteriously altering species establishment and/or drainage. The finish grade alternatives reflect trade-offs between the types of habitats to be developed. Options for scheduling the grading were based on considerations of erosion control and weed invasion.

These alternatives were discussed with TNC representatives and the following approach selected. The entire site will be graded as a single operation, with the revegetation effort designed to minimize erosion and weed invasion. A limited stockpiling and sorting effort will focus on stockpiling the chert and the soils rich in organic matter for burial and selecting the rocks needed for rare plant habitats.

Pre-Grading Activities

Several tasks are required to prepare the site for grading, including:

* clean-up of the wooden and concrete debris remaining from the military installation
* weed control of noxious perennial weeds and non-native annuals
* seed collection of both common and rare species
* rare species boundary designation to limit disturbance during grading
* subsurface geotechnical investigations to observe the quality of the fill, refine the volume estimates and determine fill compaction criteria

The site was divided into "treatment areas" that delineate vegetation management practices required prior to revegetation: pre-grading weed control, pre-grading seed collection and initial grading operations. The latter will supplement the weed control and seed collection efforts. Each of these treatment activities had 3 potential levels of management: No Management, Moderate Management or Intensive Management. The treatment categories arising from this were mapped on a Pre-Grading Treatments map or an Initial Grading Treatment map for use by the contractor and the site preparation crew.

Grading Operations

Since the terrace cuts are relatively shallow, most recontouring work can be performed without special engineering. Relatively light grading equipment, such as a D6 Caterpillar, will offer the best compromise between work efficiency and minimal disturbance of adjacent downslope pristine areas (Lewis, pers. comm.). A large "grade-all" (super backhoe) used to pull rocks back upslope will minimize disturbance to downslope areas containing rare plants. Other necessary equipment include a front-end loader, a dump truck, a water truck, and a compactor.

Haul routes will be designated to minimize damage to areas adjacent to the site and prevent compaction of those areas within the site which do not require restoration. These routes will be ripped after grading is completed.

Initial Grading Work

The sorting and stockpiling will focus on selecting rocks for creating rocky outcrops and stockpiling the chert for later placement in the sub-grade. Those topsoil areas with heavier than usual clay content, mulch accumulation, or exotic weed growth will be stripped to approximately 6 inches and stockpiled for burial in the lower subgrade profile. This will reduce later weed control efforts.

The top layer (6 inches) of all disturbed areas of pure or close to pure native plants can be scraped and stockpiled on site for use as the finish grade to serve as a supplemental seed source.

The remaining material can be developed into a soil-rock mix for constructing the finish grade. The stony phase of the dominant native Montara soil will be duplicated as closely as possible.

The soil tests indicated that existing soil fertility is sufficient for supporting a restored bunchgrass community. Thus, no special soil amendments were recommended at this phase of soil-rock mixing.

Sub-Grade Restoration

The subgrade operation will begin by placing the chert as the lower fill within the summit area and benches. Next, the existing fills composed of native materials will be moved back into place on the terraces and the summit. This will primarily be a matter of pushing the fill back up onto the cuts and compacting the material as horizontal lifts with the first layer ripped into the native subgrade. The subgrade surface will be a gentle slope wherever possible.

Finish Grade Restoration

A front-end loader will distribute piles of the soil-rock mix and piles of the "native grass seed" topsoil mix evenly over the site. This topsoil will be ripped into the compacted subgrade on sloping areas. Handthrowing all piles until the surface is level will minimize compaction and attempt to simulate the relatively low bulk density of the Montara stony phase topsoil, where the soil is loosely packed between the many rocks. To minimize weed problems arising from moisture retention, grading work will be completed so that no mounds of pure soil are left on the finish grade.

Soil depths will be set and staked to attempt to achieve a uniform final grade. This will prevent widely varying surface conditions from limiting the ability to control weeds effectively. It will still provide sufficient microtopographic variation to support a diversity of species.

Development of Special Habitats

Habitats for the rare species will be constructed as part of the topographic restoration. The rocky outcrops on which Calamagrostis ophitides and Calochortus tiburonensis grow will be created by placing groups of rocks very close together in very stony soil. These habitats will be developed near the boundaries of their existing populations to create natural extensions from their current distributional limits. The very shallow, stony substrate which Hesperolinon congestum grows on will develop wherever presently scraped bedrock areas are too steep to cover with deep topsoil.

Erosion Control

Erosion control measures that minimize rapid surface runoff on the newly graded, exposed slopes will be required. Sediment traps such as low curtains of geotextile or filter fabric may be necessary in the heads of the drainage swales to catch sediment-laden runoff. Surface erosion can be minimized by developing a gently sloped finish grade that contains a mix of rock sizes and a permeable soil surface for sufficient infiltration of rainwater.

REVEGETATION

The revegetation program consists of seven components: alternative approaches to revegetation, experimental tests, species selection guidelines, seed collection/propagation guidelines, seeding and planting procedures, maintenance and monitoring.

A number of ecological constraints were accounted for in formulating the revegetation approach, some of which are common to serpentine soils (Kruckeberg 1984). The constraints include: (1) the potential for genetic variation within the rare plant species in different areas of the Preserve, (2) the naturally low fertility of serpentine soils which limits plant growth, (3) the easily compacted nature of serpentine soils, (4) the lack of information about species life histories, (5) the extremely windy nature of the site and (6) herbivory by deer and rabbits.

Alternative Revegetation Approaches

Several alternatives are associated with each of the revegetation tasks. Species selection options consider ways of approximating the former bunchgrass community. The seed collection and scheduling options develop various approaches to completing the project given a limited amount of on-site native grass seed. Options for the establishment methods review techniques and the timing of introductions. The weed control options discussed techniques that will promote the growth of the native species while reducing competition from exotics. Fertilization, irrigation and fencing options pose trade-offs between maximizing establishment and the technical feasibility of such practices for this site.

The review of these alternatives with TNC representatives resulted in the following preferred approach. Seeding will be the main revegetation technique. Planting and a salvage operation will supplement seeding in a relatively limited portion of the study area. The rare species not currently growing on the eastern knoll are reproducing on other portions of the Preserve, so their introduction is not currently warranted (Steve Johnson, pers. comm.). As there was not extensive browsing of the transplants in the demonstration plot, fencing will not be used during the field trials. The establishment plots will test fertilization but will be conducted without irrigation. The selection of the phasing approach, the weed control regime and the requirements for irrigation, fertilizer and fencing will depend upon the analysis of the field trials data.

Experimental Studies

A two year experimental study program was developed to test and refine the general approach presented in this plan. The program involves field trials, laboratory/greenhouse testing and demonstration plots. Several potential test variables were generated for the field trials: 5 critical variables were selected for testing. The field trials involve establishment trials and management trials.

Establishment Trials

The establishment trials will evaluate establishment and survival at one windward location and one leeward location. The following variables will be tested:

* Seed Mix: control, cover crop, nurse crop
* Seed Application Rate: 20#/acre, 50#/acre
* Fertilization: fertilizer, no fertilizer

The control will provide information on natural establishment occurring from seed blown into the plot and germinating from the soil seed bank. As there is not a sufficient amount of seed available on-site to completely revegetate the site at one time, the project may be phased in two different ways. These involve two different seeding strategies which will be tested on the establishment plots: a cover crop mix and a nurse crop mix. If the "cover crop" approach is utilized, the site would be stabilized after grading with a non-persistent cover crop such as agricultural barley (Hordeum vulgare). Sections of the site would then be converted to natives each year with a mix consisting entirely of native seed. This would continue until the entire site was revegetated with natives. If the "nurse crop" approach is selected, the entire site would be seeded immediately after grading with a mix of seed collected on-site and two nurse crop species, one native (Hordeum brachyantherum, collected off-site) and one a compatible exotic (Zorro fescue). These nurse crops would occupy the spaces between the slower growing perennials. The site would be then be reseeded on an annual basis until the natives dominated the site. For a 50# application rate, the mix would consist of:

	Cover Crop	Nurse Crop
Stipa pulchra:	20#	15#
Danthonia californica:	15#	10#
Bromus carinatus:	5#	5#
Hordeum brachyantherum:	1#	8#
Zorro Fescue		4#
Other grasses:	5#	4#
Forbs:	4#	4#
	50#	50#

Each treatment will be replicated 3 times for a total of 36 plots at each location. Germination rates for each species will be calculated for each treatment. Survival and cover will be periodically monitored for a two year period. The data will be analyzed using an analysis of variance (Greig-Smith 1983) to test for statistically significant differences of establishment.

Management Trials

The management trials will be used to select a weed control regime that reduces exotic species without damaging or eliminating native forbs. The study design will be similar to that of the establishment plots. Tests will be conducted in three vegetation types: (1) an undisturbed Avena-Stipa area, (2) an area of Lolium-Stipa-Danthonia, and (3) an area dominated by forbs. Clipping times will be based on the following phenological stages:

* control (no mowing)
* early clipping (approximately February: at the bud stage, just before anthesis of the oats)
* mid-season clipping (mid-March-April: at the flowering stage just as Stipa forms)
* late clipping (May: just before anthesis of the annual ryegrass)
* all 3 times

All plots will receive a fall mowing (September) to encourage fertile tillering of the grasses. With 3 replicates, these 5 treatments would require 15 plots at each location. Species composition and frequency will be sampled on each plot before treatments begin and monitored prior to each clipping time for the two year test period.

Laboratory and Greenhouse Tests

Seed application rates are usually derived from site conditions and such characteristics of the seed as the number of seeds per pound, seed viability and germination rates. Since these latter factors are not known for most of the site's native species, they will be determined by laboratory and/or greenhouse testing. Similarly, optimum seed burial depths will be determined by greenhouse tests.

Demonstration Plots

Since the project will be visible for several years, demonstration plots for interpretive purposes will be a valuable asset to TNC's educational program. One such trial has already been developed by an interested volunteer, Steve Dowty.

Species Selection

An approximation of the original serpentine bunchgrass community was made based on Fiedler's (1984) frequency surveys of the western knoll. Her figures were adjusted by removing the exotic species and adding those native species encountered during the seed collection surveys.

These frequencies will be need to be converted into a seed mix with an application rate on a "pounds per acre" basis. The trial seed mixes for testing on the establishment plots were developed to serve as first approximations of this application rate. These trial mixes will be monitored to determine the species frequencies that establish on the windward and leeward plots. Once these mixes are adjusted to achieve the designated frequencies, the laboratory tests of germination rates will be used to calculate application rates for habitat specific mixes.

Seed Collection and Propagation

Seed Collection

A survey of the Ring Mountain Preserve identified the main stands of native grasses and forbs from which seed can be collected. The Preserve was subdivided into collecting sites which were delineated on the basis of topographic position and plant community.

A Seed Collecting Guide was developed for 25 of the common species located during the survey. The Guide describes where the more collectable stands of each species are found and gives approximate quantities of available grass seed. The seed of rare plant species will be collected on or around the project site rather than from other portions of the Preserve. This will perpetuate any genetic variation which may exist within the Preserve.

The Preserve has approximately 30 to 50 pounds of collectable native grass seed available per year (Kaplow, pers. comm.). This consists primarily of Stipa pulchra (15 to 20#/yr), Danthonia californica (5 to 15 #/yr) and Bromus carinatus (5 to 15 #/yr). Seed from other grass species will be available in lower quantities, generally under two pounds per species. The amounts of collectable forb seed were not predicted.

The collecting period for this site will range from mid-spring to mid-summer with most of the grasses ripening in April and May. The return period for seed collection of most stands will be 5 to 10 days. The collection period for grasses will be spread over a four to five week period. It will take a crew of three approximately 3 weeks labor to collect the native grass seed.

While most of the grass species are easily collected by hand, the seed of many forbs is so small that other techniques such as vacuums or nets may prove useful. Danthonia californica seed is more easily obtained as seed-bearing hay. Mowing and vacumming patches for direct use as a planting mix is another means of collecting some species.

Several of the species will need to be cleaned before they are stored. Cleaning techniques and estimated collection times were prepared. The cleaned seed will then be stored in a cool, dry, and dark place.

Propagation

The seed of many of these species will be collected in sufficient quantity to be used in the seed mix. Those species with limited seed supply (e.g., Koeleria, Calochortus) as well as some of the more common species will be propagated for planting in designated areas, such as spots where sufficient cover is not attained by seeding and on rocky outcrops.

Container size for planting will be either 2" liners (super stubbies or supercells) or 4" pots. Plants propagated in a coastal nursery will already be acclimatized to the harsh coastal environment so will have lower transplanting losses than those grown inland.

Seeding and Planting

Seed Mix and Application Rate

The estimated seed application rate for hand seeding the site ranges from a minimum of 50# per acre up to 150# per acre in the steeper areas (Dennis Rogers, pers. comm.). With a range drill, the rate could be lowered to approximately 20# per acre (Becky Green, pers. comm.). A 20# and a 50# hand seeding rate will be tested on the establishment trials to determine the minimum rate that will provide sufficient cover.

Seed collected during the first year of the project will be used for the establishment trials. During the two years of field trials, seed will be collected and stored. Approximately 100 pounds of grass and forb seed collected from the site will be available for seeding the first year following test plot evaluation. Assuming a 50# application rate, two acres could be seeded the first year under the cover crop approach with one acre seeded each year thereafter until the entire site was converted to natives. If the nurse crop approach is used, the entire site would be seeded the first year after grading at a rate of 10-12# per acre for the native grasses. About 5# per acre of native grasses would be available for re-seeding in later years under this approach.

necessary in rocky areas or where rare plants are concentrated. Once the restored bunchgrass community is stable, reproducing and sufficient litter has accumulated, the other weed control techniques may be used as the basic management tool.

Erosion Control

Spot erosion control measures will be necessary as part of the revegetation effort. Either hydromulch, straw or a photodegradable erosion control blanket will be feasible for use on the site. If straw is selected, native straw will be used to prevent weed seeds from being inadvertently introduced to the site.

Fertilization

If the establishment plots show positive results with fertilization, the chemical analysis of the soils developed during the planning process will serve as the basis for selecting the fertilizer.

Monitoring and Evaluation

Monitoring and evaluation are essential to evaluate the success of the revegetation effort. The monitoring and evaluation of the test plots will be key elements in refining the implementation approach. In addition to monitoring frequency and cover, the vigor of selected individuals will be monitored

This project will provide TNC with an opportunity to establish one of the first long-term monitoring programs of a restoration in the western US. Comparisons of the non-disturbed bunchgrass community with the revegetated areas will provide valuable information for other such restoration projects. Long-term monitoring will also provide information about the successional dynamics of the serpentine bunchgrass community. Periodic monitoring of the status of weed populations will indicate when control is required.

COMMUNITY USE AND EDUCATION PROGRAM

Trail Plan

Since Ring Mountain is a walk-on Preserve open to the public, access to and interpretation about the restoration is extremely important from both a recreational and an educational standpoint. A trail plan was developed which will link the restoration site with existing trails. From the trail, users will be able to hike to the summit, the Preserve's highest point.

One of the primary reasons for the preservation of Ring Mountain is the endangered plants. During the blooming season, spur trails leading from the main trail will provide access to these plants for interpretive purposes. The specific siting of these trails will be determined after the restoration project has progressed to the point where the new plant populations are firmly established.

Visitor Interpretation

The restoration project offers a tremendous opportunity for TNC to develop an interpretive program about the restoration process. The approach itself and the various tasks will be important interpretational subjects. Another significant focus of the interpretive program will be the discrepancy between what was a relatively minor disturbance (road construction, relatively shallow cuts and fills), and the effort involved in restoring the area to a facsimile of its original condition.

In addition to tours led by docents, many visitors use the Preserve on a self-guided basis. Interpretative material for this audience will be available in brochures at the trailheads. Signing near and within the restoration area will be developed to inform the public about the project and request their compliance in avoiding the newly revegetated areas.

Volunteers

This project will also provide an educational experience for volunteers who assist in its completion. The volunteer program will be organized at the beginning of the project and involve both individuals from the community and local conservation corps. Frequent coordination with the revegetation specialist will ensure that the tasks are completed in the prescribed manner.

Substantial opportunities exist for volunteers to assist on all project tasks, except some of the grading work. Assistance will be especially valuable in monitoring the test plots, pre-grading tasks, finish grade preparation, plant salvage, planting, and project monitoring and interpretation.

PROJECT IMPLEMENTATION

The implementation of this project will be coordinated by someone familiar with the various phases of native plant revegetation. This specialist will (1) monitor and evaluate the experimental work

Seeding

The native grass seed will be broadcast into a loose, friable surface and buried to prevent dessication from the strong winds. Smaller forb seed will be broadcast on the surface. Because of the compactive nature of serpentine soils, the usual procedure of firmly tamping the seed bed after sowing is not recommended. Seed will be covered with an organic mulch, native straw cover or screened soil. This will allow good aeration while retaining moisture under these droughty conditions.

An annual re-seeding during November may be required for one or more years in areas of low establishment. Container planting is another option for these areas.

Planting

Planting will take place only when the soil is moist. Although early plantings are most successful in stabilizing a site (Rogers 1981), the planting time will vary depending on the rainfall pattern. Planting may begin in early November during early rainfall years but will be no later than mid-January in years of late rainfall. If the year is an exceptionally dry one, planting will be postponed.

Grass container stock will be planted on approximate one foot "centers" and interseeded. The planting scheme will simulate the appearance of the native plant community rather than the conventional outplanting practice of standard spacing in rows. The planting design will also reflect each species microhabitat requirements, such as forbs growing at the base of rocks.

Since the grading work will disturb some areas which are colonized by native perennials, a salvage operation will be organized. Volunteers will assist in salvaging those areas of pure native grasses and rare perennials that are disturbed by the grading. This effort will provide plants for a relatively limited portion of the site, probably one acre or less.

Rare Species Establishment

The rare species will be introduced to the site based on their predicted ranges (Fiedler 1984) and preferred habitats. _Hesperolinon_ _congestum_ will be introduced on all bare, bedrock areas and on steep screes, primarily on south and south-east facing slopes. _Calochortus_ _tiburonensis_ and _Calamagrostis_ _ophitides_ will be reintroduced to rocky habitats on the eastern portion of the site. These latter two perennial species will be planted rather than seeded.

Maintenance

The seeding and planting effort will strive to establish a community of 100% native species. However, a mix of native and non-native species will result unless intensive weed management of the entire Preserve is undertaken. Fiedler's (1984) work on the western knoll suggests that an area with a cover of 3-9% exotic species is acceptable as a "bunchgrass" community.

The management of exotic weeds is the most important aspect of the maintenance program. Erosion control and fertilization are also addressed. Fencing and irrigation recommendations are not included here as they are not part of the selected approach.

Weed Control

Weeds will be controlled at all stages of the project. By beginning immediately to reduce the seed supply of exotic species, future maintenance will be lessened. This pre-grading weed control can be accomplished by burning, controlled grazing or mowing (with a plastic-bladed weed whipper). Burning offers the additional advantages of reducing the mulch level and the amount of seed stored in the soil. The pre-grading weed control will be followed by scraping and burying those pure exotic stands growing on piles to reduce the seed supply in the soil.

The serpentine summit is surrounded by a downslope sandstone grassland community dominated by exotic annuals. Weed control of this area prior to grading will minimize weed invasion of the newly graded area. Either prescribed burning or controlled grazing of goats will reduce the exotics in these lower grasslands.

Several noxious species will also be controlled prior to grading, including purple star thistle, yellow star thistle (_Centaurea_ _solstialis_) and fennel. Hand and herbicide control methods have been prescribed for these species (e.g., Amme 1985). The use of non-chemical control methods is preferred by TNC and will be used exclusively, providing sufficient control is obtained. These noxious species will also be controlled on other portions of the Preserve to prevent their seed from blowing onto the site after grading.

Mowing will be the basic management technique during the revegetation period. Handweeding or hand clipping will be and revegetation, (2) refine the seed mixes, (3) work with the grading contractor and engineer to set soil depths and other design details for habitat reconstruction, (4) supervise seed collection, seeding, planting and maintenance and (5) coordinate other day-to-day decision-making, including the assistance of volunteers.

TNC will also secure grading permits and go through the necessary environmental review process before beginning this work. Because of the rare plants, a Memorandum of Understanding is necessary between TNC and California State Department of Fish and Game (Susan Cochrane, pers. comm.).

A project schedule and budget were developed that outline the major tasks and their associated expenses on an annual basis. The length of the project will depend on the results of the test plots and the availability of seed. We estimate that the revegetation will take from 4-7 years after the completion of the experimental studies.

ACKNOWLEDGEMENTS

This paper is based primarily on the consultant's report prepared by DAWN for this project. We thank TNC representatives Steve Johnson and Becky Green and the following DAWN staff and consultants for input on that report: David Amme, Jim Bertenshaw, Charli Danielsen, Peggy Fiedler, Katherine Hermann, Gary van Houten, David Kaplow, Erik van Lennep, Robin Moller, David Peterson, Dennis Rogers, and Paul Zinke.

REFERENCES

Amme, David. 1985. Controlling Purple Star Thistle, A Case Study. Fremontia Vol. 13 (2): 22-23.

Fiedler, Peggy L. 1984. Natural Communities, Rare and Invasive Plants of Ring Mountain. Consultant's Report to The Nature Conservancy.

Greig-Smith, P. 1983. Quantitative Plant Ecology. UC Press, Berkeley, CA.

Kruckeberg, Arthur R. 1984. California Serpentines: Flora, Vegetation, Geology, Soils, and Management Problems. University of California Publications in Botany, Volume 78, University of California Press, Berkeley, CA.

Rogers, Dennis. 1981. Notes on Planting and Maintenance of Bunchgrasses. Fremontia. Vol 9(1): 24-28.

Zinke, P.J. and A. Stangenberger. 1978. Serpentine Soils Data Weibull probability functions. Tables, Figures, 4 fiche cards. Microfiche #27.3 California Agr. Expt. Sta. Projects 1762, 2595, 2937. 145 Mulford Hall, Univ. Calif., Berkeley, CA 94720.

Guadalupe Dunes Revegetation Program

Jacqueline L. Bowland [1]

Abstract: The purpose of this paper is to describe the design and goals of the Guadalupe Dunes Revegetation Program, developed to restore a pipeline construction corridor. To aid in the formulation of the Program, eight test plots have been established within the dunes to look at: 1) natural reinvasion by native plants; 2) potential problems with invasion by weedy exotics; 3) physical stabilization techniques; and 4) success of the proposed seed mix made up entirely of locally obtained native species. On-going literature search is incorporated and previous mistakes avoided in the ever-changing design of the Revegetation Program.

STUDY AREA

Guadalupe Dunes

The Guadalupe Dunes are a part of the largest dune complex remaining in coastal California. The dunes area encompasses approximately 18 square miles, or roughly 12,000 acres. These dunes are considered to be unique because of their limited extent in California and sensitive due to the presence of a high number of endemic plant species, with several species at the northern or southern boundary of their range. The area has undergone extensive disturbance, primarily in the form of off-road vehicles, oil field operations, and livestock grazing.

The botanic characteristics of the Guadalupe Dunes can be categorized into four general community types: coastal strand; foredune; backdune scrub; and dune swale. In general, the species composition in each of these communities is fairly homogeneous, and species diversity is low to moderate. However, the plant species that are present are highly adapted to the harsh environmental conditions ambient within the dunes, such as blowing sand, salt-laden wind, and substrate with low nutrient and moisture content.

Also present within the dunes is an unusually high number of endemic plants, many with limited distributions. The California Native Plant Society has listed at least 18 sensitive plants as occurring within the dunes. Field surveys conducted by McClelland Engineer's biologists for this project concentrated on verifying the occurrence of those sensitive species within the potential disturbance area associated with pipeline construction. Eleven plants listed by CNPS were located, along with three additional special interest plants.

Program Need

Pipeline Construction

The need for development of the Revegetation Program has resulted from a development proposal by an oil company to construct an offshore oil platform with a pipeline to an onshore pipeline to a processing facility. The onshore portion of the pipeline would be installed within a 100-foot-wide right-of-way which traverses approximately 5 miles of dune, resulting in an estimated of temporary disturbance of 70 acres. This disturbed area will require rapid restoration and physical stabilization to prevent erosion and to enhance natural revegetation.

Goals of the Revegetation Program

The three primary goals of the Revegetation Program are to:

o   Restore all disturbed areas to pre-construction conditions in as short a timeframe as possible;

o   Promote natural reinvasion of native plants; and

---

[1] McClelland Engineers, Inc.

o Provide physical stabilization in unstable areas to facilitate regrowth by native plants.

These goals consider both environmental and engineering concerns. Environmental concerns include invasion of disturbed areas by invasive non-native plants and potential erosion of unvegetated slopes. The engineering concerns overlap the environmental ones because slope stability is critical to the integrity of a buried pipeline. The mobility of sand dunes and harsh environmental conditions require special consideration in the selection of restoration methodologies. To achieve these program goals, the experimental test plot program, on which this paper is focused, is designed to study various techniques in order to select the best restoration approach for this project. Ideally, the test plots should provide sufficient data to help predict natural versus enhanced revegetation rates.

METHODS

The test plot program was developed to provide site-specific information to augment existing literature on previous revegetation efforts. Similar revegetation programs were studied and local experts were consulted during the initial design phase of this test plot program to assure incorporation of as much pertinent existing data as possible.

The experimental test plots were designed to allow observation of natural plant reinvasion and species composition compared to reinvasion and composition when native seeds are applied. Additional trials were established to look at methods of physical sand stabilization and subsequent natural versus seeded plant establishment. Various mixtures of native seeds, geared to specific plant community conditions, have been developed. These mixes include pioneer species capable of rapid growth, good sand stabilization, and endurance under the harsh environmental conditions of the dunes. This program differs from other dune revegetation projects studied, since it does not include the use of fertilizer, irrigation, propagated plants, or the use of non-native plant species.

Revegetation/Reinvasion Experimental Plots

A total of eight trail plots have been established, with three in the backdune scrub community, two in the dune swale, one on a mobile sand dune, and two in the foredune. With the exception of the mobile dune site, all other plots measure 4 ft x 4 ft (16 sq ft).

Clearing

The five backdune scrub and dune swale plots were hand cleared of vegetation and the top 6 to 12 inches of sand using shovels and picks. (The foredune plots were not cleared due to the difficulty of stabilization in that harsh environment.) The removed vegetation and topsand were windrowed around the perimeter of each plot and left for a period of two weeks prior to being returned to the plot. These methods were selected to duplicate pipeline construction conditions, wherein vegetation and topsand will be mechanically removed and windrowed to one side of the construction corridor prior to pipe laying. The vegetative materials and topsand would then be replaced over the backfilled trench after construction is completed.

Physical Stabilization

Jute Netting

One backdune plot and the two foredune plots were covered with natural hemp jute netting. The netting was directly laid over the replaced overburden on the backdune plot, and over the existing vegetation on the foredune plots.

Sand Fencing

One single-strand sand (snow) fence was placed across a 100-foot-wide mobile dune. A second fence line was placed parallel to the single line for about 50 feet of this width.

Subplots

Each plot (except the sand fencing) was subdivided into nine 1 ft square subunits utilizing stakes and string to define the areas. A 1/2 foot buffer zone was established around the perimeter outside of each plot. The subplots were intended to facilitate monitoring, and the buffer zone was planned to reduce the effects of surrounding vegetation entering the plots from outside via subsurface runners or seed dispersal.

Seed Dispersal

The seed mix developed during the planning phases of this program will be scattered over one-half of the plots after the first soaking rain occurs (Nov-Dec). Seeds are currently being collected, and commercial source investigated to obtain the needed quantities of the desired mix. Application rates are planned to be approximately 20 pounds per acre. There will be two separate seed mixes; one formulated for application within the foredunes, and one for use in the backdune scrub.

Monitoring

Ongoing monitoring was initiated after the plots were established. The timing of the monitoring visits varies in accordance with growth rates, being more frequent during spring and fall, and less frequent during the dormant periods of summer and winter. In no event does the monitoring occur more often than once per week or less than once a month.

Checklist

The monitoring is conducted by two students from Cal Poly-San Luis Obispo. The method entails completion of a checklist indicating the number of plants and species occurring within each subplot, notes on relative percent cover, indications of changes noted over time, and any problems identified (i.e., grazing, erosion, etc.).

Photodocumentation

Included in each monitoring trip are photos taken from specified control points established at each plot, and at additional random locations to illustrate important aspects or changes occurring within each plot.

RESULTS AND DISCUSSION

Limitations of Study

Two specific elements of the test plot programs are recognized as limitations. These are the size of the plots, and the duration of the study period.

Plot Size

Because one of the program design elements is to predict natural versus enhanced revegetation rates along the proposed 100-foot-wide 5 mile-long pipeline corridor, the small plots may not yield relevant (or applicable) data. The size of the plots had to be restricted to 4 x 4 ft due to existing land use restrictions. The plots are located on land leased to Union Oil Company for oil production, and are therefore under the jurisdiction of their coastal land use permit. Additionally, because of the sensitivity of the dunes, the program was designed to avoid removal of large amounts of vegetation. Although it is difficult to define optimal plot size, plots of at least 100 ft x 100 ft (1000 sq ft) would have better reflected the effects of a 100-foot-wide construction corridor over the full length of the pipeline right-of-way. Specific concerns related to the corridor width include the ability of plants to become established via underground runners and seed dispersal from adjacent undisturbed habitats, and the rate at which some natural revegetation may be expected to occur across the 100-foot disturbance width.

Duration of Study

The test plot trials will probably be underway for two full years prior to pipeline construction. This is considered a relatively short period of time to obtain applicable results due to the potential for natural variations of weather patterns. Given a good rainy season, substantial regrowth could occur during the study period. Given relative drought conditions, however, little growth would be expected, and therefore, little usable information would be obtained.

Findings From Test Plots

Backdune Scrub Plots (Plots A, B and C)

Two plots are located on a steep windward slope, and one plot is covered with jute netting. The ongoing field monitoring indicates better regrowth with faster reinvasion of natives on the plot without jute netting. This could be due to the type of jute netting used and/or the installation technique. The netting used has a tightly woven mesh of thick hemp that does not allow adequate sunlight penetration to the soil surface and may also be preventing sufficient moisture penetration to the ground by trapping water within the mesh. Both of these slope plots exhibit downslope soil creep. The jute netting, which was positioned over the replaced vegetative overburden, is apparently too high off the ground to prevent the soil creep. Such netting would have to be placed directly on the soil surface in order to retard soil erosion. Ideally, windrowed overburden could then be placed on top of the netting to provide a seed source. However, this would require "double handling" of the overburden, which would be both costly and difficult to execute. It is interesting to note that the regrowth/reinvasion of plants onto these plots is not restricted to the lower area, where soil creep has carried much of the seed material.

A third plot is located within the backdune scrub community on a gently sloping leeward exposure. This plot is primarily being invaded by native species. Non-native invasive species, although present, have not become problematic in terms of outcompeting native plants. This observation, coupled with those regarding the two plots within the dune scrub (Plots D and E), indicates that invasion of the disturbed pipeline corridor by non-native plants should only be a problem where source habitats for the invasive species are in proximity to the disturbed area.

Plot C has received some grazing pressure from deer and rabbits. This has resulted in minor changes in species composition, but does not thus far warrant fencing to preclude such disturbances.

Dune Swale Plots (Plots D and E)

Two plots are located in the dune swale community. In both plots, the dominant plants are currently weedy non-native species, whereas initially the plots contained native plants. This high frequency of invasive plant occurrence appears to be directly related to the proximity of the source habitat, because the area surrounding both plots is largely composed of non-natives, primarily mustards.

These two plots are being heavily grazed by cattle and possibly by deer. The significance of this grazing/trampling is difficult to assess at this time. However, although direct mortality of individual plants is evident, natural revegetation within plots continues and does not appear to be seriously impeded. Much of the grazing has been on invasive species, mostly the mustards, and may therefore have beneficial aspects for native plant success through the removal of competing plants. However, the trampling from cattle could damage natives and retard sprouting.

Mobile Sand Dune Trial (Plot F)

Plot F is the mobile sand dune trial where a single strand and a double strand of sand fencing is being monitored. Since the installation of these fences, sand has accreted on the leeward side as expected. The shape of the newly formed dune behind the single fence line is larger and more gently formed than the dune associated with the double strand. The latter exhibits a steeper windward face, appears more stable, and contains less sand than the former. On the leeward side of the double strand, a mat of wind-deposited leaves, seeds and other blown plant vegetative material has formed. This mat of vegetative material is surprisingly stable, and contains seeds from several different plant species. No such vegetative mat is associated with the single line of fence. This mat is the first step of natural revegetation of this mobile dune, as it provides a protected area of stability where plants can become established.

Foredune Plots (Plots G and H)

Two new plots were recently established (Oct 1986) in the foredune community. Both are covered with jute netting. No results are yet available for these trials.

CONCLUSIONS

Incorporation of Findings Into Revegetation Program

The final analysis of information obtained during the course of the test plot trials will occur as the last phase of the Revegetation Program, immediately prior to implementation. Several items have already been learned, despite the short duration of this study, which directly apply to revegetation of the pipeline corridor. These are itemized below.

Jute Netting

A different type of jute netting which has a wider mesh should be used to avoid smothering of seedlings and the trapping of moisture away from the soil surface. Additionally, unless laid directly on the ground, this netting will not retard downslope soil erosion.

Site Clearing Techniques

The current program for initial right-of-way (ROW) clearing entailes one step to windrow vegetation and a separate step to windrow the top 6 to 12 inches of sand. Based on the lack of stump sprouting to date on the test plots, it appears that less damage would result to the root stock from a combined clearing effort. This method would remove the vegetation and topsand in one cut, and windrow it together along the side of the ROW. This would prevent double handling during both the clearing operation and the restoration operation, reducing disturbance to the vegetative materials as well as cost. This change in methodology has already been recommended for incorporation into the construction bid packet.

Exclusion of Non-Native Plants

Observations of all plots indicate that only areas with an immediately adjacent source habitat of invasive species are in jeopardy of significant growth of non-natives. Very few areas are within the entire 5-mile length of the pipeline corridor where large concentrations of invasive species occur. These primarily occur within the dune swales where cattle grazing pressure is expected to be highest. It does not appear to be necessary to remove (i.e., "weed-out") these invasive plants along the entire ROW to enhance the success of the native species. In addition, the disturbance that could result from a crew walking down the ROW to hand clear weeds is probably not justifiable, given the low occurrence of invasive species anticipated to occur.

Innovative Approach

Regardless of the results obtained from the test plot program, an important part of this effort has been the willingness of the oil company to go beyond the standard requirements in their advanced planning for the restoration of disturbed areas. As a result, McClelland's biologists were able to identify environmental constraints early in the planning process. This allowed incorporation of the engineering and environmental concerns with sufficient time to allow for significant changes. This advance coordination of disciplines is essential for any resource management program.

Habitat Reclamation for Endangered Species on San Bruno Mountain

Thomas S. Reid, Raymond C. Walsh [1]

Abstract: There have been five years of progress in habitat restoration and control of exotic species under the San Bruno Mountain Habitat Conservation plan. San Bruno Mountain, in northern San Mateo County, is habitat for numerous rare, endemic and range limit plants and animals. Because of Endangered Species Act conflicts, the Mountain became the subject of the 1982 Habitat Conservation Plan and the first Section 10(a) permit issued by the US Fish and Wildlife Service. Part of the HCP calls for a program to reclaim habitat for endangered species in areas 1) disturbed by construction, and 2) infested by invasive exotic species. Although the permit focuses on the Mission blue butterfly, the implementation of the HCP has stressed the need for diversity in reclamation. This has given the opportunity to use much locally collected plant material, including several rare plants.

In 1982 the San Bruno Mountain Habitat Conservation Plan (HCP) was approved by the U.S. Fish and Wildlife Service. The HCP charges the County of San Mateo with managing over 2700 acres of natural land as habitat for rare or endangered species. The management program includes elements for control of invasive exotic species and revegetation of native plant communities. This paper reports some of the tools used and the progress made in five years of implementation.

SAN BRUNO MOUNTAIN

San Bruno Mountain comprises 3400 acres of open space on the San Francisco Peninsula, at the northern edge of San Mateo County (fig. 1). Today, the mountain is clearly an island in an urban sea, yet San Bruno Mountain has probably always been an unusual environment. The mountain's foggy, windswept rocky ridges create habitats on the Peninsula which are more similar to conditions found farther north on the California coast. The unusual conditions on San Bruno Mountain support a diverse collection of rare, endemic or range limit plants and animals.

The historical plant communities were foothill woodland, grassland, and a mixed chaparral and coastal sage brushland. All are represented on the mountain today, but non-native species skew the species composition. The non-natives present include the same pest species plaguing north coast parklands: gorse, Scotch and French broom, eucalyptus, pampas grass, and African iceplant.

Comparison of an early photogrammetric Forest Service map with recent air photos shows that the contiguous natural lands on San Bruno Mountain have diminished by 30 percent over the past 50 years, with the greatest loss in the extent of grassland (fig. 2). Of 4047 acres of grassland present around 1930, 1811 acres remained in 1981. Roughly half of the loss resulted from urban development; the other half of the loss resulted from expansion of both native and non-native brush communities.

Despite its limited area, San Bruno Mountain supports substantial species diversity. A 1968 Flora of San Bruno Mountain (McClintock, Knight, and Fahy) found representatives of 88 families; 71 percent of the 542 species noted were natives, and of these, 14 were California endemics and 10 occurred on San Bruno

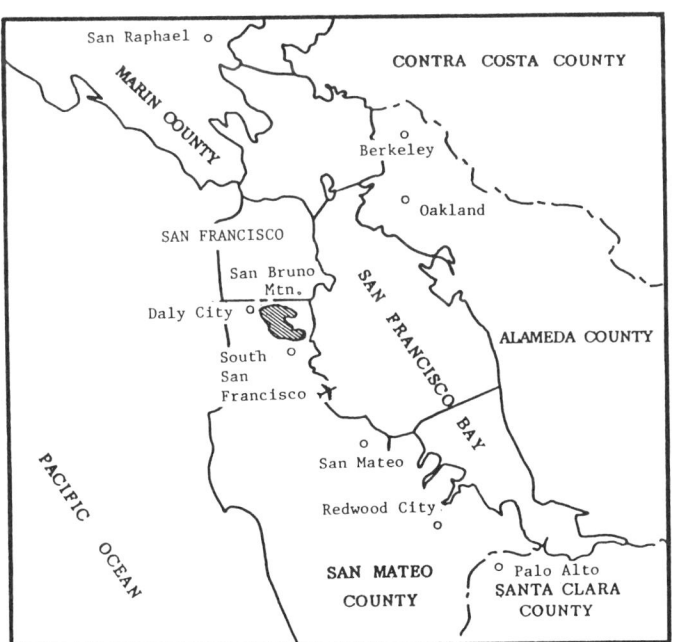

Figure 1 -- San Bruno Mountain Location

---

[1] President, Thomas Reid Associates, Palo Alto, CA; and Revegetation Consultant, Clyde Robin Seed Co. Hayward, CA.

Mountain at the southern limit of their range. Several uncommon plant species are listed in Table 1.

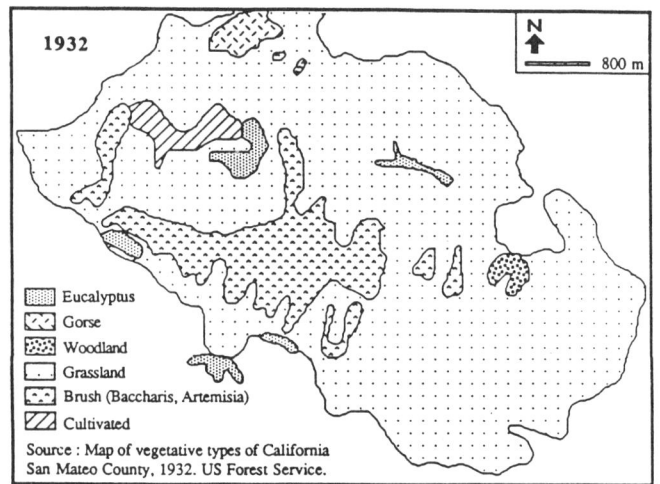 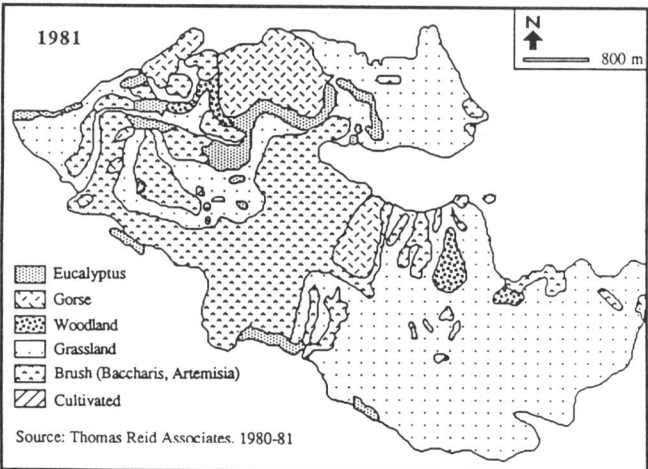

Figure 2 -- Vegetation Changes 1932 - 1981

Table 1 -- Species of Concern

Animals

The Mission Blue butterfly (Plebejus icarioides missionensis)
  - State and Federally listed endangered species
The San Bruno Elfin butterfly (Callophrys mossii bayensis)
  - State and Federally listed endangered species
The Bay Checkerspot butterfly (Euphydryas editha bayensis)
  - Proposed for the Federal endangered species list
The Callippe Silverspot butterfly (Speyeria callippe callippe)
  - formerly under Federal proposal for endangered status, expired July 3, 1980
The San Francisco Tree Lupine Moth (Grapholitha edwardsiana)
  - formerly under Federal proposal for threatened status, expired July 3, 1980

Host Plants - Larval or Adult Food Plants for Animals of Concern

Plantago erecta - larval food plant for the Bay Checkerspot
Sedum spathulifolium - larval food plant for San Bruno Elfin
Lupinus albifrons- larval food plant for the Mission Blue
Lupinus variicolor- larval food plant for the Mission Blue
Lupinus formosus- larval food plant for the Mission Blue
Viola pedunculata- larval food plant for the Callippe Silverspot
Lupinus arboreus - larval food plant for Tree Lupine Moth
Orthocarpus densiflorus - larval food plant for the Checkerspot

Lomatium utriculatum - host plant
Eriogonum latifolium - Wild Buckwheat; host plant
Brodiaea pulchella - Blue Dicks; host plant
Carduus sp. - host plants
Silybum marianum - Milk Thistle; host plant
Pteridium aquilinum - Braken Fern; host plant
Monardella villosa - Coyote Mint, Pennyroyal; host plant
Horkelia californica - California Horkelia; host plant
Scabiosa atropurpurea - Pincushion Plant; host plant

Rare, Endemic, and Range Limit Plants

<u>Silene</u> <u>verecunda</u> <u>verecunda</u> - The Dolores Campion; range limit; under federal review
<u>Erysimum</u> <u>franciscanum</u> var. franciscanum - The San Francisco Wallflower; range limit;
<u>Arabis</u> <u>blepharophylla</u> - Coast Rock Cress; range limit; under federal review
<u>Orthocarpus</u> <u>floribundus</u> - San Francisco Owl's Clover; range limit; under federal review
<u>Helianthella</u> <u>castanea</u> - endemic; under federal review
<u>Arctostaphylos</u> <u>imbricata</u> - Manzanita; endemic; under federal review
<u>Arctostaphylos</u> <u>montaraensis</u> - Montara Manzanita; endemic; under federal review
<u>Arctostaphylos</u> <u>pacifica</u> - endemic; under federal review
<u>Arctostaphylos</u> <u>uva-ursi</u> - Bear-berry; range limit
<u>Vaccinium</u> <u>arbuscula</u> - Huckleberry; range limit
<u>Lathyrus</u> <u>vestitus</u> - Pacific Pea; endemic
<u>Clarkia</u> <u>rubicunda</u> - Farewell to Spring; range limit
<u>Chorizanthe</u> <u>pungens</u> var. Hartwegii - Spine-flower; endemic
<u>Grossularia</u> <u>leptosma</u> - Bay/Canyon Gooseberry; range limit
<u>Castilleja</u> <u>franciscana</u> - Franciscan Paint Brush; range limit
<u>Ligusticum</u> <u>apiifolum</u> - Lovage; range limit
<u>Maieanthemum</u> <u>dilatatum</u> - False Lily of the Valley; range limit
<u>Allocarya</u> <u>chorisiana</u> - endemic
<u>Sambucus</u> <u>callicarpa</u> - Red Elderberry; range limit
<u>Silene</u> <u>scouleri</u> - range limit
<u>Chrysopsis</u> <u>villosa</u> - Golden Aster; range limit; host plant
<u>Cirsium</u> <u>quercetorum</u> - Brownie Thistle; range limit; host plant
<u>Grindelia</u> <u>maritima</u> - Steyermark; endemic; under federal review
<u>Layia</u> <u>hieracioides</u> - endemic
<u>Pentachaeta</u> <u>bellidiflora</u> - endemic; under federal review
<u>Senecio</u> <u>aronicoides</u> - Butterweed; range limit
<u>Tanacetum</u> <u>camphoratum</u> - Dune Tansy; endemic; under federal review

---

The invertebrate fauna has been scarcely studied, with lepidoptera receiving most of the attention. In carrying out monitoring for the HCP, Robert Langston has observed 40 species of butterflies and over 100 moths. Small vertebrates are numerous, though none are endangered (several years of survey have failed to reveal the San Francisco garter snake here). Table 1 also presents the animals of special interest along with their host plants.

THE HABITAT CONSERVATION PLAN

In the 1970's both open space and land development pressures intensified; an initial resolution came about in 1976 when roughly half of the mountain became a County and State park. The new parkland contained most of the brushland communities on the mountain, but most of the grassland community still lay in private ownership. Thus additional land use constraints arose from the Endangered Species Act prohibition against taking the Mission blue butterfly, a grassland species listed as endangered by the US Fish and Wildlife Service.

The San Bruno Mountain Habitat Conservation Plan specified an additional 800 acres to be set aside and established a perpetual management program for all open space on the mountain (fig. 3).

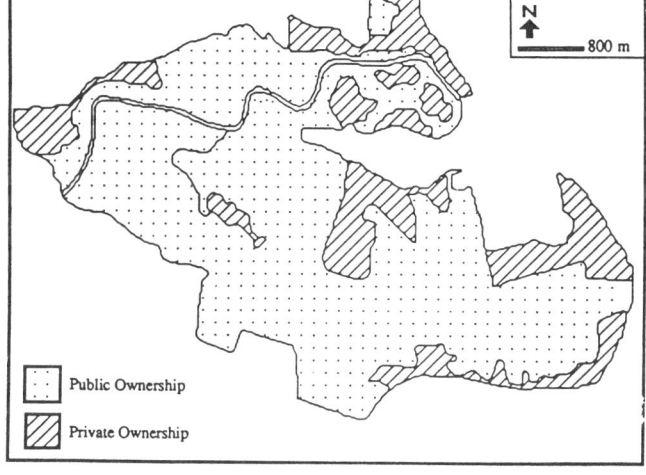

Figure 3 -- Disposition of Land under HCP

Public stewardship will ultimately extend over 2700 acres roughly equally divided between grassland and shrubland. Of the remainder, some 400 acres is subject to development and 300 acres is unplanned.

The HCP established the land division and set up a program to mitigate the habitat loss to development. The basic elements of the HCP program are monitoring, habitat restoration, and habitat enhancement. The monitoring entails both monitoring the populations of species of concern, and monitoring the development activities for adherence to the HCP provisions. Habitat restoration is required because all graded land around the development areas must be revegetated with San Bruno Mountain native species. Habitat enhancement entails exotic species control and revegetation of reclaimed land as well as expansion of their existing distribution of species of concern.

The legal focus of the HCP is the federally listed Mission blue butterfly, yet the plan acknowledges the importance of maintaining the ecological fabric of the mountain. The ecological orientation of the plan is essential to its success. It is obvious that the Mission blue itself depends on specific components of the grassland community and that any attempt to sustain the Mission blue colony must depend on sustenance of the grassland community. Beyond that mechanistic dependence, the San Bruno Mountain HCP is an opportunity to direct the management of the parklands to the general goal of establishing a valuable ecological reserve in a urban area. Developing revegetation as a tool with the greatest feasible species diversity is a first step toward that goal.

REVEGETATION METHODS

Both direct seeding and container planting are needed for revegetation on San Bruno Mountain. Because of the endangered species issues and the general need to preserve genetic identity of the species already present on the mountain, nearly all of the plant material are collected from the mountain itself. The few exceptions are species needed in hydroseed mixes for erosion control where there were inadequate stocks of mountain seed. We are fortunate that most of the species establish well from seed and can be readily collected. At the end of 1985, approximately 1600 lbs. of seed and 10,000 container plants have been collected and grown for the project over the past four years. Over 50 native plants are represented including 12 species designated as host or nectar plants for rare or endangered butterflies. Table 2 lists the species frequently collected for use in revegetation.

Table 2 -- Principal Species Collected

Achillea millefolium var. californicum
Aesculus californica
Allium sp.
Anaphalis margaritacea
Arabis blepharophylla
Arctostaphylos imbricata
Aristolochia californica
Artemisia californica
Baccharis pilularis pilularis
Castilleja sp.
Chlorogalum pomeridianum
Chrysopsis villosa
Diplacus aurantiacus
Erigeron glaucus
Eriogonum latifolium
Eriophyllum confertiflorum
Eriophyllum staechadifolium
Erysimum franciscanum
Fragaria californica
Grindelia sp.
Helianthella castanea
Heteromeles arbutifolia
Horkelia californica
Iris douglasiana
Iris longipetala
Lomatium sp.
Lupinus albifrons var. collinus
Lupinus arboreus
Lupinus formosus
Lupinus variicolor
Mimulus guttatus
Monardella villosa
Oenothera hookeri
Osmaronia cerraseformis
Phacelia californica
Rhamnus californica
Salvia spathacea
Salix lasiolepis
Sedum spathulifolium
Sidalcea malvaeflora
Silene verecunda verecunda
Sisyrinchium bellum
Solidago californica
Viola pedunculata
Wyethia augustifolia

One aspect of the program which has made collection slow is the emphasis on collecting plant material from areas designated for development in the HCP. The restriction reflects both the need to salvage genetic material from areas which will ultimately be lost to development and to the need to impact conserved areas as little as possible. The limited availability on the mountain and the program need for large quantities of seed have made the plant material fairly costly to acquire. The initial revegetation efforts are largely directed at development areas and costs are paid directly by the developer.

Because the San Bruno Mountain program is a long term undertaking, it appeared logical to attempt to place some of the San Bruno Mountain natives into cultivation, so-called "growing for increase". The most successful effort has been on the mountain itself. There, a half acre of exotics were cleared on park land. A total of 1800 plants of major host species (*Lupinus albifrons*, *L. variicolor*, *L. formosus*, and *Eriogonum latifolium* were planted, most as liners (2 inch pots), in March of 1985. Some seed was available for harvest by fall. It is hoped that the plot will increase the seed availability and reduce unit costs.

Direct seeding is primarily accomplished by hydroseeding. Hydroseeding, where seed is mixed with a wood fiber mulch and sprayed on to the ground, is a cost effective method of reseeding extensive bare slopes after construction. So far, 41 acres have been revegetated in this way. A series of seed mixes has been developed to meet various needs (table 3). The different seed components reflect both habitat requirements and relative availability of seed. In the development areas themselves, we have encouraged use of a naturalized mix in an effort to get more extensive native plantings than specified by the HCP alone.

Table 3 -- Representative Seed Mixes

HABITAT AREAS

Species	
Achillea millefolium	1 lb.
Artemisia californica	2 lbs.
Chrysopsis villosa	2.5 lbs.
Eriogonum latifolium	2.5 lbs.
Eriophyllum staechadifolium	2 lbs.
Grindelia sp.	1 lb.
Lasthenia chrysostoma	5 lbs.
Lupinus albifrons	0.5 lbs.
Lupinus variicolor	1 lb.
Lupinus formosus	.5 lbs
Phacelia californica	0.5 lbs.
Salvia spathacea	1.5 lbs.
Stipa pulchra	.5 lb.
Horkelia californica	2 lbs.
TOTAL	22.5 lbs./acre

San Bruno Mountain County Park
 ORV TRAILS

Species	
Artemisia californica	2 lbs.
Baccharis pillularis var. consanguinea	4 lbs.
Eriophyllum confertiflorum	2 lbs.
Eschscholzia californica	1 lbs.
Lupinus arboreus	3 lbs.
Lupinus albifrons	0.25 lbs.
Lupinus formosus	0.25 lbs.
Lupinus variicolor	0.25 lbs.
Mimulus aurantiacus	4 lbs.
Viola pedunculata	1.25 lbs.
TOTAL	18 lbs.

Container planting has been used to place species that do not propagate well by direct seeding and to establish selected woody plants in otherwise grassland seeded areas. We have also used container plantings in seeded areas to provide some initial age diversity. In all, 6000 containers have been planted in different microclimates on the mountain. None of the containers were watered after initial planting -- in the cool San Bruno Mountain environment, survival has been approximately 75 percent.

Container planting is also the logical choice for particular species with limited availability. Seed or cuttings from several of the rare plants on the mountain have been collected sparingly and grown in containers. Arabis blepharophylla, and Erysimum franciscanum have been successfully grown and replanted on the mountain.

The butterfly host plants reestablished in disturbed areas or spread to unoccupied natural habitats have been observed to be used by the endangered species for egg laying, larval and adult feeding. Small areas where host plants have been introduced have been monitored for several years and the distribution of both Mission blue or San Bruno elfin has shifted to include the enhanced areas. The field observations constitute a "bio-assay" of the effectiveness of the revegetation -- at least in the limited ecological context of the endangered butterflies.

EXOTIC SPECIES CONTROL

In 1982, 570 acres of the mountain were covered with dense stands of several non-native woody plants. The exotics were present in another 400 acres and clearly showed expansion toward dominance. Exotic control is an important component of the Habitat Conservation Plan.

The ultimate goal of exotic control is to reduce the threat of loss of native habitats to expanding exotics and to enlarge the area and thus the cover and diversity of native species in areas now dominated by exotics. The program has to proceed in stages: setting species priorities for control and applying control in stages.

Priority exotics are those which appear to be expanding most rapidly and which quickly dominate the microhabitats of the species of concern. Accordingly, gorse, Scotch broom, French broom and pampas grass have been set as high priority for control. Second come eucalyptus and iceplant. Priorities have not been set for numerous herbaceous species, such as fennel, introduced thistles, and European grasses, because of the indeterminate threat and the questionable practicality of control.

Control proceeds in three stages: 1) containment, where outlying colonies of an invasive species are removed to prevent subsequent expansion into an uninfested area. 2) reduction, where the standing crop or biomass of the exotic is removed to allow better ground access and to reduce exotic competition with other species. 3) elimination, where the re-establishment of the species is prevented by destroying roots, exhausting the seed bank, and barring re-introduction of seed from outside.

So far, containment has been readily accomplished for all priority species. Outlying colonies are easily found and with intensive effort over several years, the exotic can be permanently removed.

Stage two, reduction has been focused on the priority species. A variety of physical and chemical methods have been evaluated and it appears that reduction can be cost effectively accomplished even on steep slopes. Mechanical control where heavy equipment can travel is best done by disking or crushing. The tough brushy species are not easily removed by chaining; hogging or chopping works best if the material has been burned first. Fire is a natural brush reduction tool, but even large stands of gorse on San Bruno Mountain do not burn sufficiently hot while green to kill the roots or even to burn out the thick stems. Herbicides, primarily glyphosphate, Monsanto's RoundUp (tm), work well on gorse and broom when applied with sufficient wetting agent. RoundUp at 1.5 percent solution applied at 2.5 to 4.0 gallons of concentrate per acre is effective in spring and early summer.

A combination of treatments is used. On shallow slopes, thick stands 4 to 8 feet in height are first burned and then disked. Seed and stump sprouts appear within a few months and are sprayed when less than 2 feet in height, preferably before flowering. On steep slopes, initial burning scorches the shrubs and causes die-back, which actually increases the load of dead vegetation available as fuel after resprouting. Subsequent burns can reduce the standing mass to a point where an operator can gain access for herbicide application.

The third step, elimination, is a distant dream. Reports of gorse seed remaining viable for 10 to 20 years are plausible and point to a need for long term effort. The brooms are probably as persistent. Other species now set for control can probably be effectively eliminated since they are not as abundant or invasive as the legumes. One effect of burning and disking is to encourage seed germination; initial response is heavy seed sprouting, but the growth is less after a second treatment. It is obviously vain to hope for elimination as long as the invasive species are still grown as ornamentals in nearby residential areas.

CONCLUSION

Numerous factors contribute to success on San Bruno Mountain. In the opinion of the authors the most important factor is the program emphasis on species which are adapted to poor soils and which propagate readily in disturbed areas. The task of re-establishing mostly early successional species is tractable.

Moreover, the HCP is a particularly appropriate vehicle for carrying out the work on San Bruno Mountain. The foundation on the federal 10(a) permit and the Endangered Species Act gives an authority to the revegetation program that makes it easier to maintain cooperation among developers and public agencies not directly interested in the ecological value of the mountain. The permit establishes adequate funding with a life of 30 years; the long term program can accommodate experimentation and follow-up where shorter programs would be limited to tools at hand. The formality of the HCP has made it easier to get cooperative assistance from the Department of Forestry and from the California Conservation Corps.

On the other hand, several factors oppose success: A year of low or poorly distributed rainfall can significantly impair revegetation, essentially wasting a year in the program. Also, reliance on locally collected plant material means that seed is costly and not always as abundant as could be wished. The urban location provides easy access, but also carries the threat of vandalism, illegal trash dumping and off-road vehicles. The invasive exotics present include some particularly difficult species; only the long term nature of the program offers hope. Lastly, the HCP must compensate for losses from partial development on San Bruno Mountain, yet the development timetable has been difficult to predict. Fortunately, the development activities have been slower than anticipated, which has given us time to collect plant material and to perfect revegetation methods.

Five years of implementation have produced results beyond the initial expectations of the San Bruno Mountain Habitat Conservation Plan. Within the context of development costs, HCP funding and County stewardship for the park, cost effective methods have been found 1) to revegetate construction areas so as to reestablish habitat for several rare or endangered species of both animals and plants; and 2) to contain and reduce the infestation of several exotic species.

REFERENCES

McClintock, Elizabeth; Knight, Walter; Fahy, Neil: A Flora of The San Bruno Mountains, San Mateo, California. Proceedings of the California Academy of Sciences Vol. 32 No. 20 pp. 587-677; November 1968.

Habitat Characteristics of Willowy Monardella in San Diego County: Site Selection for Transplants

Gerald A. Scheid [1]

Abstract: Willowy monardella is a State of California endangered species which occurs in small populations along ephemeral streams. Critical habitat of this species has been drastically reduced in recent years. This study collected information characterizing monardella habitats to aid a transplant program of relocating populations slated for destruction to suitable "safe" sites. The data collected suggest that proper site selection depends on the local characteristics of the stream channel, the amount and type of vegetation cover, the grain size distribution of the soil, and the location of the plants relative to the stream channel. Fluvial disturbance probably plays an important role in the creation and maintenance of natural habitats. This information provided guidlines for the selection of sites to be considered for the re-introduction of monardella populations.

Willowy monardella (Monardella linodes ssp. viminea (Greene) Abrams) is a State of California listed endangered species nearly endemic to San Diego County. Recent development of roads, highways, and housing has caused losses of critical habitat and populations of this subspecies. Based on a survey conducted in 1982, it was estimated that some 1500 individual clusters existed comprising 33 distinct populations. In the fall of 1986, only 19 populations remained with a total 995 clusters (34% reduction). Some of these populations slated for destruction were removed and transferred to nursuries for a future transplanting endeavor which would attempt to re-establish these individuals back into suitable habitats.

The purpose of this project was to describe and quantify a "suitable" monardella habitat. This would be accomplished by visiting existing sites of willowy monardella populations to collect descriptive data on habitat characteristics. These data would then be used as a guide for habitat selection for the transplanting program.

A member of the mint family this monardella subspecies is a perennial plant with numerous erect stems from a woody base. The clumps of stems die back in summer to be rejuvenated by the winter rains. It is distinguished from other monardella species by its relatively longer leaves which lack pubescence below and its bracts which are often tipped with rose. The pale rose lavender flowers form dense heads on flower producing branches.

General Habitat

In San Diego County, Willowy monardella occurs in isolated populations along ephemeral streams in several canyons that support a flood disturbance type vegetation (Fig. 1). This vegetation type in San Diego County is characterized by Baccharis sarathroides, Eriogonum faciculatum, and Plantanus racemosa and nearly all monardella sites have these species as the dominant plants.

In general, Monardella populations are found growing on three major land forms characteristic of ephemeral streams. These are benches cut from the banks of major channels, stabilized midchannel sandbars, and floodplain terraces (Fig. 2). In places where channels were narrow and relatively deep sites were located on benches cut in the bank, along low banksides, and small, localized, stable sandbars. In areas of canyons where the channel was wide and relatively shallow sites were located on low, stabilized midchannel sandbars and on well dissected floodplain terraces. The distribution of sampled sites located on each of these geomorphological features can be seen in Table 1. As will be seen, the type of landform a population occurs on influences the distribution of the clusters within the habitat.

---

[1] Research Biologist, Department of Biology, San Diego State University, San Diego, CA. 92182-0057

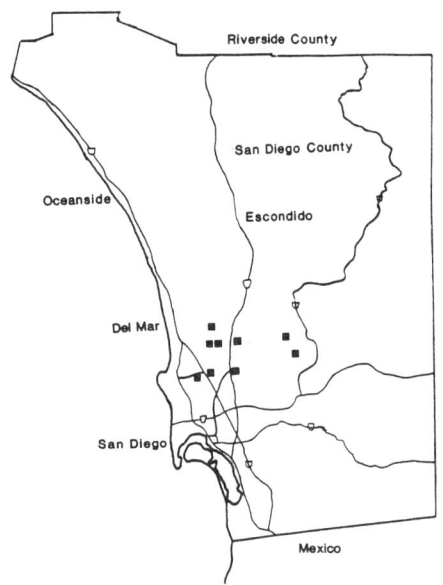

Figure 1. Distribution of <u>Monardella linoides</u> sp. <u>viminea</u> in San Diego County.

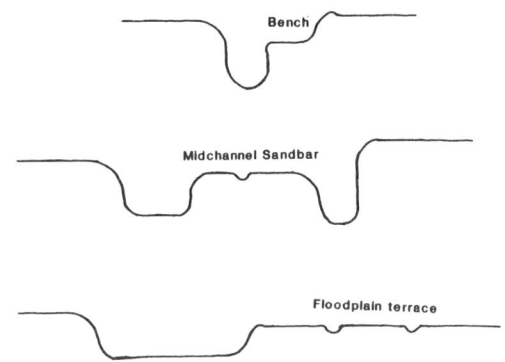

Figure 2. Stream profiles showing location of the geomorphological features on which monardella populations occur.

METHODS

The factors measured at each of these population sites can be divided into two catagories, 1) Those describing the physical and biotic aspects of the habitat (soils and vegetation), and 2) Those describing the distribution of monardella plants within the habitat. The attributes in the habitat catagory that were measured were the particle size distribution of representative soil samples from areas containing monardella plants, and the live cover by species, an estimate of total vegetation cover, and shrub height for both areas colonized and uncolonized by monardella. The attributes in the distribution catagory that were measured were the cluster height and crown dimensions, the cover over the center of a cluster and cluster canopy overlap with other species, the cluster location relative to streambed, and the nearest neighbor to the cluster.

RESULTS

Habitat Characteristics

Soils

The grain size distribution for the soil samples taken from each site show a consistently high sand content with generally low gravel and even lower silt and clay contents (Fig. 3). The percent sand and gravel were not significantly different between sites with the exception

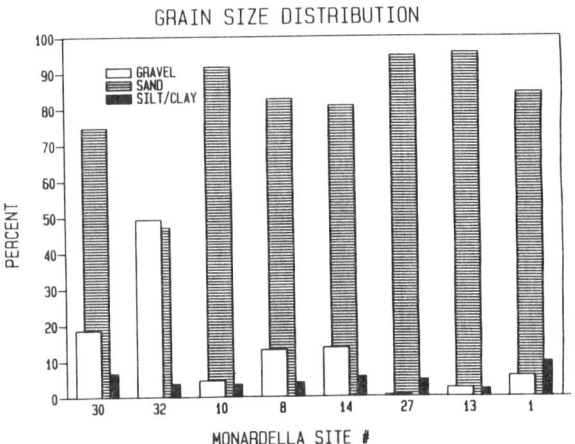

Figure 3. Frequency distribution showing the percent of soil in a particular grain size for all the monardella population sites. The clear bars represent the gravel fraction, the striped bars represent the sand fraction, and the solid bars the combined silt and clay fraction.

Table 1. Distribution of sites for monardella populations with respect to the type of landform they occur on.

SITE	#	GEOMORPHOLOGICAL FEATURE
West Sycamore Canyon	30	Bench, Channel Bottom
Opata Creek	32	Bench
Sycamore Canyon	10	Bench
	8	Sandbar
San Clemente Canyon	14	Floodplain Terrace
	27	Sandbar
	13	Sandbar
Lopez Canyon	1	Sandbar
Carroll Canyon	33	Floodplain Terrace

of site 32 which was different from all other sites for these fractions. The percent silt and clay contents were not significantly different between all sites.

Thus, with one exception, the grain size distribution of soils between sites appears to be relatively consistent. Further support for this soil consistency is seen by looking at the breakdown of the total sand content into the various sand size classes (Table 2). It shows that 1) The proportion of each sand size class was not significantly different between sites and 2) the largest proportion of sand is in the coarse sand size class.

The overall mean values for soil grain sizes indicate that when selecting a potential site for transplants the total sand content of the soil should be around 83 percent (Table 3). The dominant sand fractions should be in the coarse sand size classes with about equal proportions of medium and fine sand. Gravel, silts and clays should be a relatively small percentage of the soil.

Vegetation

Analysis of the vegtation cover comparing sites colonized by Monardella and nearby uncolonized sites revealed that there were no differences between these areas for mean shrub cover, subshrub cover, herbaceous cover, total cover, and the amount of open ground (Table 4). The lack of differences in herbaceous cover and open ground between colonized and uncolonized areas was, however, marginal and based on observations of these areas the colonized sites seem to have less herbaceous cover and more open ground. It appears that the availability of open ground might be an important factor on sites colonized by monardella. The percent cover of both dominant shrubs, Eriogonum and Baccharis, was not significantly different between and within colonized and uncolonized sites.

Thus, the overall mean total vegetation cover for potential sites should be about 75 percent with 25 percent open ground. The proportion of the total cover that is contributed by herbs should be about half that contributed by shrubs. The dominant shrub species, _Eriogonum fasciculatum_ and _Baccharis sarathroides_, should be about equal in proportion cover.

Table 2. The distribution of grain size classes within the sand fraction of typical soils from monardella habitats.

SITE #	VERY COARSE SAND (2-1mm)	COARSE SAND (1-.5mm)	MEDIUM SAND (.5-.25mm)	FINE SAND (.25-.1mm)	VERY FINE (.1-.05mm)
30	5.7	21.0	11.0	23.3	13.5
32	3.4	18.4	8.9	12.2	4.3
10	4.4	44.1	16.2	15.0	6.5
8	3.5	36.6	14.6	19.8	8.3
14	5.6	31.4	13.4	20.6	9.7
27	1.0	49.2	19.6	17.4	7.5
13	1.6	57.2	23.3	8.2	5.0
1	5.7	21.0	11.0	23.3	13.5
33	2.9	36.6	13.5	24.9	11.3

Table 3. Means and ranges of various soil grain sizes for a typical monardella habitat.

GRAIN TYPE	pct.	MAX.	MIN.
GRAVEL	11.2+3.3	69.7	0.1
SAND FRACTION			
Very Coarse Sand	3.9+0.6	12.1	0.7
Coarse Sand	37.7+2.6	60.0	8.5
Medium Sand	14.8+1.1	23.3	5.8
Fine Sand	18.3+1.6	37.2	5.0
Very Fine Sand	8.4+1.0	22.1	0.3
SAND (TOTAL)	83.2+3.2	98.2	27.2
SILT and CLAY	5.6+0.8	15.9	0.5

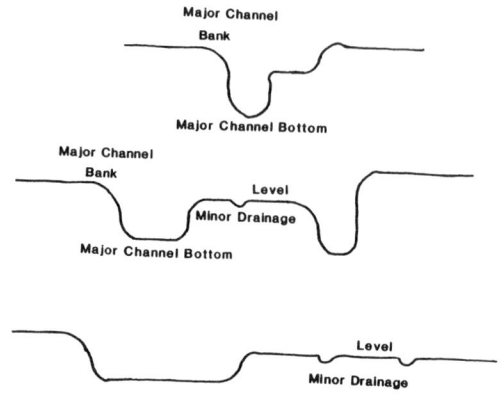

Figure 4. Stream profiles showing the locations of occurrence of monardella clusters with respect to the streambed.

Population Distribution within the Habitat

The location of the Monardella clusters relative to the stream channel is important if periodic flooding is a factor in establishing and maintaining populations. Three major types of locations were defined to describe where the individual monardella clusters were distributed. They were the major channel bank/bottom, the minor drainages, and the level areas between the drainages (Fig. 4). The frequency distribution for monardella clusters occurring in the three types of locations by site reveal characteristics consistent with the type of landform the habitat occurs on within the stream system (Fig. 5). Again with the exception of site 32, the sites located on benches (30, 32, 8) had clusters distributed mainly about the channel banks and bottoms while sandbar and floodplain terrace sites (8, 14, 27, 13, 1, 33) had clusters mainly along the drainages and level areas away from the channel. This result may be an indication of the pattern of flooding that occurs on these different landforms which appears to influence the distribution of monardella clusters.

In addition to the location of the population relative to the stream channel, information on the location of the monardella plants in relation to other shrub species present in the habitat is of importance for the relocation of transplants. The percent of the total Monardella clusters sampled having overlapping canopies with shrubs shows

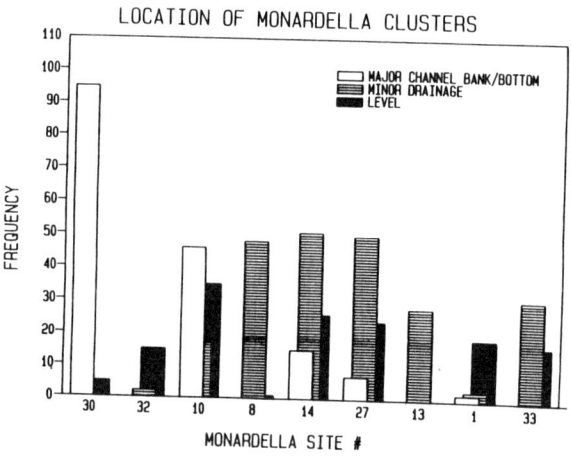

Figure 5. Frequency distribution showing the location of monardella clusters at each site. The clear bars represent those occurring along major channel banks or bottoms, the striped bars represent those occurring along minor drainages, and the solid bars those occurring on the level areas between the drainages.

that a greater percentage of clusters had overlap with Baccharis and with Eriogonum than with other species while only a small percentage of all clusters occured in the open with no canopy overlap (Table 5). The fact that 83 percent of all clusters sampled have canopy overlap with shrubs suggests a close association between the two.

Table 4. Vegetation cover for sites colonized by monardella and uncolonized sites. (* = marginal non-significance)

	MEAN (pct.)	
	Mlv	Non-Mlv
SHRUB COVER	50.2+2.7	43.8+5.8
Proportion shrub cover:		
Baccharis	18.7+3.6	
Eriogonum	22.2+2.7	
SUBSHRUB COVER	4.7+4.0	1.8+1.4
HERBACEOUS COVER *	21.1+3.4	37.2+7.6
TOTAL COVER	76.1+2.2	82.8+1.9
OPEN GROUND *	24.7+2.5	17.2+1.9

Table 5. Distribution of monardella cluster canopy overlap.

SPECIES	PCT. OF TOTAL MONARDELLA CLUSTERS
Baccharis sarathroides	37%
Eriogonum fasciculatum	29%
Other species	17%
Open	17%

In order to further elucidate this association of Monardella clusters to the dominant plants in the habitat the cover over the center of a cluster and nearest neighbor to a cluster were measured and analyzed. The results for the cover over center data show that the percentage of clusters having no cover over the center was slightly greater than those whose centers were cover by shrubs (Table 6). There was a greater percentage of clusters whose center was covered by Baccharis than Eriogonum.

Canopy overlap and cover over the center results can be summarized graphically by a simple model depicting hypothetical shrub canopies (Fig. 6). The 83 percent of all clusters having canopy overlap was divided such that 45 percent had overlap over the center of the cluster and 38 percent had some canopy overlap but the center of the cluster was not covered. Only 17 percent of all clusters sampled grew in the open with no overlapping canopies. Thus, it appears that the distribution of monardella clusters is not only linked to the landform the population occurs on but also the distribution of the dominant shrubs.

Results for the nearest neighbor data adds support to this association hypothesis (Table 7). Nearly half of all the Mlv plants sampled in this study had Baccharis as a nearest neighbor while a slightly less percentage than this were closer to Eriogonum. However, the overall mean distance from Monardella clusters to these two shrubs was not significantly different. It may be that this association with dominant shrubs somehow contributes to the survival of monardella plants, but exactly how is unknown. Ultimately, the placement of monardella transplants in relation to the dominant shrubs present should consider the amount of open space available near the shrub for further growth and establishment of the transplant.

Table 6. Distribution of cover over the center of a monardella cluster.

SPECIES	PCT. OF TOTAL MONARDELLA CLUSTERS
Baccharis sarathroides	22%
Eriogonum fasciculatum	13%
Other species	10%
Open	55%

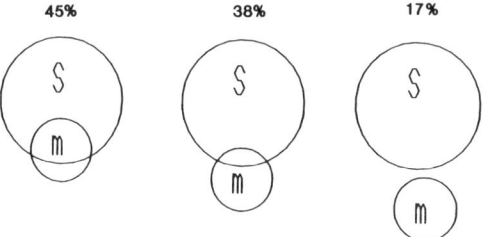

S = SHRUB CANOPY

m = MONARDELLA CANOPY

Figure 6. Simple model depicting the relation between shrub canopy and the frequency of canopy overlap and cover over the center of monardella clusters. Of the 83 percent of clusters having canopy overlap, 45 percent also had cover over the center. Only a small percentage of the total clusters grew completely in the open. (S- shrub canopy; m- monardella canopy)

Table 7. Frequency and mean distance of the dominant shrubs as nearest neighbors to monardella clusters.

	Baccharis	Eriogonum
Pct. Total Population Nearest Neighbor	45.0+5.4	33.0+7.0
Mean Distance	58.0+10.1	57.5+6.0

CONCLUSIONS

The goal of this project was to provide information about Monardella habitats to be used as background for the transplanting of this plant back into suitable areas. The data collected suggest that several factors are important for choosing proper sites although not all factors that might be important could be investigated. In general, the selection of suitable habitat for Willowy monardella plants depends on:

1) General Location within the stream system.

2) Amount and type of vegetation cover.

3) Grain Size distribution of the soil.

4) Cluster location in relation to the streambed.

5) Cluster location in relation to dominant shrubs.

Although quantitative data are lacking, observations made during field studies and information gained from overviews of stream dynamics have lead to the assumption that fluvial disturbance plays an important role in the maintenance and creation of natural habitats for this species. The selection of habitats for monardella transplants must consider the overall affect of factors acting to change these habitats in time, most importantly seasonal peak flows and flood years in addition to other habitat characteristics such as soils and vegetation.

Since the exact conditions required for germination, establishment, and exactly how the plants disperse is unknown, it becomes difficult to answer when, let alone, where exactly to place individuals in the habitat in relation to the physical and biological features present. Conditions that exist now may be different from those the Monardella plants require to become thoroughly established. Additional information concerning the population dynamics of this subspecies would provide important information of Monardella's biology and ecology needed for the success of a long term transplant program.

Acknowledgments: I thank the director of this project John Reiger, California Department of Transportation, San Diego; Dr. Paul Zedler, San Diego State University, for his consultation; and Joan Wojtan for her assistance in the data collection. This study was funded by the California Department of Transportation.

Methods of Increasing Native Populations of *Erysimum menziesii*

Jean Ferreira, Suzanne Smith [1]

Abstract: Prior to State Park acquisition, uncontrolled use in the Marina dunes reduced the native vegetation coverage by 36 percent and greatly impacted the many endangered species that exist there. As a part of a 43 acre dune restoration project at Marina State Beach, California, 3500 Erysimum menziesii seedlings were propagated from seed collected from a remnant population at the State Beach and introduced into the dune system. Natural habitat conditions were used as guidelines during greenhouse propagation to promote success during planting out and establishment. Preliminary planting out results at six months indicate an 80 percent success rate for the seedlings.

A project was undertaken by the California Department of Parks and Recreation (DPR) in July 1985 to develop methods to increase the size of the existing population of Erysimum menziesii (Hook.) Wettst. (Menzies' wallflower), an endangered plant, at Marina State Beach by introducing propagated seedlings of E. menziesii into available habitat. Marina S.B. is located on Monterey Bay, on the central coast of California.

E. menziesii is a very localized species endemic to California. It occurs in partially stabilized coastal sand dunes. It is not found in dune areas with dense competing vegetation, on beaches or on highly unstable sand dunes. The known locations are all on large dune systems.

The distribution of E. menziesii is restricted to three areas on the California coast. The Monterey County location, which includes a population within Marina State Beach, is the southernmost location. The others are found in Mendocino and Humboldt counties.

E. menziesii is a member of the Brassicaceae, the mustard family. It is a biennial or short-lived perennial, with a long taproot, a simple to multiple caudex, a basal rosette of leaves, and bright yellow petals. The population at Marina S.B., and a small population just north of the S.B., have a few characteristics that differ from the typical E. menziesii. The plants bloom two to three months later (June) than the other known populations (March-April), and are also dissimilar in blooming longevity, pubescence, and color. It has been suggested that the Marina populations are an unnamed subspecies (Yadon, Price). The plants are currently being studied to determine their status. The possibility of these populations being a subspecies increases the value and the importance of their preservation.

E. menziesii was listed in September 1984, by the California Department of Fish and Game as an Endangered Species, and is currently under review by the Federal Government for listing. It is on the California Native Plant Society's list of rare and endangered plants of highest priority.

The habitat of E. menziesii, the coastal dunes of California, is characterized by a maritime climate, high exposure to salt spray and windblown sand blast, and a shifting, sandy substrate with low water holding capacity and low in organic matter. With these harsh conditions, once any disturbance to the habitat has occurred, it is very difficult for the native vegetation to become re-established. If the disturbance continues, re-establishment is virtually impossible.

---

[1] Associate State Park Resource Ecologist, CA Department of Parks and Recreation, Sacramento, CA; and Senior Park Aid, CA Department of Parks and Recreation, Marina State Beach, Marina, CA.

Monterey Bay is uncommonly rich in endemic plant species (Stebbins and Major 1965). The increased use of the coastal strand and coastal scrub areas of Monterey Bay has taken a toll on the vegetation. Recreational, residential and commercial developments, and recreational use have caused many of the endemic species and species of limited distribution to become rare and endangered. Besides E. menziesii, seven species of plants and animals that are found at Marina S.B. are listed by government agencies or the California Native Plant Society as rare or endangered.

The dune vegetation at Marina S.B. has been subjected to human disturbance for many years. The area was popularly used by off-road vehicles from the 1950s until the county prohibited vehicular use in 1973. More recently, hang gliders have heavily impacted the dunes. Presently, a hang glider school is located at the north end of the unit.

Recreational impacts have resulted in a massive loss of vegetation and destabilization of the dunes. A few blowouts have become so massive that the shifting sand is reaching Highway 1. Aerial photographs of the Marina area were used to determine the rate and degree of dune destabilization that has occurred at the State Beach. The percentage of bare sand was found to have increased from 16 percent in a November 22, 1941 photograph, to 47 percent in a photograph dated May 6, 1978, and further to 52 percent bare sand on April 12, 1984. Of the bare sand now present on the Marina S.B. dunes, at least 36 percent has been destabilized by human use.

Sand stabilization work has been going on ever since humans first started disturbing dune environments. Revegetation work in the dunes has been, and is, the most common means of stabilization. The use of native species for revegetation has only been emphasized in recent years. Prior to this project, E. menziesii had been grown in nursery situations and had proven to be fairly easy to propagate. The development of propagation methods and transplanting techniques for this project was done by trying to mimic nature. The propagation medium, the type of containers, timing of the planting, and the location of the plantings all needed to be explored.

To perform collection and propagation work on a State listed endangered species, a Memorandum of Understanding was entered into with California Department of Fish and Game (DFG). Limitations and requirements which were placed on the DPR included that no more than 20 percent of the seed crop be collected annually, all plants propagated be planted within Marina S.B. boundaries, and a report of progress be submitted to DFG annually.

The project followed three phases of study. First, the existing natural population of E. menziesii at Marina S.B. was studied to learn the species' preferred location in the dune, the associated species, and E. menziesii's ability to compete with native and non-native species. Next, the methods of propagation were developed and implemented by mimicking what was observed in nature. Finally, the seedlings were transplanted out into the dune in untreated bare areas, and in areas that had been stabilized with straw; success rates of the plantings were monitored.

The project was developed to increase the number of individuals and populations of E. menziesii, creating a more stable existence for an endangered species and what may be a subspecies. Since all populations are in a frequently changing, easily disturbed habitat, larger population numbers will aid in insuring the survival of the species.

Materials and Methods

Fencing and Stabilization

The initial step for stabilization of E. menziesii's habitat was the installation of a four foot high wire-and-lath fencing to prevent further disruption by foot traffic. A DPR closure order closed 31 acres to public use, entry, or occupancy on May 20, 1984. The fencing delineates this area, which surrounds and includes the E. menziesii population. Appropriate signs were posted on the fence to inform the public of the closure and restoration work.

The fence installation and all physical labor connected with this project were provided by the Monterey County Court work Alternative Program. The participants perform community work in lieu of imprisonment. The "court workers" provided an estimated 6500 hours of labor to this project between May 1985 and April 1986.

Sand was stabilized in the closed E. menziesii area through a technique called "straw planting". Handfuls of straw were buried 3 to 4 inches, leaving 6 to 10 inches protruding straight out of the sand. These bundles were planted 1 to 2 feet apart in areas devoid of vegetation and on the eroding slopes of hummocks. This type of stabilization deflects wind off the surface of the sand, limiting the wind's ability to pick up the grains and move them across the dunes. Other types of stabilization methods cover the soil surface, intercepting sun and rain, competing with any vegetation attempting to colonize. The 1 to 2 foot spacing of the straw bundles allows a large percentage of the sand to remain uncovered, so the sun and rain can reach the surface, favoring plant establishment. The area first treated with straw planting was the unstable foredune in front of the existing E. menziesii population. An extra row of snow fencing was also installed in front of the population to break up wind patterns.

Seed Collection

In May 1985, the existing population of E. menziesii at Marina S.B. was surveyed and found to consist of approximately 325 plants. The majority were located in a swale behind the foredune approximately 500 feet south of the parking lot.

From July 27 to November 1, 1985, seeds from these parent plants were collected, cleaned, treated with Captan (N-((trichloromethyl)thio)-4-cyclohexene-1, 2-dicarboximide 5 percent), a garden fungicide, and stored for use in propagation. Each collection batch was stored in a separate paper bag marked with the collection date. The take of each collection was limited to 20 percent of the seed produced by each plant, and was collected by shaking the dried seeds off the pods rather than collecting the entire pod off the plant. This was done to ensure the maturity of the seeds.

Greenhouse

The ranger station at Marina S.B. was once the building for the Society for the Prevention of Cruelty to Animals for Monterey County; the back of the office is what was once the kennel area. Three 9 foot by 12 foot greenhouse rooms with planting benches were built in the kennel area. The design of separate rooms was to protect against disease spreading throughout the entire greenhouse. The rooms were constructed from redwood and corrugated fiberglass built onto the existing kennel structure. The benches in each room hold up to 25 supercell racks, or 2,450 supercells, for a total greenhouse capacity of 7,350 supercell containers.

An irrigation system was installed into the 3 rooms, each with a timer, allowing the 3 rooms to operate separately if needed. A Hydro Rain HR 6100-A was chosen because of its 6 separate timing stations and relatively low cost ($60.00). The misting system was a flat anvil type.

Once the greenhouse was constructed, all wooden surfaces were painted with copper napthlate and all other surfaces were washed with a 9:1 water-bleach solution to sterilize the interior.

The cost for the irrigation system and installation was $240.00; another system was later added to a hardening-off table outside the greenhouse at a cost of $78.00. Cost of the lumber was approximately $450.00. With tools and other supplies, the total cost for the greenhouse and the propagation supplies was $1,600.00.

Propagation

To promote easy seedling adaptation to the dune environment, sand was used as a growing medium rather than a soil mixture. Sand was collected from a rear dune area so that it would contain less salt, sifted to remove debris, placed in trays and heated in an oven to 140° for 45 minutes to sterilize. It was then stored in a sealed container until ready for use.

Seeding was done in 1.5 inch by 8 inch Leach tubes, also called supercells. These containers were chosen over others because they allowed for the development of a long taproot system. The longer the taproot when planting the seedling, the greater chance the roots will reach the permanent moisture deep in the dunes and survive the annual dry season. The supercell containers and holders were also washed in a 9.1 water-bleach mixture prior to planting to prevent disease.

A small number of 4 inch peat pots were tested for their suitability for E. menziesii propagation. The seedlings grown and planted out in peat pots showed a 50 percent survival rate; however, the pots were rejected as a planting container because the lack of depth of the pot may inhibit the taproot growth and because peat has the potential to wick soil moisture.

Each supercell was filled with 1 inch of sterilized pea gravel, a half inch layer of vermiculite, to prevent the sand from piping out the bottom of the tube, and sand. The sand was treated with a light dusting or spray of Captan.

Records were kept on each batch of seedlings including the collection date of the seed, sowing date, first germination, the timing of the fertilization and amounts, planting out date, and placement in the dunes.

Germination occurred generally 5 days after planting. A 98 percent germination rate was typical. True leaves appeared about 3 weeks later. At this stage, seedlings were fertilized with one-half strength 15-6-3 fish base fertilizer. Approximately 8 weeks after planting, when the roots began to emerge from the bottom of the planting tubes, the seedlings were put outside to harden off. At this point, the irrigation was cut back from 3 minutes twice a day to 2 minutes twice a day. Seedlings remained on the hardening-off tables from 1 to 3 weeks before being planted in the dunes. The sowing period was staggered between September 29 and December 17, 1985, to accommodate limited hardening-off facilities, the scheduling of the planters, and the weather.

The timing of the sowing of the seeds was designed to have the seedlings ready for planting in the dunes during the start of the rainy season. Fertilization of the plants while in the greenhouse was kept at a minimum to encourage easy adaptation to the naturally low nutrient level of the dune environment.

Planting Out

The planting out occurred over a period of 3 months, from December 1985 through February 1986. Approximately 3500 E. menziesii seedlings were planted out in the dunes. The average diameter size of the seedlings was 1 inch when planted, and they had germinated 8 to 10 weeks earlier. The criteria for site selection for planting out was established by attempting to duplicate the existing population habitat. Areas chosen were behind the foredune, in swales, and in bare sandy areas to lessen competition for water availability. Approximately 2400 seedlings were planted in areas stabilized by straw planting, and 1100 were planted in bare sand. No irrigation was provided for the seedlings in the dunes.

Because sand was chosen as a planting medium, special care had to be taken in the planting process, to prevent damage of the root system. The seedling was shaken loose from the supercell tube into a sling which was fashioned from a split supercell. The filled sling was placed against the edge of the planting hole and sand was filled in around the root and sling. Before the sand was compacted around the plant, the sling was removed. Using this method, approximately one hundred seedlings per person per day could be planted.

Monitoring

White plastic tags were placed near each seedling after it was planted. Many of these tags could not withstand the strong winds and were gone within 2 months. Three months after planting, an informal survey was taken to determine survival and size of the seedlings in the dunes. At 6 months, a sampling of 1000 seedlings was taken. The seedlings were retagged and measured to determine growth.

Results

The results of an informal survey taken in March, 3 months after the seedlings had been planted in the dunes, showed very low survival of seedlings in areas which had not been mechanically stabilized by straw. The primary problem in these areas was burial by sand, caused by both the advancing dune and active construction of animal burrows. Seedlings planted in areas that had been stabilized had a 95 percent survival rate. The diameter of the rosettes varied from less than 1 inch to over 3 inches.

The sampling results in mid-June, 6 months after the planting, again showed very high survival rates in areas which had been stabilized by straw. Even after the dry season, 85 percent of the seedlings planted in areas stabilized by straw had survived. The diameter sizes of the rosettes were as follows: 28 percent of the sample were less than 1 inch, 61 percent were between 1.0 and 1.9 inches, 10 percent were between 2.0 and 2.9 inches, and 1 percent was over 3 inches.

In late September, 1986, 7 to 9 months after planting, an early rain storm supplied water to the plants, the first they had received after the dry summer months. Growth started immediately. By mid October, rosettes which had measured 1.75 inches in July, increased to over 3.5 inches. Many smaller seedlings of less than 1 inch in diameter grew to over 1.5 inches.

Discussion

Success of the planting of E. menziesii seedlings at Marina S.B. varied with the placement of the seedlings in the dunes. Sand movement and competition for water were the two major factors associated with unsuccessful plantings. However, the major factor contributing to the survival rate of the planting project was the favorable rains which fell from fall 1985 through spring 1986. After the planting was completed, 7 inches of winter and spring rains fell.

Although E. menziesii is found in only partially stabilized dunes, and does not appear to compete well with other species, especially non-native species of Carpobrotus, sand stabilization has proven to be a major requirement for successful seedling establishment. A comparison of success rates between seedlings planted in areas stabilized by straw planting, and untreated areas, generally showed a higher success rate in stabilized areas.

The first step to success in planting dune species is not showy top growth but a long, well developed root system which will enable the plant to survive in the dune sand, a substrate with low water-holding capacity. Growth was observed after the first 3 months in the dunes; however, during these months rainfall was plentiful. The test of survival was the summer months, the annual dry season in Monterey County. Very little rainfall and strong afternoon winds are typical summer weather in Marina. The survival rate measured at the 6 month mark indicates that the root systems did indeed develop to the depth of year-around moisture in the dunes.

Seedlings planted in swales where water collects during rains showed more growth than those planted on the tops of hills. This statement is general and the variability great; a close survey of all seedlings in any one area has shown variation in size up to 2.5 inches.

The intent of the propagation efforts was to provide an environment which, as closely as possible, mirrored the dune environment. Heat beds were not installed in the greenhouse to speed the growing process. Fertilization of the seedlings in the greenhouse was minimized to prevent excessive top growth, which could jeopardize the plant's survival once placed out in the desicating winds of the dunes, and create difficulty in adapting to the low nutrients int he dunes. Sand was used as a growing medium to prevent an interface of two different soil types when planted into the sand, with different moisture retention capabilities and nutrient levels. The plants were transplanted to the dunes as early as possible to promote a natural growth pattern. This next year's growth and flowering will be the concrete evidence of a successful project.

ACKNOWLEDGMENTS

Besides the many people from the Department of Parks and Recreation who worked on and supported this project, a special thanks to Vernal Yadon, Pacific Grove Natural History Museum, who generously offered his knowledge about the Marina S.B. flora, and his experiences propagating E. menziesii; Robert Price, U.C. Berkeley, and Ken Berg, Humboldt S.U., for sharing their expertise on the species; and Al Grahm and Ed Hummel, Ornamental Horticulture Department, Monterey Peninsula College, for their encouragement and guidance in creating a successful greenhouse. The project could never have been completed to the extent that it has been without the hundreds of participants in the Monterey County Court Work Alternative Program who supplied the labor.

REFERENCES

Berg, Kenneth. Humboldt State University, personal communication October 1985.
Grahm, Al. Professor of Horticulture, Monterey Peninsula College, personal communication, August 1985.
Hummel, Edward. Professor of Horticulture, Monterey Peninsula College, personal communication, May through December, 1985.
Price, Robert. Univ. CA, Berkeley, personal communication, October 1985.
Stebbins, G. L., and D. Major. 1965. Endemism and Speciation in the California Flora. Ecol. Monogr. 35:1-35.
Yadon, Vernal. Pacific Grove Natural History Museum, personal communication, June 1985 through October 1986.

The Effects of Controlled Burning on Three Rare Plants

Robert Boyd [1]

Abstract: This paper describes results from a small-scale controlled burn conducted in October 1983 to determine the impact of fire on three rare plants from the Pine Hill Ecological Reserve: *Fremontodendron decumbens*, *Ceanothus rodericki*, and *Wyethia reticulata*. *Fremontodendron* proved to be a postfire resprouter. Fire also stimulated production of rootsprouts and germination of buried seeds. *Ceanothus* was killed by fire, but seedling production was 22 times greater on the burned plots and seedling survival was higher than in unburned plots. Fire did not harm *Wyethia* and stimulated flowering in 1984, which resulted in large numbers of seedlings in 1985. These three rare plants possess varying combinations of adaptations to fire, including resprouting, rootsprouting, fire-stimulated germination, and fire-stimulated flowering. Each is adapted to fire, and appropriately-timed controlled burning is not a threat to their existence but a prerequisite for successful reproduction.

For many years, fire has been viewed by land managers in a negative way. This attitude, summed up succinctly as, "The only good fire is a dead fire", has recently given way to a much more flexible policy regarding the use of fire as a management tool. Controlled burns are being used to improve wildlife habitat, decrease the hazards of wildfires, and to maintain fire-adapted plant communities in a relatively natural condition.

One such fire-adapted plant community is chaparral. Before the advent of fire-suppression policies, chaparral stands might have burned at a frequency of 3-5 times every 100 years. Burning has a number of beneficial effects: it stimulates germination of many shrub and herb species, releases nutrients bound in the litter layer for re-use by plants, and results in increased use of the burned area by wildlife. Besides these benefits, controlled burning of chaparral reduces the chances of a destructive wildfire occurring in the burned area.

Managers must weigh many factors in making vegetation management decisions. If rare plants are present in the area to be burned, the effect of fire on those plants must be considered. Specific information on the response to fire of rare plants is lacking. Most rare plants in the chaparral are, like the other members of the community, probably adapted to fire so that burning will not have a detrimental effect. However, this may not always be the case. I know of one reported case, for two species in the Red Hills of Tuolumne County, in which a controlled burning program was terminated because of perceived ill-effects on the rare plants involved (Clark, 1986). This vaccuum of knowledge poses a problem for the manager, who must then weigh the costs and benefits of a management policy without the information necessary to make scientifically-informed decisions. The most prudent policy is to conduct a small-scale experiment on the specific rare plants involved.

Pine Hill rises from an elevation of 1,600 feet to slightly over 2,000 feet in the foothills of the Sierra Nevada east of Sacramento. The Pine Hill Ecological Reserve, administered by the California Department of Fish and Game and encompassing some 240 acres, contains the majority of Pine Hill. This Reserve was established to protect the six species of rare plants found there. South-facing slopes are covered with chaparral, while the the north-facing slopes have an overstory of ponderosa pine or black oak with an understory of chaparral shrubs. The chaparral on the south-facing slopes, dominated by whiteleaf manzanita

---

[1] Visiting Post-Doctoral and Lecturer Botany Department, University of California, Davis, CA.

(*Arctostaphylos viscida* Parry), was in poor condition, with most shrubs dying. This condition was attributed to the lack of fire in the recent (past 50 years) history of Pine Hill.

Department of Fish and Game managers desired to burn the manzanita chaparral area both to stimulate reproduction among the shrubs and to decrease the chances that a wildfire originating off the Reserve would consume the entire hill. Significant populations of three rare plants occurred within the area of the proposed burn: Pine Hill flannelbush (*Fremontodendron decumbens* Lloyd), Roderick buckbrush (*Ceanothus rodericki* Knight), and Eldorado mule-ears (*Wyethia reticulata* Greene). The former two species are state-listed as rare, whereas the latter is a candidate for state listing. Because the impact of fire on these rare plants was not known, the Department of Fish and Game wanted to conduct a small test burn to determine whether a large-scale burn might harm the rare plant populations. My own studies of the reproductive biology of Pine Hill flannelbush were at a point where I also was interested in determining how fire would affect that species (Boyd, 1985). This paper reports the results of a small controlled burn and a postfire monitoring program designed to determine: 1) if fire would harm existing individuals of the three rare plant species, and, 2) if fire would be beneficial by stimulating production of new individuals of these species.

METHODS

Pine Hill Flannelbush

The area for the test burn was located on the east ridge of Pine Hill. More than 100 flannelbush shrubs were growing on that ridge, and the population was divided into a burned and an unburned portion. The unburned plants were included to act as a control for the burning treatment. The locations of 43 shrubs found within the burned area and 60 shrubs found in the control portion of the ridge were mapped prior to the burn. Beginning on 5 April 1984 and continuing thereafter on an occasional basis, the condition of the marked plants within the burned area was checked. Each time the original shrubs were checked, I checked the burned area for rootsprouts. Every rootsprout found was mapped and its condition was subsequently monitored along with the original resprouting shrubs. In July 1985, the control area was checked against the map of shrubs found in October 1983 to determine if any rootsprouts had appeared in that area.

To separate the increase in germination attributable to fire over that which would otherwise have occurred, 25 shrubs were randomly selected from the burned and control areas of the study site. The number of living seedlings found under the canopy of each shrub was counted in late March 1984, when germination in the burned area was almost at an end.

The entire burned area was censused for seedlings every 2-3 weeks following the discovery of the first seedlings in late January 1984. The location of each seedling was mapped and marked with a colored stake. The condition of each seedling was recorded during subsequent census intervals.

Roderick buckbrush

Nine plots, 2 meters long on each side and with a relatively high cover of *Ceanothus rodericki*, were selected within the burned area, and nine similar plots were selected outside of the burned area. The corners of the plots were marked with metal stakes. In order to quantify the relative amount of *C. rodericki* present in each plot, I counted the number of rooting points within each plot. A rooting point, arbitrarily defined as a relatively discrete area of rooted branches, was sometimes quite difficult to identify due to the frequent branch-layering of the plants. In order to assure burning, dried brush was piled on the burned plots to a depth of 0.75-1 meters.

All plots were checked for seedlings in March 1984. Censusing continued at irregular intervals until October 1986.

Eldorado mule-ears

Nine plots, 2 meters long on each side and containing a large number of stems of *Wyethia reticulata*, were selected within the burned area, and nine similar plots were selected outside of the burned area. The corners of the plots were marked with metal stakes. The number of stems present in each of the plots to be burned was counted in October 1983. In addition to the number of stems present, the number of flower heads produced before the fire was counted on both burned and unburned plots. The number of flower heads and stems produced on each plot was counted in October of 1984 and

1985. All plots were examined for *Wyethia* seedlings on 23 March 1984 and 16 April 1985.

Burning treatment

An area of approximately one hectare was burned on 27 October 1983. At the time of the burn, the relative humidity was 36 percent, the wind was 0-4 miles per hour, and fuel moisture (measured with a 10-hour fuel stick) was 7 percent. Fuel cut from the firebreak around the area to be burned was placed within the burned area, in many cases near flannel-bush plants. This was done to help the fire carry over thinly-vegetated rocky areas. After the fire, a flamethrower was used to ignite areas to which the fire had not carried naturally.

RESULTS AND DISCUSSION

Pine Hill flannelbush

Some of the shrubs within the burned area were not completely burned. Of the 43 shrubs within the burned area, 5 had some portion of the canopy remaining alive after the burn. These shrubs were all located on a north-facing slope which did not burn well during the fire, and were excluded from subsequent monitoring.

The total flannel bush population on this site has been increased by the fire (table 1). By early April of the following year, most of the completely-burned *Fremontodendron* shrubs had begun to send up shoots from the base of the dead crown. Mortality was low among the 38 completely-burned shrubs, with one *Fremontodendron* failing to resprout after the fire. This individual was replaced by a rootsprout which emerged from the ground about 0.5 meters from the killed crown. Thus, there actually were no losses to the original number of Fremontodendron shrubs as a result of the fire. Rootsprouts were discovered at irregular intervals from May 1984 through May 1985, and are important contributors to the overall postfire increase in the flannelbush population (table 1). As of October 1986, 14 have been discovered and all but one is still alive. Two rootsprouts were also found in the unburned area in July 1985. The proportion of rootsprouts to mature shrubs was significantly higher in the burned area (contingency table analysis, p 0.05), indicating that rootsprout production was significantly accelerated by the fire. The seedling census of the areas under 25 burned and 25 unburned shrubs turned up 145 live seedlings under the burned shrubs and 2 live seedlings under the unburned shrubs. This 73-fold difference in seedling production was highly significant statistically (Mann-Whitney U test, p 0.05), and indicated that fire stimulated germination of a seed bank of viable flannel bush seeds. A total of 1,117 flannel bush seedlings were discovered after the fire, but among them mortality was quite high. Damage by herbivores, the summer drought, and competition by resprouting shrubs killed most of them within one year (table 1).

Many of the seedlings and rootsprouts alive now will not survive to maturity (defined as the production of viable seeds). At least a few are vigorous enough now, and are far enough away from competitors, to have a good chance for long-term survival. The overall effect of the controlled burn was to stimulte both vegetative (rootsprout) and sexual (seedling) reproduction of Pine Hill flannelbush. The end result is a likely increase in the number of individuals in the population of mature plants.

Roderick buckbrush

Burned plots had an average of 61.6 ± 20.1 (S.D.) buckbrush rooting points prior to the burn, whereas the unburned plots averaged 57.0 ± 12.1 (S.D.) rooting points. These densities were not statistically significant (Mann-Whitney U test, p 0.05), indicating that the burned and unburned plots were quite similar in the number of plants present prior to the fire. After the burn, however, none of the mature *Ceanothus* plants in the burned plots resprouted.

Large numbers of *Ceanothus* seedlings were observed in the burned plots in early February 1984. On 23 March 1984, when germination was judged complete, I counted 39 seedlings in the unburned plots and 841 in the burned plots. This 22-fold difference in seedling production is significant statistically (Mann-Whitney U test, p 0.05), demonstrating that fire stimulated germination in this species of *Ceanothus*.

The survival of burned plot seedlings was significantly greater (contingency table analysis, p 0.05) than that of unburned plot seedlings at all census intervals from June until the end of the study. The number of seedlings germinating in 1984 still alive at representative dates were as follows:

Table 1 -- Number of live flannel bush individuals in the burned area before the controlled burn (October 1983), and one through three years later (1984-1986).

Type of individual	1983	1984	1985	1986
Original plants	38	37	37	37
Rootsprouts	--	6	14	13
Seedlings	--	94	56	45

	Live seedlings	
Date:	Burned plots	Unburned plots
March 1984	841	39
October 1984	278	1
July 1985	172	1
October 1986	136	1

Almost all of the seedlings in the unburned plots died by the end of summer (within seven months). Many of the burned plot seedlings died of drought or from being eaten by herbivores, but some (16 percent) have survived to the present day. The growth rate of the seedlings in the unburned plots was noticeably less than that of burned plot seedlings. At most, these seedlings had produced only a few pairs of leaves by the end of the summer of 1984. By that time, some burned plot seedlings had become multi-branched plants bearing many times that number of leaves.

The long-term prospects for recovery of this species seem good. The complete mortality of the prefire population makes this species much more vulnerable than flannel bush to unforeseen climatic events. However, in this instance, most plots have many vigorously-growing plants. The ability of this species to reproduce asexually to branch-layering will also help it to spread over the burned plots. It seems likely that all of the burned plots will eventually recover, although it will be many years until this recovery is complete.

Eldorado mule-ears

The number of Wyethia stems produced on the burned plots in 1984 was not significantly different (p 0.05, Mann-Whitney U test) than the number of stems produced the previous year (table 2). Mule-ears is a perennial that produces aerial stems from an underground rhizome. These stems are produced during the winter and die in late summer. At the time of the burn, the aerial stems had died, and the living buds of the plants were buried safely beneath the soil. However, in 1985 Wyethia stem production increased significantly (p 0.05 Mann-Whitney U test) on the burned plots while not changing significantly on the unburned plots (p 0.05, Mann-Whitney U test). Apparently, improved postfire growing conditions stimulated asexual reproduction on the burned plots, leading to this increase in the number of stems per plot.

The most striking difference between the burned and unburned plots was in the extent of flowering of the Wyethia plants in 1984 (table 2). The number of flower heads produced on the unburned plots did not change between 1983 and 1984 (Wilcoxon paired sample test, p 0.05), but the number of flower heads on the burned plots increased 23.5-fold over the number counted before the burn. This change was statistically significant (Wilcoxom paired sample test, p 0.05). The following year showed a significant decline in flower head production for both burned and unburned plots compared to the previous year (Wilcoxon paired sample test, p 0.05). However, the burned plots still produced 7.5 times more flower heads than they did in the year before the fire.

The first spring after the fire, very few seedlings could be found. Only three seedlings were found within the study plots, and all three were in unburned plots. Therefore, unlike the two previous species, there was no postfire germination from a buried seed bank. However, after the increase in flower head production on the burned plots in 1984, large numbers of seedlings appeared in the spring of 1985. Results of my count of seedlings during April 1985 in all plots showed a 54.5-fold difference in seedling production between the burned and unburned plots (table 2). Some of these seedlings will probably survive to maturity, adding

Table 2 -- Number of mature stems, flower heads, and seedlings found on the mule-ears study plots during the study. Data are mean ± S.D.

Data	Plot treatment	1983	1984	1985
Stems per plot	Burned	144±95	158±100	217±125
	Unburned	---	140±66	143±64
Flower heads per plot	Burned	6.8±7.0	160±57	51±35
	Unburned	9.3±8.0	12±4.9	5.6±9.0
New seedlings per plot	Burned	--	0	24±36
	Unburned	--	0.33±0.47	0.44±1.3

new plants to the mule-ears population on the burn.

OBSERVATIONS ON THE LARGE-SCALE BURN

This research showed that fire would not cause any lasting harm to these three rare plant species. As a result, the Department of Fish and Game and the California Department of Forestry burned the large south-facing slope in June 1985. Even though the timing of this major burn was different than for the test burn (late spring versus mid-fall), the impact on the rare plants seemed comparable. When I examined the large burn in the summer of 1986, I found seedlings of the rare buckbrush, seedlings, rootsprouts, and resprouts of the flannel bush, and most of the mule-ears plants had produced flower heads. The rare plant populations within both the small and large burned areas will apparently recover completely from the effects of the fires.

CONCLUSIONS

The data presented in this paper demonstrated that each of the three species of rare plants examined were adapted to naturally-occurring fires in some way and required fire to stimulate reproduction. Pine Hill flannelbush resprouted after fire, so that the original population size was largely unchanged. In addition, this species produced additional individuals by fire-stimulated germination from a seed bank and production of sprouts from the roots of established plants. Roderick buckbrush was completely killed by fire, but fire stimulated germination from a seed bank. Seedling survival and growth on burned areas was greater than unburned areas, so that the population eventually will recover. Eldorado mule-ears was not harmed by fire. Unlike the other species, it did not have fire-stimulated germination from a seed bank. Instead, the plant reproduced vegetatively the second season after the fire, and increased flowering after fire allowed reproduction by seed as well.

Acknowledgements: Many people contributed to this project. Scott Clemons of the California Department of Fish and Game was instrumental in organizing and getting approvals for the controlled burn, in addition to helping me set up the monitoring program. Rick York of the California Native Plant Society also helped to establish the study plots. Curt Fox of the Department of Forestry did a fine job conducting a successful controlled burn. This study was partially supported by the California Native Plant Society through their mini-grant program. The Department of Fish and Game provided supplies and other assistance in the realization of the controlled burn. Special thanks are due the Department of Forestry for providing the manpower and equipment necessary to conduct the controlled burn.

REFERENCES

Boyd, Robert S. 1985. The Pine Hill Fremontia. Fremontia 13(1): 3-6.

Clark, George M. 1986. The Red Hills of Tuolumne County - Recap of the April Meeting. Newsletter of the Sacramento Valley Chapter, California Native Plant Society. May edition.

Pediocactus knowltonii Recovery Efforts

Peggy Olwell, Anne Cully,
Paul Knight, Steve Brack [1]

Abstract: A USFWS Recovery Plan for Pediocactus knowltonii established reintroduction as a primary goal for the survival of this species. In 1985 a joint effort between the FWS, State of New Mexico, and the Nature Conservancy resulted in the establishment of a transplanted population of this species. Cuttings were acquired from the type locality, rooted in a greenhouse and moved to the reintroduction site. The survival of these transplants and subsequent flowering and fruit set indicate a successful technique.

Pediocactus knowltonii L. Benson (Knowlton cactus), listed as endangered by U.S. Fish & Wildlife Service (FWS) on November 28, 1979, is one of the rarest and most sought after of the cacti in the United States. Collection is the foremost threat followed by habitat destruction from oil and gas development and grazing.

The plants grow either as a solitary stem or in a cluster of up to 30 stems. Each stem may range up 3.8 cm in length and 3.0 cm in diameter (fig. 1). Although the plant scarcely protrudes above the soil level most of the year, from mid-April through mid-May its yellow-centered pink flowers make it much more conspicuous. The flowers open from mid-morning (approximately 10:00 AM) to early afternoon (1:00 PM), and generally last two to three days. Fruit development occurs late May to early June, with dehiscence by a vertical slit along one side of the ovary wall from mid-to-late June.

Pediocactus knowltonii is a narrow endemic limited to one known viable population located in northwestern New Mexico at the eastern edge of the Colorado Plateau (fig.2). This population covers an area of less than 15 acres with most of the estimated 9000 plants occurring within less than 2.5 acres. The species grows on the top and slopes of a single hill composed of Tertiary alluvial deposits, at an elevation of 1890 meters. The surrounding biotic community consists of elements of the Great Basin Conifer Woodland [2] dominated by species such as pinyon pine (Pinus edulis Engelm.), Rocky Mountain juniper (Juniperus scopulorum Sarg.), Utah juniper (Juniperus utahensis (Engelm.) Lemmon), big sagebrush (Artemesia tridentata Nutt.), woolly phlox (Phlox hoodii

Figure 1--Pediocactus knowltonii in flower at the type locality.

---

[1] Endangered Species Botanist, U.S. Fish and Wildlife Service, Albuquerque, NM; Botanist and Chief Botanist in New Mexico Natural Resources Department, Santa Fe, NM; Owner, Mesa Gardens, Belen, NM

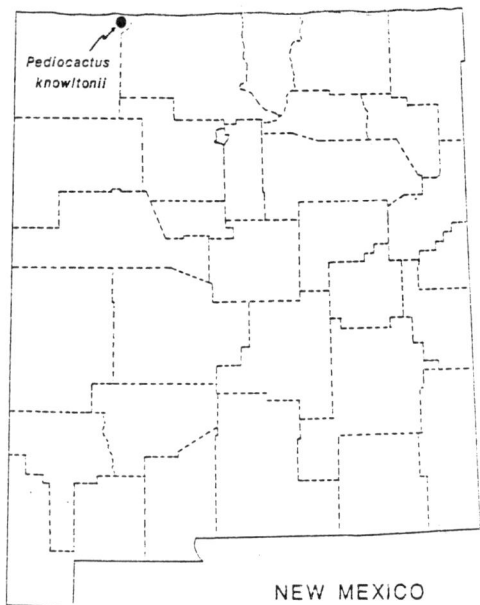

Figure 2--Distribution of <u>Pediocactus knowltonii</u>.

Richards.), beardtongue (<u>Penstemon linarioides</u> subsp. <u>coloradoensis</u> (A.Nels.) Keck), blue grama grass (<u>Bouteloua gracilis</u> (H.B.K) Lag.), galleta grass (<u>Hilaria jamesii</u> (Torr.) Benth.), and a foliose lichen (<u>Parmelia physodes</u> var. <u>vittata</u>).

A recovery plan[3] was developed for <u>Pediocactus knowltonii</u> and approved by FWS in March 1985. As part of the recovery process a reintroduction program was designed. With only one viable population it was believed that a reintroduction program would be the best method to ensure survival of the species.

METHODS AND MATERIALS

In March 1985, several areas on federal and State of New Mexico lands were surveyed to identify an adequate transplantation site. Several criteria for site selection were established prior

---

[2] Brown, D.E. and C.H. Lowe. 1980. Map, biotic communities of the Southwest (scale 1:1,000,000). Rocky Mountain Forest Range Experimental Station General Technical Report. RM-78. USDA Forest Service.

[3] U.S. Fish and Wildlife Service. 1985. Knowlton Cactus Recovery Plan. U.S. Fish and Wildlife Service, Albuquerque, New Mexico. iv+53pp.

to the search and designation of the reintrodution site. These criteria included the following: the site must be located within the probable historic range of the species; it must contain similar vegetation to the type locality; and contain approximate elevation, topographic features and soil structure to the type locality. To curtail visitation of cactus collectors, the site must be inaccessible to vehicles, and the site must also be on federally administered land so that the Endangered Species Act is enforceable. Because oil and gas development occurs throughout the historic range of <u>Pediocactus knowltonii</u>, the site needs to be fully protected from these activities.

The area selected duplicates most of the environmental parameters that exist at the type locality. The site is on Federal land within 5 miles of the type locality and access is restricted except by hiking. The elevation at the site ranges from 1890-1900 meters and a greater portion of the site contains similar soil structure and cobble density to the type locality. Although it is somewhat drier than the type locality, the dominant perennial species occur at the reintroduction site.

The reintroduction program began in May 1985, when 250 cuttings were taken from wild plants at the type locality. These cuttings were taken from single or multi-headed plants. The cutting was dipped in a rooting hormone, ROOTONE-F, which contains a fungicide. The rooting hormone was also applied to the cut surface of the wild plant to protect it from a fungal attack. The cuttings were placed in potting soil, fertilized, watered and hardened in a greenhouse over the summer. Of the 250 cuttings taken, 240 or 96 percent of the cuttings developed roots while in the greenhouse.

A grid system was established at the reintroduction site prior to the transplanting. Starting with the datum point, every two meters, north to south and east to west, a galvanized 20 penny nail with an identification tag was buried. Each point in the grid was characterized as to cover and associated species.

For comparative purposes, twenty-four 10 meter square monitoring plots were established at the type locality with apriori selection. Plots were set up depending upon aspect, placement on hill, soil type, associated vegetation type, and absence or presence of <u>Pediocactus knowltonii</u>. Soil samples

Figure 3--Average change in stem diameter over one year.

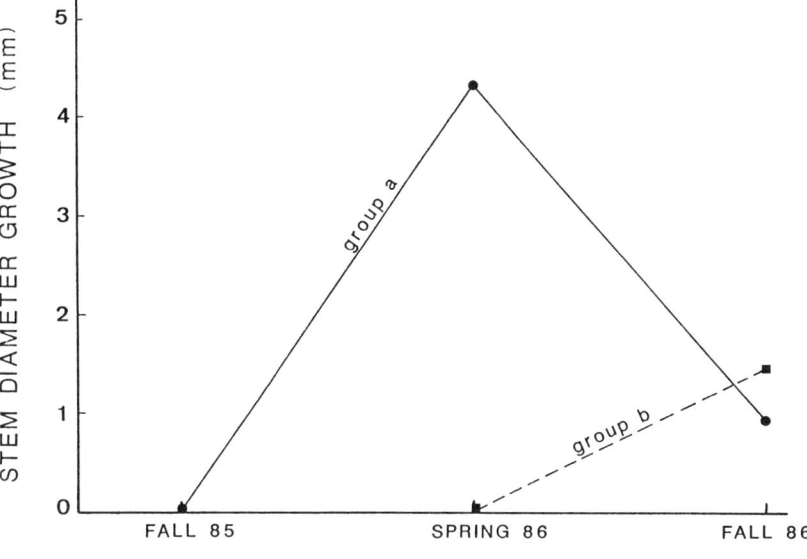

were taken from 8 of the monitoring plots. Each plant within the plot was mapped and stem diameter, number of buds, flowers or fruits was recorded. Visitations to the flowers by potential pollen vectors were noted.

In September 1985, 103 plants (Group A) were transplanted onto the reintroduction site. Each plant was situated 20 cm south of an identification tag, was watered individually, and stem diameter measurements were record. In April 1986, 47 plants (Group B) were transplanted and received the same treatment as Group A. Soil samples were taken from several points across the grid. The plot was read in Fall 1985, Spring 1986, and Fall 1986, and will be read twice annually with data taken on stem diameter, number of buds, flowers and fruits, and seed set.

CONCLUSIONS

Perhaps the most surprising change observed within the reintroduction site was the large stem diameter growth in Group A from the time of transplant, Fall 1985, to Spring 1986. It was expected that the plants would have to acclimate to the native environment after having been in a greenhouse situation for five months. As indicated in figure 3, Group A had an average growth spurt of 4.35 mm from Fall 1985 to Spring 1986 and then withdrew into the ground from Spring 1986 to Fall 1986 with a shrinkage in size of 3.88 mm. This in not unusual for

Pediocactus knowltonii. Generally, there are two times during the year when swelling and/or growth can occur. In the spring (April and May) when the temperature and soil have warmed up, the plants will grow vigorously and flower. From June through September, the plants shut down and shrink into the ground with the dry summer conditions. As soon as the soil moisture builds up from the late summer rains and the soil cools down, the plants will go into their second stage of growth. The plants may not increase in volume; however, meristematic activity is taking place, as the buds are set in the fall. A few buds may open, but usually the buds will remain unopened throughout the winter. Freezing temperatures do not damage the buds.

Group B, planted in the spring, did not have nearly the initial growth spurt which Group A had. A hot, dry climate occurs from late spring into early summer. During this time period, the plants recede into the soil, and a shrinkage in size is expected. Perhaps the reason Group B had some positive growth (1.45 mm) was the result of an application of fertilizer prior to transplant and watering at the time of transplant. These treatments may have assuaged the harsh effects of the late spring environment.

The low percent mortality of the transplants was very encouraging. Overall, there was a 5.3 percent mortality for the first year, with all of it occurring in the summer:

Mortality (percent)

	Group A	Group B
9/85-4/86	0	not planted
4/86-10/86	3.9	8.5

For Group A, there was no loss of plants from Fall 1985 to Spring 1986 and a 3.9 percent loss during the summer. Group B experienced the highest mortality rate in the summer. Although the data is very preliminary it appears that fall is a better time to transplant Pediocactus knowltonii into its native environment. Perhaps summer presents the harshest conditions for the plants and they need to be more firmly established in the habitat before encountering these conditions.

A higher frequency of anthesis and greater fecundity occurs at the reintroduction site than at the type locality:

Phenology

	Intro Site	Type Locality
Flowering (pct)	62	28
Fruiting (pct)	11	7
Flowers/plant	1.1	0.4

There are several reasons which could explain the disparity. Data from the type locality was gathered two weeks earlier than the data from the reintroduction site. Although not yet documented, it appears that the type locality is cooler and wetter than the reintroduction site and therefore the type locality population was not yet into full production at the time of data collection. In addition, the plants were fertilized prior to transplanting and may have initiated bud development in the greenhouse before being transplanted.

Although the data thus far is preliminary, a survival rate of 94.7 percent is encouraging. The 62 percent flowering level may be a result of aberrations produce by the transplanting methodology, however, the 11 percent fruiting indicates that the required pollen vectors are present at the site. The higher mortality rate of spring transplants suggests that fall is a more optimum introduction time.

The objective of this study is to conduct long term monitoring at both the type locality and the reintroduction site. Additional studies such as pollination and seed set studies will be undertaken in the future. Weather monitoring stations will be established at both sites. Those cuttings not planted in the reintroduction site will be used as a seed source for further study. An area adjacent to the reintroduction site will be seeded as a test plot. The plot will be monitored to determine if this approach to reintroduction is more successful than the transplant method. This data will be used to better understand the population biology and ecological requirements of the species for future reintroductions and for better biological decisions in the management of the species.

ACKNOWLEDGEMENTS

We would like to thank the New Mexico State Parks Department for assistance in transportation to the reintroduction site, and the Nature Conservancy for allowing us to remove cuttings from the type locality.

Genetic Conservation Issues in Land Restoration: Open Forum Discussion

Jean Ferreira, Deborah Hillyard [1]
(Topic not in conference)

Abstract: This forum discussed the biological, philosophical, and logistical problems encountered when using plant species in restoration. Solutions discussed were documentation of existing problems; education; project budgeting to include long term planning; tightening up of specifications in contract/mitigation work; alternative use of exotic species; use of sterile material; and regulation of the nursery/seed industry to require more source documentation.

The genetic problems encountered in using native plant species in any kind of restoration, salvage, or revegetation work revolve around the introduction of plants of a different genotype into an existing population. This can lead to problems within species if the introduction is not well adapted to the existing conditions; or between species if hybridization occurs which results in non-viable seeds or viable seeds which result in non-reproductive offspring. Both of these situations are of particular importance in dealing with rare species.

Other concerns voiced by the group were:
- replacement of lost populations with different or unknown genotype
- use of botanic gardens as storehouses of genetic information, especially many different genotypes or closely related species
- potential conflict of two goals in restoration: recreating an esthetic landscape vs. preserving genetics
- genetic variability testing: how reliable is it? how important are few-loci differences? how much difference is too much? how do we set limits?
- what constitutes a "local" population?
- creating a new population of rare plants: is it viable? is it a range extension?

The discussion touched on each of these problems, and solutions ranged from general to very specific. The consensus was that many of these problems had to be dealt with by educating public agencies and others involved in restoration work about the potential genetic problems involved, and by an emphasis on long term planning, to avoid creating a situation where the genetic integrity of a population is in jeopardy.

Other possible solutions to the problems outlined were much more specific, addressing particular steps in the restoration process, or aspects of industry or agency regulations and procedures.

Exotic species can be used for the initial stabilization of an area, allowing for natural invasion by, or inter-seeding or -planting of, native species; this allows for the emergency stabilization that is often needed, but cannot be planned for ahead of time. By using exotic species, preferably non-invasive ones, chances are minimized that genetic pollution will occur. The extreme of this concept is the use of only exotics for revegetation of disturbed areas. This becomes a problem when those exotics chosen for use can successfully out-compete desired natives, or are aggressive in invading established vegetation.

Development of sterile cultivars of native plant materials for use in landscaping and revegetation is another tactic. Polyploids of many species currently exist, that could be developed into non-reproducing material of commercial value. These would not present a genetic threat to existing populations, although those with the ability to reproduce asexually have the potential of posing a competitive threat to existing vegetation.

Many of the inadvertant introductions could be avoided by specifying in planning and contract documents the area

---

[1] Associate State Park Resource Ecologists, California Department of Parks and Recreation, Sacramento, CA

of known (and desired) genetic origin, indicating desired locations or methods of collection. The ability to do this hinges on having information on hand from prior projects, and from research conducted on specific problems in procuring materials. Documentation of existing problems and monitoring of successful (and not so successful) techniques are essential, to have a source to draw on for future projects.

When designing a seed collection project, it is important to designate what constitutes a "local population" for a particular species. The idea of the concentric circles approach to seed collection is a useful concept when actually procuring seed or cuttings; this involves collecting seed as close to the desired source as possible, moving out in concentric bands as the closest sources become exhausted. The shape of the "circles" is modified by topography, microclimate, or other factors that may influence the distribution of the target species.

Regulation of the nursery and seed industry was deemed important in aiding those interested in controlling genetic pollution. Requiring documentation as to the place of collection of all commercially available seed and plant materials would insure that consumers were at least informed as to the source of the materials they purchase. Establishment of seed zones for widespread species, similar to those used in the timber industry, could enhance survival of seeded or planted material. Neither of these precludes the possibility of introducing material of undesirable origin into a sensitive area, but either would serve to inform those who wish to avoid an unwanted introduction.

Regulation, of course, is only as effective as the enforcement of those regulations. Stipulation of material of known genetic origin on large-scale projects may serve to encourage the industry to undertake these measures on their own, or to make enforcement of regulations that much easier. In this way, pressure from those who are the largest consumers of native plant materials may serve to change attitudes regarding the importance of documentation.

Another source of control in procuring plant materials of known origin is to do in-house collection and propagation, or to contract specifically for the seed or plants needed. In this manner, responsibility for protecting the genetic resource is retained by the project manager, and procurement of plant materials is not as subject to less conscientious (or possibly unethical) individuals. Here again, the material will be only as good as that specified, so seed and plant needs must be communicated as explicitly as possible.

Almost all of the above specific project recommendations depend on planning ahead in order to effectively implement those recommendations. Long-term project planning can make feasible collecting of specified material on site; contract growing of desired material; designation of a specific "nurse" crop; stipulation of some form of guarantee, including a surety deposit to back it up; or any other condition that is desired, and should be specified ahead of time. Educating those involved in restoration work about the need for genetic conservation, and planning well in advance, are the keys to dealing with this ever-increasing threat to our diminishing resources.

The Restoration of California: A Practical Guide

Wayne Tyson [1]

Abstract: That the biological resources of California are being diminished and destroyed is nothing new. But it is not widely understood that much of the diminishment and destruction is not only needless, it is more expensive and less profitable than alternatives that preserve and restore natural habitats. This fact has exciting possibilities that can be realized only if government, business, environmental organizations and the public at large are aware of them and take action to move the course of development in that direction.

California is being reconstructed, as it has since the first humans arrived, and it will be as long as humans inhabit this habitat. The question is not whether, but how. Land development is not the only aspect of this culture that plays havoc with the life forms that make the California habitat so eminently habitable, but it is the quickest, most thorough destroyer of plants, animals, earth and the stability of that complex that all of us, especially developers, so justifiably value. It does not have to continue to be so. It is, in fact, in the best interest of all concerned, especially the short-term interests of developers, to reconstruct California in the least destructive way possible. That is, it makes good economic and managerial sense to structure the land and its biological systems efficiently.

No one really believes that the reconstruction of California is going to stop, and that one day we all will see the light and preserve every endangered species and every precious habitat. But many people and organizations behave as if they did. This is a dangerous delusion.

Others feel a sense of desperation, that they must salvage what they can despite the overwhelming superiority of a powerful opposition. Still others think that only if they can keep their finger in the dike long enough, that the great ocean of human indifference will cease its relentless pounding against the wall of reason. More dangerous delusions.

A few endangered plants might be caged, zoo-like, in some phantasmagorical "mitigation" scheme; a few important habitats might be preserved here and there; a few large areas, unsuitable for development anyway, might be "set aside." The rest will be rent asunder in the indifferent pursuit of "a better way of life." The majority of California's lands will continue to be reconstructed as usual--unless we decide to go about the development process in a different way.

THE MAX FACTOR

Today, as in years past, we think of the land as a structureless medium for our art. We "reform" it to suit our fantasies with no regard to its biological structure and scant regard to its physical structure. The landscaping that we impose upon the remnant sherds of land left over when the buildings have been built and the paving has been laid, is without biological structure, and we spend large sums of money on maintenance, water and other resources to keep it that way. We get the maximum possible phantasmagory from this approach, but it costs--and costs, and costs--forever.

What's wrong with landscaping? Nothing is really wrong with it, but it is only cosmetic. The trouble is, most people think that it is natural, just like Yosemite Valley, and don't recognize it for what it is--an artificial decoration on the land that happens to be constructed of living organisms. The fact that the plant assemblage does not function biologically is lost in the simple lust for the desired phantasy.

That's okay; land cosmetics can have a useful purpose, but we should realize that every time we apply land cosmetics in the usual way, we are displacing ever more

---

[1] Manager, Land Restoration Associates, San Diego, CA (619) 233-4881.

scarce biological resources. The plant assemblages employed in landscaping often consist of exotic plants that are not capable of sustaining themselves without continued maintenance and replacement. Such plants are commonly incapable of reproduction, and those that are, rarely are able to complete their life cycle. (When they do, we call them alien invaders, and they can be very destructive--biologically and economically.) Many plants are rendered impotent by horticultural practice, such as by planting only genetically uniform clones of male plants. Dead-end homogeneity is the choice of land cosmetology rather than life re-forming diversity--biological male chauvinism at its most virulent.

In some cases, we have no choice. Where people congregate in great numbers, we need a foundation of grass, and the site where our parks and yards are may not be meadowland sites. We may want the eye-shadowing utility and visual stimulation of trees where trees may not be a component of the indigenous vegetation complex. We may choose a bit of flowery rouge where only belly-flowers once raised their broods.

But in many places, such as the great acreages of the state highway system and similar places where the only functional need for a surface that can take a beating is the occasional tread of a maintenance worker, our only remaining excuse for choosing cosmetics over grafting back the living skin of earth is that we prefer the smooth consistency of a cosmetic monoculture to the stimulating diversity of the unexpected that only real Nature can do well.

THE "NATURAL" LOOK

Landscaping with native plants is becoming more common, but this fad has come and gone several times in the last century. Using native plants in landscaping may or may not bring about any real biological healing. A plant simply native to the state may be no more able to sustain itself and reproduce on a given site than an exotic species. Even a plant indigenous to the immediate vicinity of the site may have the same trouble.

Planting the widespread Toyon or California Holly (Heteromeles arbutifolia) on highway fills, for example, is nearly always futile unless continued irrigation is provided. The plant simply is not suited to those kinds of site conditions, and even with irrigation (adequate water supplies being only one of a number of its environmental requirements), it cannot be expected to thrive. It will not normally complete its life cycle of continued reproduction or regeneration on such a site. While it lives, it may produce viable seed, however, and thus it will provide some food, cover, and resting places for indigenous wildlife. Seeds may be transported to adjacent suitable sites where the plant's progeny will have a chance of survival.

While landscaping with native plants is an improvement on traditional land cosmetics, it does not replace the structure of the stable biological complex that existed before the reconstruction process was initiated. It is a better answer than iceplant, acacias and eucalyptus, but it is still expensive and only marginally effective.

RECONCILING OUR DIFFERENCES

If we are going to reconstruct California, then it makes sense to do so in a way that produces the maximum of positive results and the minimum of negative ones. Perfection cannot be attained, but we can do a lot better than we are now.

First things first. Profits. Land developers demand them. It costs money to buck environmentalists, and that money comes out of profits. It costs environmental organizations a lot of scarce money and energy to fight developers for little or no accomplishment. Expect this: (1) When developers think they can make money by fighting environmental concerns, they will fight. Usually they will win. (2) When an environmental organization thinks it might save a bit of California's biological birthright, it will mount a vigorous campaign against the development. Even if the developers win, they lose. Profits. Prestige. Image. Sometimes they go broke. (3) The process will repeat itself.

If a point of reconciliation can be found between developers and those who would speak for California's biological resources, both will be better off. Each will have more money and energy to apply to other concerns. In most cases, the plants and animals involved also will benefit, rather than merely serve as pawns in a conflict of self-righteous egos. "We have only two choices," said Kenneth Boulding. "We can have an 'I beat you down, you beat me down, I beat you down society,' or we can have an "I lift you up, you lift me up, I lift you up society.'"

RECONSTRUCTIVE SURGERY

Most land development projects can be designed to minimize destruction to biological resources. Sometimes it may be as simple as increasing density on that part of the site which is least vital biologically in exchange for leaving the most vital area as a preserve, dedicated and/or deed-restricted in perpetuity. If some graded areas such as cut slopes are to be left without structures upon them, partial or complete restoration of a suitable indigenous biological complex could be done instead of landscaping.

Areas of greater usage could be landscaped, but it might be found that a modified form of indigenous biological complex might meet developer's and user's requirements as well or better than landscaping. Where that was not sufficient, limited artificial landscaping might be integrated into a modified indigenous vegetation complex to increase its utility or to provide supplementary aesthetic enhancement. Such integrations can be temporary, with the sometimes more slowly developing indigenous vegetation providing superior performance in a few years, while the landscaping elements provide temporary satisfaction.

The advantage of this to the developer goes back to profits. The less grading, the lower the costs. The less graded surplus, the less need be spent on "erosion control" and "beautification." Landscaping costs a lot of money, and the irrigation system to support it a lot more. Since the restoration of a self-sufficient, self-regenerative vegetation complex costs much less than landscaping, eliminates the cost of an irrigation system, and is far more reliable in the bargain, the developer can effectively put those dollars in the bank--most of them at the "front-end." In so doing, the developer gets positive publicity, a better public image, the elimination of a lot of costly headaches and legal fees, and can take pride in the knowledge that some significant steps were taken toward reconstructing California in a better way. "Progress" suddenly has become less of a mere slogan and more of a reality.

The developer also saves a bundle in the cost of maintenance, repair and replacement of plants and irrigation system components, and perhaps the cost of the repair of irrigation-induced slope failures and the replacement cost of ruined landscaping and irrigation systems such failures often take downhill with them. The user of the development (e.g. homeowner) also will save significantly on maintenance costs every year due to these same economies, since a self-sufficient vegetation complex is far less costly to manage than an artificial landscape is to maintain. The development is a more attractive and easier to sell investment because of these annual savings.

HEALING OLD SCARS

These same principles can be applied to areas where the biological resources such as vegetation have been diminished or destroyed in the past. Where 100 percent mitigations are required, there is no dearth of places to accomplish it. Restoration of self-sufficient, self-regenerative vegetation complexes and their associated organisms to these sites can be accomplished in part by using biological resources such as soil from developments to redress the errors of the past. This will require a coordinated effort by government, business, concerned professions and the public.

IN CONCLUSION, A BEGINNING

Plants that are presently rare and endangered are better protected by habitat preservation. But habitat restoration is a better bet even for these sensitive organisms than transplanting them into an alien or marginal habitat. The technology of habitat restoration is in its infancy, but the state of the art is more than adequate for the kind of beginning outlined here. The thing to do is to get on with the job of maximizing the survival of the irretrievable germplasm encased in the exceedingly rare and precious, even useful, biological resources of California.

The biological resources of California do not gain by this procedure, but they stand a better chance of survival than they do now without it. Beer cans and oil are non-living resources that are merely _dispersed_ by our profligate ways. The _biological_ treasures of California cannot be recovered once they are lost. When the last individual of any species is gone, it cannot be collected and recycled--it is gone forever. Surely, some of the beer can-saving energy and money can be applied to building up our stocks of these treasures rather than throwing them away.

But we all have to _do_, not just talk. That will require the _setting_ aside of at least some of the differences that keep people, organizations, business and government apart, and a pledge to reconstruct California by taking full advantage of its biological treasures.

Mineral Acquisition in Native Plants

T. V. St. John [1]

ROOTS AND THEIR SYMBIONTS

The acquisition of water and nutrients depends on the timing and geometry of root growth as well as metabolic functions. Symbiotic microorganisms are often present. The interplay of the root system, mycorrhizal symbionts, and inherent nutrient utilization strategies of the plants form the subject of this analysis.

Nutrient uptake

Nutrients elements must be in water-soluble form, and they must be within a short distance of the root surface to be absorbed by the roots. Only a fraction of the total stock of most elements is in soluble form at a given time. Rapid removal of nutrient ions from the soil solution results in a relatively nutrient-impoverished "zone of depletion" adjacent to the root (Nye and Tinker 1977).

The most important limitation on the rate of nutrient acquisition is movement of ions through the soil. Ions move slowly because of physical and chemical interactions with the soil. As the soil dries, diffusion pathways may become discontinuous.

Because of slow diffusion, the acquisition of nutrients is influenced greatly by the density of roots. When roots are closer together, average diffusion pathways are shortened and uptake proceeds at a correspondingly faster pace (Barley 1970).

Timing of root growth

During the growth of annual plants, the root system often keeps pace with the shoot, maintaining a constant root/shoot weight ratio in the vegetative phase. Growth of new roots slows or ceases when the plant shifts to the reproductive phase of its life cycle (Scott Russell 1977).

In perennial plants, root growth is

[1] Researcher, University of California, Los Angeles, CA

Abstract: The uptake of nutrients depends in large part upon the timing and geometry of root growth. Symbiotic microorganisms greatly improve the plant's acquisition of phosphorus (mycorrhizae) or nitrogen (nitrogen-fixing symbionts). Mycorrhizal fungi are easily lost from soil in various kinds of disturbance, and do not reinvade rapidly.

Many native plants can make efficient use of the limited nutrient supply. The most important way of doing so is an intrinsically slow growth rate, which paces nutrient demand to the rate at which nutrients can be acquired.

Relatively little is known about the mineral requirements and symbioses of rare and endangered species. With knowledge of these factors, we might be able to formulate an approach that can help to increase their populations.

---

more likely to be linked to season. In apple trees, in which root growth has been studied much more exhaustively than in any of our native plants, root growth starts in the spring when soil temperature rises to $6.2°C$. Throughout the growing season, root growth is influenced by short-term changes in soil temperature and moisture. Root growth is greatest in early summer, slows considerably in late summer as the fruit are being produced, and resumes in the autumn (Rogers and Head 1969). St. John and Rundel (unpublished data) have found a similar pattern in the mid-elevation mixed-conifer forests of Sequoia National Park.

Root growth that is responsive to local short-term conditions can take advantage of nutrient availability that is extremely variable in both time and space. Reynolds (1975) suggested that there are localized cells in which root activity is followed by local quiescence, after exhaustion of nutrients in the region. St. John (1983) showed that roots of tropical forest trees grow and branch selectively in response to decomposing organic matter. Roots of crop plants are known to branch most extensively in nutrient-enriched sites (De Jager 1979, Drew 1975).

Geometry of the root system

The basic composition of the root system, again indicated by the example of apple, is established by the seedling. Invasion of new soil is carried out by thick, fast-growing extension roots (Rogers and Head 1969). Lateral roots, including the finer, short-lived rootlets that do most nutrient uptake, arise along extension roots and may bear more orders of laterals. It has been estimated that the root system of a mature Red Oak includes 500 million roots tips (Lyford 1975).

Microbial symbionts

The root system is the portion of the plant most concerned with the acquisition of mineral nutrients, but the effectiveness of the root system is greatly extended in many plant species by symbiotic microorganisms. The term symbiosis refers to a mutually beneficial partnership, with the plant providing energy and available carbon compounds to the microbial partner, and the microbe providing improved access to an important nutrient element. The most important symbioses are the plant-fungal relationships known as mycorrhizae, and the plant-bacteria or plant-actinomycete relationships localized in nitrogen-fixing root nodules.

Mycorrhizae

Mycorrhiza is a collective term for several distinct kinds of plant-fungus associations. The fungi may be higher fungi (Basidiomycetes) of the kind that produce mushrooms and similar structures, or they may be more primitive fungi that can be observed only under magnification and after special staining of the root tissues. In the first group are the sheathing or ectomycorrhizae, which may be seen with a hand lens on the rootlets of most conifers, oaks, and willows. Such fungi are also involved in certain mycorrhizae of the Ericaceae and related families. The reader is referred to Read (1983) for a full discussion of ericaceous mycorrhizae.

The more primitive fungi of the family Endogonaceae, although more difficult to observe, are much more widespread. They form the symbiosis known by the awkward name "vesicular-arbuscular mycorrhiza" (VAM). The fungi of these mycorrhizae are the most abundant microorganisms in most soils (Hayman 1978). In addition to their importance in the mineral nutrition of plants, they are one of the most important components of soil aggregation (Tisdall and Oades 1979) and play a critical role in stabilization of sand dunes (Koske and Polson 1984).

The mycorrhizal symbiosis is in most experimental conditions beneficial to the host plant. This is often demonstrated by comparing growth of inoculated and uninoculated plants in autoclaved or radiation-sterilized soil. At the end of an experiment, depending on plant species, soil type, duration of the experiment, and other factors, mycorrhizal plants may exceed non-mycorrhizal plants in size by a factor of thirty or more. Such experiments have been described by Read (1983), Kleinschmidt and Gerdemann (1972), Kormanik et al. (1982) and countless others.

The benefits attributed to the mycorrhizal symbiosis include faster growth (Hayman 1983), better tolerance of transplanting (Menge et al. 1980), and higher drought resistance (Safir et al. 1971, 1972). All of these qualities are important in revegetation efforts, but the primary role of mycorrhizae is improved uptake of phosphorus. The physiological effects of phosphorus are extensive, and all of the above benefits, even water relations, are though related to the improved phosphorus nutrition of mycorrhizal plants. Mycorrhizal fungi do not appear to make phosphorus more soluble or to extract it from organic compounds. Their effect is physical: phosphorus diffuses through soil very slowly, and mycorrhizal hyphae are able to explore soil volumes outside the zone of depletion that forms around roots. Their effect is essentially to shorten diffusion pathways, dramatically increasing the rate at which phosphate ions reach the root (Tinker 1978).

The biology of the fungal partners is important in the understanding of disturbance, since the effects on the fungi may determine the consequences of the disturbance on the plant community. Mode of reproduction, nutrition, and the way in which host roots are colonized differ markedly between the taxonomically distinct fungi of sheathing (ecto-) mycorrhizae and those of VAM. The fungi of sheathing mycorrhizae often form fruiting bodies, either above ground, as in mushrooms and similar structures, below ground, as in truffles, or in the litter layer. The fruiting bodies release spores that are easily disseminated by wind or animals, and new seedlings in the vicinity of established plant communities quickly become mycorrhizal in most cases. The fungi may have a narrow host range that includes only one or a few plant species, or they may have wide range of potential host species.

The fungi of VAM, although common in most terrestrial habitats, reproduce quite differently. Most species form large asexual resting spores that are not easily carried by wind. While some species are known to be transported by animals (Maser et al. 1978), it is likely that most species spread primarily by growing from root to root through the soil. The host range is very wide; that is, most species of fungi can potentially form mycorrhizae with any VAM host plant, and there is no such thing as a "correct" VAM fungus for a particular plant species. This nonspecificity allows the fungus to spread between unrelated host species. The fungi cannot grow in the absence of a host plant, and may die out after mechanical disturbance of the soil. Slow dispersal means that new seedlings may not find suitable fungal symbionts, and will lack their natural means of acquiring nutrients. Many weedy species have evolved alternative ways of obtaining phosphorus, and do not function as mycorrhizal host plants (Janos 1980, Reeves et al. 1979). Extensive areas of mechanically disturbed land in California, which may be occupied for years by such nonhost weedy species as Salsola kali or Brassica nigra, are in many cases probably entirely devoid of mycorrhizal inoculum. Such sites cannot be expected to support desirable mycorrhiza-dependent native plants until the symbionts are artificially reintroduced.

In the context of revegetation, it is important to understand the negative effects of fertilization on these symbioses. Mycorrhizae of both the ecto- and VA types are strongly suppressed by the addition of phosphate fertilizer and variably suppressed by nitrogen fertilizer (Hayman 1983).

It is important for our purposes to know which of our native plants are mycorrhizal hosts under natural conditions. While records have appeared for some California natives (i.e. Cordes 1975, Trappe 1981, Bethlenfalvay et al. 1984, Kumerow 1986), our knowledge of mycorrhizal condition of our flora remains spotty. We may assume that our pines, oaks, and willows are normally ectomycorrhizal, that most crucifers and chenopods are non-mycorrhizal, and that most others, including Poaceae, Asteraceae, Rosaceae, and similarly important families are VA mycorrhizal. The symbioses are probably most important to the plants during the establishment phase and during the spring season of most rapid growth.

Nitrogen-fixing symbionts

Another important group of symbionts are the nitrogen-fixing bacteria of certain legumes. These bacteria of the genus Rhizobium invade the host's roots and induce the formation of characteristic nodules. Within the nodules, atmospheric nitrogen is transformed into plant-available compounds at the expense of photosynthetically-produced energy. Some examples of nitrogen-fixing legumes may be found in the extensive tabulation of Allen and Allen (1981).

Similar in function to the legume symbiosis is the Actinorrhiza. Actinomycetes, or filamentous bacteria, of the genus Frankia form nodules with a variety of non-legumes, including alders, Ceanothus spp., Cercocarpus spp., and others. The rate of nitrogen fixation tends to be lower than that of legumes. This kind of symbiosis has been documented extensively in the pacific northwest (Rose 1980, 1981).

Effects of habitat disturbance on symbionts

Among the detrimental effects of mechanical disturbance is the loss of propagules of symbiotic microbes. The consequences of disturbance are most severe for VAM, since dispersal of their propagules is much more limited than for bacterial or basidiomycete symbionts.

Alternative strategies for phosphorus uptake

There is a certain group of plants that easily invades mechanically disturbed sites, the plants we think of as weeds. Among their most important characteristics is the ability to obtain phosphorus without the help of mycorrhizal symbionts. In the discussion of root density, root hairs were mentioned as one way of increasing phosphorus uptake. It is widely believed that mycorrhizae and root hairs are alternative strategies; plants with dense, long root hairs tend to be the least dependent on mycorrhizal symbionts (Baylis 1975, St. John 1980).

MINERAL NUTRITION AND PLANT GROWTH

The roots and symbionts discussed above are the key to bringing nutrients into the plant. Within the plant, there exists a variety of ways in which the nutrient supply can be managed. Plants that are native to impoverished soils use nutrients very efficiently, although at a cost in growth and reproductive rate. Plants of richer soils may use nutrients more extravagantly, but grow and reproduce in those habitats at rates otherwise unattainable. The relationship of nutrient utilization to niche and life history of the plant is the subject of this section.

Plant growth in relation to nutrient supply

The most important single difference between plants of nutrient-rich and nutrient-poor sites is growth rate (Chapin 1980, 1983). The photosynthetic rate of plants differs by over two orders of magnitude (Mooney and Gulmon 1979), and the maximum rate at which a plant can grow under ideal circumstances (R_{max}) differs by 12 fold between plant species (Grime and Hunt 1975). The fastest-growing plants retain their leaves only a short time, since young leaves have the highest photosynthetic rate, and are less likely to be shaded by older leaves (Chapin 1983). Rapid turnover of leaves carries a heavy cost in mineral nutrients, however. While a portion of the nutrient supply is transported to newer leaves at senescence, half or more of the nutrient stock of each leaf is lost with the leaf. Thus uptake per unit time must be rapid, a condition obtainable only in relatively rich soil. Plants capable of the fastest growth rates are usually ruderals, a term used by Grime (1978) to indicate species that invade highly disturbed but potentially productive habitats. It is interesting that most of our fast-growing crop plants were derived from ruderal ancestors (Chapin 1980).

Plants that are native to sites of low potential productivity have much lower R_{max} values. These plants, called "stress-tolerators" by Grime (1978), retain their leaves over a much longer interval, and are often evergreens. Many of our desirable native species are in this category. In an undisturbed natural community these stress-tolerators are able to grow slowly and reproduce continuously, where demanding ruderal species cannot. In a potentially productive soil, however, the ruderal strategy is clearly superior. I will show in the next section that mechanical disturbance at least temporarily creates an environment in which the desirable natives are hopelessly outmatched in growth and reproductive rate by ruderals.

Soil factors

To understand the changes that accompany mechanical soil disturbance, it is instructive to examine some processes that influence the availability of nutrients. It is a critically important point, but not always an obvious one, that disturbed soils tend to be is richer in available forms of nutrients than the same soils before disturbance. In undisturbed vegetation nutrient ions are absorbed rapidly as they are solubilized. One of the key reasons for greater availability in disturbed soils is the loss of this rapid uptake. Bormann and Likens (1979), studying the effects of clear-cutting in a northeastern forest ecosystem, reported that over a period of three years about 400 kg/ha of N was released to the soil and subsequently carried away in stream water. They attributed the loss to the lack of uptake by vegetation, and to the loss of exchange surfaces that accompanied decomposition of soil organic matter.

A second important disturbance-related process is the addition of organic matter when the vegetation is destroyed. Roots of the original plants may be left in the soil and some of the above ground portions may also be mixed in, depending on the nature of the disturbance. A large stock of nutrients is stored in newly dead biomass. These organic additions not only carry nutrients, but add carbon compounds that activate the soil microflora.

Aeration resulting from soil handling is also stimulatory to the microflora, as are higher soil temperature and increased soil moisture that usually accompany destruction of the natural vegetation. Soil moisture increases with the loss of transpiration.

Nitrification, the conversion of ammonium nitrogen to nitrate, is a microbial process that may accelerate dramatically. Bormann and Likens (1979) reported up to an eleven-fold increase in nitrification rate. Mature vegetation is thought by many re-searchers to inhibit nitrification (Vitousek et al 1982); the change in rate may result from the removal of this inhibition.

ROOTS, SYMBIONTS, AND MINERAL NUTRITION OF RARE AND ENDANGERED SPECIES

This discussion until now has been in rather general terms. It is difficult to specifically treat the subject of mineral nutrition in rare and endangered species because they are almost never studied in this context. Since rare and endangered species are diverse in taxonomic position, growth form, and habitat preferences, we may assume that among them are examples of all of the variations discussed here. For the present, the best we can do is treat them in the context of native plants in general.

When it comes time to introduce rare and endangered species to new habitats, better knowledge of the specifics may greatly improve our likelihood of success. For each species of interest, we should as a minimum know whether it normally depends on microbial symbionts.

If so, they may have to be introduced into the new habitat along with the plants. If the species in question happens to be a ruderal, we should realize that it may not outlast the effects of site disturbance. Conversely, if our rare species is a stress-tolerator, we must anticipate the same mistreatment that other such species receive from weedy invaders. If the plant in question occupies its native range because of a special tolerance of unfavorable conditions, as may be true with plants of serpentine soils, it may prove futile to introduce that species into more favorable habitats where it must compete with non-tolerant, but otherwise more vigorous species.

The reinoculation with symbionts is in itself an involved and poorly understood subject. Success depends heavily on nature of the inoculum, timing and manner of application, condition of the soil, and such cultural factors as biocide treatment and fertilization (Hayman 1983).

Some successes have been reported with mycorrhizal inoculation (Call and McKell 1984, Hall 1980), and there can be little doubt that inoculation is necessary on most disturbed sites (Mosse et al. 1981). However, mycorrhizal inoculation is not in itself sufficient to assure success. The weedy invaders that cause so much grief in revegetation efforts are commonly nonmycorrhizal, but they are still fast-growing ruderals and in a nutrient-rich soil are probably better competitors than mycorrhizal stress-tolerators. Hall (1978) grew the mycorrhiza-dependent white clover in competition with the less mycorrhiza-dependent perennial ryegrass. The performance of white clover was improved by inoculation, but not sufficiently to dominate perennial ryegrass in competition. In the field, it is clear that the presence of mycorrhizal plant species is not in itself sufficient to eliminate nonmycorrhizal species. Miller (1979) found that nonmycorrhizal species persisted at a revegetated site even when soil inoculum levels equalled those in an adjacent undisturbed community.

In order to fully exploit our knowledge of mineral nutrition strategies, we should attempt to create an environment that favors stress-tolerators rather than ruderals. Fertilization of the desirable species may be ill-advised. While growth rate of the intended species can be somewhat improved by fertilization, growth rate of the undesired volunteers will be sharply increased. I would like to suggest at this point the concept of anti-fertilization. There are various ways to actually remove nutrients from soil. By doing so, we should be able to reduce the growth rate of the undesirable species so much that they are no longer competitive. In effect, we would recreate the conditions in which stress-tolerant, mycorrhizal plants are the only ones that can grow and reproduce.

Among the possible ways to "anti-fertilize" are addition of organic carbon to immobilize nutrients in the microbial biomass and binding of soil nutrients with inorganic chemical reactions.

The effects on soil nutrients of such treatments as wheat straw or sawdust can be anticipated from what is known about microbial immobilization (Alexander 1971, Fenchel and Blackburn 1979). The effect is primarily on nitrogen: bacteria and fungi require additional nitrogen to process the newly available carbon, and draw it from surrounding soil. When the added carbon has been respired by soil microbes, available nitrogen will again be released to the soil.

The availability of several nutrient elements, especially phosphorus, is strongly dependent on soil pH and the concentrations of certain compounds in the soil. It may be possible, by adding agricultural lime, to make phosphorus unavailable to any but mycorrhizal stress-tolerators. There are upper limits to the pH that can be tolerated by both the desired plants and the fungi, so such treatment must be carried out with a foreknowledge of the acceptable range.

There are also inorganic additions that remove phosphorus from the available pool by means that are independent of pH. Bolan et al. (1984) used iron hydroxides to irreversibly bind soil phosphorus; the greater the addition of the hydroxides, the greater was the superiority of mycorrhizal over nonmycorrhizal plants. The reaction depended on dry diffusion of the very insoluble hydroxides.

The discussion in this paper was intended to show those aspects of mineral nutrition that bear on artificial reestablishment of desirable native plants. Reestablishment is clearly no substitute for the preservation of natural populations, but in view of the inevitability of continued habitat destruction in California, we must develop these and related techniques. Successful replanting should be a primary objective in our efforts to protect rare and endangered species, and an understanding of their mineral nutrition is an important component of that objective.

REFERENCES

Alexander, M. 1971. Microbial Ecology. John Wiley and Sons, New York.

Allen, O. N., and E. K. Allen. 1981. The Leguminosae. The University of Wisconsin Press, Madison.

Barley, K. P. 1970 The configuration of the root system in relation to nutrient uptake. Advances in Agronomy 22:159-201.

Baylis, G. T. S. 1975. The magnolioid mycorrhiza and mycotrophy in root systems derived from it. Pp. 374-389 in: Sanders, F. E., B. Mosse, and P. B. Tinker. (eds.) Endomycorrhizas. Academic Press, London.

Bethlenfalvay, G. J., S. Dakessian, and R. S. Pacovsky. 1984. Mycorrhizae in a southern California desert: ecological implications. Can. J. Bot. 62:519-524.

Bolan, N. S., A. D. Robson, N. J. Barrow, and A. G. Aylmore. 1984. Specific activity of phosphorus in mycorrhizal and non-mycorrhizal plants in relation to the availability of phosphorus to plants. Soil Biol. Biochem. 16:299-304

Bormann, F. H., and G. E. Likens. 1979. Pattern and process in a forested ecosystem. Springer-Verlag, New York.

Call, C. A., and C. M. McKell. 1984. Field establishment of fourwing salbush in processed oil shale and disturbed native soil as influenced by vesicular-arbuscular mycorrhizae. Great Basin Naturalist 44:363-371.

Chapin, F. S. III. 1980. The mineral nutrition of wild plants. Ann. Rev. Ecol. System. 11:233-260.

Chapin, F. S. 1983. Patterns of nutrient absorption and use by plants from natural and man-modified environments. Pp. 175-187 in: H. A. Mooney and M. Godron (eds.). Disturbance and Ecosystems. Springer-Verlag, Berlin-Heidelberg.

Cordes, C. 1975. Mycorrhizae in the chaparral of southern California. Master's thesis, Department of Biological Sciences, California State Polytechnic University, Pomona.

De Jager, A. 1979. Localized stimulation of root growth and phosphate uptake in Zea mays L. resulting from restricted phosphate supply. Pp. 391-403 in: J. L. Harley and R. Scott Russell. (eds.). The Soil-Root Interface. Academic Press, London.

Drew, M. C. 1975. Comparison of the effects of a localized supply of phosphate, nitrate, ammonium, and potassium on the growth of the seminal root system, and the shoot, in barley. New Phytol. 75:479-490.

Fenchel, T., and T. H. Blackburn. 1979. Bacteria and Mineral Cycling. Academic Press, London.

Grime, J. P. 1975. Interpretation of small-scale patterns in the distribution of plant species in space and time. Pp. 101-124 in: A. J. H. Freysen and J. W. Woldendorp (eds.). Structure and Functioning of Plant Populations. Elsevier, North-Holland, Amsterdam, New York.

Grime, J. P., and R. Hunt. 1975. Relative growth rate: its range and adaptive significance in a local flora. J. Ecol. 63:393-422.

Hall, I.R. 1978. Effects of endomycorrhizas on the competitive ability of white clover. N. Z. J. Agr. Res. 21:509-515.

Hall, I. R. 1980. Growth of Lotus pedunculatus Cav. in an eroded soil containing soil pellets infested with endomycorrhizal fungi. N. Z. J. Agr. Res. 23:103-105.

Hayman, D.S. 1978. Endomycorrhizae. Pp. 401-442 in: Y.R. Dommergues and S.V. Krupa (eds.). Interactions between non-pathogenic soil microorganisms and plants. Elsevier Scientific Publishing Company, Amsterdam.

Hayman, D.S. 1983. The physiology of vesicular-arbuscular endomycorrhizal symbiosis. Can. J. Bot. 61:944-963

Janos, D.P. 1980. Mycorrhizae influence tropical succession. Biotropica 12 (supplement):56-64

Kleinschmidt, G. D., and J. W. Gerdemann. 1972. Stunting of Citrus seedlings in fumigated nursery soil related to the absence of endomycorrhizae. Phytopathology 62:1447-1453

Kormanik, P. P., R. C. Schultz, and W. C. Bryan. 1982. The influence of vesicular-arbuscular mycorrhizae on the growth and development of eight hardwood tree species. Forest Science 28:531-539.

Koske, R. E., and W. R. Polson. 1984. Are VA mycorrhizae required for sand dune stabilization? Bioscience 34:420-424.

Kumerow, J., and W. Borth. 1986. Mycorrhizal associations in chaparral. Fremontia 14:11-13.

Lyford, W. H. 1975 Rhyzography of non-woody roots of trees in the forest floor. Pp. 179-196 in: The development and function of roots. Edited by J. G. Torrey and D. T. Clarkson. Academic Press, London.

Maser, C., J. M. Trappe, and R. A. Nussbaum. 1978. Fungal-small mammal interrelationships with emphasis on Oregon coniferous forests. Ecology 59(4):799-809.

Menge, J. A., J. LaRue, C. K. Labanauskas, and E. L. V. Johnson. 1980. The effect of two mycorrhizal fungi upon growth and nutrition of avocado seedlings grown with six fertilizer treatments. J. Am. Soc. Hort. Sci. 105:400-404.

Miller, R.M. 1979. Some occurrences of vesicular-arbuscular mycorrhizae in natural and disturbed ecosystems of the Red Desert. Can. J. Bot. 57:619-623

Mooney, H. A., and S. L. Gulmon. 1979. The determinants of plant productivity- natural verses man-modified communities. Pp. 146-158 in: H. A. Mooney and M. Godron (eds.). Disturbance and Ecosystems. Springer-Verlag, Berlin-Heidelberg.

Mosse, B., D. P. Stribley, and F. Le Tacon. 1981. Ecology of mycorrhizae and mycorrhizal fungi. Advances in Microbial Ecology 5:137-210.

Nye, P. H., and P. B. Tinker. 1977. Solute movement in the soil-root system. University of California Press, Berkeley and Los Angeles.

Read, D. J. 1983. The biology of mycorrhiza in the Ericales. Can. J. Bot. 61:985-1004.

Reeves, F. B., D. Wagner, T. Moorman, and J. Kiel. 1979. The role of endomycorrhizae in revegetation practices in the semi-arid west. I. A comparison of incidence of mycorrhizae in severely disturbed vs. natural environments. Am. J. Bot. 66:6-13.

Reynolds, E.R.C. 1975. Tree rootlets and their distribution. In: S.G. Torrey and D.T. Clarkson.(eds.) The development and function of roots. Academic Press.

Rogers, W. S., and G. C. Head. 1969. Factors affecting the distribution and growth of roots of perennial woody species. Pp. 280-295 in: W. J. Whttington (ed.) Root Growth. Plenum Press, New York.

Rose, S. L. 1980. Mycorrhizal associations of some actinomycete nodulated nitrogen-fixing plants. Can. J. Bot. 58:1449-1454.

Rose, S.L. 1981. Tripartite associations in snowbrush (Ceanothus velutinus): effect of vesicular-arbuscular mycorrhizae on growth, nodulation, and nitrogen fixation. Can. J. Bot. 59:-34-39.

Safir, G. R., J. S. Boyer, and J. W. Gerdemann. 1971. Mycorrhizal enhancement of water transport in soybean. Science 172: 581-583.

Safir, G. R., J. S. Boyer, and J. W.Gerdemann. 1972. Nutrient status and mycorrhizal enhancement of water transport in soybean. Plant Physiology 49:700-703.

Scott Russell, R. 1977. Plant Root Systems: Their Function and Interaction with the Soil. McGraw-Hill book Company, London.

St.John, T. V. 1980. Root size, root hairs, and mycorrhizal infection: A re-examination of Baylis's hypothesis with tropical trees. New Phytol. 84:-483-487.

St.John, T. V. 1983. Response of tree roots to decomposing organic matter in two lowland Amazonian rain forests. Can. J. For. Res. 13:346-349.

Tinker, P. B. H. 1978. Effects of vesicular-arbuscular mycorrhizas on plant nutrition and plant growth. Physiol. Veg. 16:743-751.

Tisdall, J. M., and J. M. Oades. 1979. Stabilization of soil aggregates by the root systems of ryegrass. Aust. J. Soil Res. 17:429-441

Trappe, J. M. 1981. Mycorrhizae and productivity of arid and semi-arid rangelands. Pp. 581-599 in: J. T. Manassah and E. J. Brishey (eds.). Advances in food producing systems for arid and semiarid lands. Academic Press, New York.

Vitousek, P. M., J. R. Gosz, C. C. Grier, J. M. Melillo, and W. A. Reiners. 1982. A comparative analysis of potential nitrification and nitrate mobility in forest ecosystems. Ecol. Monogr. 52:155-177.

Revegetation With Rare and Endangered Species: The Role of the Propagator and Grower

J. Michael Evans, Jeffrey W. Bohn [1]

Abstract: This paper examines case history nursery treatment for six endangered plant species. Certain horticultural principles for handling sensitive species can be gleaned from the experiences encountered with these six species. Revegetation with endangered plants poses challenges at three levels.
1. Collection of propagation material (seed, cutting) of sensitive species.
2. Propagation and production techniques are discussed for the species listed below.
3. Phytosanitary precautions in preparation for out-planting on the project site.
Summary: Rare and endangered plant revegetation with nursery grown container plants is a viable option for the preservation of species, when coupled with the preservation and restoration of their natural habitats.

For the purpose of environmental mitigation or for compliance with federal, state, or local laws for preservation, rare and endangered plants grown in containers offer one alternative for species preservation and habitat enhancement. The information provided for each of the species listed below can be used to establish some basic guidelines for the horticultural treatment of rare and endangered species in general. The species listed below include:

a) Four San Clemente Island endemics (Malacothamnus clementinus, Dephinium kinkiense, Lotus dendroideus var. traskiae, and Lotus argophyllus ssp. adsurgens) which are being produced under contract for the U.S. Navy under permit by the U.S. Fish and Wildlife Service. The purpose of this plant propagation is for the recovery of endangered species and enhancement of habitat pursuant to the objectives of the Endangered Species Act of 1973, as amended. The propagation and revegetation efforts are in accordance with the Service's "Recovery Plan for Endangered and Threatened Species of the California Channel Islands."

b) One San Diego County endemic (Monardella linioides ssp. viminea) is being produced under contract for the California Department of Transportation, under a Memorandum of Understanding between that agency and the California Department of Fish and Game. The purpose of this plant propagation is for an environmental mitigation for a road right-of-way.

---

[1] Co-owners, growers, Tree of Life Nursery, 33201 Ortega Highway, P. O. Box 736, San Juan Capistrano, CA 92793.

c) One species (Carpenteria californica) is a Federal candidate species, Category 1 (Smith, 1984). Interestingly, while this species is threatened in its native habitat, it is common in the horticultural trade, having been produced for the ornamental landscape industry for many years.

PLANT LIST

Plant Name	State/Fed Status
Malacothamnus clementinus	CE/FE
Delphinium kinkiense	CE/FE
Lotus dendroides var. traskiae	CE/FE
L. argophyllus ssp. adsurgens	CE/C2
Monardella linoides ssp. viminea	CE/C2
Carpenteria californica	/C1

(See Appendix 1 for explanation of status)

CASE HISTORY NURSERY TREATMENT FOR THE SPECIES

Malacothamnus clementinus (Munz & Johnst.) Kearney

San Clemente Island Bush-Mallow is a highly ornamental plant producing many, large lavender flowers over a long season. Its lush foliage and aggressive habit make it quite conspicuous when it is encountered in its natural state. The planting at the San Clemente Island Native Plant Nursery by Mitch Beauchamp, has grown very nicely and provided many stem and root cuttings for propagation.

Malacothamnus clementinus is one of the endemic species on San Clemente Island. This island has more endemics, 14, than any other member of the southern California island group. (Wallace, 1985).

As a subject for revegetation, its vigorous habit and fast growth make it ideal for out-planting in its native area. This plant also shows great potential as a landscape ornamental, especially for erosion control in coastal environments. Only plants produced by nursery propagation from cultivated stock plants, should be used for this purpose, in order to preserve the wild plants in their natural state.

Raven reported that this taxa grows in a single locality at Lemon Tank. He notes the significance of this site, in that it is near the edge of one of the few small areas of marine sediments on the island (Raven, 1963). Mills reports 5 additional sites on the southern portion of the island's west shore, in, or at mouths of canyons. (Mills, 1985). The large clumps on the island may prove to be single clone plants, due to vegetative propagation by underground stems or root shoots. This may explain the lack of viable seed set on solitary populations.

Collection

May 1985 - Seed (3, presumably sterile) Lemon Tank. Secured from M. Beauchamp.
20 May 1985 - Root Cuttings - Lemon Tank.
13 September 1985 - Seed -Horse Beach Canyon mouth.
1 March 1986 - Root cuttings, stem cuttings - Horse Beach Canyon mouth.
3 March 1986 - Root cuttings, stem cuttings - San Clemente Island Nursery planting (Lemon Tank progeny).
20 August 1986 - Root cuttings, stem cuttings - Horse Beach Canyon site.

It has been suggested that cross-pollination in spring is needed to get better seed set and maintain genetic diversity. Cross-pollination of China Canyon and Lemon Tank material should be attempted (Beauchamp, 1983). The only viable seed has come from the Horse Beach Canyon site. Seed set is not always good, due to environmental or physical conditions, not yet fully understood. The Horse Beach site was located in 1985, by Jim Mills (Mills,1985), and our first seed collection at this site was on September 19, 1985. The seed appeared to have been on the stems for at least one month. No seed was encountered upon our return eleven months later, in August of 1986. Cutting material could be collected almost year-round, although cuttings obtained in August have provided the best results.

Propagation

Seed - Three attempts: one, collected at Lemon Tank, seed was determined sterile; two others were from Horse Beach Canyon. Of the two sowings, the one closest to the collection date provided the best germination rate (35%). From both sowings, a total of 34 plants were brought to a mature out-planting stage. Soil mix is a soil-less type propagation media. Seed was sown in a standard "California Flat" and no pre-treatment of seed was used.

Cuttings - Tip and stem: three attempts from three locations, Horse Beach Canyon, Lemon Tank and SCI Nursery. The collection dates were November, 1985; March, 1986 and August, 1986, and all cuttings were "stuck" within 24 hours of being cut. Again, standard "soil-less" cutting media was used and rooting hormone 800-1000 ppm IBA (indolebutyric acid) was applied prior to being placed in the flat. Cuttings were placed under intermittent mist until rooted. Once they were rooted, they were moved to outdoor shade, to "harden-off" before being transplanted. Good rooting percentages were experienced at all three dates. One hundred percent rooting was experienced with August, 1986 cuttings, and the lowest was seventy-five percent.

Cuttings - Root: Two attempts were made at root cuttings from two sites, the Horse Beach Canyon and the Nursery. A total of 36 plants were brought up to out-planting stage. Percent of take ranged from 50% to 85%. Root cuttings ranged from pencil size diameter and 4" in length to a small "clump" of many smaller roots, six inches across. The larger clumps of small roots were 95% successful. Root cuttings were placed directly into 4" pots for small cuttings and #1 gallon pots for the larger. No treatments were made on the roots. The soil was 50% potting mix, 50% cutting mix, pasteurized. These root cuttings were ready for shifting or out-planting in three months.

Phytosanitary Precautions

Seed - Flats are given a preventative fungicidal treatment at two week intervals, with Benlate^{TM}, Chipco 26010^{TM} and Zyban^{TM} used on a rotation basis. Subdue^{TM}, Terraclor^{TM}, and Banrot^{TM}, (See Appendix 2) are also used on a once every other month, rotating basis, during the propagation period.

Cuttings - Flats are treated with the fungicides, Benlate^{TM}/Captan^{TM} or Benlate^{TM}/Dithane-m-45^{TM}, every two to three weeks, during the propagation period.

Seed/cuttings - Once seedlings and cuttings have been transplanted, fungicide treatment is reduced to a treatment of Subdue™, Aliette™ or Banol™, once every three months, as a preventative measure.

Container plants - Caterpillar damage was noted in the nursery in San Juan Capistrano in April-May. Treatment and complete eradication was achieved with Bacillus thuringiensis, a biological insecticide affecting only the larvae of Lepidoptera.

A practical precaution in the nursery is to distinguish between the different clonal populations for eventual consideration when out-planting. We have found that since plant tags are easily lost, or become faded, plants of distinct progeny should be produced in different color containers (i.e., green and black) and documented accordingly.

Summary

Malocathamnus clementinus presents no real problem for the nurseryman. It can be grown from both seed and cutting. More seed is needed to carry on further work on germination and seed longevity. Careful planning and timing is needed when a proposed out-planting date is targeted (see propagation). The use of cuttings vs. seed could facilitate a shorter lead time for the propagator to meet the out-planting "window". Less genetic diversity can be achieved with cuttings, however, and that may be a problem. It is an excellent candidate for early establishment on revegetation projects due to its rugged habit and quick response following environmental change, i.e., drought, browsing, fire and landslide.

Delphinium kinkiense Munz

San Clemente Island Larkspur is a lovely, pure white, spring-flowering perennial, endemic to the island. In bloom, it is quite conspicuous, even when viewed from a distance in its grassland habitat. The species is named after "Kinki", a Gabrielino Indian name for the island (Munz, 1969). Mills reports 20 populations of Delphinium kinkiense, all but 4 of which are on the high bluffs of the steep eastern escarpment (Mills, 1985).

Collection

15 May 1985 - Seed (6) secured from R. M. Beauchamp.

2 March 1986 - Field survey. Flowering plants were noted at Jack, near the type locality. We noted a principal pollinator to be a large, black and white solitary bee.

11 April 1986 - Seed (14) Secured from R. M. Beauchamp.

2 May 1986 - Seed (50) Dried seed capsules on dessicated (top-growth) plants were encountered and collected. This was a timely collection as the seed was very difficult to find in the grassland community and seed predation was heavy. We found holes chewed through the bottom portion of the upright seed capsules which allowed the forager access to the seeds. To date, we have been unable to determine if this little seed eater is an insect or a mouse. Only 50 seeds were collected because of stipulations in the USFWS permit.

Propagation

We treated the first few seeds we had much like the Delphinium cardinale we grow. Seed was sown within 5-7 days of collection. Standard soil-less seed media was used and seed was covered with approximately 1/32-1/16" of sand. No seed pre-treatment was used. No germination was observed. Sowing times were May 1985 and April 1986. We are more optimistic about a fall 1986 sowing season, using the 50 seeds collected on 2 May 1986, which have been in cool, dry storage. Rain has a wonderful effect on germination of seeds of this genus.

Phytosanitary Precautions

Within eight days of planting, treatments with the fungicides Benlate™, Aliette™, Banrot™, and Banol™ were started and used in rotation every other month. These treatments continued until it was determined that no germination occurred. Delphinium kinkiense will be one of the most difficult species for container culture and out-planting. We feel it is imperative that this plant be handled on a seasonal basis due to its dry-season dormancy and fleshy root. The plants will be subject to "damping-off" and other related, soil-born fungi during the dormant period, unless they are grown in a biodegradable container that allows the free exchange of air in the root zone, and judiciously watered.

Summary

We expect this species to be slow in the nursery establishment period. The most successful season for out-planting will probably be early spring when the plants are actively growing. Ideally, the age of the container out-plants will be twelve to sixteen months.

Lotus dendroideus var. traskiae=
  L. scoparius (Nutt in T.G.) var. dendroideus (Greene) Ottley
  L. scoparius (Nutt in T.G.) ssp. taskiae (Eastw. ex Noddin in Abrams) Raven.

San Clemente Island Broom, a San Clemente Island endemic, is distinguished from its close relatives on the other Channel Islands by its longer (3-5 cm.) seed pod containing more (4-8) seeds. (Munz & Keck, 1959).

Three populations of this woody perennial are known on the northeast portion of the island.

Collection

May 1985 - seed obtained from R. M. Beauchamp.

28 Feb. 1986 - Field Survey. Plants in stage of late flowering, early fruit set.

2 May 1986 - Seed from Wilson Cove. 300 seeds collected from among several plants with heavy fruit set. Since the permit limits seed collection to 300, we collected a few fruit from several plants, thereby obtaining genetic diversity and not depleting any one plant's seed crop. The fruit lot was infested with weevils. Upon return to the mainland nursery, we dusted the batch with the insecticide, Diazinon^{TM}. The beetles were eradicated and the seed was cleaned from the fruit before setting the seed into cool, dry storage in a paper bag.

Propagation

Beauchamp reports a germination rate of 30% with erratic growth. He indicates that scarification of seeds with fine sandpaper enhances the germination rate. He also noted root nodules in nursery-grown container stock and presumed that the bacterial innoculant must be present in the mainland soils (Beauchamp, 1983). We made three attempts in May 1985, the seed was 5-13 days old in two sowings and 10 years on the third. Seed was sown in sand and no seed treatment was used on one lot, a 24 hour water soak was used on the others. Germination occurred within three weeks of sowing on all lots. The 10 year old seed germinated at the same rate as the fresh seed, 65% germination. The seedlings were large enough to transplant into individual containers in 8 weeks. There should be no problem in producing several plants from the seed collected on 2 May 1986. We are waiting until the fall of 1986 propagation season.

Phytosanitary Precautions

At time of sowing: The fungicides, Benlate^{TM} and Chipco 26019^{TM} were used alternately on a bi-weekly application. Once transplanted from seed flats into containers, they received a fungicide treatment of Subdue^{TM} once every three months, as a routine preventative to water mold fungal pathogens. As with any container grown native, periodic light feedings with a balanced plant food are in order.

Summary

Only three propagation attempts were made. More seed and time could reveal better techniques from which to grow this plant. No real difficulties were encountered. During the March 1985 field trip, heavy insect predation, to the point of defoliation on some plants was noted. Our experience has shown that Lotus (and several other leguminous plants) are heavily grazed by rabbits unless they are protected in the nursery. While an old, woody shrub in the wild may be able to tolerate this kind of attack, many young nursery seedlings can be destroyed in one night by just one rabbit. The handling and protecting of rare plants in a nursery setting is a great responsibility for the propagator.

Lotus argophyllus (Gray) ssp. adsurgens Raven

San Clemente Island Silver Lotus is an extremely rare San Clemente Island endemic occurring in three isolated populations at the extreme south end of the island. Raven (1963) calls it "a beautiful silvery, suffructescent plant with densely crowded ascending leaves." Philbrick (1978) calls it "strikingly beautiful." It occurs on west-facing slopes of lava rock, with Bergocactus emoryi, Opuntia littoralis, O. prolifera, Selaginella sp., Perytile emoryi, Mirabilis laevis, Lupinus spp. and Stipa sp., with the cacti forming the highest percent of cover.

Collection

11 October 1984 - Field survey - No plants were found during a search in the Pyramid Cover area.

13 September 1985 - Seed - Hills south of Guds, R. M. Beauchamp found three plants and identified them for us. We collected 7 seeds from the rocky soil beneath the plant.

2 March 1986 - Seeds and cuttings - At Guds, 51 + plants were encountered, 16 of which were tagged and numbered in the field. The plants were flowering beautifully; we photographed and documented this presumably new population.

We planned a new trip for 8 weeks later, estimating ripe seed at that time. 42 tip cuttings were taken from 9 of the tagged plants and refrigerated in plastic bags until the time of stricking in the nursery.

3 May 1986 - Seed - Terrace below Guds (elev. 520'). 250 partially ripe seeds were collected. We plan another trip for 6 weeks later, anticipating fully ripe seed at that time.

12 June 1986 - Guds. The timing for this seed collection was perfect, but practically all of the fruit had been foraged by Peromyscus maniculatus clementus, San Clemente Island Deer mouse. The mouse cuts the entire stem with all of the fruit (and new flowers) at varying degrees of ripeness. He then carries the stem to a safe place such as the shelter of a prickly-pear cactus. There, he eats the seed in the "hard green pea" stage and discards the stem, leaves, fruit husks and flowers of the branch tips. We located 8 of our original 16 plants tagged in March. All 8 had been grazed. The duff and discarded stems could usually be found about 5-10' from the Lotus plant, in a sheltered spot. This was most discouraging for the plant propagator because we knew that the season was right for seed collection. So did the mouse. Approximately 100 slightly immature seeds were collected from one plant, 4 mature seeds were collected from a second. A total of 10 cuttings (5 each) were collected from two other plants. Deer mouse scats were collected in the interest of science.

Propagation

Seed - Only 7 seeds have been sown to date. The medium was our standard soil-less type. Seed was fresh and no pre-treatment was used. Two seeds germinated in three weeks.

Cuttings - Two attempts were made, 42 cuttings in March 1986 and 10 in June 1986. Our usual soil-less rooting medium was used and two strengths of rooting hormone were used. The best take was 10% of the latter sticking. We anticipate a fall 1986 sowing of the seed collected in June. We intend to scarify 2 lots with light sandpaper and a warm water soak for experimental purposes.

Phytosanitary Precautions

Cutting flats - Fungicidal treatments of Benlate^{TM}, Chipco 26019^{TM}, were used alternating, bi-weekly and Subdue^{TM}, once every other month, as a preventative for water mold fungal pathogens. Our single surviving plant is still in the cuttings flat at this time and it receives a solution of water soluble fertilizer once every three weeks.

Summary

Lotus argophyllus ssp. adsurgens will require further study for nursery propagation from seed and cutting. Predation of seed by the native deer mouse, and the limited number of cuttings available on the small population of plants will provide an increased challenge to the propagator. The propagator must use a great deal of discretion to preserve the natural pool of available seed and vegetative material when collecting for nursery production. Perhaps a few plants could be caged in the late winter/early spring so that viable seed could mature and be collected in spite of the deer mouse. Container plants, 12-16 months old should transplant into a native site quite readily, as Lotus is a very rugged genus.

Monardella linoides Gray ssp. viminea (Greene) Abrams

San Diego Willowy Mint is an aromatic herbaceous perennial in the mint family, endemic to southwest San Diego County. Its attractive lavender flower heads are borne profusely above the mass of small, light green leaves. The plant blooms virtually the year round, with its principle season being the summer months. In San Diego County it occurs infrequently in coastal canyons below 200 m in such places as Poway; Mira Mesa; Murphy Canyon and Sycamore Canyon (Beauchamp, 1986). Despite its very restricted natural range, this species is quite versatile in cultivation, showing no extraordinary requirements in regards to soil type or watering. The plant is being propagated and produced as part of a mitigation for a road right-of-way in San Diego County. A Memorandum of Understanding between the California Department of Transportation and the California Department of Fish and Game outlines measures to protect this species. The goal of this mitigation is not limited to mere replacement of exact numbers of impacted individual plants, but to augment the population by 3000% (Hall-Cather, 1984).

Collection

September 1981 - Seed - Murphy Canyon, San Diego. 2000 Viable seeds. (Cal Trans personnel).

18 August 1983 - Seed - Murphy Canyon. 200 dried inflorescences yields 2360 seeds, 1952 of which are dark and hard, 408 of which were light straw colored and not viable (Moore)(Cal Trans personnel).

31 August 1983 - Salvage - Murphy Canyon. 21 live plants in containers (Cal Trans personnel)

8 May 1985 - Salvage - Murphy Canyon 55 live plants in containers.

April 1985 - March 1986 - Cuttings -Taken from original seedlings and "second generation" cutting-grown plants. Original seedlings were grown from wild collected seed.

Propagation

22 September 1983 - Seed - 450 dark seeds were tested for viability. Results showed 40% germination after six weeks. (Cal Trans personnel)

24 October 1983 - Seed - 500 dark seeds were sown and showed a 40% germination after one week. (Cal Trans personnel).

26 October 1983 - Seed - 500 + dark seeds (seed collected 1981). First seedlings appeared in five days on this two year old seed lot (Cal Trans personnel). Note: The sowings listed above yielded 500 healthy "rose pot" liners after transplanting loss and seedling mortality were accounted for. The germination rate obtained and reported by Mark Moore of Cal Trans was 40% (Moore, 1983).

April 1985 - March 1986 - Cuttings - Over this time, a total of 9 crops were stuck with cuttings being taken over the range of the 500+ plants in nursery containers. We felt that propagation by cuttings would eliminate any possibility of hybridization with other Monardella species in the area. Both tip and stem cuttings were used. Rooting hormone rates ranged from 800 ppm to 1000 ppm IBA (indolebutyric acid). A soil-less cutting medium was used in standard "California" propagation flats. The flats were then placed under intermittent mist. Rooting usually occurred in 3 to 4 weeks and 85 to 90% rooting was normal.

Phytosanitary Precaution

The fungicide, Benlate™ was applied once monthly until rooted. Transplanted plants received the fungicide Subdue™, once every three months. For seed flats, Benlate™, Chipco 26019™, and Banrot™ were used alternately every three weeks as a preventative against fungal attacks.

Summary

Nursery treatment for this species illustrates the technique of "artificial propagation" that is, using nursery produced plants as a propagation source to produce more plants. When this technique is employed with rare and endangered species, care must be taken to propagate from as varied a gene pool as possible. Seed and cuttings should be obtained from several mother plants in the wild and subsequently propagation from cultivated plants should include material from several individuals. Where any possibility of hybridization exists, seed from plants grown in cultivation should be avoided entirely. Propagation and production of this species was extremely successful.

For a flowering perennial, Monardella linoides ssp. viminea would make a fine garden subject with its attractive flowers, pleasant aroma and tidy habit. If it is introduced into the trade, only artificially produced plants should be used for propagation, thereby making no impact on wild populations, and yet increasing the numbers of plants in the ground.

Carpenteria californica Torr.

Bush Anemone, an erect evergreen flowering shrub, is one of California's rarest endemics. It occurs in a few restricted areas in Fresno County, between the San Joaquin River and the Big Creek tributary of the Kings River. Its large, fragrant white flowers which appear in clusters during the summer, make it one of the finest ornamental shrubs in the California landscape. As early as the late 1800's, Carpenteria was in the American horticultural trade (Bailey, 1900). A sport selection, Carpenteria californica "Ladhams" is reported to have flowers 3 1/4" in diameter (Lenz & Dourley, 1981). A variety with clusters of small flowers, which was introduced from Tilden Park in Berkeley, is called "Elizabeth" (Dourley, 1986). While this plant receives Category 1 status (see Appendix) in the federal register, and is offered some protection in its wild state, it is quite popular in the horticultural trade and is available for planting in garden situations, both at home and abroad. It is reported as a garden subject in Edinburg, Kew and a number of private gardens in Britain and Europe, and has been in European horticulture for perhaps 150 years or more (Dourley, 1986).

Collection

Seed for Carpenteria californica can be purchased from commercial seed sources; normally collected from plants in cultivation. Seed is produced abundantly on the wild plants, yet our observations and searches have failed to produce a single seedling growing anywhere near the parent plant. Our major seed source is from collection made in September, 1983 from plants in Fresno County. A trace of seed should produce many plants because this seed is very small. With 15,010,000 to 21,460,000 seeds per pound (Schopmeyer 1974), one can see that a little seed can go a long way.

Cuttings have been taken from plants in cultivated landscapes, and stock plants growing in the ground and in nursery container plants.

Propagation

Typically, propagation is by seed sown in spring, cuttings in a greenhouse, or from suckers which are produced freely (Bailey, 1500; Lenz & Dourley, 1981; McMinn, 1939). Everett (1957), reports 12 seed lots and 1 cutting attempt at Rancho Santa Ana Botanic Garden between 1928 and 1941. The highest degree of success was obtained when seed was sown directly on sphagmum or peat moss.

Seed - Over the past 6 years we have made over 33 attempts. Germination is usually within 14 days, full germination in 30 days is at 80-85%.

Cuttings - Numerous attempts have been made in cutting propagation, using both tip and stem cuttings, 4-7" long. Rooting hormone IBA was used at rates from 500 ppm to 2000 ppm, the cuttings were placed in the greenhouse using intermittent mist. Rooting started in 30-45 days. Flats were fully rooted in 65-75 days then moved outdoors to 50% shade to harden-off. Best results, (50% success) were achieved when the cuttings were taken in the spring and 1000 ppm IBA was used.

Phytosanitary Precautions

Cleanliness, the most important part of prevention, can not be stressed enough in seedlings of Carpenteria californica. To bring a fully germinated flat of seedlings to maturity is nothing less than miraculous. Extreme care in watering must be exercised at all times. The flow rate at which water is applied is critical because large drops tend to push the tiny seedlings into the flat causing damage. All materials, flats and seed mix should be new or sterilized. Fungicides to control damp-off are also necessary, the seed should either be dusted prior to planting or the flat should be drenched once it has been sown. The fungicides PCNB, Benlate^{TM}, Chipco 26019^{TM}, and Subdue^{TM}, are all used on a bi-weekly rotation. Water and soil-borne fungal pathogens are the source of most problems encountered in the propagation from seed. Water should be as pure as possible and free of algae or fungi that could induce pathogenic conditions. Carpenteria is reported to be resistant to oak root fungus (Lenz & Dourley, 1981). Attacks by aphids disfigure the leaves and plants and make eradication by spraying difficult, due to the revolute nature of the leaves.

Summary

While seeds are abundant, they yield fewer plants due to a high mortality in the juvenile stage. Plants produced from cuttings are easier to handle and percentages are acceptable. To facilitate year-round propagation, well maintained stock beds will be of great value to the propagator. Carpinteria californica is an example of a species which, due to its restricted range, is endangered; however, it is a popular garden plant due to propagation in the commercial nursery trade. While nursery and garden cultivation offer some security for the preservation of species, they are by no means to be considered as substitutes for the preservation of habitat. Though a plant may exist worldwide in cultivation, it may still be endangered in the wild state. The genetic pool and the ecological importance of wild plants cannot be replaced by the same species grown in the landscape.

CONCLUSIONS

Collection

Collection of propagation material (seed, cutting) of sensitive species is critical in order to insure for local progeny and genetic diversity, while preserving the integrity of the propagule source by not depleting the native supply of seed or vegetative growth. This involves timely field trips, accurate record keeping, and selective acquisition of seed and cuttings from the mother plants.

Propagation

Propagation and production techniques for endangered species, place emphasis on seasonality, record keeping, transplant schedules, potting media, and container style. Many methods (including seed storage, crop staggering, container plant maintenance, and "second generation" propagation from the nursery grown plants) are considered as techniques to insure timely availability when several species are needed for the same project.

The most difficult stage in the production process, is working out how each plant may be reproduced with speed and efficiency. The insights gained in field collection have proven to be beneficial in resolving these problems, as well as determining what conditions might be duplicated in the nursery to establish stock beds from which to continue propagation and study. Further propagation from these beds, or from plants in containers will allow year-round propagation trials, to determine the best method of propagation to meet the desired results. By observing the plants in a cultivated setting, the grower can learn how susceptible the plants are to disease and insect damage and determine the proper handling methods in the nursery as well as on the out-planting site.

Phytosanitary Precautions

Phytosanitary precautions in preparation for out-planting on the project site include insect pest and disease prevention and control, weed control in the containers, natural plant vigor and non-dependence on residual influence of agricultural chemicals. It should be noted that the high percentages of success in seed and cutting propagation of dry-land plants can be attributed to modern agricultural "tools" including equipment and chemicals. Pathogenetic fungi (damp-off, water molds, etc.) which plagued native plant propagators in earlier years, can be prevented or controlled, to a large degree, with the use of fungicides. The propagator/grower of endangered species is presented the challenge of raising healthy plants and preparing them for reintroduction to the native site; "weaned" of their nursery treatment, and capable of unimpaired establishment in their "new" home. This is done by maintaining healthy standards in nursery production and reducing the frequency of chemical treatment on the plants as they grow older.

Relating to nursery plant vigor and success in out-planting, the matter of mycorrhizal inoculations should be considered. Controlled inoculation, and specialized growing methods that provide the proper environment for natural, random infection, are two areas in which we are now experimenting. We have chosen not to report on mycorrhizal fungi in container plant culture in this paper as the field is still experimental to us.

The use of steam-pasteurized soil eliminates the danger of weed infestation and reduces the possibility of pathogens. Sanitary procedures are crucial in the production of most dry-environment species.

Introduction of non-native insects, weeds or plant pathogens into the native area would be contrary to the goals of revegetation.

Horticultural Ethics

The horticulturalist dealing with rare and endangered species, grown from wild-collected propagation materials or "second generation" stock, assumes a great responsibility. Even the rather mundane chore of keeping accurate records becomes critical when handling plants from different sites or varied genetic sources. Nursery care and preparation for re-introduction to the native site has been discussed in this paper, and considered as a viable alternative for species preservation and habitat restoration.

While the programs for the management and preservation of rare and endangered plants may include nursery propagation, it should be noted that the mere preservation of the species is not the main issue. Artificial propagation and garden cultivation of sensitive species could never replace their existence in the wild state, nor justify the total destruction of their natural habitats.

The Franklin Tree, (Franklinia alatamaha Marsh.), a North American species, serves to remind us of the loss of a beautiful flowering tree, extinct in the wild, and today known only in cultivation.

Let us hope that the rare plants in California will be preserved in the wild, and when necessary, their populations enhanced by carefully planned revegetation programs.

ACKNOWLEDGEMENTS

The authors would like to express their appreciation to the agencies for which the endangered species are being produced, and the individuals mentioned below. Our thanks to the U.S. Navy, Office of the Staff Civil Engineer, Natural Resources, North Island, (San Clemente Island Plants), and John Rieger, Biologist, California Department of Transportation, District 11, (San Diego Willowy Mint) for their assistance. Mitchel Beauchamp has been an invaluable source of information on southern California and San Clemente Island botany. Lisa Iwata patiently entered this manuscript into the word processor, for which we are truly grateful.

REFERENCES

Bailey, L.H. Encyclopedia of American Horticulture. New York: MacMillan Co.;1900 Vol I. 509p

Beauchamp, R.M. Attempted Propagation of San Clemente Island Plants. 1983, Unpublished draft supplied by Pacific Southwest Biological Services and the author.

Beauchamp, R.M. A Flora of San Diego County, California. National City, CA: Sweetwater River Press; 1986. 241p

Dourley, J. Director of Horticulture, Rancho Santa Ana Botanic Garden, Claremont, CA (telephone conversation with J. Michael Evans) 28 October 1986.

Everett, P. C. A Summary of the Culture of California Plants at the Rancho Santa Ana Botanic Garden 1927-1950. Claremont, CA: Rancho Santa Ana Botanic Garden; 1957. 223p.

Hall-Cather, L. The transplantation of sensitive plants as mitigation for environmental impacts in San Diego County. 1984. Unpublished draft supplied by author.

Lenz, L.W.; Dourley, J. California Native Trees and Shrubs. Claremont, CA: Rancho Santa Ana Botanic Garden; 1981. 231p.

McMinn, H. E. An Illustrated Manual of California Shrubs. San Francisco: J.W. Stacey, Inc. 1939. Berkeley: University of California 663p.

Mills, J. (Maps locating sensitive plant species on San Clemente Island) 1985 located at Naval Air Station, North Island, San Diego, CA.

Moore, M. Progress and activity report regarding salvage and propagation of Monardella linoides viminea pursuant to a Memorandum of Understanding, 1983. 5p. Located at: California Department of Transportation, Environmental Resources, San Diego, CA.

Munz, P.A., California Miscellany - VII. Delphinium kinkiense Munz, sp. nov. Aliso 7 (1): 69-70; 1969 April.

Munz, P.A.; Keck, D.D. A California Flora and Supplement. Berkeley, CA: University of California Press; 1959. 1681; 224p.

Philbrick, R. Distribution and evolution of endemic plants of the California islands; proceedings of a multidisciplinary symposium; 1978 February 27-March 1; Santa Barbara, CA: Santa Barbara Museum of Natural History; 1980; 173-187p.

Raven, P. H. A Flora of San Clemente Island. Aliso 5 (3): 289-347; 1963 April.

Raven, P.H. The Floristics of the California Islands. In: Proceedings of the symposium on the biology of the California islands; 1965 October 29-30; Santa Barbara, CA: Santa Barbara Botanic Garden; 1967; 57-67

Schopmeyer, C.S., tech. coord. Seeds of woody plants in the United States. Agric. Handbook 450. Washington, D.C.: U.S. Department of Agriculture; 1974. 883p.

Smith, J.P. Editor; York, R. Data Entry & Management. Inventory of Rare and Endangered Vascular Plants in California. 3rd edition. Berkeley, CA: California Native Plant Society; 1984. 174p.

Wallace, G. D. Vascular Plants of the Channel Islands of Southern California and Guadalupe Island, Baja, California, Mexico. Contribution in Science No. 365. Los Angeles, CA: Natural History Museum of Los Angeles County; 1985. 136p.

APPENDIX

1. Designations of status for plants listed:

    CE = State listed, endangered.
    FE = Federally listed, endangered.
    C1 = Federal, enough data on file to support the federal listing
    C2 = Federal, Threat and/or distribution data are insufficient to support federal listing.

2. Trade names (noted,^{TM}), for agricultural chemicals mentioned in this paper imply no endorsement or recommendation whatsoever on the part of the authors.

Germination and Seedling Establishment of the Ione Buckwheat

Rodney G. Myatt [1]

Abstract: Seed germination and seedling growth of *Eriogonum apricum* were measured under controlled environmental conditions and related to the restricted distribution of the species. Optimum germination correlates with conditions in the field, although the range of conditions for successful germination is broader. Reduced root growth of seedlings under low light intensity, moist soil, and competition, as is found under shrubs nearby, most likely restricts the buckwheat to open habitats among the chaparral.

The Ione buckwheat (*Eriogonum apricum* Howell) is a narrowly restricted endemic occurring in the Sierra Nevada foothills near Ione, California. It is one of several endemics of the Ione Formation (Gankin and Major 1964), an outcrop of highly acidic, laterized soils extending from near Oroville in the north to near Friant in the south (Allen 1929). Small isolated populations of the buckwheat occur in openings among the Ione manzanita (*Arctostaphylos myrtifolia* Parry) at a few scattered sites. Environmental factors involved in seed germination and seedling establishment were investigated and related to the species' restricted distribution.

HABITAT

Eriogonum apricum was first discovered about 5 miles south of Ione by J.T. Howell in 1954 (Howell 1955), at a site referred to here as "Apricum Hill." This site was purchased by The Nature Conservancy and later by the California Department of Fish and Game. Subsequent to 1954, a few other populations of the typical form (var. *apricum*) were found, the largest just north of Highway 88. Populations of a prostrate variety (var. *prostratum*)(Myatt 1970) were later discovered north of Ione, first near Irish Hill Road and later near Carbondale Road.

The Sierra Nevada foothills are characterized by a Mediterranean-type climate, with hot, dry summers and mild winters. The Ione region, being opposite the Carquinez Straits, is under slightly more maritime influence, and thus has less continentality, than similar habitats to the north and south (Major 1967). The soils of the Ione Formation are predominantly clay to clay loam, dominated by kaolinite, low in nutrients, and acidic (Myatt 1968).

The vegetation is chaparral, in most places dominated by the Ione manzanita, with gray-leaf manzanita (*A. viscida*) and shrubby live oak (*Quercus wislizenii* var. *frutescens*) more abundant in draws and sites with better soils. The Ione buckwheat occurs only among the Ione manzanita. At the type locality (Apricum Hill), the majority of the population occurs in a single, large opening devoid of other vegetation except for some moss plants at the bases of large buckwheats.

HABIT AND PHENOLOGY

Vegetative Growth

Eriogonum apricum is an herbaceous perennial with small, ovate, basal leaves, a short, branching woody caudex, and multiple branching flowering stems. It is typical of many California foothill herbaceous species which fruit during late summer and fall, germinate seeds during the mild winter, and do most of their growing during the spring when warm temperatures and moisture availability coincide. The production of leaves continues throughout the spring and then ceases as the flowering stems develop. Most of the growth of the early seedling stage is root growth, which must be sufficient to ensure survival through the summer drought. Some seedlings produce flowering stems the first year, others take until the second.

Dispersal

The achene (with seed enclosed) is dispersed from the plant, along with the dried calyx, by simply falling to the ground. The dried calyx makes the unit floatable, thus seeds are dispersed somewhat by surface run-off. Ants also gather achenes, and may function in some dispersal.

---

[1]Associate Professor of Biology, San Jose State University, San Jose, CA

Flowering

The typical (erect) variety has an extended flowering period, beginning in early summer and continuing into November (fig. 1). Seeds mature from late summer throughout the fall. At any time during the late summer, individual plants may have unopened buds, mature flowers, and mature fruits. The prostrate variety differs significantly in flowering and fruiting sooner, and over a shorter time. Interestingly, the two major populations of the erect variety also differ somewhat in flowering times, with the more southern population (Apricum Hill) starting and peaking later. There were no differences noted between the two populations of the prostrate variety.

Seedling Mortality

Seedlings are evident in the field by February. Percent survivorship of seedlings was determined by staking out 100 seedlings in the field with toothpicks in February and noting the condition of each throughout the season. They were divided into two groups, those under the canopy of a larger buckwheat plant and those well away from any large plant. Approximately 10 percent survived the first season, with no apparent differences between the two groups (fig. 2).

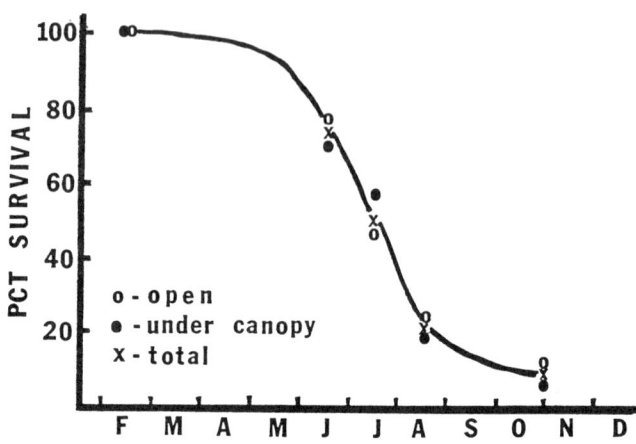

Figure 2-- First year survival of E. apricum seedlings at Apricum Hill.

GERMINATION

Germination requirements of Eriogonum apricum, as determined by tests in the lab, correlate with those conditions that occur in the field. Seeds were mass collected from each population, stored air dry at room temperatures, and germinated on wet filter paper in petri dishes. There were no differences between varieties apricum and prostratum, so most of the following results were obtained with seeds of the former.

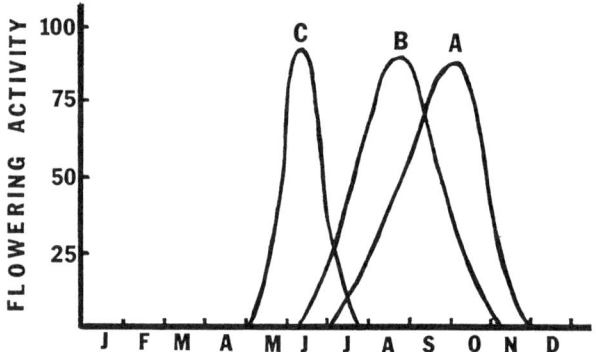

Figure 1-- Comparative flowering activity of three Eriogonum apricum populations. Flowering activity is based on estimated percent of plants with open flowers.
    A - Apricum Hill site (var. apricum)
    B - Hwy.   site (var. apricum)
    C - Irish Hill Road site (var. prostratum)

Temperature

The optimum germination temperature, considering percentage and rate (speed) of germination, is about 45°F (7°C)(fig. 3), which corresponds to the mean December and January temperatures at Ione. Given enough time, however, high percentages are reached at other temperatures except those above 65°F. Nearly 90 percent germination is reached after 60 days at 40°F. Pretreatment at 40°F for several days increases the rate at the higher temperatures (fig. 3B).

pH

Germination in response to pH was determined by applying buffered solutions to seeds in petri dishes. Contrary to the pH of the soil, seed germination was over a broad range, but with a sharp drop-off at the higher and lower ends of the scale (fig. 4).

SEEDLING ESTABLISHMENT AND GROWTH

After germination, the most critical period in a plant's life is the establishment and survival of the seedling stage, when many of the selective forces effect the genetic outcome of the population (Stebbins 1971, Solbrig 1980). *Eriogonum apricum* seedlings are exposed to a summer of virtually unavailable water and high temperatures. The most important task facing the seedling is to develop a sufficient root system as soon as possible. This means relatively fast and deep growth during the late winter and spring. Root length and degree of root branching are important criteria for potential survivability of the seedlings.

Water

Tests were conducted in which varying amounts of water were made available to seedlings to determine the effects on root growth. In one case, seedlings were grown in a sloping container (moisture gradient box) which had a continuous water table near the bottom and varying moisture levels above the water table, depending on the depth of the soil (fig. 5). The soil used was a sandy loam, made from mixing equal amounts of sand to standard greenhouse mix. Root systems did not grow well in saturated or constantly moist soil near the bottom, and the length of the roots and health of the plants correlated with the depth to the saturated soil. Seedlings planted above a certain point on the gradient died before the roots could reach sufficient moisture.

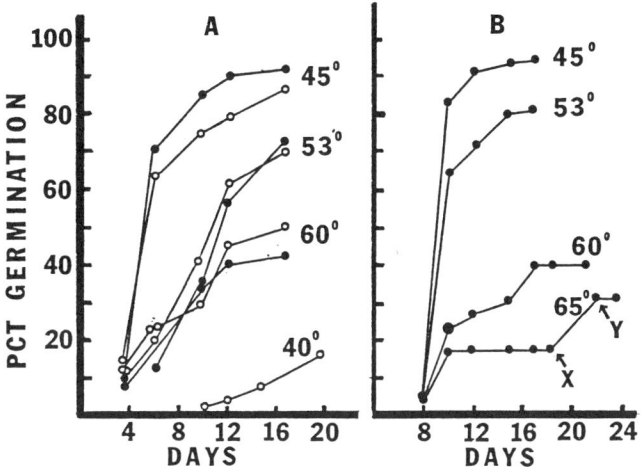

Figure 3-- Cumulative percent germination of *E. apricum* at different temperatures
A: Seeds placed directly in selected temperatures. o = var. *apricum*, ● = var. *prostratum*;
B: Seeds pretreated for 8 days at 40°F. Seeds in 65°F were returned to 40°F on the 17th day (X) and placed back in 65°F on the 21st day (Y).

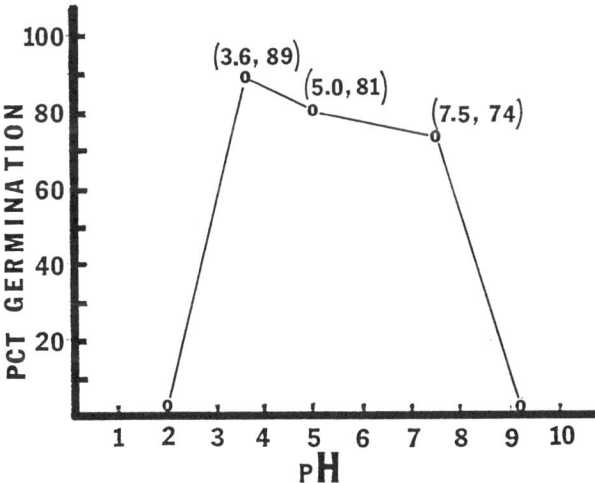

Figure 4-- Percent germination of *E. apricum* in response to pH.

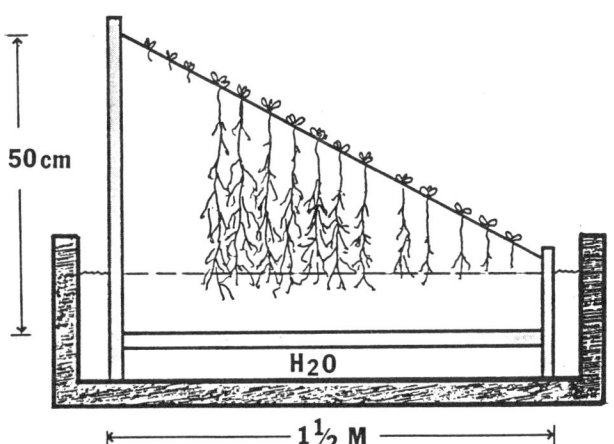

Figure 5-- Diagram of moisture gradient box, with resulting root systems. The water table is indicated by the dashed line.

Soil and Litter

Seedlings grow equally well in both native, Ione Formation (red) soil and greenhouse mixture. However, 16 of 20 plants started in the greenhouse mixture in March had flowered by June, but none growing in the Ione soil had flowered by the same time.

Seedlings were also planted in soils (both types) containing leaf litter of Arctostaphylos myrtifolia and Quercus wislizenii, either as dried litter mixed in with the soil or as an extract added. There was no measurable effect on growth in either case.

Light

The most striking observation in the field is that Eriogonum apricum plants occur only in open areas among the Ione manzanita. The most obvious interpretation is that the buckwheat is a heliophyte and the shade under the shrubs inhibits its growth. Measurements of mid-day light intensities in the field were as follows: 8000-12,000 foot candles in the open and an average of 1000-1500 f.c. under the shrub canopies.

To test the effect of reduced light intensities, plants were grown under full sunlight and three reduced light conditions. Three shade chambers were constructed with plastic screen mesh covering the top and two sides of each. The chambers were constructed so that the light intensity in each was about one-half that of the next higher set-up. Root length, degree of root branching, average petiole length, shoot length, and total plant dry weight were recorded following 13 and 31 days of growth. The amount of root growth, as evidenced by the degree of root branching and total plant dry weight, was significantly higher in full sunlight and progressively less for each reduced intensity. Figure 6 illustrates the total plant dry weights for plants grown in each soil type. The reduced intensities also resulted in evidences of etiolation (longer petioles and above ground shoots) and reduced vigor of the shoot. There were no significant differences in results between plants grown in Ione versus those in greenhouse mixture.

Competition

The restricted distribution of Eriogonum apricum suggests competition as an important factor in its seedling establishment. Grasses and other herbs,

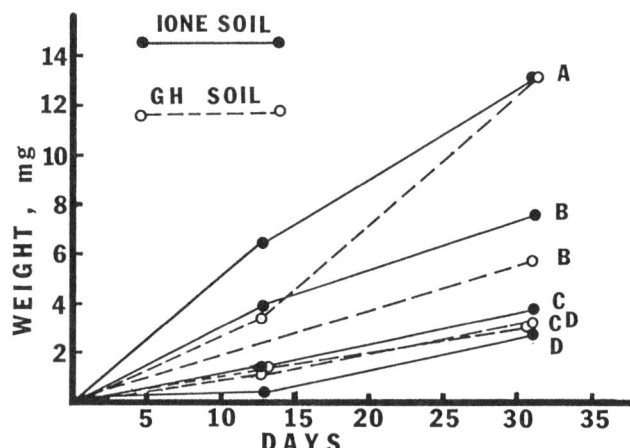

Figure 6-- Mean total dry weight of E. apricum plants grown under different light intensities. Mid-day July light intensities, in foot-candles, were:
A: 10,000-12,000
B: 4000
C: 2000
D: 700-1000

while common among the chaparral shrubs, are generally lacking in the open sites with the buckwheat. Competition experiments were done in which germinated Eriogonum seeds were planted at low and high densities, and either alone or with low or high densities of Festuca microstachys seeds, a common annual grass in the area. Plants were grown in 6 inch pots and the mean root length of the Eriogonum plants in each pot was recorded after 54 days.

When both the Eriogonum and Festuca were planted at the same time, the presence of the Festuca did not seem to affect the growth of the Eriogonum, at least for the first two months:

No. of Eriogonum	No. of Festuca	Eriogonum root length, cm
1	0	20.0
5	0	14.1
21	0	14.8
2	13	18.5
13	4	15.5
13	2	15.3

However, when the Eriogonum was planted in pots with already established Festuca plants (2 months old), the results were quite different. Eight to ten germinated Eriogonum seeds were planted in each of three attempts and none survived for more than one week. Most of the seedlings extended the cotyledons above the surface, but none produced any other leaves.

Moreover, in the pots in which the Festuca and Eriogonum were planted at the same time, although there were no differences in root growth of the Eriogonum for two months, differences in shoot growth were expressed later. By six months, Eriogonum plants grown without Festuca had well developed flowering stems and flowers, whereas those plants grown with Festuca had no flowering stems.

CONCLUSIONS

It is evident that the requirements by Eriogonum apricum for full sunlight and its reduced root growth in soils with high moisture content are the major factors in its restriction to open areas within the chaparral. The reduced light under the shrubs, the fact that the soils there remain wetter for a longer time following rains, and the presence of grasses would result in insufficient root development by the time the summer drought arrived. Even in the open areas, the vast majority of seedlings don't survive the first summer. Eriogonum apricum is similar to other edaphic endemics which, because of a broad tolerance to certain soil conditions and the inability to compete in more favorable zonal habitats, find a foothold and are thus restricted to these extreme habitats.

The restriction of Eriogonum apricum to just a few of the many potential sites within the Ione Formation indicates an apparent limitation in reproduction or dispersal. The reproductive effort, in terms of the number of seeds produced and the establishment of seedlings, seems sufficient to support and continue populations at the local sites. The extended period of flowering and fruiting, and the ability of seeds to germinate over a wide range of conditions and a long period of time, enhances the survival potential of at least a few individuals in a habitat where there seems to be a temporal variation in safe sites (Harper, et.al. 1970, Cook 1980).

Dispersal to new, unoccupied sites appears limited. Seed predation, by ants particularly, seems significant but also may be a factor in dispersal. Artificially establishing populations by sewing seeds into open sites void of Eriogonum apricum would undoubtedly be successful, whereas the transplanting of seedlings would not be effective or necessary.

It is likely that, over long periods of time, the constrictinn of open sites by invading manzanita plants might reduce the local populations of buckwheat. In the past, fires were probably important in periodically opening up areas and favoring the buckwheat, as indicated by the recent fire at the Carbondale Road site.

Besides the limited dangers of the encroaching manzanitas, the main concern is the presence of clay mining operations in the area which could completely eliminate a small population. The efforts of The Nature Conservancy and the California Department of Fish and Game have been important in conserving at least one representative habitat of the region.

REFERENCES

Allen, V. The Ione Formation of California. U. C. Public. in Geol. Sci. 1: 347-449; 1929.

Cook, Robert. The biology of seeds in the soil. In: Solbrig, Otto T., ed. Demography and evolution in plant populations. Bot. Mon. volume 15; Univ. Calif. Press, Berkeley; 1980; 107-129.

Gankin, R.; Major, J. Arctostaphylos myrtifolia, its biology and relationship to the problem of endemism. Ecol. 45(4): 792-808; 1964.

Harper, J.L.; Lovell, P.H.; Moore, K. The shapes and sizes of seeds. Ann. Rev. Ecol. Syst. 1:327-356; 1970.

Howell, J.T. Eriogonum notes IV: a new species from California. Leafl. West. Bot. 7:237-23 ; 1955.

Major, J. Potential evapotranspiration and plant distribution in western states with emphasis on California. In: Shaw, R., ed. Ground level climatology; 1967; 93-126

Myatt, Rodney. A new, prostrate variety of Eriogonum apricum Howell (Polygonaceae). Madrono 20(6):320-321; 1970.

Myatt, Rodney G. The ecology of Eriogonum apricum Howell. M.S. Thesis; Univ. Calif., Davis; 1968; 130 p.

Solbrig, Otto T. Demography and natural selection. In: Solbrig, Otto T., ed. Demography and evolution in plant populations. Bot. Mon. volume 15; Univ. Calif. Press, Berkeley; 1980; 1-20.

Stebbins, G. Ledyard. Adaptive radiation of reproductive characteristics in angiosperms, II: seeds and seedlings. Ann. Rev. Ecol. Syst. 2:237-260; 1971.

Endangered Species Conservation *Ex Situ:* The National View

Donald A. Falk [1]

Abstract: The threats to species survival are extremely complex; despite years of effort a large number of taxa remain endangered or have already become extinct. To address this problem effectively on a national scale requires a corresponding diversity of approaches to conservation, especially by combining the respective strengths of in situ and ex situ work into an integrated conservation strategy.

The primary goal of any species conservation effort must be to prevent extinctions; if the elements of diversity themselves are lost, there is little else that can be done. In addition, part of the current approach to this primary goal is to conserve as much of the genetic diversity within species as possible.

To achieve these central goals in the face of complex and intensifying threats to species survival, conservationists are employing an increasingly diverse range of approaches. In recent years, ex situ programs -- particularly botanic gardens, arboreta, and seed storage facilities -- have been called into play to contribute their respective strengths in plant research and conservation.

Viewed nationally, the question of the best approach should not be categorical ("Which is better, in situ or ex situ conservation?), for if we frame this as an "either-or" proposition we will lose sight of the potential for these two approaches to be mutually reinforcing. In reality there is already a spectrum of approaches to conservation that can be applied. In any given situation there is a particular combination of measures that will be most effective. Our task is thus to ascertain in each situation what mix of methods will yield the greatest degree of protection.

As relative newcomers to the conservation community many botanic gardens and arboreta are viewed with skepticism or suspicion by traditional conservationists. They are resources which have long been overlooked by conservationists as somehow extraneous to the preservation of species in their habitats. Yet a growing body of evidence indicates that these institutions have an increasingly valuable role to play in an integrated approach to conservation.

Can ex situ facilities single-handedly conserve species in their genetic entirety over an indefinite period? Perhaps not, and even if they could there would be some question of the utility of such an exercise, if not accompanied by preservation of natural populations in situ. But this is really the wrong question to be asking. Instead, we should be looking for ways to bring these resources to bear in any way possible, for the scale and pace of endangerment demand that we be increasingly resourceful.

AN OVERVIEW OF ENDANGERMENT IN THE U.S.

It is to a great extent the scale and complexity of plant endangerment itself which compels a more sophisticated approach to conservation. Despite our best efforts, there have been at least 103 documented species extinctions in the continental United States in the last 200 years, and over 250 in Hawaii (Mohlenbrock, 1983; Ayensu and DeFilipps, 1978). Moreover, of extinctions on the continent, 63 have occurred in this century, including 31 in the last fifty years alone. Ongoing extinction on this scale suggests a critical need to mobilize every available resource.

The Scale of Plant Endangerment

In order to fully appreciate the magnitude of the problem, it is helpful to have some understanding of the numerical scale of endangerment currently. With the cooperation of the national office of The Nature Conservancy

---

[1] Director of Administration, Center for Plant Conservation, 125 The Arborway, Jamaica Plain, MA 02130.

and the Office of Endangered Species, U.S. Fish and Wildlife Service, the Center for Plant Conservation has assembled a database of over 5100 listings of plant taxa considered to be in some danger of extinction. Given that the total continental U.S. flora is estimated at 20,000 taxa (Ayensu and DeFilipps, 1978), the presence of nearly one-fourth of the native flora on a list of potentially endangered taxa indicates the immensity of the problem. At least half of the listed taxa are found west of the Rocky Mountains and in Hawaii. The problem in Hawaii is particularly acute, with as much as 50 percent of a flora which is 95 percent endemic endangered (Ayensu and DeFilipps, 1978; Carlquist, 1980).

Of most critical concern are taxa at the specific or infraspecific rank that are listed or proposed under the Endangered Species Act, or that are represented by five or fewer sites or less than 1000 individuals in the wild.[2] As of the most recent tabulation (May 1987), nearly 800 taxa (over 15 percent of the total list) meet these criteria. Moreover, the threat is not confined to just a few taxonomic groups. There are over 1000 genera with taxa in the database, with anywhere from one to 180 endangered or threatened representatives in each. Eight genera -- _Astragalus_, _Eriogonum_, _Cyrtandra_, _Penstemon_, _Linum_, _Pelea_, _Euphorbia_, and _Arctostaphylos_ -- account for more than 14 percent of the entire list.

The Diversity of Threats

For most of these taxa we have at best an incomplete understanding of the causes of endangerment. Information is often anecdotal or out of date, especially for the many taxa which occur in remote populations not regularly monitored by a conservation agency. This uncertainty is exacerbated by our general inability to distinguish, except in a few well-documented cases, between taxa that are rare but stable in nature, and those that are declining. It is even more difficult to distinguish between true declines and long or irregular cycles, as in the Small Whorled Pogonia (_Isotria medeoloides_)(Lea, 1985).

Overall, the threats to species' survival are of sobering complexity. Causes of endangerment regularly cited (Mohlenbrock, op.cit.; Ayensu and DeFilipps, op.cit.; Endangered Species Technical Bulletin) include an array of overlapping, even contradictory factors:

    land conversion for agriculture,
        housing, commercial, industrial,
      or transportation development
    dam construction and site inundation
    soil compaction or disturbance
    erosion
    mining disturbance for coal, oil
        (including oil shale), minerals,
      sand and gravel
    wetlands draining and filling
    powerline construction
    herbicide spraying
    trampling and overgrazing by
        introduced range animals and
      other herbivores
    forest clearcutting
    forest succession
    fungal blight
    competition from introduced exotic
        plants
    fire
    fire suppression
    off-road vehicles
    trampling and picking by
        recreational hikers
    commercial collecting
    vandalism
    disappearance of symbionts and
        pollinators

In short, plants may be endangered by just about every significant economic and non-economic use of land in this country, including many effects which are difficult or impossible to stop even with protective ownership of the land. It is precisely this diversity of threats which requires a diversity of conservation strategies.

EVOLUTION IN CONCEPTS OF CONSERVATION

To a great extent, what is at issue is a shift in our notion of "correct" conservation practice. Although we tend to accept prevailing models of strategy at any given time, it is useful to recognize that both the definitions and models of conservation are continually changing. Some of these changes are

---

[2] This corresponds to FWS's LE, LT, PE, and PT categories, and TNC's G1 and T1 ranks. The author and the Center are indebted to the staff of the Conservancy and the Office of Endangered Species for their cooperation in developing these data. Some synonyms have not yet been eliminated, so that the actual number of taxa may be slightly smaller than the number of listings.

brought about by increased understanding of the workings of natural systems; others are essentially philosophical or attitudinal shifts. A brief look at how concepts of conservation have changed in this country may thus help us to understand how our current models may be changing, for a great deal of evidence suggests that we are experiencing an important change in our concepts of conservation.

To the earliest European settlers on this continent, Nature was the object of both awe and concerted efforts at destruction; it was simultaneously God's creation and an unlimited resource for Man's (sic) use. Most of the relevant early Colonial laws were intended to protect fisheries and forests from overexploitation (Geller, 1974). "Conservation" in this era was entirely a matter of resource management.

The first real calls for "wilderness preservation" did not occur until the mid-1800's (Nash, 1973). But in the latter half of the century, recognition began to spread that land was worth protecting either for its own sake or as a potentially useful resource. The protection of Yosemite Valley, followed by the creation of Yellowstone National Park and the Adirondacks forest preserve, set the stage for the era of massive land acquisition by the Federal government under Theodore Roosevelt and Gifford Pinchot of the nascent Forest Service. Much, if not most, of this acquisition was oriented to conserving natural resources such as timber and minerals for more sustained and equitable use (Hayes, 1959; Bates, 1957). Pinchot articulated the concept of government as "steward of the national interest"; it was in fact during this period that the "conservation movement" was formed and named.

Through the early twentieth century the model of land acquisition as the conservationist's primary tool encouraged the purchase of millions of acres of resource and natural areas. But already the concept was undergoing change; a new branch of biology -- ecology -- was providing insight into the workings of natural systems with a precision previously unattainable. The effect of the science of ecology soon penetrated to conservation theory, spawning the post-World War II ascendancy of the "stewardship" concept. Championed by The Nature Conservancy, the Sierra Club, and others, the stewardship philosophy regarded humanity as a visitor or borrower of nature. At the same time, however, the philosophy significantly recognized the necessity of active protection and management to achieve the goals of conservation. "Management of natural areas" ceased to be a contradiction in terms, and instead grew to become standard practice. The current approach to land management is characterized by a combination of laissez faire protection and active intervention -- to a degree that would have been considered unthinkable a century before -- into natural processes (for instance, altering succession by forest thinning or fire management). It is ironic that the tools of destruction, the chainsaw, herbicide, and bulldozer, become in the right hands the very tools of much current conservation practice.

But sound management requires good information, and by and large such information has been scarce or unavailable, especially for rare species. Although there has been no comprehensive survey, most of the rare or threatened taxa in the United States are poorly understood from the point of view of population genetics, physiology, and ecology. As a consequence, we have the least amount of information about precisely those species for which we would most want to design management practices.

This shortage of information is particularly critical in light of the other major post-War conceptual development, toward the idea of "genetic diversity" as the central conservation goal. This notion fundamentally changed the definition of conservation itself, from primarily a matter of acreage to a question of genepools. Not only were the techniques of conservation changing, but also the basic definition of what comprised conservation. Here again, however, we encounter the recurrent problem with so many rare taxa: we simply do not know the extent of intraspecific genetic diversity, and must guess or extrapolate. We recognize that a "taxon" is a genetic entity, with a certain range of variation falling within its limits. But without a clearer picture of a taxon's genetic profile, we cannot truly apply a modern concept of conservation (see Fiedler, 1986; Rabinowitz, 1981).

The trend visible through this capsule history is one of increasing integration of various techniques of land and species conservation: land acquisition. legal protection, active site management, research (Turner 1985). Viewed in this context, we can more clearly understand the emergence of a role for ex situ programs in conservation of genetic diversity: working in concert with other approaches, ex situ programs can be a powerful tool.

THE ROLE OF EX SITU CONSERVATION PROGRAMS

Individual botanic gardens and arboreta have been engaged in conservation activities for some time. However, until recently most American gardens and arboreta have devoted their attention to their traditional roles in display, education, and horticultural research. Providing optimal growing conditions for plants is traditional for gardens; collectively, they have been doing it for centuries. What is new is the incorporation of conservation as an additional priority for many of these institutions.

In the late 1970's several conferences -- at the Royal Botanic Gardens, Kew, U.K., New York Botanical Garden, and elsewhere -- began to examine to potential contribution of gardens and arboreta to species conservation (Prance and Elias, 1977; Synge and Townsend, 1979). More recently, the International Union for Conservation of Nature (IUCN) has sponsored a conference on the topic, "Botanic Gardens and the World Conservation Strategy".

Such institutions are natural allies of plant conservation in many respects, especially their:

- expertise in taxonomy and identification
- knowledge of germination, propagation, and seedling establishment requirements
- facilities for long-term maintenance of living plant material in various forms
- integration into the academic and applied botanical research communities
- high visibility and visitation in many urban communities, as loci for public awareness and education.

In recent years a number of gardens -- including The Arboretum at Flagstaff (Flagstaff, AZ), Berry Botanic Garden (Portland, OR), Bok Tower Gardens (Lake Wales, FL), Denver Botanic Gardens (Denver, CO), Garden in the Woods (Framingham, MA), Holden Arboretum (Mentor, OH), Nebraska Statewide Arboretum (Lincoln, NE), Pacific Tropical Botanical Garden (Lawai, Kaui, HI), San Antonio Botanical Gardens (San Antonio, TX), State Arboretum of Utah (Salt Lake City, UT), Waimea Arboretum and Botanical Garden (Haleiwa, HI), and others -- have incorporated conservation of native species into their charters and accession policies. Other established gardens, such as Arnold Arboretum (Jamaica Plain, MA), Desert Botanical Garden (Phoenix, AZ), Fairchild Tropical Garden (Miami, FL) Missouri Botanical Garden (St. Louis, MO), New York Botanical Garden (Bronx, NY), North Carolina Botanical Garden (Chapel Hill, NC), Rancho Santa Ana Botanic Garden (Claremont, CA), and the University of California Botanical Garden, Berkeley (Berkeley, CA), have continued and expanded their existing programs of collecting and growing native flora. Several of these institutions have been engaged in rare plant monitoring, rescue, and cultivation for years, and have established important collections (Huckins, 1983).

Moreover, gardens and arboreta are not the only ex situ sites of potential use; seed storage facilities may also play a key role. Seed storage can be a cost effective and secure method for maintaining large numbers of samples over long periods of time. The primary drawback lies in the relative paucity of information about rare native plants' orthodoxy to storage conditions, dormancy mechanisms, viability, and germination requirements. Nonetheless, seed storage may allow large numbers of collected samples -- and hence a greater sample of wild genetic diversity -- to be maintained at relatively low cost. Several gardens have established seed banks on site; Federal facilities are also becoming available for this purpose (see below).

Working individually, these and other gardens laid the groundwork for a more coordinated national program, and have illustrated some of the contributions that ex situ facilities can make. Although the range of activity is wide, for simplicity gardens' programs may be thought of in terms of three primary contributions: maintenance of living collections, research, and education.

Living Collections

Gardens can and do maintain living plant material as a genetic reserve. These captive genepools may serve as backup to the wild populations, preventing species extinctions that might otherwise follow catastrophic loss of the last wild source. For instance, Cooke's Kokio (Kokia cookei) from the island of Molokai, Hawaii had been reduced to a single living tree by 1910; by 1915 that specimen was nearly dead. Hawaiian botanist Joseph Rock collected seeds, from which the species has been rescued from almost certain extinction. Efforts are ongoing to re-establish the species in the wild, but in the meantime the Waimea Arboretum and Botanical Garden continues to safeguard some of the only remaining living material.

Botanic gardens can also serve as a safeguard against unexpected losses in the wild. The main site for the Virginia Roundleaf Birch (Betula uber) was nearly destroyed in the 1980's, even though the plants were on protected land. Fortunately the U.S. National Arboretum and other institutions had seedlings and cuttings in cultivation; had the entire species been destroyed in the wild, there would still be living genetic material available for reintroduction.

Ex situ facilities can also play a useful role in restoration of damaged sites. For example, a Vermont population of Hudsonia tomentosa on Nature Conservancy Land was nearly destroyed by off-road vehicles in the early 1980's. The Conservancy arranged for greenhouse propagation of cuttings taken from the remaining plants; once rooted, the cuttings were transplanted back to their original location, where they have helped to restabilize the population.

Living collections can be used as a source of propagules for site restoration and reintroduction carried out by an appropriate land-managing agency. A current example recommended as a recovery action by the U.S. Fish and Wildlife Service is San Antonio Botanical Garden's work with Texas Snowbells (Styrax texana). Seed and cuttings were field collected and propagated at the Garden, and will be used by Fish and Wildlife to establish a site on protected land.

Research

The traditional skills of gardens and arboreta in plant research can be beneficially applied to endangered species conservation. While this application is new, it illustrates a commodity -- information -- that gardens can develop in addition to growing and distributing live plant material.

Gardens can in some cases carry out research which may improve the effectiveness of management of the wild populations (Brumback, 1986). For instance, the Holden Arboretum (Mentor, OH) has worked with the Spreading Globeflower (Trollius laxus ssp. laxus) under contract with the Ohio Department of Natural Resources (ODNR). Arboretum staff collected seeds and measured germination under varying conditions of shading, soil moisture, pH, and stratification (Parsons and Yates, 1984). ODNR was able to incorporate these findings into their management plans for the wild populations.

A similarly positive role has been played in Desert Botanical Garden's work with Agave arizonica. The plant had been highly reduced in the wild in the 1960's when the Garden began working with propagation; at one point only a handful of clonal sites were known. With the Garden's assistance, over forty additional clonal sites have since been located. Equally important, plants in cultivation at the Garden are being used in breeding experiments designed to shed light on the plant's taxonomic status and possible hybrid origin.

In some cases, garden activities primarily contribute to scientific understanding of a taxon. An example is a cooperative program involving the Arboretum at Flagstaff's work with six rare and endangered taxa in the genus Pediocactus. In cooperation with the Center and the Institute of Museum Services, Arboretum staff have identified a mycorrhizal fungus apparently symbiotic with the plants in the wild, and are investigating its effect on seed germination and seedling growth.

Garden-based research and conservation is included increasingly in recovery actions recommended for Federally listed taxa by the U.S. Fish and Wildlife Service. One current example is the Florida Torreya (Torreya taxifolia), which is suffering heavy fungal damage at its only remaining wild sites on the Appalachicola River in Florida and southern Georgia. The regional office of the Fish and Wildlife Service has recommended as part of its recovery plan that plants could be established experimentally at botanic gardens north of the taxon's present range, to study the effect of climate on the plants' resistance to the pathogen. It is suspected that the taxon may have originally been more northerly, and that the extant population is showing evidence of physiological stress by virtue of its location near the species' extreme southern limit.

Education

American botanic gardens and arboreta receive tens of millions of visitors annually, ranging from the casual stroller to the professional botanist and researcher. These visitors represent a potentially crucial constituency for conservation in all its forms; thus botanic gardens can become a valuable means of raising public awareness of the importance of preserving natural areas. Habitat displays at the North Carolina Botanic Garden and the University of California Botanic Garden, Berkeley, for instance, illustrate fragile and unique plant communities which need conservation. Representative plantings of community types can sensitize visitors to the habitats typical of their native region.

In fact, gardens are in many respects ideal loci for large-scale conservation education. It is a sobering thought to consider the impact on our natural areas if those tens of millions of visitors were to go to the sites themselves. But in a garden setting, the visitor can see a recreation of the plant community, and begin to appreciate the importance of protection. Gardens can also serve as natural sites for symposia, workshops, and other public events in which conservation is the central topic.

DESIGNING A NATIONAL PROGRAM OF EX SITU CONSERVATION

The joining of many individual ex situ facilities into a coordinated national program has been the primary task of the Center for Plant Conservation since its inception in 1984. In thinking through the optimal structure of a national program, the organizers identified and then worked from a set of specific design criteria. Although such processes are frequently more systematic in retrospect than they seem at the time, the founding group of gardens and conservationists did devote considerable time to formulating long-range goals and program structure (see Falk and Walter, 1986; Thibodeau and Falk, 1986; Falk and Thibodeau, 1986; 1987 in press). In large part, the shape of the program has followed naturally from the primary areas in which gardens are strongest, as outlined in the preceding section. The criteria are offered here both for insight into the Center itself, and as possibly useful guidelines for creation of comparable programs elsewhere, including regionally.

1. The program should be action-oriented, stressing actual conservation of living endangered plant material. All other activities -- education, cooperative projects, even research -- are either derived from this basic activity or help support it. In the Center's case this criterion is reflected in the emphasis on building the National Collection.

2. The program should focus on the most endangered species, in particular those threatened throughout their range. In many respects this becomes the highest single decision-making criterion in developing the National Collection; directing resources to the most endangered species in the country is arguable one of the most important functions that a national coordinating group can provide.

Two tools are necessary to meet this condition. First, there must be a basic policy statement that guides the organization in its decision-making. In the Center's case, this is the Criteria for Highest Priority Taxa for Addition to the National Collection (Center for Plant Conservation, 1987); this document articulates the standards against which any proposed accession will be judged. The second tool is a database containing the key information about the plants' status in the wild, the number and distribution of populations, and coverage under Federal law. As described above, with the cooperation of TNC and the U.S. Fish and Wildlife Service, the Center has been able to develop just such a tool for species selection.

In its annual operating cycle, the gardens working with the Center propose their accessions as much as a year prior to actual field work. This enables careful review of the taxa selected by the garden, Center staff, and regional botanists and permitting authorities. The Center is also undertaking a nationwide survey of regional botanists, to attempt to capture their knowledge of taxa which may be facing a particularly imminent threat of extinction; even within the highest national rankings there are taxa at varying distance from extinction.

3. __The program should consist of a network of participating institutions__, each addressing the endangered flora of its own region. Early designs that involved centralized maintenance of the living collection were quickly discarded in favor of a network approach. A corollary of this principle is that the program should be conceived __bioregionally__ rather than along political boundaries. This allows for more consistent horticultural practice, and improves the likelihood that a garden will be able to successfully cultivate a taxon. The regional aspect also contributes significantly to the educational value of the display collections for the visiting public.

At the present time the Center's national network includes nineteen participating gardens and arboreta in fourteen regions. In addition, the seed storage facilities of the National Plant Germplasm System (NPGS) are available for storage of seeds collected through the program. Future additions to the garden network will be made where the need for additional capacity is greatest, most likely in regions of greatest botanical diversity and development pressure.

4. __The program should be scientifically valid and self-critical__. A technical Advisory Council unaffiliated with any of the Participating Institutions has been part of the Center's concept since its beginning. The Advisors formulate and recommend scientific policy, as well as reviewing every proposed accession by the Participating Institutions. Expertise on the Council is broad, including plant taxonomy, population biology, botanical databases, government regulation, conservation strategy, and horticulture.

A corollary to this principle is that the Collection should be a useful and well-documented resource. Part of its utility derives from its ability to make plant material that might otherwise be unavailable accessible for research purposes. Although the program is too new to evaluate this contribution, it is likely that the material in the participating gardens will be used regularly for pure and applied research.

5. __The Collection should meet the highest possible standards of conservation biology__ according to available data. In practice this means that the Collection must be designed to capture as much as possible a representative cross-section of the wild genome. Recognizing that some rare alleles may be missed in any sample, and that others will be lost from the Collection over time, the goal remains to represent as much of each taxon's genetic diversity as is feasible. Although the data on intraspecific genetic diversity are not as extensive as one would hope, a preliminary policy statement (Center for Plant Conservation, 1986) has provided initial guidance. This is an area needing considerably more research effort (see below).

6. __The Collection should be a permanent resource__ to the greatest extent possible, supported by institutional commitments by the gardens and the Center. Collections of lasting significance are justifiably a long-term curatorial responsibility of the institution that chooses to hold them. The irreplaceable character of endangered species collections adds a particular weight to the need for permanent commitment. Each institution must make this commitment to its collection beyond the tenure of an individual curator or director. The Center correspondingly accepts the responsibility to help each garden support its collection financially and technically.

7. __The program should allow conservationists to anticipate priorities__; instead of continually being in a reactive posture, a national program (or a good regional one, for that matter) should enable conservationists to look ahead and be proactive. For instance, knowing that a population is declining in the wild, a cooperative effort can be developed to protect and reinforce the existing population __before__ it reaches a critically low density.

8. __The program should be inherently collaborative__, and seek out the most effective combination of measures in each particular instance. In some cases the remaining wild individuals are so few in number and so threatened that the first step must be to immediately establish a protected genepool. In other cases the highest priority may be research into a particular aspect of the taxon's biology for management purposes, or propagating material for reintroduction or transplanting by a responsible agency. By its very nature, the Center represents a three-way cooperation between horticulturists, conservation agencies, and conservation biologists. Although the data for any given taxon may be insufficient in any one of these areas, it is always a goal to bring these fields together to provide an optimal strategy.

NEEDS FOR FUTURE TECHNICAL DEVELOPMENT

As ex situ programs develop, like any other approach they face particular technical difficulties that should be recognized openly. In many cases specific research may be indicated; in other cases general program growth and experience will provide the answers. A few of the current issues are:

1. Problems of genetic representation. Although the goal is to capture as much of the wild genetic diversity as feasible, so little is known about the genetics of most of the taxa that gardens are forced to either extrapolate or speculate about optimal sampling schemes and collection size. A great deal more research is needed in the area of population genetics to enable a satisfactory set of program guidelines in this area.

2. Difficulties with seed germination and other aspects of propagation. Since so few of the high priority taxa have been grown before, the gardens are continually having to discover the optimal horticultural practices needed. The situation is complicated further by the lack of a regular forum for exchange of propagation techniques with rare plants, a gap that the Center may need to fill.

3. Questions of long-term maintenance. "Permanent horticulture" may in some cases be impossible; the strategy for each taxon should reflect its the ability of specimens or propagules to be maintained. Seed storage may be invaluable in this respect, although so few taxa have been screened for viability in storage conditions that prediction is difficult.

CONCLUSION: TOWARD AN INTEGRATED CONSERVATION STRATEGY

Botanic gardens, arboreta, and other ex situ facilities are an important resource in the conservation of endangered species. Because of the complexity of threats to survival, every appropriate tool should be used in an coordinated fashion. The evolution in our concepts of conservation demonstrates an increasing emphasis on a genetic approach, and on the fundamental compatibility of in situ and ex situ methods. Whether conceived locally, regionally, nationally, or globally, conservation strategies should reflect a true commitment to an integrated strategy.

ACKNOWLEDGMENTS

My thanks to my colleagues Dr. Linda McMahan, Dr. Francis Thibodeau, and Dr. Kerry Walter (all of the Center for Plant Conservation), without whom this would all be no more than theory.

REFERENCES

Ayensu, Edward and Robert DeFilipps. Endangered and Threatened Species of the United States. Smithsonian Institution, Washington, D.C. 1978

Bates, James L. Fulfilling American Democracy: The Conservation Movement. Mississippi Valley Historical Review 44:29-57, 1957. Reprinted in Pursell, C., From Conservation to Ecology, Thomas Crowell, 1973.

Brumback, William. Endangered Plants at the Garden in the Woods: Problems and Possibilities. Arnoldia 46(3): 33-35, Summer 1986.

Carlquist, Sherwin. Hawaii: A Natural History. Pacific Tropical Botanical Garden, Lawai, Kaui, Hawaii. 1980.

Center for Plant Conservation. Criteria for Selecting Highest Priority Plants for Accession to the National Collection of Endangered Plants. 1987.

Center for Plant Conservation. Recommendations for the Collection and Ex situ Management of Germplasm Resources from Rare Wild Plants. 1986.

Falk, Donald and Francis Thibodeau. Saving the Rarest. Arnoldia 46(3):3-18. Summer 1986.

Falk, Donald and Francis Thibodeau. Building a national ex situ network: the U.S. Center for Plant Conservation. In Bramwell, D. et al. Botanic Gardens and the World Conservation Strategy. International Union for Conservation of Nature. Academic Press, London, U.K. 1987, in press.

Falk, Donald and Kerry Walter. Networking to Save Imperiled Plants. Garden January/February 1986.

Fiedler, Peggy. Concepts of rarity in vascular plant species, with special reference to the genus _Calochortus_. Taxon 35(3):502-518. 1986.

Geller, Lawrence. Pilgrims in Eden: Conservation policies at New Plymouth. The Pilgrim Society, Plymouth, MA. New England Historical Series. 1974.

Hayes, Samuel. Conservation and the gospel of efficiency: The Progressive Conservation Movement. Harvard University Press, Cambridge. 1959.

Huckins, Charles, ed. Preliminary Directory of Living Plant Collections of North America. American Association of Botanical Gardens and Arboreta, Swarthmore, PA. 1983.

Lea, Douglass. Secrets of a small Pogonia. Defenders. November/December 1985. p32-36.

Mohlenbrock, Robert. Where have all the wildflowers gone? MacMillan, New York. 1983.

Nash, Roderick. The American Wilderness in Historical Perspective. Forest History 6:3-13. 1973. Reprinted in Pursell, C. _op.cit._.

Parsons, Brian and Thomas Yates. The cultural requirements of _Trollius laxus_ ssp. _laxus_. Ohio Department of Natural Resources, Columbus, OH. 1984.

Prance, G. and Thomas Elias, eds. Extinction is forever. New York Botanical Garden, Bronx, NY. Proceedings of a conference. 1977

Rabinowitz, Deborah. Seven types of rarity. _In_ The Biological Aspects of Rare Plant Conservation (H. Synge, ed.). John Wiley and Sons, Chichester, U.K. 1981

Stebbins, G. Ledyard, Jr. The genetic approach to problems of rare and endemic species. Madrono 6:241-272. 1942

Synge, Hugh and H. Townsend. Survival or extinction. Royal Botanic Gardens, Kew. Conference proceedings. 1979.

Thibodeau, Francis and D. Falk. The Center for Plant Conservation: A New Response to Endangerment. Public Garden 1:1, January 1986. American Association of Botanical Gardens and Arboreta.

Turner, Frederick. Cultivating the American Garden. Harper's, August 1985, p.45-52.

Can Threatened and Endangered Species Be Maintained in Botanic Gardens?

Thomas S. Elias [1]

Abstract: Many threatened and endangered species can be successfully grown for short and intermediate terms in botanic gardens, although they are subject to biotic and abiotic factors which influence their survival. Management decisions and horticultural practices are major factors in the success of threatened and endangered species in cultivation and long-term survival requires a different management strategy than that commonly employed by botanic gardens. Examples and data are based on long-term cultivation of native plants at Rancho Santa Ana Botanic Garden in Claremont, California.

Botanic gardens and arboreta can be important agents in a multifaceted effort to conserve rare plant taxa. Preserving and protecting rare plants in their natural habitats is nearly always preferable to maintaining them in artificial settings or transplantation experiments. However, favorable natural conditions are not always available for many reasons. Commercial, agricultural and residential developments have displaced and will continue to alter the natural landscape so as to exclude many natural components. Displacement of pollinators and the introduction of disease, pests and aggressive introduced species can influence native species in in situ situations. Also, the availability of rare species for educational and research purposes is limited if only natural populations are maintained.

Relatively few data are available on the ability of botanic gardens to maintain individuals or populations of rare plants in long-term cultivation. The living plant collections of the Rancho Santa Ana Botanic Garden during its sixty-year history have been focused solely on the native flora of California. From the onset, many rare species were brought in as seeds, cuttings or by transplantation. This paper will examine the factors affecting the survival of living collections and discuss several examples. Recommendations will be made for a program to insure a higher success rate in the long-term survival of rare species in botanic gardens and arboreta.

Species of rare annuals or biennials should be maintained not solely as living plants in botanic gardens, but their seed should be properly prepared and stored in a seed bank. The maintenance of genetic lines in annuals growing under cultivated conditions on a long-term basis is obviously exceedingly difficult. Herbaceous perennials and shrubs are easier to maintain through a program for their culture and propagation. Trees are the easiest, provided suitable conditions including space, are available.

Many people believe that because rare plants are rare they must also be difficult to propagate and grow. This stereotypic attitude must be discarded. Some of them are indeed difficult to propagate or maintain, but others thrive in cultivated conditions and can be easily propagated. Each species presents its own requirements for propagation and culture.

Many factors can adversely affect rare plants in living collections although we most often think of the biological factors. These not only include temperature, moisture, soil and air conditions but also mycorrhizal associations, pests and disease, and the absence of specific pollinators. These can act independently of each other or in concert, sometimes coinciding while at other times not. With time, some experimenting, and careful note-taking, the biological factors can usually be overcome. While these factors are of major importance, they are not always the primary ones in the long-term maintenance of rare plants.

Abiotic or human-related factors are often responsible for the loss of many plants in botanical institutes. Often an individual or institute goes to great length to obtain a few seeds or cuttings

---

[1] Director, Rancho Santa Ana Botanic Garden, Claremont, CA

of a rare species and then turns them over to someone else to propagate and grow. Unless the recipient is given as much information as is known about the taxon including its requirements, elevation, moisture regime, and other habitat data, how can the grower be expected to know how to treat the precious commodity he or she has been given? Until recently, there has been relatively little information available about the propagation and cultivation requirements of rare native plants.

Another common factor is the loss of correct labels or mislabelling of individual specimens. During its propagation, an individual plant usually moves from a flat to a small pot, then gradates up through one or two more larger pot sizes before it is planted out in the main collection. Accidental mixing of labels is not unusual when people are on vacation or when unusually heavy work loads demand a faster processing of materials. Even in the main collections, visitors or vandals sometimes remove or switch labels and unless a separate accurate record of its precise location is kept, a plant can be lost for scientific purposes.

Botanic gardens lose numerous plants each year to the daily maintenance routine of weeding, mowing, tilling, irrigation, and other mechanical activities. While damage to plants is nearly always unintentional, it does occur. Unless the gardeners and groundspeople are aware of the importance of an endangered plant they will treat it with the same level of concern as any other plant in the garden. A shortage of trained personnel to maintain living plant collections can also lead to the loss of many plants until proper procedures are learned, usually by trial and error.

Administrative and supervisory personnel occasionally change, often accompanied by the establishment of new programs and the elimination or revision of other programs viewed as out-of-date or ineffective. Each director and chief horticulturist wants to leave his or her mark of accomplishment. Building new plant displays is one of the more visible ways of accomplishing this goal. Many valuable plants have been discarded because long-range plans had not been made when continuity between administrations ended or became disrupted.

CASE STUDIES

Agave utahensis var. nevadensis

There have been five separate introductions of this agave into our Botanic Garden. The first consisted of 204 bare-rooted plants which have been moved from the Clark Mountains in San Bernardino County to the Garden on 13 October 1936. By 24 May 1951, 50 of the original plants were still alive. During that year, the Rancho Santa Ana Botanic Garden moved from its Orange County location to new facilities in Claremont, California. An undisclosed number of this introduction was moved to Claremont and by 24 May 1981 only 16 plants had survived. Offspring of this original introduction are still growing in the garden today.

Other introductions of this taxon were made in 1950, 1960, 1971 and 1980. Plants or their offspring from the latter three dates survive today in the Garden's living collections. Succulents are among the easier plants to maintain for long periods of time.

Baccharis vanessae

Seed of this shrub was first collected in November 1978 from Encinitas in San Diego County. Twenty-four young plants were obtained, nineteen of which were planted out in the Garden on 10 December 1979. Two-thirds of the cuttings taken in May 1985 successfully rooted, and were grown in our nursery until they were large enough to be planted out. They are present today in three locations in the Garden. Baccharis vanessae is an example of an introduction which must be propagated at regular intervals to ensure survival in cultivation.

Carpenteria californica

Three different introductions of this taxon have been made since 1935 and offspring of all three still flourish in the Garden. Seed was collected in July 1935 near Auberry; from it more than 100 plants were placed in the living collection at the Orange County site. On 29 March 1951, 22 plants were moved to the new Claremont site. By the spring of 1972, 16 of these plants were still alive; however, by June 1982 the survivors had dropped to four. Cuttings were made from the remaining plants later that year and five new plants resulted. These were planted out in the Garden in March 1984.

The other two introductions were made in 1981 and 1983. This attractive shrub is easy to grow and should be propagated via cuttings when the plants reach 10 to 15 years of age.

Ceanothus floriosus var. porrectus

Three young plants of this shrub were first introduced into the Garden in 1950 and planted out the following spring. In September 1958, cuttings were taken and rooted and a year later 15 new plants were added to the living collections. Additional cuttings were made the following year with a similar high rate of success. In December 1961, 130 cuttings were taken and 128 new specimens planted out the next spring. Seven years later 110 plants were still alive, but in 1970 only 75 plants remained; in 1977 the number had dropped to 19 and by 1982 to 10.

This introduction has been maintained in the Garden due to repeated vegetative propagation. A propensity for easy rooting and minimal care make this taxon a relatively easy one to maintain on a long-term basis.

Dendromecon rigida subsp. rhamnoides

Seed of this attractive bush was collected from Catalina Island in June 1964 from which 15 plants were obtained. They were planted out into the main collection in April 1965. The number of surviving plants has gradually been declining. Thirteen plants remained in 1966, 10 in 1968, 8 in 1969, 6 in 1971, and 4 in 1972; the latter still persist. This species is difficult to propagate vegetatively. An active program of collecting fresh seeds must be an integral part of the management plan for this taxon. Further experimental work is needed to determine ways to vegetatively propagate this taxon with a higher rate of success than following old traditional methods.

Dudleya traskae

Two plants of this succulent were introduced from the type locality on Santa Barbara Island in April 1941. By 1950 they had grown sufficiently for division into 8 plants and by 1966, a total of 70 individuals resulted from the continued lifting and dividing of the clump-forming plants. Additional cuttings or divisions were made in 1970, 1971, 1981, 1984 and 1986.

This is an easy species to maintain in a garden environment. Since it can be readily propagated, literally hundreds of plants can be produced. There is no reason why this endangered species cannot be conserved in botanic gardens indefinitely.

Lavatera assurgentiflora

This large and attractive shrub has been separately introduced on four different occasions. Seeds were first brought to the Garden in November 1944 and from this, 179 plants were planted out. Regrettably, only 13 survived three years later. Several plants were then moved to the new Garden in Claremont, but the transplanting was apparently unsuccessful. The 1962 introduction of additional seeds yielded three plants which were killed by frost in 1965. In 1975, 12 cuttings were brought to the Garden 10 of which rooted. Only two were planted out in the main collection and both are alive today. Lavatera assurgentiflora is in fact, not a difficult plant to propagate and grow in a garden setting.

Lepechinia ganderi

Seed of this perennial was collected from native populations in the San Miguel and the Otay Mountains in San Diego County in 1980 and 1982 respectively. Fourteen plants from the 1980 and three plants from the 1982 introductions were added to the main collection. Both populations have been maintained by a regular program of vegetative propagation using rooted cuttings.

Lyonothamnus floribundus var. asplenifolius

In October 1958, seed was collected of this interesting tree, a native of Catalina Island. Germination occurred the following spring and in October 1959, 4 specimens were planted out. A second seed batch from this introduction resulted in an additional 21 plants. Individuals from both propagations are still present in the Garden.

We have also succeeded in propagating and growing Lyonothamnus floribundus var. floribundus. Seed of this variety was collected in October 1960, 29 plants were obtained and planted in the main living collection. Several of these continue to thrive.

Tanacetum camphoratum

Seed of this northern Californian native was first collected and brought to the Garden in July 1954 from the Humboldt lighthouse in Samoa. The seed was not sown until October 1956 and two months later, 60 young plants were placed in pots. The following spring, 57 individuals were planted out in the Garden. These were lifted, divided, and replanted in January 1962 and again in February 1984. The plants thrived and spread rather aggressively in our coastal sand dune area. They adapted readily to the southern California climate and even invaded an adjacent groundcover of *Carpobrotus*.

CONCLUSIONS

Based upon the data assembled on approximately 85 taxa of rare plants including those listed in this paper, it is clear that endangered species can be grown on a long-term basis in botanic gardens. Several important elements, however, are essential for their success. These are:

1. An institutional commitment, preferably as part of a purpose statement or policy approved by the governing board, to the proper maintenance of a living collection of rare species. Collected wild, rare plant specimens should only be entrusted to those botanical institutes with such a commitment. Rare plants propagated from specimens already in cultivation can be made available to other Gardens for use in displays or educational activities.

2. The maintenance of a living collection should be accompanied by the addition of seed lots of the same taxa to established seed storage facilities with suitable equipment to ensure maximum viability of the seeds. Rare annuals and biennial taxa should be maintained in seed storage facilities rather than as living plants.

3. In addition to the primary plant specimens, secondary collections from the same provenance should be established at other suitable locations whenever possible. This will increase the likelihood that a particular introduction will be saved if members are lost at the main center.

4. There is a need to involve all staff and volunteers in the project. It is important to fully inform the plant propagator, gardeners, tour leaders and all other staff which utilize the collection in addition to the people directly involved in the rare plant program. The greater the knowledge staff members and volunteers have on the special status and protection of these plants, the greater the level of security for these collections.

5. The need to establish a schedule to monitor the health and well-being of the living specimens and to plan a definite program for plant propagation, vegetatively if possible. All herbaceous and woody perennials have definite life spans which are curtailed if they are grown under stress. Therefore, care must be taken to propagate these plants prior to their eventual decline. Accurate and up-to-date records are essential to determine optimum conditions for propagation.

In conclusion, it is clear that botanic gardens and arboreta can propagate and maintain living collections of rare and endangered plants on a long-term basis provided adequate provisions are taken for their care. However, cultivation of rare plants should not be regarded as a satisfactory alternative to the protection and conservation of natural areas. Growing potentially doomed taxa in gardens form only one part of a multifaceted effort and drive needed to preserve the great diversity of plants in California, the United States and worldwide.

ACKNOWLEDGEMENTS

I wish to thank Mr. Walter Wisura for help in gathering data for this paper, Dr. Kit Tan for general comments, and Ms. Marilyn Finn for typing the manuscript.

The California Nature Conservancy's Landowner Contact and Registry Program: Voluntary Protection for Rare Plant Sites

Lynn Lozier [1]

Abstract: A new program of the California Nature Conservancy is helping to bridge the gap between limited financial resources and the protection needs of our state's phenomenal biological diversity. By working with private owners and providing information in a non-confrontational context, the Conservancy is able to prevent the inadvertant destruction of important rare plant sites. Owners are encouraged to make a commitment to voluntarily protect their rare species; properties of those who do are added to the California Nature Conservancy's Register of Natural Areas. Staff and volunteers provide encouragement and technical support while working toward more permanent forms of protection.

California's phenomenal natural diversity is an imposing conservation challenge. The protection and subsequent management needs of many species, were their habitats to be purchased outright, would go far beyond the resources of the Conservancy. Often a species is very vulnerable simply because of the limited number of places in which it occurs. The greatest threat to it may be the ignorance of its owner, since inadvertant destruction immediately precludes future protection. For this reason, in March of 1985, the California Nature Conservancy initiated a Landowner Contact Program and associated Register of Natural Areas based on the model described in Hoose, 1981.

THE CONCEPT

The Landowner Contact program is based on the assumption that if private landowners can be made aware of the rare species which live on their property, many can be convinced to care for them. The Conservancy makes the connection, provides the information, and reinforces it with our California Register of Natural Areas -- honorary recognition for owners who have made the decision to take on that responsibility. As described in the program brochure, "The Register is designed to honor and recognize owners of outstanding natural areas for their commitment to the protection of our state's natural heritage. The program relies on citizen-based conservation and the willingness of landowners to safeguard the best that remains of our natural world."

The California program has many features in common with similar programs in other states[2]. Through it, owners voluntarily commit to protect their rare species to the best of their ability, to contact the Conservancy if there are any threats or impacts which they are unable to deal with, and to contact the Conservancy should they decide to sell or transfer the property. In California, a fourth commitment is included: to permit the Conservancy to survey the species on an annual basis.

Owners who agree to these conditions are entered with their properties in The California Nature Conservancy's Register of Natural Areas. This is an "honor roll" of people "doing the right thing". It is not a legally binding relationship, although owners are asked to give the Conservancy 30 days notice should they wish to terminate the agreement. Neither does this have any impact on the owner's rights over his or her land. It remains their property. The key to a Registry agreement is the relationship it establishes.

The Landowner Contact program functions as a biological outreach to owners of special places letting them know that they have something rare which needs their care, and then following up with the input, feedback, and support needed to keep them involved. The program's four important functions are these:

---

[1] Director of Landowner Contact, The California Nature Conservancy, San Francisco, CA.

[2] See Natural Areas Journal 4(3) 1984.

- It <u>prevents inadvertant destruction</u> by educating landowners about the exceptional features of their property.
- It <u>encourages informed stewardship</u> by private owners working with the Conservancy in a "conservation partnership".
- It <u>builds relationships</u> between owners and the Conservancy which can be scaled up into stronger forms of protection.
- It <u>functions as a holding action</u>, buying time and reducing the need for significant cash outlays so that funds can be directed elsewhere.

THE PROCESS

Selection

Protection priorities of the California Nature Conservancy are determined by its Identification staff. A "scorecard" generated by the California Natural Diversity Data Base, in the Nongame Heritage Section of the State Department of Fish and Game highlights those species most immediately in need of protection. The selection of the best possible sites to protect those rare species involves further field work by volunteers, many of whom may be called upon later to assist the Landowner Contact staffer. Ownership of selected sites is researched, and that information passed on to Landowner Contact program where interpretive materials for the owner are prepared.

In its first 20 months, the great majority of Landowner Contact sites have been targeted because they have one or more very rare plants, or are home to a threatened natural community. Several have been only known occurrences, and many are known from 5 or fewer sites. To date, only a few sites have come to the program because of rare animals since mobility can make effective protection of an animal at a single isolated site unrealistic. Although the procedures are similar, for purposes of simplicity this paper will address only how the Landowner Contact program deals with rare plant sites.

Preparation

A packet of information is compiled which will ultimately be presented to the landowners. This folder's purpose is to provide them with the basic information they'll need to identify, plan for, and manage the rare species on their property. It serves as a focus of conversation during the staffer's visit with the owners, and is left with them as an addition to their other important personal papers.

The packet is intended to impress owners with the significance of their property, the Conservancy's professionalism, and its commitment to the rare species' protection. It provides them with information about how their activities might be tailored to benefit the rare species, or at least avoid negatively impacting it. The first page is a cover letter which sets the tone: "Certain places in our state support plants, animals, and natural communities which are so rare, threatened, or endangered, that the decision about whether they will survive for the future or disappear from the face of the earth can fall to a single individual -- you, the landowner."

The rest of the packet is designed to support that basic statement. Its second page, entitled <u>Your Property and Its Special Plant</u>, is an overview of the property covering location, acreage, the rare species present, and its status if listed. Two key headings on the page are "Ecological Significance" and "Management Considerations". They tell the owners in brief layman's language why the site is important and what they can do to maintain the species which helps make it so special. All this is stated in affirmative terms.

The next page, entitled <u>About Your Special Plant</u>, includes a drawing of the plant and a description in simple terms which emphasizes how it can be distinguished from similar, but more common species. The habitat is also described, along with range and other occurrences. The section entitled "Ecological Context" includes an explanation of why the species is thought to be rare. And finally, "Threats" outlines recent impacts to other sites and a summary of activities known to be detrimental to the species.

In addition to this information, the packet contains distant and close-up photographs of the plant, habitat shots if available, and an aerial view. Maps show the general area, the borders of the property, and the distribution of the plant on site. Pockets in the folder contain the program brochure, reprints of newspaper articles about recently registered sites, and other Conservancy literature.

Contact

Based on the material provided by the Identification Department, the Landowner Contact staffer decides whether to make a direct approach to particular property owners with a letter, or to look for an introduction through the community. If there is any evidence of belligerence on the part of an owner, then sources are explored in order to find a local contact who can provide an introduction. This could be the volunteer who did the field work on the species, or friend or neighbor who is a Nature Conservancy member.

Typically, the Conservancy staffer writes directly to the private owners. The tone of the letter is upbeat and inquisitive. Owners are told that it is the Conservancy's understanding that a rare species grows on property for which they are the owner of record. The staffer expresses an interest in knowing more about the history of the property and how the owners' "activities have resulted in the rare plant's survival to date". The letter includes references to the Conservancy's status as a private, non-profit/non-confrontational group and states that the program's function is "providing private landowners with the information they need to make important decisions about the rare species on their property". The letter ends as the staffer expresses a desire to meet with the owners for a few minutes in the near future.

About ten days later the staffer follows up with a telephone call in order to arrange for a meeting. This is the point at which the most resistance may be experienced. It is not unusual for owners to ignore or misplace the letter, or simply not to read it very carefully. Many need to be reassured that they are not going to be "raked over the environmental coals" or have their hands tied. Regardless of their initial reaction, most owners are genuinely curious about the rare species on their property, and can be convinced to meet, if only for long enough for the staffer to share some photographs and maps.

The ideal circumstance to meet with owners is on their property where the species can actually be seen. When this is possible it is extremely effective. Even out of season when an element may not be visible, meeting in the owners' home is much preferable to their place of business or other less personal site. The hospitality extended to a guest (even one who may not be immediately accepted) sets an excellent tone for the discussion that will follow.

The owners' packet is the focus of the conversation. Generally people have three basic questions they'd like to have answered: "Who are you?", "How do you know?", and "What's the big deal?"

Some conservative owners, particularly in rural areas, consider themselves conservationists but may have an "anti-environmentalist" attitude. Reprints of articles about the Nature Conservancy's "private sector" approach are reassuring here.

The second question, "how do you know?", requires an explanation of the Data Base and how it functions. In particular owners are interested in knowing when the species was first discovered on their property. (And the staffer hopes that it was an old historical site reference, or that the recent discoverers had the owner's permission to be on the property.)

Finally, some owners need to be reminded of why preserving rare species is important. For many people, just having the only site, or one of very few, is more than enough reason to maintain a resource. For others, more explanation is necessary. People vary greatly in what they respond to, from the religious argument that God put it here and we have an obligation to maintain it, to the potential future uses of its genetic resources. The staffer takes the position that it is, without question, important and that people have a lot of different reasons for why it's important to them. Then the arguments are simply enumerated.[3] Occasionally owners require a period of cultivation, and the staffer follows up with reprints and other materials supporting whatever argument they seem to be most receptive to.

The Pitch

If owners seem favorably disposed toward the presence of the plant on their property, then the Register of

---

[3] For a discussion of the arguments see Ehrlich and Ehrlich 1981.

Natural Areas is explained. They are reminded that this is a voluntary relationship which provides a structure for them to protect the species and to have The Nature Conservancy's assistance in that effort. In order to qualify for the California Nature Conservancy's Register of Natural Areas, owners are told that the following four commitments are required:

1) To protect the area and its unique natural elements to the best of their abilities.
2) To contact The Nature Conservancy if there are any threats to the area or its elements.
3) To allow the Conservancy to visit the site annually at a mutually agreeable time.
4) To notify the Conservancy of any intent to sell or transfer ownership of the area.

The Registry agreement is totally voluntary. Although 30 days notice is requested in the event that owners wish to terminate the arrangement, it is not legally binding. The significance of the agreement is the relationship it establishes -- one of good will and communication between owners and The Nature Conservancy.

Follow-Up

People who agree to add their property to the Conservancy's Register of Natural Areas, and therefore to care for the species themselves, are presented with an oak and brass plaque, which identifies them as the owners of a natural area of statewide significance. With their permission, a press release is sent to the local papers which includes a photograph of the rare species and, ideally, one of the owners with their plaque. Local publicity serves to reinforce in the owners' minds the significance of their commitment, and to provide community reinforcement. Press releases are structured to emphasize the owners' relationship with the land, to get them thinking about the long term needs of the species, and to set the stage for future commitment to more permanent forms of protection.

Following registration, the rare plant population must be monitored annually. This is coordinated by The California Nature Conservancy's Stewardship department, and depends heavily upon local volunteers. Ideally, the same people who surveyed the site, and made the introduction to the owners can be counted on to act as facilitators in their relationship with the Conservancy and to conduct an annual survey of the population to make sure that things are still going well.

Maintaining the Relationship

The Nature Conservancy has established a system of maintaining owners of Registry sites and continuing to cultivate them over time. They receive honorary membership in the Conservancy and are sent its national magazine and state newsletter automatically. An annual Landowner Contact newsletter is being prepared which will let them know what other people are doing on their sites and set the stage for subsequent upgrading. In addition, they receive VIP invitations to special events the Conservancy hosts all over the state from dedications to annual meetings and breakfasts with board members. Finally, the Landowner Contact staffer makes a point to visit each owner on an annual basis. This is generally not done in season, but worked in as possible in connection with other trips. In this way the Conservancy is able to gauge the owner's level of ongoing commitment and understanding and to plant the seeds of subsequent protection, including the possibilities of conservation easements, gifts, and bequests.

PROGRAM TO DATE

In its first 20 months, the California Landowner Contact program has brought rare species to the attention of the owners of 31 important sites. At close to half of those sites, owners have been willing to make a commitment to protect the species and add the properties to our Register of Natural Areas.

In only once case were owners so belligerent that it appeared unwise to give them the details of the rare plants on their property. In most cases, even those individuals who declined to make a commitment at the time were willing to talk again and the dialogue continues. This is definitely a positive step.

Currently in California, 23 rare plant species are protected through 17 Registry agreements covering almost 1000 acres. Some highlights include:

The Anderson Valley Cemetery District Board's agreement to protect the Rodrick's fritillary (*Fritillaria Rodrickii* Knight) population (one of three in existence) in one of their cemeteries. In this case, caring for the plants meant a change in their maintenance and mowing activities. Historically these have been undertaken just before the Memorial Day weekend. Now they are delayed for several weeks until the rare plants have completed seed set.

- The Yreka phlox (Phlox hirsuta E. Nels.) is protected at its two known sites by Registry agreements. Owners of several of the parcels making up one site, a subdivided area within the city limits, have made commitments to voluntary protection. The other known site, in a rural area, is also protected by a Registry agreement.

- The Conservancy is working with the Presbyterian Conference Center in the San Bernardino Mountains to help protect their wet meadow from vehicle impacts as a part of a Registry agreement. A wall and fence have been constructed with assistance from the City of Big Bear, the California Conservation Corps, and Conservancy volunteers. The site supports the bird-footed checkermallow (Sidalcea pedata Gray) and ten other rare plants.

THE FUTURE

The California Nature Conservancy's Landowner Contact and Registry program has a lot of potential for reducing inadvertant destruction of critical rare plant areas, and for building commitment on the part of private owners to protect them. Like most of the Conservancy's activities, it depends very heavily on volunteers. As the program expands it will need even more volunteer help.

Volunteers assist in the site selection process and follow up by mapping rare plant occurrences so that owners can be provided with the most complete information possible on what areas they need to be especially careful with. This level of volunteer participation will continue to be needed as those who live near selected sites are called upon to function as local contacts for owners.

Once a site is registered, volunteer help may be solicited for those situations in which physical improvements such as fencing are needed. Following registration, it is absolutely essential that populations be monitored over time, and assistance on the local level will be very important for this as well. Finally, local volunteers do a great deal to provide a context for private owners in which their contribution to conservation is recognized and acknowledged, and in which they get friendly, daily feedback on the effectiveness and importance of their work.

The goal of California Nature Conservancy's Landowner Contact program is to build awareness and a sense of responsibility in each owner we work with. Our Register of Natural Areas is a vehicle for developing that commitment. An owner once explained his estate planning by saying that he had arranged that his wife, his children and his dogs would be cared for after he was gone. We would like to see him add his rare plants to that list.

CONCLUSION

It has long been acknowledged in the Conservancy that owning a deed, just a piece of paper, does not in and of itself protect a rare plant. People protect rare plants, whether they be Conservancy staff, owners or managers on the ground, or volunteers in the community. California's tremendous conservation needs make it clear that active protection through purchases alone will not be adequate to prevent species from becoming extinct. We need people to help us and lots of people to do the job. Our California Landowner Contact program is aimed at just that: letting people know what they have, why it's important, what they can do to protect it, and then working with them to make it happen.

REFERENCES

California Nature Conservancy Register of Natural Areas Brochure 1986.
Ehrlich, Paul R.; Ehrlich, A.H. Extinction: The Causes and Consequences of the Disappearance of Species. New York: Random House; 1981. 35-100.
Hoose, Phillip M. Building an Ark: Tools for the Preservation of Natural Diversity Through Land Protection. Covelo, CA: Island Press; 1981. 35-68.
Natural Areas Journal. Landowner Contact 4(3) 1984 July. 34p.

Habitat Restoration by a Non-Profit Organization: A Case Study

Phyllis M. Faber [1]

Abstract: One half-mile of riparian habitat on Stemple Creek that bisects a dairy ranch near Tomales, California will be restored through an exchange: CNPS will replace a bridge, destroyed in the 1982 storm, and construct a fence on both sides of a creek in return for an access easement on the creek bed and adjacent riparian corridor. The fencing and bridge will exclude livestock from the creek bed and banks, allowing vegetation to be restored and protected in the future. The project will also provide limited public access through CNPS. The California State Coastal Conservancy has funded the project. While there are no rare or endangered plants in the project area, there are a number of interesting plants for Marin and some specially mentioned in Howell's Marin Flora. This project offers a model for habitat restoration and protection through a partnership between a private land owner, a non-profit conservation organization, and the state.

Stemple Creek drains into the Estero de San Antonio, located in Marin County near the border of Sonoma County. The Estero has been identified as an important wetland with statewide significance by both the California Coastal Commission and the California Department of Fish and Game. Typical of many coastal watersheds, erosion and sedimentation from agricultural uses in the watershed have degraded water quality and the wetland. Ranchers have been reluctant to become involved in riparian projects because of the potential for govermental restrictions which might interfere with their operation or might require large capital outlays for fencing costs.

PROJECT BACKGROUND

During the 1982 storm, a bridge washed out along Stemple Creek on the ranch of David Righetti, just east of Tomales, California. Mr Righetti's dairy herd had crossed this bridge four times daily to get to and from the pasture to the milking barn. Since the bridge washed away, cows walk down and up steep stream banks in several places to cross the creek resulting in extensive damage to many parts of the creek bank, to the creek bed, and to the vegetation in and adjacent to the creek.

For a number of years the Marin Chapter of the California Native Plant Society has had Mr. Righetti's permission to explore both the adjacent pastures and the creek for native plants. His ranch located "east of Aurora School", is cited in John Thomas Howell's Marin Flora for a number of plants and has not only a good assemblage of coastal meadow plants but a number of species that are found in Marin only near the Sonoma line. Damasonium (Machaerocarpus californicus) and Downingia concolor are examples of plants listed only "east of Aurora School" that have been found in the stream bed on or adjacent to the Righetti ranch. Ranunculus lobbii, rare in Marin, has been found nearby in the creek. Iris longipetala and camass (Camassia quamash var. linearis) grow in abundance in the meadow along with great washes of gold fields (Lasthenia californica) and other spring wild flowers. While there are no rare and endangered plants known on this property, assemblages such as this are rare. The Righetti Ranch, thus, is special because of the flora and the cooperative spirit of the owner.

PROJECT DESIGN

The Marin Chapter of CNPS wanted to prevent the ongoing degradation of the

---

[1] California Native Plant Society, Marin County Chapter, Mill Valley, California.

creek following the loss of the Righetti bridge and wanted to protect the stream from any further cow traffic. Mr Righetti was willing to work with CNPS; he was anxious to have the bridge replaced to decrease the risk of injury to his cows in going up and down the steep banks, particularly in wet weather. The watershed enhancement program of the California State Coastal Conservancy made it possible for CNPS, a non-profit organization dedicated to the protection and preservation of California's native flora, to apply for funds to replace the bridge and to construct fencing on each side of the riparian corridor for the full length (2200 lineal feet) of Stemple Creek that bisects David Righetti's 221 acre parcel.

The grant awarded to CNPS from the State Coastal Conservancy for $54,485.00 will pay for the design and construction of a wooden bridge built on pilings and for the fencing. CNPS will receive in return an easement to allow it to monitor the creek and to maintain access. Stiles will be constructed to allow entry into the creek area and there will be publicized field trips every spring led by CNPS members as well as a brochure describing the flora on the property. These trips will be carefully designed to allow for monitoring the creek restorative processes, surveying the flora, and yet, will not interfer with the dairy operation.

CONCLUSIONS

This project is the first State Coastal Conservancy project in Marin County to be implemented on privately-owned ranch land, owned by a dairy operator that is well-respected in the ranching community. It provides a good model to show that appropriate riparian restoration can occur that benefits both the natural resource and the agricultural operation. In addition, the project has been designed and carried out voluntarily through a cooperative agreement between the rancher and a non-profit organization rather than by local or state governmental mandate.

San Clemente Island: Remodeling the Museum

R. Mitchel Beauchamp [1]

Abstract: Changes in the flora of San Clemente Island since 1964 due to changes in military and feral animal use as well as to increased field investigation are discussed. The status of several endemic plants is addressed as well as management concerns for reforming vegetation associations. Two plants thought to be extinct are reported as extant.

San Clemente Island is one of the eight islands off the coast of Southern California. Geologically it is unrelated to the other islands in the archipelago. It lacks the unusual breccia and Franciscan rocks of Santa Catalina Island, its nearest neighbor, 17 miles to the northeast. San Clemente Island is composed chiefly of Miocene volcanic andesite, rhyolite and dacite. On the island's periphery, as well as at a 1500' elevation interior site, occur fossiliferous sedimentary material also of Miocene age (Olmsted, 1958). A recent soil survey of the island identified soils as largely clays (Estrada, 1983).

The vascular flora of San Clemente Island has evolved or persisted on this volcanic base. As discussed by Carlquist (1965), Raven (1963), and Thorne (1969), the native flora of the island reflects a disharmony with adjacent mainland areas of similar habitat. This disharmony, combined with the relatively high level of plant species uniqueness, suggests continued isolation of the island from mainland connections since emergence.

A recent compilation of the Channel Islands' flora by Gary Wallace (1985) allows an updated evaluation of the island flora.

Wallace's compilation, with a few additions which will be noted later, assigns 345 taxa to San Clemente Island. Sorting non-native from native gives a count of 264 native taxa. Of these 264 taxa, 14 are, as cited by Raven and Thorne, unique to San Clemente Island:

Astragalus nevinii
Brodiaea kinkiensis
Camissonia guadalupensis ssp. clementina
Castilleja grisea
Delphinium variegatum ssp. thornei
Delphinium kinkiense
Eriogonum giganteum ssp. formosum
Galium catalinense ssp. acrispum
Lithophragma maximum
Lotus argophyllus var. adsurgens
Lotus dendroideus var. traskiae
Malacothamnus clementinus
Stephanomeria blairii
Triteleia clementina

Since 1963, when Raven compiled a treatment of the San Clemente Island flora, a rather extensive amount of field work has occurred.

San Clemente Island is administered by the U.S. Navy, serving as a training and testing facility. As part of the environmental awareness of the 1970's, the Navy began, as part of its Naval Ocean Systems Center staff on the island, a Natural Resources program. A heavy program emphasis was placed on island habitat assessment, involving both plants and animals. Associated with the federal presence on San Clemente Island was the fact that the first four plants to be listed by the U.S. Fish and Wildlife Service under the Endangered Species Act were four endemic plants, Castilleja grisea, Malacothamnus clementinus, Lotus scoparius ssp. traskiae, and Delphinium kinkiense. Management focussed on the habitat for these plants, as well as a listed reptile, the Island Night Lizard, and two birds, the San Clemente Sage Sparrow and the San Clemente Loggerhead Shrike. Field work to assess the extent of listed and candidate plant and animals was started in 1976. Field work involved investigation of the several canyon systems, transects of vegetation to characterize plant associations and placement of exclosures to demonstrate the adverse effect of goat grazing and pig rooting.

---

[1] Consulting Botanist and Horticulturist, Pacific Southwest Biological Services, Inc., National City, CA; Editor, Herbertia International Journal of Bulbous Plants, American Plant Life Society, La Jolla, CA.

Several feral or non-indigenous animals, including goats, pigs, mule deer, chuckar, Gambel's quail, house cats, Norwegian rats, harvest mouse, meadow mouse, and house mouse have been introduced to San Clemente Island (Chambers, 1981). Their presence is a primary threat to indigenous and endemic plants and animals on the island.

Coincidental with the emphasis on biological investigation, a goat and pig removal program was identified in the Natural Resources program. Goats were live trapped and shipped off-island. Some recovery of plant populations was noted but this was mostly in areas near island habitations, principally Wilson Cove. The more remote island areas still contained substantial numbers of goats. Currently less than 1,000 goats remain on the island.

The recovery of the island vegetation has been quite remarkable with the lowered goat population. The most remarkable sight is the extensive stands of Stipa grassland in areas normally grazed to the bare ground. In the central island area, Baccharis pilularis ssp. consanguinea has begun to spread.

At the south end of the island the rare Lotus argophyllus ssp. adsurgens occurs in several large stands where only a few plants were known before.

Seedlings of the island trees, i.e. Prunus ilicifolia, Quercus tomentella, and Lyonothamnus floribunda, however, have yet to appear in the eroded understory of the senescent groves on the islands steep east slope.

Destruction of bulbous and rhizomatous plant habitats by feral pigs continues and pig populations appear to be expanding at the expense of the goat population and island vegetation. Several island endemics, particularly Brodiaea kinkiensis and Triteleia clementina are severely rooted-up by the pigs. The type locality of Delphinium kinkiense has been destroyed by pig rooting of Sanicula crassicaulis at that site.

The botanical field work during the last decade on San Clemente Island has added substantial information on the distribution of the flora as reported by Raven in 1963.

Malacothamnus clementinus

Raven's knowledge of the single population at Lemon Tank lead him to hypothesize that the plant survived due to its occurrence near the present limit of Pleistocene inundation, i.e. 1500'.

Seven new colonies have been located, three on the west side near Lost Point, one large breeding colony at Horse Beach Canyon, and one on a cliff in China Canyon. One colony is occasionally swept by high tide-driven waves. Ornithologists discovered the west coast population and Lt. Commander James Mills discovered the Horse Beach Canyon population while performing biological field investigation as part of his Naval Reserve training obligation.

Lithophragma maximum

Rimo Bachigalupi (1963) described this endemic species in a companion article with Raven's flora. The plant was considered possibly extinct in the U.S. Fish and Wildlife Service Endangered Species listing. The plant was rediscovered by Jan Larson, Howard Ferguson, and myself in a south branch of Bryce Canyon in 1977 and currently 3 colonies are known. Four plants were taken for cultivation in a prominent Orange County native plant nursery. The remaining plants are still vulnerable to goat predation.

Saxifraga californica

A single inflorescence of this plant was found by Larry Sward in 1976. A recheck of the site confirmed a single plant at the head of Sambucus Canyon on the east side.

Sibara filifolia

Heretofore known historically from Santa Cruz and Santa Catalina islands, this small annual was discovered at the southern end of San Clemente Island in spring of 1986. Two plants were observed and one collected so seed could be propagated away from goat predation. The plant had been considered possibly extinct until this rediscovery.

Lycium brevipes

The last known plants of this taxon were reported by Raven to have been destroyed during construction of the northern runway at the isthmus on San Clemente Island. A small population, apparently of this species, occurs near a borrow pit above the NOTS pier area. The population appears to have several young plants.

Lotus argophyllus ssp. adsurgens

This distinctive lotus seems to have evolved a very reflective pubesence and leaf orientation much like the Argyroxiphium of the Hawaiian Islands. The plants grow in dry, rocky sites exposed to full sun at the southern end of San Clemente Island. Goat predation has been severe in this area due to the remote, protected nature of this shore bombardment portion of the island. Many hundred plants flowered this year, but seed set was poor due to mouse predation of seed heads. Introgression between this and the more widespread Lotus argophyllus ssp. ornithopus may explain some of the variation recognized by Dunkle (1950).

Lavatera assurgentiflora

Only one native stand of this widely cultivated shrub is yet known on San Clemente Island. The taxon is included in Philbrick's (1980) Lavatera assurgentiflora ssp. glabra. At the site, north of the main runway, a rock quarry was recently reactivated, destroying over half the population. Seeds of this population have been used to produce plants which are to be reestablished elsewhere on the island.

Crossosoma californica

Contrasting to the extensive stands of this paleo-endemic of the Californian flora on Santa Catalina Island, only 9 shrubs are known on San Clemente Island. The plants do set viable seed, but this plant has not yet been a target for reestablishment.

Ceanothus megacarpus

A few, very vigorous shrubs of this taxon occur in China Canyon, while some very senescent individuals occur in east side canyons. Goat predation is intense on this plant where it is accessible.

Castilleja grisea

This endemic plant, listed as Endangered, is much more widespread on San Clemente Island than originally known. The east side of the island has several extensive areas of the shrub. The plant also occurs in cliffs of all canyons and was thought to be an obligate chasmophyte or cliff dweller. Field work, however, disclosed an undisturbed population at Pyramid Head where the shrub is a component of the only intact Maritime Sage Scrub on the island. Unfortunately, this unique site, which offers a better pre-feral herbivore understanding of the island vegetation, was reduced by half when a Marine Corps bulldozer operator practiced on his machine in the area.

Dudleya

Every canyon on the island has Dudleya. Historically, two taxa have been ascribed to the island, Dudleya virens and Stylophyllum albidum (Britton & Rose, 1903). A population on the island's west coast area seems to fit the S. albidum description, but the transfer of this species ephithet has yet to be made to Dudleya.

Orobanche uniflora

A single colony of this parasite was found in a Cleome isomeris stand above a sea cliff area. A similar discovery of Orobanche uniflora was made by me on San Nicolas Island in 1978 (Westec, 1978).

Cyrtomium falcatum

The discovery of this east Asian fern in a remote west side canyon by Dylan P. Hannon in 1985 suggests an interesting hypothesis on long distance dispersal, not from eastern Asia, but from coastal San Diego County where the fern is recorded as adventive in canyons at La Jolla, 65 miles east of the island. Because of its location high on a cliff in a remote canyon, human transport of the plant to the island, which is the main vector of most weeds in the flora, is not probable. Observation on the island of wind patterns during severe Santa Ana winds, i.e. blowing out to sea, suggests possible transport of spores. Some aspects of soil formation on San Clemente Island have been proposed in connection with aeolian transport from mainland source areas (Muhs, 1980).

Several plants previously collected on San Clemente Island have yet to be confirmed as extant in the island's flora. Dissanthelium californicum, Dendromecon rigida ssp. rhamnoides, Lomatum insulare, and Batis maritima are among this group.

Fire

The reduction in grazing has resulted in a greater vegetation stand on San Clemente Island. In attempting to reestablish shrublands in appropriate slope and soil conditions, the relationship between island plants and fire has become an important consideration.

Because of the routine use of live ordnance, fires are common on San Clemente Island. Recently, the island's fire fighters have begun to use burning to reduce the extent of unmonitored fires. Grassland response to fire seems to favor the *Stipa*, but other endemics are not favored, especially if they have not set seed for the season.

Shrubland response to fire is purely conjecture. No extensive stands of shrubland now occur, aside from *Lycium/Opuntia* areas which dominate the lower western sea terraces. Chaparral plants, such as *Adenostoma fasciculatum*, *Ceanothus megacarpus*, and *Dendromecon rigida*, are very uncommon on San Clemente Island. To use them as a revegetation effort would not address conservation of the vast majority of insular and island endemics which could be amalgamated into some type of sage scrub vegetation. Some credible representation of this association is seen at Pyramid Head and at Wilson Cove.

SUMMARY

The rich floral diversity of San Clemente Island appears to be on its way to preservation. Although feral herbivores have substantially disturbed the competitive relationships of plants on San Clemente Island, the current, reduced levels of some of these animals has allowed a glimpse at the manner in which recovery can occur.

Many areas need to be surveyed further on this island, especially the rugged canyons. Floristic relationships still remain to be investigated, regarding both the suite of plants on San Clemente Island as well as the inter-island relationships.

Acknowledgments: My two decades of botanical research on San Clemente Island has been due to support and cooperation by the island's Natural Resources Program and its director, Mr. Jan K. Larson. Finally, we should not forget the sacrifice of a young, undergraduate student, Tom Burns, who gave his life while investigating the unique botanical treasures of San Clemente Island.

REFERENCES

Bachigalupi. Rimo. A new species of *Lithophragma* from San Clemente Island, California. Aliso 5(3):349-350; 1963.

Beauchamp, R. Mitchel. A flora of San Diego County. California. National City. CA: Sweetwater River Press; 1986. 241 pp.

Britton, N. C.; Rose, J. N. New or noteworthy North American Crassulaceae. Bull. New York Bot. Gard. 3:1-45; 1903.

Carlquist, Sherwin. Island life. A natural history of the islands of the world. Garden City, NJ: Natural History Press; 1965. 451 pp.

Chambers Consultants and Planner. Final EIS--Feral animal removal program, San Clemente Island, California. San Diego, CA: Naval Air Station, North Island; 1981.

Dunkle, M. B. Plant ecology of the Channel Islands of California. Allan Hancock Pacific Expeditions 13(3):247-386; 1950.

Estrada, David C. Soil survey of Channel Islands anex--San Clemente Island part--interim report. U.S. Department of Agriculture, Soil Conservation Service; 1983. pp. v, 197.

Muhs, Daniel R. Quarternary stratigraphy and soil development, San Clemente Island, California. University of Colorado. Department of Geography, Ph.D. thesis manuscript; 1980. 220 pp.

Olmsted, F. H. Geologic reconnaissance of San Clemente Island, California. Geological Survey Bulletin 1071-13; 1958. 68 pp + map.

Philbrick, Ralph. Distribution and evolution of endemic plants of the California islands in The California islands: Proceedings of a multidisciplinary symposium, Powell, D. M. (ed). Santa Barbara, CA: Santa Barbara Museum of Natural History; 1980. pp 173-187.

Raven. Peter H. A flora of San Clemente Island, California. Aliso 5(3):289-347; 1963.

Thorne, R. F. A supplement to the flora of Santa Catalina and San Clemente islands, Los Angeles County, California. Aliso 7(1):73-83; 1969.

Wallace, Gary D. Vascular plants of the Channel Islands of Southern California and Guadalupe Island, Baja California, Mexico. Natural History Museum of Los Angeles County, Contributions in Science No. 365. 136 pp.

Westec. Survey of archaeological and biological resources of San Nicolas Island. Westec Services; 1978 October.

Assessment and Monitoring of Rare Plants in Alberta, Canada

Clifford Wallis, Lorna Allen [1]

Abstract: The history of efforts to assess rare plants in Alberta, including a 1986 pilot project is reviewed. Based on phenology, habitat and location information, historical locations and similar habitats were surveyed for rare species. Each rare plant location was documented and assessments of threats were made. Twenty-two priority species were located including one species not previously reported for the study area. Recovery and monitoring plans for three species were recommended, one species was tentatively classed as threatened, and 15 were regarded as rare but not threatened. For eight species, additional information is required before their status can be determined.

IN CANADA

The history of formalized efforts to conserve rare plants in Canada is not long. In the United States, the passage of the Endangered Species Act in 1973 served as an impetus for the identification and monitoring of rare species, including plants (Butler 1986). In Canada, there has been no comparable legal impetus, and plants have received little attention, especially in comparison with rare and endangered animal species. With the exception of species found on federal lands (such as National Parks), plant life is under provincial jurisdiction in Canada. Only Ontario and New Brunswick have legislation which lists specific endangered plants and prohibits their destruction. Only one species has been declared endangered in each (Tingley 1986).

Perhaps one of the best known definitions of "rare" is that of the IUCN Red Data Book: "Taxa with small world populations that are not at present Endangered or Vulnerable but are at risk. These taxa are usually localized within restricted geographical areas or habitats or are thinly scattered over a more extensive range" (IUCN ND). However, as this definition incorporates the concept of endangerment or threat, considerable knowledge of present extent, population size, factors controlling distribution and possible threats for each species is required before it can be classified as rare. For most species in Canada, the required information to determine "threat" is not available.

Some of the initial rare plant lists were Parks Canada'a lists of species not to be collected in the National Parks, begun in the 1970's. In 1973, the Canadian Botanical Association established the Rare and Endangered Plants Committee which began the task of inventorying the rare and endangered plant species of Canada. As a contribution to this initiative, in 1975 the National Museum of Natural Sciences began the preparation of a series of rare plant lists, by province and territory. Because of the lack of sufficient information to determine "threat", species were included in these lists based primarily on known distribution. A rare plant is defined by the National Museum as "one that has a small population within the province or territory. It may be restricted to a small geographical area or it may occur sparsely over a wide area" (Argus and White 1975).

The Committee on the Status of Endangered Wildlife in Canada (COSEWIC) has begun the task of developing a national listing of endangered plant species in Canada. Ten species are listed as rare, 10 as threatened and 14 as endangered (COSEWIC 1986). Species are added to this list based on information presented to the committee, and no attempt has been made to develop a comprehensive listing.

While a preliminary, comprehensive national list of rare plant species (with no determination as to threat) was completed in 1976 (Kershaw 1976) and Dr. Argus of the National Museum of Natural Sciences is working on an update, most of the rare plant lists for Canada have been developed at a provincial level. This is both the

---

[1] Environmental Consultant, Cottonwood Consultants, Calgary, Alberta, Canada; and National Areas Biologist, Natural Areas Program, Public Lands Division, Alberta Forestry, Lands and Wildlife, Edmonton, Alberta, Canada.

scale at which most data is available and the level at which any legislative action would most likely be taken.

IN ALBERTA

While there is no legislation specific to protection of endangered plants in Alberta, there is provision under the Wilderness Areas, Ecological Reserves and Natural Areas Act to protect rare plant species by establishing an ecological reserve to protect, among other things "rare and endangered plants or animals that should be preserved" (Wilderness Areas, Ecological Reserves and Natural Areas Act 1980). Although there are several sites proposed, no Ecological Reserves have as yet been established.

Despite this lack of legal protection, there are several examples in Alberta where the presence of rare species has been considered in land management decisions. A proposed highway that would have blocked off the major water supply to peatlands that support numerous rare orchid species in the Wagner Natural Area was realigned. Development of a fish hatchery at Many Springs in Bow Valley Provincial Park was halted, again because the reduced water flow would be harmful to the rare species of orchids and other species of wetland plants occurring there (Wallis and Wershler 1981). In an area of southwestern Alberta with a high number of rare plant species, a survey was done to identify populations of rare plants which could potentially be impacted by a proposed access route for a gas wellsite and to suggest possible mitigation (Loewen and Allen 1986).

The need for recognition and consideration of rare plants in land management decisions is becoming increasingly important. For example, 16 species of plants found in the wetlands of the Parkland and Grassland Natural Regions of Alberta are now classified as rare largely due to loss of wetlands through drainage and cultivation (Bradley 1986a).

Argus and White (1975) completed a preliminary listing of rare plants in Alberta, which was updated by Argus and White (1978) and Packer and Bradley (1978 and 1984). Packer and Bradley surveyed numerous Canadian herbaria and mapped the Alberta distribution of all plants which met the "rare" criteria. Only species for which there were five or fewer recorded localities or collections in the province and with one of four main distribution patterns were considered for inclusion on this list (adapted from Kershaw 1986):

1. Widespread species which are rare throughout their range.
2. Peripheral species which are widespread but only small populations occur within the area.
3. Disjunct species found as localized populations at widely scattered localities. They may occur as restricted disjunct populations throughout their range, or they may be widespread in part of their range but with some restricted, disjunct populations.
4. Endemic species which are considered rare because they are limited to a local area or are restricted geographically although, where they do occur, they may occur in large numbers.

Packer and Bradley (1984) is the most recent list of rare plants for Alberta and includes 360 species or 24 percent of the Alberta flora (Packer and Bradley 1984). Kershaw (1986) examined the species on this list that fit into each of the four categories above and found the following (defining disjunct as a population more than 500 km from the nearest population):

widespread and rare   1 pct
peripheral   84 pct
disjunct   10 pct
endemic   5 pct

These lists have aided in the identification of major concentrations of rare species and of restricted habitats which tend to support rare species. Areas identified as having a high number of endemics include southern Alberta and the Lake Athabasca vicinity. Areas with a high concentration of rare species include the Cordillera, the northeast corner of Alberta, the botanically diverse southwest corner of Alberta, and the dry Grassland region along the southern border. But many species listed as rare at present may prove not to be so. For example, comparatively little work has been done in mountain and northern areas where access is difficult. Species now listed as disjunct in these areas may in fact just be undercollected.

One of the initiatives taken in 1986 in Alberta has been to refine the rare species list. Species have been reviewed with respect to their North American range, rather than just their Alberta range, and available information on habitat has been included. The result is a detailed summary of Alberta's rare flora that ranks species based on the importance of the Alberta population to the species survival in Canada and North America (Bradley 1986b; Fairbarns and Loewen 1986; Wallis 1986).

This is the first step in compiling the information required to properly assess and manage rare plants.

PILOT ASSESSMENT AND MONITORING PROGRAM

In 1986, a pilot project was initiated to assess and monitor known populations of some of the species identified as high priority. This study is sponsored jointly by the Alberta Natural Areas Program, the Alberta Forest Service, and World Wildlife Canada's "Wild West" program. It is apparently the only rare plant monitoring project in Canada (G. Argus, personal communication).

The study area encompasses over 30,000 sq. km of varied terrain in the southwest corner of the province of Alberta. Included are three major natural regions (Rocky Mountains, Aspen Parkland, and Grassland) and six sub-regions (Alpine, Subalpine, Montane, Foothills Parkland, Foothills Grassland, and Mixed Grassland). Contained within these natural regions are a wide variety of habitats: wetlands, active sand dunes, rock outcrops, active riparian zones, mature coniferous forests, lush aspen woodland and rough fescue grassland, and dry grasslands. A high proportion of Alberta's rarest plants occur in this area.

The intent is to relocate the original collection sites of "priority" species of vascular plants which had previously been collected in the study area. From data collected in the field and a review of herbarium material, an assessment of the threats to the habitat of many species has been made. In addition, a review of the literature on rare plant monitoring is providing some direction for implementing a monitoring program in Alberta. Procedures for maintaining populations of threatened and endangered plants have been recommended.

Species Under Consideration

Twenty-eight priority species have previously been recorded in the study area:
Melica spectabilis Scribn.
Carex geyeri Boott
Allium geyeri S. Wats.
Iris missouriensis Nutt.
Polygonum engelmannii Greene
Suaeda moquinii (Torrey) Greene
Minuartia nuttallii (Pax) Briq.
Stellaria obtusa Engelm.
Draba densifolia Nutt. ex T. & G.
Saxifraga oregana Howell var. montanensis
Suksdorfia violacea A. Gray
Astragalus kentrophyta A. Gray
Lupinus pusillus Pursh
Oxytropis lagopus Nutt.
Epilobium glaberrimum Barbey
Mertensia lanceolata (Pursh) A. DC.
Castilleja cusickii Greenm.
Penstemon eriantherus Pursh
Cirsium scariosum Nutt.
Erigeron purpuratus Greene
Erigeron radicatus Hook.
Hymenopappus filifolius Hook.
Machaeranthera tanacetifolia (HBK) Nees
Prenanthes sagittata (A. Gray) A. Nels.
Senecio foetidus Howell var. hydrophiloides
Senecio megacephalus Nutt.
Stephanomeria runcinata Nutt.
Townsendia condensata D.C. Eat.

Other priority species have been collected at Waterton Lakes National Park on lands adjoining the study area. They were included in the list of species under consideration as they could possibly occur within the study area:

Botrychium paradoxum W. H. Wagner
Trisetum montanum Vasey
Cypripedium montanum
Polygonum austiniae Greene
Stellaria umbellata Turcz.
Aquilegia jonesii Parry
Papaver pygmaeum Rydb.
Epilobium mirabile Trel.
Douglasia montana A. Gray
Phacelia lyallii (A. Gray) Rydb.
Erigeron flagellaris. A. Gray

Study Methods

The study consisted of three phases:
1. literature and herbarium review
2. field assessment,
3. preparation of recommendations and monitoring plan.

Initially, Canadian herbaria containing "priority" plant species from Alberta were visited. Most of the relevant specimens are housed in the University of Alberta, Edmonton collection. Alberta collections from other Canadian herbaria had previously been recorded by John Packer for an update of the Flora of Alberta (Moss 1983). Where this information was insufficient, or where the species were not represented at the University of Alberta, other herbaria were consulted, including the Northern Forest Research Centre herbarium in Edmonton, the National Museum of Canada and Canada Department of Agriculture facilities in Ottawa and the University of Calgary in Calgary.

Specimens were examined by researchers who would later conduct the field surveys and representative herbarium material was photographed for future reference. All data from the labels was recorded to aid in relocating the former collection sites. This included general and legal descriptions, elevation, all habitat information, collection date, phenological state of the plant, and collectors.

Where possible, known collection sites were mapped on 1:50,000 scale topographic maps. Aerial photograph interpretation and analyses of bedrock and surficial geology maps were carried out to define additional areas of habitat similar to the known collection sites.

A field itinerary was constructed to ensure that most of the species could be found in the field. This was kept flexible so that changes could be made if plant phenology was advanced or delayed. Field visits were timed to coincide with the most favorable times for locating each species, usually at the height of flowering. An attempt was made to visit all known collection locales unless the available information was unclear. Representative similar habitats within the study area were also surveyed.

In the field, rare plant habitats were documented on data sheets, maps, aerial photographs, and photographically. Information noted included:
1. Species
2. General location
3. Legal description of location
4. Elevation
5. Map no.
6. Aerial photograph no.
7. Photograph no.
8. Site specific directions
9. Number of individuals
10. Distribution in area occupied
11. Habitat description including landform, soil texture, aspect, moisture, microsite location, slope position
12. Reproductive evidence (type and abundance)
13. Major natural threats
14. Human and other threats

Surveys were conducted from late May to late October 1986 with a concentration of effort from late May to early August. Concurrently, rare plant researchers were also involved in a field assessment of "environmentally significant areas" -- these included sites which were of botanical, wildlife, geological, or hydrological interest. Simultaneously undertaking the rare plants and environmentally significant areas projects reduced travel costs and facilitated more extensive surveys than was possible within the budgets of either project alone.

Results

Generally, 1986 growing conditions were excellent. This contrasted sharply with the previous few years when a series of droughts suppressed plant growth making the location of many rare plants almost impossible.

Data gathered from the herbaria review resulted in some changes to the priority listing. Three species were deleted from the list: Carex geyeri Penstemon eriantherus, and Senecio foetidus var. hydrophiloides. It was found that the habitats of these species were relatively secure; that some species were very adaptable to disturbance; and that they had been collected in numerous sites even though they were restricted to a small geographic area.

We were unable to locate the only Alberta specimen of Saxifraga oregana var. montanensis at the National Museum of Natural Sciences herbarium where it had previously been housed. As there is some ongoing taxonomic debate over this species, it is possible that the specimen has been revised to a more common species. Collection data was also unavailable for Stellaria obtusa Engelm. Neither of these species was actively searched for in 1986 field studies.

When surveys of herbaria were undertaken, an additional three priority species were noted to occur within the study area: Astragalus lotiflorus Hook. Haplopappus uniflorus (Hook.) T & G Thelesperma marginatum Rydb.

With these changes, field searches for 26 priority vascular plant species were carried out. Of these, 21 were again located in 1986 field studies. A new location was found for one species which had previously been reported for Waterton Lakes National Park but not for the study area.

The priority species have been divided into four categories:

1. Recovery and Monitoring Plans Required
Three species have been recommended for the preparation of detailed recovery and monitoring plans: Iris missouriensis, Castilleja cusickii, and Cypripedium montanum.

The first two species are confined to very small populations, their habitats often less than one hectare in size and whose Foothills Parkland and Foothills Grassland environments are still being impacted by human activities. Major features of the habitat are the presence of groundwater flow just below the surface and lush forb and graminoid meadow vegetation. Iris missouriensis appears tolerant of and may actually benefit from some grazing by cattle. Castilleja cusickii appears to have a requirement for ungrazed or lightly grazed lands. Historical populations of both species have been lost due to cultivation of habitat and planting of introduced grasses and forbs for hay crops. Modification of these habitats and heavy cattle grazing pose continuing threats.

Previously unreported, Cypripedium montanum, was found in the study area in 1986. It occurs in small numbers in mesic shrub and woodland vegetation in the Rocky Mountains. Threats include road expansion and increased vehicle access.

2. Threatened

Astragalus lotiflorus has been identified as probably threatened. The study area is peripheral to this species' main range in Alberta so it is difficult to make an accurate assessment from the 1986 studies. Previous studies (C. Wallis, unpublished field notes 1974-1985) indicate that the species is rare and local within its main range and that there has been considerable habitat loss.

2. Rare, But Not Threatened

Another 15 species are considered rare but their habitats are not known to be in any immediate danger. These include many species whose habitat within the study area is relatively well-protected in Waterton Lakes National Park (*), Writing-on-Stone Provincial Park (+), and the Prime Protection Zone (#) under Alberta's East Slopes Policy:

Melica spectabilis*
Polygonum engelmannii*
Suaeda moquinii+
Minuartia nuttallii*#
Draba densifolia *#
Astragalus kentrophyta+
Lupinus pusillus+
Oxytropis lagopus
Mertensia lanceolata*#
Cirsium scariosum*#
Erigeron flagellaris*
Haplopappus uniflorus
Hymenopappus filifolius+
Senecio megacephalus*#
Stephanomeria runcinata

In Alberta, Haplopappus uniflorus habitat is protected outside the study area in Kootenay Plains Natural Area and Wood Buffalo National Park.

Sizeable populations of Oxytropis lagopus and Stephanomeria runcinata are not found in any protected areas in Alberta but their habitat does not appear to be threatened at present.

Polygonum engelmannii is considered to be very restricted in its Alberta distribution but it is abundant within that limited range.

4. More Information Required

In addition to the two species for which collection data was unavailable (Saxifraga oregana var. montanensis and Stellaria obtusa), the status of six species could not accurately be assessed as available collection data was imprecise and populations of these plants could not be located in the field. In some cases, the lack of good label information related to early historical data where reference points were non-existent and where they have now disappeared because of human activities. Extensive searching in apparently suitable habitats for five of these species was unsuccessful. Other means of locating these species will have to be devised:

Allium geyeri
Suksdorfia violacea
Erigeron purpuratus
Machaeranthera tanacetifolia
Prenanthes sagittata
Thelesperma marginatum

Based on herbarium label data and knowledge of remaining habitat, Allium geyeri is possibly threatened, falling in the same category as Castilleja cusickii. Machaeranthera tanacetifolia, collected only once in the late 1800's along a well-traveled trail, may be the result of chance introduction. H. Scoggan, collector of Thelesperma marginatum, passed away in the spring of 1986. He had destroyed his field notes and this could make relocation of the original collection site difficult.

The status of two early-blooming species could not be completely assessed as there was an unusually early spring and the field program began somewhat later in the season. Despite intensive searches in known locations, no sign of Erigeron radicatus or Townsendia condensata could be found.

Particularly noteworthy is a link between the discovery of some significant butterfly populations and the identification of previously unknown localities of one of our rarest plants. Clouded Parnassian butterflies (Parnassius phoebus Fabr.) which feed on stonecrops (Sedum lanceolatum Torr.) were noted in an area of Milk River Ridge, far from their normal range in Alberta. The stonecrop, a common plant species elsewhere in Alberta, is an indicator of tertiary gravel exposures in an unglaciated area of the Milk River Ridge. These gravels support the major populations of hare-footed locoweed (Oxytropis lagopus) in Canada, one of our priority species. Several other rare plants also thrive there. The importance of maintaining contacts in other disciplines was amply demonstrated.

The literature review failed to uncover a wealth of published material on rare plant monitoring, however, a collection of papers (Synge 1980) from a 1980 international conference on rare plants is proving to be very useful. Topic areas covered include:

1. Techniques for assessing the status of plants.
2. Approaches to monitoring rare plant populations in a variety of different natural regions.
3. Methods of achieving rare plant conservation.

General Recommendations

Many of these recommendations may seem obvious to experienced researchers but they may be of some use to those initiating research and monitoring programs:

1. Conduct all pre-field season interviews and herbaria examination prior to the growing season, and be prepared for unusually early breaks in the weather.
2. Sample over several years if climatic conditions appear to temporarily be suppressing plant growth.
3. Focus field programs on a narrow range of habitats and species in order to obtain the most effective use of field time. Broadscale surveys help in initial determination of additional research needs but they are not the preferred method for a thorough assessment of potential habitat.
4. Cooperate with researchers in other disciplines who may be able to provide insights into rare plant habitats through identification of other environmentally significant areas.
5. Precisely label all collections to help future researchers. Species which are common now may not be in the future, therefore, this recommendation applies equally to common and rare species. The single biggest problem in initiating assessment and monitoring programs is the lack of sufficient label data.
6. Permanent plot establishment is important for a long-term monitoring program, however, other methods should also be explored. These include random and selective sampling in similar habitats and periodic re-assessment of threats to actual and potential habitat.

Recommendations Specific to the Study Area

Based on data from the various herbaria and the 1986 field program, four major recommendations are made:

1. The most pressing requirement is to initiate recovery and monitoring plans for: Iris missouriensis., Cypripedium montanum, and Castilleja cusickii.
2. Another project should devise and undertake additional field programs to identify locations of species whose habitat is being threatened, where the existing collection data is inadequate, and for which the 1986 studies were unsuccessful.
3. Protection should be provided for known populations of Oxytropis lagopus, Stephanomeria runcinata, and Haplopappus uniflorus. No suitable habitat for any of these plants is currently well protected in the study area.
4. Habitats of rare plants which are not currently threatened should be monitored on a periodic basis to assess any changes in status.

References

Argus, George W. Letter to Peter Lee, on file at Alberta Forestry, Lands and Wildlife, Natural Areas Program, Edmonton, Alberta. 1986

Argus, George W.; White, David. A preliminary list of the rare plants of Alberta. Unpublished manuscript, Museum of Natural Sciences, Botany Division, Ottawa, Ontario. 1975.

Argus, George W.; White, David. The rare vascular plants of Alberta. Syllogeus No. 17. Museum of Natural Sciences, Botany Division, Ottawa, Ontario. 1978 42pp.

Bradley, Cheryl E. Disappearing Cottonwoods, the social challenge. Unpublished draft supplied by author. 1986a.

Bradley, Cheryl E. The rare flora of Alberta, Volume 3, taxa occurring in the Rocky Mountains south of the Crowsnest Pass. Unpublished draft supplied by author. 1986b.

Butler, James R. Selected North American perspectives relevant to the conservation and management of endangered plant species in Alberta. Unpublished draft supplied by author. 1986.

COSEWIC. Species classified by Committee on the Status of Endangered Wildlife in Canada. Available from Canadian Wildlife Service, Ottawa, Ontario 1986. 2pp

Fairbarns, Matt; Loewen, Valerie A. The rare flora of Alberta, taxa occurring in the Rocky Mountains north of the Crowsnest Pass. Unpublished draft supplied by authors. 1986.

IUCN. How to use the IUCN Red Data Book categories. Threatened Plants Committee, International Union for the Conservation of Nature and Natural Resources, Gland, Switzerland. no date. 9pp.

Kershaw, Linda J. Phytogeographical survey of rare, endangered and extinct vascular plants in the Canadian flora. Ph.D. dissertation, University of Waterloo, Waterloo, Ontario. 1976. 303pp.

Kershaw, Linda J. Rare plants in the prairie provinces, a discussion of terms and distribution characteristics Unpublished draft supplied by author. 1986.

Loewen, Valerie A.; Allen, Lorna J. Survey of rare flora along the South Castle road. Unpublished draft supplied by authors. 1986.

Moss, Ezra H. Flora of Alberta second edition, revised by John Packer. University of Toronto Press, Toronto, Ontario. 1983. 687pp

Packer, John G.; Bradley, Cheryl E. A checklist of the rare vascular plants of Alberta with maps. Department of Recreation Parks and Wildlife, Provincial Parks Division, Edmonton, Alberta. 1978 468pp.

Packer, John G.; Bradley, Cheryl E. A checklist of the rare vascular plants in Alberta. Natural History Occasional Paper No. 5, Provincial Museum of Alberta, Edmonton, Alberta. 1984. 112pp.

Synge, Hugh (ed.). The Biological Aspects of Rare Plant Conservation. Proceedings of an international conference held at King's College, Cambridge, England, 14-19 July 1980. John Wiley & Sons, New York. 1980. 560p

Tingley, Donna. Endangered plants in Alberta, alternatives for legal protection. Unpublished draft supplied by author. 1986.

Wallis, Clifford A. The rare flora of Alberta, Volume 2, taxa occurring in the Canadian Shield, Boreal Forest, Aspen Parkland, and Grassland natural regions. Unpublished draft supplied by author. 1986.

Wallis, Clifford A.; Wershler, Cleve R. Natural history inventory and assessment in the Many Springs area, Bow Valley Park, Volume I. Fish and Wildlife Division, Alberta Energy and Natural Resources, Calgary. 1981. 85pp.

Wilderness Areas, Ecological Reserves and Natural Areas Act. Revised statutes of Alberta Chapter W-8. Queen's Printer, Government of Alberta, Edmonton, Alberta. 1980. 12pp.

Genetic Structure and the Conservation of California's Endemic and Near-Endemic Conifers

F. Thomas Ledig [1]

Abstract: California has 15 endemic conifers and another 13 almost uniquely Californian. The genetic structure of many of these species (i.e., the amount and distribution of genetic variation among and within populations) has been evaluated using isozyme analysis. They run the gamut from genetically depauperate to highly variable. In general, the amount of genetic diversity is related to a species rarity, or the size of its range, but the generalization is weak. Patterns make sense only within an historical context, by taking into account paleoclimatic fluctuations. A species' genetic structure has major implications for conservation.

The amount and distribution of genetic diversity has important implications for species conservation. For example, in species with high levels of diversity, inbreeding depression will probably be a major problem if populations are reduced drastically in size. On the other hand, genetically depauperate species can be managed in small populations with little reduction in reproductive capacity, but they are potentially at greater risk than genetically variable species; new stresses, such as insect or disease pests or environmental pollution, can quickly decimate genetically uniform populations.

The distribution of genetic variation is also important. It should dictate conservation priorities (i.e., which populations to preserve), and determine whether genetic interchange among populations is desirable. Genetic interchange between isolated populations may lead either to a reduction in fitness if adapted gene complexes are disrupted or to a restoration of vigor, depending on circumstances.

To aid in conservation, the Institute of Forest Genetics and the California Conifer Germplasm Conservation Project (Millar 1986) have launched major research programs, surveying the level and structure of genetic variation in many of California's endemic and near-endemic conifers. Studies of rare or endemic species contribute to conservation in two ways: 1) they provide information directly applicable to the genetic management of those species and 2) they are models, or natural experiments, that will help to predict what may happen in more widespread species if natural forest becomes fragmented and reduced in size by management practices.

California has a special responsibility for the conservation of endemic species. A recently published estimate suggests that the state is home to 1,517 endemic plants, nearly twice as many as Hawaii which is second on the list, and nearly as many as the total (1,749) for all the rest of the states combined (Gentry 1986). Of the 86 tree species in California (which excludes the willows and many desert species like the arborescent monocotyledons), 21, or one-quarter, are endemic (Griffin and Critchfield 1972). Fifteen of these are endemic conifers (table 1). Another 11 conifers can be considered primarily Californian, but extend into adjacent Oregon, Nevada, or Baja California (table 2). Therefore, almost a third of California's tree species are conifers that are more or less unique to the state. This paper summarizes our knowledge of their genetic structure, attempts to extract generalizations, and discusses the implications of genetic structure for in situ conservation and management.

METHODS OF GENETIC ANALYSIS

Genetic diversity in California's conifers has been measured and mapped using a technique called electrophoresis which separates the plant's enzymes. Enzymes are polypeptides, chains of amino acids, that function as catalysts in plant metabolism. Enzymes are under

---

[1] Geneticist, Institute of Forest Genetics, Pacific Southwest Forest and Range Experiment Station, Forest Service, U. S. Department of Agriculture, Berkeley, CA.

Table 1-- Status of research on the genetic structure of California's endemic conifers.

Species	Scientific Name	Status
Santa Lucia fir	(Abies bracteata D.Don)	Completed[1]
Santa Cruz cypress	(Cupressus abramsiana C.B.Wolf)	Planned[2]
Gowen cypress	(Cupressus goveniana Gord.)	Planned[2]
MacNab cypress	(Cupressus macnabiana A.Murr.)	Planned[2]
Monterey cypress	(Cupressus macrocarpa Hartw.)	Completed[3]
Piute cypress	(Cupressus nevadensis Abrams)	Planned[2]
Mendocino cypress	(Cupressus pygmaea [Lemm.] Sarg.)	Planned[2]
Sargent cypress	(Cupressus sargentii Jeps.)	Planned[2]
Cuyamaca cypress	(Cupressus stephensonii C.B.Wolf)	Planned[2]
Foxtail pine	(Pinus balfouriana Grev. & Balf.)	Completed[4]
Digger pine	(Pinus sabiniana Dougl.)	Completed[1]
Torrey pine	(Pinus torreyana Parry)	Completed[5]
Bigcone Douglas-fir	(Pseudotsuga macrocarpa [Vasey] Mayr)	In progress[2]
Giant Sequoia	(Sequoiadendron giganteum [Lindl.] Buchholz	Completed[6]
California-nutmeg	(Torreya californica Torr.)	Planned[7]

[1] F. T. Ledig, in preparation
[2] C. I. Millar, personal communication
[3] Conkle, this symposium
[4] J. L. Hamrick, personal communication
[5] Ledig and Conkle 1983
[6] Fins and Libby 1982
[7] J. L. Hamrick and F. T. Ledig

simple genetic control and the sequence of amino acids in each enzyme molecule corresponds to a sequence of chemical "code words" in a gene, part of the DNA molecule. Genetic variants, called isozymes, usually differ in only one or a few amino acids.

The tissue for isozyme analysis (usually seed) is crushed in a pH-controlled buffer solution and each sample of crude extract is then inserted into a slot in a slab of starch gel. An electric current is passed through the gel and the enzymes in the extract migrate in the electric field. The distance they migrate depends upon their amino acid sequence because it determines the static charge on the molecule. After a few hours, a specific enzymatic substrate is added to the gel along with a stain that colors in the presence of the compound produced by that particular enzyme as it converts substrate to product. Colored bands indicate the position of the isozymes, and isozyme variants are characterized by the relative distance they migrate in the gel. Up to 59 genes have been surveyed in some studies of conifers (Ledig and Conkle 1983).

One measure of genetic diversity is "expected heterozygosity", the proportion of the gene loci at which an individual is expected to have two isozymic forms; homozygosity is the case in which both copies of the gene are identical and only one form of the isozyme is seen. Expected heterozygosity and observed heterozygosity should be identical only in large, random mating populations, and in the absence of migration, mutation and selection; however, observed and expected heterozygosity usually differ very little in conifers. Therefore, expected heterozygosity is a good measure of diversity within populations.

Diversity or differentiation among populations can be characterized also, by partitioning total genic diversity into components among and within populations (see Nei 1975). G_{st}, the genic diversity among populations as a percent of total genic diversity, will be used in this paper to provide a relative measure of population differentiation.

Isozyme analysis is fairly simple in diploids; i.e., species that carry two copies of each gene, one derived from their maternal parent and the other from the paternal parent. Almost all of California's conifers are diploids.

With the exception of coast redwood, all of California's endemic or near-endemic conifers have either been characterized by isozyme analysis, or such analyses are in progress or planned for the near future (tables 1 and 2). Redwood has a chromosome number of 66, probably a hexaploid on the basic number

Table 2-- Status of research on the genetic structure of conifers that are predominantly Californian but range into other states.

Species and Range		Status
Range -- Alta and Baja California		
Coulter pine	(Pinus coulteri D.Don)	Completed[1]
Bishop pine	(Pinus muricata D.Don)	Completed[2]
Monterey pine	(Pinus radiata D.Don)	Completed[3]
Tecate cypress	(Cupressus forbesii Jeps.)	Planned[4]
Range -- California and Oregon		
Brewer spruce	(Picea breweriana S.Wats.)	In progress[1]
Coast redwood	(Sequoia sempervirens [D.Don] Endl.)	--
Baker cypress	(Cupressus bakeri Jeps.)	Planned[4]
Range -- Oregon south to Baja California		
Incense-cedar	(Calocedrus decurrens Torr.)	Completed[5]
Jeffrey pine	(Pinus jeffreyi Grev. & Balf.)	Completed[6]
Sugar pine	(Pinus lambertiana Dougl.)	Completed[7]
Knobcone pine	(Pinus attenuata Lemm.)	Completed[8]
Others with restricted ranges -- partly in California		
Washoe pine	(Pinus washoensis Mason & Stockwell)	In progress[9]
Port Orford-cedar	(Chamaecyparis lawsoniana [A.Murr.] Parl.	In progress[4]

[1] F. T. Ledig, in preparation
[2] Millar 1983
[3] Plessas and Strauss, in preparation
[4] C. I. Millar, personal communication
[5] Harry 1984
[6] Furnier and Adams 1986
[7] Conkle 1981 and in preparation
[8] Strauss 1985
[9] C. R. Niebling, personal communication

of 11 in the taxodiaceae. Other Californian conifers have diploid numbers of 22, 24, and 26. Because hexaploidy complicates inheritance and analysis of genetic markers, no one has undertaken an isozyme analysis of genetic structure in coast redwood.

RESULTS OF STUDIES ON DIVERSITY AND DIFFERENTIATION IN CALIFORNIAN CONIFERS

Gene Diversity

Conifers are considered the most highly heterozygous of organisms (Hamrick et al. 1979), but California's conifers run the gamut from the most genetically depauperate of plant species to some of the most variable. At the one extreme is Torrey pine and at the other, Jeffrey pine. Within either of the two populations of Torrey pine, individuals have identical isozymes; within the limits of observation, heterozygosity is zero (Ledig and Conkle 1983). Heterozygosity within populations of Jeffrey pine averages 0.30 (Furnier and Adams 1986). To put these values in context, heterozygosity for the 38 conifers tabulated in Ledig (1986) averaged 0.168. Several of California's conifers fall close to this average (table 3).

In the assemblage of Californian conifers, species with narrow ranges tend to have less variability than those with wide ranges (fig. 1). A better generalization may be that California coastal conifers have lower levels of variability than those from the Sierra Nevada or those that are distributed in both the outer and inner coastal ranges. Species restricted to the outer Coast Ranges (Monterey pine, Torrey pine, Bishop pine, Santa Lucia fir, and Monterey cypress) average 0.08 in heterozygosity compared to 0.19 for the rest. However, the relationships are weak. For example, the coastal Monterey cypress which has a restricted population, comparable in size to Torrey Pine, is as variable as several of the more widespread species. Coastal species are generally restricted to the fog belt, their probable refuge during xerothermic intervals in the recent geologic past.

Table 3-- Measures of genic diversity for some of California's endemic and near-endemic conifers (H_e is expected heterozygosity averaged across populations and G_{st} is the percent of the total genic diversity among populations).

Species	H_e	G_{st}
Santa Lucia fir	0.05	5
Incense-cedar	0.18	4
Monterey cypress	0.16	12
Knobcone pine	0.09	19
Coulter pine	0.15	--
Jeffrey pine	0.30	14
Sugar pine	0.28	--
Bishop pine	0.08	14
Monterey pine	0.13	5
Digger pine	0.13	6
Torrey pine	-0-	100
Giant Sequoia	0.14	10

Climatic changes may have repeatedly shrunk populations. Axelrod (1981) refers to several fluctuations from cold, moist to warm, dry climates. Furthermore, the presence at San Diego of relict vegetation typical of the Sonoran desert attests to occurrence of drier conditions in the recent past. Variation could have been lost during the xerothermic "bottlenecks" if populations were greatly reduced in size over a period of several generations.

In certain species, variability tends to be highest in southern populations and decreases toward the north. In Coulter pine, heterozygosity increases from a low of 0.11 at the northern extreme of its range on Mt. Diablo to a high of 0.19 at the southern extreme in the Sierra Juarez of Baja California (fig. 2). Similar patterns are seen in giant Sequoia (Fins and Libby 1982), Jeffrey pine (Furnier and Adams 1986), western white pine (<u>Pinus</u> <u>monticola</u> Dougl. ex D. Don; Steinhoff et al. 1983), and Douglas-fir (<u>Pseudotsuga</u> <u>menziesii</u> [Mirb.] Franco), and may be related to glaciation (Critchfield 1984). Following glacial retreat, conifers migrated north from southern refugia. Recolonization may have offered the opportunity for genetic erosion because only limited numbers of colonists would manage to disperse into previously unoccupied territory. They could carry only a sample of the genetic variation in the parental population, and each step northward created the opportunity for the loss of more variation.

Population Differentiation

Population structure can be either continuous or fragmented and a species may be genetically homogeneous or differentiated into genetically distinct populations, with all combinations and grades between the extremes. In conifers, most of the total genic variation is within populations, with relatively small differences among populations (e.g., see review in Guries and Ledig 1982). Usually, less than 10 percent of the total variation is among populations. Some of California's conifers are strongly differentiated, however. In Torrey pine, the statistical extreme, all variation is between its two populations and none is within (Ledig and Conkle 1983). Genetic variation among populations of knobcone pine is also greater than normally encountered; of the total diversity, 19 percent is among populations (Strauss 1985). On the other hand, Santa Lucia fir populations show little differentiation despite a highly

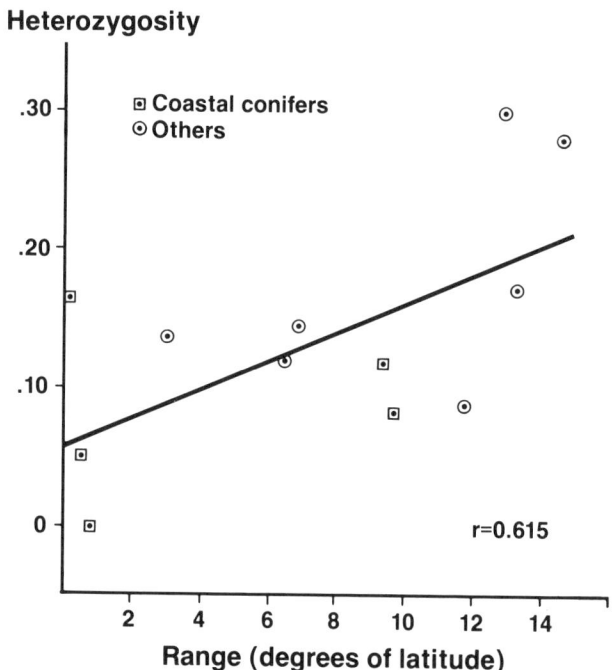

Figure 1--In Californian conifers, genic diversity within populations, as measured by expected heterozygosity, increases with an increase in the latitudinal range over which a species is distributed (▫, species restricted to the outer Coast Ranges; ⊙, species that are distributed either in inland ranges or in both outer and inner ranges), but the relationship is weak.

fragmented population structure. Values for California's other conifers are listed in table 3.

IMPLICATIONS OF GENETIC STRUCTURE FOR CONSERVATION

Conservation and Inbreeding Depression

Where genetic diversity exists, it should be maintained. It is axiomatic that a species cannot evolve in response to changing environmental conditions in the long term without diversity, but less obvious are the immediate dangers if diversity is reduced by inbreeding.

Inbreeding increases with a reduction in population size, and for most conifers, inbreeding reduces survival and reproductive capacity, which could accelerate a slide to extinction. The inbreeding coefficient is a statistic that reflects the degree of relatedness between parents. Progeny of non-related parents have a coefficient of zero, those from crosses among full-siblings have a coefficient of 0.25, and progeny that result from self-pollination have a coefficient of 0.5. The coefficient increases with each generation of inbreeding. For every increase of 0.1 in the inbreeding coefficient, height growth decreased about 4 percent in slash pine

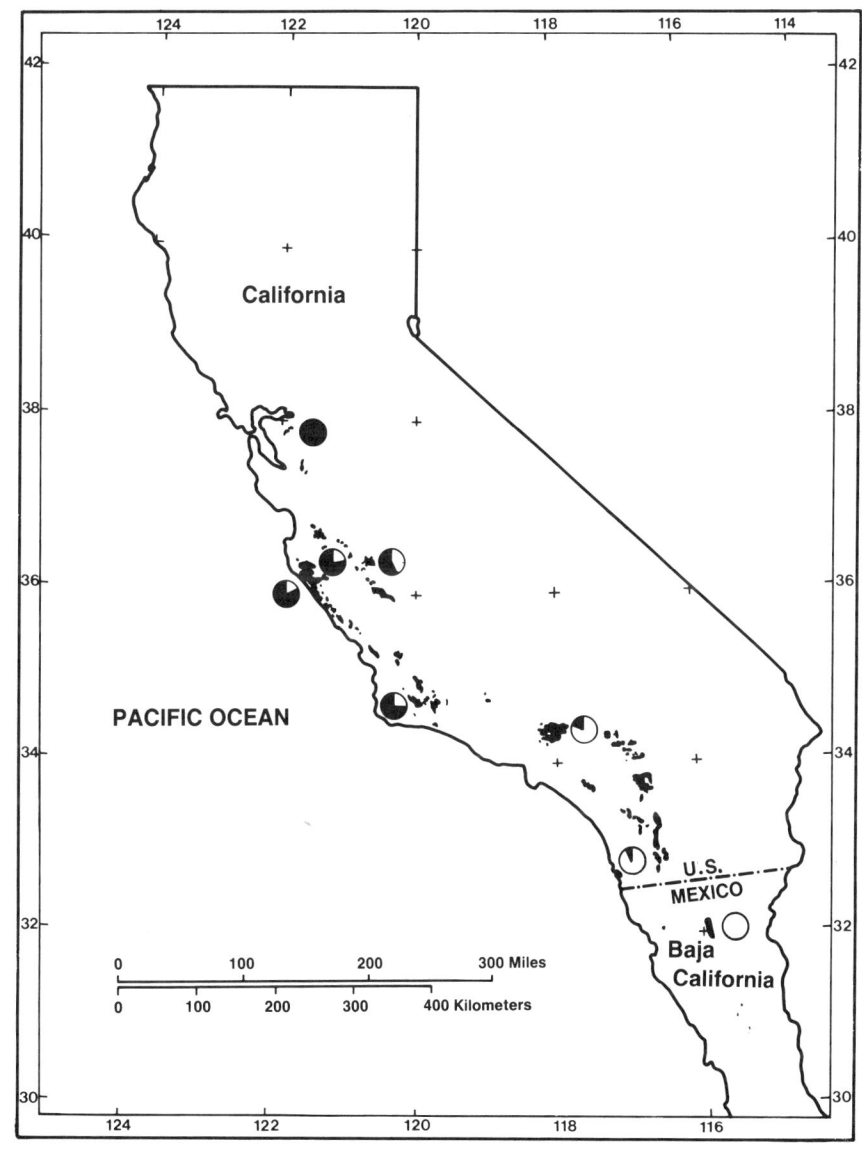

Figure 2--Genic diversity in Coulter pine, as measured by expected heterozygosity within populations, is highest in the southern portion of its range and lowest at its northern limits; pie charts show heterozygosity on a scale between 0.107 on Mount Diablo in California and 0.193 in the Sierra Juarez of Mexico.

(_Pinus elliottii_ Engelm.), and this decrease is probably typical for conifers (Squillace and Kraus 1963). As a result of inbreeding depression, chances of survival are greatly reduced because survival and the ability to compete with grass, forbs, brush, and other tree species depends on growth (see Manley and Ledig 1979 for a development of this argument). Even if inbred progeny survive, they are likely to reach reproductive age later and have smaller crowns, which will reduce their reproductive output. Even more important for species preservation than a reduction in progeny growth, inbreeding results in embryonic abortion, reducing seed yield about 15 percent for every 0.1 increase in the inbreeding coefficient (Squillace and Kraus 1963).

The impact of inbreeding in conifers is inversely related to the amount of genetic diversity, a relationship first noted by M.T. Conkle (personal communication). Diversity for enzymes reflects diversity for recessive lethals and other deleterious genes (Ledig 1986). Self-fertility in highly heterozygous species like Douglas-fir and sugar pine is much reduced relative to self-fertility in red pine (_Pinus resinosa_ Ait.). Red pine is genetically depauperate (Fowler and Morris 1977) and, apparently, completely self-fertile (Fowler 1965), whereas seed yield is reduced on the average 89 percent by selfing in Douglas-fir (Sorensen 1969).

Judging by its lack of variability for isozymes, Torrey pine has probably been purged of most deleterious genes and could be managed in greatly reduced populations without seriously damaging its reproductive capacity. By contrast, Jeffrey and sugar pines tolerate little inbreeding without adverse effects (M.T. Conkle, personal communication) and should be maintained in populations large enough to decrease the opportunity for inbreeding. Monterey pine, with intermediate levels of variability, has sufficient tolerance of inbreeding to be an aggressive colonizer in New Zealand (Bannister 1965).

Species Reintroduction and
Cross-Contamination from Alien
Populations

When populations are well-differentiated, transfers or exchange between populations should be avoided. Population diversity may result either from chance changes in gene frequency in small, isolated populations or from selection. If the latter, transfers are not likely to be as well-adapted as the local population. If it is necessary to intervene by seeding or planting, the conservative course is to use only seed or planting stock from the local population. This is especially true for species like Torrey pine and knobcone pine that have well-differentiated populations. However, for species like Santa Lucia fir, in which most diversity is within populations and one population is genetically very like every other, transfers may be as suitable as seed or seedlings regenerated _in situ_. Where the local population has been extirpated (e.g., as a result of fire), reintroduction can be guided by measures of genetic similarity.

The results of mixing two different populations is uncertain. Intercrossing may be used to enhance or restore genetic diversity, releasing vigor, as in the hybridization of inbred corn lines. Conversely, if two populations have differentiated to the point of evolving divergent, adapted gene complexes, the hybrid may be maladapted in either parental environment, and perhaps, in any environment, a situation known as hybrid dysgenesis or outbreeding depression (Templeton 1986). A natural example may be the "blue" and "green" races of Bishop pine which meet and hybridize north of Fort Ross (Millar 1983). Differences between the races may be maintained by selection against hybrids. With sensitive populations, managers are well-advised to proceed cautiously and avoid cross-contamination unless well-planned trials have shown no hybrid dysgenesis.

CONCLUSION

Surveys of the genetic structure of several of California's endemic and near-endemic conifers are completed or underway. A variety of structures exist, ranging from species with small, fragmented populations to those with large, continuously distributed populations. And on these structures is superimposed a genetic architecture; genic diversity ranges from low to high levels and may be distributed over anything from a seemingly homogeneous array to a hierarchy of genetically differentiated populations. Species with small ranges and those from coastal California tend to have less variation than those with more extensive geographic distributions that include both the Coast Ranges and the Sierra Nevada. In a number of cases, diversity has apparently been lost as species migrated north during the current interglacial period. Genetic drift has had a major role in shaping the genetic structure of many of California's conifers, particularly those with severely restricted ranges.

In the management of California's conifers, conservationists must operate within the constraints imposed by genetic structure, the patterns of genic diversity. Genetically depauperate species can be managed as small populations, but for species with greater diversity, heterozygosity is an index of population vigor and can be sacrificed only with temerity. When populations have genetically diverged, the cautious approach is to avoid intermixing or cross-contamination because of the dangers of maladaptation and the possibility of outbreeding depression.

REFERENCES

Axelrod, D.I. Holocene climatic changes in relation to vegetation disjunction and speciation. Amer. Natur. 117:847-870; 1981

Bannister, M.H. Variation in the breeding system of Pinus radiata. In: Baker, H.G. and Stebbins, G. L. eds. The genetics of colonizing species. New York: Academic Press; 1965; 353-372.

Conkle, M.T. Electrophoretic analysis of variation in native Monterey cypress (Cupressus macrocarpa Hartw.). In: Proceedings for the California Native Plant Soc. Symp., November 5-8; Sacramento, CA. 1986 (In press).

Conkle, M.T. Isozyme variation and linkage in six conifer species. In: Conkle, M.T. tech. coord. Proc. Symp. on Isozymes of North American Forest Trees and Forest Insects, 1979 July 27; Berkeley, CA. Gen. Tech. Rep. PSW-48. Berkeley, CA: Pacific For. Exp. Sta., For. Serv., U.S.D.A.; 1981; 11-17.

Critchfield, W.B. Impact of the Pleistocene on the genetic structure of North American conifers. In: Lanner, R.M. ed. Proc. Eighth North Amer. For. Biol. Workshop. Logan, UT. 1984; 70-118.

Fins, L.; Libby, W.J. Population variation in Sequoiadendron: seed and seeding studies, vegetative propagation, and isozyme variation. Silvae Genet. 31:101-148; 1982.

Fowler, D.P. Effects of inbreeding in red pine, Pinus resinosa Ait. II. Pollination studies. Silvae Genet. 14:12-23; 1965.

Fowler, D.P.; Morris, R.W. Genetic diversity in red pine: evidence for low genic heterozygosity. Can. J. For. Res. 7:343-347; 1977.

Furnier, G.R.; Adams, W.T. Geographic patterns of allozyme variation in Jeffrey pine. Amer. J. Bot. 73:1009-1015; 1986.

Gentry, A.H. Endemism in tropical versus temperate plant communities. In: Soule, Michael E. ed. Conservation Biology: the science of scarcity and diversity. Sunderland, MA: Sinauer Associates, Inc.; 1986:153-181.

Griffin, J.R.; Critchfield, W.B. The distribution of forest trees in California Res. Pap. PSW-82. Berkeley, CA: Pacific Southwest For. and Range Exp. Sta., For. Ser., U.S.D.A.; 1972. 114 p.

Guries, R.P.; Ledig, F.T. Genetic diversity and population structure in pitch pine (Pinus rigida Mill.) Evolution 36:387-402; 1982.

Hamrick, J.L.; Linhart, Y.B.; Mitton, J.B. Relationships between life history characteristics and electrophoretically -detectable genetic variation in plants. Ann. Rev. Ecol. System. 10:173-200; 1979.

Harry, D.E. Genetic structure of incense-cedar (Calocedrus decurrens). Berkeley, CA: Univ. of California, Berkeley; 1984. 163 p. Dissertation.

Ledig, F.T. Heterozygosity, heterosis, and fitness in outbreeding plants. In: Soule, Michael E. ed. Conservation Biology: the science of scarcity and diversity. Sunderland, MA: Sinauer Associates, Inc.; 1986:77-104.

Ledig, F.T.; Conkle, M.T. Gene diversity and genetic structure in a narrow endemic, Torrey pine (Pinus torreyana Parry ex Carr.). Evolution 37:79-85; 1983.

Millar, C. I. A steep cline in Pinus muricata. Evolution 37:311-319; 1983.

Millar, C. I. Gene conservation in California's forests. Fremontia 14(1):6-7; 1986.

Manley, S.A.M.; Ledig, F.T. Photosynthesis in black and red spruce and their hybrid derivatives: ecological isolation and hybrid adaptive inferiority. Can. J. Bot. 57:305-314; 1979.

Nei, M. Molecular population genetics and evolution. In: Neuberger, A. and Tatum, E.L. eds. North-Holland res. monog: frontiers of biology. New York: American Elsevier Publ. Co.; 1975. 288 p.

Sorensen, F.C. Embryonic genetic load in coastal Douglas-fir, Pseudotsuga menziesii var menziesii. Amer. Natur. 103:389-398; 1969.

Squillace, A.E.; Kraus, J.F. Effects of inbreeding on seed yield, germination, rate of germination, and seedling growth in slash pine. In: Proc., For. Genet. Workshop; 1962 Oct. 21-23; Macon, GA. So. Tree Imp. Comm. Publ. 22; 1963:59-68.

Steinhoff, R.J.; Joyce, D.G.; Fins, L. Isozyme variation in *Pinus monticola*. Can. J. For. Res. 13:1122-1131; 1983.

Strauss, S.H. The relation of heterozygosity to growth rate and stability among inbred and crossbred knobcone pine (*Pinus attenuata* Lemm.). Berkeley, CA: Univ. California, Berkeley; 1985. 148 p. Dissertation.

Templeton, A.R. Coadaptation and outbreeding depression. In: Soule, Michael E. ed. Conservation Biology: the science of scarcity and diversity. Sunderland, MA: Sinauer Associates, Inc.; 1986:105-116.

Concepts of Preserve Design: What We Have Learned

Deborah B. Jensen [1]

Abstract: Island biogeography, ecology and population genetic theory have provided insights into the best sizes and shapes for preserves designed to maintain species populations capable of responding to long-term environmental change. Empirical studies of fragmentation and isolation have verified the influence of preserve size and isolation on population extinction and emphasized the importance of edge-effects: a phenomenon not predicted by the theories. Design lessons from both ecological theory and fragmentation studies are reviewed and the limitations of current methods are discussed. Designing the outside of the preserve is recommended and three questions are presented as a framework for identifying the area to be included within the administrative boundary.

The forces causing the loss of species and their habitats are nearly as diverse as the species themselves. As a result, a successful conservation plan typically includes a variety of different protection tools. Most people agree that the surest way to conserve complex biological systems is to protect them in place (in situ) through a series of preserves. While there is agreement that preserves are necessary, there is no concurrence on how to guarantee they will work.

Scientific design of a preserve for in situ conservation requires a multidisciplinary effort. Population biology and genetics can be used to determine the number of individuals of a target species the preserve must include. However, not only the target species but also the ecological community in which it lives must be protected. Incorporating community dynamics into the preserve design requires a knowledge of ecology and vegetation succession. Finally, the effects of activities outside the preserve boundaries need to be considered using land use planning and land use controls.

Unfortunately, most of the world's existing parks and preserves were not designed to be self-contained biological preserves. They may not be adequate to protect the species found there. The methods of designing a new preserve can also be used to evaluate the effectiveness of an existing park or preserve.

---

[1] Energy and Resources Group, University of California, Berkeley, 94720

This paper reviews the applications of ecological theory and fragmentation studies to preserve design. Ecological theories provide insight into the process of extinction, but are of limited use in preserve design because they are not quantitative and not readily adapted to the analysis of specific cases. Because preserves are rarely the "islands" assumed in many modern ecological models, designing the land uses outside the preserve is likely to be as important as designing the inside of the preserve.

Establish Goals

Setting goals is the first step in designing a new preserve or evaluating the conservation merits of an existing preserve. What should the preserve accomplish? Meeting different goals requires different types of preserves. For example, preventing the extinction of a species or suite of species can be accomplished in a zoo or botanic garden. In contrast, maintaining a population capable of responding to long term environmental change, or maintaining populations of existing native vertebrate species on National Forests requires in situ conservation strategies.

Performance criteria for the preserve or conservation plan clarify the policy goal. Shaffer (1981) recommends explicitly stating the length of time the conservation plan will be in effect and defining acceptable levels of risk. The preserve design will be different if the preserve is to provide a 50 percent chance that a target species will be extant in 100 years than if it is to give 95 percent certainty, or if the species should be extant in 500 years.

This paper will focus on preserves designed to conserve species in imminent danger of extinction by maintaining the biological system of which they are a part. These are the species most in need of immediate conservation actions. Understanding the nature of extinction will make it possible to identify vulnerable taxa and determine the requirements for a preserve designed to prevent extinction.

Extinction

Extinction can be viewed as the loss of a lineage, be it a population, a race, a subspecies, or a genus. Typically, deterministic forces, many of which are anthropogenic, such as habitat loss, pollution, overharvesting, or loss of an obligate mutualist, reduce population size or simplify population structure making the population susceptible to chance events which eliminate it. The chance or stochastic forces contributing to species extinction may be intrinsic to the population, for instance the loss of alleles due to inbreeding, or extrinsic, such as environmental variation (Shaffer 1981).

Population extinction is generally believed to be due to both environmental forces and traits characteristic of the organism. The different forces contributing to extinction can be classified into two categories: extrinsic and intrinsic. Extrinsic forces include environmental changes, natural or anthropogenic, and interactions with other species. The intrinsic forces believed to contribute to species extinction include: 1) demographic stochasticity, or random fluctuations in population size, 2) social behaviors which break down at small population sizes, and 3) genetic deterioration due to the loss of genetic diversity through inbreeding and genetic drift (Shaffer 1981, Soule 1983, Soule and Simberloff, 1986).

Small populations are believed to be more vulnerable to extinction caused by intrinsic factors. Loss of genetic material through genetic drift and inbreeding increases at very small population sizes. This may reduce the species ability to evolve in response to environmental changes. Demographic events also become more important at small population sizes. Fluctuations in population number due to chance demographic events are inversely proportional to the square root of the carrying capacity (May 1974). As a result small populations suffer proportionally larger swings in total numbers of individuals.

These fluctuations in the number of individuals in the population may make the species vulnerable to other extinction forces. For example, Crampton's orcutt grass (*Tuctoria mucronata* (Crampton) J. Reeder) was reduced to one known population, and then no individuals of this annual were seen for several consecutive years. Finally, the conditions were right and a handful of individual plants were able to mature and flower. Crampton's orcutt grass declined to a small enough population that one or two bad seed production years nearly resulted in the extinction of this annual grass.

Rarity is often considered the best indicator of a species' vulnerability to extinction. However, rarity is not a term with an agreed upon definition (see Rabinowitz 1981). Definitions of species' rarity range from low population density wherever the species is found, to few populations regardless of the density or absolute number of individuals in each population. If rarity is to indicate vulnerability to extinction, a rare species should be defined as one with few extant populations each of which has few individuals. Such a species is likely vulnerable to both extrinsic and intrinsic extinction forces.

However, using any definition, rarity is not an adequate indicator of the likelihood of extinction of a species, particularly for plants. Plants which have always been rare either because they are recently evolved or because there is only a very small acreage of suitable habitat may not be especially vulnerable. They are likely to have adapted to small population sizes, hence will be less vulnerable to intrinsic extinction factors than species which were once widespread and are now quite rare. In these latter cases, an understanding of the extrinsic threats to the taxon are needed to evaluate its vulnerability.

It is important to recognize that extinctions of species may not be attributable to the same causes as extinctions of populations since community level interactions may be critical in species extinction. For example, if a pollinator goes extinct or is outcompeted by an introduced pollinator such as the honey bee (Schaffer, et al. 1979) a plant species which depends upon the native pollinator may be adversely effected and suffer decreased reproduction. Paine's (1966) classic study of a keystone predator teaches that the loss of one species in a community may result in what has been called a "cascade of extinctions" (Terborgh and Winter 1980).

Community interactions are not the only reason species extinction may differ from population extinction. As the total number of populations decreases, the species as a whole is more susceptible to extinction through extrinsic factors. Each population becomes a greater percentage of the total, and thus catastrophic loss of any population has a larger impact on the viability of the species. Both the number of populations and the number of individuals in the population are important in species survival.

The lesson from studying the process of extinction is that to prevent extinction it is necessary to:

1. Maintain a large enough population, since small populations are more prone to chance demographic problems and loss of genetic diversity through drift;

2. Guarantee that more than one population persists;

3. Identify and eliminate the causes of population decline;

4. Maintain other species in the community that may be critical to the survival of the target taxa.

In addition, understanding what contributes to making a species extinction-prone, provides some guidance about which taxa to protect first.

Habitat conversion is the greatest cause of extinction; it threatens to accelerate global extinctions to an unprecedented rate by the turn of the century (Myers 1979). This habitat conversion has two main effects: first is the outright destruction of habitat which either eliminates the species or reduces its numbers, and second is fragmentation of habitat which creates isolated populations. These habitat fragments provide the core building blocks with which to build a preserve system.

Island Biogeography

Island biogeography has influenced contemporary thinking on preserve design, because many researchers view nature preserves as islands of favorable habitat surrounded by a hostile man-made environment (e.g. Diamond and May 1976, Simberloff and Abele 1976a, 1976b, Sullivan and Shaffer 1975, Terborgh 1976, Wilcox and Murphy 1985). As land conversion and habitat fragmentation continue, the remaining areas of native vegetation begin to resemble real islands. Looking at the species dynamics of real islands may provide insight into what to expect from habitat islands where they truly are within a sea of developed land.

The theory of island biogeography (MacArthur and Wilson 1967) is a general model which explains the number of species found on an island as a dynamic equilibrium between the immigration of new species and the extinction of species already present on the island. Once equilibrium is reached, the number of species should remain constant, although the composition of the species present on the island at any time will change.

MacArthur & Wilson's island biogeography model has four findings which have been influential in the optimal design of nature preserves (e.g. Diamond and May 1976). They are briefly presented below.

1. Area effect. Species richness at equilibrium increases with the area of the island. The lesson for preserve design is that, all else being equal, big preserves support more species than small preserves.

2. Isolation or distance effect. Islands farther from the mainland source of species will have fewer species. The preserve design criteria is to consider the distance between preserves (or habitat patches). If preserves are near to each other, species may be able to migrate between them. Isolation also adds to the definition of an extinction prone-species. Species with limited dispersal capabilities should be more vulnerable than vagile taxa.

3. Species equilibrium. The equilibrium number of species is controlled by a balance between immigration of new species to the island and extinction of species on the island. Immigration is a function of the isolation of the island and extinction is function of the size of the island. Smaller islands will have a higher extinction rate than larger islands. This may make it difficult to maintain species on very small preserves.

4. Relaxation. Islands recently isolated from the mainland will be "super-saturated". This means that they will have a continental or mainland number of species (similar to a very large island) and gradually lose species through extinction until they reach an island equilibrium number of species. The preserve

design lesson is that recent isolates will lose species until they reach the equilibrium number for an area of that size, so as preserves (or any habitat areas) become habitat islands they will lose species.

Limitations of Island Biogeography

The island biogeography model has been a powerful explanation of why there are fewer species on islands than on the mainland. It has inspired hundreds of research projects which have greatly increased the knowledge of biogeographers and ecologists alike. But it cannot provide guidelines for the conservation of particular taxa. The model cannot identify how many acres are need to protect one species, because size must use a species dependent scale. 5000 Downingia could fit into one small vernal pool, but 5000 Abrahms cypress would require many acres.

For a number of years there has been a debate over island biogeography's predictions about the best size, shape and number of preserves. This controversy over one single large preserve versus several small preserves (see Soule and Simberloff 1986, for one recent paper trying to lay this to rest) is another example of the limited usefulness of island biogeography as a preserve design tool. The model provides factors which may need to be taken into account when designing or evaluating preserves and makes predictions about the number of species present at equilibrium, but it has no means of providing quantitative results for any particular case. It cannot be used to determine how many acres are needed to protect a given number of species, nor can it give predictions about non-equilibrium, or non-island cases, and these may represent the majority of parks and preserves.

Despite the lack of quantitative results the island biogeography model is important because of the questions and answers it has provoked. It has demonstrated the need for species specific research and has emphasized the importance of the habitat fragment/island analogy.

Species specific research

Because the island biogeography model cannot predict if a viable population of any particular species will be present on an island, many researchers are taking a different approach. Minimum viable population analysis is being used to determine how big a population is needed to guarantee persistence over a specified period of time (Wilcox 1986). Population viability analysis uses population biology and demography to look at the critical aspects of the population which influence the probability of extinction (Gilpin and Soule 1986).

Initially, researchers, using models which include genetic stochasticity or demographic stochasticity, thought there was a threshold value below which the population quickly succumbed to extinction, and above which the probability greatly decreased. Recent models of the importance of environmental variation in species extinction, such as the work of Menges (1986) show that there is no threshold. Rather, the probability of extinction simply decreases gradually with population size. Therefore, if environmental variation is high, only large populations can make a long time to extinction likely.

Population viability analysis is necessarily done on a case-by-case basis; there are no universal guidelines which can be applied to all taxa indicating how many individuals are needed to maintain a viable population. Careful estimates of the numbers of individuals needed will likely be completed for very few species because of the large amounts of data necessary for the analysis. Because of this some researchers eschew the species specific approach and look at the entire community.

Fragmentation, edges and community level research

Many researchers argue that most habitat islands or nature preserves are not surrounded on all sides by hostile habitat (e.g. Harris 1984, Janzen 1986, Margules et al 1982). Adjacent habitat may support the target species by effectively increasing the preserve area, or adjacent areas may support species which compete with or prey upon target taxa. Are nature preserves really analogous to islands? Do habitat fragments have the levels of species losses that island biogeography would predict? What other effects result from fragmentation and insularization?

Questions such as these have led to numerous studies of fragmentation and isolation. Studies of forest islands in anthropogenic landscapes (see Burgess and Sharpe 1981) show that the environments surrounding habitat islands may be able to support the "island" or preserve species, but that the habitat island edge is much more important than had been expected.

Research in both the Amazon rain forest (Lovejoy et al 1984, Lovejoy et al 1986) and the eastern deciduous forests of the United States (Whitcomb et al 1981, Temple 1986, Ranney 1977) have found environmental conditions at the edges of forest fragments differ from the interior vegetation. Newly created edges between forested and unforested areas create a steep gradient in wind speed, insolation, temperature and humidity (Ranney 1977). For example, in tropical forests temperature differences (in the shade) extend up to 100 meters into the interior of a forest fragment (Lovejoy et al 1986). Wind speed in an old growth stand of douglas fir surrounded by a clear cut is above normal levels for approximately three tree heights from the edge of the stand (Harris 1984). Clearly, physical differences between the edge and the interior extend into the stand altering the physical environment of the interior.

These physical factors modify the environment of the edge, making it suitable habitat for a different suite of species than in the interior of the forest. Edge vegetation is usually vegetation representative of an earlier successional stage than that of the interior. Weedy, non-native species of plants and animals are quite successful in edges. These species may outcompete native plants or may prey on native species as is the case in eastern forests where the European cowbird invades the edge and preys on the native interior forest bird species (Wilcove et al 1986).

Fragmentation studies present some tangible findings which can guide preserve design because they indicate the limitations of small habitat patches.

1. The physical environment of the edge is different from that of the interior. If the preserve is small or narrow, relative to the scale of the vegetation patterns, there may be only edge and no interior to the habitat fragment. It may be unable to support species restricted to the interior vegetation type. As a result, total acreage may not be a good measure of the functional area of the preserve.

2. The edge vegetation is often of an earlier successional stage than the interior. Large areas of edge vegetation may change the successional pattern of the interior by producing a seed rain into the interior. In addition, the edge may filter out interisland seed dispersal for interior species, particularly for animal mediated dispersal. Thus, successional patterns in the patch may be altered, and many more shade intolerant taxa found in the interior of habitat islands than would be expected from a similar acreage embedded in a larger piece of vegetation.

3. Corridors have often been touted as a way of effectively increasing the size of small preserves, or at least allowing dispersal among preserves. The edge-effects lessons lead to questions about the concept of corridors. Do corridors really work to enhance dispersal amongst preserves or do they serve only to create additional habitat for weedy and perhaps undesirable species?

4. Different organisms perceive different edges. Some species may be restricted to old growth stands and perceive the beginning of the second growth stand as an edge. Others species can utilize either plant community and therefore effectively inhabit a larger preserve. For preserves designed to protect more than one target taxon, separate analyses of the functional preserve size may be necessary for each taxon.

Preserve design: what have we learned?

Clearly there is no simple way to design preserves. A design manual with step by step instructions does not yet exist. There is, however, a growing body of literature which collectively presents a list of the concerns to be addressed in setting preserve boundaries.

The step by step approach usually recommended entails first identifying the target taxa or community to be protected and setting goals for the duration of existence and probability of extinction. Then minimum viable population analysis is used to determine the number of individuals of the target taxon to include in the preserve. Next, species ecology and community ecology are used to define the habitat requirements necessary to support the species. Defensible examples of this habitat are identified, and the habitat quality evaluated. The density of individuals found per unit area of habitat when multiplied by the desired numbers of individuals yields the number of acres necessary. Hopefully this area is smaller than the number of acres available. This area is drawn on a map, including the highest quality habitat wherever possible, and the preserve design is complete.

The literature includes an emphasis on determining the minimum viable population, but the major cause of most species' endangerment is habitat loss. Preserve design needs to focus on protecting adequate habitat which is not always defined by the area which contains the population. The Coachella fringe-toed lizard (Uma inornata) lives in moving sand dunes found on the floor of the Coachella Valley outside of Palm Springs. The major threat to the lizard was obstruction of the sand transport system in the valley; construction blocked the source of the dune sand. Without new sand, the dunes soon stabilized and became unsuitable habitat for the lizard. This habitat loss led to the federal listing of the lizard as threatened. Once the major threat to the lizard had been identified, the sand transport system became the most important concern in preserve design. As a result, the lizard preserve contains substantial acreage which is not lizard habitat, but rather is the source of sand--a large wash at the upwind end of the preserve. Including this acreage within the preserve guarantees the protection of the sand transport system which creates the blowing dunes essential to the lizard.

Too much of the preserve design literature limits the scope of the decision making process to only biological considerations. A number of nonbiological constraints such as cost, political boundaries, history, and social or cultural concerns influence the placement of the boundaries of a preserve. Another limitation of the literature is the conviction that all the area which contributes to the species' survival must be contained within the preserve. An all inclusive preserve may not be necessary. The adjacent land use may be compatible with the preserve goals, or it may be possible to implement land use controls which limit the types of land uses permissible outside the preserve. These examples create a preserve which is not analogous to an island.

An alternative approach to the step by step list of biological considerations uses geography as the interdisciplinary tool which integrates the many levels of concern: population, community, landscape or habitat, land use patterns, finances and politics. All these constraints must focus on the location of the administrative boundary.

Three questions of preserve design

There are three questions which encompass all of preserve design and which can be used as a framework for designing preserves or for evaluating the ability of an existing preserve to protect a target species.

What must be inside the boundary?

Answering this question identifies the minimum criteria for the preserve using tools such as population viability analysis. The focus is on the target species. How many individuals, are needed to allow the species to persist for a given number of years? What array of habitat patches are needed, with what essential habitat requirements in each patch? Should habitat for obligate mutualists be included or can they exist outside the preserve and cross the boundary? Physical parameters such as hydrology and appropriate substrate must be evaluated, as in the case of the fringe-toed lizard. Finally, how will this preserve function in relation to other preserves. Is this preserve to function only as core habitat; is it one of a series of preserves; or is it the only protected area for this taxa? Answers to all or as many of these questions as possible will identify those features that absolutely must be within the boundaries of the preserve.

What can be outside the boundary?

This question focuses on the factors which contribute to the target species' survival, but need not be under complete control by the managing agency. It is equivalent to asking how small the preserve can be To determine this, examine land use outside the preserve. In many case the outside is neither asphalt nor agriculture. What types of land uses can be expected in the future? Do all sides border on the same types of land uses? What threats are there? Are these threats important enough to require including more land on the inside or can they be managed or controlled some other way?

Where should the boundary be?

This question focuses on edge effects and management problems. A balance must be struck between the value of having more land inside and threat or cost of leaving it out.

The boundary can be thought of as a permeable filter across which species and people can pass. But control of this movement differs greatly from one side to the other (see Schonewald-Cox 1987). If the preserve is surrounded by hostile man-dominated landscapes, species which disperse across the boundary to the outside will often be lost (e.g. Janzen 1986). To decide where the boundary should be, focus on movement across the boundary by the target species, by beneficial species, and by harmful species, as well as movement of people or substances across the boundary. Can anticipated difficulties be best remedied by a bigger buffer or by placing the boundary in a different place?

Many of the arguments about the best shape for a preserve start with an assumption that the habitat to be included within the preserve is homogeneous. All else being equal, a circular preserve might be better, but all else is never equal. Vegetation patterns, terrain, watershed boundaries, land uses and political boundaries may differ on each side of the preserve. Focusing on the boundary and potential edge effects is much more profitable than focusing on shape per se. The object should be to minimize the edge in those areas where it is likely to contain threats such as successional species or harbor weedy non-native taxa.

The placement of the boundary can also include financial and political questions. Balance the cost of including more land against the cost of leaving it out. (Include both management costs and the cost of increased likelihood of not meeting the conservation goal). What is the existing ownership pattern? Including financial and political questions in the design is an exercise in making explicit the trade-offs between biological considerations and other constraints

Examples of designing the outside of the preserve

Most land in the world to cannot be in preserves, but it may be possible to design the land outside to contribute to species conservation. Dickert's Elkhorn Slough study is an excellent example of this. He and his students evaluated the rate of sedimentation which could be expected from the Elkhorn Slough watershed under different land uses. He then recommended land use limits (zoning) which restricted land uses outside the preserve to levels which would not cause an adverse sediment load in the estuary (Dickert 1986). Designing the land uses in the watershed outside the preserve, in combination with the preserve itself, guarantees Elkhorn slough will be a much more successful estuarine preserve.

The Greater Yellowstone ecosystem, is another example of designing outside the preserve. The grizzly bear is nearly extirpated in the lower 48 states. Considerable research effort was put into estimating the number of grizzlies necessary to maintain a viable population. Then the area needed to support a population of this size was determined. The conclusion from this research is that the Yellowstone National Park is too small to maintain a viable population of grizzly bears.

The grizzly bear is now being managed within the Greater Yellowstone Ecosystem, an area which includes Yellowstone National Park, Glacier National Park and considerable acreage in the adjacent national forests. This is possible because the grizzly uses a broad range of habitats and because these parks are not habitat islands; rather they are surrounded by similar habitat in the national forests.

CONCLUSIONS

Most of the threats to a preserve come from outside the preserve as preserves are rarely true ecological islands. Many of these threats can be mitigated by altering outside land uses. Analysis of the conservation potential of the outside of the preserve requires the same thought process as designing a new preserve. Future conservation efforts need to focus on ways to increase the effective size of existing preserves by planning the land uses on the outside of the boundary.

There are, as yet, few quantitative tools which can be applied in a generic fashion to a wide range of populations, species or preserves. Therefore the case study approach must be used. It is clear that more organismal and ecological data are needed. The more species specific data collected, the more case studies available to draw on when detailed studies cannot be done. When the data for population viability analysis is unobtainable, focusing on the habitat needs may suffice.

Most of the major preserves which will ever exist have already been "designed". They should be evaluated the goal of conservation of biological diversity, either for target species or some group of taxa. If the existing preserves are inadequate, we must determine what else can be done to improve their value as a part of a portfolio of protected areas.

Vulnerable taxa should be protected first; but rarity is often not the best indicator of vulnerability. Some species have always been rare and have be adapted to small population sizes. Such species are not particularly extinction-prone. Conservation effort may be better spent on species which have recently become rare or which are threated by current anthropogenic activities.

Political and socioeconomic constraints are extremely influential in both the design of new preserves and the management of existing preserves to enhance their conservation potential. Rather than ignoring these concerns because they are beyond one's expertise, conservation biologists should work to integrate the many different disciplines essential to protecting biological diversity.

ACKNOWLEDGEMENTS

I thank S.P. Malloch for his critical comments and editorial advice. This work was supported in part by a National Wildlife Federation Conservation Fellowship awarded for 1986-1987.

REFERENCES

Burgess, R.L.; Sharpe, D.M. eds. Forest island dynamics in man-dominated landscapes. New York: Springer-Verlag; 1981. 310 p.

Diamond, J.M.; May, R.M. Island biogeography and the design of nature reserves. In: May, R.M ed. Theoretical ecology: principals and applications Philadelphia: W.B. Saunders Co.; 1976: 163-186.

Dickert, T. Assessing cummulative impacts in watershed management planning, paper presented at Rare and Endangered Plants: A California conference on their conservation and management, Nov 5-8. Sacramento: California Native Plant Society; 1986

Gilpin, M.E.; Soule, M.E. Minimum viable populations: processes of species extinction. In: Soule, M.E. ed. Conservation biology: the science of scarcity and diversity. Sunderland, MA: Sinauer Associates; 1986: 19-34.

Harris, L.D. The fragmented forest: island biogeography theory and the preservation of biotic diversity. Chicago: University of Chicago Press; 1984. 211p.

Janzen, D.H. The eternal external threat. In: Soule, M.E. ed. Conservation biology: the science of scarcity and diversity. Sunderland, MA: Sinauer Associates; 1986: 286-303.

Lovejoy, T.E.; Bierregaard, R.O. Jr.; Rylands, A.B.; Rylands, J.R.; Quintela, C.E.; Harper, L.H.; Brown, K.S. Jr.; Powell, A.H.; Powell, G.V.N.; Schubart, H.O.R.; Hays, M.B.; Edge and other effects of isolation on Amazon rain forest fragments. In: Soule, M.E. ed. Conservation biology: the science of scarcity and diversity. Sunderland, MA: Sinauer Associates; 1986: 257-285.

Lovejoy, T.E.; Rankin, J.M.; Bierregaard, R.O. Jr.; Brown, K.S. Jr.; Emmons, L.H.; and Van der Voort, M. E. Ecosystem decay of Amazon Forest Remnants. In: Nitecki, M.H. ed. Extinctions. Chicago: Chicago University Press; 1984: 295-326.

MacArthur, R.H.; Wilson, E.O. The theory of island biogeography. Princeton: Princeton University Press; 1967. 203 p.

Margules, C.M.; Higgs, A.J.; Rafe, R.W. Modern biogeographic theory: are there any lessons for nature reserve design? Biological Conservation 24: 115-128; 1982.

May, R.M. Stability and complexity in model ecosystems. Second ed. Princeton, N.J.: Princeton University Press; 1974. 265 p.

Menges, E. Extinction probability in rare plant populations: the effects of environmental and demographic stochasticity. In: Rare and endangered plants: A California conference on their conservation and management, Nov 5-8. Conference program, abstracts and poster session.; Sacramento: California Native Plant Society; 1986: abstract no. 121.

Myers, N. The sinking ark. Oxford: Pergamon Press; 1979. 307 p.

Paine, R.T. Food web complexity and species diversity. Amer. Naturalist 100: 65-75; 1966.

Rabinowitz, D. Seven forms of rarity. In: Synge, H. ed. The biological aspects of rare plant conservation. Chichester: John Wiley & Sons Ltd.; 1981: 205-217.

Ranney, J.W. Forest island edges - their structure, development and importance to regional forest ecosystem dynamics. EDFB/IBP-77/1 Oak Ridge: Oak Ridge National Laboratory; 1977. 38p.

Schaffer, W.M.; Jensen, D.B.; Hobbs, D.E.; Gurevitch, J.; Todd, J.R.; Schaffer, M.V. Competition, foraging energetics and the cost of sociality in 3 species of bees. Ecology 60(5): 976-987; 1979.

Schonewald-Cox, C.M. The boundary paradigm, Conservation Biology 1: (In press) 1987.

Shaffer, M.L. Minimum population sizes for species conservation. Bioscience 31: 131-134; 1981.

Simberloff, D.S.; Abele, L.G. Island biogeography theory and conservation practice. Science 193: 285-286; 1976a.

Simberloff, D.S.; Abele, L.G. Island biogeography and conservation: strategy and limitations. Science 193: 1032; 1976b.

Soule, M.E. What do we really know about extinction. In: Schonewald-Cox, C.M.; Chambers, S.M.; McBryde, B.; Thomas,

L. eds. Genetics and conservation: a reference for managing wild animal and plant populations. Menlo Park, CA: Benjamin/Cummings; 1983: 111-124.

Soule, M.E.; Simberloff, D. What do genetics and ecology tell us about the design of nature reserves? Biological Conservation 35:19-40; 1986.

Sullivan, A.L.; Shaffer, M.L. Biogeography of the megazoo. Science 189: 13-17; 1975.

Temple, S.A. Predicting impacts of habitat fragmentation on forest birds: a comparison of two models. In: Verner, J.; Morrison, M.; Ralph, C.J. eds. Wildlife 2000. Madison, WI: University of Wisconsin Press; 1986: 301-304.

Terborgh, J. Island biogeography and conservation: strategy and limitations. Science 193: 1029-1030; 1976.

Terborgh, J.; Winter, B. Some causes of extinction. In: Soule, M. E.; Wilcox, B.A. eds. Conservation Biology. Sunderland, MA: Sinauer Assoc.; 1980: 119-133.

Whitcomb, R.F.; Robbins, C.S.; Lynch, J.S.; Whitcomb, B.L.; Klimkiewicz, M.K.; and Bystrak, D. Effects of forest fragmentation on avifauna of the eastern deciduous forest. In: Burgess, R.L.; Sharpe, D.M. eds. Forest island dynamics in man-dominated landscapes. New York: Springer-Verlag; 1981: 125-205.

Wilcove, D.S.; McClellan, C.H.; Dobson, A.P. Habitat fragmentation in the temperate zone. In: Soule, M.E. ed. Conservation biology: the science of scarcity and diversity. Sunderland, MA: Sinauer Associates; 1986: 257-285.

Wilcox, B.A.; Murphy, D.D. Conservation strategy: The effects of fragmentation on extinction. Amer. Naturalist 125:879-887; 1985.

Wilcox, B.A. Managing for viable populations of endangered plants. In: Rare and endangered plants: A California conference on their conservation and management, Nov 5-8. Conference program, abstracts and poster session.; Sacramento: California Native Plant Society; 1986: abstract no. 119.

Island Biogeography and Preserve Design of an Insular Rare Plant Community

Tim Krantz [1]

Abstract: Principles of island biogeography will be examined with respect to a rare plant community--the pebble plains and associated alpine meadows of Big Bear Valley in the San Bernardino Mountains --a relict alpine plant community distributed over a 260 km square area in relatively discrete "islands" in a "sea" of conifers. Using indicator species to identify and define the rare plant communities, their distributions were mapped using low-level aerial photographs checked against historic collection data. The rare plant communities are distributed among a number of populations, some consisting of single isolated islets, and others are part of complex archipelagos.

Island biogeographical principles that will be examined include distance and size from nearest neighbors; archipelago configurations relative to species diversity; habitat fragmentation and expected population trends; isolation mechanisms, speciation and endemism in island ecosystems; and applications of these principles to preserve design to optimize species diversity and survival.

The principles of island biogeography have been illustrated in classical studies such as Carlquist (1973, 1980), Diamond (1975a, 1975b), and MacArthur and Wilson (1967). They deal with Hawaiian flora and fauna, South Pacific island avifauna and theoretical island biogeography, respectively. Yet, there have been few examples of island biogeographical studies dealing with insular rare plant communities, let alone with practical applications of these principles to preserve design.

The Big Bear Valley Preserve system, situated in the San Bernardino Mountains of Southern California (fig. 1, Regional Location Map) offers an opportunity to examine these principles with respect to a rare plant community--the pebble plains and associated alpine meadows of Big Bear Valley--a relictual alpine plant community that ranges over a 260-square kilometer area (approximately 96 square miles), distributed in relatively discrete "islands" in a "sea" of conifers. Derby and Wilson (1978, 1979) first characterized the floristic composition of several highly discrete pebble plains islands, termed "pavement plains" in that study. Krantz (1981) identified two endemic species, Bear Valley sandwort (*Arenaria ursina* Rob.) and Kennedy's buckwheat (*Eriogonum kennedyi* Porter ex Wats.), as indicators of the pebble plains community, and bird-footed checker-bloom (*Sidalcea pedata* Gray), slender-petaled mustard (*Thelypodium stenopetalum* Wats.), or San Bernardino blue grass (*Poa atropurpurea* Scribn.) as indicators of the associated alpine meadows community (1979, 1980, 1981). Indicator species' distributions were mapped using low-level aerial photographs and field inspections, and checked against historic collection data. As defined by the indicator species, the rare plant communities are distributed among a number of populations, some consisting of single, isolated islets, whereas others are part of complex archipelagos (fig. 2, Rare Plant Communities Map).

FLORISTIC ORIGIN OF THE PEBBLE PLAINS

Prior to the uplift of the northeast end of the San Bernardino Mountains (about 2.5 million years ago), Big Bear was covered by a huge Pleistocene lake that left a deep clay

---

[1] Mr. Tim Krantz, Senior Ecologist, Michael Brandman Associates, Costa Mesa, California.

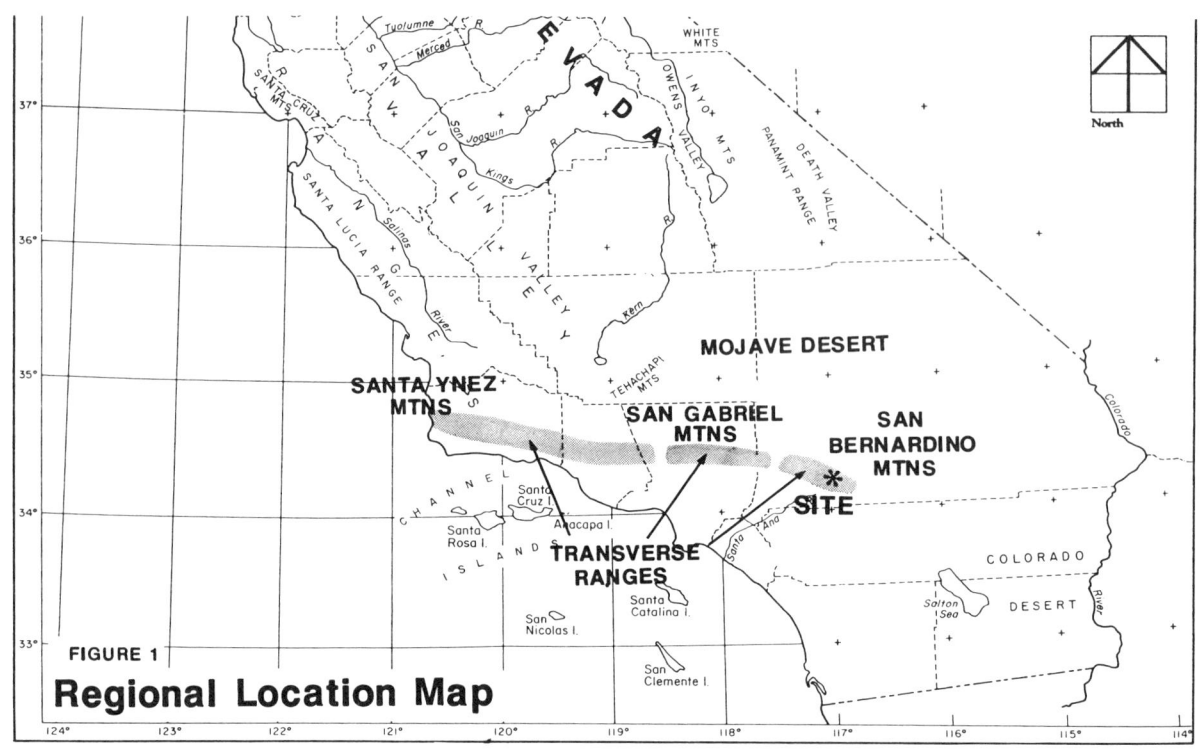

FIGURE 1
Regional Location Map

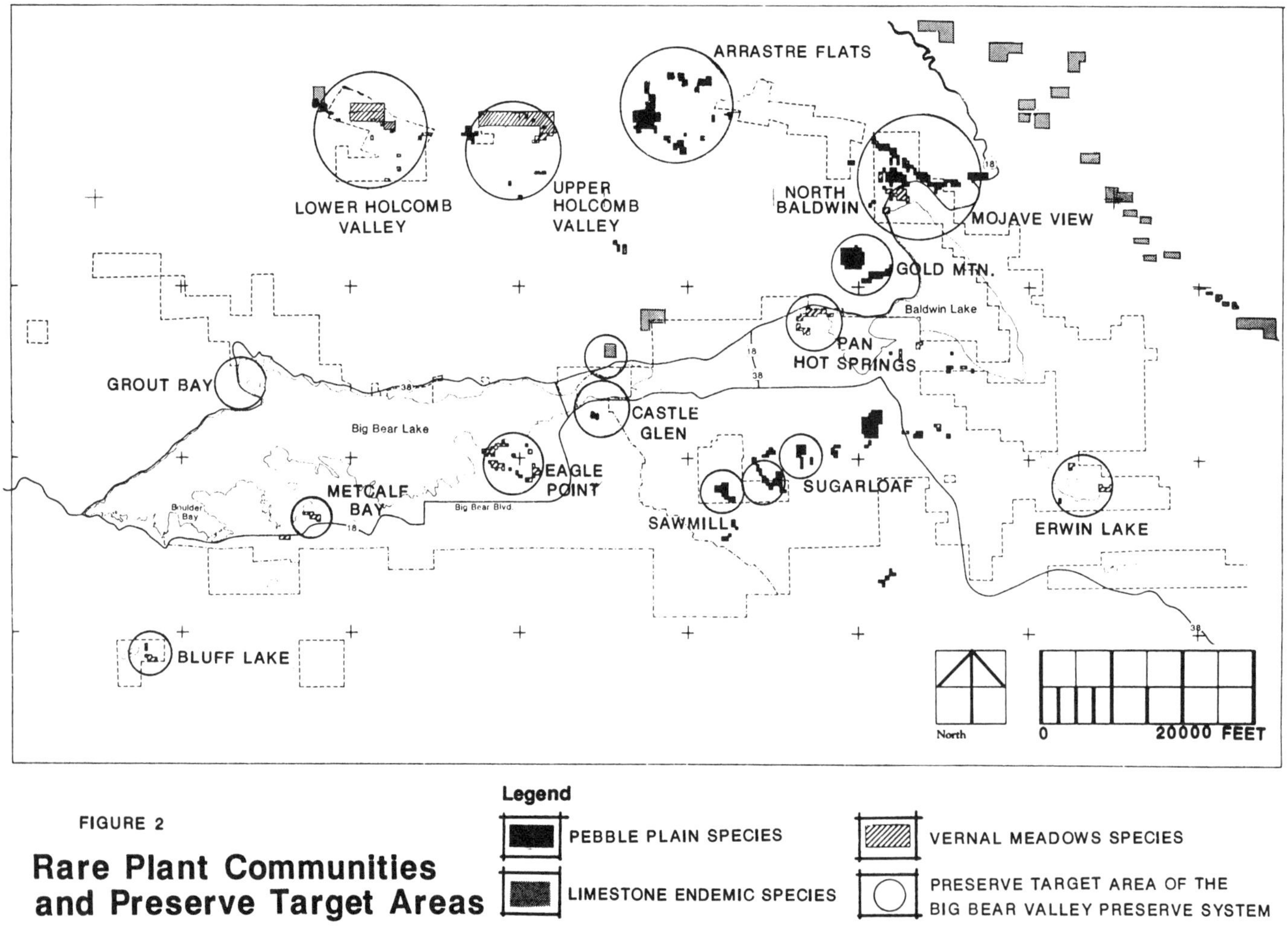

FIGURE 2
Rare Plant Communities and Preserve Target Areas

Legend:
- PEBBLE PLAIN SPECIES
- LIMESTONE ENDEMIC SPECIES
- VERNAL MEADOWS SPECIES
- PRESERVE TARGET AREA OF THE BIG BEAR VALLEY PRESERVE SYSTEM

deposit over the area. Subsequent uplift of Big Bear and Holcomb valleys has fragmented the deposit into a number of benchtop and valley clay lenses, ranging in elevation from approximately 6,500 to 7,500 feet. Frost heave pushes cobbles in the clay deposits to the surface, creating a vestiture of quartzite pebbles, hence the name "pebble" or "pavement" plains.

During the Pleistocene (18,000 to 20,000 years ago) Mt. San Gorgonio, situated at the east end of the Transverse Mountain Ranges of Southern California, was the southernmost peak on the North Pacific Coast to have held glaciers. It was not connected to the arctic continental ice sheets, but was even then a glaciated island separated from the Sierra Nevada to the north by over 100 miles (fig. 1). At that time, Big Bear Valley, just 10 miles to the north of San Gorgonio, was above timberline and was covered by an alpine flora of tufted, perennial herbs more typical of the modern Sierran alpine flora.

During the xerothermic period (8,000 to 10,000 years ago) the climate became hotter and drier. The Mojave Desert expanded to the west, further isolating the montane flora of the Transverse Mountain Ranges. Conifer forests climbed higher in elevation with the more temperate climate, generally overtaking the alpine flora of Big Bear Valley, except on the clay soils of the Ice Age lake. The clay deposits are impermeable to water, becoming very dry and hot in summer months, killing conifer seedlings before they can become established. Thus, the relict alpine flora has persisted on the clay soils to this day, now isolated from other kindred islands of alpine vegetation by conifer forest.

The combination of desert and montane floristic influences has provided a diverse palette for evolution to work with. Over 325 vascular plant species have been documented on as many acres at North Baldwin Lake, with 275 on the 50-acre Eagle Point tract alone. Species diversities can exceed 10 species per decimeter square.

Because of its relatively recent isolation, the relictual alpine flora exhibits little generic disharmony, or dissimilarity, between the pebble plains and their Sierran and Cascade Range counterparts to the north. Southern disjuncts, or species that reach their southernmost occurrences here or in Southern California mountains, represent 47 percent of the pebble plains flora (using Derby and Wilson's species list, which first characterized the pebble plains community, 1979).

Northern disjunction, representing northernmost species' occurrences and, thus, floristic influences from the south, comprises only 12 percent of the pebble plains flora (ibid). Yet, considering that the annual plant species are poorly represented in most alpine plant communities due to the ephemeral growing season, the high proportion of annual plant species (approximately 33 percent of the pebble plains flora) is probably indicative of desert or Sonoran floristic influences. The presence of four species of cactus on the North Baldwin Lake pebble plains is also anomalous in comparison to other alpine plant communities. Ironically, the desert and alpine species are both similarly adapted to drought-stress conditions. In the desert, obviously, water is unavailable for long periods; in an alpine community, available water is locked up in the form of ice or snow for much of the year. Both plant communities have developed convergent strategies of reduction of leaves and general plant morphology; development of protective solar surfaces such as white, reflective hairs; and succulence or bulbiforme water-storage capabilities.

ISOLATION MECHANISMS, SPECIATION, AND ENDEMISM

Compound Isolation

The extremes of freezing winter temperatures and hot, dry summers on the exposed pebble plains represent an environmental barrier against the more temperate-adapted species of the montane flora. This is evidenced by the disharmony of the pebble plains from the surrounding conifer forest flora.

There is an interesting example of adaptive radiation from pebble plain to forest represented by the morpho- logically plastic Kennedy's buckwheat. Kennedy's buckwheat is ideally adapted to the rigors of an alpine environment. Its silver, tufted mats are reflective of the ultraviolet rays and heat of the sun. Its matted leaves float on the heaving clay soil in the winter, well anchored with deep, penetrating roots, and protect its rootzone below the tufts in the heat of summer. On the open pebble plains, the Kennedy's buckwheats all have single-scaped flower stems and tightly matted leaves, although as one walks out into the surrounding conifer forest the plants change before one's eyes to become large, sprawling mats with long leaves and many branched flower stems, better suited to keep from being buried under pine needles and detritus. Plants in the ecotone have mixed single and branched stems. The branched form has been called _Eriogonum wrightii_ Torr. ex Benth. Ssp. _subscaposum_ (Wats.) Stokes, but more appropriately might be named _E. kennedyi subscaposum_, as it is clearly an adaptive-radiated form of the alpine relict ones on the pebble plains.[2]

With insular faunal communities, one talks about isolation in terms of dispersability and breeding barriers. With insular plant communities, dispersal can be by means of seeds, pollinators or seed-eaters. Dispersal difficulties are compounded on the pebble plains by the rapidly changing precipitation gradient from west to east. The westernmost pebble plains and meadows receive approximately 45 inches of precipitation annually, and the easternmost at North Baldwin Lake receive less than 15 inches per year. Thus, a number of species will bloom in May at North Baldwin Lake while the same species are still under snow and will not bloom until July at Bluff Lake to the west. Precipitation falling on the open pebble plains in the form of snow blows off quickly and piles up in the surrounding trees, creating a much earlier anthesis (as early as February) for species on the plains as opposed to those in the trees (generally not until April).

---

[2] It is interesting to note that an endemic subspecies, _E. K. alpigenum_ (M. & J.) Stokes, with scapes of less than 1 centimeter, occurs on the summit of Mt. San Gorgonio, 10 miles to the south of the Big Bear _E. kennedyi_ complex, whereas another similarly short-scaped form occurs on the isolated pebble plains of Burnt Flat which lies just above the Mojave Desert northwest of Baldwin Lake. This may represent divergent adaptive radiation of _E. kennedyi_ forms toward both extremes of alpine and desert climatic influences.

The more sensitive species to these anthesis isolation barriers are those with limited seed dispersal capabilities or with specialized pollination mechanisms. The endangered bird-footed checker-bloom is a good example. It is heavy-seeded, with a dispersal range measured in millimeters. It was once described as abundant in Big Bear meadows (Parish 1917), but was never collected (may never have colonized) in Holcomb Valley. Its westernmost occurrence at Bluff Lake, an isolated meadow over a mile from the nearest neighboring wet meadows in Lower Bear Creek (now almost entirely under the waters of the Big Bear Lake reservoir), has probably been a separate population since Pleistocene times. North Baldwin Lake is the easternmost population of the checker-bloom, and it, too, has probably been separate from its nearest neighbors at South Baldwin Lake for thousands of years.

The plants from these two populations at either extreme of the species' distribution are markedly different from each other. They bloom as much as 3 months apart and the plants at North Baldwin have only one or a few flowering branches, as opposed to more than 10 flowering branches on plants at Bluff Lake. Such gross phenological differences may become genetically fixed, given time and isolation of the populations. This is a reflection of a species' dispersability, or the lack of it.

One other Big Bear rare plant community deserves mention. Uplift in the northeast San Bernardino Mountains has exposed narrow ridges of limestone that dissect Big Bear and Holcomb Valleys. The limestone substrate has created an edaphic isolation mechanism that has produced 4 of the endemic plant species listed in table 1.

The Big Bear pebble plains, meadows and limestone endemic plants have undergone compound isolation events: first, the geographic isolation from the Sierran montane flora during the Ice Age and later xerothermic period. Second, the isolation from other pebble plains islands by the conifer forest barrier itself, and finally by other anthesis and edaphic barriers. The stage was set for evolution.

Table 1

Rare Plant Species List of the Big Bear Valley Preserve System

For All Rare Plant Species Occurring in the Base Map Area (fig. 2) That Are Listed in the Inventory of the California Native Plant Society (1984)

Specific Name	Species Distributions			
	1	2	3	4
Arabis parishii	X			
A. shockleyi				X
Arenaria ursina	X			
Astragalus albens	X			
A. leucolobus			X	
Castilleja cinerea	X			
C. montigena		X		
Echinocereus engelmannii munzii			X	
Erigeron parishii			X	
Eriogonum kennedyi austromontanum	X			
E. ovalifolium vineum	X			
Haplopappus uniflorus gossypinus	X			
Ivesia argyrocoma			X	
Lesquerella kingii bernardina	X			
Lilium parryi				X
Linanthus killipii	X			
Mimulus exiguus			X	
M. purpureus purpureus	X			
Orthocarpus lasiorhynchus			X	
Perideridia parishii parishii			X	
Phlox dolichantha	X			
Poa atropurpurea			X	
Sedum niveum			X	
Senecio bernardinus	X			
Sidalcea pedata	X			
Taraxacum californicum		X		
Thelypodium stenopetalum	X			
	14	2	9	2

[1] Endemic to the Big Bear Ranger District, San Bernardino National Forest.
[2] Endemic to the San Bernardino Mountains.
[3] Endemic to Southern California, but with one or two other occurrences.
[4] Rare in California, but more widely distributed elsewhere.

Endemism

The local Serrano Indians had a legend that the Creator, Kukitat, died at Baldwin Lake, and from his grave sprang the world's wildflowers. They undoubtedly recognized the tremendous diversity and uniqueness of the Big Bear flora, and, in a way, the legend was right on the mark.

Dr. Sherwin Carlquist (1973) stated that "endemism is a constant byproduct of evolutionary change, and the percentage of endemics is a measure of degree of isolation in time and space." The Big Bear flora is very well endowed with endemics. Nine species and five subspecies of plants are endemic to within the Big Bear Ranger District of the San Bernardino National Forest. Another two species are endemic to the San Bernardino Mountains, and another nine species and two subspecies are endemic to the Big Bear area, except for a few other occurrences. This represents the highest degree of floral endemism for an area of this size in California--possibly in the continental United States.

Most of the endemics are the result of isolation from alpine populations to the north, dating their origins to at least 20,000 years ago at the end of the Ice Age. Others are of more recent derivation. The relatively recent event, in geological terms, of isolation of the pebble plains and meadows from each other by trees has already spawned some differences between populations of the same species from one island to the next, as indicated by the different checker-bloom morphs discussed earlier. Another example is illustrated by the Big Bear-endemic ashy-grey paintbrush (Castilleja cinerea Gray). Its population on Sugarloaf Ridge (above 9,000 feet in elevation) has smaller, dark maroon bracts (and may be called C. c. forma rubra) as opposed to the broad, yellowish bracts of the valley populations.

In fact, the speciation that produced such endemic annuals as Baldwin Lake linanthus (Linanthus killipii Mason) and purple monkeyflower (Mimulus purpureus Grant) probably resulted from the influx of desert annual species, and would, thus, represent rapid speciation to the specific taxonomic level. The subgenus Paradanthus of Mimulus, of which both the purple monkeyflower and the near-endemic eye-strain monkeyflower (M. exiguus Gray, the tiniest monkeyflower species in the world, with only one other occurrence in Baja California) are members, has apparently undergone an explosive pulse of speciation since that time, with as many as 10 species of the Paradanthus (depending on how this difficult group of taxa is classified) occurring in the San Bernardino Mountains.

The high degree of floral endemism is reflected by several interesting relationships. For example, the Kennedy's buckwheat is the principal host for the obligate root parasite, the ashy-grey paint brush, both local Big Bear endemics. The Kennedy's buckwheat is also the food plant for an as yet unnamed subspecies of the blue butterfly (Philotes enoptes, Dr. John Emmel, pers. comm.). The larvae of the endemic Andrew's marble butterfly (Euchloe hyantis andrewsii) feeds on the endangered slender-petaled mustard and Parish's rock-cress (Arabis parishii Watson) flowers.

Archipelago Configuration

Speciation has occurred because of the differential gene pools created by the insular distribution of the plant communities. Traits that would normally be "averaged out" in larger, more homogenous populations can be expressed in isolated ones. Furthermore, hybridization of the same species but from different gene pools, or of different species produced by the conspiracy of desert and alpine floras mixing together, may undergo a genetic "concentration" of the newly created genetic entity with further isolation and possible recolonization of other islands later.

According to island biogeographic theory, this cycle of gene pool mixing and isolation takes place most effectively in a complex archipelago as opposed to a single isolated islet. This is only logical in that genetic "crossings" over the isolation barrier would take place more readily the more complex the archipelago and the nearest the neighbor island. The number of actual colonizations of one island from the next would take place more frequently, depending upon the distance between islands. The larger the island, the greater the chance of falling in the appropriate habitat to survive and reproduce.

The colonization rate by direct seed dispersal is related to the distance from, and size of, the nearest neighbor island. Similarly, the extinction rate for a given island flora is inversely proportional to the size of the island and the complexity of the surrounding archipelago. For example, an unusually prolonged drought or change in hydrology alters a spring that feeds a very small wet meadow. The chances of survival of water-dependent species are greater, given a larger population and a larger, more complex island. Larger islands tend to offer a greater diversity of microhabitats, or niches, which may act as refugia for declining species. Furthermore, given a chain equidistant islets of the same size, the central ones would be more diverse than the ones at the ends of the chain. For example, if a species goes extinct on an island in the center of the chain, it may be recolonized from islands to either side, whereas if a species becomes extinct on an island at the end of the chain, its only chance for recolonization would be from the neighbor island to the inside. Thus, one would hypothesize that the greatest diversity of species would be found on the largest of islands or most complex of archipelagos.

It is fitting, then, that the North Baldwin Lake flora is the most diverse of the pebble plains archipelagos, with over 325 vascular plant species. The North Baldwin archipelago exemplifies both principles of distance-size and configuration in that it is one of the largest and most complex of archipelagos, with hundreds of acres of pebble plains and meadows, and is centrally located in the crux of a "V" formation of the pebble plains' overall range, as it extends from North Baldwin Lake to the west and southwest through Holcomb and Big Bear Valleys (fig. 2). Conversely, the tiny pebble plains islets at the extreme northwest end of the range in Lower Holcomb Valley, situated 1.5 miles west of the next pebble plains archipelago in Upper Holcomb Valley, are relatively depauperate of other than the indicators and most common associated species.

The Sawmill series of bench-top pebble plains is another example. The largest island of the linear archipelago configuration consisted of a 90-acre plain at the east end of the chain (now mostly developed). The 14-acre Sawmill plain at the extreme west end of the chain represents the westernmost extant pebble plain of the series. Killip's linanthus hop-scotches from one island to the next, reaching its westernmost distribution on the Sawmill plain, restricted there to only a few tiny pockets. Others of the more transmontane, desert-adapted species

(*Echinocereus engelmannii munzi* Pierce & Fosb. for example) have not persisted on the smaller pebble plains to the west end of the archipelago, and are restricted to the larger, east end plains.

Fragmentation and Extinction

There has been much work done on island avifauna and equilibria of species diversity relative to distance: size from neighbor islands. With animals, the equilibrium of the colonization rate in relation to the extinction rate for a given island is easy to conceptualize--one can picture birds flying to and from islands--but surely this must happen, given time and isolation, with insular floras as well.

Short of complete extirpation of an organism from an island or islands, its habitat may be reduced, or "fragmented," by a number of natural as well as manmade events. In modern times, it is almost always hominid-induced. In the Big Bear area, the first major fragmentation event was the conifer forest overtaking the alpine plant community as the climate warmed with the recession of Ice Age.

The next major fragmentation event occurred with the construction of the Big Bear dam in 1883. A higher dam was constructed in 1911, inundating over 2,500 acres of meadows and pebble plains.

Subsequent urbanization around Big Bear Lake's shore, overgrazing, competition from introduced weeds and off-road vehicles have nearly eliminated what remained. Parish wrote that "...the lower part of the valley was formerly a green subalpine meadow, a sedgy pool in the center; now all is submerged beneath the deep waters of a great reservoir. This appears to have effected the extinction of some of the plants which formerly grew here" (1917). Indeed, the spiral orchid (*Spiranthes porrifolia* Lindl.), sea milkwort (*Glaux maritima* L.) and Bolander's quillwort (*Isoetes bolanderi* Engelm.) can no longer be found in the valley, and several meadow endemics, the bird-footed checker-bloom and the slender-petaled mustard, are reduced to less than 20 acres of extant occupied habitat.

Based upon the island biogeographical principles of distance and size discussed earlier, one would predict that the remaining fragments of wet meadow or pebble plains habitats would decline in species diversity. This would result from the greater extinction rate of the much smaller, extant fragments, as well as from a decreased colonization rate because of the greater distances between remaining fragments.

The meadow-endemics have been particularly hard hit. Following the inundation of Big Bear Lake, the remaining meadows have, without exception, undergone urbanization, intensive grazing, alteration of drainage patterns and off-road vehicle use. In just over 100 years, an entire, rich, subalpine meadow ecosystem of greater than 5,000 acres has been reduced to tiny fragments of 10 or 20 acres, totaling less than 1,000 acres in the entire region.

The Eagle Tract is one of the largest of the remaining fragments at the west end of Big Bear Valley. An undeveloped tract of 50 acres on the south shore of Big Bear Lake, it is one of the checker-bloom's last stands. Once part of the thousands of acres of lush meadowlands and pebble plains that carpeted the west end of Big Bear Valley, a small meadow of less than 10 acres is all that remains. It is now surrounded by residential neighborhoods, and is subjected to the depredations of heavy off-road vehicle recreation. Most of the extant meadow habitat is now fenced and protected, but is it enough?

Even minor upstream alterations of drainage patterns that feed the wet meadow may result in extirpation of a number of hydrology-sensitive species. Some species collected here only 8 years ago can no longer be located (Yellow owl's clover, *Orthocarpus lasiorhynchus* Gray), and others are reduced to very small occupied habitats of fractions of acres.

Even if the entire remaining meadow can be preserved, the total number of species can be expected to decline until the fragmented habitat reaches a new equilibrium of species diversity. One can only imagine how species-rich the Big Bear Valley meadowlands once were, with a remnant flora of over 275 species on such a small remaining fragment as at Eagle Point.

What will be the result of the greatly increased isolation of extant meadows, such as at Bluff Lake or Metcalf Bay? Which species will be most vulnerable to the fragmentation? And looking beyond the flora, which faunal species, dependent upon the meadow ecosystem, are going to be most affected?

PRESERVE DESIGN

The Big Bear Valley Preserve was first established by the Nature Conservancy in 1980 with the purchase of 97 acres on the north shore Baldwin Lake. Since then, the Nature Conservancy has spent over $2,000,000 for the purchase of additional parcels, and has received several other parcels as dedications by private land owners. Still other parcels have been secured through "conservation easements" or management agreements with private land owners and government agencies.

Combined, these parcels form the Big Bear Valley Preserve system, a chain of preserves that includes a wide diversity of plant and wildlife habitats throughout the Big Bear and Holcomb Valley areas.

The 15 "target areas" for preserve consideration were identified according to the indicator species for pebble plains and meadow rare plant habitats. Essentially, they include the best of what is left of these unique plant communities with their rich, endemic flora.

The resulting preserve design maintains the overall geographic distribution of the rare plant communities, from the Hitchcock meadows and pebble plains at the west end of Holcomb Valley, to the North Baldwin Lake Botanical Area, to the west end of Big Bear Valley at Bluff Lake.

Preserve design of insular biotic communities should always strive to maintain the continuity of island systems and archipelagos. To preserve only the North Baldwin Lake archipelago is not sufficient. The resultant fragmentation might so isolate it from the next archipelago in the system that it would no longer be as biologically functional with pebble plains and meadows to the south and west. This may create an even more difficult barrier to the rare event of a successful seed dispersal or pollinator crossing.

The preserve conservationist must not restrict one's view to the island, but rather, must broaden one's view to encompass the entire distribution of the rare plant community. However, this perspective is often more easily conceptualized than achieved. Plant communities rarely heed political divisions or boundaries, making a regional preserve design more complicated to put together. The Big Bear Valley Preserve system is no exception, with five governmental agencies having jurisdiction in the area. Of the 15 target areas, seven are under National Forest jurisdiction. A draft Sensitive Biotic Resources Management Plan has been developed for rare plant communities as well as wintering bald eagles, but has not yet been formally adopted and lacks a map of the designated target areas to help the Forest Service land manager with on-the-ground management and planning decisions.

The remaining eight parcels are under four different local government jurisdictions. The North Baldwin Lake Botanical Area has been purchased in fee by the Nature Conservancy, but vehicular access from surrounding Forest Service lands remains a problem. The Sugarloaf, Castle Glen and part of the Eagle Point preserves are protected by in-fee dedications or conservation easements. The Sugarloaf Preserve was created in 1982 as a "mitigation bank" for several other developments that affected sensitive plant occurrences. Still other developers have been required to provide fencing for designated target areas as a mitigation for environmental impacts of their projects elsewhere in the Big Bear area.

Finally, two of the preserve areas have been protected by entering into voluntary land owner protection agreements under the Nature Conservancy's Register of Natural Areas program. This program has worked well with several nonprofit camps, for whom tax credits or charitable contributions would not otherwise be incentives for resource protection. This leaves only two parcels without protective management agreements yet in place, and portions of several others.

The inducement for local government participation in a regional preserve program is often that of streamlining environmental processing of applications dealing with sensitive plant constraints. Though some Big Bear developers view the offsite mitigation measures, such as fencing of target areas, as a form of environmental extortion, they do so willingly, rather than prepare formal environmental impact reports at much greater cost and time spent.

The advantage of adoption of a regional biotic resources map or overlays with the local government General Plan or Forest Service Master Plan is that it can address cumulative impacts on resources, where an individual, project-by-project assessment cannot. The disadvantage is that, once resource target areas have been established, everything not indicated for protection is slated for eventual development. The bottom line is that development will continue, and that there will be a net loss of habitat. The redeeming factor is that the regional preserve plan can pick the best and most manageable areas for protection, with a pooling of mitigation programs within the targeted preserve areas.

The City of Big Bear Lake has indicated the three target areas within its jurisdiction as open space in its General Plan. A recent project there exemplifies the concept of the regional mitigation program. An application was filed for a large-scale housing project on a 1.5-acre parcel on the south shore of Big Bear Lake. The state and federally endangered checker-bloom, Sidalcea pedata, was identified in a drainage ditch of several hundred square feet, totaling about 35 plants. Despite the presence of a formally listed species, the project was given a Negative Declaration, provided that the developer entered into a mitigation program acceptable to the Department of Fish and Game and Fish and Wildlife Service. A Memorandum of Understanding was developed that established a transplantation program as part of a meadow restoration project on one of the designated target areas, and required that the target area be fenced and protected from off-road vehicles and parking (of patrons from a bar next to the target meadow). The final conservation: development equation resulted in the protection and restoration of a 4-acre parcel that could be easily managed, and with the loss of less than one-tenth of an acre of highly fragmented, unmanageable habitat.

The Big Bear Valley Preserve system protects key wintering bald eagle and waterfowl habitats on a regional basis also. By protection of target areas on both Big Bear and Baldwin lakes, the wintering bald eagles (of which the Big Bear basin supports 25 to 30 birds each year) can move from one lake to the other, depending upon conditions of ice and prey availability. Again, developments outside of target areas may provide offsite habitat improvements for bald eagles within target areas, such as trimming and limbing of trees for perching, or improvement of waterfowl and fisheries habitats. In time, the target areas may be improved to increase their habitat value for target species, while development inexorably continues elsewhere. Thus, the Big Bear Valley Preserve system was established, and in only 5 years has nearly been completed. Its success is remarkable in these times of general siege for sensitive biotic resources in Southern California, in that it has overcome the hurdles of multiple jurisdictions and their inherent tendency of narrowly focused, project-by-project environmental impact assessment.

There are still more questions than answers for the preserve manager. How small is too small, and how isolated is too isolated? What are the species diversity equilibria for the resultant fragmented preserves, and what management steps could be undertaken to counteract the fragmentation events? Only time will tell, and we can only hope that the bald eagles will continue to spend their winters in Big Bear, and that checker-blooms will continue to bloom until the next Ice Age brings a resurgence of Big Bear's relict alpine flora.

REFERENCES

California Native Plant Society. Inventory of Rare and Endangered Vascular Plants of California, Special Publication No. 1. (2nd Edition), April, 1980. 115 pps.
Carlquist, Sherwin. Hawaii, A Natural History. Printed for the Pacific Tropical Botanical Garden, SB Printers, Inc., Honolulu, Hawaii, 1980. 468 pps.
Carlquist, Sherwin. Island Biology. Columbia University Press, New York. 1973.
Derby, Jeanine A., Ruth C. Wilson. Floristics of pavement plains of the San Bernardino Mountains. Aliso 9(2): 364-378. 1978.

Derby, Jeanine A., Ruth C. Wilson. Phytosociology of pavement plains in the San Bernardino Mountains. Aliso 9(3): 463-477; 1979.

Diamond, J.M. The island dilemma: lessons of modern biogeographic studies for the design of natural reserves. In: Biological Conservation. 7: 129-146; 1975a.

Diamond, J.M. Island biogeography and the design of natural reserves. In: Theoretical Ecology, Ed. by R.M. May, 163-186 p. 1975b.

Krantz, T.P. A botanical investigation of Sidalcea pedata, a survey of the species throughout its range. Prepared for the San Bernardino National Forest. 1978. 21 p.

Krantz, T.P. Thelypodium stenopetalum, the slender-petaled mustard, a botanical survey of the species throughout its range. Prepared for the San Bernardino National Forest. August 1980. 44 p.

Krantz, T.P. A survey of two pavement plains endemics: The Bear Valley sandwort, Arenaria ursina and Big Bear buckwheat, Eriogonum kennedyi ssp. austromontanum; a study of the taxa throughout their ranges. Prepared for the San Bernardino National Forest. April 1981. 79 p.

Krantz, T.P. The Bear Valley bluegrass, Poa atropurpurea, a survey of the taxon in the San Bernardino Mountains. Prepared for the San Bernardino National Forest. August 1981. 40 p.

MacArthur, R.H. and E.O. Wilson. The Theory of Island Biogeography. Princeton, New Jersey. Princeton University Press. 1967. 203 p.

Parish, S.B. An enumeration of the pteridophytes and spermatophytes of the San Bernardino Mountains, California. Reprinted from The Plant World, 20 (6, 7, 8): 163-178, 208-223, 245-259, August 1917.

Establishment of a Vernal Pool Preserve in San Diego County

John P. Rieger [1]

Abstract: The establishment of 79 acres of vernal pool preserves in San Diego was the result of an elaborate process in evaluation and identification. Many steps were required before the vernal pool preserves could be finalized. An extensive survey of the existing vernal pools was conducted before any determinations could be made. The presence of easements and the possibility of ownership of remainder parcels had to be addressed. Delineation of the watersheds had to be known precisely to ensure the integrity of the pool system. The status of the pools and identification of rehabilitation activities needed to be evaluated. Lastly, special agreements and slope easements and rerouting of utility easements ensured protection for the pools within the boundaries established.

Since 1980 the California Department of Transportation (Caltrans) has been involved in the purchase of vernal pool habitat in the City of San Diego. These purchases were required as compensation for vernal pool impacts caused by construction of projects on Interstate 15 and a State Route 52. The two acquisitions of vernal pool habitat properties were necessitated by Section 7 Biological opinions from the U.S. Fish and Wildlife Service (USFWS) given to the Federal Highway Administration (FWHA). This paper presents the procedures and activities related to the creation of the vernal pool preserve and some of the management obligations associated with them.

The presence of the endangered vernal pool plant San Diego mesa mint (Pogogyne abramsii) on a federally funded project necessitated consultation with the USFWS under the Endangered Species Act. In August 1979 the USFWS under the Endangered Species Act. In August 1979 the USFWS rendered the first biological opinion. This opinion and the other opinions stated that destroyed vernal pools can be compensated for by the "acquisition of privately owned vernal pools containing Pogogyne abramsii of equivalent or greater value. In addition, priority should be given to those areas which are relatively large, undisturbed, well-buffered and of high quality."

METHODS

Aerial photography and an existing survey report by California Department of Fish and Game were used to identify suitable locations to conduct more detailed site evaluations. Vernal pools were measured using length and width adjusted for irregularities of the pool. Dimensions were averaged so that the fewest dimensions could be used to calculate the area of the pool. In every case the calculations are approximate and conservative. The pool areas were calculated either as a rectangle, trapezoid, triangle, oval or circle or combination of these shapes. All pools were measured by the same individual so that a degree of precision was maintained. Pools were grouped into complexes by virtue of their proximity to other pools. Pool areas were totaled by complex and treated as a unit.

Biological Data

Each pool was surveyed for key vernal pool plant species. Percentage cover of mesa mint was estimated. The percentage represents an average of two

---

[1] District Biologist, California Department of Transportation, P.O. Box 85406, San Diego, CA 92138-5406

estimates using sight estimation. In cases where estimates differed by 10% or more, a detailed estimate resolved the differences.

Management and Disturbance

Direct disturbances to vernal pools were noted. Presence of motorized two or four wheel vehicles, various forms of disturbance such as trash dumping, grading, filling and introduction of exotic plant material were also recorded. Management considerations include noting the distance to residential communities, accessibility, type of future development as indicated by community plans, zoning designations, or current proposals in the environmental process, and the extent of rehabilitative work required for pools that have been degraded.

Determination of the Vernal Pool System

The watershed of a pool system was defined as the upland area that would contribute to the water budget of the vernal pools. It was necessary to determine this area by an engineering survey crew, as some of the larger pool systems had slight topographic relief and some of the sites were near property lines. The watershed was determined for pools on the outside of the complex and plotted on 1:200 scale maps. The outside perimeter formed the minimum area for the complex.

RESULTS

Twelve vernal pool complexes were visited and a total of 119 pools totaling 261,915 square feet with 18,909 square feet of mesa mint were examined. Seven alternatives were developed ranging in size from 15 to 57 acres occurring in two to four parcels of land. Motorcycle and four wheeled vehicles had damaged portions of pools in every complex. No pools were destroyed beyond repair; however, the degree and extent of restorative work ranged from minor to extensive recontouring and dirt removal. As expected, pools near residential areas exhibited more signs of disturbance than pools farther away. Additionally influencing the disturbance level was the degree and density of vegetative growth surrounding the pools and the level of accessibility.

Development of Alternatives

Seven alternatives were developed involving from two to four parcels encompassing from 53,000 to 120,000 square feet of vernal pools. The designs were submitted to Caltrans management for selection. The alternatives analysis report included for each alternative the total pool area, area of mesa mint, general quality of the pools, estimated acreage needed to acquire the complex, and the watershed and resource management zone. Vernal pools vary in size and densities within complexes, therefore it was not possible to develop a design with only 1.3 acres of pool, the level of impact on the I-15 project. Ownerships of property affected by the design were determined by using tax assessor maps and property title searches were conducted on all properties within the candidate pool preserve selected.

First Acquisition

The alternative selected for the I-15 project is 26 acres on the Del Mar Mesa in two parcels (20.2 acres eastern parcel, 5.8 acres western parcel) with 31 pools totaling 120,000 square feet including one pool covering approximately 80,000 square feet.

Second Acquisition

A subsequent acquisition for the SR 52 project increased the holding of the eastern parcel by 52 acres to 72 acres. An additional 6.7 acre parcel was required to the south on Lopez Ridge. This parcel was designed to be located adjacent to the Los Penasquitos Regional Park, a natural park separating the two vernal pool preserve locations. This design arrangement increases the viability potential of the Lopez ridge site as it will be attached to permanently designated natural open space.

Design Constraints

The final configuration of the preserve is the result of the existing easements, ownership boundaries, and negotiation between the biologist and engineers. Title searches of the property revealed three easements for proposed facilities were on the land parcels to be acquired. These consisted of waterline, road, and full utility easement. To unencumber the land in the preserve the waterline and road easements were moved off the property to the north by acquiring additional 5.75 acres for that purpose. The third easement, a San Diego Gas and Electric Company utility system, involved complicated and lengthy negotiations with three parties, Caltrans, SDG&E, and California Fish and Game. This was necessitated by a hearing before the California Transportation Commission (CTC). Caltrans was requested to make every effort at reducing the amount of land to be purchased from a specific landowner. The solution developed allowed for above ground utilities to be left in place and to move the underground utilities to the perimeter of the preserve. The tower locations were set at the high point between the drainages of the two large pools in the eastern property. In addition a number of construction constraints were outlined to limit the type and extent of disruption to the natural vegetation. By accepting the tower sites, a substantial amount of money ($250,000) was saved. A hydrologic and soils study conducted for the pools near the tower sites indicated that some reduction of watershed and the limited construction activity would not be disruptive to the large pools to the north.

An added problem arose during the process to get condemnation approval. The owner of the largest pools threatened by letter read before the CTC "to eliminate the reason why Caltrans was buying the property". This threat was not taken lightly as other pools in San Diego have been deliberately destroyed in the past. An emergency Order of Possession (O.P.) was requested by Caltrans lawyers and granted by the local court. However, the O.P. did not take effect for three days after it was granted or on Monday. After that time the property would be legally owned by Caltrans. The grading and environmental quality offices of the City of San Diego were notified about the situation, and a warning system was developed for the upcoming weekend. The San Diego Chapter of CNPS volunteered to watch the access road into the complex for heavy equipment which would be used to destroy the pools. The owner did try to obtain a grading permit for agricultural purposes. However, the staff was able to refer him to the environmental office. He did not submit an application with the environmental office.

Another situation arose when the Caltrans Right of Way Engineering office made an error in transcribing the survey coordinates of the smaller parcel to the west. This resulted in a smaller amount of land on a parcel that was already very small (5.76 acres).

In addition the error occurred at the narrowest point of the parcel which made the design unacceptable. This required renegotiating with the landowner to increase the purchase size since a settlement in court had already been reached. This renegotiation took over 18 months to accomplish.

Another instance of an error in the design occurred at the easternmost preserve boundary. At this location no 100 foot management zone was incorporated into the preserve. Only portions of two pools were being acquired, and an additional two pools were at the property boundary with no watershed. To correct this situation an additional acre was needed which would allow for the 100 foot management zone further to the east. During the acquisition process the owner of the property expressed concern about how this additional loss would affect his future development opportunities. Again in response to the input from the CTC, a slope easement was written which will allow a two to one slope extending a maximum of 40 feet into the eastern perimeter of the new resource management area. The resulting preserve is 79 acres occurring on three parcels north and south of the Los Penasquitos Park. The total square footage of pools is 170,000 square feet including approximately 80 pools of varying quality.

The property will be fenced and management and title to the property will be turned over to a conservation agency. Several remedial actions remain to be taken such as trash clearing, pool restoration, rehabilitation, revegetation of scarred areas, and decompaction of abandoned roads.

CONCLUSIONS

The process of establishing a vernal pool preserve requires several steps and an active involvement in disciplines other than biology. The goal of an optimum preserve design as discussed by Diamond (1975) can, in reality, be difficult to achieve for non-biological reasons. Influences from ownership and financial factors can affect the ultimate configuration of the preserve design. Frequently cost will influence the decision making process. All too frequently the decisions that have to be made are done in an informational vacuum. These factors increase the possibility of error in the design process. There are many important facts that we have yet to learn about vernal pools which would help in their management. Unfortunately, public works projects rarely wait for science. Therefore, I hope the decisions that have been made are conservative and any errors in judgment will be on the side of the vernal pools and will not result in any deleterious effects. The preserve established through a public works project is the first vernal preserve established solely for the San Diego Mesa Mint. In addition to possessing very large pools this preserve also contains the northernmost population of mesa mint, which further adds to the overall value of the preserve. Active management of the preserve will be mandatory as residential development continues to encroach upon the adjacent mesas.

LITERATURE CITED

Diamond, Jared M. The island dilemma: Lessons of modern biogeographic studies for the design of natural reserves. Biol. Conserv. 7:129-146.

Opportunities for Involvement in Endangered Plant Education

Abstract: An overview of model curricula and a variety of educational projects which focus on endangered plant education. Programs offered by public and private science museums and nature centers, botanical gardens are highlighted. CNPS chapter projects are discussed and ideas for future efforts included.

Kay Antunez de Mayolo [1]

Everyone can identify the one group of extinct organisms that have captured the public's attention during the past few years. Just ask a young child who the monster with the large head and sharp teeth is and even those who are barely verbal can tell you its <u>Tyrannosaurus rex</u>! The dinosaurs have helped set unprecidented museum attendance records, produced enormous sales of life-like replicas, toys, books, T-shirts and sent many teachers searching for classroom materials to take advantage of their student's keen interest.

It would seem to follow that this curiosity and interest in dinosaurs and the process of extinction would also have a corollary in the theme of the modern process of animal and plant extinction. And with the same enthusiasm for learning the odd sounding names of the dinosaurs, children should easily be able to learn to distinguish and identify plants and therefore develop a deep appreciation and a respect for their unique place on the earth. We need to teach them, involve them and trigger their curiosity and concern.

The focus of this talk will be to discuss several types of programs which have been developed by a cross section of different educational institutions including the California Native Plant Society. I feel that good models should be repeated in order to reach a wider audience. I hope to encourage you to take these ideas home and remodel them into useful tools and programs for the groups of people you hope to inspire an interest in the preservation of endangered plants and their habitats.

In the initial organization of the education symposium, Susan Cochrane, Joe Medieros and I had several meetings to decide how to develop the program. We often got sidetracked into discussions of how one gets interested in single themes such as plant recognition and awareness of the uniqueness of species. Each of us could recall experiences in our lives where someone or some event drew our attention to the diversity of plant life. All succeeding experiences that compounded our knowledge and appreciation came from additional experiences and at some point the interest was self-perpetuating. How can we help initiate others?

As we all know, plants, especially endangered plants get much less attention than do the endangered animals, so there is much to be done in the way of creative efforts to interest and educate the public and anytime is a good time to start.

During the past months, Linda McFelter from the Great Valley Museum in Modesto and I made a telephone survey of 40 public and private educational organizations to inquire about their education programs. We selected the survey sample after searching through lists of California educational organizations and identifying a select group whose focus was associated with natural history interpretation and science education. We telephoned each organization and asked to speak with the education program director and inquired about what types of educational programs had been developed or were in the process of being developed that specifically focused on the theme of endangered habitats, species, and plants. I also sent a letter to each CNPS chapter to inquire about programs that had been developed for general plant education and specific programs in the area of endangered plant education.

---

[1] Nature Area Coordinator, Sacramento Science Center and Junior Museum, Sacramento, CA.

From the survey sample, of the organizations contacted (museums, nature centers, science academies, wildlife sanctuaries, botanical gardens, national parks), 10 have developed a program or educational tool that in some way focused on endangered plants. Of the 27 CNPS chapters surveyed, 5 responded and provided information about their chapter education efforts.

During the remainder of this presentation, I would like to discuss the types of programs which each of the 7 organizations have developed and share what the CNPS chapters are doing.

The Sacramento Science Center and Junior Museum has developed 25 different "touring one person shows" or outreach programs. One of these, adaptable to use with 4-12th grade students, focuses on the process of endangerment and what efforts are being done to help the survival of species. The lesson usually focuses on animals and displays animal skins and other items confiscated by the U. S. Fish and Wildlife Service. There is some effort to discuss endangered plants, but visual and hands-on materials as display items are in lesser supply. This classroom presentation is requested by teachers who are sent pre-visit activity ideas such as a bulletin board activity which asks students to sort groups of animal pictures into four sections: extinct, endangered, threatened, and safe. Students are asked to look for articles or pictures of species which fit into each catagory. An additional activity suggests students use wildlife maps to determine the number of endangered species in each county and to draw conclusions about where most of the endangered species tend to be and what inferences can be made to evaluate the human land use practices. There are also a series of recommended post-activities such as one called "endangered epics" in which students write a book about a particular endangered species for a younger child to read.

The Santa Cruz City Museum, in conjunction with the Santa Cruz County chapter of CNPS has held many successful spring wildflower shows. The exhibition of garden grown specimens are arranged according to their habitat. Rare plants are mixed in with their appropriate group and identified as special, but they are not emphasized in the show. Introduced weeds and exotic species are also displayed and appropriate interpretative information supplied.

In the past years, between 400-600 school age children have visited the display over a period of 4 days. They are given a half hour presentation featuring themes of plant life cycles, seed dispersal, plant anatomy and food from plants which is available to sample. This presentation if followed by a half hour tour through the display where they are shown the diversity of plant life and told how each plant fits into its own habitat. There is a separate area to enjoy the smells, shape, touch and color of plants on display.

The Santa Cruz City Museum also uses and loans out a slide-tape presentation developed by the Santa Cruz County CNPS chapter which features wildflowers of the region. The slide show is accompanied by a written script and is a model of volunteer effort to develop an educational tool useful in the promotion of public awareness of the Santa Cruz County flora.

Coyote Point Museum for Environmental Education, located in San Mateo County, is planning a spring wildflower show to be co-sponsored by the Santa Clara Valley chapter of the CNPS. This museum has had speakers and displays featuring issues involving endangered species and recently held a seven part lecture series titled "Ethics in the Environment". This program was funded by the California Council for the Humanities and surpassed all expectations in anticipated attendance. They also have planned a monthly program targeted for adults titled "Preserving Diversity of Life" which will feature a panel discussion with three speakers from the local community who will discuss the themes of tropical rainforest destruction, gene pool erosion and the endangered Monterey pine and cypress.

The Santa Barbara Botanic Garden does not have a special tour to feature the rare and endangered plant specimens located in the garden. They have had specimens of rare plants stolen when direct mention was made of their rare plant status. They attempt to do most of their interpretative work by demonstrating the importance of revegetation projects such as their bunchgrass meadow. The staff at the garden also serves as a resource for information on native plants and has given talks on rare plants to community organizations.

Strybing Arboretum in Golden Gate Park has a variety of interesting programs that could be easily developed by other organizations. Of significance is their effort to identify and mark each of the endangered or rare status specimens displayed in the garden. A green E on the label identifying the plant also communicates its uniqueness as an endangered plant species. Supplementing this is a booklet titled "California Rare and Endangered Plant Walk" which was developed by the 1983 docent class of George Washington High School. This attractive booklet outlines a self-guided tour and also presents information about the causes of endangerment, need for preservation and describes the 25 endangered California native plants grown in the garden.

The arborteum is in the process of redesigning the California native plant garden which will be ready for planting in 1987. During the planning stages, designers have taken an interest in developing plant displays which augment the arboretum's effort to provide public education concerning rare plants. In addition to this, the arboretum is planning to construct a display to feature a small demonstration garden for the 1987 San Francisco Landscape Garden Show. The theme they have chosen is a San Francisco urban garden featuring native plants of the San Francisco area, most of which are endangered species.

Strybing Arboretum has taken the position of "preservation through cultivation" and is exemplary in its imaginative ways of developing interpretative materials and programs which feature California native plants.

The Living Desert Museum in Palm Desert and the Moorten Botanic Garden and Cactarium in Palm Springs consider the issue of endangered plants to be one of their main points of focus. The Palm Desert Museum also sponsors an annual wildflower show and uses garden propagated specimens some of which are endangered species.

Many of the CNPS chapters who did not respond to the survey are involved with rare and endangered plant education. Offering talks on this theme at their chapter meetings, field trips to areas to study and observe rare species, newsletter articles and propagating garden specimens of rare plants for their plant sales are all efforts to interest and inform members and the public of this issue. Several chapters have developed unique programs which I would like to discuss.

The Napa County chapter has begun an ambitious project which will keep them busy for a period of years. Each of their newsletters to be issued in the future will include a portion of a page to be cut out and added to a rare plant notebook. Described as "build your own rare plant book" the folder size notebook will eventually include descriptions and information about the 18 rare and endangered plants of Napa County. Other chapter activities include the development of a native plant botanic garden at Skyline Park and active "periodic plant watches" involving their members. In addition, an education subcommittee has developed and trained volunteers for a group called the "Natural Science Docent Program", a chapter education outreach project. This chapter sponsored program organizes volunteers who make presentations to Napa County elementary schools, museums, nature areas and for youth and adult groups.

The Mt. Lassen chapter has members who are involved as docents working with the Chico Creek Nature Center. These members have developed displays which focus on the rare and endangered plants and habitats in the Chico area. Other chapter members serve as docents at the Nature Conservancy's Vina Plains Preserve. The chapter has always participated as a co-sponsor of the Butte County Environmental Council's "Endangered Species Faire" held each spring in Chico.

The San Diego chapter, like the Santa Cruz County chapter, has developed an educational slide show accompanied by a taped narration. Their show does not focus on rare plants, but attention is given to the value of landscape revegetation projects using native plants. The show has been presented to many garden clubs and service groups in San Diego County.

In addition, the San Diego chapter has been involved in another unique educational project. Last spring chapter members established a roadside "ramada" along a highway used by weekend sightseeing traffic during a weekend when the local newspapers had publicized that the desert was in bloom. They put up signs to identify individual plants, maintained a shaded roadside stand to distribute information and gave personal tours through the area to describe the desert vegetation and issues involved with desert habitat destruction. Although somewhat difficult to make advanced plans for such forms of public education, the group felt it was an important program and hopes to repeat it in years to come.

The Sacramento Valley chapter has developed and produced a video program which focuses on the Sacramento riparian forest. The 12½ minute videotape produced by a team of professionals and chapter members is titled "The American River Forest: A Sacramento Treasure". The program features the common riparian forest plants with an emphasis on the importance of the river in supporting the vegetation. The video lesson is aimed at upper elementary age children with the goal of developing a more complete understanding of the American River Parkway and its significance. The chapter hopes to compliment this video production with others focusing on topics such as annual wildflowers, wildlife and history of the parkway and citizen involvement in preserving the parkway.

To conclude, we can see that through any number of creative efforts, educational programs can be developed which will increase the public's opportunity in endangered plant education. You will hear about additional models from our next speakers. In addition to these, I know there are many others, but we need more slide-tape presentations that can be borrowed by groups, more chapter rare plant booklets, video programs, demonstration gardens and temporary displays. What about a special field trip program for families with young children, youth poster contests which use themes such as illustrating habitat or individual species losses? Who can design us a colorbook or prepare an endangered species lesson guide which features plants? What clever learning aids and toys can be developed to assist with the hands-on learning experiences? Just how can we capture some of the public's enthusiasm for dinosaurs and put it to work for the preservation of rare and endangered plants before they in turn become extinct.

Conservation Ethics, Animals, and Rare Plant Protection

Rolf W. Benseler [1]

Abstract: Preservation of taxa in nature is predicated upon ecosystem protection. Yet there are those perceived as environmentalists supportive of and actively involved in the protection of animals to the detriment of the associated native biota. Flagrant cases include saving feral ungulates posing direct threats to rare and endangered plant populations. Awareness and response to such destructive activities need to be addressed with the same concern and vigor given those of developers and other resource exploiters. Elementary and high school curricula must include an ecologically balanced presentation of nature and an understanding of and concern for rare species.

A primary threat to rare species, as all organisms, is habitat degradation and destruction. Too often despite our fervor (or perhaps because of it), efforts to save rare plants fail to recognize and implement this dictum. Our commitment to rare plants must be a commitment to the preservation of rare and unique ecosystems.

Many impacts, especially those perpetrated by corporate exploiters on natural communities have been addressed and, in some cases, mitigated. On the other hand, damage too often condoned or ignored for a variety of reasons are those perpetrated by protectors of native, exotic and feral herbivorous animals. Problems become especially acute when population numbers and densities exceed carrying capacities due to the absence of or inadequate predation. In many instances, human activities and mismanagement are responsible for the imbalance. Under these circumstances we are thrust into the uncomfortable and awesome responsibility of assuming the role of predator if the ecosystem is to be returned to some semblance of balance.

The havoc wrought by vertebrate herbivores is more often condoned than that of invertebrates, let alone pestiferous microbes and plants, that are dealt with using pesticides or biocontrol.

---

[1]
Rolf W. Benseler
Professor of Biological Sciences
California State University
Hayward, CA 94542

While such action may be condoned as expedient, if not totally positive, control measures of run away avian or mammalian populations are perceived as unacceptable regardless of direct threats to rare plants or the extent of environmental degradation in general.

Such beliefs and practices have a long history in our country, yet we might begin with the 60's and 70's when "save the ecology" was in vogue.

Save the ecology of coastline, forest, woodland, chaparral, vernal pools continues to be a popular battle cry; politically it is flexible.

1. It can mean saving so-called "sanitive" environments. The maintenance of unpolluted, healthy conditions. It covers a multitude of sins.
2. It can mean opposing logging, livestock, mining exploiters as well as sub-urban developers. Those that would convert, hence degrade environments to paved-over areas and weed patches.
3. It can mean doing what is necessary to keep environments as close as possible to natural conditions composed of native species forming "natural" communities.

All of the above advocate adherence to general ecological concepts with which most of us are in agreement, just as long as they do not require too much personal sacrifice or conflict with pre-conceived biases, especially those concerned with animals.

Perversion of our North American environmental ethics has deeper roots, however.

Nature--fakerism, ancient in its origins was especially popular during the latter part of the last century. The great naturalists John Burroughs and John Muir railed against story tellers and writers who modified the realities of nature in order to enliven their tales of wildlife, to suit public demand, making them more or less intelligent, appealing, violent, absurd, comic, and anthropomorphic as deemed necessary. Burroughs labeled this practice "The Yellow Journalism of the Woods". In 1907, in an article entitled Nature - Fakers, Theodore Roosevelt lambasted this appalling miscarriage of responsibility. Aldo Leopold, most notably, carried on the crusade to instill realistic perceptions of nature and conservation ethics.

With the advent, rapid rise and popularity of motion pictures, nature-fakerism experienced a revival depicting natural history with cute stories, trick photography for the purpose of titilation. Disney films carried this to perfection, influencing generations of film goers. And today, despite the excellent nature presentations on PBS, Stephen Kellert, the Yale wildlife sociologist, in his studies of public attitudes towards animals, found Merlin Perkins and his animal antics to be the most popular "nature" presentation on television.

John Livingston in his book One Cosmic Instant maintained that perception of animals and nature in general has been implanted in us much like the multiplication tables and the periodic table of chemicals via the Walt Disney-Mother Goose Table of Animal Values.

We have been taught that some organisms were created (or evolved) more equal than others. Importance values can be determined based on characteristics such as

1. Aesthetics: beautiful animals, pretty flowers vs. unspectacular, to downright ugly.

2. Utility: what are they good for? or, what do they contribute? or, what is their role in the environment? (They're food for birds seems to be a safe reply at most environmental gatherings).

3. Noxious: are they dangerous, poisonous, pathogenic, pestiferous? We're better off without them.

4. Sentience: are they capable of sensation and consciousness? Do they exhibit complex behaviors?

5. K/r Selection: are they long-lived with few offspring vs. short-lived, with many offspring, hence expendable?

Racism is perhaps too strong a term for such discrimination. Such attitudes perhaps reflect speciesism or taxism They are certainly anthropomorphic.

Higher vs. lower animals and plants are commonly misinterpreted to imply more than phylogenetic position defined by biologists. Biological complexity and sentient condition as we perceive them are what are held to be really important. We allow these value scales to override what we know to be the ecologically preferred course of action in "natural" communities and their conservation. An extreme position is that taken by animal philosophers and their disciples from diverse groups including so-called environmentalists. With missionary zeal and methods of the electronic evangelists, they expend large sums of money to save cute animals, i.e. those they deem have rights, without regard for associated populations and community components.

Familiar examples of much publicized exotic and feral animals include feral horses over much of the west, especially in the Great Basin; burros in fragile desert communities; pigs in California woodlands and goats, the scourage of Mediterranean type ecosystems throughout the world.

The December 1985 issue of BIOSCIENCE is a "keeper", containing several very interesting, important articles. One, Duties to Endangered Species by Holmes Rolston III, in particular, received widespread praise.

"Destroying species is like tearing pages out of an unread book, written in a language humans hardly know how to read," is a wonderful statement, as is "Humans ought to respect the lifelines within species that persist genetically over millions of years". Sentiments expressing the thrust of our cause. Caution is suggested in "An adequate ethic for preserving species requires an unprecedented mix of biological science and ethics."

Further reading of Prof. Rolston's duties, however, evokes suspicion. For example, he takes issue with Peter Raven's generality that dependent animals and plants become extinct with each plant taxon that goes extinct. Raven's (Presidio) manzanita (*Arctostaphylos hookeri* spp. *ravenii*), he contends, consists of a single wild individual and its extinction is not likely to trigger others. He continues "...if all 79 (only 79) plants on the endangered species list disappeared, it is doubtful that the regional ecosystems involved would measurably shift their stability." Furthermore, "Few cases can be cited where the removal of a rare species damaged an ecosystem." So it seems rare and endangered plants must earn their protection and are expendable as far as community function is concerned. He continues, moreover, "A substantial number of endangered species, have no resource value." One species, tidal shore beggar's tick, *Bidens bidentiodes* with stick-tight seeds is unlikely to be a potential resource. "As far as humans are concerned, its extinction might be good riddance." We seem to have few duties to useless, noxious weeds.

Prof. Ralston, nevertheless, continues to provide profundities like "There is something...morally naive about living in a reference frame where one species (that's us folks) takes itself as absolute and values everything else relative to its utility."

The offshore islands are especially afflicted with exploding ungulate populations--sheep, pigs, and goats. Rolston admits, not without misgivings one suspects, that species, not sentience, generate some duties; pointing out that on San Clemente Island, the U.S. Fish and Wildlife Service and the California Department of Fish & Game asked the Navy to shoot 2000 feral goats to save three endangered plant species, *Malacothamnus clementinus*, *Castilleja grisea*, and *Delphinium kinkiense*. "That would kill several goats for each known surviving plant." (Happily, the Fund for Animals rescued most of the goats...)," he added. "The National Park Service," he continues, "did kill hundreds of rabbits on Santa Barbara Island to protect a few plants of *Dudleya traskiae*, once thought to be extinct and curiously called the Santa Barbara live-forever."

Duties to even endangered plants seem less critical when compared to those of exotic, destructive animal populations, a result of human folly, crying out for mitigation.

Plant people view introduced invasive plant populations much differently. There are lovely blue gum/radiata pine forests in the Oakland Hills; an area with scattered occurrences of rare leather wood (*Dirca occidentalis*) and Alameda manzanita (*Arctostaphylos pallida*). Below freezing temperatures the winter of 1973 killed Eucalyptus shoots, causing widespread alarm that all the trees were dead. Unfortunately, not so, plus or minus a few expletives, testified the late James Roof of Tilden Botanical Garden. Nearby are lovely stands of broom with at least three species plus intergrades of *Cytisus*. They bear pretty flowers, have interesting bee pollination mechanisms, provide excellent slope stabilization and the roots have nitrogen-fixing nodules to supplement soil fertility. What could be more environmentally sound and sanitive?

Yet what did I read in my CNPS Bay Leaf? "Broom Bush." "Bring tools with which to vent your wrath on the aggressive invaders which threaten the beauty of natives...broom has crept in and must be stopped!" "...you'll feel virtuous..." Can you imagine the uproar if a southern California chapter scheduled a goat bash on an offshore island? Bring weapons with which to vent....I'll let you complete the announcement. Animal people with media in tow would launch a dramatic helicopter flotilla to intervene...you can also complete that scenario.

Garrett Hardin, upon receipt of the AIBS Distinguished Service Award addressed the annual AIBS meeting at the University of Massachusetts last summer. As usual, if you are familiar with his work, he had much to say that is applicable to this discussion. "Biology abounds in insights that call for a restructuring of popular opinions." "Whenever a population grows beyond the carrying capacity, the environment is rapidly degraded." "The ultimate goal of game management is to minimize the aggregate suffering of animals", ala Aldo Leopold.

Ledyard Stebbins has provided us with guidelines given..."Conservation is politics, whether we like it or not." "Know your enemy...bureaucrats, who are subservient to industries of exploitation: lumbering, mining and large-scale recreational development". To which we might add fossil fuel industries, agriculture and livestock businesses-plus bureaucrats who are subservient to so-called protectors of destructive animal populations.

The future rests with the youth, hence it is imperative that school curricula include an ecologically balanced presentation of nature and an understanding of and concern for rare species of all five kingdoms. Care must be taken to insure that future generations are not indoctrinated in the Mother Goose-Walt Disney Checklist of Animal Values.

An excellent beginning in this direction is via "PROJECT WILD--an interdisciplinary supplementary environmental and conservation education program for educators of kindergarten through high school age young people."

The program is not without its detractors. Advertisements purchased by the Friends of Animals depicts a coyote bash and solicits money to get Project Wild out of the schools.

They state that the goals of Project Wild are to desensitize children to animal suffering, and to promote the fur trade, and ask for public support to stop this brainwashing of children and the exploitation of animals.

Still, the program has caught on, according to Jennifer Meyer. "Teachers are going wild over WILD!"

In conclusion, to save rare plant populations, we must

1. strive to save "natural" ecosystems;

2. guard against all exploiters, even those hiding under the umbrella of environmentalism;

3. support application and implementation of ecological principles in wildland management decisions, free of taxist, anthropomorphic biases;

4. disseminate the teachings of John Burroughs, John Muir and Aldo Leopold and a love of all creatures (taxa) great and small.

REFERENCES

Hardin, Garritt. Cultural carrying capacity: a biological approach to human problems. Bioscience 36(9):599-606; 1986.

Kellert, S.R. Public attitudes toward critical wildlife and natural habitat issues. Washington, D.C. U.S. Fish and Wildlife Service; 1979.

Lever, C. Naturalized mammals of the world. London: Longman; 1985.

Livingston, John A. One cosmic instant. New York: Macmillan Co.; 1975.

McKnight, T. Feral livestock in Anglo-America. Univ. of Calif. Pubs. in Geography, Volume 16; 1964.

Meyer, Jennifer. Teachers going wild over Wild. Outdoor California 45(5):17-21; 1984.

Rolston, Holmes. Duties to endangered species. Bioscience 35(11):718-726; 1985.

Roosevelt, T. Nature-Fakers. Everybody's Magazine; 1907, September.

Stebbins, G.L. Rare plants in California's national forests: their scientific value and conservation. Fremontia 13(4):9-12; 1986.

General Index

The index indicates the page on which a main entry/title heading first appears; names of contributors are set in capitals, accepted scientific names, without citation of authority, in italic. All other entries are in roman type. Index entries for taxa referred to briefly in a particular paper would run to over several pages—thus they are omitted except where relevant to a main entry.

Agave arizonica, 305
Alameda manzanita, 447
Alien introductions, 185
ALLEN, LORNA, 579
AMME, DAVID, 447
Arctostaphylos pallida, 447
Arroyo de la Cruz, 141
Autecological monitoring, 385, 391

BARRY, JAMES W., 73
BARTEL, JIM A., 15
BAUDER, ELLEN T., 209
BEAUCHAMP, R. MITCHEL, 575
BENNETT, PETER S., 215
BENSELER, ROLF W., 623
BERG, KEN S., 351
Birds, endangered, 441
BOHN JEFFREY W., 537
Boron toxicity, 394
Botanic gardens, 563
BOWLAND, JACQUELINE L., 487
BOYD, ROBERT, 513
BRACK, STEVE, 517
BRATT, CHARIS C., 289
Bureau of Land Management, 51, 455
Burning, controlled, 513
        prescribed, 233
BUTTERWICK, MARY, 257

Cactus theft, 215
CALLIZO, JOE, 397
Camatta Canyon amole, 277
CAMPBELL, FAITH T., 7
California Natural Diversity Data Base, 181
California priority taxa, 107
        state laws, 33, 43
Chamaesyce hooveri, 239
Chaparral vegetation, burning, 233
Chlorogalum purpureum var. *reductum,* 276
CITES, 11
CLIFTON, GLEN, 397
CLIFTON, GLENN L., 239
CNPS listing, 40, 41
CNPS Rare Plant Program, 1
Coastal sage scrub, 133
        salt marshes, 441

COCHRANE, SUSAN A., 33
Collomia rawsoniana, 225
CONKLE, M. THOMPSON, 249
Conservation ethics, 623
        non-profit exchange project, 573
        programs, 7, 99, 401, 553
        case studies, 23
        strategies, 553
        voluntary action, 567
CULLY, ANNE, 517
CUMMINGS, EARL W., 43
Cupressus guadalupensis var. *forbesii,* 367
Cupressus macrocarpa, 249

DaVILLA, WILLIAM B., 167, 225, 239
DAWSON, BRUCE E., 455
de BECKER, SALLY, 391
de BENEDETTI, STEVEN H., 193
de LAMATER, RICK, 305
de MAYOLO, KAY ANTUNEZ, 619
Dichanthelium lanuginosum var. *thermale,* 391
DUNN, ANTHONY T., 367
DUNN, PATRICK V., 441

Ecosystem management, 73
Education programs, 619
ELIAS, THOMAS S., 563
Endangered Species Act, 15, 33, 43, 49
Endemic conifers, genetic diversity, 587
Endemism, 1
Eriogonum apricum, 547
Erysimum menziesii, 351, 507
EVANS, J. MICHAEL, 537

FABER, PHYLLIS M., 573
Facultative biennials, 351
FALK, DONALD A., 553
FARVE, REYNAUD M., 425
FAULL, MARK R., 429
Federal listing, 15, 23, 39
Feral pigs, effect on ecosystems, 193
Feral pigs, eradication and control, 189, 193
FERREIRA, JEAN, 507, 523
Fire impact, 367, 513
Floristic exploration, 91
Forest Service sensitive plant program, 61
Fynbos, 283

GAWITH, E.L., 283
Geothermal areas, 391
Gold mining activities, 397
Golden Gate National Recreation Area, 471
GRENELL, PETER, 401
Government funding, 67
Guadalupe Dunes Revegetation Program, 487
Guarantees, 405

Habitat Conservation Plan, 493
HALL, LAUREN A., 413
HASTEY, EDWARD L., 51
HAVLIK, NEIL A., 421, 447
Hemizonia arida, 429
HENNESSY, LINDA L., 181
Highways, 79
HILLYARD, DEBORAH, 405, 523
HODGSON, WENDY, 305
HOLLAND, ROBERT F., 129, 329
Holocarpha macradenia, 295, 421
HOWALD, ANN M., 409
Humboldt Bay salt marshes, 263
Hybrid taxa, endangered, 305

Insular rare plant communities, 605
Ione buckwheat, 547
Island biogeography, 605

JENSEN, DEBORAH B., 595
JOHNSON, R. ROY, 215

KEIL, DAVID J., 141
Keystone species, 137
Kings Canyon Jewel Flower, 282
Kings Canyon National Park, 279
KNIGHT, PAUL, 517
KNUDSEN, MONTY D., 461
KRANTZ, TIM, 605
KRUCKEBERG, ARTHUR K., 121
KUNZMAN, MICHAEL R., 215

Land Restoration, genetic problems, 523
　　　　　　　　public action, 525
LEDIG, F. THOMAS, 587
LEITNER, BARBARA M., 391
Lespedeza leptostachya, 359
Lichens, 289
Livestock grazing effects, 199
Lupinus ludovicianus, 276, 278
Lupinus nipomensis, 276
LOZIER, LYNN, 567

MARANGIO, MICHAEL S., 267
MARTZ, CRAIG, 79
McCARTEN, NIALL F., 335
McCLINTOCK, ELIZABETH, 185
McLEOD, MALCOLM G., 141, 275

McMAHAN, LINDA R., 23
Menzies' wallflower, 351
MESSICK, TIMOTHY C., 99
Midget Milk-vetch, 279
Mineral requirements and acquisition, 529
Monardella linodes subsp. *viminea,* 501
Monardella, willowy, 501
Monitoring programs in Alberta, Canada, 577
Monterey cypress, genetic analysis, 249
MORGAN, RANDALL, 267
Mouse Buckwheat, 280
MYATT, MONA M., 173
MYATT, RODNEY G., 547

NABHAN, GARY P., 377
National forests, 61
NELSON, JAMES R., 159
NEWTON, GAIL A., 263
NICOLA, STEPHEN J., 67
Nipomo lupine, 275, 277
NORRIS, LARRY L., 279
NUGENT, SUSAN, 341
Nurse plant ecology, 377

Oil development, impact of, 409
OLWELL, PEGGY, 517
Orcuttia viscida, 329
Orcuttieae (Gramineae), 239

PALMER, REXFORD E., 295, 321, 341
PARKER, V. THOMAS, 233
Parks and preserves, design concepts, 595
PAVLIK, BRUCE M., 311, 385
Pediocactus knowltonii, 517
Pediocactus peeblesianus var. *peeblesianus,* 257
Peebles Navajo Cactus, 257
Performance bonds, 405
Pinnacles National Monument, 193
Poa marcida, 341
Population dynamics, 351, 359, 367
　　　　　　　 fluctuations, 329
　　　　　　　 monitoring, 397
Potential research natural areas, 85
Prairie Bush-Clover, 359
Public lands, 51
Purple Mountain Parsley, 280

Quercus lobata, 129

Rare plant surveys, 159
Recovery plans, federal role, 461
Red Hills Management Area, 167
Red Hills Management Area Plan, 425
REID, THOMAS S., 493
Reproductive ecology, 321
Resource conservation programs, 401
RIEGER, JOHN P., 615

Ring Mountain Preserve, 477
Roadside management programs, 79

St. JOHN, T.V., 529
Salmon Mountain conifers, 155
Salt marsh bird's beak, 441
San Bruno Mountain, 493
San Clemente Island flora, 575
San Francisco Bay Region, 335
San Luis lupine, 275
San Luis Obispo County, 275
Sandhill plant communities, 267
SAWYER, J.O., 155
SCHEID, GERALD A., 501
SCHMEIDLER III, N.J., 283
SCHOFIELD, LARRY, 341
SCHOOLCRAFT, GARY, 85
Sensitive plant management plans, 455
Sequoia Gooseberry, 281
Sequoia National Park, 279
Serpentine communities, 335, 477
Serpentine endemics, 121
SHEVOCK, JAMES R., 91, 181
Silene invisa, 321
SMITH, SUZANNE, 507
SMITH, WELBY R., 359
SMITH, Jr. JAMES P., 1
SMITH, Jr. ZANE G., 61
South-western Cape Province, 283
Species preservation, propagator's role, 537
Stable populations, 311
State Coastal Conservancy, 401
State listing, 40
STEBBINS, JOHN C., 225, 239
STONE, R. DOUGLAS, 167, 239
STRAHAN, JAN, 477

Tarweed, 295, 429
       preservation, 421
TAYLOR, DEAN Wm., 167, 225, 239, 321
Tecate Cypress, 367
THOMAS, TERRI, 471
Torrey pine, 249
Transplantation, case histories, 413
Tuctoria mucronata, 329
TYSON, WAYNE, 525

VANBIANCHI, RONALD, 341
Vegetation Habitat Relationship System, 173
Vernal pool plants, 329
       preserves, 615
Vernal pools, threats to, 209

WALLIS, CLIFFORD, 579
WALSH, RAYMOND C., 493
WESTMAN, WALTER E., 133
WILLOUGHBY, JOHN W., 167, 199
WILLY, ALISON G., 189
Witsenia maura, 477
WOLLEY, GREGORY J., 477

YORK, RICHARD P., 4, 39, 109

Acknowledgements

This conference was organized by the California Native Plant Society with joint financial sponsorship from the following agencies, organizations, and individuals. Without this joint effort, the conference could not have happened. Their insight and commitment to the protection of botanical resources is gratefully acknowledged.

California Department of Fish and Game
California Energy Commission
California Department of Parks and Recreation
U.S. Bureau of Land Management
U.S. Fish and Wildlife Service
Southern California Edison
Pacific Gas and Electric Company
Chevron Inc.
The Nature Conservancy
California Botanical Society
Rancho Santa Ana Botanic Garden
Jones and Stokes Associates
Scott and Jenny Flemming
Darl Dumont
Ellen Bauder

Grateful recognition is due the members of the Coordinating Committee, who gave unselfishly of their time, expertise, and encouragement and actually seemed to enjoy themselves during periods of hard labor and high stress.

Jim Nelson	- Conference Coordinator
Rosemary White	- Administrative Assistant
Susan Cochrane	- Program
Mark Stopher	- Logistics Coordinator, Facilities Management
Craig Martz	- Press Liaison, Conference Merchandise
Rick York	- Publicity
Thomas Elias	- Proceedings Editor, Program
Deborah Jensen	- Program Assitance
Deborah Hillyard	- Poster Session
Jean Ferreira	- Banquet, Field Trips
Linnea Hansen	- Open Forum Discussions
Joe Callizo	- Exhibits, Sales
Arthur Hayler	- Finances

We also wish to thank the members of the original steering committee who contributed much in shaping the conference in its infancy and whose support actually made the conference possible. James Bartel, Dan Cheatham, Susan Cochrane, Charli Danielsen, Sally de Becker, Mary de Decker, Thomas Elias, Peggy Fiedler, Linnea Hansen, Deborah Jensen, James Jokerst, Harlan Kessel, Monty Knudsen, Barbara Leitner, Craig Martz, Tim Messick, Mona Myatt, James Nelson, James Shevock, James P. Smith, Jr., John Willoughby, and Rick York.